INTERNATIONAL MARKETING NINTH EDITION

Vern Terpstra

Ravi Sarathy

Lloyd Russow

INTERNATIONAL MARKETING NINTH EDITION

Vern Terpstra
University of Michigan

Ravi Sarathy
Northeastern University

Lloyd Russow
Philadelphia University

NCP
NorthCoast
Publishers, Inc.

Published by: Northcoast Publishers, Inc.
                  5063 Turney Road, Garfield Heights, OH 44125
                 (216) 332.0323 (V) • (216) 332.0324 (Fax)
                 cservice1@northcoastpub.com

Address inquiries to:
College Permissions: Northcoast Publishers, Inc.
5063 Turney Road, Garfield Heights, OH 44125.

Printed in the United States of America
B C D E F G E
ISBN 1-933583-22-3

This publication is designed to provide accurate and authoritative information with regard to the subject matter involved. It is sold with the understanding that the publisher is not engaged in rendering legal, accounting or other professional advice.

If legal advice or other expert assistance is required, the services of a qualified professional person should be sought.

—From: *A Declaration of Principles*, jointly adopted by a Committee of the American Bar Association and a Committee of Publishers and Associations.

Visit our home page at: http://www.northcoastpub.com

Contents

Contents – Expanded

Part 2: Global Marketing Management

Part 3: Coordination and Control of Global Marketing

List of Cases by Chapter

Preface

International marketing has become a necessary way of life for firms that want to survive and grow in the dynamic world economy of the new millennium. New markets are opening, and old markets are evolving. The majority of the world's population lives in the so-called "bottom of the pyramid." They represent an increasingly growing and important market that requires innovative responses by international marketers. New competitors are appearing; and old competitors are growing through alliances, acquisitions, and mergers. China and India have become major players, both as markets and as competitors. The global village is becoming a global marketplace. To paraphrase, "No company is an island unto itself." This continuing globalization has forced businesses and business schools to become more sophisticated about international marketing. *International Marketing*, 9th edition, has evolved accordingly.

This new edition reflects recent developments in the world economy and their implications for international marketing. The text continues to address the challenges and opportunities facing small exporters as well as large multinationals. The text covers economic and cultural environments, the continuing changes occurring therein, and the implications for firms that want to survive and succeed in this dynamic environment. The authors have broad international experience. Between them, they have taught on every continent. That experience has given them a real-world feel for the developments analyzed in *International Marketing*. The text has been used around the world and has been translated into Chinese; new editions have also been published for Taiwan, Indonesia, and India.

Key Features

The text adopts a practical approach to understanding the international marketplace. Material is organized according to the types of daily decisions marketing managers face in the international context.

Economic, political, cultural, and technological environments are introduced early on, setting the stage for the functional areas, which follow.

Chapters contain "Global Marketing" features. These features spotlight specific international firms and situations to provide students with interesting examples of international marketing in action.

Changes in This Edition

All of the chapters and tables have been revised. Many new tables and illustrations have been added as well. New examples illustrate current business practices and problems. New cases have been included, which are tied to web sites. Tables are linked to databases for potential update.

International Marketing, 9th edition, contains new conceptual material on the cultural environment (Triandis, Hall, Hofstede, et al.) and its relevance for international marketing. The text stresses the increasing importance of technology and the WWW to all aspects of marketing—and provides suggestions and examples of how students and instructors can use it as they study international marketing. Recognizing that the development of information technology networks has made the management of global business easier, Chapter 5, "Information Technology and Global Marketing," discusses how companies such as Benetton and Mast use information technology to plan and control business operations.

International Marketing, 9th edition, contains a new chapter, Chapter 6, "Ethics and Global Marketing." Along with the foundational material, this theme is carried throughout the text in terms of challenging examples and case material to stimulate in-class and online discussion. New material on logistics and global distribution is also presented.

Instructional Resource Package

The learning supplements provided with *International Marketing*, 9th edition, have been updated and revised to provide instructors with effective and valuable teaching tools. The supplements reflect the environmental changes seen in this twenty-first century and the latest technology. For example, PowerPoint presentations are linked to spreadsheets. Over 150 universities, businesses, and public institutions use/refer to the web-created material.

Instructor's Manual

This comprehensive and valuable teaching aid includes chapter summaries, chapter learning objectives, lecture illustrations, questions and answers, case teaching notes, transparency masters, and a comprehensive test bank. The Instructor's Manual has been rigorously revised in this edition to provide instructors with a thorough and up-to-date teaching tool.

Testing Resources

This valuable resource provides testing items for instructors' reference and use. The new edition of the test bank has undergone substantial changes. Approximately half of the test items have been edited or rewritten. The test bank contains over 1,300 multiple-choice, true/false, short-answer, and extended-essay items that vary in difficulty. The test items are also available in a computerized format, allowing instructors to select problems randomly by level of difficulty or type, to customize or add items, and to scramble items to create up to 99 versions of the same test.

Acknowledgments

Like earlier editions, this edition benefited from the contributions of many people. We thank the hundreds of American, Asian, European, and Latin-American executives who we consulted, who conducted research, and who we met at seminars over the years. They provided many practical insights and examples. Our students, both in the United States and abroad, challenged and stimulated us to sharpen our analyses.

Many faculty colleagues provided cases, materials, and constructive suggestions. We gratefully acknowledge them and especially thank the major reviewers of this edition:

Andrew C. Gross, Cleveland State University
Attila Yaprak, Wayne State University
Dharma de Silva, Wichita State University
Richard Hise, Texas A&M University
Mohammad Elahee, Quinnipiac University

Special thanks goes to Thomas Lloyd of Westmoreland Community College for his superb revision of the instructor's manual, test bank, and transparency masters.

We also want to thank our creative team:
Marianne Miller, copyedit
Tia Andrako, interior design and production
James Fedor, cover design
Micah Putman, IT support

Finally, we welcome comments and suggestions from users of this edition. Through such feedback, we can continue to provide an up-to-date and useful product.

Vern Terpstra, Ravi Sarathy and Lloyd Russow

September 2005
cservice1@northcoastpub.com

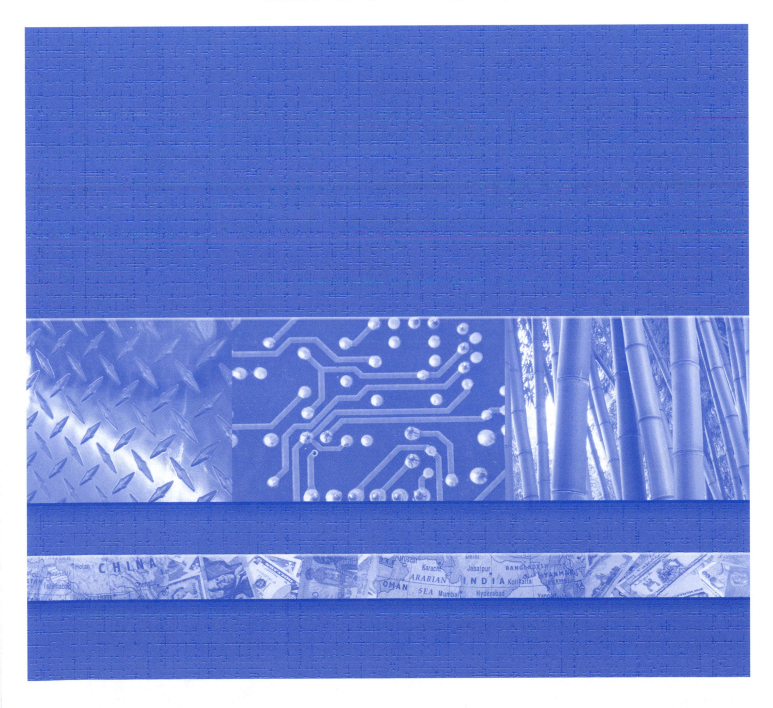

PART 1

The International Environment

CHAPTER 1

Introduction

The Concept of Global Marketing

International marketing has become important to companies around the world for three reasons: (1) Foreign markets constitute an increasing portion of the total world market. (2) Foreign competitors are increasing their market share in one another's markets. (3) Foreign markets can be essential sources of low-cost products, technology, and financial and human capital. In a word, the United States and other major economies are more interdependent with world markets.

The main goals of this chapter are to

■ Show how interdependent nations have become.

■ Distinguish between international and domestic marketing.

■ Describe the global environment in which marketing takes place.

■ Show a variety of ways in which a firm may practice international marketing.

■ Illustrate how the Internet has played a role in reshaping global marketing.

■ Emphasize that global marketing is a matter of perspective in which firms consider the whole world as their market, making few distinctions between domestic and foreign markets.

"The world is too much with us," said Wordsworth. In a different sense, that could be the complaint of many domestic firms that are threatened by the loss of market share from imported goods. Import competition has been increasing, for example, imports were only 1 percent of U.S. gross domestic product (GDP) in 1954; they were 6 percent of GDP in 1964, 10 percent in 1984, and 13.4 percent in 2002. Exports and imports, as a proportion of GDP, have been increasing in similar fashion in most of the world's major economies. In the last 25 years, the amount of total world output accounted for by trade in goods and services rose over 20 percent, to 54 percent in 2002.[1] This means that over half of what is produced every year is to be sold in a foreign country. This book deals with the significance of this international interdependence for the business firm.

As data in Table 1-1 indicate, U.S. imports have been steadily growing, contributing to a worsening balance of trade. Although U.S. interdependence with the world economy is still less than that of many other nations listed in Table 1-1, that interdependence is likely to increase. Many more U.S. firms, whether they like it or not, will be forced to become part of world markets and global competition. At the same time, countries such as China are becoming a major force in the world economy. Meanwhile, nations such as South Korea and Germany have had open economies for some time; their firms are more accustomed to selling in international markets. Hence, some U.S. firms may have to catch up to compete effectively and to gain market share in world markets.

Table 1-1. International Trade Profiles, Selected Countries

Country	1998 ($US Billions)	2002 ($US Billions)	Comments
United States			Major trading partners: Canada, Mexico, Japan, and EU.
GDP	7,921.3	10,207.0	Major exports: capital goods and industrial supplies.
Exports	922.5	966.5	Major imports: capital goods, industrial supplies, consumer
Imports	1,108.5	1,408.0	goods, and automobiles.
Germany			
GDP	2,122.7	1,876.3	Major trading partners: U.S., EU, and China.
Exports	621.7	712.7	Major exports: machinery and automobiles.
Imports	595.7	642.8	Major imports: machinery, minerals and fuels, and food.
Japan			
GDP	4,089.9	4,323.9	Major trading partners: EU, Central Europe, and U.S.
Exports	449.7	481.6	Major exports: machinery and vehicles.
Imports	391.2	443.8	Major imports: vehicles, aircraft, and chemicals.
(South) Korea, Rep.			
GDP	369.9	473.0	Major trading partners: U.S., China, and Japan.
Exports	156.2	190.0	Major exports: electrical/electronic products, automobiles,
Imports	116.8	187.3	and semiconductors.
			Major imports: machinery and transport equipment,
			petroleum, and chemicals.
China			
GDP	928.9	1,234.2	Major trading partners: U.S., Argentina, and Europe.
Exports	207.8	365.0	Major exports: commodities.
Imports	169.0	341.3	Major imports: fuel, machinery, and chemicals.

Sources: World Bank, *World Development Report* 1999/2000, Table 1, pages 230–231; *World Development Report*, 2000/2001, Table 20, pages 312–313; *World Development Indicators*, 2004, Table 1.1, pages 15–16; Table 4.5, pages 198–200; Table 4.6, pages 202–204; Table 4.7, pages 206–208; and Table 4.8, pages 210–212.

Economist Intelligence Unit, Country Reports, various issues.

Note: Exports and imports data are trade in goods and services combined. GDP is calculated using World Bank Atlas method.

Global Marketing and Domestic Marketing

International marketing is best explained by briefly reviewing marketing in a domestic context. In this book, **marketing** is defined as "the collection of activities undertaken by a firm in order to assess and satisfy customer needs, wants, and desires." This broad definition of marketing encompasses both for-profit and not-for-profit organizations, whether public or private. When discussing products, this textbook refers not only to manufactured goods, but also to services, ideas, and people (as in political campaigns or movies). A firm's ultimate success depends primarily on how well it performs in the marketplace, requiring knowledge of the market. Marketing involves many responsibilities, including the following:

- A firm must identify and study its consumers: Who are they? Where are they? Who are prospective buyers? Are they similar to or different from current consumers? What factors are important in consumers' decisions to purchase (or not purchase) the product?
- The firm must develop the products that satisfy customer needs and wants.
- The company must set prices and terms on the products so they seem reasonable to buyers and return a fair profit to the company.
- The company must distribute the products so they are conveniently available to buyers.
- The firm must inform the market about its wares; it must use marketing communications to raise awareness, increase interest, and increase sales. With the Internet, distance and time have become less important, while delivery and service have become more important.
- There is an implied warranty of satisfaction with the product, which differs from country to country. Firms must reassure customers and may need to perform a variety of after-sale services. The firm's marketing responsibility does not end with the sale.
- Firms must monitor the marketing activities of their domestic and international competitors and develop appropriate organizational structure and long-term marketing strategies and competitive responses.

Marketing management, therefore, is the planning and coordinating of all of these activities to achieve a successfully integrated marketing program.

International marketing is, by definition, the act of marketing across national boundaries. One difference between domestic and international marketing is that the latter includes the task of marketing between countries, as well as within each country, as shown in Figure 1-1. That is, the international marketer has an additional responsibility—moving products across national boundaries—in addition to moving products within each of the markets the company serves.

Figure 1-1. Domestic versus Global Marketing

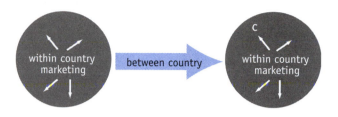

International Marketing: A Closer Look

The activities just described—market research, product development, pricing, distribution, and promotion—together constitute the essence of marketing. What then is **international marketing**? International marketing consists of identifying, understanding, and satisfying global customer needs better than the competition (both domestic and international). It also consists of coordinating marketing activities within the constraints of the global environment. Table 1-2 examines this definition in greater detail and breaks down the main components of international marketing into five objectives:

- Identifying and understanding global customer needs
- Satisfying customer needs
- Being better than the competition (domestic and international)
- Coordinating marketing activities
- Recognizing the constraints of the global environment

Identifying and Understanding Global Customer Needs

Customer needs can be identified by carrying out international marketing research. Such research helps a firm understand customer needs in different markets and determine whether those needs are different from those of the customers it currently serves. For example, a U.S. company seeking to sell washing machines in Europe must know that Europeans often wash their clothes with hot water (at a temperature of 60 degrees Centigrade—140 degrees Fahrenheit), whereas most washing in the United States

---

Table 1-2. International Marketing: The Essentials

Objective	Corresponding Action
Identifying and understanding global customer needs	Carrying out international marketing research and analyzing market segments; seeking to understand similarities and differences in customer groups across countries.
Satisfying customer needs	Adapting manufactured goods, services, and elements of the marketing mix to satisfy different customer needs across countries and regions. Including in manufacturing and technology decisions the implications of costs and prices, development of global customer information databases, and distribution channel and logistics information.
Being better than the competition	Assessing, monitoring, and responding to global competition by offering better value and developing superior brand image and product positioning; broader product range; low prices; high quality; good performance; and superior distribution, advertising, and service.
	Recognizing that competitors may include state-owned enterprises, other multinationals, and domestic firms, each having different goals, such as market share over profits.
Coordinating marketing activities	Coordinating and integrating marketing strategies and implementing them across countries, regions, and the global market, which involves centralization, delegation, standardization, and local responsiveness.
Recognizing the constraints of the global environment	Recognizing that the global environment includes: • Complex variation due to governmental, protectionist, and industrial policies. • Cultural and economic differences. • Differences in marketing infrastructure. • Financial constraints due to exchange-rate variation and differences in inflation rates.

---

is done at lower water temperatures. Companies also need to analyze market segments across countries in order to position their products appropriately for entry into international markets.

Satisfying Customer Needs

If needs differ across countries and regions, a company must consider how to adapt its products and the various elements of the marketing mix to best satisfy customers. If a company needs to lower prices, it should consider how to cut manufacturing costs and whether to shift manufacturing to a country where manufacturing costs are lower. A well-articulated distribution and logistics system is needed to make sufficient quantities of goods and services available at the point of sale (POS). Ideally, firms also should develop global customer databases and information systems in order to understand and respond to customer needs and purchasing decisions.

Being Better Than the Competition

Firms must contend with both domestic and global competitors. Global competitors may include large multinationals and state-owned enterprises that are not profit-oriented, as well as small local firms. Multinational enterprises have operations in more than one country.

Whether large or small, they have a more extensive set of experiences to draw upon and generally have access to resources a domestic firm may not, including labor, financing sources, and managers with a broader perspective. Long-term success comes, in part, from assessing, monitoring, and responding to actions by global competitors, especially in the understanding of competitive and comparative advantages that competitors enjoy.

Coordinating Marketing Activities

International marketing creates a new level of complexity because firms must coordinate their marketing activities across countries. This may involve staffing and allocating responsibilities across marketing units in different countries and deciding which decisions to decentralize and which to control from headquarters, whether to develop standardized campaigns and plans, and how much local responsiveness is appropriate.

Recognizing the Constraints of the Global Environment

The **global environment** is complex, and this complexity increases as the number of markets served by a firm increases. As firms attempt to market in the international arena, they must cope with cultural and economic differences that exist in the marketing infrastructure. These costs include factors such as the structure and sophistication of the distribution system (people who prefer or have time to purchase food daily tend to rely less on refrigeration and purchase smaller quantities of products than people who purchase on a weekly basis), the financial constraints imposed by exchange-rate changes and varying inflation rates (which, in turn, depend largely on the state of a nation's economy), and the impact of government policies (especially protectionist and other policies that unfairly benefit competitors and create difficulties in market entry).

At its simplest, international marketing involves **exporting** products to a few countries. A firm becomes more of an international marketer as it increases its direct involvement in overseas markets by controlling more of the decisions regarding pricing, promotion, distribution, and product design.

Manufacturing abroad may be a strategy undertaken to enlarge the customer base. A company may begin manufacturing overseas to lower its costs so it can match the lower prices of strong international competition. Sometimes a company manufactures and sells in the same market. However, a firm may not find it feasible to enter foreign markets alone, instead seeking a partner to share some of the risks. Such a partner could contribute capital, add new products (to broaden a product line, for example), or provide a new distribution channel. The local government may prohibit the foreign company from operating in its country unless the firm has a local partner.

Companies unwilling to commit capital and management resources to marketing in foreign countries might be happy to settle for less risk, less involvement, and lower returns by **licensing** their product or technology to a foreign company. The goal of these companies is still to earn profits from foreign demand, but the approach is indirect. Management is saying, "We'll take fewer headaches in return for lower profits." A firm may seek to license its products or enter into a **franchise** agreement. These approaches, where someone pays a firm to use its patents and to sell its products, allow firms such as McDonald's to open more outlets and gain access to more customers than they could if they were to rely solely on their own capital to build new stores.

Foreign customers can force a company to change the ways it does business. A foreign buyer may insist that the selling firm accept payment in kind: orange juice or wine or chickens in return for machinery. If the firm accepts the offer, it then finds itself peddling orange juice and chickens around the world, a consequence of the growing trend toward **countertrade** in international marketing.

Thus, for a company entering foreign markets, international marketing may include exporting and importing (foreign sourcing), manufacturing overseas (with or without partners), countertrade, licensing, and franchising.

International Marketing Management

The complexity of international marketing is due largely to two factors: global competition and the global environment. Customer needs vary across countries. Competitors with different strengths now come from all over the world. Likewise, the global environment presents a bewildering variety of national governments, cultures, and income levels. Domestic marketing management is often portrayed as the task of responding to the uncontrollable factors in the firm's environment while manipulating the controllable factors. International marketing management is infinitely more complex.

Figure 1-2. Global Environment

As depicted in Figure 1-2, the global environment is multifaceted. The controllable elements of the global environment include the 4 Ps of marketing: product, place, promotion, and physical distribution. The uncontrollable elements are those things marketers cannot control, such as the legal environment. However, marketers can exert pressure on and affect change in these "uncontrollable" elements. For example, by introducing products such as computers and the Internet, marketers change how people communicate (a part of culture). The so-called "controllable" elements are not always totally under the marketers' influence. Governments place price floors on products such as cigarettes (or add to the price of the product through taxes). International marketing management has the same task as that of a domestic marketer, but must view the environment in broader terms. Thus, price, product, channels of distribution, and promotion vary across, say, France, Brazil, India, and the United States. While marketers must consider the laws of a nation when marketing domestically, in the international environment, they must take into account the laws of many nations. Furthermore, they must contend with the possibility that the laws of one country may conflict with those of another.

An added dimension of international marketing management is the need for a firm to coordinate and integrate its many national marketing programs into an effective multinational program. Indeed, a principal rationale of multinational business operations (as opposed to the alternative of independent national companies) is that the division of labor and the transfer of know-how in international operations enable the whole to be greater than the sum of its parts.

A practical result of these differences is that an international marketing manager needs broader competence than domestic marketing managers or managers marketing in a specific foreign country. In other words, the international marketing manager has a dual responsibility: **foreign marketing** (marketing within foreign countries) and **global marketing** (coordinating marketing in multi-

ple markets in the face of global competition).

Of particular interest is what international marketing managers think are the most important aspects of their duties and responsibilities. Professor Kashani at IMD, Switzerland, conducted a survey of marketing and general managers.[2] The sample was predominantly European (72 percent) and split among industrial products (45 percent), consumer goods (21 percent), pharmaceuticals (14 percent), and services (20 percent). Their main concerns are presented in Table 1-3.

The Global Marketplace

To get a sense of the range of activities that constitute international marketing, consider some examples of companies operating in the global marketplace. It is helpful to see how different companies make decisions regarding products, prices charged, distribution channels, countries sold to, and partners chosen—all in an attempt to increase sales and profits.

Table 1-3. Marketing Managers' Concerns

Concern	Contributing Factors and Explanation
Developing new products	The pace of innovation is so high that every firm must be capable of launching new products in a timely fashion. Time-to-market is a critical variable in determining competitive advantage.
Developing relationships with suppliers, distributors, and customers	The complexity of technology and markets demands that companies develop long-term partnership relations with suppliers to jointly develop products and processes, with distributors to launch detailed marketing campaigns in many countries, and with customers to learn about the utility of their products and to cooperatively develop product modifications and new products.
Fewer but stronger global competitors	The resource and scale needs of global markets are leading to mergers, acquisitions, and greater industry concentration. Larger competitors have greater resources and the ability to implement global strategies over a longer time horizon; this places pressure on firms to grow, seek alliances, and constantly seek partners and acquisition candidates. The alternative is to become a takeover candidate of other companies.
Growing price competition	Products become commodities more rapidly. This, coupled with scale economies, leads to severe price competition. Firms must either reduce costs or innovate constantly to compete on the basis of differentiated products rather than price.
Greater regional integration and government regulation	Increasing regionalization, examples of which include the European Union, NAFTA, and ASEAN trading blocs. Other important influences on strategy include government regulations, such as local content laws and trade barriers (tariff and non-tariff barriers).
Developing a marketing culture	Listening to the customer is paramount; enhancing and using communication capabilities are essential to successful international marketing, as is recognition of other important constituencies, such as the environmental lobby.

Source: K. Kashani, "Marketing Futures: Priorities for a Turbulent Environment," *Long-Range Planning* 28(4), 1995, 87–98.

Nintendo in the Global Video Game Market

Is there a teenager in America who has not played a Nintendo game? This 100-year-old Japanese company of the same name, which originally sold playing cards, began marketing the Nintendo game machine as Famicom, a family computer, in Japan in 1983. Meanwhile, in the United States, Atari was leading the computer game industry. Despite waning interest in Atari games, Nintendo was aware of the huge potential in the United States and test-marketed its computer in New York in 1984. By 1991, the product had achieved greater penetration than any other home computer or personal computer: 30 million Nintendo machines had been sold to U.S. consumers.

The Nintendo machine was simple and was designed to be connected to the home TV set. Despite having similar capabilities to early computers, Nintendo called it a "game" rather than a "computer." (The unit had no keyboard and no functions other than to play games.) The units were sold through toy stores and were priced at just under $100, much less than the price of computers at that time.

Nintendo's U.S. sales increased from $800 million in 1987 to $3.3 billion in 1990, with a U.S. market share of nearly 80 percent. Nintendo was able to capture one of every $5 spent on toys in the United States.

Since Nintendo had such a large share of the market, it was slow to introduce new technologies. Meanwhile, in 1991, its competitor, Sega, in an attempt to capture some of this lucrative market, introduced a 16-bit system called Genesis about a year before Nintendo introduced its own machine. (Sega did not achieve much success until it introduced a new game, Sonic the Hedgehog, which was wildly attractive to game players.)

Nintendo followed suit; but because Sega had introduced its machine first, Sega and Nintendo split the emerging market for 16-bit systems, with each firm selling between 5 million and 6 million new systems by 1992.

Competitive pressure is typical for profitable industries: Nintendo, in 1990, earned profits of $350 million on sales of $2.5 billion. Such profits attract competition; therefore, Nintendo later found it difficult to maintain its 80 percent share of the market.[3]

Sony decided to enter the market with an even more advanced technology machine, the Sony PlayStation, which used 32-bit graphics and played games from a CD-ROM. These two features allowed for more complex and faster games with breathtaking graphics, colors, and sound. Again, because Nintendo was slow to introduce a newer-technology machine, Sony was able to gain considerable market share with its Sony PlayStation. This competitive edge continued with Sony's next generation PlayStation 2 (PS2).

Large profits also attracted Microsoft's attention, which saw the video game system as a source of profits as well as an avenue to attract new consumers into a networked gaming world. Microsoft's Xbox was launched at considerable investment—and with the likelihood of large initial losses as it attempted to play catch-up with Sony and Nintendo.

By 2003, video game industry revenues in the United States exceeded revenues from movie ticket sales. Sony had about 60 percent of the video game consoles in the world, with the remaining 40 percent split nearly equally between Microsoft and Nintendo.

The computer gaming business is a fascinating example of how technology and marketing can interact to form a profitable worldwide consumer-oriented industry and how technological and environmental changes can threaten market leadership. Evolving customer needs, competition, and technological change led to the successive market leadership of first Atari, then Nintendo, Sega, and Sony, followed by Microsoft, which made a large investment with the next technology cycle of network gaming.[4]

Disney with a Foreign Accent

With Disney characters such as Mickey Mouse having been shown in movies and cartoons all over the world for 50 years, Tokyo Disneyland was a logical creation. It began in 1983 as a joint venture between Mitsui Real Estate Development and Keisei Railway companies. The Walt Disney Company, however, had no ownership share; it designed the amusement park and it supplies its managerial expertise, receiving in return royalties of 10 percent of gate and 5 percent of concessions.

With this foreign success, Disney expanded into Europe. Construction of Euro Disneyland began in the summer of 1989, 20 miles east of Paris, at a cost of $2.8 billion for the first phase. The Paris location was chosen, in part, because 109 million people lived within a six-hour drive and because, as part of the deal, France agreed to build a high-speed train between the theme park and Paris (with travel time estimates of just 30 minutes each way). Unlike its stake in Tokyo Disneyland, Disney owns 49 percent, the maximum permitted by the French government.

Disney began promoting the Disney characters with French corporate partners such as Renault and Banque Nationale de Paris. Disney also started a Disney Channel on European television in a joint venture with media entrepreneur Rupert Murdoch and aired Disney entertainment specials in Europe. Disney even adapted the park to reflect European culture. Fantasyland focused on the Grimm Brothers' fairy tales and Lewis Carroll's *Alice in Wonderland*. Discoveryland focused attention on European greats such as Jules Verne, Leonardo da Vinci, and H. G. Wells. Signs are in multiple languages, and employees are expected to speak at least two languages.

In its first year of operation, attendance at Euro Disney was about 20 percent lower than targeted. High European admission prices (about 30 percent higher than at Walt Disney World in Orlando), recession in Europe, and roads blocked by protesting farmers have been cited as some reasons for lower-than-planned attendance. Disney also encountered some labor problems because French workers were less willing to comply with stringent Disney standards pertaining to dress, hairstyle, and general appearance.

Euro Disney opened to high hopes in April 1992, but it incurred continual losses for the next three years prior to registering a minuscule profit of 2 million French francs before extraordinary gains on a debt restructuring.

Why did this park perform poorly when Disneyland operations in the United States and Japan were so successful? Reasons include (1) location—a 20-minute train ride from Paris with little else in the area to hold tourists' interest and cold weather much of the year; (2) relatively high prices; (3) a limited number of rides, allowing tourists to go through the park in a day and providing them with little incentive to stay overnight at Disney-owned hotels; (4) little cultural adaptation to familiar childhood characters (Goofy in the United States versus Asterix in France) and a ban on wine sales (later rescinded); and (5) a European recession that resulted in a decrease in the number of visitors (attendance dropped from around 9.8 million in the first year to 8.8 million from 1993 to 1994, with about 9 million in the third year of operation). The Disney Corporation also learned that tourists preferred to bring their meals as picnic lunches rather than purchase fast food and that few customers bought souvenirs. This meant that attendees spent less per person at Euro Disney than at the firm's other parks. Competitors also emerged, such as Blackpool Pleasure Beach, Tivoli Gardens in Copenhagen, and Anheuser-Busch's Port Aventura in the sunnier climate near Barcelona, Spain.[5]

For all of these reasons, the highly leveraged amusement park, with over $3.4 billion in debt, incurred over $750 million in losses its first three years and was forced to restructure its operations. Disney had spent heavily on creating a hotel complex around the park outside of Paris. However, since the park was only a short train ride away from the center of Paris, many tourists avoided staying at park hotels, opting instead to combine a day trip to the park with a hotel stay in Paris. This is quite unlike Orlando, where Disney is the major attraction and tourists, principally Americans, seem to enjoy planning their holidays around entertainment provided by Disney.

Walt Disney, the parent company of Euro Disney, attempted a variety of cost-cutting strategies in the 1990s and early part of this century, including postponing expansions, deferring royalty payments, lowering admission prices, reducing hotel rates, and cutting costs. Yet French labor laws made it difficult to reduce costs by cutting the work force. (Plans were to reduce the number of workers from 17,000 to about 12,000.)

In 2002, the $600 million Walt Disney Studio Park opened; but as with the original theme park, attendance figures and profits were much lower than expected. Among other things, Disney had incorrectly forecasted that a large number of Germans would vacation at the park. Moreover, the timing of the grand opening took place just six months after the September 11, 2001, terrorist attacks, which discouraged travel from other European locations. Losses through mid-2004 increased to $134 million, and the firm accumulated $2.7 million in debt. As part of a refinancing deal by Euro Disney creditors, Disney initiated a second round of restructuring in 2004.

The European market has been tough on the theme park industry. Besides Disney, Universal Studios and Six Flags have encountered similar difficulties.[6]

Profiting from the Newly Rich

To succeed in international marketing, one must form as well as understand consumers' tastes in different countries. Dickson Poon of Hong Kong has made a fortune estimated at over $1 billion by selling luxury brand-name goods to the newly rich from Japan and the fast-growing countries of Southeast Asia; namely, Hong Kong, Malaysia, Singapore, South Korea, and Taiwan. While working as an apprentice in Geneva at Chopard, a jeweler and maker of fine watches, Poon absorbed the ambience of high-fashion, high-price retailing. Stores were understated, refined, and luxurious; and there was no hard sell. Poon took this style back to Hong Kong, opening a European-type store in Hong Kong's most upscale shopping center. He emphasized attentive service and carefully selected merchandise, concentrating on brands such as Chopard, Rolex, Hermes, and Audemars Piguet. The concept worked. Poon then obtained the Charles Jourdan fashion franchise (adding names such as Polo/Ralph Lauren and Guy Laroche) and, in some cases, obtained licensing rights to manufacture and distribute franchise products in the Far East (and worldwide). Poon's signature is an elegant shop in a prime location; he now operates over 70 such stores. But his winning insight is the appeal of famous brand names to newly rich customers. About one-third of Poon's sales are to traveling Japanese businesspeople and tourists. In November 1987, he purchased S. T. Dupont, which makes luxury lighters and pens. Poon's aim was to use the Dupont name to introduce new lines of menswear, luggage, and watches. His business is vanity, making a profit from it wherever it can be found.[7]

The Asian economic crisis that began in June 1997 hurt retail sales all across Asia, and Dickson Poon was no exception. Sales dropped sharply as the newly rich lost their assets in the stock market and were threatened with job losses and recession. Even so, Poon continued to expand in Asia, developing larger stores, focusing on major brands such as Tommy Hilfiger and Ferrari, and selling off a portion of his ownership in major European luxury goods firms such as Austin Nichols (U.K.) and DuPont (France). These equity sales allowed Poon to raise capital for further expansion in Asia at a time when the economy was reeling and competitors were running for cover. What Poon was banking on was the long-term continued growth of Asia as the recession wound down and incomes started rising again and new fortunes were made. Poon continues to expand rapidly across Asia and to look for additional acquisitions, even investing in Harrods, the famed up-market U.K. retailer.[8]

Korean Furs (for Less)

Similar thinking drives the world's largest fur manufacturer, Jindo Fur Company of South Korea. Jindo's goal is to develop a chain of stores selling furs worldwide. It targets the low end of the market—furs selling under $2,000. This figure was chosen because approximately 60 percent of all fur sales are at or below that price. To sell profitably at this price, Jindo uses Korean labor and vertical integration. It buys pelts at auctions in North America, Scandinavia, and Russia. Jindo then treats and assembles the pelts in its Seoul factories before selling them in its worldwide outlets. Forty-five Jindo fur salons are located in South Korea, Hong Kong, Europe, North America, Hawaii, and Guam. Although tropical islands may seem like odd locations, Jindo markets furs to tourists on vacation.[9]

Jindo began its worldwide marketing by selling in duty-free shops to Japanese tourists and advertising in in-flight magazines. Jindo's discounted prices were appealing to Japanese tourists when compared with the high prices charged at home, as Dickson Poon also discovered. Recently, a joint venture, Jindorus, was established with Interlink of Russia. The first store opened in the Intourist Hotel in Moscow, with additional stores to be opened as the Russian economy improves. Jindo sees a huge untapped market potential for furs, but attention to costs and global marketing expansion is essential to its long-term success.

Where the Buyers Are

Sometimes foreign markets may be the only markets in which a company's products can be sold. Consider water desalination, for instance. About two-thirds of the world's water desalination plants used to convert salt water into freshwater are in Saudi Arabia. These plants use considerable energy and are expensive to run. Saudi Arabia has plentiful energy and high incomes; it is also a country

GLOBAL MARKETING

Dolls for Chinese Children

China has over 1 billion people, of whom about one-third are between the ages of 3 and 16, totaling about 375 million. Because population-control practices in China typically restricted families to one child, parents and grandparents lavish much love and attention on their only child or grandchild. Among other things, this means they are willing to splurge on toys, despite the average income of only $1,100 in 2003 (versus $37,600 in the United States). Anthony Chirico, who founded Nanuet Entertainment, had been selling to China such U.S. TV shows as G.I. Joe and Teenage Mutant Ninja Turtles. He saw an opportunity to increase his markets in China by selling Western toys, teaming up with a client who had been marketing the Robotech line of plastic figures in the United States. Chinese children traditionally played with toys made of wood and metal; and the newer, colorful plastic figures priced between $1.60 and $30.00, Chirico speculated, might be attractive to the children and their families.

The U.S. toy introduction was accompanied by an 85-episode cartoon series. Chirico began by licensing the TV cartoon show for nominal fees and by persuading the Chinese TV stations to allow his company to insert TV commercials for Robotech toys in the middle of programs. (Chirico also had to overcome the Chinese preference for showing commercials in five-minute blocks at the end of programs.) Those negotiations took three years. The programs also were dubbed in Mandarin Chinese and were attractive to Chinese stations because their themes—family values and world cooperation against aliens—were not in conflict with Chinese values. A Hong Kong-based toy company supervised production of the toys in China and distributed them. Chirico was able to convince the Chinese TV stations to start showing the Robotech cartoon series shortly after the toys went on sale in department stores.

The toys were first introduced into Shanghai and Guangdong, the most prosperous areas of China, then into other provinces. As children in Guangdong became exposed to Hong Kong TV, however, their tastes evolved to the likes of Batman. As a result, Robotech toys began to sell better in the distant provinces in northeast China, where newer fads such as Batman had yet to catch on.

continued

Chinese parents' preoccupation with their only child is not limited to buying toys. Chinese parents play English language tapes to their unborn child, hoping to give the child a head start. Later, the child might hear Tang dynasty poetry, music, and the Roman alphabet and numbers, all of which could provide Western marketers with new global marketing opportunities. As China becomes more affluent, Chinese scholars have begun to worry about the possible impact of such lavish attention on their children. A study by Kara Chan notes, with relief, that even young children are not overtly affected by materialism.

Sources: Andrew Tanzer, "China's Dolls," *Forbes*, December 21, 1992; "Study This, Baby: Chinese Fetuses Bear Heavy Course Loads," *Wall Street Journal*, February 8, 1994; Kara Chan, "Materialism among Chinese Children in Hong Kong," *International Journal of Advertising & Marketing to Children*, July 2003, Volume 4, Issue 4, pages 47–62.

Data query: http://devdata.worldbank.org/data-query; accessed January 27, 2004.

where salt water is plentiful, while freshwater is scarce. Ionics, Inc., of Watertown, Massachusetts, has built its business around water desalination, with considerable sales coming from North Africa and the Middle East, not the United States.

Where the Ideas Are

Overseas markets can also be a source of new product ideas. Environmentalists in the United States and Europe have been pushing for cleaner, less-polluting electric cars to replace gasoline-powered vehicles in order to reduce dependence on imported oil. California has even mandated that 2 percent of cars sold in 1998 and after be emission-free. The practical problem is that electric-car batteries retain only enough energy to be driven about 60 miles before requiring a recharge. A battery that promises extended ranges—180 to 250 miles—and that can be recharged in minutes rather than hours is understandably generating much excitement. One such producer is Electric Fuel, which conducted a two-year field test in Germany with the German phone and postal services, car companies Mercedes-Benz and Opel, and Siemens to help decide whether 40,000 phone and postal services delivery vehicles could switch to electric batteries. Recharging is quickly accomplished by removing spent fuel cassettes and replacing them with new ones, the used fuel cells being reprocessed chemically at regeneration plants. These batteries are also safe; Electric Fuel's zinc-air batteries, for

example, operate at ambient temperatures and use a combination of zinc, zinc oxide, and air instead of dangerous molten chemicals used in batteries from other developmental efforts.[10] Together with DaimlerChrysler, Electric Fuel successfully completed a multiyear government-funded program to demonstrate the viability of zinc-air fuel cells in an all-electric passenger taxi hybrid van.

How the World Would Like to Smell

Gillette wanted to create an "intentionally global" fragrance—that is, a line of deodorants, shaving gels, aftershave, and related products that would appeal to men in the United States and Europe. However, Carl Klumpp, Gillette's chief perfumer, knew that European men were heavier users of fragrances, starting with shower gel, then using a deodorant body spray, and perhaps finishing off with eau de toilette (similar to a light cologne). American men own cologne and aftershave but don't wear them routinely—"less than one-quarter had a killer cologne for attracting women," and most thought that the subject was too personal to discuss with friends.[11] Klumpp, who might begin the day spending 30 minutes smelling different substances for practice, decided on a citrusy chypre family of fragrances for starters; then he asked four of the world's major fragrance supply houses to come up with a formula using his preferred smell. After much testing, Gillette launched the Cool Wave line of deodorants in 1992. It and the similarly conceived and launched Wild Rain line were enormous successes in both the United States and Europe. And while Klumpp swears by his nose, he also uses a gas chromatograph to analyze the aroma molecules in different substances, making it easier to combine fragrances and to copy specific smells. Givaudan, a Swiss chemical company, undertakes regular expeditions to the rain forest in search of rare and unusual flavors and exotic aromas. In 2003, Givaudan scientists visited Madagascar and came back with 150 samples, including the scent of the previously unknown rara flower, whose aroma is combination of natural strawberry, floral, jasmine, and honeysuckle.[12]

Risks and Differences of Foreign Markets: Russia

Getting the product to the consumer can be quite a feat in emerging markets. Ben & Jerry's, the manufacturers of superpremium ice cream in unusual flavors, began a 70 percent joint venture with the company Iceverks, manufacturing and selling ice cream in Karelia, Russia, 700 miles north of Moscow. The companies deliberately waited two years before expanding into Moscow, as they did not want quality to suffer because of poor logistics and supply problems. There were shortages of refrigerated trucks, which had to be imported. Franchisees lacked freezers, and Iceverks had to sell or lease equipment to them so that ice cream could be kept frozen. Franchisees and their employees had to be taught to be polite to customers and to restock inventory before completely running out of certain flavors. Franchisees were selected based on personal contacts and trust. Iceverks chose a small Moscow distributor, Vessco, because key managers at the two companies had been classmates. Despite these efforts, continued Russian economic difficulties made profitable operation a distant dream, ultimately leading Ben & Jerry's to divest from their Russian venture and consider U.S. expansion instead.[13]

A somewhat different tack was taken by Mary Kay in selling cosmetics in Russia. With economic liberalization, Russian women began to seek Western cosmetics. At the same time, several Russian state-owned enterprises privatized and Russian women were often getting laid off in downsizings. These women were seeking new jobs and stable income sources. Mary Kay thus found a ready-made environment for its products—reasonably priced American cosmetics—as well as for its sales approach of multi-layered marketing. Relying on women acting as independent representatives, buying cosmetics for themselves at 40 percent off retail and then selling them in small groups of friends and acquaintances, Mary Kay found Russian women avid to take on the job of selling its products. This was particularly true since a Mary Kay representative could earn $300 to $400 a month compared to an average salary for Russian women of a little over $100 a month. Mary Kay has had to train its representatives, of course, with more experienced representatives training new recruits in areas such as understanding the quality and use of products, being well groomed, being polite and complimentary to potential clients, and doing basic bookkeeping. Representatives from more distant locales face further difficulties, having to come to Moscow to replenish their cosmetics supplies. Sales continue to grow, from US $90 million in 2000 to nearly $150 million by 2003—a whopping 40 percent increase![14]

Timken in China

Timken entered China in 1996, planning to manufacture automotive bearings in a joint venture in China and sell the output to local Chinese firms. But the company had difficulty collecting receivables from Chinese state-owned firms. Timken then attempted to sell products to foreign auto firms, which were beginning to locate and manufacture in China. But the 1997 Asian financial crisis and low volumes led Timken to re-examine its strategy.

International Marketing: Planning Upstream and Downstream Linkages

*T*ate & Lyle (T&L), *a UK-based food multinational that specializes in ingredients such as sugar, starches, proteins, and animal feed, is constantly scouring the world for new sources of supply. T&L had experience in sugar manufacturing around the world and had worked with joint ventures in Thailand and China. When the firm identified Vietnam as a new Asian source for sugarcane and saw the potential for increasing local demand (for growing consumption of products such as soft drinks), management agreed that it would be a good place to expand its sugar operations. Another factor was the Vietnamese government's interest in expanding domestic sugar operations so the nation would become self-sufficient in sugar, rather than rely on imports.*

T&L placed great importance on careful site selection for its sugar refinery, with the goal of locating plants close to local cane growers. It chose a remote location inside Vietnam, the central Nghe An province, because of suitable soil and large-acreage farms. But Nghe An had few good roads, and few farmers had experience growing sugarcane. The farmers were reluctant to plant sugarcane until T&L had built its factory, then waited until other farmers planted the new crop. Despite these difficulties, T&L was able to convince enough farmers to plant sugarcane. However, a drought in the initial year of production lowered yields and meant another setback, resulting in the factory operating at just over 5 percent of capacity (65,000 tons compared to a target of 1.1 million tons).

continued

The company decided to begin manufacturing in China for export, sending 70 percent of output to Europe. The goal was eventually to export 100 percent of production. At the same time, Chinese economic growth and equipment needs in manufacturing allowed Timken to begin importing newer technology products for sale in China, with the potential for after-sales service and revenues. Strategic flexibility in response to performance shortfalls and the changing environment were key to Timken's gradual success.

T&L obtained a loan from the International Finance Corporation (IFC) of $50 million. It designed a highly automated refinery, with quality and throughput in mind. The firm had to continuously work on developing relationships with farmers, who wanted cash on delivery, not staggered payments as was T&L's custom. T&L adapted, though, and paid cash on delivery of the sugarcane. It also developed software to help farmers decide when crops should be harvested, when fields should be fertilized, and where to plant improved seedlings. The farmers had to be persuaded to accept such advice. In running its operations, it used few expatriates, preferring to train local management.

Source: "Tate & Lyle Is Well Placed in Vietnam," *Wall Street Journal*, May 5, 2004.

Piracy Lives On!

William Tay, owner of the Hye Mieko, saw his ship leave Singapore, headed for Cambodia with photographic supplies and general cargo. He lost contact with the ship when it was about 180 nautical miles from Cambodia. Already having had another ship hijacked and $2 million of cargo stolen, he hired a Lear jet to search for his ship. Searching in international waters off the coast of China, he found the ship 60 miles from Vietnam. The ship, which seemed to have a naval vessel in its wake, did not respond to signals; so Tay took pictures and flew to Shanwei, 120 kilometers from Hong Kong, where the ship was expected to land. The hope was that the Chinese authorities would help recover the ship and its cargo. China launched a campaign against sea pirates and in 1994 alone, investigated 209 cases of piracy, recovering 22 ships.[15] The problem is a continued headache for shippers, with the International Maritime Bureau reporting a 37 percent increase to 234 pirate attacks worldwide in the first six months of 2003, compared to 171 in the corresponding period in 2002.[16]

Learning from the Examples

Companies market their products internationally for several reasons:

- They want to take advantage of the potential of world markets. Nintendo, Disney, the Japanese motorcycle industry, and Jindo Furs have all benefited from expanding their foreign market potential.
- They want to diversify geographically.
- They want to use excess production capacity and

take advantage of a low-cost position due to experience-curve economies and economies of scale. The Japanese motorcycle industry's thrust into the United States was aided greatly by its superior low-cost position.

- A product can be near the end of its life cycle in the domestic market while just beginning to generate growth abroad. Dickson Poon's export of brand-name luxury goods to the Far East is an example of taking advantage of the general rise in conspicuous consumption that accompanies prosperity. Selling Robotech toys to China is an example of responding to lagging product cycles in developing countries.
- Sometimes overseas markets are a source of new products and ideas. Companies in foreign markets can become joint-venture partners, providing capital and market access.
- Tested market entry methods can work in emerging markets, as shown by Mary Kay in Russia. Emerging markets, however, require patience and sometimes innovative market entry modes, as in the case of Ben & Jerry's in Russia. International marketing can bring expected risks, such as international currency risk, but also unexpected risks, such as piracy in the China Sea.
- One of the most difficult aspects of international marketing is developing products with universal appeal, as illustrated by Disney. Success in one country does not always translate to success in another country, as Euro Disney illustrates. In the face of competition from video games, LEGO is faced with trying to make its bricks appealing to children in the Far East.
- Any successful international marketing effort will attract competition. Nintendo has seen its 90 percent video game market share erode as competitors innovate with new products, price cutting, alliances, and persistence.
- There are many ways to enter foreign markets, as the examples suggest, ranging from simple exporting to more complex and risky investments involving manufacturing, marketing, and top management.

The U.S. Firm in the Global Marketplace

Although the global market is attractive, U.S. firms have been slow to take advantage of it. The United States has always been one of the world's largest markets. It is also a self-contained, continent-sized market. For about 30 years after World War II, little foreign competition existed in the United States. Today, however, foreign firms from all over the world vie for a piece of the U.S. market. At the same time, other countries have grown so fast and become so prosperous that their markets have become more attractive than the U.S. market. An example is the fax machine, which grew rapidly in Japan before becoming popular in the United States as the Japanese market was reaching saturation. Likewise, the market for railroad cars is small in the United States as compared to Europe, where train transportation is more popular. Also, the building of nuclear power plants in the United States has become strictly regulated, even though foreign countries readily accept them as a source of energy.

Ignoring foreign markets and foreign competition presents two risks for U.S. companies: losing market share at home and not profiting from higher growth in overseas markets. These dual pressures have led more and more to the establishment of multinational corporations, as defined below.

Export Sales versus Sales from Foreign Subsidiaries

Larger U.S. firms have generally been able to participate in global marketing due to their superior financial and managerial resources. Table 1-4 lists **multinational companies** with significant foreign sales from their overseas operations. For the purposes of this text, a **multinational corporation** (MNC) is one in which the company manufactures and markets its products or services in several countries. Almost every company on the list finds it more efficient to sell from their foreign manufacturing subsidiaries than through exports. In addition, exports, strictly defined, may have no chance to succeed because they are too highly priced in relation to local competition or they are kept out by government barriers. Most of the firms on the list could not maintain their market share in foreign markets without establishing a foreign subsidiary.

The question of how much a firm should obtain from foreign revenues and how much it should export is unresolved. As market conditions and the product life cycle change, companies may find that effective selling overseas requires foreign subsidiaries and that such foreign subsidiary sales may replace exports over time.

Importance of Foreign Direct Investment (FDI)

Companies can generate international sales from exporting or by selling goods made by their subsidiaries in foreign countries. As a method of market entry, foreign sales subsidiaries or foreign manufacturing facilities are preferred over other alternatives for a variety of reasons:

- To lower costs, such as manufacturing expenses, by using cheaper inputs such as labor (*outsourcing* is a familiar term for this strategy); to lower distribution costs by shortening the number of channels; and to reduce transportation costs by shortening the distance that products or components need to be shipped
- To get around trade barriers, such as tariffs, by manufacturing locally or bypassing government disincentives, such as *buy local* or *buy member* legislation (as one might see among members of NAFTA [North American Free Trade Agreement] and the EU [European Union])
- To serve customers better by learning about local needs through closer contact
- To forgo at least some foreign exchange risk by off-

Table 1-4. Foreign Sales of Major MNCs, 2003

Company	Total Sales ($ billions)	Foreign Sales ($ billions)	Foreign Sales as a % of Total Sales (%)
Wal-Mart Stores	256.3	47.6	18.6
BP (U.K.)	232.6	184.7	79.4
General Motors	185.5	51.6	27.8
DaimlerChrysler (Germany)	171.9	142.0	82.6
Ford Motor	138.4	54.8	39.6
General Electric	134.2	60.8	45.0
Total (France)	131.6	105.6	80.2
Toyota Motor (Japan)	129.0	73.9	57.3
ChevronTexaco	120.0	64.2	53.5
Carrefour Group (France)	96.9	47.5	49.0
Allianz Worldwide (Germany)	96.9	67.8	70.0
ING Group (Netherlands)	94.7	71.0	75.0

Source: Forbes 2000—The World's Leading Companies, 2004; company web sites and annual reports (for complete list, see Instructor materials).

setting foreign income with foreign liabilities (for example, using local sales to purchase local supplies)

Table 1-5 shows foreign direct investment (FDI) flows, which provide some indication of the level of firm market entry activity via FDI, as a result of either foreign sales facilities or foreign manufacturing facilities. Note that most of the FDI goes to rich or developed nations, which number fewer than 50 countries, rather than the 150 developing nations. When looking at the FDI inflow among the top ten host nations, note the figures on China (both the People's Republic of China and Hong Kong), which is considered a developing nation.

Table 1-5. Foreign Direct Investment Inflows

Country	1998 ($ billions)	2001 ($ billions)
World	694.5	735.1
Developed Nations	484.2	503.1
United States	103.4	124.4
United Kingdom	33.2	53.8
France	23.2	52.6
Netherlands	11.1	50.5
Germany	12.2	31.8
Developing Nations	187.6	204.8
China, PRC	44.2	46.8
Mexico	14.0	24.7
China, Hong Kong	11.4	22.8
Brazil	19.0	22.5
Poland	4.9	8.8

Sources: Foreign Direct Investment Inflows in Country Groups (http://www.unctad.org/Templates/WebFlyer.asp?intItemID=2111&lang=1); accessed July 22, 2004; Top Ten Foreign Direct Investment Host Economies in 2001 (http://www.unctad.org/Templates/WebFlyer.asp?intItem ID=2087&lang=1); accessed July 22, 2004; United Nations Conference on Trade and Development (UNCTAD).

The Role of the Internet in Reshaping International Marketing

The Internet impacts strategic marketing decisions about promotion, physical distribution, pricing, and the product... the "4P's" of marketing. It also impacts all communication among a firm's employees, its customers, its suppliers, and other stakeholders. For example, with respect to physical distribution, web sites provide firms with a nonstore retail outlet and provide retailers with a wholesale outlet. The Internet can also be a means of product delivery in the case of electronic or digitized products such as music, video, and software. Strategic decisions about promotion are also affected by the Internet. When promoting products, firms need to decide when to place advertisements. (Why do windshield wiper ads air on the

GLOBAL MARKETING

LEGO and Strategic Adaptation

LEGO comes from the Danish words leg godt, or "play nicely." LEGO toys seem out of place in today's world of video games, where putting together colorful little plastic bricks to build castles appears childish. But LEGO, founded in 1949, thrives, perhaps, because young children use their imagination and build pirate ships, bridges, and fortresses. Parents also like LEGOs, finding the toy wholesome and considering it something they might have played with when they were children. In fact, LEGO found that about 13 percent of LEGO sets in the Netherlands were bought for use by adults! About 80 percent of all children who play with LEGOs are boys. The company has been experimenting with pastel colors and themes that appeal more to girls, such as dollhouses and nurseries. (See http://www.lego.com/scala.) Its recent line, Clickits, is aimed squarely at girls. As explained by Raymond Hastings, LEGO's marketing research manager: "Clikits fits into girls' interests and their desire to control their immediate surroundings. It is open-ended, process-oriented and consistent with Lego's principles of appealing to people's creativity."

The newer Mindstorm line incorporates motors and batteries and computer chips inside the familiar LEGO bricks so that creations can be programmed and made to spring into action. Robots are the logical and latest evolution of these trends.

LEGO, which is a privately owned and secretive company, is enormously profitable. Its Danish-registered companies

continued

radio only when it is raining?) Advertising—information about products, services, etc.—is available all of the time. Geography is no longer a problem. (Compare Internet advertising to billboards; for example, a billboard on Route 76 is not seen by people on Route 23.) As long as a server is running and connected to the Internet, anyone can view the material on a web page, regardless of location. Promotion via the Internet can act as mass personal selling, where the communication is tailored to the individual. The technology exists to personalize information for each viewer (My MSN page, for example).

Internet marketing is more interactive than other avenues, with consumers and nonconsumers having the power and control to select what they see; to compare prod-

alone show profits after taxes of around $70 million on sales of about $900 million. LEGO has another 23 companies registered outside Denmark, about which information is scant. However, LEGO is finding that markets in Europe and the United States are mature. A lower-priced U.S. competitor, K'NEX, in partnership with Hasbro, had gained share. LEGO has naturally turned to the East, with sales in Japan growing 14 percent and sales in Korea growing 50 percent (though from a small base). As families in India and China reach middle class, LEGO hopes they, too, will buy the bricks. Counterfeiting is a problem, though, as the bricks are easy to copy and the lower prices appeal to the generally lower-income consumers in Asia.

LEGO's LEGOLAND theme park near its Billund, Denmark, headquarters opened in 1968 and attracts a million visitors a year. The park features miniature versions of famous landmarks, such as the Statue of Liberty, as well as animals and rides—all built from LEGO bricks. More recently, LEGO built a theme park near Windsor Castle in London, called LEGOLAND Windsor, which is entirely made of LEGO bricks. The park is aimed at children 2 to 13 years old and stresses that learning is fun. For example, guests "ride" in cars built out of LEGO bricks and focus on learning responsible driving. A similar theme park opened in 1999 in California.

Sources: C. Darwent, "Lego's Billion-Dollar Brickworks," *Management Today*, September 1995; "LEGO Interlocks Toy Bricks, Theme Parks," *Wall Street Journal*, December 27, 1994; "Playing Well with Others," *Technology Review*, May 15, 1998; Greg Johnson, "Legoland Contented to Build Slowly; New Theme Park Not Billing Itself as Rival to Bigger Neighbors," *Los Angeles Times*, December 17, 1998; Ruth Mortimer, "Building a brand out of bricks," *Brand Strategy*, April 2003; Ravi Chandiramani, "Lego Moves In on The Girls' Market," *Marketing* (UK), February 13, 2003.

uct, price, and delivery offerings among competitors quickly and easily; and to have access to a broader set of alternatives in nearly every product category. (Firms must put a lot of information on the Web and make it easily accessible, allowing consumers to pick and choose.) Consumers rely on the Internet as a search tool in large part because it is cheaper, it is less time-consuming, and it offers a broader assortment than conducting a search by driving around or calling or writing companies with questions. Consumers can become better informed (or ill-informed depending on the source) quicker. Consumer power comes from the ability to direct the message received.

Segmentation may be more difficult, but that is changing as technologies allow computer users to deter-

mine who is accessing information on their computer.

The Internet can be used to collect and disseminate vast amounts of information. Collection of information on people who are connected to the Internet is under constant scrutiny for ethical and moral reasons. Controls and guidelines are being developed and refined regularly.

Companies must incorporate their domain name, which is a firm's URL (Internet address), into their branding strategy. No one wants to key in an address such as http://www.getabettermousetrapforlessmoney.com. Consumers must also be able to find a company's web site easily, using search engines, which is partly a function of design (meta tags, for instance). Locating a site easily also has to do with how useful people find the site—the more a site is referenced, the more likely it is to be near the top of search engine results.

Despite the claim that promotion via the Internet is relatively cheap compared with other methods, it is costly to design, upgrade, and maintain a web presence. Small companies do compete more directly with large firms. However, with their limited resources, small companies must spend the necessary time, energy, and money to design an effective web site that is easy to navigate, that is stimulating, and that provides the content consumers are seeking. Bulk e-mail may be cheaper to send than bulk land-based mail, but carefully designing the message and harvesting or purchasing e-mail addresses is not cost-free.

Consumers can also use the Internet as a tool to extol or vilify a company, the company's products, or the company's actions using chatrooms and discussion forums. People are able to gain access to a broad population almost instantaneously. This complicates the public relations aspect of marketers' responsibilities. The Internet allows people to test the boundaries of freedom of speech and good taste, whether they are posting their opinions about vendors or DVDs.

Market research opportunities go beyond sending e-mail messages to customers, asking about new features or products. Virtual malls and stores can be created to simulate certain live conditions and to perform experiments while controlling many exogenous variables not possible in a real-world setting. Marketers can use white boards, discussion groups, and chat rooms to elicit opinions and advice from people around the globe, making the research as anonymous as people like (which tends to affect the types of responses that market researchers get).

The Internet permits businesses to expand consignment-like models, which means they can offer a broader product line to consumers. For example, Amazon.com sells books and DVDs that it carries in its own inventory, but it also allows others to advertise and sell books and DVDs. (Amazon collects and forwards the charges for the merchandise, shipping, and handling and provides a measure of warranty about the other sellers.) While the Internet allows consumers to "shop the world," it also allows businesses to form vast geographic areas in which to combine resources in a synergistic manner. Amazon. com quickly expanded from being a seller of books to a company in the entertainment business to a firm that fulfills a variety of shopping needs.

International Marketing: The Trade Barrier of the Mind

As its trade deficit shows, the United States lags behind other nations in the general level of export trade activity. This poses a question: How does a U.S. firm approach overseas markets? The answer is, in many cases, reluctantly.

A statement made nearly two decades ago by Kenneth Butterworth, chair of Loctite Corporation, still holds true for far too many U.S. managers. Mr. Butterworth said that "the problem really lies in the mind. That is the greatest trade barrier in America."[17] In other words, long insularity and overdependence on the American market have made American firms unsure about their ability to capture markets overseas. Culture, language, and environmental differences are sometimes intimidating. Firms from other countries, however, have overcome such differences, and many U.S. companies are following suit.

Due to continued U.S. trade deficits, small- and medium-sized businesses are being urged, both at the federal and state levels, to export. They can get help by signing up for trade missions sponsored by the U.S. Department of Commerce and other organizations. Export finance is available to carry export receivables for longer periods and to offer favorable interest rate financing. The large number of foreigners and immigrants hired by these companies helps them learn about opportunities in foreign markets, as well as efficient ways to approach the markets. A weaker dollar also makes exporting easier. From its peak in 1985, the dollar declined by 60 percent in 1995 against currencies such as the yen, the German mark, and the Swiss franc before appreciating once again through 1997. Dollar depreciation makes U.S. products more competitive and allows U.S. firms to raise prices while offering goods and services priced lower than those of foreign competitors. The dollar began depreciating again by the end of 2001, losing about one-third of its value in relation to the yen and the euro by October 2003.

Ultimately, international marketing is a matter of perspective. The term *global marketing* best captures this perspective of the world as a market, with individual countries being submarkets. For those companies that hold such a view, the distinction between domestic and international marketing disappears and the focus is on market opportunities, wherever they may be.

The Approach of This Book

The sources of the differences between international and domestic marketing are to be found not in the functions themselves, but in the parameters that determine how the functions are performed. Therefore, students of international marketing should be able to identify the relevant parameters and understand how they affect the marketing program. This book assumes that readers have that ability from their background in other marketing courses. Part 1 discusses the world environment in which international marketing is practiced. Part 2 analyzes the management of marketing in this multinational context. Part 3 deals with planning and coordinating the international marketing program.

Part 1: International Environment (Chapters 1–6)

In domestic business studies, consideration of the environment plays a critical though somewhat unrecognized role in the behavior of a firm. A number of "environmental" courses deal with topics such as business and society, business and government, business conditions, and business law. In the functional courses, too, much attention is paid to the external environment of the firm. Marketing, for example, discusses buyer behavior, demographic trends, competition, laws regulating pricing and promotion, developments in retailing, etc. Technology (and in particular, the Internet) is changing customer/ firm relationships. Networks facilitate communication for the firm and all of its constituents. The global environment involves similar issues, but it is broader and more complex because of interactions among nations. The global environment, its impact on marketing, and the way marketing affects the global environment are the focus of Part 1.

Part 2: Global Marketing Management (Chapters 7–13)

The various functions of marketing as they are performed in the international environment are discussed in Part 2. An examination of the problems peculiar to international marketing should also help broaden students' general understanding of marketing. The foreign environment dealt with in Part 1 is seen as the key variable in international marketing. A large part of the discussion centers on international marketing by manufacturers. However, the specific international marketing problems of service industries are covered in Part 2. In addition, Part 2 stresses the importance of an overall marketing strategy to shape and guide the formulation and implementation of specific international marketing tasks.

Part 3: Coordination and Control of International Marketing (Chapters 14–15)

A second critical international aspect of marketing management, covered in Part 3, is the task of integrating and coordinating many individual national marketing programs into an effective multinational operation. This section discusses and illustrates (with many examples) the strategy and marketing practices of large multinational firms. However, small firms are not excluded. Using the Internet, even the smallest of firms are reaching into the global marketplace. Simply by posting their web sites, firms allow people, wherever they are located, to learn about their company and their products. Much of the discussion applies to small as well as large firms.

Summary

As foreign economies continue to grow and account for a larger portion of the total world market and as foreign competitors actively seek market share in the United States, many U.S. firms are being forced into some degree of international marketing. More and more, this has led to the establishment of multinational corporations, defined as those firms which may extend to manufacturing, carrying out joint ventures with local partners, licensing, importing, and taking part in countertrade transactions. The varied strengths of foreign competitors, the ramifications of dealing with different national governments, and economic and cultural differences in foreign markets contribute to the complexity of international marketing.

Companies compete globally because (1) strong market potential exists overseas; (2) international sales allow them to enhance their long-run profitability; (3) low-cost production and quality are critical to competing successfully in global markets; and (4) they can achieve success by carefully choosing certain market segments, as witnessed by Dickson Poon's success in profitably marketing luxury goods to the growing numbers of newly rich in the Far East.

Large multinationals are likely to get more of their foreign revenues through sales of their foreign subsidiaries than through exports. This can be a key element of strategic success in international marketing. More important, though, is a global marketing perspective of the world as one market, with individual countries treated as submarkets and a focus on exploiting market opportunities wherever they occur.

Questions and Research

1.1 What is international marketing? How does it differ from domestic marketing?

1.2 Why is international marketing important to most firms?

1.3 Consider the examples described in the section "The Global Marketplace." Compare and contrast the international marketing actions of the firms discussed. Focus on their choices in the areas of products, market segments, the sequential choice of countries to sell to, pricing, the growth of and response to competition, and the use of licensing and joint ventures.

1.4 How do large U.S. multinationals compete in the global marketplace? Why do most of them sell more from their foreign subsidiaries than through exports?

1.5 "The greatest trade barrier to exporting lies in the mind." Explain that statement.

1.6 "Global marketing is a shift in perspective." Explain this statement.

1.7 Choose a prominent publicly held company in your geographic area. Find out what its total foreign revenues have been for the past five years and how much of its foreign sales come from overseas operations and how much come from exporting from the home market. Also study the comments about international markets made by the chair of the company in its annual report. How important is international marketing to this firm?

Endnotes

1. The World Bank, *2004 World Development Indicators*, NY, 2004, page 303.

2. Kashani, K. "Marketing Futures: Priorities for a Turbulent Environment," *Long-Range Planning*, Volume 28, Issue 4, 1995, pages 87–98.

3. "Just Like the Computer Games It Sells, Nintendo Defies Persistent Challengers," *Wall Street Journal*, June 27, 1989; "Atari Tests Technology's Antitrust Aspect," *Wall Street Journal*, December 14, 1988.

4. See Wilson, Johnny. "Bad Moon Rising: A Primer on PC Game Industry Myopia," *Computer Gaming*, January 1999; "Nintendo Unveils 64-bit Game Player in Bid to Top Sony, Sega CD Machines," *Wall Street Journal*, November 27, 1995; "Older Machines Win Video-Game Crowd," *Wall Street Journal*, December 26, 1995; "3-D Video Games: The Next Generation," *Business Week*, October 16, 1995; "Nightmare in the Fun House," *Financial World*, February 21, 1995; "Sega," *Business Week*, February 21, 1994; "Sony's Big Bazooka," *Fortune*, December 30, 2002; "A Grown-up's Guide to Games," *Wall Street Journal*, November 21, 2002; Dean Takahashi, *Inside the Xbox*, Prima, 2002.

5. "Step Right Up, Monsieur," *New York Times*, August 23, 1995.

6. See "Euro Disney's Fiscal Loss to Spur Study of Woes by U.S. Concern," *Wall Street Journal*, July 9, 1993; "Euro Disney's Loss Narrowed

in Fiscal 1994," *Wall Street Journal*, November 4, 1994; "Euro Disney's Prince Charming?" *Business Week*, June 13, 1994; "A Faint Squeak from Euro-Mickey," *The Economist*, July 29, 1995; "Euro Disney Posts First Annual Profit," *Wall Street Journal*, November 16, 1995; "California; For Struggling Euro Disney, Help from Abroad," *Los Angeles Times*, June 10, 2004; "Disney Gives Plans to Aid European Parks," *New York Times*, July 1, 2004.

7. Tanzer, Andrew. "Keep the Calculators Out of Sight," *Forbes*, March 20, 1989; Lucas, Louise, "Dickson Concepts Faces Loss As Recession Bites," *Financial Times*, December 11, 1998.

8. "Dickson on Lookout after Big Profit Rise," *Hong Kong IMail*, June 24, 2003; "Dickson in $100m Expansion," *Hong Kong IMail*, August 27, 2003.

9. "Jindo to Set its Export Goal," *Korea Economic Daily*, December 8, 1994.

10. "Electric Fuel of Israel Poised to Draw Two More European Concerns to Project," *Wall Street Journal*, May 30, 1995.

11. "Thank Carl Klumpp for the Swell Smell of Right Guard," *Wall Street Journal*, May 11, 1995.

12. Black, Jane. "It's All in the Nose (and Tongue)," Businessweekonline. com, July 8, 2003.

13. "Ben & Jerry's Is Trying to Smooth out Distribution in Russia As It Expands," *Wall Street Journal*, September 9, 1995; The History of Ben & Jerry's Ice Cream (http://www.benjerry.com/our_company/about_us/ our_history/timeline/index.cfm); Unilever Company History (http:// www.unilever.com/company/unilevertoday).

14. "For Mary Kay Sales Reps in Russia, Hottest Shade Is the Color of Money," *Wall Street Journal*, August 30, 1995; "Mary Kay's Eastern Front," Forbes.com, September 13, 2003; Mary Kay, Russia (http://www.marykay.ru).

15. "Owner Hires Plane for Search and Spots Vessel," *Straits Times* (Singapore), June 27, 1995.

16. Marine Watch Keeps Straits Safe," *New Straits Times-Management Times*, August 5, 2003; Hodge, Neil, "Attacks by Sea Pirates Up Markedly This Year," *Business Insurance*, July 28, 2003, Volume 37, Issue 30.

17. "You Don't Have to Be a Giant to Score Overseas," *Business Week*, April 13, 1987.

Further Readings

Cateora, Philip and John L. Graham. *International Marketing*, 12th edition. Boston: McGraw-Hill/Irwin, 2005.

Jeannet, Jean-Pierre and H. David Hennessey. *Global Marketing Strategies*, 6th edition. Boston: Houghton Mifflin, 2004.

Kaynak, Erdener, editor. *Strategic Global Marketing: Issues and Trends.* New York: International Business Press, 2002.

Kotler, Philip, Dipak C. Jain, and Suvit Maesincee. *Marketing Moves: A New Approach to Profits, Growth, and Renewal.* Boston: Harvard Business School Press, 2002.

Ricks, David. *Blunders in International Business*, 3rd edition. Oxford, UK; Malden, MA: Blackwell Publishing, 1999.

Ronkainen, Ilkka A. and Michael R. Czinkota, editors. *Best Practices in International Marketing.* Fort Worth, TX: Harcourt College Publishers, 2002.

Shanklin, William L. and David A Griffith. "Crafting Strategies for Global Marketing in the New Millennium." *Business Horizons*, September–October 1996, pages 11–16.

Terpstra, Vern and Lloyd C. Russow. *International Dimensions of Marketing*, 4th edition. Cincinnati, OH: South-Western College Publishing, 2000.

Wind, Yoram (Jerry) and Vijay Mahajan with Robert E. Gunther. *Convergence Marketing: Running With the Centaurs.* Upper Saddle River, NJ: Financial Times, Prentice Hall, 2002.

Case 1.1

AGRO INDUSTRIA EXPORTADORA S.A. (AI)

Agro Industria Exportadora S.A. (AI) was founded in 1973. Its original owners were from Zamora and Michoacan, in Mexico; and they planned to buy agricultural produce and process it for sale, using labor-intensive processes. AI's operations, employing as many as 450 people, lasted until 1982. During this early period, the founding partners invited Mr. Gonzalez, from Guadalajara, to join the company as manager. Over time, he received an ownership interest; and in 1978, he decided to buy out the original owners, a process that was completed in 1982. At this point, however, the Mexican economy was in a perilous state, with the peso heavily devalued after a long period of being tied to the dollar at a fixed parity of 12.5 per dollar. The difficult economic situation led Mr. Gonzalez to cease operations.

However, given Mexico's potential in agriculture and agribusiness, IFC, which is a division of the World Bank, decided to make agribusiness investments in Mexico. IFC invited a Mexican national, Mr. Ojeda, who was also a director of Banamex, to become involved in such a venture. He, in turn, contacted Mr. Gonzalez to restart operations, with a greater focus on exporting.

The reborn company slowly progressed; and in 1986, Mr. Ojeda quit Banamex to become a partner in the company, with additional investment from the venture capital arm of Banamex. The company decided to focus on exporting frozen vegetables and sought another partner, Mr. Polari, a big grower of vegetables. Mr. Polari's association with the company lasted three years, until 1989, when he sold his share in the company. By then, AI had its ownership divided as follows: Mr. Gonzalez held 25 percent, Mr. Ojeda had 35 percent, and an investor from Mexico City held the balance. IFC, which had held an ownership stake in the company during its difficult years, sold out, as was its custom once the company stabilized and did not require continued IFC capital or support.

Initially, the company had canned Anaheim chilies for export to the United States. Once the United States opened its market to the import of fresh Mexican chilies, however, prices shot up and selling canned chilies was no longer viable. Hence, AI had to find another product line for its canning plant, which had started initial operations in 1987.

Mr. Gonzalez had been invited to Japan; and when scouting business opportunities there, he noticed that the Japanese were heavy users of grapefruit segments in jellies, cakes, pies, etc. He returned to Mexico, thinking that this represented a potential opportunity for AI. However, some practical problems immediately arose. Whereas chilies are high in acidity, fruit is generally low in acid and high in sugar content. As a result, cans are likely to explode easily. Hence, AI had to experiment with new canning methods and processes. However, Japanese canning technology as applied to grapefruit was not useful to AI because of differences in weather, altitude (Guadalajara is about 3,000 feet above sea level), and humidity. Further, fresh fruit is soft and has a different texture than frozen produce. Therefore, AI had to adapt its production processes. Its initial exports to Japan were of poor quality, and shipments suffered from spoilage. Consequently, AI had to request time from its Japanese clients to solve its production problems.

In 1990, AI decided to begin importing U.S. cans. The cans needed a special enamel coating to accommodate citrus products. Further, the Mexican cans oxidized easily (even before use) and were not of uniform quality, as different kinds of steel imported from Spain and Venezuela were used in production. Consequently, AI decided to import cans from Florida, even though this meant paying for transporting empty cans to be shipped to the AI plants. But the U.S. cans were of superior quality, and soon AI stopped experiencing problems with exploding cans and other problems of uneven quality. AI had learned that the Japanese were continually seeking quality improvements at continually lower prices.

At first, AI exported on an exclusive basis to the Marubeni Corporation. However, when Marubeni began lowering the quantities it purchased, AI began to seek additional Japanese distributors, including the Japanese trading companies Mitsui and Toshoku. Because AI had established a good name in Japan, it had actually been approached by Marubeni about becoming a distributor. AI's competition came from Mexico, Israel, and South Africa. AI had the best quality (or so it claimed), though its prices were slightly higher. AI thought it was too difficult to sell directly to the final Japanese consumer firms, who numbered about 50 in all: major grocery chains, food processors, and others.

AI typically processed the fruit in Mexico, packed it in cans without labels, and used a Mexican shipping line for transportation to Japan. It shipped about one container every ten days to Japan, with the final customer price about double the FOB Manzanillo price.

A critical point in export success is the quality of the produce. AI took care in its purchasing. Japanese customers wanted all of the grapefruit segments to be of the same size. Hence, AI had two people permanently stationed at the growers' sites, where they made commitments to purchase fruit at the bloom stage, picking producers based on taste, freshness, and fruit size. Once fruits were ready to pick, picking was done every day, with AI's two people supervising. Once the fruit was received, it was graded by size, with the smaller units sold off to juice firms. Only fruit of the requisite size was exported to Japan. On average, for fruit with a value of 100 pesos, transportation costs added another 120 pesos. Since the cans were destined for re-export, imported cans were stored in-bond to avoid duties. Most of the fruit exports to Japan were in #10 cans, containing 2 kilograms of product and 1 kilogram of syrup. As was to be expected, AI faced seasonal cycles and had to develop multiple fruit lines to remain busy year round. For example, in the 1992 fiscal year, AI exported the following:

Grapefruit	August–December	1.575 million pounds
Valencia oranges	January–March	1.470 million pounds
Lemons	May–August	.4 million "cell sacks"[a]

a lemon juice in lemon-shaped containers.

AI believed that it had to pick produce lines that were not chosen by its competitors. Its most recent produce addition was strawberries, with a target of 7 million pounds annually. To enter this line, AI made an agreement with Congeladora de Samora, whereby it took over operations of its factory in return for a 50-50 split of the profits. Strawberries are generally sold in 30-pound plastic pails, in Pure-Pak cartons, or in 425-pound drums for use by jam manufacturers.

Foreign Markets

AI has a U.S. food broker, World Food Sales, which it owns. World Food's sales director, a former partner of AI in its earlier incarnation, has over 30 years of experience in the frozen produce industry. AI pays a 6 percent sales commission to World Food. World Food also represents other Mexican food produce companies, such as growers of broccoli and cauliflower. Sometimes the U.S. broker served as an alternative export conduit to Japan, enabling AI to export incremental quantities if demand from its (then) exclusive distribution arrangement in Japan was low. As part of operating procedures, all sales are made on letters of credit and quotes to all international customers are priced in U.S. dollars.

In addition to Japan and the United States, AI also sells to Europe, principally to Germany. Like Japan, Germany requires quality and is willing to pay a high-er price if necessary. Mr. Gonzalez's wife is German and was instrumental in helping AI break into the German market, achieved gradually by repeated visits to the World Food Fair held every third year in Cologne. German exports are to IC Frozen Foods, the German distributor, who also exports to Sweden and Denmark, where it has representatives.

The United Kingdom is a more difficult market, as lower-quality, highly discounted products compete with AI's produce. AI has also considered Korea as a market, though a 1991 visit indicated that while AI quality was considered superior, its prices were considered high.

New Directions

AI's goal is to diversify its export markets. In 1990, its export sales were 70 percent to the United States and Canada, 25 percent to Japan, and 5 percent to Europe. In 1992, the respective percentages were 60, 30, and 10. In 1993, targeted percentages were 50, 40, and 10, respectively. AI notes that each market has peculiarities and presents a different set of challenges. For the U.S. market, AI is experimenting with new lines such as broccoli, cauliflower, romanesco (a hybrid of cauliflower and broccoli), brussels sprouts, and cucumbers (pickled and fresh). Cucumbers represent its latest success, which it buys from 92 growers who devote 205 hectares to the crop, with exports totaling 4.4 million pounds. AI is renting a plant to process cucumbers. It houses three grading machines, where the cucumbers are first sorted by size. They are then hydro-cooled; loaded onto 40-ton trailers in green plastic bags (along with 2 tons of ice); and exported at a temperature of 38 degrees to the United States, with more ice added after the trucks cross the border. The cucumbers continue on to Colorado, where they are washed, packed, and sold as fresh produce. The entire cycle averages 17 hours from receipt of cucumbers to the crossing of the border, with a total elapsed time of 24 hours to Colorado. The central, critical element is freshness.

Role of Logistics

Logistics are extremely important. AI uses the Mexican carrier Aguilas de Oro, with a handoff at the border to Middleton Trucking, which has a fleet of 110 trucks. The crossing point is Laredo, Texas, which is extremely hot. Therefore, the produce has a high risk of perishing. Success is partly a matter of minimizing transportation costs. In July and August, at the height of the cucumber pickling season, trucking rates are seasonally low due to excess capacity. Therefore, AI is able to negotiate rates averaging 1 cent per pound for ordinary cargo to Laredo and 2 cents for cooled cargo—a savings of almost 33 percent over normal tariffs. AI negotiated directly with trucking companies, choosing Middleton over competitive bids from Freymiller and Prime.

Another bottleneck is the availability of containers, but major clients such as Vlasic guarantee the availability of containers at the border. In general, it is important for AI to arrange the U.S. transportation leg with Middleton first, before closing the link by entering into a contract with its Mexican partner. An alternative is to sell cucumbers in a brine solution for pickling, with cucumbers in brine sent to the United States for further processing: washing, slicing, and then selling to clients such as McDonald's or to major pickling companies such as Vlasic Foods. In 1992, AI cucumber sales reached 2.75 million pounds of brine pickles.

For shipment to Europe, the company contracts for a certain number of containers each month to transport its products (currently 10 to 12 containers a month) on terms typically set out separately as FOB plant, plus freight, in-bond expenses, transloading, and ocean freight. In 1993, shipping estimates were for 150 containers of produce, split 70 percent broccoli and 30 percent romanesco, which is gaining a market. Three hundred tons of romanesco were shipped in 1992, with an estimated 1,000 tons shipped in 1993. Romanesco is costlier to grow, however, with a pound of seed costing $2,500, versus $200 for a pound of broccoli seed; but the potential return is greater.

Costs and Regulations

AI's food processing is labor-intensive, though seasonal. For example, the grapefruit segment preparation requires an assembly line of about 2,250 workers who cut, peel, segment, and can the grapefruit. A key is intelligent buying of raw materials, signing contracts with growers in advance, and never growing its own produce. In 1992, AI sales were $16 million, yielding a profit of $1.5 million. In 1993, sales were $27 million, with a net profit of about 8.5 percent.

Because AI is a Mexican company, capitalization is also critical, especially in export markets where working capital requirements are high. To enable AI to take a longer-term perspective on export markets, AI's partners contributed an additional $1.5 million in capital in order to reduce borrowing costs (over 30 percent on an annual basis on peso-denominated debt in Mexico).

A complication is divergent agricultural standards in different export markets. Regulations differ among countries about permissible levels of chemical additives and fertilizers. Hence, the two supervisors assigned to grower relations must monitor the farming process. AI often supplies chemicals and fertilizers to facilitate certification of additive levels in the exported produce. In addition, AI carries out the necessary inspections prior to export, as in the case of strawberries destined for the U.S. market, where permissible chemical parts per million have been lowered from .5 to .05.

Duties are a concern, as most advanced nations protect agricultural products. For example, U.S. duties have averaged 17 percent on vegetables and 14 percent on strawberries—on average, about 13 percent of shipment value. With the passage of the NAFTA, these tariffs will be lowered but will not disappear. In comparison, Central America enjoys duty-free access to Europe and the United States, a considerable advantage over AI produce. Similarly, in Japan, there is a 17 percent duty on products in a sugarcane-based syrup, but syrup with a corn base can enter duty-free. At the same time, quality standards are such that exports to Japan must meet higher quality standards than exports for the U.S. market.

The Future

AI is serious about expanding its export business. Its owners believe that in international business, once they make a deal, they must honor it. In one case, they bought lemons out of season at six times the regular price and air-freighted the cell-sack product to meet a commitment to a customer. The customer's satisfaction led to a large order the next year. The partners are convinced that AI can succeed only by building long-term relationships in export markets. Timely delivery is also a must, given the perishable and seasonal nature of the products. AI knows that it must deliver the best-quality products, both to win customers and to get repeat orders.

QUESTIONS AND RESEARCH

1. How did AI first enter export markets? What factors enabled it to compete in the U.S. market?
2. How did AI enter the Japanese market? What were the challenges in exporting to Japan?
3. Trace the evolution of AI's expansion into international markets in terms of product lines and geographic market scope.
4. Do you think that AI has been successful in entering international markets? Discuss the factors critical to AI's success.
5. What are the challenges facing AI as it seeks to continue expanding internationally? What recommendations would you give AI in terms of products, markets, and the way it conducts international business?

Case prepared by Professor Ravi Sarathy, Northeastern University, for use in class discussion. © 2003, all rights reserved.

Global Economic Environment

The World, Regional, and National Economies

When a firm leaves its home market to market internationally, it must deal with the challenges of the larger, more complex world economy. In Chapter 2, we introduce the various dimensions of that environment.

The main goals of this chapter are to

- Present an overview of world trade to re-emphasize the economic linkages among nations.

- Describe how the World Trade Organization (WTO), the United Nations Conference on Trade and Development (UNCTAD), and other global organizations influence trade.

- Explore the developments in regional trading blocs and other areas such as Eastern Europe.

- Discuss the national role in global trade and identify some key countries for business in the coming decade.

- Present information on population, urbanization, income, natural physical endowments, and infrastructure; then provide an overview of how those characteristics impact marketing.

Marketing is an economic activity affected by the economic environment in which it is conducted. International marketing has an impact on two interrelated economic environments: (1) the global, or world, economy and (2) the economy of individual countries.

It is reasonable to speak of the "world economy" because the nations of the world affect one another economically. Nations, of course, also relate to each other politically, diplomatically, militarily, and culturally. Many of these other elements of international relations are intertwined with economic considerations. For example, Marco Polo's travels and the Crusades had significant economic impacts. The great voyages of discovery and the building of colonial empires were motivated by economic as well as political aspirations. More recently, economic considerations have played a role in regional cooperative movements such as the EU, the economic amalgamation of 25 European nations. International economic concerns are also frequent items on the agenda of the United Nations (UN) and its affiliated agencies.

The existence of this world economy is critical for the business firm. Because nations relate to each other economically, international business operations are possible. Today, in fact, international marketers are major participants in international economic relations. For that reason, it is necessary to examine the world economy to see how it aids and constrains international marketing. This chapter begins with a discussion on international trade, a major element in international economic relations.

A Picture of World Trade

The interrelated nature of the world economy is most easily seen by examining trade among nations and by closely scrutinizing the nature of the trade taking place.

Global Volume

Total world trade in 2002 exceeded $13.0 trillion in merchandise ($6.5 trillion in exports and $6.7 trillion in imports) and $3.1 trillion in commercial services ($1.6 trillion in exports and $1.5 trillion in imports). Gross world product was approximately $32.3 trillion in 2002; thus, the world's nations exported about 25 percent ($8.1 trillion) of what they produced in 2002. (See Table 2-1.)

According to the World Bank, global interdependence, fostered by increasing trade and the associated relationships among nations, has played a significant role in the decline in world poverty over the past 15 years.[1]

Internationalism is increasing as a way of life. Nations moving in the direction of trade expansion can raise their standard of living, while countries that restrict trade increase their political separation and isolation and slow economic progress (and see Thurow, Lester: *Fortune Favors the Bold*, 2003). Firms, like nations, must recognize that they are in the world marketplace when considering opportunities for growth and when facing new competition. The isolationist position is difficult for firms as well as nations to maintain. One can't just say, "Stop the world—I want to get off."

Foreign Trade of Individual Nations

The United States is the world leader in trade. In 2002, U.S. trade in merchandise totaled $1.84 trillion ($640 billion in exports and $1,202 billion in imports) and trade in commercial services totaled $478 billion ($273 billion in exports and $206 billion in imports). This translated into a $496 billion trade deficit in 2002. Trade balances are calculated by subtracting that which is purchased abroad (imports) from that which is sold (exports). A trade deficit exists when imports exceed exports and a surplus exists when exports exceed imports in the time period being measured.

Germany was second in trade volume with $1.11 trillion in merchandise trade ($613 billion in exports and $494 billion in imports) and trade in commercial services of $249 billion ($100 billion in exports and $149 billion in imports). Japan traded $754 billion in manufactured goods ($417 billion in exports and $337 billion in imports) and $172 billion in services ($65 billion in exports and $107 billion in imports).

Note also that in China, with a population of over 1.2 billion (20 percent of the world's population), trade has been growing rapidly and now accounts for approximately 5 percent of world trade in manufactured goods and 3 percent in commercial services. What surprises many people is that China is experiencing a trade *deficit* in both goods and services. Many attribute growing demand for imports to enormous infrastructure projects (for example, the Three Gorges Dam), increasing imports of oil and other fuels to run new factories, and the rapid increase in consumerism that is taking place. Table 2-1 highlights trade among the world trade leaders and other selected nations.

Top products traded in 2002 were in the machinery and transportation equipment category, which accounted for about 41 percent of world trade ($2.5 trillion). Office and telecommunications equipment (one of the product categories within machinery and transportation equipment) accounted for over 13 percent of trade ($838 million), while other major merchandise categories such as chemicals (11 percent, or $660 billion) and fuels (10 percent, or $615 billion) remain on the "top traded merchandise" list. Services show a trend toward declining importance of travel and transportation relative to other commercial services (for example, accounting, advertising, and consulting). In 1995, travel and transportation accounted for nearly 60 percent of all services traded; in 2002, those categories accounted for just over 50 percent.[2]

Some nations are more dependent on trade. That is, rather than earning most of their income from national sales to domestic consumers, some countries earn 10, 20, even more than 50 percent of national income by selling what they produce to foreigners. For example, Japan exported $482 billion worth of goods and services in 2002, which accounted for 12 percent of its gross national product (GNP). Germany depends on trade for 36 percent of its GNP; Belgium exports over 70 percent of what it produces every year. (A large proportion of Belgian trade, two-thirds, occurs with other EU nations.) By contrast, the United States exports only about 9 percent of what it produces.[3]

Foreign Trade of Individual Firms

Foreign trade is just as important to a firm as it is to a nation. In fact, much of international marketing involves

GLOBAL MARKETING

Ford—Made in Japan (and Spain and England and Mexico and even the United States)

*M*ost people would say that a Ford is an American car company and might assume that most of the parts that go into making a Ford car or truck are American-made. An analogous case could be made for Volvo (a Swedish company), Jaguar (English), and Mazda (Japanese).

Surprisingly to some people, all of those auto brands are owned and managed in part or whole by the Ford Motor

continued

Table 2-1. Foreign Trade of Individual Nations

Area or Nation	Gross National/World Income (current)[a]	2002 $US billion and (percent)	
		Exports (percent of world total)	Imports (percent of world total)
World	$32,312.2 (100.0)		
Manufactured Goods[b]		6,455.0 (100.0)	6,693.0 (100.0)
Commercial Services		1,570.0 (100.0)	1,545.0 (100.0)
Brazil	$452.4 (1.4)		
Manufactured Goods		60.4 (0.9)	49.7 (0.7)
Commercial Services		8.8 (0.6)	13.6 (0.9)
China	$1,266.1 (3.9)		
Manufactured Goods		295.2 (4.4)	325.6 (5.0)
Commercial Services		39.4 (2.5)	46.1 (3.0)
Germany	$1,984.1 (6.1)		
Manufactured Goods		613.1 (9.5)	493.7 (7.4)
Commercial Services		99.6 (6.3)	149.1 (9.6)
Mexico	$637.2 (2.0)		
Manufactured Goods		160.7 (2.5)	173.1 (2.6)
Commercial Services		12.5 (0.8)	17.0 (1.1)
Russian Federation	$346.5 (1.1)		
Manufactured Goods		106.9 (1.7)	60.5 (0.9)
Commercial Services		12.9 (0.8)	21.5 (1.4)
United States	$10,383.1 (32.1)		
Manufactured Goods		639.9 (10.7)	1,202.4 (18.0)
Commercial Services		272.6 (17.4)	205.6 (13.3)

a The World Bank currently uses gross national income (GNI) rather than gross national product (GNP) as a measure of wealth.

b These contain significant reexports; for example, total exports of Singapore and Hong Kong in 2002 totaled $326.3 billion, but $240.3 billion (74%) were reexported.

Sources: GNI data: World Bank Group; Data Query performed on July 16, 2004 (http://devdata.worldbank.org/data-query); Trade data: World Trade Organization, *International Trade Statistics*, 2003 (http://www.wto.org/english/res_e/statis_e/its2003_e/its03_bysubject_e.htm) (files: i05.xls [merchandise]; i07.xls [commercial services]).

Company, as are Aston Martin, Land Rover, Mercury, and Lincoln. Ford and other companies account for much of the world's trade as they ship parts and supplies between partners and subsidiaries for their products all over the globe. Companies pay less attention to national borders as they seek to cut costs in an increasingly competitive and interdependent global economy.

Mazda and Ford announced a new "Global Engine Family Strategy," which will rely on plants in Hiroshima (Japan), Dearborn (the United States), Chihuahua (Mexico), and Valencia (Spain) to produce inline engines for passenger cars and light trucks for its assembly facilities around the world. Ford will also get about 20,000 engines per year for its Ikon, a midsize car model that uses a 1.3- and 1.6-liter gasoline-powered engine, from Hindustan motors (India), with parts coming from Ford plants in South Africa and Spain. This plan is consistent with Ford's strategy to increase its reliance on India as a sourcing hub. Some Mazda models manufactured in the United States will be built with engines from a Ford plant in Mexico, but will get transmissions from a Ford plant in the United States. Other Mazda models, also made in the United States, get engines from Mazda plants located in Japan, the United States, and Spain.

How do companies keep all of this straight and the supplies running smoothly? Ford uses Vastera, Inc., a U.S. company in Dulles, Virginia, to provide logistics services. Third-party logistic companies (3PLs) – such as United Parcel Service, Deutsche Post, and APL Logistics – and 4PLs (those that select and manage 3PLs), such as Vastera and Kuehne & Nagel, can ship, store, truck, and provide whatever logistical network services are needed to ensure that components and supplies move efficiently from plant to plant worldwide.

Sources: Ford Motor Company web site (http://www.ford.com/en/ourVehicles/allVehicles/default.htm);

"Mazda Announces Sourcing for New Global Engine Family" (http://www.Mazda.com/mnl//200002/engine_e.html); "Ford Enters Sourcing Deal with India's Hindustan Motor," January 15, 2002, *Asia Pulse*, New Delhi, Northern Territory Regional; "Ford Seeks to Make India Sourcing Hub," November 18, 2001, Indian Express Online Media, Financial Express; "Year of the 3PLs," February 18, 2002; *Journal of Commerce*, Logistics, page 12.

international trade—the cross-border movement of goods and services. In relation to this subject, "Global Marketing: Ford—Made in Japan (and Spain and England and Mexico and even the United States)" shows how one company, Ford, sources the products they make.

Composition of World Trade

A study of the commodity composition of world trade gives further insight into international economic relations. Considering just four commodity categories—food, fuel, other primary commodities, and manufactured goods—long-run shifts in market share are seen.

Agricultural/Food Products

In 2002, trade in agricultural products accounted for 9 percent of total world trade. Yet at $583 billion that year, agricultural exports accounted for 43 percent of total world exports of primary products. Of the $583 billion, $189 billion, or over 32 percent, was accounted for by intra-Western European trade; nearly $65 billion (11 percent) was traded among Asian nations; and $34 billion (6 percent) was accounted for by intra-North American trade. Conversely, in 2002, agricultural products accounted for 11 percent of all North American exports, nearly 20 percent of exports from Latin America, and 16 percent of African exports. Despite some recent declines, the value of agricultural trade increased by 6 percent between 2000 and 2002.

Fuel

The WTO (described later in this chapter), categorizes fuel as a mining product. While mined products also include ores, minerals, and metals, 78 percent ($615 billion) of trade in mined products was attributed to fuels in 2002. Ten percent of total world trade is accounted for by fuel, which is expected to increase primarily because of high demand in the large Chinese market.

On the importing side, the EU (15 nations) led the way with $190 billion (30 percent of total trade in fuels in 2002), followed by the United States with $122 billion (20 percent), and Japan with $66 billion (10 percent). China imported only $19.3 billion in fuels in 2002, but this was up from $1.3 billion in 1990; fuel now constitutes 6.5 percent of total imports by China.

Middle Eastern nations are highly dependent on fuel (70 percent of merchandise exports). This is followed by African nations (50 percent) and Central European, Baltic, and Commonwealth of Independent States (CIS) nations (25 percent of exports come from fuels). Nearly 30 percent of the world's fuel comes from the Middle East. Twenty percent comes from Western Europe, followed by Africa, Asia, and Central Europe, each accounting for approximately 11 percent of the annual trade in fuels.

Manufactured Goods

This large category includes iron, steel, chemicals, machinery and transport equipment, textiles, and other consumer goods. Trade in manufactured goods grew at an annual rate of 7 percent from 1990 to 2000, but has leveled out since 2000, accounting for 75 percent ($4.7 trillion) of all merchandise exports in 2002. The largest subcategory, machinery and transport equipment, accounted for $2.5 trillion of exported manufactured goods. Within that subcategory, office and telecommunications equipment accounted for $838 billion while automotive products totaled $621 million in exports in 2002. Trade in office and telecom equipment was led by Asian nations, accounting for 50 percent of the world's exports ($422 billion) and 35 percent of imports in 2002. Western Europe imported nearly the same amount as Asia, but only exported 28 percent of total world exports for 2002. North America accounted for approximately 15 percent of the exports and 21 percent of the imports.

One trend worth noting is the decline in exports from the EU (36 percent of world share in 1980 but 28 percent in 2002), Japan (21 percent in 1980 but 10 percent in 2002), and the United States (20 percent in 1980 but 13 percent in 2002). On the importing side, the overall trend is for increased imports in developing nations and for decreased imports in developed nations. (The United States is an exception. In 1980, this market accounted for 16 percent of world imports; and in 2002, it accounted for 20 percent of imports.)

Commercial Services

Tracking of service trade is still in its infancy, and this is reflected in the poorly defined categories used by the WTO. Commercial services are classified into three categories: transportation, travel, and other commercial services. Other commercial services accounted for 47 percent of total commercial service exports in 2002 ($740 billion of the $1.57 trillion total). The second largest category, travel services, accounted for $480 billion, or 31 percent, of service exports in 2002. The largest exporting regions were Western Europe with a 43 percent share, followed by North America with 20 percent and Asia with 19 percent. The United States had $85 billion in travel service exports in 2002, more than the next two largest exporters, France ($34 billion) and Spain ($33 billion), combined. The largest importers that year were the United States ($61 billion), Germany ($53 billion), and the United Kingdom ($42 billion). Transportation services accounted for 22 percent ($350 billion) of exports of services in 2002. The largest exporters included the United States ($46 billion), Germany ($26 billion), and Japan ($24 billion). The largest importers of travel services in 2002 were the Unit-

Trading Services

According to the WTO, trade in services accounted for nearly 24 percent of world trade in 2002, up nearly 4 percent in the last two years. Four trends will drive the proportion of trade in services to manufactured goods still higher—cross-border mergers and consolidations, increased online usage of services, reduction of barriers to trade in services, and better measurement of service trade. Each of these is explained below.

1. *Continuing mergers and consolidations in key service areas such as accounting (Deloitte Touche Tohmatsu), banking (Credit Suisse First Boston), entertainment (AOL and Time Warner), and travel (Carnival and Princess Cruise lines). These mergers will create global companies that serve their clients and customers wherever they may be.*
2. *Increased service usage among consumers, particularly among Internet users of e-business. All estimates predict phenomenal growth for business-to-consumer (B2C) service e-commerce in the next few years. Business-to-business (B2B) service, while attracting less attention, will continue to dominate Internet activity.*
3. *WTO and others' efforts to reduce trade barriers for services. The goal of the General Agreement on Trade in Services (GATS) is freer trade in services—accountancy, advertising, architectural and engineering services, education, postal and courier services, sporting services, telecommunications, and tourism.*
4. *Better measurement. Advances in hardware, software, and data analysis techniques, as well as adoption of standards such as the Harmonized System of product classification, will make it easier to measure the flow of services from nation to nation.*

Using financial services as an example, the following are a few noteworthy headlines and statistics that relate to the worldwide increase in trading in the services sector:

- *The Check Clearing for the 21st Century Act allows American banks to use electronic facsimiles of checks rather than to physically send checks around the nation. This is another factor leading to rapidly declining use of checks as a payment method in the United States, where check use is declining by 3 to 5 percent per year. ("Banking Law Mints*

continued

Tech Windfall," CNET News.com, *July 16, 2004)*

- *Oracle is focusing on China, where the information technology (IT) market is growing by 20 percent annually. The driving forces are telecommunications, financial services, and high-tech manufacturing (in that order). ("Oracle Counts on Success in China,"* Reuters, *July 18, 2004; ZDNet.com)*

- *By 2007, online banking accounts in Germany are expected to reach 32.6 million, an annual growth rate of 11 percent. Online trading accounts will increase from 2.7 million in 2002 to 4.8 million by 2008. ("Online Banking on the Rise in Germany,"* IDC Research, *March 14, 2003)*

- *In the United States, 17 percent of Americans were using online banking services by the end of 2002. Forecasts indicate that 67 million, or 30 percent, of U.S. citizens will be using online banking by the end of 2007. ("Online Banking Goes Mainstream in U.S.,"* Gartner Group, *March 10, 2003)*

Certain legal factors will negatively affect trade in services. Antitrust laws aimed at curtailing the formation of huge companies that dominate an industry will rise as a result of megamerger trends. Antitrade laws designed to protect industries that play an important role in the nation's economy or industries that are considered vital to defense will continue to be enacted. Consumer protection laws are likely to become more elaborate and labyrinthine as countries within the EU and other regional groups attempt to coordinate these laws. Finally, intellectual property protection (IPP) is an important topic in most trade negotiations. With respect to piracy of entertainment, movies, software, and music are at the top of stolen intellectual property (IP) lists in nearly every country of the world.

ed States ($59 billion), Japan ($32 billion), and Germany ($30 billion). As the statistics show, trade in services is dominated by industrialized nations; but China and Thailand are now on the list of top 15 importers with 3 percent and 2 percent, respectively, of world import share in 2002.[4]

For international firms, a detailed study of the composition of world trade reveals *what* is being traded as well as *who* is buying and selling. **Trend analysis** shows which products are growing and which are fading, indicating potential threats and opportunities. The interest of less developed countries in industrialization may also create investment opportunities for firms in manufacturing or processing. For developed countries, investments in manufacturing or processing abroad could help less developed

countries increase manufactured exports by adding items to their export line or by refining or processing their primary commodities.

Patterns of World Trade

Which countries are the major players—and winners—in the game of international trade? Trade statistics show that in any given year, 50 of the world's nations account for between 90 and 95 percent of merchandise trade. Conversely, only 40 of the more than 200 nations in the world account for over 90 percent of the trade in services – the latter is more concentrated. As shown in Table 2-1, the three top traders (the United States, Germany, and Japan) supply nearly 30 percent of the total exports of goods and services while the top ten account for more than 55 percent of trade in both merchandise and services.

Historically, the industrial nations supply three-quarters of all exports and nearly 80 percent of the services traded annually. (See Table 2-2.) The low-income nations, by contrast, supply a mere 3 percent of the world's trade in goods and services. Considering there are approximately 200 nations, those figures show the lopsided nature of trade. Poorer nations get a small percentage of their income from few products and few sources. A poorly diversified economy makes the economy more vulnerable to downturns in the industry it depends on most. Accepting the argument that trade leads to higher gross national income (GNI), the historical trends in trade, if they continue, will lead to a wider economic gap between rich and poor nations. In discussing GNI (above) the assumption is made that such income is largely derived from export sales.

After rapid growth in the 1990s, world trade actually declined in 2001. (Merchandise trade declined by 4 percent in value, while trade in services merely stagnated.) In 2002, world trade grew again in nearly all regions and sectors, enough to offset the loss from the previous year. Observers noted that growth was coming not so much from the wealthy nations, but from China, other developing nations, and the transition economies in Europe.

The overall picture of world trade patterns shown in Table 2-2 provides necessary background for understanding world trade. However, it is often more important to identify the trading patterns of the particular nations. For example, Table 2-3 shows the major trading partners of the United States. Of particular importance is that China replaced Mexico as the second most important supplier of the United States in 2003. (China also moved from ninth to sixth place on the export side between 2001 and 2003.) France, historically one of the largest trading partners of the United States, may soon fall off the list of top ten traders. To complement this information, a firm might use

Table 2-2. World Trade Export Shares 2002

	Merchandise Exports ($US billion)	Merchandise (percent)	Service Exports ($US billion)	Service (percent)
World	6,454.9	100.0	1,511.2	100.0
Economic Development				
Low	211.2	3.3	41.0	2.7
Middle	1,447.0	22.4	225.6	14.9
High	4,796.7	74.3	1,244.6	82.3
Geographic Area				
Africa	140.0	2.2	31.0	2.0
Asia	1,620.0	25.8	322.0	20.5
Central & Eastern Europe	314.0	5.0	60.0	3.8
Western Europe	2,657.0	42.4	763.0	48.6
Middle East	244.0	4.0	29.0	1.8
Latin America*	350.0	5.6	56.0	3.6
North America	946.0	15.1	309.0	19.7

Sources: Economic development category data: World Bank, *World Development Indicators*, 2004, Table 4.5, pages 198-200; Table 4.7, pages 206-208; Geographic area and individual nation data: World Trade Organization, *International Trade Statistics*, 2003, Tables 1.3 and 1.4, page 20; Table 1.5, page 21; Table 1.7, page 23.

*Note: WTO includes Mexico in Latin America, not North America.

In reporting the geographic area data, the WTO *excluded* re-exports; therefore, the merchandise trade total of $6,272 and service trade of $1,570 is different from the WTO-reported world totals in other tables. The trade shares shown in the geographic areas above are calculated on the basis of these lower total figures.

a product breakdown by country to provide a more complete profile of a nation's trade.

The statement that most trade is with industrial countries is borne out by the figures for the United States, but the importance of other factors becomes evident as well. For example, the role of Canada and Mexico as trading partners of the United States cannot be explained very well in terms of their size or degree of industrialization. **Geographic proximity** is an important consideration. In general, countries that are neighbors are better trading partners than countries that are distant from each other. The lower transportation costs are accompanied by greater familiarity and ease of communication and control.

Surprisingly, recent research suggests that the Internet may not have a major impact on trading patterns of manufactured goods and that geographic proximity will continue as a major factor in explaining trading patterns. This is borne out by some recent surveys and statistics showing that Europeans prefer to purchase from local merchants and to make purchases offline, as do many other consumers, because of lack of trust and the desire to see or touch the merchandise. This requires a trip to the local store. Recent reports also show that, with the exception of the United States and Europe, Internet traffic is highest among nations within the same region. While far from conclusive, these findings show that the role of geographic proximity explains a lot about trading patterns.[5]

Political influences continue to be a critical factor in trade relations and may be borne out by reviewing trade statistics such as those presented in the previous tables. One explanation for the declining trade between the Unit-

Table 2-3. Major Trading Partners of the United States in 2003

Top 10 Purchasers	U.S. Exports ($US billions)	Top 10 Suppliers	U.S. Imports ($US billions)
Canada	169.5	Canada	224.2
Mexico	97.5	China	152.4
Japan	52.1	Mexico	138.1
United Kingdom	33.9	Japan	118.0
Germany	28.8	Germany	68.0
China	28.4	United Kingdom	42.7
Korea, Republic	24.1	Korea, Republic	37.0
Netherlands	20.7	Taiwan	31.6
Taiwan	17.5	France	29.2
France	17.1	Ireland	25.8

Note: Merchandise exports only.

Sources: *Top Trading Partners:* Total Trade, Exports, Imports; U.S. Census Bureau, Foreign Trade Statistics (http://www.census.gov/foreign-trade/statistics/highlights/toppartners.html); accessed July 26, 2004; Trade Stats Express, Office of Trade and Economic Analysis (OTEA), Trade Development, International Trade Administration, U.S. Department of Commerce (http://ese.export.gov); accessed July 26, 2004.

ed States and France over the 2000–2003 period is that France did not support the United States in the war on Iraq. Another long-standing example is U.S. trade with Cuba. Although Cuba is a close neighbor of the United States, practically no trade exists between the two countries. This controverts the statement about geographic proximity made earlier. While speaking in Miami to an audience of mostly Cuban-Americans on May 20, 2002,

President Bush announced that the United States would not lift trade sanctions that were first imposed in 1962.[6] These sanctions constitute a near complete embargo, allowing Americans to sell only agricultural goods and then for cash only. Even attempts to allow travel and imports of medicine were quashed in Congress. These decisions put the United States in a lonely position. Other nations expanded travel and trade with Cuba as Fidel Castro neared his eightieth birthday. The point here is that an analysis of trade patterns both on an aggregate and national basis can be useful to a firm when it is planning its global marketing and logistics systems. Examination of the causes of trade patterns suggests possible approaches to adapting to the patterns or to modifying them.

International Trade Theory

Domestic marketing places a good deal of emphasis on the analysis of buyer behavior and motivation. For the international marketer, knowledge of the basic causes and nature of international trade is important. It is easier for a firm to work with the underlying economic forces than against them. To work with them, however, the firm must first understand them.

Essentially, international trade theory seeks the answers to a few basic questions: Why do nations trade? What goods do they trade? Nations trade for economic, political, and cultural reasons. But the principal economic basis for international trade is *difference in price*; that is, a nation can buy some goods more cheaply from other nations than it can make them. In a sense, the nation faces the same "make-or-buy" decision as the firm does. Just as most firms do not seek complete vertical integration, but buy many materials and supplies from outside firms, so most nations decide against complete self-sufficiency (or **autarky**) in favor of buying cheaper goods from other countries.

An example given by Adam Smith helps illustrate this point: When discussing the advantages to England in trading manufactured goods for Portugal's wine, he noted that grapes could be grown "under glass" (in greenhouses) in England but that to do so would lead to England's having both less wine and fewer manufacturers than if it specialized in manufacturers.

Nations—and, in fact, people—have an **absolute advantage** when it comes to making or doing certain things. Florida has a climate that is better suited for growing oranges than Alaska does and, therefore, can grow oranges less expensively. Japan has a more skilled workforce than the Philippines does for producing highly sophisticated robots. And while a physician may be able to install a new light fixture, a licensed electrician is likely able to do it better and faster. In fact, Smith's major conclusion was that the "wealth of nations" is derived from the division of labor and specialization (Adam Smith: *Wealth of Nations*). Applied to the international picture, this means trade rather than self-sufficiency.

Comparative Advantage

It has been said that price differences are the immediate basis of international trade. The firm that decides whether to make or buy also considers price as a principal variable. But why do nations have different prices on goods? Prices differ because countries producing the goods have different costs. And why do countries have different costs? The Swedish economist Bertil Ohlin came up with an explanation generally held to be valid: Different countries have dissimilar prices and costs on goods because different goods require a different mix of factors in their production and because countries differ in their supply of these factors. Thus, in Smith's example, Portugal's wine would be cheaper than England's wine because Portugal has a relatively better endowment of wine-making factors (for example, land and climate) than England does.

This discussion has dealt with the principle of **comparative advantage**; namely, that a country tends to produce and export those goods in which it has the greatest comparative advantage and import those goods in which it has the least comparative advantage. As Smith suggested, the nation maximizes its supply of goods by concentrating production where it is most efficient and trading some of those products for imported products where it is least efficient. An examination of the exports and imports of most nations tends to support this theory.

Product Life Cycle

A refinement in trade theory is related to the **product life cycle**, which in marketing refers to the consumption pattern for a product. When applied to international trade theory, it refers primarily to international trade and production patterns. According to this concept, many products go through a trade cycle wherein one nation is initially an exporter, then loses its export markets, and finally may become an importer of the product. Empirical studies have demonstrated the validity of the model for some kinds of manufactured goods.

Outlined below are the four phases in the production and trade cycle, with the United States as an example. Assume that a U.S. firm has come up with a high-tech product. What follows is:

Phase 1: The United States exports the product.

Phase 2: Foreign production starts.
Phase 3: Foreign production becomes competitive in
      export markets.
Phase 4: Import competition begins.

In Phase 1, **product innovation** is likely to be related to the needs of the home market. The firm usually serves its home market first. The new product is produced in the home market because, as the firm moves down the production learning curve, it needs to communicate with both suppliers and customers. As the firm begins to fill home-market needs, it starts to export the new product, seizing on its first-mover advantages, and to increase sales (assuming the U.S. firm is exporting to Europe).

In Phase 2, importing countries gain familiarity with the new product. Gradually, producers in wealthy countries begin producing the product for their own markets. (Most product innovations begin in one rich country and then move to other rich countries.) Foreign production will reduce the exports of the innovating firm. (Assume that the U.S. firm's exports to Europe are replaced by production within Europe.)

In Phase 3, foreign firms gain production experience and move down the cost curve. If they have lower costs than the innovating firm, which is frequently the case, they export to third-country markets, replacing the innovator's exports there. (Assume that European firms are now exporting to Latin America, taking away the U.S. firm's export markets there.)

In Phase 4, the foreign producers now have sufficient production experience and economies of scale to allow them to export back to the innovator's home country. (Assume that the European producers have now taken away the home market of the original U.S. innovator.)

In Phase 1, the product is "new." In Phase 2, it is "maturing." In Phases 3 and 4, it is "standardized." The product may become so standardized by Phase 4 that it almost becomes a commodity. This modification of the theory of comparative advantage provides further insight into patterns of international trade and production and helps the international company plan logistics, such as when it will need to produce—or source—abroad.

Technological advances have changed many aspects of international marketing, and the impact on the product life cycle is the speed at which products move through these stages. Information is more readily available, and ideas are exchanged more rapidly; so the time between product introduction in one country and its introduction in other nations has grown much shorter. Competitors are also entering industries more quickly—which means that firms must seek lower production alternatives more quickly—so movement to Stage 4 occurs more rapidly as well.

Balance of Payments

In the study of international trade, the principal source of information is the **balance-of-payments** (BoP) statement of the trading nations. These are summary statements of all of the economic transactions between one country and all other countries over a period of time, usually one year. As an accounting of all transactions between one nation and the rest of the world, the BoP is a double-entry report in which the total of all payment and receipts are equal. Deficits (spending exceeds earnings) or surpluses (earnings exceed deficits) occur in specific BoP accounts. The accounts most often discussed are the **current account** and the capital account.

The **current account** includes a list of trade transactions in manufactured goods and services, as well as a list of unilateral transfers. Unilateral transfers, as the term suggests, are one-way transfers. Assume that a firm exports a manufactured good, such as a book, and in exchange gets the value of that book in some currency. Those actions are offsetting parts of the transaction (outflow: book; inflow: money). But when someone earns money during the year, purchases a gift, and sends it to a relative in another country, the transaction is only one-way. (The gift is shipped or exported, but no money flows back into the country.) Where there are large numbers of foreign workers, as in Germany and Saudi Arabia, these transfers can be substantial.

The **capital account** includes flows such as direct and portfolio investments, private placements, and bank and government loans. Again, in countries that receive a lot of investment funds (such as those in Eastern Europe and China) or in countries that supply a lot of funds (such as the United States, the Netherlands, and the United Kingdom), the capital account can be a significant component in the total BoP accounting statement.

The international marketer usually is more interested in the details of current account transactions; that is, in the nature of the goods being traded and their origin and destination. Careful examination of the current account can identify the source of competing products as well as potential markets. A more detailed explanation of the usefulness of balance of payments is provided below.

Marketing Decisions

The BoP is an indicator of the international economic health of a country. These data help government policymakers plan monetary, fiscal, foreign exchange, and commercial policies. The data can also provide information for international marketing decisions. By reviewing import data, marketers can determine the major sources of foreign-made products and, from this, gain some idea of competitors' locations. Export data, on the other hand, can be used to identify where a nation's products are being shipped and thereby divulge some information about *consumers'* locations.

For those companies facing severe import competition, another useful aspect of the data in the BoP records is that they may aid a firm in arguing for protection of its industry. This would be the case if imports are rising rapidly and displacing workers or if imports are threatening strategic industries. Companies supplying products to a foreign nation should also review the BoP statistics for warning signs of impending trade legislation. For example, rapidly rising imports might presage government regulation of trade for that particular product. This means that watching trends in the BoP data for a few years is also critical.

Data in Table 2-4 presents a snapshot of current account information for one U.S. product. The data are taken from the *World Trade Annual*, a comprehensive five-volume publication of the UN. The publication provides details of exports and imports by Standard International Trade Classification (SITC) category. (Partial data are provided for illustrative purposes.)

The first part of the table lists some of the major *importing countries* for typewriters (yes, people still buy them) and the countries that supplied them. The second part of the table shows a similar list of the *exporters* and the markets to which they exported.

Financial Considerations

Up to this point, the text has dealt primarily with the current account in the BoP, especially the movement of goods reflected in that account. A look at the capital account is also useful.

A nation's international solvency can be evaluated by checking its capital account over several years. If the nation is steadily losing its gold and foreign exchange reserves, there is a strong likelihood of a currency devaluation or some kind of exchange control. An exchange control means that the government restricts the amount of money sent out of the country as well as the uses to which it can be put. With exchange control, a firm may have difficulty obtaining foreign exchange to **repatriate** (send home) **profits** or import supplies needed to manufacture its products. If the firm is importing products that are not considered necessary, the scarce foreign exchange will go instead to goods on which the nation places a higher priority.

The firm's pricing policies, too, are affected by the balance-of-payments problems of the host country. If the firm cannot repatriate profits from a country, it tries to use its transfer pricing to minimize the profits earned in that country, gaining its profits elsewhere – where it can repatriate them. If the exporting firm fears devaluation of a currency, it hesitates to quote prices in that currency, pre-

ferring to give terms in its home currency or another "safe" currency. Thus, the BoP is an important information source, particularly for international marketing and international finance decision makers.

Commercial Policy

One reason international trade is different from domestic trade is that it is carried on between different political units, each one a sovereign nation exercising control over its own trade. Although all nations control their foreign trade, they vary in the degree of such control. Each nation invariably establishes laws that favor its nationals and discriminates against traders from other countries. This means, for example, that a U.S. firm trying to sell in the French market faces certain handicaps from the French government's control over its trade. These handicaps to the U.S. firm are in addition to any disadvantages resulting from distance or cultural differences. By the same token, a French firm trying to sell in the United States faces similar restrictions when competing with U.S. firms selling in their home market.

Commercial policy is the term used to refer to government regulations bearing on foreign trade. The principal tools of commercial policy are tariffs, quotas, exchange control, and administrative regulation (the "invisible tariff"). Each of these terms will be discussed as it relates to the task of the international marketer. Governments often use trade barriers to protect domestic industries and the jobs they provide. (This is the reason some individuals refer to this intervention as *protectionism*.) For instance, if a government placed a tax (tariff) on all foreign-made cars, making the cars more expensive, simple rules of supply and demand will show people buying more domestic-made cars than foreign-made cars. People with jobs (for instance, auto-workers) are happier than people without work because they can provide for themselves and their families. When people are happy, they tend to support the government and the officials who impose the protection.

Tariffs

A **tariff** is a tax on products imported from other countries. The tax may be levied on the quantity—such as 10 cents per pound, gallon, or yard—or on the value of the imported goods—such as 10 or 20 percent *ad valorem*. A tariff levied on quantity is called a *specific duty* and is used especially for primary commodities. *Ad valorem* duties are generally levied on manufactured products.

Governments may have two purposes in imposing tariffs: They may want to earn revenue, *and/or* make foreign goods more expensive in order to protect national producers. When the United States was a new nation,

Table 2-4. Examples of Import/Export Statistics from Balance-of-Payments Data, 1998-2000

Imports (partial table at four-digit product code level)

SITC Number Importer Provenance	Quantity Units	Value Thousands of U.S. Dollars	SITC Number Importer Provenance	Quantity Units	Value Thousands of U.S. Dollars
751.1 Typewriters, Cheque Writers			**751.1 Typewriters, Cheque Writers (Cont.)**		
Canada..............Tot	N	25102	2770	Ireland..............Tot	W	41	1041
USA	N	16058	1861	USA	W	1	53
Mexico	N	2123	141	Japan	W	4	181
Japan	N	824	128	Asia, other, NS	W	1	55
Indonesia	N	1331	241	United Kingdom	W	27	624
Germany	N	3838	270				
United Kingdom	N	358	67	Italy..............Tot	W	494	6596
				USA	W	-	165
USA..............Tot	N	570723	46063	Bermuda	W	7	80
S.Africa Cus. Union	N	710	277	Mexico	W	299	3276
Mexico	N	389103	25723	Japan	W	5	149
Japan	N	19634	4673	China	W	23	359
China	N	82595	4499	India	W	38	339
Indonesia	N	36883	6636	France	W	5	126
Korea Republic	N	3490	175	Germany	W	56	1290
India	N	1222	540	United Kingdom	W	49	604
Germany	N	5400	128	Switzerland	W	5	93
Italy	N	794	235				
United Kingdom	N	8133	2551	Netherlands..........Tot	W	59659	9541
Bulgaria	N	21600	501	USA	N	6260	708
				Japan	N	7477	2992
Israel..............Tot		-	117	China HK SAR	N	1953	173
				Indonesia	N	2538	324
Japan..............Tot		-	48636	Korea Republic	N	1532	446
USA		-	679	Philippines	N	7197	1345
Mexico		-	65	Belgium-Lux	N	4571	842
China		-	25441	France	N	8727	760
Malaysia		-	201	Germany	N	2752	616
Asia, other, NS		-	2172	Sweden	N	253	55
Germany		-	65	United Kingdom	N	15470	1397
Italy		-	64				
United Kingdom		-	192	Portugal..............Tot	W	56	904
				Mexico	W	10	157
Austria..............Tot	W	241	3797	Japan	W	4	89
USA	W	4	171	India	W	6	77
Mexico	W	37	598	Singapore	W	3	52
Japan	W	2	98	Germany	W	3	59
China	W	15	197	Italy	W	4	108
Indonesia	W	4	54	Spain	W	15	204
Germany	W	19	298	United Kingdom	W	6	97
Italy	W	10	259				
United Kingdom	W	148	2045	Spain ....Tot	W	490	7540
				USA	W	1	112
Belgium-Lux..........Tot	W	152	3191	Mexico	W	320	4680
USA	W	12	449	China	W	78	988
Mexico	W	32	643	Indonesia	W	23	293
France	W	3	110	Asia, other, NES	W	5	219
Germany	W	10	331	Thailand	W	11	434
Italy	W	29	419	Germany	W	5	99
Netherlands	W	16	330	Italy	W	10	204
United Kingdom	W	37	774	United Kingdom	W	25	323
				Slovenia	W	5	55

W: weight, metric tons; N: number; "-" indicates the data are not available; this is a partial list of statistics for this product category.

Source: United Nations, *World Trade Annual* 1998, 2000, Volume 5, New York: Walker & Company, pages 267, 997, 998.

Table 2-4. Examples of Import/Export Statistics from Balance-of-Payments Data (continued)

Exports (partial table at four-digit product code level)

SITC Number / Importer / Provenance	Quantity Units	Value Thousands of U.S. Dollars	SITC Number / Importer / Provenance	Quantity Units	Value Thousands of U.S. Dollars
751.1 Typewriters, Cheque Writers			**751.1 Typewriters, Cheque Writers (Cont.)**		
Canada.................Tot	N 1878	160	Germany (Continued)		
USA	N 1783	157	Austria	W 23	777
			Belgium-Lux	W 14	538
USA.....................Tot	N 161749	32401	Denmark	W 4	211
S.Africa Cus. Union	N 1070	496	Finland	W 4	184
Canada	N 6188	1829	France	W 29	1017
Brazil	N 387	192	Greece	W 19	574
Chile	N 11038	1408	Italy	W 16	565
Colombia	N 3393	1388	Netherlands	W 26	1264
Ecuador	N 1055	117	Portugal	W 2	79
Mexico	N 71435	6849	Spain	W 16	699
Peru	N 97	108	Sweden	W 6	331
Uruguay	N 6580	593	United Kingdom	W 24	778
Venezuela	N 6773	1152	Switzerland	W 6	246
Costa Rica	N 309	99	Bulgaria	W 3	238
El Salvador	N 1365	350	Czech Republic	W 48	753
Guatemala	N 3593	1125	Hungary	W 3	87
Honduras	N 572	286	Poland	W 82	1864
Dominican Repub.	N 718	277	Romania	W 8	190
Trinidad & Tobago	N 819	283	Slovak	W 8	181
Panama	N 8488	1047	Belarus	W 5	100
Japan	N 685	395	Latvia	W 2	64
United Arab Emir.	N 377	175	Lithuania	W 6	142
China	N 658	668	Russian Federation	W 84	1878
China, HK SAR	N 104	113	Ukraine	W 51	850
Korea Republic	N 165	270	Croatia	W 6	110
Malaysia	N 43	67	Slovenia	W 2	88
Asia, other, NS	N 466	196			
Mongolia	N 282	99	Italy ....Tot	W 400	9174
Philippines	N 1304	451	S.Africa Cus. Union	W 13	317
India	N 2683	604	Algeria	W 9	114
Singapore	N 748	290	Libya	W 55	1625
Thailand	N 121	69	Morocco	W 11	162
Austria	N 203	86	Cote D'Ivoire	W 3	67
Belgium-Lux	N 1331	442	USA	W 17	451
Denmark	N 830	290	Brazil	W 20	512
France	N 11024	3552	Chile	W 10	252
Germany	N 1429	661	Venezuela	W 2	62
Ireland	N 236	80	Israel	W 8	53
Italy	N 41	169	United Arab Emir.	W 4	120
Netherlands	N 1435	198	Turkey	W 6	109
Spain	N 85	407	Korean Republic	W 2	105
Sweden	N 645	379	Austria	W 10	212
United Kingdom	N 9530	3773	Belgium-Lux	W 11	269
Norway	N 11	72	Denmark	W 17	315
Switzerland	N 12	59	France	W 11	243
Australia	N 816	350	Germany	W 17	320
New Zealand	N 1556	382	Portugal	W 1	78
			Spain	W 30	733
			United Kingdom	W 10	243
			Czech Republic	W 5	129
			Romania	W 10	243
			Russian Federation	W 68	1584
			Bosnia Herzegov.	W 4	73
			Australia	W 3	202

W: weight, metric tons; N: number; "-" indicates the data are not available; this is a partial list of statistics for this product category.

Source: United Nations, World Trade Annual 1998, 2000, Volume 5, New York: Walker & Company, pages 267, 997, 998.

most government revenues came from tariffs. Many less developed countries today earn a large amount of their revenue from tariffs because they are among the easiest taxes to collect. Today, however, the protective purpose generally prevails over straight revenue collection. One could argue that with a tariff, a country penalizes its consumers by making them pay higher prices on imported goods; also, it penalizes producers that import raw materials or components. The countervailing rationale is that a policy that is too liberal with imports may hurt employment in that country's own industries.

Tariffs affect pricing, product, and distribution policies of the international marketer as well as foreign investment decisions. If a firm is supplying a market by means of exports, the tariff increases the price of its product and reduces competitiveness in that market. This necessitates a price structure that minimizes the tariff barrier. A greater emphasis on marginal cost pricing could result. This examination of price is accompanied by a review of other aspects of the firm's approach to the market. The product may be modified or stripped down to lower the price or to get a more favorable tariff classification. For example, watches could be taxed as timepieces at one rate or as jewelry at a higher rate. The manufacturer might be able to adapt its product to meet the lower tariff.

Another way the manufacturer can minimize the tariff burden is to ship products "completely knocked down" (CKD) for assembly in the local market. The tariff on unassembled products or ingredients is usually lower than that on completely finished goods in order to promote the use of local labor. This establishment of local assembly operations is a form of the phenomenon known as **tariff factory**, the term used when the primary reason a local plant exists is to get behind the tariff barriers of protected markets that it can no longer serve with direct exports. The assembly operations may eventually lead to completely manufacturing the product in the host market. This generally requires the use of additional local labor, the goal of the government in imposing a tariff.

All trade barriers raise prices of targeted goods and services. *Ad valorem* tariffs are more effective against high- and low-priced products, while specific tariffs are more effective at keeping low-priced goods out. Nations wanting to keep out low-priced vehicles could impose a specific duty of $2,500 on every auto. This amount is relatively large for a car that costs $25,000 versus a car that costs $250,000. An *ad valorem* duty of 10 percent, however, would raise the relative price of all imported cars by the same amount.

There is another aspect to the debate about using different trade barriers. The tariff collected goes back into the coffers of the nation that imposed the duty. This money can be distributed to consumers and others in the home country. *Non-tariff barriers* (NTBs), described below, raise prices for consumers, but the additional money does not go to the government or other home national parties. Instead, the money flows out of the country and may even go to the exporter in the form of higher profits.

Tariffs used to be the most effective and easiest tool for countries to use in reducing or eliminating foreign-made goods. Over the past 50 years, though, the WTO, bilateral trade agreements, and agreements among nations (such as NAFTA) have significantly reduced and even eliminated tariffs. Tariffs are easily identifiable as trade barriers and, therefore, are one of the main targets of free-trade proponents. Protecting local industries remains a goal of many government leaders, though; so innovative ways were—and still are—being invented to stem the tide of imports. Increasingly, as governments agreed to reduce tariff barriers, they turned to NTBs, such as quotas, to affect changes in the flow of trade.

Quotas

Quantitative restrictions, or **quotas**, are barriers to imports. They set absolute limits on the amount of goods that may enter a country. An import quota can be a more serious restriction than a tariff because a firm has less flexibility in responding to it. Price or product modifications do not get around quotas the way they might get around tariffs. The government's goal in establishing quotas on imports is obviously not revenue. Rather, government's goal is the conservation of scarce foreign exchange and/or the protection of local production. About the only response a firm can make to a quota is to assure itself a share of the quota or to set up local production if the market size warrants doing so. Since the latter is in accord with the wishes of government, the firm might be regarded favorably for taking such action.

In April 2002, U.S. President Bush unveiled a plan to protect the steel industry that included tariffs of up to 30 percent on imported steel. Since the WTO now prohibits the use of so-called voluntary restraints that were used to protect the industry, quick-acting tariffs were imposed.[7] For political reasons, including the desire for support for the war in Iraq and WTO pressure, the United States lifted these tariffs in December 2003, 18 months after imposing them.

Fallout from the steel tariffs imposed by the United States includes foreign producers finding other markets for the products barred from entry. In an effort to find new markets, these producers compete more heavily in markets with fewer trade barriers. In an effort to prevent potential dumping of diverted U.S. imports, the EU imposed quotas on imported steel to protect its market. Furthermore, the EU threatened to impose retaliatory restrictions on American-made goods such as Harley Davidson motorcycles and Tropicana orange juice. Clearly, imposing trade barriers in one country can and often does have negative global repercussions.[8]

Exchange Control

The most complete tool for regulation of foreign trade is **exchange control**, a government monopoly of all dealings in foreign exchange. Exchange control means that foreign exchange is scarce and that the government is rationing it out according to its own priorities. A national company earning foreign exchange from its exports must sell this foreign exchange to the control agency, usually the central bank. In turn, a company wanting to buy goods from abroad must buy its foreign exchange from the control agency.

Firms in the country must be on the government's favored list to obtain exchange for imported supplies. Alternatively, they may try to develop local suppliers, running the risk of higher costs and indifferent quality control. The firms exporting to that nation must also be on the government's favored list. Otherwise, they will lose their market if importers can get no foreign exchange to pay them. Generally, exchange-control countries favor the import of capital goods and necessary consumer goods but not luxuries. While the definition of "luxuries" varies from country to country, it usually includes cars, appliances, and cosmetics. If the exporter does lose its market through exchange control, the only option may be to produce within the country if the market is large enough for this to be profitable.

Another implication for a firm when foreign exchange is limited is that the government is likely to restrict companies' profit remittances as another way of keeping the country's scarce foreign earnings within its borders. In this situation, the firm tries to use transfer pricing to get earnings out of the host country or to avoid accumulating earnings there. It accomplishes this by charging high transfer prices on supplies sold to the subsidiary and low transfer prices on goods sold by that subsidiary to affiliates of the company in other markets. The firm's ability to do this depends on the plan's acceptance by tax officials of the country.

Invisible Tariff and Other Government Barriers

There are other government barriers to international trade that are hard to classify; for example, administrative protection, the invisible tariff, and **NTBs**. As traditional trade barriers have declined since World War II, the NTBs have taken on added significance. They include customs documentation requirements, marks of origin, food and drug laws, labeling laws, antidumping laws, "buy national" policies, subsidies, and many other means. For example, nations can make goods more expensive simply by adding the requirement that all incoming products must have additional forms or paperwork. This documentation takes time and costs money for the exporter. Another example of an NTB

is subsidies. (See "Global Marketing: Subsidies and Retaliation.") There are many types of NTBs. Because these barriers are so diverse, their impact cannot be covered in a brief discussion. But some idea of what nations are doing to impede trade can be gained by reading the disputes under consideration by the WTO (http://www.wto.org).

Other Dimensions and Institutions in the World Economy

The global business environment is complex and includes many players—national, regional, and local governments; private and publicly held firms; and innumerable international organizations, special interest groups, and individuals. The following discussion includes some of the more widely known institutions (and, in some respects, most important institutions). We also discuss other aspects that have an impact on the global business environment.

World Trade Organization (WTO)

Because each nation is sovereign in determining its own commercial policy, the danger is that arbitrary national actions will minimize international trade. This was the situation in the 1930s, when international trade was at a low ebb and each nation tried to maintain domestic employment while restricting imports that could help foreign rather than domestic employment. The economic reality of tariffs is that if one nation erects trade barriers, other nations are likely to follow suit by erecting their own barriers, most typically retaliating by imposing duties on products it purchases from the other nation. The bankruptcy of these "beggar my neighbor" policies was evident in the worldwide depression to which they contributed. This unhappy experience led the major trading nations to seek better solutions after World War II. One outcome of their efforts was the General Agreement on Tariffs and Trade (GATT), now called the World Trade Organization **(WTO)**.

Although GATT's initial membership consisted of only 23 countries, it included the major trading nations of the Western world. Today, WTO is more than ever the world's trading club, accounting for over 90 percent of world trade. It has approximately 150 members with two dozen applicants currently negotiating membership. The WTO has contributed to the expansion of world trade. Since 1947, it has sponsored eight major multilateral trade negotiations, the latest being the Uruguay Round, which lasted from 1986 to 1994. As a result of these conferences, the tariff rates for tens of thousands of items have been reduced and a high proportion of world trade has seen an easing of restrictions on most manufactured goods with respect to manufactured goods, and many services (apparel, textiles, and agricultural products have traditionally involved difficult negotiations).[9]

Providing a framework for multilateral trade negotiations is a primary reason for WTO's existence, but there are other WTO principles that further trade expansion. One is the principle of **nondiscrimination**. Each contracting party must grant all others the same rate of import duty; that is, a tariff concession granted to one trading partner must be extended to all WTO members under the most-favored-nation (MFN) clause.

Another WTO principle is the concept of **consultation**. When trade disagreements arise, WTO provides a forum for consultation. In such an atmosphere, disagreeing members are more likely to compromise than to resort to arbitrary trade-restricting actions. All in all, world trade cooperation since World War II has led to a much better trading policy than the world might have expected. WTO has been a major contributor to this.

Some indication of the scope of WTO's activities in this area can be seen in "Global Marketing: "Disputes Brought Before the WTO." In 2005, world-wide, economic troubles are making further contributions from WTO very difficult. Unemployment in the industrialized nations, large trade deficits in the United States, and heavy debt in many developing countries are causing nations to give more attention to national concerns than to international cooperation.

United Nations Conference on Trade and Development (UNCTAD)

Although WTO has been an important force in world trade expansion, benefits have not been distributed equally. Less developed countries, many of which are members of the WTO, have been dissatisfied with trade arrangements because their share of world trade has been declining and prices of their raw material exports compare unfavorably with prices of their manufactured goods imports. These countries believed that the organization accomplished more to further trade in goods of industrialized nations than it did promote the primary products produced by developing nations. It is true that tariff reductions have been far more important to manufactured goods than to primary products. The result of these countries' dissatisfaction was the formation of **UNCTAD** (United Nations Conference on Trade and Development) in 1964. UNCTAD is a permanent organ of the United Nations General Assembly and counts over 190 member countries.

The goal of UNCTAD is to further the development of emerging nations—by trade as well as by other means.

Subsidies and Retaliation

*A*fter September 11, 2001, travelers were understandably shaken and reluctant to get back into airplanes. Airlines, already facing poor earnings in a highly competitive industry, faced collapse. In hindsight, the number of passengers actually declined very little. Yet airlines slashed prices dramatically in an attempt to regain customers in the months following the attacks on New York and Washington.

Drastically lower revenues produced global industry losses of $2.5 billion in 2001, and losses in subsequent years dwarfed this amount. To support the hard-hit airline industry, the U.S. government provided over $15 billion in aid, including subsidies and loan guarantees, to the U.S. airline companies. Even though the EU provided similar, although smaller, subsidies to its industry, it filed a charge with the WTO, stating that U.S. companies were abusing the government aid to unfairly lower prices in Europe to make up for lost revenue at home.

In response, the EU proposed that a surcharge be placed on foreign airline tickets for non-EU companies that were using subsidies to unfairly lower their prices. This action, referred to as a countervailing duty or tariff, caused a reaction among affected firms. The United States threatened to counter the EU surcharge with surcharges on European-carrier tickets. Just like two children fighting, this sort of behavior can easily escalate. Given the number of jobs at stake in the global airline industry, these subsidies and related issues were important agenda items at future WTO GATS talks.

Sources: "EU Ponders Duty on Foreign Airlines," March 13, 2002, *Financial Post*, World, page FP14;

"Airlines Face More Heavy Losses," May 28, 2002, *South China Morning Post*, Section: Business Post, page 5; "U.S. Carriers Could Incur Large Costs From EC Tariff Plan," March 25, 2002, *Airline Financial News*, Volume 20, Number 12.

Note: The reference to EC is the European Commission.

Documents on Air Transport Services, World Trade Organization, Air Transport Services (http://www.wto.org/english/tratop_e/serv_e/transport_e/transport_air_e.htm), December 22, 2004.

Under WTO, trade expanded, especially in manufactured goods, creating a growing trade gap between industrial and developing countries. UNCTAD seeks to improve the prices of primary goods exports through commodity agree-

Disputes Brought Before the WTO

The WTO addressed approximately 300 complaints between 1995 and 2004. All of the member countries are or were involved in some dispute at one point in time; but the most commonly named complainant or respondent is the United States, followed closely by the EU. Disputes are as likely to rise between developing countries as they are between developed and developing nations; and disputes cover every imaginable good, service, and law—from alcohol, apples, and auto parts to grapefruit, macaroni, pet food, and polypropylene, as well as underwear and water. Telecommunication services, patent codes, tariff preferences, and subsidies, as well as film revenue and sound recordings, are the basis of other disputes. The most commonly cited areas, though, remain agricultural, steel, and textile goods. A representative selection follows.

Mexico: Measures Affecting Telecommunications (filed by the United States); 6 June 2004

India: Anti-dumping measure on batteries from Bangladesh (filed by Bangladesh); 2 February 2004

Dominican Republic: Measures affecting the importation and internal sale of cigarettes (filed by Honduras); 13 October 2003

United States: Definitive Safeguard Measures on Imports of Certain Steel Products (filed by Brazil); 23 May 2002

Turkey: Import Ban on Pet Food from Hungary (filed by Hungary); 7 May 2002

Slovakia: Safeguard Measure on Imports of Sugar (filed by Poland); 17 July 2001

Mexico: Measures affecting telecommunications services (filed by the United States); 27 August 2000

Trinidad and Tobago: Provisional anti-dumping measure on imports of macaroni and spaghetti from Costa Rica (filed by Costa Rica); 20 January 2000

Canada: Measures affecting film distribution services (filed by EU); 22 January 1998

Peru: Countervailing duty investigation against imports of buses from Brazil (filed by Brazil); 9 January 1998

Turkey: Taxation of foreign film revenues (filed by the United States); 17 June 1996

European Union: Import duties on rice (filed by Thailand); 11 October 1995

Source: WTO web site
(http://www.wto.org/english/tratop_e/dispu_e/dispu_status_e.htm).

ments. If the commodity-producing countries of e.g., oil, minerals and food products, could get together to control supply, higher prices and higher returns would result.

UNCTAD has also worked to establish a tariff preference system favoring the export of manufactured goods from less developed countries. Since these countries have not been able to export commodities in a quantity sufficient to maintain their share of trade, they want to expand in the growth area of world trade: industrial exports. They believe they might achieve this if manufactured goods coming from developing countries faced lower tariffs than the same goods coming from developed countries.

UNCTAD has made modest progress. One achievement is its own formation, a new club for world trade matters that is a lobbying group for developing country interests. Former Tanzanian president Julius Nyerere called it "the labor union of the developing countries." Through UNCTAD, developing countries have also received preferential tariff treatment from the EU, Japan, and the United States, as they requested. Overall, UNCTAD has focused world attention on the trade needs of developing countries and has given them a more coherent voice. UNCTAD's committees and studies have also made for a more informed dialogue.

WTO, UNCTAD, and the Firm

WTO's success in reducing barriers to trade has meant that a firm's global logistics can be more efficient. Further, the firm, through its subsidiaries in various markets, can help protect its interest in trade matters through discussions with governments in advance of trade negotiations. In the United States, for example, a committee holds hearings at which business representatives can present their international trading problems. These problems are noted for consideration in WTO negotiations. Firms in the EU usually work with trade associations that channel industry views to the EU negotiators. Brazil also looks to trade associations for industry views.

UNCTAD can have a more direct impact on a firm than WTO. International firms can play a major role by relating to the tariff preferences granted by the industrialized nations. Developing countries have limited experience in exporting manufactured goods. By itself, elimination of tariffs is not sufficient to help those countries. In these cases, the multinational firm can be a decisive factor. If the firm combines its know-how and resources with those of the host country, it can offer competitive exports. Included in the firm's resources is its global distribution network, which could be the critical factor in gaining foreign market access. Also, the firm supplies the foreign marketing know-how lacked by most developing country producers. For example, if Ford had the choice of importing engines from its plant in Britain or its plant in Brazil, it might choose Brazil if engines from Brazil had a zero tariff and engines from Europe faced a 15 percent duty.

International Financial System

A major goal of business is to make a profit, so firms pay close attention to financial matters. International companies must be even more concerned with financial matters than national firms because international companies deal with many currencies and many national financial markets where conditions differ. Marketing across national boundaries involves financial considerations, which will be discussed next.

EXCHANGE RATE INSTABILITY

International payments are one aspect of the financial side of international trade. In most cases, international transactions occur in different currencies. Dealing with multiple currencies is not a serious problem in itself, but difficulties arise because currencies frequently change in value with regard to each other and in unpredictable ways.

A **foreign exchange rate** is the domestic price of a foreign currency. For the United States, this means that there is a dollar rate, or price, for the British pound, the Swiss franc, and the Brazilian real, as well as every other currency. If one country changes the value of its currency, firms selling to or from that country may find that the altered exchange rate is sufficient to wipe out their profit or, on the brighter side, to provide a windfall gain. In any case, the firms must be alert for currency variations in order to optimize their financial performance. (See "Global Marketing: That Will Cost You A Little More, Sir.")

If you ever traveled abroad and used a foreign currency, you participated in a foreign exchange transaction. You bought or exchanged your currency for another currency. From a tourist's perspective, it's good when your currency is strong and you can purchase a lot for your (domestic) currency; it's bad when your (domestic) currency is weak and you have to spend more for a good meal or nice jacket. But if you are a manufacturer who depends on exports, when your domestic currency is expensive, demand for your products will likely decrease. Supply and demand for goods and services are affected by the price of the currency that people use and by the volatility of the currency. The more a currency changes in value, the more volatile the currency is and the harder it is to predict the cost of whatever people buy with that currency.

Major currency traders include banks and other financial institutions, which trade currencies in the hundreds of billions of dollars every day. Trading is used in business transactions (for example, Dell may need yuan to pay suppliers in China), but also for speculative reasons. Just as traders in stock exchanges seek profits, foreign currency traders gamble on whether the price of a currency will rise or fall.

GLOBAL MARKETING

That Will Cost You a Little More, Sir

Imagine that the $300 stereo equipment you are looking at suddenly goes up in price to $500. When buying products that are made abroad (and so many things are made abroad), you don't usually think about the exchange rate between your currency and that of the manufacturer. Do you own a Toyota or a Volkswagen? Did you look up the exchange rate between the U.S. dollar and the Japanese yen or German euro? Probably not. If you ever traveled to a country that uses a different currency, you undoubtedly watched the exchange rate, which probably changed a few cents or more between the time you planned your trip and the time you returned. So whether buying a hamburger in Paris or a jacket in Hong Kong, you are likely to calculate the cost in dollars or some other home currency.

When companies manufacture something in another country, even if the item consists of only one of the components of a product, the firm must consider the cost of doing so in the local currency because that is how the locals expect to be paid. Or, if a firm makes something in one country and sells it in another country, the exchange rate is important because the price must be stated in a foreign currency (like the stereo sold in the United States and the hamburger sold in Paris). When the exchange rate changes, costs and prices change, too. Sometimes currency prices relative to one another are very stable and change little over time; sometimes, though, the change can be substantial and sudden. Consider the following:

Change in Price Relative to $US

Country/Area	Currency	Change over 3 Months (%)	Change over 1 Year (%)
Euro-zone	Euro	-2.82	-10.72
Mexico	Peso	-1.80	+4.69
South Africa	Rand	-2.10	-11.03
Switzerland	Franc	-2.77	-11.36
United Kingdom	Pound	-2.17	-13.96

August 20, 2004, was used as end date. Source: http://www.uta.fi/~ktmatu/rate-datamenu.html (University of Tampere).

continued

To put this in perspective, imagine that firms making the following products decided to pass along to the consumer the entire 10 or 15 percent increase in their prices.

Change in Price ($US)

Item	Original Price	10% Increase	15% Increase
Jeans	$50.00	$55.00	$57.50
Textbook	$110.00	$121.00	$126.50
Computer	$1,500.00	$1,650.00	$1,725.00
Car	$18,000.00	$19,800.00	$20,700.00

Sometimes that "little bit more" can be a lot.

Whether a currency increases or decreases in value relative to another currency is important. When the Canadian dollar is strong or strengthens relative to other currencies, you can buy more euros for each Canadian dollar, for example. That is good for tourists traveling to the Euro-zone. It is not good for Canadian manufacturers, though, because Canadians will buy foreign-made goods and services instead of those produced in Canada. When the Canadian dollar is weak or weakens, you can purchase fewer units of foreign currency. That generally means that tourists will spend less time abroad and purchase fewer souvenirs. Businesses that use foreign suppliers also have to pay more Canadian dollars for the foreign currency used to pay for their foreign-made components and supplies.

Currency prices also reflect the overall health of an economy and, in part, explain why people believe a strong currency is good and a weak currency is bad for the consumer. A nation that has a positive **balance of trade**, or trade surplus, is exporting more products than it is importing. That means traders need to purchase the nation's currency to pay for those products. The more demand there is for a currency, the higher the price. Countries that are growing or that have a stable economy attract investors. Investors need the local currency to buy property, build factories, etc., which, in turn, increases demand for the currency and raises its price.

Added exchange stability within the EU was a major reason behind the adoption of the **euro** (€). This process involved cooperation and coordination of fiscal and monetary policies among the EU member participants, the creation of a European Central Bank, and the loss of substantial national sovereignty on policies that had a direct impact on employment and economic growth.

A Brief History

The following historical perspective is helpful in understanding the global organizations that formed shortly after World War II, the goals of which included fostering an environment of exchange rate stability.

In the days of the gold standard, exchange rates did not change in value. The stability and certainty of the international gold standard came to an end, however, with the advent of World War I. The international financial system of the 1930s had no certainty, stability, or accepted rules. Instead, there were frequent and arbitrary changes in exchange rates. This chaotic and uncertain situation contributed to the decline in international trade during that period. The worldwide Depression of the 1930s was reinforced by the added risks in international finance.

At the conclusion of World War II, nations met to address some of the problems that were believed to be contributing factors leading up to the war. In 1944, some of the allied nations met at Bretton Woods, New Hampshire, to design a better international economic system for the postwar world. One element of this system dealt with international trade, resulting in the formation of the WTO. Another element – concerned with the need for international capital led to the formation of the World Bank. A third aspect ,involving the international monetary system, resulted in the establishment of the International Monetary Fund (IMF), to which we turn next.

INTERNATIONAL MONETARY FUND (IMF)

The **IMF** was originally designed to help nations control exchange rate fluctuations by having members agree on a specific exchange rate (U.S. dollars per British pound, for example) and then using vast stores of gold to buy and sell currencies to maintain those exchange rates. (For instance, buying U.S. dollars with gold—taking dollars out of circulation—would make dollars scarce and force the price up; selling dollars for gold—releasing dollars into the world supply—would force the price to decline.) This worked well. Trade increased dramatically after World War II, in part because currency prices were stable, making it less risky to buy and sell products and services denominated in other currencies.

The system failed in the early 1970s because there was too little gold to offset the tremendous amount of foreign currency being used. In essence, the system fell victim to its success. Since then, currencies "float" freely in price relative to one another, with prices being determined by supply and demand. There is only occasional intervention by the IMF or central banks of various nations.

In the new millennium, the IMF plays a slightly different role. The organization and some of its members still occasionally intervene in foreign exchange markets; but this intervention, while it does affect currency prices, cannot control prices to the degree that was first established under the Bretton Woods agreement. Most often the IMF acts as a forum for monetary and fiscal discussions that affect the world economy, much as the UN acts as a forum for initiatives designed to promote peace. In addition to providing a forum for discussion, the IMF supplies financial assistance in the form of loans (usually for stabilizing a currency or for balance-of-payment problems) and technical assistance in the form of economic consultants (who provide advice to governments on designing effective economic and financial policies). All of their initiatives are designed to support the core IMF goals, which have remained the same since its inception: the promotion of worldwide financial stability and economic growth.

Financial stability and economic growth lead to more customers for the world's products and remove some of the risks associated with international trade.

The importance of currency prices is that international marketers must contend with exchange rates that are continuously changing, which complicates decision making about international pricing and logistics.

The World Bank Group

The **World Bank** is another institution conceived at Bretton Woods. Originally called the International Bank for Reconstruction and Development (IBRD), its primary mission was to assist war-torn countries of World War II in rebuilding their cities and infrastructure through loans with very favorable terms. Like the IMF, the World Bank plays a different role today. The goals of promoting economic growth remain, and the World Bank still provides many loans for infrastructure development. However, instead of helping countries such as England and other developed nations, assistance goes primarily to developing nations. Today the World Bank Group includes the IBRD, the International Development Association (IDA), the IFC, and the Multilateral Investment Guarantee Agency (MIGA). The activities of these organizations support the main goal of the World Bank Group, which is to improve the living conditions of the world's population, especially among the poorest countries. Loans for schools, roads, and telecommunication projects create potential consumers and an environment better able to support the needs of businesses.

Regional Economies

Nations have agreed to work together to pursue common economic goals. Formal agreements have been signed among nations that are similar in terms of culture and religion (such as ALADIA), among neighbors (ECOWAS), and among countries that are similar in terms of relative wealth and economic development (CARICOM). When discussing these agreements or groups of nations, the term *regional economic integration* is used. While the countries invariably sign these agreements because of the potential or perceived economic benefits, they are not always comprised of nations from a specific region. For instance, in late 2004, the EU began accession talks with Turkey that may eventually lead to EU membership. However, many believe that the culture of Turkey is too different from that of other EU members and that because Turkey is an Asian, not a European, nation, it is not an appropriate EU candidate. The next section highlights some of these regional groups.

Regional Economic Integration

As stated previously, another major development since World War II has been the growth of regional groupings. The EU is best known and most successful, but it is only one of many. Regional groupings result from agreements between nations in the same region; their goal is to cooperate in various economic matters. There may also be political ties between these nations, but it is the economic aspect that is important. **Regionalism**, or economic cooperation within regions, is an attempt by nations to attain goals they cannot achieve in isolation. The North Atlantic Treaty Organization (NATO) is a counterpart in the military field. Some major regional groupings are shown in Table 2-5.

There are costs to a nation in joining a regional group, the chief one being that it must give up some **national sovereignty**, which is a nation's right to govern itself without outside interference. Nations do this only because they hope the benefits will be greater than the costs. The major benefit sought through economic integration is faster economic growth. By joining together, member nations gain additional resources, larger markets, and economies of scale for their industries. Another objective of regional groupings is *countervailing power*. For example, the EU seeks a stronger position against the economic power of the United States and Japan.

The reduction of trade barriers within the group adds dynamism to member economies by increasing competition. Sluggish national firms and monopolies lose their protective walls and are forced to change in a more competitive direction. Furthermore, the group of countries together may be able to afford an industry too large for any individual member country. Thus, industrialization can be aided by regional integration. All of this may mean greater wealth, progress, and self-sufficiency for the region. Various forms and degrees of economic integration are possible.

Forms of Economic Integration

Economic integration takes many forms. Among the most common types is the free-trade area. Distinguishing characteristics and examples of various types of economic integration are presented in the following section.

FREE-TRADE AREA

Although all regional groupings have economic goals, the various groups differ in organization and motivation. There are three basic kinds of organization for economic integration. The simplest is a **free-trade area**, in which the member countries agree to have free movement of goods among themselves; that is, no tariffs or quotas are imposed against goods coming from other members. The European Free Trade Association (EFTA) is a major example. The EFTA agreement was signed on January 4, 1960, and included Austria, Denmark, Norway, Portugal, Sweden, Switzerland, and the United Kingdom. Today EFTA is an international organization that includes Iceland, Liechtenstein, Norway, and Switzerland. The original EFTA members, except for Switzerland, decided to take more comprehensive steps to unify trading and other policies by forming what was to become the EU or by joining the EU at a later date. Because of the manifest benefits to members in cooperating, in 1992, EFTA and the EU agreed to form an even larger country grouping called the European Economic Area (EEA); it contains all of the EU and EFTA members except Switzerland. Signing these agreements requires that nations give some of their national sovereignty to the parent organization or group. Switzerland and the other EFTA members do not agree with all of the EU policies and clearly demonstrated their desire to maintain their independence by not joining the EU.[10]

In the 1960s, Latin Americans responded to European integration moves by forming regional groupings of their own. In Central America, they formed the Central American Common Market (CACM); in South America, they formed the Latin American Free Trade Area (LAFTA). The Andean countries broke away from LAFTA to form the Andean Common Market. Unfortunately, none of those groups has made rapid progress. In the early 1990s, the Southern Cone countries (Argentina, Brazil, Paraguay, and Uruguay) formed Mercosur, which has made some progress.

During the Vietnam War, a number of Southeast Asian nations formed the Association of Southeast Asian Nations (ASEAN). ASEAN includes over 500 million people, with a collective GNI of more than US$750 billion. In 1992, ASEAN launched the ASEAN Free Trade Area (AFTA), the strategic objective of which is to increase the ASEAN region's competitive advantage as a single production unit. The elimination of tariffs and NTBs among the member countries is expected to promote greater economic efficiency, productivity, and competitiveness.[11]

The United States is a member of two free-trade areas, one with Israel and one with Canada and Mexico. The latter is known as **NAFTA** (North American Free Trade Agreement). NAFTA is very important because it creates a free-trade area of 410 million consumers—as large as the EU-EFTA grouping. As with any regional grouping, NAFTA has encountered some rough spots; but its importance can be seen in the fact that the three member countries are each other's largest customers and suppliers. (The United States also has agreements on free trade with many other nations, including Chile, Jordan, and Australia; but these are not the same as free-trade areas.)

In December 1994, Canada, the United States, and Mexico, as well as other nations in the Americas, established the Free Trade Agreement of the Americas (FTAA). FTAA has 34 members (800 million people), stretching from Alaska to Tierra del Fuego. The goal was to complete negotiations for the agreement by December 2005.[12]

Table 2-5. Selected Regional Economic Groupings

ALADIA: La Asociación Latinoamericana de Integración (Latin American Integration Association [LAIA])
Argentina, Bolivia, Brazil, Chile, Columbia, Cuba, Ecuador, Mexico, Paraguay, Peru, Uruguay, and Venezuela

ASEAN: Association of Southeast Asian Nations
Brunei, Cambodia, Indonesia, Laos, Malaysia, Myanmar, Philippines, Singapore, Thailand, and Vietnam

CAN: Comunidad Andina (Andean Community)
Bolivia, Columbia, Ecuador, Peru, and Venezuela

CARICOM: Caribbean Community
Antigua and Barbuda, Bahamas, the Barbados, Belize, Dominica, Grenada, Guyana, Haiti, Jamaica, Montserrat, St. Kitts and Nevis, St. Lucia, St. Vincent and the Grenadines, Suriname, Trinidad, and Tobago

ECOWAS: Economic Community of West African States
Benin, Burkina Faso, Cape Verde, Ivory Coast, Gambia, Ghana, Guinea, Guinea Bissau, Liberia, Mali, Niger, Nigeria, Senegal, Sierra Leone, and Togo

EU: European Union
Austria, Belgium, Cyprus, the Czech Republic, Denmark, Estonia, Finland, France, Germany, Greece, Hungary, Ireland, Italy, Latvia, Lithuania, Luxembourg, Malta, the Netherlands, Poland, Portugal, Slovakia, Slovenia, Spain, Sweden, and the United Kingdom

Mercosur
Argentina, Brazil, Paraguay, and Uruguay

NAFTA: North American Free Trade Agreement
Canada, Mexico, and the United States

CUSTOMS UNION

Though similar to a free-trade area in that it has no tariffs on trade among members, a **customs union** adds the more ambitious requirement that members also have a uniform tariff on trade with nonmembers. Thus, a customs union is like a single nation not only in having internal trade, but also in presenting a united front to the rest of the world with its common external tariff. A customs union is more difficult to achieve than a free-trade area because each member must yield its sovereignty in commercial policy matters—not just with member nations, but with the whole world. Its advantage lies in making the economic integration stronger and avoiding the administrative problems of a free-trade area. For example, in a free-trade area, imports of a particular good would always enter the member country with the lowest tariff, regardless of the country of destination. To avoid this perversion of trade patterns, special regulations are necessary.

The leading example of a customs union is the EU. Although the EU is often referred to as the Common Market, it has successfully achieved customs unions status. As it continues to put into practice the 1992 Maastricht Treaty directives, the EU will possess many common market characteristics. Furthermore, with the implementation of a common currency in 12 member states and the formation of a European Union Central Bank, the EU has begun to adopt properties of an economic union. Though this has taken longer than EFTA, it represents a more ambitious endeavor because it includes not only a free-trade area among members, but also a common external tariff. In addition, it covers agricultural products, which were omitted by EFTA.

COMMON MARKET

A true **common market** includes a customs union but goes significantly beyond it because it seeks to standardize or harmonize all government regulations affecting trade. These include all aspects of government policy that pertain to business; for example, corporation and excise taxes, labor laws, fringe benefits and social security programs, incorporation laws, and antitrust laws. In such an economic union, business and trade decisions would be unaffected by the national laws of different members because the laws would be uniform. The United States is the closest example of a com-

mon market. Even in the United States, however, the example is not perfect because different states have different laws and taxes pertaining to business. U.S. business decisions, therefore, are somewhat influenced by differing state laws.

As mentioned earlier, the EU is the best contemporary example of a common market undergoing formation; but there are added dimensions that go beyond even a common market classification. The diverse cultures make it difficult to implement some initiatives. It took nearly ten years to implement an EU passport because, among other things, there was disagreement over the color and emblem to use on the cover. On the other hand, the implementation of the currency switch in 2002, from national to European euro, took less than the six months originally expected because of careful planning and intense marketing. In the years and months leading up to the conversion, companies and consumers were exposed to television and radio advertisements, information sessions at their workplaces, prices printed in both national and euro denominations, web sites, brochures, and billboards, all explaining the seemingly mundane. On January 1, 2002, the first day the new currency was available, people were so anxious to get it that many ATMs ran out of euros.

There is still a good deal of work to accomplish. Not all members of the EU wanted to give up their national currency (Denmark, Sweden, and the United Kingdom). This makes expansion of the Euro-zone more difficult because initiatives, particularly those related to monetary and fiscal policy, cannot be applied throughout the entire EU until all members join the monetary union. Enlargement is another issue; and in some respects, it is the most important one the EU faces. On May 1, 2004, ten nations were admitted to the EU (Cyprus, the Czech Republic, Estonia, Hungary, Latvia, Lithuania, Malta, Poland, Slovakia, and Slovenia); and other nations, such as Bulgaria and Romania, are awaiting admittance into the union. One major concern is that some of these nations will require extraordinary assistance because they are not as well off economically as many of the current members. In addition, some of these countries have considerable infrastructure needs. This means that the richer nations will have to underwrite or support some of their poorer neighbors.

German unification in the early 1990s was an example of this phenomenon on a smaller scale. Former West

Table 2-6. Forms of Economic Integration

Stage of Integration	Elimination of Trade Barriers among Members	Common Trade Barriers among Members	Free Factor Mobility	Coordination of Economic Policies	Coordination of Political Policies
Free-Trade Area	Yes	No	No	No	No
Customs Union	Yes	Yes	No	No	No
Common Market	Yes	Yes	Yes	No	No
Economic Union	Yes	Yes	Yes	Yes	No
Political Union	Yes	Yes	Yes	Yes	Yes

Germans complain about the high taxes they continue to pay for integrating the former East Germans into the economy. On the other hand, the former East Germans did not automatically become rich overnight; nor did they have the ability to purchase everything they wanted. Goods in the former West Germany were not subject to the price controls the people had come to expect under the Communist regime. While more goods were available, they were also relatively expensive. Few people are completely happy.[13] A summary of differences among various forms of integration is presented in Table 2-6.

OTHER GROUPINGS

Economic unions among nations are characterized by a common currency. Underlying this obvious aspect is the coordination of fiscal and monetary policies (establishment of prime lending rates of interest, size of reserves banks must retain, etc.). This form of integration is uncommon because of the impact on inflation and unemployment rates. A review of the discussions surrounding the adoption of the euro among EU members highlights some of these issues and the difficulties in obtaining Euro-zone consensus. The requirement that members of an economic union adopt harmonized fiscal and monetary policies is a major reason behind some EU members opting out of the Euro-zone. (For an overview of some of the issues involved, see "The Euro, Our Currency" at http://europa.eu.int/comm/economy_finance/euro/our_currency_en.htm.)

As shown in Table 2-6, political unions require adoption of the principles behind the other forms of integration, as well as the adoption of a governing structure that supercedes individual national or state interests. One characteristic that indicates a group is moving in this direction is when the members of the union agree to the jurisdiction of the same governing body. Other characteristics include a common army and common foreign policy related to international issues. Political unions are actually more common than many people realize. Many nations in the world today are federations of smaller geographic areas that at one time or another believed they would be better off if they cooperated. Germany, a federation of 16 states, is a good example. The United States is a grouping of what were once independent states, some of which minted their own currency, manned their own militias, and collected tolls or duties at their borders. Vestiges of this state independence in the United States include drivers' licenses and driving laws that differ from state to state and licensing requirements for lawyers, doctors, and other professions, which are regulated at the state, not the federal, level of government.

There are also a number of examples of looser forms of economic cooperation. Many of these are of interest because they can affect the operations of a firm. Many nations of Africa are associate members of the EU and enjoy preferential entry of their goods into EU countries.

EU producers, in turn, have an advantage over non-EU producers in selling to the associated states. Association agreements exist between the EU and other nations, including Algeria, Egypt, Israel, Jordan, Lebanon, Morocco, Syria, Tunisia, Turkey, and the Palestinian Authority.

The appearance of regional economic groupings is a promising development both for the regions and for multinational firms. For example, in August 2004, Russian President Vladimir Putin announced plans for a "Unified Economic Space" that included Russia, Ukraine, Belarus, and Kazakhstan. The unfortunate reality is that, except for the EU and Mercosur, these groupings have made very little progress. (See "Global Marketing: African Unity.")

While NAFTA has its problems, it should be a solid performer. Efforts elsewhere have done little, though ASEAN holds promise for the future. Where integration is successful, it offers opportunities for firms that can operate within the group, but challenges for those on the outside.

Devolution, the decomposition of national and regional groupings, is a reflection of diverse points of view and counteracts some of the regional and global cooperation sought by the EU, NAFTA, and organizations such as the WTO, the IMF, and others. Consider the breakup of the Soviet Union into a multitude of new nations, the creation of new countries from the former Czechoslovakia and Yugoslavia, the continuing call by separatists for more autonomy for Corsicans from France, and the near-national division of the Flemish and Walloons in Belgium. Those examples should serve as a reminder to marketers to consider the diversity of needs within regional groups and to proceed with caution when developing regional strategies.

REGIONALISM AND THE MULTINATIONAL COMPANY

The rise of regional groupings means that fewer but larger economic entities are gradually replacing the multitude of national markets. When a firm is considering an investment decision, the relevant market area may include up to 25 countries rather than just one national market. For example, the "United States of Europe" and "Euro-land" are expressions used to describe the new Europe. An indication of the importance of the EU to American investors is provided by the following statistic: Over 65 percent of all capital flowing out of the United States in 2003 ($99 of $152 billion) went to Europe. Analysts attribute the amount and the growth in foreign investment flowing into the EU to harmonization of product specifications, lower foreign exchange risk, and other steps taken in the economic integration of the nations that make up the EU.[14]

A firm's logistics will be modified by regional groupings. There will be pressures to supply a region from within rather than to export to it. A firm will have the added incentive of the larger market; but it will also benefit by getting behind the tariff barrier, where it will be able to compete better with local producers and be protected from outside competition. At the same time, these local producers will become stronger competitors due to economies of scale in the larger market, the alliances they are forming, and the stronger competition in the free-trade area. A firm's operations within a regional group will tend to be more uniform and self-contained than they would be in ungrouped national markets.

In response to global forces and economic integration, a firm's marketing program will be modified over time. As the differences in markets diminish, greater uniformity will occur in marketing to member countries. A firm will gain economies of scale in product development, pricing, distribution, and promotion. For example, as member nations harmonize their food, drug, and labeling laws, a firm can eliminate product and packaging differences that were required by different national laws. Similar modifications will occur in the other functional areas. The first of the following examples illustrates how firms reacted to the formation of the EU. The second is a success story of a firm that increased its marketing because of lower trade barriers among NAFTA members.

The New Eastern Europe

One of the major developments in recent history was the fall of the Berlin Wall and the decline of Communism. The fragmentation of the Communist bloc reduced the threat of war between East and West and significantly improved economic relations between the two groups. Each side considered the other to be the enemy until about 1990. Today they share friendly relations, and Western nations are providing substantial financial assistance to Eastern European nations. On May 1, 2004, eight former Communist nations were admitted into the EU.

FDI into these former Communist nations is soaring as well, averaging $25 billion annually between 1998 and 2002. Given these nations' rich oil and natural gas reserves, large investments continue to be made in their petroleum industries.[15]

The countries of Eastern Europe provide a very attractive potential market of 400 million people, which is more than that of all of Western Europe. Generally, there is also a familiarity with and a desire for Western goods and a Western standard of living. And the people in these countries are relatively rich compared to markets in developing nations. (See summary profile in Table 2-7.)

Although the markets look attractive, potential problems in Eastern Europe suggest caution. After years of Communist rule, Eastern European countries need to establish a legal system that can deal properly with a market economy and property rights. In addition, they lack hard currencies and stable monetary systems. After decades of a

GLOBAL MARKETING

African Unity

In the early 1960s, a number of African nations established the Organization of African Unity (OAU). The OAU did not meet many of its economic goals in the ensuing 40 years. As a result, in July 2000, 53 African nations agreed to disband the OAU and replace it with a new organization, the African Union (AU). The AU is based on the "New Partnership for Africa's Development" and the EU model. Fifty-three nations have agreed on the general terms of the agreement, which include good governance, free press, and fiscal transparency. Their goals include creating an environment in which the nations of the African continent can enter the mainstream of worldwide economic development. Through establishment of peacekeeping forces, a security council, and a legislature, the focus in the immediate future is to mediate wars and internal strife and to begin to address the abject poverty common to many nations by seeking debt relief so the nations can use funds to feed and meet other needs of their people. The ultimate goal is to create an EU-like structure, including monetary union under one currency and a central bank.

While the announcement was accompanied by dancing in the streets (literally), the obstacles to success seem almost insurmountable. These 53 nations have highly diverse ethnic groups within their national boundaries. The differences are sharp enough to be at the center of the warfare and genocide that has been all too common throughout Africa over the past few decades. Furthermore, independence is fiercely guarded after a history of colonial rule. Those factors will make it difficult for the AU to reach any agreements by which all can abide. With few financial resources and crushing levels of debt, there is not enough money to build schools, roads, and other infrastructure. In turn, economic development will be difficult if firms do not have a ready resource of skilled local labor and if they cannot get their products to market. More importantly, without the funds needed to supply basic health care, food, and housing, large numbers of people will continue to die and there will be little hope of focusing much beyond survival. It is vital that the AU succeed in reducing strife and debt levels if economic development and global integration is to occur, and it is a wise leadership that realizes this.

Sources: Jon Jeter, "New Organization Replaces African Post-Colonial Relic," Tuesday, January 9, 2002, *Washington Post*, page A15; see also NEPAD, the document upon which AU is founded (http://www.nepad.com).

command economy, people and institutions lack a commercial or market mentality. Problems in adjusting to a market economy have caused political instability. The Russian crisis of 1998, corruption, and other difficulties in the petroleum and banking industries are examples. Another legacy of the command economy is a weak distribution infrastructure. In other words, reaping the Eastern Europe potential is as much a challenge as it is an opportunity.

Despite these problems, many Western firms have entered Eastern European markets. They believe that the potential is too great to ignore and that there are first-mover advantages: The first firm to become well established as the market is developing could be difficult to compete with later.

The U.S. government has recognized the potential promise of Eastern Europe and has established a service to encourage and assist American firms in doing business there. Its acronym, appropriately, is BISNIS. (See "Global Marketing: Commerce Promotes Business with Business Information Services for the Newly Independent States [BISNIS].")

Table 2-7. GNI in Central Europe and Former Soviet Union (USSR) Nations, 2002

Area/Nation	Population (millions)	GNI (billions $US)	GNI Growth (annual %)	GNI per Capita ($US)
Central Europe				
Albania	3.2	4.8	4.7	1,450
Bosnia & Herzegovina	4.1	5.6	3.9	1,310
Bulgaria	7.9	15.5	4.8	1,770
Croatia	4.5	22.4	5.2	4,540
Czech Republic	10.2	69.5	2.0	5,480
Hungary	10.2	65.8	3.3	5,290
Macedonia, FYR	2.0	3.8	0.7	1,710
Poland	38.2	189.0	1.4	4,570
Romania	22.3	45.7	4.3	1,870
Serbia and Montenegro	5.4	23.7	4.7	3,970
Slovak Republic	8.2	15.7	4.0	1,400
Slovenia	2.0	22.0	3.0	10,370
Total	**118.0**	**483.6**		
Average			3.5	**$3,644**
Former USSR				
Armenia	3.1	2.4	12.9	790
Azerbaijan	8.2	6.1	10.6	710
Belarus	9.9	14.3	4.7	1,360
Estonia	1.4	6.5	6.0	4,190
Georgia	5.2	3.4	5.6	650
Kazakhstan	14.9	24.6	9.8	1,520
Kyrgyz Republic	5.0	1.6	-0.5	290
Latvia	2.3	8.4	6.1	3,480
Lithuania	3.5	13.8	7.2	3,670
Moldova	4.3	1.6	7.2	460
Russian Fed.	144.1	346.5	4.3	2,130
Tajikistan	6.3	1.2	9.1	180
Turkmenistan	4.8	7.7	14.9	1,090
Ukraine	48.7	41.5	4.8	780
Uzbekistan	25.3	7.9	4.2	310
Total	**286.7**	**487.5**		
Average			7.1	**$1,441**
Total of All Nations	**404.7**	**971.1**		
Average of All			5.5	**$2,420**

Note: GNI is calculated in current $US; GNI per capita is calculated using World Bank Atlas method in current US$. As defined by the World Bank, Gross National Income (GNI) is the sum of value added by all resident producers plus any product taxes (less subsidies) not included in the valuation of output; plus net receipts of primary income (compensation of employees and property income) from abroad.

Source: World Bank, *2003 World Development Indicators*, Data Query (http://devdata.worldbank.org/data-query); accessed July 27, 2004.

National Economies

In a discussion of international marketing, some nations bear special consideration because of their population or the amount or growth rate of their trade. Economic-related characteristics also affect what is marketed and how it is marketed. National data about population, income, infrastructure, and natural endowments are presented in the following passages to illustrate their impact on marketing.

The United States

Although the international environment of a firm is important, the global influence of its home base cannot be ignored. In ways varying from country to country, the home government affects the international operations of a firm, both positively and negatively. A Swedish or Dutch multinational company operates under a set of advantages and constraints different from those that affect a U.S. or a Japanese firm or a firm from one of the former colonial powers of England or France. Using the United States as an example, the text will discuss the advantages and constraints peculiar to a U.S. multinational company. The pattern can be applied to international firms domiciled in other nations.

One impact on a firm's international operations is its home government's policies toward such business. Most governments encourage exports. The United States is no different: U.S. government assistance is offered through the information and promotional services of the Department of Commerce. Furthermore, the Export-Import Bank helps finance American exports and offers a government-assisted program of export credit insurance and political-risk insurance.

The U.S. foreign aid program has helped U.S. companies export to markets that otherwise would have been closed because of their lack of foreign exchange. Those foreign aid programs that have a favorable effect on recipient nations' attitudes toward the United States improve the environment for the firms. A critical determinant of a firm's ability to export is, of course, the resource endowment of its home country. Furthermore, the business environment at home may have taught the firm skills that aid its performance abroad. Each state in the United States also maintains economic development agencies, the goals of which are to promote state exports and attract foreign investors. The type and level of assistance varies but generally includes market assessment, identification of trade leads, and trade missions to other nations.

Other U.S. policies relate to international business. The government has encouraged investment in less developed countries by its investment-guarantee program. Although not as favorable as in the past and undergoing

G L O B A L
MARKETING

Commerce Promotes Business with Business Information Services for the Newly Independent States (BISNIS)

*S*ince the nations of the former Soviet Union hold a lot of potential, Business Information Services for the Newly Independent States (BISNIS) was established in 1992 as a separate and special entity of the U.S. Department of Commerce's International Trade Administration. BISNIS is charged with promoting and facilitating trade and investment between the United States and the former Soviet Union states of Armenia, Azerbaijan, Belarus, Georgia, Kazakhstan, the Kyrgyz Republic, Moldova, the Russian Federation, Tajikistan, Turkmenistan, Ukraine, and Uzbekistan. (The United States classifies Estonia, Latvia, and Lithuania as the Baltic States and does not include them in this initiative.) BISNIS has ten offices in Russia and one in each of the other nations. Services offered include market information, counseling, electronic market updates and trade lead information, the monthly newsletter (BUSINESS Bulletin), and postings on its English- and Russian-language web pages. BISNIS Expolink Eurasia, an electronic exhibition area for U.S. companies, was recently added. While they are free to post, American firms must have their company information translated into Russian. BISNIS efforts have resulted in over $3 billion in U.S. exports and investment between 1992 and 2002.

Source: http://www.bisnis.doc.gov.

changes, government tax policy is favorable to business in foreign countries.

The government's commercial policy can help or hinder a firm internationally. As was previously stated, when a nation adopts free-trade policies rather than a protectionist stance with other nations, firms of that nation generally find it easier to conduct business in foreign countries. Firms are not completely helpless; they may be able to influence their nation's commercial policy by lobbying the appropriate government officials.

Other government actions and national achievements

can affect a firm internationally. U.S. antitrust policy has constrained U.S. companies abroad. American technological and space achievements aid U.S. companies in sales of high-technology products. In part, these technological advances are supported by government funds for research and development (R&D). On the other hand, foreign dissatisfaction with the U.S. role in the world can threaten foreign operations of U.S. firms. Dissatisfaction over some U.S. action may lead to a march on the U.S. Embassy abroad—or the local Goodyear plant or the local Coca-Cola bottler.

The size and wealth of the U.S. economy are a source of both envy and resentment. They affect the image of U.S. companies abroad, often considered to have an unfair advantage over local companies. The United States is the world's leading exporter and importer. This lends weight to U.S. commercial policy negotiations, which favor foreign sales by U.S. firms. Since the U.S. market is so attractive, other countries must open up their markets if they want to sell to the United States. In those and other ways, a company's nationality affects its international marketing.

Table 2-8. 20 Markets to Watch

Nation	Population (millions)	GNI (millions $US)	2002 Trade (billions $US)	FDI Inflows (millions $US)	Investment Climate
Chile	16	64.2	43.6	1,603	143.3
China	1,280	1,266.1	706.2	52,700	138.8
Czech Republic	10	69.5	92.5	9,319	143.9
Greece	11	132.8	72.1	50	156.7
Hong Kong	7	161.5	111.9	13,718	162.6
India	1,049	510.2	151.2	3,449	123.9
Italy	58	1,184.3	614.8	14,545	166.9
Korea, Republic	48	476.7	376.8	1,972	148.5
Malaysia	24	94.9	204.1	3,203	137.4
Mexico	101	637.2	363.3	13,627	132.6
Philippines	80	78.0	78.7	1,111	120.6
Poland	38	189.0	115.1	4,119	139.0
Portugal	10	121.6	80.4	4,276	162.8
Russian Federation	144	346.5	201.7	2,421	124.0
Singapore	4	87.0	230.8	7,655	176.6
South Africa	45	104.2	68.6	754	129.2
Spain	41	653.1	373.6	21,193	167.2
Thailand	62	126.9	231.6	1,068	136.0
Turkey	70	183.7	105.2	1,037	108.0
Vietnam	80	35.1	41.7	1,200	117.6
United States	**288**	**10,383.1**	**2,374,500**	**30,030**	**172.4**
World	**6,199**	**32,312.2**	**16,263,600**	**651,189**	**108.5**

Notes: Criteria used in selecting these markets include those shown as well as GNI growth rate, trade in goods and trade in services (exports and imports evaluated separately), and business environment—three separate variables. Most statistics were also compared to world totals. Of the criteria shown, GNI is reported in current $US; trade is the total of all merchandise and service imports and exports (Hong Kong and Singapore trade data do not include reexport or reimport data, which is substantial) and is reported in current $US; and investment climate is calculated by using the 2003 *Composite International Country Risk Guide* (ICRG) and the Euromoney country creditworthiness rating ranks as reported in the *2004 World Development Indicators*. The score can range from 0 to 200.

GNI growth rates in some countries (Italy and Portugal) were below 1 percent over the previous year but over the long run, showed better-than-average growth. China and Turkey had GNI growth rates of 8 percent in 2001–2002; many others were in the 4 to 7 percent range.

One criteria used was "time to enforce a contract" measured in days. The time period measures the number of days from filing a lawsuit until payment or settlement. Poland was exceptionally poor in this respect, with the number of days reported to be 1,000! Time to enforce contracts in Italy also requires a substantial amount of time, 645 days. Most countries' enforcement takes less than 12 months. (As a basis of comparison, the United States is listed as taking 365 days.)

The data for the United States and the world are included for comparative purposes.

Sources: World Bank Data Query (http://devdata.worldbank.org/data-query); World Bank, *2003 World Development Indicators*, accessed July 24, 2004; Investment climate: World Bank, *2003 World Development Indicators*, Table 5.2, pages 258-261; Trade data: World Trade Organization, *International Trade Statistics 2003* (http://www.wto.org/english/res_e/statis_e/its2003_e/its03_toc_e.htm) (Appendix Tables A4-A7); FDI data: UNCTAD–*Handbook of Statistics* (Part Six, International finance, Table 6.2 Foreign direct investment: inward and outward flows) (http://www.unctad.org/Templates/webflyer.asp?docid=4324&intItemID=1397&lang=1&mode=toc).

Markets to Watch

Rising personal fortunes from Internet and high-technology ventures in the 1990s was followed by the "dot-com bubble burst," a general decline in economic well-being, and negative economic growth rates in the industrialized world. Not every nation followed this trend, however; and there are some bright areas on the horizon with regard to trade and economic development. Besides those already mentioned—the so-called Triad (the United States, the EU, and Japan), the transition economies in central and Eastern Europe, and the developed nations that are members of the Organization for Economic Cooperation and Development (OECD)—potential markets can be found in almost every corner of the globe. Table 2-8 identifies a few of those potential markets. Depending on the types of products and the goal (whether to increase a firm's sales or identify markets for sourcing the firm's goods), some of these markets are better than others. However, all are already major trading powers or hold a good deal of promise for the near future.

The second dimension of the economic environment of international marketing includes the domestic economy of every nation in which a firm is selling. Thus, an international marketer faces the traditional task of economic analysis, but in a context that may include 100 countries or more. The investigation will be directed toward answering two broad questions: How big is the market, and what is the market like? Answers to the first question help determine the firm's market potential and priorities abroad. Answers to the second question help determine the nature of the marketing task.

Size of the Market

A firm's concern in examining world markets is the potential the markets offer for the firm's products. The international marketer must determine market size not only for present markets, but also for potential markets. This helps to allocate effort among present markets and to determine which markets to enter next. **Market size** for any given product is a function of particular variables, and its determination requires analysis. Certain general indicators are relevant for many goods. This section will discuss how world markets are described by the following two general indicators: (1) population—growth rates and distribution, and (2) income—distribution, income per capita, and GNI.

Population

People are needed to make a market; and other things being equal, the larger the population in a country, the

New Markets in China

Many people would argue that China, with a per capita income of less than $4,000 per year, is not a good market for high-technology merchandise. Like many other nations, though, China's income is not evenly divided among its people. One recent Chinese report states that the country will displace Japan as the world's largest personal computer market by 2006. This is good news for Mr. Sim, the CEO of Creative Technology of Singapore. His firm has developed Prodikeys, which combines a special keyboard and software that allows people to learn to play music at the computer. The plan is to introduce the product in China first, then Japan, South Korea, Taiwan, Hong Kong, and Singapore. Priced at $175 per unit, the Prodikey also requires that the user have a computer with a high-end sound board and speakers. Again, given the per capita income, trying to sell this product may not seem to be the best strategy. Yet Mr. Sim is relying on the projections for computer sales and the overall size of the Chinese market. He is also relying on acceptance because Creative Technology developed the product in China for the Chinese, and he expects the high value placed on education to carry over into learning to play music.

The market for wireless communication is increasing in China, too. With China Unicom recently launching a cellular network based on the U.S. standard and the Chinese purchasing 5,000 cellular phones a month in 2003, the market looks terrific, particularly for U.S. companies. Since China joined the WTO, it has also agreed to open its borders to service providers for Internet data service, call centers, mobile service, and a host of other wired and wireless services. Time and persistence are still necessary to break into the market, but many predict that China will be a leading market for the forseeable future because of its vast population and economic growth rate.

Sources: "Creative to Pitch Keyboard Combo at China Market," Monday, April 29, 2002, *Business Times*, Singapore; "A Lucrative New Market Is Calling: TELECOMS," Friday, March 15, 2002, *Financial Times*, page 4.

better the market. Of course, other things are never equal; so population figures in themselves are not usually a suf-

Table 2-9. Population and Life Expectancy (2003), Annual Average Population Growth Rates (2002-2015), and Projected Population (2015)

Nation or Income Group	Population (2003)	Life Expectancy (born in 2003)	Population Growth Rate 2003-2015 (%)	Population (2015)
Low-Income	2,311.9	58.1	1.6	2,794.9
Lower-Middle Income	2,305.8	69.2	0.8	2,918.3
Upper-Middle Income	333.1	73.7	1.1	380.6
High Income	887.2	78.5	0.3	1,007.0
World	6,272.5	66.8	1.0	7,100.9
China	1,280.4	70.7	0.6	1,389.5
India	1,048.6	63.4	1.2	1,231.6
United States	288.4	77.3	0.8	319.9
Indonesia	211.7	66.7	1.1	245.5
Brazil	174.5	68.5	1.1	201.0
World	6,198.5	66.7	1.0	7,090.7

Sources: World Bank, *2004 World Development Indicators*, Table 2.1 Population Dynamics, pages 38–41; Table 2.19 Mortality, pages 108-111.

ficient guide to market size. Nevertheless, the consumption of many products is correlated with population figures. For many "necessary" goods, such as ethical drugs, health-care items, some food products, and educational supplies, population figures may be a good first indicator of market potential. For other products that are low in price or that meet particular needs, population also may be a useful market indicator. Products in these second categories include soft drinks, ballpoint pens, bicycles, and sewing machines.

Population figures are one of the first considerations in analyzing foreign economies. One striking fact is the tremendous differences in size of the nations of the world. The largest nation in the world has about 10,000 times the population of the smallest countries. Well over half the people of the world live in the ten countries that have populations of more than 100 million. On the other hand, as many as one-half of the countries have populations of less than 10 million and more than 50 have fewer than 1 million people. (See "Global Marketing: New Markets in China.")

The marketer is concerned primarily with individual markets, but regional patterns can also be important for regional logistics. For example, Asia contains six of the ten most populous markets. By contrast, Africa, the Middle East, and Latin America are rather thinly populated. Nigeria is the largest African nation with over 125 million people; but the Democratic Republic of Congo, Egypt, and Ethiopia all have populations that exceed 50 million. Latin America has only two relatively populous countries: Brazil with 175 million and Mexico with 100 million. Europe, much smaller in land area but more densely populated, has three countries with populations over 60 million. The five most populous nations will account for nearly 50 percent of the world's population by 2015. (See Table 2-9.)

Population Growth Rates

The international marketer must be concerned with population trends as well as the current population in a market. This is because many marketing decisions will be affected by future developments. Although most countries experience some population growth, the rates among the world's richest nations are typically low.

The World Bank projects that global population will exceed 7 billion people by 2015 even though population growth rates are expected to decline further, to an average of 1 percent per year. The population of high income nations are expected to grow by an average of 0.3 percent annually, while low income nations are expected to grow by approximately 1.5 percent. As the most populous nations, China and India are expected to grow at a slower rate, but will still add almost 300 million people to their combined populations. (Population growth rates are provided in Table 2-9.)[16] The data in the table reflect the strong correlation between level of economic development and population growth. The richer countries have more stable populations; the poorer countries are growing rapidly.

Distribution of Population

Understanding population figures involves more than counting heads. The population figures should be classified by age group, gender, education, or occupation, for example, or in other ways that show the relevant segments of the market. Religious, tribal, educational, and other attributes will be discussed later. Here, such population characteristics as age and density are considered.

AGE

People in different stages of life have different needs and present different marketing opportunities. In the U.S. market, many firms recognize different market segments related to age groupings. Each country has a somewhat different profile as to age groupings. Generally, however, there are two major patterns—one for developing countries and one for industrialized countries.

Developing countries are experiencing population growth and their people have relatively short life expectancies. This means that nearly 35 percent of their population is in the 0-14 age group and approximately 60 percent is in the productive 15-64 age group (only 4.4 percent is in the 65+ category). Contrast that with the rich industrialized countries, which have less than 20 percent in the 0-14 group, 67 percent in the 15-64 group, and over 15 percent in the over-65 category. The large senior markets are important in the high-income countries, but also in some developing markets such as China, even though the proportion of elderly is somewhat smaller, with over 85 million citizens in that group. By 2050, over 20 percent of the world's population is expected to be over the age of eighty. Even in poorer nations, people are living longer due to better health care and better living conditions than in years past. In Angola, the life expectancy is now 47, which is low compared to developed nations; but it is nearly twice what it was a half century ago, when life expectancy was only 25 years.

DENSITY

The concentration of population is important to the marketer in evaluating distribution and communication problems. The United States, for example, had a population density of 31 people per square kilometer in 2002, which was only a small fraction of the population density in the Netherlands (477 people per square kilometer) or in Singapore (6,826 people per square kilometer). Even with a modern transportation network, distribution costs in the United States are likely to be higher than in the Netherlands. Promotion is facilitated where population is concentrated; but land prices, and consequently rent for office space, will be higher in denser markets.

Even when the density figure for a given country is used, careful interpretation is necessary. For example, Egypt is listed as having 64 people per square kilometer. That is very misleading because Egypt's population is among the world's most concentrated, located almost entirely along the Nile River. The rest of the country is desert. Canada provides a similar example. It has a density of three people per square kilometer; but most of the population is concentrated in a narrow band along the U.S. border, leaving the major portion of the landmass unoccupied. In such cases, the population is more concentrated and reachable than the statistics indicate.[17]

When evaluating a particular country, a firm is interested in the figures not only for that country, but also for a potential regional market that could be served by common production facilities.

Density is often closely linked with **urbanization**, the number of people living in cities rather than rural locations. Numerous cultural and economic differences exist between people in cities and people in villages or rural areas. Those differences are reflected in the attitudes of the people. Modern transportation and communication have greatly reduced the differences between urban and rural populations in the United States; but in much of the world, the urban-rural differences persist. Because these differences are important determinants of consumer behavior, the international marketer needs to be aware of each market's particular situation.

People living in rural communities tend to be more self-sufficient (since trading is often more difficult and time-consuming). They also tend to rely more heavily on agriculture for income, rather than manufactured goods or services.

Several reasons exist for the contrasting behavior of urban and rural populations. Research shows that products aimed at rural markets in developing countries required more adaptation than products sold in urban markets.[18]

Cities are the places in an economy where communications media are most developed. Cities also offer more possibilities for formal and informal education, which affect the literacy, skills, and attitudes of their inhabitants. Urbanites, therefore, tend to be less conservative and less tradition-oriented than rural dwellers. There is a stronger demonstration effect of new products and consumption patterns in urban areas, which leads to stronger markets in those locations.

The international marketer must study the relationship of urbanization to the consumption of the firm's product. Several factors may favor the urban markets: income and consumption patterns, distribution facilities, and communications possibilities. Cities such as Bangkok, Istanbul, and Jakarta, for example, possess a highly disproportionate share of their countries' consumption of many consumer goods.

There is a strong correlation between degree of urbanization and the level of economic development. A relationship between the level of economic development of a nation and the agrarian nature of its economy also exists. Poorer nations tend to earn more income from agriculture than rich nations.

Developing countries are generally less urbanized, especially the low-income nations. Combined with low incomes in these regions, the lack of urbanization makes these markets unattractive to many marketers of consumer goods. Not only are these poor markets small, they are also difficult to reach when most of the population is rural. Thus, the degree of urbanization is an indicator of the size of the market and the nature of the marketing task. Though this kind of data is especially significant for marketers of consumer goods, even companies that produce industrial goods find a correlation between their market potential and urbanization.

Parallels also exist between economic development and pollution. Increased crop yield can be had, but it generally results from the use of modern powered equipment and the use of pesticides and fungicides with associated risk factors. Increased income leads to more purchases of appliances, automobiles, and other pollution-generating devices. Developed countries call for restraint and the use of more energy-efficient and environmentally friendly products within their own borders and by developing nations. The poorer countries counter that the expense associated with these product attributes are high. Why should they be conservative when they have had to endure the results of a century or more of developed nations' pollution?

The rise in gasoline prices in 2004 was due in part to the war in Iraq, terrorism, and uncertainties surrounding the Russian oil industry; but there was a longer-term reason as well. With falling prices for autos and rising affluence in China, sales of autos rose 76 percent in 2003; and this growth is expected to continue at double-digit rates for the next several years.[19] With rising demand for autos, as well as electric appliances and other products requiring power, China is the second largest oil-consuming nation behind the United States. More power means more pollution. China is getting larger amounts of oil from Chad and exchanging arms to get the oil they need to supply their burgeoning energy needs. Some people question the ethical nature of this arrangement and cite numerous human rights concerns associated with this trading relationship.[20]

The watchword is **sustainable economic development** the use of environmentally sound practices to reach their economic goals. Perhaps the most visible of initiatives are those undertaken by the UN (e.g., United Nations Conference on Environment and Development in 1992 and the World Summit on Sustainable Development held in South Africa in August 2002). Yet other global organizations, such as the World Bank, as well as developed nations and multinationals are coming to the realization that they must help developing countries by paying or subsidizing. Some nations, such as Costa Rica, are on the front lines of this battle. While supporting the practice of establishing national parks for their burgeoning tourism industry, the government is countering that support with the desire to build large hydroelectric dams for energy exports. Doing so would flood large tracts of land that support the wildlife that tourists come to see, thus exemplifying the "growth versus protection of the environment" dilemma.

Income

Income is also a factor that firms use when selecting markets. Wages and wealth are not related to the size of a market (Hong Kong, Switzerland, and Qatar are wealthy but small nations), yet firms want to identify markets or segments of markets that are willing *and* able to buy their goods or services. Firms use measures of income to select potentially good markets, as well as to develop strategies to meet the needs of people with different incomes.

DISTRIBUTION OF INCOME

One way of understanding the size of a market is to look at distribution of income. **Per capita income** figures are averages; and they are meaningful, especially when most of the population is near the average. Frequently, however, this is not the case. Few nations have an equal distribution of income among their people, but the high-income economies are somewhat better in this respect than the other country categories. Marketers must be attentive to differences in income levels if their product is at all income-sensitive.

Most countries have an uneven distribution of income. For example, the poorest 40 percent of the people in the Russian Federation account for less than 15 percent of the income generated. The richest 20 percent generate over 50 percent of the income. In Sierra Leone, the poorest 40 percent of the population account for 3 percent of the income; the richest 20 percent account for 63 percent. In developed nations in general, the amount of assets income held by the poorest 20 percent of the population ranges from 5 to 10 percent and the amount held by the wealthiest 20 percent ranges from 35 to 45 percent. Nevertheless, income distribution is not equal in any nation. According to the World Bank's Gini index, Sweden, Norway, and Belgium are among the nations with the most unequal income distribution in the world.[21]

The more skewed the distribution of income, the less meaningful the per capita income figure. When most people are below the per capita income figure and there is a small wealthy group above it, the country has a **bimodal income distribution** but no middle class.

A bimodal income distribution means that the marketer must analyze not a single economy, but a dual economy. The poor group must be studied separately from the wealthy group. One might find, for example, that the two groups are not different segments of the same market, but are actually different markets. Brazil, India, and Mexico are examples of countries with sizable groups of affluent consumers living alongside a majority of the population who live in poverty. As was already mentioned, income is not evenly distributed in industrial markets, either. Products designed for affluent consumers in developing nations can be marketed to these upper-income groups as well as to

Table 2-10. Total and Per Capita Income in 2003

Income Group	Number of Countries	GNI ($U.S. billions)	Population (millions)	GNI per Capita ($U.S.)
Low Income	59	1,022	2,311.9	440
Lower-Middle Income	54	3,944	2,655.5	1,490
Upper-Middle Income	40	1,812	333.1	5,440
High Income	55	27,806	972.1	28,600
World	208	34,578	6,272.5	5,510

Source: World Bank, *2004 World Development Indicators*, Table 1.1 Size of the Economy, pages 14-17.

Note: Data are in current U.S. dollars converted using the World Bank Atlas method; World Bank, *2004 World Development Indicators*, page 21.

Number and names of countries in each income group: World Bank Data. Statistics for country groups (http://www.worldbank.org/data/countryclass/classgroups.htm); accessed August 5, 2004.

industrial nations. This characteristic is a major reason why firms should pay less attention to national or geographic borders and more attention to consumers' needs and desires. (And it's one of the reasons the Tiffany Company has been successful in expanding beyond New York City.)

PER CAPITA INCOME

GNI has earlier been defined in the text (p. 48) as "The sum of value added by all resident producers....plus net receipts of primary income from abroad (absent tax considerations)".The statistic most frequently used to describe a country economically is its per capita income (above), utilizing GNI as a measure of per capita income. This figure is used as a shorthand expression for a country's level of economic development. Partial justification for using this figure in evaluating a foreign economy lies in the fact that it is commonly available and widely accepted. A more pertinent justification is that it is, in fact, a good indicator of the size or quality of a market.

The per capita income figures vary widely among the countries of the world. Many nations of the world have an average annual per capita income below $500, the poorest of which are in Africa (Burundi, the Democratic Republic of Congo, and Ethiopia—all with an annual per capita income of only $100 in 2002). To put that in perspective, it takes the average Ethiopian one year to earn what a lawyer who charges $300 per hour earns in 20 minutes. People in high-income countries have average annual per capita income nearly 70 times that of the average person in low-income countries, with European nations being among the richest. (In Norway, per capita income is $38,730; in Switzerland $36,170.) The people in the World Bank categories of "upper-middle income" and "high income" nations account for 15 percent of the population, but they accounted for 80 percent of the world's GNI in 2002.[22] This emphasizes the need for marketers not only to identify those people who are willing to purchase their products, but also to recognize that potential cus-

Table 2-11. Per Capita Income in 2002, Measured Two Ways

Country	GNI per Capita ($U.S.)	PPP[a] Adjusted per Capita ($U.S.)	Multiplier[b]
Ethiopia	100	780	7.8
Tajikistan	164	930	5.7
Bangladesh	380	1,770	4.7
India	470	2,650	5.6
Belarus	1,360	5,500	4.0
Columbia	1,820	6,150	3.4
China	4,250	9,420	2.2
Hungary	5,290	13,070	2.5
Greece	11,600	18,770	1.6
Australia	19,530	27,440	1.4
World	5,120	7,820	1.5

a Purchasing power parity.

b Column 2 divided by Column 1.

Source: World Bank, *2004 World Development Indicators*, Table 1.1 Size of the Economy, pages 14-17.

tomers must also have the ability to pay for the products.

Table 2-10 provides a summary of the data for all of the countries tracked by the World Bank. Because per capita income figures are relied on so extensively, however, the following words of caution are in order.

Purchasing Power Not Reflected

Per capita income comparisons are expressed in a common currency—often in U.S. dollars—through an exchange-rate conversion. The dollar figure for a country is derived by dividing its per capita income figure in national currency by its rate of exchange against the dollar. The resulting dollar statistic for a country's per capita income is accurate only if the exchange rate reflects the relative domestic purchasing power of the two currencies. There is often reason for doubting that it does.

As mentioned earlier, exchange rates are predominantly determined by the demand for and supply of a country's imports and exports—plus speculative demand. A country's external supply and demand have quite a different character from supply and demand within the country. Thus, it is not surprising that the external value of a currency (the exchange rate) may be different from the domestic value of that currency. Table 2-11 illustrates the differences between the exchange-rate value of a currency and its real purchasing power. In some cases, the real purchasing power is nearly eight times the exchange-rate value.

The limitations of an exchange rate in indicating relative purchasing power can be illustrated further. Take the experience of tourists, who soon learn that that some prices appear high; others low. In other words, the value of their own currency abroad depends on what they purchase.

If tourists want to live in the same style abroad as they do at home, their expenses will probably be higher than if they live like the residents of the host country. For example, the price of white bread in Germany is twice as much as it is in France. Of course, the Germans do not consume as much white bread as the French. This indicates another aspect of prices and purchasing power—that is, people tend to consume more of the things that are inexpensive in their country. However, the exchange rate reflects the *international* goods and services of a country, not its *domestic* consumption. (See "Global Marketing: Buying a Burger Abroad: A Basic Lesson in PPP".)

A further example is the case of exchange-rate changes, as with a devaluation or currency appreciation. An extreme case involves Japan. In 1985, the Japanese yen was 240 to the U.S. dollar. In 1988, the yen was 120 to the dollar. This meant that, in dollar terms, the Japanese market was twice as large in 1988 as in 1985. This was obviously not true in real terms, as American marketers to Japan learned. Their sales to Japan rose only modestly.

Lack of Comparability

Another limitation of the use of per capita income figures is that there is a lack of comparability for two reasons. First, many goods entering into the national income totals of developed economies are only partially accounted for in less developed countries. A large part of a North American's budget, for example, goes for food, clothing, and shelter. In many, less developed nations, those items may be largely self-provided and, therefore, not reflected in national income totals. Second, many goods that figure in the national income of developed nations do not figure in the national incomes of poorer countries. For example, a significant amount of U.S. national income is derived from such items as snow removal, heat for buildings and homes, pollution control, military and space expenditures, agricultural support programs, and winter vacations in Florida or other warm states. Many less developed nations

Buying a Burger Abroad: A Basic Lesson in PPP

*I*t was 2 pm, and we had just departed our hosts after a wonderful four-course luncheon meeting at La Défénse, a major business district on the outskirts of Paris. A colleague asked us to wait while he made a quick stop in one of the stores before we went back to our hotel. Much to our surprise, he returned with some French fries from McDonald's. Even after a full meal, he wanted a "taste of home" after being on the road for the last ten days.

Since McDonald's operates in nearly every country of the word, the Big Mac Index was devised in the mid-1980s as a humorous way to measure purchasing power. The idea was that if the theory of purchasing power parity was accurate, a Big Mac ought to cost the same in every country. If the price was significantly different, the index could be used to predict changes in exchange rates. A Big Mac that cost more in London, for example, would indicate that the British pound is overvalued and that it would fall in the near future. A substantially lower price would indicate that the currency is undervalued and would likely rise. If the cost of Big Macs was nearly the same—Price McParity—the price of the currency would likely remain the same. The following table shows a partial list of the cost of Big Macs around the world.

continued

are in tropical areas, and their citizens are not necessarily poorer for not having the above-mentioned items of consumption. However, their national income figure is lower because of the absence of these items.

The primary author of this text spent eight years in a rural area of Congo. Although not living entirely in the African manner, he found his food, clothing, and housing expenses to be a fraction of those he incurred while living in the northern part of the United States. This meant that a given income went much further for consumption of basic items.

Sales Not Related to Per Capita Income

A third limitation to using per capita income figures to indicate market potential is that the sales of many goods show little correlation with per capita income. Many con-

Country (currency)	Ex-change Rate[a]	Big Mac Price ($US)[b]	Implied Purchasing Power[b]	Under/ Over Valued[b]
United States ($)	1.0	2.90	...	...
Argentina (Peso)	2.9	1.48	1.50	-49
Australia (A$)	1.5	2.27	1.12	-22
China (Yuan)	8.3	1.26	3.59	-57
Euro Area (€)	0.9	3.28	1.06	13
Hong Kong	7.8	1.54	4.14	-47
Japan (¥)	114.4	2.33	90.3	-20
Russia (Ruble)	29.0	1.45	14.5	-50
Switzerland (SFr)	1.3	4.90	2.17	69
Turkey (Lira)	1,530,000.0	2.58	1,362,069	-11

a Average exchange rate in various markets on May 15, 2004.

b "Food for Thought," *The Economist*, May 29, 2004, pages 71–72.

c Calculated (2.90/price $US), where 2.90 is the price of a Big Mac in the United States.

If there is parity in purchasing power in the country, vis-à-vis the United States, the expected exchange rate and the actual exchange rate should be the same.

Sources: "Food for Thought," *The Economist*, May 29, 2004, pages 71–72; XE.Com; historical rates (http://www.xe.com/ict); accessed, August 6, 2004; see also http://www.economist.com/markets/Big-mac/index.cfm.

With so many currencies undervalued (those with a minus sign), what does that say about the U.S. dollar?

Table 2-12. Countries with Gross National Income over $250 Billion (2002)

Country	GNI ($US billions)[a]	Percent of World Total
United States	10,207	32.2
Mexico	597	1.9
Japan	4,324	13.6
Spain	597	1.9
Germany	1,876	5.9
India	495	1.6
United Kingdom	1,511	4.8
Korea, Rep.	473	1.5
France	1,362	4.3
Australia	384	1.2
China	1,234	3.9
Netherlands	378	1.2
Italy	1,101	3.5
Russian Federation	304	1.0
Canada	702	2.2
Switzerland	264	.8
Brazil	495	1.6
World	31,720	100.0

a Current $US.

Source: World Bank, *2004 World Development Indicators*, Table 1.1 Size of the Economy, pages 14–17.

sumer goods sales correlate more closely with population or household figures than with per capita income. Some examples include Coca-Cola, jeans, bicycles, computers, and stereo equipment. Industrial goods and capital equipment sales generally correlate better with the industrial structure or total national income than with per capita income. For example, the airport and office buildings in Kinshasa, Congo, are equipped in much the same way as similar structures in New York City. Extractive or manufacturing industries tend to use similar equipment wherever they are located. Where governments run health and education programs, per capita income is not necessarily a useful guide to the national potential of goods supplied to the health and education industries.

Gross National Income (GNI)

Another useful way to evaluate foreign markets is to compare their GNPs. As first introduced in Table 2-1, **Gross national income (GNI)** measures *the total domestic and foreign value added by residents*. For certain goods, total GNI is a better indicator of market potential than per capita income. Where this is true, it is useful to rank countries by GNI. Table 2-12 lists the economies with a GNI of at least $250 billion in 2002. The fact that only 17 nations qualify for this list (and that they account for more than 80 percent of total world income) gives further insight into the poverty in the world and the limitations of most economies.

It is helpful to contrast the GNI approach to measuring market potential with the per capita income approach. For example, in 2002, Iceland's per capita income was $27,380 and India's was $2,340. Those figures have been adjusted for purchasing power. Without purchasing power parity adjustment, the actual figures are more distant— $470 for India and $27,960 for Iceland. Using those data alone, Iceland is 100 times as attractive economically as India. However, that same year, India's GNI was more than 60 times as large as Iceland's ($495 billion versus $8 billion); and India's population is over 3,000 times as large (1.05 billion versus 284,000).[23] This is an extreme example, but it illustrates the need for proper comparisons.

At this point, consider another view of the per capita income approach. For goods that require high consumer income, it may be true that a small country such as Belgium (about 10 million people) is a better market than India, even though Belgium's GNI is less than that of India. For example, in 2002, Belgium had more cars and personal computers than India. On the other hand, India consumed four to six times as many trucks, buses, and tons of cement and steel. Obviously, the relevant income figure for evaluating a market depends largely on the product involved.

Nature of the Economy

In addition to their size and market potential, foreign economies have other characteristics, including those produced by the nation's physical endowment, the nature of their economic activity, their infrastructure, and their degree of urbanization—all of which affect a marketing program.

Physical Endowment

A nation's resources play a major role in economic development. Countries with large land mass tend to have more natural resources, both in terms of quantity and breadth. Australia, China, Russia, Canada, Mexico, and the United States are among the world's largest in terms of land mass; they also have a wealth of natural resources. However, smaller nations such as Japan must buy much of the raw materials they consume and must buy much of what goes into the production of goods and services. Although there are exceptions, generally, the richer and more diverse the endowments, the higher the country's potential for favorable economic development.

NATURAL RESOURCES

A nation's **natural resources** include its actual and potential forms of wealth supplied by nature—for example, minerals and waterpower—as well as its land area, topography, and climate. The international marketer needs to understand the economic geography of a nation in relation to the marketing task at hand. Land area is not very important, except as it figures in population density and distribution problems. Local natural resources can be important to the international marketer in evaluating a country as a source of raw materials for local production. Merck, for example, built a compounding plant in India and received the Indian government's permission to ship key ingredients from the United States. This permission was later withdrawn, and Merck had to locate a new source of raw materials in India to keep the plant operating.

Another reason for exploring a country's resource base is to evaluate its future economic prospects. Some countries that currently have relatively weak markets might develop more rapidly than other countries because of their richer resource endowment. New technologies and discoveries can revolutionize a nation's economic prospects. Oil changed the outlook for Libya and Nigeria, for example.

By the same token, technological change can also impoverish an economy that is largely dependent on just one export commodity. For example, the development of rayon, nylon, and synthetic rubber did great damage to the countries exporting silk and natural rubber. What would be the impact on Brazil if a good synthetic coffee were developed? A glance through the maps in an atlas will show how the various natural resources are distributed among the nations of the world.

TOPOGRAPHY

The surface features of a country's land, including rivers, lakes, forests, deserts, and mountains, are its **topography**. These features interest an international marketer, for they indicate possible physical distribution problems.

Flat country generally means easy transportation by road or rail. Mountains are a barrier that raises transportation costs. Mountains also may divide a nation into two or more distinct markets. For example, the Andes Mountains divide many South American countries into entirely separate areas. Although these areas are united politically, a marketer often finds them to be separate markets culturally and economically. Deserts and tropical forests also separate markets and make transportation difficult. An international marketer analyzes data on the topography, population, and transportation situation in order to anticipate marketing and logistical problems.

Navigable rivers are desirable because they enable economical transportation. The Mississippi River and the St. Lawrence Seaway are North American examples. In Europe, river and canal transportation are more important than anywhere else in the world. Even landlocked Switzerland can ship by river barge to Atlantic ports. The accessibility of a market should also be determined by its ports and harbors—contact with sea transportation.

Landlocked countries such as Bolivia, Zambia, and Zimbabwe are more costly to reach than neighboring countries with seaports. These countries have transportation problems other than cost (for instance, customs inspections) if there are political differences with the neighbors whose seaports and railroads they must use. Finally, the existence of lakes, seashores, rivers, and mountains can indicate particular marketing opportunities. Suppliers to the tourist, recreation, and sporting industries find markets in countries endowed with places for boating, skiing, and other recreational activities.

CLIMATE

Another dimension of a nation's physical endowment is its climate, which includes not only the temperature range, but also wind, rain, snow, dryness, and humidity. The United States is very large and has great climatic variations within its borders. Smaller nations have more uniform climatic patterns. Climate is an important determinant of a firm's product offerings. An obvious example is the heater or air conditioner in an automobile. Climate also affects a whole range of consumer goods—from food to clothing and from housing to recreational supplies. Even medical needs in the Tropics are different from those in temperate zones.

Extremes of climate may dictate modifications in product, packaging, or distribution. For example, electric equipment and many packaged goods need special protection in hot, humid climates. There is great international variation in climate; for example, in July, India has 13 inches of rainfall, Guinea has 51 inches, and New York City has 4 inches.

Climate may have another, more subtle effect on the nature of the market. Although insufficient evidence exists to prove cause and effect, most less developed countries are tropical or subtropical. Tropical countries generally have low per capita incomes and a high percentage of the population in agriculture. A marketing manager needs to be aware of climate to the extent that it affects people as consumers and workers.

Infrastructure of the Nation

A manufacturing firm generally divides its activities into two major categories: production and marketing. These operations depend on supporting facilities and services outside the firm. These external facilities and services are called the **infrastructure** of an economy. They include paved roads, railroads, energy supplies, and other communication and transport services. The commercial and financial infrastructure includes advertising agencies and media, distributive organizations, marketing research companies, and credit and banking facilities. The more adequate these services are in a country, the better a firm can perform its production and marketing tasks. Where these facilities and services are not adequate, a firm must adapt its operations (or avoid the market altogether).

When considering the potential profitability of operations in a given country, an international marketer must evaluate the infrastructure constraints as well as the market potential. As might be expected, tremendous variation exists internationally. Generally, the higher the level of economic development, the better the infrastructure.[24] Case 2.3 at the end of the chapter, "The Lifeblood of the World's Economies—Electricity" provides an indication of the variation in energy supplies available. The feature "Global Marketing: Infrastructure: Building Bridges to Close the Digital Divide" highlights the importance of infrastructure and its many components in the development of a *truly* World Wide Web as opposed to a developed-country Web.

ENERGY

The statistics on energy production per capita serve as a guide to market potential and to the adequacy of the local infrastructure. Marketers of electrical machinery and equipment and consumer durables are concerned about the extent of electrification throughout the market. In countries with low energy consumption, a marketer will find that power is typically available only in the cities, not in the villages or countryside where most of the population lives. Energy production is also closely related to the overall industrialization of an economy and thus is correlated

Infrastructure: Building Bridges to Close the Digital Divide

*F*or the digital divide to shrink, technology must be made available to those people who currently do not have it. There are three requirements for e-commerce to take place, whether B2B or B2C: content, income, and infrastructure. All transactions require that the parties involved be willing and able to participate in the exchange process. **Content** (music, videos, e-mail, telephony, and information, for example) is what drives people to want to have an Internet connection; income and infrastructure are the "capability" components that enable people to participate in e-commerce. With literally billions of web sites and the addition of more every hour, content exists. Its access is limited only by entities that charge for the material or by governments and other interested parties who want to protect consumers from fraud and subversive or obscene information.

Income, as previously discussed, is still very low in some nations, which means that even old technology—three- or four-year-old computers and software that may cost only $100 for a complete PC and the software necessary for an Internet connection—is beyond the reach of many, such as the average Ethiopian, who earns $100 per year.

This is a small part of the picture, however, when one considers the time and money needed to build the infrastructure required to connect to other computers, the financial infrastructure that must be in place to allow people to enter into transactions on the Web (worldwide is a bit premature), and the ability to deliver manufactured goods once they are purchased.

Infrastructure at a basic level requires roads for delivering goods, computers and software, and electricity to power the connecting electronics (even if going wireless, power is needed to recharge power packs). Very often financial institutions are needed to complete a transaction—transferring funds from one account to another and sometimes supplying credit (in the form of a credit card, for example). If the parties live in different countries, banks may also provide the service of exchanging currencies. Without a commercial infrastructure, many transactions would not take place.

continued

Perhaps most important, though, is a connection to the Internet. If the industry standard remains land-connected – using traditional telephone lines, coaxial cable, or fiber optics for DSL or cable connections – large amounts of capital and labor are needed to build the infrastructure to link computers in cities and nations with the rural populations prevalent in so many areas of the world. If the standard becomes wireless, scores of additional satellites and transmission towers must be built. Different compression software would also be needed to send pictures, sound, and gigabytes of other data between wireless components.

There are some encouraging signs of people finding solutions to these problems. In Laos, the head of the Jhai Foundation, Mr. Lee Thorn, is distributing sturdy PCs that have no moving parts and cost around $400, including all of the hardware and wireless capabilities needed to connect to the Internet. Farmers can check the prices they get for their crops before they make a long trek to the nearest sales office. The PCs also help farmers make decisions about future crop allocations.

Even with these encouraging statistics and isolated signs of improvement, much needs to be done in terms of building infrastructure and providing the tools needed to reduce the digital divide.

Sources: "Emerging Market Indicators," *The Economist*, November 3, 2001, Volume 361, Issue 8245, page 106; "High-Speed Internet Access; Broadband Blues," *The Economist*, June 23, 2001, Volume 359, Issue 8227, page 62;

Joane E. Oxley and Bernard Yeung, "E-Commerce Readiness: Institutional Environment and International Competitiveness," *Journal of International Business Studies*, 2001, Volume 32, Issue 4, pages 705-723; Srilata Zaheer and Shalini Manrakhan, Concentration and Dispersion in Global Industries: Remote Electronic Access and the Location of Economic Activities," *Journal of International Business Studies*, 2001, Volume 32, Issue 4, pages 667-686; "Making the Web World-Wide," *The Economist*, September 28, 2002, Volume 364, Issue 8292, page 76.

to the market for industrial goods there. Finally, energy production per capita is probably the best single indicator as to the adequacy of a country's overall infrastructure.

TRANSPORTATION

The importance of transportation for business operations needs no elaboration. Transportation capabilities, infrastructure, and modes vary significantly from country to country depending on the topography and level of economic development. The transportation infrastructure is vital to a firm that must move people, components, services, and finished goods to another country or within a nation's borders. Information on railways (miles and gauge), highways (paved and unpaved), waterways, pipelines, airports, and seaports is available from the U.S. Central Intelligence Agency's *The World Factbook*.[25] The International Institute for Management Development (IMD) publishes a competitiveness ranking for 60 nations that includes a comparison of the basic infrastructure as well as scientific and technological infrastructures across nations.[26] Transportation companies and associations are other good resources for such data.

COMMUNICATIONS

In addition to being able to move its goods, a firm must be able to communicate with various audiences, especially workers, suppliers, and customers. Communications with those outside the firm depend on the communications infrastructure of the country. Intracompany communications between subsidiaries or with headquarters depend on local facilities. Table 2-13 shows the distribution and availability of several communications media in major regions of the world.

In general, variations in communications infrastructure follow variations in the level of economic development. Thus, Japan and the countries of Western Europe are well supplied with all kinds of media; whereas the developing countries in Africa, Asia, and Latin America are weak in all of the media, except perhaps for radio. Analysis of communication options identifies promotional possibilities in foreign markets.

COMMERCIAL INFRASTRUCTURE

Equally important to a firm as the transportation, communication, and energy capabilities of a nation is the nation's **commercial infrastructure**. Commercial infrastructure refers to the availability and quality of supporting services such as banks and financial institutions, advertising agencies, distribution channels, and marketing research organizations. Firms accustomed to strong supporting services at home often find great differences in foreign markets. Wherever the commercial infrastructure is weak, a firm must make adjustments in its operations, which affect costs and effectiveness.

No comparable table on commercial infrastructure is available (as with communication and other indicators), and data in this area are more difficult to find. Nevertheless, a firm can get reasonably good information about the commercial infrastructure of a country. The best sources are commercial attachés in embassies and domestic service organizations with foreign operations; for example, banks, accounting firms, and advertising agencies.

Table 2-13. Distribution of Communications Media per 1,000 Persons

Country or Region	Daily Newspapers[a]	Radios[b]	Televisions[c]	Telephone Mainlines[c]	Mobile Telephones[c]	Personal Computers[c]
United States	213	2,117	938	646	488	659
Europe						
France	201	950	632	569	647	347
Germany	305	570	661	651	727	431
Hungary	465	690	475	361	676	108
Italy	104	878	494	481	939	231
Poland	102	523	422	295	363	106
Spain	100	330	564	506	824	196
United Kingdom	329	1,445	950	591	841	406
Latin America						
Argentina	37	681	326	219	178	82
Brazil	43	433	349	223	201	75
Colombia	46	549	303	179	106	50
Mexico	94	330	282	147	255	82
Uruguay	293	603	530	280	193	110
Venezuela	206	294	186	113	256	61
Asia						
China	339	350	167	161	28	
India	60	120	83	40	12	7
Indonesia	23	159	153	37	55	12
Japan	578	956	785	558	637	382
Malaysia	158	420	210	190	377	147
Philippines	82	161	182	42	191	28
Thailand	64	235	300	105	260	40
Africa, Mideast						
Algeria	27	244	114	61	13	8
Egypt	31	339	229	110	67	17
Israel	290	526	330	467	955	243
South Africa	32	336	177	107	304	73
Syrian, Arab Rep	20	276	182	123	23	19
Turkey	111	470	423	281	347	45

a 2000; b 2001; c 2002.

Source: World Bank, *2004 World Development Indicators*; Table 5.10 Power and Communications, pages 290–293; Table 5.11 The Information Age, pages 294–297; except for newspapers and radios, the data comes from the *International Telecommunication Development Report, 2003*; the number of personal computers does not include those located in educational facilities.

Other Characteristics of Foreign Economies

The previous survey of foreign economies has been introductory rather than exhaustive. It should be helpful, however, in giving the market analyst a feel for the relevant dimensions of national economies. The last section of this chapter will cover one other characteristic of economies that can be important in operations in foreign markets, inflation.

INFLATION

Each country has its own monetary system and monetary policy—except for the 12 European countries in the Euro group. The result is differing financial environments and rates of inflation among countries. In general, inflation rates declined in the last ten years, in part because of the bursting of the dot-com bubble as well as the financial and ethical business crises. Yet, of all of the nations analyzed by the World Bank, more than one-half had single-digit annual inflation rates in 2002, which means that the other countries had more serious challenges with double- or triple-digit rates. As with most statistics, inflation rates ought to be viewed over time in order to gain a better perspective. The inflation rates for the period covering 1990–2002 ranged from -0.3 (prices actually declined at a rate of 0.3 percent per year) in Japan to triple-digit rates of 121 in the Russian Federation and 139.8 in Brazil (average annual percent growth).[27] In general, inflation rates turned much lower between 1999 and 2004.

Some interesting regional patterns appeared in the inflation picture in 2002. The United States and Canada had low inflation during this period, as did Western Europe, thanks in part to the adoption of the euro, which lowered transaction costs. Hungary, with an inflation rate of 11 percent, and Romania, with inflation at 24 percent, were more similar to the former Soviet Union economies than to the other European nations. Many of the former Soviet economies were experiencing double-digit inflation rates in 2002, the worst of which was Uzbekistan with a 46 percent rate of inflation.

Latin American and the Caribbean nations were generally in the single digits, with some exceptions: Ecuador reported 12 percent; Paraguay reported 15 percent; Uruguay reported 18 percent; and Argentina, Suriname, and Venezuela faced inflation rates over 30 percent in 2002. This was quite a change from the beginning of the 1990s, when Brazil was experiencing more than 2,000 percent inflation at one point and many other nations in the area had double- and triple-digit inflation rates for sustained periods of time.

The Asian nations had low rates, with Papua New Guinea being the only nation with inflation in the double digits (12 percent). As was already mentioned, Japan is one nation where prices actually declined through 2004.

In Africa, as in years past, a number of countries experienced double-digit inflation rates in 2002. Yet there were exceptions. Angola's inflation rate in 2002 was only 103 percent, which is one of the lowest in a decade, coming off an inflation rate of 150 percent in 2001 and over 4,000 percent in 1996. Zimbabwe also had a triple-digit inflation rate of 107 percent in 2002. More than a dozen nations in Africa had inflation rates in double and triple digits in 2002, but the rates were down dramatically from previous years. For example, the Democratic Republic of Congo had an inflation rate of 299 percent in 2001, better than earlier rates of 500 and 600 percent and the unimaginable 23,760 percent in 1994! In 2002, the inflation rate was a relatively modest 23 percent. To put this in context, imagine paying a monthly rent of $1,500, then the landlord increases the rent to $2,250 for the coming year. That's an example of a 50 percent inflation rate.

The Central and Eastern European nations and former Soviet countries continue to substantially reduce inflation rates, too. In some places, double-digit rates are still found (Turkmenistan, 12 percent; Russian Federation, 15 percent; Tajikistan, 22 percent; Romania and Serbia and Montenegro, 25 percent; Belarus, 42 percent; and Uzbekistan, 45 percent); but none of the countries are showing signs of triple-digit or greater inflation rates experienced in the early to mid-1990s.

Of particular note is the fact that inflation means a further complication for operating in foreign markets. High rates of inflation complicate cost control and pricing. Differential rates of inflation also influence how a firm moves funds and goods among its various markets. Marketers must also address the consumers' perception of price gouging or unfair profit taking, which often occurs when rising costs force a company to raise product prices.

Summary

International trade, the economic link between nations, is one of the largest and fastest-growing aspects of the world economy. A study of the subject should include the composition of trade—that is, the shifting shares of manufactured goods and services versus other various commodities—and the patterns of trade, both globally and within individual countries, to help a firm's international logistics planning.

The theory of international trade helps in understanding a nation's comparative advantage and is useful for locating supply or production sources. The international product life cycle theory can help a firm know when to source, or produce, abroad.

The BoP is a summary statement of a nation's economic transactions that can be analyzed to determine market potential and competition in a country.

All countries have regulations on their international trade (commercial policy), usually to protect employment in home industries. Tariffs and quotas are the major tools used by industrial countries to control their trade. These affect a firm's pricing, product, and logistics decisions. Exchange control is a more comprehensive and rigid form of trade control.

WTO, as the world's trading club, works to liberalize the exchange of goods and services between countries. To the degree it is successful, WTO facilitates a firm's international marketing. UNCTAD is the lobby for developing countries' interests in trade. Its efforts, too, can affect a firm's international marketing and influence the firm's logistics.

After the decline of Communism and the fragmentation of the Communist bloc, the countries of Eastern Europe offered a large potential market. However, some economic, cultural, legal, and political problems may need to be solved before that potential is fully realized.

In the growing interdependence of the world economy, many nations are finding economic integration with their neighbors desirable. This offers more resources, larger markets, and economies of scale to help the countries compete in the world economy. The EU is the major successful integration story. Efforts elsewhere have made little progress, although NAFTA is a bright spot. Where integration is successful, it offers opportunities for firms that can operate within the group, but challenges for those on the outside.

The major world currencies have been floating since 1973. The resulting instability and uncertainty disrupt the sourcing patterns and pricing decisions. The IMF, though no longer able to maintain stable currencies, is still a force for moderation and stability in international finance. By lending to deficit countries, IMF helps to keep the markets viable and open to the international marketer. The World Bank, through its development loans, provides resources to help poor countries strengthen their economies and become more prosperous, thus providing more attractive markets for international firms. World Bank projects themselves can provide attractive marketing opportunities.

A firm's home country is an important determinant of its international marketing success. U.S. regulations, for example, can limit a firm's international marketing; but the government also supports international business by supplying information, insurance, financing, and other kinds of assistance. Moreover, the large, competitive U.S. domestic market is a good training ground for international marketing. The U.S. image in the world, however, can be an advantage or a disadvantage for a firm's international marketing.

The two main areas of investigation for a company evaluating a foreign market are (1) the size of the market and (2) the nature of the economy. Population is one of the primary indicators of market size. Two-thirds of the world's countries have less than 10 million people and represent small markets, especially compared to the United States. Growth rates vary widely and are generally inversely correlated with the attractiveness of a market. The marketer is concerned with the distribution of the population among different age groups with different purchasing power and consumption patterns. Population density is important for evaluating distribution and communication problems.

Markets are "people with money," so income figures on a country are necessary for market evaluation. One dimension is the distribution of income among the members of a society. Countries with a bimodal distribution of income represent dual economies with two major market segments, generally one rich and one poor. Countries with a more even distribution of income or a large middle class represent more of a mass market.

Per capita income is the most widely used indicator of market potential. Figures vary widely, with the poorest countries reporting less than 1 percent of the per capita income of the richest countries. World Bank studies show that these figures are often inaccurate, however. Actual purchasing power in many poor countries is three to eight times as high as that indicated by the per capita income figure expressed in dollars. Per capita income figures are a useful indicator of potential for some consumer goods but misleading for other consumer goods and for industrial goods.

Total GNI gives an idea of the total size of a country's market and is a helpful indicator of potential for some kinds of products. The range of GNI figures between the largest and smallest economies is over 10,000 to 1.

A country's physical endowment affects the nature of its economy. Its natural resources are one indicator of its economic potential and raw material availability. Its topography helps determine physical distribution problems and market accessibility. Its climate influences the kinds of products offered and the kinds of packaging needed.

Countries can be grouped according to the nature of their economies or level of economic development. Such groupings can be a useful form of segmentation for international marketers. For better analysis, countries' economies can be divided into agricultural, manufacturing, and service sectors.

A firm's ability to operate in a country depends on the supporting facilities and services available, collectively called its infrastructure. The transportation and communication facilities in a country affect a firm's ability to get its goods to consumers and to communicate with customers, suppliers, and the home office. Energy availability affects the kinds of products that can be sold to consumer and industrial markets. A country's commercial infrastructure (ad agencies, wholesalers, etc.) constrains a firm's marketing task and capability.

Generally, major differences exist between urban consumers and rural consumers. Countries differ greatly in their degree of urbanization, with the number of city dwellers declining with the level of economic development. The marketing task varies between the city and the countryside.

Inflation complicates the marketing task; and its incidence varies, generally being much higher in developing countries. The role of government as regulator, customer, and partner is another variable affecting a firm's marketing in a country.

Questions and Research

2.1 What can be learned from studying the composition and patterns of world trade?

2.2 How can an understanding of international trade theory help the international marketer?

2.3 What is a BoP? Of what use is it to international marketing?

2.4 What is an MNC, and why are they on the rise?

2.5 What is WTO, and what does it do for the environment of international marketing?

2.6 Why might a U.S. exporter feel threatened by the formation of regional economic groupings? How might the firm react?

2.7 What economic characteristics would you look for in an emerging potential market?

2.8 What does the euro mean for U.S. firms already operating in the EU? What impact does the euro have on those countries considering entering the EU?

2.9 What are the potential benefits of World Bank activity for international marketing?

2.10 Discuss the use of population size as an indicator of market potential.

2.11 Why is the international marketer interested in the age distribution of the population in a market?

2.12 Discuss the limitations of per capita income in evaluating market potential.

2.13 What can topography tell an international marketer about a foreign market?

2.14 Marketing opportunities and problems in a country vary according to its level of economic development. Explain.

2.15 What marketing differences might be encountered in an agricultural versus an industrialized country?

2.16 Discuss a nation's infrastructure as a marketing constraint.

Endnotes

1. The World Bank, *World Development Indicators*, 2004, pages 1-2.

2. World Trade Organization, *International Trade Statistics*, 2001, Table IV, Trade by Sector (http://www.wto.org/english/res_e/statis_e/its2003_e/its03_bysubject_e.htm).

3. GNI data: World Bank Group; Data query performed on July 16, 2004 (http://devdata.worldbank.org/data-query); Trade data: World Trade Organization, *International Trade Statistics*, 2003 (http://www.wto.org/english/res_e/statis_e/its2003_e/its03_bysubject_e.htm) (files: i05.xls [merchandise]; i07.xls [commercial services]).

4. World Trade Organization, *International Trade Statistics*, 2003, Section IV; Table IV.1, page 103; Tables IV.3-IV.5, page 105; and Tables IV.15-IV.19, pages 114-116; Chart IV.9, Tables IV.43 and IV.45, pages 132-133, 136; Table IV.2, page 104; Charts IV.14 and IV.16, pages 113-114; and Tables IV.74 and IV.77, pages 160-163.

5. Leamer, Edward E. and Michael Storper. "The Economic Geography of the Internet Age," 2001, *Journal of International Business Studies*, Volume 32, Issue 4, pages 641-665; "Europeans Opt for Local eMerchants," October 4, 1999, *Nau/Jupiter Communications Internet Surveys*; "Europeans Research Online, but Buy Offline," August 26, 2002, *Forrester Research*; "Interregional Internet Bandwidth 2000-2001," *TeleGeography Research*.

6. DeYoung, Karen. "Bush: No Lifting of Cuba Policies," Tuesday, May 21, 2002, *Washington Post*, page A01.

7. Barro, Robert J. "Big Steel Doesn't Need Any More Propping Up," *Business Week*, New York, Issue 3776, page 24.

"Europe Responds with Its Own Steel Tariff," April 1, 2002, *Construction Week*, Volume 248, Number 12, page 7.

"Leaders: George Bush, Protectionist; Tariffs on Steel," *The Economist*, London, Volume 362, Issue 8263, page 13.

"Steel in The Melting Pot," April 18, 2002, *Financial Times*, Global News Wire—Asia Africa Intelligence Wire.

"Trade Scene: Steel Yourself—It's a Mess," December 14, 2001, *Journal of Commerce*, JoC Online.

8. "EU Trade Ploy Threat to Recovery," April 18, 2002, *Australian Financial Review*, Section: International News, page 143.

9. "Members and Observers" (http://www.wto.org/english/thewto_e/whatis_e/tif_e/org6_e.htm); "Accessions" (http://www.wto.org/english/

thewto_e/acc_e/acc_e.htm); "Trading into the Future: Introduction to the WTO" (http://www.wto.org/english/thewto_e/whatis_e/tif_e/agrm0_e.htm); accessed December 23, 2004.

10. European web site (European Economic Area) (http://europa.eu.int/comm/external_relations/eea/index.htm); The Secretariat of the European Free Trade Association web site (http://secretariat.efta.int/euroeco).

11. Association of Southeast Asian Nations (ASEAN) web site (http://www.asean.or.id/1024x768.html; http://www.us-asean org/asean.asp).

12. North American Free Trade (NAFTA) web site of the U.S. Department of Commerce, International Trade Association (http://web.ita.doc.gov/ticwebsite/naftaweb.nsf; http://www.nafta-sec-alena.org/english/index.htm); Free Trade Area of the Americas (FTAA) web site (http://www.alca-ftaa.org/alca_e.asp).

13. The Euro (http://europa.eu.int/euro/html/entry.html); Euro Essentials (http://europa.eu.int/comm/economy_finance/euro_en.htm, http://europa.eu.int/comm/enlargement/report2001/, and http://europa.eu.int/comm/enlargement/pas/ocp/ocp_index.htm).

Ms. Harriet Barseghian Marsh of the EU Enlargement Information Centre, personal communication (enlargement@cec.eu.int); January 9, 2003.

With respect to the other three nations, Bulgaria and Romania are not expected to enter the EU before 2007 and Turkey started accession discussions in late 2004.

14. U.S. Bureau of Economic Analysis, U.S. Direct Investment Abroad: Country and Industry Detail for Capital Outflows (http://www.bea.doc.gov/bea/di/usdiacap.htm#2003).

15. NATO web site, "Members" (http://www.nato.int/structur/countries.htm); UNCTAD, NATO (http://www.nato.int/structur/countries.htm); UNCTAD, Foreign Direct Investment inflows (http://www.unctad.org/Templates/WebFlyer.asp?intItemID=2111&lang=1); World Bank, *2003 World Development Indicators*, Data Query (http://devdata.worldbank.org/data-query); accessed July 27, 2004.

16. The World Bank, *2004 World Development Indicators*, Table 2.1 Population Dynamics, pages 38-41.

17. The World Bank, *2004 World Development Indicators*, Table 1.1 Size of the Economy, pages 14-17.

18. See, for example, Hill, John S. and Richard R. Still. "Effects of Urbanization on Multinational Product Planning," Summer 1984, *Columbia Journal of World Business*, 62-67. See also Roth, Martin S. "Effects of Global Market Conditions on Brand Image Customization and Brand Performance," Winter 1995, *Journal of Advertising*, Volume 24, Number 4, pages 55-75.

19. Johnson, Tim. "China's Car Owners Get Crash Course in Driving," *Philadelphia Inquirer*, Wednesday, July 21, 2004; Business section, page 1C.

20. "Fueling Prices? China's Huge Oil Consumption May Add to Soaring Costs," ABC News, May 28, 2004; "China Invests Heavily in Sudan's Oil Industry," *Washington Post*, Thursday, December 23, 2004, page A1.

21. The World Bank, *Global Economic Prospects and the Developing Countries 2003* (http://www.worldbank.org/prospects/gep2003/ index.htm) and *World Development Indicators*, 2004, Table 2.7 Distribution of Income or Consumption, pages 60-63. The Gini index can be used to measure the distribution equality of an item. In this case, the index measures the extent to which the distribution of income among individuals deviates from a perfectly equal distribution. The lower the value, the more inequitable the distribution. Belgium, Norway, and Sweden

all had Gini indexes below 30. Be aware, though, that this is *not* an indication of wealth. Swaziland, with a GNI of $1,240 in 2002, has a Gini index over 60. (The implication is that much of the population earns near or close to the average income.)

22. The World Bank, *2004 World Development Indicators*, Table 1.1 Size of the Economy, pages 14-17.

23. The World Bank, *2004 World Development Indicators*, Table 1.1 Size of the Economy, pages 14-17.

24. See, for example, Mitra, Arup, Aristomene Varoudakis, and Marie-Ange Veganzones-Varoudakis. "Productivity and Technical Efficiency in Indian States' Manufacturing: The Role of Infrastructure," January 2002, *Economic Development and Cultural Change*, Chicago. Volume 50, Issue 2, pages 395-426.

25. *The World Factbook* is published annually and is available in print form as well as online (http://www.odci.gov/cia/publications/factbook/index.html).

26. The competitiveness rankings are available online at the International Institute for Management Development web site (http://www01.imd.ch/wcy/ranking).

27. The World Bank, *2004 World Development Indicators*, Table 4.14 Monetary Indicators and Prices, pages 234-237; The World Bank, *2003 World Development Indicators*, Data Query (http://devdata.worldbank.org/data-query); accessed August 6, 2004.

Further Readings

Altman, Daniel. "Small-Picture Approach to a Big Problem: Poverty," Tuesday, August 20, 2002, *Wall Street Journal*, Section C, page 2.

Baldacci, Emanuele, Luiz de Mello, and Gabriela Inchauste. "Financial Crises, Poverty, and Income Distribution," June 2002, *Finance & Development*: Washington, Volume 39, Issue 2, pages 24-27.

Caplanova, Anetta, Marta Orviska, and John Hudson. "Eastern European Attitudes to Integration with Western Europe," *Journal of Common Market Studies*. Oxford: June 2004. Volume 42, Issue 2, pages 271-288.

De Matteis, Alessandro. "International Trade and Economic Growth in a Global Environment," *Journal of International Development*. Chichester: May 2004. Volume 16, Issue 4, pages 575-588.

Haynal, George. "Building North America," Summer 2002, *Harvard International Review*, Cambridge. Volume 24, Issue 2, pages 88-89.

Lamont, James. "Companies Court Partners Among World's Poor," August 29, 2002, *Financial Times*, page 7.

Moore, Stephen and Julian L. Simon. *It's Getting Better All the Time: 100 Great Trends of the Last 100 Years*, October 2000, Cato Institute (http://www.cato.org).

Pastore, Michael. "At-Home Users Approaching Half Billion," March 6, 2002, *CyberAtlas* (http://cyberatlas.internet.com/big_picture/geographics/article/0,,5911_986431,00.htm).

"PC Market Headed for Geographic Shift," March 11, 2002, *CyberAtlas* (http://cyberatlas.internet.com/big_picture/hardware/article/0,,5921_988841,00.html#table).

Prahalad, C. K. and Allen Hammond. "Serving the World's Poor Profitably," *Harvard Business Review*, September 2002, Volume 80, Issue 9, pages 48-57.

Schaede, Ulrike. "What Happened to the Japanese Model?" *Review of International Economics*. Oxford: May 2004. Volume 12, Issue 2, pages 277-294.

Schiff, Maurice and L. Alan Winters. *Regional Integration and Development*, World Bank, 2003.

Talukdar, Debabrata, K. Sudhir, and Andrew Ainslie. "Investigating New Product Diffusion Across Products and Countries," Winter 2002, *Marketing Science*, Linthicum. Volume 21, Issue 1, pages 97-114.

"The Americas: Waiting for the IMF to Tango; Argentina's Crisis," March 30, 2002, *The Economist*, Volume 362, Issue 8266, pages 31-32.

Thurow, Lester. *"Fortune Favors the Bold,"* 2003. Harper Collins Publishers, N.Y., N.Y.

Yu, Tyler T., Miranda M. Zhang, Lloyd Southern, and Carl Joiner. "An International Comparative Study of Economic Development: The Recent Evidence," *Journal of American Academy of Business*, Cambridge. Hollywood, FL: September 2004. Volume 5, Issues 1/2, pages 1-7.

Recommended Web Sites

Regional Economic Integration:

Association of Southeast Asian Nations (ASEAN): http://www.aseansec.org

Economic Community of West African States (ECOWAS): http://www.ecowas.int

European Union (EU): http://europa.eu.int/index.htm

Global Organizations:

International Monetary Fund (IMF): http://www.imf.org

United Nations (UN): http://www.un.org

The World Bank Group (IBRD): http://www.worldbank.org

World Trade Organization (WTO): http://www.wto.org

Data Sources:

World Bank, World Development Indicators, Data Query (http://devdata.worldbank.org/data-query)—selected World Development Indicators (over 200 economic entities and 14 economic country groups; 54 indicators of approximately 550 available with online version or 600 in print edition [for most recent five-year period])

Strategis, Industry. Create your own comparative reports on commercial policies, foreign investment, geography, government, people, trade, and many other indicators, using a variety of reliable resources; Dynamic Document Creator

(http://strategis.ic.gc.ca/sc_mrkti/ibin/compare.html).

International Data Base (IDB) is an interactive data bank containing statistical tables of demographic and socio-economic data for 227 countries and areas of the world. The population statistics are collected and compiled by the U.S. Census Bureau

(http://www.census.gov/ipc/www/idbnew.html).

Population Reference Bureau (http://www.prb.org), in particular the "Quick Facts" and the "World Population Data Sheet" (data can be accessed online as well as purchased). The data includes population statistics—birthrates, death rates, contraception, life expectancy, and urbanization.

U.S. balance of payments tables are available on the Bureau of Economic Analysis web site (home page: http://www.bea.gov); BoP reports (http://www.bea.doc.gov/bea/di/home/bop.htm) and data (http://www.bea.gov/bea/uguide.htm#_1_22). See also the Library of Economics and Liberty web site (http://www.econlib.org/library/Enc/BalanceofPayments.html).

Case 2.1

FOREIGN EXCHANGE RATES

Country	Currency	Exchange Rate (per $US, August 2, 1999)	Exchange Rate (per $US, Sept. 1, 2005)
Argentina	Peso	2.98	2.9160
Brazil	Real	3.047	2.3576
Britain	Pound	0.619819	0.5548
Canada	Dollar	1.50753	1.1873
China	Renminbi/Yuan	8.2772	8.1098
Euro zone	Euro	0.938031	0.8106
India	Rupee	43.2917	44.1300
Indonesia	Rupiah	6,804.00	10,425.0000
Japan	Yen	114.374	110.7100
Mexico	Peso	11.4229	10.7570
Philippines	Peso	38.5483	56.3500
Russia	Ruble	24.24	28.4920
South Africa	Rand	6.17527	6.3817
Switzerland	Franc	1.4983	1.2543
Turkey	Lira	430,375.00	—

Source: http://www.xe.com/ucc/; http://www.xe.com/ict/; http://www.x-rates.com.

QUESTIONS AND RESEARCH

1. Find the latest quotations for these currencies.

2. Calculate the approximate changes in the value of these currencies. Show the increase or decrease in relation to the U.S. dollar.

3. Why have these changes occurred? (Give a general explanation.)

4. What are some of the implications of changing exchange rates for marketers?

Case 2.2

U.S. PHARMACEUTICALS, INC. (A)

U.S. Pharmaceuticals (USP) is a U.S. firm with about 30 percent of its sales outside the United States. USP concentrates on the ethical drug business but has diversified into animal health products, cosmetics, and some patent medicines. These other lines account for about one-fourth of USP's $800 million sales.

USP's international business is conducted in some 70 countries, mostly through distributors in those markets. In six countries, however, it has manufacturing or compounding operations. (*Compounding* refers to the local mixing, assembling, and packaging of crit-

ical ingredients shipped from the United States.) USP's only Latin American manufacturing/compounding operations are in Latinia, a country with a population of about 30 million. Some products are shipped from Latinia to other Latin American markets.

USP's Latinian plant is operated by the pharmaceutical division. It is engaged in producing and compounding USP's ethical drug line. It does no work for other USP divisions (cosmetics, proprietary medicines, and animal health). All of the other divisions, which also sell in Latinia, export their finished products from plants in the United States. The Latinian plant employs 330 people, of whom only two are North Americans—the general manager, Tom Hawley, and the director of quality control, Frixos Massialas.

USP's cosmetics and toiletries business accounts for $150 million in sales and is handled by a separate division—Cosmetics and Toiletries. The division sells in only 38 of USP's 70 foreign markets. One of the division's better foreign markets is Latinia, where it has sales of over $8 million and an acceptable market position. Cosmetics and Toiletries has a marketing subsidiary in Latinia to handle its business there. Jim Richardson, an American, heads the subsidiary. The rest of the staff are Latinians.

Jim Richardson was very disturbed by news received from the Latinian Ministry of International Trade. Tariffs were being increased on many "nonessential products" because of the balance-of-payments pressures the country had been experiencing for the past year and a half. For USP's Cosmetics and Toiletries specifically, this meant a rise in the tariffs it pays—from 20 percent to 50 percent ad valorem. The 20 percent duty had posed no particular problem for Cosmetics and Toiletries because of the prestige of the imported product and the consumer franchise it had established, Richardson explained. He believed, however, that the 50 percent duty was likely to be an insurmountable barrier.

Cosmetics and Toiletries' competition in Latinia was about evenly divided between local firms and other international companies from Europe and North America. Jim believed that local firms, which had about 40 percent of the market, stood to benefit greatly from the tariff increase unless the international firms could find a satisfactory response. When Jim received the news of the tariff increase, which was to be imposed the first of October—one week away—he called a meeting to consider what Cosmetics and Toiletries could do. Deborah Neale, manager of Cosmetics Marketing, and Emilio Illanes, manager of Toiletries Marketing, met with Jim to discuss the situation.

Several different courses of action were proposed at the hastily called meeting. Deborah suggested, "We could continue importing, pay the high duty, and change the positioning strategy to appeal to a high-price, premium market." Another idea was to import the primary ingredients and assemble (compound) and package them in Latinia. (Duties on the imported ingredients ranged between 10 percent and 35 percent ad valorem.) Emilio suggested asking Cosmetics and Toiletries in the United States for a lower price on the products shipped to Latinia so the duty would have a lesser impact on the final price in the local market. Jim mentioned the alternative that none of them wanted to consider. "If we can't compete at those high prices, we may have to give up the market."

QUESTIONS AND RESEARCH

1. Evaluate the alternatives that were brought up at the meeting.

2. Are there any other possible courses of action? Explain.

3. Propose and defend a course of action.

4. How would your response differ if, instead of a tariff increase, Latinia had imposed a quota, cutting the imports of these products by 75 percent?

Case 2.3

THE LIFEBLOOD OF THE WORLD'S ECONOMIES—ELECTRICITY

Electricity is a critical part of any nation's infrastructure. Without it, people would not have computers, telephones (even wireless need to be recharged), televisions, and (perhaps most importantly), electric lights and refrigeration—all of which are an important part of people's lives. There is also, of course, the electricity needed to run the machines for industries. Businesses need electricity to function, so researching a nation's ability to provide electricity is important.

Consumption of electricity also gives some indication of a nation's wealth. Assuming that the electricity consumed goes toward powering appliances in homes as well as in manufacturing, the higher the consumption, the larger the middle class—those who can afford electric appliances. The following table provides some recent statistics on average energy use around the world. (Consider that an average energy-efficient refrigerator requires approximately 600 kilowatts of energy per year.)

Annual Electric Consumption, 2001

Country or Income Group	(KwH/person)
Low income	317
India	365
Kenya	117
Nicaragua	268
Nigeria	82
Pakistan	358
Lower middle income	1,304
Brazil	1,729
China	893
Indonesia	404
South Africa	3,793
Thailand	1,508
World	2,159
Upper middle income	2,505
Argentina	2,107
Czech Republic	4,977
Estonia	3,764
Gabon	814
Mexico	1,643
High income	8,421
Canada	15,385
Germany	6,093
Korea, Republic	5,288
Norway	24,881
Spain	4,933
United States	11,714

Source: The World Bank, Data Query, *2004 World Development Indicators*, Table 5.10 Power and Communications, pages 290–293.

These data tell only part of the story, though. In the United States and other developed nations, on rare occasions, the ability to supply electricity still does not meet local demand. On a particularly hot day, when people are running air conditioners and fans in addition to using electricity for other needs, the population may be subject to a brownout (when lightbulbs grow dim because they and other electrical devices are not getting sufficient power to run at designed levels). California, among other places, has experienced rolling blackouts, where power is available only to a specific area at certain times of the day. Total blackouts are also possible when a storm or another unexpected occurrence completely cuts power to a region.

In India, the problem of getting enough power to run trains, manufacturing plants, and home appliances is becoming severe in some areas. Power outages may last only an hour; even more common, though, are power outages that last five or ten hours (sometimes even longer). In the town of Purnea, for instance, power was out on one occasion for 34 days. While the problems in India have existed for decades, they are becoming acute as more people can afford to purchase computers, refrigerators, televisions, and air conditioners. The shortages are blamed not only on the inability of the power companies to generate enough electricity, but also on the theft of electricity. India's Power Minister, Suresh Prabhakar Prabhu, estimates that half of all power generated is subsequently stolen by people who illegally tap overhead power lines. (Do not attempt this at home!)

Comparing populations and power consumption provides intriguing bases for discussions about major environmental issues facing the world. The United States has a large middle class and uses a lot of electricity. America, with a population that is one-fourth that of India, consumes more than 30 times the electricity. Access to electricity may be as high as 40 or 50 percent in urban areas of India, but available only to between 3 and 10 percent of people living in rural locations. Comparing India or China to Norway, with only 5 million people, is even more dramatic.

China, projecting a rapid increase in demand for electricity, is building the second largest dam in the world, the Xiaolangdi Dam. This is just one of ten dams planned for the Hongshui River. Where is the largest dam? The largest dam, the Three Gorges Dam, is also located in China. Behind this dam sits a lake, created by damming the Yangtze River, that will be 400 miles long and nearly 600 feet deep. Once completed, the dam will be capable of generating 18,200 megawatts of power. The average middle-income electric consumption is approximately 1,400 KwH per person. With a population of 1.3 billion, China would need 1,820 gigawatts (billion watts) of power to satisfy the demand of an average middle-income nation. On the bright side, the Chinese also hope that by building the dam, they will be able to control flooding and the associated loss of life—in the last century, approximately 300,000 people died due to floods.

Across the globe in Costa Rica, the government is eager to sell electricity to neighboring countries as a source of income. As a result, it has been studying the feasibility of building a dam in the Boruca territory. The estimated yield of the plant would be 1,500 megawatts, most of which would be exported to Mexico and the United States (since Costa Rica is already meeting the demands of its population). Preliminary plans call for a dam over 800 feet tall that would result in the flooding of more than 50,000 acres. Local residents would be displaced; and property destined to be flooded is home to flora and fauna that, if not endangered, are certainly rare. Unique wildlife and plants attract tourists; and building this dam would hurt the tourism industry, one of Costa Rica's major "exports."

While hydroelectric power is seen as a cleaner alternative than coal-burning or nuclear plants, it also presents unique problems. Flooding large tracts of land requires that many people and companies move or be displaced. If the land that is flooded contains dangerous chemicals or by-products from industries, waste treatment plants, and abandoned vehicles (with oil and gasoline left inside), the pollutants must be cleaned or cleared; otherwise, the water will be contaminated. New water treatment plants, factories, roads, housing, and other construction must occur to take the place of the submerged properties. There is also the ecological impact on plant and animal life within the flooded region and the impact of support infrastructure (transmission towers, for example).

Whatever the solutions, as nations develop and people want more power-driven products, economic and ecological consequences will result. Companies that provide the plans for these projects and build them, as well as the firms that produce energy-consuming products (from automobiles to refrigerators), have a responsibility to take these important issues into account when they design, build, and market their products.

QUESTIONS AND RESEARCH

1. Why would frequent brownouts or prolonged blackouts have an impact on after-sales service costs for electrically powered products?

2. How much power will India need in five years (consider current population, population growth rates, and current electricity/power consumption)?

3. How would intermittent power access like that in India and other parts of the world affect sales of electrically powered products?

4. There are vast opportunities for many companies in developing markets. What can companies do to help developing nations plan for the infrastructure needs associated with economic development?

Sources: "China Builds Second Biggest Dam," July 1, 2001, BBC News; "China's Three Gorges Dam—Eco-Boon or Cesspool?" November 4, 1997, CNN Interactive, CNN.com, accessed August 14, 2002; "Costa Rica: Indigenous Territory Threatened by Hydroelectric Dam," *World Rainforest Movement* (http://www.wrm.org.uy/bulletin/4/CostaRica.html), accessed July 15, 2002; "Indians Can Only Wait On Government as Blackouts Strike," August 2, 2002, *Philadelphia Inquirer*, page A21; The World Bank, Data Query, *2002 World Development Indicators* (http://devdata.worldbank.org/data-query), accessed August 14, 2002; The World Bank, *2002 World Development Indicators*, page 130.

Case 2.4

UNICOLA

Unicola is a medium-sized beverage and snack food company based in the United States. Annual sales are $450 million. The firm has developed some special enriched beverage and snack foods that offer high nutritional value as well as convenience and refreshment. Unicola is interested in foreign markets for these new products. (Its present business is confined to the United States and Canada.) The company believes that these products should not be promoted as "health foods," but as traditional soft drinks and snacks because consumers do not like to buy products just because "they are good for you."

Because promotion is so important to the successful introduction of these products, George Horton, Unicola's advertising manager, has been looking at promotional possibilities in various foreign markets. One of these areas is Southeast Asia. His preliminary screening includes four variables: (1) newspaper circulation per capita, (2) radio receivers per capita, (3) television receivers per capita, and (4) population. The markets being investigated have already been screened on the basis of political criteria. After the political screening, the following Southeast Asian nations remain on the list for further screening on the basis of promotional possibilities: Bangladesh, Hong Kong, India, Indonesia, Malaysia, Pakistan, the Philippines, Singapore, South Korea, Sri Lanka, Taiwan, Thailand, and Vietnam.

QUESTIONS AND RESEARCH

1. Prepare a table showing the scoring for these 13 countries on the four criteria suggested.

2. Which five countries would you choose as offering the best possibilities for promoting Unicola's products? Explain and defend your choices.

3. What other information would you need about these countries? How would you get it?

CHAPTER 3

The Cultural Environment

The People of the World

Economic factors are important in determining a consumer's ability to purchase a product. Whether a purchase actually occurs, however, depends largely on cultural factors. Therefore, to understand markets abroad, a marketer must have an appreciation for the cultural environment of buyer behavior. This chapter presents the major ingredients of that cultural environment.

The main goals of this chapter are to

- Show how a country's material culture determines whether a firm's products fit in with the way of life for a group of people, and if not, what adaptation may be necessary.

- Explain the role of a culture's language in shaping the marketing task.

- Explore the subject of a society's aesthetics—its sense of beauty, proportion, and appropriateness—in connection with a firm's products and communications.

- Describe how the local educational system can impact a firm's marketing and staffing situation.

- Discuss the effect of religion on consumer behavior.

- Distinguish characteristics among different values and among different attitudes that influence purchasing decisions.

- Explain how the social organization in a given country (family, age group, class, etc.) affects consumer behavior.

Marketing has always been recognized as an economic activity involving the exchange of goods and services. Only in recent years, however, have sociocultural influences been identified as determinants of marketing behavior, revealing marketing as a cultural as well as economic phenomenon. Because an understanding of marketing is culture-bound, one must acquire knowledge of diverse cultural environments in order to be successful at international marketing. It is necessary to remove one's culturally tinted glasses to study foreign markets.

The growing use of anthropology, sociology, and psychology in marketing is explicit recognition of the noneconomic bases of marketing behavior. It is not enough to say that consumption is a function of income. Consumption is a function of many other cultural influences as well. Furthermore, only noneconomic factors can explain the different patterns of consumption of two individuals with identical incomes—or, by analogy, of two different countries with similar per capita incomes.

A review of consumer durables ownership in EU countries shows the importance of noneconomic factors in determining consumption behavior. For example, you could compare penetration levels of home appliances (white goods) among EU members. Slovakians, new members of the EU, own the most refrigerators (40 per 1,000 people) but have the fewest microwave ovens (3/1,000) and few dishwashers (3/1,000). Austrians own more refrigerators than most other EU members (31/1,000) and a lot of microwave ovens (36/1,000) but few clothes dryers (5/1,000). Greeks own more refrigerators than their EU counterparts (32/1,000); but purchases of microwave ovens (9/1,000), clothes dryers (2/1,000), and dishwashers (7/1,000) are among the lowest in the EU. There appears to be some relationship between income and the purchase of white goods when looking at higher-order convenience items such as dishwashers and clothes dryers versus items that might be considered more of a necessity, such as refrigerators and ovens.[1]

Nevertheless, it is remarkable that the same countries can be at high-penetration levels for some appliances and at low-penetration levels for other appliances. People in Luxembourg and Denmark have the highest income of EU members ($40,000 and $30,000, respectively) but only moderate levels of consumption of white goods. People living in Latvia, Lithuania, and the Slovak Republic have lower income levels ($3,500, $3,700, and $4,000, respectively); but as mentioned in the case of the Slovakians, they have the highest per capita consumption of refrigerators among other EU members.[2] Differences in consumption patterns for these and other consumer products cannot be explained by different levels of income alone. However, they can be better explained when cultural differences are taken into account.

What is Culture?

Culture is too complex to define in simple terms. It seems that each anthropologist has a definition. The anthropologist John Bodley succinctly brings together the major points of agreement in his description of the term: "Culture is learned behavior; a way of life for any group of people living together in a single, related and interdependent community."[3] One fundamental aspect is that culture is a total pattern of behavior that is consistent and compatible in its components. It is not a collection of random behaviors, but behaviors that are related and integrated. A second fundamental is that culture is learned behavior. It is not biologically transmitted. It depends on environment, not heredity. It can be called the man-made part of the environment. The third fundamental is that culture is behavior that is shared by a group of people, a society. It can be considered as the distinctive way of life of a people. The elements of culture will be discussed after the role of cultural analysis in U.S. marketing is considered.

Much of what follows is based on work performed by Dr. Geert Hofstede.

Nearly 40 years ago a psychologist named Dr. Geert Hofstede studied cultural characteristics in individuals from around the world. It was a landmark study that involved over 100,000 people. In essence, the study attempted to classify people and define cultural characteristics that shaped work-related values and impacted the work environment. Originally, there were four dimensions: power distance, individualism, masculinity, and uncertainty avoidance. In a subsequent study, Dr. Hofstede added long-term orientation as a fifth dimension.

Power distance is the degree to which power in a group is shared and is the relative distance between the "most" and "least" powerful people. In cultures with low power distance, there is a tendency toward egalitarianism and group decision making. In cultures characterized as high power distance, rank and title are more important and authority is accepted rather than questioned.

Societies that score high on Hofstede's **individualism** dimension, tend, as the term suggests, to place more emphasis and importance on individuals than on collectivistic cultures. Praise and blame are placed on the individual, and family ties and friendships tend to be weak. Independence is a trait associated with high individualism. Collectivists, on the other hand, place much importance on family and friends, having many long-term relationships and an extended notion of family. (When asked "How large is your family?" an individualist would tend to provide a small number [4—that includes parents, brother, and sister], whereas a collectivist would respond with a larger number [20—that includes grandparents, cousins, and many other family members].)

Masculinity versus femininity recognizes that some societies are male-dominated and that a large separation exists between men and women. Gender roles in a masculine society are very different, often more structured. Manifestations of this separation can be seen in education levels (women do not attend school at the same rate and level as men), in upper-level government posts held by women (women hold no or few positions of power), and in the wage gap that exists between women and men performing the same job (and in the fact that men and women do not hold the same jobs).

Whether a person or group can be characterized as high or low in terms of **uncertainty avoidance** is a matter of how entrepreneurial they are, whether the culture generally can be referred to as risk takers, or whether the group avoids change or prefers structured, lock-step instructions. Those who are entrepreneurial, who gamble, who embrace change, and who appreciate diverse opinions but don't like to follow rules are low on Hofstede's uncertainty avoidance scale. On the other hand, when a person or a group of people is likely to avoid uncertain situations, they are less likely to gamble or try new things but are apt to follow instructions.

In studying Chinese managers, Hofstede also identified a fifth cultural dimension or characteristic he called **long-term orientation**. People who believe that wisdom comes from age or longevity, that tradition and elders are to be valued, and that rewards come to those who make long-term commitments are classified as having a long-term orientation. Those who "live for today," have little savings, and focus on short-term gains and ill-defined plans are ranked low on this dimension. For example, cab drivers in the Czech Republic shortly after the fall of Communism often charged tourists double, sometimes triple, the fare they charged locals because the tourists were unlikely to return, were rich, and could afford it.[4]

Hofstede's work has been expanded, duplicated, tested, and contested in a wide body of research that has spanned a large portion of the last century. His work is important to international business because it laid the groundwork for viewing the role of culture in the work environment. Hofstede helps explain how to motivate people in the work world and why people react differently to the same circumstances or objects. In marketing, people are often classified on the basis of demographics—income levels, size of family, and geographic location. When marketers refer to baby boomers, Generation Xers, and Millenniums, they use psychographics (age, certainly, but also people's interests, values, and beliefs) to classify people into those groups. Taking the step from demographics to psychographics takes research like that conducted by Hofstede to identify characteristics that are commonly held across international boundaries. The influence of Hofstede's research is seen in the profusion of scholarly articles that identify his characteristics in today's research.

Cultural Analysis in U.S. Marketing

In approaching the cultural environment of international marketing, it is revealing to see how cultural analysis is used in marketing. If you scan textbooks in marketing, you see that they all have one or more chapters on the contributions of the behavioral sciences to marketing. In addition to chapters on consumer behavior, concepts derived from the behavioral sciences occur in chapters on marketing research, promotion, and pricing. Even the product is defined in terms of psychic as well as physical utility. For example, if marketing managers are to be successful, they must be familiar with the following concepts: (1) reference groups, (2) social class, (3) consumption systems, (4) family structure and decision making, (5) adoption-diffusion, (6) market segmentation, and (7) consumer behavior.

More evidence of the role of cultural analysis in marketing is the number of people trained in anthropology or sociology who are working in marketing. Major companies employ them, or they may work in advertising agencies and consulting firms. University consultants to industry come not only from schools of business and engineering, but also from departments of anthropology and sociology. Such attention to cultural analysis is notable. More importance is placed on cultural analysis in foreign markets, where the international marketer generally knows little about the local culture. (See Figure 3-1.)

Elements of Culture

Varying definitions exist pertaining to the elements of culture, including one that counts 73 "cultural universals." This book uses a simpler list that encompasses eight major areas: (1) technology and material culture, (2) language, (3) aesthetics, (4) education, (5) religion, (6) attitudes and values, (7) social organization, and (8) political life. (The political aspect of culture is reserved for discussion in Chapter 4.) A broad definition of culture would include economics as well; however, the subjects are often treated separately, as is done in this book. The discussion of culture here is not definitive and perhaps would not satisfy the anthropologist. Nonetheless, the material should contribute to an understanding of the cultural environment as it affects a firm's foreign marketing.

Aesthetics

Aesthetics refers to the prevalent ideas in a culture concerning beauty and good taste, as expressed in the arts—music, art, drama, and dance—and the appreciation of color and form. International differences abound in aesthetics, but they tend to be regional rather than national.

Figure 3-1. Culture Shapes Marketing

Culture is that which you can sense (hear, see, smell, taste, and touch) as well as that which is hidden (assumptions, attitudes, beliefs, and values).

What you can sense: music, art, architecture, fashion, food, dance

What is hidden: feelings about work, wealth, religion, future, family, friends, time

What you can see is a manifestation of what you can't see. People's reactions to the same marketing campaign, for example, are likely to be different from culture to culture. Marketers must recognize this fact if they are to develop effective marketing strategies and accept that they must adapt the movies, watches, cars, insurance, and other products that they market to accommodate the differences among cultures.

For example, Kabuki theater is exclusively Japanese, but Western theater includes at least all of Western Europe in addition to the United States and Canada in its audience.

Musical tastes, too, tend to be regional rather than national. In the West, many countries enjoy the same classical and popular music. In fact, due to modern communications, popular music has become truly international. Nevertheless, obvious differences exist between Western music and music of the Middle East, Africa, or India. Likewise, the dance styles of African tribal groups or the Balinese are quite removed from Western dance styles. The beauty of India's Taj Mahal is different from that of Notre Dame in Paris or the Chrysler Building in New York City.

Design

The aesthetics of a culture probably do not have a major impact on economic activities. In aesthetics, however, lie some implications for international business. For example, in the design of its plant, product, or package, a firm should be sensitive to local aesthetic preferences. This may run counter to the desire for international uniformity, but the firm must be aware of the positive and negative aspects of its designs. Generally, Asians appreciate complex and decorative styles, particularly when it comes to gift wrapping, for instance.

A historical example of lack of cultural sensitivity is illustrated by early Christian missionaries from Western nations who were often guilty of architectural "imperial-

ism." The Christian churches built in many non-Western nations usually reflected Western rather than indigenous architectural ideas. This was not done with malicious intent, but because the missionaries were culture-bound in their aesthetics; that is, they had their own ideas about what a church should look like.

The U.S. government faces a similar problem in designing its embassies. The U.S. Embassy in India received praise both for its beauty as a building and for the way it blended with Indian architecture. The U.S. Embassy in London, however, has received more than its share of criticism, including comments about the size of the sculpted American eagle on top of the building. Some Britons also took exception to the architecture of the London Hilton. For a firm, the best policy is to design and decorate its buildings and commercial vehicles to reflect local aesthetic preferences. In its thousands of outlets abroad, McDonald's has learned to adapt its facilities to local tastes.

Color

The significance of different colors also varies from culture to culture. In the United States, for instance, people use colors to identify emotional reactions; people "see red," they are "green with envy," and they "feel blue." Black signifies mourning in Western countries, whereas white is often the color of mourning in Eastern nations. Green is popular in Muslim countries, while red and black have a negative connotation in several African countries. Red is an appealing and lucky color in China, blue sometimes suggests evil, and yellow is often associated with authority. Certain colors have particular meanings because of religious, patriotic, or aesthetic reasons. The marketer needs to know the significance of colors in a culture when planning products, packages, and advertising. For any market, the choice of colors should be related to the aesthetic sense of the buyer's culture rather than that of the marketer's culture. Generally, the colors of the country's flag are safe colors. Japan has a Study Group for Colors in Public Places. It wages war on "color pollution." Its mission is "to seek out better uses for color, to raise the issue of colors."

Music

There are also cultural differences in music. An understanding of these differences is critical in creating advertising messages that use music. The music of nonliterate cultures is generally functional, or has significance in the people's daily lives; whereas the music of literate cultures tends to be separate from people's other concerns. For example, a Western student has to learn to "understand" a Beethoven symphony, but aborigines assimilate musical culture as an integral part of their existence. Ethnomusicologist William Malm stated that understanding the symbolism in different kinds of music requires considerable cultural conditioning. Therefore, homogeneity in music throughout world cultures is not possible. There are exceptions, of course; but one implication for a firm is that wherever it utilizes music, it should use music of the local culture. Recognizing the importance of music in popular culture, companies such as Coca-Cola, PepsiCo, and Nike are frequent sponsors of events such as MTV Video Music Awards Latin America and WOMAD (Festival of World Music, Arts & Dance).

Paul Anka provides an example of the value of "going native" in music and language. Anka has recorded ten albums that have sold, collectively, 10 million copies, none of which has been heard in the United States. The secret is that the songs in the albums were sung in Japanese, German, French, Spanish, and Italian—songs that Anka composed strictly for those countries in a style indigenous to their musical cultures.

Anka isn't fluent in those languages. For months, he worked with native musicians on music and lyrics that would appeal to each nation. He sang in the local language phonetically. Mr. Anka succeeded because of his broad appeal, but also because he recorded his music in so many other languages.

Brand Names

The choice of brand names is also affected by aesthetics. Frequently, the best brand name is one in the local language, pleasing to local taste. This leads to a multiplicity of brand names, which some firms try to avoid by searching out a nonsense word that is pronounceable everywhere but that has no specific meaning anywhere. Kodak is one example. In other cases, local identification is important enough that firms seek local brand names. For example, Procter & Gamble has 20 different brand names for its detergents in foreign markets.

The aesthetics of a culture influence a firm's marketing abroad, often in ways that marketers are unaware of until they make mistakes. A firm needs local input to avoid ineffective or damaging use of aesthetics. This input may come from local marketing research, local nationals working for the firm, and local advertising agencies or distributors.

Material Culture

"What do you do?" If you live in or visit America, you hear that question quite frequently. The question says much about the culture. Instead of "you are what you eat," "you are what you do." The focus of many conversations in the United States is about one's work, not about family, weather, world events, or politics. A person's job title, earnings, car, house, clothes, and other possessions help define that individual in America. While some people view this as overindulgence and self-absorbed behavior, others argue that this behavior reflects a competitive and entrepreneurial spirit. Americans are not alone in the world in terms of material acquisition; they are merely an example. As is discussed next, attitudes toward material wealth differ markedly across cultures.

Technology and Material Culture

Material culture includes the tools and artifacts—the material or physical things—in a society, excluding those physical things found in nature unless they undergo some technological transformation. For example, a tree as such is not part of a culture, but the Christmas tree is. **Technology** refers to the techniques or methods of making and using that which surrounds us. Technology and material culture are related to the way a society organizes its economic activities. The term *technology gap* refers to differences in the ability of two societies to create, design, and use that which exists in nature or to use that which has been transformed in some way.

When referring to industrialized nations, developing nations, the nuclear age, or the space age, one is referring to different technologies and material cultures. One can also speak of societies being in the age of the automobile, the bicycle, or foot transportation—or in the age of the computer, the abacus, or pencil-and-paper calculation. The relationships between technology, material culture, and the other aspects of life are profound but not easily recognized because people are the products of their own culture. It is primarily as people travel abroad that they perceive such relationships.

When discussing this topic, Karl Marx went so far as to say that the economic organization of a society shapes and determines its political, legal, and social organization. His view was termed "economic determinism," his materialistic interpretation of history. Few people today would take such a strong position, but they may recognize many examples of the impact of tools, techniques, and economic organization on the nature of life in society. For example, people's behavior as workers and consumers is greatly influenced by the technology and material culture.

The way people work (and how effectively they work) is determined in large part by their technology and material culture. Henry Ford's assembly line revolutionized U.S. productivity and, ultimately, the standard of living. The U.S. farmers' use of equipment and technology has made them the world's most productive agriculturalists. Ironically, agriculture is one of the most capital-intensive and technology-intensive industries in the United States. The R&D is not done by the farmer, however, but by land-grant universities, equipment manufacturers, and seed and chemical companies. The computer, as one of the newer artifacts, affects the way people work, the kind of work they can do, and even where they work. If you consider the nature of the factory and agricultural methods and the role of the computer in an African nation, you can see technology and material culture as a constraint on work and productivity in a culture. In developed economies, tractors are able to cultivate many acres every day; while in developing countries, where farmers may have only hand tools, it takes days (even weeks) to plant or tend an acre of land.

How people consume and what people consume are also heavily influenced by the technology and material culture. For example, the car has helped to create the conditions that made suburban living possible, with the accompanying lifestyle and consumption patterns. The car has also shaped dating behavior. Television has a wide-ranging impact on consumer and voter behavior. The microwave oven influences not only the preparation of food, but also the nature of the food consumed. Considering artifacts such as the digital camera and the cellular telephone, you can imagine further ramifications of each new product on the life of the consumer. Knowing the impact of these products in the U.S. culture, you can conjecture how consumer behavior might be different in countries with much lighter penetration of such products. For example, the number of cars in use in 2002 ranges from 486 per 1,000 people in the United States to 110 in Mexico, 23 in Egypt, 8 in Nigeria, 5 in India, 5 in China, and 2 in Vietnam.[5]

Material Culture as a Constraint

Managers need to develop insight into how material culture in foreign markets affects their operations abroad. In manufacturing, foreign production by a firm may represent an attempt to introduce a new material culture into the host economy. This is usually the case when a firm builds a plant in a less developed country. The firm generally checks carefully on the necessary economic prerequisites for such a plant; for example, raw-material supply, power, transportation, and financing. Frequently overlooked, however, are the other cultural preconditions for the plant.

Prior to making foreign production decisions, a firm must evaluate the material culture in the host country. One aspect is the economic infrastructure; that is, transportation, power, and communications. Other questions are these: Do production processes need to be adapted to fit the local economy? Will the plant be more labor-intensive than plants at home? The manager discovers that production of the same goods may require a different production function in different countries.

MATERIAL CULTURE AND MARKETING

It is equally important for marketers to understand the material culture in foreign markets. For example, the industrial marketer finds it useful to obtain and analyze input-output tables, which show how materials and components are used in making products. Where these tables can be even partially constructed, a firm has a better idea of how its products relate to the material culture and industrial structure of the country. Such information helps identify customers and usage patterns.[6]

In large diversified markets such as the United States, almost any industrial product can find a market. In developing nations, however, industrial goods marketers find increasingly limited markets in which they can sell only part of their product line—or perhaps none of it. The better the picture of the material culture in world markets, the better able a firm is to identify the best prospects. The prospects in countries where the principal agricultural implement is the machete differ from those countries in which farmers use tractors.

Consumer goods marketers are also concerned with the material culture in foreign markets. Such simple considerations as electrical voltages and use of the metric system must be taken into account. Product adaptations may also be necessitated by the material culture of the family. Does the family have a car to transport purchases? Does the family have a stove to prepare foods or a refrigerator in which to store food? If electrical power is not available, electrical appliances will not be marketable unless they are battery-powered. To those people who wash clothes by a stream or lake, detergents and packaged soaps are not useful; the market is for bar soaps only.

Large multinationals are learning from entrepreneurs in developing countries that the key to success in markets where income is low is to market products that come in small sizes, are relatively cheap, and are easy to use. Unilever packages its shampoo in single-use sizes, selling it for a few cents in India. Other examples include 3-inch square packages of margarine in Nigeria that don't need refrigeration and an 8-cent tube of Close-Up with enough toothpaste for about 20 brushings. Unilever expects that developing markets will account for 50 percent of all sales by 2010, up from 32 percent in 2005.

There are other examples of firms catering to markets in developing nations, where over half of the world's population is located. Scojo Vision of Brooklyn, New York, provides training and $75 loans to entrepreneurs in Latin America and Asia to purchase kits containing eye charts and glasses. The glasses come in three strengths and sell for only $2. Freeplay Energy in London designed and sold 3 million hand crank radios. Since many people in developing countries have no electricity and cannot afford to purchase batteries, these units are popular for listening to farm and health reports. Phillips Electronics of the Netherlands has developed its own version, which the firm is now selling in India for around $20. Indian firms located in Madras and Bangalore are developing wireless kiosks that allow users to access the Internet for as little as 3 cents an hour and computers with voice recognition software, which is aimed at users who cannot read.[7]

Other parts of the marketing program are also influenced by the material culture. For instance, the promotional program is constrained by the kinds of media available. The advertiser wants to know the availability of television, radio, magazines, and newspapers. How good is the reproduction process in newspapers and magazines? Are there advertising and research agencies to support the advertising program? The size of retail outlets affects the use of point-of-purchase displays. The nature of travel and the highway system affects the use of outdoor advertising.

Modifications in distribution may also be necessary. These changes must be made on the basis of the alternatives offered by the country's commercial infrastructure. What wholesale and retail patterns exist? What warehouse or storage facilities are available? Is refrigerated storage possible? What is the nature of the transport system—road, rail, river, or air? What area does it cover? Firms that use direct channels in the United States, with large-scale retailers and chain-store operations, may have to use indirect channels with a multitude of small independent retailers. These small retailers may be relatively inaccessible if they are widely dispersed and transportation is inadequate.

If local storage facilities are insufficient, a firm may have to supply its own packaging or provide special packaging to offer extra protection. Whereas highways and railroads are most important in moving goods in the United States, river transport is a major means in other countries.

GLOBAL MARKETING

Material Culture Matters

The per capita income in Mexico in 2002 was $5,920. Fewer Mexicans own cars, trucks, telephones, and personal computers than people in the United States and other developed nations own. Because of this fact, it's difficult and expensive to ship goods, to travel, and to communicate with customers and suppliers.

Over 11 million cars are on the roads of Mexico. Approximately 33 percent of roads are paved; and although they are expensive to use, the best of these roads are the toll roads (las cuotas). Traveling 200 miles by car between Mexico City and Acapulco costs a little over $40, but the toll for a large truck is $115.

Telephone service was privatized in 1990 and opened to competition in 1997. However, there are still only about 15 telephone lines for every 100 people and installing a new line may take a month or two. Mobile phone usage is considerably higher, with 25 cellular phones for every 100 people. Local telephone service is still unreliable in some areas; and in general, the cost of making calls is expensive because of high government taxes on phone services.

Independent messenger services should be used to deliver important correspondence since mail service is slow and, at times, unreliable. Sending mail electronically is an option in some areas, but it reaches only the relatively wealthy segment of the population who own computers. Only 5 million computers are in use in Mexico, or an average of 20 people for every computer. Ten percent of the population of 101 million people were classified as Internet users in 2002. In 2003, the ISP and connection charges were $23 for one month of service.

Sources: World Bank, *2004 World Development Indicators*, Tables 1.1, 5.9, 5.10, 5.11, and Data Query (http://devdata.worldbank.org/dataquery); *Mexico Country Commercial Guide*, 2004; U.S. Department of Commerce, International Trade Administration (http://www.buyusa.gov/mexico/en/22.html); Autotransport Administration of Mexico, Division of Secretary of Transportation and Communication (http://www.sct.gob.mx/autotransporte/index.htm).

And in still other countries, air is the principal means of transport. Thus, in numerous ways, management is concerned with the material culture in foreign markets. (See "Global Marketing: Material Culture Matters.")

Table 3-1. Major World Languages

Language	Speakers (millions)	Language	Speakers (millions)
Chinese, Mandarin	874	Russian	167
Hindi	366	Japanese	125
English	341	German	100
Spanish	322	Korean	78
Bengali	207	French	77
Portuguese	176	Chinese, Wu	77

Source: *World Almanac 2003*; World Education Corporation, page 633.

IMPERIALISM?

Perhaps the most subtle role of international marketing is that of agent of cultural change. When a firm introduces new products into a market, it is, in effect, seeking to change the country's material culture. The change may be modest—a new food product—or it may be more dramatic—a machine that revolutionizes agricultural or industrial technology in the host country. The product of the international firm is alien in the sense that it did not originate in the host country. The firm must consider carefully the legitimacy of its role as an agent of change. It must be sure that changes it introduces are in accordance with the interests of the host country. When the product is coming from a developed nation and marketed in a developing country without modification, people may resent the firm's product as a form of "neo-colonialism," "westernization," or "imperialism." Along this line, someone coined the term *Cocacolonization* in regard to U.S. cocoa business abroad. More recently, the use of Mc as a prefix to words or expressions (usually with a negative connotation) refers to McDonald's as an institution that represents American cultural influence.

In Canada, foreign sources—especially American—account for 95 percent of movies shown and 83 percent of magazines sold, as well as books and records.[8] Partly because of this fact, there is a Ministry of Canadian Heritage, whose director is pushing legislation to limit the share of U.S. movies and magazines. There are also regulations requiring TV stations to offer 60 percent "Canadian content" and radio stations to include 35 percent "Canadian content" in their popular music broadcast.

Language

Language is perhaps the most obvious difference between cultures. Inextricably linked with all other aspects of a culture, language reflects the nature and values of that culture. For example, the English language has a rich vocabulary for commercial and industrial activities, reflecting the nature of the English and U.S. societies. Many less industrialized societies have only limited vocabularies for those activities but richer vocabularies for matters important to their culture.

An Indian civil servant, Nabagopal Das, commented on the important role of the English language in India's development. He said it would be a serious error for India to replace English with Hindi or other Indian languages because none of them gives adequate expression to the modern commercial or technical activities necessary for India's development. On the other hand, these other languages are more than adequate, indeed rich, for describing the traditional culture. Similarly, Eskimo has many words to describe snow, whereas English has one general term. This is reasonable because the difference in forms of snow plays a vital role in the lives of Eskimos. The kinds of activities they can engage in depend on the specific snow conditions. Of course, in the United States, the subculture of skiers has a richer vocabulary for snow than that of nonskiers.

Because language is such an obvious cultural difference, everyone recognizes that it must be dealt with. It is said that anyone planning a career in international business should learn a foreign language. Certainly, if a person's career involves dealing with a particular country, he or she will find learning the country's language to be very useful. However, learning German or Japanese is not a great help to those people whose careers do not involve Germany or Japan. Because it is usually impossible to predict to which countries a career will lead, it is best to study a language spoken by many people (Mandarin) or a language that is commonly used as a first or second language in many nations (English, French, and Spanish). Whether or not it is a primary language of the parties involved, English is frequently used in negotiations, legal documents, and business transactions. Table 3-1 shows the number of speakers of the major world languages. (The figures for English are misleading because for almost every country, English is the first choice as a second language.)

Americans should not to be complacent, however. More than 340 million of the estimated 566 million Internet users in 2002 (or approximately 60 percent) speak a language other than English. While English-speaking users are the largest group (228 million), Chinese Internet users are the second largest group with 56 million, followed closely by Japanese-speaking users at slightly more than 52 million. Other important languages are Spanish (41 million users), German (39 million), and French and Italian (each with about 20 million users).[9] Despite the large number of European users, the majority of web sites of the largest companies are still available only in the English language.[10]

Language as a Cultural Mirror

A country's language is the key to its culture. Thus, if an individual is to work extensively with any one culture, he or she must learn the language. Learning a language well means learning the culture because the words of the language are merely concepts reflecting the culture. For a firm to communicate well with political leaders, employees, suppliers, and customers, it must assimilate this one aspect of culture more than any other.

Studying the language situation within foreign markets can yield useful information about them. The number of languages in a country is a case in point. In a real sense, a language defines a culture; thus, if a country has several spoken languages, it has several cultures. Belgium has two national languages, French in the South and Flemish in the North. This linguistic division goes back to the days of Julius Caesar, but even today political and social differences exist between the two language groups.

Canada's situation is similar to Belgium's, with Canada having both French and English languages and cultural groups. Many African and Asian nations have a far larger number of languages and cultural groups. Africa has one-tenth of the world's population but one-third of its languages. To communicate midst this diversity, a *lingua franca* (a hybrid language) must be used for communication between the groups. (The term *lingua franca* was originally coined for the commercial language Sabir, which was used along the Mediterranean during the Middle Ages; it was a mixture of Italian, French, Spanish, and other languages.) There are also language bridges, usually the language spoken by the largest group. In China, it is Mandarin; in India, it is Hindi; in many countries, it is the colonial language.

The Republic of the Congo serves as an example of this situation in many third world countries. Separate tribal languages are spoken by the numerous tribes living there. Some local dialects are *lingua franca* trade languages (Lingala, Monokutuba, and Swahili), but the official national language is again a European one—French. Such situations present real obstacles to learning the "language of the people." The usual approach in these situations is to rely on the European language and the *lingua franca* for business and marketing communications. Unfortunately, they are not the mother tongue of most nationals.

DIVERSITY: LINGUISTIC AND SOCIAL

Other problems accompany language diversity within a nation. Many tribal languages are not written. All inter-tribal communications are in the *lingua franca*, which is a written language. However, because the *lingua franca* is not everyone's native tongue, it does not communicate as well as the parties' native languages. The European languages used in former colonies have the virtue of covering a wide

Language and Translation

*A*ccording to Worldwatch, 6,800 languages are spoken in the world today—over 1,000 in the Americas, 1,300 in the Pacific and Australia, 230 in Europe, over 2,000 in Africa, and nearly 2,200 in Asia. The most linguistically diverse countries are Papua New Guinea with 832 languages, Indonesia with 731, India with 398, Nigeria with 515, Mexico with 295, Cameroon with 286, and Brazil with 234. Many of these languages are spoken by few people and do not have a written form, which, unfortunately, means they are likely to be extinct within the next generation. However, all reflect the culture of the people speaking them.

Many say that U.S. firms have it easy, but more than 25 languages are spoken in American homes by 125,000 or more people. The fact that there are nearly 7,000 languages coupled with the fact that 5 or more languages may be spoken in any one country makes it difficult for a company to develop an effective marketing campaign. As more firms expand their markets to additional areas of the world, more material will need to be translated if customers are to understand advertisements, instruction manuals, and warranties.

Translation is expensive, too. Consider some of the global organizations that include members from all around the world—where ideas rather than products are marketed. The WTO spent $16 million, or 22 percent of its operating budget, in 2000 translating the documents it generated. The EU employs more than 4,000 translators and interpreters. In 1999, the EU spent about €600 million of its €85.5 billion budget (0.8 percent) for these services, and that didn't include the paper used to print the documents translated.

Never mind that Coca-Cola has to produce advertisements for its products in over 100 countries. Imagine what it must cost for the translation of technical manuals for medical equipment manufacturers such as Siemens or what SAP and Microsoft spend to produce software in different languages or the training and repair manuals that Airbus and Boeing provide to their customers around the world. It gives new meaning to the phrase spread the word.

Sources: Payal Sampat, "Last Words," *Worldwatch*, 2001; U.S. Census Bureau (language usage: http://www.census.gov/population/www/socdemo/lang_use.html); "Tongue-tied" *The Economist*, April 7, 2001, page 83; "Tongue-tied" *The Economist*, October 19, 2002, page 84; Mr. Robert Rowe, Translation Services, European Commission, Brussels e-mail correspondence, September 23, 2002.

English in Italy

Mr. Silvio Berlusconi, the flamboyant prime minister of Italy, promised a government of three I's: Inglese, Internet, e Imprese (English, Internet, and business). In an attempt to foster two of these, biographies of Italian ministers were posted in English on the government's primary web site (http://www.governo.it). Unfortunately, they were not translated well. The Defense Minister graduated with a maximum of ballots (graduated at the top of his class). The Communication Minister was the former Undersecretary to the Inside (Undersecretary of Internal Affairs). The Technology Minister was born to Lucera; conjugated; graduated in Economy near the University Mouthfuls of Milan; and in 1994, moved newly to Paris to cover loads with President of IBM Europe (was born in Lucera, is married, earned a degree in economics from the Bocconi University in Milan, and moved to Paris in 1994 to become president of IBM Europe.) All of these mistakes were attributed to the use of a computerized translation program.

There are legions of stories like this. The recommendation from experts is to use parallel translation (have two people translate the same message and compare the differences) or back-translation (translate into the target language, translate back into the original, and compare with the intended message). The advice is to focus on the intent and not to attempt a literal, or exact, word-for-word translation.

Source: Deborah Ball, "Lost in Translation: Italy's First Attempts at English Prove Less Than Meaningful," *Wall Street Journal*, December 17, 2001.

territory. However, they are foreign to the culture and spoken by only a small part of the population.

Language differences within a country may indicate social as well as communication divisions. In both Canada and Belgium, the two linguistic groups have occasionally clashed to the point of violence. Angola, Nigeria, and India are examples of less developed countries where differing linguistic groups have also engaged in hostilities.

The United States is not exactly a linguistic melting pot either. Spanish accounts for over half of all of the foreign-language speakers, but several of the other groups provide segmentation for marketing and media purposes. While the United States is more homogeneous than the EU, the melting pot is not complete.

Even in China, where 1 billion people "speak Mandarin," more than ten sociolinguistic groups exist. Among the Han Chinese, many Sinitic sublanguages and dialects exist, whose speakers are often unable to understand one another. These linguistic variations are related to cultural differences.

Many former colonies have some linguistic unity in the language of the former colonial power, but even this is threatened in certain countries. For example, in India, Hindi is an official language along with English. Hindi has the advantage of being an Indian language but the drawback of belonging to just one segment of India's population. When it was declared an official language, riots broke out, occasioned by the other language groups.

It is said that a language defines a cultural group—that nothing distinguishes one culture from another more than language. But what does it mean when the same language is used in different countries? French, for example, is the mother tongue not only for the French, but also for many Belgians and Swiss. Spanish plays a similar role in Latin America. The anthropologist, however, stresses the spoken language as the cultural distinction. The spoken language changes more quickly than the written language and reflects the culture more directly. Although England, the United States, and Ireland use the same written English, they speak somewhat different dialects. These three cultures are separate yet related, as are the Spanish-speaking cultures of Latin America.

Even where a common language is spoken, different words signifying the same meaning are occasionally used, as are different pronunciations. In Latin America, for example, the word for *tire* is not the same as that used in other Spanish-speaking countries. In England, people say "lorry," "petrol," and "biscuits"; but in the United States, people say "truck," "gasoline," and "cookies." Incidentally, even within one country—for example, the United States, where almost everyone speaks "American" English—there are different cultural groups, or subcultures, among which the spoken language varies.

Language as a Problem

In advertising, branding, packaging, personal selling, and marketing research, marketing is highly dependent upon communication. If management is not speaking the same language as its various audiences, it is not going to enjoy much success. In each of its foreign markets, a company must communicate with several audiences: its workers, its managers, its customers, its suppliers, and the government. Each of these audiences may have a distinctive communication style within the common language. The number of language areas in which a firm operates approximates the number of countries in which it sells. Any advantage gained by the fact that one language may be used in more than one country is partly offset by the fact that in many countries, more than one language is necessary.

Taiwan's garbage trucks blare English phrases as they pass through neighborhoods because the mayor, Mr. Hsu Tain-tsair, is seeking U.S. foreign investors. The mayor believes that "we'll attract more investors if the local population speaks the foreign language."[11] If an employee wants to get promoted at Matsushita Corporation (the makers of Panasonic and other global brands), he or she must pass a proficiency test in English. Toyota Motor Corporation, Komatsu Ltd. (earth-moving equipment), and NEC (computers) have also tied promotions to English-speaking abilities. The reason for this is explained by the director of human resources for Matsushita: "Japanese are insulated by their language and do not have a global mentality because of this language barrier."[12] Other companies can learn from this as well. There is an old international business joke: "What do you call someone who can speak three languages? (Answer: trilingual) What do you call someone who can speak two languages (Answer: bilingual) What do you call someone who speaks one language (Answer: American)" (See "Global Marketing: English in Italy.")

Language diversity in world markets could be an insuperable problem if managers had to master the languages of all of their markets. Fortunately, that is not the case. To be effective, any person assigned to a foreign operation for a period of a year or more should learn the local language. However, cultural bridges are available in many markets. For example, in countries where a firm is operating through a distributor, the distributor may act as the bridge between the firm and its local market. In advertising, a firm may be able to rely on a local advertising agency. Agency personnel, like the distributor, probably speak the advertising manager's language—especially if the firm communicates principally in English. For example, the Dutch firm Philips uses English as the official company language even though it is domiciled in the Netherlands. Because of its widespread operations, the company finds English to be the most useful language for its markets. In the Chrysler/Daimler-Benz merger, American English was made the corporate language.

In countries where a firm has subsidiaries, the language requirement becomes even greater. Then a firm has more direct communication with its audiences. Even in this case, however, the burden is lessened because among its national managers, the firm can usually count on people of the "third culture." The expression *third culture* is used to describe nationals who have become so familiar with another culture that they become a bridge between the two. This is the best solution to both the language gap and the culture gap.

As has been suggested, there are ways to circumvent the language problem. However, language is a critical factor. It is the key to understanding and communicating with the local cultures around the world. An international firm needs language capabilities not only among its distributors and other collaborators, but also among its own personnel.

Canada provides an illustration of a situation requiring linguistic sensitivity by international firms. In labor negotiations in Quebec, General Motors helped underwrite the cost of an interpreter to provide documentation in both French and English. GM agreed to recognize the French-language version of the contract as official. Other guidelines recommended to alleviate potential tension between the two groups included (1) bilingual labeling and advertising, (2) bilingual annual reports and press releases (French in Quebec), and (3) bilingual executives for operations in Quebec.

Education

In developed nations, education usually means formal training in school. In this sense, those people without access to schools are not educated; that is, they have never been to school. However, this formal definition is too restrictive. Education includes the process of transmitting skills, ideas, and attitudes, as well as training, in particular disciplines. Even so-called "primitive" peoples have been educated in this broader sense. For example, regardless of formal schooling, the Bushmen of South Africa are well educated in relation to the culture in which they live.

One function of education is to transmit the existing culture and traditions to the new generation. (The role of women in Afghan society—particularly their access to formal education under Taliban rule—and the subsequent changes instituted when President Hamid Karzai was elected illustrate the role of education in the process of cultural change.) Education plays an important role in cultural change in the United States, as it does elsewhere. For example, in the past, developing nations' educational campaigns were carried out with the specific intent of improving techniques used in farming and in reducing the population explosion. In Britain, business schools were originally established to improve the performance of the economy. Hall and Petzall attribute the rapid economic development of Singapore to formal apprenticeship programs.[13]

International Differences in Education

When looking at education in foreign markets, the observer is limited primarily to information about the formal process; that is, education in schools. This is the only area for which the United Nations Educational, Scientific and

Cultural Organization (UNESCO), the World Bank, and others have been able to gather data. Traditionally, literacy rates have been used to describe educational achievement; recently, however, international agencies have been measuring inputs as well as educational system outputs other than literacy. For example, the World Bank still includes adult and youth illiteracy rates in its reports. (Now it has begun measuring participation in education, which includes enrollment ratios in primary, secondary, and tertiary levels of education, and education efficiency, which includes completion rates at different levels of education and average number of years of school.) The World Bank also reports on inputs such as expenditures per student, teachers' compensation, number of faculty with appropriate qualifications, and pupil-teacher ratios. Perhaps most importantly, the goals of the World Bank have changed—from activities aimed merely at increasing literacy rates to measures designed to ensure that "all children complete a full course of primary education," a target it hopes is achieved by 2015. (See Table 3-2.)

The education information available on world markets refers primarily to national enrollments in the various levels of education—primary, secondary, and college or university. This information can give an international marketer insight into the sophistication of consumers in different countries. There is also a strong correlation between educational attainment and economic development. Hanushek and Kimko argue that qualitative measures such as math and science scores on international achievement tests should also be used as indicators of human capital development and long-term economic prospects. Because U.S. students consistently score lower on these exams than students in other countries, Hanushek and Kimko warn that the United States may lose its technological edge in the future.[14]

Because only quantitative data are available, there is a danger that the qualitative aspects of education might be overlooked. Furthermore, in addition to the limitations inherent in international statistics, the problem exists of interpreting them in terms of business needs. For example, a firm's needs for technicians, marketing personnel, managers, distributors, and sales forces must be met largely from the educated population in the local economy. When hiring people, the firm is concerned not only with the level, but also with the nature of the applicants' education.

Training in law, literature, or political science is probably not the most suitable education for business needs. Yet in many nations, such studies are emphasized almost to the exclusion of others more relevant to commercial and economic growth. Too often, primary education is preparation for secondary, secondary education is preparation for university, and university education is not designed to meet the needs of the economy. In many nations, university education is largely preparation for the traditional prestige occupations. Although a nation needs lawyers and philosophers, it also needs agricultural experts, engineers, managers, and technicians. The degree to which the educational system provides for these needs is a critical determinant of the nation's ability to develop economically.

Education and International Marketing

The international marketer must also be something of an educator. The products and techniques a firm brings into a market are generally new to that market. The firm must educate consumers about the uses and benefits. Although a firm may not make use of a formal educational system, its success is constrained by that system because its ability to communicate depends in part on the educational level of its market. An international marketer is further concerned about the educational situation because it is a key determinant of the nature of the consumer market and the kinds of marketing personnel available. Some implications for businesses include the following:

Table 3-2. World Education

Country by Income Group	Primary School Teacher-Pupil Ratio	Secondary School Enrollment (%)	Adult Literacy Rate (%)	
			Male	Female
Low-Income	40	46	72	53
Lower-Middle Income	22	75	92	82
Upper-Middle Income	21	81	95	92
High Income	17	100	99	99
World Average	28	70	84	71

Notes: The teacher-pupil ratio data are for the period 2001–2002; secondary school enrollment is male and female enrollment combined for 2000–2001; literacy rates are for people over age 15 in 2002.

Sources: World Bank, *2004 World Development Indicators*; Table 2.10 Education Inputs, pages 72–75; Table 2.1 Participation in Education, pages 76–79; Table 2.13 Education Outcomes, pages 84–87; UNESCO, Institute for Statistics, July 2004.

- When consumers are largely illiterate, existing advertising programs, package labels, instructions, and warranties need to be adapted to include fewer words and more graphics and pictures.
- When women are largely excluded from formal education, marketing programs may differ from those aimed at female segments in developed nations. When a firm is targeting women audiences with less education, messages need to be simple, perhaps with less text and more graphics.
- Conducting marketing research can be difficult, both in communicating with consumers and in getting qualified researchers. If few people are able to read, written surveys would be an ineffective tool in gathering data. Personal interviews, although more costly, would tend to increase response rates and accuracy.
- Cooperation from the distribution channel depends partly on the educational attainments of members in the channel and of other partners and employees. When overall levels of education are low, finding and hiring local qualified marketing employees for certain service or managerial positions may be difficult and very competitive. Long-term training programs and commitments to employee education may raise local operating costs.

Religion

This chapter is concerned with the cultural environment of business. You have already reviewed several aspects of culture. The material culture, language, and aesthetics are, in effect, outward manifestations of a culture. If you are to gain a full understanding of a culture, however, you must become familiar with the internal behavior that gives rise to the external manifestations. Generally, it is the **religion** of a culture that provides the best insights into this behavior. Therefore, although an international company is interested primarily in knowing how people behave as consumers or workers, management's task will be aided by an understanding of *why* people behave as they do.

Numerous religions exist in the world. This section presents brief overviews of animism, Hinduism, Buddhism, Islam, the Japanese following of various faiths (Shinto, Buddhism, and Confucianism), and Christianity. These religions were selected on the basis of their importance in terms of numbers of adherents and their impact on the economic behavior of their followers. Adherents to these religious beliefs account for over three-fourths of the world's population. Estimates for the major religions in 2002 were as follows: Christianity, 2.0 billion; Islam 1.3

billion; Hinduism, 900 million; and Buddhism, 360 million. There are also those people who are described as "secular" (including agnostic, atheist, and nonreligious), which includes approximately 850 million people, and followers of "Chinese Traditional Religion" (a combination of Confucianism, Buddhism, and Taoism), which has approximately 225 million adherents. The number of animists, described as various forms of primal-indigenous religions (tribal, ethnic, etc.), is common but difficult to determine—with the reported number of adherents varying from 100 to 245 million. (Most estimates are in the range of 150 million followers.)[15]

Animism or Nonliterate Religion

Animism is the term used to describe the religion of indigenous peoples. It is often defined as spirit worship, as distinguished from the worship of God or gods. Animistic beliefs have been found in all parts of the world. With the exception of revealed religion, some form of animism has preceded all historical religions. In many less developed parts of the world today, animistic ideas affect cognitive behavior.

Magic, a key element of animism, is the attempt to achieve results through the manipulation of the spirit world. It represents an unscientific approach to the physical world. When cause-and-effect relationships are not known, magic is given credit for the results. The same attitude prevails toward many modern-day products and techniques.

For example, during the author's years in Congo, he had an opportunity to see reactions to European products and practices that were often based on a magical interpretation. In one instance, a number of Africans affected the wearing of glasses, believing the glasses would enhance the intelligence of the wearer. Some marketers of consumer goods in Africa have not hesitated to imply that their products have magical qualities. Of course, the same is sometimes true of marketers on television.

Other aspects of animism include ancestor worship, taboos, and fatalism. All of them tend to promote a traditionalist, status quo, backward-looking society. Because such societies are more interested in protecting their traditions than in accepting change, marketers face problems when introducing new products, ideas, or methods. Marketers' success in bringing change depends on how well they understand and relate to the culture and its animistic foundation.

Hinduism

There are over 900 million Hindus in the world, most of them in India. In a broad sense, about 80 percent of India's population is Hindu; but in the sense of strict adherence to the tenets of Hinduism, the number of followers is smaller. A common dictum is that Hinduism is not a religion, but a way of life. Its origins go back approximately 3,500 years. It is an ethnic, noncreedal religion. A Hindu is born, not made; so a person cannot become a Hindu or convert to Hinduism, although he or she may become a Buddhist, for example. Modern Hinduism is a combination of ancient philosophies and customs; animistic beliefs; legends; and more recently, Western influences, including Christianity. A strength of Hinduism has been its ability to absorb ideas from outside; Hinduism tends to assimilate rather than exclude.

Despite this openness, many in India are unhappy about marriages between Christians or Muslims and Hindus because it is viewed as a threat or dilution of Hindutva (Hindu-ness) of the culture. Much violence has occurred between the Hindu and Muslim populations, with one instance of over 500 people killed in Gujarat in early 2002.[16] Because Hinduism is an ethnic religion, many of its doctrines apply only to the Indian situation. However, they are crucial in understanding India and its people.

Sikhism is a religion also practiced in India that represents a combined form of Hinduism and Islam, featuring a much debated aspect, the **caste** system. While the Indian government officially abolished it over a half century ago and instituted quotas and job-preferment policies, there are still examples of separate *gurdwaras* (houses of worship) for Sikhs and the *Dalit*, or scheduled caste (formerly called "untouchables"), some of whom are converting to Buddhism, Christianity, and Islam to escape the caste system.[17, 18]

Another element—and a strength of Hinduism—is *baradari*, or the "joint family." After marriage, the bride goes to the groom's home. After several marriages in the family, there is a large joint family for which the father or grandfather is chief authority. In turn, the older women have power over the younger. The elders give advice and consent in family council. The Indian grows up thinking and acting in terms of the joint family. If a member goes abroad to a university, the joint family may raise the funds. In turn, that member is expected to remember the family if he or she is successful. *Baradari* is aimed at preserving the family.

Veneration of the cow is perhaps the best-known Hindu custom: Gandhi called this the distinguishing mark of the Hindu. Hindu worship of the cow involves protecting it, but eating the products of the cow is also considered a means for purification. Another element of traditional Hinduism is the restriction of women, following the belief that to be born a woman is a sign of sin in a former life. Some marriages are still arranged by relatives. Traditionally, a man may remarry if widowed, but a woman may not. This attitude toward women makes it all the more remarkable that India placed a woman, Indira Gandhi, in its highest office.

Nirvana is another important concept, one that Hinduism shares with Buddhism. This topic is discussed in the following section.

Buddhism

Buddhism springs from Hinduism, originating about 2,600 years ago. Buddhism has approximately 360 million followers, mostly in South and East Asia from India to Japan. There are, however, small Buddhist societies in Europe and America. Buddhism is, to some extent, a reformation of Hinduism. It did not abolish caste, but declared that Buddhists were released from caste restrictions. This openness to all classes and both sexes was one reason for Buddhism's growth. While accepting the philosophical insights of Hinduism, Buddhism tried to avoid its dogma and ceremony, stressing tolerance and spiritual equality.

At the heart of Buddhism are the Four Noble Truths:
1. The Noble Truth of Suffering states that suffering is omnipresent and part of the very nature of life.
2. The Noble Truth of the Cause of Suffering cites the cause of suffering to be desire; that is, desire for possessions and selfish enjoyment of any kind.
3. The Noble Truth of the Cessation of Suffering states that suffering ceases when desire ceases.
4. The Noble Truth of the Eight-Fold Path that leads to the Cessation of Suffering offers the means to achieve cessation of desire. This is also known as the Middle Way because it avoids the two extremes of self-indulgence and self-mortification. The eight-fold path includes (1) the right views, (2) the right desires, (3) the right speech, (4) the right conduct, (5) the right occupation, (6) the right effort, (7) the right awareness, and (8) the right contemplation. This path, though simple to state, is a demanding ethical system. **Nirvana** is the reward for those who are able to stay on the path throughout their lifetime or, more probably, lifetimes.

Nirvana is the ultimate goal of the Hindu and Buddhist. It represents the extinction of all cravings and the final release from suffering. To the extent that such an ideal reflects the thinking of the mass of the people, the society's values would be considered antithetical to such goals as acquisition, achievement, and affluence. This is an obvious constraint on marketing. Of course, not all Buddhists are so nonmaterialistic.

Islam

Islam dates from the seventh century AD. It has over 900 million adherents, mostly in Africa, Asia, and the Middle East. Most of the world of Islam is found across the northern half of Africa, the Middle East, and throughout parts of Asia to the Philippines. Islam is usually associated with Arabs and the Middle East, but non-Arab Muslims outnumber Arab Muslims by almost three to one. The nations with the largest Muslim populations are all outside the

Middle East. Indonesia, Pakistan, Bangladesh, and India all have over 100 million Muslims. Although there are two major groups in Islam (Sunni, 85 percent, and Shi'ite, 15 percent), they are similar enough on economic issues to permit identification of the following elements of interest to marketers.

Muslim theology, *Tawhid*, defines all that one should believe; whereas the law, Shari'a, prescribes everything one should do. The Koran (Qur'an) is accepted as the ultimate guide. Anything not mentioned in the Koran is likely to be rejected by the faithful. Introducing new products and techniques can be difficult in such an environment. An important element of Muslim belief is that everything that happens, good or evil, proceeds directly from the Divine Will and is already irrevocably recorded on the Preserved Tablet. This belief tends to restrict attempts to bring about change in Muslim countries; to attempt change may be a rejection of what Allah has ordained. The name *Islam* is the infinitive of the Arabic verb to *submit. Muslim* is the present participle of the same verb; that is, a Muslim is one submitting to the will of Allah.

The Five Pillars of Islam, or the duties of a Muslim, include (1) the recital of the creed, (2) prayer, (3) fasting, (4) almsgiving, and (5) the pilgrimage. The creed is brief: There is no God but God, and Mohammed is the Prophet of God. The Muslim must pray five times daily at stated hours. During the month of Ramadan, Muslims are required to fast from dawn to sunset—no food, no drink, no smoking. Because the Muslim year is lunar, Ramadan sometimes falls in midsummer, when the long days and intense heat make abstinence a severe test. The fast is meant to develop self-control and sympathy for the poor. During Ramadan, work output falls off markedly, which is attributable as much to the Muslim's loss of sleep (from the many late-night feasts and celebrations) as to the rigors of fasting. The average family actually spends more money on the food consumed at night during Ramadan than on the food consumed by day in the other months. Other spending rises also. Spending during Ramadan has been said to equal six months of normal spending, corresponding to the Christmas season elsewhere. Sales increases of 20 to 40 percent of furniture, cars, jewelry and other large or expensive items are common. One firm stated that between 35 and 40 percent of all auto sales take place during Ramadan.[19]

By almsgiving, the Muslim shares with the poor. It is an individual responsibility, and there are both required alms (*zakat*) and freewill gifts. The pilgrimage to Mecca is a well-known aspect of Islam. The thousands who gather in Mecca each year return home with a greater sense of the international solidarity of Islam. Spending for the pilgrimage is a special form of consumption directly associated with religious behavior.

There is a relationship between religion and culture, as is discussed here; but there is also a relationship between culture and laws, which will be discussed later in the text. Behavior deemed acceptable or not acceptable is often reflected in the laws of a nation or group of people. The tie between religion and law is perhaps most clear in Islam. With respect to business, Muslims are not allowed to consume pork or alcohol. Furthermore, people are not allowed to invest in firms whose primary business involves alcohol, defense, entertainment, gambling, or the manufacture of or processes using pork products. Under shariah law, investors are not allowed to hold any stake in conventional banks or insurance companies because these institutions are believed to engage in usurious practices that are illegal. Even the ability to own stock or shares in companies with large amounts of debt or that make annual interest payments is being called into question. While there is some tolerance for investing in these companies, devout Muslims point out that this is a breach of shariah rules against usury. Some marketing implications of Islam are noted in Table 3-3.

Table 3-3. Islam and Marketing

Islamic Element	Marketing Implication
1. Daily prayers	Work schedules; hours of peak/off-peak customer traffic; timing of sales calls
2. Prohibition on usury and consumption of pork and alcohol	Prohibition of or difficulty in selling certain products (insurance, banking and financial services); processes used in manufacturing of food and other products for human consumption or use; inappropriateness of layaway and other credit tools
3. *Zakat* (mandatory alms)	Spending patterns; attitude toward charity; social consciousness; excessive profits used for charitable purposes
4. Religious holidays (e.g., Ramadan) and other religious or sacred periods	Sales and special promotions; lavish gift periods; food distribution and restaurant hours; Muslim "weekend" is Thursday and Friday.
5. Public separation of sexes	Access to female customers; direct marketing to women; mixed-gender focus groups

Japan: Shinto, Buddhism, and Confucianism

Japan is a homogeneous culture with a composite religious tradition. The original national religion is Shinto, "the way of the gods." In the seventh century, however, Japan came under the influence of China and imported an eclectic Buddhism mingled with Confucianism. In 604, Prince Shotoku issued a moral code based on the teachings of both Confucius and Gautama Buddha. Its 17 articles still form the basis of Japanese behavior. The adoption of the religions from China was only after the authorities decided they would not conflict with Shinto. Traditional Shinto contains elements of ancestor and nature worship; state or modern Shinto added political and patriotic elements. Official estimates of 90 million Japanese Buddhists are somewhat misleading. An old refrain is that Japanese are born as Shinto, get married as Christians, and die as Buddhists.[20] Depending on whom and how you ask, figures on followers of Buddhism in Japan vary widely, from 20 to 90 percent of the total Japanese population of 127 million people. (The high figures are based on birth records and on Buddhism being the "preferred religion" in a response to research questions posed to Japanese; the low figures incorporate the response of up to 75 percent of Japanese who claim to be nonreligious or follow no religion.)

Among the more important aspects of modern Shinto are (1) reverence for the divine origin of the Japanese people and (2) reverence for the Japanese nation and the imperial family as head of that nation. The term *modern* Shinto is used because when the imperial powers were restored in 1868, state Shinto became a patriotic cult, whereas sectarian Shinto was purely religious. Of course, sectarian Shinto, through ancestor worship, also affects Japanese attitudes. In many houses, there is a god-shelf (*kamidana*) on which the spirits of the family ancestors are thought to dwell and watch over the affairs of the family. Reverence is paid to them, and the sense of the ancestors' spirit is a bulwark of the family's authority over the individual. (See "Global Marketing: Shinto in Japan.")

The impact of modern Shinto on Japanese life is reflected in an aggressive patriotism. The mobilization of the Japanese of World War II and their behavior during the war are examples. One longtime observer said, "Nationalism is the Japanese religion." More recently, the economic performance of Japan is due, at least in part, to the patriotic attitude of those working in the economic enterprise. The family spirit carried over to the firm, which has meant greater cooperation and productivity. Some Eastern religions seek virtue through passivity. Shinto, by contrast, stresses the search for progress through creative activity. Japan's economic performance clearly seems to follow the Shinto path. The aggressive Japanese attitude is reflected in the company song of Kyocera, a Japanese firm.

GLOBAL MARKETING

Shinto in Japan

Shinto rituals play an important role in Japanese culture, as demonstrated by the naming ceremonies attached to the new Princess Aiko born in December 2001, the first child of Prince Naruhito and Princess Masako. Mother and father did not get to name her. Rather, the child was taken to a Shinto shrine, where she was bathed while two scholars played wooden stringed instruments to ward off evil spirits and the household's chief of protocol recited from the eighth-century Chronicles of Japan. Naruhito's father, Akihito, the emperor of Japan, then revealed the child's name—the little girl was to be called Princess Toshi during her youth. The following year was filled with many other ceremonies, including one to ensure that she had enough to eat throughout her lifetime.

Shinto temples contain many shrines devoted to various deities (kami) from various religions, such as the Kangiten or Shoten. These shrines are used to intone marital harmony and fruitful marriages, which is believed to have been adapted and adopted from the Hindu deity Ganesha. Thousands of Shinto shrines are found throughout Japan. Perhaps the largest and most elaborate ceremonies take place at New Year, when as many as 70 million people seek good health, good fortune, and other blessings for the coming year.

continued

As the sun rises brilliantly in the sky,
revealing the size of the mountain, the market,
oh, this is our goal.
With the highest degree of mission in our heart,
we serve our industry,
Meeting the strictest degree of customer requirement.
We are the leader in this industry and our future
path, Is ever so bright and satisfying.

Christianity

Christianity is a major religion worldwide, and little time will be spent describing its general teachings. The emphasis here is the impact of the different Christian religious groups (Roman Catholic and Protestant) on economic

Kirigami *are white paper cutouts of cranes and other auspicious forms meant to connect humans with the Shinto gods. Although not as popular an art form as it once was,* kirigami *can still be found in household shrines. One of the more important duties for the imperial family is presiding over the annual* Niinamesai (Festival for the New Tasting) *Shinto rite in late November. This ceremony involves an offering of rice to ensure a good harvest and has, over the years, become a part of other traditions, including the grand opening of new businesses. Also, many businesses have a shrine to a deity whose customary symbol is a pair of foxes, and Japanese companies generally choose a patron god or goddess.*

Other signs reflect the importance of the Shinto religion and the unique way in which the Japanese incorporate other beliefs. The new luxury hotel Nikko Kumamoto in Kyushu, on the southern island of Japan, includes a Northern Italian-style chapel for those couples who want to get married under the sun or stars, as well as a Shinto shrine for Shinto-style weddings.

Sources: "Cutting Out a Spiritual Tradition," *Daily Yomiuri,* January 5, 2002; "JAWOC Looks to Cure Transportation Headache," Global Newswire, February 2, 2002; "Princess Aiko Taken to Imperial Palace Buildings," Japan Economic Newswire, March 12, 2002; "Nikko Hotels International to Open Hotel in Kumamoto, Japan," PR Newswire, May 29, 2002.

attitudes and behavior. Two studies have dealt with this subject: Max Weber's *The Protestant Ethic and the Spirit of Capitalism* and R. H. Tawney's *Religion and the Rise of Capitalism.* The Eastern Orthodox churches are not discussed in this section, but their impact on economic attitudes is similar to that of Catholicism.

Roman Catholic Christianity traditionally has emphasized the Church and the sacraments as the principal elements of religion and the way to God. The Church and its priests are intermediaries between God and human beings; and apart from the Church, there is no salvation. Another element is the distinction between the members of religious orders and the laity, with different standards of conduct applied to each. An implicit difference exists between the secular and the religious life.

The Protestant Reformation, especially Calvinism, made some critical changes in emphasis but retained agreement with Catholicism on most traditional Christian doctrine. The Protestants, however, stressed that the Church, its sacraments, and its clergy were not essential to salvation: "Salvation is by faith alone." The result of this was a downgrading of the role of the Church and a consequent upgrading of the role of the individual. Salvation

became more an individual matter.

Another change by the reformers was the elimination of the distinction between secular and religious life. Luther said that all of life was a *Beruf,* a "calling," and even the performance of tasks considered to be secular was a religious obligation. Calvin carried this further by emphasizing the need to glorify God through one's calling. Whereas works were necessary to salvation in Catholicism, works were evidence of salvation in Calvinism.

Hard work was enjoined to glorify God, achievement was the evidence of hard work, and thrift was necessary because the produced wealth was not to be used selfishly. Accumulation of wealth, capital formation, and the desire for greater production became Christian duty. The Protestant Reformation thus led to greater emphasis on individualism and action (hard work), as contrasted with the more ritualistic and contemplative approach of Catholicism.

Although it is useful to recognize the separate thrust of Roman Catholic and Protestant Christianity, it is also important to note the various roles Christianity generally play in different nations. Some nations reflect varying mixtures of Catholic and Protestant, and the resulting ethic may be some combination of both doctrines. Of course, within Christianity (as with Buddhism, Hinduism, and Islam), wide variations exist in the degree to which adherents follow the teachings. In all groups, segments range from fundamentalist to conservative to casual.

Religion and the Economy

In discussing various religions, the text suggested some economic implications that are elaborated on here. Religion has a major impact on attitudes toward economic matters. The following section, "Attitudes and Values," will discuss the different attitudes religion may inspire. Besides attitudes, however, religion may affect the economy more directly, as in the following examples.

- Religious holidays vary greatly among countries—not only from Christian to Muslim, but also from one Christian country to another. In general, Sundays are a religious holiday where Christianity is an important religion. In the Muslim world, however, the entire month of Ramadan is a religious holiday for practical purposes. A firm must see that local work schedules and marketing programs take into account local holidays, just as American firms plan for a big season at Christmas.
- Consumption patterns may be affected by religious requirements or taboos. Fish on Friday for Catholics used to be a classic example. Taboos against beef for Hindus or pork for Muslims and Jews are other examples. The Muslim prohibition against alcohol has been a boon to companies such

as Coca-Cola. Heineken and other brewers sell a nonalcoholic beer in Saudi Arabia. On the other hand, dairy products find favor among Hindus, many of whom are vegetarians.

- The economic role of women varies from culture to culture, and religious beliefs are an important cause. Women may be restricted in their capacity as consumers, as workers, or as respondents in a marketing study. These differences may require major adjustments in the approach of a management conditioned to the U.S. market.

    Procter & Gamble's products are used mainly by women. When the company wanted to conduct a focus group in Saudi Arabia, however, it could not induce women to participate. Instead, it used the husbands and brothers of women for the focus group.

- The caste system restricts participation in the economy. A company may feel the effects not only in its staffing practices (especially its sales force), but also in its distribution and promotional programs because it must deal with the market segments set up by the caste system.

- The Hindu joint family has economic effects. Nepotism is characteristic of the family business. Staffing is based more on considerations of family rank more than on any other criteria. Furthermore, consumer decision making and consumption in the joint family may differ from those in the U.S. family, requiring an adapted marketing strategy. Pooled income in the joint family may lead to different purchase patterns.

- Religious institutions themselves may play a role in economic matters. The Church, or any organized religious group, may block the introduction of new products or techniques if it sees the innovation as a threat. On the other hand, the same product or technique can be more effectively introduced if the religious organization sees it as a benefit. The United States has seen the growing role of religious groups. "Global Marketing: Marketers Get Religion" provides some examples from other countries.

- Religious divisions in a country can pose problems for management. A firm may find that it is dealing with different markets. In Northern Ireland, there is strong Catholic-Protestant hostility. In India, Muslim-Hindu clashes led to the formation of the separate nation of Pakistan; but the animosity continues. In the Netherlands, major Catholic and Protestant groups have their own political parties and newspapers. Such religious divisions can cause difficulty in staffing an operation or in distributing and promoting a product. Religious differences may indicate market segments that require separate strategies and media.

Marketers Get Religion

The U.S. Post Office sells stamps for Christmas, Chanukah, Kwanza, and a host of other holidays and events. On September 1, 2001, it released the first Islam-themed American stamp. The new first-class postage EID stamp commemorates the end of Ramadan and the end of the pilgrimage to Mecca.

In Moscow, the Holy Land Exhibition Company is planning a $38 million religious theme park that is expected to open in 2005. Visitors will be able to dine on "Last Supper" meals, visit a replica of the Church of the Nativity in Bethlehem, or see a miniature version of the Red Sea. This park is based on the Scriptorium, a $25 million Christian Foundation theme park that opened in Florida in 2002. Included in the park is a re-creation of ancient Jerusalem, animatronic robots that "talk" about the Bible, and a fiber-optic finger of God that writes the Ten Commandments on a rock.

Coca-Cola and PepsiCo held special promotions for Ramadan in Turkey. PepsiCo offered free 600-milliliter bottles of soda with the purchase of larger 2.5-liter bottles so customers could "get through iftar and sahur in one purchase." (Iftar is the meal at the start of the day before the fast begins, while sahur is taken in the evening to end the fast.) Coca-

continued

Clearly, an international firm must be sensitive to religious differences in its foreign markets and be willing to make adaptations. To cite one example, a firm that is building a plant abroad might plan the date and method of opening and dedicating the building to reflect the local religious situation. In particular, a firm's advertising, packaging, and personal selling practices need to take local religious sensitivities into account.

Attitudes and Values

People's attitudes and values help determine what they think is right or appropriate, what is important, and what is desirable. The attitudes that relate to marketing will be presented. It is important to consider attitudes and values

Cola offered special commemorative Ramadan plates for consumers who sent in bottle caps.

McDonald's agreed to pay $12 million to settle a class-action suit filed by Hindus, Sikhs, and Jews for not disclosing that beef flavorings were used in the McDonald's French fry recipe. American Muslims also want a portion of the funds since the use of beef likely violated the halal food code (specifies how the beef is to be prepared).

There are banks, mortgage companies, and other financial institutions in Muslim nations, despite the prohibition on earnings through interest payments (riba). If someone wants to purchase a car, a typical deal might go something like this: The person buying the car would go to the local Jaguar dealer and pick out the model and features. Then, through a transaction referred to as murabaha, the buyer would ask his bank to purchase the car (for, say, $50,000), which would then resell the car to the buyer for $55,000, paid in monthly installments.

There are many other examples of how marketers have attempted to address religious-based opportunities, as well as many cases where they have failed to do so. Further Readings, at the end of this chapter, includes recommendations that will enlighten and entertain.

Sources: "Banking on Allah," *Fortune,* Volume 145, Issue 12, June 10, 2002, pages 154–164; "Holy Robots Give Bible Buzz in Pond's 8m Theme Park," *Sunday Times,* August 18, 2002, page 18; "Muslims Making Push to Join McDonald's Fries Settlement," *Dallas Morning News,* July 5, 2002; "Sale of Islamic-Themed Stamps Shouldn't Be Affected by September 11 Attacks," *Patriot News,* November 27, 2001; "This Europe: Russia Drops Disney for Biblical Dancers," *The Independent,* July 16, 2002, page 10.

because, as someone said, "People act on them." Douglas North, the Nobel Prize-winning economist said, "People act on the basis of ideologies and religious views." People have attitudes and values about work, money, time, family, age, men, women, and a host of other topics that have an impact on marketing. The list is long and goes beyond the scope of this book; only a few will be highlighted here.

Marketing Activities

Ever since Aristotle, selling activities have failed to gain high social approval. The degree of disapproval, however, varies from country to country. In countries where marketing is looked upon unfavorably (a wicked or immoral profession), marketing activities are likely to be neglected and underdeveloped. Capable, talented people are not drawn into business. Often marketing activities are left to a special class or to expatriates. One is reminded of the medieval banking role filled by Jews or the merchant role of the Chinese in Southeast Asia. In any case, depending on a country's attitude toward business, an international firm may have problems with personnel, distribution channels, and other aspects of its marketing program. There is a bright side to this picture, however. Because marketing is well developed in the United States, a U.S. firm abroad may have an advantage in marketing.

Wealth, Material Gain, and Acquisition

The United States has been called the "affluent society," the "achieving society," and the "acquisitive society." Those somewhat synonymous expressions reflect motivating values in society. In the United States, wealth and acquisition are often considered signs of success and achievement and are given social approval. In a Buddhist or Hindu society, where nirvana or "wantlessness" is an ideal, people may not be so motivated to produce and consume. Marketers obviously prefer to operate in an acquisitive society. However, as a result of rising expectations around the world, national differences in attitudes toward acquisition seem to be lessening. For example, Buddhist Thailand is proving to be a profitable market for many consumer goods firms.

Work may be an end unto itself for some people, and one's position with a particular organization may be an important measure of the person's social status. For others, family, leisure time, and friends take precedence over money and position. German and French workers have gone on strike, even rioted over plans to extend their workweek beyond 35 hours, to cut paid vacation time, or to raise the age that one becomes qualified for retirement benefits.[21]

Change

When a company enters a foreign market, it brings change by introducing new ways of doing things and new products. In general, North Americans accept change easily. The word "new" has a favorable connotation and facilitates change when used to describe techniques and products. Many societies are more tradition-oriented, however, revering their ancestors and traditional ways of consuming.

The marketer as an agent of change has a different task in traditional societies. Rather than emphasizing what is new and different about a product, the marketer might relate the product to traditional values, perhaps noting that it is a better way of solving a consumer problem. In seeking acceptance of its new product, a firm might try to get at least a negative clearance—that is, no objection—

from local religious leaders or other opinion leaders. Any product must first meet a market need. Beyond that, however, to be accepted, the product must also fit in with the overall value system.

The Campbell Soup Company met this kind of obstacle when it introduced its canned soups into Italy. In conducting marketing research, it received an overwhelmingly negative response to the question, would you marry a user of prepared soups? Campbell had to adjust its marketing accordingly.

Risk Taking

Consumers take risks when they try a new product. Will the product do what they expect it to do? Will purchasing or using the product prejudice their standing or image with their peers? Intermediaries handling the untried product may also face risks beyond those associated with their regular line. In a conservative society, there is a greater reluctance to take such risks. Therefore, a marketer must seek to reduce the risk perceived by customers or distributors in trying a new product. In part, this can be accomplished through education; guarantees, consignment selling, and other marketing techniques can also be used.

Risk avoidance is a major factor in the low number of online shoppers. While the number of users is growing exponentially, a recent survey found that one-third of Internet users did not shop online because they did not want to risk providing credit card information over the Internet. One-quarter of those surveyed believed it was safer to purchase at a retail shop. The number of Internet users who are also online shoppers is highest among developed nations (generally between 15 and 25 percent of users purchase something online) and lowest among developing nations (generally below 5 percent of users shop online).[22] Recent research indicates that this differs from one culture to another,[23] but this may also be a reflection of different use patterns (that is, some people use the Internet for entertainment or research, while others use it for shopping).

Consumer Behavior

The attitudes just discussed are relevant to understanding consumer behavior in the markets of the world. International managers must have such an understanding to develop effective marketing programs. Because of the impossibility of gaining intimate knowledge of a great number of markets, they must rely not only on company research, but also on help from others. Those who can assist managers in understanding local attitudes and behavior include personnel in the firm's subsidiary, the distributor, and the advertising agency. Although a firm is interested in changing attitudes, most generally it has to

adapt to them. As Confucius said, "It is easier to move mountains than to change the minds of men."

Social Organization

The **social organization** of a group of people helps define their roles and the expectations they place upon themselves and others in the group. Concepts such as family vary from group to group, which becomes evident when talking about these concepts to people from other cultures. The nature of people's friendships with others—how quickly the relationships develop, how the friendships are nurtured, and how long they last—also reflect on the social organization within the culture or group. Social organization is formally defined in the government and the laws that proscribe certain behavior among people. The nature of social organization and the impact on marketing is discussed next.

Kinship

Kinship includes the social organization or structure of a group—the way people relate to other people. This differs somewhat from society to society. The primary kind of social organization is based on kinship. In the United States, the key unit is the family, which traditionally included only the father, the mother, and the unmarried children in the household. Of course, the definition is changing, as is reflected in each census. The family unit elsewhere is often larger, including more relatives. The large joint family of Hinduism was discussed previously. A large extended family is also common in many other less developed nations. Those who call themselves brothers in Congo, for example, include cousins and uncles.

In developing countries, the extended family fulfills several social and economic roles. The family unit is not prescribed or defined by a specific religious restriction, as does the *baradari* of Hinduism. The extended family provides mutual protection, psychological support, and economic insurance or social security for its members. In a world of tribal warfare and primitive agriculture, this support was invaluable. The extended family, still significant in many parts of the world, means that consumption decision making takes place in a larger unit and in different ways. Pooled resources, for instance, may allow larger purchases. (For this reason, per capita income may be a misleading guide to market potential.) The marketer may find it difficult to determine the relevant consuming unit for some goods. Is it a household or a family? How many members are there?

As Table 3-4 demonstrates, the size of households varies greatly around the world. An interesting comparison is the United States and Japan. The United States has slightly more than twice the population as Japan but 25

Table 3-4. Average Number of Occupants per Household

Saudi Arabia	8.21	Nigeria	5.23	Czech Rep.	2.71
Gabon	6.87	Mexico	4.43	Japan	2.63
Pakistan	7.59	Turkey	3.97	United States	2.63
India	5.94	Ireland	3.12	Sweden	1.99

Source: *International Marketing Data and Statistics,* 2004; *European Marketing Data and Statistics,* 2003, Euromonitor.

times the land mass. (The United States has approximately 293 million people and covers 9.6 million square kilometers, while Japan has 128 million people and covers an area about the size of California—378 thousand square kilometers). With relatively less land but so many people, it is reasonable to expect that the number of occupants per dwelling is higher in Japan than in the United States.[24]

Common Territory

In the United States, **common territory** can be a neighborhood, a suburb, or a city. In many countries of Asia and Africa, common territory is the tribal grouping. In many countries, the tribe is often the largest effective unit because the various tribes do not voluntarily recognize the central government. Unfortunately, nationalism has not generally replaced tribalism. Tribalism and religious or ethnic divisions often lead to bloody conflict, shown by such examples as Congo, Ireland, Israel and Palestine, Pakistan, the Philippines, Rwanda, and Sudan. Even in Europe, the Scots and the Welsh are not happy about being under British rule. For the marketer, in many countries, groupings based on common territory may be a clue to market segmentation.

Special Interest Group

A third kind of social grouping, the **special interest group** or association, may be religious, occupational, recreational, or political. Special interest groups can also be useful in identifying different market segments. For example, in the United States, the American Association of Retired Persons (AARP), the Sierra Club, and the National Rifle Association (NRA) represent market segments for some firms.

Other Kinds of Social Organization

Some kinds of social organization cut across the three categories just discussed. One is **caste** or **class groupings**. These may be detailed and rigid, as in the Hindu caste system; or they may be loose and flexible, as in U.S. social classes. The United States has a relatively open society, but

there is still concern about social standing and status symbols. While social class is more (or less) important and rigid in comparing countries, each country has its own social and ethnic groupings that are important for its society and the economy. These groupings usually mean that some groups are discriminated against and others are favored. A firm needs to know this social organization because it will affect the company's marketing program. Different groups may require different marketing strategies, for example.

Other groupings based on age occur especially in affluent industrialized nations. Senior citizens usually live as separate economic units with their own needs and motivations. They are a major market segment in industrialized countries. And although teenagers do not commonly live apart from their families, they still compose a significant economic force to be reckoned with. (See "Global Marketing: Teens—Truly Global Consumers.")

As noted in the discussion of the extended family, much less separation between age groups exists in less developed areas. Generally, strong family integration occurs at all age levels, as well as a preponderant influence of age and seniority, which is in contrast to the youth motif prevalent in the United States. Of course, Generation X and baby boomers are important age groupings in the United States.

A final aspect of social organization concerns the role of women in the economy. Women seldom enjoy parity with men as participants in the economy; and their participation is related to the economic development of nations—the poorer the nation, the fewer women seen in jobs outside the home. The extent to which women participate in the money economy affects their role as consumers and consumption influencers. Even developed countries exhibit differences in attitude toward female employment. For example, significant differences in female employment exist between the United States, several European countries, and Japan. These differences are reflected both in household income levels and in consumption patterns.

In spite of the constraints noted, the economic role of women is undergoing notable change in many countries. Many believe this change is occurring too slowly, however. Some of the differences in women's role in society are highlighted in Case 3.2 at the end of the chapter.

Teens—Truly Global Consumers

"*Cultural convergence continues to transform the marketplace as borrowing among cultures accelerates.*" This is the opening sentence in a recent article comparing teenagers in the United States and Korea. The authors look at many attitudes of young people in those two nations and come to the same conclusion that many others have. The findings of many cross-cultural studies are that young people, because of their exposure to new ideas and to one another through television and the Internet (as well as their willingness to take risks and try new things), are similar in those respects that are not confined to a particular geographic area or culture. That is, certain characteristics, beliefs, attitudes, and behaviors are common to teenagers; and because of that, marketers can get teenagers' attention in similar ways. Something else marketers do not miss is the fact that teenagers are more affluent than in the past. Those factors are also highlighted by Parmar, who refers to a "homogeneous global youth customer segment."

Look in teens' bedrooms in cities around the world—Des Moines, Los Angeles, Jakarta, Mexico City, Paris, Santiago, Singapore, and Tokyo. You will find an amazing similarity of items: Nikes and Reeboks, Levis, MP3 players, PCs, and NBA jackets. Teens everywhere watch MTV and the World Cup, and most of them shop in malls that look amazingly alike.

These are promising developments for international consumer goods marketers. Caution is necessary, however, before firms implement a one-size-fits-all strategy. Many seasoned observers note that cultural differences persist. For example, one survey found that American teenagers prefer to eat on the run, while teens elsewhere prefer meals they can savor. The same survey showed that American teenagers use fewer features on their cell phones than their European and Japanese counterparts. So despite similarities among teenagers around the world, marketers are unable to use identical practices to reach teenagers in all markets.

Sources: Mark Mitchell, Barbara Hastings, and Faruk Tanyel, "Generational Comparison: Xers in the United States and Korea," *International Journal of Commerce and Management*, 2001, Volume 11, Number 3/4, pages 35–53; Arundhati Parmar, "Global Youth United; Homogeneous Group Prime Target for U.S. Marketers," *Marketing News*, October 28, 2002, pages 1, 49.

Cultural Variables and Marketing Management

Culture is an integrated pattern of behavior shared by people in a society. This chapter has presented several dimensions of culture. These cultural variables are important to firms marketing internationally. What firms are able to do in marketing to a particular society and what they want to do are shaped by these variables. In other words, international marketing is a function of culture. (See "Global Marketing: Culture Is Dynamic—Something Marketers Need to Remember.")

Summary

Culture is an integrated pattern of behavior and the distinctive way of life of a people. The various dimensions of culture influence a firm's marketing.

A country's worker behavior and consumer behavior are shaped by the technology and material culture. The kinds of products a firm can sell and its distribution and promotional programs are constrained by the country's infrastructure. This includes not only the country's transportation and communications systems, but also things such as the availability of media and advertising agencies.

Communication is a major part of the marketing task, so a firm must communicate in the languages of its markets. This may require adaptation in packaging and labeling, advertising and personal selling, and marketing research. Fortunately, national employees, distributors, and advertising agencies can help with the language barrier.

Each society has its own ideas about beauty and good taste—its own aesthetics. When a firm is considering the design and color of its products and packaging, is advertising, and is selecting music and brand names, it must try to appeal to those tastes.

Differences in literacy and consumer skills, as a result of a country's educational system, determine what adjustments in products and marketing communications are necessary. The quality of marketing support services (advertising and marketing research) in a country is also affected by the output of the educational system there.

Religion is a major determinant of attitudes and behavior in a society. Each country has its own religious profile; but major world religions such as Buddhism, Christianity, Hinduism, Islam, and secular (agnostic, animism, atheist, and nonreligious) include approximately 85 percent of the world's population. Each of those religions has its own impact on the attitudes and behaviors of consumers who follow the religion. For example, a traditional animist might be reluctant to accept new products and a devout Buddhist who is seeking an absence of desire,

GLOBAL MARKETING

Culture Is Dynamic—Something Marketers Need to Remember

People's behavior changes in response to changes in the environment, which emphasizes the dynamic nature of culture. In certain situations, these statements may seem obvious. Fashion changes from year to year, and popular songs change from week to week. Foods eaten today might have seemed strange a decade or two ago, and the language includes new words to describe new things in the environment. The dynamic nature of culture is not always noticeable, though. If marketers fail to recognize these changes, they may lose opportunities—or worse.

Demand for kitchen appliances is changing in Europe; people want larger refrigerators. What's behind this change? Europeans are working longer hours; and they're moving farther from cities and their jobs, which requires a longer commute. With fewer hours in the week for shopping, people are purchasing larger quantities of food. Because Europeans generally have small families and prefer bottled water, they don't need or want in-the-door water and ice dispensers commonly found on American refrigerators. Consequently, appliance

continued

manufacturers have to adapt designs, rather than send the large models common in the U.S. market.

The picture of the aging is also changing, thanks in part to marketers. No longer the toothless, doddering, rocking chair-bound image of yesterday, older citizens are traveling, dancing, rock climbing, and even sky diving. People who retire at sixty or sixty-five can expect to live another quarter century or more. In 2002, more than 23 million Japanese, or 18.5 percent of the population, was over sixty-five. In the United States, Americans over fifty own 75 percent of all financial assets, control over 80 percent of money invested in savings and loan associations, and own 67 percent of all shares sold in the stock market. Because older people are one of the largest, fastest-growing populations that control a lot of wealth, marketers are making more adaptations to products to cater to this group. Japan is leading the way with universal design products—goods that are easier to use, not just for older people, but for all age groups. Examples include OXO Good Grip utensils, Fiskars Soft Touch scissors, and the NTT (Nippon Telephone & Telegraph) Raku Raku ("easy easy") cellular phone with large key pad. Ford Motor company has its designers dress in "'third-age suits" that add age to the wearer by stiffening their joints and making their waists bigger; this is done so they can design car seats that are easier to get in and out of.

Sources: "Over 60 and Overlooked," *The Economist*, August 10, 2002, pages 50–51; Allyson Stewart-Allen, "U.S. Kitchen Goods Makers Find Euro Market Worth Courting," *Marketing News*, American Marketing Association, September 24, 2001, page 8.

or a state of wantlessness, is not a strong potential consumer. Other religious impacts on marketing include religious holidays and product taboos, the role of women in the economy and society, and the caste system. Finally, religious divisions in a country may indicate market segments that require different marketing programs and sales forces. Even Japan's composite religious tradition has affected the economy of that country.

Attitudes and values greatly affect consumer behavior. Attitudes about wealth and acquisition, change, and risk taking are especially important for the international marketer who may be introducing innovation to a society in the form of new products—and new lifestyles.

Social organization refers to the way people relate to one another and to the various groups and divisions in a society. The size and nature of the family, tribalism and ethnic divisions, and different roles for women or age groups (such as senior citizens) can all influence a marketing program.

Questions and Research

3.1 What is culture?

3.2 Give examples of cultural concepts used in U.S. marketing.

3.3 How can a nation's technology and material culture affect a firm's marketing in that country?

3.4 Discuss the role of the international marketer as an agent of cultural change. Is this role legitimate? Explain.

3.5 Why are international marketers interested in the linguistic situation in their markets?

3.6 How can an international firm deal with the language challenges in its foreign markets?

3.7 How can the aesthetic ideas and values of a society influence a firm's marketing in that country?

3.8 How is international marketing constrained by the educational level in a market?

3.9 What, if anything, does a country's religious situation have to do with a firm's marketing in that country?

3.10 Discuss the marketing implications of the following religious phenomena: (a) religious holidays, (b) taboos, (c) religious institutions (church and clergy), and (d) nirvana.

3.11 Identify some constraints in marketing to a traditional Muslim society.

3.12 What is the marketing significance of these aspects of social organization: (a) the extended family, (b) tribalism, (c) the role of women in the economy?

3.13 Convenience Foods Corp. has asked you to do a cultural analysis of a South American country in which it is considering operations. How would you go about completing this task?

Endnotes

1. European Marketing Data and Statistics, 2003; 38th Edition, Euromonitor, Tables 13 and 14.

2. World Bank, *2002 World Development Indicators* (http://www.worldbank.org/data/countrydata/countrydata.html), Tables 1.1 and 1.6.

3. Bodley, John H. Cultural Anthropology: Tribes, States, and the Global System. Mountain View, CA: Mayfield, 1994.

4. Drakulić, Slavenka. *Café Europa: Life After Communism*, 1999, Penguin Books.

5. International Marketing Data and Statistics, 2004; 28th Edition, Euromonitor, Table 4.2, pages 167–169.

6. United States input-output tables are available on the Bureau of Economic Analysis web site (http://www.bea.gov/bea/uguide. htm#_1_15).

7. Kirpalani, Manjeet and Pete Engardio. "25 Ideas for a Changing World," *Business Week*, August 26, 2002, Issue 3796, page 112.

8. *Wall Street Journal*, September 24, 1998, B1.

9. "English Is Not the Net's Only Language," *Global Reach*, NAU Internet Surveys, May 24, 2002; "Non-English Speakers Dominant Online," *Global Reach*, October 31, 2002.

10 ."Europemedia: Multinationals Fail European Internet Users," NAU Internet Surveys, April 5, 2002.

11. Dean, Jason. "Throwaway Phrases: Taiwan's New Way to Pick Up English," *Wall Street Journal*, September 25, 2002, page 1.

12. Voight, Kevin. "Japanese Firms Want English Competency," *Wall Street Journal*, June 11, 2001.

13. Hall, Kenneth and Stanley Petzall. "The Making of Technicians for a High-Technology Future: The Singapore Apprentice," *Journal of Asian Business*, Volume 16, Number 4, 2000, pages 39–56.

14. Hanushek, Eric A. and Dennis D. Kimko. "Schooling, Labor-Force Quality, and the Growth of Nations," *American Economic Review*, 2000, Volume 90, Issue 5, pages 1184–1208.

15. Adherents.com, Major Religions of the World Ranked by Number of Adherents (http://www.adherents.com/Religions_By_Adherents.html); accessed September 3, 2004.

16. "Religious Violence in India Ebbs After 4 Days of Killing," *Wall Street Journal*, March 4, 2002, Section A, page 12.

17. "Caste in India, Still Untouchable," *The Economist*, June 16, 2001, Volume 359, Issue 8226, page 42.

18. "Quitting Hinduism," *Christianity Today*, December 9, 2002, pages 22–23.

19. "Oman's Auto Distributors Gearing Up for Ramadan," *Times of Oman*, September 1, 2002.

20. "Japan's Mori Adds Religion Card to Hand," *Wall Street Journal*, June 23, 2000, page A16.

21. "Longer Workweeks Likely in Europe," *USA Today*, Tuesday, July 27, 2004, page 4B.

22. "Cyber-Nervous," *Marketing News*, August 19, 2002, page 3.

23. "Information Sensitivity and E-Commerce: A Cross-National Study of Japan, the U.S., and France," *2001 AMA Educators' Proceedings: Enhancing Knowledge Development in Marketing*, Volume 12, pages 255–264.

24. U.S. CIA Factbook, 2004 (http://www.odci.gov/cia/publications/factbook); accessed January 19, 2005.

Further Readings

Ahn, Se Young and Jeon, Bang Nam. "The Association of Individual Attitudes toward Foreign Firms: A Korean Case Study," *Journal of Asian Business*, Volume 17, Number 1, 2001, pages 45–68.

Axtell, Roger E. *Dos and Taboos of Humor Around the World*, 1999, New York: John Wiley & Sons.

Blanton, Karen Kniep and John E. Barbuto, Jr. "Cultural Constraints in the Workplace: An Experiential Exercise Utilizing Hofstede's Dimensions," *Journal of Management Education*, Volume, 29, Issue 4, August 2005, pages 654–667.

Carvalho, Sergio W. "Assessing the Role of Nationalistic Feelings in Consumer Attitudes toward Foreign Products: An Exploratory Study in Brazil," *2002 AMA Educators' Proceedings: Enhancing Knowledge Development in Marketing*, Volume 13, pages 261–262.

Chaney, Lillian H. and Jeanette S. Martin. *Intercultural Business Communication*, 2d Edition, 2000, Upper Saddle River, NJ: Prentice Hall.

Chen, Ming-Jer. *Inside Chinese Business: A Guide for Managers World-Wide*, 2001, Boston, MA: Harvard Business School Press.

Dicle, I. Atilla and Ulku Dicle. "A Cross-Cultural Study of Managerial Work Values in Singapore," *Journal of Asia-Pacific Business*, Volume 3, Issue 1, 2001, pages 63–82.

Doran, Kathleen Brewer. "Lessons Learned in Cross-Cultural Research of Chinese and North American Consumers," *Journal of Business Research*, October 2002, Volume 55, Number 10, pages 823–829.

Dwyer, Sean, Hani Mesak, and Maxwell Hsu. "An Exploratory Examination of the Influence of National Culture on Cross-National Product Diffusion," *Journal of International Marketing*, June 2005, Volume 13, Issue 2, pages 1–27.

Ezzell, Carol. "Clocking Cultures," *Scientific American*, September 2002, Volume 287, Issue 3, pages 74–75 (http://proquest.umi.com/ pqdweb?Did=000000148764391&Fmt=3&Deli=1&Mtd=1&Idx=1&Sid=1&RQT=309).

"Fast-food Firms Hope to Get More Bucks with Clucks (Chicken Takes Increasing Portion of Menu Space," *USA Today*, July 28, 2004, page B1.

Ferraro, Gary P. *The Cultural Dimensions of International Business*, 4th Edition, 2002, Upper Saddle River, NJ: Prentice Hall.

Hewlett, Sylvia Ann. *Creating a Life: Professional Women and the Quest for Children*, 2002, New York: Hyperion/Talk Miramax Books.

Hofstede, Geert. *Culture's Consequences: Comparing Values, Behaviors, Institutions, and Organizations Across Nations*, 2d Edition, 2001, Thousand Oaks, CA: Sage Publications.

Hofstede, Geert. *Culture's Consequences: International Differences in Work-Related Values*, 1980, Thousand Oaks, CA: Sage Publications.

Lere, John C. and Kris Portz. "Management Control Systems in a Global Economy," *CPA Journal*, September 2005, Volume 75, Issue 9, pages 62–66.

Luna, David and Susan Forquer Gupia. "An Integrative Framework for Cross-Cultural Consumer Behavior," *International Marketing Review*, Volume 18, Issue 1, 2001, pages 45–69.

Milner, Laura M. "Sex-Role Portrayals in African Television Advertising: A Preliminary Examination with Implications for the Use of Hofstede's Research," *Journal of International Consumer Marketing*, 2005, Volume 17, Issue 2,3, pages 73–91.

Neelankavil, James P., Anil Mathur, and Yong Zhang. "Determinants of Managerial Performance: A Cross-Cultural Comparison of the Perceptions of Middle-Level Managers in Four Countries," *Journal of International Business Studies*, Volume 31, Issue 1, 2000, pages 121–140.

Raymond, Mary Anne, John D. Mittelstaedt, and Christopher D. Hopkins. " Perceptions of Consumer Needs Levels and Implications for Standardization—Adaptation Decisions in Korea," *2002 AMA Educators' Proceedings: Enhancing Knowledge Development in Marketing*, Volume 13, pages 376–377.

Trofimov, Yaroslav. *Faith of War*, 2005, Henry Holt, N.Y., N.Y.

Recommended Web Sites

Women Watch: Information and Resources on Gender Equality and Empowerment of Women (http://www.un.org/womenwatch); for gender-specific statistics, see the UN Statistics Division—statistics and indicators on women and men (http://unstats.un.org/unsd/demographic/products/indwm); United Nations Statistics Division.

What Is Culture? (http://www.wsu.edu:8001/vcwsu/commons/topics/culture/culture-index.html); created by faculty and staff at Washington State University.

Statistical tables and culture indicators (http://www.unesco.org/culture/worldreport/html_eng/tables2.shtml) and Youth and Culture (http://www.unesco.org/culture/youth); United Nations Educational, Scientific and Cultural Organization (UNESCO).

YourDictionary.com (http://www.yourdictionary.com); translate words and phrases, play games (crossword puzzles in English, French, German, and Spanish), write your name in hieroglyphs, and learn about dead and dying languages.

World Religions: Adherents.com (http://www.adherents.com); includes brief explanations of religions and statistics on adherents.

Case 3.1

BOTTLED SPIRITS

The Hopi are the westernmost tribe of Pueblo Indians, located in northeastern Arizona. There are fewer than 10,000 of them. They typically live in terraced pueblo structures of stone and adobe and are clustered into a number of small, independent towns. Like all Pueblo Indians, the Hopi are peaceful, monogamous, diligent, self-controlled, and very religious.

The most conservative tribe in the Southwest, the Hopi want no tourists to photograph, sketch, or record their dances. They do, however, allow visitors to observe their ceremonies by watching masked Kachina dancers impersonate Hopi gods. The Hopi also invite tourists into their homes to buy Kachina dolls and Hopi pottery.

Kachinas are the Hopi Indians' holy spirits. They are sometimes personified by masked dancers and sometimes represented by wooden dolls. There are roughly 250 different Kachinas. Although the Hopi will sell Kachina dolls to tourists, they are sensitive to how others may use the Kachina costume or idea. For example, in 1987, Miss New Mexico won the costume competition in the Miss USA competition, wearing a Kachina costume. Hopi religious leaders complained that that use was sacrilegious.

In another incident, the Hopi protested when Kentucky's Ezra Brooks distillery began marketing its bourbon in bottles shaped like Kachina dolls. As a Christmas promotion, the Brooks distillery had planned to distribute 5,000 of the Kachina doll bottles in Arizona and the Southwest. It had already shipped 2,000 bottles when it learned of the Hopi complaint. Reflecting the Hopis' anger, a tribal leader asked, "How would a Catholic feel about putting whiskey in a statue of Mary?" The Hopi not only complained, but also received assistance from the Arizona senator to have production halted.

QUESTIONS AND RESEARCH
1. What should the distillery do? What courses of action might it take?
2. Propose and defend your solution to this problem.

Case 3.2

THE ROLE OF WOMEN IN SOCIETY

Look around the classroom or think about the people in your class. If you are in the United States, approximately half of the students are probably women. Did you ever consider why? People's attitudes and expectations about family and friends are a part of culture. So are their attitudes and expectations about the role of men and women in society. What is of added interest is that these attitudes are not the same from culture to culture, and they change over time.

In the United States, dual-income households and single parenthood are not new or extraordinary; but in other nations, those situations would be unexpected. Consider Japan, where, on average, women are paid less for performing the same jobs as men. In fact, in 2001, women earned only 65 percent of what their male counterparts earned. That may not surprise you, but the expectations of Japanese over the age of forty might. The typical family in Japan consists of a working father, a stay-at-home mother, and one child. One transplanted American working in Japan said that the culture is like the 1950s in the United States—something out of the old television show of that era, *Leave It to Beaver*. Until recently, women were expected to work until they found a husband, then devote their lives to raising a child and overseeing other domestic responsibilities. Once the child was grown, some women would return to the workforce, but only for part-time or temporary work, often cleaning others' homes, caring for children, or teaching.

This is changing, though, in part by decree. In June 1999, the Japanese government enacted a law designed to create an environment in which men and women are treated equally and participate jointly in all aspects of society. Attitudes are changing, but very slowly. Younger men want to participate in the raising of their children and want to spend more time at home than in the past. Younger women want to finish college, have a career, and get married later. Miyuki Yasuo, a public relations and advertising manager for L'Oreal, started using a house cleaning service to reduce the stress associated with caring for her home and child, in addition to pursuing her career. Her housekeeper is paid ¥100,000 per month (approximately $850) to do the shopping, prepare meals, clean the house, and pick up Mr. and Mrs. Yasuo's child from child care every evening.

Men and women over forty hold more traditional Japanese values. In addition, many Japanese business-

Table 3-5. Women in Society

Country or Region	Literacy Rate				Distribution of Labor Force					
	Illiterate (ages 15–24)		Illiterate (ages > 24)		Wage & Salaried[a]		Self-Employed[b]		Family Worker[c]	
	W	M	W	M	W	M	W	M	W	M
Africa										
Benin	73	45	88	67	3	7	64	54	29	32
Egypt	46	29	79	50	35	55	12	29	36	10
Kenya	14	8	54	26	12	32	17	19	56	30
Namibia	10	14	35	27	36	60	20	16	28	10
South Africa	10	9	…	…	70	78	5	8	…	…
Latin America										
Brazil	10	15	25	22	64	61	22	29	10	6
Columbia	4	5	12	11	70	61	28	38	2	1
Honduras	20	23	43	40	48	46	42	41	11	12
Mexico	5	4	20	13	58	58	23	32	19	10
Venezuela	4	5	14	11	70	58	23	34	2	1
North America										
Canada	…	…	…	…	90	88	9	12	1	0
United States	…	…	…	…	93	91	6	10	0	0
Asia										
Bangladesh	62	41	…	…	9	15	8	43	77	17
Indonesia	5	3	34	16	24	32	29	52	45	14
Malaysia	5	4	31	15	72	71	14	25	15	4
Philippines	3	4	9	7	41	42	30	40	19	10
Turkey	12	3	40	13	25	49	8	39	67	12
Europe										
Finland	…	…	…	…	90	81	10	18	1	1
Greece	<1	1	8	3	58	53	19	42	24	5
Ireland	…	…	…	…	91	72	8	27	2	1
Poland	<1	<1	…	…	74	70	20	26	7	4
Portugal	1	1	19	11	73	71	26	28	2	1

Sources: The UN Statistics Division—statistics and indicators on women and men (http://unstats.un.org/unsd/demographic/products/indwm/table5e.htm); World Bank Data Query (http://devdata.worldbank.org/data-query); accessed September 3, 2004.

a. Wage and salaried workers are those who work for a private or public entity for which the workers/employees receive a salary.

b. Self-employed are those who operate their own business.

c. Family workers are those who are unpaid employees of a family-run enterprise of another person in the same household.

… indicates that data is not available; but in all cases, except for illiteracy rates associated with people over twenty-four in South Africa (around 14 percent for men and women over fifteen years old according to the World Bank), all are near zero.

es are still slow to reward women by promotion or pay; nor do they allow husbands more time off to be with their family and help raise their children. Yet more Japanese households are calling on housekeeping services to help care for their homes and children, creating a whole new industry in Japan. While some see the change as beneficial—leading to equal treatment of women and men, with a side benefit of helping create jobs and improving the economy of Japan—others see this as cause for alarm. As more women work and put off having a family, there will be fewer children to take care of an aging population, which has been the tradi-

tional method of caring for the elderly.

The role of women in society and business is important because interactions between men and women are affected by expectations about what is and is not acceptable behavior. From one culture to the next, differences exist about expected gender roles; and people working in these environments must have some appreciation for or understanding of the differences if they are to succeed in relationships with coworkers. Sensitivity to this situation will affect how a person is perceived as a manager, negotiator, business partner, and colleague.

One way of determining how cultures view women and their role in society is to review statistics on education and the distribution of men and women in the workforce. Generally, the more even the distribution between men and women in work and education, the more likely it is that women are treated equally in business. Table 3-5 shows illiteracy rates (the lower the rate, the more educated the group) as well as distribution of the labor force.

QUESTIONS AND RESEARCH

1. Review the figures on illiteracy rates in Table 3-5 and discuss the disparity between the rates for men and women. The rates seem most different among developing nations. Why?
2. A large disparity in pay still exists between men and women, even in industrialized nations. Countries such as Japan and the United States have laws about equal pay for equal work. What activities can the people of a nation engage in to reduce the inequity more quickly? What roles can schools and companies play?
3. Men and women are depicted differently in advertisements that are shown on television and that appear in magazines. Identify some stereotypes from these ads.

Sources: Brian Bremner, "Japan Overlooks the Power of Its Women at Its Own Peril," *Business Week*, November 1, 1999, Business Week Online; William Hall, "The Status of Women in Japan," J@pan.inc, December 2000; "More Working Women Employing Housekeepers," *Financial Times*, June 15, 2002.

Case 3.3

AFLAC

AFLAC became the official name of the American Family Life Assurance Company in 1989. It entered the Japanese market in 1975 and soon became one of the most successful foreign companies in any industry operating in Japan. By 1982, 1 in 20 Japanese households was an AFLAC policyholder. By 1988, the ratio was 1 in 6. And by 1995, about 1 in 4 Japanese households had an AFLAC policy, which is still true today. AFLAC is the second largest insurance company in Japan and the number one foreign life insurance company. It is the second most profitable foreign company operating in an industry in Japan. In 2001, Japan accounted for 78 percent of the total company sales of $9.6 billion.

Founded in the United States in 1955, AFLAC specializes in cancer insurance (about 54 percent of its policies are in this field). Although AFLAC was the second foreign insurance company to enter the Japanese market, it was the first company, either Japanese or foreign, to introduce a policy for cancer protection in Japan. Two Japanese firms also issued independent health insurance coverage, but they had a much smaller number of policies outstanding.

Cancer insurance is a controversial product in the United States because consumer advocates argue that disease-specific policies are an inefficient, costly form of coverage. Bans on the sale of these policies were only lifted in Connecticut and New York in the late 1990s. Attitudes in Japan are somewhat different. When AFLAC hired Nomura Research to see what its customers wanted, the answer was more coverage. On the government side, company president John Amos had developed a strong relationship with the powerful Japanese bureaucracy. Indeed, in 1988, John Amos was named by *Forbes* magazine as the insurance industry's most innovative executive for his success in penetrating the Japanese market. (The company has won many other prestigious awards since then, too.)

Japan is one of the largest insurance markets in the world. About 90 percent of Japanese households carry life insurance with a relative contract value much higher than that in either Europe or the United States. Japan also has rather comprehensive national health insurance; so private company plans supplement the government program in such areas as private rooms, costly major disease, and lost income. AFLAC's cancer insurance sales grew rapidly, in part because cancer is the major cause of death in Japan and because cancer is usually associated with costly treatment and long stays in the hospital. Thus, the Japanese perceive cancer as the most threatening and the most expensive disease they can encounter, wanting to provide for it as best they can.

Most Japanese insurance companies use homemakers as a part-time sales force for door-to-door sales. Amos came up with another idea—use retired Japanese workers to sell to their former colleagues. "Their retirement benefits weren't good enough to last them forever, so AFLAC became a little like their social security," he recalled. AFLAC uses different methods for distributing its products, which also helps to reduce operating costs.

Japanese corporations agreed to encourage their workers to buy the insurance and to deduct the premiums from their monthly paychecks. Retired executives from each corporation are often enlisted to do the actual selling. Over 17,000 such payroll groups have been established. Over 92 percent of the corporations listed on the Tokyo Stock Exchange use AFLAC's payroll deduction plan, although less than half of their employees subscribe to it. Even Nippon Life and Dai-ichi Mutual Life, two of Japan's largest life insurance companies, offer AFLAC's cancer policies to their employees.

Another part of AFLAC's approach is "bank set sales." With this program, a bank automatically deducts the annual premium from the accumulated interest on a policyholder's savings account and transfers it to AFLAC's account. Some 250 banks are participating in this program, serving about 500,000 policyholders. The Japanese have a favorable attitude toward saving, and this program appeals to their orientation to save and to their strong desire for insurance coverage. Because the banks enjoy a good reputation, AFLAC's insurance program gains further credibility by this association with them.

AFLAC has not relied on advertising in Japan, depending instead on its strong sales network and full-time sales force. Because the company innovated cancer insurance and because of the company's different marketing approach, however, it received a lot of publicity in various media.

In 1994, AFLAC expanded its product line with Super Care, a policy for nursing home care, and Super Cancer, an upgrade on its original policy. Super Cancer allows for a cash payment when cancer is first diagnosed. Nursing home costs are another major concern in Japan because the population has a very long life expectancy.

One indicator of AFLAC's success is a first-year renewal rate of 90 percent—and 94 percent after the second year. Both of those figures are higher than in either the Japanese or U.S. life insurance industries. AFLAC views those figures as corroboration of its product and marketing program.

Some changes are taking place. In 2000, sales of accident/disability policies surpassed those for cancer policies in the United States. As a result of an aggressive marketing program, the CEO, Dan Amos, is on his way to meeting his goal of increasing U.S. sales as a percentage of total sales. (In 2001, 70 percent of the firm's earnings and 80 percent of its assets were Japanese.) Deregulation in the Japanese insurance industry has led AFLAC to form an alliance with the largest Japanese insurer, Dai-ichi Mutual Life; and noncancer products now account for 60 percent of new sales. AFLAC also uses new technologies, such as processing claims on the Internet, to increase profitability. It costs the firm about $72 to write and process new policies, versus a cost of $120 for Japanese insurance firms, giving AFLAC a big advantage over its competitors.

QUESTIONS AND RESEARCH

1. Describe AFLAC's marketing program in Japan—product policy, pricing, promotion, and distribution.
2. Explain how this marketing program relates to the Japanese culture and economy and why it is so successful.
3. To view the "Duck Campaign" commercials (in English), which are being used to promote the debut of AFLAC's first accident policy in Japan, access http://www.aflac.com/about_us/corp_overview_commercials.asp.

Sources: AFLAC corporate web site (http://www.aflac.com); Hoover's Company Profile Database, 2002; "How AFLAC Laid a Golden Egg in Japan," *Business Week*, November 11, 2002, page 56.

CHAPTER 4

The Political-Legal Environment

The political environment of international marketing has three dimensions: the host country, home country, and international environments. The many laws affecting international marketing fall into three categories: U.S. law, international law, and foreign law.

The main goals of this chapter are to

- Discuss concepts critical to nations, such as sovereignty, security, and prestige, in order to understand political risk.

- Describe the role of firms in the political and legal environment—how firms are shaped by it and how firms shape the laws and politics of a nation.

- Identify the areas of the home country environment that affect a firm's international marketing.

- Explain how U.S. export controls, antitrust laws, and tax laws affect the feasibility and profitability of a U.S. firm's international marketing.

- Discuss the effect of international organizations such as the IMF and the WTO and regional groups such as the EU on the international legal environment.

- Describe international conventions designed to protect intellectual property.

The politics and the laws of a nation obviously influence the practice of international marketing. This chapter examines the nature of the political-legal environment and its impact on international marketing.

The Political Environment

The **political environment** of international marketing includes any national or international political factor that can affect its operations. A factor is political when it derives from the government sector. The political environment comprises three dimensions: the host country environment, the international environment, and the home country environment. Surveys have shown that dealing with problems in the political arena is the number one challenge facing international managers and occupies more of their time than any other management function. Yet international managers' concerns are different from those of political scientists. Managers are concerned primarily about political risk—the possibility of any government action adversely (or favorably) affecting their operations.

Host Country Political Environment

By definition, an international firm is a guest, a foreigner in all of its markets abroad. Therefore, international managers are especially concerned with nationalism and dealings with governments in host countries.

HOST COUNTRY NATIONAL INTERESTS

One way to gain an understanding of the situation in a foreign market is to see how compatible a firm's activities are with the interests of the host country. Although each country has its own set of national goals, most countries share many common objectives. Nationalism and patriotism refer to citizens' feelings about their country and its interests. Such feelings exist in every country. The celebration of a major holiday in recognition of a country's birthday and its achievement of independence or nationhood reinforces the sense of national identity and nationalism.

All countries want to maintain and enhance their national sovereignty. Foreign firms, individually or collectively, may be perceived as a threat to that sovereignty. The larger and more numerous the foreign firms, the more likely they are to be perceived as a threat—or at least an irritant. In times of turmoil, foreign firms and foreign embassies may be targets.

Countries want to protect their national security. Although a foreign firm is not a military threat as such, it may be considered as being potentially prejudicial to national security. Governments generally prohibit foreign firms from involvement in "sensitive" industries such as

defense, communications, and perhaps energy and natural resources. For example, when Libya nationalized the service stations of foreign oil companies, the reason it gave was that this commodity was too important to be in the hands of foreigners. When a firm is from a country deemed unfriendly to the host country, the firm may have difficulty operating or may even be denied admission.

Countries are also concerned about their national prestige. They establish national airlines and send their best athletes to the Olympics as ways of gaining international recognition. Economically, they may foster certain industries for the same reason. Foreign firms may be prevented from entering those industries or from acquiring a national firm in a certain industry. Many countries seek "national solutions" to help troubled companies retain what are perceived to be national champions. International firms need to be sensitive to these issues and must be careful not to be too "foreign." This includes their advertising and branding policies as well as ownership and staffing. Establishing local R&D would be perceived favorably in this context.

All countries want to enhance economic welfare. Generally, this means increasing employment and income in the country. Foreign firms contribute by generating employment. They can contribute further by using local suppliers and having local content in their products. They can contribute further still by exporting from the country and generating foreign exchange. They can contribute in a different way by supplying products, services, and/or training that enhance productivity.

HOST COUNTRY CONTROLS

Host countries don't depend entirely on the goodwill of foreign firms to help them achieve their national goals. To try to ensure desirable behavior by foreign firms—and to prevent undesirable behavior—governments use a variety of tools, some of which are explained here.

Entry restrictions. If allowed to enter a country, a firm may be restricted in terms of industries it can enter. A firm may be prohibited from acquiring a national firm. It may not be allowed 100 percent ownership, instead being required to enter a joint venture with a national firm. It may be restricted as to the products it can sell. For example, the United Kingdom, Australia, Brazil, and Canada are debating whether to reduce foreign ownership restrictions on media, while the post-9/11 United States is not likely to loosen (and may even tighten) current ownership regulations. (A domestically-owned free press is viewed as critical for imparting an unbiased view of local and global events.)

Price controls. Once in a country, a foreign firm may encounter a variety of restrictions. One of the most common is price controls, whic.h in inflationary economies, can severely limit profitability. For instance, instead of reducing the dosage they are supposed to take or foregoing needed medications altogether, U.S. citizens (particularly seniors) are going to Canada by the busloads for their medications and ordering them from foreign sources via the Internet to take advantage of price-controlled pharmaceuticals. Companies selling drugs in the United States argue that if price controls are imposed in the United States, they would have to reduce R&D budgets for new drugs.

Quotas and tariffs. A country's quotas and tariffs may limit a firm's ability to import equipment, components, and products, forcing a higher level of local procurement than the firm may want.

Exchange control. Many countries run chronic deficits in their balance of payments and are short of foreign exchange. They ration its use according to their priorities. Foreign firms may be low on that priority list and have difficulty getting foreign exchange for needed imports or profit repatriation. Ballooning foreign debt and an inflation rate of 200 percent in 2002 led Zimbabwe President Mugabe to centralize all foreign exchange transactions and force exporters to surrender all hard foreign currencies in return for the official rate of 55 $Zimbabwe for 1 $US (versus 600 $Z to the $US on parallel black market rates).[1]

(Forced) asset transfer. This can take the form of confiscation (government seizure of assets with no remuneration), expropriation (seizure with some compensation, though typically less than fair market value or a firm's valuation), or nationalization (seizure of entire industries, such as banking and railroad, regardless of nationality). Other forms of asset transfer typically target non-native firms and owners. Domestication, another form of asset transfer, generally takes place over a longer period of time and is often a planned part of an investment. This occurs when a firm wants to transfer ownership to locals to increase their stake, thereby increasing local interest in protecting its assets.

Fortunately, expropriation, confiscation, and nationalization are occurring less often as developing countries begin to see FDI as desirable. From a peak of 83 cases in 1975, the number declined as the 1980s progressed, with only one case in 1985. It is a rare phenomenon today. In fact, many governments are going through privatization of key industries, which is a transfer of state-owned property into private hands.

This decline does not mean that expropriation or nationalization should not be a concern to investors. There are still many examples of government-enforced transfer of assets of both individuals' and companies' investments and holdings. Some experts argue that this downward trend of expropriation can be reversed quickly and easily. (See, for example, Comeaux and Kinsella in "Further Readings" at the end of this chapter.) Reasons provided by governments for these asset transfers include protection of its citizens against terrorism (where assets may be frozen or confiscated), restitution for former human rights violations (farm property seizure and redistribution in Zimbabwe and gold mine ownership in South Africa), and the potential of nationalization to protect vital industries such as banking (Japan) and utilities (England).

Host country controls take many forms. Future regulations will likely focus on the protection of individuals and national security, protection of privacy rights, corporate ethical behavior, and environmental protection. These are complicated issues that will lead to different, often conflicting laws. Mexico's "opt-in" program is one example of a privacy rights law. In Mexico, direct marketers are required to purchase a list of people who have expressed an interest in receiving direct mail. There are also the European Data Protection Directive and the U.S. anti-spam initiatives.[2]

Increasingly, individuals are being held liable for their own and for their company's actions. Ignorance is not bliss, and it is no longer accepted as a defense by many courts. As the officers of Enron, Arthur Andersen, Tyco, WorldCom, and a host of others discovered, the penalties can be severe. Prosecution can be long-sought, as in the ongoing case of India versus Warren Andersen (Union Carbide's chair at the time of the Bhopal disaster in 1984); and no one is immune from investigation or above scrutiny, as Martha Stewart (ImClone stock sale) and even the President of the United States, George W. Bush, discovered (Harken Energy stock sale).

POLITICAL RISK ASSESSMENT

In a matter of hours, some form of political unrest (Nigeria), a short statement ("We have a viable nuclear weapons program."—North Korea), or an act of terrorism (a bomb exploding in a Bali nightclub) can alter the relationship between nations. Such events underscore the importance of continuous monitoring of host country political environments because they can change rapidly. Terrorism occurs worldwide and, alarmingly, with increasingly devastating results. (See "Global Marketing: Terrorism—Taking Its Toll.") A change in leadership, whether through coup, appointment, or election, likely means a change in regulations, many of which have an impact on business.

A firm must develop political and diplomatic skills in-house but may also use consultants who have expertise with particular countries. The U.S. Department of Commerce Commercial Services branch provides useful information and has a staff of country-specific advisers. Some private firms provide evaluations about the political risk environment of specific countries. These services are moderate in cost in some cases, but, depending on coverage, may cost several thousand dollars a year. Firms use different methods and come up with somewhat different ratings of a country's political risk, although many ratings are comparable. Table 4-1 provides information on one firm's country risk service. A recent article questions the accuracy of country risk assessment measures, though.[3]

In its own study of the political environment, a firm can include a preliminary analysis of its political vulnerability in a particular host country. Elements in such an analysis may include external and company factors, which are described in the sections that follow.

External Factors

Political risk is also affected by factors beyond a company's control:

Firm's home country. A firm is usually better accepted in a country that has good relations with the firm's home country.

Product or industry. Sensitivity of the industry is an important consideration. Generally, raw materials, public utilities, communications, pharmaceuticals, and defense-related products are most sensitive.

Size and location of operations. The larger the foreign firm, the more threatening it is perceived to be. This is especially true when the firm has large facilities and is located in a prominent urban area, such as the capital, which serves as a constant reminder of the foreign presence.

Visibility of the firm. The greater the visibility of the foreign firm, the greater its vulnerability. Visibility is a function of several things, including the size and location of the firm's operations in the country and the nature of the firm's

GLOBAL MARKETING

Terrorism—Taking Its Toll

*T*errorism takes a terrible toll, not just because of the death and destruction, which is horrific, but also because of the loss of a sense of security that people everywhere feel. Examples include the killing of the Olympic athletes in Munich in 1972; the embassy bombings and other attacks in Africa in 1998 (nearly 6,000 dead); the attacks on the eastern United States on September 11, 2001, when approximately 3,000 people were killed; the bombing of a Balinese nightclub that resulted in nearly 300 casualties in October 2002; and the hostage taking in a Moscow school in September 2004 that resulted in over 300 deaths, many of whom were children. The locations of these events; the nationalities, ages, and occupations of the victims; and the reasons cited for the attacks clearly show that no one is safe—whether going

continued

Table 4-1. The Economic Intelligence Unit (EIU) Country Risk Service

Category of Risk and Description

Political risk—The factors in this category relate to the threat of war, social unrest, disorderly transfers of power, political violence, international disputes, regime changes, and institutional ineffectiveness, but also include the quality of the bureaucracy, the transparency and fairness of the political system, and levels of corruption and crime in the country in question.

Economic policy risk—Open economies with low inflation and low fiscal deficits are rated more favorably. Among the criteria considered are monetary policy, fiscal policy, exchange-rate policy, and trade and regulatory policies.

Economic structure risk—Measures include economic variables central to solvency. Among the subcategories of risk are growth and savings, the current account, and debt structure.

Liquidity risk—This risk measure is indicative of potential imbalances between resources and obligations that could result in disruption of the financial markets. Among the factors considered are the direction of reserves, import cover, M2/reserves, the degree of a country's dependence on portfolio inflows, and the size of a country's direct investment inflows.

Currency risk—A score and ratings are derived to assess the risk of devaluation against the dollar of 20 percent or more in real terms over the forecast period.

Sovereign debt risk—A score and ratings are developed to assess the risk of a buildup in arrears of principal and/or interest on foreign-currency debt that are the direct obligation of the sovereign or are guaranteed by the sovereign.

Banking sector risk—A score and ratings are used to assess the risk of a buildup in arrears of principal and/or interest on foreign-currency debt that are the obligation of the country's private banking institutions.

Notes: EIU assesses four types of general political and macroeconomic risk (political risk, economic policy risk, economic structure risk, and liquidity risk) independently of their association with a particular investment vehicle. Each risk is given a letter grade. These factors are then used to compile an overall score and rating for the country. EIU also evaluates risk exposure associated with investing in particular types of financial instruments; namely, specific investment risk. This includes risk associated with taking on foreign-exchange exposure against the dollar, foreign-currency loans to sovereigns, and foreign-currency loans to banks.

Source: *Country Risk Service, April Handbook,* 2002; Economist Intelligence Unit, Ltd., pages 10–13 (http://www.eiu.com).

Company Factors

The risk factors listed here are more controllable, since firms are the decision makers.

Company behavior. Each firm develops some record of corporate citizenship based on its practices. Some firms are more sensitive and responsive to the situation in the host country than others. Goodwill in this area is a valuable asset.

Contributions of the firm to the host country. Many of these contributions are objective and quantifiable. How much employment has been generated? How much tax has been paid? How many exports has the firm generated? What new resources or skills has the firm brought in?

Localization of operations. Generally, the more localized a firm's operations, the more acceptable the firm is to the host country. There are several dimensions to localization, including having local equity, hiring local managers and technical staff, using local content in the products (including local suppliers of goods and services, for example), developing local products, and using local brand names.

Subsidiary dependence. This factor somewhat contradicts the preceding point. The more a firm's local operation depends on the parent company, the less vulnerable it is. If a firm cannot function as a separate, self-contained unit but is dependent on the parent for critical resources and/or for markets, it will be seen as a less rewarding takeover target.

Political monitoring and analysis are continuing tasks for a firm. A firm must use the information that these analyses provide to manage its political relations. Table 4-2 suggests some approaches to managing potential political risk, both before and after entering a country.

International Political Environment

The international political environment involves political relations between two or more countries. This is in contrast to the previous concern for what happens only within a given foreign country. An international firm almost inevitably becomes involved with the host country's international relations, no matter how neutral it may try to be. It does so, first, because it is a foreigner from a specific home country and, second, because its operations in a country are frequently related to operations in other countries, on the supply side, the demand side, or both.

One aspect of a country's international relations is its relationship with a firm's home country. U.S. firms abroad are affected by a host nation's attitude toward the United States. When a host nation dislikes any aspect of U.S. policy, it may be the U.S. firm that is bombed or boycotted along with the U.S. Information Service office. English and French firms operating in the former colonies of those countries are affected by that relationship, favorably or

---

products. Consumer goods are more visible than industrial goods. Finished goods are more visible than components or inputs that are hidden in the final product. Heavy advertisers are more visible than nonadvertisers. International brands are more provocative than localized brands.

Host country political situation. The political situation can affect a firm. The company should thus evaluate a country's political risk.

Table 4-2. Managing Political Risk

Pre-entry Planning

1. Perform research; assess potential risks.
2. Avoid threatening countries.
3. Negotiate with host government. (Include planned domestication.)
4. Purchase insurance—government agencies such as OPIC (Overseas Private Investment Corp.) and MIGA (Multilateral Investment Guarantee Agency), as well as private providers.
5. Adjust entry method.
6. Use local capital.

Post-entry Planning

1. Have a monitoring system.
2. Develop a corporate communications program.
3. Develop local stakeholders (employees, suppliers, customers).
4. Have appropriate national executives and an appropriate advisory board.
5. Change operations over time as perceived host country cost-benefit ratio changes; for example, new products and processes, more local equity and management, new exports, and local R&D.
6. Have contingency plans.

---

otherwise. In 2002, Arabs continued their call for a boycott of all American goods for policies viewed as pro-Israeli. Coca-Cola, McDonald's, Procter & Gamble, and KFC were among the firms that expected the boycott to negatively impact sales.

A second critical element affecting the political environment is a host country's relations with other nations. If a country is a member of a regional group, such as the EU or ASEAN, that fact influences a firm's evaluation of the country. If a nation has particular friends or enemies among other nations, a firm must modify its international logistics to comply with how that market is supplied and to whom it can sell. For example, the United States limits trade with various countries. Arab nations have boycotted companies dealing with Israel.

Another clue to a nation's behavior is its membership in international organizations. Besides regional groupings, other international organizations also affect a member's behavior. Members of NATO, for example, accept a military agreement that may restrict their military or political action. Membership in WTO reduces the likelihood that a country will impose new trade barriers. Membership in the IMF or the World Bank also puts constraints on a country's behavior. Many other international agreements impose rules on their members. These agreements may affect patents, communication, transportation, and other items of interest to the international marketer. As a general rule, the more international organizations a country belongs to, the more regulations it accepts—and the more dependable its behavior.

Home Country Political Environment

A firm's home country political environment can constrain its international as well as domestic operations. The political environment can limit the countries that an international firm will enter. The *U.S. Bureau of Industry and Security* (BIS—formerly the Bureau of Export Administration) provides information on export limits regarding specific products and recipients and destinations of U.S. exports. (The most recent *Export Administration Regulations* [EAR] can be found in the Federal Register.) There are broad trade restrictions for exports to Cuba, Iran, Iraq, Libya, North Korea, Sudan, and Syria. As well, there are restrictions on certain products, such as those incorporating short-range wireless technologies, open cryptographic interfaces, beta test software, and encryption source code. (See "Global Marketing: Government: Friend or Foe?") Governments of nearly every nation have limits on what products they will sell and to whom they will sell them. In the U.S., the guiding principles of the BIS parallel other nations' reasons for these limits, including the following:

- The Bureau's paramount concern is the security of the United States. The Bureau's mission is to protect the security of the United States, which includes its national security, economic security, cybersecurity, and homeland security.
- Protecting U.S. security includes not only supporting U.S. national defense, but also ensuring the health of the U.S. economy and the competitiveness of U.S. industry.[4]

The best-known example of the home country political environment affecting international operations used to be South Africa. Home country political pressures induced more than 200 American firms to leave that country in the latter decades of the 20th century. After U.S. companies left South Africa, the Germans and the Japanese remained as the major foreign presence. German firms did not face the same political pressures at home that U.S. firms did. However, the Japanese government was embarrassed when Japan became South Africa's leading trading partner. As a result, some Japanese companies reduced their South African activity. Matsushita closed an office there; Sanyo and Nissan reduced their exports to South Africa; NEC and Pioneer Electronics agreed to suspend exports.

A more recent example occurred when pressure from American human rights groups induced some U.S. firms to leave Myanmar. PepsiCo, for example, pulled out of a joint venture even though it held 85 percent of the soft drink market there.

One challenge facing multinationals is that they have a triple-threat political environment. Even if the home country and the host country pose no problem, multinational firms can face threats in third markets. Firms that do not have problems with their home government or the host government, for example, can be bothered or boycotted in third countries.

The Legal Environment

In addition to the political environment in a nation, the **legal environment**—that is, the nation's laws and regulations pertaining to business—also influences the operations of a foreign firm. A firm must know the legal environment in each market because those laws constitute the "rules of the game." At the same time, a firm must know the political environment because it determines how the laws are enforced and indicates the direction of new legislation. The legal environment of international marketing is complicated, possessing three dimensions. For a U.S. firm, these are (1) U.S. laws, (2) international law, and (3) domestic laws in each of the firm's foreign markets.

Law and International Marketing

U.S. marketers are familiar with domestic regulations affecting marketing, such as the Pure Food and Drug Act and the Robinson-Patman Act. These are not the U.S. laws that affect international marketing, however. Numerous other laws are relevant to international marketing and relate to exporting, antitrust, and organization and ownership arrangements.

EXPORT CONTROLS
Export control laws have changed significantly in response to increased concerns over security and personal safety. One clear indication of this is the U.S. government renaming in 2002 one of the main export control offices, from the Bureau of Export Administration to the Bureau of Industry and Security (BIS), which "better reflects the broader scope of the agency to include homeland, economic and cyber security."[5]

There have always been trade regulations about "dealing with the enemy," policies that dictate what and to whom people may sell. As in the past, U.S. businesses may not sell sophisticated aircraft; biological, nuclear, or conventional weapons; computer hardware and software; telecommunications equipment; and a host of other products to people in nations such as Cuba, North Korea, Iraq, and Sudan. But there are also limits on certain optical

Government: Friend or Foe?

National leaders and lawmakers believe that trade is good for the economy and that exports mean more jobs and a better chance of getting re-elected. The U.S. government has various initiatives and programs to encourage exports, such as the Gold Key Service provided by the Commercial Service of the U.S. Department of Commerce. Trade missions are a common component of trade promotion, and they often lead to positive results. An aerospace trade mission to Vietnam in the fall of 2002 led by the Department of Commerce included Boeing and a dozen other manufacturers. Potential deals from meetings with Vietnamese firms were worth billions over the next few years.

Export-promoting activities are undertaken by state and local development offices as well. Denver, Colorado, opened an office in Shanghai and sponsored a trade mission to China for Denver firms to assist China with security and other aspects of hosting of the 2008 Olympics.

In 1993, the United States created the Advocacy Center, a department within the Department of Commerce's International Trade Administration. Its role is to assist American firms that believe they are facing unfair competition because of foreign government support. The Advocacy Center investigates such claims and, if well-founded, provides representation for the firm on a nation-state level in discussions with other governments and international agencies, such as the WTO.

On the other hand, governments also enact legislation to limit trade to protect consumers against certain products (genetically modified foods, for example), as well as to support specific ideas. American President George Bush supported a continued embargo against Cuba because of the Communist regime in that country. Annual votes in the UN show that most other nations around the world do not support the 40-year-old embargo, and some of them openly trade with Cuba. Embargo critics in the United States and abroad argue that it has failed to lead to the downfall of Communism or its leader, President Castro, and that it hurts the people of Cuba by denying them access to many essentials. It also denies Americans free access to Cuban cigars and cheaper sugar. One recent report indicated that the embargo costs U.S. businesses

continued

between $1 billion and $2 billion each year in travel-related industry alone!

Sources: "Denver Mayor to Lead China Trade Mission," *Denver Post*, October 18, 2002; "Lifting Travel Ban to Cuba Would Generate $1.18 Billion to $1.61 Billion for U.S. Economy," PR Newswire, July 15, 2002; "U.S. Aerospace Contingent Flies to Talk to Business," *Vietnam Investment Review*, September 2, 2002; The Advocacy Center web site (http://www.ita.doc.gov/td/advocacy); accessed September 10, 2004.

equipment, sensing devices, flow control equipment, and advanced textiles (for example, those that can change color to mimic surroundings). While there may be very few U.S. trade restrictions to Canada, the United Kingdom, Sweden, and other nations that are long-term allies, there are always exceptions.

How do exporters know what and to whom they may ship? There are many agencies in the U.S. government with trade oversight responsibilities, as shown in Table 4-3. Three important agencies are: the U.S. Department of Commerce and its many agencies (including the BIS, which was mentioned previously); and

1. the U.S. Customs Service, the agency responsible for ensuring that imports and exports enter and exit the country in accordance with U.S. regulations; and

2. the U.S. Department of the Treasury, particularly the Office of Foreign Assets Control (OFAC), which provides information on sanction programs and country summaries (restrictions on shipments to specific countries and areas of the world).

A relatively small number of U.S. exports require a special license (98 percent of all exports require only a general license for which no application is needed or they must qualify for NLR—no license required—status). BIS relies heavily on exporters to ensure that the products they sell are not dual-use items (items that have both commercial and military applications) going to someone on their "denied persons" or "entity" list. The latter list is comprised of end users who have been determined to constitute an unacceptable risk or who are considered unreliable in handling sensitive products. For the transactions that do require an export license, an application for an individually validated license, issued on a case-by-case basis, must be filed.

The BIS also has a list of "red flags"—items that should raise suspicion when being exported (for example, the buyer is willing to pay cash for expensive items normally purchased through some form of financing). When an order is placed by someone on the denied persons list or there is a red flag, exporters are expected to report this fact to the BIS.

There are fines and other penalties for those firms that do not adhere to the export control regulations. A New Jersey firm paid $30,000 because it violated U.S. regulations by shipping chemicals through the United Arab Emirates to Iran. The company also violated Arab antiboycott rules by verifying that the goods did not originate in Israel. In another case, a fine of $52,500 was imposed on a firm for illegally selling to Singapore, Taiwan, and Thailand sophisticated measuring devices used in constructing military hardware. In November 2001, a $2.12 million penalty was imposed on McDonnell Douglas for allegedly exporting machine tools to China, while the Chinese firms that accepted shipment of the tools were slapped with a $1.32 million penalty and a denial of export privileges order. And in August 2002, the Department of Commerce imposed a fine of $30,000 on Hans Wrage & Co. for re-exporting nearly $500,000 worth of shotguns from Germany to Poland. While Hans Wrage is a German firm, the guns originated in the United States and the company shipped them to Poland without the required U.S. authorization. The U.S. Department of Commerce, through the BIS, administers and enforces export controls. Violations of Export Administration Regulations may result in fines, as in the examples provided (typically being settled rather than going to court), but can also lead to criminal penalties and administrative sanctions.[6]

ANTITRUST CONTROLS

It might seem strange that U.S. antitrust laws would affect the foreign business activities of U.S. companies. However, that is a fact. The opinion of the U.S. Justice Department is that even if an act is committed abroad, it falls within the jurisdiction of U.S. courts *if the act produces consequences within the United States*. Many activities of U.S. businesses abroad have repercussions on the U.S. domestic market. The question arises primarily in three situations: (1) when a U.S. firm acquires a foreign firm, (2) when it engages in a joint venture with a foreign firm, or (3) when it enters into an overseas marketing agreement with another firm.

The two agencies in the U.S. government that have jurisdiction over antitrust regulations for most industries are the *Department of Justice* (DOJ) and the *Federal Trade Commission* (FTC). There are many antitrust regulations; but perhaps the most familiar are the Sherman and Clayton acts, both of which were written in the late 1800s. When a U.S. firm expands abroad or when a foreign corporation enters the U.S. market by acquiring an existing company, the DOJ and FTC are concerned about the possible impact on competition in the United States. If it is determined that the activity is anticompetitive, it will not be approved; or if the activity is already underway, it may be halted. As shown in the following examples, there are

Table 4-3. U.S. Government Departments and Agencies with Export Control Responsibilities

Department of State, Office of Defense Trade Controls (DTC): DTC licenses defense services and defense (munitions) articles.

Department of the Treasury, Office of Foreign Assets Control (OFAC): OFAC administers and enforces economic and trade sanctions against targeted foreign countries, terrorism-sponsoring organizations, and international narcotics traffickers. The OFAC web site provides information on these sanctions as well as the Specially Designated Nationals and Blocked Persons list (SDN list).

Nuclear Regulatory Commission, Office of International Programs: It licenses nuclear material and equipment.

Department of Energy, Office of Arms Controls and Nonproliferation, Export Control Division: It licenses nuclear technology and technical data for nuclear power and special nuclear materials.

Department of Energy, Office of Fuels Programs: It licenses natural gas and electric power.

Defense Threat Reduction Agency—Technology Security: This agency of the Department of Defense (DoD) is responsible for the development and implementation of policies on international transfers of defense-related technology. It also reviews certain dual-use export license applications referred by the Department of Commerce.

Department of the Interior, Division of Management Authority: This agency controls the export of endangered fish and wildlife species.

Drug Enforcement Administration, International Drug Unit: It oversees the export of controlled substances.

Drug Enforcement Administration, International Chemical Control Unit: It controls the import and export of listed chemicals used in the production of controlled substances under the Controlled Substances Act.

Food and Drug Administration, Office of Compliance: This agency licenses medical devices.

Food and Drug Administration, Import/Export: This agency licenses drugs.

Patent and Trademark Office, Licensing and Review: It oversees patent filing data sent abroad.

Environmental Protection Agency, Office of Solid Waste, International and Special Projects Branch: This agency regulates toxic waste exports.

Source: Bureau of Industry and Security (formerly Bureau of Export Administration) (http://www.bxa.doc.gov/about/reslinks.htm).

civil and criminal penalties, including officer liability, for corporate violations. Government action is more likely when the firms are in the same industry.

The acquisition of Princess Cruise Line (United Kingdom) by American rival Carnival had to be brought before the FTC. While the European Commission approved a takeover bid, the FTC initally had not decided how to classify the market in which these firms operate—as "holiday industry" or "high-end cruise industry." If it had been the latter, approval was unlikely since that classification is more specialized and has fewer firms. Subsequently, the acquisition was approved.

Joint venturing, alliances, and other forms of cooperation among firms can lead to government intervention, too. The reasoning by the government is the same—competition in the U.S. market will be reduced by a particular marriage of a U.S. and foreign firm, regardless of location.

Laws in the United States can reach foreign countries and affect the international marketing of U.S. and foreign firms. These laws also affect international marketing by foreign firms operating in the United States; foreign firms are also subject to U.S. antitrust regulation.

Three of the world's largest Dynamic Random Access Memory (DRAM) chip makers are part of an industry-wide investigation into anticompetitive predatory pricing.

Micron Technology (United States), Samsung Electronics (Korea), and Infineon Technologies (Germany) are suspected of keeping prices artificially low in order to drive smaller competitors out of the industry. The commodity-like price for 128 megabit chips rose from $1 to over $2, but it was still considerably less than the estimated $4 it cost to manufacture them.

Elf Atochem of France is one of the largest chemical firms in the world. An executive of the company, Patrick Stainton, has pled guilty to a DOJ charge of antitrust conspiracy, the penalty being 90 days in jail and a $50,000 criminal penalty. Mr. Stainton had participated in suppressing competition in the sales of an important compound used in making pharmaceuticals, herbicides, and plastics.

The U.S. Department of Commerce imposed a $30,000 fine on Sun Microsystems of California, Ltd., for arranging for shipments of computers to the People's Republic of China that did not adhere to conditions of the export license issued to the firm.

Businesses must contend with U.S. laws that are applied both in the United States and in firms' foreign markets. Companies must also be aware of the counterparts to the FTC and DOJ in other parts of the world, which may have their own perspective on the importance of competition and what might be viewed as anticompetitive behavior. A dramatic example of this was the attempted merger of General Electric (GE) and Honeywell in 2001. The proposed $43 billion acquisition of Honeywell by GE had been approved by the U.S. government, but it was blocked by the European Commission antitrust division. In other cases, companies face different penalties or requirements in different markets. For example, as part of the settlement in its antitrust cases, in 2005, Microsoft was fined $650 million and had to unbundle its Media Player software and Windows operating systems for the European market, but not in the United States or elsewhere.[7]

ORGANIZATION AND OWNERSHIP ARRANGEMENTS

The organization of a firm can be influenced by specific laws that are designed to promote foreign trade. In general, more restrictive laws may, indeed, allow certain exceptions to firms meeting specified conditions.

Webb-Pomerene Associations and Export Certificates of Review

The Webb-Pomerene Act of 1918 permits competing firms to form Webb-Pomerene Associations in order to cooperate when engaged in export trade. It specifically excludes them from antitrust prosecution in the development of foreign markets; that is, even though the firms compete domestically, they can collaborate when exporting. Today there are only a handful of Webb-Pomerene Associations still in existence (in chemical, cotton, film, paper, and wood products). A more commonly used vehicle is the Export Trade Certificate of Review (**COR**, or "export certificate" as it is sometimes called). Under the Export Trade Act of 1982 (Title III), certain American firms, associations, and individuals are granted immunity from federal and state antitrust laws and unfair competition lawsuits for their export activities. COR applications are jointly reviewed and certified by the U.S. Department of Commerce and the DOJ, while the Webb-Pomerene Associations are administered by the FTC.

Foreign Sales Corporation (FSC)

Since the early 1970s, the U.S. government has attempted to provide exporters with some form of tax relief on profits earned from exports. The WTO has ruled that the U.S. FSCs (Tax Reform Act of 1984), which allowed American firms to pay less tax on their profits from exports, is an export subsidy and is not in keeping with WTO goals of reducing trade barriers. The United States responded by enacting the Extraterritoriality income Exclusion Act (ETI, signed in 2000), which allowed non-U.S. firms the same treatment. In 2002, responding to a complaint filed by the EU, the WTO ruled that the ETI did not eliminate the subsidy and that the U.S. tax law must be changed, otherwise, contended the WTO, the United States faced up to $4 billion in retaliatory tariffs. Barring an (unlikely) change in

the U.S. tax law, these changes will result in higher tax bills for some firms (for example, Boeing and GE would have gained approximately $4 billion in annual tax savings under ETI), but will still provide some beneficial treatment of profits on active business transactions earned abroad for U.S. and non-U.S. firms.[8]

Export Trading Company Act of 1982

This was another effort by the United States to aid exporters. The **export trading company (ETC)** that was to result from this legislation was supposed to emulate Japanese and Korean trading companies. To reach the size and sophistication of Japanese ETCs, the legislation permitted banks to invest in these entities and eased antitrust restrictions on export activities. Participation by banks has not materialized, though. Instead of the huge conglomerates that were supposed to result from this act, most ETCs provide marketing and transportation services for a particular region of the world or focus on a particular set of products. While sophisticated in many respects, these ETC's are unlike the Korean or Japanese counterparts in terms of size and scope of services.

Yet, American firms have benefited from the Export Trading Company Act of 1982. The Office of Export Trading Company Affairs (OETCA) was created by Congress as part of the act. OETCA administers two programs available to all U.S. exporters or potential exporters—the COR program, which was described previously, and the *MyExports* program. The MyExports program gives U.S. exporters and export service providers a convenient way to establish contacts and to market their products and services through postings with the *U.S. Exporters' Yellow Pages* and the *U.S. Trade Assistance Directory*. OETCA also provides export news and information on exporting resources and sponsors special events such as trade missions and export-related conferences.[9]

OTHER CONTROLS

Examples of other controls include U.S. laws against bribery by U.S. firms, antiterrorism initiatives, and laws against the support of Arab boycotts.

Foreign Corrupt Practices Act (FCPA)

As a result of public outcry in the late 1970s about the ethical behavior of firms and bribery, the U.S. government passed the Foreign Corrupt Practices Act (FCPA) to prohibit U.S. firms from using bribery in any business transactions (although "grease payments" are still allowed). At first, the problem for U.S. firms was that their competitors from Japan and Western Europe were not forbidden to use bribes. U.S. firms complained that the act put them at a serious competitive disadvantage because bribery has often been the most effective form of persuasion in business and government markets abroad. Fortunately, in

December 1997, the members of the OECD, a group of 30 industrialized nations, and five nonmember countries signed the Convention on Combating Bribery of Foreign Public Officials in International Business Transactions. All participants have ratified the agreement, and all except Turkey adopted legislation to implement enforcement of the convention's articles.

This does not mean the end of bribery or similar behavior, though. Transparency International publishes the *Bribe Payers Index*, which provides information about business sectors and nations in which businesses are prone to instances of corruption, as well as suggested solutions to bribery. (See "Global Marketing: Bribery around the World.")

Antiterrorism Regulation

After September 11, 2001, the United States and other governments became aware of the need to monitor and halt financing of terrorism. An example of an initiative to address this growing problem is the Uniting and Strengthening America by Providing Appropriate Tools Required to Intercept and Obstruct Terrorism Act of 2001 (**USA PATRIOT Act**). It expands reporting requirements by financial institutions and those businesses that conduct financial transactions with clients that might attract criminals or terrorists (a broad spectrum that includes banks, casinos, and mutual fund investment houses, but may also soon include others, such as precious metal dealers, pawnbrokers, and travel agencies). Activities that are illegal or suspicious (for example, transferring large funds or purchasing many money orders in small amounts) must be reported to the government. This means that smaller transactions and more kinds of transactions will come under scrutiny and will require customers to give up privacy that many associate with firms in financial industries. Failure by businesses to comply with reporting these transactions can result in million dollar fines and other penalties.[10] Yet disclosure requirements where one nation (for example, the United States) requests information on transactions that took place in another nation (for example, Switzerland) is a challenge to national sovereignty (Swiss in this example) and would undoubtedly raise issues of extraterritoriality.

Antiboycott Rules

Antiboycott laws were enacted to prohibit U.S. firms from participating in foreign boycotts that the United States did not sanction. While the Arab League boycott of Israel is the principal foreign economic boycott that U.S. companies must be concerned with today, the laws apply to all boycotts imposed by foreign countries that are unsanctioned by the United States.

The oil wealth of the Arab states has given them power that they use in several ways. One way is to try to force companies that sell to lucrative markets not to have any dealings

GLOBAL MARKETING

Bribery around the World

Which nations and business sectors are most prone to bribery?

Most Likely Nations	Most Likely Sectors
Russia	Public works/ construction
China (PRC)	Arms and defense
Taiwan	Oil and gas
South Korea	Real estate/property
Italy	Telecommunications
Hong Kong and Malaysia	Power generation/ transmission
Japan and the **United States**	Mining
France	Transportation/storage
Spain	Pharmaceutical/medical
Germany and **Singapore**	Heavy manufacturing
United Kingdom	Banking and finance
Belgium and the **Netherlands**	Civilian aerospace
Canada	Forestry
Austria	Information technology (IT)
Switzerland and **Sweden**	Fishery
Australia	Light manufacturing

Most Likely Nations: In response to "How likely are companies from the following countries to pay or offer bribes to win or retain business?" Nations in bold print have ratified the OECD convention against bribery; the others have not. Countries listed together are perceived to be approximately equal in terms of bribery potential.

Most Likely Sectors: In response to "How likely is it that senior public officials would demand or accept bribes in the following business sectors?"

Notes: Interestingly, according to perceptions of "well-informed" people (*Corruptions Perception Index, 2003*), Finland, Iceland, and Denmark are the least corrupt nations; while Bangladesh, Nigeria, and Haiti are most corrupt. *The Corruption Perceptions Index* (CPI) is a composite of data from 17 organizations (including the World Economic Forum and the Economist Intelligence Unit) and 13 indexes over three years (2001–2003) and includes more than bribery. For more information on the CPI, including when and how it was developed, see the Internet Center for Corruption Research (http://www.icgg.org).

Sources: *Global Corruption Report, 2004*, Transparency International (http://www.globalcorruptionreport.org); *Bribe Payers Index 2002*, Transparency International, (http://www.transparency.org/cpi/2002/bpi2002.en.html); accessed, September 10, 2004.

with Israel. In other words, the Arabs boycott firms that sell to Israel. Because the Arab markets are much larger collectively than the Israeli market, many firms are tempted to drop the Israeli market and sell to the Arabs. This is counter to U.S. foreign policy. An example of a request to violate the antiboycott rules is provided by the BIS: "Importation of goods from Israel is strictly prohibited by Kuwait import regulations; therefore, certificate of origin covering goods originating in Israel is not acceptable."

Companies found to be violating the antiboycott regulations must desist and may be subject to civil penalties, but these penalties are often less than $10,000. There are some exceptions. Two subsidiaries of L'Oreal were fined nearly $1.5 million in 1995; and in 1993, Baxter International (medical equipment) agreed to pay a civil suit that exceeded $6 million for violating the anti-Arab boycott rules.

International Law and International Marketing

No international lawmaking body corresponds to the legislatures of sovereign nations. What then is international law? For this discussion, it is defined as "the collection of treaties, conventions, and agreements between nations that carry, more or less, the force of law." International law in this sense is quite different from national laws that have international implications, such as the U.S. antitrust laws. The international extension of U.S. law is on a unilateral basis. International law involves some mutuality, with two or more countries participating in the drafting and execution of laws or agreements.

Discussion of the impact of international law begins here with those international agreements having a general effect on international business and then addresses those dealing with more specific marketing questions. Then, the legal implications of regional groupings will be presented.

FCN, TAX, AND OTHER U.S. TREATIES

The United States also has many multilateral and bilateral treaties and agreements with other nations. Among them are the *Treaty of Friendship, Commerce and Navigation* (FCN Treaty) that the United States has entered with approximately three dozen other nations. FCN treaties cover commercial relations between two nations. They commonly identify the nature of the rights of U.S. companies to do business in those nations with which the United States has such a treaty, and vice versa. FCN treaties usually guarantee "national treatment" to the foreign subsidiary; that is, it will not be discriminated against by the nation's laws or judiciary.

Tax treaties that the United States has signed with a number of nations are also generally bilateral. The purpose of such treaties is to avoid double taxation; that is, if a company has paid income tax on its operations in a treaty nation, the United States will tax the firm's income only to the extent that the foreign tax rate is less than the U.S. rate. Thus, if the corporate income tax rates are equal in the two countries, there is no tax to pay in the United States on income earned in the other country. Obviously, tax treaty nations are, in general, better places for a subsidiary than countries that do not have such a treaty.

The Wassenaar Arrangement on Export Controls for Conventional Arms and Dual-Use Goods and Technologies is a multilateral treaty that the United States and 32 other nations have signed. The purpose of the agreement is to deny transfer of goods that could be used for military purposes and that might threaten the security of the participating nations.

Many other treaties exist between the United States and other nations. The examples provided here emphasize the need for careful evaluation of opportunities and the recognition that home rules as well as foreign regulations may have an impact on how, what, and where business is conducted.

IMF AND WTO

The IMF and the WTO were discussed in Chapter 2, but both agreements are part of the limited body of effective international law. Both agreements identify acceptable and unacceptable behavior for member nations. Their effectiveness lies in their power to apply sanctions. The IMF can withhold its services from members that act "illegally"; that is, contrary to the agreement. WTO allows injured nations to retaliate against members who have broken its rules.

International marketers are interested in the IMF and WTO because of a shared concern in the maintenance of a stable environment conducive to international trade. These firms are concerned about the IMF's ability to reduce restrictions on international finance, and they support WTO's efforts to free the international movement of goods.

The legal reach of WTO and IMF does not extend to an international marketer's behavior, but rather to the behavior of the nations to which the firm is marketing. The environment for international marketing is more dependable and less capricious because of these two organizations.

UNITED NATIONS COMMISSION ON INTERNATIONAL TRADE LAW (UNCITRAL), OECD, WORLD HEALTH ORGANIZATION (WHO), INTERNATIONAL LABOR ORGANIZATION (ILO), AND OTHER INTERNATIONAL ORGANIZATIONS

The UN, the OECD, the WHO, the ILO, and other international organizations do not have legislative rights or responsibilities over nations; but they are concerned about the behavior of firms and the impact their activities have on the economic and social well-being of the world. They also recognize that multinational businesses make a large contribution economically and socially and that an environment conducive to conducting international business is essential. To address these concerns, these bodies have developed *codes of conduct*, or guidelines, for ethically and socially responsible corporate behavior that promote the fair treatment of corporate entities. While these international bodies do not formally coordinate or consult with one another in developing these guidelines, it is safe to assume that the people in each organization do review one another's work. Emphasis should be on the word guidelines, since these do not constitute any form of international law.

Two organizations described previously focus on specific aspects of world economics—trade (the WTO) and financial stability (the IMF). The UN and the OECD take a more general perspective in the guidelines they have developed.

The UN established a United Nations Commission on International Trade Law (UNCITRAL) with a goal to "promote the adoption of new international conventions and model laws and the wider acceptance of uniform international trade terms, provisions, customs and practices."[11] With respect to the conduct of firms, UNCITRAL is concerned with the following main areas:

- International Commercial Arbitration and Conciliation
- International Sale of Goods and Related Transactions
- Cross-Border Insolvency (where the debtor has assets in more than one state)
- International Payments
- International Transport of Goods
- Electronic Commerce
- Public Procurement and Infrastructure Development

The OECD has only 30 members, but they are the home countries to nearly all of the largest multinationals and constitute the largest markets for firms' products. The *Corporate Governance Principles* were adopted by the OECD in 1999. The principles are now used as a benchmark by international financial institutions and are the focus of roundtable discussions taking place around the globe. The World Bank Group and OECD, using these principles as a framework, established the Corporate Governance Forum, the mission of which is to "assist nations to improve the standards of governance for their corporations, by fostering the spirit of enterprise and accountability, promoting fairness, transparency and responsibility."[12]

Other global bodies focus on specific topics and occasionally propose codes. Often they hold discussions on topics that, if or when legislation is adopted on a national level, have an impact on business transactions. For example, the WHO has adopted a code of conduct surrounding the marketing of infant formula that, in essence, serves as international law on the subject. The ILO has developed

international labor standards, being especially mindful of how children in the workforce are treated. The Financial Action Task Force (FATF) of the OECD has developed the FATF Forty Recommendations as the international definition of money-laundering enforcement procedures, which are designed to curtail criminal and terrorist activities.[13]

Still supportive of the concept of a code of conduct, the World Bank launched a somewhat different program in 2000 called Corporate Social Responsibility and Sustainable Competitiveness, under which is the CSR for Future Leaders Program, which is aimed at young future entrepreneurs. The goal of these World Bank programs is to promote the idea that corporate social responsibility is a vital component of an effective corporate strategy.

STANDARDS ORGANIZATIONS

Numerous other international organizations have a semi-legal influence on international marketing. One group of special interest is the *International Standards Organization* (ISO). The ISO is a nongovernmental organization (NGO) that is a network of the national standards institutes of nearly 150 countries. ISO specifications are system standards about materials, products, processes, and services used in manufacturing products and supplying services. Industry groups in most of the major industrial countries participate in the work of ISO, and many firms require that their partners be ISO-certified.

Perhaps because foreign markets are relatively small compared to the domestic market, U.S. industries have been less active in the ISO than other nations. This lack of interest may be costly in the long run; the United States may find itself closed out of many markets because its products do not meet more widely accepted standards.

Other standards organizations include the International Electrotechnical Commission (IEC), which develops standards for all electrical, electronic, and related technologies. The International Telecommunications Union (ITU), which is part of the United Nations System, is the international body that assists with coordination of global telecommunications networks and services.

Differing national standards are a major hindrance to international trade. The standards developed by these organizations, while not binding, serve as a basis for national standardization and as references when drafting international tenders and contracts. It is important that firms be aware of these organizations and their standards and that firms participate in designing these standards, rather than merely reacting to regulations that eventually result.

It would also be appropriate for firms to conduct business in a manner that is consistent with the *Universal Declaration of Human Rights*, which was adopted by the UN shortly after the organization was formed. In essence, the General Assembly of the UN proposed that all must recognize that "the inherent dignity and equal and inalienable rights of all members of the human family is the foundation of freedom, justice and peace in the world."[14]

INTELLECTUAL PROPERTY (IP)

Intellectual property (IP) is created in the human mind. It includes thoughts and ideas that are turned into paintings, music, software, and architectural designs and the processes used to create products. It may be debatable whether someone "owns" an idea, and the protection of IP takes on ethical dimensions when questions such as how much an idea is worth and how long it should be protected are considered. Clearly, IP is a complicated topic that one could devote an entire semester discussing. Here, however, the concerns associated with the marketing implications of IP are what it is, why it's important, and how to protect it.

IP usually brings to mind "inventions," which are defined as "products or processes that provide a new way of doing something or that offer a solution to a problem, and which require a patent to have some protection from theft."[15] IP does include inventions, but it also refers to trademarks (branding, which includes names, marks, and characters used in identifying products and companies), industrial designs (ornamentation and aesthetic aspects of something), and geographical indications (GIs). (See "Global Marketing: GIs: Consumer Protection or Trade Barrier?")

IP is important, but it is difficult to state how much is created each year. Not only is it challenging to assign a value to IP, it is difficult to count the number of IP creations since so much of what is created is not reported or registered. Statistics on the number of applications for patents, copyrights, and other forms of protection are often used to provide an indication of the number of new inventions and other IP created each year. The International Intellectual Property Alliance, which tracks computer software, films, television programs, music, and books, conducted a study that showed that the aforementioned IP products contributed about 8 percent ($800 billion) to the U.S. GDP in 2001; they represent the fastest-growing sectors in the economy.

Why is IP protection necessary? One problem is that rather than purchase a product from the producer, many consumers merely copy the product (for example, downloading music from the Internet or copying software) or buy the product, sometimes unknowingly, from individuals who have copied the product without the permission of the IP owner and are selling unlicensed, counterfeited, or pirated copies. Lost revenue for the companies owning the IP is substantial. Estimates vary considerably, but the projected loss to businesses because of piracy is between $25 and $50 billion worldwide.[16] One study found that 92 percent of all software in China is unlicensed—with little or no enforcement of IP laws and relatively small fines and no jail time for those caught making counterfeit products![17] This is despite China's membership in the WTO.

GLOBAL MARKETING

GIs: Consumer Protection or Trade Barrier?

You may want to hurry and buy some domestic Swiss cheese, Budweiser beer, and Kraft Grated Parmesan cheese. If the WTO gets agreement among its members to adopt all of the recommended GIs, the only Swiss cheese you will be able to buy is the cheese imported from Switzerland; Budweiser will be an expensive Czech beer; and the only Parmesan cheese will come from Parma, Italy.

GIs are signs used on products that have a geographically distinctive characteristic or association and may be used by all producers in the designated area. This is different from a trademark, which only a single producer may use. Generally, GIs are applied to food or agricultural products. Examples include champagne, which comes only from the Champagne region of France; Roquefort, which is made in Roquefort, France (the rest is blue cheese); feta, which comes from certain areas in Greece; and, of course, the one and only Tuscany olive oil. Yet GIs may also be used when marketing Swiss watches, for example. Support for GIs is based in part on the belief that consumers should know where the products are produced so they are better informed and better protected from false or misleading marketing. A counterargument is that many of these terms have become synonymous with an entire product class and should be available to all. If GIs were to become regulations, they would act as trade barriers and limit competition. According to GI proponents, if a wine is referred to as "champagne," customers should be assured that it comes from the region of Champagne in France. Opponents argue

continued

Illegal as the practice may be, people have no reservations about copying a song or an article or piece of software. From a business perspective, this is not just lost revenue because it does not take into account the added liability and other costs, such as losing future sales. If someone copies a designer pair of jeans and sells them to you and they fall apart in the washing machine, who gets the returned merchandise? Not the pirate. If a pair of brakes fail on your car or the medication you take does not work, the pirate cannot be held liable because that

that common use of the term champagne *should allow its use for all sparkling wines; and if not allowed, customers would be confused by the different terms.*

The use and adherence to GIs is voluntary among WTO members, at least for now. The EU is pushing hardest for acceptance of GIs and is seeking more formal protection under the WTO Agreement on Trade-Related Aspects of Intellectual Property Rights (TRIPS).

Examples of GIs that are protected in selected countries include the following:

- *Bulgaria: Bulgarian yoghurt and Merlou from Sakar (wine)*
- *Canada: Canadian Rye Whisky, Canadian Whisky, and Vancouver Island*
- *Czech Republic: Pilsen and Budweis (beers)*
- *EU: Champagne, Sherry, Porto, Chianti, and Moselle Luxembourgeoise (wines)*
- *Hungary: Eger (wine) and Szatmar (plum)*
- *Slovak Republic: Modranská majolika (hand-painted pottery)*
- *United States: Idaho (potatoes and onions), Real California Cheese, and Napa Valley Reserve (still and sparkling wines)*
- *Other products: Newcastle brown ale, Kentish ale, Scottish beef, Scotch Whisky, Irish Whiskey, Jersey Royal potatoes, Cornish clotted cream, Roquefort, Gorgonzola, Olive de Kalamata, Opperdoezer Ronde, Danablu, Lübecker Marzipan, and Coquille Saint-Jacques des Côtes-d'Amour*

Sources: The World Intellectual Property Organization (WIPO), "What is a geographical indication?" (http://www.wipo.int/about-ip/en/about_geographical_ind.html); accessed, November 27, 2002; "What are Geographical Indications?" Slide Show (http://www.wto.org/english/thewto_e/whatis_e/eol/e/wto07/wto7_19.htm); "Discussion develops on geographical indication" WTO News Release, TRIPS Council 1–2 December 1998 (http://www.wto.org/english/news_e/news98_e/pu_e.htm).

individual is not identified. But the person making the repairs to your car, the pharmacist, and the owner of the IP can be, and often are, held liable. Consumers may also lose confidence (or blame) the IP holder for shoddy products and not return to make purchases in the future.

Perhaps most serious of all is that when the owners of IP are not paid for their inventions and other creations, they have little incentive to invest more time, effort, and money into creating and commercializing other new ideas. In the end, the consumer has fewer choices. That may not be so important when it comes to the latest video games or style of automobile; but it may be an issue for, say, the development of a cure for a deadly disease.

INTELLECTUAL PROPERTY PROTECTION (IPP)

IP without **intellectual property protection (IPP)** is not worth much because others could take and use a product and there would be no need to compensate the inventor. Registration of trademarks and patents are common methods used to protect a firm's IP. The U.S. Patent and Trademark Office (USPTO) tracks information on applications filed in the United States and makes this information available, as do other national agencies in other countries. The USPTO granted its six millionth patent in 1999 (granted to 3Com Corporation for its HotSync Technology) and in 2003 received over 350,000 patent and nearly 270,000 trademark applications.[18] The *World Intellectual Property Organization* (WIPO) and other international organizations provide similar data. Most patents, trademarks, and copyrights are granted to companies and individuals in developed countries. For example, of the 9.4 million patent applications recorded in 2000, the five countries with the most applications were Japan (486,000), the United States (332,000), Germany (263,000), the United Kingdom (233,000), and Sweden (205,000), accounting for 16 percent of all patent applications.[19] The importance of protection can be seen in "Global Marketing: Pirates at Large."

Patent and Trademark Protection Systems

Many firms have patented and trademarked products to sell. When selling outside their home market, they want to protect their intellectual rights in those markets as well. Generally, applications for patents and trademarks must be filed separately in whatever country the firm wants protection. This can be a time-consuming and expensive process.

Because of the expense and inconvenience of applying for patents and trademarks in multiple countries, various efforts have been made to develop a multilateral approach. The main feature is a simplified application system, which can be a major convenience for firms wanting protection in many countries, although individual national filing fees generally must still be paid. The benefit is the elimination of duplicate procedures. Developing countries will tend to accept the preliminary search and evaluation findings of industrialized countries.

Several efforts include global and regional agreements and conventions that are designed to eliminate some duplication in applying for IPP. There are also some multinational bodies whose mission encompasses IPP.

The most significant of the conventions is the Paris Union (officially called the Paris Convention for the Protection of Industrial Property) because of the broad scope of protection and the number of contracting member nations. The Paris Union includes 164 nations and allows a six-month protection period in the case of trademarks and a one-year period for patents. That is, registration of a trademark in one member country gives the firm six months in which to register in other member countries before it loses its protection in those countries. There are many other conventions, such as the Berne Convention that focuses on Literary and Artistic Works and currently has 149 members.

Another important convention is the Madrid Agreement Concerning the International Registration of Marks, or simply the Madrid Agreement (not to be confused with the Madrid Agreement for the Repression of False or Deceptive Indications of Source on Goods, which was signed in 1994). This treaty, originally signed in Madrid in 1891, focuses on trademark registration and protection among the 70 member nations.

In addition, the Patent Cooperation Treaty (or International Patent Cooperation Union) signed in Washington, D.C., in 1970 is a cooperative union for the filing of applications for the protection of inventions among 120 member nations. WIPO reported that over 100,000 patent applications were filed under the Patent Cooperation Treaty in 2003—39,250 applications (or 36 percent) coming from the United States, 16,774 (15.2 percent) coming from Japan, and 13,979 (12.7 percent) coming from Germany. The number of patents filed under this treaty indicates its popularity and nations' belief in the enforcement of IPP when disputes arise, as specified in the treaty. International protection of IP is critical for the expansion of world trade and investment.

There are many other conventions and agreements, the goal of which is to bring some order to IPP. WIPO is an agency of the UN, which coordinates the protection of IP on a global scale through information services and administration of many of the international IPP conventions. The mission of WIPO is "the maintenance and further development of the respect of intellectual property throughout the world" and "that the acquisition of the protection and its enforcement should be simpler, cheaper, and more secure."[20] This must be balanced with the needs of developing nations, though. Because the vast majority of patents originate in industrialized countries, less developed nations argue that for them, patents mean high prices for products, import monopolies rather than local manufacturing, and high royalty payments for the use of patents. Those nations are expected to attempt to change the patent system to give them less expensive access to technology.

The WTO, within its TRIPs agreement, contains a Most-Favored Nation (MFN) clause regarding trademark registration. This agreement includes WTO members, some of which are not Paris Union members, thereby extending protection to other nations.

Regional counterparts provide similar protection, registration, and information. The European Patent Office (which

Pirates at Large

*P*iracy on the high seas still takes place, as indicated by the International Chamber of Commerce (ICC) headlines "Pirates Attacks Against Ships Increase" and "Shipping Warned to Steer Clear of Pirated-Infested Somali Coast." This type of piracy, which involves boarding a vessel, stealing the multimillion-dollar cargo, and sometimes killing the crew, is a serious commercial risk. However, another type of piracy involves the illegal copying of trademarks and the manufacturing of fake products for resale.

Many companies fall victim to piracy of IP and counterfeiting of their products. With over 1 billion people, China is an attractive market for companies, but it is also a market in which a large percentage of trademarked goods are counterfeited. Procter & Gamble estimates that 15 percent of its soaps and detergents bearing the brand names Tide, Head & Shoulders, and Vidal Sassoon that are sold in China are fake (cost: $150 million per year). For Gillette, the situation is even worse—as many as 25 percent of all Gillette razors, Duracell batteries, and Parker pens are bogus. One raid in the Chinese district of Yiwu netted 4 million fake razors. The following week the distributors were back selling more. Anheuser-Busch representatives walked into a store to make an initial sales call only to find their beer on the shelves—identical in package, but not in taste. Converse shoes had millions of loyal followers in Brazil; the problem was that Footwear Acquisition (the owner

continued

includes the EU members and other European nations) and the Office for Harmonization in the Internal Market (which provides a single system for trademark registration throughout the EU, called Community Trade Mark—CTM) are European examples. The Inter-American Convention for Trademarks and Commercial Protection (also known as the Pan-American Convention) and the Buenos Aries Convention for the Protection of Trade Marks and Commercial Names are examples in the Western Hemisphere.

When marketing products abroad, firms must pay attention to IPP and the agencies and conventions that provide assistance and information. The most interesting question in brand and trademark protection concerns the countries that are not members of one of these arrangements.

of the Converse name and shoe style) wasn't selling the shoes—they were all fakes. Pirates of Microsoft software have become so sophisticated that even experts have a difficult time telling what is real from what is fake. (The counterfeiters use a million-dollar machine to copy the CDs and have figured out how to duplicate the holograms used as an antitheft device.)

Yamaha, recognizing the enormous potential in the Chinese market, entered into a joint venture with a state-owned motorbike manufacturer, investing $93 million to update three plants. Not only was the excess plant capacity used to produce copies of the Yamaha motorbikes, the latest engine technology used in new products quickly showed up in the products of Yamaha's competitors. Yamaha suspected that its Chinese partners were selling the technology. It is believed that as many as five of every six "Yamaha" motorbikes in China is a fake.

There are thousands of examples of piracy. All one needs to do is walk down a crowded city block in any part of the world, where he or she is likely to see peddlers selling "Rolex" watches, "Kate Spade" handbags, and videos or DVDs of new movie releases. Piracy is a serious problem with potentially serious consequences beyond lost income. The ICC has reported on fake eyedrops that contained untreated tap water rather than sterile solution and contraceptive pills made from flour. According to the WHO, 10 percent of all pharmaceuticals are fake and may contain harmful ingredients or little or no medication at all.

Sources: "New Service Will Help Firms Fight Fake Drugs," International Chamber of Commerce (http://www.iccwbo.org/home/news_archives/2002/stories/drugs.asp); accessed November 26, 2002; International Chamber of Commerce web site (http://www.iccwbo.org); "China's Piracy Plague," *Business Week*, June 5, 2000, pages 44–48; "In Wooing Brazil's Teens, Converse Has Big Shoes to Fill," *Wall Street Journal*, July 18, 2002, pages B1–B2.

REGIONAL GROUPINGS AND INTERNATIONAL LAW

Many nations have felt the need for larger market groupings to accelerate their economic growth. Such regional groupings have developed on all continents. What each grouping has found, however, is that economic integration alone is not sufficient without some international legal agreement. Initially, this takes the form of a treaty that establishes the regional grouping. Inevitably, however, as integration proceeds, further legal agreements are necessary. In this way, the body of international (regional) law grows. Because these groupings are primarily economic alliances, the international law that develops relates primarily to economic and business questions. Therefore, regional groupings provide a development of international law that is of interest to multinational companies.

The EU Example

The basic laws of the EU are contained in the Treaty of Rome. Under this international law, the member countries succeeded in forming a customs union and harmonizing certain economic regulations. The Single European Act (SEA) of 1985 and the Treaty on European Union (or Maastricht Treaty) in 1992 considerably expanded the EU's law-making ability. Adoption of a common currency among most EU members in 2002 makes foreign exchange easier and less risky in Europe. But it also has far-reaching monetary and fiscal policy implications. This, in turn, has an impact on laws governing the banking industry. Furthermore, the ten new members that joined the EU in 2004 will adopt EU laws. Business and marketing in the EU will largely be governed by the new international laws rather than by national laws of the member countries.

An example of the impact of European law is when Japanese video games maker Nintendo and seven of its distributors were fined 167.8 million for colluding in an attempt to control market prices of video games. The rejection of GE's bid to merge with Honeywell in 2001 is another instance of the substantial impact of EU laws, though GE later pulled out of the deal. Note that references in both cases are to laws and a court with jurisdiction across EU member nations.

Reinforcing the strength of international law in the EU is the European Court of Justice, which is more effective in dealing with supranational legal questions than the famous World Court in The Hague.

Experience Elsewhere

The EU has, by far, made the most progress of all of the regional groupings. This is especially true in the area of regional law. The CACM made great strides in its early years, even proposing a monetary union similar to the EU adoption of the euro. CACM was unable to achieve many of its goals because of disagreements among members and became stagnant between 1969 and 1990. Since 1991, CACM has discussed the possibility of joining other economic groups in the area, including the North American free trade area. The idea is to enlarge the community into a more effective, more economically diverse group. None of these initiatives has gotten much further than the discussion stage, however.

Mercosur and the Andean Community are examples of other regional groupings in the Western Hemisphere. While they, too, made progress in their early years, the members had difficulty achieving the groups' economic and trade goals.

NAFTA continues to make hesitant strides to freer trade. Proposed changes in U.S. laws are always underway to strengthen, or at times counteract, NAFTA goals. One initiative would allow Mexican trucks on American roads, which had been banned because of safety and pollution concerns (shipments had to be transferred to U.S. carriers at the border). Another recent proposal was the elimination of all tariffs on imported manufactured goods by the year 2015. Those changes will have an impact on laws in the other member nations as well.

In Asia, ASEAN has also made halting steps toward freer trade and harmonization of laws. The Asian crisis in the mid-1990s hit ASEAN heavily, of course, but it continued to add new members (Vietnam in 1995, Myanmar and Laos in 1997, and Cambodia in 1999). Members are also cooperating in the building of a trans-ASEAN transportation network for road, air, and sea traffic; the coordination of telecommunication networks to increase compatibility; and the beginning stages of trans-ASEAN power grid and gas pipeline projects.

Coordination of economic and social goals among nations means that the laws of the members will overlap. In some cases (as within the EU), they may be administered by a central body. Similar laws, coordination, and cooperation across national boundaries have an impact on how products are marketed in every part of the world.

THE WORLD OF INTERNATIONAL LAW

The body of international law is small compared to domestic law. Nevertheless, examples of international law and the ways it can impinge on international marketing have been presented. International law, whether regional or global, is the growth area in the legal environment of international marketing.

Because agreement is easier to obtain with a small number of countries, regional law grows faster than other international law. International law generally facilitates international trade. When a change in law is unfavorable, however, firms want to be informed about the change so they can optimize performance within the new constraints.

International marketers need to scrutinize two other areas of international law. One is the codes of conduct developed by international groups already mentioned. While these guidelines are not binding and cannot be strictly considered international law, they are often used to steer national and, in the case of the EU, regional legislative activities.

The second development affecting the internationalization of law is the increasing cooperation between countries with regard to legal matters. As one example, Britain and the United States have a treaty spelling out situations in which judgments of the courts of one country are enforced in the courts of the other country. Most commercial disputes will be covered. Broader than that treaty is the informal cooperation between regulators in different countries. Regulators visit various countries and exchange information in the formulation of new regulations concerning business. In the antitrust area, there have been exchanges of personnel between the United States and the EU.

Legal cooperation exists among industrialized countries. Nations work together in UNCITRAL, WIPO, OECD, and the World Bank, where mechanisms exist for the exchange of information about multinationals. The rapid transplantation of regulatory initiatives from one country to another means that companies can no longer deal with regulations on a country-by-country basis, but must devise coordinated strategies.

Foreign Laws and International Marketing

U.S. laws play a ubiquitous role in U.S. business practices. The laws of other nations play a similar role with regard to the activities of businesses within their boundaries. The importance of foreign laws to a marketer lies primarily in domestic marketing in each foreign market. Problems arise when the laws in each market are somewhat different from those in every other market.

DIFFERING LEGAL SYSTEMS

Before considering national peculiarities in marketing law, a brief discussion of the predominant legal systems that underlie individual national law is in order. Legal systems are most often based on common law, civil or code law, or Islamic traditions. When categorizing nations, one must exercise care because many nations are best classified as a mixture of one or more types of legal systems. For example, Quebec province uses both civil and common law traditions, while in Nigeria, Islamic law is applied in the northern, predominantly Muslim areas, but common law is used in other parts of the country.

Common law is English in origin and is found in the United States and other countries that have had a strong English influence, usually a previous colonial tie (about 40 nations). Common law, often called "case law," is tradition-oriented; that is, the interpretation of what the law means on a given subject is heavily influenced by previous court decisions as well as by usage and custom. If there is no specific legal precedent or statute, common law requires a court decision. To understand the law in a common law country, one must study the previous court decisions in matters of similar circumstance, as well as the statutes.

Civil or **code law** is based on an extensive and, presumably, comprehensive set of laws organized by subject matter into a code. The intention in civil law countries is to spell out the law on all possible legal questions rather than rely on precedent or court interpretation. The "letter of the law" is very important in code law countries. However, this need to be all-inclusive may lead to some rather general and elastic provisions, permitting application to many sets of facts and circumstances. Because code law countries do not rely on previous court decisions, various applications of the same law may yield different interpretations. This can lead to some uncertainty for a marketer.

Code law is a legacy of Roman law. It is predominant in Europe and in nations of the world that have not had close ties to England. Thus, code law nations are more numerous than common law nations. Many civil code systems are influenced by the French, German, and Spanish systems because of previous colonial or other relationships. For example, the German code has had an influence on the Teutonic and Scandinavian countries. There are about 90 civil law countries.

Islamic law represents the third major legal system. About 35 countries follow Islamic law in varying degrees, usually mixed with civil, common, and/or indigenous law. The Islamic resurgence in recent years has led many countries to give Islamic law, Shari'a, a more prominent role. Shari'a governs all aspects of life in areas where it is the dominant legal system, as in Saudi Arabia. Rules not defined by Shari'a are decided by government regulations and Islamic judges. Although it has harsh penalties for adultery and theft, Islamic law is not dramatically different from other legal systems with regard to business. In Saudi Arabia, for example, the Committee for Settlement of Commercial Disputes operates in a manner that would not be uncongenial to a Westerner.

The differences in legal systems are important to international marketers. They must study the legal systems and seek appropriate local legal advice when necessary. The following section merely alerts the marketer to some of the variations in legal systems abroad.[21]

FOREIGN LAWS AND THE MARKETING MIX

Anyone who is familiar with regulations in the United States will not be surprised at the range of laws affecting marketing in other nations, although he or she may be surprised at the lack of regulation in some less developed countries.

There are also laws about taxes on Internet sales, royalty payments for downloading songs and software, privacy, what marketers may or may not do with the information they gather, protection of minors, use of screening or blocking software, and a host of other concerns that were unheard of ten years ago. While the Internet and e-commerce advancements have opened a broad spectrum of opportunities for businesses (and individuals), many new legal and ethical issues must be addressed (and see chapter 6). Discussions about these issues highlight the differences in how they are viewed from country to country. For example, privacy laws in the United States and the EU are quite different and clearly show that some subjects are long-standing and culturally related. These differences make it more difficult to come to an international agreement about how to treat the issues.

Instead of presenting a catalog of foreign laws, the following material deals with how laws influence the four Ps

GLOBAL MARKETING

Pirates at Large To Fight the Pirates

Holograms were an early high-tech solution used to prevent piracy and counterfeiting. They appeared on credit cards, CD and DVD packages, and on some currencies (the euro paper money). Now, though, the machines used to produce the prototypes have fallen in price to about $2,500—well within the reach of serious counterfeiters.

New high-tech solutions are being developed to combat piracy, though. An Israeli firm, Bsecure (formerly Pitkit Technologies), offers a variety of products that can tell what is genuine and what is fake. The company manufactures inks that contain signature chemicals, microwires thinner than a human hair, and unique polymers with embedded codes used to coat identification badges and packaging—all of which can be detected with special scanners to make sure the products are genuine. Bsecure also makes tamperproof packaging substances that prevent counterfeiters from opening product packages and substituting imitations. Bsecure's clients include New Balance Athletic Shoe, Inc.; Intel; Seagram's; and the motor vehicle departments in Israel and Belarus.

Wal-Mart and Procter & Gamble have been investigating radio-frequency identification (RFID) tags, currently used by Mobil in their Speedpass program and the E-ZPass toll system. The idea is to track shipments more closely and ensure arrival of genuine goods by putting small RFID tags in product cases. The problem is cost. The price of the microchips would have to fall to 5 cents or less to make them a cost-effective option.

Mention "Los Alamos" and many people think of the atom bomb, first developed and tested in the United States in this remote part of New Mexico. It was also the home of Isotag, manufacturer of nanotechnology isotags. These unique and identifiable single molecules can be added to a variety of products (including cosmetics, gasoline, and pharmaceuticals) to help firms distinguish real from counterfeit. (Isotag merged with other firms to form Authentix, a company that specializes in technologies designed to combat counterfeiting and piracy.) Scanned products that do not contain the isotags can be

continued

removed from store shelves—and possibly traced to their source so the pirates can be caught. What's the best part? Isotags cost less than 1 cent per unit.

There are other product defense techniques: ink that becomes visible when copied (the word counterfeit appears), tamper-evident glue, self-destruct technologies for sound and video recordings, and activation and deactivation codes for software.

Bsecure estimates that the amount of counterfeit products sold annually totals $1 trillion. While the market for products to defend against piracy was only about $24 billion in 2002, it is growing by 16 percent per year.

Sources: "Forgery Fighters," *Jerusalem Report*, October 7, 2002, page 36; "Tech Goes Undercover," Optimize, November 1, 2002, page 15; "Beam Me Up Some Ivory Soap," *Fast Forward*, October 2002, Issue 12 (http://www.optimizemag.com/issue/012/fast.htm); accessed December 6, 2002; Authentix site (http://www.authentix.com); accessed February 26, 2005.

of marketing; that is, product, price, place (distribution), and promotion. The treatment is brief and suggestive of the problem areas. A more extensive study is in order when considering a specific market. For example, Japan has more than 10,000 laws to regulate business.

Product

If **product** is everything the consumer receives when making a purchase, the international marketer will find many regulations affecting it. The physical and chemical aspects of a product are affected by laws designed to protect national consumers with respect to its purity, safety, and performance. As the thalidomide tragedy showed, nations differ as to strictness of their controls. The Food and Drug Administration (FDA) had not cleared the drug for sale in the United States; but many deformed babies were born in Europe, where it was legal.

In a similar vein, European manufacturers were disturbed by U.S. safety requirements for automobiles, which had to be modified to meet the needs of one market. Because the U.S. market is large, the adaptation was not as serious as that needed to meet the peculiar requirements of a small market. There are exceptions. The EU ban on hormone-treated beef effectively closed the market of over 375 million people to American cattle ranchers. American farmers rely on hormone treatments to get their cattle to market quicker and cheaper than producers in other countries and, therefore, have been unwilling to change their husbandry practices. This example highlights what fre-

quently appears to be the protectionist use of these laws. Although consumers should be protected, different safety requirements are not necessary for consumers of every country. By maintaining different standards, nations imply that consumers in other countries are not being adequately protected. One reason nations often persist in demanding particular legal requirements is to protect their own producers. For example, Britain kept French milk out of the country by requiring it to be sold in pints rather than metric measures. German noise standards kept British lawn mowers off German lawns.

Fortunately, in the late nineties, the United States and the EU drafted an agreement to accept each other's standards for a wide range of products. This Mutual Recognition Agreement will save millions of dollars on both sides of the Atlantic. Automobiles were not included, and the FDA retained its control over pharmaceuticals.

China now has a product liability law to protect its consumers. Some, unfortunately, have used the law to target foreign companies. Procter & Gamble was sued by a woman who said its shampoo melted her hair. It turned out the shampoo was counterfeit.

Labeling is subject to more legal requirements than packaging. Labeling items that are covered include (1) the name of the product; (2) the name of the producer or distributor; (3) a description of the ingredients or use of the product; (4) the weight, either net or gross; and (5) the country of origin. As to warranty, a marketer has relative freedom to formulate a warranty in all countries.

Brand names and trademarks also face different national requirements. Most nations are members of the Paris Union or some other trademark convention, which ensures a measure of international uniformity. However, differences exist between code law countries (ownership by priority in registration of a brand) and common law countries (ownership by priority in use) in their treatment of a brand or trademark.

Cybersquatting—registering domain names and not using them—is a common practice, especially with the release of new extensions such as .biz, .name, and .info. Companies around the world are fighting over Internet addresses and domain names. WIPO arbitrates and provides details of many of these disputes, one of which was the use of the address HardRockCasinos.com. The case was brought by Hard Rock Café International (USA) against WW Processing, "an entity of unknown legal status, with headquarters in Nevis, Saint Kitts and Nevis," which had already registered the domain. There were many issues in the case. One deciding factor was the fact that Hard Rock Café owned the name "Hard Rock Casino" and had been using it in other business activities, while the respondent, WW Processing, had not been using the name or the Internet address. ("Neither Respondent nor its predecessors-in-interest is making or made a legitimate non-commercial or fair use of the disputed domain name.") In April 2002, WIPO ordered that the domain name be transferred to Hard Rock Café International.[22]

Other recent cases have involved well-known names and companies such as Toyota, Intel, Air France, Coca-Cola, Playboy, and Victoria's Secret.

Pricing

Price controls are pervasive in the world economy. **Resale price maintenance (RPM)** is a common law relating to pricing. Many nations have some legal provisions for RPM, but with numerous variations. Another variable is the fact that some countries allow price agreements among competitors.

Another law in many nations is that of government price control. The price controls may be economy-wide or limited to certain sectors. For example, France has had a number of economy-wide price freezes. At the other extreme, Japan controls the price on only one commodity—rice. Generally, price controls are limited to "essential" goods, such as foodstuffs. The pharmaceutical industry is one of the most frequently controlled, sometimes taking the form of controlled profit margins.

For example, at one time, Ghana set manufacturers' margins at between 25 and 40 percent, depending on the industry. Argentina allowed a standard 11 percent "profit" on pharmaceuticals, whereas Belgium fixed maximum prices and wholesale and retail margins on pharmaceuticals. Germany did not set margins but had an obligatory price register, making prices and margins available for public scrutiny. In 1998, China introduced price controls on pharmaceuticals, cutting prices of imported and joint venture-produced drugs by over 20 percent. The pricing formula restricted profit margins.

Two other pricing issues that firms face are dumping and transfer pricing. **Dumping** occurs when a firm sells products below the cost of manufacture or when it sells products for a lower price abroad than at home. The basis for the latter is that selling internationally costs more because of added risks, additional transportation and distribution costs, and numerous other factors. The nation being subjected to dumping often applies antidumping or countervailing duties to raise the price of imports to more closely match the domestically made products. Typically, the cases are brought by developed nations (such as the United States) against developing nation manufacturers (China, for instance) who have access to cheap labor. But developing nations have also charged developed nation producers with dumping, such as the steel manufacturers in India who claimed that South Africa, the EU, and Australia were dumping steel products in their country.[23]

There is also the issue of **transfer pricing**, the price at which intercompany transfers take place. Governments are vigilant about these transfers and do what they can to curtail tax avoidance strategies that involve transfer pricing. A recent case was that of British Petroleum, which was charged with taking excessive profits from its operations in Russia via transfer pricing.[24]

Distribution

Distribution is an area in which an international marketer has fewer constraints. A firm has a high degree of freedom in choosing distribution channels from among those available in the market. Of course, one cannot choose channels that are not available. For example, France had a specific prohibition against door-to-door selling, but the Singer Company received a special exemption from this law. One major question is the legality of exclusive distribution. Fortunately, this option is allowed in most markets. In fact, the strongest legal constraint does not apply to firms managing their own distribution in foreign markets, but rather to exporters who are selling through distributors or agents.

Careful selection of an agent or a distributor is critical for two reasons. First, the quality of the distributor helps determine a firm's success in the market. Second, the contract with the distributor may bind the exporter to a commitment that is difficult and costly to terminate. The challenge for the exporter is to be aware of national laws concerning distributor contracts in order to avoid potential problems. It is much easier to enter an agency agreement than to end one. (See "Global Marketing: Distributor Divorce: Including an Escape Clause.")

Promotion

Advertising is one of the more controversial elements of marketing; and it tends to be subject to more control than product, price, and distribution. Most nations have some law regulating advertising, and advertising groups in many nations have self-regulatory codes. Advertising regulation takes several forms. One pertains to the message and its truthfulness. In Germany, for example, it is difficult to use comparative advertising and the words *better* or *best*. In Argentina, advertising for pharmaceuticals must have prior approval of the Ministry of Public Health. Even China brought foreign firms to court over their advertising claims under its new law.

Another form of restriction relates to control over the advertising of certain products. For example, Britain allows no cigarette or liquor advertising on television. Finland is more restrictive and allows no newspaper or television advertising of political organizations, religious messages, alcohol, undertakers, diet drugs, immoral literature, or intimate preparations. Another restriction is through the taxation of advertising. For example, Peru once implemented an 8 percent tax on outdoor advertising; Spain taxed cinema advertising.

Some markets institute greater restrictions on sales promotion techniques than what is found in the United States. In the United States, there is often no constraint on contests, deals, premiums, and other sales promotion gimmicks. The situation is quite different in other countries. As a general rule, participation in contests must not be predicated on purchase of the product. Premiums may be restricted with regard to size, value, and nature. A premium may be limited to a certain fraction of the value of the purchase and may be required to relate to the product it promotes; that is, steak knives cannot be used as a premium with soap or a towel with a food product. Free introductory samples may be restricted to one-time use of the product rather than a week's supply. In the infant formula controversy, sampling was completely forbidden. Variations are great; but in most cases, the U.S. marketer is more limited in host countries than at home.

ENFORCEMENT OF THE LAWS

A firm needs to know how foreign laws will affect its operations in a market. It is not sufficient to know only the laws; a firm must also know how the laws are enforced. Most nations have laws that have been forgotten and are not enforced. Other laws may be enforced haphazardly, and still others may be strictly enforced.

An important aspect of enforcement is the degree of impartiality of justice. Does a foreign subsidiary have as good a standing before the law as a national company? Courts have been known to favor national firms over foreign subsidiaries. In such cases, biased enforcement means that a law is interpreted one way for the foreigner and another way for a national. Knowledge of such discrimination is helpful in evaluating the legal climate.

The Firm in the International Legal Environment

Firms that have little experience with international transactions may not realize that there may be little recourse when another party in a contract does not pay for goods or services received, the product received is defective, or the service is not up to agreed-upon standards. Whatever the resolution of a contracted dispute, the time it takes to reach that point is often much longer and more costly than expected.

WHOSE LAW? WHOSE COURTS?

Domestic laws govern marketing within a country. Questions of the appropriate law and the appropriate courts may arise, however, in cases involving international marketing. As noted, few international laws apply to international marketing disputes. Nor is there an international court in which to try them, except for the European Court of Justice for the EU.

When commercial disputes arise between principals of two different nations, each would probably prefer to

Distributor Divorce: Including an Escape Clause

Escape clauses are designed to protect the parties of an agreement in the event a disagreement or circumstance arises that prevents completion to the expectations of those involved. In the case of hiring sales representatives in other countries, the desire to get out of a contract is most commonly due to the salesperson not meeting the company's goals. The U.S. Department of Commerce and an American export compliance firm, Unz & Co., have formulated some advice about sales representative agreements.

In international contracts, escape clauses may be limited by local laws, regardless of what the parties agreed to, whether verbal or written. Therefore, one should learn as much as possible about appropriate commercial laws and seek local legal advice. When talking to a lawyer, one should consider asking the following questions:

• What is the required advance notice for termination? (possibly 180 days or more)

continued

have the matter judged in its own national courts under its own laws. By the time the dispute has arisen, however, the question of jurisdiction has usually already been settled by one means or another. One way to decide the issue beforehand is by inserting a jurisdictional clause in a contract. Then, when the contract is signed, each party agrees that the laws of a particular nation (or state in the case of the United States) govern the content of the contract.

If the parties do not have a prior agreement as to jurisdiction, the courts in which the appeal is made decide the issue. One alternative is to apply the laws of the nation in which the contract was signed. Another is to use the laws of the country where contract performance occurs. In one of those ways, the issue of which nation's laws shall govern is already out of the company's hands when a dispute arises. Most companies prefer to make that decision themselves. Therefore, they insert a jurisdictional clause into the contract, choosing the more favorable jurisdiction. Of course, the choice of jurisdiction must be acceptable to both parties.

The decision as to which nation's courts will try the case depends on who is suing whom. The issue of which

- *What are justifiable reasons for termination? (Not meeting a sales objective may be insufficient grounds.)*
- *What compensation is due on termination? (Cost can be substantial, including lost potential sales.)*
- *In what language are contracts to be written? (Careful translation is a necessity.)*
- *Whose laws apply? (Even with a written contract, some nations do not allow the salesperson [or the firm] to waive the nation's jurisdiction.)*
- *Is the representative to be referred to as an agent? (In some instance, "agent" implies power of attorney and more authority than desirable.)*
- *What happens to proprietary property upon termination (including sales records, customer data, patents, trademarks, and similar materials)?*
- *Are the host country laws in conflict with home country laws? (Sales exclusivity, labeling, and other components may be in violation of antitrust regulations, antiboycott laws, or other home country regulations.)*

Source: *A Basic Guide to Exporting*, 1998, prepared by the U.S. Department of Commerce with the assistance of Unz & Co., Inc. (http://www.unzco.com/basicguide/c4.html#negotiating); a more recent counterpart is the *Exporting Guide* produced by Team Canada, Inc. (http://exportsource.ca/gol/exportsource/interface.nsf/engdocBasic/0.html) or the *Export Programs Guide*, published by the U.S. Department of Commerce, International Trade Administration.

courts have jurisdiction is separate from the issue of which nation's laws are applied. Suits are brought in the courts of the country of the person being sued. For example, a U.S. company might sue a French firm in France. This kind of event often leads to the situation in which a court in one country tries a case according to the laws of another country; that is, a French court may apply the laws of New York State. This would happen if the parties had included a jurisdictional clause stating that the laws of New York State govern; it would also happen if the French court decided that the laws of New York State were applicable for one of the other reasons mentioned.

Some U.S. laws have a particularly long reach. Corporate fraud and embezzlement of millions, sometimes billions, of dollars by executives at Enron, Tyco, WorldCom, Allegheny Health System, and others led to new corporate reporting and personal liability laws in the United States. Those laws apply to all publicly traded firms, even those whose headquarters are in other nations. This means that foreign firms listed on the New York Stock Exchange must also comply. The European governments and companies

are asking that they be subject to looser rules; but so far, the Securities and Exchange Commission (SEC) is standing firm. The Japanese, on the other hand, are less concerned since some of their laws are similar and since they, too, went through recent fraud cases involving giants such as Mitsui and the Tokyo Electric Company.

The Economic Espionage Act of 1996, designed to protect trade secrets, is far-reaching in that it applies to the theft of trade secrets or corporate espionage by U.S., as well as non-U.S. individuals or entities, and that "the district courts of the United States shall have jurisdiction of civil actions." Penalties may include fines of $500,000 and jail sentences of 15 years.[25]

ARBITRATION OR LITIGATION?

An international marketer must be knowledgeable about laws and contracts. Contracts identify two things: (1) the responsibilities of each party and (2) the legal recourse to obtain satisfaction. Actually, however, international marketers consider litigation a last resort and prefer to settle disputes in some other way. For several reasons, litigation is considered a poor way of settling disputes with foreign parties. Litigation usually involves long delays, during which time inventories may be tied up and trade halted. Further, it is costly—not only in money, but also in customer goodwill and public relations. Firms also frequently fear discrimination in a foreign court. Thus, litigation is seen as an unattractive alternative, to be used only when all else fails.

More peaceful ways to settle international commercial disputes are offered by conciliation, mediation, and arbitration. Conciliation and mediation are informal attempts to bring the parties to an agreement. They are attractive, voluntary approaches to the settlement of disputes. If they fail, however, stronger measures (such as arbitration and litigation) are needed. Because of the drawbacks of litigation, arbitration is used extensively in international commerce.

Litigation costs are high, particularly in the United States, which is a litigious society (suing someone is a common way to resolve disputes). The *American Arbitration Association* (AAA) provides alternatives; it administered over 200,000 cases in 2001 via mediation, arbitration, and less formal *alternate dispute resolution* (ADR) formats. While the AAA claims to be the largest full-service ADR provider, other agencies in the United States, such as the Better Business Bureau (BBB), handle a large number of arbitration cases as well. The savings to the U.S. court system and to the parties involved in the disputes are incalculable.[26]

Arbitration generally overcomes the disadvantages of litigation. Decisions tend to be faster and cheaper. Arbitration is less damaging to goodwill because of the secrecy of the proceedings and its less hostile nature. This means that the climate for conciliation is better so that almost one-third of the cases are settled in direct talks before the judgment stage is reached. Decisions are more equitable and informed because of the expertise of the arbitrators, who are not judges, but people with practical experience. Arbitration allows business to continue while the dispute is being settled. It neutralizes the differences between legal systems because decisions are not based on points of law, but on practical considerations of equity. Each party also has the satisfaction of avoiding the courts of the adversary's country.

In an increasing number of countries, including the United States, arbitration awards have the status and enforceability of court decisions. This practice is supported by the large number of arbitral awards that are upheld in courts around the world. There are even examples of cooperative international arrangements, such as the one recently reached between the AAA and the Malta Arbitration Centre for the use of ADR to resolve commercial disputes between American companies and those located throughout Europe and North Africa.[27]

The arbitration procedure is relatively straightforward. If firms want to settle disputes by arbitration, they include an arbitration clause in the contract. A common form is the one suggested by the AAA:

> Any controversy or claim arising out of or relating to this contract, or the breach thereof, shall be settled by arbitration administered by the American Arbitration Association under its Arbitration Rules, and judgment on the award rendered by the arbitrator(s) may be entered in any Court having jurisdiction thereof.

Because of its advantages, arbitration is increasingly popular for settlement of commercial disputes. A number of examples support this trend. One is from UNCITRAL, which formulated the Model Law on International Commercial Arbitration. Because of its multinational source, this law could be used to combine national arbitration rules into a single global standard.

Another development is the increase in the number of centers for hearing arbitration. The ICC in Paris is one of the leading, more well-established and well-respected centers in the world, receiving more than 500 arbitration cases every year. The ICC also supplies samples of arbitration clauses, but in a variety of languages, and allows users to access an "arbitration cost calculator" to estimate the cost of pursuing a claim. All of those resources are available on the ICC web site at http://www.iccwbo.org. Estimates are that fewer than 10 percent of the ICC decisions are challenged.

In 2001, the International Centre for Dispute Resolution (ICDR), a division of the AAA, handled over 600 cases involving 63 countries and claims in excess of $10 billion. The ICDR has cooperative arrangements with more than 50 arbitral agencies in 40 countries, including the Permanent Court of Arbitral Awards at The Hague. Many

resources and agencies for ADR are helpful in reducing the costs and other problems often associated with litigation, but the following offer a starting point.

China created its own arbitration tribunal in 1989, and Beijing is now one of the busiest arbitration centers in the world. Even with this tribunal's problems, foreign firms find it far superior to going into a Chinese court. Although it does not recognize awards of other tribunals, the AAA signed a cooperation agreement with China's International Economic and Trade Arbitration Commission in 2001. With a goal of capturing more of the large arbitration cases, in 2002, the Singapore International Arbitration Centre drastically reduced the fees it charges for its services. The management fees are lower than those charged by the arbitration associations in Stockholm, Kuala Lumpur, China, and the ICC in Paris. For example, the fee for a case involving a $10 million claim was lowered from nearly $24,000 to $14,000. The maximum fee for a case is now $25,000, versus $68,375 the previous year in Singapore.[28]

The International Centre for Settlement of Investment Disputes (ICSID), an autonomous unit of the World Bank, provides facilities for arbitration of disputes between member countries and investors of other member countries. It is especially useful when a government is a party in the dispute.

The advantages of arbitration and other forms of ADR over litigation have been emphasized. Although it is very important, arbitration should not be considered a *panacea*. Cases can take as long as two years and can cost over $100,000. (Rates vary according to the amount in dispute and the arbitral board.) Nevertheless, if disagreements do arise, arbitration is a preferred alternative to litigation.

There is another way of dealing with disputes among business partners. Rather than relying on "fixing" the problem after it occurs, businesses are taking time before a contract is signed to more carefully evaluate potential partners. This trend is supported by the findings of one study of the English court cases between 1990 and 2001. Despite a significant decline in suits, the researcher did not find a corresponding increase in arbitration, but did find that businesses took more care in establishing partner relationships initially and put more effort into resolving disputes before involving third parties. Reasons cited for more careful prearrangement assessment included the expense of litigation, but also the distraction to the businesses' personnel and the cost in terms of partner and consumer relations.[29]

E-LAW

E-commerce is not new, but it certainly becomes more pervasive every year. New opportunities and challenges face businesses and marketers, whether they are considering new methods of distribution for software, videos, and reading material; advertising using a relatively new medium (the Internet); dealing with transparent pricing; developing new products such as Internet security; or developing interactive gaming software, web site consultant services, or the Combined DNA Index System (CODIS) data management system.

E-commerce also introduces new legal issues. Marketers must deal with topics such as privacy. Also difficult to contend with are the differences between countries. For example, the United States wants to reduce privacy in order to combat terrorism (the establishment of the Directorate for Information Analysis and Infrastructure Protection), while the EU, Canada, Singapore, and other nations have enacted rules such as the Consumer Credit Directive to ensure that consumer information is carefully regulated. Fraud, spam (junk e-mail), and IP theft take place on an unprecedented scale—all made easier by the Internet. Examples of e-terrorism include the theft of customer records and subsequent threat of release unless a ransom is paid, spy software capable of snooping competitors' records, and virus attacks that destroy vital records or close web sites—all becoming much too common. Laws establishing punishments for those crimes and the way perpetrators are to be prosecuted must also cross national boundaries if they are to be effective.

Governments are particularly interested in the issue of taxation. With billions of dollars in transactions taking place on the Internet, governments are losing money because of uncollected sales tax and value-added tax (VAT). Attempts to regulate or control sales and taxes have not been successful, but the United States and the EU are at the forefront of designing and implementing new regulations. It may become the responsibility of firms such as eBay to collect the sales taxes and distribute them to the appropriate authorities.

Whether marketing products through e-mail, offering promotions on its web site, or making statements about its products, a firm's after-sales responsibilities and liability are issues being debated in the press, in courts, and in international agencies around the world.

The topics mentioned here are only a few of those likely to occupy lawmakers for years to come, but marketers must keep abreast of new developments and the regulatory impact those developments can have on marketing.

The Marketer Is Not a Lawyer

What are the implications for the international marketer of all of the legal parameters discussed in this chapter? There are methods to reduce political and legal risks, some of which were shown in Table 4-2. Hiring an expert is usually a good idea. Keep in mind however, that many lawyers do not have detailed knowledge about all of the domestic, international, and foreign legal aspects involved in international marketing. While international marketers cannot know all of the relevant laws, they do need to know what

decisions are affected by the laws. A firm can call in legal counsel when special expertise is needed. Expertise includes not only the domestic legal staff, but also legal representatives from the firm's foreign markets.

A firm's need for legal expertise is related to its international involvement. If a firm only exports or licenses, it has fewer legal needs than if it has foreign subsidiaries and joint ventures. Where it operates through licenses or distributors, these parties relieve the firm of some of its legal burden. When a firm has subsidiaries, however, it needs local legal counsel.

With the growth of international business and the proliferation of national and international regulation, the international legal function is becoming more complex. Firms need an international legal staff at headquarters and local lawyers in foreign subsidiaries. In host countries, the task will be largely decentralized because of local practices. However, some coordination and exchange of experience will be necessary to optimize performance of a firm's international legal function.

Summary

A host country's behavior is guided by its national interests, such as security, sovereignty, prestige, and economic welfare. To achieve its goals, a country uses a variety of controls over a firm, such as entry restrictions, price controls, quotas and tariffs, exchange control, and even expropriation. These national interests and controls constitute the political environment of an international firm.

A firm needs to evaluate the host country environment and assess the political risk in every country in which it enters into business transactions. Then the firm needs a plan for managing host country relations, both before and after entering the country.

An international firm often becomes involved in international relations, usually against its will. It needs to know how a given host country relates to its own country and to other nations, as well. Also, a firm's home country may restrict its international marketing activities. The United States, for example, is especially attentive to these issues.

Many U.S. laws affect U.S. firms. These laws relate to the regulation of exports and to antitrust implications of overseas ventures and even help the firms get involved in international marketing. One example is the U.S. Export Certificates of Review.

Still other U.S. laws concern the behavior of U.S. firms abroad. The FCPA prohibits bribery, and antiboycott provisions are meant to prevent U.S. firms from cooperating with the Arab boycott of Israel.

The FCN Treaty ensures that U.S. firms will not receive discriminatory treatment in a foreign legal system. UNCI-

TRAL's Convention for the International Sale of Goods facilitates the international selling task. IMF and WTO, each in its own way, help to create an environment more favorable to international marketing. ISO is creating standards for international products that a firm must incorporate into its product planning.

International patent conventions help international firms protect their most valuable IP.

Regional economic groupings, especially the EU, are writing new multicountry laws covering many aspects of business. These laws facilitate international marketing in a region.

Each foreign country has its own legal system, which is shaped by the common law, by code law, or by Muslim law tradition. These foreign laws affect all aspects of product policy, including the physical product, the package and label, the brand name, and the use of warranty.

Pricing and promotion programs are generally more strictly regulated in foreign markets than in the United States.

In cases of legal disagreements, each party usually prefers its own country's courts. A jurisdictional clause should be included in all international marketing contracts in case a problem arises. However, rather than litigate in a foreign court, many international firms prefer to settle differences by arbitration. Arbitration is often more efficient, more equitable, and less damaging to continuing relations.

E-commerce is causing lawmakers to review current laws about privacy, liability, and taxation in a new light. These regulations will have an impact on how marketers collect and use information about their consumers, what warranties they include with their products, and how they promote their products over the Internet.

Questions and Research

4.1 Explain the threefold political environment of international marketing.

4.2 Discuss the various kinds of host country controls over an international firm.

4.3 How might a firm analyze its own political vulnerability in a particular host country?

4.4 What can a firm do to help manage its host country relations?

4.5 Identify the elements of the international political environment.

4.6 Explain the foreign policy concerns with regard to U.S. export controls.

4.7 Discuss the various aspects of international marketing that can be affected by U.S. laws.

4.8 Discuss the ambivalent attitude of the U.S. government toward antitrust in international business.

4.9 Give examples of the kinds of international laws that can influence a firm's international marketing.

4.10 Explain a firm's concerns relating to international patent and trademark law.

4.11 Discuss the influence of regional groupings—especially the EU—on the development of international law.

4.12 Explain how foreign laws can affect the four Ps of marketing.

4.13 Why is arbitration preferred to litigation?

4.14 Discuss how the Internet will shape marketing regulations in the future.

Endnotes

1. "Bank Lending Rates for Exporters Drop to 15%" *Financial Gazette*, August 1, 2002.

2. "Mexican Bill Could Affect U.S. DMers," *Marketing News*, October 14, 2002, page 5.

3. Oetzel, Jennifer M., Richard A. Bettis, and Mark Zenner. "Country Risk Measures: How Risky Are They?" *Journal of World Business*, Summer 2001, Volume 36, Number 2, pages 128–145.

4. Guiding Principles of the Bureau of Industry and Security (http://www.bxa.doc.gov/ManagementTeam/BISGuiding Principles.html); accessed November 8, 2002.

5. Commerce Department Renames Agency "Bureau of Industry and Security," Bureau of Industry and Security News Release, April 18, 2002 (http://www.bxa.doc.gov/press/2002/CommerceRenamesAgencyBIS.html).

United States Department of Treasury, Export License Requirements (http://www.itds.treas.gov/licenseinfo.html); accessed November 12, 2002.

6. "Commerce Department Imposes Civil Penalty on Minnesota Firm in Settlement of Exportiolations," BIS Press Page (http://www.bxa.doc.gov/press/Archive2001/MinnFirmFined.html); accessed November 12, 2002.

"Commerce Department Imposes $2.12 Million Civil Penalty on McDonnell Douglas for Alleged Export Control Violations," BIS Press Page (http://www.bxa.doc.gov/press/Archive2001/McDonnellDouglasFined.html); accessed November 12, 2002.

"German Company Fined for Illegal Shotgun Sales," BIS Press Page (http://www.bxa.doc.gov/press/2002/GermanFirmFined. html); accessed November 12, 2002.

"New Jersey Company Pays $30,000 to Settle Charge of Illegal Exports to Iran," BIS Press Page (http://www.bxa.doc.gov/press/2002/MercatorExports2Iran.html); accessed November 12, 2002.

7. "Carnival Bid for P&O Falls Beneath Royal Caribbean," *Financial Times*, Global News Wire, July 28, 2002.

"Infineon Contacted About U.S. Probe Into Chip Makers," Financial Times, *Global News Wire*, June 20, 2000.

"European Executive Agrees to Plead Guilty for Participating in an International Antitrust Conspiracy," U.S. Department of Justice News Release, Wednesday, August 7, 2002.

"Monti Defends EU After Blocking General Electric-Honeywell Merger," *Financial Times*, July 10, 2001, page 8.

"EU Told to Reconsider Microsoft Case," *Financial Times*, Global News Wire, May 16, 2002.

"A Welfare State for Aggrieved Market Losers," *Financial Times*, Wednesday, March 24, 2004, page 17.

8. "U.S. Dam Says Bush Administration to Work on International Corporation Tax Overhaul," *AFX European Focus*, Economic News, November 14, 2002.

9. Rasmussen, C. (Economist, Office of Export Trading Company Affairs, personal communication; November 19, 2002); The Office of Export Trading Company Affairs (OETCA) web site (http://www.ita.doc.gov/td/oetca); accessed November 19, 2002.

10. Ensminger, John J. "September 11 Brings New Anti-Terrorism and Anti-Money Laundering Responsibilities to Financial Institutions," *Review of Business*, Volume 23, Number 3, Fall 2002, pages 29–34. In the United States, the agency responsible for coordinating activities among the 25 or so other federal bodies and enforcing the regulations is the Financial Crimes Enforcement Network (FinCEN).

11. United Nations Commission on International Trade Law (UNCITRAL) (http://www.uncitral.org/en-index.htm); accessed November 22, 2002.

12. Corporate Governance Forum (http://www.gcgf.org); accessed November 22, 2002.

13. Ensminger, John J. "September 11 Brings New Anti-Terrorism and Anti-Money Laundering Responsibilities to Financial Institutions," *Review of Business*, Volume 23, Number 3, Fall 2002, pages 29–34.

14. The United Nations, *Universal Declaration of Human Rights* (http://www.un.org/Overview/rights.html); accessed February 9, 2005.

15. The World Intellectual Property Organization (WIPO) (http://www.wipo.int/about-ip/en/patents.html); accessed November 26, 2002.

16. "Description of the IIPA," International Intellectual Property Alliance (IIPA) (http://www.iipa.com/aboutiipa.html); accessed November 26, 2002.

17. "High Prices Encourage Software Piracy," *Australian Financial Review*, September 4, 2002, page 52; "China Faulted for Rampant Product Piracy," *Philadelphia Inquirer*, September 17, 2004, section B, page D3.

18. United States Patent and Trademark Office (USPTO), Performance and Accountability Report: FY 2003 (http://www.uspto.gov/web/offices/com/annual/2003/index.html).

19. Calculated based on World Intellectual Property Organization (WIPO) patent application statistics for 2000—"25 Years of Industrial Property Statistics (1975–2000)" (downloaded in MS Excel format from http://www.wipo.int/ipstats/en/index.html on November 27, 2002).

20. *Yearly Review of the PCT: 2003*, World International Property Organization, 2004, pages 3–4; memorandum of the Director General, World Intellectual Property Organization (http://www.wipo.int/about-wipo/en); accessed December 1, 2002.

21. There are different classification schemes and criteria used in classifying countries' legal systems. Most sources include a number of types; but one of the more trustworthy and clear is that developed by the law faculty at the University of Ottawa (http://www.uottawa.ca/world-legal-systems), which is used here.

22. WIPO Arbitration and Mediation Center; ADMINISTRATIVE PANEL DECISION; Hard Rock Café International (USA), Inc. v. WW Processing; Case No. D2002-0021

(http://arbiter.wipo.int/domains/decisions/html/2002/d2002-0021.html); accessed December 16, 2002.

23. "Essar Steel, SAIL Move Court Against Dumping," *Financial Times*, Global News Wire, March 27, 2004; accessed September 17, 2004.

24. Russian Arm of BP to Meet Minority Shareholders' Demands," *Sunday Business* (London), August 22, 2004.

25. United States Code, Title 18; see, in particular, sections 1831–1832 and section 1837; for an explanation of the Federal Protection of Trade Secrets and the Economic Espionage Act of 1996, see http://www.cybercrime.gov/EEAleghist.htm and the *Washington State Bar News* (http://www.wsba.org/media/publications/barnews/archives/sep-97-federal.htm).

26. American Arbitration Association 2001 annual report.

27. "American Arbitration Association Announces Cooperative Agreement With Malta Arbitration Centre" (http://www.adr.org/index2.1.jsp?JSPssid=15780&JSPsrc=upload\LIVESITE\About\..\NewsAndEvents\Press\Malta%20Coop%20Release.htm); accessed December 18, 2002.

28. "Fees Slashed to Attract 'Big-Ticket' Arbitration Cases," *Business Times Singapore*, September 21, 2002.

29. Ede, Justin. "It's Good to Talk—Rather Than Sue," *The Times* (London), November 26, 2002, page 7.

Further Readings

Anspacher, Jeff. "Export Trade Certificates of Review," *Export America*, August 2002, Volume 3, Number 8, pages 14–15.

"Brussels Extends Powers to Crack Down on Cartels," *Financial Times*, November 27, 2002, page 8.

"Customs Solution," *Forbes*, May 24, 2004, page 172.

"Clear Sailing for Pirates," *Business Week*, July 15, 2002, page 53.

Comeaux, Paul E. and N. Stephen Kinsella. *Protecting Foreign Investment Under International Law: Legal Aspects of Political Risk*, 1997, Dobbs Ferry, NY: Oceana Publications.

Finkel, David. "Crime and Holy Punishment," *Washington Post*, Sunday, November 24, 2002, page A01.

"Fixing a Lock and Key to Your Identity," *Financial Times*, December 5, 2002, page 24.

Hadjikhani, Amjad and Pervez N. Ghauri. "The Behaviour of International Firms in Socio-Political Environments in the European Union," *Journal of Business Research*, 2001, Volume 52, Number 3, pages 263–275.

"India Court Rejects Union Carbide," *Washington Post*, August 28, 2002.

Keillor, Bruce D., Gregory W. Boller, and Robert H. Luke. "Firm-Level Political Behavior and Level of Foreign Market Involvement: Implications for International Marketing Strategy," *Journal of Marketing Management*, 1998, Volume 8, Number 1, pages 1–11.

Kobrin, Stephen. "Territoriality and the Governance of Cyberspace," *Journal of International Business Studies*, 2001, Volume 32, Number 4, pages 687–704.

"Making Sense of Transfer Pricing," *Financial Express*, *Global News Wire*, August 14, 2004.

Mewhirter, Erin and Michael Fullerton. "The Trade Act of 2002," *Export America*, November 2002, pages 20–21.

"Russia May Restrict Beer Advertising," *Philadelphia Inquirer*, August 8, 2004, page E2.

"Taxing Multinationals: The Donnybrook Ahead," *Business Week*, September 9, 2002, pages 86–89.

"Washington Alters Line on U.S. Investor Protection," *Financial Times*, October 2, 2002, page 13.

Recommended Web Sites

Antiboycott laws (http://www.bxa.doc.gov/AntiboycottCompliance/Default.htm) for U.S. firms. The U.S. Bureau of Industry and Security maintains information about antiboycott rules.

Bribe Payers Index 2002 (http://www.transparency.org/cpi/2002/bpi2002.en.html). Transparency International (TI) is an international nongovernmental organization "devoted to combating corruption by bringing civil society, business, and governments together in a powerful global coalition." Its founder and chair is a former World Bank official, and members include journalists and academics. Among other activities, TI publishes the *Corruption Perceptions Index* for 91 countries and the widely referenced *Bribery Index* that is the result of surveys of business executives in 21 nations.

International Standards Organization (http://www.iso.ch/iso/en/ISOOnline.frontpage)—information about the organization, ISO 9000, and 14000 certification; "In the beginning" is especially descriptive (http://www.iso.ch/iso/en/ iso9000-14000/basics/general/basics_2.html).

Laws for nations of the world (http://www.loc.gov/law/guide/nations.html). The U.S. Library of Congress provides many resources for country-specific legal information.

The International Chamber of Commerce (ICC) (http://www.iccwbo.org); organization information, dispute resolution services, documentation, information, and standard arbitration clause—MS Word documents in Arabic, Bulgarian, Dutch, English, French, German, Greek, Italian, Spanish, Vietnamese, and other languages.

Organization for Economic and Cooperation and Development (OECD)—the Convention on Combating Bribery of Foreign Public Officials in International Business Transactions (http://www.oecd.org/EN/home/0,,EN-home-86-3-no-no-no,00.html).

United States Government sites:

- United States Department of Commerce:

  - Bureau of Industry and Security (BIS) provides information about export controls (http://www.bxa.doc.gov/licensing/exportingbasics.htm). The BIS is a department within the Department of Commerce that is the primary licensing agency for "dual use" exports—items that can be used for private or legitimate business applications as well as for military purposes. This site provides information on the type of export controls U.S. businesses are subject to as well as the best way to comply with the regulations.

  - United States Department of Commerce, Office of Export Trading Company Affairs (OETCA), Export Trade Certificates of Review (COR) information (http://www.ita.doc.gov/td/oetca/etc.html).

- United States Customs Service (http://www.customs.ustreas.gov) is the agency responsible for ensuring that U.S. imports and exports enter and exit the country in accordance with all U.S. laws and regulations.

- United States Export Administration Regulations (EAR) web site (http://w3.access.gpo.gov/bis/ear/ear_data.html) provides information about current changes to export regulations, general export prohibitions, special reporting requirements, applications (classification, advisory, and license), and documentation.

- United States Federal Trade Commission (FTC) (http://www.ftc.gov).

- United States Copyright Office at the Library of Congress (http://lcweb.loc.gov/copyright) provides copyright information, including "copyright basics," fees, and more.

- United States Department of Justice (DOJ), Antitrust Division (http://www.usdoj.gov/atr/index.html). It also maintains a portal of Internet links to antitrust agencies in other nations (http://www.usdoj.gov/atr/contact/otheratr.htm).

- United States Patent Office (USPTO) for patent information, including "patent basics," fees, statistics, and more (http://www.uspto.gov).

- United States Department of State's annual *Patterns of Global Terrorism* report (http://www.state.gov/s/ct/rls/pgtrpt) provides statistics and information on worldwide terrorism.

- United States Department of the Treasury, Office of Foreign Assets Control (OFAC) (http://www.treas.gov/offices/enforcement/ofac) administers and enforces economic and trade sanctions based on U.S. foreign policy and national security goals against targeted foreign countries, terrorists, international narcotics traffickers, and those engaged in activities related to the proliferation of weapons of mass destruction. Application instructions for export licenses and a description of the Export Control Commodity Number (ECCN) and Commodity Control List is available on a Department of Treasury web page (http://www.itds. treas.gov/licenseinfo.html).

The World Intellectual Property Organization (WIPO) is an international organization dedicated to promoting the use and protection of intellectual property. Headquartered in Geneva, Switzerland, WIPO is one of the 16 specialized agencies of the United Nations system of organizations. It administers 23 international treaties dealing with different aspects of intellectual property protection. The Organization counts 179 nations as member states (http:// www.wipo.int). WIPO also supplies detailed information on the IPP treaties (http://www.wipo.int/treaties/en/index.jsp) it administers, which include, among others, the Paris Union, Berne Convention, Brussels Convention, Madrid Agreement, and Rome Convention. See also "Global Protection Treaty Systems" (http:// www.wipo.int/treaties/registration/index.html) for information on the Madrid Agreement Concerning the International Registration of Marks as well as the Patent Cooperation Treaty (PCT).

Case 4.1

THE LEGAL AND POLITICAL ENVIRONMENT OF CIGARETTE MARKETING

Tobacco has been used in one form or another—seemingly for as long as humans and the plant coexisted, but certainly as long as recorded history. Humans have had a love-hate relationship with tobacco—the product sometimes being extolled as a cure-all and other times being labeled a wicked, insidious killer. To curb its use, or sometimes as a means of financing wars, governments have banned, taxed, and regulated tobacco. Typically, banning tobacco products affects demand and, ultimately, sales, while taxes or tariffs are passed along to consumers as higher prices. Other regulations have been aimed at the distribution or promotional aspects of marketing.

North and South America

Americans smoke over 450 billion cigarettes every year (more than 2,255 per capita), making it the largest market in the world. In Canada, the per capita consumption is also high, nearly 2,000; but with a population of 31 million, total annual consumption is only one-tenth that of the United States. Most countries in Latin and South America are currently experiencing annual per capita consumption rates of between 500 and 1,500 cigarettes.[1]

New York City has recently adopted a ban on smoking in public places that is perhaps the toughest in the nation. Other than in a handful of places (such as private clubs), smoking is prohibited. It will even affect inmates, since the no-smoking policy also applies to New York jails.[2]

We Card, the placard that is (or should be) present in stores selling tobacco, tells people that if they want to buy cigarettes or other tobacco products and they look under the legal age to buy them, the sales agent is supposed to ask for identification that includes a birth date. This is simple compared to the requirements under the Tobacco Free Internet for Kids Act. Under this law, anyone selling tobacco on the Internet and shipping to a consumer in the United States must verify the age of the purchaser. One idea being tested includes requiring customers to provide their name, age, and driver's license number (subject to verification). Internet tobacco vendors must be able to supply hard evidence that they are not selling to underage smokers. Anyone selling to minors would be subject to a fine of up to $5,000, but only if the sale was made unintentionally. If vendors intentionally sell tobacco to minors, they could get even stiffer fines and face prison terms of up to five years![3]

A study conducted in the United States by the National Cancer Institute concluded that ultra light, light, mild, and similarly labeled cigarettes are no less harmful than regular cigarettes because smokers inhale harder and longer and they smoke more cigarettes to make up for lower nicotine levels. Philip Morris is taking a proactive stance by including literature with their cigarettes that explains this fact to smokers, although doing so is not a law in the Unites States. Other firms in the industry are likely to follow suit.[4]

The DOJ wants new regulations to limit tobacco promotions to black and white, with no "alluring" and "lifestyle" images (no woman reclining on a couch or no bare-chested men). The law would also require that warning messages cover at least 50 percent of the package and would include a ban on all point-of-purchase promotion (no racks or display signs). All of the following are examples of how promotion of tobacco products is being regulated in the United States: prohibition of the use of cigarette brand names or trademarks on clothing and other nontobacco products, cease-and-desist orders for advertising on newspaper home-delivery bags, fines for giving too much TV exposure to billboards at baseball games and car races, and penalties for ads placed in magazines that have teenage audiences.[5]

Huge awards, such as the Master Settlement Agreement of 1998 that awarded over $200 billion to 46 states (and the earlier four-state award of $40 billion), as well as individual awards, such as the one for Ms. Betty Bullock of California (the $28 billion award against Philip Morris was later reduced to *only* $28 million), have an impact on firms' profits; and as with taxes, these expenses are generally passed along to consumers in the form of higher prices. Even though tobacco products are addictive and therefore relatively *demand-insensitive* to price increases, multimillion and multibillion dollar awards and steep tax increases have more than tripled cigarette prices to consumers in many areas. Demand is declining, especially among younger smokers (the prime target of antismoking campaigns and, some would argue, the tobacco firms); and high prices seem to be an effective deterrent for young smokers. Since smoking in this age group causes the most concern, lawmakers will likely keep using tax hikes as one tool in the arsenal to reduce smoking.[6]

Aside from the regulations, special interest groups are pressuring governments, lawyers, and even intermediaries for change. One example is the recent call from religious groups for Wal-Mart to explain inconsistent marketing of cigarettes in the United States, where Wal-Mart has minimal point-of-purchase display material, and in Mexico and South Korea, where banners, large cardboard displays, and other marketing items are aggressively exhibited.[7]

On every pack of cigarettes, Canada requires graphic pictures that depict diseased lungs, yellow teeth, a hospital patient on a respirator, or one of another dozen or so explicit photographs to remind people of the dangers of smoking. The concept is designed to reinforce the text messages that warn of lung disease, cancer, and death. Legislators in the United States (as well as in Brazil and other nations) are contemplating similar laws.[8] A ban on cigarette manufacturers' sponsoring sport and cultural events took effect in October 2003.[9]

Nova Scotia's Act to Protect Young Persons and Other Persons from Tobacco Smoke, which became effective on January 1, 2003, makes it illegal for anyone under the age of 19 to possess a cigarette.[10]

In Mexico, despite an increase in population between 1985 and 2002, from 60 million to 100 million people, cigarette consumption declined from 54 billion to 49 billion per year. Cigarette consumption is expected to decline further as new regulations take effect, especially the ban on television and radio advertisements and the 100 percent increase in cigarette tax.[11]

Middle East and Africa

In the Middle East, average cigarette consumption is between 500 and 1,500 cigarettes per year per person. In Bahrain, Israel, and Jordan, cigarette smoking is higher (2,000); but in Kuwait, smoking is higher than in the United States, Japan, and nearly anywhere else in the world—over 3,000 cigarettes annually for every person! Statistics from the last half of the 1990s indicate that except for South Africa, where cigarette consumption is slightly over 1,500 per person per year, most African nations have per capita consumption rates below 500. Trends indicate that these numbers are rising rather quickly. Within this region, people in Morocco, Libya, Algeria, Egypt, and other Northern African nations smoke an average of three times more, 1,500 per capita annually, than people in other nations. Somewhat surprising is the fact that it was the officials of African nations, not those in rich, developed countries, who provided the leadership behind the WHO's Framework Convention on Tobacco Control in 2002.[12]

Relatively few restrictions exist on cigarette consumption in Africa and the Middle East. Algeria, Iraq, Israel, and the Sudan have comprehensive advertising bans; and smoking is prohibited in some public areas in Benin, Botswana, Israel, Mali, Morocco, Nigeria, Sudan, South Africa, Syria, and Zambia. Voluntary employer restrictions are in place in a handful of other nations (including Kuwait, Lebanon, and Tunisia). In 2002, there were calls for bans on public smoking in Ghana, Kenya, and Uganda. That same year, Nigeria enacted advertising bans on billboards, print, and electronic media for tobacco products and banned public smoking in movie theaters, on public transportation, in offices, in schools, and in a host of other areas.[13]

Europe

Consumption trends across Europe are in some respects regional. Those people who smoke the least are found in the northern European nations of Norway (725 per capita), Sweden (1,200 per capita), and Finland (1,350 per capita). Most other nations in both east and western Europe (including France) have consumption rates of between 1,500 and 2,500 cigarettes annually. There are some exceptions. Heavy smokers exist in Spain (2,800 per capita) and Switzerland (2,700 per capita), as well as in Bulgaria, Belarus, Slovenia, Hungary, and Modova. Worst, though, is Greece, where consumption is over 4,300 cigarettes for every man, woman, and child, which is the highest rate in the world according to the WHO.[14]

The United Kingdom, Germany, and Romania have the laxest rules about smoking in public areas; while the rest of the European nations have varying degrees of regulations about smoking in public spaces. Advertising bans exist in Finland, Iceland, Italy, Norway, and Portugal.[15]

An attempt to impose a near complete ban on all tobacco advertising across the EU in 2000 was halted by Germany, which saw the restrictions as too harsh. In 2002, though, a revised ban was approved by the EU Parliament that prohibited sponsorship of sporting events and limit advertising to tobaccophile journals (such as Cigar Today) and magazines for executives in the tobacco industry.[16]

Effective January 2003, smokers in France began paying an additional 17 percent for a pack of Marlboro cigarettes. The money raised from the new tax on tobacco, the largest increase ever in that country, is to be used to help fund the country's health-care system.[17]

Sweden has had strict restrictions on cigarette advertising for over 25 years, including prohibition on print and electronic media ads, as well as point-of-purchase requirements that allow promotion in "moderation." Now, however, the Swedish government is working on laws that would require harsher messages on tobacco product packaging (such as "smoking kills" and "smokers die younger"), a ban on tobacco-branded merchandise (clothing, for example), and further limits on point-of-purchase displays. If passed, virtually all tobacco advertising would be outlawed. Besides packaging and promotion, Swedish laws include limits on product content, specifying the number of milligrams of nicotine allowed in cigarettes.[18]

Asia-Pacific

Three of the top five cigarette markets in the world are in Asia. The Chinese smoke 1.6 trillion cigarettes each year. Add to this the Japanese (325 billion) and Indonesian (215 billion) markets, and these three nations account for over 2 trillion (or 40 percent) of the total 5.5 trillion cigarettes sold in the world each year. In Asia, consumption rates for cigarettes vary from relatively low rates of fewer than 150 per person in India to rates over 3,000 per person in Japan. More alarming are the statistics about China, where per capita consumption is 1,800 annually. According to the WHO study, consumption has increased by over 50 percent between 1990 and 2000 and the Chinese now smoke more that one-third of all of the world's cigarettes![19]

While tobacco advertising has been banned in Malaysia for about ten years, a new law also forbids cigarette manufacturers from sponsoring sporting and entertainment events. New laws would also prohibit the showing of movie scenes that depict smokers.[20]

Tougher new laws in Australia include banning public smoking in restaurants and bars while food is being served. Establishments must provide smoke-free areas for nonsmokers when food is not being served, and designated no-smoking areas must be made available around counters and bars (admittedly difficult to enforce). Tobacco companies that violate advertising regulations will also face million-dollar fines, rather than the $9,000 "slap on the wrist" that Philip Morris received for hosting a rave at Fox Studios.[21]

The Smoke-Free Environments Act in New Zealand prohibits tobacco promotion in most forms. This includes print/electronic advertising, sponsorship (cultural or sporting events as well as scholarships), and the use of trademarks or other identification on nontobacco products and items (clothing, for example).[22]

India is also concerned with the number of smokers in the country. Its sentiments are conveyed in a recent award-winning promotion. Ogilvy & Mather won the 2002 Gold Outdoor Award at the International Advertising Festival in Cannes for its antismoking ad that shows a cowboy standing over a dead horse with the copy "secondhand smoke kills."[23]

Global

The WHO is calling on the nations of the world to make a concerted effort to reduce smoking and to take a unified stance against promotion of tobacco products. In its Framework Convention on Tobacco Control, the WHO suggests that (much) higher prices and less promotion would reduce tobacco consumption and it asks that nations enact stricter rules about promotion (bans preferably), raise prices by instituting higher taxes, and help fund training and other costs associated with getting tobacco farmers to grow other crops.[24]

How will tobacco be marketed in the future? Some new cigarette slogans are hinted at in pamphlets and from tobacco executives. Witness advertising copy for Advance cigarettes: "All of the taste, less of the toxins!" A possibility for Omni cigarettes: "Will not kill you as quick, or as much!" The former statement is an excerpt from the pamphlet included with Advance cigarette packages; the latter is a statement made by Bennett LeBow, CEO of the Vector Tobacco Company, about the advantages of the firm's new Omni cigarettes.[25]

According to the WHO, the future holds some interesting possibilities. Its predictions: by 2020, more cigarettes will be sold illegally (smuggled) than legally and tobacco advertising will be illegal. A decade later cigarettes will be sold only by prescription in developed nations and 75 percent of the price of cigarettes will be its tax. Tobacco-related costs in health care, insurance, and other expenses will reach $1 trillion annually by 2040.[26]

QUESTIONS AND RESEARCH

1. Enter buy cheap cigarette in any search engine and see how many hits you get. What kind of proof of age is required? Are you able to identify the seller's location? Explain.
2. Identify in some detail the legal, political, and other challenges facing cigarette marketers in the United States and abroad.
3. Identify the various interest groups, organizations, and institutions that companies must consider as they market cigarettes.
4. Identify in detail marketing and other strategies and tactics that cigarette companies are using to meet the challenges confronting the industry. Suggest some other approaches.
5. Apart from the legal and political dimensions, do you see any ethical dimensions to these issues? If so, what questions would you raise and how would you respond to them?

CASE ENDNOTES

1. Mackay, Judith and Michael Eriksen. *Tobacco Atlas*, 2002, Geneva, Switzerland: World Health Organization (available free of charge in PDF format: http://www5.who.int/tobacco/page.cfm?sid=84), Table A, pages 94–101.

2. "Smoking Bill Is Adopted as Council Ends Year," *New York Times*, December 19, 2002, page 3B; "A Smoking Ban in City's Jails Worries Correction Officers," *New York Times*, January 5, 2003, page 27.

3. "New Bill Aims to Separate Kids, Cigs Online," *Marketing News*, February 4, 2002, pages 6–7; Tobacco Free Internet for Kids Act (HR 2914 IH); *Tech Law Journal* (http://www.techlawjournal.com/cong106/tobacco/hr2914ih.htm); accessed December 6, 2003.

4. "Philip Morris Tells Smokers 'Light' Cigarettes Aren't Safer," *Wall Street Journal*, November 20, 2002, page B3.

5. "U.S. Seeks Tough Tobacco Restrictions," *Wall Street Journal*, March 11, 2002, page A1; "Bold Promotions Land R.J. Reynolds in Controversies," *Wall Street Journal*, September 6, 2002, pages A1, A6.

6. "Accepting $28 Million in Tobacco Suit," *New York Times*, December 25, 2002, page A21; "RL30058: Tobacco Master Settlement Agreement (1998): Overview, Implementation by States, and Congressional Issues," National Council for Science and the Environment, November 5, 1999 (http://www.ncseonline.org/NLE/CRSreports/Agriculture/ag-55.cfm); accessed January 6, 2003.

7. "Wal-Mart Rejects Shareholder Call to Explain Policies on Tobacco Ads," *Wall Street Journal*, March 1, 2002, page B2.

8. "Canada Hopes Photos Will Coax Smokers to Kick the Habit," *Washington Post*, October 6, 2002, page A30.

9. "Tobacco Companies Appeal Quebec Court Ruling On Law Banning Advertising," cnews (http://www.canoe.ca/NationalTicker/CANOE-wire.Tobacco-Ruling.html); accessed January 12, 2003.

10. "Cigarette possession becomes illegal for Novia Scotia's under 19," *British Medical Journal*, January 11, 2003.

11. "Mexico Strives to Snuff Out Tobacco Use Among Youths," *San Diego Union-Tribune*, June 2, 2002, page A24; "Tobacco Ads to Be Banned on Mexican TV and Radio," *Bloomberg News*, May 31, 2002 (http://quote.bloomberg.com/fgcgi.cgi?T=marketsquote99_news.ht&s=APPftXxM4VG9iYWNj); accessed January 6, 2003.

12. Mackay, Judith and Michael Eriksen. *Tobacco Atlas*, 2002, Geneva, Switzerland: World Health Organization (available free of charge in PDF format: http://www5.who.int/tobacco/page.cfm?sid=84);Table A, pages 94–101.

13. Mackay, Judith and Michael Eriksen. *Tobacco Atlas*, 2002, Geneva, Switzerland: World Health Organization (available free of charge in PDF format: http://www5.who.int/tobacco/page.cfm?sid=84), pages 74, 75.
"Ban Smoking in Public, KNH Boss Urges Government," *Africa News*, October 14, 2002.
"Muhwezi Wants Ban on Smoking in Public," *Africa News*, August 22, 2002.
"Ban Smoking in Public Places," *Africa News*, June 17, 2002.
"*House of Representatives Bans Tobacco Advertisement,*" *Africa News*, March 22, 2002.

14. Mackay, Judith and Michael Eriksen. *Tobacco Atlas*, 2002, Geneva, Switzerland: World Health Organization (available free of charge in PDF format: http://www5.who.int/tobacco/page.cfm?sid=84); pages 74–77.

15. "Europe Curbs Cigarette Promotion," *Wall Street Journal*, November 21, 2002, page B10.

16. "Europe Curbs Cigarette Promotion," *Wall Street Journal*, November 21, 2002, page B10.

17. "France Passes Largest Tobacco Tax Increase in Its History," Tobacco Reporter (http://www.tobaccoreporter.com/news/LateBreak.asp#france); accessed January 12, 2003.

18. "Match Game: Globally Speaking, U.S. Tobacco Laws Relatively Lax," *Marketing News*, November 11, 2002, pages 1, 11–12.

19. Mackay, Judith and Michael Eriksen. *Tobacco Atlas*, 2002, Geneva, Switzerland: World Health Organization (available free of charge in PDF format: http://www5.who.int/tobacco/page.cfm?sid=84), pages 74–77. Note that the Chinese market is tightly controlled and largely closed to foreign-made cigarettes. One concern is that if the market is opened to sophisticated foreign manufacturers, the allure of foreign-made tobacco products may increase overall consumption.

20. "Malaysia Bans 'Sly' Tobacco Ads," *Marketing News,* September 16, 2002, page 7.

21. "Tough New Law Stays on Pub, Club Cig Bans," *Sunday Mail*, March 17, 2002, page 3. "Huff Away, Just Don't Puff," *Sydney Morning Herald*, December 18, 2002, page 13.
Million Dollar Fines for Tobacco Ads," *Sydney Morning Herald*, November 21, 2002, page 6.

22. Hoek, Janet and Robert Sparks. "Tobacco Promotion Restrictions—An International Impasse?" *International Marketing Review*, 2000, Volume 17, Number 3, pages 216–230.

23. "Applause for Commercial Breaks," *Philadelphia Inquirer*, November 16, 2002.

24. World Health Organization, "Intergovernmental Negotiating Body on the WHO Framework Convention on Tobacco Control, Fifth Session; New Chair's Text of a Framework Convention on Tobacco Control," June 25, 2002.

25. "Tobacco Industry Unleashes New Generation of Deceit," *USA Today*, November 11, 2002, page 1A

26. Mackay, Judith and Michael Eriksen. *Tobacco Atlas*, 2002, Geneva, Switzerland: World Health Organization (available free of charge in PDF format: http://www5.who.int/tobacco/page.cfm?sid=84), pages 90–91.

WEB SITES

Advertisements (http://tobaccofreekids.org/adgallery); examples of tobacco ads around the world.

American Medical Student Association Comprehensive List of Tobacco Texts (http://www.amsa.org/hp/tobtexts.cfm).

Smithsonian Institute, Marlboro Advertising Oral History and Documentation Project, ca. 1926–1986 (updated in 2000) (http://americanhistory.si.edu/archives/d7198.htm).

Parker-Pope, Tara. "Safer" Cigarettes: A History—PBS, NOVA presentation (http://www.pbs.org/wgbh/nova/cigarette/history.html).

Tobacco.org (http://www.tobacco.org) for the latest tobacco news and resources;

World Health Organization (WHO) (http://www.who.int/health_topics/tobacco/en); and the WHO Tobacco Control Country Profiles (http://www5.who.int/tobacco/page.cfm?sid=57)?see especially Appendix B (PDF file) on legislation by nation.

World Bank (http://www1.worldbank.org/tobacco); tobacco control, including PowerPoint presentation on smuggling, tobacco controls in developing countries, health-related issues, and economic concerns.

Case 4.2

U.S. PHARMACEUTICALS, INC. (B)

U.S. Pharmaceuticals (USP) is a U.S. firm with about 30 percent of its sales outside the United States. USP concentrates on the ethical drug business; but has diversified into animal health products, cosmetics, and some patent medicines. Those other lines account for about one-fourth of USP's $800 million sales.

USP's international business is conducted in some 70 countries, mostly through distributors in those markets. In six countries, however, USP has manufacturing or compounding operations. (Compounding refers to the local mixing, assembling, and packaging of critical ingredients shipped from the United States.) USP's only Latin American manufacturing/compounding operations are in Latinia, a country with a population of about 30 million. Some products are shipped from Latinia to other Latin American markets.

Recently, USP has run into a problem in Latinia with its newest drug, Corolane 2. This drug is effective in treating certain intestinal diseases and infections. The drug has been under development for several years. Three years ago, when it showed considerable promise in the extensive testing process, USP registered the name *Corolane 2* in the United States and several other major world markets. Last year USP introduced Corolane 2 in the United States and several large foreign markets. Its early promise was confirmed by its quick acceptance by the medical profession in those countries.

Because of Corolane 2's initial success, USP plans to introduce the drug in all of its foreign markets. It planned to both manufacture and market the drug in Latinia. A problem arose, however, because Jorge Rodriguez, a Latinian citizen, had already registered local rights to the name *Corolane 2*. Though a questionable procedure, this is perfectly legal, for Latinia is a code law country that gives exclusive rights to trade names according to priority in registration rather than to priority in use, which is the basis for exclusive rights in the United States. Furthermore, Latinia is one of several countries around the world that is not a member of the international patent and trademark agreements.

The problem for USP was that it could not sell Corolane 2 under that name in Latinia because Rodriguez owned the rights. Of course, Rodriguez was quite willing to sell his rights to the Corolane 2 name for $20,000.

Registering foreign brand names was Rodriguez's way of supporting himself. He made a good living by subscribing to foreign trade and technical publications (especially in the medical field) and registering all of the new names he found. Not all of the names would be exploited in Latinia, but enough of them were to make it profitable for him. Corolane 2 was an atypical case. Early in the drug's development process, journal articles told of successful tests and applications. As soon as the name *Corolane 2* was mentioned in one of the articles, Rodriguez registered it in Latinia, beating USP lawyers by just two weeks.

USP had encountered problems like this before in Latinia and other countries. It conducted R&D on many projects, most of which never reached the market. Some company officials believed it was not profitable to register every new product name in every market.

QUESTIONS AND RESEARCH

1. Identify and evaluate the alternatives open to USP in Latinia.
2. What variables are important in this decision?
3. How could this kind of problem be avoided?

Case 4.3

WHAT IS INTERNATIONAL LAW?

If you were to ask someone for a straightforward definition of *international business*, the person might say something like "it is business conducted across national boundaries." So international law must be "law that is conducted across national boundaries." That might be possible were it not for **national sovereignty**, which, in simplest terms, can be described as a nation's inalienable right to govern itself without outside interference.

National sovereignty was at the heart of the Gulf War in the 1990s and the dispute between Iraq and the UN about weapons inspection. The allied coalition (the United States, France, the United Kingdom,

Saudi Arabia, and other countries) defended Kuwait because Iraq sent in troops, which was a violation of Kuwait's sovereignty. The rationale for the Iraqi invasion, to some extent, was that Kuwait had been taking oil from Iraq's Rumaila field (theft of Iranian property and a violation of Iraqi national sovereignty). Iraq states that the subsequent weapons inspections are a violation of its national sovereignty—that it had the right to do whatever it wants within its own borders.

China, France, and Mexico enact laws to which they hold their corporate and individual citizens responsible. Perhaps the best or truest form of international law takes place in the EU. The EU is a group of nations, each with its own national sovereignty; but the nations have agreed to policy making and legal restrictions that supersede national laws in certain circumstances and areas. No other international entity has the right to govern the activities of citizens from different nations.

Controversy over the use of child labor, poor working conditions, and exploitation in manufacturing products around the globe are issues raised by nations and consumers alike. Response may take the form of product boycotts, demonstrations, or government-imposed sanctions. The response from the offending nation is that these actions violate national sovereignty. It is an important issue that has consequences for everyone—consumers, CEOs, wage earners, policy makers, marketers, and responsible global citizens.

Recently, however, much to the dismay of American firms, lawyers representing foreign claimants have been using an arcane 1789 U.S. statute to sue American companies. The Alien Tort Claims Act was originally intended to reassure Europeans that the new United States of America would not provide protection to pirates and assassins. Recently, however, the law was used in a suit brought by Burmese citizens against Unocal, a southern California energy giant. In essence, the complaint was that Unocal was "vicariously responsible" for the Burmese government's use of peasants (forced at gunpoint, some of whom were tortured and killed) to build a pipeline to be used by Unocal to transport natural gas. Even though Unocal did not participate in building the pipeline, it was being held accountable for "providing practical assistance or encouragement" to the Burmese government. The terms were not disclosed, but the case was settled out of court in April 2005. Had the case gone to trial and Unocal lost, the amount of monetary award would have been enormous and, more importantly, would have laid the foundation for similar claims against multinationals. More disturbing to American

firms is that U.S. law is based on precedence; therefore, if this law had been successfully applied in the Unocal case, it would have been used in other cases as well. Coca-Cola and Citigroup are also facing suits under this law. It is estimated that over 1,000 American and foreign firms could be facing similar suits. The awards would be in the trillions of dollars, likely forcing some firms into bankruptcy.

What does this mean for international marketers? If someone breaks a contract with them in their own nation, marketers can often sue for restitution. Between parties of different nationalities, though, this may be difficult or impossible because of national sovereignty and the refusal of one nation to allow its citizens to be subjected to the laws of another nation. In essence, it means that any contract that involves parties from different nations requires careful scrutiny and that all methods of reducing commercial and political risk should be considered—from using forward exchange contracts, arbitration clauses, and political risk insurance to withholding proprietary information and being a good corporate citizen.

Source: "Making a Federal Case of Overseas Abuses," *Business Week*, November 25, 2002, page 78.

QUESTIONS AND RESEARCH

1. Identify an EU law that has an impact on marketers. Discuss how it might best be addressed.
2. Review ways the in which contract disputes can be managed.

Case 4.4

SWOT ANALYSIS

New laws need not mean new threats to marketers; rather, the laws should be evaluated as potential opportunities. For example, newly required security measures and regulations have been a boon to some companies. Consider Iridian Technologies, a company that has developed a relatively low-cost biometric iris recognition system that can be used at airports, sensitive installations, and other areas where security is a concern and access must be limited. This unobtrusive, fast, and accurate identification process is currently in use at Schiphol, JFK, and Heathrow airports, as well as at the Pentagon. The UN uses the Iridian system to allow fairer distribution of supplies by identifying double-dippers at food aid stations in Pakistan.

Environmental concerns spurred by conservationists, multilateral agreements such as the Kyoto Accord, and host government regulations have increased incentives to develop green products. Examples include hybrid vehicles, such as the Toyota Prisus, Honda Insight, and Civic Hybrid, and concepts that will likely arrive to market shortly, including Honda's RDX (a sport utility electric and gasoline hybrid) and the Acura DN-X (a 400-horsepower muscle car that gets a reported 42 miles per gallon versus the more traditional 10 to 15 miles per gallon for similar cars).

To help power the natural gas hybrid vehicles, the FuelMaker Corporation of Toronto, Canada, has developed a home fueling system that connects a car to a natural gas line in an owner's home. Initially priced at $2,000, "Phill" allows consumers to "gas up" the Honda GX or a similar vehicle at home rather than hunt for a station with the equipment needed to fuel hybrid gas cars.

Sources: "Eyes Have It for Identification," *Philadelphia Inquirer,* Wednesday, October 24, 2002, pages C1, C4; "Green Garage," *Los Angeles Times,* Wednesday, October 16, 2002, page 1.

QUESTIONS AND RESEARCH

1. Research, identify, and discuss new products being developed to reduce piracy.
2. What are some potential threats facing marketers as new, stricter environmental laws are enacted? What if the laws are relaxed or adherence is postponed (for example, car emissions)?

CHAPTER 5

Information Technology and Global Marketing

Information technology (IT) has changed the way marketing is conducted, and information has become a strategic weapon.

The main goals of this chapter are to

- Describe recent IT innovations, focusing on global linkages with customers and suppliers.

- Provide examples of how the Internet and electronic data interchange (EDI) are used effectively to communicate with customers and coordinate transactions between customers and suppliers.

- Develop information about customers around the world, using Internet-based interaction and point-of-sale information-gathering techniques.

- Demonstrate how firms involve customers in new product design and interact with them after the sale, enhance customer loyalty, and stimulate repeat business.

- Present new international market research techniques, such as using virtual shopping environments to collect data and tracking customer behavior on the Internet.

Global Linkages: An Overview

IT has dramatically changed the way companies conduct their international marketing. Global IT linkages can be considered a form of virtual international marketing.[1] Significant linkages, which are summarized in Figure 5-1, include the following:

1. The company can *monitor the POS* to obtain detailed information on consumer purchase behavior. **Point-of-sale** (POS) information systems include data on sales sorted by brands, quantities, prices, package size, time of day and day of week, and month. Data may also be collected on whether coupons were used and competing products were purchased, providing instant feedback about customer decisions, letting a firm know exactly what was sold, at what prices, in what quantities, and at which location. The company can use that information to update inventory records, make decisions about additional production runs, adjust prices and launch sales, and design new products.

   The information collected feeds into **database marketing**, where vast stores of knowledge about customers and potential customers are analyzed and utilized to develop products and marketing strategies. Information, aggregated by individual store and then by larger groupings such as city, region, and sales territory, allows marketing managers to relate actual sales to historical data, competitive market share, advertising, promotion and, pricing. In turn, this leads to better information about the effectiveness of the marketing mix strategy.

   For example, a company can collect general information about visitors who access its web site—frequency of visits, number of unique visitors, length of time spent at the site, frequency of downloads, etc. Firms can use the web statistics they collect through tracking software to redesign the site (suggesting the addition or deletion of content) or to change site navigation. Since a company can identify the locations of users, it may offer different products (more beach wear in coastal areas, for example) or change the language of its site. If a company finds that it receives repeated requests for information, it may decide to add a link or a section of frequently asked questions. The data from the tracking software may also indicate that the firm should emphasize after-sales service.

   Data mining (analysis of data to identify patterns for predictive purposes) is not an easy task, in part because of the vast amounts of data involved. Data mining is akin to getting 10,000 hits, using a web search engine—no one has time to look at all of the results. Data, if not used in a timely fashion, becomes useless; and the money spent on collecting it is wasted. Software manufacturers are addressing this issue by making it quicker and easier to analyze data. Enterprise Miner software, developed by SAS, used in conjunction with a new version of Predictive Model Markup Language (PMML), allows users to integrate predictive and descriptive models more easily. IBM's DB2 Information Integrator provides an efficient means of caching data from a variety of sources that permits users to maintain data in a way that is more easily and quickly accessible. Microsoft is competing with its Analysis Services, which is being purchased by smaller firms because of the database's ease of use and compatibility with other components of the data mining functions.

2. The company can *interact with the customer*, both pre- and postsale: at presale by allowing customers to communicate wants and desires and to be involved in designing and testing the product; at postsale by collecting and using information about customer satisfaction and about events and problems surrounding pre- and postsale service. The goal is to enhance customer loyalty and encourage repeat purchase behavior.

3. The company can use IT to *develop new international market research techniques* like those based on simulated, or virtual, shopping environments. The company can monitor consumer behavior in the virtual shop to trace the effects of marketing variables such as price, packaging, and promotions in a simulated environment.

4. The company can *use information networks, principally the Internet, to sell and develop a new direct channel of distribution* to the customer, allowing customized shopping at the convenience of the customer. The Internet allows even small firms to interact directly with customers around the world who have access to the Internet.

5. The company can u*se the Internet and EDI to deal directly with business partners, customers, and suppliers.* The Internet is the central medium for that purpose—ubiquitous, inexpensive, and available nearly all over the world to small as well as large companies. Combining the Internet with the intranet (internal corporate networks) allows firms to communicate both internally and externally. Companies can use those networks to send orders, negotiate prices, set up auctions at which prequalified suppliers submit bids, exchange product specifications, track production status, track shipments, and handle billing and payments.

Advanced use of the Internet would include interaction at the product design phase where suppliers and customers interact with a firm in developing new products, with a view to reducing time to market and reducing cost to manufacture. **Electronic Data Interchange** (EDI) is the principal technical communication vehicle for such information exchange between a company and its business partners in the world today, displacing the telephones, faxes, and memorandums of yesteryear! Corporate data networks and EDI facilitate accurate interaction, simplifying the use of techniques such as quick response production planning based on up-to-date sales figures. Another major innovation has been just-in-time supply chains, with EDI allowing communication of quick-response production schedules and required delivery quantities.

Figure 5-1. Information Technology and International Marketing

Information Technology as a Strategic Marketing Tool

↓ ↓

Global Customer Linkages:
Point-of-Sale Data
Collection

Presale and Postsale
Interaction with Customers

Marketing Research Using
Virtual Shopping Techniques

Global Supplier Linkages:
Development of Direct
Distribution to the
Customer, Primarily
Internet-Based

EDI to Deal Directly
with Business Partners

Changes in the information environment, technological infrastructure, and communication culture and related factors have had dramatic implications for marketing strategies. Those changes have affected a firm's evaluation of market attractiveness, its competitive position, and all other aspects of marketing planning and implementation. Information systems development also influences a firm's marketing organizational structure, dissolving boundaries between the firm and its environment, its suppliers, and its competitors and customers, as well as boundaries within the firm (reducing barriers between marketing and manufacturing, for example). Information content also becomes a feature of the product and even becomes a product in its own right. Applied systematically, information systems can affect the performance and delivery of elements of the marketing mix (such as service, distribution, marketing communication and promotion) and marketing research.

Democratization of Technology

This information transformation is comparable to the industrial revolution in the nineteenth and twentieth centuries in that it impacts nearly everything people do. How they live and interact with one another is changing dramatically. But technological advances and new ways of using technology are taking place at a more rapid pace than what occurred during the industrial revolution. Not only is the cost of connecting to others decreasing rapidly, but wireless technologies are allowing people in even the most remote regions (those without the traditional infrastructure) to tie in to the information systems if they so choose. Thomas Friedman, in *The Lexus and the Olive Tree*, refers to this as the democratization of technology and information.[2] The advances in information availability afford greater interactivity and transparency for anyone participating in the global business environment. Furthermore, the relationships between a company and its customers are changing dramatically, with the balance of power shifting toward well-informed consumers who are seeking long-term integrated solutions rather than a one-time product purchase.[3] Companies that recognize the shift will thrive, while those stuck in the marketing perceptions of the last quarter-century will be replaced by savvy competitors. Relationship marketing will become increasingly important, which may, at times, go counter to outsourcing of customer service.[4, 5]

At the core of many of the advances in IT is the Internet, allowing people to exchange information at a rate and volume not possible only a short while ago. While speed of transmitting data has increased, more importantly, perhaps, is the rapid penetration of devices and software that allow people access to the technology. More people are using the Internet every day, whether they are sending pictures to relatives around the globe or downloading maps to the car for directions to the nearest electronics store. Marketing is communication, and the Internet has changed how people communicate with one another. The Internet has altered the nature and process of making strategic and tactical decisions. The Internet impacts everything that marketers do—whether dealing with price, promotion, the physical distribution of goods and services, or the products they sell. Marketers also shape the Internet, acting as **change agents** when they allow customers to print out cents-off coupons for groceries rather than clip coupons or to download a movie rather than go to a theater or video rental store.

Consumers are also becoming more powerful. Internet marketing is more interactive than other avenues, with consumers having the power and control to select what they see; to compare product, price, and delivery offerings among competitors; and to access broader sets of alternatives in nearly every product category. (Firms must put a lot

Table 5-1. Web-Based Global Marketing

Foci of Web-Based Marketing:
• Development of a presence
• Potential sales outlet and distribution
• Product and services information
• Collection of customer/visitor information
• Communication and interaction with customers
• After-sales service, user support

Web Marketing Strategy Issues:
• Web site design and positioning
• Infrastructure for web-centric marketing
• Coexistence with other distribution channels
• Product range for Internet site sales
• B2B marketing
• Data use and protection

IT also raises new issues, perhaps the most controversial of which is personal privacy. Security against theft and destruction of data, accuracy of information, morality, taxes, and cultural invasion are also concerns that accompany enhanced IT capabilities. Table 5-1 provides some of the issues surrounding web-based marketing, which is inherently global in nature.

A Global Network Illustrated

Figure 5-2 shows global linkages at Mattel, providing an example of global networks. This U.S.-based toy designer depends on feedback from customers around the world for new product ideas. Mattel takes new toy ideas and selects independent Far East-based companies as manufacturing subcontractors. Inventory statistics from a network of global warehouses are analyzed at the U.S. headquarters to arrive at follow-on orders that are given to the manufacturing subcontractors. Finished products ship directly from the Far East subcontractors to the various global warehouses, with allocations based on sales figures attained from global customers, which are analyzed at headquarters and at regional offices. Sales figures and inventory levels are also relayed to and analyzed by management for monitoring and changing prices, when indicated, to achieve increased sales in an industry where the bulk of demand is concentrated in a short selling season. Management's twin imperatives are (1) to ensure that popular toys are avail-

of information on the Web, making it easily accessible and allowing consumers to pick and choose.) Consumers rely on the Internet as a search tool in large part because it is cheaper, is less time-consuming, and offers a broader assortment than conducting a search by calling companies or writing to providers with questions. Consumers are able to become better informed (or ill-informed depending on the source) quicker. Consumer power comes from the ability to direct the message received.

Figure 5-2. Global Linkages at Mattel

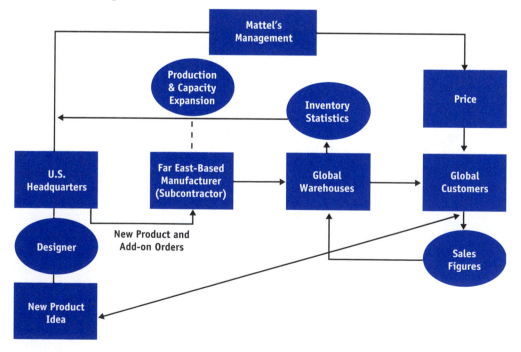

able in sufficient quantities around the world to satisfy demand (hence, the need to transmit rush follow-on orders to distant manufacturing subcontractors) and (2) to price efficiently enough to clear toy inventories to prevent losses from obsolescence of outdated toy inventories. Without the global marketing information network in use at Mattel, such market responsiveness would be difficult.

Developing global networks is complicated by the very nature of the international environment. Difficulties arise from:

- Differences in the level of infrastructure across countries, including (1) the depth and sophistication of computer networks; (2) the availability, reliability, and cost of telephone systems; and (3) the penetration of computer hardware and software usage across companies. Arguably, those three areas are fundamental to the development of IT–based marketing.
- Traditional barriers, such as tariffs, quotas, and NTBs (for example, customs formalities and local content laws).
- Cultural differences such as those created by language and business practices.
- Legal differences that complicate the establishment of commercial relationships with overseas partners and require close attention to questions of data security and network access.
- Geographical distance and different time zones, which make communication difficult.

- Barriers created by government regulation, such as limits on transborder data flows and on use of **value-added networks** (VANs).
- Differences in the level of technological sophistication of overseas partners, such as in the use of information systems, computer hardware and software, incompatible standards, and differences in managerial expertise brought to bear on subjects such as quality control, inventory management, customer service and support, and market research. Those differences complicate efforts to tie partners into the global network.

Global Networks: A Conceptual Framework

Figure 5-3 outlines an idealized framework for global marketing networks that would include the following major elements:

1. Linkages between a firm and its customers and suppliers around the globe.
2. Integrated marketing communications (principally advertising and promotion) aimed at global markets and global service needs that connect a multinational sales force with distributors and suppliers

Figure 5-3. A Conceptual Framework for Global Marketing Networks

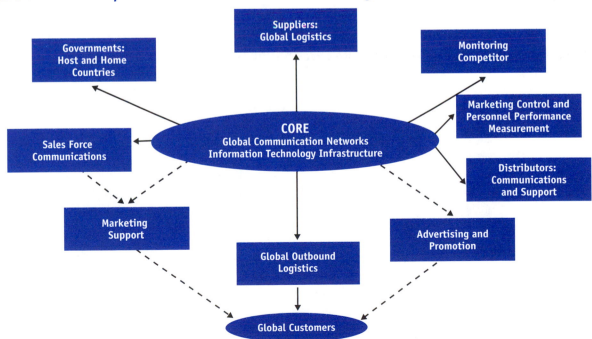

3. A set of major environmental linkages with outsiders, including host governments, multinational competitors, and the global logistics infrastructure, with both in-house entities and independent third parties.

4. Linkages to the implementation aspects of such global marketing networks. This is principally comprised of marketing control, organizational structure, and personnel. Equally important are technical issues crucial to the smooth functioning of such global networks.

The remainder of this chapter will examine in greater detail the various elements of such a global marketing network.

Linkages With Customers

As IT becomes more closely intertwined with the very fabric of doing business, information becomes a critical resource – both enabling a company to compete in the marketplace and a service in its own right that the company can offer and sell to its customers. A company competes in two arenas: the physical *marketplace* and the virtual *marketspace*. Information changes the way a company creates value and competes within the virtual value chain. A well-known example is Federal Express's system, which allows its customers to access the FedEx database and verify where a letter or parcel is in the system: whether it is en route, whether it has been delivered, who received it, and when it was delivered. Providing that information allows FedEx to provide an additional service of value to the customer, differentiating itself from the competition, building customer loyalty, and increasing repeat business. Value chain activities in the virtual world include *gathering, organizing, selecting, synthesizing, and distributing information*. Often those steps result in a company entering a new business. Table 5-2 summarizes the information needed for specific strategic decisions.

Consider the opportunities offered by a central database of books, music, videos, and other forms of digital material:

- Customers can preview or "try out" the product before deciding whether to buy it. As part of the interactive experience, customers can also contribute reviews and suggestions for other potential buyers.

- A distributor can construct customer profiles based on customers' previous choices or searches and suggest additional items that are likely to be of interest. Thus, the distributor can customize the marketing message for each customer. Coupled with customer reviews and suggestions, a firm can direct its product development and acquisition to meet changing buyer patterns.

- A company can offer to act as a reseller for other providers for materials they do not carry (for example, used books and DVDs).

- A company can store all of its recorded movies, music, and books in digital archives, particularly when the files are compressed. The material, now a new product, requires little in terms of inventory

Table 5-2. Global Marketing Networks and Information Needs

Strategy Area	Information Needs
Global Sourcing	Manufacturing lot sizes of parts and subassemblies by location; monitoring inventory, costs, and quality; allocating production; exchanging design information; and changing product specifications
Global Logistics	Servicing overseas subsidiaries: up-to-date information on inventory, manufacturing output, demand in various markets, shipping details, and delivery dates, all categorized by finished goods and parts numbers
Global Servicing	Achieving service quality levels; offering warranty and after-sale services; providing worldwide personnel and parts; and providing training and documentation, including service updates
Global Competitors	Monitoring competitive new product offerings and analyzing competitor market share, cash flow, and profits
Strategic Partners	Exchanging R&D results; communicating strategic goals and tactics; and coordinating transfer of technology, manufacturing, and marketing
National Governments	Providing local output and value-added statistics, company-specific export and import flows, local pricing, promotion, and service and complying with national interests
Global Customers	Coordinating multinational marketing (adapting products, offering discounts, coordinating pricing and credit, and allocating product to markets), developing and maintaining customer and sales leads databases, and utilizing global sales force and distributor management

carrying costs and affords customers a broader array of products from which to choose.

- With direct links between store and customer, traditional intermediaries become less important, reducing distribution costs.

Amazon is one firm that uses this technology effectively. The virtual marketspace opportunities described previously are available to consumers anywhere in the world who have access to the Internet and who can access a company's databases and home page. Suddenly, a company is close to customers in distant lands—to teenagers in Tokyo as well as in Tucson. Imagination and creativity are a firm's only limits in using the virtual marketspace to attract and serve international customers. As illustrated, companies can:

- Develop new products and services tailored to the needs of small customer segments—even individual customers.
- Interact directly with customers to capture and store information about them and to use that information to better serve them. A major gain is that such information allows a firm to more precisely forecast demand and shifts in preferences, avoiding both stockouts and excess inventory that could become obsolete and have to be discounted.
- Move a product's utility (the reason for purchasing a product) from the physical to the virtual world, affecting scale and scope economies. In general, such a move makes it easier for small companies to sell in world markets. Information-based products and services have low or no variable costs of production while the fixed costs of production are high, resulting in a disproportionate investment in infrastructure. Such products are often patentable, and a patent can serve as a barrier to entry.
- Provide access when and where customers want it. As long as a server is running and connected to the Internet, anyone can view the material on a web page, regardless of location. Promotion via the Internet can act as mass personal selling, where communication is tailored to the individual. No longer is promotional timing a problem (the policy of advertising windshield wipers only when it rains); the Internet is "on" 24/7/365. No longer is geography a problem (a billboard on Route 76 is not seen by people on Route 23, for example); the information is available for individuals in Toledo, Ohio (in English), and in Toledo, Spain (in Spanish).

Virtual Shopping Environments and Experiments

Virtual shopping environments allow market researchers to observe consumers under near-real circumstances. Those experiments provide firms with an opportunity to gather valuable information, incurring fewer competitive risks and lower costs than traditional field marketing research, which uses controlled field experiments and focus groups.

In a virtual shopping environment, a customer interacts with a grocery store or any other retail outlet as simulated on a computer. The customer can survey the layout of the store, pick directions to walk, stroll down an aisle, and watch the display of goods on shelves unfold. The customer can stop and examine a product more closely, read the label, and peruse product literature. The customer can see the price, conduct comparison shopping, look for promotions, and perhaps buy the product. The computer records many aspects of customer behavior, including the time spent shopping, alternatives compared, the order in which products and categories were examined, the decision to purchase, as well as the quantity purchased and the price paid.

The simulation can be quite realistic, offering 3D representations of products. Such tests may be costly to set up; but once the store layout and product assortment have been digitized and stored in a simulation database, companies can conduct experiments that monitor customer response to variables such as changes in price, packaging, and promotions; new display techniques; and new products. Companies can explore questions such as the drawing power of a brand under different competitive conditions, the impact of price cuts, and expanded offerings. Researchers can study whether a firm's product line meets customer needs and understand which display mode (arraying a firm's products all together next to the competition's or according to size of package, for example) best elicits a desired customer purchase behavior.

Virtual shopping experiments have many advantages: They are easy to set up and can be modified easily. They can be kept secret from the competition. Experimental design methodology can be used to study the effects of key variables such as price cuts and package size. Such experiments can also help marketers understand the shopping process; that is, how customers buy products. Virtual shopping makes international marketing relatively easy because the virtual shop can be presented to customers in different countries via a computer network. In addition, the shop can be modified to offer local products priced in local currencies and in the local language. Comparing standardization versus adaptation strategies is more easily accomplished using this approach.

Of course, not all products can be tested or sold in virtual shopping environments; products that customers want to touch or smell or taste are harder to simulate. It has been shown that sensory input has an impact on the purchase decision.[6,7] The capability of equipment and software is improving, though; and the improvements will allow the senses to play a part in these virtual spaces in the near future. Work is being conducted to improve a virtual haptic display device—a glove that connects to the computer—that will allow consumers to "feel" soft objects such as fabric. Adding smell to visual displays, such as movies, has been attempted for decades; and progress is being made in this area as well. VirTra Systems (http://www.virtrasystems.com) offers virtual reality market testing and promotion that promises total "immersive virtual realty," including a 360 degree visual experience and simulations that include tactile sensations and real-life smells. In summary, virtual shopping illustrates the gains to be realized from using IT in conducting market research.

Online and Internet-Based Shopping

With the creation of virtual shops, it is a short step to allowing customers to do their shopping in these online stores. The difference is that in virtual shops, customer shopping is simulated; in online shopping, actual transactions take place, with money being exchanged for goods and services. As issues such as confidentiality and security of payment are addressed to customers' satisfaction, more people will shop online. According to the Association of National Advertisers, 80 percent of U.S. companies are selling products online—providing a wide array of services and goods.[8] Recent trends in Internet shopping include the following:

- Large retailers such as Wal-Mart are influential in determining which products are made available to consumers, and they can squeeze suppliers to get better margins for themselves. Online shopping allows suppliers to bypass the retailer, go directly to the customer, and offer consumers a wider array of choices.
- The Internet allows businesses to expand consignment-like models, which means e-businesses can offer a broader product line to consumers. For example, Amazon.com sells books and DVDs that it carries in its own inventory, but it also allows other firms to advertise and sell books and DVDs through its web site. (Amazon collects and forwards the charges for the merchandise, shipping, and handling and provides an assurance about the sellers' products.) While the Internet allows consumers to shop the world, the Internet also allows businesses from different geographic areas to combine resources in a synergistic manner. Amazon.com quickly expanded from being a seller of books to a

company in the entertainment business to a firm that fulfills a variety of shopping needs.
- Firms must be aware, though, that the nationality of users is expanding and changing. While the majority of people with Internet access currently reside in the United States (30 percent), 23 percent are now Europeans and nearly 15 percent reside in Asia. In 2003, Spain posted a 23 percent increase in the number of its population that used the World Wide Web, versus 3 percent in the United States. Increasingly, this will force companies to "go global" if they are to remain competitive.
- Online shopping offers convenience, allowing customers to shop 24/7/365, and affords more choices in products and suppliers. Time and place become less relevant. Online shopping also increases value because part of the savings from not incurring retailers' margins can be passed on to shoppers. Online shopping also allows customizing based on customers' needs in product areas as diverse as computer systems, clothing, and home furnishings—referred to as "customerization."[9]

The Internet's Impact on Marketing[10]

Firms find that as customers gain increased access to the Internet, it becomes a more viable approach to interacting with customers and their households. Through the Internet, a company can:

- Develop a presence on the Internet, enhancing its image and using the Internet as a vehicle for advertising—both broad corporate image advertising as well as product- and service-specific advertising. A company's image is a precious asset, difficult to replicate but easy to lose.[11] However, customers on the Internet typically approach sites because they are looking for information, interaction and communication, or entertainment or because they want to close a transaction. Customers are likely to bypass advertising unless the message is informative and helps them in the decision-making process. A danger is that online shoppers may have difficulty separating advertising from objective content, leading consumers to question the validity of information provided at a company's web site.[12] More on the topic of web site design will be discussed in a later section.
- Provide information about products and services, prices, product availability, order status, access to its databases, and links to other useful sites on the Web.

The more useful such information is to customers, the more customers will visit the site and the longer they will stay, making the site "sticky" and allowing the company more time to capture their business.

- Communicate and interact with customers by handling queries from them, responding to complaints and feedback about products, and conducting market research by persuading customers to respond to queries and forms on the Web (giving the firm the ability to conduct market research in real time and continuously update its market information).
- Provide after-sales service, product upgrades, and access to online experts and facilitate the formation of user groups. Firms can offer a chat room in which users communicate with one another about product use and new features desired, make complaints, and ask questions. This value-added service enhances customer loyalty and encourages repeat business even as it builds confidence in the company. Adding free e-mail service is an example of providing clients with a reason to keep coming back to a company's web site.
- Sell to the customer. The most enticing aspect of the Internet is a firm's ability to close commercial transactions with clients and obtain payment. The news and music industries are leading the way with micropayments (sales involving prices below $1 per unit). Other payment technologies—such as use of cell phones to make purchases from vending machines (payments are collected by the cell phone service provider or are prepaid and stored on cell phone microchips), advances in biometrics (allowing account access via fingerprint or retinal scan), and acceptance of digital checks to speed transaction processing—are changing marketing practices. Technologies that provide convenience to consumers; cost-effective transaction processing for firms; and, perhaps more importantly, security for all participants will make buying and selling via electronic means increasingly attractive and profitable.

Pricing on the Internet

The Internet allows customers to be fully informed. They can use search agents to learn about competing products' features, warranties, return policies, prices, shipping and handling costs, and taxes. This means that in many instances, companies will find themselves competing more on price than on features. How does this help firms selling products that are differentiated by superior quality and service? Those companies must be able to communicate to customers that the lowest price may not provide the desired bundle of attributes. Firms that compete on attributes other than price must also realize, though, that price competi-

tion will only intensify. This means they must develop business models that allow profitable operations at lower prices by seeking lower manufacturing costs, reducing distribution costs (bypassing channel intermediaries), and cutting costs by carrying smaller inventories. Closer and faster communication between company and consumer allows firms to practice just-in-time manufacturing and better customization of product. As mentioned previously, new payment technologies are allowing firms to profitably unbundle products such as music and news and deliver specific songs and stories to individual users.

In the United States, another issue is sales tax. Most U.S. Internet sales do not require payment of sales tax. However, Wal-Mart and other large retailers with physical locations in many states are lobbying that sales tax be applied to all online sales so they can compete in price with retailers that have no brick-and-mortar outlets.

Can the Internet Coexist with Other Channels?

Many large firms that dominate their industry have assiduously developed close channel relationships with distributors, wholesalers, and retailers. The major U.S. car companies are an example, relying on a nationwide network of car dealers who sell in a time-honored ritual of haggling over car price, an options package, and financing. The dilemma faced by automobile manufacturers is that, by developing Internet-based marketing for their consumers, they cannibalize sales from existing channels, taking sales from existing outlets (such as the car dealer up the street). They are not generating additional sales. (This would anger the bricks-and-mortar dealers and the salespeople that work, having no impact on total sales.)

Using the Internet as a channel of distribution can also upset corporate culture, which has been built up over a long period of time. Yet firms have no alternative. Companies that delay or make a desultory attempt because they are afraid of the impact on current channel relationships simply allow newcomers to obtain first-mover advantages with the new channel (the Internet). For example, in book retailing, Barnes & Noble was a "late mover," slow to recognize the Internet as a new channel; a newer firm, Amazon, became an industry leader very quickly. The Internet will become a dominant new channel. Therefore, firms must establish their position while working with existing channels and salespeople, perhaps by giving them a portion of sales commissions during a transition period. Otherwise, firms are likely to disappear.

Firms are also learning to use both traditional and online outlets by offering the convenience of online shopping with instant delivery for products that cannot be downloaded. Best Buy, for instance, encourages consumers to shop online, order and pay for the merchandise, and pick up the purchase at the bricks-and-mortar store (convenient because the stores are nearly ubiquitous).

Can Everything Be Sold on the Internet?

Products such as books, airline tickets, hotel rooms, vacations, computer hardware and software, and stocks and bonds are some of the products that first made a splash using the Internet as a channel of distribution. Those products still dominate Internet sales. But as customers become more comfortable with shopping on the Internet, other products are being sold online: homes, flowers, mortgages, insurance, office products, home furnishings, and apparel, to name a few. Certain products are better suited to Internet sales—products whose features can be assessed online; products for which competing offerings can be ranked; products that are nonperishable, light in weight, and easy to ship; and products that are familiar to customers. But if you include what is available on auction web sites, *anything* can be purchased on the Internet (including, purportedly, a human liver). Consumers must also be willing to postpone consumption gratification until the product arrives; for example, buying a bottle of wine to take to a dinner that evening would still be purchased at the corner store. But the expanding range of products sold online suggests that merchants are using their ingenuity to adapt their products for sale on the Web.

B2B Marketing on the Web

Even while firms grapple with consumer marketing on the Web, over half of all Internet transactions are between businesses (i.e., **B2B transactions**). Businesses find that they can more easily procure product inputs, supplies, and components on the Web. Firms can clearly lay out specifications, prequalify suppliers, and post projects for bids. Such procurement saves immensely on product purchasing costs and can be speedy. EDI allows for rapid interchange of information and payment.[13] Integrated web-based sourcing, production, and tracking systems allow manufacturers to manage production, movement, and storage of products in ways not possible previously. Smaller inventories, fewer stockouts, and less obsolete merchandise mean higher profits.

Infrastructure for Web-Centric Marketing

Secure networks are a must for preserving company confidentiality and for providing peace of mind to customers as they arrange to pay for their purchases. Speed of Web response is also important because customers are likely to become impatient when secure transaction processing networks are slow. Consumers also worry about the integrity of the companies they buy from; arrangements that guarantee customer rights, the ability to effect product returns and exchanges, and the ability to settle disputes will help alleviate such worries and win the customers' trust. To better understand consumer behavior and trends, firms use measurement tools to gather data on visitor traffic and interest. Services such as Media Metrix, tracking software such as DeepMetrix, feedback on customer satisfaction surveys, and cookies (small bits of information stored on visitors' computers) are ways in which companies learn more about their consumers, both actual and potential.

Web Site Design and Positioning

Attractive, well-designed web sites are important if a firm expects to get and maintain customers' attention, ultimately resulting in purchases. Sites that load quickly are essential, as are sites that are structured so that clients can quickly and easily find the information they are seeking. A web site is an advertisement as much as it is a source of information about the company and its products. Thus, the same level of attention and graphic design expertise that is devoted to print and other media ads should also be given to web site design. (See Table 5-3.)[14] Major firms attempt to make their sites comprehensive so that visitors stay as long as possible; for example, Microsoft provides one-stop access from its msn.com site to e-mail; chat facilities; and travel, brokerage, news, and entertainment links—all under its aegis. Smaller companies often form consortia, linking each other's sites, such as those between purveyors of books and CDs, software, movies, travel services, toys, and brokerage services.

Portals that contain narrow but deep coverage of a particular topic (such as the EU) are expensive to construct and maintain, whether updating statistics, stories, and other content or linking to other resources (since web addresses, or URLs, change constantly, which leads to user frustration because the hyperlinks no longer work). The other extreme is represented by firms such as Amazon, which tries to be a one-stop shop on the Internet, having expanded from books into movies, music, and games, then beyond entertainment into jewelry, electronics, and more. The chief competitive advantage is not so much the range of product offerings as it is a base of shoppers who like to shop online, were early adopters of this technology, and are repeat buyers, likely to exhibit loyalty as long as their shopping experience is satisfying.

Companies must incorporate their domain name, which is part of the URL, into their branding strategy. No one wants to key in an address such as http://www.getabettermousetrapforlessmoney.com. A firm's web site must

Table 5-3.
Developing a Global Web Presence

1. Use simple language.
2. Avoid complicated sentence structures.
3. Use the active voice.
4. Avoid humor.
5. Use graphics to help communicate written concepts.
6. Avoid complicated and unnecessary graphics.
7. Translate the web site into selected target languages.

also be easily found using search engines, which is partly a function of how a web site is designed (meta tags and the like) as well as how useful people find the site (the more a site is referenced, the more likely it is to be near the top of search engine results). And as multinationals have learned, language is important when branding. For example, in a Hispanic market, General Motors used the brand name Nova, meant to illicit an image of a bright star. Unfortunately, in Spanish, the brand name means "'doesn't go"—not a good name for a car.

Despite the claim that promotion via the Internet is relatively cheap compared with other methods, it is costly to design, upgrade, and maintain a web presence Even though their resources may be somewhat limited, small companies can compete more directly with larger firms. Small companies must spend the time, energy, and money needed to design an effective web site that is easy to navigate, is stimulating, and provides the content consumers are seeking. Sending bulk e-mail may be a less expensive option than sending bulk land-based mail, but designing the message and harvesting (or purchasing) e-mail addresses is not cost free.

Customization

One of the most exciting aspects of using IT in marketing is the ability to find out exactly what customers want, then customizing to meet individual customers' needs. What can be digitized can be customized! The new hybrid consumers expect to be able to customize the products they buy and the information they seek at a price they are willing to pay.[15]

Customization requires continuous learning by both a company and its customers. Firms that listen to their customers create a sense of caring, which leads to customer loyalty. Of course, this built-in loyalty advantage must be supplemented with competitive, quality products; in addition, products must evolve to accompany technological improvements.

An example of such customization is Peapod, a company that allows customers to buy groceries online. Peapod works with grocery chains to present the available assortment of goods and services online. The products are displayed in whichever format the customer requests: displayed by produce category, by items on sale at that time, by brand name, by package size, etc. Then the customer indicates what items he or she wants to buy. Peapod's buyers purchase and deliver the groceries for an additional charge. Despite the higher price, customers find that they save time and money by taking advantage of sales, doing comparison shopping, and avoiding impulse purchases. Peapod has a high rate of repeat business; and by asking customers to rate their shopping experience, it learns from its customers. This allows Peapod to modify and improve its service, particularly in critical areas such as handling customer complaints and correcting erroneously filled orders.

Who controls and learns from interaction with customers—the retailer or the manufacturer? Whichever party controls the information gains power. One solution is an alliance, as in the auto industry, where car manufacturers work with dealers to deliver mass customization. In such instances, dealers receive special training that allows them to deal effectively with customers who are armed with information about buying cars and to respond quickly to customers' e-mail queries.

What are some key steps in developing an information-based mass customization approach? In adapting to today's consumer, firms must address four key areas:

1. Companies must gather information to learn about their customers, recognizing, however, that not all customers are equally important. Initially, companies need to concentrate on large-volume customers and customers who are at the user frontier, enabling the company to learn from them (for example, customers who are willing to test prerelease software). Companies can benefit from collaborating with such customers in creating new products. Involving customers in the design process can result in a better product and win their loyalty and their willingness to buy the new product, reducing the time it takes for product acceptance. Beyond individual product design, companies can maintain a continuous dialogue. This implies accepting and encouraging interaction instead of employing a one-way broadcast.

Therefore, it is important to train the frontline sales force and others who interact with customers to gather and transmit information. Not unsurprisingly, customers are resistant to providing personal information because of their all-too-realistic fears of being deluged with junk mail. "**Micromarketing**," the customization of marketing messages for small groups of people, can lose their effectiveness when many companies, armed with the same databases, bombard customers with multiple direct mail pieces. Companies need to make a special effort to respect customers' privacy if they are to gain the customers as allies. The information gathering needs to focus on two areas

- How hard is it for a customer to do business with the company (customer sacrifice)?
- How much of a customer's total business does the company get (customer share)?

2. IT can be used to facilitate the purchase and delivery of goods and services. This suggests that there are two distinct skill sets that are relevant to satisfying customers. One set focuses on what new products and services should be offered and customized; while the other skill focuses on how to deliver the goods, whether delivery is possible, and whether the newly customized offerings should be produced in-house or subcontracted.

3. Companies can offer IT-based follow-up services, including handling of complaints and customer retention campaigns. Customer problems can form the basis of modifications and better service. But increased customer access raises customers' expec-

tations, resulting in customers becoming frustrated when a response is not immediately forthcoming.

4. Using database management, companies can organize and store information for ease of retrieval and for use in distinct phases of the marketing process (such as new product development, information gathering prior to purchases being made, current product purchases, and postpurchase follow-up). The latter can be categorized into after-sales training and service, the generation of repeat business, and enhancement of retention. Successful database marketing requires that the database design be linked to marketing decisions that use such information. As mentioned, one well-known example of that approach is FedEx, which offers Internet-based tracking of packages so customers and suppliers know exactly where a critical shipment is and when it is scheduled to arrive at a customer's site.

The Internet's Impact on Marketing

The studies and concepts reviewed previously suggest that customer linkages can be divided into two broad categories: customer interaction variables and customer information

Table 5-4. Variables Affecting Global Linkages with Customers

Customer Interaction	Customer Information
Relationship: one-time; ongoing	Customer database and buying history; market demographics
Product complexity: straight sales versus after-sales support and complex service	Customer segment positioning; vertical industry segments
Length of selling cycle: necessary for repeated interaction to close the sale? team selling effort?	Key decision makers; team buying?
Intensity of competition for order; first-time or repeat sale?	Client importance: size and frequency of order; lead user Competitive presence among the following: • Existing customers • New prospects/sales leads
Price: fixed or negotiated; volume and use-based pricing	Differences across country markets
Upstream involvement: customer participation in product design, modification, and customization	Customer input and feedback during product design; role in prototype (beta site) testing; feedback on product performance
Distribution channel in reaching customer: independent distributors, personal selling, direct mail, telemarketing, or an original equipment manufacturer (OEM) arrangement?	Channels used to reach customer: alternative distribution approaches, volume and efficiency
Downstream involvement: customer participation in joint selling; promotion	Customer capabilities; convergence of interests; perceived strategy development
Service relationship: extent of service interaction, quality of service, and parts shortages; debriefing service personnel	Customer service: monitoring of service quality
Other: exchange rate risk and risk-sharing	Monitoring exchange rate changes and effects on customers; development of risk-sharing formulas based on exchange rate bands

variables. *Customer interaction* variables affect the nature of the relationship established with a customer and shape the parameters of the network to be developed. *Customer information* variables are concerned with the information content of the network; that is, what kinds of information will flow from the firm to the customer and vice versa. The information content aspect is concerned mainly with understanding the buyer and the role the firm's product plays in helping the buyer improve his or her business performance. Strong **customer relationship marketing** is based on the purposeful development of systems and processes that allow for close contact between a firm and its customers—from product design through sales, warranty, and repurchase. Table 5-4 summarizes how those two categories of variables shape global linkages with customers.

Examples of Global Customer Linkages

Liz Claiborne has been developing links with retailers that allow buyers to view new fashion lines and specific styles on a high-resolution graphics computer. The high-definition image is digitized and transmitted to a retailer, saving the person time and providing for feedback as the design process is occurring. The retailer does not have to wait for visits from a factory representative, but can view the line whenever he or she chooses. The system also allows the retailer to zoom in on details of a product, such as the detailing over pockets or the weave of the fabric, and then transmit an order. Similar CAD/CAM-based linkages transmit design information to Liz Claiborne's overseas suppliers, which allows retail buyers, executives, and representatives of manufacturing subcontractors to interact in shaping the final product.

Gould Pumps has been manufacturing pumps for more than 150 years. Today it produces many varieties of industrial pumps; and because pumps wear out, replacement demand is a major component of sales. Gould had five geographically separated product divisions, which meant that salespeople might have to place five separate orders (with each manufacturing division) for one customer order. The 34 sales offices, including 7 international offices, were widely dispersed, which further delayed order processing and sometimes resulted in nonstandardized price quotes. Gould wanted to create a system to retain customers, increase sales, and speed up shipping and delivery. It wanted to provide customers with immediate information on pricing, order status, inventory availability, and shipping schedules. Further, Gould wanted to allow customers to dial into the company's computers and look up the information themselves. The goal was a centralized system that would bypass and reduce the load on local sales offices, agents, and distributors. Lastly, Gould wanted an international order-entry system that would eventually be integrated with inventory, plant scheduling, and shipping systems.

The global network would link markets in the United States, Canada, Italy, West Germany, and Hong Kong. A planned next stage would link the customer order to the factories producing the pumps, thus automating purchasing and providing links with preferred suppliers for components and subassemblies. In turn, this could lead to integrating all of the manufacturing plants to provide just-in-time deliveries to customers. In short, an attempt to provide better customer service could lead to integration of several parts of the company, including purchasing, material requirements planning, outside sourcing, production control, and costing.

In summary, an understanding of the buyer, together with interaction variables as depicted in Table 5-3, helps shape a global network that can aid a firm in improving the quality of its marketing relationship with industrial customers worldwide. A supplementary benefit is that aggregating information gathered from customers scattered around the world will result in data about individual country markets, as well as about individual products in a product line.

Linkages with Suppliers

After customer influence, the second major focus of global networks is linkages with suppliers. Several factors mediate this relationship. Foremost is the intent behind the business purchase transaction. Is the relationship intended to be long-term; that is, a strategic partnership? Why does the client firm seek a supplier? A strategic orientation arises out of a mandate by the client firm to reduce fixed costs and investments while seeking quality and lowered outsourcing costs. In turn, this often leads to favoring a few suppliers in an effort to gain improved quality and closer coordination in design and manufacturing, as well as the traditional economies of scale. Table 5-5 outlines the variables affecting global linkages with suppliers.

Arising out of such a strategic orientation in seeking suppliers, the next question is this: "When does the supplier become involved?" A critical concern is whether the supplier should be involved at the design stage of a product's development—affecting a final product, manufacturing costs, quality, ease of service, etc. Other kinds of involvement may include supplying a long-term open order, guaranteeing incremental product performance improvements over the life of the order, providing customer support and warranty services, and engaging in joint promotion.

Most shirt buyers have never heard of TAL Apparel Limited, but this company supplies all of the shirts sold by

Table 5-5. Variables Affecting Global Linkages with Suppliers

Strategic Orientation	Subcontractor or Partner
Stage of Involvement	At design? (designs for ease of manufacture)
Pricing Relationships	Sharing of cost reductions achieved by supplier (volume-based discounts)
Delivery Terms	Just-in-time
Quality Standards	Contracted for targeted improvement
Compatibility of Capital Equipment and Communications Network	CAD/CAM standards; EDI; transparent document interchange
Service Responsibilities	Subassemblies replaced by suppliers; joint service teams; spare part provisions; service data interchange
Technology Transfer	Safeguarding technology; technical assistance in implementing technology; second sourcing

JCPenney. TAL, a company based in Hong Kong, collects point-of-sale information from all JCPenney retail outlets around the world; analyzes the data using a software model designed by TAL; and manufactures the sizes, colors and designs specified. TAL has the shirts shipped directly to each store, bypassing the JCPenney buyers, shippers, and warehouses. JCPenney was able to cut inventories from thousands of shirts that they would hold for as long as six months to zero.[16]

Favoring more efficient inventory management, JCPenney leaves many marketing decisions to the supplier. This practice is in contrast to a typical North American pattern, where suppliers perform mainly as subcontracting manufacturers, with all product design and test phases carried out by the client (OEM) firm itself. Outsourcing is a strategic decision that requires supplier involvement; it is the first and most important question that firms need to ask. Several other consequences follow from that strategic decision.

Li & Fung, which began as a Chinese import-export business in 1906, is a supply chain management firm that orchestrates the manufacture and delivery of a vast array of consumer goods, including garments, fashion accessories, toys, sporting goods, promotional merchandise, handicrafts, shoes, travel goods, and household items. The firm's network of suppliers spans 40 nations; while Li & Fung customers are located throughout North America, Europe, Africa, and Asia. While the company still focuses on trade as a core competency, it has continuously updated its supply chain technology and today uses BizTalk and the Supplier SCMTalk Solution to manage the huge amount of data that pass through its network every day.[17]

Examples of Global Supplier Linkages

To provide evidence of the previous concepts, the following examples highlight recent corporate efforts in developing global networks with overseas suppliers.

Mast Industries

Mast is the manufacturing and sourcing arm of The Limited, responsible for supplying Limited subsidiaries such as The Limited, Lerner, Abercrombie & Fitch, Victoria's Secret, and various catalog businesses. Mast does not generate clothing ideas itself. Instead, buyers for the various Limited retail subsidiaries come to Mast with garment ideas for their stores. Mast's job is to get the clothing produced and make it available on time for the various Limited subsidiaries. Mast works with independent factories in Hong Kong, Taiwan, Singapore, Korea, and Europe. One of its objectives is to reduce the turnaround time necessary to get the items into the stores (that is, reduce the offshore production and sourcing time). The MAST Connection is the network of suppliers, transport companies, and retailers that allows apparel orders to be filled within 30 to 60 days—compared to 3 to 10 months taken by competing specialty and department stores. The reduced turnaround time allows buying decisions to be delayed until consumers' needs can be more clearly assessed. The short production time also means that smaller repeat orders can be placed, instead of one large order early in the buying season. In turn, this process reduces the risk of having excess unsold inventory at the retail stores, which obviates the need for end-of-season sales at discount prices. Thus, initial prices need not be set at high levels in order to cover losses on unsold end-of-season merchandise. The lower initial prices can translate into increased market share. Figure 5-4 details the workings of Mast's global supply network.

Mast's system uses EDI bar coding, product data management, and event management to facilitate global coordination of orders. Mast uses videoconferencing and high-definition TV (HDTV) to facilitate global discussions on fabric colors and textures. The 35mm photograph quality of HDTV allows fabric comparisons to take place between the Far East and the United States. The technology allows buyers and suppliers to zoom in on a complex print, seeing enough detail to count the stitches in the cloth. Using this technology cuts down on travel time and, more importantly, allows for quick decisions; a decision about fabric can be made in a few hours instead of five days. Quick results also come about through use of an e-mail system that links Mast to its suppliers. An employee can request a quote from the company's overseas production network and receive a cost sheet overnight. Communicating via e-mail increases overall responsiveness while it deals with the major time difference between Mast's East Coast U.S. offices and the company's Far East suppliers.

Developing such global networks means overcoming several problems—one being the building or leasing of high-speed communication facilities, which are not available worldwide. Countries that do not develop the communication infrastructure needed to conduct business place their firms in the position of being unable to compete in global trade.[18] There are also regulatory problems, ranging from government controls over the kind and type of equipment to be used on a network to controls over the transmission of data across borders (transborder data flows). Customs clearances can also hold up shipments. In response to this, Mast has developed artificial intelligence systems to automatically determine the tariff classification of a garment and its duty rate. Those systems expedite the import and export of garments between Hong Kong and the United States (since trade barriers are commonly found in the apparel and textile industries).[19]

Benetton

Figure 5-5 shows one of the more advanced systems linking a firm with suppliers and customers. The system is found at Benetton, another apparel retailer. Benetton's network includes company-owned retail outlets and franchisees, and the firm uses both in-house and subcontract manufacturing. Benetton analyzes sales from its owned outlets to forecast sales by product lines. That information is relayed to independent agents who use the information to increase orders from franchisees. Such orders are grouped and transmitted to Benetton factories and to subcontractors. Up-to-date information allows orders to be closed closer to the selling season, cutting down on unsold goods; and the speed of the system allows smaller orders to be placed later in the season. Close ties to manufacturing allows headquarters to respond to order status inquiries; and a subsystem allows Benetton to automate preparation of shipping and customs documents for a large number of countries, each with its own import, tariff, and shipping rules.

Benetton uses RFID—technology-embedded shipping labels—to help its retailers keep track of shipments, man-

Figure 5-4. Global Supply Network at Mast Industries

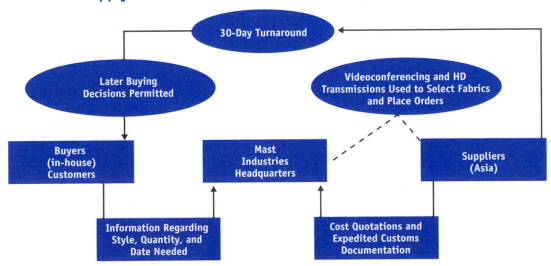

Figure 5-5. Supplier-Customer Linkages at Benetton

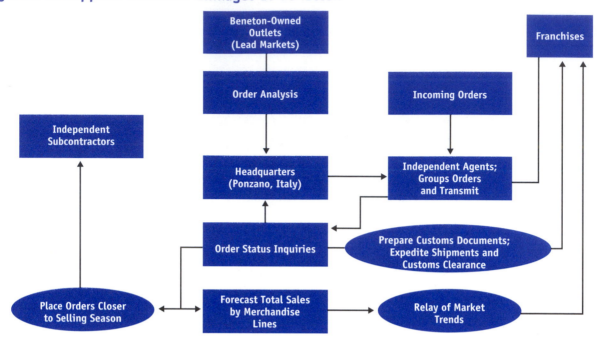

IT and the Obsolete Inventory Problem

IT can help alleviate a serious problem that marketers of consumer goods face: goods with short product life cycles that become obsolete, resulting in large losses to firms because they must write off excess inventories that cannot be sold through regular channels at normal retail prices. Firms have typically responded to that problem by reducing production quantities, in which case they run the risk of lost sales on popular products whose demand exceeds the supply.

Quick response production planning techniques, in which early market sales figures are used to adjust subsequent production schedules, rely on IT. For example, in the case of apparel, losses from obsolescence for a company selling fashion-conscious clothing were traditionally very high. Lead times in the garment industry were generally long—ordering fabric, zippers, buttons, and other notions; contracting with manufacturers in Asia or Eastern Europe; and shipping finished goods well in advance of

age inventory, and cut costs. The system includes an antenna and semiconductor that are less than a millimeter in size and, therefore, can be sewn directly into clothing tags. While discreet, they are more durable than the paper bar codes that consumers often see hanging from the sleeves of new garments.[20]

the season. Exacerbating the problem was the fact that potential sales were often misjudged, blamed in part on the length of time between demand estimate and receipt of the merchandise (often separated by as much as 8 to 12 months). Markdowns and lower profit from end-of-season merchandise was the result.

Increasingly, sophisticated application of IT is leading to shorter time periods between the design and delivery of apparel. One solution is a **risk-based multistage production sequencing**, which allows for development of production plans for the manufacturing process based on predictability or stability of demand. It is graphically displayed in Table 5-6. The process, which is described in the following steps, shows how an apparel firm can shorten the time between concept design and sales to consumers.

1. Divide the product line into two major categories, with one category containing items with more predictable demand and the other category including products with more volatile demand.
2. Develop a team of seasoned marketing professionals, each one asked to develop a sales forecast by color and style for the more volatile products.
3. Statistically analyze the forecasts to develop a group mean or average forecast and identify the variance among the forecasts. Forecasts that are substantially different (variance is high) indicates a product with highly volatile demand.
4. Use the initial forecasts to develop a production schedule. The firm then contracts to buy a certain

Table 5-6. Multistage Production Sequencing

Predictive Demand Criteria
1. Manufacture goods in advance of season based on internal forecasts.

September–March	March	March–April	September–October	September–December
Design	Show samples to retailers	Place orders with suppliers	Receive goods at distribution center	Ship to retailers
	Receive orders			

Volatile Demand Criteria
2. Use averages and variances of team member forecasts to order items with predictable demand in November. Obtain advance orders from select retailers in February to fine-tune forecasts and place orders for items with less predictable demand.

September–December	November	February	March	March–April
Design Develop internal team forecasts	Place advance orders with suppliers based on team forecasts	Receive advance orders from retailers	Receive orders	Place remainder of orders with suppliers

August–October	August–December
Receive goods at distribution center	Ship to retailers

amount of production capacity to be used over a period of months. Some of that reserved production capacity is used during the initial months to produce products with less volatile demand as well as a portion of the total forecasted demand for the more fashionable items; that is, not all of the forecasted demand is scheduled for production.

5. Obtain advance orders from a select group of influential retailers who together account for a significant portion of annual sales. Use the early orders as additional information to help team members develop revised forecasts. Based on those revised demand forecasts, allocate the remaining production capacity among the various fashion products in accordance with the revised demand figures.

The net result of the above system is fewer losses due to the write-off of obsolete goods in inventory. At the same time, point-of-sale information and order-taking systems allow a firm to keep track of stockouts (unmet demand) so the forecasting system can be continually revised. This ensures that foregone profits, because of stockouts, are balanced against losses caused by excess inventory. The heart of the system is developing timely information and letting production schedules react to that timely market information.

Using models and techniques such as those described above, industrial buyers throughout the world are seeking to reduce the number of suppliers they buy from, while negotiating longer-term agreements. They seek to link manufacturing with product design, inventory and shipping, and customer information. In some industries, designers seek closer links to suppliers to reduce excess inventory that may become obsolete. A firm not only has to communicate with outsiders, but also must break down functional barriers within the organization. Given the hybrid consumer and demands for customization, marketing and manufacturing must work together to design products that can be manufactured at low a cost and to choose and coordinate outside suppliers. Such networks are complex and costly, but they are quite necessary to doing business as a multinational firm.

Subsidiary Linkages: Sales Force, Distribution, and Service

While buyers and suppliers represent two principal nodes of the global network, other interests must also be integrated. They include sales force interests, distribution and other aspects of the marketing system (promotion, for example), and service.

Sales force interests concentrate on sales leads, up-to-date customer profiles and sales histories, a sales call scheduling and monitoring system, inventory availability and shipping dates, prices and discounts or deals allowable, and competitive pressures pertinent to each sales lead. In global industrial markets, a special issue is the use of multinational and multifunctional leads, with a drawn-out selling cycle. Necessary elements of the network are a reporting subsystem to monitor and summarize progress made through a sales lead at each visit as well as communication capabilities between members of the sales team.

Service has emerged as a major element of successful industrial selling. Hence, global networks must include service subsystems. Basically, there are two central service issues: providing field service to enhance customer satisfaction at a reasonable cost and using service feedback to enhance product design and quality of next-generation products. Related issues include maintaining failure and service records, forecasting future failures from the service history of a product or parts family, keeping track of the cost of service, facilitating feedback about product design in order to implement incremental product improvements, and facilitating similar feedback about parts and subsystem suppliers for similar corrective action. Also important is record keeping with regard to the cost of providing service; customer satisfaction with service; an adequate parts inventory in the field, used for service calls; and comparative competitor performance in the service area, including comparative warranty information and comparative "mean time between failure" statistics. Providing service in the international arena is complicated by distance, the number of locations from which service is provided, the location and availability of warehouses and parts, training and the dispatching of technical personnel, and technical information available to enhance the quality of service performed.

When reconsidering outsourcing, firms are learning that outsourcing to reduce costs sometimes leads to other kinds of costs—frustrated customers. Both Web.com and Dell moved their call centers for after-sales support back to the United States after months of customer complaints.[21]

Global Networks and Management Control Issues

The shape of global networks is also affected by organizational structure and management control needs.[22] The management control and organizational issues that surround the implementation of global marketing systems are summarized in Table 5-7. Critical points outlined in the table include the following:

- **Enhancing management efficiency** through applications in areas such as order entry, sales calls, expense reporting, analysis of product profitability by region and customer, and databases of technical product specifications.

Table 5-7.
Implementing Global Marketing Systems

Managerial Issues	Managing customers and suppliers
	Marketing efficiency: sales force control; forecasting, analysis, and planning; statistical capabilities; competitive assessment
	Environmental monitoring: governments, consumers, competition, technology, and legal aspects
	Database commonality
Organizational Issues	Opening up the firm: • Externally, with customers/suppliers • Internally, with manufacturing and others Sharing data: value of information; availability of information, access levels, and frequency of access
Technological Issues	Use of EDI; data transfer problems; transmission protocols
	Data networks: use of third-party VANs and VSAT private data (satellite-based) networks
	Data security: controlling access—hackers and viruses
	Government regulation on transborder data flows; data privacy issues
	Compatibility of equipment: computers and data transmission
	Legal responsibilities in using computer linkages with suppliers and customers

Note: VANs = Value-Added Networks; VSAT = Very Small Aperture Terminal

- **Managing the selling process** through information that permits client and product profitability analysis, comparing actual sales with targets or quotas, and sales trend forecasting.
- **Managing the manufacturing subcontracting process** with data on costs, quality, and delivery performance; spending on joint design and research; and comparative information on product and process improvement.
- **Managing the customer relationship** through databases of customer purchases, customer complaints, and other feedback and through direct links with customers, using approaches such as EDI (covered in detail in a subsequent section).
- **Facilitating management control** with immediately accessible, up-to-date information that allows

managers to perform the computer equivalent of "management by walking around." "Strolling" through successive levels of a customer database can help trace causes of sales declines. For example, a shortfall in a regional quota may be traced to a particular customer, where a change in a manufacturing process led to a switch in the raw material specifications, resulting in the customer's preference for a competitor's product. While the salesperson may know this information, placing the information in a central database can ensure a faster reaction and a more appropriate response at a higher level of the organization.

- **Environmental monitoring** is particularly important when a firm is dealing with diverse country markets and national differences in regulations and standards.

- **Statistical analysis capabilities** in areas such as market share shifts; isolation of market segments across countries; and customer reactions to management actions such as promotions, new product improvements, changes in service levels, enhanced delivery, and the like. For example, Frito-Lay, the snack foods company, used such capabilities to trace reduced market share in a region to the introduction of a generic store brand. Possessing such data allowed a quick counterresponse and eliminated the problem.

Management control draws on a set of databases and statistics that is also relevant to linkages with customers and suppliers. The difference is in the level of aggregation and analysis to which such data are subject; timeliness and speed of response are what interests management. Hence, from a management control perspective, greater emphasis will be placed on the communication network itself and on cost/benefit trade-offs in articulating the database and communications network configuration. Implementation is always a management preoccupation, and it is clear that a full-blown global network is a major corporate undertaking, requiring considerable analysis and commitments of time and money. Hence, management is more likely to opt for implementation in phases—building a full-scale global network for one product line, then using the learning from that effort to extend the concept to other product lines. Such an approach more clearly identifies the difficulties involved in extending global networks to various countries and in coordinating the tie-in of suppliers and customers to such a network.

The Valuation of Information

An important question is the value of information. Firms must decide how much information to make available to outside partners such as customers and suppliers (while the technology needed to create and maintain a large, complex database that contains sensitive information about the partner firms and clients has existed for many years). Equally important is software that restricts access to specific areas within a complex database, allowing database managers to control what each user can view, change, add, or delete. The access control provides firms with the ability to maintain one database for all users, rather than have separate databases that may contain the same data. Entering and updating data in multiple locations is expen-

Figure 5-6. Supply and Distribution Network at Pier 1 Imports

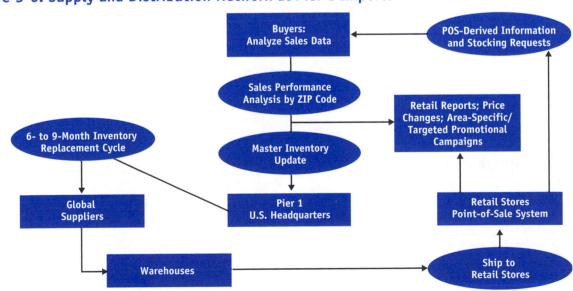

Figure 5-7. A Basic Approach to EDI

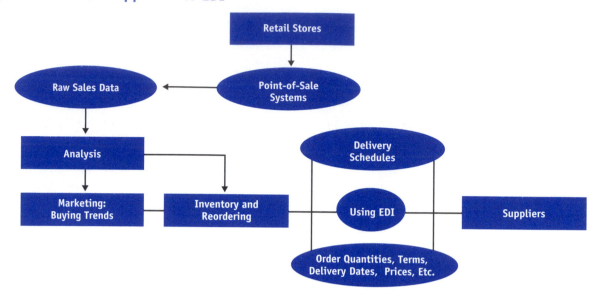

sive and increases the likelihood that mistakes will be made. Therefore, the software that controls access adds considerable value to the data and the database.

Firms must also be concerned about the cost and time required to implement such networks, including finding or designing appropriate software and getting partner collaboration in implementing such efforts. In addition, technologies and management styles inherent in using a global network are being adopted at different rates in various overseas markets. As a consequence, overseas suppliers may be unable to successfully implement their end of a network. Their unfamiliarity or resistance to change may also lead them to oppose such networking attempts. Such reluctance slows down the pace of implementing a global network. Technology and access to technology is uneven worldwide. Thus, firms must spend time and effort on training their partners to make full and effective use of global networks. One such example is Pier 1 Import's approach to supply and distribution networks, which is illustrated in Figure 5-6.

Technological Issues in Developing Global Networks

Developing global networks is partly an exercise in developing a global information and communications network. Several computer-related technical issues affect such network development. Foremost is the growing global use of EDI and of third-party VANs. Figure 5-7 summarizes the basic characteristics of using EDI.

EDI DEFINED

EDI can be described as business being conducted between computers or, more accurately, the direct transfer of business transactions between computers. EDI is a process used to automate standardized data exchange between business partners. Thus, a buyer could set up EDI with vendors to buy on a just-in-time basis, with all orders being electronically transmitted directly to the vendor's computer systems. In turn, the buyer could query the vendor's manufacturing database to ascertain what the status of the order is, how far along it is, and when delivery is likely to be scheduled. Then upon shipment, the buyer could use EDI to instruct their bank to electronically transfer funds in payment.

A major advantage of EDI is the decrease in duplication of data entry, which decreases the possibility of errors and raises productivity. EDI can reduce pipeline inventory and the length of time goods wait at loading docks and in warehouses. The problem in implementing EDI globally is that foreign suppliers, who may be small in relation to the client firm, often do not have EDI capability and must make an effort to learn how to do business using EDI. EDI, of course, requires a telecommunications network that can connect users on disparate computer systems. Such networks are available to a far greater extent in the United States than in Japan or Europe, with the smaller emerging markets lagging.

Implementing an EDI system has its difficulties, including the following:
- User access to hardware and software must be compatible with others using the system.
- There is a high cost of telecommunications infrastructure development and maintenance (hardware

Table 5-8. EDI: A Checklist

Managerial Issues

- Correct orders (timely receipt of and acknowledgement of orders).
- Accurate remittance notices, advising that a payment has been made.
- 100 percent accuracy of payments made with EDI to suppliers (correct amount credited to the correct account on time).
- Separation of payment details from remittance data (information on what is being paid for, which account should be credited, etc.). Separation creates a reconciliation problem: payments to client accounts.
- Ample time for implementation, permitting a careful evaluation before move from pilot use to full-scale volume and time for installation and training.
- Expandability, to be able to add new trading partners (necessity of low cost of adding partners facilitated by VAN support programs to educate new trading partners and get them up and running).
- Confidentiality and data ownership issues (preserving confidentiality since sensitive firm and client data are being sent over the network).
- Security, prevention of unauthorized access, error correction, and audit trails.
- Legal responsibility: When errors are made, who is responsible for consequences? the firm? the client? the provider of the physical VAN?
- Government regulations governing access to and the cost of using data networks and satellite communications; also, national data privacy laws affecting the database design of such networks.
- Build your own or use a third-party network (VAN)? As the volume of EDI transactions increases, larger EDI users find it more economical to develop their own EDI transmission networks, though this means investing in special fault-tolerant hardware and software combinations.

Technical Network Issues

- Volume of data transmitted: network must be able to handle peak data traffic.
- 24-hour access to the network, 24-hour uptime (that is, using alternative routes to avoid parts of the network that are defective, guarding against disasters such as power outages, electrical storms, hurricanes, etc.).
- Storage and forwarding capabilities (users must be able to access data and documents at their convenience), which requires developing fast search and query capabilities when dealing with diverse databases and database software.
- Ability to handle different physical data characteristics, such as SNA and asynchronous.
- Ability to handle different rates of data transmission speeds.
- Data standards and security of payment because of competing and sometimes incompatible standards between the United States and Europe.
- Cost: Generally, a fixed fee plus charges based on volume of data traffic and software to handle EDI, covering the technical issues outlined above.
- EDI software supporting multiple software platforms, such as workstations, mainframes, Windows, and Unix, and integration with in-house financial software so that one company's purchase order system can communicate with another company's order receipt and processing system.
- Internetworking capability (a trading partner working through a different third-party EDI network), which is crucial for global EDI since local VANs often provide EDI services in their countries and may have incompatible equipment and standards.

and software and upgrades of both).

- Adoption of a new system is easier and quicker when it is compatible with the existing order-entry and inventory systems.
- Data must be secure (outsider access to a host computer via a network).

Table 5-8 outlines some of the managerial and technical network issues relevant to EDI implementation. However, the biggest factor hindering EDI's widespread adoption is a lack of confidence in a system that does away with paper forms in triplicate and with tried and trusted accounting systems. In conducting such data interchanges, a common data format is essential.

When Greenwood Mills, a fabric producer, used EDI to link up with customers, an impediment was fabric bolt sizes. Greenwood used standard measurements, such as 36-inch and 48-inch fabric sizes (minimum measurements). But customers who used numerical control machines needed to communicate exact sizes to their fabric-cutting machines, whether the bolt was actually 37 or 37.5 inches wide. Hence, they had to remeasure the shipments. Fabric color required similar standardization. (Greenwood used names for different colors, while customers measured fabric color by its variance from a standard color, such as red.) In order to use EDI with customers, Greenwood had to reconfigure the product database for exact bolt sizes and color variances. A Textile Apparel Linkage Council (TALC) has been formed to standardize terminology among the various companies, suppliers, and customers in the U.S. textile industry. Similar vertical industry groups have formed across industries in the United States, Europe, and the Far East. Thus, a major implementation problem is that standards are incompatible within and across industries.

Summary

Multinational corporations face an increasingly complex task of communicating and coordinating with their global customers and suppliers. The main components of such a network include linkages with customers; suppliers; the sales force; and other elements of the marketing system, including distribution, promotion, and after-sales service. Factors such as customer profiles, the complexity of the product and the selling cycle, the strategic nature of the partnership, and the level of interdependence all influence the design and detail built into the network. Another set of influences on the network are managerial issues such as efficiency, market research needs, forecasting, analysis and planning, environmental monitoring and competitive assessment, and sales force and marketing control. Just as important are organizational issues, since creating such a network forces greater openness with customers and with other functional areas within a corporation. Also important are technical issues such as the value of information made available to outsiders, the use of technologies such as EDI, third-party VANs, data security problems and controlled access, and government regulations limiting freedom of transborder data flows.

Questions and Research

5.1 How can IT change the practice of international marketing?

5.2 What are some principal features of a global marketing network? What obstacles make it difficult to create such a network?

5.3 What are the different kinds of information needed by global marketing networks?

5.4 How can a company be said to compete in both the marketplace and the marketspace?

5.5 What is a virtual shopping environment? How can it be used by international marketing managers?

5.6 How does IT help implement the concept of mass customization?

5.7 Distinguish between customer information and customer interaction variables.

5.8 What variables should a company keep in mind when designing global supplier linkages?

5.9 How can IT help firms reduce losses from obsolete goods?

5.10 What are some management control and organizational issues underlying the implementation of global marketing networks?

5.11 What is EDI? How can it help a firm's international marketing efforts?

Endnotes

1. Speier, Cheri, Michael G. Harvey, and Jonathan Palmer. "Virtual Management of Global Marketing Relationships," *Journal of World Business*; Volume 33, Issue 3, September 22, 1998, page 263.

2. Friedman, Thomas L. *The Lexus and the Olive Tree*, 2000, New York: Farrar, Straus, Giroux, pages 41-88.

3. Wind, Yoram, Vijay Mahajan, and Robert E. Gunther. *Convergence Marketing: Running With the Centaurs*, Upper Saddle River, NJ: Prentice Hall, 2002, pages 205-214.

4. "Philippines, India, China to See Sharp Rise In Call Centers," *Company News*, Thursday, September 25, 2003.

5. "Hang-ups in India: Call Center Backlash! India Isn't the Answer, Say Some Firms," *Fortune*, December 2, 2003, page 44.

6. Citrin, Alka Varma, Donald E. Stem, Eric R. Spangenberg, and Michael J Clark. "Consumer Need For Tactile Input: An Internet Retailing Challenge," *Journal of Business Research*, Volume 56, Issue 11, November 2003, page 915.

7. "New Luxury-Car Specifications: Styling. Performance. Aroma," *New York Times*, Saturday, October 25, 2003, section A, page 1, column 5, Business/Financial Desk.

8. "The Internet and Business," *Internet Indicators* (http://www.internetindicators.com/facts.html); accessed December 29, 2003.

9. Wind, Yoram, Vijay Mahajan, and Robert E. Gunther. *Convergence Marketing: Running With the Centaurs*, 2002, Upper Saddle River, NJ: Prentice Hall, pages 205-206.

10. "The Internet: Selling Points," *Wall Street Journal*, Special Report, December 7, 1998; Hamel, Gary and Jeff Sampler, "The E-Corporation," *Fortune*, December 7, 1998.

11. Kanner, Bernice. "The Bad Man Cometh: Interview with Saatchi and Saatchi Worldwide CEO Kevin Roberts," *Chief Executive*, December 1998.

12. Fellman, Michelle Wirth. "Globalization: Worldwide Economic Woes Force Global Marketers to Seek New Opportunities—or Ways to Ride Out the Storm," *Marketing News*, December 7, 1998.

13. Smith, Gwendolyn. "Mastering the Art of Global Marketplace Exposure," *Marketing*, July 20, 1998.

14. Terpstra, Vern and Lloyd Russow. *International Dimensions of Marketing*, 4th Edition, 2002, Cincinnati, OH: South-Western Publishing, page 140.

15. Wind, Yoram, Vijay Mahajan, and Robert E. Gunther. *Convergence Marketing: Running With the Centaurs*, 2002, Upper Saddle River, NJ: Prentice Hall, pages 205-206.

16. "Made to Measure: Invisible Supplier Has Penny's Shirts All Buttoned Up," *Wall Street Journal*, September 11, 2003, A1.

17. Li & Fung Limited web site (http://www.lifung.com); accessed September 25, 2004.

18. Friedman, Thomas L. *The Lexus and the Olive Tree*, 2000, New York: Farrar, Straus, Giroux.

19. Mast Industries web site (http://www.mast.com/about/mastconn.htm); accessed December 30, 2003.

20. "Benetton to Add Electronic 'Smart Tags' to Clothing Line," *ComputerWorld*, (http://www.computerworld.com/printthis/2003/0,4814,79286,00.html); accessed September 25, 2004.

21. "Hang-ups in India," *Fortune*, December 22, 2003, Volume 148, Issue 13, page 44.

22. Schultz, Don E. "Structural Straitjackets Stifle Integrated Success," *Marketing News*, March 1, 1999.

Further Readings

Anderson, Alex. "The language of e-Business: Microsoft partnership blends XML and EDI," *MSI* (Manufacturingsystems.com), September 2003, Volume 21, Issue 9, page 14.

Bishop, Bill. *Global Marketing for the Digital Age*, 1999, Lincolnwood, IL: NTC Business Books.

Dann, Susan and Stephen Dann. *Strategic Internet Marketing*. 2002, Hoboken, NJ: John Wiley & Sons.

Darrow, Barbara. "IBM Speeds Up Information Integration," *Financial Times*, June 21, 2004 (Global News Wire).

Farhoomand, Ali and Peter Lovelock. *Global e-Commerce: Text and Cases*, 2001, Upper Saddle River, NJ: Prentice Hall.

Forrest, Edward. *Internet Marketing Intelligence: Research Tools, Techniques, and Resources*, 2003, Boston: Mc-Graw Hill/Irwin.

Hayes, Frank. "'Wal-Mart says so," *Computerworld*, November 17, 2003, Volume 37, Issue 46, page 70.

Jesdanum, Anick. "Erecting Borders on the Web" *Philadelphia Inquirer*, July 11, 2004, Business, E03.

Lee, Sangjae and Gyoo Gun Lim. "The impact of partnership attributes on EDI implementation success," *Information & Management*, Amsterdam, December 2003, Volume 41, Issue 2, page 135.

Miller, Thomas W. *Data and Text Mining: A Business Applications Approach*, 2005, Upper Saddle River, NJ: Prentice Hall.

"Plugging in with Gary Thompson, Highlights from Talks with IT Strategists," *Intelligence Enterprise*, August 7, 2004, page 48.

Roberts, Mary Lou. *Internet Marketing: Integrating Online and Offline Strategies*, 2003, Boston: McGraw-Hill/Irwin.

Senn, James A. *Information Technology: Principles, Practices, and Opportunities*, 3rd Edition, 2004, Upper Saddle River, NJ: Prentice Hall.

Taylor, David A. "Supply chain vs. supply chain," *Computerworld*, November 10, 2003. Volume 37, Issue 45, page 44.

Thomas, Jerry W. "Brave New World: Strategic Impact of the Internet," *Communication World*, Issue 4, March 1998, pages 15, 38.

Turban, Efraim. *Electronic Commerce 2004: A Managerial Perspective*, 2004, Upper Saddle River, NJ: Pearson/Prentice Hall.

Wind, Yoram, Vijay Mahajan, and Robert E. Gunther. *Convergence Marketing: Running With the Centaurs*, 2002, Upper Saddle River, NJ: Prentice Hall, pages 205-206.

Zimmerman, Ann. "B-2-B—Internet 2.0: To Sell Goods To Wal-Mart, Get on the Net," *Wall Street Journal*, November 21, 2003, B.1.

Recommended Web Sites

European Society for Opinion and Marketing Research (ESOMAR) (http://www.esomar.org).

StatSoft (http://www.statsoft.com/), particularly the description of data mining, data mining techniques, and terminology (http://www.statsoft.com/textbook/stdatmin.html).

Thearling.com (http://www.thearling.com) for information about data mining, data mining defined, recommended readings, ethical issues, and uses.

CHAPTER 6

Ethics and Global Marketing

vents over the past five years have high-lighted dramatic instances of firms' uneth-ical, irresponsible, and illegal activities. This behavior is not beneficial for the firms; or for their constituents, who include customers and stockholders; or the public at large. This chapter explores how ethical standards should govern global business. It discusses ethical principles and how they affect the development of moral stan-dards. The chapter then discusses the variety of ethical dilemmas that affect international market-ing and ways corporations have attempted to resolve them, using numerous examples.

The main goals of this chapter are to

- Identify recent instances of unethical behavior and the consequences of that behavior.

- Describe ways in which industries are respond-ing to the call to halt irresponsible activities undertaken by upper-level managers and industry leaders.

- Present laws and legal actions taken by various governments to legislate ethical behavior.

- Identify efforts under way by international agencies to address the need for morally responsible behavior.

- Discuss the positive long-term impact of good corporate citizenship.

The Effect of Ethical Behavior on Global Business

Consider the following instances:

- A firm increases its sales of cigarettes in countries such as Indonesia because of growing restrictions and liability issues placed on them in markets such as the United States.[1]
- Pharmaceutical firms have rarely focused R&D dollars on developing drugs to fight diseases such as malaria, a disease that kills millions of children around the world, as such diseases are not prevalent in the firms' principal markets in Europe and the United States. Sanofi has offered to sell at cost on a nonprofit basis a new antimalarial drug in a late stage of development; Novartis has similarly started selling its antimalarial drug on a nonprofit basis in poor countries.[2]
- A firm markets its Internet gambling services to U.S. citizens and fights attempts to regulate such activities, taking its case to the WTO.[3]
- The European Commission began investigating Apple after receiving complaints from consumers that downloading songs from the iTunes music service in the U.K. was more expensive than in other parts of Europe;[4]
- Activists accuse toy and clothing manufacturers of sourcing their products from suppliers who do not respect labor rights and protest against such practices (those protests have a possible negative effect on the manufacturers' reputations and brands); independent agencies are asked to audit and certify the manufacturing practices of toy firms such as Mattel.[5]
- In the United States, there are many well-documented cases of unethical behavior on the part of individuals and corporations that led to the Sarbanes-Oxley Act of 2002, as well as the antifraud actions being pursued by the European Commission, the OECD, and the International Federation of Accountants. Names such as Enron, Adelphi Communications, Parmalat, Nortel Networks, Ahold NV, and WorldCom are forever associated with unethical, unscrupulous, and illegal behavior.

As the above examples suggest, ethical dilemmas abound in international marketing. This chapter explores these dilemmas and suggests approaches for companies interested in practicing ethical international marketing.

The Environmental Investigation Agency has noted that Indonesia is losing an area of forest the size of Switzer-

land every year. The Indonesian government estimates that illegal logging costs $3 billion a year in lost revenue in addition to environmental damage. A problem is the corrupt army, police, and bureaucracy that abet illegal timber trade. China is a major market for Indonesian timber, but the country does not assume responsibility for the illegal logging and cutting down of forests in Indonesia.[6]

Should international marketing managers focus just on making a profit, let governments regulate their behavior, and practice compliance with the letter of the law? This is an extension of the classic free-market Friedman position—that the job of business is to make a profit. However, there are several reasons why international businesses should be concerned with ethics.

All firms need to worry about their legitimacy. Corporations are granted permission by society to operate with legal limited liability, to raise capital, etc.; and if they do not behave responsibly, their existence might be threatened.

Multinational corporations (MNCs) have more power compared to local firms, local consumers, and perhaps local governmental authorities; they also have accumulated more knowledge about products, markets, consumer behavior, and societal consequences of their actions. Therefore, multinationals must be careful to use this power ethically.

Culture and local context influence local values and local moral standards. MNCs may find that they have to balance conflicting local values and corporate values. They must judge, then, when to adapt to local standards and when to hold on to their moral standards—which may be Western, but they consider to be universal.

Another issue is one of agency. MNCs have a multitude of executives and employees carrying out actions on behalf of the corporation. Corporations need to ensure that abstract and laudable moral standards they hold are implemented by their employees in all markets.

Economic ideology may also play a part in affecting the ethical standards of a firm. Capitalism elevates the role of consumption, wealth accumulation, and the right to private property. This, in turn, colors how firms in a capitalist system view their social responsibility and affects how much they believe they should concern themselves with social justice, environmental pollution, and the like. Capitalism also assumes perfect competition and the lack thereof may lead to a higher level of unethical behavior. (There are no or few competitors who can gain from being more ethical, and collusion is possible when an oligopoly exists.) In such a situation, governmental regulation to promote competition and antitrust regulations may be a necessary complement to gradually enhancing ethical behavior.

Therefore, firms must make a diligent effort to understand moral principles from which to draw ethical standards. Those standards will govern their behavior and help them bridge the gap between profit-oriented actions and greater corporate social responsibility.

Developing Ethical Standards

Corporations need to be ethical. Corporations are a creation of society and are allowed to exist, to carry on business, to bear limited liability, and to be granted legal protection in areas such as contract law, all at the sufferance of society. In return, society expects corporations to keep societal interests in mind when conducting business. In a sense, business exists in cooperation with society and cannot survive for the long term if it practices continual unethical behavior. Such unethical behavior hurts society, consumers, suppliers, workers, and the general social welfare (for example, the consequences of pollution). Unethical behavior will result in a gradual erosion of society's acceptance of and patience with the corporation. It is in the long-term self-interest of the corporation to practice ethical behavior. Firms have to obey the law, and legal compliance may be seen as satisfying society's expectations of ethical behavior. In many cases, however, legal compliance represents a bare minimum, a floor for ethical behavior (and see: "Global Marketing: Beyond Compliance"). Hence, firms need to explore and establish for themselves the ethical standards that will govern their behavior. Questions typically arise over what is ethical behavior and how far ethics must govern corporate behavior. Developing **ethical standards** is a gradual process—one corporations can develop over time through a process of learning, dialogue, and reflection with their workers and customers, with other businesses, and with other societal institutions.

In judging whether corporate actions meet an ethical standard, firms may need to assess legal compliance in light of their own ethical standards. A firm that is in compliance with the law may decide that it does not need to concern itself further with ethics. However, in the international arena, local laws may be at odds with universally accepted moral principles—apartheid laws in South Africa being an egregious example. Hence, firms seeking to develop and uphold ethical standards may find it necessary to go beyond legal compliance and assess whether their actions meet ethical standards. Firms may want to pay particular attention to the consequences of their actions and how the outcomes of their actions affect various individuals and groups. (This perspective is further explored in the next section in a discussion of rights and justice as moral principles governing ethical actions.)

To conduct business activities in an ethical manner, a firm needs to develop moral standards that will serve as a foundation for all of their behavior. Several moral principles can help shape ethical standards for a corporation. Those principles include utilitarianism, justice, human rights, and caring for others.

Utilitarianism and concerns with rights and justice stem from the two dominant schools of thought in ethics—**teleological** and **deontological** theories. Utilitarianism stems from teleological roots, while deontological thinking yields the "rights" approach. The teleological school focuses on ends, choosing actions that maximize good and minimize harm for most people. In contrast, the deontological school emphasizes means and the fact that people are entitled to be treated as ends in themselves. Therefore, actions may not transgress a person's basic rights; hence, the results are less important than respecting individual rights.[7] These approaches are presented next.[8]

Utilitarianism

Utilitarianism judges behavior in terms of the costs and benefits to society; it suggests choosing actions that result in the greatest net benefit or the lowest net cost. Such judgment also results in efficient behavior, in using resources efficiently. Implementing utilitarianism means being able to measure costs and benefits. The measurement may be subjective in that the benefit of a meal or a job may have different values for different people; hence, two people may not agree on the precise cost and benefit of an action. Some of the most important aspects of life (quality of life, for example) are also the most difficult to measure. Another difficulty involves trade-offs; that is, how much of a certain cost to accept in return for other benefits. Further, the costs may fall disproportionately on certain segments of society while the benefits accrue to other (distinct) segments of society. Utilitarianism does not easily accommodate the impact of these costs on a segment that may be disadvantaged. That is, the distribution of costs and benefits is not a paramount consideration under the utilitarian perspective. The eventual distribution of costs and benefits that results may conflict with the notion of an individual's rights and with the concept of justice for an individual or group. Hence, moral principles built on rights and on justice are equally important.

Rights and Justice

Theories based on rights and justice have many roots. Immanuel Kant's *categorical imperative* is a useful starting point, stating that people should not be treated as means, but as ends. This means that people are beings whose existence as free, rational individuals should be promoted, that everyone should be treated as a free person equal to everyone else.[9] The possibility arises, however, that individual rights will conflict. In such cases, society must decide whose rights take precedence. Hence, justice and fairness become important in determining ethical behavior.

Reference was made earlier to evaluating trade-offs under the utilitarian perspective and the possibility that some segment of society may be burdened with costs while the benefits accrue to other segments. Bringing justice into the perspective helps reassess actions. A *distributive justice* approach can be used, the goal being to achieve a fair distribution of society's benefits and burdens. Under this approach, people who are similar in relation to the issue being considered (for example, those experiencing a job loss) should be granted similar benefits and bear similar burdens. An alternative view is *compensatory justice*, which holds that justice involves compensating people for wrong done to them or for loss suffered.

A complicating factor is the weight given to need, ability, and effort when assessing the justness of distributive outcomes. Capitalism assumes that the benefits an individual receives should be proportional to his or her contribution. Socialism, in contrast, is biased towards needs and distributes benefits according to need, while expecting people to work according to their ability. This can offend an individual's sense of fairness, as there may be little relation between work and reward and little freedom to choose what kind of work one might want to do.

John Rawls has attempted to develop a theory of justice that takes into account equality, needs, ability and effort, minimum standards of living, and preservation of freedom.[10] He asserts that the distribution of benefits and burdens in a society is just:

1. If everyone has the same degree of liberty; that is, one's liberties are protected from infringement by others—the Principle of Equal Liberty.
2. If there are inequalities in society, efforts are made to improve the position of the most needy members of society—the Difference Principle.
3. If everyone has the same opportunity to qualify for the most privileged positions in society's institutions—the Principle of Fair Equality of Opportunity.

Caring for Others

One characteristic of the ethical principles discussed thus far is that they are impartial; they do not take into account specific individuals. However, most individuals assess their acts partly in terms of the impact their acts have on people they know—their family; friends; coworkers; neighbors; community; even city, state, and nation. The question arises, should individuals show special consideration for those with whom they have a close relationship; that is, parents, children, spouses, relatives, and close friends? Is showing favoritism ethical? Cultural differences may play a part here, with cultures that favor collectivism over individualism; for example, accepting and requiring special consideration for others with whom one has a close relationship.

G L O B A L
MARKETING

Beyond Compliance

In light of widespread, well-documented lapses in corporate ethical behavior at the outset of the twenty-first century, more and more firms and nonprofits are coming to realize that it is necessary to manage and conduct corporate affairs "beyond mere compliance" with legal norms. That is, as defined by Marcus and Kaiser:

> *In the continuum of ethics (political consciousness) law, this gap where the law ends or does not yet speak to regulate conduct is the area "beyond compliance." For corporations to function in an ethically responsible manner, business managers must recognize that the technical limits of law do not set a moral floor for behavior. Operating beyond compliance requires recognition that, though some moral obligations to others may not be codified, yet that does not make their observance any less imperative.*

> *Managing beyond compliance requires the members of an organization to progress beyond the at-any-cost corporate culture of previous decades. It will require a move beyond the gamesmanship of hyper-technical parsing and the what-can-be-gotten-away-with mentality by business managers, their attorneys, accountants and other professionals guiding and advising the corporation.[14]*

Furthermore, given legal decisions that have traced corporate liability back two, three, or more decades, managing beyond compliance is a pragmatic stance for twenty first-century corporations. As Marcus and Kaiser stated:

> *The advantages of such progressive leadership will be myriad. The risk that unethical behavior poses to the vitality and perpetuity of a company cannot be overestimated. Pushing the legal envelope into arguably unethical territory at various stages in the process or levels in the entity invariably produces a cumulative end result well outside of the legal obligations of compliance. This approach was the cause of many of the financial disasters that beset some of the largest and oldest US firms in the beginning of this century. Further, given that the*

continued

law is continually evolving, mere compliance with the letter of the law can be dangerous. Unless a company has its finger on the precise pulse of where the law is going, it can get stung by mere compliance, particularly where personal harm is caused by corporate action or inaction. Tobacco companies did not violate any legal regulation when they failed to warn the public of the known health risks posed by cigarettes. Nonetheless, they now face billions of dollars in punitive damage judgments for their negligence. Companies that dispose of toxic waste in water or soil in a manner that causes personal injury or property damage can be held legally liable for such harm regardless of the legality of the original dumping. Examples abound of situations where a company's activities result in financial liability that far exceeds the cost-benefit calculation factored into corporate decision making.

There is also an apparent trend toward conferring legal reward for companies operating beyond compliance. Principles of organizational accountability impose indirect vicarious liability on a corporation for the actions of its agents (managers, employees). Increasingly organizations are held accountable for the actions of their agents whether management knew of the misdeeds or not. To alleviate some of the harshness of such strict liability on the entity, some statutes and court decisions have recognized that a company's financial damages may be mitigated to the extent that the organization affirmatively attempted to prevent the illicit behavior—that is, to the extent that it operated the entity beyond the bare floor of legal compliance.[15]

Integrative Social Contracts and Hypernorms

As suggested in the previous discussion, cultural differences can be a source of ethical conflicts because of the underlying multiple value systems. An effort to reconcile such conflicts is Donaldson and Dunfee's **Integrative Social Contracts** theory and their **hypernorms** approach.[11] They suggest that in the context of most local cultures, managers can apply ethical standards derived from the local context, principally from domestic firms, industries,

professional associations, and other organizations. However, there will be instances when hypernorms take precedence. Hypernorms are manifest, universal norms that represent principles so fundamental to human existence that they are reflected in a convergence of religious, philosophical, and cultural beliefs.[12] These norms represent standards that are in some sense universal, most likely negative injunctions against murder, deceit, torture, oppression, and tyranny.[13] An example of a hypernorm, suggested by Donaldson and Dunfee, is informing employees about dangerous health hazards, a universal ethical standard that should override any local practice that contradicts this ethical injunction.

Given these different approaches to developing moral principles, how should a firm incorporate such principles as it seeks to develop its own ethical standards? One approach might be to accept that different ethical principles have arisen because of drawbacks in one of the approaches. Thus, a *pragmatic* approach may require drawing on the implications of all of these theories as specific policies and actions are tested. Further, discussion of the ethicality of a firm's policies and actions in light of the various principles is necessary to arrive at reasoned moral judgments that are shared across a firm, thus helping to derive moral standards.

In the international arena, why does unethical behavior happen? Job pressures, lack of personal ethics, flawed corporate culture and leadership, a complaisant government and national culture, poor governance processes, lack of sanctions, ease of using intermediaries and hiding one's tracks, large stakes (size of orders, profits)—all of those can create a breeding ground for unethical behavior. Hence, internal discussion is essential to help develop an individual's ethical outlook, since the ethical standards of a firm are nothing but the collective acting out of the ethical beliefs of all of the employees of the firm. Thus, examining and debating ethical principles can result in individuals with a shared ethical outlook and a firm with high moral standards underpinning collective ethical actions. Such a discussion might embrace the following typology, shown in Figure 6-1.

In the next section, a variety of ethical dilemmas that face the international firm and that apply the methodology outlined in Figure 6-1 are presented to illustrate how they can be used to develop ethical standards.

Types of Ethical Conflicts

To understand the range of ethical conflicts that may arise when MNCs conduct international business activities, it is useful to consider the marketing value chain and assess where conflicts may occur at each step of the chain. (See Table 6-1.)

Figure 6-1. Developing Ethical Standards

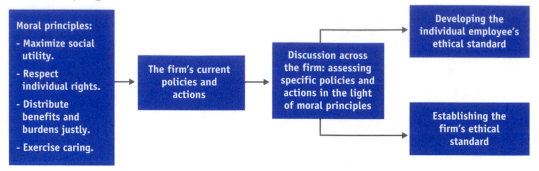

Source: Adapted and developed from Figure 2.1, Manuel Velasquez, *Business Ethics*, 5th Edition, Prentice-Hall, 2002, page 131.

Table 6-1. Ethical Conflicts in the Value Chain

Value Chain Activity	Example
Global strategy: competing for market share	Bribery to obtain contracts
International marketing research	Testing new drugs in emerging markets
New product and service development	Ignoring low-income segments and populations in new product development
Global manufacturing; supply chain and logistics and linkage to international marketing	Supply chain manufacturing outsourcing partners who exploit local labor, negatively affecting the reputation of the company
International pricing	Price discrimination across markets
Global branding	Accusations that brands charge premium prices, create barriers to entry, shut out local competitors, and create cultural homogeneity
International distribution	Exclusive distributors that raise prices and reduce competition
Staffing international marketing positions; control and incentive systems	Hiring family members to fill supervisory positions
International advertising	Inappropriate appeals that clash with cultural values
Multiple stakeholders and societal consequences	SUVs and their impact on global warming

Global Strategy and Competing for Market Share

Part of global strategy is deciding which markets to compete in, then developing strategies and actions to win market share in those markets. An ethical problem arises when bribery is used to win business and market share and to influence public officials, co-opt consumer agencies, and consumer rights watchdogs.

For example, Monsanto agreed to pay fines of $1.5 million to settle bribery charges. The company had made $750,000 in payoffs to Indonesian officials to get permission to sell its genetically modified seeds (permission that it ultimately did not receive).[16] The bribes were paid by local executives and lobbyists working for Monsanto but were apparently done without the knowledge of Monsanto's top management. Upon learning about the transgres-

sion, Monsanto voluntarily informed U.S. authorities and accepted sanctions, though prosecutors did attribute the occurrence of the bribes to careless oversight by the company. In another example, the U.S. firm Fidelity National Financial was accused by its Taiwanese competitor of paying bribes through its Alltel Information Services subsidiary (which it had recently acquired) to secure software contracts worth around $176 million.[17] (See Figure 6-2.)

The example of Alltel provides some insight into the gradual process by which large-scale bribery unfolds. The sales effort in question began in January 2001, and major contracts were closed only in September and October 2004. During this lengthy period, there were changes in top management at the client firm, a suspension of the initial contract (leading to pressure to obtain reinstatement), the authorization of illegal payments, and the trail of evidence needed to establish illegal behavior.

Figure 6-2. Anatomy of a Bribe—Fidelity National and the China Construction Bank

2001

June	Alltel Information Services (AIS) and Grace & Digital Information Technology (GDIT) agree to help sell Fidelity National Financial (FNF) software to China Construction Bank (CCB).
July	CCB and AIS sign an interim software licensing agreement.
December	CCB and AIS sign a long-term licensing agreement.

2002

January	The chairman of CCB is fired and replaced; the contracts with AIS are suspended.
March	AIS terminates its agreement with GDIT.
May	AIS hosts the new CCB chairman and others to a golf outing at Pebble Beach.

2003

April	FNF takes over AIS and renames it Fidelity Information Services.
September	CCB agrees to license FNF's software.

2004

October	Fidelity announces that CCB will use its software to process loans.

2005

March	The CCB chairman resigns for "personal reasons."

Source: "Suit Alleges US Firm Paid Bribes for China Contracts," *Wall Street Journal*, March 21, 2005.

Clearly, such bribery and corruption do have indirect costs, such as unfair competition, misallocation of resources, inefficiency, the long-term impact on slowing growth, and reduced entrepreneurial drive. If seen as pervasive and arbitrary, bribery and corruption can reduce the motivation to set up business and enter new markets. How should firms respond? Doh and others have suggested a gamut of activities. They range from avoiding such markets to changing entry mode (using joint ventures, licensing, arms length distribution), developing and adhering to corporate codes of conduct against bribery (a concern being that local firms might refuse to join such an agreement, thus gaining a temporary advantage), and being thoroughly trained and educated about bribery, as well as by developing laws and agreements governing such behavior.[18]

It is useful to see how the principles and methodology in developing ethical standards can be applied to specific corporate actions. Consider the common problem of bribery in international markets described previously. Bribes can be paid to facilitate routine transactions, such as obtaining expedited customs clearance of goods that have been legally imported, or to be chosen over a competitor to receive, for example, a sizable government contract.

- The first kind of bribe, grease payments, may be seen as maximizing social utility. It preserves jobs and speeds the transit of scarce goods to customers, though it may favor the rights of the individual receiving the bribe over others. It also somewhat distorts the distribution of benefits in favor of the person receiving the bribe. It burdens society with the additional costs of the bribe, especially when they are passed on to customers or shareholders. **Grease payments** probably have little positive impact on the principle of caring for others; though in many emerging markets, government jobs may be handed as favors to close relatives and friends of senior political figures. A firm might judge grease payments to be justifiable on the grounds of greatest social benefits at minimum social costs with little (hence, acceptable) injury to social justice and individual rights. In another firm, the same discussion could come down on the side of branding such bribes as unethical on the grounds that social justice should take precedence over any additional net benefit that society might receive.

- However, in the case of the bribe to obtain business over a competitor, the same application of the moral principles of utilitarianism, rights, social justice, and hypernorms might result in most firms agreeing that such bribes are unethical and unjustifiable. The key point is that firms need moral principles and a reasoned discussion to judge their policies and actions and to arrive at ethical standards that are acceptable to them—policies they can abide by and implement.

Legal Regulation and Compliance

National and supranational laws and regulations may clarify what constitutes minimal ethical behavior and may constrain the range of legal actions that a firm can undertake in its international operations. As stated in Chapter 4, attempts to forge supranational laws governing business conduct are counter to traditional legal notions and respect for national sovereignty. **National sovereignty** means that a country can conduct its own affairs without interference from other governments or the laws of any other country. Thus, when the EU was formed, individual European nations had to agree to accept European laws and pass enabling legislation to mirror those laws. The alternative is to create voluntary associations such as the OECD, the UN, and the WTO and to voluntarily agree to accept and abide by their rules and guidelines, such as those against bribery and corruption.

The UN, as part of its **Global Compact**, announced in June 2004, "Businesses should work against corruption in all its forms, including extortion and bribery." The UN Convention against Corruption stresses that corruption is damaging to national economic growth. It has recommended codes of conduct for public officials, transparency of public procurement, the prevention of bribery to influence public officials, and generalized anticorruption crime-fighting efforts. While the UN stops short of policing efforts, it does recommend the sanctioning of such unethical behavior. Transparency International, a supranational NGO that seeks to eradicate corruption in international trade and business, similarly notes in its "Business Principles for Countering Bribery" that

> The enterprise shall prohibit bribery in any form whether direct or indirect. . . . The enterprise shall commit to implementation of a Programme to counter bribery.[19]

U.S. Law

The FCPA specifically bans payments to gain business, though it does allow facilitating payments. The difficulty in allowing some level of bribery is that it may become a slippery slope leading to larger and more frequent payments. Hence, corporations may prefer to ban all such payments. For example, Sealed Air Corporation (manufacturer of Bubble Wrap® cushioning and other packaging products) has developed a **code of conduct**, sections of which are provided below.

> Sealed Air Corporation has a reputation for conducting its business on a highly ethical level. It is important that we continue this record of integrity in the future.
>
> Each and every employee of the Company and its subsidiaries throughout the world is responsible for the maintenance of our fine reputation. We expect that each employee will support the Company's principles of business ethics and

behave in a manner consistent with these high standards. No employee in a supervisory position has the authority to instruct a subordinate to violate the ethical guidelines of the Company.

> Each of our employees is expected to comply with the law, but our standard of business ethics goes beyond compliance with law. No list of rules can substitute for the exercise by anyone who represents our Company of basic morality, common decency, high ethical standards and respect for the law. If an employee is in doubt about the acceptability of a particular course of action, the following test should be applied: Assuming full public disclosure of the action, would both the employee and the Company feel comfortable from a moral, ethical and legal standpoint? If the answer is "Yes," then the action is very probably consistent with our corporate philosophy. If not, then the action should be reviewed with the employee's manager or with the Company's Law Department before proceeding.
>
> Our products and services will be sold on their merits. We will compete vigorously and fairly in the markets we serve. We will afford our competitors the degree of respect that we expect them to afford us. We will not enter into illegal arrangements nor engage in illegal concerted activities with our competitors or with others. . .
>
> Sealed Air requires its employees to comply fully with anti-corruption laws in the United States and similar laws in other countries. Sealed Air forbids its employees to make or offer illegal bribes or kickbacks intended to secure favored treatment for the Company from customers, suppliers, domestic or foreign government officials or others. This rule also applies to the use of intermediaries to make such payments.[20]

Sealed Air's Code of Conduct is clear in stating the company's explicit ethical standard that "goes beyond compliance with law." It further suggests an easy-to-understand generalizable test: "Assuming full public disclosure of the action, would both the employee and the Company feel comfortable from a moral, ethical and legal standpoint?" Such unequivocal and clear statements from top management help create a climate of regard for ethical standards and a strong desire to comply with them. Such a commitment is the necessary first step to developing ethical standards that pervade a company.

International Research

A particular issue with international research, particularly in emerging markets, is that a firm or its agencies may be working with research samples and with underlying populations whose members may be less informed, less educated, and less powerful when compared with the foreign firm. Hence, ethical standards dictate that a firm insist that permission of the research subject, informed consent, confidentiality, and restrictions on using and sharing information gathered from research be in place before the research begins. As in the home country, a firm needs to be especially attentive when using children as subjects for its international research effort. Pharmaceutical drug testing in emerging markets is an example of the kinds of ethical issues that firms need to take into account when conducting international market research, as discussed below.

DRUG TESTING IN EMERGING MARKETS

Before they can be certified by the FDA and other drug certification agencies worldwide for use in treating ill patients, newly developed drugs require extensive testing for toxicity, effectiveness, side effects, and interactions with other drugs. Drug companies have begun testing new drugs among populations in countries such as India, Africa, and Eastern Europe. The attraction for researchers is a larger pool of patients to draw from who have not received much medical treatment involving new drugs ("drug-naïve") as well as the low costs of administering the drug trials. For instance, Covance, one of the world's largest drug development service companies, has considerably expanded its clinical trials services in Central and Eastern Europe. To find potential recruits for its new drug studies, Covance draws on a population of over 470 million people in 20 countries in this region. In return, the countries and their health-care systems gain access to advanced medical treatments and new drugs under development. The drug companies and Covance clients benefit from "high patient recruitment rates and excellent data quality." The Central European region also has well-trained medical investigators; and the drug trials can be done at a low cost, which may explain the five-fold increase in clinical trials in the Czech Republic, Poland, and Hungary over the past ten years. Another attraction is the "high incidence of many of the diseases most targeted by the pharmaceutical industry"; for example, Bulgaria has one of the highest rates of cardiovascular disease and strokes.[21]

Ethical conflicts can arise when the only access to health care for low-income patients is through participation in such clinical trials. Some of the difficulties of conducting these trials include recruiting patients for whom English is not a native language. Their understanding of English is often limited. In such a case, questions can be raised about their giving informed consent when signing a liability release in English. In India and other countries with a patriarchal bent, women may be pressured by male relatives to sign releases and enter new drug trials. To be sensitive to possible exploitation, the contract research organization should use local and regional ethics committees at the hospitals and local facilities to evaluate patient recruitment practices and the proposed features of the clinical trials. Joseph Herring, president of Covance, notes that certain principles govern such collaboration, with the most important principle being the dictum "Aspire to a good that is greater than the individual or the group."[22]

One such drug trial on a new AIDS-prevention remedy was abruptly halted in Cameroon on the grounds that drug trial participants were not being fairly treated. A nonprofit public health organization, Family Health International (FHI), was conducting a study on the efficacy of an AIDS antiviral drug, Viread, also known as tenofovir. At a high risk for AIDS, the people in the study were from the five countries of Ghana, Nigeria, Malawi, Cameroon, and Cambodia. The drug was being supplied free by Gilead Sciences. If the drug tests were successful, Gilead planned to make Viread available at cost to poor countries.

The Cameroon study had recruited 400 women, including prostitutes at a high risk of contracting the AIDS virus. As is customary in drug trials, half the patients in the study were randomly assigned to receive a placebo pill, while the other half received a daily dose of tenofovir. The participants received monthly health exams, including liver and kidney function exams to test for drug toxicity. The women had given informed consent and in the presence of a multilingual patient advocate, had received advice about practicing safe sex. The study had been approved by Cameroon's National Ethics Committee and by FHI's own review board. If a patient in the trial contracted AIDS, he or she was to be referred to a Cameroon AIDS treatment program for antiviral drugs. However, a French AIDS activist group, Act Up-Paris, managed to get the study halted on the grounds that the patients in the trial were "utilized as veritable guinea pigs" in an attempt to promote the drug's commercial prospects. In turn, the New York-based AIDS activist group Treatment Action decried Act Up-Paris's actions as "ethical imperialism." The five-country study had been funded by the Bill and Melinda Gates Foundation with a grant of $6.5 million. Act Up-Paris's protests had also halted the study in Cambodia. A similar study was being carried out in the United States to test the efficacy of the drug in AIDS prevention among gay men in Atlanta and San Francisco.[23]

New Product Development (NPD)

New product development (NPD) for foreign markets usually involves product adaptation and segment identification. Firms have to decide how to adapt their products, which segments they will adapt products for, and whether to develop entirely new products for those markets and segments. Given the fact that large portions of the developing world are poor, affordability is an issue; keeping affordability in mind, firms have to consider whether to adapt products. In emerging markets, firms should be attentive to the impact on the user—in terms of health, welfare, and value. The oft-held view is that low-end products are commodities with limited profit prospects. While low-margin products sold in sufficiently high volumes may yield adequate returns on investment, firms may be concerned that entry into such segments runs counter to their chosen strategy of concentrating on highly differentiated niche products sold at high prices for high profit margins.

Product development focusing on the needs of low-income populations can be a controversial choice within a firm. Making such a choice has particular significance in the global pharmaceutical industry. Diseases such as AIDS and malaria are scourges that have a huge effect in Africa, in India, and in other tropical countries—with lives lost and debilitating effects on the ability to work.[24] A well-known example is Merck's work on a drug for river blindness in the highlands of Africa.[25] This disease affects about 20 million people, primarily poor, in remote parts of Africa. The disease is transmitted by black flies whose habitat is swift-flowing water. Merck spent over $100 million of its R&D funds on developing a potential treatment for this disease, but would not be able to market it commercially given the low purchasing power of the affected population. They decided to make their treatment for river blindness, ivermectin, available free of charge for distribution by numerous agencies, including the UN.[26]

Merck's development and subsequent donation of a treatment for river blindness is an example of **Global Public Good (GPG)**.[27] The World Bank defines GPGs as "commodities, resources, services and systems of rules or policy regimes with substantial cross-border externalities that are important for development and poverty reduction, and that can be produced in sufficient supply only through cooperation and collective action by developed and developing countries." With regard to pharmaceutical drugs, given the paucity of drug development efforts directed toward affordable drugs for diseases such as river blindness, private philanthropies have often stepped up their efforts. For example, in 1999, the Global Alliance for Vaccines and Immunization (GAVI) donated over $750 million to promote the development of vaccines. GAVI gave an equal amount again in 2004 to help develop vaccines against malaria, AIDS, tuberculosis, and other diseases (yellow fever, influenza, and hepatitis).

Segmentation and the Poor

Market segmentation focuses on identifying segments that are sizable and fast-growing, that offer profit opportunities, and that are relatively less intensely competitive. For firms, this has generally translated into seeking niche markets and selling higher-priced, value-added products and services. Low-end products are avoided because they offer slim margins, are volume-driven, and are likely to become commodity businesses. Yet most of the world's consumers are poor, and global marketers must confront the issue of selling to the world's poor.

In his book *The Fortune at the Bottom of the Pyramid*, C. K. Prahalad emphasizes that profits are possible in this segment.[28] By practicing what he terms "inclusive capitalism," companies can do well financially and develop new sources of value. He notes that in much of India and China, single-use packages account for the bulk of sales. For example, 60 percent of the value of all shampoo sold in India is in single-serve packages that sell for about a penny a piece. The product is profitable for global multinationals such as Unilever and Procter & Gamble, as well as for myriad, small local firms.

Another example of market segmentation is that of providing subsistence farmers in rural villages with access to PCs, allowing them to track weather, source agricultural inputs at competitive prices, and track commodity price fluctuations so they can market their crops at fair prices and retain a reasonable share of the profits. To develop such PC kiosks, companies have to innovate along several dimensions, including developing the following:

- Rugged PCs
- Back-up power supply to manage power outages
- Solar panels to provide inexpensive energy
- Satellite-based telephone hookup to allow Internet access

What is interesting is that potential entrants into such markets are not creating just "single-serve" equivalents of their standard products, but are creating innovative solutions that can serve as a platform for additional products capable of being marketed globally.[29] As companies strive to manufacture affordable products, they may rethink design, feature sets, functionality, materials, and the like, resulting in price-performance breakthroughs that can serve as powerful entry points in challenging incumbents in developed markets. As an example, Prahalad refers to an effort in India to develop a car for under $3,000 to cater to India's vast numbers of lower-middle class consumers (the recently poor). While such cars may lack many of the features demanded by consumers in Germany or Japan, they will be built utilizing significantly lower-priced parts and subsystems, which will inevitably affect the global market and competition in the auto parts industry. It is entirely possible that nascent car companies in India and China will develop significant competitive advantages in products, logistics, and service capabilities, gradually enabling them to compete successfully in the advanced nation markets.[30] What is noteworthy is that a firm's ethical impulse not to marginalize low-income consumers can lead to its enhanced long-term global competitiveness—another example of "managing beyond compliance."

Global Manufacturing and the Supply Chain

Mattel (see the discussion in Chapter 5) and other toy companies manufacture the bulk of their toys in China and other Asian countries. By doing so, they can take advantage of low-cost labor and an efficient logistics system that allows them to raise or lower procurement quantities as demand evolves in the United States and Europe. It allows them to rapidly design and manufacture new toys in response to competitors' successes. It also allows them to quickly adapt their toys to changing tastes among their primary market—children and parents. Thus, overseas manufacturing is critical to the toy companies' global procurement strategy. Further, linkages between their global manufacturing and global marketing help preserve international competitiveness. These companies have come under attack from public interest groups for not paying enough attention to the welfare of their overseas workers, particularly when those workers are employed by subcontractors in China, Vietnam, and elsewhere. In response, Mattel has developed a set of **Good Manufacturing Practices** (GMP) that govern their overseas manufacturing practices and provides an overarching ethical framework for such decisions. The elements of their GMP are listed below.

Mattel Good Manufacturing Practices (GMP) Highlights

(The firm must comply with local laws as a minimum standard.)

Management Systems. Facilities must have systems in place to address labor, social, environmental, health and safety issues.

Wages and Working Hours. Employees must be paid for all hours worked. Wages for regular and overtime work must be compensated at the legally mandated rates and all overtime must be voluntary.

Age Requirements. All employees must meet the minimum age for employment as specified by country and Mattel requirements.

Forced Labor. Employees must be employed of their own free will. Forced or prison labor must not be used to manufacture, assemble, or distribute any Mattel products.

Discrimination. The facility must have policies on hiring, promotion, employee rights, and disciplinary practices that address discrimination.

Freedom of Expression and Association. Each employee must have the right to associate, or not to associate, with any legally sanctioned organization.

Living Conditions. Dormitories and canteens must be safe, sanitary, and meet the basic needs of employees.

Workplace Safety. The facility must have programs in place to address health and safety issues that exist in the workplace.

Health. First aid and medical treatment must be available to all employees.

Emergency Planning. The facility must have programs and systems in place for dealing with emergencies such as fires, spills, and natural disasters.

Environmental Protection. Facilities must have environmental programs in place to minimize their impact on the environment.

Source: Mattel Inc.'s Corporate Social Responsibility Report, 2004, page 18 (http://www.mattel.com/about_us/Corp_Responsibility/csr_final.pdf).

To obtain widespread adoption of its GMP principles, Mattel has to be persuasive in motivating its suppliers to implement such practices and must be willing to accept the higher procurement costs that follow. Mattel can feel comfortable knowing it is following ethical principles in its procurement only when its far-flung supply network can be swayed to adopt such principles themselves. Mattel's actions, if successful, could burnish its reputation in the eyes of parents and children. Setting a high ethical standard within its supplier network will also raise the bar for the rest of the industry. They will become aware of Mattel's sourcing principles and may be expected to follow similar ethical principles. One possible consequence is the betterment of working conditions worldwide for workers in similar factories in a variety of industries beyond toys and apparel.

Pricing

A generalized problem is one of high prices relative to incomes in specific markets. An extreme example is the cost of the AIDS "cocktail" of drugs, which arrests the progress of AIDS and allows patients to attain a semblance of normalcy. But this course of treatment averages over $10,000 a year (far beyond the reach of most Africans) and Africa has one of the highest rates of AIDS infections. One response has been the development of copycat drugs by Indian pharmaceutical companies, which are sold for less than one-tenth the price of regular drugs. This development was made possible because India recognized process patents only until 2005, allowing Indian firms to legally manufacture similar drugs using noninfringing processes, thus underpricing Western competitors in the markets of Africa.

Other pricing problems may include price fixing, unfair discounts, discriminatory discounts, and premium pricing in poor neighborhoods (such as offering high-interest payroll loans). All of those practices are possible because of a lack of competition, allowing the foreign firm to exercise market power through pricing control. Another factor is the desire to maximize profits from the higher margins that result from higher prices, without much concern for affordability. In the long run, those practices can be self-defeating, as the higher prices create an umbrella that allows for the emergence of competitors who can develop and offer products suited to local needs at affordable prices.

Global Branding

Corporations develop global brands as one of the bases for product differentiation in the global marketplace. The intent is for consumers to learn to trust the brand and purchase it with confidence that the company behind the brand will deliver quality and value. Firms build brands by extensive advertising and promotion. Extensive investment in a brand is often rewarded with premium prices and brand loyalty, resulting in repeat purchases and higher long-term income. Brand loyalty also translates into increased sales volume and sustainable market share, creating a barrier to entry.

However, these very qualities of a global brand—namely, premium prices, barriers to entry, and brand loyalty—are also held against the company and the brand as negative consequences that prevent smaller local companies from competing and winning market share. The argument is that brands delude customers into believing that consuming certain brands provides a superior lifestyle. Furthermore, the emotional attachment to a brand promotes a "vapid lifestyle" and an increasingly consumerist economy. Brand power is also seen as allowing companies behind the brand to use low-cost labor in developing economies, to ignore workers' rights, and to use materials and create consumption habits (for example, the SUV) that are harmful to the environment.[31] The No Logo movement, which first gained prominence in the U.K. and Europe, is the foremost proponent of such an argument, blaming global brands for creating cultural homogeneity and creating "a Barbie world for adults."[32]

Local policy makers and international executives both need to consider whether strong global brands crowd out local brands (for shelf space and mind space) and whether global brands represent a battle between unequals (between large global brand companies and smaller, underfinanced competitors from developing countries). At the same time, a company that makes massive investments in building and sustaining global brands is likely to want to safeguard its reputation with vigor and avoid unethical actions, whether it is selling shoddy quality and dangerous products, harming the environment, or exploiting workers in poor countries. The company has to worry that consumers will take their business elsewhere it if it undertakes such actions. Enlightened, long-term self-interest may, in fact, motivate a company with a global brand to behave more ethically, if only because it is more in the global limelight.

Ethical Behavior and Brand Value

A company with a strong brand has to worry that its brand reputation and strength will be hurt because of perceived or real ethical missteps. A brand is powerful and profitable precisely because consumers develop a preference for and choose to purchase a brand. Repeat purchases by brand-loyal customers provide the underpinning for brand equity and recurring income and profits. However, brand strength can also be a magnet for activists, who see corporations as the root of many of society's ills. Activists are quick to target major brands, using antisocial behavior. For example, Gap is held responsible by some activists for exploitative labor practices undertaken by its network of global suppliers. Unilever is accused of contributing to overfishing and depleting fishery stocks worldwide because of its global procurement of fish. The danger is that consumers will remember such accusations, whether founded or not, and drop their preference for the brand, sapping the brand's ability to be successfully marketed internationally.

A company can respond to such threats by inculcating values across the firm, subscribed to by all employees, which are consonant with its customers' values. For example, Gap can show its concern for fair labor practices by developing and auditing fair labor standards for all of its suppliers, then making clear to all of its global consumers that its garments are procured only from suppliers who adhere to the company's global code for treatment of labor. Its **Social Responsibility Report** summarized the results of over 8,500 visits to its 3,000 supplier factories in 50 countries. These visits led Gap to revoke its approval of 136 factories and also led to its rejection of contract manufacturing bids from many more factories for serious violations of minimum wage, safety, environmental, and other standards (such as use of underage laborers).[33]

A company following Gap's path should be careful to ensure that its public pronouncements on values are reflected in its behavior; that is, all of its employees understand and implement the company's values through their actions, in choosing suppliers, and in continuing to do business with them. In analogous fashion, Unilever responded to accusations that it contributed to overfishing by joining with the Worldwide Fund (WWF) to form the Marine Stewardship Council (MSC). The MSC certifies well-managed fisheries and preserves surrounding ecosystems as being compliant with environmentally sound practices. There are similar organizations for other industries, such as fair-trade coffee and eco-friendly wood.

When thinking about values, companies also need to distinguish between values that are central to the company's core businesses and values that may be somewhat peripheral. Companies need to ensure that they closely monitor values that are crucial to their business. In the case of Gap, this clearly points to the need to monitor suppliers who provide the company with clothing and other fashion accessories.

Where peripheral issues are concerned, a company's actions may have less impact on the outcomes; hence, the company may be better served by working with industry groups and broader initiatives, as in the example of De Beers' condemnation of conflict diamonds.[34] **Conflict diamonds** are diamonds that are sold to raise resources to purchase weapons and prolong conflict. These diamonds come from mines in areas held by rebel armies and by warring nations. De Beers, along with other diamond-producing-industry companies, diamond-consuming nations, and other interested parties have worked together under the auspices of the UN in a set of talks known as the Kimberley Process. The goal has been to halt trade in conflict diamonds.

International Distribution

The issue here is restraint of trade, with undue pressure put on channels to prevent discounting. Firms may argue that discounting undercuts their value-based strategy. In response to such channel and pricing control, smuggling and gray markets emerge. **Gray markets** arise when goods destined for a particular geographic market are diverted to other markets, often through unauthorized distribution channels (sometimes through smuggling), to meet the needs of the alternative markets. Prices are often below those set in official distribution channels. Gray markets exist in markets as diverse as automobiles, brand-name apparel, cosmetics, and electronic consumer goods. Some of the consequences of gray market emergence include dilution of exclusivity, free riders, damage to channel relations, undermining pricing strategy, creating liability risk, and possibly damaging reputations.[35]

For example, Kubota tractors destined for the U.S. market are specifically designed to meet OSHA standards and other safety regulations. Kubota found that some of its tractors sold in the Japanese market were refurbished and then resold in the United States. With inadequate warranties, the tractors were not compliant with U.S. safety regulations. This activity has serious consequences for Kubota's brand equity and customer satisfaction—and possibly product liability. But the underlying reason for the practice is price. A segment of the market is willing to accept flawed warranties and compromised safety standards in return for gray-market tractors at lower prices. Companies faced with gray-market competition have to be willing to develop solutions that balance their profit interests with those of emerging price-conscious customer segments.

Global Promotion

A general problem in global promotion is a lack of cultural sensitivity that results in offending local mores and values. An example is the controversial series of Benetton clothing ads that featured interviews with convicted killers.

The campaign was called "We, on Death Row." With respect to this and other campaigns, Benetton believes that "campaigns are not only a means of communication but an expression of our time."

Beyond the themes and content of ad campaigns, other treacherous areas are false advertising, advertising to children, and not respecting religious and other cultural values. A larger question is the power of advertising to influence consumption, a point referred to earlier as part of the No Logo movement. One can indeed question the long-term consequences of advertising that promotes consumption at the cost of ever-increasing indebtedness and personal bankruptcy. But it would be difficult for a marketing executive to question whether promoting conspicuous consumption and a throwaway culture is ethically suspect.

Multiple Stakeholders and Societal Consequences

As corporations move beyond a narrow focus on customers and shareholders as paramount, other stakeholders such as employees, the government, and society at large begin to matter.[36] Considering multiple stakeholders suggests that businesses should be managed with the long-term well-being of all stakeholders in mind. From that perspective, factors such as the good of society, the needs and rights of workers, the need to preserve jobs, and the need to train youth for jobs later in life are all seen as equally important relative to profits. Table 6-2 shows the reciprocal nature of interests between the firm and its multiple stakeholders. Thus, the utilitarian perspective with multiple stakeholders might well justify a reduction of profits to preserve long-term worker welfare.

An example of the impact of multiple stakeholders is the Green movement and the growing demand that firms pay attention to the environmental pollution consequences of their actions. Customers and the public at large are more aware of and pay attention to recyclability, the nature of packaging used, and the problem of electronic waste. For instance, the EU has regulations in place requiring firms to be responsible for recycling end-of-life products that they manufacture. Green seals of approval, now common, are a factor that influences consumers' buying behavior. An example of the kind of dilemma created by weighing consumer demand and acting environmentally responsible is presented in the next section.

Ford Motor Company solicited input from insurance companies for the design of its autos. The reason for this seemingly unlikely pairing is that Ford wanted to design cars that would be less expensive to repair when they were involved in accidents. Ford thought that doing this could result in less expensive insurance premiums for its customers, which it could use in promoting its cars.[37]

Table 6-2. The Firm and Stakeholders Reciprocity

Constituent	Threat to Constituent	Threat to Company
Shareholders	Investment—expectation of economic success	Source of capital resources
Employees	Wages, benefits, and job security	Skills, labor, and loyalty
Customers	Reliable, affordable, quality products and services	Revenues to keep the firm profitable
Business Partners	Potential economic success	Dependent on partners for business operations
Community	Tax base and economic/social benefit to the community and its members	Right to build facilities and to operate in an environment conducive to a productive and competent workforce

Source: Adapted from A. Marcus and S. Kaiser, *Managing Beyond Compliance*, Garfield Heights, OH: NorthCoast Publishers, 2006.

The Ethical Nature of Promoting Large SUVs

Cars emit carbon dioxide, which is thought to contribute to global warming. Such emissions can be reduced when fewer people purchase large SUVs, which are generally fuel-inefficient vehicles. CAFE (corporate average fuel economy) rules are set at only 20.7 miles per gallon for SUVs as compared to 27.5 mph for full-size cars.[38] Hence, SUVS have come under attack as making the United States more dependent on imported oil, as well as for their poor safety record. The industry, by manufacturing and promoting more fuel-efficient cars and trucks, could help reduce dependence on energy imports. Should car companies, therefore, promote fuel-efficient cars and encourage the public to buy them at the expense of pricier, more profitable, large, fuel-guzzling SUVs?[39] In Canada, the answer has been a resounding "yes." Canadian automobile companies signed an agreement with the Canadian government, agreeing to reduce greenhouse gas emissions by 17 percent over five years, which would involve using fuel-saving technologies and alternative fuels such as ethanol, clean diesel, and biodiesel.

Prioritizing Values

When there are multiple stakeholders, corporations need guidance as to how to prioritize values. A puzzle for corporations is that there are many worthy causes and constituencies. A firm's consumers and its shareholders might ask what it is doing about global warming, terrorism, governmental corruption, and poverty, among other issues. An automobile company might well argue that its products have little to do with terrorism, governmental corruption, and poverty. The company may go on to state that it is working on reducing emissions and is devoting funds to research to develop an engine that is clean-burning, thus helping to reduce global warming. In rebuttal, activists might point out that the company imports thousands of containers full of parts every year and that its manufacturing processes in other countries, coupled with these shipments, contribute to pollution and global warming. The company may find out that it markets its cars in countries with high levels of corruption and that its dealer network in those countries resorts to questionable business practices in fleet sales to government agencies. It may discover that its factories hire employees whose families live in substandard housing and are unable to find good schools for their children, who are thus growing up poorly educated. Through such a discovery process, firms will gradually realize that their very prominence makes them the target of consumers and activists who hold them responsible for and expect them to ameliorate societal ills.

A recent effort, the **Copenhagen Consensus**, is an example of how firms might prioritize their social responsibilities.[40] The Copenhagen Consensus project has attempted to (1) rank some of society's major problems and (2) prioritize the problems based on the costs and benefits of developing solutions, then ranking the solutions based on what results in the greatest benefit for the least cost. (See Table 6-3.) This is an example of the utilitarian approach to ethical dilemmas.

To analyze the costs and benefits of solutions to each of the major problems, the project assembles nine of the world's leading economists, including four Nobel laureates. This approach accepts the fact that resources are scarce and that society does not have unlimited resources to tackle all of society's problems at once. Therefore, is it better to spend marginal resources on promoting primary education, reducing global warming, or fighting the spread of communicable diseases? The Copenhagen Consensus attempts to come up with answers to that question and in the process, develops and gains acceptance for its methodology of making trade-offs between "causes." Firms that are similarly pulled in different directions could well employ prioritizing methodologies to focus first on issues and values that affect the core of their business.[41]

Table 6-3. The Copenhagen Consensus "Top-Ten Problems"

1. Climate change	6. Governance and corruption
2. Communicable diseases	7. Malnutrition and hunger
3. Conflicts	8. Population and migration
4. Education	9. Sanitation and water
5. Financial instability	10. Subsidies and trade barriers

This review of ethical issues that arise in international marketing has attempted to be wide-ranging. There are no absolute, single answers to ethical conflicts that arise in international business. However, firms must be prepared with a set of ethical standards that are agreed to by all employees. The firms and their employees can then apply those ethical standards to help resolve ethical conflicts in an honorable manner.

Summary

Ethical dilemmas abound in international business, ranging from the advisability of developing products for low-income consumers to price discrimination across countries.

Because they are societal institutions that exist with the permission of the various societies and markets they serve, firms need to act ethically across international markets.

Firms also have to consider cultural differences and how they may reflect different ethical standards. Firms need to factor those differences into their own behavior.

Several moral principles are useful in arriving at ethical standards. These moral principles include utilitarianism, theories of rights and justice, Kant's categorical imperative, the notion of caring for significant others, and the Integrative Social Contracts theory.

In addition, a recent perspective includes the notion of **"managing beyond compliance"**: the recognition that a gap exists where the law ends or does not yet speak to regulate corporate conduct. Operating beyond compliance means that although some moral obligations to others may not be codified, that fact does not make their observance any less imperative.

To develop ethical standards, a firm must apply the moral principles to its policies and actions, discuss them among the its employees, and then arrive at its (mutually agreed and enforceable) ethical standards. At the same time, individual employees should use the moral principles and discussion of the firm's policies and actions to develop their own ethical standards.

Ethical dilemmas pervade a firm's international marketing value chain.

Major problems include bribery to compete for busi-ness and market share, market research, development of new products for low-income segments of the population, assurance that subcontractors manufacturing products marketed globally adhere to working standards that safeguard worker welfare, international price discrimination, consequences of global branding and the backlash against global brands as contributing to high prices and a consumerist culture, problems in international distribution and advertising, and pressures from multiple stakeholders (the Green lobby, for example) over the environmental consequences of a firm's products and marketing.

Firms need some guidance on how to prioritize the values of multiple stakeholders. The Copenhagen Consensus project offers one example of how such priorities can be set.

Questions and Research

6.1 How can concerns over ethical behavior affect global business practices? Provide examples.

6.2 Why should a firm be concerned about ethics in international marketing activities?

6.3 What are some fundamental moral principles that are relevant to assessing global business actions?

6.4 How can a firm connect moral principles to the development of ethical standards that would govern its international activities?

6.5 Describe some ethical conflicts that can arise along the value chain.

6.6 How can ethical standards help overcome problems associated with bribery and corruption in international markets?

6.7 Discuss Sealed Air Corporation's Code of Conduct discussed in the text. How can such codes of conduct be implemented? How can other firms learn from Sealed Air Corporation?

6.8 How do ethical issues affect the clinical testing of new pharmaceutical drugs in emerging markets?

6.9 How can firms develop successful business models to use in offering products and services for the poorest segments of the population in emerging markets? Why is it ethical for firms to concern themselves with "the bottom of the pyramid"?

6.10 How can a multinational firm be affected by unethical manufacturing practices among its suppliers? How has Mattel handled such conflicts?

6.11 How can unethical behavior affect brand equity and brand value? How have firms such as Gap and Unilever addressed such ethical concerns? What can be learned from them?

6.12 How does the presence of multiple stakeholders affect conduct? Focus on the issue of reducing environmental pollution globally to discuss how the green lobby affects global business practices.

6.13 Multiple stakeholders may have different goals that conflict with each other. How can a firm prioritize multiple conflicting goals as it attempts to practice ethical behavior?

6.14 Discuss the concept of GPGs in the context of developing new drugs for treating illnesses found primarily in poor emerging nations whose populations cannot afford the cost of new pharmaceutical drugs, even when proven highly effective. What broad lessons are learned from such an example for the practice of global business?

Endnotes

1. "Cigarette Deal Sets Market Rolling," *Financial Times*, March 16, 2005, page 30.

2. "Affordable Drug to Treat Malaria 'Ready Next Year,' *Financial Times*, April 8, 2005, page 6; "Sanofi to Sell Cheap Malaria Drug: French Company Decides Against Patent Protection, Reducing Number of Deaths," *Wall Street Journal*, April 8, 2005, page B3.

3. "House of Cards: The WTO and Online Gambling," *The Economist*, November 20, 2004, Volume 373, Issue 8402, page 82.

4. "EC Launches iTunes Pricing Investigation," *Guardian*, February 24, 2005.

5. "Independent Monitor Completes Follow-Up Audit of Mattel Facilities and Suppliers in China and Mexico," *Yahoo! Finance*, December 17, 2004.

6. "Tackling Wood-Nappers: Illegal Logging in Indonesia," *The Economist*, May 7, 2005, Volume 375, Issue 8425, page 63.

7. Adapted from Marcus, A. and S. Kaiser, *Managing Beyond Compliance*, 2005, Garfield Heights, OH: NorthCoast Publishers.

8. This section draws on Velasquez, Manuel, *Business Ethics*, 5th Edition, 2002, Upper Saddle River, NJ: Prentice Hall.

9. Velasquez, Manuel. *Business Ethics*, 5th Edition, 2002, Upper Saddle River, NJ: Prentice Hall, pages 97–99.

10. Rawls, John. *A Theory of Justice*, 1999, Harvard Press; Velasquez, Manuel, *Business Ethics*, 5th Edition, 2002, Upper Saddle River, NJ: Prentice Hall, pages 116–120.

11. Donaldson, T. and T. W. Dunfee. "Towards a Unified Conception of Business Ethics: Integrative Social Contracts Theory," *Academy of Management Review*, Volume 19, 1994, pages 252–284.

12. Donaldson, T. and T. W. Dunfee. "Towards a Unified Conception of Business Ethics: Integrative Social Contracts Theory," *Academy of Management Review*, Volume 19, 1994, page 265.

13. Spicer, A., T. W. Dunfee, and W. J. Bailey. "Does National Context Matter in Ethical Decision Making? An Empirical Test of Integrative Social Contracts Theory," *Academy of Management Journal*, Volume 47, Issue 4, 2004, pages 610–620.

14. Marcus, A. and S. Kaiser. *Managing Beyond Compliance: The Ethical and Legal Dimensions of Corporate Responsibility*, 2005, Garfield Heights, OH: NorthCoast Publishers, page vi.

15. Marcus, A. and S. Kaiser. *Managing Beyond Compliance: The Ethical and Legal Dimensions of Corporate Responsibility*, 2006, Garfield Heights, OH: NorthCoast Publishers, pages vi–vii.

16. Seed Money: In Indonesia, Tangle of Bribes Creates Trouble for Monsanto,? *Wall Street Journal*, April 5, 2005, page A1.

17. "Suit Alleges US Firm Paid Bribes for China Contracts," *Wall Street Journal*, March 21, 2005.

18. Doh, Jonathan P., Peter Rodriguez, K. Uhlenbruck, J. Collins, and L. Eden. "Coping with Corruption in Foreign Markets," *Academy of Management Executive*, Volume 17, Issue 3, 2003, pages 114–129.

19. Transparency International, *Business Principles for Countering Bribery*, 2003.

20. Sealed Air Corporation Code of Conduct (http://www.sealedair.com/corp/conduct.html); accessed April 7, 2005.

21. Vrabevski, Milan. "Clinical Trials in Bulgaria, Parts 1 and 2," *European Pharmaceutical Contractor (EPC) Magazine*, Summer 2002 and Autumn 2002.

22. Herring, Joseph L. "A Winning Prescription for Drug Development Outsourcing," *European Pharmaceutical Contractor*, Autumn 2004.

23. "Cameroon Halts AIDS Study," *Wall Street Journal*, February 8, 2005, page D7.

24. "The Menace of AIDS," *The Economist*, July 8, 2002; "Four Horsemen of The Apocalypse," *The Economist*, Volume 367, Issue 8322, May 3, 2003, page 85.

25. "Merck Corporation and the Cure for River Blindness: Case 5-3, page 132 in LaRue Tone Hosmer, *The Ethics of Management*, 4th Edition, 2003, Boston: McGraw-Hill.

26. World Development Report, 2000/2001, Box 10.1, page 182, Washington, DC: The World Bank, 2001.

27. Kaul, Inge, Pedro Conceicao, Katell Le Goulven, and Ronald U. Mendoza, eds. *Providing Global Public Goods*, 2003, New York: Oxford University Press; Kaul, Inge, Isabelle Grunberg, and Marc Stern, *Global Public Goods—International Public Cooperation in the 21st Century*, 1999, New York: Oxford University Press.

28. Prahalad, C. K. "The Fortune at the Bottom of the Pyramid—Eradicating Poverty through Profits," *Financial Times*, 2004, Upper Saddle River, NJ: Prentice Hall.

29. Wind, Yoram and Vijay Mahajan. "Convergence Marketing: Strategies for Reaching the New Hybrid Consumer," *Financial Times*, 2002, Upper Saddle River, NJ: Prentice Hall.

30. Prahalad, C. K. "Why Selling to the Poor Makes for Good Business," *Fortune*, Volume 150, Issue 10, November 15, 2004, pages 70–73.

31. "The Case for Brands," *The Economist*, Volume 360, Issue 8238, September 2001, page 9.

32. Klein, Naomi. *No Logo: Taking Aim at Brand Bullies*, 2000, New York: Picador USA.

33. The Gap, Incorporated, *2003 Social Responsibility Report* (http://www.gapinc.com/social_resp/social_resp.htm); accessed May 14, 2005.

34. Allen, James and James Root. "The New Brand Tax," *Wall Street Journal*, September 7, 2004, Section B, page 2.

35. Antia, K. D., Mark Bergen, and Shantanu Dutta. "Competing with Gray Markets," *Sloan Management Review*, Volume 46, Issue 1, Fall 2004, pages 63–70.

36. Garriga, Elisabet and Domenec Mele. "Corporate Social Responsibility Theories: Mapping the Territory," *Journal of Business Ethics*, Volume 53, 2004, pages 51–71.

37. "Ford Designed Mustang to be More Insurance Friendly," *USA Today*, Tuesday, August 9, 2005, Section B, page 1.

38. "Roadroller: Sport-utility Vehicles," *The Economist*, Volume 366, Issue 8307, January 18, 2003, page 62.

39. "Greening of The Boardroom—Socially Conscious Investors Get Results on Global Warming," *Boston Globe*, March 31, 2005, page E1; "Car Makers Reach Canadian Accord to Cut Emissions," *Wall Street*

Journal, April 5, 2005, page B1.

40. Copenhagen Consensus (http://www.copenhagenconsensus. com); accessed June 15, 2005.

41. Lomborg, Bjorn. Prioritizing the World's To-Do List," *Fortune*, Volume 149, Issue 10, May 17, 2004, pages 60–62.

Further Readings

Donaldson, T. and T. W. Dunfee. "Towards A Unified Conception of Business Ethics: Integrative Social Contracts Theory," *Academy of Management Review*, Volume 19, 1994, pages 252–284.

Garriga, Elisabet and Domenec Mele. "Corporate Social Responsibility Theories: Mapping the Territory," *Journal of Business Ethics*, Volume 53, 2004, pages 51–71.

Machan, Tibor R., editor. *Business Ethics in the Global Market*, 1999, Stanford, CA: Hoover Institution Press.

Marcus, A. and S. Kaiser. *Managing Beyond Compliance: The Ethical and Legal Dimensions of Corporate Responsibility*, 2006, Garfield Heights, OH: NorthCoast Publishers.

Prahalad, C.K. *Fortune at the Bottom of the Pyramid*, 2005, Pearson Education/Wharton School Publishing, Upper Saddle River, NJ.

Rawls, John. *A Theory of Justice*, 2005, Cambridge, MA: Belknap Press.

Review of Business, Special Issue: *Global Regulatory and Financial Reporting Reform and the Convergence of Accounting and Auditing Standards: The Time Has Come*, Volume 26, Issue 2, Spring 2005.

Spicer, A., T. W. Dunfee, and W. J. Bailey. "Does National Context Matter in Ethical Decision Making? An Empirical Test of Integrative Social Contracts Theory," *Academy of Management Journal*, Volume 47, Issue 4, 2004, pages 610–620.

U.S. Dept. of Commerce, International Trade Administration. *Business Ethics: A Guide to Responsible Business Enterprise in Emerging Markets*, 2003, Washington DC: Government Printing Office.

Velasquez, Manuel. *Business Ethics*, 6th Edition, 2006, Upper Saddle River, NJ: Prentice Hall.

Wartick, Steven L. and Donna J. Wood. *International Business and Society*, 1998, Malden, MA: Blackwell Business Publishers.

Recommended Web Sites

Business Ethics (http://www.business-ethics.com), especially "100 Best Corporate Citizens for 200x" (select 2000–2005) (http://www. business-ethics.com/whats_new/100best_2005.html) and Resources for Educators (http://www.business-ethics.com/For-Educators.htm).

Business Ethics, Canada (http://www.businessethics.ca).

Corporate Ethics (Washington Post—http://www.washingtonpost. com/wp-dyn/business/specials/corporateethics).

Corporate Fraud Task Force (U.S. Government, Office of Deputy General, U.S. Department of Justice)—(http://www.usdoj.gov/ dag/cftf). For specific cases, see the Significant Criminal Cases and Charging Documents web page—

(http://www.usdoj.gov/dag/cftf/cases.htm).

Corporate Social Responsibility (http://www.csrwire.com).

E-Business Ethics (Colorado State) (http://www.e-businessethics. com); play the Gray Matters game (developed by Lockheed Martin).

Case 6.1

WAL-MART AND ITS CRITICS

Wal-Mart is the world's largest retailer. With 2005 sales of around $300 billion and profits exceeding $10 billion, it accounts for about 8% of U.S. retailing. Economists would consider retailing a fragmented industry, as Wal-Mart, the biggest firm in the industry, accounts for less than one-tenth of the industry. However, Wal-Mart exercises a global influence on retailing. It has pioneered the concept of providing a wide variety of low-priced, quality goods to its customers. It is responsible for pushing its competitors to lower their prices and match the value that Wal-Mart provides its customers. It is in the forefront of a movement to use overseas sourcing of goods, particularly from China, in an effort to lower the cost of goods sold in retail stores. And it has pioneered the spread of superstores, with more than 3,700 stores in the United States, dwarfing football fields in size and offering a large assortment of goods and services.

As Wal-Mart has continued to grow, it has attracted several critics. Robert Greenwald's documentary, Wal-Mart: The High Cost of Low Prices, is an example of such criticism. Critics focus on its antiunion stance; the low wages it pays; its increasing use of foreign sourcing, contributing to job losses in U.S. manufacturing; and its impact on small retailers, often driving them out of business. Finding itself the target of negative publicity, Wal-Mart may have to reassess how it balances achieving corporate goals with the impact it has on the United States and other countries in which it does business.

The Wal-Mart Formula for Success

The key points of Wal-Mart's retailing strategy include the following:

- Everyday low prices. Customers are attracted to Wal-Mart because it has built a reputation for low prices.
- Superstores. Very large stores are usually located on the outskirts of town. They offer ample parking and the space to carry a wide assortment of products.
- An emphasis on listening to the consumer. Wal-Mart emphasizes listening to and pleasing the customer.
- An emphasis on keeping costs low and continually cutting costs. This allows Wal-Mart to sustain and continually lower prices.
- Low wages that help keep labor costs low. Wal-Mart indicated that its average hourly wage for U.S. full-time employees was $9.68 an hour and about a dol-

lar higher in major urban areas such as Chicago and Atlanta.
- No unions. Wal-Mart believes that "only an unhappy associate would be interested in joining a union." Thus, Wal-Mart actively sought to prevent unions from being formed.
- An emphasis on volume sales, with low margins per unit compensated for by the high volume of units sold.
- The importance of a wide and expanding assortment of goods and services.
- A constant search for lower-cost suppliers. This put pressure on suppliers to constantly lower prices; otherwise, they could be supplanted.
- A growing reliance on overseas sourcing to lower procurement costs.
- Low overheads, almost Spartan in its General and Administrative (G&A) spending—spare offices, simple furniture, shared hotel rooms, and economy-class travel.
- Entrepreneurial store managers and limited bureaucracy at headquarters, which allows individual managers greater autonomy.
- State-of-the-art supply chain management. This allows Wal-Mart to manage a global widely dispersed supply chain and ensure that goods arrive just in time at warehouses and stores across the United States and around the world.
- Excellence in information technology. This allows Wal-Mart to gauge consumer demand and shifts in demand and to manage inventories, pricing, and sourcing.
- Expansion overseas. This ensures that Wal-Mart can maintain growth rates as the U.S. market nears saturation, thereby exporting the Wal-Mart retailing and management model (though with mixed results).

Wal-Mart is a major U.S. employer, with over 1.2 million workers in the United States. It describes itself as a leading employer of Hispanic Americans, with more than 139,000 Hispanic employees. It is also one of the leading employers of African Americans, with more than 208,000 African-American employees. Of its 1.2 million U.S. workers, over 220,000 are 55 or older. It sees itself as providing jobs for minorities, new immigrants, and older employees. Based on the company's policy of promoting from within, entry-level low-paying jobs can be a stepping stone for promotion if workers exhibit drive and performance.

Wal-Mart also asserts that it helps improve the living standards of lower-income consumers by allowing them to buy goods they could not otherwise afford.

Wal-Mart stresses that its relentless drive to lower costs and to lean on suppliers helps increase productivity in the U.S. economy. Wal-Mart also suggests that the savings from low prices reduce U.S. inflation and that the savings consumers incur from shopping at Wal-Mart allows them to use the money in other ways, such as saving for home ownership and making mortgage and car payments.

Complaints about Wal-Mart

Wal-Mart's critics point to several negative consequences of the company's policies. Critics have asserted that:

- Wal-Mart's volume-based, low-price strategy makes it difficult for mom-and-pop retailers to compete, driving them out of business.
- By creating large superstores on the outskirts of cities, Wal-Mart hollows out inner cities and despoils the environment, gobbling up land for its stores, creating the need for parking lots and highways.
- Wal-Mart pays low wages to keep costs down, making it difficult for workers to support a family. In its desire to keep overheads low, the company offers limited health care and requires co-payments that make health care unaffordable to low-paid employees. The company has been accused of exploiting its workers. It has also been the target of lawsuits over its treatment of workers, accusing it of requiring employees to work "off the clock," not paying overtime to workers, hiring illegal immigrants (indirectly through a floor-cleaning subcontractor), and discriminating against female workers.
- Wal-Mart is antiunion. In response, unions have joined together in an attempt to organize Wal-Mart workers and move Wal-Mart to recognize and accept unions. The Union Network International, a federation of 900 unions in 150 countries, has focused on Wal-Mart. It has tried to influence Wal-Mart workers in Germany who are unionized to initiate sympathetic work stoppages and has tried to organize workers in South Korea, where Wal-Mart has 16 stores. It is also trying to convince teachers who belong to unions to boycott Wal-Mart as a source of back-to-school supplies.
- Wal-Mart has contributed to manufacturing activity moving out of the United States. This has resulted from the company's continued pressure on U.S. suppliers to lower costs, forcing them to manufacture overseas in order to get access to low-wage labor, thus being able to meet Wal-Mart demands for low prices.
- Wal-Mart's suppliers follow lax labor policies, such as using child labor, paying substandard wages, conducting business in hazardous factories and workplaces, and not respecting workers' rights. Wal-Mart, like other corporations, has responded with codes of conduct for suppliers, conducting internal audits to ensure compliance with their rules for fair treatment and employment of workers. However, Wal-Mart has not used outside independent agencies to audit the workplaces and labor practices of its overseas suppliers.

One consequence of the criticisms has been opposition to Wal-Mart's expansion in areas such as California and the eastern states. Wal-Mart has been able to expand rapidly and successfully in some parts of the United States, such as the southwest. Opposition to and support for Wal-Mart seems somewhat divided along geographic lines within the United States.

Wal-Mart Overseas

In its recent expansion into China, Wal-Mart has been enthusiastically received. When it opened a store in Chongqing, it had over 120,000 customers the first day. Customers asked the managers why they waited so long to open a store. Shoppers avidly purchased the merchandise on display, marveling at the quality, the assortment, the low prices, the freshness of the produce, and the eye-catching displays of wares. Most of what Wal-Mart sold in China was also sourced in China. Wal-Mart took care to adapt to Chinese cultural needs. The store increased the amount of space devoted to food and produce; allowed customers to touch the goods and to examine open packages; and sponsored cultural activities at the stores for all age groups, including the elderly. Wal-Mart has attempted to ensure that it develops a positive image in China. It faces considerable competition in China from local state-owned retailing chains and from Carrefour, the French superstore retailer, which has twice as many stores and has partnerships with local governmental and state-owned firms.

Wal-Mart has had somewhat mixed results in its expansion into Europe, where it attempted to acquire existing retail chains in Germany and the UK. Most of its overseas success has come from the UK, Canada, and Mexico. It has been less successful with its acquisitions in Germany, with its expansion into Brazil and Argentina, and with its one-third ownership of the Seiyu Japanese retail chain. It has cautiously moved into China, opening just over 40 stores and earning under $1 billion in sales in China in 2004.

Wal-Mart's Future

As complaints about Wal-Mart mount, it cannot afford to ignore them, hoping they will disappear. The issue is whether the complaints are justified and whether Wal-Mart can respond to them without sacrificing some of its commercial success. But Wal-Mart needs to develop an effective response to its critics if it wants to preserve its reputation and continue to grow around the world.

QUESTIONS AND RESEARCH

1. What is Wal-Mart's impact on customers, suppliers, competitors, workers, communities, and the overall economy in the United States?
2. What is the impact of Wal-Mart on the global economy and on individual countries where it sources from and where it has stores (China, for example)?
3. What should Wal-Mart's goals be with regard to its different constituencies—customers, suppliers, employees, shareholders, and society at large?
4. In your view, how well has Wal-Mart fulfilled its' social responsibilities in the United States? In the world as a whole?
5. What changes might you recommend to Wal-Mart? What are your reasons for recommending such changes?

Sources: "Labor Leaders Say Multination Effort Targets Wal-Mart," *Wall Street Journal*, August 23, 2005; Clay Chandler, "The Great Wal-Mart of China," *Fortune*, July 25, 2005; "Special Report: Wal-Mart: How Big Can It Grow?" *The Economist*, April 17, 2004; "Learning to Love Wal-Mart," *The Economist*, April 17, 2004; "Wal-Mart," *Forbes 2000*, April 12, 2004; Abigail Goldman and Nancy Cleeland, "An Empire Built on Bargains Remakes the Working World," three-part series, *Los Angeles Times*, November 23, 24, and 25, 2003; http://www.walmartfacts.com/newsdesk/wal-mart-fact-sheets.aspx#a22.

Case prepared by Professor Ravi Sarathy, for use in classroom discussion. Copyright 2006, Professor Sarathy.

Case 6.2

NUTRISET AND PLUMPY'NUT

Starvation is unpleasant to think about. As the body starves, it turns on itself, beginning to consume muscle and tissue. Starvation is agonizing for the crying child and for his or her mother who is frantically trying to save her child. Starvation follows war and famine in places such as Darfur, Sudan, where thousands of families have been attacked by Arab militias and driven away from their arable lands in what the U.S. government has termed *genocide*. How can a company help in such a situation? Nutriset, a French company, is focused on humanitarian nutrition programs. It seeks to develop products that can help children and adults recover from malnutrition and starvation.

Nutriset is a small company based in Normandy, with $15 million in sales. Its founder and managing director, Michel Lescanne, had worked in a French aid agency, attempting to develop an enriched chocolate bar for malnourished children. However, the taste was not pleasant. The chocolate bar melted quickly in warm weather, a climate common in much of Africa and other tropical locations. It was also costly to produce and unlikely to suit straitened budgets of aid agencies. When Lescanne founded Nutriset, he continued to work on food products for humanitarian relief.

The traditional approach to countering starvation was to give patients enriched milk powder drinks. A UN formula, F-100, was mixed with water to give to a child or an adult. This approach presented several difficulties. Water, clean water, was scarce in famine-ridden areas. If the milk powder was not mixed with clean water, it could become contaminated and cause other diseases. If the milk was not consumed immediately, bacteria could form in the warm temperatures. Getting the milk powder often meant making a trip to a refugee camp, which sometimes meant leaving other children behind with no adult to care for them. Refugee camps were possible vectors for disease, and a weakened child could easily be infected. Aid workers who had to administer the milk and water mixture were often overwhelmed by the number of children and families seeking treatment and help.

Andre Briend, Lescanne's colleague and a consultant to Nutriset, had also been working on the problem of finding foods for the treatment of starvation. At breakfast one day, he noticed a jar of Nutella and immediately called Lescanne to ask, "Why not a spread?" As a result, Plumpy'nut was born.

Plumpy'nut is a peanut butter-based spread, a

peanut butter paste that comes in small packets, each weighing 92 grams and costing an aid agency 35 cents. Diets to combat starvation are dependent on the weight of the child, as the overtaxed digestive system cannot handle too much rich food. The packets are small enough to ensure that the correct amount can be given to a child over the course of a day. Three to four packets a day for several weeks can overcome severe malnutrition and nourish starving children back to health.

Peanuts are common in much of Africa and a regular part of the diet; hence, few children are allergic to peanut products. Because the paste comes in a sealed sachet, it can be torn open and given to a child immediately without risk of contamination or the need for clean water. Aid workers are not needed to mix the food, as was the case with the enriched milk powder. A mother can take care of the child herself, does not need to visit a refugee camp or aid station, and does not need to leave her other children behind or expose her children to the risks of infection at the camp.

Nutriset has distributed over 300 tons of Plumpy'nut in Darfur and in places such as Ethiopia, Sudan, and Malawi. It is not "big business," with relatively small orders. An exception is a big customer such as the United Nations High Commissioner for Refugees (UNHCR), which placed ten orders for Plumpy'nut, totaling $400,000. Since its "customers" reside in remote places that are difficult to access, Nutriset has to pay attention to logistics. It needs to be able to respond to emergencies, shipping the requisite quantities as quickly as possible. Nutriset, wary of being seen as profiting from tragedy, does not seek to develop commercial products such as energy bars. Its other products include a 20 mg zinc tablet for use in treating acute diarrhea in infants and young children under the age of 5. It also makes Vitapoche, an enriched food that has been used by the French government in helping homeless people. Its R&D also focuses on improving Plumpy'nut. For example, its research helped develop a version of Plumpy'nut with a longer shelf life. The company has developed the ability to give Plumpy'nut a two-year shelf life, with new packaging and a new formula. Longer shelf life is important, as it may take several months to ship products to reach remote famine and treatment sites. Plumpy'nut may also be stored for use in possible emergencies, which cannot be forecast. And longer shelf life helps optimize scarce aid agency funds. The Plumpy family of products is covered by an IRD/Nutriset patent. Nutriset has also been considering the development of similar nourishing foods using corn or wheat as a base.

Plumpy'nut's success, the difficulties in delivering it to famine-torn countries, and the need to conserve aid agency funds have resulted in requests to manufacture Plumpy'nut locally. In response, Nutriset has helped some aid workers to source local peanut ingredients and combine them locally, using vitamins and nutrients supplied by Nutriset. Nutriset plans to set up a network of franchisees to help ensure quality, optimal production levels, and lower costs, while earning a fee for its advice. Those initiatives have led to local production in places such as Dakar and the Democratic Republic of Congo. An aid worker rhapsodized that the most beautiful thing about Plumpy'nut was that it puts the mother in charge of feeding the child.

Nutriset is an interesting example of a company that can balance commercial activity while having a social conscience. Its challenge is to continue to grow while being socially responsible.

Source: Thurow, Roger. "Famine Relief," *Wall Street Journal*, April 12, 2005; Briend, Andre, "Highly Nutrient-Dense Spreads: A New Approach to Delivering Multiple Micronutrients to High-Risk Groups," *British Journal of Nutrition*, Volume 85, Supplement 2, 2001, S175–S179; Nutriset web site (http://www.nutriset.fr) (in English: http://www.nutriset.fr/en_index.php).

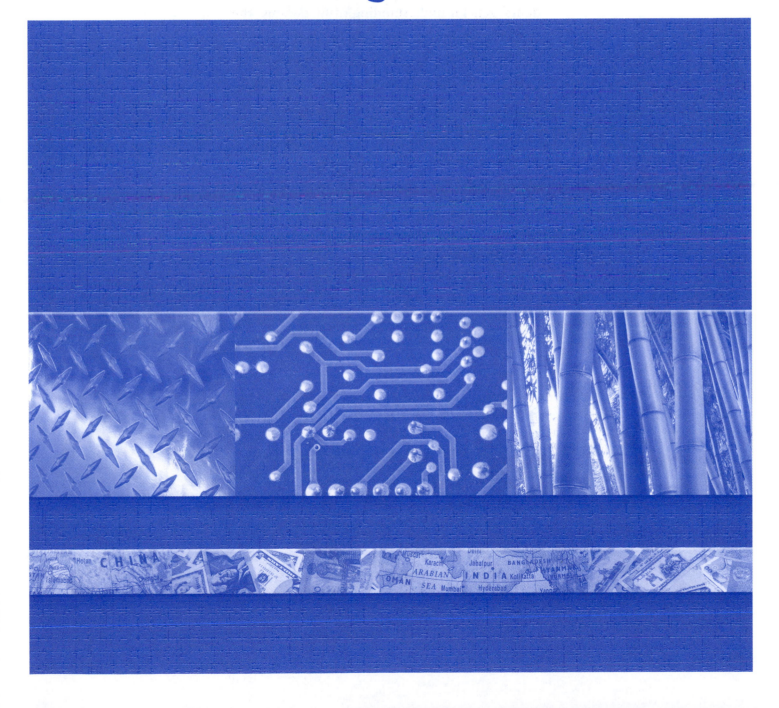

PART 2

Global Marketing Management

The various functions of marketing as they are performed in the international environment are discussed on Part 2.

An examination of the problems peculiar to international marketing should also help broaden students' general understanding of marketing. The foreign environment dealt with in Part 1 is seen as the key variable in international marketing. A large part of the discussion centered on international marketing by manufacturers. However, the specific international marketing problems of service industries are covered in Part 2.

In addition, Part 2 stresses the importance of an overall marketing strategy to shape and guide the formulation and implementation of specific international marketing tasks.

CHAPTER 7

Researching Foreign Markets

When a firm initially considers marketing to the world, it finds world markets to be "foreign" in several senses: They are located outside the firm's home country; they have different cultures, languages, currencies, and customs; and they are unfamiliar to management. Thus, lack of knowledge about world markets is the first barrier to overcome in marketing internationally. Marketing decisions cannot be made intelligently without knowing the environment and the specific characteristics of foreign markets. For this reason, this chapter's presentation of international marketing management begins with the nature and scope of international marketing research.

The main goals of this chapter are to

- Review the range of tasks involved in international marketing research by outlining typical problems encountered in conducting research overseas and discussing ways to solve those problems.

- Present techniques for conducting research, including analysis of demand, regression analysis, and cluster analysis.

- Discuss the screening of international markets and give an example of the typical steps involved.

- Explain how to evaluate information collected through international marketing research.

- Discuss the role of models in marketing research and present examples of models (for deciding the mode of market entry)—analyzing cross-cultural, household purchasing behavior; the effects of religiosity on consumption; and the impact of country-of-origin effects.

Global Market Research: Breadth of the Task

International marketing research is more comprehensive than domestic marketing research. Although all of a firm's domestic marketing research studies have potential for international application, they are not sufficient to provide all of the information necessary to make sound international marketing decisions. The firm needs an *information system* to identify and measure the market potential of foreign markets and to assess multiple cultural, political, and macroeconomic variables that are generally assumed to be constant in domestic markets. The objective of the marketing information system is to allow firms to take a proactive rather than reactive position to their constantly changing surroundings.

One group of international parameters affecting marketing decisions includes the economic factors considered in Chapter 2. A second group encompasses the political-legal aspects of international relations as discussed in Chapter 4. A third element is the analysis of competition. Although a firm must analyze the competitive situation in each market, this kind of analysis alone is not sufficient. Because competition in many industries is now international, the study of the competitive situation must also be multinational. It cannot be limited to studies of individual markets.

Finally, international comparative studies are an additional dimension of analysis. The distinctiveness of international marketing research arises from the fact that a firm is operating within a number of foreign environments. These differences necessitate not only the adaptation of domestic techniques, but also the development of new methods of analysis. The scope of the international researcher's task is apparent in the following notice:

> The International Division is seeking a research analyst to work on broad-scope individual projects involving . . . international economic and marketing research…. *The general subjects that will be researched are economic statistics, sales and marketing forecasts, distribution methodology, market planning on existing and new products,* and related subjects that would have an impact on aggregate marketing plans for given geographical areas…. Because of the scope of the projects, it is necessary to have a much broader familiarity with economic and marketing subjects than may be normally required for a marketing research professional.* [Italics added for emphasis.]

A small international marketing firm has information needs similar to those of larger firms. It can contract with specialized international marketing research firms that cater to the needs of smaller firms, or it can collaborate with its distributors, licensees, or joint venture partners to gather information on international markets and environments.

What Information Is Needed?

A key early decision that most firms face is deciding which world markets to enter. A firm needs a way of ranking the markets according to their attractiveness. This requires an investigation of their market and profit potential, their growth rates, and the local competitive situation. Once a firm has identified desirable target markets, it must decide how to serve those markets—by exporting, licensing, or producing locally, for example.

Once a decision has been made to market in a particular country, standard marketing questions arise—questions regarding product, pricing, and channel. Those decisions can be further broken down until, eventually, a specific local issue is resolved—the kind of package and label that should be used for a firm's floor wax in the Philippines, for example. The information needed to make those decisions is frequently provided by marketing research. (See Table 7-1.)

Table 7-1. Information for Marketing Decisions

Marketing Decisions	Intelligence Needed
1. Go international or remain a domestic marketer?	1. Assessment of global market versus domestic market (demand and competition)
2. Which markets to enter?	2. Assessment of individual market potential (demand, local competition, political environment)
3. How to enter target markets?	3. Market size, trade barriers, transportation costs, requirements and standards, and political environment
4. How to market in target markets?	4. Buyer behavior, competitive practices, distribution channels, promotional media, market experience, and company expertise

The Information Provided by Marketing Research

What information should international marketing research provide? Obtaining information about consumer behavior and product-related information may be considered typical marketing research objectives, but the objectives of international marketing research should be broader. Figure 7-1 summarizes the principal tasks of global marketing research.

Being in a global market means that a firm must seek information so it understands the country and regional environment, as well as the consumer and the product. The firm must assess the global competitors that it will face so it can better compete with them. Only then does information about the industry and the product make sense, and better research on and resulting decisions about the marketing mix can result.

Marketing Environment

Research should emphasize the gathering of information about the country and region of interest, and the evaluat-

ing of comparative information across countries. Both political information and economic information are relevant. The political dimensions of information gathering include data on the following:

- *Political structure and ideology.* What does the political leadership of the country seek? What roles do major institutions such as business, labor, the educational sector, and religion play in shaping national goals? How do legal systems and differences affect markets?
- *National objectives.* What are the country's goals for the defense sector; its fiscal, monetary, and investment policy; and the foreign trade sector? What are its industrial and technology policies for sunrise or burgeoning industries and its social policy? (For example, how do the policies affect income distribution and conspicuous consumption?) Is autonomy a goal, does the nation seek to reduce import dependence, and is developing national champions in industries considered critical?

The *economic dimension of information gathering* is more familiar. It includes obtaining data on economic performance, covering indicators such as GNP, per capita income levels and growth rates, stage of the business cycle, balance of trade and balance of payments, productivity, labor

Figure 7-1. Reasons for Conducting Global Marketing Research

costs and capital availability, capacity utilization, inflation rates, savings and investment, employment levels, educational attainment, population demographics, age distribution, public health, and income distribution.

Marketing infrastructure is also of interest, including the structure of wholesaling and retailing, laws concerning pricing and promotion, the physical distribution infrastructure, and the extent of development of consumer protection. All of those issues help determine the attractiveness of the market, as well as obstacles to entry and marketing of goods and services and the long-term profit potential.

Technology and culture form part of the environment. Thus, a firm should note how the use of technology, the level of technology available, and cultural differences affect the environment and influence market growth and attractiveness.

Government regulation is another area for market research, particularly with regard to product and safety standards, barriers to entry (affecting foreign companies and their products), and controls over managerial and marketing autonomy. Does the government implement industrial policies that benefit domestic companies and industries at the expense of foreign firms?

Competition

Assessing foreign competitors involves developing additional levels of understandin,g since foreign competitors may have distinct and different objectives that shape their strategy and tactics. They may also possess hidden resources and strengths that are culture- or nation-specific and not apparent to an outside firm. For example, close family and other ties may exist between a competitor's top management and influential individuals in government and the political arena. In conducting its assessment, a firm must first investigate its assumptions about foreign competitors' objectives and capabilities (and see: Chapter 8). Then the firm can assess potential strategies and make plans for what new markets to enter, what modes of entry to take, how vulnerable the market will be, and what the reaction of the competition will be to the firm's moves in the market. Essentially, the firm must be able to anticipate how its foreign competitors will act or react and to use that information to prepare contingency plans for a quick response as appropriate. Managers must broaden their concept of industry—for example, from providing railroad transportation to transportation of goods (and/or people) and from providing theme parks to providing leisure entertainment.

Every nation has a way of classifying firms by the products they produce or by the things they use in the production process. The United States used the *Standard Industrial Classification* (SIC) system for many years; but since 1997,

it has collected data on industries using the *North American Industry Classification System* (NAICS). Researchers who want to perform longitudinal studies that include data from American companies prior to 1997 may have to use data classified in these two different systems. Unfortunately, other nations use different industry and product classifications systems; for instance, the EU collects product data using *Classification of Products by Activity* (CPV). This leads to an oft-cited secondary complaint, that data from one source is not comparable to data from another entity. Furthermore, concordances, which are used to convert data from one system to another, are not fool-proof. One solution to the difficulty of comparing data from different sources and to limiting the competitor set by using narrow industry categories is to investigate firms as competitors by reaching out to broader product categories.

Once the codes for an industry and its products have been identified, it is somewhat easier to obtain data about them. Secondary industry data can be obtained from some government agencies, such as the Department of Commerce, which produces the *Industry Market Reports*; but the data are accessible to American firms only. And while the agencies provide information on many industries and nations, the focus is U.S.-centric. That is, the data tend to be created with a specific agenda in mind, such as the promotion of domestic jobs through exports. Trade associations, including the World Trade Centers, provide aggregate data either as a member benefit or for a fee. The firm can obtain data from specialized agencies that furnish corporate reports and related information; for example, CAROL (Company Annual Reports On-Line), Euro pages, and Corporate Direct (information on Japanese firms). There are also fee-based, private firms (such as Kompass and Business.com) and consulting and research firms that will sell data previously collected or perform the necessary research for a fee.

Consumers and Consumer Needs

A firm must understand users—users of its product and users of its competitors. A paramount consideration is documenting and understanding cultural differences as they affect customer needs, products demanded, and purchasing behavior. Analysis and market research can focus on end-user industry categories and, if relevant, on unique characteristics of consumers. Information to help in *segmentation* should be gathered, using parameters such as age, sex, size, income levels, growth rates of consumption, regional differences, purchasing power, influence over purchasing and purchasing intentions, and the role of credit-granting in purchasing behavior. Another major area of research is *product benchmarking* (or quality comparisons), which enables a firm to obtain objective comparisons of its products with those of its competitors. A firm can use that information to understand its competitors' product positioning issues within the industry. The information also is helpful to the firm for determining its positioning across countries, customer response to new product introductions, and the likelihood that customers will purchase its brands instead of competitors' brands. Finally, research should identify market trends for the medium and long term, rather than providing information for decision making only on immediate marketing plans and actions.

Marketing Mix

As you will see later, a company can standardize or adapt its product as well as its marketing mix to different country markets. Hence, it is also necessary for a firm to research its choice of marketing mix in international markets. A firm should investigate the following areas:

- *Distribution channels* — Their evolution and the firm's and its competitors' comparative performance in different channels
- *Comparative pricing strategies and tactics* — The price positioning by all competitors, price elasticity, and customer response to differential pricing behavior
- *Advertising and promotion* — The range of choices available, differences in the allocation of promotion expenditures, delineation of the advertising response function in different markets, and comparison of competitor choices in advertising and promotion
- *Media research* — Useful in determining where to advertise in order to reach target audiences; major market research firms such as Arbitron and the Kantar Group (part of WPP) provide media research and media measurement services
- *Service quality issues* — Relative to positioning by competitors and customers' reactions to higher levels of service

Marketing Intermediaries

Channel availability and capabilities can vary across markets. International markets, separated by distance, make use of extensive supply chains, with over 90 percent of goods transported by ocean carriers through use of containers and bulk cargo ships. Hence, understanding the logistics network capabilities is critical. Meeting promised delivery dates, carrying lower inventory quantities, and reducing lost sales from stockouts are examples of market-

ing outcomes affected by the quality of channel intermediaries. Firms also need to research the availability and reliability of information systems to manage delivery and customer service. This relatively new area of marketing concern results from increased emphasis on just-in-time inventory systems and customer-direct delivery, bypassing retail inventories. Other key research issues are comparative performance of competitors and customer requirements.[1]

Performance Measurement and Firm-Specific Data

Forgotten in marketing research is the role of a firm's internal information system in providing data for making marketing decisions. Marketing research often can be facilitated by setting up the required database outline and implementing internal data collection. This is particularly necessary for international markets because information that could be generated within a firm is often ignored or lost. Useful data could include sales history by product and product line, by customer and sales force, by distribution channel, and within a country and across countries. The data could also be used to analyze trends across countries and regions; to derive and analyze contributions by product, product line, customer, and region; and to develop market response functions across countries for comparing past marketing mix decisions and for suggesting future mix decisions that differ from country to country, within a country, or across regions.

Once marketing research has been completed, the resulting information must be analyzed so questions about future marketing plans and actions can be answered. Major questions that are relevant in international marketing fall into two categories: (1) market and competition decisions and (2) product and marketing mix decisions. With respect to market and competition, a firm should be concerned primarily with the following issues:

- Understanding how customers rate the company compared to the competition
- Determining the company's chances to attract customers
- Deciding whether to compete or cooperate with the competition
- Choosing which products to introduce, which distribution channels to use, and how to advertise and promote the product (product and marketing mix)
- Identifying barriers to attractive markets and finding ways to overcome them

Marketing research can also play a role in helping a firm formulate its global strategy. While strategy sets a path

Table 7-2. The Task of Global Marketing Research

The Marketing Environment	The Competition	The Product	Marketing Mix	Firm-Specific Historical Data
Political context: leaders, national goals, ideology, and key institutions	Relative market shares	Analysis of users	Channels of distribution: evolution and performance	Sales trends by:
	New product introductions	Who are the end-user industries?		- product and product line
Economic growth prospects and business cycle stage	Pricing and cost structure	Industrial and consumer buyers characteristics;	Relative pricing, elasticities, and pricing tactics	- Sales force
	Image and brand reputation	Size, age, sex, and segment growth rates		- Customer
Per capita income levels and purchasing power			Advertising and promotion: choices and impacts on customers	Trends by country and region
End-user industry growth trends	Quality: its attributes and positioning relative to that of competitors	Purchasing power and intentions		Contribution margins
		Customer response to new products, price, and promotion	Service quality, perceptions, and relative positioning	Innovation, experience, and results
Government: legislation, regulation, standards, and barriers to trade	Competitors' strengths and favorite marketing tactics and strategies			Customer retention
		Switching behavior	Logistics networks, configuration, and change	
		Role of credit and purchasing		
		Future needs	Marketing mix used and marketing response functions across countries and regions	
		Impact of cultural differences		

Analyzing the Findings: Answering Questions from the Market Research Information

- Which markets are attractive in the short and long run?
- How do we attract customers?
- What do customers think of our product and that of the competition?
- What do we do about competition? Cooperate or compete? With whom?

- What new products should we introduce?
- What should the price be?
- Which distribution channels should we use?
- How much advertising and promotion is necessary?
- Which countries should we target next?
- How should we overcome barriers to entry?

for how a firm should interact with its customers, competition, and environment, market research can provide information and analyses on environmental trends, changes in competitive behavior and government regulation, and shifting consumer tastes. In other words, market research can provide strategic information by focusing on futures research and scenario development. Market researchers who pride themselves on quantitative modeling and statistical rigor might disdain this "soft" world. However, qualitative market research can resolve strategic planning issues such as:[2]

- Determining the firm's mission, scope, and long-range objectives.
- Anticipating environmental changes and their effects—and the resulting opportunities and threats that they pose.
- Understanding the firm's capabilities versus the strengths and weaknesses of competitors.

The ideas listed above are quite different from "merely" gathering information about consumer responses to new products, prices, and advertising. Yet, just as good information is necessary for tactical marketing, so, too, is good information needed to develop and assess long-range plans. Table 7-2 summarizes these various tasks.

Problems in International Marketing Research

Because of its complexity, international marketing may encounter difficulties that are uncommon in domestic marketing research. One problem is that research must be gathered for many markets—dozens of countries in some cases—and each country poses a unique challenge. A second problem is the frequent absence of secondary data (data from published and third-party sources). A third problem is the frequent difficulty of gathering primary data (data gathered firsthand through interviews and field research).

Problems of Numerous Markets

Multiplying the number of countries in a research project multiplies the costs and problems involved, although not in a linear manner. Because markets are not identical from one country to another, the research manager must be alert to the various errors that can arise in replicating a study on a multinational basis. Five kinds of errors to look for in multinational research are:

- *Definition error,* which is caused by the way the problem is defined in each country.
- *Instrument error,* which arises from the questionnaire and the interviewer.
- *Frame error,* which occurs when sampling frames are available from different sources in different countries.
- *Selection error,* which results from the way the actual sample is selected from the frame.
- *Nonresponse error,* which results when different cultural patterns of nonresponse are obtained. Response rates can vary significantly by age or gender. For example, if selected randomly, car buyers in the United States who are asked why they purchased a car will include a large percentage of women. Ask car buyers in Argentina the same question, and a large percentage of respondents will be men. This difference will have an impact on the responses that researchers obtain.

Using Secondary Data

Secondary data for market analysis are less available and less reliable for many foreign and emerging markets. Secondary sources of information are relatively inexpensive to acquire, however, and can help prevent a firm from making major mistakes in its international marketing. Major steps in using secondary data include:[3]

- Determining research objectives.
- Clarifying what information is needed.
- Identifying where such secondary information can be found.
- Deciding whether the information source is reliable (who put out the information and what hidden agenda there may be).
- Assessing the quality of data (accuracy, timeliness,

and representativeness) and the compatibility of data from different sources.
- Interpreting and analyzing the information.
- Drawing conclusions, then relating those conclusions to the marketing problem at hand to see if they suggest courses of action or support planned decisions or actions.

Comparing Several Markets

When data for several markets are compiled, the researcher may find that many gaps exist. For example, current data on the number of automobile registrations may be available only for a few countries in the group of interest—and often, not for the same time period. Data quality may vary, and the estimates may not be reliable. The underlying definitions may not be the same, with some countries excluding light trucks from automobile registrations while others include them, for example. Many countries lack specialized firms that develop industry data for specific industries such as automobiles and air conditioners.

Table 7-3 shows the top market research firms. In 2002, the ten largest market research firms had global revenues of $8.67 billion; just over $6 billion of their sales (approximately 74 percent) were derived from outside the United States. For comparison purposes, only 9 of the top 50 firms did any international business in 1989—a clear indication that international marketing research has increased in significance, a consequence of the growing importance of global markets. These firms perform a variety of marketing research services, such as:

- Forming consumer panels to use as focus groups and to monitor purchasing behavior.
- Offering media measurement services to audit use of media and to relate expenditures to sales.
- Measuring the size of audiences for media such as TV and radio.
- Identifying sales and market share for a number of firms in specific industries, notably the pharmaceutical and health-care industries and computers and electronics.
- Conducting multicultural consumer research.
- Determining how marketing communication affects brands.
- Conducting brand equity studies.

Problems with Primary Data

Marketing research involves getting information from people about their perceptions, intentions, and actual behavior concerning a company's products, brands, prices, or promotion. People differ from country to country in

Table 7-3. Top Market Research Firms

RANK 2002	RANK 2001	Organization	Headquarters	Parent Country	Web Site	No. of Countries w/ Subsidiaries/ Branch Office[1]	Global Research Revenues (U.S. $ in millions)[2]	Revenues from Outside Home Country (U.S. $ in millions)	Percent of Global Revenues from Outside Home Country
1	1	VNU	Harrlem, Netherlands	Netherlands	http://www.vnu.com	81	$2,814.0	$2,787.0*	99.0%*
2	2	IMS Health Inc.	Fairfield, CT	U.S.	http://www.imshealth.com	75	1,219.4	731.6	60.0
3	3	The Kantar Group	Fairfield, CT	U.S.	http://www.kantargroup.com	62	1,033.2*	720.5*	69.7*
4	4	TNS (formerly Taylor Nelson Sofres plc)	London	U.K.	http://www.tns-global.com	54	908.3	732.2	80.6
5	5	Information Resources, Inc.	Chicago	U.S.	http://www.infores.com	20	554.8	143.3	25.8
6	6	GfK Group	Nuremberg	Germany	http://www.gfk.com	51	528.9	335.7	63.5
7	8	Ipsos Group SA	Paris	France	http://www.ipsos.com	35	509.0	423.2	83.1
8	7	NFO WorldGroup	Greenwich, CT	U.S.	http://www.nfow.com	40	466.1	297.7	63.9
9	10	Westat	Rockville, MD	U.S.	http://www.westat.com	1	341.9	-	-
10	9	NOP World	London	U.K.	http://www.nopworld.com	6	320.0	225.2	70.3
11	11	Synovate	London	U.K.	http://www.synovate.com	46	317.6	298.8	94.1
12	12	Arbitron Inc.	New York	U.S.	http://www.arbitron.com	2	249.8	7.9	3.2
13	13	Maritz Research	Fenton, MO	U.S.	http://www.maritzresearch.com	4	183.3	59.8	32.6
14	14	Video Research Ltd.**	Tokyo	Japan	http://www.videor.co.jp	4	152.0	1.8	1.2
15	15	Opinion Research Corporation	Princeton, NJ	U.S.	http://www.opinionresearch.com	6	132.7	45.9	34.6
16	16	J.D. Power and Associates	Westlake Village, CA	U.S.	http://www.jdpa.com	5	132.1	20.8	15.8
17	21	Harris Interactive Inc.	Rochester, NY	U.S.	http://www.harrisinteractive.com	3	120.9	25.6	21.2
18	18	The NPD Group, Inc.	Port Washington, NY	U.S.	http://www.npd.com	11	115.5	16.8	14.6
19	17	INTAGE Inc.**	Tokyo	Japan	http://www.intage.co.jp	2	105.4	3.5	3.3
20	20	Dentsu Research Inc.	Tokyo	Japan	http://www.dentsuresearch.co.jp	1	62.0	2.0	3.2
21	–	AGB Group	Milan	Italy	http://www.agb.com	19	61.1	47.5	77.7
22	31	Wirthlin Worldwide	McLean, VA	U.S.	http://www.wirthlin.com	4	54.2	12.3	22.7
23	22	Abt Associates Inc.	Cambridge, MA	U.S.	http://www.abtassociates.com	3	53.8	8.1	15.1
23	–	Market & Opinion Research Int'l	London	U.K.	http://www.mori.com	2	53.8	2.7	5.0
25	–	Lieberman Research Worldwide	Los Angeles	U.S.	http://www.lrwonline.com	1	52.7	8.3	15.8
		TOTAL					**$10,542.5**	**$6,958.2**	**66.0%**

1. Includes countries that have subsidiaries with an equity interest or branch offices or both.

2. Total revenues that include nonresearch activities for some companies are significantly higher. This information is given in the individual company profiles.

See company profiles for explanation. Rate of growth is based on home country currency and includes currency exchange effects.

* Estimated by Top 25; ** For fiscal year ending March 2003; NC No change from previous year

Source: American Marketing Association (http://www.marketingpower.com/live/content19311C5542.php); accessed March 26, 2004.

Table 7-4. Types of Cross-National Equivalence

Equivalence	Description
Construct	The construct must exist and be meaningful in all cultures studied.
Functional	Similar activities/products must have similar functions in different cultural settings.
Conceptual	The meaning of what is studied must be comparable across cultures.
Category	The category in which objects, stimuli, and behaviors are grouped is the same across cultures.
Instrument	The instrument used must measure the same phenomenon uniformly across cultures.
Item	Each item of an instrument should mean the same thing across the cultures studied.
Translation	The wording of the instrument must mean the same thing to respondents in every culture studied.
Sample	Comparability and representativeness of samples exist across countries.
Contextual	The relationship and expectations between experimenter and subject are the same across countries.
Temporal	This determines whether different times at which studies were conducted across countries affects the results.
Measurement/ Measure	The same measurement model must hold across countries; that is, the relationship between observed scores and latent constructs.
Calibration	Comparable measurement units and correct conversion exist from one domestic norm to another.
Scalar/Metric	The same distance between scales and rank orders is maintained; that is, individuals with the same score have the same value on a construct and this relationship.

Source: Derived from Anne Smith and Nina C. Reynolds, "Measuring Cross-Cultural Service Quality," *International Marketing Review*, 19(5), 450–481a.

income levels, culture, attitudes, and understanding of business issues, including specific items on surveys and questionnaires. Hence, skilled interviewers are needed to conduct personal interviews.

A fundamental problem in doing international marketing research is making sure that the same construct is being studied across cultures. For example, does the word *quality* mean approximately the same thing to consumers in different countries and cultures? Different types of equivalence are outlined in Table 7-4.

Telephone surveys may work poorly and give biased results in countries with low rates of telephone penetration, such as in much of Africa. A different problem is the growing dislike of telemarketers in advanced industrial economies and skewed nonresponses. The use of mall-intercept techniques to obtain personal interviews may give erroneous results. Malls are not as widespread in many countries, even in Europe, and the subgroup of people visiting a mall may be unrepresentative of the broader audience. Mail surveys require a developed postal system, good mailing lists, and an educated population. Accurate and complete street addresses are necessary to provide representative samples for mail questionnaires.

Often mail and telephone surveys are not practical, in which case the researcher is left with personal interviewing as an alternative. With a largely rural population in poorer countries, the problem then becomes one of physically reaching the people. Poor roads and lack of public transportation may make interviewing people economically unfeasible. In tropical areas, many roads are impassable during the rainy season. Surveys may be limited primarily to urban areas. However, in urban areas, densely populated high-rise apartment living may make sampling homogenous and the pattern of people not at home may create unintended sampling bias.

The use of probability sampling is limited where the nature of the relevant universe cannot be reliably determined; quota sampling is limited for the same reason. Therefore, the most frequently employed technique is the *convenience sample*. This type of survey is defensible primarily because of a lack of alternatives.

In addition, the environment may favor distinct research methodologies, such as instruments with a diversity of questions; use of physical stimuli, such as a product, an advertisement, or a jingle; and control of the data-collection environment, including use of simulations or tests of products in use. Other relevant factors include the perceived anonymity of the respondent. The sensitivity of the information requested, the experience of the personnel conducting the survey, and the quality of the data desired also suggest specific research approaches. Privacy considerations are important, with Europe generally having stricter privacy protection laws than the United States. Respondents may feel pressure to respond with answers they perceive to be "socially correct." Speed, cost, and control for bias also affect the choice of technique.

Languages

Language, discussed at length in Chapter 3, is the initial cultural difference that comes to mind when one thinks of foreign markets. At the very least, language difference poses problems of communication; and solutions to those problems may be expensive. The research design and specifications must be translated twice, first (in the case of a U.S. firm) from English into the language of each country where the study is to be conducted. Then, upon completion of the study, the results must be translated back into English. More important than translation expense is the communication problem. Concepts and phrases widely understood in one language may be incomprehensible in others; for example, concepts such as a home equity, line of credit, value-added tax, and bride price.

Social Organization

Much of marketing research involves gaining insight into buyers' decision processes. That research is predicated on the assumption that the decision makers and influencers have been identified. In foreign markets, a researcher usually finds that the social organization is different enough to warrant identifying anew the decision makers and influencers. (This subject, including the varying roles of women, was discussed in Chapter 3.) Differences in social organization affect the industrial market as well as the consumer market. The nature of the decision-making structure in foreign companies may be different from that in U.S. companies. This difference may be due to a bigger emphasis on family business and a greater emphasis on relationships in other countries.

Obtaining Responses

Respondents and businesspeople may be reluctant to participate in marketing research for various reasons. Respondents may suspect the questioner of being a government tax representative rather than a legitimate market researcher, or they may be reluctant to respond for fear of giving information to competitors. In addition, one of the researcher's greatest problems is trying to demonstrate the value of the research to the respondent personally. Unless that can be done, little will be accomplished with many business respondents.

Consumers, too, may be reluctant to respond to marketing research inquiries. This reluctance may be, in part, the result of a general unwillingness to talk to strangers. Foreign respondents are often more reluctant to discuss personal consumption habits and preferences than Americans are. In contrast to the reluctant respondent is the cooperative respondent who feels obliged to give responses that will please the interviewer rather than state his or her true opinions or beliefs. In some cultures, this is a form of politeness; but it obviously does not contribute to effective research.

Reluctant or polite responses are not the only barriers. Occasionally, a respondent is not able to answer meaningfully. For example, illiteracy is a barrier when written material is used. That problem can be avoided through the use of oral interviews. Even when the interview is oral, however, a communication problem called "technical illiteracy" may arise. That is, the terms or concepts used might be unfamiliar to respondents, even though the wording is phrased in the respondents' native language. Respondents may not understand the questions and, thus, be unable to answer; or they may answer without understanding, giving a useless response.

Apart from the terms used, respondents may be unable to cooperate effectively because they are asked to think in a way that is foreign to their normal thought patterns. They may be asked to react analytically rather than intuitively. Whatever the cause of a respondent's inability to respond, it is basically a translation problem. The research designer must be able to translate not only the words, but also the concepts. The cultural gap must be bridged by the research designer.

Researching Consumers: Impact of Cultural Differences

International marketing research invariably comes up against cultural differences that affect the use and efficacy of standard Western methods and may lead to erroneous interpretation of findings because of cultural misunderstandings. Professionals must then turn for help to experts who can help bridge cultural gaps. For example, Hispanics may generally be alike. However, researchers need to keep in mind differences among Hispanic subgroups of Spanish, Portuguese, Cuban, Mexican, Puerto Rican, and Central and South American origin. In addition, researchers must consider how those differences affect the way participants are identified in the conducting of research. Misidentification and mislabeling can affect response rate and a willingness to participate, replicability, and the generalizability of studies. Other pertinent issues include how to gain access to survey participants, how to enhance completion of survey instruments, and how to get beyond socially desirable responses. Such cultural differences require that standard, culturally appropriate instruments be adapted. Questionnaire translation is equally important, as often there is no one correct way to translate an English word into another language. Multiple attempts at validation with different native speakers may also be necessary.

A study of consumer behavior of Hispanics identified immigrant Mexicans as having different consumption patterns from Hispanics who had immigrated to the United States years earlier.[4] As an example, the study cites the initial unwillingness of Mexicans to buy frozen produce or meat, based on the custom of buying it fresh on a daily basis.

The international marketer's job is made easier when concepts and measurement instruments have been developed and validated across several cultures. An example is a scale used to measure the strength of national identity. The scale has been validated with a series of mall-intercept and convenience samples in the United States, Japan, Sweden, Mexico, and Hong Kong. The findings show that the United States has a relatively strong national identity; Sweden, relatively weak; and Japan, Mexico, and Hong Kong falling into a "neither strong nor weak" category.[5]

Convergence of Consumer Behavior across Countries

Just as one might expect significant divergence among consumers because of cultural and religious differences, a growing convergence of consumer behavior is occurring across countries. This is caused by multinational media and the standardized global marketing strategies of multinationals. For example, a 1995 study from Roper Starch Worldwide (see Table 7-5) suggests that four broad types of consumers exist—types generalizable to 1.97 billion consumers worldwide.[6] Another 2002 study by RoperASW studied consumers in 30 countries. Ssome interesting findings of that study included the following:

- 54 percent of parents worldwide had fun with their children every day.
- The average workday of full-time employees was 8.6 hours.
- 53 percent of the sample read newspapers every day.
- The global average of time spent with the TV, radio, and Internet was 42.3 hours per week, or roughly the same amount of time spent working in a five-day week!
- 45 percent said they cooked almost daily, with 18 percent visiting grocery stores every day.[7]

In the same vein, a Gallup poll was conducted in the major cities of Argentina, Brazil, Chile, Colombia, and Mexico, dividing consumers into eight segments across countries. The poll was based on questions about income, education, occupation, type of home, and ownership of automobiles and durable goods.[8] The survey excluded low-income workers (about 17 percent of the working population) and ignored rural markets. Based on its sample of 17,564 people, Gallup divided Latin American consumers into eight categories:

Emerging professional elite: 14%	Skilled middle class: 9%
Traditional elite: 11%	Self-skilled lower middle class: 13%
Progressive upper-middle class: 13%	Industrial working class: 14%
Self-made middle class: 11%	Struggling working class: 15%

Table 7-5. Roper Starch's Four Major Types of Consumers

Consumer Type	Percent of Global Sample	Percent of U.S. Sample	Major Features of Group	Sample Comment
Deal makers: Negotiate and haggle before buying	29%	37%	Well educated; average income and employment levels; negotiation viewed as "fun" predominantly in developed nations	"I feel really satisfied with myself, even excited, when I get a really good deal."
Price seekers: Obtain product at lowest cost	27%	36%	Predominantly in developed nations; discount retailing is not widespread; low levels of education, retirees, and women	
Brand loyalists: Shop by brand	23%	17%	Least affluent group; mostly male; median age 36; average level of education and employment	"Once I find a brand that satisfies me, I usually don't experiment with new ones."
Luxury innovators: Focus on prestigious brands	21%	11%	Most educated and affluent group; mostly male; median age 32; highest proportion of executives and professionals	

Results are based on feedback from 37,743 respondents in 40 countries.

Source: Roper Starch Worldwide 1995 Global Consumer Trends Survey, March/April 1995, as summarized in "Portrait of the World," *Marketing News*, August 28, 1995, 20–21.

Another study of Hispanic consumers in the United States found that Hispanics could be subdivided into three groups:[9]

- Isolated (primarily first-generation, mainly Spanish speaking Latin Americans)

- Acculturated (self-identified as Hispanic American or Latino)

- Assimilated (those who see themselves as Americans of Hispanic heritage)

The study estimated that by 2010, 67 percent of about 41 million Hispanic consumers in the United States would fall into the assimilated group (approximately 30 million Hispanics—the largest subgroup); 25 percent would be in the isolated group; and only 8 percent would be in the acculturated group. Interestingly, about half of all those Hispanic consumers live in California or Texas. The key segment for marketers is the acculturated group; the consumers in that group retain key aspects of their Hispanic heritage, but adopt many of the behavioral norms of the general market. While they speak Spanish among family and friends and are comfortable with both the Spanish language and English media, they tend to live in multiethic suburban neighborhoods. Marketers have to consider whether their products or services are consistent with dominant Hispanic values and experiences and what portion of the addressable market is from one of the three Hispanic segments outlined above. Then marketers need to decide how to tailor their products and the corresponding marketing mix to the needs of the identified subsegments.

Improvisation

To some degree, improvisation is probably used in all marketing research; but a higher degree is needed in international markets. Improvisation may be loosely defined as "unconventional ways of getting desired market information and/or finding proxy variables when data are not available on the primary variables."

One such approach is the use of national consumption statistics, by volume or units, for various items. Those statistics filter out exchange-rate anomalies that arise in the use of currency-based economic indicators. Examples of such information include the number, in units, of mobile telephones, televisions, and DVD players used; life expectancy at age one; number of hospital beds available and doctors per 100,000 people; consumption of various food items on a per capita basis; per capita availability of goods such as telephones, cars, and motorcycles; number of airline and train revenue passenger miles sold per year; consumption of electricity and steel; and average number of years of schooling completed by the population. All of

those indicators are generally available for a variety of countries, can be used to group countries, and can be correlated with market-size information.

New Services to Aid the International Firm

As international business continues to grow, more international marketing research services are available to aid firms. Existing international marketing research organizations are expanding into more countries, offering more services; and new organizations are entering the field. It is not possible to catalog all of these organizations; but an example is International Information Services Ltd. (IIS), a global product pick-up service for consumer-packaged goods manufacturers. IIS has 400 clients in over 30 countries, including Coca-Cola, General Foods, and Unilever. Each day supermarkets in 120 countries are "raided" by IIS shoppers who are buying products or searching for information needed by clients. They provide samples of competitive products, client products for monitoring of quality, and/or information on competing brands (ingredients, varieties, sizes, prices, etc.).

Learning by Doing

If the costs of primary marketing research are too great, another way to evaluate a market is by becoming an exporter. After a year or two of export experience, a firm will know more about actual market behavior than it could learn from a preliminary market study. If the market proves difficult or unprofitable, the firm can withdraw without incurring major losses. If the market proves attractive, the firm might consider a making a bigger commitment to the country.

Other Research Techniques to Use in Developing Countries

Four techniques that are commonly used for researching small, lower-income markets are (1) analysis of demand patterns, (2) multiple-factor indexes, (3) estimation by analogy, and (4) regression analysis. There are many other techniques; and as research continues, wider acceptance of factor analysis, neural network analysis, and other new applications will take place.

Analysis of Demand Patterns

Countries at different levels of per capita income typically have different patterns of consumption and production. For example, poorer nations tend to have a larger proportion of the population involved in agriculture, consumption of energy tends to be directly related to economic development, and trade in services is higher among richer nations than poorer ones. That data is widely available at the macro level for most countries. A simple technique known as the *multiple-factor index approach* allows insight into the consumption and production profiles of many countries. Though relatively crude, it gives a clue to a country's present position and the direction it is going. That information, in turn, helps a firm identify possibilities for export or for local production in the market.

Multiple-Factor Indexes

A *multiple-factor index* indirectly measures market potential by using a number of variables that intuition or statistical analysis reveals as being closely correlated with the potential market for the product in question. For example, a manufacturer of modular housing may look at:

- The rate of household formation.
- Population demographics to gauge the percentage of the population in the age bracket from 20 to 30 years, a prime household-forming segment.
- Income-level segments, with some minimum per capital household income, such as $2,000 per year being used to gauge purchasing power.

Smoothing out those numbers over several time periods and relating them to historic house sales and new housing construction may provide useful estimates of potential market size for the modular housing construction industry.

Estimation by Analogy

For countries with limited data, estimating market potential can be a precarious exercise. Given the absence of hard data, one technique—estimation by analogy—can be helpful in gaining a better understanding of market potential in such countries. This estimation is done in two ways: (1) through cross-section comparisons and (2) through the displacement of a time series trend to a different time period.

The **cross-section comparison approach** involves taking the known market size of a product in one country and relating it to some economic indicator, such as disposable personal income, to obtain a ratio. That ratio (in the illustration, product consumption to disposable personal income) is then applied to another country (where disposable personal income is known) to derive the market potential for the product in the country. Assume that a firm was attempting to gauge demand for do-it-yourself retailers in a potential market; it found that in Germany, the average annual per capita purchase for do-it-yourself projects was the equivalent of $1,200 (about 925 euros in 2004) and that the average per capita disposable income was $19,000. The company's proposed expansion into Poland, where the disposable income average is $5,500, would lead the researcher to believe that the average per capita purchases for do-it-yourself projects in Poland would be approximately $350.

The **time-series approach** estimates the demand in the second country by assuming that it has the same level of consumption that the first country had at the same level of development (or per capita income). This technique assumes that product usage moves through a cycle. The product is consumed in small quantities (or not at all) when countries are underdeveloped and in increasing amounts when economic growth is occurring. Thus, looking at meat and egg consumption in Taiwan in the late sixties and early seventies can provide a rough estimate of the demand for meat and eggs in mainland China in the 1990s, with Chinese incomes similar to those prevalent in Taiwan 20 years earlier.

Both approaches have limitations. The cross-section method assumes a linear consumption function. Both assume comparable consumption patterns among countries. When those assumptions are not true, the comparisons are misleading. When more sophisticated techniques are not feasible, however, estimation by analogy is a useful first step.

Using Long-Term Trend Data to Estimate Market Size

Supply and demand of tankers is an interesting market to study. Supply is relatively inelastic in the short run, with new ships on order taking three years to be delivered. Demand, on the other hand, is closely related to world economic and industrial growth; for example, changes in world oil and energy demand translate directly into demand for oil tankers and liquefied natural gas (LNG) tankers. As the imbalance of supply and demand grows, with demand outstripping supply, freight rates are likely to rise, with TCE (time charter equivalent) rates being a good indicator of the scarcity or abundance of tanker capacity.

Figure 7-2 shows the relationship between the TCE freight rate for Aframax, a type of tanker containership, and the tanker fleet utilization rate. As demand gets closer to supply, utilization rates go over 90 percent, causing sudden spikes in the daily charter rates for such ships. Ninety percent utilization is considered to be close to full use as tankers need periods for maintenance and may, at times, operate partially loaded. The tanker spot market price rose sharply in October 2004, to $97,000 per day for this type of container ship.[10] The sharp increase reflected a rise in oil price as fears of oil shortages engulfed the market due to the uncertainty of supplies from Russia and the Middle East and strife in Nigeria. Projected oil shortages are expected to last several years because of the fast-growing economies of India and China.

Ship owners, for instance, TeeKay Corp., can use such data to decide whether to order new ships. Ships are expensive, costing between $100 million to $200 million for large tankers, LNG ships, and container ships. Given that ships take three years to be delivered, ship owners have to forecast the market several years ahead in order to make sound investment decisions. Figure 7-2 is an example of the data and analysis used to make decisions on ordering ships.

Net changes in availability or supply of tankers must take into account the total number of ships on order and older ships likely to be scrapped for safety reasons, as mandated by the International Maritime Organization. (See Figure 7-3.)

This data can then be combined with derived future demand for tankers, based on forecasted trends in oil demand and demand for other forms of trade such as bulk container trade. Table 7-6 shows how Teekay puts together the relevant information in order to make a decision.

Regression Analysis

Regression analysis provides a quantitative technique for sharpening estimates derived by the estimation-by-analogy method just discussed. Cross-section studies using regression analysis benefit from existing predictable demand patterns for many products in countries at different stages of growth. A researcher studies the relationship between gross economic indicators and demand for a specific product for countries with both cross-section and time series data. To estimate likely demand, the derived relationship can be applied to countries that have only the gross economic data but not the product-consumption data. Multiple regression models use additional independent variables. For example, a model for forecasting air traffic growth could use two factors—per capita GNP growth and the yield in cents per mile (*yield* meaning the air fare for a route divided into the distance, or the number of miles on the route). Over long periods, the regression model has proved to be reasonably accurate, showing air traffic growing as incomes grow and air traffic dropping as fares rise.

There are limitations to using regression analysis, however. For example, as a product approaches saturation levels, the rate of consumption declines, requiring a different equation to explain the relationship. Nevertheless, regression analysis can provide useful insights.

Figure 7-2. World Tanker Fleet Utilization

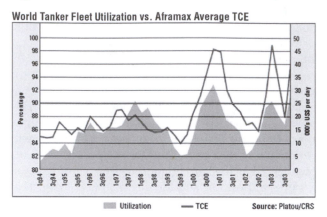

World Tanker Fleet Utilization vs. Aframax Average TCE

As reported in Teekay Shipping Corporation's First-Quarter 2004 Earnings Presentation (http://www.teekay.com/PDFs/Teekay_Q1-2004_Earnings_Presentation(1).pdf).

Figure 7-3. World Tanker Fleet Net Changes

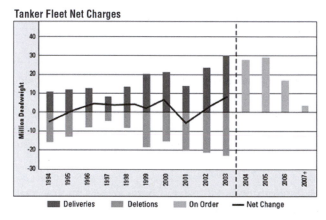

Tanker Fleet Net Charges

As reported in Teekay Shipping Corporation's First-Quarter 2004 Earnings Presentation (http://www.teekay.com/PDFs/Teekay_Q1-2004_Earnings_Presentation(1).pdf).

Table 7-6. World Tanker Fleet Utilization

	2004/2005 (MDWT)[1]	2006 (MDWT)[1]
New tankers to be delivered	59	19
Less mandatory scrapping	34	1
Net fleet growth	25	18
Tanker demand growth (estimated)[2]	29	12
Change in supply/demand balance	–4	6

1. MDWT—millions of deadweight tons.

2. Based on oil demand growth of 2.6 percent and 2 percent in 2004/2005 and 2006, respectively.

Source: Teekay Shipping, 2004.

Cluster Analysis

Firms often want to generate a short list of potential markets first, which they can then analyze more intensively. Cluster analysis is a favored technique for identifying similar markets. For example, the following variables (or some variation thereof) are commonly used by researchers to identify similarities among countries:

- *Production and transportation variables*—measured by items such as air passenger and cargo traffic, electricity usage, number of large cities, and population
- *Consumption variables*—based on income and GNP per capita; number of cars, televisions, hospital beds, radios, and telephones per capita; and educational levels of the population
- *Trade data*—derived from import and export figures
- *Health and education variables*—based on data such as life expectancy, school enrollment, and doctors per capita

Once "scores" for those four variables are developed for each country, the countries can be classified into groups, using cluster analysis. The implication is that when countries within the groups are similar, similar marketing strategies can be used.

Similar cluster analysis techniques are used by the Economist Intelligence Unit (EIU) to group markets based on the opportunities they offer. EIU's indices cover market size, market growth rates, and market intensity (which measure the relative concentration of wealth and purchasing power in those countries). For example, the market-size index is derived from data on population; consumption statistics; steel consumption; cement and electricity production; and ownership of telephones, cars, and televisions.

Clustering Countries by Product Diffusion Patterns

A problem with clustering countries on the basis of macro-economic variables is that international marketers may not find the resulting segments helpful; acceptance and diffusion of new products may vary within the proposed segments. An alternative is to segment countries based on how similar they are in the rate at which new products are adopted (the product diffusion rate). (See Table 7-7.) If such segments could be derived, managers might use information from the lead market about variables such as growth in market size when sales reach a peak to make inferences on the same variables for lagging markets. This allows a country to belong to more than one segment at

Table 7-7. Country Segmentation

Segmentation Using Macroeconomic Data
Production and transportation variables; personal consumption data; health and education statistics

Segmentation Using Product Diffusion
Long-term series product sales data; macroeconomic data (see other column); lifestyle data

the same time. For example, the United States could be in the leading markets segment for a product such as advanced personal computers, while lagging in the use of products such as smart cards or high-speed trains.

Macroeconomic data, such as standard of living, are important in explaining the readiness of a country's market to accept innovation. In addition, a diffusion-based segmentation approach uses data about factors such as lifestyle (use of phones per capita, for example) and cosmopolitanism (tourist expenditures and receipts). One study included an examination of the relationship between country-level variables and sales growth over a 14-year period for three consumer durables— TV sets, VCRs, and CD players—for 12 advanced industrial nations from Europe, Japan, and the United States.[11]

The study showed that segments based on product adoption rates did not agree with segments derived from broad macroeconomic data alone. Those results suggest that countries that look similar from a broad macroeconomic perspective may differ in the rate at which they are willing to adopt and buy new products. Cultural factors such as language and religion, which were not specifically included in the study, may play an important role in explaining differences in the product diffusion rate. Numerous studies have noted the importance of culture, mobility, and sex roles as important factors in explaining differences in product adoption rates.[12]

Screening Potential International Markets: An Example

Another marketing research screening technique useful for obtaining a short list of key country markets is described here. The screening technique is applied to the market for kidney dialysis equipment.[13] The first step is to determine what countries can afford the medical equipment. The high cost of kidney dialysis equipment and necessary supplies and personnel limit the market to wealthy countries. Hence, a first screen might be based on the wealth of a country, measured by the following (current) indicators:

- A total GDP of over $15 billion
- GDP per capita of at least $1,500

That screen alone reduces the number of potential markets to 28 countries outside North America.

Next, the markets must have specialized hospitals and doctors who can competently administer dialysis treatment. In addition, the treatment is expensive and requires a certain level of government support and subsidy; otherwise, the market for private patients alone would be too small to justify attempts at market penetration. Thus, a second screen would include other criteria:

- No more than 200 people per hospital bed (nationwide availability of hospital beds)
- No more than 1,000 people per doctor (nationwide access to doctors)
- Government health-care expenditures of at least $100 million (minimum total market size)
- Government health-care expenditures of at least $20 per capita (affordability floor)

The resulting calculation provides a set of 19 countries as potential markets. A third screen analyzes the markets in terms of the current market for dialysis equipment. Two factors are used:

- At least 1,000 deaths per year due to kidney-related causes (A lower number might indicate that the market for dialysis equipment is already being well served by competition.)
- At least 40 percent growth in the number of patients being treated with dialysis equipment

This results in just three markets for detailed consideration: Italy, Greece, and Spain.

A fourth screen consists of carefully evaluating the three countries in terms of existing competition, political risk, and other factors. Management subjectivity can come into play here because some managerial judgment is required to evaluate the strength of competition and political risk. Management may well decide to enter more than one of the three markets identified thus far. It may also go back to the third screening step and reduce the required rate of growth to, say, 30 percent in order to add some additional potential markets.

Once a short list of potential markets has been compiled, individual markets must be studied more carefully. At this point, information can be obtained from the Department of Commerce's Comparison Shopping Service (CSS). A CSS survey covers a product in a particular country's market, indicating the product's overall marketability, chief competitors, comparative prices, customary entry, distribu-

tion and promotion practices, trade barriers, and degree to which the company's product competes. About 50 key countries are covered by this low-cost and timely service.

Gap Analysis

The goal of gap analysis is to analyze the difference (gap) between estimated total market potential and a company's sales. The gap can be divided into four categories.

- *Usage gap* refers to total industry sales being less than the estimated total market potential. These gaps may be explained by estimation errors or by unpredictable changes in consumer tastes and behavior; for example, eggs being in less demand than expected. In the United States, that usage gap would probably be traced to health-related concerns.
- *Competitive gap* refers to existing market share compared to expected market share. Analysis is needed to indicate why market-share shifts have taken place and what is needed to regain market share from competitors.
- *Product-line gap* arises because a company does not have a full product line when compared to its competitors; thus, it loses sales. For example, in the mobile phone industry, part of the product line includes phones with tiny cameras. To the extent that a mobile telephone company such as Nokia or Motorola was late in marketing or did not have the camera features available, its market share might be less than it would have been if it had fielded a full product line.
- *Distribution gap* is a company's failing to target part of the market because of a lack of distribution facilities or agents. Closing that gap would require that the firm extend distribution and product availability to cover all regions and segments of the market and all channels of distribution.

Input-Output Tables

Input-output tables provide an analytical tool of great value in studying demand in foreign markets. They are becoming increasingly available for more countries, particularly for advanced industrialized nations and newly industrializing countries such as Brazil, Taiwan, and India. Input-output tables are useful for industrial product analysis and for analysis of market demand for intermediate components and materials. The tables highlight how production functions vary among nations, thus allowing the researcher to adjust market forecasts to account for country differences.

Information Sought by Marketing Research Professionals

When making decisions, marketers typically focus on four areas:

- Information for making new product development decisions
- Pricing decisions
- Setting and allocating sales efforts
- Market segmentation

A survey of 166 American and 37 Japanese market research firms showed that marketing research practices were surprisingly similar in the two countries.[14] Japanese firms conducted more research projects focusing on marketing information system design, import and export strategy development, and forecasting. Given the greater emphasis on exports in Japanese international business strategy, the focus on exports seems warranted. More Japanese research was done on distribution channel issues, perhaps because Japanese distribution is many-layered, inefficient, and more complex, with many more intermediaries between customer and firm. Japanese firms also seem to outsource sales research studies (usually done in-house by U.S. firms) to firms with greater access to databases and the ability to store data. The result is studies characterized by greater confidentiality and privacy.

Going Beyond Market Demand: Cost and Technology Trends

Market research focuses mainly on market potential and consumer behavior. In international marketing, researching cost and technology trends is also essential. In addition, if a firm considers establishing a sales subsidiary, warehouses, service centers, and manufacturing operations, then political risk analysis (See Chapter 4) is necessary to assess whether the firm will be able to stay in the market for some length of time.

Cost trends shed light on relative cost competitiveness. For example, raw materials or components may be available at a lower cost from some sources than others. Similarly, information about substituting newer low-cost materials—such as plastics for metal—and redesigning products to use fewer parts is relevant to a cost research study.

Technology trends reveal the future direction of new products and ultimately affect sales and market share. This research generally focuses on markets in which technological innovations are first presented. It aims to establish directions the industry is likely to take and the relative position of key competitors in key technologies. For example, an innovation in the video game industry is the growing use of

networked gaming, wherein individuals play games on a network against unseen opponents. How soon the network-based games become standard, how fast the current customer base demands the networked games, and how quickly competition introduces the games are questions that research into technology trends might attempt to answer.

Information Sources for International Marketing

Generally speaking, three basic sources of foreign market information exist: (1) secondary sources or published information, (2) knowledgeable individuals within the domestic market, and (3) primary data, gathered through empirical research in foreign markets.

U.S. Department of Commerce

The Department of Commerce is the chief government source of foreign market information, and it actively seeks to aid U.S. firms in selling abroad. The umbrella organization for that purpose in the Department of Commerce is the International Trade Administration (ITA). It manages the U.S. Commercial Service, a network of district offices in major cities around the country. Those offices offer personal consultation to U.S. firms interested in doing business internationally.

Another service of ITA is the publication of information on many topics of interest to the international marketer. *Export America*, ITA's biweekly magazine, is an excellent source of trade leads and information on developments in world trade. The ITA web site provides a large number of free reports on markets in different countries, such as a series of reports on the IT industry and prospects for countries as diverse as Brazil, Western Europe, China, and Japan. Information covered in the reports includes economic and marketing data on each country, industry trends, guidelines on how to do business in the countries, copyright and trademark laws, and business and import regulations. In addition to international market information, the Department of Commerce offers specific guidance in locating customers, agents, and licensees in foreign markets.

The resources provided by the Department of Commerce are a good starting point for foreign marketing research. First, the resources cover a wide range of subject matter as well as countries. Second, all materials and assistance are available at a modest cost; for example, the National Trade Data Bank information on CD-ROM. (See Global Marketing, "The National Trade Data Bank: Marketing Information for Exporters.")

Other U.S. Government Resources

Other government departments also provide information on international trade matters. Among these are the Agency for International Development, the FTC, the Department of Agriculture, and the International Trade Commission. The Department of Labor publishes a periodical titled *Labor Developments Abroad*. These examples merely indicate the extent of the U.S. government's interest in foreign countries and the way its information services can benefit the international marketer.

Non-U.S. Governments

Many foreign governments have a large amount of data available on their own economies, much of which is available from the country's embassy or consulate and their web sites. In some cases, information can be obtained from a distributor or subsidiary within the country. If the country is seeking to attract foreign investment, its information services are likely to be especially good. It probably has a development office in the United States, such as the Indian Investment Center in New York City. Many countries have web sites maintained by their foreign investment bureaus; the central bank; and other major trade organizations, such as JETRO, the Japan Trade Research Organization, in the case of Japan.

International Organizations

Chief among international organizations, of course, is the UN and its affiliated organizations. There is no doubt about the UN's major role in gathering and disseminating information about all aspects of the world economy. Its economic commissions conduct numerous studies and issue regular publications, such as the *Economic Survey of Europe* and the *Economic Survey of Latin America*. The United Nations Statistical Yearbook is an invaluable source of data on over 200 countries.

Many UN agencies are relatively unknown to the public, but they are doing work that is important to international corporations. For example, manufacturers of pharmaceuticals, foodstuffs, and hospital equipment must be up to date on the activities of the WHO. Personnel managers in international companies need to be informed about the publications and services of the ILO. Companies producing foodstuffs, fertilizers, or farm equipment are interested in the activities of the Food and Agriculture Organization (FAO). Other international organizations also provide useful information. The OECD is the most active. Its bimonthly *General Statistics* gives major economic indicators for the member countries (the industrialized countries of the West). The OECD also publishes studies on many other topics of interest to the international marketer and now sells subscriptions to its valuable economic data.

Other regional organizations supply information on their regions. The EU, for example, is especially useful for information on developments affecting that area. A number of U.S. companies have located their European headquarters in Brussels, partly to be near its power center. In addition, the IMF issues the monthly *International Financial Statistics*, while the WTO publishes world trade data. Also quite useful is the World Bank, with its annual *World Development Report* and its reports on missions to countries and studies of sectors and industries.

Online Databases

Secondary data-collection effort can be pursued online, using the Internet and commercial-service provider access to a wealth of databases. For example, the STAT-USA web site, which is fee-based, allows users to examine a host of economic data and market research reports prepared by U.S. government agencies. Nearly every major government organization maintains a web page, allowing users to access published reports by these agencies. For example, the United States Department of Agriculture has a web site, FASonline, which offers detailed information about agricultural exporters, market studies, price trends, government regulations, and tariffs.

A relatively recent entry is the website/portal globalEDGE™, maintained by the Center for International Business Education and Research at Michigan State University. It boasts information on about 200 countries with over 2,000 online resources and diagnostic tools (globalEDGE.msu.edu).

Access to these online databases, particularly commercial ones, is not cheap; but with practice and advance formulation of a search strategy, including a careful delineation of key search terms, researchers can quickly put together a vast set of material from diverse sources pertinent to the research question at hand. Aside from the standard sources such as Dow Jones, Lexis/Nexis, *The Economist*, and *The Wall Street Journal*, there are many specialized industry-specific sources. Many industries have their own trade associations that serve as clearinghouses for information related to international business. For example, the Aerospace Industries Association in Washington, D.C., prepares an annual report that includes information on the international business performance of the industry, international business prospects for the coming year, international business historic time series, and relevant government legislation and industry events. It also serves as a lobbying agency for the industry. Similar organizations exist for nearly every major industry, including telecommunications, the semiconductor industry, machine tools, and the software industry.

Beyond a narrow, single-industry focus are national associations such as the Chamber of Commerce and the National Foreign Trade Council, composed primarily of larger U.S.–based firms. Similar organizations exist in other countries (for example, the Keidanren in Japan), and their newsletters and libraries serve as important repositories for relevant secondary information. Individual cities and states also have foreign-trade associations and agencies. One example is Massport in Boston, Massachusetts, which leads trade missions to foreign markets and serves as a rallying point for international business initiatives at the state level. Every state has some form of a "state development agency," its mission being to promote state exports and entice foreigners to invest in the state. (Both parts of the mission create jobs.) While these state agencies vary in the services they provide, examples of initiatives include training seminars, networking conferences, counseling and market research, sales leads, and trade shows. Small Business Development Centers (an arm of the U.S. Small Business Administration) also have offices in many colleges and universities. They use graduate students to help businesses with specific international business problems or concerns. A strong point of those associations is the self-help feature; their members are often businesspeople with international business experience who can help their colleagues with specific details of international business in a specific country.

In addition, advertising agencies, banks, airlines, express package services, shipping organizations, freight forwarders, and major accounting and management consulting firms are also useful sources of international business information. As business has expanded abroad, these groups have followed their clients. Many offer services abroad that are as good as those they offer at home. Foreign market research is not limited to U.S. firms; more and more, local organizations in major industrial countries compete with U.S. consulting and research groups. Other examples include publishing bank newsletters and periodic reports, such as accounting firms' information guides to taxation and doing business in a variety of overseas markets.

As international business expands, a researcher can expect foreign market information services to grow as well. A basic reference book is ESOMAR's *Marketing Research Glossary*, published by the European organization ESOMAR, the World Association of Research Professionals.[15] The book's main feature is its alphabetical list of marketing research terms in English. Another useful publication from ESOMAR is a *Handbook of Marketing Research.*[16]

The Company's In-House Expertise

Companies frequently forget their own in-house expertise. Over the years, a company may build up databases and acquire informed personnel with field experience who

GLOBAL MARKETING

The National Trade Data Bank: Marketing Information for Exporters

The Department of Commerce's National Trade Data Bank (NTDB) supplies data monthly on CD-ROM; monthly updates include the full text of thousands of documents useful in international marketing. Major data sources contained on the CD-ROM include Annual Industrial Outlook *and the* World Factbook. *These contain country profiles; marketing research reports on specific products, industries, and countries; economic statistics for foreign countries, including interest and exchange rates, labor costs and rates, export and import statistics, and foreign investment figures. The Foreign Trader's Index contains lists of organizations in foreign countries, their product line interests, and ways they might help American exporters.*

For example, a company that is considering industrial food service equipment for hotels, restaurants, hospitals, and company cafeterias might begin its search on CD-ROM with the keyword industry *and then request marketing research reports from the next menu; information about a particular country could then be requested. From the list of countries, the company could pick India, which would bring up a list of nearly 100 marketing research reports available for India. Selecting restaurant catering equipment from the list would give the full text of a study by U.S. foreign commercial service personnel in Delhi, providing information on size of the market, sales in recent years, U.S. market share, principal competitors, upcoming trade shows, major customers, and other useful information.*

The NTDB service is relatively inexpensive ($60 for a single copy of the NTDB CD-ROM or $575 for an annual subscription from STAT-USA, U.S. Department of Commerce, Washington, DC 20230). The information from the two CD-ROMs available each month can be printed out, copied to a hard drive, and read into other spreadsheet software (such as Excel) or word processing packages. It is a useful and essential first step for any company beginning its marketing research into foreign markets.

return to domestic postings after foreign assignments. Any company could benefit from developing a systematic framework for inventorying the overseas knowledge and experience of its personnel in a centralized database. Doing so would enable the company to access "the wealth" through an in-house "knowledge intranet" when projects require a certain kind of knowledge. Failure to utilize such expertise is exacerbated as a company grows and develops multiple regional and national units, each with its own staff, projects, and historical databases. Of course, turnover in personnel is another way to lose accumulated knowledge and expertise, the tacit knowledge embedded in key personnel being lost when they leave the company. Consideration should be given to transforming personnel's knowledge into information that can be stored and accessed through corporate intranets.

Related parties such as suppliers, distributors, and even major customers can be another source of information for a company's secondary data gathering. One way a firm can enhance its international market information is to develop a detailed plan under which its distributors provide headquarters with information about a product market in their territory. That data may extend to pricing policies of competitors, new product introductions, brand image, customer satisfaction, and market growth rates.

Information for Sale

Many of the previous information sources are free or are offered at nominal cost. In the case of governments, the information service is subsidized. In the other cases, the supply of information is incidental to the main business of the supplier. Domestic examples of such organizations are AC Nielsen, Ward's (automotive reports), and Dodge (construction reports). Those organizations have extensive international coverage.

One important source of foreign business is found in the numerous directories of foreign firms in manufacturing, retailing, and other lines of business. Some directories cover just one country; others are international in coverage. Even guides to these directories are available, allowing a researcher to locate all directories relevant to a particular need. An example is *Trade Directories of the World*, a loose-leaf volume by Croner Publications.

A number of companies publish information about international trade. Dun & Bradstreet is one company that actively provides international financial and marketing information to those who buy its services, including banks and manufacturers. Among its important publications are *International Market Guide, Continental Europe*, and *International Market Guide, Latin America*.

Two widely used services have an entirely internation-

al focus. The Economist Intelligence Unit (EIU), which is associated with *The Economist* magazine, is one. EIU's services include providing quarterly reports on economic and political matters for most countries of the world, as well as regular reports on marketing in Europe and other special topics. EIU also conducts specialized market studies for individual firms; but in this capacity, it competes with other consulting firms.

EIU publishes weekly newsletters on developments affecting international business, as well as on companies' international experiences and problems. The weekly letters specialize by area—Europe, Asia, China, Latin America, and Eastern Europe. Other EIU publications are on the topics of investing, licensing, and trading conditions (in over 50 countries) and the topic of financing foreign operations (annual services with loose-leaf supplements).

Marketing Research Models

Prior development of models of marketing phenomena can help guide market research and make the results more useful. This section reviews a number of market research models. It covers consumer behavior, household buying behavior, country of origin effects, and the impact of religious and cultural factors on consumer behavior.

Modeling Consumer Behavior

Why do U.S. consumers buy foreign-made cars? Market research professionals often seek to model consumer behavior in the international marketplace. One model attempts to explain why U.S. households buy Japanese cars. Developed by Dardis and Soberon-Ferrer, this model hypothesizes that buying Japanese cars is affected by household characteristics that, in turn, determine the weight given to different product attributes, leading eventually to the decision to buy or not buy a Japanese car.[17] Specifically, the variables used to profile *household characteristics* include the following: income; age; sex; marital status; race; education of the head of the household; geographic location within the United States. They add another variable, labeled "the origin of disposed stock," meaning whether a previous car sold (if any) was of Japanese or other origin (that is, whether the household had previously owned a Japanese car).

The model includes *product attributes*, variables that primarily capture automobile quality: cost of repair; frequency of repair; operating efficiency (miles per gallon); weight (a means of gauging comfort and safety); depreciation rate (a reflection of the resale value of the car); and, finally, purchase price of the car, which is held constant so as to isolate the effect of the quality variables.

As the above illustrates, It is important for marketers to develop a model on which to base their data collection and analysis efforts. The model can be modified to include additional variables, such as social class, religion, and occupation. The bottom line is that an explicit model allows for the gathering and analyzing of data by a directed research effort, which permits validation and modification of the model. For example, the Dardis and Soberon-Ferrer model showed that lowering the depreciation rate of the car by 1 percent a year increased the probability of buying a Japanese car from 22 percent to 26 percent. Similarly, lowering the fuel economy (miles per gallon) by 10 percent dropped the probability of buying a Japanese car from 22 percent to 14 percent.

The implications for marketing strategy are clear. For a U.S. company trying to catch up to the perception of Japanese cars, several methods exist to lower the probability that a household will buy a Japanese car: Rather than rely on vague appeals to "buy American," companies should improve U.S. cars so that they depreciate slower, cost less to own and operate, and require repair less frequently. Of significance, the proposed model, when applied to past car-purchasing decisions, was able to correctly predict whether households would buy a Japanese or non-Japanese car 96 percent of the time.

Household Buying Behavior: A Study from Saudi Arabia

For many products, buying decisions are made jointly—by households; by husbands and wives; and, in some cases, by children. Products such as houses, automobiles, furniture, and consumer durables (for example, refrigerators and stoves) fall into this category. Understanding whether households in different countries approach major purchasing decisions differently is critical in making international marketing decisions. These can be decisions about product positioning, advertising appeals, direct-mail and telemarketing campaigns, and ways to build product loyalty. Marketers are interested in who makes the buying decisions in a family and what his or her influence is during the critical decisions of whether to buy, when to buy, where to buy, and how much to pay. Several competing theories exist to explain family purchasing behavior, as follows:

- *Culture-defined behavior*, whereby cultural norms prescribe which spouse has more power in influencing purchase decisions
- *Resource contribution*–based power, whereby the spouse who contributes more resources—be it income, status, education, etc.—is more powerful in influencing decisions

- *Relative involvement*, whereby the spouse who has the greater interest and involvement in a product or service will have more influence over its purchase

Countries and societies are male-dominated in many nations, or they are in some transition where women are gaining more rights (for example, from Japan at one end of the scale to Afghanistan at the other), or they are egalitarian where men and women are treated equally (or nearly so). Household purchasing behavior can be expected to differ across different kinds of societies.

A study on family purchasing behavior in Saudi Arabia shows how role behaviors of husbands and wives differ significantly across countries.[18] Limited to a sample of 249 upscale, married Saudi women, the study is interesting as a study of family purchasing behavior in a developing country. The study found that (1) husbands dominate consumer decision making in Saudi Arabia, as is the case in many developing countries; (2) husbands are dominant in deciding on buying a car and on "where to buy," except in the case of women's clothing; and (3) in many cases, Saudi wives who work and/or are more educated, have more influence over purchasing decisions. Overall, husbands dominate purchase decisions in what is a predominantly Islamic, patriarchal Saudi society.

Country-of-Origin Effects

An important variable affecting consumer purchase in international marketing is the country of origin (CoO). There are many products where the CoO is important to consumers, such as perfumes, cars, high-fashion clothes, consumer electronics, and software. For all of those products, country-specific stereotypes exist, with certain countries being associated positively with certain products. Examples are French perfumes and German cars. For those products, knowing the CoO affects how consumers evaluate a product. In many cases, the country of manufacture (CoM) is also relevant. For example, in India, consumers often want to look inside TV sets to see where the components have been manufactured. Figure 7-4 presents a conceptual scheme showing how CoO and CoM affect purchasing behavior, product-line decisions, and profitability.

As Figure 7-4 illustrates, once consumers are aware of CoO, their familiarity with brand, level of involvement in the purchase decision, and existing preference for domestic products become relevant, as do product- and market-level influences such as type of product and brand image. In industrial product buying, "rational purchasing" might be more prevalent; and, thus, greater credence might be given to CoM effects. Product attributes may be relevant, such as

Figure 7-4. Assessing Country-of-Origin Effect

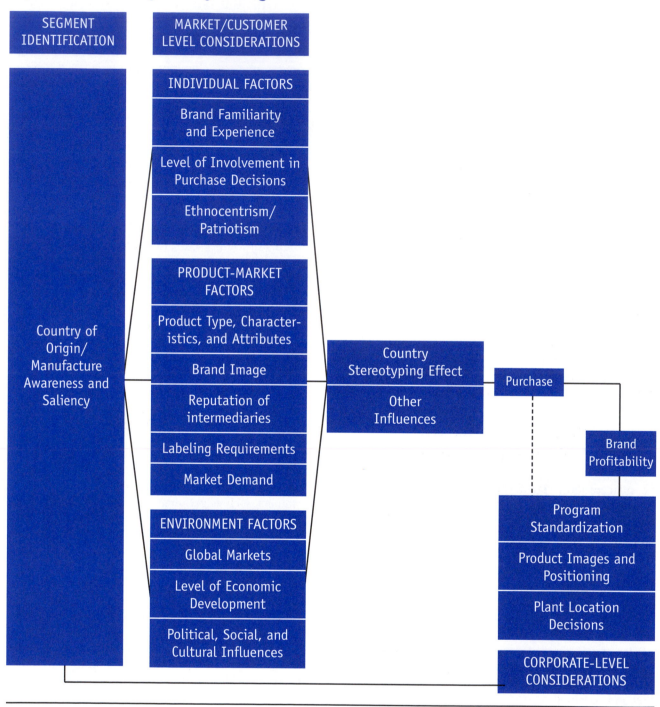

quality, performance, design, aesthetics, price, and prestige. A powerful brand image may be associated with a company and overcome the area of origin or manufacture. Reputation of the dealer or intermediary may muffle or enhance the CoO or CoM effect, and truth-in-labeling requirements as well as demand conditions can mediate the effect of CoO.

Environmental influences also come into play. These include the existence of global markets (when CoO may

become less important); level of economic development of the countries from which products come; and political, social, and cultural influences favoring certain nations. Together, these influences result in a country stereotyping effect and ultimately affect the purchase decision.

What does this mean for a firm? CoO and CoM effects have implications for standardizing marketing programs (whether to source from one or more locations and how

Table 7-8. Religion and Consumer Behavior

Variables Measuring the Importance of Religion to Consumers

- Belief in religion
- Religious practice (for example, church attendance)
- Moral consequences of being religious
- Religious socialization in the family and at schools
- Self-described level of religiousness
- Consequences of religion for society

Aspects of Consumer Behavior Likely to Be Affected by Religion

- Owning (many) material possessions
- Enjoyment of shopping
- Consumption versus thrift
- Paying more for quality or brand names
- Status derived from buying higher-priced goods
- Searching for bargains
- Reaction to advertising appeals (based on sex, power, glamour, speed, and social acceptance)
- Religion-based prohibitions and sanctioned behavior (for example, avoiding alcohol and being charitable)
- Importance of longer product warranties and guarantees; service
- Country-of-origin and country-of-manufacture effects

to adapt), for positioning the product, for selecting the image in advertising—even for deciding plant location, all other things being equal. Together, these disparate decisions affect overall brand profitability.[19]

Religious Beliefs and Consumer Behavior

Cultures differ in many ways, with a central difference being religion. It is natural to ask whether religion affects consumer behavior. For example, are devoutly religious people different from more secular people with regard to enjoying shopping and buying a large variety of material goods? What sorts of advertising appeals are more likely to resonate with a religious person? To answer such questions, a firm must first define religious beliefs and then attempt to relate them to different aspects of marketing and consumer behavior. Table 7-8 summarizes these ideas.

A research study attempted to trace the effects of religiosity on consumption behavior for a sample of Japanese and U.S. consumers.[20] The study found that consumer shopping behavior did not seem significantly different between devout and casually religious Japanese individuals. However, in the United States, devout Protestants were "more economic," buying products on sale, shopping in stores with lower prices, being open to buying foreign-made goods, believing that there was little relation between price and quality, and tending not to believe advertising claims while preferring subtle and informative advertisements. Differences also existed at the national level, with Japanese shoppers preferring to buy domestically made products, visiting many stores to find the right brand, enjoying shopping, and preferring stores with bet-

ter service. As an exploratory study, with a total sample of fewer than 250 respondents drawn from just two cities (Tokyo and Washington, D.C.) and with none of the respondents having progressed beyond a high school education, generalizations cannot be made from this study. The study is useful, though, in suggesting directions for international marketing research, particularly when marketing to countries with distinct religious systems, such as India, the Middle East, Japan, and China.

Culture and Consumer Behavior

Do cultural differences affect the acceptance of new products? Researchers found that power distance and uncertainty avoidance hinder the acceptance of new products, while individualism has a positive effect. The specific study focused on Internet usage, cellular phone usage rate, and PC usage rate as examples of receptivity to innovation.[21] Another study focusing on culture and innovativeness obtained similar results, while also noting that there was a positive effect of masculinity on innovativeness in a market.[22]

In attempting to relate cultural values to consumer behavior, though, most researchers rely on Hofstede's cultural dimensions (see Chapter 3). However, Hofstede's dimensions are derived from an examination of employees at the workplace; cultural values underlying consumer behavior may be different. Further, Hofstede's dimensions refer to a whole country as a homogenous group, whereas consumer behavior is concerned essentially with segments and subsets, subcultures within the larger culture.

Researchers have also examined whether Chinese children are materialistic, an issue that might be of interest to toy companies deciding how to position their toys and accompanying ads targeted to that group.[23] The study examined the level of materialism among children between the ages of six and thirteen in Hong Kong. It found that, in general, the children sampled were not highly materialistic, with materialism greater among younger children. Materialism among children seemed to be affected by their perception of the function of TV ads, the perceived truthfulness of those ads, and the children's general liking of TV ads. The authors also note the impact of the Chinese culture and environment in affecting attitudes towards materialism, citing traditional habits of thrift, emphasis on good social relationships and academic achievement, and good mass transportation systems that allow children to shop with their peers from a young age.

Simultaneous Approach to Forecasting Market Segments and Market Shares

Agarwal develops a simultaneous approach to determining global market segments and forecasting market shares. He integrates survey-based discrete choice methodology with latent-class models that relate an outcome, the customer's choice between competing product offerings, to a set of independent variables such as price.[24] This approach is used to identify global segments for a new service, resulting in seven distinct segments in terms of price responsiveness, size, and market potential.

Agarwal first develops key product attributes and competitors, then develops **choice cards** in an experimental design format so respondents can indicate their preference. This primary data is combined with secondary country data. These data are analyzed using experimental design data analysis techniques and factor analysis, yielding characteristic factors by country. The next step is to develop a segmentation model and decide on the number of segments, using logit models, to display the number of distinct segments and their response elasticities. This step also includes linking country and consumer specific variables to differences in response elasticities.

Agarwal then develops multiple simulation scenarios ranging from pessimistic to realistic and optimistic, and he develops forecast market shares and demand in each scenario. The result is market shares for the firm and its competitors and variations in demand in each segment under different scenarios. That data allows the firm to decide what segments to target and what specific marketing strategy to use for chosen segments based on the simulation results. Thus, the firm develops and executes a target segment strategy and an overall market strategy, all within a competitive context.

Because Agarwal's method requires the firm to obtain a large amount of detailed discrete-choice data from the sam-

G L O B A L
MARKETING

Ethics in International Marketing Research

International marketing research asks questions of individuals in foreign markets. Those questions may breach an individual's privacy. Individuals might misunderstand questions because of language barriers. In some markets, less-educated subjects may be unable to give informed consent. The researchers may seem to have power over the intended subjects, leading individuals to cooperate involuntarily. Therefore, international market researchers should keep ethical considerations in mind when planning and conducting research in foreign markets.

Ethical considerations may conflict with pragmatic research execution. An example of this is clinical trials done by pharmaceutical companies in foreign countries to test the validity of new drugs. To market a new drug, pharmaceutical companies must convince the FDA that their remedy is safe, that it does not cause harmful side effects in humans, that it is not toxic, and that it is effective in curing the illness—all while having manageable, safe side effects. Drug companies conduct trials on human subjects and gather information to prove those points. It takes time to recruit patients and to conduct the trials, which are costly. In addition, companies have to ensure that data are gathered in a scientific fashion so they can demonstrate statistically sound results to the FDA. By bringing a new drug to market six months sooner, a drug company can realize several hundred million dollars of additional sales and profits.

To save time and money, pharmaceutical companies have conducted tests of the efficacy of new drugs on patients in foreign markets, including countries such as Russia and India. The FDA is interested in receiving drug test results based on ethically diverse populations. Patients in those countries do not have access to good health care, and they may not be able to afford the cost of going to private doctors and buying imported medicines. They may also unquestioningly accept a doctor's suggestions. They may have limited education and not be able to give fully informed consent, particularly if language barriers further complicate communication. For those reasons, if a doctor suggests that they join a trial of a new medicine, they are likely to do so.

At the same time, doctors in those countries sometimes earn more money for recruiting patients and managing clinical trials of new medicines than from practicing medicine within the national medical system. (They may be paid a fee for each patient they recruit for the test, as well as a fee for managing the trial, administering the medicine on a regular basis, conducting tests, keeping a database of test results and treatment outcomes, etc.). In many countries with centralized medical care systems, patients with a particular illness are treated at the same facility, leading to a concentration of patients. This makes it easy for doctors practicing at a facility to recruit patients with a certain pro-

file (diabetic complications, for example) into a study for a client who might be seeking to test a new medicine to treat diabetics.

In one instance, a hypertension drug trial attracted only 20 qualified patients in Belgium over a two-week period. Within the same time period, 2,400 patients were recruited for the trial in Russia. Moreover, Russian patients may have had little access to modern health care and medicines. Therefore, they may not have built up a tolerance to a family of drugs, such as drugs for hypertension. In those circumstances, the clinical tests can show more clearly if the proposed drug is effective. The ability to recruit "treatment-naïve" patients draws clinical testing in foreign markets. Recruiting and managing patients is also less costly; the cost per patient of a trial in Russia may be $3,000, whereas a similar cost in the United States might be ten times that amount. Important drugs, including Zocor, a cholesterol-reducing drug from Merck, were approved by the FDA after being tested in Russia.

The general procedure is for pharmaceutical companies to work with Contract Research Organizations (CROs) to conduct these trials. In turn, the CROs work with specialized smaller firms in the foreign countries. Those firms may recruit doctors to bring in the patients and to manage the trial operations. Sometimes, the doctors set up their own CROs to work with foreign pharmaceutical companies. The FDA has the power to conduct spot inspections of these sites. However, it inspected only about 100 sites around the world in 2004 (while over 500 trials were conducted at 3,000 sites in Russia alone).

Clinical trials are subject to examination by local review boards before being submitted to the FDA. Pharmaceutical firms and their subcontractors are also bound by the internationally accepted guidelines for Good Clinical Practice, though compliance is voluntary. There are also nonprofit organizations, such as Family Health International (http://www.fhi.org/en/index.htm), that run clinical drug trials in emerging markets, primarily in Africa. The WHO and the U.S. National Bioethics Advisory Commission have raised concerns about ethical conflicts: whether the clinical trial data was derived as a result of the use of ethical conduct and sound scientific designs. In one case, Pfizer was accused of administering doses of its experimental new drug Trovan (for treating bacterial meningitis) to children in Nigeria without parental consent. Other companies have been caught in ethical conflicts: Gilead Sciences for testing the retroviral drug Viread (for HIV prevention) in Cameroon, Cambodia, and other developing countries and Boehringer Ingelheim for testing a drug in Uganda to prevent mother-child HIV transmission.

The number of clinical trials conducted in overseas markets will continue to grow because of the savings in cost and time and because of the ease of conducting the trials. Therefore, pharmaceutical companies and their partners will have to implement stronger ethical safeguards to ensure that the tests are ethically and scientifically impeccable.

Sources: "Drug Testing Goes Offshore", August 8, 2005, Fortune, pages 66–72; "Cameroon Halts AIDS Study", February 8, 2005, Wall Street Journal.

ple respondents, care must be taken in designing the choice cards. This method is useful in the case of new products and services where previously known market segments do not exist. And given the previous discussion on equivalence, it is possible that the way individuals respond to the choices presented may not be the same within identified segments.

Summary

International marketing research is complex primarily because of the difficulty of gathering information about multiple, different foreign environments. The first step is to determine what information to gather. Other problem areas include the availability and quality of primary and secondary data, the comparability of data on different markets, and hindrances in gathering information about areas such as social organization and culture. Although new services are available to help deal with those problems, improvisation and learning from experience are still important.

Quantitative techniques for market research include analysis of demand patterns, use of multiple-regression models, estimation by analogy, use of comparative analysis, and use of cluster analysis. Gap analysis, input-output tables, estimation of cost and technology trends, and clustering by product diffusion patterns are other useful tools.

The information gathered through research must be evaluated for quality, accuracy, and relevance. Data should be gathered at local, regional, and headquarters levels; a more difficult question is where data-gathering efforts should be supervised.

Sources of information for foreign markets include the U.S. government (particularly the Department of Commerce); international organizations such as the UN, the OECD, and the World Bank; industry and business associations; consulting houses; and online databases. A resource often ignored is information scattered within a company and derived from the company's own experience in various markets.

Models are an essential part of market research. A model explaining why U.S. consumers buy Japanese cars is illustrative of market research models, as are other consumer behavior models, household buying behavior models, and models of CoO effects.

Questions and Research

7.1 Explain the following statement: International marketing research is more comprehensive than domestic marketing research.

7.2 Can domestic marketing research techniques be used in researching foreign markets? Explain.

7.3 Why is it often more difficult to get responses to marketing research in other countries than it is in the United States?

7.4 Explain how the economic and commercial infrastructure in a country can affect the marketing research task there.

7.5 Define the "data problems" in international marketing research.

7.6 How can international marketing researchers deal with the problems encountered in their task?

7.7 How can international marketers prepare a comparative analysis of their foreign markets?

7.8 How might comparative analysis and groupings of foreign markets aid in solving international marketing research problems?

7.9 Discuss the U.S. government as a source of information for markets abroad.

7.10 List some of the business and trade associations that provide assistance to international marketing researchers. Explore the kinds of information provided by one such association in your area.

7.11 Identify several firms in your community. What kind of foreign marketing assistance is available to them locally or within the state?

7.12 What are some criteria for evaluating information in international marketing research?

7.13 How should a firm decide whether to gather its own research or to buy it?

7.14 Why is the screening of foreign markets important? Explain how screening was used in identifying key markets for kidney dialysis equipment.

7.15 Your company has developed a new video game based on the NBA and its players. Develop a screening procedure to develop the top five markets on which to focus. (Follow the approach outlined in screening for kidney dialysis markets.)

7.16 How can models be used in international marketing research? Discuss the information gathering implications of models encompassing (a) the purchase of foreign cars, (b) household buying behavior, (c) country of origin and manufacture, and (d) religion.

7.17 Can ethical problems arise in planning and conducting international marketing research? Explain your answer, making reference to the clinical testing of experimental new pharmaceutical drugs in foreign markets.

Endnotes

1. Roberts, John H. and James M. Lattin. "Review of Research and Prospects for Future Insights", *Journal of Marketing Research*, Volume 34, August 1997, pages 406–410.

2. See Figure 4 in N. Zabriskie and A. B. Huellmantel, "Marketing Research As a Strategic Tool," *Long Range Planning*, Volume 27, Number 1, 1994, pages 107–118.

3. Czinkota, M. R. and I. A. Ronkainen. "Using Secondary Sources of Research: Market Research for Your Export Operations," *International Trade Forum*, July 1994.

4. Peñaloza, Lisa. "Atravesando Fronteras/Border Crossings: A Critical Ethnographic Exploration of the Consumer Acculturation of Mexican Immigrants," *Journal of Consumer Research* 21, June 1994, pages 32–54.

5. Keillor, Bruce and G. Tomas M. Hult. "A Five-Country Study of National Identity," *International Marketing Review*, Volume 16, Issue 1, 1999, pages 65–82.

6. "Portrait of the World," *Marketing News*, August 28, 1995, pages 20–21.

7. Roper ASW 2002 Worldwide Time Study, November 4, 2002.

8. "Gallup Offers New Take on Latin America," *Advertising Age*, November 13, 1995.

9. Arjona, Luis D., Adam Weiss, Rajesh Shah, and Alejandro Tinivelli. "Marketing to the Hispanic Consumer," *McKinsey Quarterly*, 1998, Number 3.

10. INTERTANKO, The International Association of Independent Tanker Owners, Research and Statistics (http://www.intertanko.com/research); accessed November 15, 2004.

11. Helsen, K., K. Jedidi, and W. S. DeSarbo. "A New Approach to Country Segmentation Utilizing Multinational Diffusion Patterns," *Journal of Marketing*, Volume 57, October 1993, 60–71.

12. See, for example, Sengun Yeniyurt and Janell D. Townsend, "Does Culture Explain Acceptance of New Products in a Country? An Empirical Investigation," *International Marketing Review*, Volume 20, Issue 4, 2003, 377–397.

13. This technique is described in Kate Gillespie, Jean-Pierre Jeannet, and H. David Hennessey, *Global Marketing: An Interactive Approach*, 2004, Boston: Houghton-Mifflin.

14. Naumann, E., D. W. Jackson, and W. G. Wolfe. "Examining the Practices of U.S. and Japanese Market Research Firms," *California Management Review*, Issue 36, Number 4, Summer 1994.

15. Hastings, Raymond. ESOMAR *Marketing Research Glossary*, 2001; see http://www.esomar.org/content/pdf/GlossMaster.pdf.

16. *The ESOMAR Handbook of Market and Opinion Research*, 4th edition, 1998.

17. Dardis, Rachel and H. Soberon-Ferrer. "Consumer Preferences for Japanese Automobiles," *Journal of Consumer Affairs*, Volume 28, Number 1, Summer 1994, pages 107–129.

18. Yavas, Ugur, E. Babakus, and N. Delener. "Family Purchasing Roles in Saudi Arabia: Perspectives from Saudi Wives," *Journal of Business Research*, Volume 31, 1994, pages 75–86.

19. Samiee, Saeed. "Customer Evaluation of Products in a Global Market," *Journal of International Business Studies*, Volume 25, Number 3, Third Quarter 1994, pages 579–604.

20. Sood, James and Yukio Nasu. "Religiosity and Nationality: An Exploratory Study of Their Effect on Consumer Behavior in Japan and the U.S.," *Journal of Business Research*, Volume 34, 1995, pages 1–9.

21. Yeniyurt, Sengun and Janell D. Townsend. "Does Culture Explain Acceptance of New Products in a Country?" *International Marketing Review*, Volume 20, Issue 4, 2003, pages 377–396.

22. Steenkamp, Jan-Benedict E. M., Frenkel ter Hofstede, and Michel Wedel. "A Cross-National Investigation into the Individual and National Cultural Antecedents of Consumer Innovativeness," *Journal of Marketing*, Volume 63, Issue 2, 1999, pages 55–69.

23. Chan, Kara. "Materialism among Chinese Children in Hong Kong", *Advertising and Marketing to Children*, July–September 2003, World Advertising Research Center.

24. Agarwal, Manoj K. "Developing Global Segments and Forecasting Market Shares: A Simultaneous Approach Using Survey Data," *Journal of International Marketing*, Volume 11, Issue 4, 2003, pages 56–80.

Further Readings

Bock, Timothy. "A New Approach for Exploring Multivariate Data: Self-Organising Maps," *International Journal of Market Research*, Volume 46, Second Quarter 2004, page 189.

Craig, C. Samuel and Susan P. Douglas. "Conducting International Marketing Research in the Twenty-First Century," *International Marketing Review*, Volume 18, Issue 1, 2001.

Cui, Geng and Man Leung Wong. "Implementing Neural Networks for Decision Support in Direct Marketing," *International Journal of Market Research*, Volume 46, Second Quarter 2004, page 235.

Douglas, Susan P. and Samuel Craig. *International Marketing Research*, Chichester, UK: Wiley & Sons, 2000.

Dow, Douglas. "A Note on Psychological Distance and Export Market Selection," *Journal of International Marketing*, Volume 8, Issue 1, 2000, pages 51–65.

Farley, John U. and Patrick Barwise. "Marketing Metrics: Status of Six Metrics in Five Countries," *European Management Journal*, Volume 22, Issue 3, June 2004, page 257.

Gillespie, Kate, Jean-Pierre Jeannet, and H. David Hennessey. *Global Marketing: An Interactive Approach*, Boston: Houghton-Mifflin, 2004.

Hoffman, James. "A Two Stage Model for the Introduction of Products into International Markets," *Journal of Global Marketing*, Volume 11, Issue 1, 1997, pages 65–87.

Howell, Julian. "The Why and How of U.S. Market Entry: A Qualitative Study of Non-U.S. Pharmaceutical Companies," *International Journal of Medical Marketing*, Volume 4, Issue 3, July 2004, pages 235–251.

Keillor, Bruce and G. Tomas M. Hult. "A Five-Country Study of National Identity, *International Marketing Review*, Volume 16, Issue 1, 1999, pages 65–82.

Malhotra, Naresh K. "Cross-Cultural Marketing Research in the Twenty-First Century," *International Marketing Review*, 2001, Volume 18, Issue 3, 230–235.

Malhotra, Naresh K. *Marketing Research: An Applied Orientation*, 3rd Edition. Englewood Cliffs, NJ: Prentice-Hall, 1999.

Steenkamp, Jan-Benedict E. M. "The Role of National Culture in International Marketing Research," *International Marketing Review*, Volume 18, Issue 1, 2001, pages 30–39.

Thelen, Shawn T. and Earl D. Honeycutt, Jr. "Assessing National Identity in Russia Between Generations Using the National Identity Scale," *Journal of International Marketing*, Volume 21, Issue 2, June 2004, page 58.

Recommended Web Sites

There are many useful, well-organized web sites for data of interest to the global business researcher. Some of the major sites can be found at http://faculty.philau.edu/russowl/mega.html; but also consider the UN (for example, its CyberNations Project and the related country data). Useful sites include:

(http://www.un.org/Pubs/CyberSchoolBus/index.html), the World Bank's World Development Reports

(http://econ.worldbank.org/wdr), and Data Query (http://devdata.worldbank.org/data-query). There are also non-U.S. resources, such as Strategis, a Canadian government-sponsored agency that provides comparative country reports

(http://strategis.ic.gc.ca/sc_mrkti/ibin/compare.html).

(http://globaledge.msu.edu), is a knowledge web portal that connects international business professionals and students worldwide to a wealth of information, insights and learning resources on global business activities.

(http://janavaras.com), Janavaras and Associates International (JAI), is a global management training and consulting firm offering international marketing/management software (fee-based).

U.S. federal agency data resources include the CIA's annual Factbook (http://www.odci.gov/cia/publications/factbook/index.html) and NationMaster (http://www.nationmaster.com/).

For a current list of state development agencies and their web addresses, see http://faculty.philau.edu/russowl/market.html#Economic-development.

Manufacturers can find assistance through the Manufacturing Extension Partnership (MEP) at http://www.mep.nist.gov; for MEP Center locations by state, see http://www.mep.nist.gov/about-mep/center-info.html.

Information about the U.S. Commercial Service (a department within the Department of Commerce) offices abroad can be found at http://www.buyusa.gov/home/worldwide_us.html.

Competitive Information: Standard Industrial Classification (http://www.theodora.com/sic_index.html); North American Industry Classification System (NAICS) (http://www.census.gov/epcd/www/naics.html).

Industry Market Reports: http://www.export.gov/OneStopConsumer/OneStop/mrllogin.jsp; CAROL/Company Annual Reports On-Line (http://www.carolworld.com); Euro pages (http://www.europages.com); Corporate Direct (http://www.c-direct.ne.jp)

Case 7.1

THE INDIAN AUTOMOBILE INDUSTRY, 2005

Two-lane blacktops serve as national highways. Buses list dangerously to one side because riders are hanging onto the doors, yet the buses stop on the highway to pick up more passengers. Traffic slows down behind herds of cows and sheep or behind a farmer driving home a team of ducks. A cordoned-off area of the highway, blocked by paving stones, is given over to the drying of wheat and other grains. The only way to pass is to swing into the opposite lane against ongoing traffic. A truck or bus bears down on a car, the driver of the car having no option but to swerve onto the dirt shoulder, threatening the vendor of sweets or the squatting villagers exchanging gossip. A powerful car rarely reaches cruising speeds as it crawls along at 30 or 40 miles an hour behind an ancient truck belching black smoke, a camel caravan, or elephants carrying grass. Could such a market attract the world's premier car companies? Table 7-9 lists foreign automobile company investments in India.

Does this surge of foreign investment into India's auto industry make sense? As Table 7-10 shows, car sales (new vehicle registrations) were about 615,000 units from 1999 to 2000, with car sales rising to 736,000 in 2003–2004 after some years of stagnation. Production similarly registered strong increases, with exports also increasing significantly since 1999. Interestingly, luxury cars are forecast to account for an increasing proportion of total car sales. India, of course, is not the only emerging market receiving attention from multinational car manufacturers. China's market, about four times larger than India's, has seen investments from all of the major global auto companies. China also is developing several domestic companies that introduce domestic models often based on copied designs, but offered at lower prices.

Manufacturers such as Ford envisage building a mass-market global car with a global network of component manufacturing and assembly plants. Doing so would allow for parts and subassemblies interchange,

TABLE 7-9. FOREIGN AUTOMOBILE INVESTMENT IN INDIA

Foreign Investor	Local Partner	Details of Investment
Suzuki	Maruti Udyog	First foreign joint venture established in 1983; small car models, a van, and a utility vehicle; cost of basic Maruti: $6,000; a 57% market share in 2003–2004
Ford	Mahindra	Ford Escort and newer models, Orion and Ikon
Fiat	Premier Auto	License the Fiat Uno; to be produced and sold locally
GM (Opel)	Hindustan	General Motors began in 1995; manufacture the Opel Astra (large sedan)
Mitsubishi	Hindustan Motors	Mitsubishi minority ownership; manufacturing facility to produce Lancer units
Daimler-Benz	Tata Engineering	Assemble luxury E-Series models; 51/49 joint venture with production facilities in Pune; production equipment imported from Germany as part of Daimler's equity contribution
—	Tata/Telco	Broad line including Indica, the first "Indian" car, and Safari, Estate, and Sierra
Daewoo	DCM Group	Cielo Matiz and Nexia models to compete with Maruti
Honda	SriRam Industrial Group (SEIL)	$280 million 60-40 joint venture near New Delhi

TABLE 7-10. INDIAN AUTOMOBILE MARKET: PRODUCTION, SALES, AND MARUTI'S MARKET SHARE

	1999–2000	2000–2001	2001–2002	2002–2003	2003–2004	2004–2005 (estimate)
Sales ('000) units	615	568	571	594	736	900
Production ('000) units	577	513	564	609	842	1,000
Exports ('000) units	23	23	50	71	126	
Maruti Sales ('000) units	377	330	336	327	417	
Maruti Market Share (%)	61	58	59	55	57	

thereby lowering costs through economies of scale and reducing risks through geographical production and market diversification. Fiat launched a Project 178, under which suppliers in Brazil, for example, would be able to supply the same part to a factory in India as it would to a neighboring plant. The 178 is a family of cars based on a modified Uno platform—3- and 5-door hatchbacks, 4-door sedan, wagon, pick-up, and van. Project 178 purchasing chief Fabrizio Ceccarini said, "We want to be able to build the same car in any country to the same level of quality and are asking our suppliers to ensure that we can do that. They must be able to meet our cost and quality criteria and be able to supply a part anywhere in the world."

The Indian government had formerly frowned on developing a domestic car industry, forcing out both Ford and GM in the 1950s. A Socialist government thought cars were wasteful, preferring to invest in the building of public transportation systems. However, after 40 years of indifferent economic progress, during which time India saw many of its Asian neighbors prosper, including its one-time nemesis, China, the Indian government decided to begin promoting private enterprise. It liberalized the entry of foreign auto companies into India, lowered tariffs and taxes, and made financing available for new car purchases.

Car manufacturing has a broad multiplier effect on the economy, creating more jobs in parts manufacturing and support industries such as car dealerships, repair, and aftermarket parts supply and retailing. India is also a reasonably stable democracy, with GDP forecasted to grow nearly 6 percent a year over the next decade and with a population of about 1 billion people. India is still poor, however, with per capita income of less than $1,500 annually (even after adjustments for differences in purchasing power). However, the distribution of income is skewed. Economists estimate that about 2 million Indian households have an annual income in excess of $30,000. Given low Indian wages (for example, a chauffeur costing only $80 a month and a two-bedroom apartment renting for about $200 a month), a $30,000 income has much greater purchasing power, perhaps equal to an income three times as high in the United States. Thus, there is more disposable income to spend on luxury goods. Cable and satellite TV brings home messages about Western brands and conspicuous consumption. The spate of outsourcing to India in the software, business processing, and manufacturing industries has created significant numbers of educated young men and women. They earn good salaries, live in cities, and seek to replicate the lifestyles of their counterparts in the United States and Europe.

The automobile market is dominated by Maruti, which owns over half the market. In 2004, lower-priced cars, described in India as Segment A and B, accounted for about 78 percent of the market in units sold. Market shares were as follows:

Maruti: 55 percent
Hyundai: 18 percent
Tata Telco: 13 percent
Fiat: 4 percent
Ford: 3 percent
Hindustan Motors and Honda SIEL:
    2 percent each
GM, Skoda, and Mitsubishi: 1 percent each
Toyota: 0.3 percent
DaimlerChrysler: 0.2 percent

In response to Maruti's success, the Tata companies, India's largest conglomerate and one of its oldest company groups, decided to launch the Indica, "India's first indigenously designed and manufactured car." It sold 100,000 units within 18 months of launch. The Tata product line includes both diesel and gasoline engine Indicas, as well as newer, larger car models.

In addition to the automobile manufacturing sector, India's automobile components industry has also exhibited striking growth. When the Indian government liberalized foreign firm entry into the auto industry, it required new entrants to achieve high levels of local content within a specified period of time. In consequence, foreign car companies began purchasing Indian auto components, leading to a rapid rise in the number of companies in the industry as well as in the quality of products manufactured. The UN Human Development Report 2005 noted, "Over the past decade, Indian firms have emerged as a powerful force, especially in the components sector. Indian companies—such as Bharat Forge, Brakes India and Sundaram—have moved into high value-added areas of production." Production in the auto components industry for 2005–2006 was forecasted at $6.4 billion, as compared to actual production of $5.1 billion for 2002–2003; exports in 2002–2003 were $800 million, forecasted to rise to $1.3 billion in 2005–2006.

Many foreign auto companies in India aim to produce cars for the higher-income population segments, pricing the automobiles at two to three times the price of the basic Maruti autos. Maruti, manufacturing cars since 1983, currently has about 55 percent of the market share. Are there too many competitors in the Indian car market? How much room is there for expensive cars? Are foreign auto companies misguided in ignoring India's mass market? How should individual car companies develop their product and distribution strategy for the Indian market? Foreign auto companies in India may want to conduct additional market research to decide which segments of the market to focus on.

Case prepared by Professor Ravi Sarathy, Northeastern University, for use in class discussion. © 2005, all rights reserved.

QUESTIONS AND RESEARCH

1. Is the Indian automobile market an attractive market? Why or why not?

2. Compared to Maruti, are foreign auto companies well positioned in India? Explain your answer.

3. Which segment offers the most promise for sales and profits in India's growing middle class—developing higher-priced luxury cars or developing and marketing a car for under $5,000?

Case 7.2

WHIRLPOOL: THE EUROPEAN MARKET

Whirlpool is a major U.S.–based appliance manufacturer. The company moved aggressively into Europe when it purchased a 53 percent interest in the Philips major home appliance line. In 1990, Whirlpool bought out the remaining 47 percent, thus obtaining a wholly owned home appliance subsidiary in Europe. However, Europe experienced a recession shortly thereafter; and European operating margins were disappointing, at 3.3 percent in 1991, about 4 percent below comparable U.S. levels. Table 7-11 presents Whirlpool sales and operating profits.

TABLE 7-11. WHIRLPOOL CORPORATION REVENUES ($ MILLIONS)

	1991	1990	1989
Revenues			
North America	$4,236	$4,165	$4,116
Europe	2,540	2,456	2,269
Operating Profits			
North America	326	277	311
Europe	83	73	101

To improve its European business, Whirlpool needed to gather additional information about the European home appliance market. Table 7-12 summarizes 1990 market share for Whirlpool and its major competitors, a useful starting point. What else is needed to develop appropriate and comprehensive plans for European marketing?

TABLE 7-12. 1990 MARKET SHARE IN EUROPE (PERCENT)

Electrolux	19%
Bosch-Siemens	13%
Whirlpool	10%
Miele	7%
Temfa	6%
AEG	5%
Merloni	4%
General Domestic	4%
Candy	4%
Other	28%

The Wish List

The following represents a wish list of information that managers might find useful in preparing European marketing plans. It is based on information typically gathered in the United States.

- *The European economy.* A recovery from recession in Europe will stimulate economic activity in many fields, including the market for home appliances. Within European countries, the macroeconomic growth rates vary. Beyond the European Union, growth rates in the Eastern European countries are also important.

- *Housing starts.* In the U.S. market, information on housing starts is useful in predicting the demand for major home appliances. However, given the large base of installed appliances, only about 25 percent of appliances are sold directly to builders. Whirlpool would find it useful to understand how European housing starts can help predict appliance sales.

- *Replacement demand.* Approximately 75 percent of U.S. sales are through the retail channel, representing primarily replacement sales. Brand loyalty is an important consideration in determining whether a company such as Whirlpool can increase its sales by taking away customers from competitors. Different from appliance to appliance, the length of the replacement cycle also affects when and how often the appliance is replaced.

- *Appliance-specific information.* Major home appliances include clothes washers and dryers, refrigerators, dishwashers, and kitchen ranges (stoves). This category also includes microwave ovens. On the horizon is the microwave clothes dryer. For each appliance, a different set of product features may affect market size, competition, market share, and profits. Table 7-13 summarizes the relative penetration rates for major household appliances in Europe and the United States. The market for each appliance may be growing at different rates. Each appliance has its own price point, representing high-, medium-, and low-priced appliances. Understanding how prices are evolving in a segment of the appliance market is useful to Whirlpool, helping the company decide how to price its appliances, whether to lower prices, and at what rate. Different competitors have different strengths in each area of major home appliances, and profit margins can be significantly different from appliance to appliance. Cost structure can also differ among appliances, although in general, home appliances are raw materials- and parts-intensive. About 70 percent of cost of goods sold is in materials: steel, plastics, motors, timers, etc; another 10 percent is in labor; and the rest is in fixed overhead costs.

- *Distribution channels.* In the United States, retail sales are evenly split between Sears (33 percent), major national and regional dealers (33 percent), and smaller local shops (the remaining 33 percent). In the United States, there is a move to free retail dealers from the need to carry inventories. Instead, a retailer relays an order to the company, which ships the appliance directly to the customer within a few days. Whirlpool is experimenting with a Quality Express program that would supply customers within 48 hours. When such an innovation was tried by Shaw Industries in the carpet business, low-inventory, cut-to-order retailers took 50 percent of the distribution channel. The advantages to the manufacturer are higher margins, more information about customer preferences, and the possibility of stealing competitors' customers.

- *Competition.* The European industry is fragmented, as shown in Table 7-13.

TABLE 7-13. APPLIANCE MARKET PENETRATION (PERCENT)

	Europe	United States
Dishwasher	25%	54%
Range	92%	104%
Refrigerator	97%	100%
Washer	88%	75%
Dryer	18%	66%

Understanding competitors' plans in areas such as price setting, cost structure, and plans for product introduction is important. Some competitors are having financial difficulties. They are experiencing problems with quality or with dealer networks who are dumping their brands on the market, representing both a threat and an opportunity. Such short-term discounting by weak competitors is relevant to setting short-term marketing responses and long-term marketing plans. Acquisitions and consolidations continue to be important in Europe. By using such information, Whirlpool can grow by "buying" market share through the acquisition of competitors that may have specific strengths; for example, a strong local brand or significant market share in one or two European countries.

Opportunities in Europe

European markets have the potential to grow faster than U.S. markets. The main reason is because the level of penetration of some major appliances, such as dishwashers and dryers, is far lower than in the United States. (See Table 7-13.) There may also be opportunities for trading up as European incomes grow, houses become more spacious and energy-efficient, and multiple features and ease of use become driving considerations in replacement purchase decisions.

However, the European market differs from the U.S. market. Design differences exist between European countries; the features that make a model a top-selling item in one country may leave customers in another country feeling quite indifferent. Currently there are local brands specific to each country; while pan-European advertising is increasing. Whirlpool faces a special problem: ensuring that current Philips brand users switch to Whirlpool brand appliances when Whirlpool's rights to the Philips brand name end. Whirlpool's competition may not be the same company in every European country market. Whirlpool needs to design and carry out marketing research that provides the information necessary for the company to compete successfully in the more competitive EU.

QUESTIONS AND RESEARCH

1. What market research information does Whirlpool typically gather in the U.S. market?

2. Should Whirlpool be gathering the same information for Europe? Explain.

3. Design a marketing research plan for the major home appliance market in Europe. Specifically, how should Whirlpool identify differences between European countries that are germane to product design and marketing mix choices?

4. Try to obtain some information you listed in your answer to Number 3. What difficulties exist in gathering information about the European market?

5. Looking beyond Europe, for what other countries or regions should Whirlpool be gathering information? Why? How should it go about gathering that information?

6. Recently, European consumers have become concerned with environmental matters, giving rise to green parties and green products. Is this fact relevant to the marketing of home appliances? If so, how could Whirlpool incorporate environmental considerations in its marketing research? If not, explain your reasoning.

Case prepared by Professor Ravi Sarathy, Northeastern University, for use in class discussion. © 2005, all rights reserved.

CHAPTER 8

Modes of Entry and Global Distribution

Once a firm has chosen target markets abroad, the question arises as to the best way to enter those markets. This chapter presents the major entry methods and the criteria for selecting them. Once in a market, a firm also must identify and manage the internal distribution channels to ensure that its products are delivered when and where they are needed. This chapter discusses the major elements in managing foreign channels.

The main goals of this chapter are to

- Discuss the advantages and disadvantages of exporting, contract manufacturing, licensing, joint ventures, and wholly owned operations as ways of entering foreign markets.

- Explore types of indirect exporting, including piggybacking, and provide information on the role of selected export intermediaries.

- Review common export documentation, financing, insurance, and sources of information for trade promotion events.

- Give reasons for assembling products abroad as a way to enter markets.

- Discuss ways in which wholesalers and retailers differ internationally, requiring adjustment by the international marketer.

- Identify distribution trends that should be monitored by the international marketer.

- Explore major questions facing a firm, including the following: Should the firm duplicate its domestic approach? Should it use direct or indirect channels, selective or intensive distribution? How does a firm develop effective channel relationships? How can it keep distribution up to date?

This chapter focuses on the selection of market entry methods, the development and management of channels of distribution, and the coordination of global logistics.

How to Enter Foreign Markets

The choice of method for entering foreign markets is crucial because it has long-term implications. That is, when a firm chooses a level of involvement in foreign markets, it is also making decisions about the location and capacity of its manufacturing facilities. For example, when a firm decides to export, inherent in that decision is to leave the manufacturing plants where they are and keep plant capacity at existing levels. On the other hand, if a firm licenses its processes or brands to others, the amount of product produced increases and the worldwide location of the facilities now includes the licensees' plant. Plant location and capacity are strategic, long-term issues; they are not tactical, short-term decisions.

Furthermore, the market entry decision impacts overall marketing strategy in other ways. If a firm enters a market through a distributor or licensee, it is limiting its freedom in areas such as marketing research, product policy, pricing, and promotion. The constraining influence of the level of involvement will be a recurring theme throughout this chapter's discussion of a firm's international marketing.

The range of alternatives is wide enough that almost any company in any product area can find an appropriate way to reach foreign markets. The nature of entry ranges from indirect exporting to wholly owned production in foreign markets. (See Figure 8-1 for selected major methods of market entry.)

Before exploring these alternatives, a firm should consider managers' expertise and desired level of involvement and control in the market. The higher the expertise and the more important the market is in relation to other mar-

kets a firm serves, the more direct the level of involvement. Those factors will help in choosing an intermediary or a partner that best meets a firm's objectives.

Decision Criteria for Entry Method

Selection of the method of entry to foreign markets depends on factors peculiar to the firm and its industry:

- Company goals regarding the volume of international business desired, geographic coverage, and the time span of foreign involvement
- Size of the company in sales and assets
- Product line and the nature of the products (industrial or consumer, high or low price, technological content)
- Competition abroad, which a firm must evaluate for itself
- Saturation of local markets

Other criteria also affect the choice of entry method. Some are industry-specific (for example, power generation), which require some form of financial investment that is typically substantial. At times, the choice of entry mode is also dependent upon the geographic environment and the potential market's level of economic development.[1,2]

Those extraneous factors are included here because the decision model will not help in evaluating them—that is, a case-by-case approach is necessary.

Other criteria relate more generally to the method of entry to foreign markets, such as demand for a class of products that are less firm- and industry-specific.

NUMBER OF MARKETS

The number of markets a company serves differs from firm to firm within an industry, as does the way a firm decides

Figure 8-1. Market Entry Strategy

Single or Multiple Strategies

- Production in Home Market
- Foreign Production Sources

- Indirect Exporting
  - Piggybacking
  - Export Management or Trading Company
- Direct Exporting
  - Foreign Distributor
  - Foreign Agent
  - Foreign Marketing Subsidiary
- Foreign Production Sources
  - Contract Manufacturing
  - Licensing
  - Assembly
  - Joint or Mixed Venture
  - Wholly Owned

to enter each market. Different entry methods offer markedly different results in market risks and rewards. For example, wholly owned foreign operations are not permitted in some countries, licensing may be impossible in other markets because a firm cannot find qualified licensees, or a trading company might cover certain markets quite well but have no representation in other markets. To obtain the international market coverage it wants, a firm may have to combine different entry methods. In some markets, it may have wholly owned operations; in others, marketing subsidiaries; in yet others, local distributors.

PENETRATION WITHIN MARKETS

Related to the number of markets covered is the quality of coverage. An export management company might claim to give access to 60 countries. The producer must find out if that "access" is to the whole national market or if it is limited to the capital or a few large cities.

MARKET FEEDBACK

If a firm wants to know what is going on in its foreign markets, it must choose an entry method that will provide that feedback. Although the more direct methods of entry generally offer better market information, feedback depends, in part, on how a firm manages a particular form of market entry.

LEARNING BY EXPERIENCE

Experience is the best teacher. Typically, as a firm obtains more international marketing experience, the more directly it gets involved in foreign markets. A firm with international ambitions should choose an entry method that provides experience and that assists in realizing corporate goals.

CONTROL

Management control over foreign marketing ranges from none at all—for example, selling through a trading company—to complete control, as in a wholly owned subsidiary. A firm may want a voice in its foreign marketing; for instance, pricing and credit terms, promotion, and servicing of its products. The extent to which such control is critical to a firm bears heavily on the firm's choice of entry method.

INCREMENTAL MARKETING COSTS

Costs are associated with international marketing, no matter who does it. However, a producer's incremental marketing outlays and working capital requirements vary with the directness of the channel. For example, with indirect exporting, a producer has practically no additional outlays.

PROFIT POSSIBILITIES

In evaluating the profit potential of different entry methods, the long-term sales and costs associated with each entry method must be estimated. Costs and profit mar-

GLOBAL MARKETING

Entry Strategies for China

Formal admittance into the WTO means that China must allow easier access to its market.

China is the largest beer market in the world, recently passing the United States in consumption. To capture some of that fast-growing market, Anheuser-Busch increased its holdings in Tsingtao Brewery to over 25 percent and has one of only two foreign breweries in China.

The telecommunications industry in China was broken up in the early 1990s. It took nearly ten years, but AT&T entered a joint venture with Shanghai Telecom to provide Internet services.

Dell Computers built a manufacturing facility in Xiamen, China—not to export computers to the United States, but to supply the growing local market. The plant is larger than the one in Penang, Malaysia, that supplies 40 nations in the Pacific area. By 2003, Dell had become the third largest computer equipment supplier in China in terms of market share.

BP, ExxonMobil, and Royal Dutch/Shell are breaking into the Chinese retail gasoline and petroleum production markets by forming joint ventures with local giants Sinopec and PetroChina, as well as partnerships with local governments.

McGraw-Hill, Bertelsmann, and Cambridge University Press are a few of the publishing houses seeking marketing licenses in China. By May 2003, book retailers were poised to open superstores that are open 24 hours a day, offering 100,000 to 200,000 titles, coffee and snack bars, reading areas, and Internet connections.

Sources: Annual reports and corporate news web sites; "Foreign Bookshops Combat China Market by 24-Hour Service," *Global News Wire*, May 27, 2003.

gins are less important than total profit possibilities. For example, one entry method may offer a 25 percent margin on a sales volume of $2 million, but another may offer a 17 percent margin on a sales volume of $10 million. The latter entry method would probably be more attractive.

INVESTMENT REQUIREMENTS

Investment requirements are highest in wholly owned foreign operations. Plant investment, however, is not the only consideration; capital also may be required to finance inventories and to extend credit. Because the amount of capital required varies greatly by method of entry, this financial need can be an important determinant of what entry method a firm selects.

ADMINISTRATIVE REQUIREMENTS

The administrative burdens and costs of international marketing vary by entry method. They include documentation and red tape, as well as management time. For example, indirect exporting or licensing may involve little additional burden on management.

PERSONNEL REQUIREMENTS

Personnel needs also vary by method of entry. Generally, the more direct kinds of involvement require a number of skilled bilingual international personnel. If a firm is short of "internationalists," it is constrained in its alternatives.

LEGAL AND POLITICAL ENVIRONMENT

The more directly a firm is involved in foreign markets, the more management must deal with new kinds of legislation, regulation, taxes, labor problems, and other foreign-market peculiarities. If a firm is unable or unwilling to deal with those problems, it must choose an entry method that lets someone else handle them. FDI can, and often does, have a substantial impact on the economy. It can be in the form of creating new jobs, increasing the economic diversity of a nation, and introducing new (hopefully congruent) technologies. Country rulers, especially those in developing nations, are aware of the potential positive impact of FDI and often require that firms include FDI as part of their market entry plan.[3]

FLEXIBILITY

If a firm expects to be in foreign markets for the long run, some flexibility in its method of entry is important. Any entry method that is optimal at one point in time may be less than optimal five years later. In addition to the environment and market changing, a company's situation and goals change as well. Therefore, a firm wants flexibility—the ability to change to meet new conditions. It may want to expand to take advantage of growing markets or to contract because of adverse developments.

Although not easy to achieve, this flexibility is greater when a firm has planned for it in choosing its method of entry. For that reason, firms sometimes gain experience with limited forms of involvement before committing themselves heavily to a market.

RISK

Foreign markets are usually perceived as being riskier than domestic markets. The amount of risk a firm faces is not only a function of the market, but also of the firm's method of involvement in that market. In addition to its capital investment, a firm risks inventories and receivables. A firm must perform a risk analysis of the market and its method of entry. Exchange rate risk is another variable, as discussed in Chapter 2.

Besides economic risks, there are also political risks. A firm's political vulnerability may differ from market to market. The firm's level of involvement is one factor in that variability. Generally, the more direct and visible the entry, the more vulnerable a firm is politically.

A Simple Decision Model

The criteria for evaluating foreign-market entry methods are numerous, but they can be summarized as shown in Table 8-1. In applying the criteria, a firm seeks to answer two questions: (1) How well can the firm market through any particular entry strategy? (2) What are the costs and benefits of different entry strategies? Depending on its needs, a firm can use the matrix to select an entry strategy for individual markets, for regions, or for the whole international market. A large firm could apply that approach by product line or division. The criteria are also useful for evaluating specific channel candidates in a given country. For example, a firm could modify the matrix and use it to decide between a distributor, a licensee, and a joint-venture partner in Brazil.

Table 8-1. Market Entry Method Selection Criteria

Number of markets served	Marketing costs	Manufacturing flexibility
Level of desired market penetration	Administrative costs	Risk propensity
Desirability of consumer feedback	Competitive risks	Level of control desired
Available financial resources	Financial risks	Managerial biases

Usually, the decision facing a manager is having to choose one entry method from among several alternatives. However, many times a firm will use a combination of several entry methods—different entry methods for different countries or different product divisions, for example.

Alternative Methods of Market Entry

As pointed out earlier, there are many methods of market entry. Methods range from indirect exporting, which typically requires the least risk and level of involvement, to FDI in sales and manufacturing facilities—or perhaps a combination of those entry modes. (See Figure 8-1.) Selected methods are explored in more depth in the discussion that follows.

Exporting

Exporting is manufacturing a product in one nation and shipping it to another for sale to a final consumer. A component product can also be exported for use in producing another good or service. In those transactions, the nation of origin and the manufacturing firm are referred to as the "exporter," while the nation of destination and the buyer are referred to as the "importer."

When a manufacturer has little control over the marketing strategy (price, promotion, distribution, or even product modification) and when there is little or no contact between the buyer and manufacturer, the transaction is considered a form of **indirect exporting**. For example, Ford Motor Company installs glass, from a Mexican firm, in its cars assembled in Mexico and subsequently exports the cars to the United States. That process is considered indirect exporting of the glass. The glass firm may not even be aware that its products are leaving the country.

Piggybacking is one form of indirect exporting that is a viable alternative for many firms that make components for sophisticated products and large projects. As the term implies, one product "rides" on the back of another from one national market to another. For example, a construction firm that builds dams teamed up with a firm that manufactures industrial rakes used to clean the debris that inevitably collects at the base of a dam. The construction firm offered its customers a more complete project without getting into heavy equipment manufacturing or adding to its financial commitment. Entering a market in that fashion allows the rake manufacturer the benefit of expanding its sales internationally with little effort. The carrier is generally the larger entity and tends to have more of the human and financial resources needed for a specific market. The rider is the firm that makes a complementary product.

Firms that have limited sales or that are inexperienced in a market may rely on an intermediary such as an export trading or export management company to perform many of their marketing functions. Agents and brokers focus their attention on providing export marketing services to firms that either lack the resources or prefer to focus on core competencies rather than hire or train personnel for the technical and complicated tasks. The scope of the services can range from market research to customs clearance to inventory management and even financing.

Direct exporting also requires the use of intermediaries, but a firm typically retains title (and assumes responsibility) for a longer period of time and has closer contact with the foreign buyer. The intermediaries may be sales agents who work exclusively for the firm or who have other firms as clients. A firm may establish a sales subsidiary in other countries. Or it may ship products from one of its manufacturing facilities to another somewhere else in the world for internal consumption or for use in the production or assembly process. B2B exporting accounts for much of the trade in the world economy.

Intermediaries

Export management companies (EMCs) provide a variety of marketing services for a firm. Those services range from making simple shipment arrangements to conducting sophisticated marketing surveys, preparing market reports, developing promotional strategies, and providing financing. The scope and breadth of EMCs vary but may focus on a particular geographic region, industry, or service. EMCs are usually separate and unrelated to the firms they serve.

In practice, EMCs are occasionally confused with Export Trading Companies (ETCs) and may even be cross-listed in export directories. True ETCs, though, tend to be large, vertically or horizontally integrated entities, the most sophisticated of which can be found in Asia, particularly in Japan and South Korea (sometimes referred to as *sogo shosha* or *keiretsu*). They are what some would consider conglomerates, firms with partners that form an extensive vertical (and times horizontal) network. People might associate the name Mitsubishi with automobiles. While Mitsubishi Motors does make cars and SUVs, Mitsubishi Electric manufactures components for car entertainment systems, as well as transmission control and automotive navigation systems. (Mitsubishi Electric also manufacturers parts and components that are used in making elevators, escalators, computers, space vehicles, and display boards for stadiums.) The Mitsubishi group of companies includes a metals group that makes the steel used to manufacture automotive body parts; the Mitsubishi machinery group makes the machinery that makes the parts that go into the cars and trucks; and the energy group makes petrochemicals, the stuff that makes cars go! Names of a few of the other *sogo shosha* you might recognize are Hitachi, Honda-Matsushita, Mitsui, Nissan, Sony, Sumitomo, Toshiba, and Toyota. Banks and other financial institutions play an important role in the ETC relationships and often finance the cars, trucks, boats, and anything else the ETCs might make and sell. (For a more complete list and description of selected *sogo shosha*, see the list of recommended web sites at the end of this chapter.)

The U.S. Export Trading Act of 1982 was enacted to allow American firms to establish ETCs modeled after their large Japanese counterparts. Yet the American ETCs have not been successful, primarily because of competing interests of the firms involved. Cooperation among exporters in the form of ETCs, Webb-Pomerene Associations, or the use of Domestic Sales Corporations to reduce taxes have been less useful than originally imagined or have come under WTO scrutiny as subsidies (special tax treatment or legal treatment of domestic producers – See Chapter 4.) For a discussion of ETCs/EMCs, see *Basic Guide to Exporting* at http://www.unzco.com/basicguide/c4.html.

In summary, outside of Asia, as technology makes the development of rational sourcing strategies and establishing and maintaining relationships easier, the inflexible, long-term alliances associated with ETCs seem to offer fewer competitive advantages.

Identifying, Evaluating, and Selecting Intermediaries

Intermediaries are important in all forms of market entry; but by choosing exporting as the method of foreign market entry, intermediaries generally play a more critical role in a firm's success.

When working with intermediaries, perhaps the easiest part of the process is identifying them. A marketer can simply enter a term such as *export trading company in*to an Internet search engine (or search printed telephone directories) and get many hits in return. Trade associations, foreign business directories, commercial banks, steamship companies, airlines, business groups (the equivalent of BBBs and Chambers of Commerce are present in most areas), and the like are other sources for identifying intermediaries.

Finding a partner to represent a firm in another market *in the manner* expected is another matter. Keep in mind that just because an intermediary fails to meet sales goals, a firm may not be able to end the relationship. And if they are able to do so, it may be extremely expensive. So-called **divorce laws**, regulations that dictate the terms of separation between firms, differ widely from nation to nation. It may be possible to fire an intermediary salesperson or agency; but there may be heavy fines (loss of expected income), waiting or trial periods (which may extend into years), or other disincentives that make the firing expensive. Common advice among experts is to put a lot of effort in selecting an intermediary and to treat the intermediary

as if the relationship is destined to be a long-term one.

The evaluation a firm performs when hiring someone as its representative in the home market should also be carried out abroad, but with even more diligence. The skepticism you employ at home should be increased when dealing with someone you may have had little prior contact with other than sharing a meal on a plane. If the potential intermediary states that he can market all of your products throughout Africa, be suspicious, especially if the firm has only ten employees. Credit reporting agencies such as Dun & Bradstreet offer reports on companies in all major markets of the world as well as in countries that are quite small. American businesses can turn to the Department of Commerce's U.S. Commercial Service branch to find potential overseas agents, distributors, sales representatives, and business partners. Its Gold Key and Platinum Key services, its Partner Match (sometimes referred to as matchmaking), and the International Company Profile services provide marketers with lists of prescreened firms. The organization also provides the opportunity to participate in trade missions or one-on-one meetings with prospects. (See "Global Marketing: Golden Key to Export Opportunities.") State Development Agencies, such as New York's Empire State Development Agency's Export Marketing Assistance Service (EMAS), is one example of a state-level counterpart that also offers distributor identification and evaluation services.

After a firm obtains a list of candidates, it must secure information about each candidate in order to select the best one. For instance, in the case of potential distributors, a firm needs to know the method of operation—whether the distributors buy for their own account, whether they carry inventory, how many on are on their sales staff, what product lines they carry—and their effectiveness and reliability in marketing and in paying their bills.

ON-SITE PRESENCE

After all of this information has been gathered, the exporter should visit the market before making a final choice. That visit provides a feeling for the market that written reports can't convey. But more importantly, it provides further insights about the distributor—probably the most important single factor in export performance. Finally, the choice of a distributor is important because the company may play a role in the future as joint-venture partner or acquisition candidate. For example, when 3M established a marketing subsidiary in the Netherlands, it did so by acquiring a distributor there. For those reasons, the initial selection must be made very carefully.

Paying a visit to the better candidates and viewing their operations help the export manager make the best choice. Establishing personal familiarity makes future communication more meaningful. In some markets, a firm may not be able to develop a list of acceptable distributor candidates, in which case it might be happy even to find one that is being used by a competitor.

CONCLUSIONS ON EXPORTING

Discussion here has been primarily from the viewpoint of the firm whose only involvement is by exporting. Of course, exporting is a continual part of a firm's international business and is done by those who also engage in licensing, joint ventures, and other kinds of involvement. The focus has been on direct exporting because it is the most common form of international marketing.

Exporting includes many market entry options, but it is only one category of entry alternatives available to firms expanding internationally. Attention now turns to some options.

Foreign Manufacturing as Foreign-Market Entry

So far the assumption has been that a firm entering foreign markets is supplying the markets from domestic plants. This is implicit in any form of exporting. However, sometimes a firm may find it impossible or undesirable to supply all foreign markets from domestic production.

Several factors may encourage, or even force, a firm to produce in foreign markets if it wants to sell in them. For example, transportation costs may render heavy or bulky products noncompetitive. Tariffs or quotas can prevent entry of an exporter's products. In many countries, government preference for national suppliers can also shut the door to goods produced outside the country. (See Chapter 2.) When such preferences exist, a firm that sells to governments must produce locally. Any of those conditions could force a firm to manufacture in foreign markets in order to sell there.

Other factors may also encourage a firm to produce abroad. Because they are so large, regional groupings such as the EU and populous nations such as India, China, Russia, and the United States warrant entry via investment in local production facilities. In addition, local production allows better understanding of customer needs concerning product design, delivery, and service. Sometimes foreign production costs are lower, especially when transportation and tariff savings are added. A firm might undertake foreign production to gain any of those advantages even though it has the option of serving the market, at least partly, by exports. Britain's chemical firm ICI gave all of these reasons for beginning production on the European continent.

Once a firm has decided to enter certain markets by manufacturing in them, it has several alternatives. Foreign

GLOBAL MARKETING

Golden Key to Export Opportunities

The U.S. Department of Commerce, in cooperation with the ITA and the U.S. Commercial Service (CS) offers its Gold Key services to American firms that want to expand operations internationally. The type of assistance is broad—market research, arrangement of meetings with industry and country specialists, assistance with travel, access to interpreter service, and clerical support. If a firm cannot find the time or money to participate in a trade show, the U.S. government representatives will present the company's materials at the show or provide video services. The ITA also provides assistance to firms involved in e-commerce. (See E-Commerce Toolbox: A Guide for Going Online at http://www.export.gov/sellingonline.)

One feature of the Gold Key service is the International Partner Search, which connects firms with potential joint venture partners, licensees, agents, and distributors. The Gold Key and other services are available through Export Assistance Centers located throughout the United States and in nearly 100 countries abroad. Finding partners with help from the government is not foolproof and still requires careful assessment of the partners' capabilities, needs, and reliability. Yet Gold Key matching does perform much of the prospecting for potential partners—a very time-consuming part of the process. The Department of Commerce was cited as a particularly good resource for small- and medium-sized enterprises (SMEs) seeking to expand or enter markets via exporting.

Sources: http://www.export.gov/comm_svc/goldkey.html; http://www.export.gov/comm_svc/intl_partner_search.htm; accessed September 5, 2005. Sowinski, Lara L. "Going Global in a Flash," *World Trade*, Troy, August 2005, Volume 18, Issue 8, pages 28-33.

production may range from assembly plants, contract manufacturing, licensing, or joint ventures to wholly owned plants. In each approach, foreign manufacturing is the source of a firm's product in the market; but the extent of the company's involvement in production and marketing varies with the approach it chooses.

In **foreign assembly,** a firm produces domestically all or most of the components or ingredients of its product and ships them to foreign markets for assembly. Assembly operations involve less than full-scale manufacturing but still require that significant value be added in the local market. Notable examples of foreign assembly are the automobile and farm equipment industries. When transportation costs on a fully assembled vehicle or piece of equipment are high, a firm might be more competitive by shipping CKD and assembling in the market. Another reason for local assembly is the tariff barrier. Many countries have much lower tariffs on unassembled equipment; by forcing local assembly, governments increase local employment.

The pharmaceutical industry also uses extensive assembly operations, although they should be called compounding or mixing operations. Again, because of transportation or tariff barriers, a firm ships key ingredients to foreign markets and adds bulky liquids or other ingredients (and the capsule and packaging) locally. In a similar fashion, Coca-Cola ships its syrup to foreign markets, where local bottlers add the water and the container. The assembly or mixing plants abroad represent partial local manufacturing; they are a compromise between exports and local production.

If an assembly plant involves foreign investment, a firm must make an investment decision as well as a decision on how to enter the market. However, the investment commitment is not necessarily included in a decision to assemble abroad. A firm can assemble its products in foreign markets through licensing arrangements without making a capital outlay. For example, Jeep licensed Renault to assemble its cars in Belgium.

Contract Manufacturing

Foreign manufacturing by proxy abroad can be accomplished through **contract manufacturing**. That is, a firm's product is produced in a foreign market by another producer under contract with the firm. Because the contract covers only manufacturing, marketing is handled by the firm. Contract manufacturing is feasible when a firm can locate foreign producers capable of manufacturing its product in satisfactory quantity and quality. In some markets, that capability cannot be found.

Contract manufacturing may be attractive when a firm's competitive advantage lies in marketing rather than production. For example, in Italy, Procter & Gamble had several products manufactured under contract; Unilever did the same thing in Japan for some products. Both firms concentrated on marketing the products. Contract manufacturing obviates the need for plant investment, something a firm may want to avoid if the market is politically uncertain or if the firm is short of capital.

With contract manufacturing, a firm can avoid labor and other problems that may arise from its lack of familiarity with the country. At the same time, the firm gains the advantage of advertising its product as being locally made.

That fact may be useful in public relations or for government procurement purposes. If a market proves too small or risky for a firm, it is easier and less costly to terminate a manufacturing contract than to shut down a plant. Other advantages include transportation savings (compared to exports), occasionally lower production costs abroad, and possible exports of components or supplies to the contract manufacturer.

Drawbacks to the contract manufacturing approach may limit its application. For one, the manufacturing profit goes to the local firm rather than to the international firm. That is not serious if sufficient profit remains in marketing activities. For another, finding a satisfactory manufacturer in a foreign market may be difficult. Quality control, too, is usually a greater problem when production is done by another firm.

Licensing

Another way a firm can establish local production in foreign markets without capital investment is through **licensing**. Licensing differs from contract manufacturing in that it is usually for a longer term and involves greater responsibilities for the national party. A licensing agreement is an arrangement wherein the licensor gives something of value to the licensee in exchange for specified performance and payments from the licensee. The licensor (the international company) may give the licensee (the national firm) one or more of the following: (1) patent rights, (2) trademark rights, (3) copyrights, or (4) know-how on products or processes. Any of those may be given for use in a particular foreign market, or a licensee may have rights in several countries or on a whole continent.

In return for the use of the know-how or rights received, the licensee usually promises (1) to produce the products covered by the rights, (2) to market the products in an assigned territory, and (3) to pay the licensor some amount related to the sales volume of the products. The licensee assumes a much greater role than the contract manufacturer, taking over marketing in addition to production. Thus, the licensee is the complete foreign-market presence of an international firm for the products covered.

EVALUATING AND MANAGING LICENSING AGREEMENTS

Several features of licensing are attractive. First, it requires no capital and, thus, need not deter even small companies. Second, it is often the quickest and easiest way to enter a foreign market. Even a firm that has capital may face a slow process establishing local production and distribution. Third, a firm immediately gains local knowledge.

A fourth advantage is that many governments favor licensing over direct investment because licensing brings technology into the country with fewer strings and costs attached. Thus, licensing may gain government approval more quickly than direct investment. And from a licensor's viewpoint, there is no investment to be expropriated. Finally, the general advantages of foreign production also apply to licensing—savings in tariff and transport costs, local production where national suppliers are favored, etc.

The disadvantages of licensing are less numerous, but they may carry greater weight. The biggest fear about licensing is that the licensor may establish its own competitor. During the five or ten years of the licensing agreement, the licensor may transfer enough expertise that the licensee can go it alone. Thus, the licensor may lose that market, and perhaps neighboring markets, to the former licensee. That is less likely to occur where strong brands or trademarks are involved.

Another reason for hesitancy about licensing is the limited returns it provides. Although no capital outlay is necessary, royalties and fees from licensing are not cost-free to the licensor, which must invest management and engineering time. A direct investment approach to the foreign market requires much effort and many resources, but it may yield greater profits. Licensing returns are limited primarily to a percentage of licensee sales, commonly 3 to 5 percent. Indeed, less developed countries are trying to reduce even further the royalties and fees paid to licensors.

Yet another possible drawback is the problem of controlling the licensee. Although the contract should spell out the responsibilities of each party, misunderstandings and conflicts can arise in its implementation. Frequent areas of conflict are quality control, the marketing effort of the licensee, and interpretation of the exclusiveness and extent of territorial coverage.

Firms that are successful at licensing have developed certain techniques for minimizing the pitfalls of licensing and accentuating its potential benefits. The following is a list of some of those techniques.

- Have a deliberate policy and plan for licensing; that is, give it proper attention.
- Fix licensing responsibility in the firm by means of a licensing manager or department. Pfizer had nine licensing directors, one for each major business unit.
- Select licensees carefully.
- Draft an agreement carefully and review it with the licensee. Some items to include are territorial coverage, duration, royalties, trade secrets, quality control, and a minimum-performance clause.
- Supply the licensee with critical ingredients.
- Obtain equity in the licensee.
- Limit product and territorial coverage.
- Keep patent and trademark registration in the licensor's name.
- Be a reasonably important part of the licensee's business. Canon deliberately chose a smaller firm for its copier licensee in India in order to get better performance.

International licensing can be an important part of company strategy; U.S. firms receive over $10 billion a year from licensing agreements. It should be noted that licensing income is not limited to royalties, but also includes such items as (1) technical assistance fees, (2) sale of materials or components to the licensee, (3) lump-sum payments for transfer of rights or technology, (4) technology feedback, (5) reciprocal license rights, (6) fees for engineering services, (7) sales of machinery or equipment, and (8) management fees. The typical company receives five different types of return on its licensing agreements, but most of the income tends to be from royalties.

Joint and Mixed Ventures

Joint ventures and licensing forms of market entry have some common elements. Both involve manufacturing and distribution by a foreign firm. The major difference is that in the joint venture, the international firm has equity and a management voice in the foreign firm. The equity share of the international company can range from 1 to 99 percent, but generally is between 25 and 75 percent. Instead of our seeking a technical definition of a joint venture, however, a practical one is used:

"A **joint venture** is a foreign operation in which the international company has enough equity to have a voice in management but not enough to completely dominate the venture."

Note that the only joint ventures considered are those between an international firm and a firm that is native to the country in which the venture is located. Mixed ventures, on the other hand, are joint ventures with government entities.

Contract manufacturing and licensing are joint ventures of a sort; so is an exporter working with a foreign distributor. But none of those relationships have ties as strong as a joint venture's. As in the progression from going steady to being engaged to being married, each step represents a stronger tie. With the expansion of international operations, joint ventures have become increasingly important.

ADVANTAGES AND DISADVANTAGES OF JOINT VENTURES

The joint-venture approach must be compared with both the lesser commitments of contract manufacturing and licensing and the greater commitment of wholly owned foreign production. Whatever benefits are derived from foreign manufacture will, of course, be obtained in the joint-venture approach. As compared with a lesser commitment, joint ventures have the following advantages: (1) potentially greater returns from equity participation as opposed to royalties, (2) greater control over production and marketing, (3) better market feedback, and (4) more experience in international marketing. Disadvantages include a need for greater investment of capital and management resources and a potentially greater risk than with a nonequity approach.

When joint ventures are compared with wholly owned foreign production, a different picture emerges: (1) A joint venture requires less capital and fewer management resources and, thus, is more open to smaller companies. (2) A given amount of capital can cover more countries. (3) The danger of expropriation is less when a firm has a national partner than when the international firm is sole owner.

Many governments prefer or even demand joint ventures. They believe that their nations receive more of the profits and technological benefit when nationals have a share. Also, finding a national partner may be the only way to invest in some markets that are too competitive or crowded to admit a new operation. This latter point is important for many Japanese firms in the U.S. market.

Joint ventures compare unfavorably with wholly owned operations on only a few, but critical, points. The interests of one partner may conflict with those of the other. The interests of the national partner relate to the operation in the local market. The international firm's interests relate to the totality of its international operations; actions it takes to further global operations may not appear beneficial to the national partner. Some points of potential conflict are (1) transfer pricing, (2) earnings—pay out or plow back, and (3) product-line and market coverage of the joint venture.

Shared equity may also involve an unequal sharing of the burden. Occasionally, international companies participating in 50–50 joint ventures believe they are giving more than 50 percent of the technology, management skill, and other factors that contribute to success, but are receiving only half of the profits. Of course, the national partner contributes local knowledge and other intangibles that may be underestimated. Nevertheless, some companies believe that the local partner gets too much of a "free ride."

Compared to 100 percent ownership, the major complaint about joint ventures is the difficulty of integrating them into a synergistic international operation. When an international firm wants to standardize product design, quality standards, or other activities, its various national partners may not agree. Thus, when standardization, international exchange, and integration are important to a company, the joint-venture approach can be a hindrance. Conversely, when national operations present different product lines and localized marketing—as in packaged foods—joint ventures pose less of a problem.

Lack of knowledge about a market is a frequent reason for partnering with local firms. While the domestic firm brings knowledge about the product, the foreign firm brings its experience with local consumers.

Strategic Alliances

Almost every entry method involves an alliance with a partner. It may be an export management company, a distributor, a licensee, or a joint-venture partner. In the 1980s, however, a new term arose to describe a different kind of international cooperative venture. "Strategic alliance" has no precise definition but covers a variety of contractual relationships. Those agreements may involve competitors and usually do not involve equity. The global auto industry provides numerous examples of firms that have formed strategic alliances, some of which later developed into mergers and acquisitions (Ford-Mazda; GM-Toyota). In those and many other examples, competitors from different countries contract together to meet a strategic need of each party. Because the relationship often does not fit the definition of a licensing arrangement or a joint venture, the looser term *strategic alliance* is used.

Cross-border strategic alliances take many forms. They have become the most popular method of international expansion as firms face internationalization pressures and find that they need foreign help. The Chinese have been very active in alliance formation, as have firms that want to enter the Chinese market. Firms are finding that in most cases, if they want to enter world markets, frequently the best (and sometimes the only) way is through an alliance. Examples exist in industries ranging from cars to computers to communications.

Strategic alliances have a variety of objectives; a frequent one is market entry. Many firms find that a contractual arrangement with a foreign competitor is a better way to enter a market than the traditional distributor, licensee, or joint-venture approach.

Why would a firm help a competitor enter its home market? The answer is because the local firm is getting a new product, one that is complementary rather than directly competitive. In effect, market entry strategic alliances are a form of piggybacking. Stated differently, piggybacking is an early form of strategic alliance. Finally, although these alliances are called "strategic," every entry method a firm uses should be equally strategic.

Wholly Owned Foreign Production

The greatest financial commitment to foreign markets is wholly owned foreign production. In principle, *wholly owned* means 100 percent ownership by an international firm. In practice, a firm usually achieves the same results by owning 95 percent or even less. The chief practical criterion for wholly owned ventures is not the completeness of ownership, but the completeness of control by the international company.

Make or Buy?

A firm can obtain wholly owned foreign production facilities in two ways: (1) buy out a foreign producer—the acquisition route—or (2) develop its own facilities from the ground up. As a variation on the acquisition route, a firm can buy out a joint-venture partner. The acquisition route is especially popular, and it offers certain advantages.

Acquisition is a quicker way for a firm to get into a market than building its own facilities. Acquiring a going concern usually means acquiring a qualified labor force, national management, local knowledge, and contacts with local markets and government. And in some markets, acquisition may be the only way to enter if the industry has no room for a new competitor.

Rubbermaid was having trouble in Europe, where it had entered through a joint venture with a Dutch chemical firm. Finally, in 1998, it decided to acquire French and Polish plastics producers and the Dutch chemical firm. That acquisition gave Rubbermaid the existing products and markets of those firms, in addition to the ability to integrate their European marketing.

Buying brands is another way to break into a new market. To gain entry into the U.S. market, BP purchased Amoco (but waited a few years to incorporate BP signage) and Philips of the Netherlands purchased Magnavox. In some parts of the United States, Russian Lukoil signs are replacing signs at Mobil stations and China's bid for American brands have included Unocal (unsuccessful), TLC's purchase of RCA, and Haier's bid for Maytag (which owns the Hoover, Jenn-Air, and Amana brands).[4,5]

The alternative to acquisition is the establishment of a new facility, a method that may be desirable or necessary in certain circumstances. For example, in some markets, a firm will not be able to find a national producer willing to sell or the government will not allow a firm to sell to the international company. In other markets, producers may be willing to sell, but they lack the caliber of facilities needed by an international firm.

For its part, an international firm may prefer a new facility over an acquisition. If the market has no personnel or management shortages, a firm feels less pressure for acquisition. Furthermore, if a firm builds a new plant, it can not only incorporate the latest technology and equipment, but also avoid the problems of trying to change the traditional practices of an established concern. A new facility means a fresh start and an opportunity for an international company to shape the local firm into its own image and to get its requirements met.

A SUMMARY EVALUATION

Evaluating the sole ownership approach is easier now that you have considered the other alternatives. The advantages of wholly owned ventures are few but powerful. Ownership

Strategic Alliances

*A*lliances among firms have advantages similar to those that accrue to firms who license or franchise their name, products, and processes. A company can expand into new markets more quickly and offer its customers a broader array of products and services (all with less financial and time commitment) than trying to undertake those activities on its own.

Samsung Electronics teamed up with XM Satellite Radio so Samsung could offer its customers MP3 players with satellite radio reception (play favorites and find new ones). XM Radio subscribers will be able to download music and other content for "on-demand listening." XM Satellite is available in over 100 car, SUV, and truck models, thanks to agreements the firm has with major auto manufacturers such as Volkswagen and General Motors.

Citibank and China Union Pay (CUP) formed an alliance that will allow Chinese customers to get cash in the local currency as they travel around the world. With Citibank branches and ATMs in more than 50 countries, with one stroke of a pen, CUP is able to provide nearly worldwide customer service.

Li & Fung began as an export trading firm in China 100 years ago. Today it is one of the most sophisticated supply chain and sourcing management companies in the world. It orchestrates the manufacturing and delivery of apparel, toys, and electronic goods worldwide. Recently, Li & Fung expanded its retail operations by forming a strategic alliance with Daymon Worldwide, a global leader in the private label food industry. The deal is expected to yield an additional $1 billion annually for Li & Fung in a few years. The idea is that Li & Fung would market its products within a new retail setting—grocery stores. Daymon, with its reputation and established networks, would provide the leverage Li & Fung needs to break into this traditionally difficult retail market.

Sources: "Samsung Electronics Partners With XM Satellite Radio to Offer Samsung's First MP3 Players With XM Satellite Radio," PR Newswire Association LLC, July 26, 2005; "Citibank, China Union Pay Tie Up to Allow Chinese Access to Forex Abroad AFX," News Limited AFX—Asia, September 13, 2005; "Li & Fung Links Up with Daymon Retail," *Financial Times*, August 12, 2005; Li & Fung web site (http://www.lifunggroup.com); accessed September 15, 2005.

of 100 percent means 100 percent of the profits go to the international firm, eliminating the possibility that a national partner gets a "free ride." Complete ownership also gives a firm greater experience and better market contact.

With no national partner, no inefficiencies arise from conflicts of interest. Perhaps the overriding argument for complete control, however, is the possibility of integrating various national operations into a synergistic international system. Lesser degrees of involvement are more likely to lead to suboptimization because national partners have goals that conflict with those of the international firm. For those reasons, complete control was important for Rubbermaid, above..

The limitations to the 100 percent ownership approach are several. First, it is costly in terms of capital and management resources. The capital requirements prevent many firms from practicing a complete ownership strategy. Although large firms do not often find capital availability a constraint, they may face a shortage of management personnel.

Another drawback to 100 percent ownership is the probable negative host-government and public relations effect. Most nations believe that their participation in the venture should not be limited to supplying just labor or raw materials. Some governments go so far as to prohibit 100 percent ownership by an international firm, demanding licensing or joint ventures instead. A further risk occurring from such nationalistic feelings is outright expropriation, which is more likely and more costly with wholly owned operations.

Finally, 100 percent ownership may deprive a firm of the local knowledge and contacts of a national partner. A local collaborator often serves as a buffer between the international firm and its various national audiences. This role of the national partner as a cultural bridge can be its major contribution, helping a firm avoid mistakes in its encounters with nationals in business and government. By taking the acquisition route, a firm has more chance of getting such nationals than it does in setting up a new operation. The same applies to a wholly owned operation developed from a joint venture. With a new establishment, a firm can develop nationals who become a culture bridge; but the process is slower.

Market Entry—Related Marketing Activities

Certain peculiarities are associated with entering a different national market, not unlike the requirements people face when traveling from country to country. Products that are shipped abroad must be accompanied by various documents (similar to passports and visas) and must undergo screening and inspection for security and accounting

reasons (just as travelers have to pass through security in airports, at seaports, and elsewhere when crossing borders). If products are being shipped among good trading partners, the paperwork and inspections are likely to be less stringent, just as someone traveling from Austria to Germany may not have to show any documentation to border guards. Activities related to market entry, including documentation are discussed next.

PHYSICAL DISTRIBUTION AND DOCUMENTATION

Once in a particular market, firms must get their products to the distributors, who will get the product to the ultimate consumers. This distribution task differs from that performed in the domestic market. The shipping companies and modes of transportation are likely to be dissimilar; for example, the use of ships and airplanes is more common in getting products to foreign markets than in delivering goods within a country. Packaging costs for export are usually high because the distances and numerous changes in modes of transportation require that the product be handled more frequently. Of course, air shipments eliminate some of those problems; but that shipping method is more costly. Spoilage, pilferage, and national security are also concerns that must be taken into account. Those considerations may require special handling, special packaging, and additional documentation.

The paperwork required for shipping products across borders is greater than for domestic shipping. The importing nation requires documents of its own, particularly with heightened border security. The UN estimates that 7 percent of international trade represents documentation cost, eventually involving 40 documents and 27 parties per transaction. That fact is not unmanageable, however, as witnessed by the trillions of dollars of goods and services traded annually. Finally, insuring shipments to foreign markets is more involved than insuring domestic shipments.

The complications noted here, combined with firms' lack of familiarity with foreign markets, have deterred many managers from giving adequate consideration to foreign opportunities. Although paperwork and other complications involve extra work and cost, many sources of expertise are ready to help the exporter. Overseas freight forwarders are skilled in handling physical distribution and documentation; banks take care of the international financial aspects; insurance companies handle foreign shipments and can even insure credit to foreign customers. Also, some companies handle export packaging.

Most firms use some outside expertise, the amount often depending on the volume of export sales. The marketer has, in effect, a make-or-buy decision. Can these tasks be done more efficiently in-house, or should they be purchased outside? As sales volume increases, a firm tends to do more and more in-house.

OTHER MARKETING TASKS

Additional responsibilities associated with market entry include market intelligence, pricing, and promotion. **Marketing information** is often gathered by a firm's partners abroad, and as stated earlier, represents a major reason for seeking local partners. The firm supplying the goods may receive little market feedback. A firm needs continuing market information. While some data are available from secondary sources (for example, the U.S. Department of Commerce, the WTO, and others) and some information is provided by local partners, ultimately, there is no substitute for visiting, living, and working in the markets that a firm serves.

Pricing for foreign markets involves new dimensions. First, a manager must decide whether to quote in U.S. dollars or other currencies. If goods are priced in foreign currencies, how can the risk of fluctuating currencies be mitigated? Should the price be quoted FOB (free on board—plant or port of exit), CIF (cost, insurance, freight) to foreign port, or one of several other possible options? Should exports be at full cost or marginal cost? How should a firm handle tariffs and other add-ons to the plant price? If promotion is needed, the export manager is responsible for it. One may work with an export advertising agency and/or with national distributors in cooperative advertising programs. (All of those questions are important. They are addressed in the chapters devoted to promotion (Chapter 11) and pricing (Chapter 12).

Conclusions on Foreign-market Entry Methods

Selecting an entry method is one of the more crucial decisions marketers make, and it is a crucial strategic decision. The advantages and disadvantages of many methods of foreign-market entry have been presented. There is no one best way to enter a foreign market. The "best way" for one firm depends on its size, capabilities, and needs, as well as the opportunities and conditions in the target markets. A firm must analyze its situation and consider how the variables discussed here apply. Optimal results come from a careful analysis of alternatives rather than by merely responding to pressures. A firm is most likely to use different approaches for the various markets it serves and the way it serves markets over time. Too often in the past, firms have carried out their international business plans by responding to outside forces.

Flexibility is an important aspect of a firm's choice of entry strategy. Rather than rigidly following a single approach, a firm may want variation, depending on conditions in different markets. Larger markets may permit more direct approaches, whereas smaller markets may be better served by less direct entry. It may be appropriate to use different entry strategies for different product lines or divisions. Flexibility over time is also a major consideration. As conditions change, the optimum strategy may change. A firm can gain only by anticipating developments and adapting to them, rather than fighting them. Finding creative answers to such developments is the key to an international firm's viability.

Financial risks are typically lowest for exporting entry methods and higher for investment modes of market entry. As is the general case, higher risk yields higher returns. Marketers must remain keenly aware of the enormous competitive risks associated with contractual entry methods. Consider a firm that licenses its technology or franchises its brands abroad. In essence, a firm using that entry method is passing along proprietary company information. (It may be identifying a secret ingredient or the cooking process for its French fries.) There is less stopping foreign firms from using the knowledge once the licensing or franchising agreement expires. ("We have the knowledge, why should we keep paying you?"). The advantages and disadvantages are highlighted in Table 8-2

Table 8-2. Advantages and Disadvantages of Selected Market Entry Strategies

	METHODS OF ENTRY		
	Exporting	**Contractual**	**Investment**
Advantages	Limited financial risk	Rapid market penetration	High exposure to new markets
	Limited competitive risk	Limited commitment of time and effort	High return
	Limited commitment of time and effort	Limited financial commitment	High market penetration
			High control
Disadvantages	Limited exposure to new markets	High competitive risk	High financial risk
	Limited return (profit)	Moderate return (profit)	Moderate proprietary risk (if partnering)
	Limited market penetration	Limited control over quality, marketing, and manufacturing	Big commitment of time and effort
	Limited control		

Table 8-3. Ten Major Factors in Determining Market Entry Success

Develop a global strategic plan	Develop a long-term commitment to all intermediaries—foreign and domestic
Secure top management commitment	Be prepared to alter domestic marketing strategies.
Make a careful intermediary selection	Be willing to adapt products for cultural and regulatory reasons
Fulfill orders that match strategic plan (not merely fulfill unsolicited orders)	Provide print and promotional materials in local language
Develop a long-term commitment to all markets—foreign and domestic	Offer pre- and postsale support for products in all markets

LONG-TERM STRATEGIC DECISIONS

Factors that have a major impact on long-term market entry strategies are presented in Table 8-3. Internationally inexperienced managers are likely to overlook these considerations and make short-term, suboptimal decisions. For example, in cases of firms selling goods abroad because they have excess capacity at home, without upper level management's commitment to global marketing plans, those firms often cut off foreign sales as soon as the domestic market picks up again.

Level of Involvement—A Two-Way Street

The "internationalization theory" posited by Theodore Levitt in the mid 1980s stated that firms went through a step-wise progression in market entry, from exporting to contractual to foreign direct investment.[6] That theory has fewer followers than in the past, in part because the Internet has made it easier for firms to promote their product to the world, supplying certain products electronically to wherever and whenever they are needed. The term **Born Global** refers to companies that begin operations with both domestic and foreign sales from the outset.

However, just as products have life cycles with a decline phase, a firm's involvement in a market may undergo retrenchment and a regression to lesser forms of involvement. That results because of shifting consumer tastes, changing demographics, and an increasing competitive environment. There is also the extreme case of expropriation or another political action forcing a firm to leave wholly owned operations, having nothing left in the country. That occurred in both Cuba and Iran. A more common situation is when changes in a market or in a firm's position there cause a strategic reassessment. The factors that made a firm seek a certain level of involvement may have changed, or the firm may not have been successful in maintaining that involvement. The appropriate strategy,

then, is to accept lesser involvement in the market.

Those strategic withdrawals or retreats are not necessarily defeats. They are often merely sensible business responses to new situations. Just as discretion may be the better part of valor in some military situations, so, too, may strategic changes of involvement be the most profitable response of a firm to certain problems in foreign markets. A few examples illustrate some of these situations.

- Bulova, a strong international marketer of traditional watches, was being buffeted by the price pressures of new electronic and quartz watches. Losses overseas caused Bulova to change from its own marketing subsidiaries to less expensive independent agents.
- Unilever is one of the most powerful multinationals. In Mexico, Unilever had wholly owned production facilities for soaps and detergents. Severe competition from Colgate, Procter & Gamble, and La Corona (a Mexican firm) prevented satisfactory profits for Unilever. The company decided to sell its factory, maintain a marketing subsidiary, and contract-manufacture its product with La Corona.
- Maytag, which is headquartered in Newton, Iowa, decided to go international by purchasing Hoover in 1989. Hoover's main attraction was its strong appliance business in England and Australia and a (modest) presence on the European continent. In 1995, beset by fierce competition and a long recession in Europe, Maytag sold Hoover Europe to Candy SpA, an Italian appliance firm. One year later, obviously flexible and quick to adapt, Maytag entered a joint venture established between Maytag and Hefei Rongshida Group to manufacture washers and refrigerators for Chinese markets. Maytag International coordinates global ventures and sales in 86 countries. Maytag maintains manufacturing facilities throughout the United Sates and in two Mexican locations.

Foreign-market Channels and Global Logistics

Once a firm has chosen a strategy to get its products into foreign markets, its next challenge is distribution of the product within foreign markets. The following discussion focuses on major elements in managing foreign channels—the management of foreign distribution and international logistics.

Managing Foreign Distribution

Some firms that sell in foreign markets choose not to manage distribution within those markets. For those firms, the question was resolved when they decided on their method of entry. Firms that sell through trading companies, export management companies, or other indirect methods must accept the foreign distribution offered by the intermediaries. The same is true for firms that sell through licensing and, generally, for companies engaged in direct exporting. The firms retaining direct responsibility for foreign-market distribution are those having marketing subsidiaries or complete manufacturing and marketing operations in the markets. Possessing responsibility is different, of course, from having complete control. For example, the manager in a joint venture is constrained by the desires of the national partner. The wholly owned venture that resulted from an acquisition also finds its distribution options affected by the practices inherited from the acquired firm.

The first step in managing foreign distribution is for a firm to identify its goals in the foreign market. The marketing program, including distribution, is a means toward achieving those goals. Then the marketer must identify the specific tasks to be performed by the channel in the market. What role is the channel expected to play—inventory, promotion, credit extension, physical distribution, service? Finally, the marketer must match the job description with the channel possibilities available in the market. There is seldom a perfect match between a firm's specifications and the choices available in the market. Compromise is often necessary.

Consider how exporters might manage foreign distribution. Although they work through independent distributors abroad, export managers can have an impact on the foreign marketing of their products.

Marketing Through Distributors in Foreign Markets

Direct exporting through distributors abroad is the major form of international marketing. In every country, it is the primary method used by smaller firms that lack the resources for a greater commitment to reach foreign markets. It is also an important form of international marketing for large multinationals that do not have their own marketing presence in all of their global markets—and most do not.

A firm's success in export markets depends largely on the performance of the distributors it uses there. The challenge for a firm, then, is determining how to get the distributor to do a good job. The key is to make the relationship continually rewarding to the distributor as well as to the international marketer. In addition, distributors should be carefully selected, the agreement carefully drawn up, and marketing support offered.

Initial Distributor Selection

In distributor selection, as in marriage, choosing the right partner is the major factor to achieving success. Distributor selection was discussed earlier, but a few other items are noted here. First, carefully specifying what it wants from a distributor will help a firm choose the most suitable candidate. Not all candidates will match a firm's specifications equally well.

Second, a firm should evaluate the distributor's track record. Past performance is the best predictor of future behavior. This can be determined, in part, by talking with other clients of the distributor.

Third, a firm should try to assure that its line will be a reasonably important share of the distributor's business. The more important the firm is to the distributor, the better treatment its products will receive. One example is Avery International's goal to account for at least 10 percent of its distributors' business. Another example mentioned earlier is Canon's deliberate selection of a smaller distributor as part of its entry strategy into India.

Distributor Agreement

The distributor agreement is a legal document that should spell out the responsibilities and interests of each party, protecting both. Carefully preparing the agreement and reviewing it with the distributor should help minimize later misunderstandings. Though it is a legal document, the agreement is too important to be left to lawyers. Managers from both sides should review it and agree on its provisions. Finally, the contract should be a "living" document that can adjust to new circumstances, allowing the relationship to grow beyond the original agreement.

Financial and Pricing Considerations

A distributor wants to make as much money as possible and to work as conveniently as possible. A firm's use of financial and pricing variables will affect a distributor's ability to reach those goals. For example, a firm must determine what *margins* or *commissions* are needed. Should the firm just match the competition, or are higher margins needed to break into the market or to overcome competitive disadvantages? Conversely, a firm may offer lower margins because of competitive strengths in its total offering—a form of nonprice competition. The same questions apply to credit terms. Does a firm need to be generous on credit or merely competitive?

A firm's use of *price quotations* will also have an effect. For example, a distributor would generally prefer a CIF quote to an FOB plant quote. The CIF quote gives a clearer picture of landed cost and also means less work and responsibility for the distributor. (See Chapter 12 for more details on pricing.)

A second aspect of export pricing is *choice of currency* for the quotation. A distributor generally prefers a quote in the currency of its own country rather than a quote in U.S. dollars. This facilitates accounting and eliminates foreign-exchange exposure for the distributor.

One other financial consideration is the *payment terms* specified. For example, the use of open account terms shows trust in the distributor—and saves the several hundred dollars required to open a letter of credit. An exporting firm must balance its need for financial security with its need to satisfy the distributor.

Marketing Support Considerations

A number of other considerations will encourage distributor performance. A well-established brand name and customer franchise will make a distributor's marketing task easier. Names such as Coca-Cola, IBM, Philips, and Sony mean that the product is partially presold. Heavy advertising and promotional support by a producer also make a distributor's job easier. In addition, there may be cooperative advertising with a distributor. Another kind of support is participation in *trade fairs*, preferably in cooperation with distributors in the region.

Exporters usually train a distributor's sales force as a necessary aid to marketing. That would be done at the beginning of the relationship and as new products are added to the line. Distributors should be supplied on a timely basis with *product* and *promotional materials* from the home office. Establishing a regional warehouse (for example, for Europe or Asia) can ensure better product supply and service to the distributor.

Communications

If a distributor is to be an effective member of a firm's international network, communication is important. Telephone contact, preferably through an international toll-free number, can ensure timely responses to problems and opportunities. E-mail and computer links are also powerful, necessary tools. In addition, visits by the home office allow the face-to-face contact that humanizes a long-distance relationship. Corporate travelers could include the export manager; the product engineer; and, occasionally, the CEO.

Establishing a regional headquarters allows closer contact and support of all distributors in a region. A company newsletter can help create a corporate spirit among the "family" of distributors. That newsletter or magazine could include news and pictures about the distributors as well as the company.

Regional meetings of distributors can further encourage a family spirit, in addition to providing economies of scale for training or motivation sessions. A computer link with distributors means online communication that can result in instant information, reduced transaction time, and fewer errors. General Motors realized those benefits when it established a computer system with its European dealers. The dealers benefited from quicker, more accurate service and better availability of product and supplies. Levi Strauss & Co. implemented a similar system with major department store accounts in Europe.

Toro held its first international sales conference in Switzerland. The conference was attended by Toro distributors from 13 Western European countries. Those distributors had previously attended annual meetings in the United States, but thought the meetings were not oriented to their particular needs. The face-to-face contact between Toro personnel and European agents helped the company gain better insight into the marketing problems of each country represented. The language problem was solved by the use of simultaneous translations.

Other Considerations

Some firms use contests to provide excitement and motivation for distributors. Rewards for superior performance offer recognition and encouragement to distant distributors. One popular reward is a trip to the supplier's home country. Such visits are especially popular with Chinese partners. The trips usually include a visit to the home office and plant in addition to other tourist spots. For U.S. firms, it often means a trip to Disneyworld. Indeed, some American firms hold distributor meetings in Orlando, Florida, to take advantage of that area's popularity.

Giving a distributor an exclusive territory means that the efforts in that market will redound to the distributor's benefit. But caution should be used in granting exclusivity since it may be overoptimistic and exceed a distributor's capabilities. Another way to exert leverage over a distributor is to take an equity position in the distributor. Doing so gives a firm a different but useful kind of influence. Establishing a good communications system allows distributors to inform and advise the parent company about local conditions. A firm ought to consider adapting practices as circumstances change and involve intermediaries in major distribution decisions.

Marketing Through a Firm's Own Presence

When a firm has its own staff in a market, it generally is responsible for local distribution. However, it still must deal with the existing distribution infrastructure (that is, the wholesale, retail, and transport system), which will differ in some ways from that of the home market. A marketer must become familiar with a market's distribution environment in order to fashion an appropriate distribution strategy therein.

Wholesaling in Foreign Markets

The wholesaling functions (gathering assortments, breaking bulk, distributing to retailers) are performed in all countries, but with varying degrees of efficiency. Differences in the economy, its level of development, and its infrastructure all cause variation in the wholesaling function.

SIZE

One notable difference in international wholesaling is the size and number of wholesalers from country to country. Generally, industrialized countries have large-scale wholesaling organizations serving a large number of retailers; developing countries are more likely to have fragmented wholesaling—firms with small numbers of employees serving a limited number of retailers. Finland and India illustrate that generalization. Finland has one of the most concentrated wholesaling operations in the world. Four groups account for most of the wholesale trade. The largest, Kesko (the Wholesale Company of Finnish Retail-

ers), with a market share over 20 percent, services over 11,000 retailers. India, on the other hand, has thousands of stockists (like wholesalers) serving hundreds of thousands of small retailers. Because of the large number of small stockists, manufacturers frequently use agents to sell to the stockists, adding an extra step in the channel.

Unfortunately, there are many exceptions to the large-scale generalization. In other words, some industrialized countries have small-scale wholesaling much like some developing countries. Italy and Japan are examples. Because of Italy's fragmented distribution system, Procter & Gamble had to use an intermediary to reach the wholesale level, much like firms in India have to do. Japan is notorious for its fragmented distribution system, with wholesalers selling to other wholesalers. Half of Japan's wholesalers have fewer than four employees. Japan has almost as many wholesalers as the United States does, with only half the population. Wholesaler sales are five times retailer sales in Japan, four times the U.S. ratio.

The size of wholesaling operations around the world exhibits no easily determined pattern. Fragmented wholesaling structures can be found in Europe as well as Asia, Africa, and Latin America. One African country, Kenya, has some of the largest wholesalers in the world; and many former African colonies have large trading houses established during the colonial period. A Unilever subsidiary—the United Africa Company—has large-scale operations in many African countries. Given this unpredictable pattern, a marketer must evaluate each country individually.

The varied wholesaling picture in world markets presents a challenge to international marketers. For efficient wholesalers, it presents an opportunity to internationalize. As of 1995, American wholesalers were earning over 10 percent of their revenues outside the United States. The leading international wholesaler by far, however, is Makro, a Dutch firm. With more know-how and better economies of scale compared to local wholesalers, Makro has large operations in Latin America (Argentina, Brazil, and Colombia) and Eastern Europe (in Poland); and it is looking for new markets.

SERVICE

The most important differentiating factor in wholesaling abroad is in the services offered to a manufacturer. The quality of service usually relates to the size of operations. Smaller operators generally have limited capital and less know-how, as well as small staffs, meaning they are unable to give the same service as large wholesalers.

In some markets, manufacturers are tempted to bypass wholesalers because of their costs or inefficiencies. Although doing so might lead to more efficient distribution, its feasibility needs to be carefully evaluated. Various factors—such as the power of wholesalers or the critical functions they perform—may preclude bypassing them.

In Germany, for example, Kraft Foods found it would be more efficient to ship directly to the retailer. However, the wholesaler's control over the channel was strong enough to force Kraft to pay the wholesaler, even though its services were not being used.

In Japan, international firms have encountered problems that have led some of them to ship directly to larger retailers. This did not work, however, because the wholesalers would not cover the other outlets. Some firms such as Coca-Cola and Nestlé have gone completely to direct sales; but the cost is high. Because many small dealers are financially weak, Japanese wholesalers extend them liberal credit, sometimes as long as ten months. A manufacturer who wants to go direct may then assume the financial burden instead of the wholesaler.

Levi Strauss worked with wholesalers in Japan for ten years. Capitalizing on the craze for jeans, the company decided to set up its own direct sales force. Levi Strauss normally demanded monthly payment, but Japanese department stores paid vendors on a six-month basis. Reconciling those differences was critical to the success of the company's new distribution system.

Clearly, in a majority of world markets, wholesaling is small-scale and fragmented compared with operations in the United States and other industrialized countries. Where that is true, less service is offered by wholesalers. The following problems can arise when a marketer faces a fragmented wholesaling structure.

- Where the number of wholesalers is large, a manufacturer's contact and transaction costs may be high. This raises the consumer price, too, further limiting market penetration.
- Instead of providing credit to the channel, a wholesaler may be a demander of credit, placing a financial burden on the manufacturer.
- Small wholesalers carry a narrow assortment of goods. This may force a manufacturer to omit some products from its line or to seek other wholesalers to carry them.
- Small wholesalers provide limited geographic coverage. A marketer can postpone covering the whole national market or can try to find other wholesalers for the neglected regions.
- Small wholesalers give limited service in other ways, too. They carry less inventory. They provide less-effective selling and promotional efforts. They provide less market feedback to the producer.

In markets with fragmented wholesaling, a firm must resign itself to incomplete market coverage or try to overcome the weakness by a "pull strategy," by company distribution, or by other means. (A pull strategy involves heavy consumer advertising to "pull" products through the channel.) When facing fragmented wholesaling in Italy, Procter

& Gamble took a twofold approach. It emphasized its traditional pull strategy and inserted an extra level in the channel, using a master wholesaler that reached smaller wholesalers that contacted the retailers. In Japan, Procter & Gamble uses no less than 17,000 wholesalers, a great challenge in distribution management.

China is a particularly problematic market. Indeed, in China the large government-owned department stores help to fill in the wholesaling void by engaging in wholesaling themselves. Some Chinese department stores earn up to 70 percent of their revenues by wholesaling. Giordano and Ports International, two retailers with some success in China, do their own wholesaling, supplying their own retail outlets from their own warehouses.

Many of the considerations discussed here also apply to industrial goods, but a producer's need for know-how and service are greater than with consumer goods. This might keep industrial marketers out of certain countries or force them to seek other solutions. For example, Unisys uses United Africa Company in several African nations and piggybacks with Plessey, a British electronics firm, in Southeast Asia.

Retailing in Foreign Markets

International differences in retailing are as extensive and unpredictable as they are in the case of wholesaling. A marketer must study retail patterns in each market. Some of the major differences will be noted below.

GREATER NUMBERS, SMALLER SIZE

The major variable in retailing in world markets is the great difference in numbers and size of retail businesses. The United States and other advanced industrial countries tend to have larger retail outlets and a smaller number per capita than the developing countries do. That means the industrialized nations enjoy greater economies of scale and efficiency. Some industrialized countries do not have an extensive modern retail sector, however. Among them are Japan, Italy, Belgium, and France. Japan has more retailers than the United States, with only half the population. In Germany, 75 percent of retailing is done by large units; whereas in Italy, over 75 percent is done by small independents. Italy has four times as many retailers as Germany.

A major reason for the lack of growth in efficient large-scale retailing in Belgium, Japan, France, and Italy is the countries' legislation. Though France was one of the creators of the hypermarket (a giant supermarket), in 1973, France passed the Loi Royer, a law regulating the establishment or expansion of retail stores. The effect of the law (and of similar laws in Belgium and Italy) is to give existing retailers a veto over the establishment of any new large-scale retailers. Naturally, existing retailers don't want to see a big, new competitor come in; so they don't give out many licenses. Japan has a similar law, Daiten Ho. France illustrates the restrictive effect of such laws. Between 1985 and 1995, France built 12,000 stores on 16 million square feet; the United States built 124,000 stores on 430 million square feet.

Japan's law states that no one can open a store larger than 5,382 square feet without permission from the community's store owners. Formerly, it took eight to ten years for a store to receive permission. Apart from the law, there can be other problems. When the Lawson chain built a store in Shizuoka, Japanese shopkeepers beat up a construction worker. Later they stormed the store at night, screaming at employees and intimidating customers. Late-night calls harassed the owners' families. Finally, someone dumped excrement outside the store. Under pressure from large Japanese retail groups and U.S. trade negotiators, the government set a one-year deadline for new store approvals. Changes are occurring more quickly now.

Some international differences in retailer size are reported in Table 8-4. One would expect an increase in retailer size with economic development; but as the table indicates, some developed countries have as much small-scale retailing as less developed countries. For example, in some European countries, retailing is as fragmented as in China or Mexico. Japanese retailing is as fragmented as that in Brazil and more so than in Venezuela. Caution is necessary when using bare statistics from the table, however, because France and Japan also have modern retail developments that can't be identified in such a simple listing. For example, Seven-Eleven Japan operates more than 10,000 retail outlets, making it the largest convenience store outlet in Japan. Giant American consumer goods makers Kimberly-Clark and Procter & Gamble recognize that if they are to succeed in Europe, they need to work more closely with the super retailers Lidl and Aldi (Germany) and the Ed discount unit of Carrefour in France.

Visiting just the capitals or largest cities of developing nations does not give a true picture of the retailing structure of a country. The cities may have department stores and supermarkets like those a tourist sees at home. Such evidence in the small, modernized sector of the economy, however, is not typical of the nation as a whole. Rather, the infrastructure and amenities present in the larger cities represent one side of the "dual economy" phenomenon. That is, the same country has two different economies, one that includes the majority of the population in the villages and rural areas and the other that includes the large cities where some industrialization and commercial development has taken place.

RETAILING SERVICES

Another variable in world markets involves the services provided by the retailer to the manufacturer. A producer might want the following services from retailers: stocking, displaying, and selling the product; promoting the product (by word of mouth, by display, or by advertising); extending credit to customers; servicing the product; and gathering market information.

Carrying Inventory

Stocking products is a basic function of retailers in every country. The services offered, however, are not identical. Small retailers carry limited inventories and frequently may be out of stock of certain items. That is lost business for the manufacturer. Limited inventory means a limited line of products. New entrants to the market can have difficulty getting their products accepted by retailers.

Because they are financially weak, small retailers may carry certain products only if they do not have to invest in them; that is, the retailer carries the inventory physically, but the wholesaler or manufacturer carries it financially. That is a problem even in Japan, where small dealers may receive credit up to ten months. Consignment sales are one possible answer to this retailer inventory problem. An American firm selling prepared foods partially dealt with the problem by changing from 48-can cases supplied in the United States to 24-can and 12-can cases distributed in other markets.

Product Display

When the package plays a role in persuading consumers, display is important. The kind of display a product gets in a retail outlet depends on the physical facilities (space, shelves, and lighting). The producer will find great international variations in these facilities. At one extreme, an African duka may have less than 200 square feet of store

Table 8-4. Size of Retailers in Selected Countries

Country	Average Employment per Retailer
Colombia	1.6
Peru	1.9
Mexico	2.2
Taiwan	2.8
Netherlands	3.3
Japan	4.4
France	4.5
Australia	4.9
South Africa	6.6
Malaysia	7.7
Indonesia	11.2
United States	13.3
Germany	14.5

Source: *International Marketing Data and Statistics 1998*, 22nd edition (London: Euromonitor Plc, 1998); *European Marketing Data and Statistics 1998*, 33rd edition (London: Euromonitor Plc, 1998).

space, no electric lighting, one door and one window, a few shelves, and one or two tables. A seller in an open market or a bazaar would have equally limited facilities. Retail facilities range from those examples all the way up to a 250,000-square-foot hypermarket, a large department store found in the United States and Europe.

In Brazil, General Foods had to deal with mom-and-pop stores, usually having less than 200 square feet of space and almost no room for displays. A customer asks for an item, and the retailer retrieves it from under the counter. Local General Foods managers hoped to develop a display counter that could be suspended from the ceiling with wires. They also investigated self-dispensing units that could be nailed to the wall. A customer would take a piece of candy or gum, and gravity would replace it.

Merchandising skills correlate somewhat with the level of economic development, although many retailers in poorer countries have a flair for product display. Few firms in the United States rely on retailers for the display of their product, except for shelf space. Representatives of manufacturers arrange the displays themselves. However, that is not possible in many markets because of the small size and dispersion of retail businesses and because the firm may have a narrower line in a market, offering too small a base over which to spread its costs. Cooperation is also affected by a retailer's overall relationship with the producer, as in the case of Kimberly-Clark. It was distributing Kotex in France through the *pharmacie*, which differs from a U.S. drugstore in that it is limited to dispensing medicines and related items. The company wanted to add Kotex to supermarket outlets, as in the United States. The supermarkets were willing to handle the product, but the *pharmaciens* were angry about the competition. As a result, the *pharmaciens* put all Kimberly-Clark products under the counter and refused to display them.

Promotion of a Product

Product display is frequently all that a manufacturer can expect. Occasionally, however, retailers might do some personal selling or advertising. That is more likely when retailers have a favorable attitude toward a product and it is an important part of their sales. Use of point-of-purchase materials is another form of retailer promotion, but the small size of retail outlets makes most of those displays impractical. Product advertising by retailers is a form of promotion that also tends to be limited in many markets because of the small resources of retailers. Those limitations force a manufacturer to rely on its own advertising.

Other Retailing Services

Credit extension, product service, and market information are other services a manufacturer might want from retailers. Given the limited resources available to retailers in most countries, a manufacturer is more likely to be involved in extending credit than in finding retailers who can help. When product service is necessary, the ability of retailers to perform that service depends on their resources and technical skills. Usually, the smaller the retailers, the less able they are to provide the service. Thus, the burden of assuring product service falls on the producer. When a manufacturer is unable to assure service, it may have to forgo entering some markets.

In Turkey, at one time, about 60 percent of all farm tractors were estimated to be incapacitated. International Harvester could find only about 50 qualified mechanics in its own Turkish organization and in the government equipment centers. To maintain its franchise with consumers and the government, International Harvester undertook an extensive training program.

Acquiring market feedback for a manufacturer is not something retailers consider to be their job. Only to the extent that a manufacturer has contacts with retailers can it get market information from them. In large markets, a producer often has contact with retailers or retail organizations. Furthermore, retail audit services are available in some large markets. In small markets and in rural areas, little retailer contact is practical.

Another problem may arise when a producer wants cooperation from retailers to conduct marketing or advertising testing. Retailers may be reluctant to cooperate because they do not understand how the information can benefit them or because they are suspicious of outsiders looking at their business. Retailers in many countries are secretive about their operations and afraid of tax investigators. That secretiveness affects their relationships with producers. For example, one cosmetics firm wanted to do "before and after" retail product audits to test an advertising campaign in a Latin American country. Only after great difficulty did the firm finally secure the participation of enough retailers to conduct the test.

Distribution Trends in World Markets

Because most countries are experiencing economic and social change, to observe the wholesale or retail structure at just one point in time is not sufficient. Channel decisions must be based on what the structures will be like tomorrow as well as what they are like today. Statistics on distribution are limited for most less developed nations, but one can still get an idea of distribution trends there. Because the nature of wholesaling and retailing is related to economic development, a marketer can follow economic growth indicators as a rough guide to predicting distribution changes.

For the international marketer, a review of the development of wholesaling and retailing in the United States is instructive. Developments elsewhere often parallel those in the United States in earlier periods. That is because those nations are experiencing economic and social changes similar to those that occurred in the United States. Another reason is that U.S. retailers have carried their techniques abroad. For example, Jewel Companies, the Chicago-based retailer, entered a joint venture with Aurrera, a Mexican retailer. At that time, Aurrera was tenth in Mexican retailing. By adopting many of Jewel's techniques, Aurrera rose to the number one position in Mexico.

Another aid to the marketer is the comparative study approach. Studies of markets in which a firm is already operating should provide insight into markets with similar characteristics. For example, sales of cell phones in Japan that allow users to make purchases from vending machines might be extrapolated to predict sales in the United States or the United Kingdom.

There are five major distribution trends in world markets: (1) the growth of large-scale retailing, (2) the continuing internationalization of retailing, (3) the growth of direct marketing, (4) the spread of discounting, and (5) electronic distribution. Each of those trends will be discussed next.

LARGER SCALE, GREATER RETAILER POWER

In affluent nations, distribution developments are similar to the U.S. pattern of recent decades. Of course, not all retail developments originate in the United States. The hypermarket, for example, was a French invention. The trend in industrialized countries is toward larger units and more self-service. Globally, the number of retail outlets is dwindling, but the average size is increasing. Sweden, for example, had 30,000 food stores in 1955 but 5,000 in 1990. The trends, although they proceed at different rates, are the same. The causes of the changes are (1) rising affluence, (2) increased car ownership, (3) more households with refrigerators, and (4) more dual-income families.

Even Japan and Italy are joining the bandwagon. Italy was experiencing a yearly 5 percent drop in the numbers. And Japan is seeing a steady drop in the number of mom-and-pop stores. Many 7-Eleven franchisees in Japan were former mom-and-pop store owners. Recently, Metro AG, a German retailer, opened a hypermarket in Moscow.[7]

Some developing nations, especially the newly industrializing countries, are seeing a growth in large-scale retailing. In Korea, the first supermarket appeared in 1971. The number increased to over 1,500 in one decade. In Hong Kong, the number of supermarkets has increased more than sixfold, while the number of traditional grocery stores declined by more than one-third. The forces behind those developments are the same as those that led to modern retailing in the United States and Europe: rising incomes, more automobiles, and more working wives. Thus, the life cycle of retailing works its way around the world.

Those trends mean stronger retailing and greater countervailing power vis-à-vis the manufacturer. The power of channel members is further reinforced by the growth of large-scale cooperative wholesaling, often on an international basis. For example, Spar International is a voluntary chain of several hundred wholesalers and about 40,000 retailers in 12 Western European countries. As a result of larger operations and greater power, European retailers are demanding more private (distributor) brands. Those groups also bargain strongly on prices. Private brands already have a greater share in Europe than in the United States, and the EU has strengthened distributors in Europe.

INTERNATIONALIZATION OF RETAILING

Continuing integration of the world economy is internationalizing not only the advertising, banking, and manufacturing industries, but also retailing. The typical life cycle of today's large retailers began with a store in one city, which slowly grew into a national operation and today is going international. Retailers in the United States, Europe, and Japan are expanding their international ties with respect to procurement and marketing. Macy's of New York has buying offices in more than 30 countries.

Leading examples of retailing internationalists are U.S. franchisers, about 450 of them. McDonald's alone has more than 21,000 outlets in 104 countries. McDonald's has 8 percent of the restaurant business in France. The Japanese-owned Southland has over 13,000 7-Eleven outlets around the world. H&R Block and Pizza Hut each have over 2,000 outlets abroad. Amway, Avon, and Tupperware retail abroad. Goodyear, IBM, and Tandy-Radio Shack are U.S. producers that are also retailers abroad. Kmart and Sears are more traditional retailers operating internationally. Hard Rock Café is a well-known American establishment abroad.

Internationalism is also pushing newer U.S. retailers abroad early in their life cycle. Wal-Mart has expanded rapidly into the Americas and Asia. (See "Global Marketing: Wal-Mart Marches On.") Blockbuster Video has expanded even faster, with 2,000 outlets abroad. Toys "R" Us is in Japan and Europe. Starbucks has stores in over 30 countries outside the United States (including ten Asian markets) and over 2,500 stores (company-owned establishments as well as license and joint venture arrangements), in addition to its nearly 7,000 American outlets. Gap is in six countries. American retailers make up 40 of the top global 100 firms in the industry. India, which promises market huge potential, has long been closed to foreign retailers. To persuade the Indian government to relax some of its restrictions, retailers are using the argument that much of what they sell worldwide is made in India; therefore, the retailers are critical to the economic development of the nation.[8] Grocery stores account for a substantial portion of retailing dollars. They are breaking into new retailing ventures in other formerly closed markets such as Finland. In addition, Wal-Mart is expanding its traditional hard goods lines and now includes grocery items on its shelves in China.[9,10]

U.S. retailers are not the only internationalists. Europeans own over 10 percent of the U.S. grocery business and have important department and specialty store holdings. IKEA, the Swedish furniture retailer, and boutique retailers such as Benetton and Laura Ashley are increasingly visible in the United States. Carrefour, in Europe and the United States, is the retailing leader in Latin America. Printemps has grown from Paris to Japan, Korea, Saudi Arabia, Singapore, the United States, and Turkey. Ahold, a Dutch retailer, is in the Americas, Asia, and Europe.

The Japanese are relative newcomers to the internationalization of retailing, but they are becoming deeply involved. Jusco has supermarkets in Hong Kong, Thailand, and Malaysia. Given the geographic proximity, Southeast Asia seems to be the natural zone of influence for Japanese retailers. Indeed, while Japanese retailers account for one-half of all retail sales in Hong Kong, they have not limited themselves to that area. Wacoal, the lingerie firm, has boutiques in the United States. Major Japanese retailing groups such as Daiei, Seibu, and Jusco have ties with U.S. retailers such as Kmart, Kroger, Safeway, and Sears. Yaohan even has a Yaohan Plaza in London.

DIRECT MARKETING

In its various forms, direct marketing is a big international growth area. Mail order is growing in Europe, Japan, and developing economies such as Mexico. European mail-order sales have long surpassed those in the United States, and the large French and German mail-order firms have gone international. Each year American-based firms such as L.L. Bean, Land's End, and Eddie Bauer sell several billion dollars worth of merchandise in Japan. Along with their catalogs, they use the Internet, toll-free 24-hour international phone numbers, and fax lines.

Personal selling direct to consumers continues to be important internationally. Amway, Avon, and Tupperware are famous U.S. examples abroad; but Sara Lee is also doing it in Indonesia. With its direct sales force, Amway is the second largest foreign firm in Japan. In Brazil, Avon has 470,000 sales reps, compared to the Brazilian army's 200,000 members. Electrolux, the Swedish appliance firm, has direct sales forces in ten Asian countries, including Japan and India. Because of the international success of direct marketers, other firms have begun to piggyback with them. For example, Mattel used Avon to introduce Barbie in China; in Latin America, Avon ladies sell Duracell batteries; Rubbermaid sells through Amway in Japan; and Waterford Crystal uses Amway in the United States.

Telemarketing is another growth area in direct marketing. Harrods of London has an international 800 number

Wal-Mart Marches On

After becoming No. 1 in American retailing, Wal-Mart looked abroad for further expansion. For several years, it has also been No. 1 in global retailing, with revenues of over $100 billion. With some 2,800 stores in the United States, Wal-Mart now has over 500 stores in nine countries around the world—in Asia, Europe, and Latin America.

1991: Wal-Mart goes international via a joint venture to open a Sam's Club retail outlet in Mexico City. In 1997, Wal-Mart acquired its Mexican partner Cifra.

1992: Wal-Mart opened five stores in Puerto Rico to gain an understanding of operations outside the United States.

1994: Wal-Mart acquired 122 Woolco stores in Canada to gain a large initial market position there. In Thailand, in a joint venture with the Charoen Pokphand Group (CP), the overseas Chinese conglomerate in Thailand, Wal-Mart began operations there. Again with CP, this time in Hong Kong, Wal-Mart opened a number of Value Club stores in large apartment complexes that characterize that city. The stores are small versions of Sam's Clubs to fit the Hong Kong environment.

1995: In Brazil, Wal-Mart joined with the nation's largest discount retailer to open its first stores. In Argentina,

continued

for U.S. customers, for example; and IBM uses telemarketing in Europe. However, telemarketing has been attacked by some groups in the Netherlands and Britain for invasion of privacy and high-pressure tactics. Specialized organizations have cropped up to help firms with direct marketing. Usually, they are ad agencies, such as McCann Erickson and Ogilvy & Mather.

DISCOUNTING

Among other distribution trends is the increasing popularity of discount merchandising. "Discounters" in this case may mean anything from small shops to giant warehouse clubs. Several factors have contributed to the popularity of discounting, including the demise of resale price maintenance. In Japan, discount chain stores have replaced *another large Mercosur market, Wal-Mart began with its own operations.*

1996: In Indonesia, Wal-Mart made a modest beginning with just two stores. Wal-Mart made another modest start in China's giant market, with just two stores.

1997: Wal-Mart's first step into Europe was to acquire 21 stores in Germany.

1998: Expanding its Asian presence in South Korea, Wal-Mart buys a majority interest in four stores, in addition to six development sites. Wal-Mart also acquired nearly 100 outlets in Germany.

1999: Wal-Mart acquired 229 stores through its ASDA Group acquisition in the United Kingdom.

2002: Wal-Mart purchased a minority interest in a leading Japanese retailer (The Seiyu). In Puerto Rico, it acquired Supermercados Amigo, a chain with 32 stores. On Black Friday, the day after Thanksgiving, Wal-Mart's sales exceeded $1.4 billion—a one-day record.

2005: Wal-Mart's rumored acquisition target, France's Carrefour, the world's second largest retailer, is generating serious antitrust concerns among EU officials.

Wal-Mart's march abroad has not been an unqualified success. It separated from its partnership with CP, causing some losses. It faces strong competition in several markets; for example, the UK's Tesco and the Netherland's Makro. It also finds that each market has unique characteristics requiring adaptations from its U.S. model. Still, sales are growing rapidly.

Source: http://www.walmartstores.com; accessed September 2, 2005.

department stores as the country's largest retailers. Their share of the household products market was expected to reach 75 percent, eliminating more mom-and-pop stores. In Europe, discounters are also increasing their market share at the expense of department stores. For example, Britain's supermarket giants Sainsbury's and Tesco have seen their profit margins decline because of discounters.

As more and larger discount stores, mail-order operations, and retailer or wholesaler organizations are formed, pressure will be exerted on manufacturers' pricing and distribution practices. Firms that have become acquainted with those organizations in the United States should have an advantage since the same developments occur in other countries.

ELECTRONIC DISTRIBUTION

While ordering products online has expanded the distribution networks of even the smallest firms, some products lend themselves to electronic distribution. Anything that can be digitized (for example, music and videos) can be distributed to distant locations almost instantaneously—software, blueprints for a new kitchen or home, reports, data, and a myriad of other products. Marketers' goals include getting products to customers where and when they are wanted. Electronic distribution allows marketers to satisfy those two aspects of marketing in a manner not possible before. Of course, distribution via the Internet lowers distribution costs to nearly zero, which competitive firms use to lower prices to consumers.

Marketing Through Foreign Distribution Channels

Having considered some of the principal constraints on distribution in foreign markets, the focus turns now to strategic decisions facing the international marketer:

- Should a firm extend its domestic distribution approach to foreign markets or adapt its distribution strategy to each national market?
- Should a firm use direct or indirect channels in foreign markets?
- Should a firm use selective or widespread distribution?
- How can a firm manage the channel?
- How can a firm keep its distribution strategy up-to-date?

International or National Patterns

The important question is not whether a firm should have uniform distribution patterns in foreign markets, but which channels in each market are most profitable. A few factors may favor a standardized approach, particularly the possibility of economies of scale. Although economies of scale are not as easily attainable in distribution as they are in production, there may be some. For example, an international marketing manager may work more efficiently when tasks are similar in different markets. Particularly with the continuing integration of Europe, the more similar the conditions, the more easily experience in one country can be transferred to another country.

It can be argued that channels used in one market should be tried in another because they have been tested. Although success in one market does suggest trying the same thing elsewhere, that success is not a sufficient reason for using the same strategy in every market. Market analysis should be done before deciding on local channels.

Numerous pressures deter a firm from standardized distribution. One is the distribution structure in a country; that is, the nature of wholesale and retail operations. Because distribution structure varies from country to country, a firm's alternatives also vary. Storage and transportation possibilities in addition to the market's dispersion also help to determine channel alternatives. For example, Pepsi-Cola uses similar channels all over the world—that is, local bottler to truck driver/sales representative to retailer. However, in sparse areas, the truck driver/sales representative is too expensive, forcing the company to find another method.

Another channel determinant is the market. Consumer income and buying habits are important considerations in deciding on distribution, as is the strength and behavior of competitors. On the one hand, competitors may force a firm to use the same channel they are using because they have educated the market to that channel. On the other hand, competitors may effectively preempt that channel and force a newcomer to find some other way to the market.

The initial application of Allstate Insurance in Japan was rejected. Its entry "would disrupt existing firms." In a different approach, Allstate joined with Seibu, the Japanese retailer. That alliance gave Allstate a powerful sales channel. It also fulfilled a requirement that it "provide something new to customers"—the opportunity to buy insurance over the counter.

Finally, differences in a manufacturer's situation might suggest channel differences from market to market. An important determinant is a firm's level of involvement in a market. Where a firm supplies a market through an importer-distributor, the company has less freedom than it does in cases where it has a local plant. Similarly, working through a licensee or joint venture is more restrictive of channel selection than a wholly owned operation. Even where the level of involvement is the same in two markets, a firm's product line and sales volume may differ. The smaller the line and volume of sales, the less direct the channels a firm can afford to use.

A firm generally tries to use the same channels from market to market. Although adaptations are frequently necessary, a firm's channels will be similar around the world, especially with industrial goods. Even with consumer goods, there can be some carryover from country to country.

Direct sales has been successful for some U.S. companies entering foreign markets. When Tupperware entered Japan, the only channel it knew was parties in the home, with a hostess. It used that direct channel in Japan and found it successful. Avon is another direct seller at home and abroad. In Taiwan, for example, 11,000 Avon ladies sell to customers at home. And Amway has a force of 1.2 million direct sellers in Japan.

Another example is Shaklee Pharmaceuticals. Because vitamin pills are not "drugs" in Japan, they can be sold door-to-door. Shaklee uses that channel in the United States and entered Japan the same way. It was the only firm in that channel and became No. 1 in vitamin sales. Japanese firms hesitated to follow suit for fear of offending the traditional channels in which they sold prescription drugs.

Direct versus Indirect Channels

Because direct channels are usually more effective than indirect channels, firms like to be as direct as they can. The major determinant is the volume of sales attainable. Where volume is large, a firm can afford to go direct. When a U.S. firm considers foreign markets, it usually finds less possibility of going direct than in the United States. Many elements, such as lower incomes, a firm's narrower product line, and fewer large-scale buying organizations, combine to make most other markets smaller.

When foreign markets are small, many firms accept indirect distribution as the only feasible alternative. In India, for example, Unilever and other consumer goods companies sell through agents, who reach the stockists, who reach the retailers. Procter & Gamble in Italy used a similar three-stage channel. As you have seen, channels in Japan may be even more indirect than those in India and Italy. In such cases, fragmented wholesaling and retailing force a firm to go less direct than it would like. Those conditions characterize most world markets.

Some firms, however, insist on trying for more direct distribution as the best way to get a strong market position. That is especially true of consumer durables and industrial goods producers. Goodyear established its own franchised dealers in Europe, just like its dealers in the United States.

IBM has always gone direct to customers with its large equipment. When the company began selling smaller equipment (copiers and computers) to smaller customers, it found its direct sales force too expensive. IBM experimented with its own retail outlets, first in Europe and Argentina. When those proved successful, IBM began opening its own retail outlets in the United States.

In Japan, the Erina Co. defied conventional wisdom by going direct to consumers with its pantyhose. It developed a sales force of about 200,000 agents (99 percent are homemakers). Because that was more efficient than traditional methods in Japan, Erina's price was about half that of pantyhose sold in other channels; and Erina quickly got one-sixth of the market. The company then began looking for other products.

As noted above, the growth of the Internet, multimedia, and interactive TV are giving a new meaning to "direct marketing." Both manufacturers and retailers will have to follow and adapt to those developments.

Selective versus Intensive Distribution

Intensive distribution refers to the policy of selling through any retailer that wants to handle the product. **Selective distribution** means choosing a limited number of resellers in a market area. A firm usually wants to offer its product in as wide a market as possible. However, the company may need to select a limited number of distributors to make it worthwhile to carry inventory and provide service and promotion. For shopping or specialty goods, retailers may demand selective distribution, which protects their market by limiting competition. For industrial goods or consumer durables, selective distribution may be the only way to induce intermediaries to cooperate in providing service.

Marketing abroad, manufacturers usually give exclusive franchises to importers or wholesalers at the national level. However, selectivity at the retail level depends on local market conditions. With a multiplicity of small retailers, a firm might have difficulty locating retailers that can handle its product effectively. Low consumer mobility also limits the value of selective distribution.

In the 1980s, Benetton expanded rapidly in the United States, opening some 700 outlets. Because many of the outlets were in overlapping territories, stores began to cannibalize one another. As a result of dealer dissatisfaction, the number of Benetton outlets dropped to about 300. Benetton was forced to become more exclusive in its distribution. Of course, competition from Gap and Express took some of Benetton's clientele.

General Motors in Belgium tried to hinder the import of its cars by anyone other than the company-owned distributor in Belgium. However, the European Commission ruled that the General Motors distributor charged excessive prices for inspections and conformity certificates for cars bought outside the General Motors channel. The commission levied a fine for "abuse of a dominant position." Thus, General Motors was effectively prevented from having an exclusive distributorship in Belgium.

As the General Motors example suggests, governments are beginning to have greater influence on distribution decisions. Outboard Marine in Norway tried to implement a selective distribution system; but the Norwegian courts ruled against the company, saying that the practice would reduce competition in outboard engines. The European Bureau of Consumer Unions asked the European Commission to investigate the selective distribution practices of Grundig, Telefunken, and Saba, saying that such distribution seriously harmed the interests of consumers. The Commission agreed to examine whether their practices raised prices "artificially."

In countries with uneven income distribution, a firm might use selective distribution if it sells only to a group above a certain income level. For consumer durables or industrial products, the distribution in smaller markets might be more selective because of the thinness of the market and its relative concentration. The channel follows the market.

Working with the Channel

When a firm sells directly to a retailer or to consumers, the costs of direct distribution bring the benefits of control as well as the flexibility to respond to market conditions and better market feedback. When a firm cannot afford to go direct, it must deal with independent intermediaries. The problem then becomes one of getting cooperation rather than maintaining control. Although that problem is not peculiar to foreign markets, a firm's situation and market conditions will vary from country to country, making channel management a somewhat different task in each market. (See "Global Marketing: Innovators Abroad: Avon, McDonald's, and Oskar Mobile.")

A firm's success in a market often depends on how well independent intermediaries do their job. Thus, helping them to do their job becomes a major responsibility of the marketer. Coca-Cola ran into trouble in Japan, a market accounting for 10 percent of company sales. Its response was to put in a new manager whose *forte* was dealing with franchised bottlers. He practiced this in Japan by visiting, listening to their problems, improving inventory service, and introducing better training programs.

Manufacturers have developed many techniques for encouraging cooperation from members of a channel. Those techniques include offering margins, exclusive territories, a valuable franchise, advertising support and cooperative advertising, financing, a sales force or service training, a business advisory service, market research assistance, and missionary selling. All of those are known to students of marketing. Only their international application will be discussed here.

Levi Strauss provides a European example. When the company found a weakness in the retail link of its channel in Europe, it decided to use more selective distribution and give more support to retailers that were willing to emphasize Levi products. That extra support included special discounts, local advertising help, merchandising assistance, and training of retailers' sales staff. Levi Strauss also began computer links with retailers, which led to just-in-time ordering, lower inventory costs, and faster restocking of shelves.

A firm needs to be competitive on *margins* in each of its markets. To break into a market, a firm is sometimes tempted to beat competitors' margins, a form of price cutting and the easiest form of competition to imitate. Usually, a weak firm that has no other advantages will try this approach; but once the firm has made its entry, it may have difficulty adjusting its margins.

An international firm may or may not have a valuable *franchise* to offer its channel members. When a firm enters a new market, its brand is usually unknown. Intermediaries may be reluctant to carry the product unless the firm gives strong advertising support. Some large international companies (for example, Philips, Unilever, IBM, and Sony) are in a different position. Because of their size and reputation, they are usually considered desirable suppliers in any market they enter.

Strong *advertising support* makes intermediaries more cooperative. International firms have an advantage over national firms in that respect. First, international firms have the financial resources to advertise extensively; second, they have more expertise in advertising than most of their national competitors. A German competitor of Procter & Gamble noted that the company was able to enter any European country and "buy" a 15 percent market share just on the strength of its advertising. The resources and experience of an international company also help in cooperative advertising with channel members. The same financial resources make an international company more competitive in extending credit to the channel.

Rosenthal, the German porcelain maker, created a subsidiary called Table Top Retail. Its purpose is to support Rosenthal dealers by preventing erosion of market coverage. The company was losing some of its best dealers due to a variety of forces, including retirement. The Table Top fund will keep these specialty stores in operation until new management can be found. Faced with similar problems, Grundig, the electronics firm, formed its own franchising system to maintain and support its dealer network. Grundig's moves are especially important in view of the increased competition in the Single Market.

The size and experience of multinational companies help them obtain cooperation in other ways; for example, *training* sales or service personnel, *business advisory service*, and *market research* assistance. A firm with operations in several countries can draw on its experience when helping another market. It enjoys economies of scale in training personnel or in operating a centralized training center for several countries. Most national firms cannot match those advantages. Furthermore, an international firm can provide additional prestige through regional meetings with representatives from several countries.

An auto firm found a new way to train its far-flung network of dealers. It leased a plane and outfitted it as a classroom with cutaway training units of rear axles, engines, transmissions, etc., in addition to movies, slides, and other visual aids. The first trip was an 18-stop swing

GLOBAL MARKETING

Innovators Abroad: Avon, McDonald's, and Oskar Mobile

Avon, with sales of $7.7 billion in 2004 and as one of the world's top ten cosmetic firms and the world's largest direct marketer, is now able to hire sales representatives to go door-to-door in China. Until the fall of 2005, Avon, like other firms that depend on direct sales in other markets, had to rely on owner-operated kiosks to market its products in China.

In early September 2005, the Chinese government published new laws on direct sales and pyramid sales (where representatives earn commissions on sales made by others they hire and train). Rulings on those types of sales had been a condition of acceptance into the WTO. China now permits direct marketing, but still bans pyramid sales arrangements. The difficulty Avon faces is an army of discontented kiosk owners who must now compete for the same Avon customers to be supplied by the door-to-door sales force.

Reading through Avon's publications, a reader learns that the company's focus is on its sales force as much as its products. Avon provides a good example of how marketing shapes culture. Avon is hiring and training young women about selling and keeping track of costs and profits. In doing so, in China, Turkey, and Mexico (where the traditional role of women is marriage and child rearing), Avon is shaping entrepreneurs and creating new perceptions of women in the workforce.

MCDONALD'S WI-FI

Burgers and fries are no longer enough. McDonald's in other nations may be adding new menu items; but in Switzerland, all of the outlets also provide wireless connections. In an attempt to lure trade from competitors, McDonald's is providing additional nonfood services. The reason for selecting Switzerland as a wireless frontier is the country's reputation as a popular destination for business travelers, who want access to the wireless communication infrastructure. The hope is that they will also want a hamburger, fries, and a soft drink to go with their wireless access. Future designs of the traditional McDonald's outlets may include features other than dining tables, chairs, and cooking stations if this experiment is a success.

OSKAR SPEAKING

Oskar, an upstart Czech mobile telephone company that began operations in 2000, provided 98.4 percent market coverage by December 2004. Shortly before the company was purchased by Vodafone in 2005, Oskar began experimenting with new retail outlet designs that included music, bright colors, and individual sales stations where customer and salesperson would stand and discuss alternative phone styles and calling plans. These cylindrical stations, approximately 4 feet tall and 2 feet in diameter, function as a combination computer stand and sales cabinet. A touch screen linked to a computer allows users to view and compare models and plans, access technical information, and download ring tones and other software. Salespeople access the small, locked, built-in cabinet, where fully charged, full-featured phone models are kept for demonstration purposes—to make calls, listen to ring tones, test built-in cameras, feel the weight, and test other attributes. This atmosphere is much different from stores that display phones with batteries and sim cards removed (lest someone steal them), locked to a heavy display unit on a short cable. It's an experience, not a store—as much for existing customers as new ones.

Oskar also launched "Oskarena" for its customers and "OskarZone" for its suppliers. Essentially, they are market spaces (not places) on the Web that offer answers to common questions and chat rooms to discuss new features and uses and to air problems. These are additional marks of innovative marketing strategies designed to develop stronger company relationships with and among customers and suppliers. Largely because of its innovative ideas, Oskar won the "Most Dynamic Company in 2004" and "100 Most Significant Companies in the Czech Republic" awards.

Sources: Avon: Company Overview (http://www.avoncompany.com/ investor/companyoverview/index.html); Avon Annual Report, 2004. McDonald's: "Boingo Wireless Partners with Monzoon Networks to Expand Roaming System in Switzerland," PR Newswire U.S., January 31, 2005. Oskar: http://www.oskarmobil.cz/en and http://www. oskarmobil.cz/en/business/about_oskar/facts.php. Personal visit, Prague, March 10, 2005. See also https://www.oskarzona.cz for additional information on OskarZone.

through Central and Latin America, with four days at each stop. The six-person training team gave sessions (in Spanish) on technical and product training, as well as sales and management methods. The dealers and their sales and service personnel were included in the training.

A unique way an international firm can increase intermediaries' cooperation is by increasing its commitment to the local market. When a firm changes from imports to local production, it increases its involvement in the market and reassures local dealers. The firm's reliability and image are enhanced in the dealers' eyes, and it can give better delivery and service. Transportation, customs, inventory, and communication problems all decrease once an international firm establishes local production.

Keeping Channels Up to Date

The unique challenge of management is to keep on top of change. In international marketing, the problem is compounded when changes in the environment and the firm are occurring at different rates in different markets. Even if a firm had an appropriate strategy when it entered each market, that strategy is unlikely to remain the most desirable over time.

The variables affecting channels are numerous. In any market, the situation of a firm evolves, as was stated earlier in the discussion of product life cycle. Generally, the volume of sales increases, the product line expands, and the level of involvement changes from importer-distributor to marketing subsidiary or from licensee to joint venture. Developments in wholesaling and retailing are taking place. Technological changes in distribution as well as evolution of purchasing behavior exert pressure on a firm's channels. Laws affecting distribution are being changed.

GROWTH OF A FIRM IN A MARKET

The international firm is expanding in most of its markets. As it becomes established in a market, its sales volume should increase, which will lead to expansion of its product line. At some level of sales, the firm will find it profitable to increase its involvement in the market. Where that growth occurs, the firm is able to go more direct. In fact, that is the strategy of many international companies.

Union Carbide had been selling its consumer products in the fragmented Philippines market through one national distributor, an indirect channel. When the company expanded its involvement by building a plant in the Philippines, it wanted a more vigorous sales effort. To get that, it established 4,000 Class A dealers who, while functioning as retailers, served primarily as wholesalers to Class B and C dealers. Then, Union Carbide appointed 100 of its own salespeople to work with the Class A dealers. That system resulted in more aggressive marketing with more control.

ENVIRONMENTAL CHANGE: LARGE-SCALE RETAILING

Changes in the environment have a complex impact on a firm's marketing. The trends toward retail concentration and the buying of co-ops in Europe, for example, have a twofold impact. The concentration of the market means not only a greater possibility of direct distribution, but also increased demand for private brands. The growth of mail order has the same result. The bargaining power of those large groups affects the pricing policy of the manufacturer. Even large Japanese retailers such as Daiei and Takashimaya buy direct from foreign producers.

The strategic response of a firm to large-scale retailing may be direct channels or dual channels; that is, selling directly to large retail groups and indirectly to small retailers. Use of private brands may become necessary. In other cases, private branding may be the way to open up new markets. For example, some U.S. firms had been unable to enter the German market because German wholesalers were unwilling to carry their products. The wholesalers' associations in Germany were often strong enough to prevent the manufacturer from bypassing them. German manufacturers agreed to this restriction on the condition that the wholesalers, in turn, act as a sort of buffer against foreign firms coming in. The rise of large retail groups buying directly opens the way for non-German firms to break into the market, although perhaps with private branding. As another example, Kodak expanded its market share in Japan by private branding for a large Japanese retailer.

Large-scale retailing organizations have caused manufacturers to make other adaptations as well. The situation in the United Kingdom, which is a leader in European distribution trends, is one example. Manufacturers have increased their promotional activities to the large retailers, using missionary selling; but at the same time, they have reduced their efforts with smaller retailers. Even as manufacturers sell more directly to large retailers, they leave small, independent retailers to be serviced by wholesalers, which is, in effect, a dual-channel strategy. The strategy is used not only by food companies such as Heinz, but also by consumer durables firms such as Philips. For example, when Heinz found that fewer than 300 buying points controlled over 80 percent of the market for its products, it stopped deliveries to the small independent retailers, leaving the deliveries to wholesalers.

OTHER CHANGES

A firm must monitor other developments affecting distribution. In some markets, rising wages are drawing people out of low-wage retailing. More self-service retailing is one result. That situation caused Nissan to change its distribution channel in Japan. The company was sending sales representatives door to door, but the diminishing availability of labor for that kind of retailing caused the company to consider switching to U.S.-style automobile showrooms.

Technological developments such as the cold chain (the availability of refrigeration in warehouses, trucks, and retail outlets) in Europe and Japan will enlarge product-line possibilities. Unilever found that the major deterrent to growth was the retail link of the cold chain. Many retailers could not afford the freezer unit. Unilever helped retailers finance a frozen food unit, expecting that the growth in the company's frozen food sales would be enough to cover financing costs.

Managing distribution often requires changing the channel when conditions change; for example, a firm may add a new channel or type of outlet. After World War II, the leading U.S. producer of ice cream faced a dilemma. Its traditional outlets were drugstores, but the new supermarkets were beginning to sell ice cream. Because adding supermarket outlets would irritate the members of the existing channel, the company decided to stay with its traditional channel. Eventually, of course, supermarkets became the overwhelming favorite outlet for ice cream. That is the kind of challenge facing firms in many markets. Multinational operating experience helps resolve such dilemmas in individual markets. Although a firm may reap ill will from existing channels, it also may gain goodwill and a strong place in the new outlet by being the first to change.

There were many predictions about the conversion to the euro, including the rounding up of prices and the enlargement of the EU (which is slated to continue to grow over the next ten years). In terms of distribution, some events have occurred that altered how products move among the member nations. Mega retailers have become more popular, as have massive distribution centers for shippers (for example, UPS) and retailers (for example, the UK giant, Tesco). Movement of goods and people is easier in the last decade, despite increased security due to antiterrorism efforts. Infrastructure problems still exist in some of the new member countries that were former Soviet-bloc nations, but the amount and speed of investment to upgrade the shortcomings is an EU priority.

Logistics For International Marketing

Up to this point, the discussion has centered on distribution from the viewpoint of the financial flow and ownership flow of goods, touching only incidentally on the physical movement of goods, usually called physical distribution. A somewhat broader term—*logistics*—has become popular. As part of the marketing chain, logistics can be defined as "those activities involved with the choice of the number and location of facilities to be used and the materials or product to be stored or transported from suppliers to customers in all the firm's markets."

The important point about logistics is that it is much more than transportation or the mere physical movement of goods. International logistics decisions affect the number and location of production and storage facilities, production schedules, inventory management, and even a firm's level of involvement in foreign markets. When products are shipped abroad, there are added costs in handling increased documentation and dealing with more and different types of insurance (commercial and political risks as well as exchange rate fluctuation in the form of forward contracts). Another cost involved in shipping abroad is determining the creditworthiness of foreign buyers (or the bank service charges associated with those payments and credit instruments such as letters of credit).

Physical distribution problems can limit market opportunities on the supply side as severely as low incomes do on the demand side. By the same token, improvements in logistics can open up new markets. **Logistics management** can offer the international marketer two ways for increasing profits: cost reduction and market expansion.

Logistics within a Foreign Market

In each market where a firm has a subsidiary, the firm must seek to optimize its physical distribution. In countries where a firm is represented by distributors or licensees, it has only a limited role in local logistics. Its approach abroad can vary according to the size of the market, the way the market is supplied, the degree of urbanization, the topography, and the transportation and storage facilities.

Congo provides an illustration of physical distribution problems within a national market. Imported goods destined for the eastern part of Congo take the following path: (1) Ocean shipping arrives inland on the Congo River at Matadi, where it is unloaded and put on a train. (2) The train goes to Kinshasa, the capital, bypassing the falls between Matadi and the capital. (3) At Kinshasa, the goods are put on a boat for a 1,000-mile river trip to Kisangani, where the river again is unnavigable. (4) There, the goods are put on a train for Kindu. (5) At Kindu, goods are transshipped by truck. It is not hard to imagine, therefore, that for many goods, physical distribution costs constitute the largest element in the price. That fact is reinforced by inadequate storage facilities and adverse climatic conditions causing damage and loss en route. The rebel fighting in Eastern Congo, of course, completely disrupted all logistics there.

As discussed earlier in the text, nations differ in transportation and communications infrastructure. Developing nations generally have a weak infrastructure; and this, combined with poorer markets, forces logistic adjustments

GLOBAL MARKETING

Trouble on the Highway

*T*uck shipments are regarded as an inexpensive and flexible means of getting a firm's products to market. While air is quicker, it is more expensive; and while ocean freight is cheap, it cannot deliver to a customer's doorstep.

Despite free trade agreements and other country associations such as NAFTA and the EU, trucking companies and drivers face numerous hurdles. It took a long time before the United States and Mexico could come to an agreement on which trucks could cross the border to make deliveries and which trucks could not. Drivers who had to stop at the border were obliged to offload the truck's contents and load the goods onto the partner country's truck. That process delayed shipments and added to shipping costs.

For whatever reason, differences in driver training and licensing practices or dissimilar pollution regulations (or even where the toll roads lead) endanger multinational country agreements. Less than one year after joining the EU, the Czech Republic was calling for an end to the German Maut truck toll because it had increased truck traffic (on an already strained Czech road infrastructure) by 50 percent. It seems truckers quickly learned of alternative routes to get across various parts of Europe that took them through the Czech Republic—all to avoid paying German tolls.

Source: "Czech Trek to Dodge Maut," *Commercial Motor*, April 28, 2005, page 16.

by a firm. (See "Global Marketing: Trouble on the Highway.") At one time, PepsiCo acquired a Mexican company whose "fleet" was 37 bicycles. Over the years, PepsiCo expanded the operation, now covering Mexico with over 7,000 vehicles. Even in industrialized countries, a fragmented wholesale-retail structure can lead to distribution inefficiencies, as you have seen. Because of the difficulty of covering the whole Japanese market, for example, many firms limit their initial efforts to just the Tokyo and Osaka metropolitan areas. On the other hand, Coca-Cola believed it was necessary to cover the whole Japanese market. So the company circumvented the existing multitiered wholesale system by franchising 54 bottlers who distribute from 500 warehouses on 8,500 trucks.

You also learned that topography is one aspect of a nation's physical endowment. The existence of rivers, deserts, mountains, or tropical forests can pose opportunities or challenges to physical distribution. Some Latin American countries, for example, are divided into almost inaccessible regions by the Andes Mountains. Because those markets are not affluent, some firms do not even try to cover the whole country. Instead, they content themselves with reaching major urban areas. Bata Shoe Company in Peru is one of the rare firms that does more business in rural areas than in major cities. To cover those areas, Bata uses air, truck, rail, and occasionally mule or launch to reach distant outlets. In Europe, inland waterways can have the opposite effect, tying several nations together for the physical movement of goods.

Multimarket Logistics

If there were one world market, the logistics problems of international marketing would be basically the same as those in the domestic market. The world, however, is not one market, but a collection of individual national markets, each under the control of a sovereign government. Governments have various methods of separating their markets from others—tariff barriers; import quotas and licenses; local content laws; national currencies, monetary systems, and exchange control; different tax systems and rates; different transportation policies; and different laws on products (food, drug, labeling, and safety).

Because the world is composed of national markets, logistics management must adapt to or overcome the barriers in order to achieve an integrated world market strategy. The goal is not merely reduction of costs, but greater sales. Sales will increase if logistics improvements lead to improvements in the level of customer service. The appropriate customer service level varies among countries because of competition and customer expectations. (**Customer service level** refers to delivery times, availability of parts and service, and other elements required to meet customers' wants and needs.)

A firm's ability to develop a logistics system is affected by its level of involvement. Where a firm has wholly owned subsidiaries, it has the most control of the customer service level; joint ventures offer less control, and licensee and distributor markets offer the least control. That is one reason many firms prefer wholly owned ventures.

If a firm had a choice, its favored logistics arrangement would be to concentrate production at home and export to world markets. That allows economies of scale in production and eliminates many international business problems, such as dealing with foreign labor or governments or operating in an unknown environment. The Japanese had success with this approach. Several factors work against it, however:

(1) high transportation costs, (2) trade barriers, (3) foreign exchange risk, (4) customer service needs, and (5) political resistance. Those factors often force a firm to choose a deeper commitment to the foreign market.

For example, the Japanese built auto plants in the United States and Europe because of protectionist pressures. U.S. firms expanded production in Europe also because of protectionist fears. Coca-Cola built a concentrate plant in India because of trade restrictions. And Wacoal, a Japanese lingerie firm, built a factory in Puerto Rico to avoid U.S. tariffs. In each case, it was an involuntary change from exporting from home.

There are some signs that these trends are reversing to a limited degree, though. For example, Intel recently chose Arizona over Mexico, China, and India as the location of its newest plant.[11]

The Dynamic Environment

Designing a logistics system for international markets is a continuing task. Almost every parameter of the system is subject to change. Besides markets and competition being dynamic, transportation also is in continuous evolution. It cannot be assumed that current transportation achievements represent the end of technological change. Rather, continuing improvements are probable, opening up new logistics possibilities.

Government barriers also change, not always for the worse. As was stated in Chapter 2, tariff barriers have been reduced significantly through WTO negotiations. Other trade restrictions have been lessened because of the WTO, IMF, and similar organizations. The formation of regional groupings has had a favorable effect, allowing greater rationalization of a firm's logistics, at least on a regional basis.

Mercosur, NAFTA, and the EU are continuing dynamic developments. Other developments include government changes in import quotas and local content requirements. Also, many nations require exports from the foreign firms in their country. Changing international relations (for example, Arab-Israel and East-West) also affect physical distribution.

Another favorable development is the opening up of large new markets in such places as Eastern Europe, China, and Vietnam. Those markets pose large logistics challenges, however, because of their inadequate infrastructure. Weaknesses include roads, railroads, warehouses, and distribution organizations, in addition to other problems. In Russia, for example, security is a serious problem. Colgate has its own warehouses in Moscow with security guards posted 24 hours a day, seven days a week. When shipping by truck, an armed escort follows. When shipping by rail, Colgate has an armed guard inside the locked car.

The Flexible Response

Considering the dynamic nature of the international logistics environment, a marketer might conclude that there is no definitive solution. That conclusion is a useful guideline if it helps avoid large investments aimed at a definitive answer. A firm might better seek *ad hoc*, temporizing solutions that meet present constraints. They can then be changed as the situation changes without major new investment. Although they may represent second-best answers at any given time, in the long run, they may add up to the best feasible solution.

A firm can make major investments in facilities on the basis of a currently ideal system. However, as changes occur in technology, the political situation, or its own goals, a firm may have to make costly adjustments. Ideally, a firm should make investments in such a way that they can be adjusted to a variety of possible future environments. A manager must keep as many options open as possible. Contingency planning must be an inherent part of the *modus operandi*.

Management of International Logistics

Physical distribution is a major cost in international marketing, and profits can be increased through cost reductions in the movement of goods. Profits can be increased further if sales rise because of an improvement in customer service. For those reasons, logistics deserves close attention. This section considers the principal elements in the management of international logistics, as well as the need for international coordination.

Facilities and Technology

The facilities available in international logistics include (1) service organizations such as transportation companies and freight forwarders; (2) institutions such as free-trade zones (FTZs) and public warehouses; and (3) modern hardware such as computers, the telex, containerization, and jumbo jet planes.

FREIGHT FORWARDER

Foreign freight forwarders are specialists in both transportation and documentation for international shipments. The full-service foreign freight forwarder can relieve the producer of most of the burdens of distribution across national borders. Foreign freight forwarders handle all documentation and provide information on shipping and foreign import regulations. They arrange for shipment and insurance and consolidate shipments for lower costs. Because of their expertise in this technical area, they are used by a majority of companies to take care of overseas shipment. Their efficiency makes them valuable to both large and small companies. Electronic tracking hardware that is built into containers and sophisticated software such as Cargo-Wise allow freight forwarders to provide 24-hour advance notice on shipments (imposed post 9/11 for national security reasons) and to assist in counterterrorism activities.[12]

FTZS

Aware of the problems posed by their barriers to trade, some 50 nations have established over 500 FTZs, free ports, bonded warehouses, and similar devices to overcome some of the self-created problems. There are over 300 FTZs in the United States. The facilities are usually government owned and are supervised by customs officials. They permit a firm to bring merchandise into a country without paying duties as long as the merchandise remains in the zone or bonded warehouse. Many FTZs allow processing, assembly, sorting, and repacking within the zone. Countries provide these zones because they gain employment that would normally be driven away by their trade barriers.

FTZs offer several potential advantages:

- They permit economies of bulk shipping to a country without the burden of custom duties. Duties need to be paid only when the goods are released on a small-lot basis from the zone.
- They permit manufacturers to carry local inventory at less cost than in facilities they own because in those facilities, manufacturers must pay the duty as soon as the goods enter the country. If duties are high, the financial burden is significant.

  Bausch & Lomb leased 500 square meters in the public bonded warehouses at Netherlands' Schipol Airport and shipped merchandise there at bulk rates from the United States. The company used Schipol as its European distribution center. It realized big savings by concentrating European inventories at one spot, yet it provided two-day delivery in Europe. This system also permitted Bausch & Lomb's distributors and agents to reduce their inventories, thereby improving distributor relations.

- U.S. FTZs offer the same advantages as other FTZs and are used by U.S. and foreign firms, though more by the latter. Among the major U.S. users are General Motors and Ford, with over ten zones each.

  One advantage for firms is that they can import ingredients or components into the zone without paying the U.S. duty on them. After assembly, the complete product can be shipped into the U.S. market at the lower rate applying to the finished good. Thus, AOC, a Taiwanese TV producer, shipped tubes and components into a U.S. zone without paying the 22 percent U.S. duty on them. After assembly, it shipped them out at the lower 11 percent duty on complete sets.

- The ability to engage in local processing, assembly, and repacking can mean savings to a firm. It can ship to the market in bulk or CKD for advantageous freight rates. Then it can process, assemble, or repack for local distribution. In addition, local labor costs may be less than at home. Mercosur's growth has caused FTZs to boom in that region, but the Dominican Republic has 42 zones—the most of any Latin American country.

A variation on FTZs allows a company to have all or part of its own plant declared an FTZ or bonded warehouse. The advantages are the same, but it is more convenient for a firm. Honda's motorcycle plant in Ohio and Olivetti's Pennsylvania typewriter plant are located in FTZs. In a similar manner, Brazil permitted Caterpillar to have an on-site free zone. The savings are significant for Caterpillar because duties on its imports average 50 percent and goods have to be financed for about one year. Because such zones attract or keep companies in a country, they are a growing development. Olivetti, for example, had been threatening to leave the U.S. market until it received an FTZ. Firms from over 20 countries are operating in U.S. FTZs.

Evaluation of Free Zones

A firm should consider FTZs to see if their advantages apply to its situation. The usefulness of FTZs depends on duty rates. Since free zones are aimed primarily at overcoming tariff barriers, they are less important for products with low duties. Furthermore, the economies of bulk shipments and the use of low-cost local labor are benefits that can be obtained apart from the use of free zones.

A logistics planner must decide in which markets free zones can play a useful role. Each zone must be individually evaluated because not all deliver the promised advantages. A review of Latin American free zones found some that were excellent and some that were unsatisfactory. Other benefits are that they minimize the investment needs of a firm and have built-in flexibility. If an FTZ does not work out well, other alternatives can be tried; and a firm has lost little.

TRANSPORTATION TECHNOLOGY

Technological advances in the development of supertankers, Fastships, containerization, and tracking capabilities have altered the costs of moving goods in international marketing. Physical distribution is dependent on state-of-the-art transportation and storage. Therefore, logistics planners must make sure that a distribution

system reflects the economies possible with the technology available.

In view of increased European integration, Philips spent heavily on superautomated Eurodistribution centers for each product division. Comprehensive computer systems run the entire operation on an ordering-to-forwarding basis.

COORDINATION OF INTERNATIONAL LOGISTICS

In international marketing, logistics usually involves more than one country. That means that some coordination is necessary. Some ITT Europe companies lost major orders because their distribution costs were too high. The company studied the problem and found some interesting results. Managers perceived their distribution costs to be about 1 to 1.5 percent. In reality, they were at least 6 percent, or over $700 million for ITT Europe. A reporting and cost-control system was installed, leading to significant savings in all aspects of physical distribution—from deliveries by suppliers, warehousing, and transportation to the design of a new cardboard box for shipping.

INDIVIDUAL NATIONAL MARKETS

Within each market, physical distribution is handled primarily by a subsidiary or distributor there. However, corporate headquarters should provide assistance in planning local physical distribution. It can contribute ideas and analytical techniques, such as distribution cost analysis, so the best technology is available in each market. Furthermore, some governments may require a firm to balance each dollar of imports with a dollar of exports. Obviously, a local subsidiary cannot solve that problem on its own.

To improve its level of customer service in North America, BMW established three parts distribution centers for its 420 auto dealers and 290 motorcycle dealers. By calling the nearest center, dealers can now hook into BMW's inventory network.

REGIONAL MARKETS

Operations within regional groupings also need coordination. As those groups achieve economic integration, a subsidiary or distributor in one member country cannot be considered merely a national operation. It becomes part of the larger regional market. For example, in the EU, physical distribution must be organized on an EU-wide basis. In Mercosur, there is increasing rationalization of both production and logistics.

As expected, the Single Market in the EU is encouraging manufacturers to rationalize and centralize their logistics. One result is a reduction in the number of warehouses used. Whirlpool went from 30 warehouses to 8 regional centers; Bosch, from 36 to 10; and Eaton, from 5 to 2. 3M claimed savings of $80 million a year by reducing the number of warehouses and reorganizing and centralizing its logistics.

SKF, a Swedish firm, is the world's largest producer of ball bearings. SKF chose Singapore as its sales, service, and distribution center for Southeast Asia. Singapore was chosen because it has excellent shipping and air-freight services; and it offered a free port, enabling SFK to avoid tariffs and sales taxes on transshipments.

GLOBAL MARKET

Firms with many markets and supply sources need overall coordination for optimum integration of supply and demand. Besides wanting each plant to operate at an efficient level, a firm wants adequate inventories and customer service in each market. Such coordination is possible only on a centralized basis.

Centralized control of exports is one way to achieve coordination. One office, not necessarily at company headquarters, coordinates all export orders and assigns production sources for the orders. Eaton, for example, produces in 43 countries. All products are exported to more than 100 countries through a marketing organization based in Switzerland.

Centralized control of exports is often tied in with regional distribution centers, where inventories are held for faster local delivery. For example, Caterpillar has a parts depot in the Far East from which it ships inventory and provides services to dealers and customers in 19 Asian countries. Texas Instruments (TI) stocks materials in 16 major market areas. It uses a computer-teletype-telephone hookup to coordinate its global network. With appropriate planning, distributors and licensees can be included in the integrated logistics program. Automatic Radio International has successfully accomplished integrated logistics with 160 distributors and licensees in 80 countries.

A firm can ensure integrated international logistics under various arrangements, but some centralized control will be necessary if overall corporate interests are to be satisfied. In review, the benefit of efficient international logistics planning should be increased profits produced by (1) more stable production levels at plants in different countries; (2) lower-cost distribution resulting, in part, from the possibility of combining small orders into container or planeload lots (for example, Squibb does this by using five major exporting points with intermediate break-bulk points around the globe); and (3) better customer service levels in international markets. An extended example follows.

In one year, The Dow Chemical Company processed 25,000 foreign orders and made 12,000 export shipments. Ocean freight costs came to $12 million. Dow handled those shipments from its Midland, Michigan, headquarters through its International Distribution and Traffic Department, which had 55 employees. Dow had overseas manufacturing in 20 locations and bulk terminals or package storage facilities in more than 35 locations.

One of the department's projects was the preparation of price lists enabling sales representatives to quote a price on any chemical in more than 100 markets. Information necessary for the lists included insurance and freight costs, consular fees, and duties. Since some of that information is constantly changing, maintaining a currently valid list is difficult. Computerizing helped in this task, and updated computer lists are available to sales representatives in each country.

One reason freight rates were changing was that the department was bargaining with over 30 steamship conferences on rates and classifications of its chemicals. By getting one chemical, Dowpon, reclassified, Dow cut its freight rate from $64 to $42 per long ton. That opened new markets by making Dowpon competitive with a similar German product.

Because of the importance of shipping bulky chemicals in volume, Dow operated three vessels under long-term contract. That was in addition to its regular spot- and medium-term charter arrangements. Dow's engineers also collaborated with marine engineers on the design of specialized vessels so shipments could be made in bulk to overseas terminals.

Although Dow did its own logistics planning, it did use the service of freight forwarders—two on the Gulf Coast and one each on the East Coast, West Coast, and Great Lakes. One exception to Dow's centralized physical distribution management was the European market. As its manufacturing and marketing operations grew in Europe, Dow found that decentralization was appropriate for control of shipments within Europe.

Summary

Firms with limited resources can find quick and easy entry to foreign markets through indirect exporting. For small U.S. firms, hey can make a domestic sale to companies with buying offices in the United States. Those buyers may be foreign retail groups, foreign trade organizations, or corporations supplying foreign subsidiaries from the United States.

EMCs are another form of indirect exporting, but they are specialized intermediaries who sell their export marketing services. Use of EMCs is a low-cost way to obtain an export department without setting one up in a firm. They offer instant market access as well as economies of scale by serving several producers. These miniversions of a foreign trading company are used by thousands of U.S. firms.

Piggybacking is a form of cooperation between two producers wherein one carries the other's product(s) to export markets. This is a popular form of exporting because the rider gets instant, inexpensive export marketing while the carrier gets a complementary product to round out its line.

Direct exporting, in which a firm does the whole exporting job in-house, is more demanding than indirect exporting. There are greater personnel, administrative, and financial requirements. A firm must choose its foreign markets, find representatives in those markets, arrange the logistics, and then try to manage its foreign marketing by working with independent distributors.

Product assembly in foreign markets is a blend of exporting and local production, as a firm ships parts or ingredients from home, which are then processed locally. Foreign assembly maintains current production facilities but may allow more favorable tariff treatment, lower shipping costs, lower labor costs, or some combination.

Contract manufacturing allows a firm to produce abroad without plant investment by contracting to use a local firm's production facilities. It saves on transport and tariff costs and avoids local investment and labor problems. It is useful when governments and/or customers favor local supply.

Working with a licensee means a firm doesn't have to make a major commitment to a foreign market. A local licensee produces and markets a firm's product. Working with a licensee provides the advantage of local supply at a low cost, but a disadvantage is that it limits the control and returns of a firm. What's more, it may mean training a competitor.

Joint ventures—producing and marketing abroad with a local partner—can be an effective market entry. In addition to the advantages of local production, a firm may gain local market knowledge and contacts as well as potential conflicts. Joint venturing is more costly than other forms of entry except for wholly owned operations. Today, looser forms of partnering, called strategic alliances, are popular. These contractual, nonequity links may offer some of the advantages of joint venturing but with less commitment.

Wholly owned operations involve the greatest commitment to a foreign market. In return for that commitment, a firm receives complete control, greater international integration, and usually greater profits, but also greater exposure to foreign problems. Wholly owned operations can start with a new establishment or with the acquisition of a local firm. Acquisitions are currently very popular because they allow quicker entry and an established market position. They may also be necessary in markets that have no room for new entrants. In Eastern Europe, entry methods usually have to be adapted to the peculiar situation in each emerging market.

Exporters can influence foreign distributors' market-

ing in several ways. The first step is careful distributor selection. That requires a job specification and evaluation of a distributor's track record according to an exporter's criteria. The second step is writing the distributor agreement to recognize the interests of both parties. The third step is making suitable financial arrangements. An exporter must choose margins, price quotes, currency, and payment terms to satisfy both parties. The fourth ingredient is marketing support, which may include a strong brand, advertising support, distributor sales force training, promotional materials, and the establishment of a regional warehouse. The fifth dimension is communication, which may include an 800 telephone number, computer links, visits, a regional headquarters, and a company newsletter. Other potential motivators include holding contests, giving rewards for good performance, offering an exclusive territory, and taking equity in the distributor.

Wholesalers around the world differ greatly in size and capability. Wholesaling efficiency generally rises with the level of economic development, but there are many exceptions to that trend. When wholesaling is fragmented and small in scale, it constrains a firm's local marketing by increasing transaction costs and credit requirements and by limiting the product line and geographic coverage and services offered.

Retailing shows great international variation, with a majority of countries having large numbers of small retailers. In those markets, a firm may find it difficult to secure retailer cooperation in carrying inventory, displaying the product, promoting the product, and providing market feedback.

An international marketer must monitor distribution trends. As economies develop, their distribution structures change as wholesaling and retailing become modernized and the channel members become more powerful. The internationalization of retailing is predicted to continue, with U.S., European, and Japanese retailers spreading their wings abroad. Direct marketing remains important and mail order and telemarketing are growing. Discounting and retail price competition are spreading to more countries. Marketing via the Web is the most dynamic development to watch.

A firm would like to use the same channels in every market, but exact duplication is never possible. Differing wholesale and retail structures and consumer income and buying behaviors force adjustments. Also, a manufacturer's situation varies from market to market. Finally, in deciding on selective or intensive distribution coverage, a firm may find that what it wants is overruled by political or economic conditions.

Questions and Research

8.1 Identify the ways to reach foreign markets by making a domestic sale.

8.2 Why might a small, new-to-export company be interested in using an EMC?

8.3 How can the carrier and the rider both benefit from a piggyback arrangement?

8.4 What procedures should a firm follow when selecting a distributor?

8.5 What are the benefits to local manufacture as a form of market entry? What are the costs?

8.6 When is contract manufacturing desirable?

8.7 What are the pros and cons of licensing as a form of market entry?

8.8 How do successful licensors manage their licensing program?

8.9 Why is acquisition often the preferred way to establish wholly owned operations abroad?

8.10 Discuss the financial and pricing techniques for motivating foreign distributors.

8.11 What are some of the international differences in wholesaling?

8.12 Many markets have relatively large numbers of small retailers. How does this constrain the local marketing of an international firm?

8.13 Discuss the implications for the international marketer of the trend toward larger-scale retailing.

8.14 Why do U.S. firms tend to have somewhat different distribution channels abroad?

8.15 What are the advantages to using a foreign freight forwarder?

8.16 Discuss the potential benefits of using FTZs.

Endnotes

1. Claver, Enrique and Diego Quer. "Choice of Market Entry Mode In China: The Influence of Firm-Specific Factors," *Journal of General Management*. Volume 30, Issue 3, Spring 2005, pages 51–71.

2. Bhaumik, Sumon Kumar and Stephen Gelb. "Determinants of Entry Mode Choice of MNCs in Emerging Markets: Evidence from South Africa and Egypt," *Emerging Markets Finance & Trade*, Volume 41, Issue 2, March/April 2005, pages 5–24.

3. Sylwebster, Kevin. "Foreign Direct Investment, Growth and Income Inequality in Less Developed Countries," *International Review of Applied Economics*, Volume 19, Issue 3, July 2005, pages 289–299.

4. Balfour, Frederik. "The State's Long Apron Strings," *Business Week*, Issue 3948, August 22, 2005, page 74.

5. Fowler, Geoffrey A. "Buying Spree by China Firms Is a Bet on Value of U.S. Brands," *Wall Street Journal*, June 23, 2005, page B.1.

6. Levitt, Theodore. "The Globalization of Markets," *Harvard Business Review*, Issue 61, May–June, pages 92–102.

7. "Asia: Wal-Mart Still Waits; Indian Retail Reform," *The Economist*, Volume 376, Issue 8435, July 16, 2005, page 54.

8. Field, Alan M. "Uneven Progress," *Journal of Commerce*. August 22, 2005, page 1.

9. Uusitalo, Outi. "Competitive Reactions to Market Entry: The Case of the Finnish Grocery Retailing Industry," *British Food Journal*, Volume 106, Issue 8/9, 2004, pages 663–671.

10. Elliott, Dorinda and Bill Powell. "Wal-Mart Nation," *Time*, Volume 165, Issue 26, June 27, 2005, pages 36–39.

11. Hoffman, William. "Home Field Advantage," *Traffic World*, August 15, 2005, page 1.

12. Biederman, David. "Forward Progress," *Journal of Commerce*, August 22, 2005, page 1.

Further Readings

Agarwal, Sanjeev. "Socio-Cultural Distance and the Choice of Joint Ventures," *Journal of International Marketing*, Volume 2, Number 2, 1994, pages 63–80.

Aulakh, Preet S., Tamer Cavusgil, and M. B. Sarkar. "Compensation in International Licensing Agreements," *Journal of International Business Studies*, Volume 29, Issue 2, 1998, pages 409–420.

Baird, Alfred. "Investigating the Feasibility of Fast Sea Transport Services," *Maritime Economics & Logistics*, Volume 6, Issue 3, September 2004, page 252.

Gimeno, Javier, Robet E. Hoskisson, Brent D. Beal, and William P. Wan. "Explaining the Clustering of International Expansion Moves: A Critical Test in the U.S. Telecommunications Industry," *Academy of Management Journal*, Briarcliff Manor, April 2005, Volume 48, Issue 2, pages 297–319.

Howard, Douglas. "The Challenges of Importing a Franchise Concept to America," *Franchising World*, Volume 37, Issue 6, June 2005, pages 66–69.

Isaac, Grant E., Nicholas Perdikis, and William A. Kerr. "Cracking Export Markets with Genetically Modified Crops: What Is the Entry Mode Strategy?" *International Marketing Review*, Volume 21, Issue 4/5, 2004, pages 536–547.

Jiang, Fuming. "Driving Forces of International Pharmaceutical Firms' FDI into China," *Journal of Business Strategies*, Huntsville, Spring 2005, Volume 22, Issue 1, pages 21-40.

Karavdic, Munib and Gary Gregory. "Integrating E-commerce into Exiting Export Marketing Theories: A Contingency Model," *Marketing Theory*, London, March 2005, Volume 5, Issue 1, pages 75-103.

Ling, Florence Yean Yng, C. William Ibbs, and Javier C Cuervo. "Entry and Business Strategies Used by International Architectural, Engineering and Construction Firms In China," *Construction Management and Economics*, London: June 2005, Volume 23, Issue 5, page 509-519.

"Of Mouse and Shark's Fin," *Wall Street Journal*, August 26, 2005, page A.12.

"Online-Payment Firms Target China: Immature Market Has Slew of Companies Popping Up in Effort to Gain Foothold," *Wall Street Journal*, August 11, 2005, page B.4.

Rasheed, Howard S. Foreign Entry Mode and Performance: The Moderating Effects of Environment," *Journal of Small Business Management*, Milwaukee: January 2005, Volume 43, Issue 1, pages 41-54.

Samiee, Saeed. "Exporting and the Internet," *International Marketing Review*, Volume 15, Issue 5, 1998, pages 413–426.

Sengupta, Sanjit and Monica Perry. "Antecedents of Global Strategic Alliance Formations," *Journal of International Marketing*, Volume 5, Number 1, 1997, pages 31–50.

Shama, Avraham. "Entry Strategies of U.S. Firms to Eastern European Countries," *California Management Review*, Volume 37, Issue 3, 1995, pages 90–109.

"Soga Shosha Business Model," Sumitomo Corporation of America (http://www.sumitomocorp.com/about/soga_shosha.html); accessed August 22, 2005. You may also want to refer to the term *kieretsu*; some would argue that Wal-Mart and Daimler-Chrysler possess characteristics that mimic the *soga shosha* model.

Tihanyi, Laszlo, David A. Griffith, and Craig J. Russell. "The Effect of Cultural Distance on Entry Mode Choice, International Diversification, and MNE Performance: A Meta-Analysis," *Journal of International Business Studies*, Volume 36, Issue 6, 2005, pages 270–283.

Timmor, Yaron and Jeheil Zif. "A Typology of Marketing Strategies for Export," *Journal of Global Marketing*, Volume 18, Issue 3/4, 2005, pages 37–78.

Vasquez-Parraga, Arturo Z., Reto Felix, and Aberdeen Leila Borders. Rationale and Strategies of Latin American Companies Entering, Maintaining or Leaving US Markets," *The Journal of Business & Industrial Marketing*, Santa Barbara, 2004, Volume 19, Issue 6, pages 359-370.

Yamawaki, Hideki. "The Determinants of Geographic Configuration of Value Chain Activities: Foreign Multinational Enterprises in Japanese Manufacturing," *International Economics and Economic Policy*, Heidelberg, December 2004, Volume 1, Issue 2/3, pages 195-104.

Recommended Web Sites

Documentation:
General resource: http://faculty.philau.edu/russowl/market.html#DOCUMENTATION

U.S. Department of Commerce, International Trade Administration: http://www.export.gov/documentation.html

Export Management Companies:

Federation of International Trade Association list: http://database.binex.com/Fita

Financing exports:
General resource:
http://faculty.philau.edu/russowl/market.html#FINANCING

Intermediary Identification:
(U.S.) State Development Agencies: http://faculty.philau.edu/russowl/market.html#Economic-development

New York State Export Marketing Assistance Service (EMAS): http://www.empire.state.ny.us/International/Export_Marketing_Assistance_Service.asp

"Basic Guide to Exporting: Locating and Evaluating Foreign Representatives and Buyers (http://www.unzco.com/basicguide/c4.html#locating) and Table 3 for a list of criteria (http://www.unzco.com/basicguide/table3.html).

International Company Profiles: http://www.export.gov/negotiating.html; conduct a search on "International Company Profiles".

U.S. Department of Commerce, U.S. Commercial Service, Gold Key Matching Service: http://www.export.gov/comm_svc/goldkey.html; also U.S. Commercial Service, Partner and Trade Leads: http://www.export.gov/partners.html; and U.S. Department of Commerce International Partners Search(approximately $600/country): http://www.export.gov/comm_svc/intl_partner_search.html.

Shipping Terms Glossary:
http://www.ups.com/content/us/en/resources/glossary/index.html

Fast Ship:
http://www.fastshipatlantic.com

Sogo Shosha:
Mitsubishi companies: http://www.mitsubishi.com/php/users/category_search.php?lang=1

Mitsui: http://www.mitsui.co.jp/tkabz/english/index.html

Sumitomo: http://www.sumitomocorp.com/industry/index.html and Sumitomo-Mitsui Banking Groups: http://www.smbc.co.jp/aboutus/english/profile/group/index.html

Case 8.1

METRO CORPORATION: TECHNOLOGY LICENSING NEGOTIATION1

The Licensor Firm

Metro Corporation is a diversified steel rolling, fabricating, and construction company based in the Midwest. The company considers itself to be in a mature industry. Innovations are few. With transport and tariff barriers and the support given by many governments to their own companies, exporting as a means of doing foreign business is limited. Similarly, given the large investment, modest return, and political sensitivity of the industry, direct foreign investment is all but a closed option. In a global strategic sense, then, Metro Corporation has more frequently focused on licensing as a market entry method, with technologies confined to (1) processes and engineering peripheral to the basic steel-making process (for example, mining methods, designs of coke oven doors, and galvanizing) and (2) applications of steel in construction and other industries (for example, petroleum tank design, welding methods, and thermo-adhesion).

All of Metro's licensing is handled by its international division, International Construction and Engineering (ICE), which is beginning to develop a reputation in Western Europe and South America as a good source for specialized construction technology.

The Proposed Licensee

Impecina, a private firm, is the largest construction company in Peru and operates throughout Latin America. Impecina has a broad range of interests, including residential and commercial buildings, hydraulic works, transportation, and maritime works. Employing several thousand personnel, including engineers and technicians, its sales have doubled in the last five years. It was still primarily a Peruvian business with most turnover in Peru, but was in the process of expanding into Colombia, Argentina, Brazil, Venezuela, and the North African Mediterranean countries. Impecina has advanced computer capacity with a large IBM computer and other computers at its branches. In oil-storage tanks, Impecina's experience was limited to smaller, fixed-cone roof designs under 150 feet in diameter.

The Technology

National Tank, Inc., a fabrication division of Metro, had designed a computerized design procedure for floating-roof, oil-storage tanks, which minimized the use of steel within the American Petroleum Institute or any other oil industry standards. Particularly for larger tanks (for instance, 150-foot diameter and above), this program would confer upon the bidding contractor a significant cost advantage. National Tank had spent one worker-year, at a direct cost of $225,000, to write the computer program alone. Patents were involved in an incidental manner only for the seals on the floating roof. Metro had not bothered to file for the patent except in the United States.

The Market

Peru's indigenous oil output is very low, but it imports and refines 50 million tons annually, mostly for domestic demand. Following the escalation of oil prices and tightening of supplies in 1973, the Peruvian government determinedly set about formulating a program to augment Peru's oil storage capacity. At a preliminary meeting with ICE at U.S. headquarters, Impecina's representatives said that their government planned $200 million in expenditures on oil-storage facilities over the next three years (mostly in large-sized tanks). Of this, Impecina's "ambition" was to capture a one-third market share. That this appeared to be a credible target was illustrated by Impecina's existing 30 percent share of the "fixed-cone type under 150-foot diameter." Additionally, Impecina estimated the value of private-sector construction over the next three years to total $40 million.

Approximately half of a storage system's construction cost goes toward the tank alone, the remainder being excavation, foundation, piping, instrumentation, and other ancillary equipment, all areas of expertise with Impecina's engineers.

Neighboring Colombia was building a 12 million-ton refinery, but the tank installation plans of other South American nations were not known, according to the Impecina representative.

Each of Impecina's competitors in Peru for this business was affiliated with a prominent company: Umbertomas with Jefferson, Inc., in the United States, Zapa with Philadelphia Iron & Steel, Cosmas with Peoria-Duluth Construction Inc., etc. Thus, association with Metro would help Impecina in the bidding process.

The First Meeting

National Tank Division had, in the past year, bid jointly with Impecina on a project in southern Peru. Though that bid was unsuccessful, Impecina had learned about Metro's computerized design capabilities and initiated a formal first round of negotiations that were to lead to a licensing agreement. The meeting took place in the United States. Two Impecina executives of subdirector rank were accompanied by a U.S. consultant. Metro was represented by the vice president of ICE, the ICE attorney, and an executive from National Tank Division.

Minutes of this meeting show that it was exploratory. Both genuine and rhetorical questions were asked. Important information and perceptions were exchanged and the groundwork laid for concluding negotiations. Following is a bare summary of important issues gleaned from the somewhat circular discussion:

1. *Licensee Market Coverage.* Impecina tried to represent itself as essentially a Peruvian firm. It reviewed its government's expenditure plans and its hoped-for market share. Yet throughout the meeting, the issue of the license covering Libya, Algeria, Morocco, Colombia, Argentina, Brazil, and Venezuela kept cropping up.

2. *Exclusivity.* For Peru, Metro negotiators had no difficulty conceding exclusivity. They mentioned that granting exclusivity to a licensee for any territory was agreeable in principle, provided a minimum performance guarantee was given. Then the question was deferred for future discussion. At one point, a Metro executive remarked, "We could give Impecina a nonexclusive—and, for example, we wouldn't give another (licensee) a license for one year (in those nations)," proposing the idea of a trial period for Impecina to generate business in a territory.

3. *Agreement Life.* Impecina very quickly agreed to a ten-year term, payment in U.S. dollars, and other minor issues.

4. *Trade Name.* The Impecina negotiators placed great emphasis on their ability to use the Metro name in bidding, explaining how their competition in Peru had technical collaboration with three U.S. companies. (See above.) "Did that mean Metro's National Tank Division could compete with Impecina in Peru?" they were asked rhetorically. (Actually, both sides seemed to have tacitly agreed that it was not possible for Metro to do business directly in Peru.)

5. *Licensee Market Size.* Attention turned to the dollar value of the future large tank market (floating-roof) in Peru. Impecina threw out an estimate of $200 million in government expenditures and $40 million in private sector spending over the coming three years, of which it targeted a one-third share. Later a lower market size estimate of $150 million (government and private), with a share of $50 million received by Impecina over three years, was arrived at. (Memories are not clear on how the estimates were revised.). "Will Impecina guarantee us it will obtain one-third of the market?" brought the response "That's an optimistic figure that we hope we can realize." Impecina offered as evidence its existing one-third share of the "fixed roof under 150-foot" market, an impressive achievement.

6. *Product-Mix Covered by License.* It became clear that Impecina wanted floating-roof technology for all sizes and fixed-roof over 100-foot in diameter. It suggested that the agreement cover tanks over 100 feet in size. "Would Impecina pay on all tanks (of any size)" to simplify royalty calculation and monitoring? After considerable discussion, Metro seemed to have acceded to Impecina's proposal (to cover both types, only over 100 feet) based on consensus over three points.

   a. The competition probably does not pay (its licensors) on small tanks; therefore Impecina would be at a disadvantage if it had to pay on small tanks also.

   b. The market in floating-roof tanks was usually over 100 feet anyway.

   c. Impecina claimed that customers normally dictated the dimensions of the tanks, so Impecina could not vary them to avoid paying a royalty to Metro.

7. *Compensation Formula.* Metro proposed an initial lump-sum payment (in two installments, one when the agreement was signed and the second upon delivery of the computer program and designs) plus engineers and executives for bid assistance on a per diem rate plus a royalty on successful bids based on the barrel capacity installed by Impecina. Impecina's U.S. consultant countered with the idea of royalties on a sliding scale, lower with larger-capacity tanks, indicating talk about "1 million barrel capacity tanks." The (rhetorical?) question, "What is Peru's oil capacity?" seemed to bring the discussion down to earth and veered it off on a tangent, while both sides mentally regrouped.

   Upon returning to the topic, Impecina's executives, when asked, ventured that as a rule of thumb, their profit markup on a turnkey job was 6 percent. (However, on excluding the more price-sensitive portions such as excavation, piping, and ancillary equipment, which typically constitute half the value, Impecina conceded that on the tank alone, markup might be as much as 12 percent, although executives kept insisting 5 to 6 percent was enough.) Impecina's executives later offered only royalties (preferably sliding) and per diem fees for bid assistance from Metro's executives and engineers. Metro countered by pointing out that per diem fees of, say, $225 plus travel costs amounted, at best, to recovering costs, not profit.

The compensation design question was left at this stage, deferred for later negotiation, the broad outlines having been laid. Metro's starting formal offer, which would mention specific numbers, was to be telexed to Lima in a week.

8. *The Royalty Basis.* Metro entertained the idea that Impecina's engineers were very familiar with excavation, piping, wiring, and other ancillary equipment. Metro was transferring technology for the tank alone, which typically represented half of overall installed value.

9. *Government Intervention.* Toward the end of the discussions, Impecina brought up the question of the Peruvian government having to approve the agreement. This led to its retreat from the idea of a ten-year term, agreed to earlier; Impecina then mentioned five years. No agreement was reached. (Incidentally, Peru had, in the last two years, passed legislation indicating a "guideline" of five years for foreign licenses.)

Internal Discussion in Metro Leading to the Formal Offer

The advantages derived by the licensee would be acquisition of floating-roof technology time and money saved in attempting to generate the computerized design procedure in-house, somewhat of a cost and efficiency advantage in bidding on larger tanks, and the use of Metro's name.

1. It was estimated that National Tank Division had spent $225,000 (one workyear = two executives for six months plus other costs) in developing the computer program. Additionally, it could cost $40,000 (three-quarters of a workyear) to convert the program into Spanish and the metric system and to adapt it to the material availability and labor cost factors peculiar to Peru. Simultaneously, there would be semiformal instruction of Impecina engineers in the use of the program, petroleum industry codes, and Metro fabrication methods. All this had to be done before the licensee would be ready for a single bid.

2. It was visualized that Metro would then assist Impecina for two workweeks on the preparation of each bid and four workweeks on successful receipt of a contract award. Additionally, if Metro's specialized construction equipment were used, three workmonths of on-site training would be needed.

As the licensee's personnel moved along their learning curve, assistance of the type described in paragraph 2 would diminish until it was no longer needed after a few successful bids.

The following additional considerations went into determining the initial offer:

1. Metro's obligations (and sunk costs) under paragraph (1.a) above were fairly determinate; whereas its obligations under (1.b) depended on the technical sophistication and absorptive capacity of the licensee's engineers, their success rate in bidding, etc.

2. If Impecina's market estimates were used, over the next three years, it would generate large-tank orders worth $50 million, on which it would make a profit of $3 million (at 6 percent on $50 million or 12 percent on $25 million).

3. The market beyond three years was an unknown.

4. Exclusive rights might be given to Impecina in Peru and Colombia, with the possibility of ICE reserving the right of conversion to nonexclusive if minimum market share were not captured.

5. While Impecina's multinational expansion plans were unknown, its business in the other nations was too small to justify granting it exclusivity. Impecina might be satisfied with a vague promise of future consideration as exclusive licensees in those territories.

6. Metro would try for an agreement term of ten years. It was thought that Impecina's computer and engineering capabilities were strong enough that it would not need Metro's assistance after a few bids.

Surprisingly, the discussions reveal that no explicit consideration was given to the idea that Impecina might emerge some day as a multinational competitor.

In view of the uncertainty about how successful the licensee would actually be in securing orders and the uncertainty surrounding the Peruvian government's attitude, a safe strategy seemed to be to try and get as large a front-end fee as possible. Almost arbitrarily, a figure of $400,000 was thrown out. (That amount was roughly 150 percent of the development costs plus the initial costs of transferring the technology to the licensee.) There would be sufficient margin for negotiations and uncertainties. To ensure that the licensee's competitiveness would not be diminished by the large lump-sum fee, a formula might be devised whereby the first five years' royalties could be reduced. (See below.)

The Formal Offer

The formal offer communicated in a telex a week later called for the following payment terms:

- $400,000 lump-sum fee payable in two installments.
- A 2 percent royalty on any tanks constructed of

a size over 100-foot diameter, with up to one-half of royalties owed in each of the first five years reduced by an amount up to $40,000 each year, without carryovers from year to year. The royalty percentage would apply to the total contract value less excavation, foundation, dikes, piping, instrumentation, and pumps.

- Agreement life of 10 years.
- Metro to provide services to Impecina described in paragraph (1.a) above, in consideration of the lump-sum and royalty fees.
- For additional services, described in (1.b) above, Metro would provide, on request, personnel at up to $225 per day plus travel and living costs while away from their place of business. The per diem rates would be subject to escalation based on a representative cost index. There would be a ceiling placed on the number of workdays Impecina could request in any year.
- All payments to be made in U.S. dollars net after all local withholding and other taxes.
- Impecina would receive exclusive rights for Peru and Colombia only and nonexclusive rights for Morocco, Libya, Algeria, Argentina, Venezuela, Brazil, and Colombia. Those rights could be converted to an exclusive basis upon demonstration of sufficient business in the future. For Peru and Colombia, Metro would reserve the right to treat the agreement as nonexclusive if Impecina failed to get at least 30 percent of installed capacity of a type covered by the agreement.
- Impecina would have the right to sublicense only to any of its controlled subsidiaries.
- Impecina would supply free of charge to ICE all improvements made on the technology during the term of the agreement.
- Impecina would be entitled to advertise its association with Metro in assigned territories, with prior approval of ICE as to wording, form, and content.

The Final Agreement

ICE executives report that the Peruvians "did not bat an eyelid" at their demands and that an agreement was reached in a matter of weeks. The only significant change was Metro agreeing to take a lump sum of $300,000 (still a large margin over costs). In return, the provision for reducing one-half of the royalties up to $40,000 per year was dropped. The final arrangement called for a straight 2 percent royalty payment (on tank value alone, as before). Other changes were

minor: Impecina to continue to receive the benefit of further R&D; ICE to provide, at cost, a construction engineer if specialized welding equipment were used; the per diem fee fixed at $200 per day (indexed by an average hourly wage escalation factor used by the U.S. Department of Labor); and the $300,000 lump-sum fee to be paid in installments over the first year.

In other respects (territory, royalty rate, exclusivity, travel allowances, etc.), the agreement conformed to Metro's initial offer.

An Upset

The Peruvian government disallowed a ten-year agreement life. By then, both parties had gone too far to want to reopen the entire negotiations. Metro appeared to have resigned itself to an agreement life of five years, with a further extension of another five years subject to mutual consent. Given Impecina's in-house engineering and computer capability, extension of the agreement life was an open question.

QUESTIONS AND RESEARCH

1. Analyze the negotiations from each party's perspective.

2. List what each party was offering and what it hoped to receive.

3. Identify the elements in each list that were musts and those that were flexible, stating why.

4. Compute net cash flows for each party under several scenarios. For example: Licensee fails to get a single order; licensee gets one-third market share in Peru for three years, no orders thereafter, and no orders in any other nation; licensee gets one-third share in Peru for ten years and half again as much in business in other nations.

When computing the licensor's cash flows, remember that, in addition to the direct costs of implementing an agreement, sometimes there are substantial indirect costs. What are they? How would you apply the licensor's development costs to this exercise?

What do you think of the rule of thumb encountered in licensing literature that licensors should settle for roughly one-quarter to one-half of the licensee's incremental profit? Describe negotiating tactics or ploys each party used or could have used. Discuss the role of government intervention in licensing negotiations in general.

1. These negotiations took place between Metro Corporation and Impecina Construcciones S.A. of Peru for the licensing of petroleum tank technology.

Case prepared by Professor Farok Contractor, Rutgers University, as a basis for class discussion rather than to illustrate effective or ineffective handling of an administrative situation. © by Farok J. Contractor. Used with permission.

CHAPTER 9

International Product Policy and Global Branding

The Basic Product and its Attributes

International marketing involves satisfying consumers' needs in foreign markets. The question often asked is, "Can I sell my product in international markets?" A better question would be, "What products should I be selling in international markets?" International product policy should be the cornerstone around which other aspects of the global marketing mix are designed and integrated. Two main questions should be addressed:

- What policies and actions should accompany the marketing of existing products in international markets?

- How can new products be developed for global markets, including domestic and foreign markets?

This chapter looks specifically at companies with existing products and product lines that they seek to market internationally.

The main goals of this chapter are to

- Delineate the influences that lead a company to standardize or adapt its products.

- Discuss the product attributes that are considered, in addition to the basic product itself, in formulating international product policy.

- Discuss the characteristics of a global brand and the approaches to establishing and maintaining a global brand.

- Examine approaches to market segmentation in foreign markets.

A central issue in approaching global markets is whether products sold in the home market should be adapted or standardized for international markets. This issue raises the question of whether a company can successfully design and market a global product. Developing a global brand represents a major challenge, and delineating well-defined international market segments can help in the achievement of successful international marketing. Other issues related to the international product decision are packaging and labeling, brands and trademarks, and warranty and service policies.

Chapter 10 considers complementary aspects of international product policy: (1) new product planning and R&D for international markets and (2) configuration and management of an international product line.

What to Sell Abroad: Product Policy for International Markets

The easiest course for a firm just beginning to go international is to sell in foreign markets the same product designed for the home market. As the firm meets with success in foreign markets, it has two choices to consider: whether to adapt to the point of creating an entirely new product or whether to keep the product the same.

Standardization is more appropriate, of course, when customers are similar overseas and when the standardization can apply to services as well as to products. An interesting example is the Swatch watch collection made by the Swiss company SMH. Inexpensive and mass-produced in Switzerland, the watches are plastic fashion items selling for about $40 worldwide. The product concept involves manufacturing and marketing a striking, low-cost, high-quality watch. The watch is designed to appeal to the low-end segment of the market, accounting for 450 million units out of a total market of 500 million. SMH decided to enter this segment where Swiss companies had zero market share, making and selling an "emotional" product that would allow the wearer to convey an image, a fashion statement.

Two Swatch collections are launched each year, for a total of 140 models. A team of approximately 20 designers from Europe, the United States, Japan, Australia, and elsewhere develop designs that are then culled and presented to a management committee, which selects the items for each season's line. The watches have become collectors' items and are inexpensive enough that an individual can own several—in fact, the average customer in Italy owns six watches.

Having established a brand name and an image, Swatch launched a joint venture with Volkswagen to make a minicar with replaceable panels that permit an ever-changing appearance. Swatch later switched partners, working with DaimlerChrysler. The two-seat Smart, as the Swatchmobile was dubbed, was launched in October 1998 through a limited number of dealers scattered across Europe. The Smart is an ultralight, highly fuel-efficient two-seater, with plastic doors, hoods, and trunks. The lightweight materials allow fuel efficiency to reach nearly 60 miles per gallon. It takes under five hours to assemble a Smart because only a quarter of the Smart's value is added at the assembly stage. Smart's suppliers provide entire subsystems as modules, even installing the module—be it the door, front end or dashboard. The suppliers are also given development responsibility for their subsystem. Thus, Daimler becomes a coordinator of a factory network, acting as an integrator. The Smart was marketed as the ideal city car for old European cities with narrow streets and relatively compact city centers.[1]

Another innovative idea by Swatch involved adding a microchip to its watches. Doing so allowed the Swatch to be used as a "credit-card on the wrist." The watch could serve as a pass at ski resorts, as a pass to gain access to a variety of city attractions such as museums, and as a pass to events such as rock concerts. It was used at the XVI Commonwealth Games in Kuala Lumpur as the official timekeeper and as a means of access to VIP areas, adding further to the distinctive Swatch brand image.

Table 9-1. Factors Favoring Product Standardization versus Adaptation

Standardization
- High costs of adaptation
- Primarily industrial products
- Convergence and similar tastes in diverse country markets
- Predominant use in urban environments
- Marketing to predominantly similar countries (that is, the triad economies)
- Centralized management of international operations when mode of entry is mainly exports
- Strong country-of-origin image and effect
- Scale economies in production, marketing, and R&D
- Standardized products marketed by competitors

Adaptation
- Differences in technical standards
- Primarily consumer and personal-use products
- Variations in consumer needs
- Variations in conditions of use
- Variations in ability to buy—differences in income levels
- Fragmentation, with independent national subsidiaries
- Strong cultural differences, language, etc., affecting purchase and use
- Local environment-induced adaptation: differences in raw materials available and government-required standards and regulations
- Adaptation strategy successfully used by competitors

Adaptation versus Standardization of the Product

Table 9-1 summarizes the main factors that influence a firm to pursue standardization or adaptation strategies when introducing products into new international markets. The goals of reducing costs and complexity lead companies to consider standardization, while a customer orientation sways them toward product adaptation.

Factors Encouraging Standardization

The attractions of standardization are obvious. It can result in lower costs and economies of scale in manufacturing, product development, and marketing. Managerial complexity is reduced, and export marketing is facilitated when the same product is exported to several countries.

HIGH COSTS OF ADAPTATION

Low-volume markets and the specific nature of the adaptation contemplated can contribute to an increase in overall manufacturing costs. The result makes it difficult to sell the product at a reasonable price (that covers costs) and yet be attractive enough to garner market share and ultimately render profits. In the case of washing machines and dryers, Whirlpool found that the colder Scandinavian countries required more powerful heating elements to dry clothes compared to Italy, where it was common to hang clothes out to dry, especially in good weather. Adding a different drying module raised costs and made the dryers less competitive, especially when European economies experienced a slowdown in their economic growth.

INDUSTRIAL PRODUCTS

Products for which technical specifications are critical tend to be uniform internationally. In general, industrial goods are more standardized than consumer goods. Even when industrial goods are modified, the changes are likely to be minor—an adaptation of the electric voltage or the use of metric measures, for example. Of course, differences may be forced on a company by distinct and different national standards in areas such as environmental protection. Differences that are significant enough to encourage adaptation are "people differences"; that is, cultural differences.

CONVERGENCE AND SIMILAR TASTES IN DIVERSE COUNTRY MARKETS

As countries obtain similar income levels and develop at the same pace economically, their consumption patterns are likely to converge. Europe is a good example of this trend, with the creation of the EU and the euro resulting in a single large market with growing similarity of tastes and incomes. This convergence of consumption patterns allows firms to sell products that are standardized for much of Europe. To succeed, of course, the standardized products must offer value beyond that available from the competition.

Levitt sees globalization succeeding because of the appeal of lower prices coupled with world-standard technology, quality, and service—all of which persuade consumers to drop local preferences. Global competition spells the end of domestic territoriality. When a global producer offers lower costs internationally, patronage expands exponentially. The producer not only reaches into distant markets, but also attracts customers who previously held to local preferences and now capitulate to the attractions of lower prices.[2]

Washing Machines in Europe

An example of such convergence behavior again comes from the European washing machine industry. Marketing research conducted by Hoover, a major producer of washing machines, showed that consumers from various European countries had distinct preferences. With regard to dimensions, Italians wanted a shorter machine, while most others wanted a 34-inch height. The French, Italians, and British opted for a narrow machine and enamel drums; but West Germans and Swedes wanted a wide machine and stainless steel drums. The British wanted a top-loading feature, but the others preferred front-loading washing machines. With regard to washing machine capacity, Italians wanted 4 kilos, the British and French wanted 5 kilos, and West Germans and Swedes expressed a need for 6 kilos. Spin speed ranged from a preference for 60 rpm in France to medium speed (400 rpm) in Italy to high speed (700 to 850 rpm) in Britain, Sweden, and Germany. The British and Swedes did not want a water-heating module in the washing machine (because their homes have central hot water); but Italians, Germans, and the French did want that feature. The French and British preferred an agitator washing action; the others wanted a tumble washing action. Each country also had a distinct preference with regard to external styling: British respondents wanted an inconspicuous appearance, Italians wanted brightly colored machines, Germans wanted an indestructible appearance, the French opted for elegance, and the Swedes preferred a "strong" appearance.[3] However, to satisfy national preferences, implementing changes to the machine produced in England would have increased cost by about $18 per unit, as well as required an investment of additional capital.

Research also showed that both the heavily promoted top-of-the-line German washing machine and the inexpensive Italian machine at half the price were best sellers. In fact, the Italian machine was selling well to the German market. Levitt inferred from this that an aggressively promoted, low-priced washing machine with standard features would be the correct product choice. He noted, "Two things clearly influenced customers to buy: low price regardless of feature preferences, and heavy promotion regardless of price." That means the low price can convince customers to accept the absence of certain features. Low price alone is not enough, however. Aggressive promotion, quality, and service are equally important ingredients of the marketing mix.

Washing Machines for Emerging Markets: "The People's Washing Machine"[4]

Whirlpool launched its people's washing machine project with the goal of developing an affordable washing machine for low-income consumers in developing countries. The price had to be between $150 and $200, with initial markets of focus being Brazil, India, and China. About 25 percent of Brazilian households have a washing machine, with penetration rates in China of 8 percent and in India of 4.5 percent. Whirlpool chose to design the low-cost machine in Brazil, and then roll it out, with modifications, to China, India, and other developing countries.

With the average Brazilian worker making $220 a month, Whirlpool decided to develop a new washing machine from scratch, talking to Brazilian households and forming focus groups. A technological (and cost-reducing) innovation was a single-drive system whereby clothes are washed and spun without switching gears. While clothes might emerge somewhat damp, consumers can accept that trade-off. Another modification to lower costs included a smaller capacity of 9 pounds—acceptable to Brazilians since they did laundry more frequently. Further, Brazilians preferred a machine that sat on legs so they could clean the floor underneath; they also wanted a long soak cycle, which was the preferred Brazilian method to get clothes clean. They wanted a transparent acrylic lid so they could see the machine operate. White was the preferred color, but with bold styling.

When taking the machine to the Chinese market, designers incorporated folding lids so the Chinese user could hang shelves above the washer. Gray and green were the preferred colors, and the machine had to look attractive. (It was often kept in living areas since Chinese flats were small.) Special features requested were a grease removal option (many Chinese rode bicycles, which left grease marks on their trousers) and many different rinse options. When sold in India, the machine had to have a sari cycle, with the ability to wash 6 yards of delicate fabric. The Indian version offered castors so the machine could be wheeled from the living area to the washing area.

Hoover's and Whirlpool's experiences with washing machines suggest that standardization can work as part of a well-thought-out marketing mix. Judicious adaptation is sometimes necessary because of local market considerations. Standardization probably works best with products that do not directly influence a consumer's well-being. Products such as clothing, food items, cosmetics, and footwear may be less amenable to standardization than industrial products and machines. Standardization is probably foolhardy for food products.

An opposite and extreme reaction to standardization is the concept of mass customization. The idea here is to make individually customized products at the low cost of standardized mass-produced goods. This can be accomplished through modularity, with different processes and tasks coming together in a dynamic, changing fashion to accommodate the needs of different customers. Therefore, an organization is constantly developing new products. Companies such as Toyota are at the forefront of this mass customization drive, evolving from the continuous improvement approach typical of Japanese organizations. Mass customization also requires organizational changes, flexible and quick response teams, as well as information systems and computer networks to bring together product design teams to fit changing customer demands and to monitor progress toward meeting customers' needs.[5] That philosophy is captured in Nissan's motto for the year 2000: "Five A's—any volume, anytime, anybody, anywhere, anything."

PREDOMINANT USE IN URBAN ENVIRONMENTS

An intriguing study by Hill and Still showed that products targeted to urban markets in developing countries required only minimal changes from those products marketed in developed countries. Products targeted for semiurban markets required more changes. Products targeted for national markets in developing countries needed even further adaptation to accommodate the requirements of the poorer, more culturally diverse population. These three levels of product adaptation were identified through a study of 61 subsidiaries operating in 22 less developed countries.[6] This suggests that urban environments are similar across countries. It also suggests that products such as compact cars, which are designed to be used primarily in large cities, could be standardized across groups of countries that share similar levels of income and economic development.

MARKETING TO PREDOMINANTLY SIMILAR COUNTRIES

As suggested in Chapter 7, cluster analysis groups similar countries on a number of aspects. Using the results of cluster analysis, firms can market standardized products within groups of similar countries. The aspects used to group countries vary depending on the product and include variables such as income, language, degree of urbanization, and phone penetration.

CENTRALIZED MANAGEMENT AND OPERATING VIA EXPORTS

If a firm markets overseas principally through exports, it is likely to sell standardized products. There are two reasons a firm might choose export markets that are more likely to accept standardized products: the costs of adaptation and the lack of detailed knowledge about differences between consumers in the export markets.

COUNTRY OF ORIGIN EFFECTS

Items considered to be typical U.S. products might advantageously retain their U.S. character in foreign markets. Wrigley's chewing gum, Coca-Cola, and Levis are examples, as are French products such as perfumes and women's fashion clothing. Electronic products, cameras, and small cars seem to benefit from a Japanese home-country image. In those cases, firms may experience real gains from selling standardized products the same way they its sell the products in their home markets.

ECONOMIES OF SCALE IN PRODUCTION

Standardizing a product at a production site allows a firm to gain scale economies in manufacturing. As a company multiplies production facilities around the world, that advantage decreases. Similarly, as the output of an optimum-sized plant becomes a smaller proportion of world demand, pressure toward product uniformity decreases.

ECONOMIES OF SCALE IN RESEARCH AND DEVELOPMENT SPENDING

If a firm offers an identical product around the world, it gets more mileage out of its R&D efforts. Less research is directed toward the individual desires of national markets, allowing efforts to be focused on the development of the next-generation product. Thus, standardized products yield an advantage in product-development costs and may shorten the time to develop new products.

ECONOMIES OF SCALE IN MARKETING

Even when marketing is done on a national basis, economies of scale are possible with standardized products. Sales literature, sales force training, and advertising may vary somewhat from country to country; but they will be more similar when the product is uniform than when it must be adapted for different national markets. Satisfying after-sales service requirements and stocking spare parts inventories are easier with a standardized product. When a promotional carryover from one market to another occurs because of common language and media spillover, the carryover is not wasted, but is an extra return on the advertising.

Factors Encouraging Adaptation

The greatest argument for adapting products is that by doing so, a firm can realize higher profits. Modifying products for national or regional markets may raise revenues by more than the costs of adaptation. Specific factors encouraging product adaptation include differences in technical standards, products intended for consumer and personal use, variations in consumer needs and consumer use conditions, different income levels, independent national marketing subsidiaries, cultural differences, and government regulations.

DIFFERENCES IN TECHNICAL STANDARDS

Firms must meet technical standards to sell in different national markets. For example, agricultural products sold into the United States must meet guidelines for maximum levels of chemical additives and fertilizers used in growing the products. Europe has restrictions on the sale of beef from cows treated with growth hormones.

CONSUMER AND PERSONAL USE PRODUCTS

Products sold for personal use are likely to be successful when adapted to local markets. Products such as food, clothing, and entertainment cater to highly individualistic tastes and, hence, must be adapted to the differing needs of local populations. For example, Coca-Cola found itself losing market share in Japan to companies marketing a variety of new soft drinks: sugarless blended Asian teas, fermented milk drinks, and fruit-flavored noncarbonated drinks with less sugar. Rather than stick with its cola soft drinks, Coca-Cola began imitating its Japanese competitors. It offered its own version of Asian tea under the brand name Sokenbicha and its fermented milk drink called Lactia to compete against Calpis's Calpis Water. As a result, Coca-Cola's newer drinks outsold traditional cola drinks by a 3:2 margin. Coca-Cola was able to push its late-entry competing drinks in Japan because it controlled over 40 percent of Japan's vending machines, which are found on nearly every street corner and train platform. It could stock its drinks in the vending machines, bypass Japan's inefficient and tightly controlled traditional hierarchical distribution system, and use its advertising and marketing clout to win back younger customers who had been forsaking cola drinks for the newer variety of beverages.[7]

VARIATION IN CONSUMER NEEDS AND DIFFERING USE CONDITIONS

Although a given product can fulfill a similar functional need in various countries, the conditions under which the product is used may vary greatly from country to country. Climate, for instance, has an effect on products sensitive to temperature or humidity, making it necessary to modify these products for tropical or arctic markets. Consider, for example, the differences in oil drilling in the Sahara compared with offshore drilling in Alaska. Another factor is the difference in the skill level of users, especially between consumers in industrialized nations and those in less developed countries. With regard to cars, trucks, and tires, different road and traffic conditions may require product changes.

Variations in national habits of wearing and washing clothes may necessitate different kinds of washing machines or soaps and detergents, for example. In some countries, clothes are worn longer between washings than they are in the United States. Thus, a different washing process is needed. In some European countries, boiling water is used for washing; so the washing machine must have a special heater built in. In many countries, washing is done with tap water, in a bucket, or by a stream—not within some closed machine or container. To meet those needs, Procter & Gamble and Unilever sell soap and detergent bars.

The importance of use conditions is apparent for European car manufacturers. An American family may own multiple cars—a minivan for weekend family trips and a small car for the daily commute to work. Both the United States and Japan have speed limits, so that cars typically travel at 55 to 75 miles per hour on highways. Europe's laws are different, however, with speeds allowed in excess of 100 miles per hour on German highways, for example. A single car may be owned but commonly used for multiple purposes. Moreover, buyers of small cars are demanding luxury features traditionally found in bigger cars. In response, manufacturers intending to sell cars in Europe are trying to develop products for what they perceive to be distinct segments. Ford envisages four segments: traditionalists, who look for wood and leather in their cars; environmentalists; "life survivors," who seek the cheapest options; and adventurers, who like cars and pick them to match their self-image. Other companies such as Volkswagen, Peugeot, and BMW rely on a corporate brand image because their studies show that buyers of their "brand" of cars are loyal repeat buyers. All of the branding and niche adaptation may not be enough, however. The reason is because of a global automobile market where production capacity and supply exceed demand and new sources of competition are emerging from China and India, in addition to intensifying competition from Japan and Korea.

VARIATIONS IN ABILITY TO BUY— DIFFERENT INCOME LEVELS

The income per capita of the world's nations ranges from over $40,000 to under $1,000. This range affects not only the demand for consumer durables but also for inexpensive consumer products. Product features may have to be adapted to make a product affordable at lower income lev-

els. In Western countries with high incomes, bicycles are leisure products and consumers look for advanced features such as lightweight alloys, a large number of gears, and detachable wheels. All of those features add to the cost of the bicycle, with the average price hovering around $400 for a higher-end bicycle. In contrast, bicycles are used as basic transportation in countries such as China. Bicycles there are heavy, rugged machines, with an average selling price of under $50. Similarly, developing countries can best afford small cars that sell for less than $10,000, with a desirable price point perhaps being as low as under $5,000.[8] In India, government officials have challenged auto manufacturers to launch cars with a price of 100,000 rupees, under $2,500!

FRAGMENTED INDEPENDENT NATIONAL SUBSIDIARIES

Many firms have developed their international operations under a culture of decentralization and local autonomy. As a result, their foreign subsidiaries act as self-contained national operations. Many of those foreign subsidiaries develop products for their markets without regard to international product uniformity within the company. Those subsidiaries have grown accustomed to their independence and may press to be allowed to develop their own national products, even when standardized product development is the best course of action. Some multinationals may deliberately follow a policy of decentralization as a fundamental aspect of their overall strategy. In those cases, product adaptation is likely to be the norm.

When Ford sought to develop its world car, the Focus, it had to merge product development units in North America and Europe. The reorganization required fiercely independent national teams to agree to begin cooperating and to shed some of their autonomy.[9] A firm that has production facilities in several countries can adapt its products more easily than a firm that must rely on exports from domestic plants. National subsidiaries also can exert pressure on the parent firm to localize products. Because national subsidiaries are interested in profits, they seek the product that will sell best in their market. And because they want to prevent having their functions taken over by a headquarters office, they try to be as "national" as possible.

THE IMPACT OF CULTURAL DIFFERENCES

Cultural differences affect tastes, the acceptance of products, and consumption habits. Food is an area in which cultural differences dominate. Introducing food products into foreign markets when the food is unknown to the population can be challenging. Of course, over the past four decades, U.S. consumers have embraced Chinese and Thai foods and Mexican hot sauces; so gradually refining consumer tastes is possible.

Such a challenge faces Ocean Spray, a marketing cooperative that has begun marketing cranberry fruit-based drinks to world markets. Since cranberry juice has an unusual, almost astringent aftertaste, Ocean Spray must follow a patient strategy of giving away free samples, letting consumers taste the juice. In the United Kingdom, for example, Ocean Spray began mixing cranberry juice with black currant juice. The company has also publicized the health benefits of the cranberry (based on a Harvard University study indicating that cranberry juice helps fight urinary tract infections). Additionally, Ocean Spray has used influential opinion shapers such as Australian chef Iain Hewitson to cook with cranberry sauce on their TV shows. Ocean Spray hopes to convince customers to try and repeatedly use cranberry juice.[10]

ENVIRONMENTALLY INDUCED ADAPTATION: THE INFLUENCE OF GOVERNMENTS

Nations may forbid certain goods to be imported or manufactured in their country. Conversely, they may require that a product be manufactured locally, not imported. Demand for local production or a high degree of "local content" in a product will often lead an international firm to modify the product. A government's taxation policies can affect the nature of products offered in the market. An example is the European tax on car and engine size that has been a predominant influence on European car design.

Product adaptations may be required by local market regulations. Islam, for example, prohibits the consumption of alcohol. European and U.S. firms have been attempting to sell nonalcoholic beer in the Middle East, targeting Saudi Arabia, a hot, dry desert country. While Western nonalcoholic beer typically contains about 0.5 percent alcohol, nonalcoholic beer sold in Saudi Arabia must be totally alcohol-free; this requires reformulation and special manufacturing. To avoid using the word beer, the drink is called a malt beverage and cannot be advertised. Therefore, marketers must rely on in-store promotions and contests. The target market segment is younger Saudis who have traveled and perhaps lived abroad. Saudi Arabia is a potential future market that attracts many Western firms.[11]

Government regulations on products, packaging, and labeling are an important cause of product variation among countries, especially in food and drugs. Italy, for example, allows only spaghetti made from durum wheat to be called pasta. Government specifications affect some industrial goods, too. Trucks, tractors, and tires often must meet different government specifications in different markets.

The rise of regional groupings provides a modifying influence, but the differences do not disappear rapidly as long as national producers find government regulations to be an effective form of protection against foreign firms.

CORPORATE STRATEGY AND COMPETITIVE ACTIONS

A different approach to the standardization versus adaptation debate is to consider successful firms, understanding what they did and how their success was influenced by their strategic choices. One study looked specifically at what determined product adaptation and promotion adaptation in export operations, considering variables such as packaging, labeling, product positioning, and promotional approach.[12] The researchers suggest that company characteristics, product and industry characteristics, and specific features of the export market all determine the extent of product and promotion adaptation. That approach is set out in Figure 9-1.

Figure 9-1. A Testable Framework of Product and Promotion Adaptation

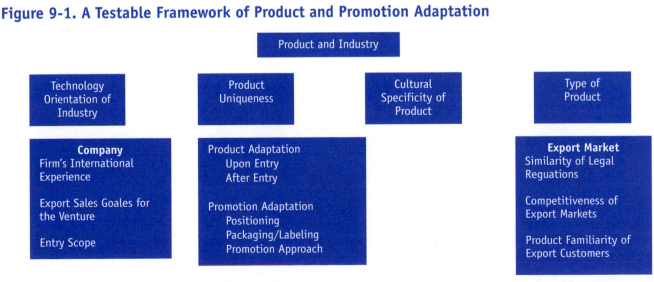

Source: S. T. Cavusgil, Shaoming Zou, and G. M. Naidu, "Product and Promotion Adaptation in Export Ventures: An Empirical Investigation," *Journal of International Business Studies* (24)3, 1993, page 485.

Factors Governing Product Adaptation

From the foregoing examples, variables that tend to foster product adaptation can be summarized as follows:

1. Most important are variations in customer needs, conditions of use, and ability to buy. They can influence adaptation in the basic product and its attributes and features, as well as in ancillary areas such as packaging.

2. Next in importance are market idiosyncrasies, such as different technical standards. A similar thrust toward adaptation is created by the existence of different languages, as illustrated by the Windows operating system software adaptation for Asian markets.

3. If competition has introduced adapted products that are well received, a similar response might be tactically correct.

4. If the costs of adaptation are not high, adaptation is more likely. Thus, because of its high R&D costs, a high-tech product may be adapted less than another type of product.

5. Local production parameters such as available raw materials, skill level of labor force, and nature of equipment might force adaptation when local manufacturing is required to enter the market.

6. Government regulations leading to differences in standards might also force product adaptation. Thus, cars imported into the United States must meet its emission controls. This is one reason why companies such as Renault and Peugeot do not sell in the United States.

7. Cultural preferences are an important reason for adaptation, especially in personal-use products such as clothing and food and in products or services for which design and taste are prominent.

Global Branding

Sooner or later the international marketing manager has to decide how important branding will be in the overall marketing mix. Brands allow for differentiation and premium pricing; and they create customer loyalty, leading to repeat purchases. Further, the profits from premium pricing, coupled with steady market share and repeat purchases, result in measurable cash flow, which is at the heart of brand equity calculations. Since acquiring customers is costly for a firm, loyal customers who buy regularly are valuable.

The Relevance of Brands

Once developed and recognized, a brand can have a long life. Major brands such as Lipton, Ivory, Gillette, and Coca-Cola have been popular for over 70 years. A big question, then, is how to build brand recognition in international markets. Brands can be built up through advertising; but advertising merely builds on the brand's foundation, which rests on quality, innovation, superior service, customer satisfaction, and value. With regard to consumer products, brand personality is also relevant; namely, how a brand creates and reinforces a buyer's self-image in products such as designer clothing brands, cars, and shoes. Furthermore, brands provide customers with a guarantee of value and quality, making customers' choices easy. It frees them from the confusion and message fatigue endemic to a competitive marketplace. Brands become a shortcut to consumption, allowing customers to make safe choices. Customers are secure in knowing that by purchasing the brand, satisfaction and value will result. Conversely, breaking this compact with the customer can quickly result in a brand's decline.

But developing and maintaining a brand's position is costly, particularly as the number of major international markets proliferate. A manager has to decide:

- Whether to aim for a global brand for the product and product line.
- Whether to offer one international brand or different national brands for a given product.
- What the role of private branding is in international marketing.
- Whether to use multiple brands in the same market to target different customer segments (though this results in higher costs).

The main question is whether to promote local country-specific brands or to establish global and regional brands with appeal across countries.[13] Table 9-2 sets out the major branding choices in international marketing and summarizes their advantages and disadvantages.

Global Brands: Why the Move to Global Brands?[15]

"A brand is a promise that has to be fulfilled everywhere, at any time."[15]

Building a global brand is inherent in marketing a standardized product. Its success depends on a growing convergence of consumer tastes and the coordination of global advertising and promotion. Mass media and telecommunications make it easy to communicate a single message simultaneously, effectively, and efficiently to a large num-

Table 9-2. A Perspective on Branding

Advantages	Disadvantages
NO BRAND	
Lower production cost	Severe price competition
Lower marketing cost	Lack of market identity
Lower legal cost	
Flexible quality and quantity control	
BRANDING	
Better identification and awareness	Higher production cost
Better chance for product differentiation	Higher marketing cost
Possible brand loyalty	Higher legal cost
Possible premium pricing	
PRIVATE BRAND	
Better margins for dealers	Severe price competition
Possibility of larger market share	Lack of market identity
No promotional problems	
MANUFACTURER'S BRAND	
Better price due to more price inelasticity	Difficulty for small manufacturer with unknown brand or identity
Retention of brand loyalty	
Better bargaining power	Brand promotion required
Better control of distribution	
MULTIPLE BRANDS (IN ONE MARKET)	
Market segmented for varying needs	Higher marketing cost
Creation of competitive spirit	Higher inventory cost
Lower inventory cost	Loss of economies of scale
Avoidance of negative connotation of existing brand	
More retail shelf space gained	
No damage to existing brand's image	
SINGLE BRAND (IN ONE MARKET)	
Marketing efficiency	Market homogeneity assumed
More focused marketing permitted	Harm to existing brand's image when trading up/down
Elimination of brand confusion	Limited shelf space
Advantage for product with good reputation (halo effect)	
LOCAL BRANDS	
Meaningful names	Higher marketing cost
Local identification	Higher inventory cost
Avoidance of taxation on international brand	Loss of economies of scale
Quick market penetration by acquisition of local brand	Diffused image
Variations of quantity and quality across markets allowed	
WORLDWIDE BRAND	
Maximum marketing efficiency	Market homogeneity assumed
Reduction of advertising costs	Problems with black and gray markets
Elimination of brand confusion	Possibility of negative connotation
Advantage for culture-free product	Quality and quantity consistency required
Advantage for prestigious product	LDCs' opposition and resentment
Easy identification/recognition for international travelers	Legal complications
Worldwide uniform image	

Source: Sak Onkvisit and John J. Shaw, "The International Dimension of Branding," *International Marketing Review* (6)3, 1989, Table 1, 24.

ber of geographically dispersed markets; for example, the simultaneous transmission of the Summer Olympics around the world. In such cases, because the same transmission is received around the world, firms benefit when the brands featured are familiar to the entire audience. Also, the growing importance of the youth market and its convergence of tastes and purchasing power motivate a reliance on global brands. Global branding also offers the emotional value of identifying with a well-known global brand to people who want to belong to a group that cuts across countries. Global branding can also be cost-effective, providing economies of scale by reaching a large number of potential consumers with the same message. In addition, a global brand can serve as an umbrella brand, support line extensions, and lend a halo to local and national brands intended for a different market segment. For all of those reasons, MNCs need both a global brand and a local brand. Further, the overall quality of the global brand-based marketing campaign can benefit from cross-border learning by transferring successful best practices and approaches from one market to another. This is possible because all markets are based on the same global brand.

The advantages of global branding include economies of scale in advertising. The uniform image can appeal to globe-trotting consumers. Global brands are also important in securing access to distribution channels. In cases where shelf space is at a premium, as with food products, a company has to convince retailers to carry its products rather than those of competitors. Having a global brand may help persuade retailers because, from the retailers' standpoint, a global brand is less likely to languish on the shelves. Finally, a hidden benefit of a global brand is that it adds to the reputation and image of the company, makes the company better known, and may help attract marketing managers and other executives who want to work for a global company.

What Characterizes a Global Brand?

There are seven common features to a global brand, as follows:

- The brand is strong in the home market. That strength and cash flow from repeat sales funds the push into new foreign markets and the investment in creating a global brand.
- Geographic balance exists; that is, the brand has reasonable levels of sales in the key markets of North America, Europe, Japan, and Asia-Pacific. A brand cannot be considered global unless people in different parts of the world have heard of it.
- The product addresses a similar need worldwide, providing a basis for a standardized message delivered globally.
- Every global brand has a country of origin that is part of the global brand's identity. If consumers do

not place high value on a brand's country of origin, a firm will have difficulty creating a strong intangible attribute for the brand.
- The brand's main focus is on a single broad product category, such as IBM, Coca-Cola, Sony, and BMW.
- Consistent positioning occurs so the brand represents the same set of practical and emotional attributes everywhere.
- There is a link to the corporate brand, with the global brand name and the corporate brand often being the same.

How to Build a Global Brand?

As Figure 9-2 suggests, a global brand follows standard, uniform brand positioning (and a strategy) across all of its key markets. That is achieved through four building blocks: advertising copy tone and content, brand slogan, brand logo, and brand icons such as packaging. Together the four components form an integrated communication plan that needs to be executed and then maintained over many years (perhaps decades) to build on the global brand. The communication plan is then linked to users and desired users: who they are, how they look and behave, and in what situations the product or service is used. As Figure 9-2 illustrates, heritage, quality, user images, and user situations stress the enduring values that must be associated with a brand in order to build a bond with the customer, leading to brand loyalty, repeat purchases, and the long-lasting value of a global brand.

Relationship with Advertising Agencies

For a global brand, it may be easier to deal with a single advertising agency that has a global network and thus can help implement and deliver a global branding strategy and the related global advertising campaign. Using one agency may help get some of its best talent committed to the global campaign. However, when a product is adapted to a local market or region, it may be prudent to employ a local agency that will work in combination with the lead agency.

WHAT PRODUCTS ARE MOST SUITED TO A GLOBAL BRANDING APPROACH?

Some products, such as food, are harder to brand globally because they are more culturally dependent. Industrial products with relative product uniformity more easily lend themselves to global advertising. So, too, does the luxury goods market, where consumers are a select upper income group that cuts across country markets to form a distinct multicountry segment.

Figure 9-2. Building Global Brands

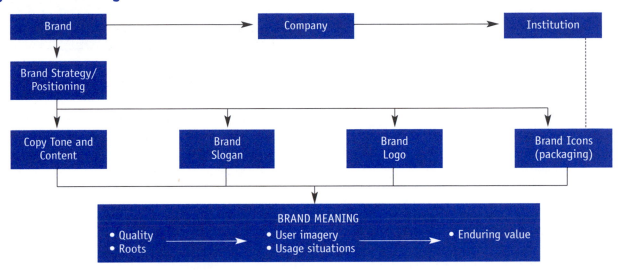

Source: John Quelch, "Global Brands: Taking Stock," *Business Strategy Review* 10(1), Spring 1999, Figure 1, page 5.

DANGERS OF GLOBAL BRANDING

Global branding does have some negatives. Managers, particularly in subsidiaries, may complain about too much standardization, rigid control from headquarters, and the inability to make allowances for the stage of market growth in each country (proving that there may be a divergence between the country's market evolution and the brand's overall worldwide development). Such possible divergence is particularly important when an established global brand begins entering emerging markets such as India or China. A firm may also have difficulty imposing the same brand image that underlies the global brand campaign in all markets. Markets in developing countries may want more practical attributes stressed; while higher-income markets may welcome a campaign built around intangible attributes that stress status, style, and well-being.

VARYING BRAND IMAGE

In developing global brands, a marketing manager has to decide what brand image to project across markets. For example, Reebok blends lifestyle and athletic prowess in its U.S. ads, while its European image is focused mainly on athletics.

To learn more about brand image, Roth examined the links between a country market's cultural and socioeconomic factors and the nature of brand image chosen, whether functional or sensory.[16] He then related those choices to product performance in the market, after adjusting for a firm's experience with the market, the nature of competition, and the choices made by the firm across the marketing mix. He found that in countries such as China, France, and Belgium, where the degree of separation between high- and low-power-status individuals is high, brand images should stress social and sensory needs. Similarly, in countries where individualism is low, as in much of Asia, brand images that stress group membership and affiliation are likely to be more successful.

Creative approaches to building brand recognition are helpful. A distributor of British skiwear, Nevica USA, offered photographers free skiwear and a fee each time one of their photographs was published in a ski magazine showing Nevica-clad skiers. Similarly, Franklin Sports Industries built name recognition by giving batting gloves to baseball players. The Franklin name appeared in large letters on the back of the gloves, making them visible to TV viewers when a camera focused on a batter. When photographs of batters appeared in newspapers or on the cover of magazines such as Sports Illustrated, the Franklin name was often visible.

A Brand's "Image Power"

Landor Associates, in association with Louis Harris Associates, has been conducting "image power" surveys for over a decade. Image power is a way to measure a brand's strength, developed by combining five separate elements:
- Share of mind (awareness and familiarity)
- Share of heart (high regard)
- Value (value for money)
- Momentum (potential for future growth or success)
- Singularity (business choice)

An ImagePower Index of 100 represents perfect brand strength (100 percent share of mind, share of heart, value, momentum, and singularity). On the other hand, an ImagePower Index of 0 represents no brand strength (0 percent share of mind, share of heart, value, momentum, and singularity). Table 9-3 reports the results of an Image Power survey.

Table 9-3 concerns only U.S. firms and focuses solely on industrial marketing, which is why familiar names such as Coca-Cola, Daimler-Benz, Gillette, and Sony do not appear. (Different companies would appear on the list depending on the nature of the survey and in which countries the surveys are done.) Such surveys are helpful in understanding the power of brands and in determining the value of brands—brand equity. For instance, a survey of Latin American brands shows that brands from companies such as Bimbo (Mexico: bread and snacks), Brahma (Brazil: beer) and Maseca (Mexico: tortillas and corn flour) enjoy high recognition and sustainability.[17] A Gallup sur-

Table 9-3. Landor Associates U.S. Business-to-Business ImagePower Survey, 1998

	Image Power Rank
Microsoft	84
U.S. Postal Service	41
UPS	72
Hewlett-Packard	40
VISA	72
Delta Airlines	39
AT&T	71
Compaq	37
FedEx	67
Dell Computer	36
Xerox	64
Chase	36
IBM	57
MCI	36
Master Card	53
Southwest Airlines	36
American Express	51
Citibank	34
Hertz	47
American Airlines	33
Canon	47
Novell	33
Marriott Hotels	45
Budget Rent a Car	32
Anderson Consulting	44
Allstate Insurance	32
State Farm Insurance	44
Pitney Bowes	32
Avis	42
Holiday Inn	31

Source: Landor Associates web site (http://www.landor.com).

GLOBAL MARKETING

LEGO's Brands

LEGO was awash in a variety of products and market segments. It had developed numerous line extensions, including clothing, shoes, and amusement parks. Since the company was incurring losses, it decided to restructure its brand architecture and product portfolio. LEGO has been known for decades as a toy company, the maker of colorful interlocking bricks that children can turn into creative constructions, including castles, space stations, and pirate islands. Adults all over the world fondly remember LEGO as a source of countless hours of engrossing play. LEGO wanted to draw on that heritage, that nostalgia, and build on it in order to grow and sell its product line into the next decade.

LEGO divided its products into four brand portals as follows:

- *The Explore brand, formerly DUPLO, is aimed at the preschool market.*
- *Make & Create, which is the traditional LEGO brick, constitutes the pure construction category, the roots of the LEGO company. In this segment, children build things and building is playing.*
- *Stories & Action is based on action toys, on story lines and role playing. Children build action figures, the BIONICLE action figure family, and then play with them. Children can make up stories about the action figures, melding virtual with physical play.*
- *LEGO Next, which is more abstract, allows children to build robots from MINDSTORM kits and then program the robots to determine and control how they will act.*

LEGO has taken pains to get its employees to understand and accept the brand restructuring. The company began with an internal process to gain an understanding of how employees saw the company, what they thought the company stood for. Franco Ciccolella, the senior vice president for global branding, said, "If our (brand) identity was to be the real thing, we had to believe in it first." Only then did LEGO approach consumers to learn about their views of the LEGO brand, bringing the information back to the company to work

continued

with employees on the brand restructuring. Employees went through the "LEGO Brand School," in which they discussed the brand and questioned it, while also getting detailed information on the company's intended approach to branding.

The new brand portfolio facilitates orderly brand extensions. LEGO has taken the BIONICLE brand of action figures into movies with the film BIONICLE: Mask of Light. Few toy firms can take their toys into film; it is usually Hollywood that takes successful films and develops toy action figures from them. Another natural continuation is comic books and trading cards.

An untapped segment for LEGO is girls over the age of six. Below that age, girls and boys are equally drawn to LEGO blocks. After that, girls may be drawn more to fashion, music, and sociable relationship-based toys (although that finding may be the result of toy industry distribution beliefs). But the end result is the same, with boys accounting for over 80 percent of all LEGO customers. Hence, LEGO is launching a female-oriented brand, CLIKITS, a range of arts and crafts materials from which girls can make jewelry, picture frames, and hair and fashion accessories. LEGO is also launching football, basketball, and hockey kits into which children can introduce LEGO figures to simulate games; LEGO has licensed the NBA brand to use with its basketball game. LEGO has licensed the LEGO name for clothing and for a line of BIONICLE shoes with Nike. The shoes have interchangeable masks on the front, like the action figures.

Because the United States is the world's largest toy market, LEGO naturally concentrates on that market, having built its third amusement park in California. However, with Japan

as the second-largest market, LEGO is looking to enter the Japanese market for the long haul. A cultural divide may be at work, however. LEGO construction toys have no rules; children use their creativity to assemble the bricks. LEGO wonders if that approach fits into a culture that emphasizes rules and conformity. Not surprisingly, some of the early adopters of LEGO's newer MINDSTORM line are young Japanese adults.

Learning how to deal with the future is why LEGO started the LEGO Vision Lab—to look into the future by researching families with children, bringing into play ideas from disciplines as varied as sociology, anthropology, architecture, and technology.

A new direction is its Executive Discovery line, which uses LEGO toys in a concept called LEGO SERIOUS PLAY. The bricks are used in executive development seminars to build confidence, develop ideas, stimulate creativity, and enhance team building. LEGO is making LEGO kits available to schools in Moscow and Madrid. However, the company has to balance education with fun. Children have fun with LEGOS and learn at the same time, while parents and adults need reassurance that LEGOs are educational toys.

The toy market is competitive. Large firms such as Mattel, Hasbro, and Bandai sell toys worldwide; makers of video games compete for the time and wallets of children from a very young age. LEGO has to innovate, to market effectively, while keeping at its core the fundamental values of creative play, of fun and education. How LEGO manages its brand, its identity, will affect everything it does in the next few years.

Source: Ruth Mortimer, "Lego: Building a Brand out of Bricks," Brand Strategy, April 2003, pages 16–19.

vey in China found the most popular brands to be Coca-Cola, Head & Shoulders, Honda, Mercedes-Benz, and Pepsi, followed by Philips, Motorola, Daihatsu, Playboy, and Star TV.[18]

Branding and China

China's rapid economic growth has been driven by Chinese manufacturers adept at making a large variety of high-quality, low-cost goods for Western companies in a number of industries. But the manufacturers found that they became dependent on the marketing success of their clients for repeat orders and that margins declined as manufacturing capacity and competition increased. Two solutions that a number of Chinese firms have adopted is to

acquire or license Western brands and to establish direct relationships with retailers such as Wal-Mart and Home Depot.[19]

As an example, Techtronic Industries of Hong Kong used to make vacuum cleaners for the Cleveland, Ohio, U.S.-based Royal Appliance Mfg. Co., which owned the popular Dirt Devil brand. As Royal faced difficulties competing in the United States, it turned to Techtronic for lower-priced products, including the Broom Vac (which sold 800,000 units for $40 apiece via two-minute infomercials advertised during Super Bowl games). When Royal became available for sale, Techtronic had to make a quick decision on whether to acquire Royal, which it did. The U.S. subsidiary now handles most U.S. marketing, but Techtronic's head-office staff in Hong Kong is more involved with product design and marketing. Other brands Techtronic has acquired include Ryobi power tools and Homelite outdoor products from Deere. Techtronic is not unique in this regard, and other companies have similarly acquired or licensed well-known brand names. For instance, Grande Holdings, Ltd., acquired consumer electronic brands, including Nakamichi, Akai, and Sansui.

Of course, acquiring a brand is the first step; companies then have to master marketing, developing relations with retailers, understanding consumers in major Western markets, and coping with ever-changing tastes while taking more risk. Rather than make products for others and let those clients worry about marketing, companies now seek to manufacture and market products, getting higher margins in return. The risk is that they may read the market incorrectly and get stuck holding large amounts of unsalable goods in inventory. The marketing risk is now theirs.

Instead of acquiring brands, Chinese firms can begin to develop their own.[20] Chinese multinationals have begun to develop brand names and capture market share in U.S. and European markets. For example, with its own brand, the Haier Group captured almost half the U.S. market for small refrigerators. Brands have been difficult to establish in China because of regional income disparities, infrastructure inadequacies that make national distribution difficult, and dominance of Chinese markets by state-owned companies. But newer Chinese multinationals, hybrids with a combination of state and private ownership, are developing major international brands. Several different kinds of Chinese companies are developing international brands, as follows:

- National champion companies, which dominate the Chinese market and use this position as a springboard to overseas markets; for example, the Haier Group.
- Dedicated exporters who have developed the necessary scale economies to compete overseas and are now supplementing their manufacturing advantage with brand-based differentiation. Examples include China International Marine Containers, which became the world's largest producer of standard freight containers by 1996, and then, after purchasing Hyundai's refrigerated container manufacturing operations, gradually captured half the world market for refrigerated containers.
- Groups of small entrepreneurial companies located in a specific geographical region of China, such as Guangdong or Zhejiang Province. The companies work together to respond to markets in which demand changes quickly, such as markets in which style affects demand. An example is the shoe cluster located in Wenzhou, in which the companies begin to codesign products with foreign companies, sometimes licensing foreign brands.

- Technology-based companies taking advantage of Chinese government-funded basic research and breakthroughs. Examples are Shanghai HealthDigit, which is commercializing a protein chip to diagnose several types of cancer with a single test, and Beijing Founder Electronics, which dominates the market for electronic systems. By using Chinese characters and drawing on state-funded research and achievements at Beijing University, Beijing Found Electronics has begun to challenge established firms in the high-resolution electronic publishing systems market.

Many of these companies will make mistakes, but will learn from them. The goal is to develop a branded differentiated position that can deliver higher margins and that is defensible in the face of competition. That strategy is strongly supported by Chinese government policies promoting foreign investment, bank credit, and reduction of foreign exchange controls.

The role of brands in shaping preferences among Chinese auto companies is an example of the intricacies of implementing branding policies in an emerging market.[21] Chinese customers differentiate between auto brands, making choices based on both the practical and the emotional or intangible attributes of a brand. Auto firms in China need to understand and exploit those preferences because the market is crowded. More than 24 brands of compact cars are available to a market estimated at 3 million compact cars a year by 2015. Intangible attributes accounted for six of the top ten attributes of an auto brand, as shown in Table 9-4.

At the same time, Chinese consumers are price-sensitive because the price of a car may represent two or three years of income. Hence, branding communications must straddle the line between delivering the price/value mes-

---

Table 9-4. Top Ten Attributes Influencing Car Purchase

1. "For people like me"
2. Attractive styling
3. Friends say it is a good car
4. A pleasure to drive
5. Good maintenance record/ rarely breaks down
6. A good family car
7. Reliable
8. Makes me feel safe
9. Makes me feel attractive/ successful
10. Manufacturer is industry leader

Source: J. Hoffe, K. Lane, and V.M. Nam, "Branding Cars in China," *McKinsey Quarterly*, Number 4, 2003, Ex. 1.

sage and avoiding the possibility that a lower price suggests lower status. As Chinese car ownership is still in its early stages, there is room to create a brand image that can foster brand loyalty. Many Chinese consumers plan or want to trade up to larger cars. This implies that brand messages referring to intangibles such as industry leadership, air of success, and style should cover individual car brands as well as corporate brands. Of course, which brand attributes are important can also change, for example, as more Chinese drive and become aware of the importance of safety features in a car. Auto firms will need a continuous program of market research to keep abreast of changing consumer tastes.

Premium Brands and Low-Priced Competition[22]

In the late 1980s, Peru was under attack from Shining Path guerillas, who often hijacked trucks carrying Coca-Cola soft drinks to retail outlets. A small family business run by the Ananos, which had moved to the city after its family farm had been destroyed by guerillas, began making a soft drink alternative in its backyard and supplying local outlets. From those beginnings emerged Kola Real, a low-priced alternative to Coke. Kola Real has captured a 19 percent market share in Peru (with 10 percent in Ecuador and 4 percent in Mexico)—against Coke's share of 35 percent in Peru, 78 percent in Ecuador, and 70 percent in Mexico.

How did Kola Real make such inroads? Its formula is low prices and big bottles.

Kola Real took advantage of the growth of outlets such as Wal-Mart, which attracts a price-conscious clientele and looks for low-priced products to stock. The advent of plastic bottles also helped, as this lowered the cost of entry and competitors could offer large nonreturnable bottles at low prices.

Kola Real's tactics include:
- Offering value. A bottle of Kola Real's Mexican brand Big Cola sells for $0.75 for a 2.6-liter bottle versus $1.30 for a Coke 2.5-liter bottle.
- Making its own concentrate, while Coke bottlers buy concentrate from Coca-Cola at a cost of about 20 percent of their revenues.
- Utilizing third parties for delivery rather than owning and operating a trucking fleet.
- Doing little advertising, relying on word of mouth from price-conscious house wives.
- Taking advantage of the increasing role of supermarkets in selling soft drinks, obtaining distribution in those outlets.
- Launching more sizes and flavors.

Of course, Coca-Cola does not take this lying down. Mexican per capita consumption of cola drinks is the highest in the world and Coca-Cola bottlers' income from Mexico consistently exceeds a 20 percent return on invested capital. So Coca-Cola fights back by offering incentives to retailers to carry Coke, rewarding points that allow a retailer to "earn" a DVD player, a private refrigerator, or a large-screen TV, for example. Coca-Cola buys insurance for shop owners, offers free classes on how to run a business, and provides several free cases of Coke a year. Coca-Cola also supplies mom-and-pop stores with coolers in which to store Coke, asking the stores not to stock rival drinks in them. These 1 million-plus small outlets account for about 75 percent of Mexico's soft drink sales. Salespeople may also threaten to stop delivery unless stores stop carrying rival Big Cola (though this may break antitrust rules and thus be illegal).

Mexico's antitrust commission has ruled that Coca-Cola was abusing its Mexican dominance of retail channels and had to stop practices designed to keep out competitors, such as using exclusive contracts. Coke now offers returnable plastic bottles, which lowers the final price to price-conscious consumers by 20 percent. Coke's salespeople also help take care of Coke displays in stores, keeping them stacked and clean, something Kola Real and its limited staff cannot do. Private brands and inexpensive rival brands ("B" brands), such as Kola Real and El Gallito from Ecuador, are capturing more market share—in Brazil, the private and "B" brands have captured 30 percent of sales. Profit margins from Coke and other premium brands are also falling as more sales come from supermarket and Wal-Mart-type outlets that can demand lower prices. The heart of Coke is its brand image. That image allows Coca-Cola to charge premium prices for its soft drinks and make profits from its sales of concentrate to bottlers. Those profits, in turn, allow for massive investments in building and maintaining the Coca-Cola brand name and brand equity around the world. With the saturation of both soft drink markets and consumption in countries such as the United States, Coca-Cola has a battle on its hands to maintain dominance in the global soft drink market.

Just as products may have to be adapted for different markets, a global brand campaign may also have to be modified for the needs of consumers, particularly in developing countries. This is outlined in Figure 9-3. A study of global brands' performance problems in developing country markets—ranging from lower-than-expected levels of profitability, lower-than-expected market share, and difficulties in the conversion of customers from competitors' products—showed that those problems may stem from a variety of causes, including poor market assessment and improper communication.[23]

Figure 9-3. Understanding Global Product Brand Performance in Developing Markets

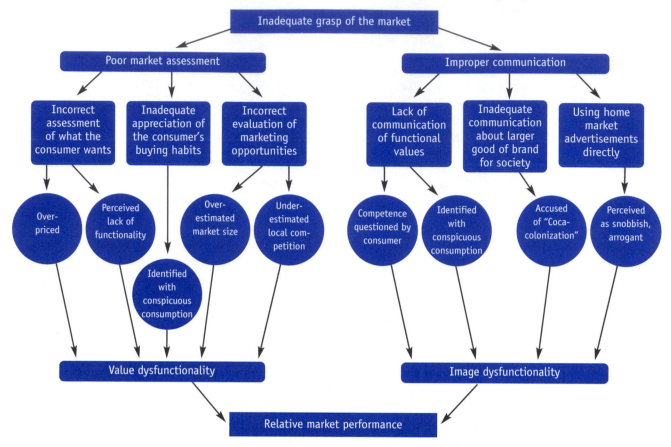

Source: K. L. Keller and Y. L. R. Moorthi, "Branding in Developing Markets," *Business Horizons*, May–June 2003, Figure 1, page 50.

The multinational company may not fully understand consumer needs, such as their overriding desire for value, for functionality, for fair prices. In turn, this lack of understanding affects branding and communication. If a brand focuses on aspirational rather than functional values, it may not communicate with the consumer. For example, aspirational values of Levis jeans may include original, masculine, sexy, youthful, rebellious, individual, free, and American; while functional values might be simple, strong, reliable, and durable. Consumers in developing countries might respond more favorably to the functional values than to the aspirational values. Global brands may also have to fight perceptions that the companies are promoting frivolous or wasteful consumption and that they represent foreign control of the economy rather than positive and socially relevant values.

Implementing Global Branding: Organizational and Team Issues

Successful implementation of a global branding strategy requires an organizational effort, including:[24]

- Procedures to obtain and share insights and best practices from different markets. This means providing motivation for people to share and use information; creating a culture that promotes sharing of information; and utilizing practices such as regular meetings of brand executives, a global branding "university" (such as "Motorola University"), intranets, and field visits, as well as shared international marketing research.
- A global planning process, a set of steps that encompasses the target segment, brand identity, brand equity goals, brand building programs, and

measurements used to judge success and achievements. The process should begin with an analysis of the brand and its associations, as well an analysis of competitors and customers. A brand audit is the starting point. A brand manual for outlining common approaches for communicating brand identity is useful, answering questions such as these: What does the brand stand for? What are the timeless elements of the brand? The brand equity measurement effort should help managers judge the profitability of the global branding effort, a brand-based profit and loss statement that takes into account market share and repeat business. The process should also help tie the global brand effort with steps taken by local managers, thus ensuring consistency and progress.

- Identification of who will be responsible for managing the global branding effort. Companies can and have used many approaches, including creating a Brand Champion, a Global Brand Manager, a Global Brand Team, and a Business Management Team. In the Business Management Team approach, a product category is managed by a team with representatives from R&D, manufacturing, and marketing; whereas the other organizational structures put marketing people in charge.

- A balance of a global approach with departures from the global standard to take into account local differences so as to create "brilliant" global brand efforts.

Brand Extensions

Brand extension allows a firm with an existing presence in overseas markets to quickly establish its new products. Using a well-known brand name with a reputation for quality can extend an aura of high quality to the new product. Brand extension can allow the new product to be introduced with lower incremental advertising expenditures. The comfort level and familiarity associated with a well-known brand can motivate customers to choose the new product over a competitor's. Brand extensions can include launching the same product in a different form, adding a brand name to related products often used together ("companion" products), building on company image and expertise, and communicating unique or designer attributes. However, there are dangers. The original brand and product may be damaged when the brand image is extended to undesirable products and settings. There must be a fit—some complementarity—between the original product and the proposed product/brand extension.[25]

Hewlett-Packard, for one, was successful in extending its brand image to the home computer market. Because Hewlett-Packard's inkjet printers were cheap and allowed low-cost color printing, the company first obtained a foothold in this segment by selling them to home computer users with children. It helped that Japanese firms that dominated the previous generation of dot-matrix printers stuck with them too long, slowing down their entry into the inkjet market because of Hewlett-Packard's strong patent position. With its strong brand association in the home segment due to its printer sales, Hewlett-Packard was able to launch multimedia personal computers intended primarily for the home market. It was able to get retail shelf space because it already supplied retailers with large numbers of inkjet printers. This allowed for the bundling of personal computers with printers. Finally, Hewlett-Packard's size and extended product range in addition to high margins from inkjet cartridge sales meant that the company could undercut home computer prices, even accepting losses in the interest of building long-term market share.[26]

Brand Protection: When and Where?

Given the value of brands, competition may choose to develop their own competitive brands. A shortcut is to copy a brand name, making slight modifications in logo or spelling, in the hope of "free riding", or capturing sales from deceived customers. Those actions hurt the original brand and bring it into disrepute. Hence, managers seeking to develop and maintain global brands must vigorously protect the brands from being copied and pirated. For a firm, brand piracy can result in sales lost to imitators, who are seen as competing unfairly. In turn, the reduced sales and cash flow reduce investment in innovation. Consumers may ultimately suffer from a lack of new high-technology and innovative products. Countries dependent on technology, such as the United States, will see their exports decrease; and job losses can result in the affected industries. U.S. firms will lose overseas sales to foreign companies that copy technology, brand names, or copyrighted material with impunity. In the short run, foreign industry and foreign consumers are the beneficiaries.[27] Overall, welfare worldwide is likely to decline unless regulations allow for a fair return to investments in technology and product differentiation.

Protecting a brand in international markets can begin with registering the brand with the appropriate authorities in the countries of interest. Blanket registration in all countries may be wise when the costs of registration, which can be significant, are within the budgetary means of the firm. Smaller firms may choose to be more selective.

Brand protection can come about through use of the brand name in common law countries or through legal registration of the brand name in code law countries.

However, use should follow registration and vice versa. While a firm must incur registration costs—primarily legal fees and administrative payments—use costs are higher. Use costs involve importing material quantities of a product and the development of distribution channels and marketing campaigns. Less-than-diligent registration and use of a brand name or trademark may result in a firm having to buy back the rights to its name (sometimes at an inflated sum), depending on the emerging market potential in the country.

Another problem is the local reaction to well-known international brands. Phonetic equivalents of English-language brands may not translate well into foreign languages, sometimes resulting in an undesirable meaning. An example is the U.S. candy bar Snickers, which is similar to the commonly used British word knickers, ladies undergarments.

A third problem may be that the English brand name is too similar to an existing brand name in the local language. For example, Sears, when spoken by a Castilian Spanish speaker, sounds remarkably similar to Seat, the Spanish automobile company. To avoid confusion, the solution was to use the full Sears Roebuck name. Sometimes a brand name will be changed to make it easy for the native speaker to pronounce. Ocean Spray cranberries, for example, when translated into Chinese characters that are pronounced as "Hoshien Pei," has the added advantage of meaning "healthy refreshment." When first entering the U.S. market, Matsushita could not use its National brand because the name was already taken. In addition, the name of the Japanese parent company was deemed too difficult for U.S. consumers to pronounce. A new brand name, Panasonic, was generated and promoted.

Product Piracy and Counterfeiting

As trade becomes more technology-intensive, Intellectual Property Protection (IPP) is essential to maintaining a competitive advantage. Firms spend large amounts of money creating technology through R&D. It takes investment in people—programmers, musicians, directors, and actors—to produce software, a best-selling CD, or a successful film. Pharmaceutical companies can easily spend $100 million over ten years in the development of a new pharmaceutical drug. Patent copyright law protects those investments.

Different nations have different regulations on what can be protected, the extent of protection, and the period of protection. Developing nations need technology and are unwilling to pay large royalties to multinationals, but the triad economies increasingly depend on technology-based exports. Even within developed nations, major differences exist in how technology is protected. A celebrated instance is the end of copyright protection in Japan for the

GLOBAL MARKETING

Protecting Brand Names and Trademarks

*T*imberland is a U.S. company with a reputation for rugged outdoor-use footwear and clothing. Its logo is a tree, and its name and logo have developed a strong image connoting high quality and durability. When the company began registering its name and logo around the world, it found that a Brazilian company, Samello, was using the Timberland name on its products. Timberland sued to prohibit Samello's use of the name. However, because winning such suits is difficult, Timberland's lawyers chose an unusual approach. Instead of requesting that the product name be protected, they argued that Timberland was the actual name of the company, and hence, as a trade name, was protected even without registration.

Another problem arose in Brazil when Timberland contracted with a Brazilian firm to manufacture shoes. The contract stated that an order was not final until samples had been inspected and approved. Timberland canceled the order because the samples were not sized properly. Then it learned that the Brazilian subcontractor had already made over 5,000 pairs of shoes with the Timberland logo. The Brazilian company was given permission to sell the shoes in the United States provided Timberland's name and logo were removed. Shortly thereafter, Timberland found the shoes on sale in the United States, deeply discounted but with the tree logo intact. Timberland's reputation for quality had been affected by the sale of substandard shoes, an action that could have destroyed the carefully built brand image and company reputation.

To avoid those problems, Timberland's lawyer, Ethan Horwitz, with the law firm of Darby & Darby, recommended that firms register their trademarks wherever they manufactured (even if the country was used only as an export platform), apply for a trademark in countries that the firm expected would be good markets the next ten years, and trademark and aggressively protect trademarks through lawsuits in countries where piracy and counterfeiting were rampant.

The fear of losing rights to brands is not an idle one. South Africa's Supreme Court ruled that McDonald's did not own the rights to its trademark in South Africa because it had not used its name there in the previous five years. McDonald's

continued

had registered its name in South Africa and had renewed its rights but had not opened operations there because of apartheid sanctions (which were lifted in 1991). The judge also decided that McDonald's trademark was not well known among South Africa's majority black population. Therefore, two small South African companies that wanted to open their own McDonald's restaurants in Durban and Johannesburg were free to do so.

A similar problem faced Grand Met, which marketed Smirnoff vodka worldwide, selling 5 million cases and spending $10 million annually in promoting the brand. Its right to the Smirnoff name came under attack in Russia from Boris Smirnoff, a descendant of Pyotr Smirnoff, who founded the Smirnoff vodka business over 100 years ago. With the Bolshevik Revolution, the Smirnoffs lost their business, as did most holders of private property. In the 1930s, Grand Met's Heublein division acquired the rights to the Smirnoff name from one of Pyotr's sons, Vladimir. A lawsuit by Boris Smirnoff claimed that Vladimir had no right to sell the name. In December 1995, the Russian Patent Office Chamber of Appeals invalidated Heublein's trademarks. Grand Met pointed out that it had spent millions over the past 50 years, building the value of the Smirnoff brand, and that when Heublein acquired the name, total U.S. sales were only about 5,000 cases. Grand Met estimated the brand's value to be about $1.4 billion, and the brand's value could diminish if Grand Met could not claim to be the "Official Purveyor to the Russian Imperial Court."

Advances in technology have allowed counterfeiters to copy brand name products to the extent that they are "indis-tinguishable from the genuine article." China is the largest source of counterfeited goods sold internationally. U.S. Customs seized nearly $50 million worth of counterfeited goods from that country in 2002. Other sources identified by the Office of the United States Trade Representative (USTR) include Ukraine (bootleg optical disks) and Russia (software). The USTR estimated losses to U.S. firms from counterfeiting at $200 billion to $250 billion a year. The Counterfeiting Intelligence Bureau of the ICC estimates that between 7 percent and 9 percent of world trade involves counterfeit products. Some of the big-name brands most likely to be counterfeited include Nintendo, Nike, Adidas, Nokia, and Louis Vuitton. The WHO estimates that 5 percent to 7 percent of the pharmaceuticals sold worldwide may be counterfeit, raising the possibility of health hazards. Counterfeiting of car parts and aviation parts can be similarly dangerous, causing mechanical failures. Hence, corporations are including identification features in their products, such as the use of RFID tags that indicate source and authenticity of parts, holograms, molecular (DNA) tags, encryption, and other covert approaches. One aspect of the fight against counterfeiting is that laws need to be enforced and sanctions need to be applied. When law enforcement is weak and the sanctions are toothless, counterfeiters flourish. Firms and nations will have to work together to reduce the plague of counterfeit goods.

Sources: "In Praise of the Real Thing," *The Economist*, May 15, 2003; "Imitating Property Is Theft," *The Economist*, May 15, 2003; "Hunting the Big Mac in Africa," *The Economist*, November 11, 1995; "Who Owns the Smirnoff Name?" *Business Week*, January 15, 1996; "U.S. MNC Wins Some Rounds against Trademark Pirates," *Business International*, June 8, 1992.

Beatles' Sergeant Pepper album, one of the best-selling records of all time. Japanese law limits copyright protection for record companies to 20 years. Hence, in 1987, when the copyright expired, a Japanese compact disc manufacturer introduced nine discount-priced collections of Beatles songs.[28] In another example, a branch of Marubeni Corporation, a giant trading company, was able to buy master tapes and issue recordings of jazz classics by artists such as Miles Davis, John Coltrane, and Nat King Cole. In contrast, the U.S. copyright law provides 75 years of protection to producers, performers, and record companies. The WTO now requires signatories to agree to abide by and implement TRIPS. TRIPS requires member countries to abide by IP laws and protect IP with laws, enforcement, and sanctions.

Private Branding

In *private branding*, which is common in consumer goods marketing, a manufacturer cedes control over marketing to a retailer or distributor. That is, the manufacturer supplies goods, but the retailer sells those goods under its brand names. Thus, a marketer such as Limited Brands might order quantities of dresses, linens, towels, lamps, and accessories, all to be sold under The Limited, Gap, and related brand names. Most of those purchases are from Far East clothing subcontractors, principally China. The original manufacturer's identity is lost, and its margins tend to be lower on sales of private brands.

Private branding provides a quick and relatively low-cost approach to penetrating foreign markets, though the seller fails to establish any relationship with the ultimate buyer and, therefore, has little control over the marketing relationship. The manufacturer has no say on the prices charged and receives little direct feedback from the market. Nor can service and after-sales support be used as a means of forging long-term ties with the ultimate buyer. However, private branding is a useful means of test-marketing products in markets whose potential is likely to grow in the future. Positioning is also important in selling those private brands. Low prices alone are not enough, however, because profitability is restricted due to lower profit margins. The goals are to match branded product quality and to offer prices that are sufficiently below that of branded products to convince customers to switch to the private label. For manufacturers who supply firms such as Sears, careful sourcing is necessary to lower procurement costs without diminishing quality, while also meeting delivery deadlines and supplying the quantities contracted for.

When product specifications are provided by buyers, sales of private brands become a window on an emerging market, allowing the manufacturer to better position itself for future direct entry. Companies such as The Limited and Sears benefit from their name becoming a well-known brand.

However, that experience with a private label may not easily transfer across national markets. For example, Britain's largest supermarket operator, Sainsbury's, has been successful in the United Kingdom, selling private-label products such as smoked salmon and its own brand of champagne. When Sainsbury's expanded into the United States, it decided not to push its private-label approach until it learned how private-label products in those product categories would be evaluated by U.S. consumers.

An interesting trend is the proliferation of private brands in supermarkets and chain stores in Europe. Most sales in the German low-price food chain ALDI are its private brand of food products. It contracts the manufacturing of basic products such as flour, rice, and noodles and aims for margins of about 12.5 percent, lower than the 16 percent margin typical in French hypermarkets or the 25 percent margin of British supermarkets. At the same time, ALDI concentrates on quality equivalent to brand-name products, but at a lower price. As neighborhood shops disappear across Europe and more customers shop at chain stores and hypermarkets, such private branding could increase.

How serious is the threat to established brands from private labels? Private-label sales are increasing in importance, accounting for about 15 percent of U.S. supermarket sales, more-so in recession years. The proportion is considerably higher in Europe, where large grocery and supermarket chains such as the Sainsbury's and Tesco dominate and, accordingly, provide more shelf space to their in-house private brands. Sainsbury's, for example, had Cott Corporation manufacture its Classic Cola and was able to capture 15 percent of the U.K. cola market,

accounting for 65 percent of cola sales within Sainsbury's.

Private labels have increased in prominence because their quality has gone up. Premium private labels have emerged, such as Loblaws President's Choice line of over 1,500 grocery items. With private labels available for a wide variety of goods, consumers may be willing to buy them over higher-priced national brands. As those European retailers begin to expand into the United States, private-label merchandise could increase in importance in the U.S..

Store brands and private labels are more of a threat when national brands do not command high market shares uniformly across a national market. In those cases, efficient retailers can win market share for their private label or store brands depending on the following:[29]

- Demographics of the local markets
- Scale and scope economies of the retailer
- Retailer pricing, promotion, and assortment (product range) tactics
- Retailer expertise in the category (frozen foods, soft drinks, etc.)
- Extent of competition in the local retail sector
- Extent of competition from all brands in the category
- Promotion and advertising strategies of national brand manufacturers

However, manufacturers of branded goods have fought back with the following tactics:[30]

- Convincing retailers of the greater overall profitability of carrying branded goods—greater turnover and more repeat buying make up for lower retailer margins
- Reducing the price gap between the national brand and the private label, while realizing that some premium is necessary to pay for brand advertising and for the greater reassurance of quality and performance that a brand conveys
- Combining brand marketing with complementary sales promotions and enhanced channel relationships
- Continuing to improve the brand so it offers value commensurate with pricing; in other words, manufacturers continuing to invest in and build up brand equity

Country-of-Origin Effect

Numerous studies have shown that consumers evaluate a product not only by its appearance and physical characteristics, but also by the country in which it was produced. This is the *country-of-origin effect*. Certain countries have a good image for certain kinds of products—Germany for cars, France for women's fashion, and Britain for men's fashion. If a firm is producing a product in a country that does not have a favorable image for the product, the company may have a difficult time marketing it. (See Chapter 7 for a model for measuring the country-of-origin effect.)

Some products are binational in origin, such as the Honda Civic made in the United States. How do consumers rate those products? That is, which country of origin do consumers give more weight to? A study of color TVs and subcompact cars with binational origins found that the source country and the brand name both affect perception of quality, although source country seems more important than brand name. Further, the country of origin does not influence a consumer's perception of all attributes of the product in the same way. German products, for example, were rated high on quality but low on economy. The country effect may carry across product categories, so a product from Germany may be regarded as high-quality whether it is a car or a toaster.[31]

Product Standards

Product standards in different markets determine whether a foreign product should be adapted to conform to local standard before being sold. Standards can be technical ones or government-mandated ones. Technical standards are enforced by the market. The best technical standards receive the approval of customers in the form of purchases; and over time, the industry settles on a certain standard. An example is the worldwide acceptance of Intel chips and the Microsoft Windows operating system software as standards for the IBM-compatible personal computer market. Apple's Mac system has been an opposing standard. However, it has gradually lost global market share, falling to below 5 percent of the market as the Wintel standard took hold. Mac's nonstandard equipment was particularly harmful in the business environment, where most companies, for cost and compatibility reasons, opted for the Wintel standard. However, consumers care more about ease of use. Thus, Apple was able to recover some ground with its iMac. Consumers were attracted to the iMac's unusual design, as well as the integrated system approach and relatively low price. Apple was able to make inroads with a segment of the market that valued design and ease of use and that were less price-conscious.

The power of adhering to a global standard is discernible in the global mobile phone industry. About 70 percent of the world uses mobile phones. The majority of mobile phones use the GSM protocol for wireless conversation, with only about 15 percent using the CDMA standard developed by the U.S. firm Qualcomm. Most CDMA users are in the United States (Verizon and Sprint) and in South Korea, the first country to adopt the CDMA standard. Europe accepted GSM since it was developed by a Europe-wide consortium of government agencies, telecommunication firms, and consumer groups.

As the industry moves to 3G wireless networks, GSM users will likely migrate to a new standard, WCDMA, while the original CDMA users migrate to CDMA2000, an upgraded version of CDMA. While WCDMA borrows some features of CDMA, it is distinct enough to provide an advantage to firms that market network equipment and handsets for the original GSM standard. Widespread adoption of the newer standards has been slow to take hold. Telecommunication firms have found that consumers are reluctant to move to 3G phones, with their higher monthly fees.

Differences in product standards can act as trade barriers, with governments enacting those standards in the public interest. In some cases, it is conceivable that the market would stop buying goods of dubious quality, making government regulation and passage of standards unnecessary. Other regulations, such as those that ensure the safety of children's toys and clothes, may be justified. Because people's preferences and incomes vary, consumers in richer countries may be willing to spend more of their incomes on assuring themselves of higher levels of safety or environmental cleanliness.[32]

In another example, the EU raised antipollution standards for small-car engines, making the cars more expensive. The new standards impact heavily on manufacturers such as Peugeot and Renault, whose small cars make up about one-third of total output. The same standards benefit German automakers, who already met stricter German antipollution standards. Hence, they gain on the competition, as do U.S. companies such as Ford and General Motors. The new standards also create increased demand for catalytic converters and fuel injection systems, which are needed to control emissions.

Often government standards can become a means of keeping out foreign competition. With new pharmaceuticals, Japan demands that tests be conducted in Japan before marketing approval is given. The fact that U.S. companies have already met rigorous FDA standards is not sufficient. One consequence is that U.S. pharmaceutical companies must spend additional time and money getting Japanese approvals, which acts as an impediment to entering the Japanese market. Those regulations also give Japanese competitors additional time to study new products from overseas and develop a response.

In many third world markets, the process of setting standards is just beginning. These countries often lack technical expertise and the financial resources to do an adequate job on their own. Therefore, they may turn to authorities in Europe, Japan, and the United States. U.S. industries would certainly gain from participating in this process, facilitating sales of U.S.-made products.

For example, the Saudi Arabian Standards Organization (SASO) received help from experts in Japan, the United Kingdom, France, and West Germany in updating product standards for more than 42,000 products. The standards seemed to favor manufacturers from those countries. Once Saudi standards are set, they are likely to be copied by the smaller neighboring countries of Bahrain, Kuwait, and the United Arab Emirates, all oil-producing countries with rising incomes.

The Saudi example is not unique. Brazil received a gift of several volumes of literature on German product standards written in Portuguese. European interests have helped India build a $16 million laboratory to certify that Indian electronic components meet European standards. The hope is that the labs will help India meet European standards and thus increase exports to Europe. Then India might use its hard currency earnings to import European telecommunication products. Japan initiated a training program for standards personnel from 28 developing countries, sending out Japanese standards experts to provide training in developing countries.

Although U.S. products may be safe and technically excellent, it is not enough that they meet only Underwriters Laboratories (UL) standards. U.S. firms as a group must influence other nations to accept UL standards as their own. Otherwise, the firms may lose markets to foreign competitors that have become more adept at influencing and adhering to different national standards. Another way standards can serve to exclude foreign products is the cumbersome certification requirements that some countries enforce, raising costs prohibitively.

Sometimes companies can take advantage of the fact that standards have yet to coalesce in key markets. Summit Technology is a small manufacturer of laser systems used in eye surgery. The company makes excimer lasers. These lasers emit light in the deep ultraviolet range and allow shallow and precise cuts to be made, permitting removal of tissue as thin as one-third the thickness of a human hair. Summit submitted to tests in the United States to receive FDA approval, which can take several years. In the meantime, Summit was able to sell 90 excimer laser systems in Europe, Japan, and Korea. Those sales were instrumental in generating cash flow so Summit could survive the slow process of obtaining FDA approval.

Standards for Hybrid Cars[33]

Consumers have begun to accept the environmentally friendly hybrid car. The car uses a combination of the traditional gasoline engine with an electric motor, deriving power from batteries that are charged when the car is running and when it is braking. The cars are expensive compared to similar-sized traditional cars because they are produced in small volumes, resulting in the high cost of parts. The current premium is estimated at about $5,000 for a small hybrid car, about one-third more expensive than its traditional gasoline engine counterpart. Consumers in the United States, the main market, may receive tax incentives, which bring down the premium. Also, the cars get excellent gas mileage and, therefore, are economical to run. In addition, initial consumers are prepared to pay a premium price to drive an environmentally friendly car. As gasoline prices near $70 a barrel worldwide, drivers have even more incentive to adopt these fuel-economic hybrid engine automobiles.

Hybrid cars have unique parts, including the power train design, the transmission, and the software to deliver power to the wheels. The major producers of hybrid cars, which include General Motors, Toyota, Honda, and Ford, are eager to see their solutions for these different subsystems become the industry standard. This would allow them to control the future direction of the industry and generate additional sales and royalty payments.

Power train: Hybrid cars use both gasoline and electric motors. Toyota has a large electric motor for powering the car and a smaller one for charging the battery. General Motors uses two electric motors of the same size to do both jobs.

Transmission: General Motors uses an automatically shifted manual transmission, which is fuel-efficient on the highway. Toyota uses a complex electronically controlled transmission.

Software: Software, which controls the power train, optimizes how power is delivered to the wheels from the electric and gasoline motors. General Motor's software is oriented to highway driving, while Toyota's software is based on city driving patterns.

Each company wants to make its systems the industry standard. Therefore, each company is trying to convince other auto companies to use its approach by offering to share technology and by developing joint R&D programs. Companies such as Ford and Honda are experimenting with their own systems. It will be some time before industry standards develop.

Product Policy and International Competition

Part of a product development and launch campaign is the investment made in strategic marketing to ensure that the product captures long-term market share. That is, new products need strategic nurturing over time if they are to wrest market share from existing product leaders. An example is Glaxo, which launched its antiulcer drug Zantac when SmithKline's Tagamet had a near monopoly in the marketplace. A carefully targeted six-year marketing campaign allowed Glaxo to get 50 percent of the market.

Glaxo's objective for its marketing investment was to achieve sustainable market share. It needed to identify customers for Zantac and to ensure their retention so that sales recurred while customer acquisition costs were reduced.

For companies playing catch-up, as Glaxo did against an entrenched competitor, that means identifying a group of competitors' customers who are ready to switch and who could generate high levels of sales and profits. Those customers might be less sensitive to price and more concerned with service and product innovativeness. Another element is to seek customers who are "share determiners," such as medical residents, who turned out to be the key to allowing Glaxo to win long-term market share. The stage of the product cycle also matters.

Customer Satisfaction and Loyalty

Understanding why customers switch is an integral part of formulating a marketing plan, particularly in competitive markets at later stages of the product cycle. Satisfied customers are generally loyal, providing a firm with significantly higher volumes of business. However, a loyal customer may be so because of other factors, such as monopoly conditions among suppliers, high switching costs, and loyalty promotion programs such as frequent flyer plans. Those customers would probably desert if they could. To complicate matters, not every customer will experience the same level of satisfaction, even when the product and service received is identical. Hence, great importance is attached to understanding what results in satisfied and loyal customers. Customer satisfaction results from several conditions:

- Basic product attributes meet customer expectations
- Customer support services increase product effectiveness and enhance ease of use
- Prompt and satisfactory procedures exist for dealing with customer dissatisfaction
- Unusual service appears to customize the product or service for the customer

Horst Schulze, president of The Ritz-Carlton Hotel Company, summarizes: "Unless customers are excited about what you are doing, you have to improve."[34]

Mode of Entry and New Product Success

The success of the international marketing of a product or service is influenced partly by how a firm chooses to enter the market—whether directly or indirectly and whether through overseas manufacturing, licensing, the use of distributors, etc. (See Chapter 8 for a detailed discussion of entry modes.) Three sets of variables influence a company's decision about how to carry out its international marketing.[35]

- *Global strategic variables* include the level of global concentration, the global synergies between national market entry and market shares, and the global strategic motivations of the firm and its competitors.
- *Transaction-specific variables* include the importance of proprietary knowledge within a firm. Is that knowledge relevant to successful overseas market entry; and is the knowledge implicit, unwritten, and tacit so that it cannot be easily transferred in arms-length negotiations to independent parties?
- *Environmental variables* are specific to each country. These variables include country risk, cultural distance, and unfamiliarity associated with each location; the forecasted distribution and uncertainty of demand from each market location; and the intensity of competition at each site. All of those variables affect the desirability of adopting entry modes that involve a firm more closely with the market. Figure 9-4 summarizes these associations.

An example of such an integrated approach to market entry is provided by Procter & Gamble. That company's efforts resulted in its becoming the largest consumer products company in China, with half of the shampoo market. Procter & Gamble began with its Head & Shoulders shampoo, using advertising to draw attention to dandruff in a country of black-haired people. It followed with intensive distribution. It then rolled out two additional brands, Rejoice and Pantene, also with antidandruff formulas. Despite a 300 percent price premium to local brands, Procter & Gamble was able to capture a 57 percent market share in three major cities. The company's goal was to be No. 1 from the start, gradually introducing other products after shampoo and detergent had been established. Procter & Gamble used several tactics:

- It spent more on TV advertising than any other company in China.
- It brought in over 100 American expatriate managers to implement and train local managers in American marketing techniques.
- It obtained total retail coverage by developing detailed maps of 228 major Chinese cities, visiting nearly every small retail shop and big department store, and getting them to stock its products.
- It handed out free samples of detergent with every washing machine sale and sold detergent in small packages.
- It offered incentives to distributors for early payment and cut off those who would not pay within 40 days.

Figure 9-4. An Eclectic Framework of the Entry Mode Choice

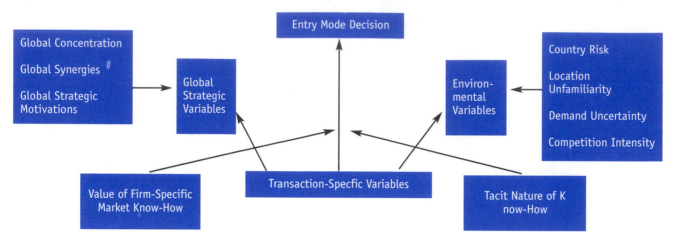

Source: W. Chan Kim and Peter Hwang, "Global Strategy and Multinationals' Entry Mode Choice," *Journal of International Business Studies* (23)1, 1992, page 33.

• It acquired three of China's major detergent man-ufacturers and two of the top Chinese brands.

Procter & Gamble showed conclusively that a coordi-nated marketing campaign can establish Western brands in China, that China is a fast-growing mass market, and that no major brand—be it cognac or soap or computers—can afford to be out of the Chinese market.[36]

Other major multinational companies have been equally creative in approaching the Chinese market. Kodak made China into its second-largest market by paying atten-tion to marketing and manufacturing. It established Chi-nese manufacturing in 1998 by acquiring debt-laden, state-owned firms for over $1 billion. By doing so, Kodak was able to supply Chinese-manufactured film, cameras, and chemicals. This gave the company a cost advantage. Kodak also started a campaign, "99,000 will make you a boss," allowing it to set up photo stores all across China. Given China's vast size, Kodak needed such dispersed and far-flung distribution channels. Kodak promised to set up individuals who wanted to run their own businesses by fur-nishing them with equipment, training, and a license—all for a one-time fee of 99,000 yuan (approximately $12,000).

Danone, the French food conglomerate famous for its yogurt, entered China somewhat late, in 1996. It pur-chased a controlling interest in Hangzhou Wahaha, which manufactured vitamin-enriched milk for children. Danone expanded Wahaha across China, building manufacturing plants, developing national distribution, and funding extensive advertising. Those actions helped Danone increase volume five-fold in two years. Once the company had developed scale, national distribution, and a brand, it

used those assets to bolster its move into a bottled water product line, achieving similar success. In Danone's plan-ning, it assumes that prices will fall 50 percent within three years because of intense competition within China. Hence, its goal is to achieve payback before price wars intensify. Danone's success led the Chinese government to ask for its help in developing a Chinese manufactured soft drink, "Future Cola," to compete with Coca-Cola.[37]

IKEA: Integrated Strategy for New Product Launch across Multiple Markets

An historical example of adapting various facets of market-ing strategy to export markets can be seen in IKEA's approach to the U.S. market. IKEA pioneered the idea of low-cost, ready-to- assemble furniture in Sweden at a time when furniture was priced high, made to order, and dis-tributed through small retailers specializing in furniture. IKEA's Scandinavian design and low prices appealed to young couples and families with children. IKEA grew rap-idly and gradually extended across Europe. It found suc-cess by emphasizing its Scandinavian origins and persuading customers of its quality, yet acknowledging its unorthodox self-service approach to selling furniture. It also began sourcing its furniture from Eastern Europe to ensure low production costs. However, it was slow to expand in the United States, knowing that the United States had often been the stumbling block for other suc-cessful European retailers. When IKEA did open in the

United States, it realized that some adaptation, as follows, would be necessary.

- It had to adapt its furniture to larger American physiques; for example, Americans found its beds too narrow.
- It had to specify product dimensions in inches rather than the metric system.
- It had to develop suites of furniture to cater to the American penchant for buying furniture as a group for the bedroom, dining room, living room, kitchen, etc.
- It had to redesign its furniture for U.S. use patterns; for example, deeper cabinets to hold larger dinner plates and larger glasses, as Americans preferred.
- Because long queues and out-of-stock items led to disgruntled customers, IKEA upgraded its point-of-sale systems and added more checkout stations to speed up customer processing. It also increased local manufacturing to prevent inventory shortages caused by a lengthy supply chain.
- Exchange rate appreciation could render its imported furniture more expensive and at odds with its marketing message of selling affordable furniture. The solution was to increase its sourcing of locally-made furniture, working with and developing U.S. suppliers to the point where they accounted for 45 percent of products sold at U.S. IKEA stores, up from 15 percent formerly.
- It matched U.S. customer service expectations by accepting a more generous returns policy than in Europe and by offering next-day delivery to attract customers who did not want to transport their own furniture, a key aspect of the IKEA model in Europe.

With those modifications, IKEA expanded its number of U.S. stores and was able to increase North American sales. Figure 9-5 summarizes how the various interlinked aspects of IKEA's strategy contributed to its overall distinctive competence and market success.

Product Attributes in International Markets

Product policy goes beyond the product itself. Attributes such as brands and trademarks, country of origin, packaging and labeling, and warranty and service policies represent key decision areas.

PACKAGING

Packaging is an important part of a product's attributes. Companies expend considerable effort developing packaging that is recognizable and distinctive, as well as functional. Examples of factors that require packaging adaptation:

- Changes in climate across countries require more protective packaging against extremes of cold and heat.
- Lengthy, difficult transportation and logistics networks require that packaging protect goods against breakage and damage.
- Lengthy periods on retailers' shelves before final sale require that packaging be protective and maintain freshness.
- Varying sizes of packaging are needed, with smaller-sized packages required in lower-income countries to make the products more affordable. Smaller size may also be common in countries where frequent shopping trips are made and shoppers carry their purchases on foot back to their dwellings.
- Differences in packaging are needed because of consumer preferences; for example, toothpaste sold in squeeze tubes versus upright cans and fruit juices packaged in glass containers versus cardboard boxes
- Utilization of standard packaging helps a product be recognized, such as Kodak's familiar yellow boxes.
- With a growing environmental consciousness on the part of consumers, purchasers attempt to persuade firms to use biodegradable and/or recyclable packaging materials that cause the least harm to the environment. Packaging adds bulk to a product and takes up more space during shipment. It might be more economical to ship the products in bulk and package them upon arrival at the destination markets. Whether that practice is feasible depends on the capabilities of the domestic packaging industry, particularly in terms of quality, use of advanced technology packaging and printing processes, cost and timely delivery, and availability of quality materials.

LABELING

Primary considerations in labeling are providing information to the consumers and using multiple languages. Regulations in many countries require that detailed product composition and nutritional information be provided. Also required are warning messages for products that may be harmful or hazardous. Firms may also want to provide instructions for the proper use of a product, in which case readability and quality of communication matter. Merely translating text from the home country's language may not be sufficient. Country regulations may require that information be presented in all of a country's or region's official languages. In Europe, this means compressing information in microscopic-sized fonts on the exterior of packages or including an insert with detailed information and instructions inside packages. This information is necessary for products such as consumer electronics devices, tools, pharmaceuticals, and food products. In those cases, the manu-

Figure 9-5. IKEA: Linking Competencies and Customers

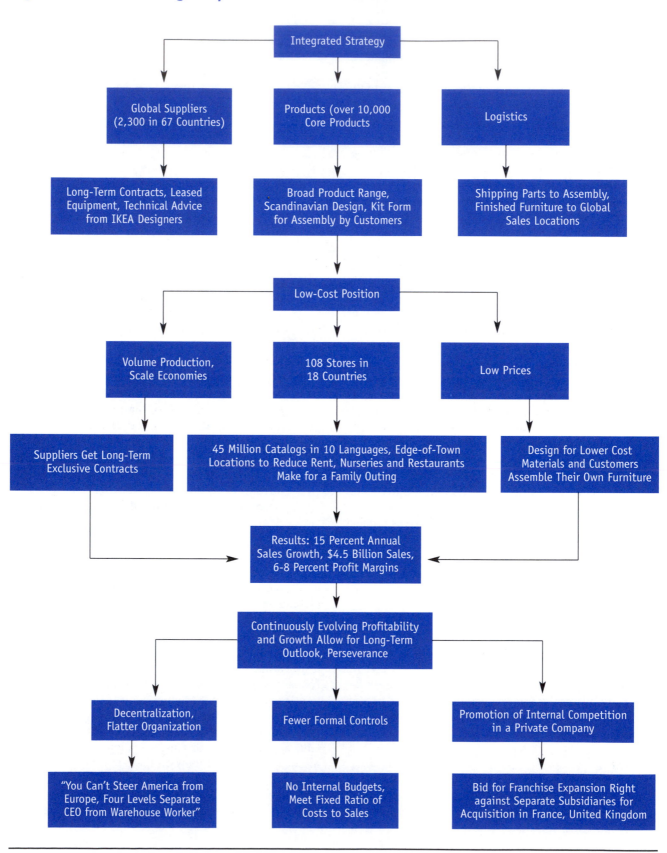

facturer wants to communicate detailed information about setup, energy consumption levels, recommended dosages, and recipes. The language complexities motivate manufacturers to use icons, diagrams, and cartoons to instruct consumers in the use of their products. Those pictorial descriptions transcend language and make it easier for a firm to introduce products into new markets.

WARRANTY AND SERVICE POLICIES

When customers buy products, they are purchasing utility, function, and performance as much as image and status. With products that have a clear function or utility (such as washing machines, hair dryers, hiking boots, and cars), customers want reassurances that the products will work as promised. Firms entering international markets are faced with the choice of standardizing their warranty policies. In other words, do firms offer the same warranty worldwide or change the terms of the warranty for specific countries or regions? A related question is that of matching or exceeding the competition. Should warranties be used as a differentiating factor in gaining market share against the competition? Should warranties be used to overcome other product attributes that may hinder international market share, such as a negative country-of-origin effect?

STANDARDIZATION

Several conditions encourage the standardization of warranties, as follows:

- Multinational customers may not accept warranties with lower standards compared to warranties they receive in other, perhaps more advanced, industrial markets.
- Goods purchased in one market may be used elsewhere. For example, cars purchased in Germany are often driven across Europe. If different levels of warranty exist in different European countries, customers may decide to switch models.
- Some products affect human health and safety, such as aircraft, pharmaceutical drugs, and food products. In those case, for ethical reasons, a firm cannot justify offering a lower level of warranty.

When a firm offers standardized products worldwide, warranty standardization is likely to follow.

LOCALIZATION

Warranties may be adapted to different local markets in several cases:

- Competition is weak, and firms do not feel pressure to incur the additional costs that a standardized warranty policy might entail. This is likely in near-monopoly markets. Examples involve travel policies and denied boarding compensation to passengers on foreign routes with little competition.

- When multiple sources of production exist, different quality levels may make offering uniform warranties difficult. This reflects a weak response to a flaw in a firm's sourcing policies, however.
- A product may fail sooner because it is used differently. Warranties may be adapted to make allowances for such use. For example, warranties differ for cars used as taxicabs compared to cars used as private vehicles.
- A lack of an international service network can make meeting warranty promises difficult. Cutting warranties in this case would be an inadequate response. A preferable approach would be to build up service capabilities worldwide so that uniform warranty policies could be offered and met.

Stronger warranties may be offered in markets in which a firm is new. This may be done to overcome customer unfamiliarity with the product and to build an installed base and market share against entrenched incumbents. The higher warranty levels would typically revert to the worldwide norm after an introductory period.

After-Sales Service

While warranties represent the front end of a marketing bargain with customers, following up and delivering on the implied warranty promise is facilitated by a company's after-sales service network. Thus, a strong level of consistency must exist between a company's warranty policies and its worldwide after-sales service network. Building that network requires choosing locations from which to offer the service; investing in physical facilities, equipment, and parts; staffing and training qualified service technicians; and instituting a logistics and information network to keep track of service performance and customer complaints so that they are handled in a satisfactory manner.

Providing and proving the existence of a service capability may ensure that a firm wins new clients in overseas markets in industrial product settings. Clients worry, justifiably, about committing resources and critical processes to products from a distant supplier with an unproven record in the marketplace. Caterpillar has built up a strong international market position by promising to deliver service parts within 48 hours anywhere in the world. That promise is appreciated by users of expensive earth-moving equipment, for whom equipment failure can mean being late in completing a project—the result being serious negative financial consequences.

Firms must decide whether to offer the international service capability themselves, offer it through their distributors and agents, or contract it to independent third parties. A central issue here is goal congruence. Are distributors interested in investing the necessary capital for building up a strong service network, or are they interested in short-term sales gains before moving on to the next hot product? Given distributors' capital shortages and lower commitments to long-term market share, firms may have to offer their distributors both financial and technical support to ensure a high level of service capability. That support could include carrying a supply of parts to ship to distributors as needed or offering ongoing training to a distributor's service personnel at the firm's expense. Offering ongoing training raises practical questions—where to conduct the training, how often to conduct it, how to ensure effective training, what language to offer the training in, whether to use online computer-based support to service personnel in distant locations, and whether to offer incentives to enhance motivation and quality of the service personnel.

Offering efficient service does not mean maintaining multiple service sites in every major market and city, however. Using operations research techniques and modeling the demand for services, multinational firms can develop optimal configurations of parts depots, service centers, and levels of staff. Doing so ensures that targeted service efficiency levels can be met for a minimum investment while high levels of customer satisfaction are maintained. An interesting development is the offering of graded service plans to customers. Clients can choose the level of service they want, with higher charges accompanying higher levels of service. That practice is illustrated by the computer software business. "Basic service" may mean a few free hours followed by a per-minute charge for phone consultation. "Total service" may mean a blanket lump-sum, fee-based, year-round, on-site service for all of a firm's users and all of its installed bases of computers. The difficulty is striking a balance between offering the requisite level of service to stay competitive and keep customers and offering higher levels of fee-based service for customers who use a product or service more intensively and see economic value in paying for premium service.

Segmentation across National Markets

Marketing managers must decide, based on a product's attributes, which segments of the market they will target. Will segmentation decisions made for the domestic market be carried over to foreign markets? A firm also must decide whether to standardize the positioning or image of a product across countries. Does the firm want to sell to the same customer segment across countries? Or does it want to sell the same (standardized) product but to different segments in various countries (because a standardized product may appeal to different segments in different countries)?

Canon's positioning of the AE-1 camera (an electronic auto-exposure single-lens reflex camera) during its glob-

al introduction illustrates that concept. Although the AE-1 was targeted to replacement buyers in Japan, it was intended for upscale first-time buyers in the United States and for older, technologically knowledgeable buyers in West Germany. The differences in segments targeted dictated accompanying changes in other elements of the marketing mix, as shown in Table 9-5.

Cameras have now become digital, but digital camera buyers are still segmented. Similar segmentation reasoning can be used as Canon and other manufacturers launch new-generation digital cameras that are technologically complex, higher-priced, and capable of taking pictures in a simple automatic operation mode, yet offering greater control and a variety of features.

Summary

When deciding what products it should sell overseas, a firm should question whether to standardize or adapt the products for foreign markets.

Factors encouraging standardization include economies of scale in manufacturing, R&D, and marketing; preserving the country-of-origin image; and serving globetrotting customers.

Factors encouraging adaptation include greater profit potential; different use conditions, income levels, and consumer tastes; local market laws; operating plants in many countries; consumer profiles; and competition. Adaptation is more likely when costs are low and do not force a company to raise prices.

Consumer tastes are converging in developed nations, leading to greater acceptance of a standardized product in those countries. The example of the washing machine industry shows how careful standardization of product features and some elements of the marketing mix can be a successful strategy.

An important decision in international markets involves brand policy. The major question is whether to opt for local brands or global brands. Global brands are consistent with a standardization approach to world markets.

Issues important to brand policy in international markets include protecting against brand piracy, paying attention to the cultural connotations of brand names, and dealing with government regulations that pertain to brands and trademarks.

Another decision is whether to use private branding. Although it may facilitate sales, a company has little contact with the ultimate consumer and learns little about changes at the consumer level.

A product's country of origin affects how the product is perceived and accepted in foreign markets. Both technical and government-mandated standards affect a compa-

Table 9-5. Diverse Segment Positioning of Canon's AE-1 Camera

Marketing Activities	Japan	United States	Europe
Target audience	Replacement buyers among young people	First-time buyers of SLR cameras who can be converted from box cameras to SLR	Replacement buyers who can be converted from old-fashioned cameras to SLR
Advertising message	"Continuous-shooting SLR": single-lens reflex that allows sequences of two frames per second	"So advanced, it's simple": Using sports celebrities to show the camera's ability to meet the challenge of fast-paced sports action and its suitability for nonprofessional photographers	No catchphrase used in Europe: ads stress technological superiority resulting from the use of a microprocessor in the central processing unit, or "brain," of the camera, as well as speed and ease of use
Advertising media	Newspaper, television, magazine	Evenly split between television and newspaper/magazine; official sponsor of Winter Olympics Games, Avon Tennis Championship, and Professional Golfers Association; substantial increase in promotional budget	Magazines, billboards, cinemas, bus/trains; substantial increase in promotional budget
Distribution	Specialty stores	AE-1 used as a means of shifting distribution from specialty stores to mass merchandisers; extensive dealer promotions and dealer training programs	Multiunit specialty chains; some dealer promotions
Price	Retail list price of 85,000 yen (with 50 Fl.4 lens and case) or US$290 upon introduction	Determined locally; retail list price of $430 upon introduction; actual selling price below $300	Different from country to country

Source: H. Takeuchi and M. Porter, "Three Roles of International Marketing in Global Strategy," in Competition in Global Industries, M. Porter, ed., Boston: Harvard Business School Press, 1986, page 140.

ny's ability to market products in various foreign markets. When product standards are set by consumer acceptance, a company can benefit immensely when its standard becomes the global standard (like the Windows operating system did in the personal computer market).

The introduction of new products by international competition can force a company to reexamine its product introduction policies. Relevant factors include building customer loyalty to retain customers; revisiting the chosen mode of market entry based on strategic-, environmental-, and transaction-specific variables; and focusing on long-term goals.

Packaging adaptation may be necessary to protect a product because of differences in climate or because of longer-than-average time spent in the distribution channel. A firm may also need to meet the package-size prefer-ences of local consumers, as well as cultural preferences regarding color, style, and materials.

Labeling may have to be adapted because of language differences, the need to inform consumers, and government requirements. Multilingual labels are one solution.

Warranties are standardized when possible. Multinational customers, competitive pressures, the nature of the product itself, and common sources of production are factors leading to standardization. However, cost savings, competitive actions, and inconsistent quality in the global service network may lead a firm to offer different warranties in different countries.

Worldwide after-sales service must be offered for certain products. Offering service training, using third parties (for example, distributors), and maintaining satisfied customers are some of the major factors a firm must keep in mind.

Another interesting decision for a firm is whether to sell to the same segment in different foreign markets. That decision depends on product characteristics. A standardized product may require a company to target different segments in different countries.

Questions and Research

9.1 What does selling a standardized product in global markets imply?

9.2 In what ways might a product be adapted for global markets?

9.3 What factors encourage global standardization of a product?

9.4 What factors encourage firms to adapt their product for foreign markets?

9.5 Explain whether consumer tastes are converging around the world. If they are, what is the implication of this trend for international marketing?

9.6 Discuss the example of the washing machine discussed in the text in terms of the standardization versus adaptation debate.

9.7 What are some approaches to brand policy in international markets?

9.8 Should a firm have one brand worldwide? Explain. Would your answer change depending on the product (for example, perfume, photographic film, credit cards, and computers)?

9.9 Why are trademark piracy and brand piracy important? How can a firm protect itself against those actions?

9.10 What are the pros and cons of private branding in international markets?

9.11 What is the importance of country of origin in international product marketing?

9.12 How do product standards affect international marketing? What can a firm do with respect to standards to bolster its foreign market position?

9.13 Discuss the promotional and protective aspects of packaging in international markets.

9.14 Evaluate the international labeling situation facing a pharmaceutical firm and a manufacturer of razor blades.

9.15 What considerations are involved in establishing a warranty policy for international markets?

9.16 Is offering worldwide service essential to international marketing? Explain your answer.

9.17 Industrial Controls Corp. began exporting to Europe and Latin America two years ago. Now service problems are beginning to hurt its reputation and threaten future sales. What might the company do to improve its situation?

9.18 How does the existence of different customer segments overseas affect international marketing?

9.19 Discuss how Canon positioned its AE-1 camera worldwide in the face of divergent customer segments.

Endnotes

1. Taylor, William. "Message and Muscle: An Interview with Swatch Titan Nicolas Hayek," *Harvard Business Review*, March–April 1993, pages 98–110; "Can Daimler's Tiny *Swatchmobile* Sweep Europe?" *Wall Street Journal*, October 2, 1998.

2. Levitt, T. "The Globalization of Markets," *Harvard Business Review*, May–June 1983.

3. Levitt, T. "The Globalization of Markets," *Harvard Business Review*, Exhibit 1, May–June 1983.

4. "Machines for the Masses," *Wall Street Journal*, December 9, 2003.

5. Pine II, B. Joseph, B. Victor, and A. C. Boynton. "Making Mass Customization Work," *Harvard Business Review*, September–October 1993, pages 108–119.

6. Hill, John S. and Richard R. Still. "Effects of Urbanization on Multinational Product Planning," *Columbia Journal of World Business*, Summer 1984, pages 62–67.

7. "For Coca-Cola in Japan, Things Go Better with Milk," *Wall Street Journal*, January 20, 1997.

8. "Would They Really Rather Have a Buick?" *Wall Street Journal*, December 16, 1998.

9. "Ford Hopes Its New Focus Will Be a Global Best-Seller," *Wall Street Journal*, October 8, 1998.

10. "Unknown Fruit Takes on Unfamiliar Markets," *Wall Street Journal*, November 9, 1995.

11. "Nonalcoholic Beer Hits the Spot in Mideast," *Wall Street Journal*, December 6, 1995.

12. Cavusgil, S. T., Shaoming Zou, and G. M. Naidu. "Product and Promotion Adaptation in Export Ventures: An Empirical Investigation," *Journal of International Business Studies*, Volume 24, Number 3, 1993, pages 479–506.

13. Onkvisit, Sak and John J. Shaw. "The International Dimensions of Branding: Strategic Considerations and Decisions," *International Marketing Review*, Volume 6, Issue 3, 1989.

14. Quelch, John. "Global Brands: Taking Stock," *Business Strategy Review*, Volume 10, Issue 1, Spring 1999, pages 1–14.

15. BMW CEO Helmut Panke as quoted in the *The Wall Street Journal*, November 20, 2003.

16. Roth, Martin S. "The Effects of Culture and Socioeconomics on the Performance of Global Brand Image Strategies," *Journal of Marketing Research*, May 1995, pages 163–175.

17. "Staying Power," *Business Latin America*, November 23, 1998.

18. Gallup China survey, *Business China*, November 10, 1997, page 11.

19. "After Years Behind the Scenes, Chinese Join the Name Game," *Wall Street Journal*, December 26, 2003.

20. Zeng, Ming and Peter J. Williamson. "The Hidden Dragons," *Harvard Business Review*, October 2003.

21. Hoffe, J., K. Lane, and V. M. Nam. "Branding Cars in China," *McKinsey Quarterly*, Number 4, 2003.

22. "A Low-Budget Cola Shakes Up Markets South of the Border," *Wall Street Journal*, October 27, 2003.

23. Keller, Kevin Lane and Y. L. R. Moorthi, "Branding in Developing Markets," *Business Horizons,* May–June 2003.

24 Aaker, David A. and Erich Joachimsthaler. "The Lure of Global Branding," *Harvard Business Review,* November–December 1999.

25. Aaker, David. "Brand Extensions: The Good, the Bad, and the Ugly," *Sloan Management Review,* Summer 1990, pages 47–56.

26. "Hewlett-Packard: Big, Boring, and Booming," *The Economist,* May 6, 1995.

27. Globerman, Steven. "Addressing International Product Piracy," *Journal of International Business Studies,* Volume 19, Number 3, Fall 1988; Higgins Richard S. and Paul Rubin, "Counterfeit Goods," *Journal of Law and Economics,* October 1986; Harvey, M. and I. Ronkainen, "International Counterfeiters: Marketing Success without Cost or Risk," *Columbia Journal of World Business,* Fall 1985.

28. "A Cruel Cut for Sergeant Pepper," *Business Week,* June 22, 1987.

29. Dhar, Sanjay K. and Stephen Hoch. "Why Store Brand Penetration Varies by Retailer," *Marketing Science,* Fall 1997.

30. Hoch, S. and S. Bannerji. "When Do Private Labels Succeed?" *Sloan Management Review,* Summer 1993, pages 57–67; Quelch, John and D. Harding, "Brands versus Private Labels: Fighting to Win," *Harvard Business Review,* January–February 1996, pages 99–109.

31. Some interesting studies on the country-of-origin phenomenon include the following: Samiee, Saeed, Terence A. Shimp, and Subhash Sharma, "Brand Origin Recognition Accuracy: Its Antecedents and Consumers' Cognitive Limitations," *Journal of International Business Studies,* Volume 36, July 2005, pages 379–397; Olsen, Svein Ottar and Ulf H. Olsson, Multientity Scaling and the Consistency of Country-of-Origin Attitudes, *Journal of International Business Studies,* Volume 33, March 2002, pages 149–167; Han, C. Min and Vern Terpstra, "Country of Origin Effects for Uni-National and Bi-National Products," *Journal of International Business Studies,* Volume 19, Number 2, Summer 1988; Bilkey, Warren J. and Erik Nes, "Country of Origin Effects on Product Evaluations," *Journal of International Business Studies,* Volume 13, Number 2, Spring–Summer 1982.

32. Sykes, Alan. *Product Standards for Internationally Integrated Goods Markets,* Washington, DC: Brookings Institute, 1995.

33. "When Hybrid Cars Collide," *Wall Street Journal,* February 6, 2003.

34. Jones, T. O. and W. Earl Sasser, Jr. "Why Satisfied Customers Defect," *Harvard Business Review,* November–December 1995, pages 88–99.

35. Kim, W. Chan and Peter Hwang. "Global Strategy and Multinationals' Entry Mode Choice," *Journal of International Business Studies,* Volume 23, Number 1, 1992, pages 29–53.

36. "P&G Viewed China as a National Market and Is Conquering It," *Wall Street Journal,* September 12, 1995.

37. "Cracking China's Market," *Wall Street Journal,* January 9, 2003.

Further Readings

Aaker, David A. and Erich Joachimsthaler. "The Lure of Global Branding," *Harvard Business Review,* November–December 1999.

Brouthers, Lance Eliot, Steve Werner, and Erika Matulich. "The Influence of Triad Nations' Environments on Price-Quality Product Strategies and MNC Performance," *Journal of International Business Studies,* Volume 31, March 2000, pages 39–62.

Cavusgil, S. T., Shaoming Zou, and G. M. Naidu. "Product and Promotion Adaptation in Export Ventures: An Empirical Investigation," *Journal of International Business Studies,* Volume 24, Number 3, 1993, pages 479–506.

Dominguez, Luis V. and C. Sequeira. "Determinants of LDC Exporters' Performance: A Cross-National Study," *Journal of International Business Studies,* Volume 24, Number 1, 1993, pages 19–40.

Doyle, Peter, J. Saunders, and V. Wong. "Competition in Global Markets: A Case Study of American and Japanese Competition in the British Market," *Journal of International Business Studies,* Volume 23, Number 3, 1992, pages 419–442.

Globerman, Steven. "Addressing International Product Piracy," *Journal of International Business Studies,* Volume 19, Number 3. Fall 1988.

Han, C. Min and Vern Terpstra. "Country of Origin Effects for Uni-National and Bi-National Products," *Journal of International Business Studies,* Number 19, Volume 2, Summer 1988.

Hewett, K., M. S. Roth, and K. Roth. "Conditions Influencing Headquarters and Foreign Subsidiary Roles in Marketing Activities and Their Effects on Performance," *Journal of International Business Studies,* Volume 34, November 2003, pages 567–585.

Hoch, S. and S. Bannerji. "When Do Private Labels Succeed?" *Sloan Management Review,* Summer 1993, pages 57–67.

Hoffe, J. K. Lane, and V.M. Nam, "Branding Cars in China" *McKinsey Quarterly,* Number 4, 2003

Hopkins, David M., Lewis T. Kontnik, and Mark Turnage. *Counterfeiting Exposed: How to Protect Your Brand and Market Share,* 2003, Hoboken, NJ: John Wiley & Sons.

Jones, T. O. and W. Earl Sasser, Jr. "Why Satisfied Customers Defect." *Harvard Business Review,* November–December 1995, pages 88–99.

Keller, Kevin Lane and Y. L. R. Moorthi. "Branding in Developing Markets," *Business Horizons,* May–June 2003

Kim, W. Chan and Peter Hwang. "Global Strategy and Multinationals' Entry Mode Choice," *Journal of International Business Studies,* Volume 23, Number 1, 1992, pages 29–53.

Knight, Gary A. and S. Tamer Cavusgil. Innovation, Organizational Capabilities, and the Born-Global Firm, *Journal of International Business Studies,* Volume 35, March 2004, pages 124–141.

Levitt, T. "The Globalization of Markets," *Harvard Business Review,* May–June 1983.

Mortimer, Ruth. "Lego: Building a Brand Out of Bricks," *Brand Strategy,* April 2003, pages 16–19.

Olsen, Svein Ottar and Ulf H. Olsson. "Multientity Scaling and the Consistency of Country-of-Origin Attitudes," *Journal of International Business Studies,* Volume 33, March 2002, pages 149–167.

Onkvisit, Sak and John J. Shaw. "The International Dimensions of Branding: Strategic Considerations and Decisions," *International Marketing Review,* Volume 6, Number 3, 1989.

Pine II, B. Joseph, B. Victor, and A. C. Boynton. "Making Mass Customization Work." *Harvard Business Review,* September–October 1993, pages 108–119.

Quelch, John. "Global Brands: Taking Stock," *Business Strategy Review,* Volume 10, Issue 1, Spring 1999, pages 1–14.

Quelch, John and D. Harding. "Brands versus Private Labels: Fighting to Win," *Harvard Business Review,* January– February 1996, pages 99–109.

Roth, Martin S. "The Effects of Culture and Socioeconomics on the Performance of Global Brand Image Strategies," *Journal of Marketing Research,* May 1995, pages 163–175.

Samiee, Saeed, Terence A Shimp, and Subhash Sharma. "Brand Origin Recognition Accuracy: Its Antecedents and Consumers' Cognitive Limitations," *Journal of International Business Studies,* Volume 36, July 2005, pages 379–397.

Sykes, Alan. *Product Standards for Internationally Integrated Goods Markets,* Washington, DC: Brookings Institute, 1995.

Taylor, William. "Message and Muscle: An Interview with Swatch Titan Nicolas Hayek," *Harvard Business Review,* March–April 1993, pages 98–110.

Zeng, Ming and Peter J. Williamson. "The Hidden Dragons," *Harvard Business Review,* October 2003.

Case 9.1

DAVILA-BOND AND THE LATIN AMERICAN SWEATER MARKET

In the summer of 2003, Charlie Davila-Bond was at yet another crossroads. As the general manager of a major sweater exporter, Davila & Bond, Inc., based out of Quito, Ecuador, he was facing a number of international strategic issues. Since 1999, his importer in Chile had lost interest in Davila & Bond products, and there was a serious future risk of a continued sales decline in Chile. The Chilean dilemma stemmed from stiff international competition in the Chilean market. The economic crisis in Argentina had trickled over to Brazil, and the devaluation of the Brazilian real to the U.S. dollar (now Ecuador's currency) had made the continuation of sales to Brazil unprofitable. Due to extremely high fixed costs (such as loan payments on new equipment and employee salaries), Davila-Bond's factory in Ecuador needed to operate at a high level of capacity to maintain profitability. A drop in sales would have a major impact on Davila & Bond's performance. To diversify his international sales portfolio, Davila-Bond's decided to place more emphasis on Mexico, a large and potentially lucrative market. Sales to Mexico instantly jumped to over 25,000 sweaters (about 12 percent of total sales), which was promising.

Yet as Davila-Bond looked at the numbers, he noticed that his firm's reliance on the Ecuadorian market was still extremely heavy. Over 50 percent of the firm's sales were coming from Ecuador. The climate in the Ecuadorian mountains was ideal for lightweight sweaters.[1] However, the economic uncertainty of the country was, at times, mystifying. Ecuador was also corrupt and was experiencing political unrest.

Would increased sales to Mexico help alleviate some of the uncertainty that Davila & Bond was experiencing? And were there underlying issues related to Ecuador's adoption of the U.S. dollar that could dampen the potential in the Mexican market? Davila-Bond knew that the time had come to redefine his international strategy. For years, he and his family had dreamed of exporting to the United States. Yet with limited plant capacity and intensely narrow margins, it seemed unrealistic. Perhaps Mexico could be a solid stepping stone toward the ultimate goal of entry into the U.S. market.

Company History

In 1974, Fernando Davila, a native of Ecuador, and his Scottish wife, Rosalind Bond, opened a factory in a valley just east of Quito, the national capital. They made high-quality yarn. Fernando had studied textile management at the University of Leicester, where he met Rosalind. They named the yarn manufacturing company Hilacril, which still exists today. Their idea was to take various sizes of high-quality imported acrylic yarn and spin it into a professionally woven product that could be used by other firms for clothing, upholstery, and car seat covers. By 1980, in order to increase sales, Hilacril began exporting to Colombia. Although the margins were not very favorable, the company began to turn a reasonable profit.

After struggling with tight margins for a number of years, in 1990, Fernando and Rosalind decided to open a weaving department. The objective of the weaving department was to utilize Hilacril yarn to create finished products, which would eventually be sold directly to consumers and retailers. The strategy proved effective; and in 1997 (now with their three sons home from university), Davila and his wife created the retail firm Davila & Bond to take further advantage of stronger margins by getting closer to the consumer.

While Fernando continued to head up the Hilacril arm of the family business, Rosalind assumed the position of president of the final product-oriented Davila & Bond. Charlie, the oldest son, served as production manager for Hilacril and general manager for Davila & Bond. He spent the majority of his time in the factory, designing new products and ensuring that the firm's quality standards were being met. As his parents began to step aside, preparing for retirement, Charlie essentially took over the leadership position of the firm. Eduardo, the second son, was the salesman of the family. He headed up all sales-related activities for both Hilacril and Davila & Bond. The youngest son, Fernando, a lawyer by training, was in charge of the Davila & Bond upholstery division. The final member of the management team was Jorge Perez, a veteran accountant and the CFO of the firm.

It was Charlie's energy, vision, and zeal that brought Davila & Bond into international markets. While spending eight years in Scotland between prep school and university, Charlie became anxious to return home and expand the family business. It took only four years for Charlie's vision of a more integrated firm to come to fruition. And since the inception of the sweater retailer Davila & Bond, Charlie was instrumental in signing franchise agreements and pushing the product into new international markets.

As a manager, Charlie had many strengths. He was upbeat and energetic and could be found joking with employees on the factory floor. Yet at the same time, he commanded respect due to his intricate knowledge of the retail sweater business. He used that knowledge and his open communication style to motivate workers. Charlie was also extremely creative, and the majority of the firm's sweater designs were based on Charlie's ideas. He made a point of attending industry conferences, many in Europe, where he could learn about new manufacturing, design, and marketing techniques. Despite the fact that Davila & Bond was located in a poor developing country with chronic economic problems, Charlie ran the company as if it were located in Milan, New York, or Paris. As a result of his accomplishments in Ecuador, Charlie was recognized in 2003 as an industry expert and appointed to a seat on the Ecuadorian Board of Textile Producers.

Background of the Ecuadorian Market[2]

Ecuador has been a presidential democracy since 1979, but its institutions have been fragile. Economic deterioration helped undermine the functioning of democracy. Lucio Gutiérrez, backed by left-wing and indigenous organizations, was inaugurated as president on January 15, 2003, taking over for Gustavo Noboa. At one point in 1999, the country held four different presidents in one 24-hour period. Despite reforms designed to prevent the proliferation of forces, the country had a fragmented and polarized political system with numerous parties. Ecuador's largest political parties in terms of congressional representation are the centre-right PSC, the PRE, and the centre-left Izquierda Democrática (ID). All have held power at some time since the transition to democracy in 1979.

Economic Conditions/Business Environment

Ecuador had a long road in becoming a stable international investment target. To that end, Ecuadorian officials recently made important developments regarding economic openness. They also pursued a strategy that included improving competitiveness and efficiency and matching their goals to international requirements. The Ecuadorian government also tried to consolidate its policy of openness by improving microeconomic management strategies in the productive and financial sectors, opening the real estate sector and the financial system to foreign investment, fostering a transparent privatization process, improving the administration of the state sector, and eliminating state interventionism.

Ecuador is a member of the Andean Community, which consists of Bolivia, Colombia, Ecuador, Peru, and Venezuela. The Andean Community was in the process of formally establishing a free-trade zone. The Ecuadorian government signed complementary economic agreements with several Latin American countries: Argentina, Uruguay, Chile, Brazil, and Cuba.

U.S.-Andean Free Trade Agreement negotiations were under consideration, the goal being to sign a deal by the end of 2004. The accord would benefit the Andean nations by more permanently locking in the special access to the U.S. market that Andean nations enjoyed under the Andean Trade Preference Act, which was set to expire in 2006. The free-trade agreement also would encourage reforms for attracting investment to the region and would allow the Andean nations to remain competitive with other nations in the U.S. market.

Mexico and Ecuador started free-trade negotiations in 1996. The same year they drafted an agenda of issues related to market access, rules of origin, customs procedures, technical regulations, safeguards, and unfair trade practice. Ecuador withdrew from the talks, saying the terms of the agreement were not favorable. Both countries planned to restart talks to negotiate a free-trade agreement.

Structure of the Economy

Oil and export agriculture were the main pillars of the Ecuadorian economy. During the 1990s, agriculture, forestry, and fishing accounted, on average, for 12.5 percent of GDP, 45 percent of exports, and over 33 percent of employment, respectively. The share of the oil and mining sector (dominated by the extraction of crude oil) as a proportion of national output averaged 12.1 percent of GDP from 1997 to 2001. Oil earnings represented 28 percent of central government fiscal revenue in 2001, and oil attracts the majority of long-term foreign investment. In the mid-1990s, a border dispute with Peru evolved into a brief military conflict. The territory in question was known to have deep oil reserves. In general, the export sector is more developed than the rest of the economy. Exports accounted for an average of 35 percent of GDP from 1997 to 2001, which increased the economy's vulnerability to external shocks, such as downturns in commodity prices.

Foreign Trade

About 60 percent of Ecuador's export earnings come from oil and bananas, as shown in Table 9-6. Other primary products account for most of the remainder, leaving the country vulnerable to external and climatic shocks. Dollarization exposed a lack of competitiveness in some export industries; and export volume growth has been weak in recent years due, in part, to rising labor costs. Since 2000, Ecuador has benefited from high oil prices. Recovery in consumer demand

Table 9-6. Ecuador's Exports/Imports[3]

Major Exports, 2002	% of Total	Major Imports, 2002	% of Total
Oil and oil products	41.0	Raw materials	36.1
Bananas and plantain	19.3	Capital goods	31.4
Tinned fish	6.8	Consumer goods	28.0
Shrimp	5.0	Fuels and lubricants	4.4

Leading Markets, 2002	% of Total	Leading Suppliers, 2002	% of Total
United States	40.8	United States	23.0
Peru	7.4	Colombia	14.0
Colombia	7.2	Brazil	6.3
Italy	5.8	Japan	6.1

and the construction of a new oil pipeline, which was planned to traverse the Andes, led to a rapid rise in imports of both capital and consumer goods, pushing the trade balance into a deficit.

TRADE POLICY

According to the World Bank, Ecuador's weighted average tariff in 1999 was 11.1 percent.[4] Prior authorization from the corresponding Ministry was still needed to import processed foods, cosmetics, and other commodities. Agricultural commodities were occasionally prevented from entering Ecuador through the arbitrary use of sanitary rules as a way to restrict import quantities (and a method for soliciting bribes).

The customs system had three main problems: inefficiency, tax evasion, and outright corruption. Unless the process was greased with money or influence, getting an imported container out of customs took weeks or months. Some importers used loopholes to place merchandise in lower tariff categories. Some imports were passed through a tunnel, where they bypassed duties and entered the market as contraband. According to the Internal Revenue Service, those and other skullduggeries cost the government between $600 million and $800 million each year—let alone the millions they cost business.

DOLLARIZATION

Early in 2000, Ecuador, confronted with a serious economic and governance crisis, adopted the U.S. dollar as its national currency. The economic situation was appalling, with high inflation, government intervention in the banking system (which included the freezing of deposits to prevent further flight from the country), and large fiscal deficits. Politically, then-President Mahaud was being challenged by a lack of congressional support for measures to stabilize the economic situation, a radicalized indigenous movement, and an agitated armed forces. In that environment and as a policy of last resort, the government decided to adopt the U.S. dollar as its currency.[5] Another factor that related to dollarization was the tax structure. Taxes were subject to frequent change. The main taxes in Ecuador were a progressive income tax levied at a rate of up to 25 percent and a VAT levied at 12 percent.

Dollarization seemed to have a positive impact on employment and income per capita figures, yet labor costs soared with the newly adopted dollar. The average labor cost more than tripled between 1999 and 2002, partly due to the strength of the dollar and the creation of new midlevel jobs by multinational firms in Quito. Although Ecuador's income per capita, $3,680 in 2002, was below that of Colombia, Mexico, Brazil and Chile, the average labor cost, $3.31 per hour, was well above the labor cost in each of the other four countries.

CORRUPTION

Weak democratic institutions, particularly judicial, had permitted endemic and widespread corruption to occur. That fueled discontent among the country's poor majority and led to significant increases in crime rates, particularly on the coast.[6] Efforts to crack down on corruption and nepotism in Ecuador had been a top priority of President Gutierrez's government. Recently, a number of high-profile figures in politics and the judiciary have been dismissed.

Ecuador is ranked 113th in the world by Transparency International,[7] a nongovernmental organization that monitors and tracks corruption. That ranking suggests that Ecuador is one of the most corrupt countries in Latin America. While the dollar has eliminated exchange rate risk for MNCs, Ecuador is consistently a

Table 9-7. Davila & Bond's Main Markets: Economic Indicators from 1999–2002

	1999	2000	2001	2002
GDP per head ($ at PPP)				
Ecuador	3,340	3,585	3,585	3,680
Colombia	6,288	6,367	6,367	6,420
Mexico	8,322	8,939	8,986	9,040
Brazil	6,905	7,295	7,500	7,640
Chile	9,080	9,730	10,150	10,373
Labour costs per house (UDSD)				
Ecuador	0.94	1.71	2.75	3.31
Colombia	1.77	1.51	1.47	1.43
Mexico	1.26	1.57	1.74	1.79
Brazil	3.46	3.58	3.02	2.58
Chile	2.37	2.33	2.07	1.99
Recorded unemployment (%)				
Ecuador	15.14	14.1	10.42	8.6
Colombia	13.2	13.9	14.98	15.65
Mexico	2.51	2.22	2.46	2.7
Brazil	14.12	13.33	11.27	11.68
Chile	9.69	9.22	9.18	8.95

From the Economist Intelligence Unit Source: Country Data

challenging destination for FDI not only because of corruption, but also because of the uncertainty that surrounds the government.

THE GROWTH OF DAVILA & BOND

By September 2003, Davila & Bond was exporting sweaters and other woven items to five other countries in Latin America: Colombia, Mexico, Brazil, Bolivia, and Chile. At the same time, the firm had also pursued an aggressive retailing strategy with a combination of company-owned and franchised stores. Fourteen Davila & Bond retail stores (eight firm-owned) were operating in Ecuador, Colombia, and Bolivia. Three additional stores were scheduled to open in Ecuador by the end of 2004. As a result of the strong brand image and reputation that Davila & Bond built through its high-quality sweaters, a number of franchising opportunities developed. In addition to the seven retail shops in Quito, Davila & Bond also owned a store in Ambato, a small city about 50 miles south of Quito. In Cuenca, a colonial city in southern Ecuador, two stores were owned under a franchise agreement. Franchised retail stores were also present in other markets: three in Colombia and one in Bolivia. Reflective of Davila & Bond's high-quality image, the stores were tastefully decorated with a European ambiance accentuated by British flags and classical music.

The basic terms of a franchise agreement were as follows: $40,000 was required up front for 120 days worth of merchandise; a $15,000 fee was charged to use the Davila & Bond name for four years; and approximately $20,000 to $30,000 was needed to set up the retail stores according to company standards (typically, Davila & Bond would front the store setup money with the promise that the store would repay within four years). In addition, Davila & Bond charged franchisees 3 percent of purchases for monthly publicity.

Refer to Table 9-8 and Table 9-9, which follow, for Davila and Bond's 2000–2002 profit and loss information.

A decision was made in 2000 to gradually reduce emphasis on yarn production as a raw material and to place more emphasis on finished product sales, primarily sweaters and shawls. From 2000 to 2002, yarn sales dropped from 42 percent of total sales to 4 percent. Sweaters and shawls experienced significant increases over the same period, with sweaters jumping from 40 percent to 57 percent and shawls up from 7 percent to 33 percent. The theory was that through vertical integration and the sale of finished products, profits would increase over time. Yet it was production costs that increased due to the labor-intensive nature of sweater manufacturing, and profits remained relatively flat.

Davila & Bond's marketing budget was close to $100,000, or 2 percent of total sales, during the last

Table 9-8. Davila & Bond's P&L

P&L (in US$ thousands)

	2000	2001	2002
Revenues	4,895	5,800	4,959
Cost of Goods Sold	2,961	3,687	3,043
Gross Profit	1,934	2,113	1,916
Gross Margin	40%	36%	39%

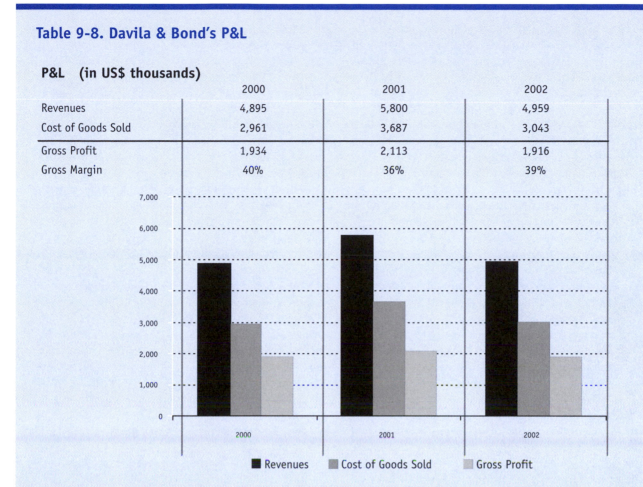

Table 9-9. P&L by Product Line

	Year 2000					Year 2001					Year 2002				
Products	Units Sold (000)	Net Sales (US $000)	Cost of Goods Sold (US $000)	Gross Profit (US $000)	Gross Margin	Units Sold (000)	Net Sales (US $000)	Cost of Goods Sold (US $000)	Gross Profit (US $000)	Gross Margin	Units Sold (000)	Net Sales (US $000)	Cost of Goods Sold (US $000)	Gross Profit (US $000)	Gross Margin
Sweaters	199	1,952	1,011	941	48%	253	2,405	1,417	988	41%	285	2,816	1,647	1,169	42%
Chales	42	319	155	164	51%	230	1,797	1,075	722	40%	215	1,622	1,026	596	37%
Fabrics	201	536	325	211	39%	237	406	283	123	30%	96	310	211	99	32%
Yarns	454	2,088	1,470	618	30%	268	1,192	912	280	23%	51	211	160	51	24%
Total		4,895	2,961	1,934	40%		5,800	3,687	2,113	36%		4,959	3,043	1,915	39%

few years. Since 2004, the company has added new products to its Ecuadorian stores. That new approach involved other products that were not manufactured at their own factory—

Cumberland jackets, chinos, and women's shirts. Charlie noted that the company was trying to leverage its name recognition in the home market. He also considered more of a push in the teenage market, prima-

rily through magazine and television advertising.

International sales hovered between 40 percent and 50 percent between 2000 and 2002. The one major change was a sixfold increase in sales to Mexico and a 10 percent decline in Colombian sales. Still, Colombia was the top export destination, accounting for 24 percent of sales in 2002, followed by Mexico with 12 percent, Brazil with 3 percent, and Chile and

Bolivia with 2% each. Political unrest and a weak economy in Bolivia meant an end to that market in the short run. And poor economic conditions throughout Latin America made market entry risky and complicated.

The increase in sales in Mexico highlighted the potential of that market and how important it was to future growth. In 2003, Davila & Bond had only one store, with the company engaged in developing distribution channels. In 2004, Charlie said the following:

> We are developing our distributors. One of them sells with our brand name (Davila & Bond) and also with their private label to big wholesale chains like Liverpool, Palacio de Hierro, Costco and Wal-Mart.[8] Our second distributor tackles the lower market all over Mexico, which has given us a great boost on sales. We have not decided on franchises yet. We sell over 90,000 items a year to the Mexican market. For the year 2005 we expect a sales increase of 20% for this market.

The relevance of the Mexican market would imply a new approach in regards to the production strategy. In that respect, Charlie mentioned, "We have had some talks on the possibility in producing in Mexico, but nothing is definite yet. Mexico's labor costs are pretty similar to the Ecuadorian's, but labor laws are very difficult to handle."

Although Davila & Bond was clearly the market leader in Ecuador, Charlie perceived a number of small threats within the country. First, importation of sweaters from China, South Korea, and Taiwan was on the rise. Producers in those countries had a major competitive advantage in labor costs, yet the quality of their sweaters was typically below that of Davila & Bond's. One local competitor, Fashionlana, had made a minor surge by copying the business model and manufacturing technique of Davila & Bond. Fashionlana had the same supersoft technology that Davila & Bond utilized and had recently opened three retail stores in Quito.

PRODUCTION

Technology was a key ingredient to Davila & Bond's success. Through keen long-term vision, the firm decided to purchase sophisticated weaving machines from Germany. Each machine cost over $100,000. However, in the mind of Charlie, the investment was well worth it since the machines ran 24 hours a day, 364 days a year (every day but Christmas). Davila &

Bond had plans for expanding its knitting department in 2004 by acquiring six new machines from the German firm Stoll. Charlie commented, "The whole knitting project will increase our production 20% with a total investment of US$ 600.000." That investment was to be financed directly by the German supplier over a period of three years. Also, for the year 2005, the company planned to buy a new weaving machine at a cost of $250,000. The machine would increase yarn production another 20 percent.

The raw synthetic yarn was also imported (typically from Peru or Germany), which enabled the firm to produce a high-quality range of products. Using supersoft technology and materials, the Davila & Bond's sweaters that looked and felt like cashmere, yet could be washed in a washing machine due to their synthetic nature. Moreover, Charlie and his staff of sweater designers traveled to seminars and fashion shows in the United States and Europe to generate ideas for new designs. The company also purchased a new state-of-the-art computer software design program to enhance the creation and production of new styles. Quality was a huge priority for Davila & Bond. Each final product went through a seven-point quality check prior to shipment to ensure that the company's excellent reputation and positive image were maintained.

In the factory, the firm employed 130 workers in the Davila & Bond knitting department, another 50 in weaving, and 70 in the Hilacril yarn division. In addition, about 40 employees worked in the company-owned retail stores around the country. The typical factory worker worked 50 hours a week and earned $250 a month ($300 to $350 if production goals were met). That compared well to the local minimum wage of just under $150 a month, and turnover was virtually nonexistent.

THE MEXICAN MARKET[9]

Charlie was convinced that with just over 100 million consumers and a rising per capita income, Mexico would be an excellent market for the company's sweaters. The plan to open a Davila & Bond store was in place, and the potential to engage in franchising looked promising. Charlie was extremely pleased with the distributor he had selected and agreed to take on a second distributor for "lower-end sales."

Mexico was the largest trading nation in Latin America and the eighth largest in the world. GDP growth had been strong since 1996. In addition, FDI had surged, partly due to Mexico's friendly investment climate, competitive labor costs, fully convertible currency, low taxation, and duty-free access to the United

States and Canada. Investment had been particularly strong from major multinational manufacturers who set up operation in Mexico to supply the U.S. market free of duty. More investment was expected with the recent entry into the EU/Mexico Free Trade Agreement. Mexico was now uniquely positioned to supply the two largest markets in the world tariff-free, the EU and North America.

Investors had few restrictions, and investment approaches ranged from a branch office to a fully owned subsidiary. Most investors set up a corporation (S.A). That required a minimum share of capital, at least two shareholders, and registration in the public register. All foreign investments had to receive prior authorization from the Ministry of Foreign Affairs.

Labor costs in Mexico were very competitive. Skilled and semiskilled labor was plentiful. However, some pressure came from the border regions with the United States, with their many job vacancies and high turnover of staff. There were no controls on the remittance of profits or the repatriation of capital. In some strategic areas of the economy, such as the oil industry, satellite communications, postal services, and minting, foreign investment is prohibited.

There were no restrictions on a foreign investor's access to capital. Most financing from local sources was obtained from privatized commercial banks. Interest rates were very high by international standards. Most investments, however, both domestic and foreign, were sourced from private capital.

Mexico had a number of important ports on both its Atlantic and Pacific coasts, including Altamira, Ensenada, Mazatlan, Progreso, Salina Cruz, and Veracruz. There were plenty of warehouse facilities at most ports. Joint-venture contracts were easily set up in Mexico. Those contracts did not create a business entity, and operations were carried out by the active party. However, income and losses were divided between the two partners according to the contract.

With respect to patents and trademarks, Mexico was a signatory to the 1983 Union of Paris Convention for the Protection of Industrial Property. Patents are protected for a term of 20 years from filing. Nonuse (unless justified by technical or economic reason) may result in the issue of a compulsory license. Trademarks are registered for ten years, renewable for further ten-year periods indefinitely. Mexico did have a significant problem with piracy in the music, alcoholic beverage, clothing, and software industries and some counterfeit/contraband difficulties with other consumer goods.

LOOKING TO THE FUTURE

Although Charlie Davila-Bond knew that the emphasis on international sales was an important factor in the growth of his firm, he also acknowledged that the Ecuadorian market was a mature cash cow. He clearly stated, "First, Davila & Bond must maintain its number one position in the Ecuadorian market." Yet at the same time, he went on to say, "We must also expand our image overall and increase our international sales." Indeed, the trade-off between balancing the risk of relying too heavily on Ecuador with aggressively pursuing international sales while possibly losing ground at home was the key to the future.

As Charlie examined his existing markets, he thought more growth in Mexico was almost a certainty. With a market of 100 million people and an income per capita triple that of Ecuador, the potential of selling more sweaters in Mexico was promising. Charlie mentioned that he even had talks with a Mexican producer about the possibility of manufacturing there. But he was somewhat concerned about the complexity of Mexican labor laws. Elsewhere in Latin America, Brazil and Argentina seemed like viable possibilities. Being relatively large, wealthy nations with a European fashion sense and an amenable climate, those markets looked like reasonable places to bolster future sales. For the moment, Charlie wanted to determine the best possible strategy for further penetration into the Mexican market. Would finding a stronger distribution partner there be essential? What were the benefits and drawbacks of getting involved in manufacturing in Mexico, possibly through one of the Mexican maquilas? Compared to other potential markets in the world, Mexico's profile seemed to be an excellent fit, both culturally and economically, with Davila & Bond's international.

Finally, the production issue was something Charlie had to address. Typically, all of the sweaters for the year were sold by August. Expanding the plant was certainly an option, yet labor costs in Ecuador had been creeping up and were no longer a competitive advantage. Did it make sense to outsource some part of production to Mexico? If so, could Davila & Bond's quality reputation be maintained? Also, franchising had gone well in recent years, and the potential for establishing stores in Mexico, Europe, and elsewhere remained strong. As the end of 2003 approached, Charlie knew that the time had come to take Davila & Bond to another level. The decisions he made would set the firm's trajectory for years to come.

ENDNOTES

1. In Quito, the people say that there are four seasons in every day: morning is like spring, noon is like summer, early evening is like fall, and midnight is like winter.

2. Part of this section has been drawn from The Economist Intelligence Unit Research.

3. www.economist.com

4. Index of Economic Freedom—Heritage Foundation.

5. World Bank: Crisis and Dollarization in Ecuador.

6. U.S. Agency for International Development 2002.

7. Transparency International: Corruption Perceptions Index 2002.

8. Wal-Mart is the most important retailer in Mexico. Sales in 2003 were $11.8 billion, and 671 units were distributed over 68 cities nationwide. It employs approximately 110,755 people, has 24,378,536 square feet in supermarket space, and has 60,342 restaurant seats.

9. Part of this section was based on research drawn from the UK Trade and Investment Office.

Case prepared by Professor Christopher Robertson (Northeastern University) for use in classroom discussion, with assistance from Mr. Charlie Davila-Bond. Copyright @2005, all rights reserved.

Case 9.2

IKEA

IKEA, founded in Sweden in 1953, designs and sells inexpensive furniture and accessories. It operates its no-frills furniture stores in over 40 countries, and its sales have increased rapidly from ?1.2 billion in 1984 to ?8.2 billion in 1999 to over ?13 billion in 2004. In 2004, it stores received over 400 million visitors, up from 220 million in 1999. IKEA's stores are in 24 countries across Europe, in the United States, in Canada, in seven Asian countries, and in four countries in the Middle East. IKEA's concept is straightforward: sell functional, well-designed furniture at prices so low that everyone can afford it, thus creating better living for its customers. On the marketing side, IKEA sells inexpensive, ready-to-assemble, well-made furniture to customers who are willing to transport it home. On the manufacturing side, IKEA designs the furniture, then subcontracts manufacturing to low-cost sources around the world that can produce high-quality products. As the furniture itself is sold in kit form, the pieces actually are made in different locations, with IKEA purchasing from manufacturers offering the lowest prices.

IKEA's furniture comes boxed and must be assembled by the customer at home. Customers pick up the boxed kits from an adjacent self-service warehouse. IKEA stores tend to be located near freeway exits and outside cities, where space is available at low rates. That allows the firm to provide ample parking, and customers can easily get in and out of the store without encountering traffic jams. IKEA also cooperates with local car rental companies to help customers rent small trucks to transport their purchases.

The furniture design is Scandinavian modern, with textiles in pastel colors. The international product line is less varied than that sold within the home markets of Scandinavia. Over the years, IKEA has won design awards, designed furniture based on eighteenth-century Swedish furnishings, and designed special furniture for children. IKEA's market is the "young of all ages." It has a flair for marketing to young couples with children. Its warehouses are festively decorated, it provides day care for children, and it features inexpensive restaurants. The focus on child care and in-store restaurants is to keep people in the stores until they buy something, preventing their exit because of bored and unmanageable children or the desire to get a meal.

The emphasis is on low-priced furniture, priced 30 to 50 percent below the competition's fully assembled furniture. From market to market, prices vary somewhat for the same basic product, but not greatly.

IKEA's founder, Ingvar Kamprad, grew up on a farm in southern Sweden and began a business selling flower seeds and ballpoint pens through mail-order catalogs. He insists that employees be "cost-conscious to the point of stinginess." He has written, "Too many new and beautifully designed products can be afforded by only a small group of better-off people. We have decided to side with the many."

IKEA has always been innovative in selling furniture. When it entered Sweden in the early 1950s, furniture retailers were small, purchasing furniture to customer specifications and placing orders with a manufacturer only after receiving a commitment from customers. Furniture was expensive and bought in sets (for example, a dining room suite), and credit was an important sales tool. IKEA entered the market with large showrooms outside cities, the option to buy one piece of furniture at a time, self-service for cash, and low prices.

When IKEA entered Switzerland with its first store near Zurich, it had to decide whether to rely on the IKEA company name, to position itself as a Scandinavian furniture company (in which case it might be confused with Danish furniture), or to identify IKEA as a distinctive Swedish company. IKEA knew it would have to address Swiss concerns (the Swiss were perceived to be a conservative group) about a Swedish company and its way of selling furniture.

IKEA prepared a set of ads that showcased typical conservative Swiss opinions of and reactions to IKEA. The ads consisted of letters sent by a conservative Herr Bunzli to IKEA, saying what he thought of the company's ideas and way of selling furniture in Switzerland. The aim of the campaign was to joke about the old-fashioned values of the Swiss and appeal to those who wanted to change. The ads exemplified IKEA's philosophy: to take advantage of being a foreigner and to use attention-getting and provocative advertising. Managers in all countries are required to follow that advertising strategy, though they can use local agencies, following guidelines from headquarters.

The first year IKEA was in Switzerland, 650,000 people visited its stores. The next year IKEA entered the huge West German market and subsequently France, drawing on its experiences with the German- and French-speaking parts of Switzerland. IKEA continues to open stores at a rapid rate, a dozen new stores opened at the beginning of its 2005–2006 fiscal year, between May and August 2005. Two of those stores were in the United States; the rest were in Europe.

IKEA has a special organization structure dedicated to smooth and speedy entry into foreign markets. This foreign-expansion group has several key subunits: a European deco-manager, a manager of construction, and a first-year group whose responsibility is to create and manage new overseas outlets during the first year. The construction manager selects a site and supervises the creation of the new store, overseeing inventories, installation of fixtures, communications networks, etc. The first-year manager oversees hiring, reassignment of experienced employees from other IKEA locations, training, and advertising campaigns and decides on the "assortment" of product line to be carried. Furniture is typically ordered from a central warehouse in Sweden and starts arriving three months before opening day.

Planning of a new outlet begins about ten months before opening day. Since IKEA has expanded rapidly, the first-year group cannot spend a whole year nurturing new outlets, as originally envisaged. Training has to be speeded up to allow local management to take over sooner. The staff begins working about two months before opening day to familiarize themselves with IKEA's mode of operations and product line, which ensures a smooth opening. Advertising begins at about the same time. The staff generally takes a trip to IKEA's outlets in Scandinavia, culminating in a press conference the day before store inauguration.

IKEA and the United States

IKEA entered Canada in 1976. With nine stores in Canada by 1985, the United States seemed like the next logical market. California was its first pick; Boston, its second choice. Executives who set out to study the California market encountered some obstacles, however. California had unique standards for upholstered furniture that would have raised costs by 15 percent. California's system of unitary taxation by which it taxed its "share" of IKEA's worldwide income was unpalatable.

Boston was attractive because of its huge itinerant student and yuppie populations. However, government regulations and lack of responsiveness on the part of state officials led the company to establish its first warehouse and retail operation in suburban Philadelphia, instead

Philadelphia made special efforts to help IKEA. Why? Jobs and tax revenues. Through the Greater Philadelphia International Network, a small-business-backed office that tries to attract foreign investment, IKEA officials were introduced to bankers and real estate brokers, given a helicopter tour of the city, and invited to cocktail parties every evening of their three-day stay.

Location, of course, is critical to this kind of company. The Philadelphia market area, which includes Delaware and southern New Jersey, had large numbers of young middle-income families and relatively inexpensive commercial real estate. The Network helped IKEA find space in a mall next to a turnpike exit in the suburb of Plymouth Meeting. "Pennsylvania Turnpike, Exit 25" is the sort of address it seeks. (Forty percent of its customers were likely to be from out of state.)

IKEA shifted its North American headquarters from Vancouver, British Columbia, to Philadelphia. Opening a second store in the Virginia suburb of Dale City (near Washington, D.C.) in the spring of 1986, IKEA found that it had underestimated the market by 50 percent. Consequently, severe inventory shortages developed. By 2005, IKEA had opened 24 stores across the United States, with seven stores in California alone. New stores were scheduled to open in Chicago and Boston, among other locations, as of this writing.

IKEA clearly focuses on customer value. It is concerned with two questions: How can the product be improved? How can we become a better place to work? The company expects all of its employees to be thrifty; even the head of its North American operations flies economy class to Scandinavia. The point is that anything that does not add to customer value is to be avoided.

QUESTIONS AND RESEARCH

1. Analyze IKEA's international expansion. Why was it successful?

2. To what extent does IKEA's product line need to be adapted to foreign markets?

3. Did IKEA have to adapt other aspects of the marketing mix when entering foreign markets? Explain.

4. Prepare a time chart showing how IKEA proceeds in opening a new international store.

5. How did IKEA enter the United States? Why did it choose Pennsylvania? Comment on its subsequent US expansion.

6. IKEA's U.S. web site is http://www.ikea.com/ms/en_US. Browse its online catalog and map of store locations. Comment on its product adaptation for U.S. markets and its geographic distribution in the United States.

NPD and Product-Line Policies

Chapter 9 discussed how a firm's basic product fits into global markets. Chapter 9 also dealt with global branding and its implementation. Product features such as packaging, labeling, brand name, and warranties were discussed, as well as how those features may change as they encounter global markets. Chapter 10 considers additional aspects of product policy surrounding NPD and product-line policies.

The main goals of this chapter are to

- Discuss diverse approaches to product development for international markets.

- Consider how technology-intensive industries approach global product development.

- Present Japanese views and examples of international product development.

- Discuss how policies on conducting global R&D and global acquisitions and divestitures contribute to global product development.

- Analyze the role of benchmarking and quality improvements in developing world-class products.

New Product Development (NPD)

NPD for multiple international markets is based on two major ideas: (1) understanding consumer needs in different countries and (2) drawing on a firm's knowledge base and assets to develop products that can satisfy consumer needs in different countries.

Importance of Consumer Needs

Consumer needs are the starting point for product development, whether for domestic or global markets. Consider pianos, for instance. Many pianos are gathering dust in living rooms around the world—40 million of them by one estimate. Yamaha, with 40 percent of the global market but declining demand, had to rethink customer needs. It chose to retrofit pianos (for about $2,500) with a computer board that can capture music from the piano as it is played; the piano can then be used as a playback instrument. It can even play back performances by great piano artists. The piano is linked to a computer that "reads" disks of piano music and then causes the piano to play the music back. This is the player piano concept all over again, with disks substituting for paper rolls.[1] What was a dead business is being revived by creating a value-added product in response to consumer needs.

Products for Foreign Markets: A Conceptual Framework

In addition to consumer needs, conditions of use and ability to buy the product form a framework for decisions on NPD for foreign markets. The strategy may be product extension, with or without significant product adaptation, new products for specific foreign markets, or design of a global product for all markets. In using that framework, the development process encompasses the product itself as well as communication about the product (that is, advertising). Table 10-1 summarizes the implications of that concept.

When consumer needs and conditions of use are not taken into account, failure is the result. For example, Heinz was attracted by the size of the Brazilian market. As a result, it set up a joint venture with Citrosuco, an orange juice exporter, to launch its first product, Frutsi, a fruit drink that had been successful in Venezuela and Mexico. Every street corner in Brazil, however, has a small store selling freshly squeezed orange juice at low prices. Although Heinz could keep pure fruit juice content at 10 percent in most countries, Brazilian regulations set a minimum of 30 percent. This raised prices and made Frutsi uncompetitive with the fresh-squeezed variety. To complicate matters, the additional fruit juice shortened shelf life, necessitating new packaging.

To penetrate the market, Heinz gave cases of Frutsi to retailers on consignment, to be paid for after the product was sold. This led to overstocking, and many cases of spoiled product had to be returned. (Brownouts and electric supply interruptions are common in Brazil, and the hot climate hastened product deterioration when refrigeration failed). Then Heinz spent $200,000 on TV advertising featuring a robot character that wasn't considered friendly enough. Although a name change to Suco da Monica, based on a popular Brazilian cartoon character, helped to increase sales, Heinz decided to pull out. All three of the factors in Table 10-1—customer need, conditions of use, and ability to buy—were unfavorable to Heinz in Brazil.[2]

General Motors also saw a market decline for its Buick in the United States. The image of Buick for middle-class American senior citizens contributed to the eroding market share. However, Buick has been a growing market for General Motors in China, with sales of the car in China

Table 10-1. Market Characteristics and Product-Line Strategies

If:			Then:
Customer *Need*	Conditions *of Use*	Ability *to Buy*	**Product-Line Strategy**
Same	Same	Exists	Product and Communications Extension
Different	Same	Exists	Product Extension and Communications Adaptation
Same	Different	Exists	Product Adaptation and Communications Extension
Different	Different	Exists	Product and Communications Adaptation (with new products in the future)
Same	Not Applicable	Low to None	New Product and Communications

Source: Warren J. Keegan, "Multinational Product Planning: Strategic Alternatives," *Journal of Marketing* 33(1).

likely to exceed U.S. Buick sales by around 2006. Buick was sold in China before the country's Communist revolution, and China's last emperor owned two of them. Buick was known as the car of the elites, a symbol of status and affluence. When General Motors wanted to return to China in the mid-eighties, as China was opening up to the West and Western multinationals, it sought Chinese government permission to establish a Buick factory.

Buick appealed to small business owners, the emerging middle class, and older Chinese who could finally afford a car. One buyer in his sixties purchased Buick's entry-level Sail by pooling funds with his daughter, a schoolteacher. He referred to the Buick as "a luxury brand that brings social status." The Buicks are adapted to local tastes, with large chrome grills and slanted headlights. The interior features leather seats and roomy backseats (as drivers may be ferrying important officials and businesspeople who sit in the back). DVD players are built into the backseats. Lower-end Buicks have six-CD changers, wood-style panels, coolers to hold drinks, and drawers to store comfortable driving shoes for women who wear high heels. Those product details focus on psychological needs because they are seen as adding to perceived value.[3]

Adoption and Diffusion of New Products

New product introduction entails adoption and diffusion (use). There are five stages: awareness, interest (knowledge), evaluation (of information to decide whether to try), trial, and adoption (continuing use).[4] The first stage, **awareness**, involves communicating the existence of a new product or innovation to potential adopters/consumers. The second stage of deepening **interest** relates to obtaining detailed knowledge about the new product or innovation. Next, consumers must **evaluate** the knowledge they've gathered to decide whether to break old habits and take the risk of trying the new product. The trial phase is when the new product is actually being used for the first time. Finally, consumers assess their experience from first use and decide whether to continue using the product—**adoption**.

Mirroring the stages by which consumers decide to adopt new products are the stages of decision making that firms go through in introducing the products. The first stage involves **concept generation** and the **screening** of competing new product ideas. Next comes evaluation of a short list of ideas in view of consumer needs, costs of production, current revenues, and competitive actions. Next, the firm enters the **prototype** stage, in which trial runs of the new product are made. After ascertaining product viability and quality from an engineering and production standpoint, the firm then moves to **product testing** in the marketplace. If testing is successful, the product is **launched** into the wider market, perhaps with additional modifications based on results from the testing phase. Results from the product launch are then evaluated and the product is kept on the market, completing market entry. Competition is a complicating factor, since retaliatory moves by competitors can hinder an accurate assessment of market acceptance. Success breeds imitation, so rarely does a new product have the market to itself unless protected by strong patents and copyrights (as in the case of new pharmaceutical drugs).

Product Development

The next section reviews some of the variables that influence product development.

INTERFACE OF CUSTOMER NEEDS AND THE COMPANY'S KNOWLEDGE BASE

One conception of NPD in rapidly changing environments views new products as the outcome of a meeting of "relationships and knowledge."[5] Every company has a relationship with its existing customer base. Companies also possess knowledge, skills, resources, and competencies. That **knowledge base** can consist of technology, accumulated experience, business processes, and methodologies. Companies wanting to create new products or services can ask themselves how their customers are going about creating value. Companies can then assess whether their competencies allow them to develop products that can be inputs to the customers' new value-creating business directions. Therefore, companies must constantly increase their knowledge base and competencies. If that process results in knowledge that exceeds customer requirements, they can go further afield in search of new customers and new markets. Witness companies such as Microsoft, Hewlett-Packard, and Intel, whose product mix completely changes virtually every 18 months, as previously mentioned.

CORE COMPETENCE, PRODUCT PLATFORMS, AND PRODUCT FAMILIES

Meyer and Utterback[6] extend the relationship between a company's core competencies and new products. They suggest that effective product development has distinct layers, with a bedrock of **core competencies** upon which are built **product platforms** and then product families marketed to customers. The concept of a product family built on a platform rising out of core competencies suggests a clear product development path for next-generation products. It also stresses new product compatibility with the product family and the constant need for innovation and strengthening of the underlying core competencies. The diagram in Figure 10-1 illustrates the product platform concept.

Halman and his coresearchers[7] focus on the risks and problems connected with the development and management of platforms and product families that emerge from

Figure 10-1. A Framework to Integrate Markets, Platforms and Competencies

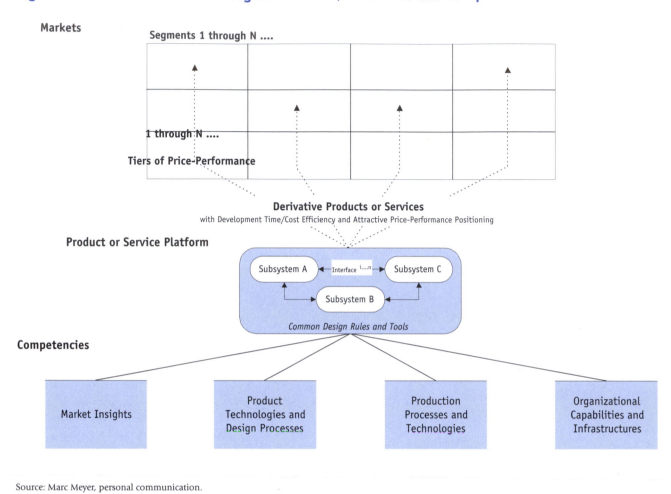

Source: Marc Meyer, personal communication.

them. Costs and time are associated with developing a platform. Platform thinking requires the formation and collaboration of multifunctional groups. It also requires deliberate planning for the sequence of products that will emerge from the existing platform and planning for platform regeneration and next-generation platforms. Generating additional products from an existing platform may be easiest, even though the platform may be nearing architectural obsolescence, which creates a barrier to architectural innovation.

Halman explored three European firms, including ASML, a leading supplier of semiconductor manufacturing (microlothography) tools; Skil, a division of Bosch and a manufacturer of power tools; and Stork Digital Imaging, a supplier of digital print and preprint applications to the graphics arts and textile printing markets. The three companies had a similar understanding of the complexities

and application of the product platform approach. All three focused on product architecture rather than process as the basis for defining and creating their platforms. They resorted to platform approaches to gain increased flexibility in product design, greater efficiency in product development and realization, and improved effectiveness in market positioning and communication.

Table 10-2 provides a summary of how the three companies viewed their experience using platform approaches to product development. The table provides a practical window on the difficulty, costs, and benefits of implementing the product platform concept. Some of the trade-offs from using platforms included platform-constraining flexibility in product development, higher initial time and cost to develop platforms, and lower differentiation resulting from sticking to a common platform. Clearly, choosing the wrong platform can negatively affect an entire product family and reduce market success. Interestingly, the common lesson the three companies derived from their experience with product platforms was the necessity—first and foremost—of focusing on consumer *needs*.

Robertson and Ulrich address the different perspectives of differentiation and commonality inherent in a platform approach to product development. They note that a platform-based product plan incorporates attention to the entire portfolio and timing of the introduction of its various components. A platform-based plan also offers detailed differentiation—how the various products in the family are different internally (within the firm) and externally (in the eyes of the customer and the market). Similarly, a commonality plan lays out the extent of shared technology, modules, subsystems, software, interfaces, and standards.[8]

Two French Examples

The connection between a firm's knowledge and competencies on the one hand and relationships with existing customers on the other hand is illustrated in the history and growth of two of France's largest companies, Générale des Eaux and Lyonnaise des Eaux. In the mid-1800s, the companies started providing water and sewer services to French cities. Over time, they expanded by providing additional services required of cities: railroads, canals, electricity generation and supply, and all manner of public infrastructure. The companies benefited from a unique French law of "concessions" that grants private companies

the right to provide public infrastructure projects for a fixed term—30 to 60 years, for example—during which time they can make a profit. What is interesting about these two companies is that they have grown by seeing themselves as managers of cities.

Providing public services at a profit is a tricky and complex business. The success of these two firms lies in their ability to provide "the financial, social, legal, managerial, and technical engineering" that allows public infrastructure projects to be efficient and profitable. What is also interesting is that as cities evolved, these firms were able to provide new services. For example, they have branched out into waste management services, and they provide electricity to 10 percent of Paris, generating electricity by incinerating the garbage they collected. They have adopted environmentally safe technologies and have expanded overseas, managing water distribution networks and wastewater treatment in 50 cities on six continents, including many small cities in the United States. Their product development strategy is summed up in the view of a Générale executive, "Our people have no a priori right to say no to a client request. If one of the companies in the group cannot produce what the client wants, then we will create a company that can."[9]

COMPRESSION AND EXPERIENTIAL STRATEGIES

Eisenhart and Tabrizi looked at 72 product development projects from 36 Asian, U.S., and European firms operating in the global computer industry.[10] They contrasted two

Table 10-2. Risks and Lessons Learned from Platform-Based Product Development

	ASML	Skill	SDI
Risks	• Development time and costs of platform • Rigidity in design • Restrictions on the integration of new technologies • Incorrect forecast of future user needs • Change from one platform to another	• High cost and time for integration of existing elements • Platform development easily becomes a goal in itself • Mistakes made in the beginning have a high impact • Failure to forecast customer needs correctly	• Development time and costs to meet specifications of all target markets. • Development process becomes more complex • Restrictions for all market segments • Selection of the right platform
Lessons Learned	• Definition of a platform requires choosing from alternatives • Development of a platform is a strategic decision • Understanding of market requirements is necessary	• Development of a product family needs a clear concept • A product family makes communication clear • Customer needs have to be identified early	• Having one platform for two markets is difficult for the stability of the platform • Market requirements have to be tested before platform development

Source: Johannes, I. M. Halman, Adrian P. Hofer, and Win van Vuuren, "Platform-Driven Development of Product Families: Linking Theory With Practice," *Journal of Product Innovation Management* 20, 2003, pages 149–162, Tables 4 and 5.

different approaches:

- The *"compression" strategy* assumes that the steps to developing new products are known. and that rapid product development is crucial. Product development can be speeded up by planning, using CAD, involving suppliers, empowering project leaders, and using multifunctional teams.

- The *"experiential" strategy* is based on the notion that NPD is an uncertain process and what matters is creativity, a process relying on factors such as real-time experience, flexibility, and improvisation.

The authors argued that both perspectives, compression and experiential strategies, are necessary for successful product development.

A different approach to product development suggests postponing product definition as long as possible. By delaying product specifications until close to product launch, a firm can take advantage of the latest developments in core technologies and consumer preferences.[11]

SENSORY SEGMENTATION

Another approach to international product development is *sensory segmentation*, which divides customers according to their responses to sensory product characteristics. Such cross-country segments allow the development of a limited range of products within a product line to satisfy a large number of product needs across countries. This approach is most useful in consumer product development, as illustrated by the following example.

A multinational marketer of various fruit-flavored sodas in over 50 countries found that the sheer number of flavors led to problems in sourcing; quality control; variable acceptance criteria; and, consequently, lower product-line profitability. The company characterized sensory perceptions along the following dimensions: flavor type, flavor level, color, use of a sweetener, acidity, and cloud. The company had to choose sensory variables that could be controlled through changes in product formulation and in the manufacturing process. That way, the company could respond to consumer preferences with product modifications or new products. Products were chosen or specially blended to conform to the different sensory packages desired. When the product was tested against competitors' products in different countries, consumer panel preferences yielded three sensory segments: "low-impact" seekers who wanted mild products, "medium-impact" seekers, and "high-impact" seekers who wanted robust products with the sweetest taste and the darkest color. Developing products to meet the needs of each sensory segment across countries allowed the company to reduce the number of products marketed internationally while still meeting the needs of large numbers of customers in each country.[12]

TECHNOLOGY UPHEAVALS: THE SILICON GRAPHICS APPROACH[13]

Companies in high-tech industries face the certainty that current-generation technology will become obsolete. Their dilemma is balancing incremental improvements to the current technology-based product line while focusing on next-generation technology that will make their current products obsolete, dramatically reducing sales. Companies can't avoid next-generation technology because their competitors will innovate and, inevitably, cause the company's current markets to vanish. Hence, the challenge is how to manage new technologies in product development.

Technology executives have emphasized the need to cannibalize themselves. That is, they deliberately seek to supplant their products (even if the products are still selling well) with newer products and product lines. Otherwise, a company's mature-technology products will become commodities. And with shrinking margins, the company will not be able to spend on R&D and on changing customer needs. Compressing the time it takes to develop new products allows companies to start NPD initiatives later and thus factor in the latest customer perceptions and wants.

Silicon Graphics (SGI) is a leader in high-performance computing, visualization, and storage technologies. The company's approach to NPD, for example, is based on six fundamentals:[14]

1. *Form product development teams focused on specific customer segments.* Base the teams on their needs; then let the engineers design new products in cooperation with customers. Market research is useless in that context. Instead, the best technology and R&D staff must work with leading-edge customers, sometimes referred to as lead users. Those users constantly "push the envelope" of the capabilities of current products, suggesting a NPD direction for the company.[15]

2. *If new products cannibalize existing products that are still growing, so be it.* The paralysis caused by fear of cannibalization of existing product lines can be deadly to long-term growth.

3. *Use new technology and capabilities to address high-end frontier customers* in a rapidly changing technology environment. Use older technology to develop cheaper, low-end, mass-market products.

4. *To create chaos, build on core capabilities,* which SGI defined as:
   - Advanced microprocessors.
   - Intuitive interfaces, requiring less customer training.
   - Symmetric multiprocessing, allowing SGI supercomputers to use microprocessor arrays to manipulate vast volumes of graphics data at high speeds.
   - A shared architecture and operating system across

all SGI machines. Proprietary but open architecture allows a company to set technical standards for an entire industry and consolidate its market share.[16]

- Bright technological people; as a technology company, SGI's fortunes are determined by its people. The technical merits of ideas rather than hierarchy or status should determine new product directions.

5. *Alliances are essential* to maintaining an accelerated pace of innovation.

6. *Financial targets provide control over the NPD process,* such as insisting on gross margins of 50 percent, R&D at 12 percent of sales, and 15 percent growth in sales per employee.

VISION IN PRODUCT-LINE DEVELOPMENT: SANDOZ AND NUTRITION

Sandoz, a Swiss pharmaceutical company, merged with Ciba to form one of the world's largest drug companies, Novartis. Prior to the merger, Sandoz diversified out of the drug business by buying the U.S. baby food company, Gerber, for $3.7 billion. You might question such a diversification on the grounds that margins are lower in the nutrition food business than in pharmaceuticals. Sandoz's chair Marc Moret, however, offered some interesting insights into why Sandoz acquired Gerber Foods, noting that nutrition and pharmaceutical products are appropriate and complementary products for a health-care company: "Our vision of nutrition is one of a continuum from diet and medical nutrition to treating highly complex diseases with innovative compounds." Nutrition contributes to health; and by acquiring Gerber, Sandoz could provide both nutrition products and drugs. Gerber possesses databases and research facilities oriented to infants and young children, while Sandoz's drug development experience can help Gerber develop medically nutritional products, particularly for an aging population. Sandoz is a leading distributor of nutrition products to nursing homes in the United States and can develop baby food markets in emerging developing nations. Novartis has continued these acquisition-based product diversification efforts. It bought Bristol-Myers' U.S. business in generic and over-the-counter drugs for $660 million in 2005, giving it control of brands such as Excedrin (a pain reliever), Comtrex (to alleviate cold and flu symptoms), and NoDoz (a sleep medicine). Then the company announced a $7 billion acquisition of two European generic drug companies, HEXAL and Eon Labs. Such complementarity provides some balance to the income stream from pharmaceuticals, which is beset by growing health-care regulation and cost and price reduction pressures.[17]

Multinational Partnerships in Biotech Firms

A technological revolution has hit pharmaceutical drug development. As a result, the former emphasis on synthe-sizing new compounds in labs and then testing for human efficacy is being replaced by biotechnology processes and genetic engineering to develop or imitate disease-fighting substances in humans. For example, researchers agree that cancers, whether genetically inherited or episodic, are caused by gene breakdown. Certain genes function as green lights and red lights, starting and stopping cell growth. Impairment of those functions causes uncontrolled growth and cancerous cell mutations.

Swiss pharmaceutical companies have responded to industry changes by buying controlling stakes in U.S. biotech companies for two main reasons: (1) The United States is rich in small biotech start-ups that require capital and a hands-off atmosphere in which to do research. (2) Switzerland is hedged in by environmental legislation that displays a fear of genetic engineering. Switzerland has repeatedly tried to ban the use of genetically modified animals for new drug-testing purposes, a cornerstone of biotech research. Furthermore, it is a small country with just a few large companies that dominate the industry. Scientists are unlikely to take risks in such an environment or to find the free-wheeling culture required for breakthrough work typical of biotech start-up firms in the United States. Finally, Switzerland has a strong currency, a low cost of capital, and concentrated shareholdings. Therefore, Swiss firms can afford to take a long-term view, ignoring pressure from institutional money managers seeking short-term share price rises. For those reasons, Swiss firms have spent billions of dollars investing in U.S. companies instead of utilizing their capital for internal R&D. They have invested in major U.S. research institutions such as the Dana Farber Cancer Institute in Boston and the Scripps Research Institute in La Jolla, California. They have also set up U.S. venture-capital firms to invest in start-up biotech companies. Continuing that trend, Novartis acquired 20 percent of a biotech start-up, Alnylam Pharmaceuticals, to gain access to its RNA interference (RNAi) knowledge and patents. RNAi is a naturally occurring gene silencing mechanism that could have great promise in treating cancer and other diseases.[18]

A similar approach can be seen in the partnership between Bristol-Myers Squibb and Otsuka of Japan. Otsuka used the low-tech approach of having good scientists, chemists, and biologists conduct painstakingly slow lab work. In contrast, many U.S. pharmaceutical companies have moved to using robots to conduct large-scale drug experiments. The robots search millions of slightly different variations of a single molecule in an attempt to find the molecule that performs best against an illness. Otsuka's approach relied more on having superior scientists use their long years of experience to make informed guesses about what compound might work best. That was the case with the schizophrenia-fighting drug Abilify, which had fewer side effects. Otsuka was able to develop the drug in its labs. Squibb was able to license the drug and get FDA approval in a three years, agreeing to pay Otsuka 35 percent royalties on sales.

In recent years, other drug companies have also begun to market in the United States drugs that were first discovered in Japan. As a result, in recent years, Japanese drugs have accounted for about 13 percent of new drugs approved for sale in the United States. Such partnerships allow U.S. firms to bring new drugs to market more quickly, leveraging years of Japanese effort, and exploiting two different approaches to drug discovery. While these represent divergent approaches to NPD, at the same time, Japanese companies can tap larger U.S. markets while wending their way through the slower Japanese drug approval process.[19]

A Step-Wise Approach to Screening Efforts in NPD

As the costs of developing new products go up, projects are screened several times to ensure that only viable projects receive continued funding. The outline of a modern biotech company's multiple-stage approach to NPD is summarized below.[20]

The company manufactures biotech materials and equipment for use by researchers and testing labs. The company's Project Approval Team (PAT) is composed of the heads of manufacturing, quality assurance, finance, R&D, and marketing, with two additional rotating members from R&D and marketing. The PAT evaluates projects in several phases:

1. *Idea generation* begins with pilot funding for a project generated by any R&D scientist. The results of the initial investigation are documented in an idea-evaluation report and screened by the PAT cochairs, usually from marketing and R&D. If deemed promising, the idea is investigated further with additional funding. Then another report is generated with a proposal suggesting a feasibility study and possible product development. That report is screened by the PAT.
2. The *feasibility* study, resulting in product definition, includes specifications, market potential, and estimates on return on investment. It is reviewed by the PAT.
3. *Product development* includes a specifications stage that establishes components used, packaging, fitness testing, and hazard and stability evaluation. Cost estimates and sales forecasts are used to refine rates-of-return calculations, and test marketing is conducted. If PAT approval is positive at this stage, *final optimization* begins. An initial batch of the drug is made, with attention to documentation, quality-assurance specs, regulatory compliance, and final design. Marketing is called in to develop product promotion and advertising.
4. *Product launch* occurs as the product is handed off to the operating divisions.

It is interesting to observe the evaluation criteria used by the PAT:

- Potential for patent-protected market position
- Long-term market potential and long-term impact on the company
- Possibility of alliances and external funding
- Estimated financial returns
- Fit with company core competencies and with manufacturing, marketing, and distribution capabilities
- Probability of technical success

While the model described above represents the needs of product development in a technology-intensive industry, several of the concerns are relevant to NPD in a variety of industries. One of those concerns includes the balancing of technological, financial, and marketing issues

Japanese Approaches

It is interesting to study the NPD process in Japan, given the capture of significant market share in global markets by Japanese industries. Two examples are considered: the automobile industry and the copier industry.

New Car Development

Broadly speaking, American cars provide comfortable transportation; German cars provide speed; and Japanese cars traditionally offer quality, reliability, and value. Major Japanese producers have approached new car development through a series of important steps.

1. Developing the product concept. Japanese car companies begin with the premise that customers want more original products, but cars have different levels of meaning for different people. Therefore, the focus is on expanding the minds of designers.
2. Specific R&D projects in areas such as new materials and processes
3. Market analysis, including consideration of investment needs, competition, and profit analysis
4. Planning production and supplier choice
5. Planning marketing strategy and product launch.

Table 10-3 summarizes how Japan's major auto manufacturers approach those five critical steps.[21]

Canon and the Personal Copier

In the mid-90s, another Japanese company, Canon, decided that its goal would be to develop a copier for offices with

Table 10-3. Japanese Company Approaches to New Car Development

Product Concept

Customers want more original products, but cars have different levels of meaning for different customers. Therefore, the focus is on expanding the minds of designers.

Nissan: Developed the concept of cars as the "production of a mobile life stage" and "presentation of new life space."

Toyota: Targeted a car concept, the Lexus, for a segment of the U.S. car-buying public characterized as a 43-year-old male living in Los Angeles with a $100,000 income. To satisfy that customer, Toyota conceived three design goals: a maximum speed of 250 km per hour, fuel economy of more than 22.5 mpg, and the quietest car in production.

Honda: Based the Civic on a "man maximum, machine minimum" principle so that there would be more space for passengers. The Civic also pioneered a revolutionary clean-engine technology.

R&D

The broad focus is on new materials, processes, and increased use of electronics

Nissan: Focused on "development of the world's best suspension."

Toyota: Concentrated on aluminum and composite material engines and electronic controls for air intake and exhaust.

Honda: Developed Civic's clean engine through teams of researchers submitting different solutions to the same problem.

Product Design

Multiple parameters are involved: performance, comfort, fuel efficiency, safety, environmental controls, and different national regulations; different consumer tastes and segments, computer-aided design (CAD) with shared designs across models, and links to computer-aided manufacturing (CAM)

Nissan: Developed three segments/divisions: full-size, compact, and subcompact; developed a merit system to promote younger workers in product development.

Toyota: Formed a new product development committee to replace the chief examiner system: two committee chairs, a design engineer at the development stage, and a production engineer at the product preparation stage.

Honda: Gave employees of the Civic responsibility and a project management focus on teamwork; used guest engineers at product development stage to bring in ideas from different company cultures.

Source: T. Sasaki, "How the Japanese Accelerated New Car Development," *Long Range Planning* 24(1), pages 15–25.

---

fewer than five employees who did not currently use copiers. Utilizing existing technology, however, the cheapest copier would cost more than 500,000 yen to produce, would need service by professional engineers, and would be expensive because it would be sold through dealers and the manufacturer's direct sales force. For those reasons, existing copiers were too expensive for the small-firm market.

With all of that in mind, Canon came up with its Personal Copier Product Concept:[22]

Goal:	A copier priced under $1,000.
Issues:	Defining the target market segment, quality level required for personal use maintenance, target price and cost, size and weight, and new functions to be added.
Product Concept:	Compact, lightweight, priced less than $1,000, maintenance through exchange of disposable parts, and added functions for ease of use and versatility.
Approach:	While incorporating cost and reliability issues, study disposable photoreceptors, development apparatus, instant toner fuser, and new materials and compo-

nents. Study other electronic consumer products, such as fans and TVs, to learn about cost versus reliability. Obtain compactness through outer structural design, using foam plastics, piston-motion mechanism utilizing mechanical clutch, and small diameter (60-mm) photoreceptor drum.

Organization Structure:	Task Force X for prototype model; engineering model inspired by Team X for AE-1 camera. The composition of this task force is shown in Figure 10-2.
Slogan:	"Let's make the AE-1 of copiers."

Canon attributed its success in developing the personal copier to several factors:

- Senior management's vision of an under-$1,000, maintenance-free copier.
- Company-wide cooperation as exemplified by the setting up of Task Force X (illustrated in Figure 10-2).
- Use of young engineers, average age 27.
- Designation of a product champion, Hiroshi Tanaka (Director of Reprographics Products Develop-

Figure 10-2. Canon's New Personal Copier

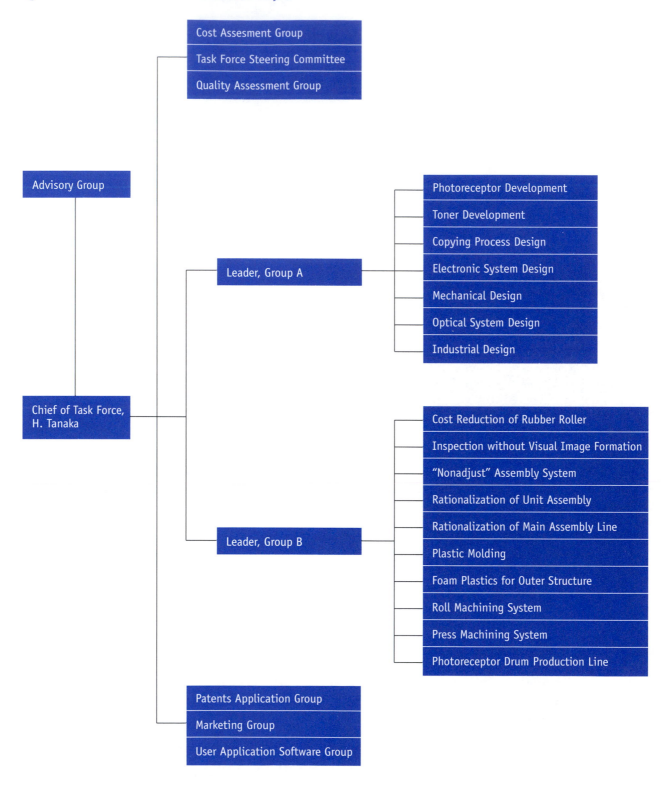

Source: Teruo Yamanouchi, "Breakthrough: The Development of the Canon Personal Copier," *Long-Range Planning* 22, no. 5 (1989).

ment Center), who acted as a bridge between top management and young engineers.

- Balance of cost versus reliability, leading to invention of cartridge-based technologies.
- A well-structured development process, allowing chronology of product concept through sales launch to be completed within three years.

Additional factors specific to Japanese product development are discussed by Harryson in a comparison of Sony and Canon. Pertinent factors include job rotation of engineers, direct transfer of R&D teams to production as their products reach commercialization, and the role of centers of excellence.[23]

Supplier Relationships

Supplier relationships are a critical element of Japanese approaches to NPD. Japanese companies such as Toyota and Nissan make complex products that require mass production, assembly, and integration of several subsystems and thousands of parts. Typically the companies (1) work with few suppliers; (2) develop long-term partnerships with suppliers; (3) require continuous improvement from suppliers in quality, speed, and time to supply; (4) require lower prices and fewer numbers of parts; and (5) most importantly, involve a limited number of key suppliers early in the design and development of new products. Large companies such as Toyota have several tiers of suppliers. Those companies deal directly only with tier-one suppliers, who, in turn, work with the next tier, etc.[24]

Not all suppliers are capable of being full-fledged partners. They may lack the necessary people skills, technology, prototype-building ability, and knowledge base. Hence, some first-tier companies may not be equal partners. Instead, they may have considerable responsibility for developing a complex assembly to meet customer specifications. Other companies with lesser skills may execute instructions from clients, even building commodity parts on a per-order basis. A supplier firm cannot be a partner to every client, and it may be better off serving as order taker and supplier for some clients.

An example of the supplier-partner approach to NPD comes from Nippondenso, a major supplier of parts to the global auto industry. (Toyota is one of Nippondenso's principal customers.) In developing a new line of alternators, Nippondenso used several years of basic research and a survey of customer preferences toward size and performance. Different alternator housing types, wire specifications, regulators, and terminals added up to 700 variations from which a customer could choose. Once chosen, Nippondenso would work with the customer to customize certain product aspects, such as where the alternator mounts would be located. In this way, Nippondenso took over all of the alternator research and product develop-

ment function, supplying Toyota and other major auto manufacturers on a global basis.

THE HUMAN FACTOR AND SUCCESSFUL PRODUCT DEVELOPMENT ACROSS PRODUCT GENERATIONS

An interesting study focused on the Japanese auto industry asks how knowledge can be passed on from one NPD team to the next as teams work on successive product generations. Aoshima divides the knowledge needed to carry out successful NPD into two types: (1) knowledge needed at an integrative level to combine modules and subsystems into a new product and (2) lower-level knowledge, perhaps at the component level, where parallel and separate development can take place.[25]

Aoshima studied NPD teams at a variety of Japanese auto companies across several product generations. He focused on the extent to which project personnel stayed constant, moving from one NPD team to the next-generation product NPD team. He suggests that such personnel transfer, which might be easier in the then-prevalent pattern of loyalty and lifelong employment within one company, facilitated the higher-level integrative tasks. The reason may be because such knowledge can be more easily retained and is harder to codify and pass along from person to person. On the other hand, Aoshima notes that component-level knowledge can be more easily standardized and taught to new project personnel. Therefore, there is less need to ensure continuity of personnel as a new NPD team is formed to develop a next-generation product. (See Figure 10-3.)

Aoshima's research was conducted in the context of the auto industry, with the car companies developing new automobiles within a brand family such as the Celica. Aoshima does raise the question of whether similar transfer of personnel from one NPD project to the next is necessary for products that are more modular in nature and require less integration.

Role of Global Sourcing

If low-cost, timely development and high-quality, state-of-the-art components are desired, global sourcing is often a necessary step. Kotabe and others[26] have offered interesting insights into the strategic role of offshore sourcing by multinationals. They point out that a firm that shifts from supplying a market through exports to supplying through a manufacturing plant in the market's country also has to rethink its component sourcing decisions. New choices must be made because of tariffs, transportation costs, lower costs from local supply sources, and greater familiarity with new local-supplier capabilities.

Several variables affect the sourcing decision:

- Tariff and nontariff barriers
- Nationality of the parent multinational

Figure 10-3. Systems Knowledge Transfer in the Japanese Auto Industry

Year	Corona Project — Sub-Product Manager (Shusa-tsuki, Shu-tantoin)	Corona Project — Project Managers (CE or Shusa)	Celica/Carina Project — Project Managers (CE or Shusa)	Celica/Carina Project — Sub-Product Manager (Shusa-tsuki, Shu-tantoin)	Product Generation
1907		(Amano)	Hasegawa		
70	(Hirai)	(Takahashi))	Nishida	Wada	
					1st
75		(Hirai)	Moriya		
77					2nd
80				Kuboji	
81			Wada	Nakagawa	
	Konishi	Adachi			3rd
84					
85					
			Kuboji		4th
88					
89					
90		Konishi			5th
92			Nakagawa		
93					
94					6th

Product Management Groups of the Celica/Carina/Corona Projects

October 1970 (Celica/Carina)
• A platform was derived from the Corona.

August 1977 (Celica/Carina)
• A platform became independent of the Corona.

July 1981 (Celica), September 1981 (Carina)

May 1984 (Carina)
August 1985 (Celica, Carina ED, Corona Coupe)
• The Carina and the Corona were integrated (FF). The Celica became independent.

May 1988 (Carina)
August 1989 (Celica, Carina ED, Corona EXIV)

May 1992 (Carina)
October 1993 (Celica, ED, EXIV)
February 1994 (Carren)

People in parentheses are not in the text.

Source: Yaichi Aoshima, "Transfer of System Knowledge Across Generations in New Product Development: Empirical Observations from Japanese Automobile Development," *Industrial Relations* 41(4), October 2002, Figure 1, pages 605–628.

• Stage of the product in the product life cycle
• Exchange rate
• Transportation costs
• Production costs
• Growth of sales in local market
• Profitability in local market

Thus, a firm will be motivated to begin local sourcing because of high tariff barriers; mature products or components; an appreciating exchange rate in the parent country; high transportation costs; low local-market production costs; and an attractive local market, as reflected in growth rates and profitability. However, Japanese firms, for instance, may be predisposed to Japanese sourcing because of supplier infrastructure, relationships, and belief in the superior quality of products made in Japan.

Environmental factors also play a key role in the sourcing decision. They often affect global product-line performance, as captured by variables such as market share, sales growth, and returns on sales and on investments. The important mediating environmental factors are product and process innovation and asset specificity. That is, advanced technology components may be affected by product and process innovations. In-house or third-party sourcing may be determined by where the most innovation has occurred. Also, components requiring specialized assets might have to be sourced from organizational units where the specific assets already exist. In-house sourcing is more likely for components that require specialized assets, such as proprietary software or machinery. Overall, technology intensity—measured by the levels of R&D spending—affects the transfer of equipment and components between units of a multinational. Technology intensity also affects decisions about whether to source offshore and, ultimately, market share and a firm's profitability.

OUTSOURCING PROBLEMS

Outsourcing can bring problems with design, manufacturing, costs, and quality. Compaq experienced difficulties with its outsourced supplier of laptop computers, Japan's Citizen Co. The problems arose because no Compaq employees were in charge of the Compaq order at Citizen. Compaq now has a separate management group to supervise outsourcing. The group requires control information such as daily quality data and output from product integrity audits. Similarly, both U.S. and Japanese car firms were hurt when they had to recall cars because of flaws in seat belts made by a Japanese supplier, Takata Corp.

A deeper problem might be a company's use of outsourcing to achieve short-term cost savings—a strategy that can be costly in the long run. Outsourcing should be used only as part of a long-term strategy. Unions dislike outsourcing because it reduces union membership and undermines their authority. Changes in marketing relationships, such as the move to mass customization (see Chapter 9), also require firms to bring back in-house that which was formerly outsourced.

There has been a significant increase in the outsourcing of some of the tasks associated with NPD. Researchers have used transaction cost theory and resource-based views of a firm to suggest that outsourcing occurs as firms (1) focus on core tasks that best suit their resources and capabilities and (2) outsource other tasks to increase efficiency and speed up the process. Tasks and subsystems outsourced at six sample firms identified by the researchers included microprocessors, operating systems, software, peripherals, networking properties, control systems, handling systems, and design of components such as pumps and standard modules.[27]

JOINT PRODUCT DEVELOPMENT BY A FIRM AND ITS CUSTOMERS

A recent innovation is the growing involvement of customers in designing next-generation products. Lead users often understand best the features they would like in a next-generation product. Hence, firms have begun involving customers in NPD. Firms now provide toolkits that allow customers to design products. The customers return the toolkits to the firm for prototype manufacture. That process cuts development time and increases the likelihood that customers will readily accept the new products.

Customer-oriented product development toolkits should have the following features:

- Allow users to carry out complete cycles for trial-and-error learning. This involves building, simulating, and testing and evaluating, ultimately choosing between alternative trials to arrive at the best design.
- Provide users with a solution space (constrained by the manufacturer's capabilities and production

system) from which users can create the designs they want.
- Provide user-friendly toolkits so that little time is invested in learning and training.
- Allow users to supplement libraries of standard solution modules with their own add-ons, which leads to unique and customized solutions.
- Ensure that user-designed solutions following the rules of the toolkits can be "translated"; that is, easily manufactured by the toolkit supplier without additional engineering intervention and modification.[28]

Location of Product Development for Global Markets

Where a global product is developed and who participates in developing it are both important. Product development may be centered in one country, perhaps at headquarters. Because a product is to be a global one, it is important to acquire information from key markets around the world. Hence, involving foreign subsidiaries at the early stage of product concept development is crucial to success. That way, features of importance to a variety of consumers in different markets can be considered.[29]

Firms must recognize, however, that development teams tend to "own" products. The teams are reluctant to accept designs from other teams, even when the designs originate within the company. In theory, a firm should assign central responsibility for the design of a particular product to a particular team in a particular country. The assumption is that that team's design will then be adopted globally. Organizational conflicts can undermine that plan, however. In that case, a company may be forced to compromise and accept two versions of what was meant to be a global product.

Benefits of Decentralized Product Development

Companies with well-established foreign subsidiaries usually encounter demands for increased local autonomy. Those demands may be reinforced by the nationalistic feelings of subsidiary personnel, most of whom are probably citizens of the local country. Participation in the fundamental corporate activity of developing new products is a forceful way of showing employees that they have "a piece of the action." In that situation, a firm must weigh the payoff in improved morale against any loss of efficiency in product development.

In industries in which product development is slow and costly, companies may be forced to go outside for new products. The pharmaceutical industry serves as a good illustration. Although most firms in the industry are research-intensive, none can derive a complete product line from internal research only. It takes too many years and vast financial resources to bring a new drug to market, for instance. Therefore, in the pharmaceutical industry a four-fold approach to product development is seen:

1. Internal R&D
2. Acquisition of firms with new products
3. Licensing of new products from firms that developed them for markets where the firm is not represented
4. Joint-venturing with a firm that has complementary products

Unilever is one international company that deliberately seeks the advantages of international research development. The company has development activities in four European countries, as well as close research liaisons with its associated companies in the United States and India. As one vice chair said, "By locating research and development activities in a number of countries, an international company can take advantage of its unique ability to do research in a variety of national environments. . . . The probability of success is increased if there is good liaison between the laboratories. . . . There is a greater chance of sparking off new ideas."

Local Market Needs

Another encouragement to decentralized product development is local market need. Some products require continuous local testing during the development process, when they are being designed primarily to meet market specifications (tastes, use conditions, etc.) rather than technological standards. Development close to the market is practical because use conditions usually cannot be simulated in a firm's domestic laboratories. According to that reasoning, one would expect to find consumer goods developed locally more often than industrial goods. Furthermore, when demand for a product is limited to one market, the product is usually developed in that market.

Other Local Market Considerations

Perishability raises the question of the adequacy of the local transportation infrastructure and the ability of local distribution channels to store and display the product effectively until sale. Lack of refrigerated trucks, supermarket freezers, and cold-storage warehouses, as well as brownouts, are common problems that restrict the sale of products such as ice cream, frozen fish, and meat in developing countries.

Local markets may also differ in the strength of local consumer movements and the degree of product liability that the international marketer must bear in that market. While local laws may permit reduced product liability when compared to the home market, companies seeking a global image will set an internal standard that applies to all country markets. Such conflicts are apparent in products such as cigarettes, toys, pharmaceuticals, and consumer appliances. Of course, it is also possible that excessively onerous product liability in markets such as the United States will deter firms from manufacturing and selling in those markets. An example comes from the general aviation industry. Makers of small four-seat-and-under aircraft have all but left the U.S. market because of product liability laws that place the manufacturer at risk even after a decade of product sale and use. Legislation has found fault with manufacturers even in the face of irresponsible user behavior. (See Chapter 6.)

Given the importance of local market considerations, firms often use bidirectional approaches, whereby both headquarters/local market issues and personnel help shape NPD. The outline of such a concurrent bottom-up and top-down process is described in Table 10-4.

Table 10-4. Concurrent Headquarters and Local Market Influences on Product Development

Headquarters Influences

- Recognition by marketing unit of the need for a new or modified product
- Initiation of product development process, including cost and market (sales) analysis and lab tests
- Test marketing in local market
- Local market product launch

Local Market Influences

- Suggestion by local manager of customer need for a new or modified product
- Suggestion by preliminary market analysis of further development
- Contact with headquarters to receive information on and permission to develop modified or adapted version of existing product
- Ensuing development, with help from headquarters labs as necessary
- Test marketing to decide whether to proceed
- Approval from headquarters for new product launch, with standards for quality, brands, and packaging

Cooperation in Developing Products

As the costs of developing new products rise and diverse technologies are needed, consortium approaches have increased in appeal. Consortium partners typically have complementary assets in design or technology, and the alliance is initiated to develop new products more speedily. For example, because IBM and Toshiba had complementary technologies, they began collaborating on the design of lightweight computer screen displays used in laptop computers. Because small color screens that use low energy are essential for the next generation of laptops, IBM joined Toshiba. IBM's goal was to learn from Toshiba's expertise in manufacturing. Ultimately, IBM used the color screens in its laptop computers. Over time, IBM's strategic priorities changed; and they divested their personal computer business to a Chinese company, Lenovo. IBM may no longer need Toshiba's computer screen technologies, but that fact does not negate the initial impetus that led to their collaboration several years ago.

CREATING A COMMON STANDARD

Collaboration can also result in a common standard being adopted. Palmtop devices are widely used by executives for tracking appointments and phone numbers, taking notes, etc. These devices need to be compatible across manufacturers and with other technology; for example, desktop and laptop computers, cellular phones, and the Internet. Hence, manufacturers are trying to coalesce around common standards, with groups of manufacturers attempting to establish their standards as the world standard. Microsoft, a relative latecomer to this palmtop product area, is trying to establish its Windows CE standard against more established standards set by firms such as Symbian. (See "Global Marketing: Standards and Global Product Matters.")

NATIONAL CONSORTIA

Governments have formed national consortia to develop new products in the face of global competition. The best-known and most successful example is Airbus, which was a collaboration between the national governments of France, Germany, Spain, and the UK. The consortium was originally formed in 1972 to develop a new commercial aircraft for the European market, thus competing with Boeing. It is still in business as a consortium, having successfully developed several commercial aircraft models over the past 30 years. In the past several years, it has captured about half the global market for commercial jets. Thus, it has emerged as a serious competitor to Boeing, raising complaints that its success is owed, at least in part, to product development subsidies granted by the consortium owners; that is, the nation states. (See Case 10.1, Boeing and Airbus: Competing Product Lines, at the end of the chapter.)

GLOBAL MARKETING

Standards and Global Product Markets

*S*tandards can cast a long shadow. Two decades ago Microsoft pulled out of its partnership with IBM and the joint OS2 standard to focus on its proprietary Windows standard. The result? The Windows operating system dominates the world of personal computer software, installed on over 90 percent of all computers around the world. To try and break that stranglehold, Hewlett-Packard announced plans to sell personal computers in Asia. Those computers run on Linux, an open and cheaper alternative to Windows. This move could have been in response to joint plans by governments of China, Japan, and South Korea to push open-source software.

Microsoft, in turn, is trying to break into the market for next-generation smart mobile phones. It is forming a partnership with Motorola in which Motorola phones will work with Microsoft Windows Mobile software. Although Motorola is the second-largest manufacturer of mobile phone handsets, handset manufacturers have generally been wary of using Microsoft software. Their fear has been losing sales and profits as Microsoft leverages its dominance and experience in areas such as e-mail, music downloads, and game playing. Nokia and other partners, including Siemens and Samsung, own large stakes in Symbian, a handset software company. It is a means of shaping and controlling a standard not dominated by Microsoft. Recently, Motorola sold its 19 percent stake in Symbian as Nokia moved to take a controlling interest in Symbian. That move might make Nokia's consortium members wary of relying on Symbian for handset software since they would be indirectly relying on one of their chief competitors.

A similar standards battle is shaping up around next-generation high-definition DVDs. High-definition DVDs can store and play back high-quality images. That, in turn, requires more storage capacity as the images are more data-intensive; that is, the higher the definition, the larger the file size. DVDs have become the medium of choice for viewing movies at home. Consumers own DVD players and buy movies in DVD format. Movie rental companies offer movies in DVD format, the videocassette having become almost obsolete.

continued

Further, DVDs are a favored storage medium for use with computers and video game machines, likely to extend their sway with other personal electronic devices as well. All of these devices are converging, which means domination of the next-generation DVD standard is very important—and looks to be quite lucrative. The new DVD standard will affect not only DVD sales, but also sales of computer software, video game consoles, organizers, smart mobile phones, etc.

DVD manufacturers care about the standard as it affects their ability to dominate the market, to obtain leading market share, and to keep out competitors. By controlling the technology standard and the underlying patents, manufacturers can avoid paying royalties and can receive royalties from competing manufacturers, resulting in a competitive advantage. High-end manufacturers such as Sony are beset by low-priced competition from China and Taiwan. Those manufacturers would like to render the competition ineffectual by moving to a next-generation proprietary standard that they control.

Companies such as Microsoft are interested in the emergent standard because they hope to become part of it. For example, using video compression software, companies can reduce the size of files, which results in movies and other content being stored on a single DVD in high-definition.

Microprocessor manufacturers such as Intel have a big interest in making sure that their next-generation microprocessors are compatible with high-definition DVDs. They hope to play a part in shaping the format so they have an advantage in designing their proprietary microprocessors.

This standards battle is being played out by two opposing camps. On one side is Sony, which lost out in the videotape generation when its Betamax standard was sidelined. Sony technology also is not represented, for the most part, in current-generation DVD players. Hence, Sony, allied with Matsushita, has developed an extremely thin high-definition DVD format. The new DVD format has a protective plastic layer just one-tenth of a millimeter thick (about the thickness of a human hair). It is capable of storing 50 gigabytes of data, using a blue laser with a narrower beam that allows more data to be stored on a DVD. The newer technology would be more difficult to copy, thus reducing the threat from low-end Chinese and Taiwanese manufacturers. This is the Blu-ray camp, and other members include Dell, Hewlett-Packard, Hitachi, and Philips.

In the other camp are Toshiba and NEC, who wanted to avoid the difficult manufacturing problems of making DVDs with a protective plastic layer 0.1 mm thick. Instead, their DVDs would have a 0.6 mm thick plastic layer. The advantage is that 0.6 mm is the same thickness as current-generation DVDs. That means manufacturing is easier, and it allows for backward compatibility with current-generation DVDs. From a consumer viewpoint, old DVDs might still be able to be read on new-generation DVD players and recorders. While storage capacity would be lower, at about 30 gigabytes, video compression algorithms could reduce the need for additional storage capacity. Not coincidentally, Microsoft sought to ally with this group, known as the HD-DVD team, but offered its WMV-9 video compression software to both camps. Microsoft preferred not to be locked out of whichever standard ultimately prevailed.

An industry organization, the DVD Forum, has the role of choosing a standard for the next generation. Politics plays a role in choosing a standard, with both Intel and the Taiwanese manufacturers hoping to sway the Forum to their benefit. Intel was able to influence the rules of voting so that abstentions did not count as no votes. Some of the Blu-ray camp were persuaded to switch sides. The result was that a version of the Toshiba HD-DVD standard was tentatively approved in an 8-6 vote. A second rewritable disk standard was subsequently approved; it favored Microsoft's compression technology along with two other approaches.

Ultimately, it is content that will anoint a standard as a winner. And that outcome rests on whether movie studios and other content producers (for example, video game software manufacturers) will choose one standard over another in which to release their products. This process could drag on while competing teams seek to convince content producers (for example, moviemakers) that their standard is best. Consumers might hold off buying new-generation DVD players until the standards issue is settled. That trend would mean that volume sales and profits appear further out in time from when the new investments were made. Given the size of the market and the stakes involved, it is not surprising that, for now, Sony is unwilling to compromise. The standards battle will continue.

Source: "Technology Titans Battle over Format of DVD Successor," *Wall Street Journal*, March 15, 2004; "H-P to Sell PCs Running on Linux in Asian Market," *Wall Street Journal*, March 17, 2004; "Microsoft Partners with Motorola on Mobile Phones," *Wall Street Journal*, September 15, 2003; "As Microsoft Eyes Their Turf, Electronics Giants Play Defense," *Wall Street Journal*, February 23, 2004.

Another example of a national consortium is the GSM organization created in Europe to develop mobile telephony standards for the entire European market. That common standard would facilitate "roaming" across Europe for businesspeople and travelers. They could use one mobile phone to stay in touch with colleagues and friends. Access to the resulting large, single European market would help firms achieve economies of scale. It would also serve as a barrier to entry for mobile phones and networks from other countries such as the United States and Japan, which were developed on different standards (for example, TDMA and CDMA).

Incremental Innovation

Much of NPD consists of small but steady improvements to existing products. This is especially true of industrial products. As product use increases, customer feedback provides suggestions for additional features that should be incorporated. Similar competitive products provide another source of ideas. A firm can periodically evaluate its product in relation to those of the competition. Doing so can result in the development of a checklist to determine in what areas competitors' products have an advantage. That activity is essential to keeping and gaining market share. By the same token, incremental innovations based on information from existing customers and focus groups allow a company to stay one step ahead of the competition. The firm is able to continually provide differentiated products for a higher price rather than have to compete on the basis of lowest cost.

NPD: Preserving Options for the Future

The heart of NPD is choosing between projects, then gradually narrowing the number of projects until a few (or perhaps just one) are taken to market. This development funnel, with projects passing through stage-gates, is critical to the success of NPD. How the stages are defined and set, how projects are evaluated, and which projects are passed through affect the likelihood of eventual success.

New Product Project Termination

Not every project will result in successful NPD. Over a two-year period, Green and others studied 80 NPD projects in four divisions of a U.S. chemical firm. Interviews were repeated every six months to gauge changes in the project's progress and in project evaluation. The goal was to understand what factors influenced decisions to terminate a project. The research findings, summarized in Figure 10-4, are interesting. They emerged from a study of NPD projects while the projects were being carried out, not after the projects were completed or terminated. The study found the following variables to be influential:

- *Management advocacy:* If management does not champion or diminishes support for a project, increases pressure on project personnel, and deems the project to be of low priority, the project may not receive resources and, thus, will be terminated.
- *Performance:* This is the likelihood that a project

Figure 10-4. Factors Influencing the Termination of New Product Development Projects

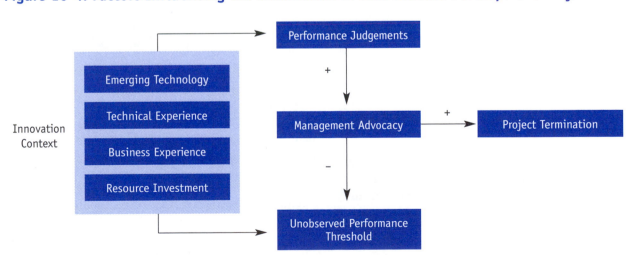

Source: Stephen Green, M. Ann Welsh, and Gordon E Dehler, "Advocacy, Performance, and Threshold Influences on Decisions to Terminate New Product Development," Academy of Management Journal 46(4), 2003, pages 419–434, Figure 1.

will meet technical and commercial objectives in a timely fashion, be manufactured at a reasonable cost, and achieve desired market share.

- *Innovation context:* Innovation encompasses (1) the nature of the underlying technologies, whether they are established or new or even radical; (2) the firm's or division's technical background, capabilities, and experience with the technology; (3) the firm's or division's business experience with the technology; and (4) the level of investment in the project, including human as well as physical capital and monetary investments.

- *Performance threshold:* The assumption is that different types of projects have unstated but different performance thresholds that they have to exceed in order to continue. It is possible that new projects in emergent technologies will excite scientists and managers and be allowed to continue for longer periods, implicitly meeting lower thresholds. The authors suggest that those projects bring psychic rewards to the people involved, allowing the projects to continue despite subpar performance judgment. Based on the above, Green and his coresearchers developed a framework to explain the myriad influences affecting new product project termination.

Product Testing

As part of the development process, a product must be tested under realistic use conditions. Another reason for testing in a number of markets is to meet national requirements on product specifications and performance. For example, in the case of food products, drugs, and electrical or transportation equipment, some local testing may be necessary to receive government authorization to sell. In the case of pharmaceuticals, there is often a special factor. Obtaining FDA approval of new drugs is a very time-consuming process. Drug manufacturers often test and certify their drugs in other markets. They begin marketing there before getting final approval in the United States, thus expediting international introduction of the product.

Finally, local product testing may be advisable for promotional reasons. Although a firm must test its products vigorously, there may be advantages in having local testing done outside the firm. It may improve the firm's public relations locally by using national testing organizations. That certification may be valuable to an international firm in its efforts to demonstrate adaptation to local market conditions.

For example, Abbott Laboratories develops new drug products and then sends them to universities and hospitals around the world for testing. Findings are reported in various national medical journals. Those actions have the dual advantages of extensive international testing under different conditions in addition to publicity value when findings are reported.

Role of Acquisitions and Divestments

As market environment and customer preferences change, firms are faced with two choices: (1) evolve the product line to stay abreast of customer needs and address competitiveness issues to maintain market share in a changed industry environment or (2) divest product lines because industry conditions have diminished the product's attractiveness or because changes in the customer base and customer preferences make the current products less satisfactory. Sometimes acquisitions are a necessary step in expanding market share in key regional and national markets. Doing so permits viable competition against the market leader.

Allied Domecq's expansion into wine is an example of how companies use corporate divestment and acquisition strategies to reformulate their product lines and develop a global presence. Allied Domecq is one of the world's leading liquor companies. It saw its competitors, Diageo and Pernod Ricard, buy the Canadian Seagram Company, thus increasing their market share in the global liquor business. In reply, Allied Domecq made major acquisitions in the wine industry, thus balancing its liquor portfolio (consisting of brands such as Beefeater gin and Kahlua liqueur) with a wine segment. It spent over $1.7 billion acquiring wine companies in different countries, including Spain's Bodegas y Bebidas, New Zealand's Monata, and the well-known and regarded champagne houses Mumm and Perrier Jouet. This allowed Allied Domecq to become the world's third largest wine distributor. The company chose to expand via acquisition into wine because it viewed wine as an attractive business with rapid growth prospects (with consumption of higher-priced premium wines rising even faster in the UK and North America).

Wine is a capital-intensive business. It requires owning land and maintaining inventories of wine while the wine is being aged. If companies choose not to grow their own grapes, they must buy them from vineyards. That means they will be unable to control the quality of the grapes, possibly resulting in uneven quality. Allied Domecq took care to buy companies in countries with low costs, such as New Zealand and Argentina. It also acquired companies in areas such as Spain's Rioja region and France's Champagne region, where quantities are controlled by local regulations. Those regulations limit wine gluts and maintain premium prices as well as cachet and quality.[31]

Product-Line Diversification

Management theorists such as Meyer and Utterback (cited earlier in this chapter) have suggested for some time that product-line diversification should relate to a firm's unique competitive advantages, its core competencies. Firms in Southeast Asia do not seem to be guided by those principles in their product-line expansion, however. An example comes from Uni-President Enterprises of Taiwan. This highly vertically integrated food company not only manufactures products such as instant noodles, yogurt, and beverages, but also sells them through its own distributors and retailers. As a Chinese firm, it may have a better understanding of its Chinese customers' food tastes. It also has been able to develop some premium brands. What is intriguing, however, is the close relationship between its product-line expansion and the increased purchasing power of its Taiwanese customer base.

It is interesting to consider how a brand's personality can change as the brand moves from country to country. Brand personality includes facets such as sincerity, excitement, competence, sophistication, and ruggedness, each appealing differently to customers in countries as diverse as China and the United States.[32]

Over time, as Taiwanese GDP per capita climbed, Uni-President branched out from basic products such as vegetable oil and flour into instant noodles. Then as the phenomenon of the working spouse became more common in Taiwan, the company opened convenience stores to cater to harried working couples. Uni-President Enterprises subsequently diversified into finance and insurance services to cater to the growing financial needs of its clientele.

Uni-President Enterprises uses alliances with different companies (for example, Japan's Kikkoman and U.S. PepsiCo) to enter product lines such as soy sauce and snack foods. The company sees future growth coming from mainland China, where it sells instant noodles, adapting them to different regional tastes.

A similar approach to diversification guides the activities of the Thailand-based Charoen Pokphand Group (CP Group) in China. The firm sees that its years of experience in China and its network of contacts with Chinese officials are critical to its future. Hence, it has formed alliances with other firms to bring in product-based expertise: with Honda for motorcycle technology, with Heineken for beer brewing, and with NYNEX for telephone projects. Once a source of product-specific technology is obtained, CP Group brings in experienced Chinese managers from its operations around Asia. The firm also brings in as local partners high-level officials from local companies and municipal governments. Thus, CP Group's formula for product expansion is based on its Chinese experience and contacts, as well as a patient, long-term view of opportunities in China. The actual product-specific competence seems secondary.

The question arises, how can firms from Southeast Asia disregard factors such as core competence in expanding willy-nilly? The answer may lie in two areas. The first is that competition is stunted in these regions. As a result, large, well-established firms have an edge in entering new industries. As economic development proceeds, a shakeout may occur, at which point companies may decide to focus their strategies more closely and follow their core competencies. The second explanation is that knowledge of Chinese culture and contacts within China, managerial talent, and access to capital are the scarce factors. Companies such as Uni-President Enterprises and CP Group have all three. They possess experienced managers who can use cash flow from profitable Taiwanese and South Asian operations to fund their rapid product line and geographic expansion. As Chinese, they have family and clan connections across Southeast Asia. Those competencies might be part of the tacit knowledge base on which Uni-President Enterprises and CP Group build their expansion. What their experience suggests, then, is this: In economies in relatively early stages of development, core competence may stem from cultural knowledge and access to scarce resources as well as from more traditional factors such as technology and brand names.

Product-Line Success and Downstream Value Activities

NPD development and eventual success may hinge on careful planning of downstream marketing activities. An example is the product-line evolution of Tat Konserve Sanayii (TAT), a Turkish tomato processor. TAT enjoys the comparative advantages of Turkey's soil, good growing climate, and relatively cheap labor. It exports 70 percent of its output from three factories processing 7,000 tons of raw vegetables a day. It works closely with small contract farmers to whom it provides selected seeds, fertilizer, and finance. TAT uses reverse-osmosis processing technology to retain vitamins and enzymes in fruit. Perhaps its most important step, however, was to develop an exclusive distribution arrangement with Kagome, which controls half the Japanese tomato paste market. TAT sold a 7 percent stake to Kagome in 1987, later raised to 15 percent. While Japan is TAT's main market, the company also exports to North Africa and the Middle East and supplies the main food companies in Malaysia (for example, Nestlé) and Brazil (for example, Unilever). If Turkey joins the EU, TAT's access and sales there could be enhanced. TAT demonstrates the importance of structuring the value chain in order to obtain success in international marketing of commodity product lines.[33]

Table 10-5. The Pros and Cons of Product-Line Extension

Advantages

- Allows narrow customer segments to be satisfied; for example, offering a cereal formulated with added bran and a low-fat, healthy oil might attract health-conscious older consumers.

- Making minor product modifications to add a "new" product allows firms to claim that they are innovative and to target customers who are looking for something new.

- Allows a firm to cover high and low price points, putting out both premium-priced products and a lower-priced, bare-bones product.

- Multiple and similar products allow excess capacity to be used without costly setup and product changeover costs.

- Allows additional sales, at least in the short run; is also cheaper than launching and establishing a new brand, which could cost as much as $30 million.

- Permits additional shelf space, which can keep out a competitor's products.

- Distribution channels often demand unique variations on the basic product line so that they can differentiate themselves, such as a larger package or added features to attract customers.

- Allows response to competitive threat; for example, "me-too" products to match the success of Chrysler's minivan or of baking soda-based toothpaste.

Negative Aspects

- Having too many items in the product line muddies image, leading distribution channels to unilaterally decide what items in the product line they will stock.

- Reduces brand loyalty by encouraging customers to experiment and switch.

- Crowds out genuine new product ideas.

- Cannibalizes demand from other items in the product line and does not enhance overall demand.

- As total products in the line grow faster than shelf space, retailers control what is displayed; disappointing performance may give impetus to a private label usurping the company's brand.

- Increased complexity leads to higher costs, stockouts at the retail level, manufacturing problems, errors in forecasting demand, material shortages, and less management and R&D attention to new product efforts.

- Customers and retailers may be turned off by too many product-line items and opt, instead, for brands with one or two all-purpose offerings.

Product-Line Extensions[34]

A review of the various corporate examples cited suggests that firms use product-line extension to broaden their appeal to customers and to offer additional products to domestic and international markets. At the end of the chapter, Case 10.1, Boeing and Airbus: Competing Product Lines, notes that product-line extensions, termed derivative aircraft, have been the mainstay of the aircraft industry over the past decade. However, product-line extensions do have a downside. Quelch and Kenny, for example, found that at one company, "filler" products were 65 percent of the line but only 10 percent of sales. Reducing the number of those items could increase shelf space for core products in the line. Of course, the company must plan to drop customers of "filler" products, attempting to move them to core products, perhaps through special incentives. Table 10-5 summarizes the positive and negative aspects of a policy of product-line extension.

Competitive Influences on the Product Line

Competition serves as a benchmark in assessing how to satisfy customer needs worldwide. The competition's product line is particularly relevant. If a firm wants to be one of the top three or four players in an industry, it must match competitors' product lines. A recent example comes from rivals for Apple's iPod. (iPod is a portable music player that can hold about 10,000 songs as digital files; a mini version has lower storage capacity but can still hold several hours of music.) Rivals such as Thomson Electronics, Rio Audio, Creative Labs, and Samsung have offered similar models. Their products have 1.5 to 4 gigabytes of storage capacity and a battery life of 15 hours. They are half the cost of the iPod, while equally compact. They are differentiated by their shape, display and its readability, colors, and control buttons and features.[35]

Other Influences on the Product Line

Product-line choices for individual markets are affected by additional factors. Those factors include government regulations, the market's level of economic development, the company's growth patterns, and the length of time the firm has been in a particular foreign market. The mode of entry into a foreign market, whether through exports or licensing or joint ventures, also plays a role.

Government regulation, domestic and foreign, often affects product lines. Some governments prohibit export of certain products for national security reasons. That regulation keeps some domestic products from being included in foreign product lines. The Export Control Act, for example, gives the U.S. President power to restrict exports to Communist countries. However, with better East-West relations, those controls are being relaxed.

Host-country governments have shown increasing interest in local product lines of multinationals and may bar certain products from their markets. Islamic countries, for instance, bar liquor; as a result, Anheuser-Busch has created a nonalcoholic beer for Islamic markets. Host-country pressures can also encourage firms to enter new product areas to please the local government. International Protein Corporation (now known as The Scoular Company), for example, began a boat-building operation in Panama as a condition for participating in fishmeal and shrimp operations. And because of the Indian government's restrictions on foreign involvement in low-technology industries, Hindustan Lever (Unilever's Indian subsidiary) switched its emphasis from toilet articles to animal feeds and chemicals.

The level of economic development in a country also affects the choice of products to be sold there. Established firms usually have a domestic product line that ranges from mature products to advanced, higher-technology products. Firms from industrialized countries find that the choice of products from the line for foreign markets depends on the level of development of those markets. This is as true for consumer goods, such as those from CPC International or General Foods, as for industrial marketers, such as Dow Chemical and GE. A GE executive remarked:

> We're placed to track right up the development curve with countries growing economically. Our first businesses in a country are those necessary for infrastructure building such as power generation and transmission and locomotives. As light industry starts, we can take in our small motors and other low-technology industrial products. As electrification spreads, our consumer house-wares find a market. Finally, when advanced manufacturing begins, we can take in our engineering plastics and other high-technology products.

Impact of Method of Entry

The nature of a firm's involvement in foreign markets is another product-line determinant. Theoretically, if a firm enters a market through exports only, it has freedom to choose as many or as few products as it wants in each market. Once it establishes an export operation, however, it will feel pressure to expand the product line to gain economies of scale. If the firm uses an export agent, there is less pressure because the intermediary can spread the cost over the other products carried. "Buy national" policies, tariffs, and transport costs are other restraints on the export line.

Licensing offers less freedom in product selection. Appropriate licensees may not be available for all products a firm wants to enter in a market. Licensees may not have satisfactory technology, or the best candidates may be licensed to competitors. Even if a firm finds suitable licensees, the firm may be producing products that compete with those of the licensor. Therefore, the licensee's product line can limit the licensor's product line in the market. Occasionally, a firm can overcome such limitations by using different licensees in a country. The feasibility of that depends on the availability of licensees and the divisibility of the licensor's product line. If the licensor's products are competitive, the licensee would not want another firm in the country to be involved.

The joint-venture approach can restrict a firm's foreign product line, too. Most joint ventures of international firms bring together two companies, each with a particular product line, just like licensing does. When the national partner has complementary products, the product-line possibilities of the international partner are confined.

Wholly owned foreign operations offer the greatest product-line flexibility. A firm can initially produce products in its foreign plants—products deemed best suited to local market needs, use conditions, competitive situation, and purchasing power. With initial success and market evolution, additional products can be introduced and adapted for the foreign market.

Foreign-Market Choice: Matching Products to Markets

Each international marketer has to decide what products to sell to what countries. There are several approaches to help in making that decision.
- Using the international product life cycle (IPLC) to identify potential markets.
- Screening markets to extract a short list of those

with the highest potential.

- Assessing individual markets in terms of how well they meet the firm's objectives (market share, return on investment, or matching competition).
- Conducting a competitive audit to isolate markets in which risk-return trade-offs are most attractive.
- Deciding on realistic market-share objectives for the markets chosen.

International Product Life Cycle (IPLC)

The IPLC comprises stages of demand growth. Those stages are staggered in time across countries, representing lags in income and development of consumer demand in the various countries. Typically, demand first grows in the innovating country and in other advanced industrial nations similar to the innovating country. Only later does demand begin in less developed countries (LDCs). Consequently, production first takes place in the innovating country, with excess production (greater than domestic demand) being exported to satisfy demand elsewhere. As the product matures and technology is diffused, production occurs in other advanced industrialized countries and then in LDCs. A further implication of this life cycle is that as products become mature in a firm's home market, they may be dropped there but continue to be sold in other markets. In other words, the sequence for dropping products generally follows the same order as for adding products, again leading to different product lines in different countries. The ability to selectively market and match products to markets is a strength of the international marketing firm. It can continue to exploit its mature products, even when they are no longer sold in its home country or other industrialized nations.

A concrete example of product life cycles is seen in Figure 10-5. It illustrates the demand curves for the video game industry from 1980 through fall 2003 and includes a forecast through 2007. The industry began with Atari, in its heyday from the late 1970s through about 1983. Then came Nintendo, which captured over 90 percent market share worldwide with its 8-bit machine, superior graphics, and popular games that included Super Mario Brothers and Zelda. Nintendo lost market share to Sega, which launched a 16-bit machine capable of playing somewhat more complex games. Sega had a hit with its Sonic the Hedgehog game. Sony then entered the market with its CD-ROM-based PlayStation, which became the market leader. Nintendo followed with its N64 and GameCube; then Microsoft entered the market with its Xbox. The chart illustrates how each generation's decline accompanied the rise of the next-generation product, even as the total mar-

ket size as a whole increased. IPLC charts such as the one shown in Figure 10-5 raise several interesting questions for the international marketer.

- How does a company determine the emerging obsolescence of a product generation?
- How does a company forecast the length of a cycle and the inflexion point when demand starts declining?
- When will demand start taking off in emerging markets, even as it declines in advanced industrial nations?
- Will demand in newer markets leapfrog generations, as happened with the wild success of mobile phones and the leapfrogging of hardwired telephony (land lines)?
- Should manufacturing of video games be shifted around the world in response to demand cycles?
- How should a company selling video games develop its global marketing strategy?
- How can a company continue to be a major player across several generations of a changing industry, as Nintendo seems to have accomplished in the video game business?

Figure 10-5. The Video Game Industry Product Cycles

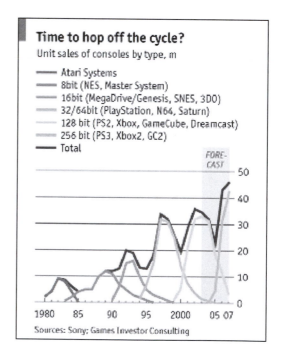

Source: "Changing the Game," *The Economist*, December 4, 2003.

Table 10-6. Competitive Audit of a Foreign Market

Basic Information

1. Which competitive products are sold in country X?
2. What are the market shares of competitive products?
3. How do competitive products compare with our own in reputation, features, and other attributes?
4. Which support facilities (production, warehousing, sales branches, etc.) do competitors have in country X?
5. Which problems do competitors face?
6. What relationships do competitors have with the local government? Do they enjoy special preferences?

Marketing Information

1. Which distribution channels are used by competitors?
2. How do competitors' prices compare with our own?
3. What credit terms, commissions, and other compensation are extended by competitors to their channel members?
4. What promotion programs are used by competitors? How successful are those programs?
5. How good is the postsales service of competitors?

Market Supply Information

1. How do competitive products get into the market?

If they are imported:

2. Who are the importers?
3. How do importers operate?
4. What credit, pricing, and other terms are extended to importers by foreign suppliers?
5. How long has each importer worked with a foreign supplier? Is the importer satisfied with the supplier?

If they are produced locally:

6. Who are the producers?
7. Are the producers entirely locally owned, or is there foreign participation?
8. What advantages do local manufacturers have over importing competitors?

Source: Franklin R. Root, *Entry Strategies for International Markets*, Lexington, MA: Lexington Books, 1987, pages 42–44.

Market Potential and Market-Entry Decisions

When a firm is considering what markets to enter, a key issue is unrealized market potential. In general, companies might be better off targeting markets in which significant market shares are likely to be achieved. In those fast-growing markets, new customers do not have preestablished links with suppliers that are emerging; growth makes the established competitors slack and inattentive to new entrants; and demand may exceed supply from established suppliers, leading to openings for other firms seeking entry. Ryans[36] found that firms adapting a product achieve highest market share in the introductory and growth phases of the market and less during maturity and decline phases.

The market-entry decision must weigh unrealized market potential against the strength of competition. Multinationals within an industry are likely to have similar data, leading to their similar rankings of individual country market attractiveness. Hence, the strength of competition likely to be encountered is important. Competitive audits are a formal way of judging the strength of competition in markets of interest. Table 10-6 presents the basic questions that form part of a competitive audit.

A company can combine the results from a competitive audit with an assessment of market potential to begin estimating the market share they are likely to achieve. Then, depending on objectives, the company assesses whether a specific market represents an attractive opportunity for entry.

Government regulations and attitudes may also be factors that affect market attractiveness. Import-substituting governments often use tariffs and regulations to keep out foreign multinationals and to foster the growth of domestic companies. In such instances, foreign firms must decide whether they want to participate in local markets by licensing technology to the local firm. The hope is to eventually secure entry once the government liberalizes its economic policies regarding foreign multinational participation in the domestic economy.

Table 10-7 presents a framework for analyzing a government's role in influencing market attractiveness in LDCs. The analysis was designed to assess attractiveness for export opportunities, but it can also be used in judging market attractiveness for other modes of entry.

Table 10-7. Consumer Product Export Opportunities to Liberalizing LDCs: A Life-Cycle Approach

Stage	Government Policies	Market Characteristics	Foreign Exporter Opportunities
Preliberalization	• Encouragement of import substitution • Severe restrictions on consumer imports • Possible production limitations on consumer products • Heavy taxation on consumption and/or higher incomes; discouragement of conspicuous consumption	• Sellers' market • Restricted competition • Pent-up consumer demand	• Very restricted
Liberalization	• Greater encouragement of free enterprise and competition • Encouragement of export orientation • Allowance of wider income disparities	• Greater availability of consumer products • Wider choice of products • Increased consumption of consumer products	• Substantially increased
Partial Retraction	• Reenactment of higher tariffs and quotas and/or decreased importer access to foreign exchange • Reenactment of import substitution	• Slower consumption growth likely • Competition from local production	• Curtailed or threatened • Continued access via foreign investment may be possible

Source: Kate Gillespie and Dana Alden, "Consumer Product Export Opportunities to Liberalizing LDC's," *Journal of International Business Studies,* Volume 20, Issue 1, pages 93-112.

Thus, a firm evaluates risk, competition, probable returns, and resource commitments before deciding whether to launch a product in a particular market. Questions used to screen for product launch into a foreign market might include the following:

- What is the product's competitive position at home? (What is transferable to overseas markets?) Is the product new?
- Is there a market? What is its size? How does the product relate to consumers' needs, ability to buy, and conditions of use in the market? Is adaptation necessary in product attributes, the physical product, and packaging?
- Is the market growing? How attractive is it? What is the level of product saturation?
- Is there much competition? What does the competitive audit show?
- Will government regulations diminish chances of success?
- Will the product require much training and after-sales service? Are complementary products needed?
- Is the product likely to become obsolete soon? (That is, is this type of product undergoing rapid technological change?)
- What resources (management time, financial resources) will have to be committed to the market?
- What are the potential returns from the market, and what is its level of risk? Where does the market rank when compared with alternatives?

- What are the objectives for this market? (Possible objectives include market share, profits, defense against a competitor, response to local government, and maintenance of a presence in lead markets.) A firm also must distinguish between strategic and short-term objectives for the market.
- If entry into a market is through a partnership, such as a joint venture or strategic alliance, is there agreement on objectives? Is there likely to be conflict over goals?
- How patient is the company? How long will top management be prepared to wait until success is achieved? For example, if a firm has few managers who speak Japanese, have little knowledge of day-to-day management problems of doing business in Japan, and have few personal business contacts there, it cannot expect early success from Japanese market entry.

Based on the foregoing list, companies are generally selective in introducing new products into foreign markets. Answers to the questions above should lead to a short list of potentially attractive markets. After exhaustive investigation, one or two are chosen for product launch. The process is, of course, not static. Markets discarded as being unattractive can be assessed more favorably with the passage of time and with changes in economic conditions. This constant revaluation of markets is seen in Coca-Cola's approach to certain foreign markets.

COCA-COLA: RETHINKING FOREIGN-MARKET ENTRY

Coca-Cola has traditionally been content with supplying the syrup needed to prepare the soft drink and letting the local bottlers market the product. However, as Coca-Cola grows more dependent on foreign earnings (about 80 percent of total earnings) and as the U.S. market becomes saturated (5 percent growth a year versus foreign growth at about 16 percent a year), managing growth in foreign markets becomes more important. Coca-Cola has devised several ways to tailor its strategy to match product penetration and future potential of each market. Those market strategies are described below.

- *Japan.* Coca-Cola continues to rely on a dozen bottlers that are Japan's largest food and trading companies; for example, Kirin, Mitsubishi, Mitsui, and Kikkoman. Coca-Cola also developed unique drink products for the Japanese palate, such as milk- and yogurt-based drinks.
- *United Kingdom.* Coca-Cola formed a 49 percent owned joint venture with Cadbury Schweppes and took over bottling from franchises held by Grand Met and Beecham.
- *France.* Coca-Cola bought back bottling rights from Pernod Ricard, which had sold Coke in France for 40 years. Because consumption in France is only 13 percent of the U.S. average of 46 gallons per person, Coca-Cola hopes to raise consumption by controlling the marketing directly. Paris may also have an important role as the center from which to ship concentrate and cans to other parts of Europe, an important capability in the Single Market.
- *Brazil.* In the world's third-largest market for soft drinks, with a hot climate, and with 140 million thirsty people, Coke is being challenged by Pepsi. Pepsi had formed an alliance with Brahma, Brazil's largest beer company, capturing 25 percent of the cola market in São Paulo within a year. Because Brazil's per capita consumption is only about a quarter of U.S. consumption, there is much potential. Coca-Cola began introducing large plastic bottles of Coke (2 liters compared to Pepsi's 1.5 liters) and diet versions of Coke. Heavy investment and advertising are seen as the key to maintaining a 50 percent market share in this fast-growing market.
- *Australia.* Coca-Cola purchased a 41 percent interest in Amatil, Australia's largest Coke bottler. Australia has the third-largest per capita consumption of Coke after the United States and Mexico, and Coca-Cola has a 53 percent market share there. Coca-Cola also formed a joint venture to buy out its bottler in New Zealand, a small market.
- *India.* Coca-Cola has been focusing recently on India. The company purchased soft drink brands from Parle, India's leading soft drink manufacturer.

Coca-Cola also entered into a joint venture for bottling and marketing with Parle's company owners. This was intended to give Coke a 60 percent market share and access to distribution through Parle's 60 bottlers. Subsequently, Coca-Cola has had problems with its joint-venture partner over its desire to bottle Pepsi drinks in its plants.

- *China.* Another recent focus of Coca-Cola has been China. The company has been careful to form joint ventures with state-owned bottling plants in key cities, gradually developing production capabilities and market share. The share of foreign soft drink manufacturers in China has increased rapidly, with Coca-Cola getting about two-thirds of the growth. By allying with powerful and well-connected government companies, the company obtains some insurance against a local backlash, which is inevitable as local soft drink manufacturers find their market share eroding.

Coca-Cola's current focus is on developing countries. After leaving India because of government controls over brand name usage, it returned to the country. (In India, soft drink consumption is growing 20 percent a year, partly in response to PepsiCo's 39.9 percent share in a joint-venture local bottling operation.) Coca-Cola awarded its Coke bottling franchise in China to several government companies in order to win market share. Clearly, the company will do what it takes in each market to be successful. Thus, the fact that Coke is a global brand does not imply standardization of the entire marketing mix.

Benchmarking Products and Product Performance

A common-sense approach to improvement is for a company to compare its products to those of the competition, note the dimensions along which competitors' products are superior, and use knowledge of those gaps to guide product improvement and future development.[37] Product-line **benchmarking** can be divided into four main areas:

Focus (market segmentation, product specifications, service levels)

- Relative value (understanding end use in order to add value)
- Market dominance (market share and relative return on investment)
- "Looking end to end" (improving flow of information and physical product)

Benchmarking actually took root in the auto industry when U.S. automakers decided to study the manufacturing and quality management practices of their Japanese competitors. U.S. carmakers wanted to gauge the magnitude of quality gaps, then use Japanese practices as guidelines for improving their operations, catching up to the Japanese. Motorola was another early user of benchmarking, defining it as a way for a company to compare its products and practices against a best-in-class standard, then use that information to improve its operations. Since benchmarking can be difficult to do and can raise fears of competitive spying, several independent agencies have sprung up to conduct industry-wide benchmarking. One example is the International Benchmarking Clearinghouse, part of the American Productivity & Quality Center in Houston, Texas.

Quality as a Marketing Edge: ISO 9000

In Europe, customers often ask suppliers if they have received ISO 9000 certification.[38] In the United States, firms that win the Baldridge Quality Awards trumpet their feat in full-page ads in the business press. The Japanese are known for their attention to quality and their insistence that suppliers reduce defective parts per million on incoming parts. In all of those cases, the link between product quality and marketing is a strong one, as better quality produces:

- Superior performance.
- Reliability.
- Durability.
- Ease of maintenance.
- The matching or exceeding of competitors' product features.
- Superior service: speedy, courteous, and competent after-sales service.

Ultimately, superior quality can reduce a customer's life-cycle ownership costs, enhancing customer loyalty, repeat buying, and word-of-mouth advertising. This section briefly examines ISO 9000 as a key quality standard in international marketing.

ISO 9000 subsumes a series of standards promulgated by the International Organization for Standardization in Geneva. Those standards allow a customer to specify the level of quality expected from suppliers while allowing independent third parties to certify that the required levels of quality are being achieved. The EU has mandated that certain product categories meet ISO 9000 guidelines; for example, medical devices, telecommunications products, and construction products. As more European customers gave preference to ISO 9000-certified suppliers, U.S. and Japanese firms also sought certification under the ISO 9000 guidelines and began to require that their suppliers do the same.

ISO 9000 has, therefore, become a de facto global standard. Firms, however, can go beyond ISO 9000 in areas such as responsiveness to customer requests (outlined in ISO 9004). There are also the ISO 14000 family of standards pertaining to environmental management. It is useful to review how marketing considerations can be blended with more manufacturing-oriented quality processes.[39] ISO 9004 suggests the roles that marketing should play.

- Take the lead in establishing quality requirements for the company by determining customer needs and communicating them throughout the company.
- Translate customer needs into specifications, including performance and sensory characteristics, installation configuration, statutory and technical standards, packaging, and quality assurance.
- Set up an information system to monitor customer satisfaction and dissatisfaction and feed back any pertinent information to facilitate design and manufacturing changes.
- Develop early warning systems to spot performance problems with new product introductions, continuously monitor product performance against quality specifications such as reliability and safety, and track and analyze customer complaints so corrective action can be taken in design and manufacturing.

Global R&D Management

Investing R&D in technology-based industries is risky because the money spent may not result in a commercially viable product. As an example, pharmaceutical industries typically spend more than $300 million over a ten-year period to develop a new pharmaceutical drug. Seven out of ten drugs developed do not recover their R&D costs. In the pharmaceutical industry, large firms such as Ciba, Glaxo, and Merck must conduct in-house research as well as buy ownership rights to R&D being conducted in small research boutiques. The firms must fund the research in return for rights to the ensuing product, if it is successful. In such cases, two approaches pioneered at Merck are useful:[40]

1. View the funding of R&D projects as the buying of options. A small and limited downside risk (the loss of the R&D investment) is balanced by a large unlimited upside risk (the project resulting in a successful blockbuster drug). That is, the company providing the funding has the right to back out of the project at any time if it deems that progress is unsatisfactory or, continuing funding at the next stage, to retain its rights to the fruits of the research. Using that methodology, traditional-option pricing models can be used. The necessary data points are (a) the total amount of investment in the R&D project; (b) the estimated value of future

cash flows from the project if it successful; (c) the time period over which the company (Merck) can exercise its option; (d) an internal investment hurdle rate (the cost of capital for projects of such a risk class); and (e) a variable that measures the volatility of investment in such a class of R&D projects, averaged across the company's and industry's experience over the recent past. That analysis allows the pharmaceutical firm to determine whether the value of the option is greater than the investment to be made in the R&D project.

2. View and analyze several R&D projects as a group, subjecting them to probabilistic analysis to ascertain the range of likely future outcomes from funding one or more specific R&D projects. This approach is set out in Figure 10-6, a computer simulation model that analyzes pharmaceutical R&D projects. It uses as input estimated ranges (that is, optimistic, average, and pessimistic numbers rather than point estimates) for a number of variables:

- Scientific and therapeutic effectiveness variables
- R&D project investments and downstream capital expenditures
- Profit models based on product prices and quantities, production, and selling costs
- Macroeconomic variables such as interest rates, inflation, and exchange rates

Using the model and the variables, the computer generates several iterations, each time drawing a number for each variable from the probabilistic distribution stored in its database. The final output is a series of probability distributions showing the range of expected outcomes. This exercise allows a firm to make better decisions about funding projects, continuing investment in projects, and deciding on the overall size of the R&D effort.

While health-care reform creates uncertainty about the demand environment, the pharmaceutical industry in the United States and Europe provides sound lessons in how to innovate in an information-intensive industry whose fundamental technology is changing rapidly. Rebecca Henderson's study of U.S. and European pharmaceutical companies suggests that innovative success is due to three characteristics:[41]

1. Maintaining close ties to the scientific community at large so companies continue to be knowledgeable about new information
2. Betting on a wide variety and mix of projects across several technologies, disciplines, and fields
3. Innovating in their R&D organization so both product line and functional interests are borne in mind and are balanced.

Figure 10-6. Merck's R&D Planning Model

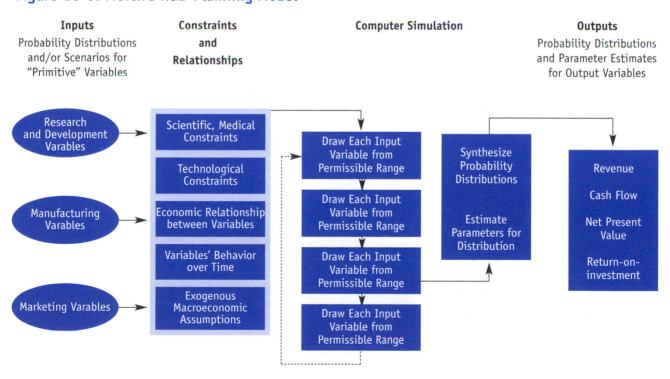

Source: Nancy Nichols, "Scientific Management at Merck," *Harvard Business Review*, January-February 1994, 95.

Rationale for Global R&D

Most multinationals are increasing the amount of R&D they carry out at multiple locations around the world. One reason is that a firm's ability to innovate globally contributes to its overall international competitiveness.[42] Conducting global R&D also helps a firm meet host-country interests as it facilitates technology transfer. Multinational foreign R&D is possible because of the increased availability of skilled scientific talent and technology resources in other countries, enhanced IPP, and better communication capabilities that allow integration and supervision of a dispersed global R&D effort. Comparative advantage comes into play in the sense that different countries may have world-class capabilities. For example, top-notch scientists in specific areas of expertise such as the development of robotics or pharmaceutical drug development might be found in Japan and Switzerland, respectively.

Government incentives may also make it cheaper to conduct overseas R&D when specific program funding exists for technologies deemed to be in the national interest. One example is Project Esprit, which promotes advanced technology computing in Europe. Availability of low-cost, high-quality research personnel, such as Russian research scientists, as well as the success of some multinationals with foreign R&D, may motivate other multinationals to attempt the same. Conducive government regulation and a hospitable climate to specific kinds of R&D may also play a part in deciding where to locate a R&D effort.

Key Issues in Developing a Global R&D Capability[43]

Linking product development for international markets to a global R&D network raises several critical issues for management.

- *Where should a firm carry out the foreign R&D?* Relevant factors in selecting overseas R&D sites include integration with existing manufacturing and sales operations; host government regulations and requirements; and the quality of local research infrastructure, including availability of scientists and the level and sophistication of the research efforts of local universities.

- *How much autonomy should a firm grant the local R&D operation?* This important variable determines, to some extent, who decides what research is carried out at the overseas R&D facilities. Whether operations are centralized may depend on the overall orientation of the firm, its tendency to centralize authority in most areas of multinational management, and the competency of local R&D facilities, as well as their previous history of contributing research to the firm. Criticality of the underlying technologies being investigated, the amount of resources committed and the time constraints in completing the research may also influence the degree of centralization. Whether the research is creative and groundbreaking or more an extension and diffusion of previous research may also contribute to the decision of using central control or granting greater autonomy.

For example, a study of R&D labs of multinationals in the UK showed that most of the labs had a limited role in carrying out basic research. However, they

Figure 10-7. International R&D at Kao Corporation

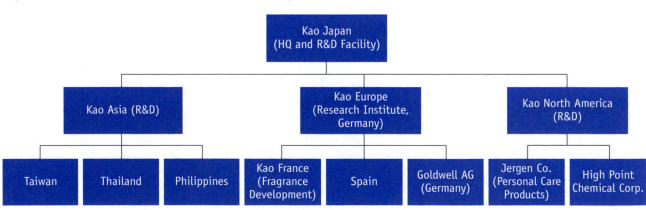

played a major role in developing new products and in adapting existing products and processes for their markets.[44] One approach sets up specific research mandates for major overseas labs, with a specific lab functioning as a global clearinghouse for the multinational's research efforts in that area. An example of that approach is shown in Figure 10-7, illustrating Kao Corporation's organization of global R&D.

- *How should a firm coordinate global R&D?* A major goal of global R&D is the sharing of information. Information communication among scientists and engineers is critical to enhanced research productivity. Measures include periodic meetings and presentations, stage-gate and milestone achievement monitoring systems, travel and telephone contacts, the creation of multinational project teams, job rotation across R&D labs in different countries, and a company culture that fosters open cross-national research communication.

Stage-gate systems are procedures in which product development is broken up into a series of steps or stages. At the end of each stage are milestones that must be achieved in order to move to the next stage. These milestones function as gates: hence, the term stage-gate system.[45] In evaluating NPD projects, stage gates are one avenue for weeding out undesirable projects, a means of narrowing the development funnel. To implement such a stage-gate approach, companies need evaluation criteria to judge how projects are performing and whether they pass the gate. A 2003 study compared Dutch and British companies in their use of evaluative criteria in applying stage-gate processes in NPD. The typical stages, or phases, at which projects are reviewed include the following:

- Idea Screening (technical feasibility)
- Concept Screening (customer acceptance, product performance, technical feasibility)
- Business Analysis (sales and profits)
- Product Testing (product performance and quality)
- Test Marketing
- Post-Launch, Short-Term (customer acceptance, customer satisfaction, sales levels)
- Post-Launch, Long-Term (sales, market share, margins, customer satisfaction)

Used to evaluate projects at each stage, the criteria broadly include product, market, and finance criteria. However, the criteria differ and change as the project moves from one stage to the next. Figure 10-8 sets out the stages and criteria used and their relative importance in Dutch and British companies.[46]

By reading across the rows, you can see the differences in how UK and Dutch companies approach the screening process. For example, UK companies use Market Potential as a criterion more often than Dutch companies. The UK similarly uses IRR (Internal Rate of Return) and ROI (Return on Investment) criteria more intensely in the Business Analysis phase. Figure 10-8 provides insight into what stages to use in NPD processes as well as what criteria to use at different stages.

Also relevant to coordinating global R&D is whether a scientific culture prevails across a company (overcoming national culture differences) or whether local cultural norms prevail in affecting operations and the effectiveness of overseas R&D labs. Arnoud de Meyer[47] studied communication within the global R&D operations of 14 multinationals that together manage several thousand R&D employees. He summarized communication and coordination mechanisms into several categories, as follows:

- *Socialization efforts* to create a corporate-wide R&D culture, using devices such as temporary assignments in other labs, relatively constant traveling to facilitate face-to-face meetings, clear rules and procedures for matters such as documentation of work, and training programs.
- *Formal communication procedures* emphasizing meticulous reporting and documentation, databases of findings to facilitate researcher access to results in far-flung locations, and planning procedures involving researchers and managers from multiple sites.
- *Boundary-spanning roles* through the identification and use of special individuals who can facilitate transfer of information across R&D labs. Those people do so through travel, presentations, and special conferences. The individuals are technologically able as well as experienced. They rank relatively high in the hierarchy so they know what informal channels to use and who has information or should receive it.
- *Organization structures* include the use of central coordination staff and a network organization facilitated by electronic communication.
- *Electronic communication* includes the use of videoconferencing, e-mail, and shared databases. (However, de Meyer suggests that periodic face-to-face meetings are essential to supplement the use of electronic communication technologies.)

- *Where do overseas R&D units fit into the organization structure?* Approaches include using matrixes, subordinating overseas R&D to headquarters R&D, and making R&D part of existing product-line or geographic divisions. The decisive factor should be whether the organization structure contributes to effectiveness and efficiency.

- *What staffing and personnel issues must a firm confront?* How are people chosen for the overseas R&D labs? Who is the R&D manager? How important are criteria such as

Figure 10-8. Evaluation Criteria Used in New Product Development Gates

The Netherlands

NPD Evaluation Gates	Customer Acceptance	Customer Satisfaction	Sales Objectives	Sales Growth	Market Share	Sales in Units	Break-Even time	Profit Objectives	IRR/ROI	Margin	Stays within Budget	Introduced in Time	Product Performance	Quality	Time-to-Market	Prdocut Uniqueness	Market Potential	Marketing Chance	Technical Feasilibility	Intution
Idea Screening	46	31	24	27	31	38	11	24	5	27	8	19	51	36	17	51	52	28	70	54
Concept Screening	48	37	11	1	4	14	6	10	9	8	9	14	48	36	9	18	22	14	47	20
Business Analysis	31	22	51	28	37	62	27	46	26	46	16	22	25	18	20	20	50	39	27	20
Product Testing	36	37	6	2	5	22	11	9	6	16	39	34	65	67	21	28	10	6	36	20
Test Market	68	66	9	7	12	24	8	12	8	16	17	29	61	56	18	23	19	17	43	19
Post-Launch S/T	54	39	41	28	33	59	15	41	19	44	12	32	45	35	14	26	35	22	8	16
Post-Launch L/T	31	52	38	42	36	51	7	38	17	40	10	9	31	23	4	14	27	13	3	13

United Kingdom

NPD Evaluation Gates	Customer Acceptance	Customer Satisfaction	Sales Objectives	Sales Growth	Market Share	Sales in Units	Break-Even time	Profit Objectives	IRR/ROI	Margin	Stays within Budget	Introduced in Time	Product Performance	Quality	Time-to-Market	Prdocut Uniqueness	Market Potential	Marketing Chance	Technical Feasilibility	Intution
Idea Screening	54	38	46	27	27	27	11	32	16	35	19	14	33	22	35	75	71	40	75	62
Concept Screening	60	45	20	10	10	23	10	15	8	23	25	22	45	32	23	42	53	35	70	28
Business Analysis	31	25	60	52	55	70	42	67	67	23	31	31	27	22	46	36	69	48	33	19
Product Testing	45	39	20	14	13	16	13	20	16	27	59	45	73	60	47	42	30	17	59	19
Test Market	77	66	27	16	16	20	16	20	17	25	33	41	83	79	36	36	38	19	48	11
Post-Launch S/T	73	75	70	64	52	71	32	53	29	71	16	43	54	61	32	32	36	23	9	14
Post-Launch L/T	57	76	68	72	71	68	28	72	49	79	6	13	55	64	0	30	32	17	8	8

Source: Susan Hart, Erik Jan Hultink, Nikolaos Tzokas, and Harry R. Commandeur, "Industrial Companies' Evaluation Criteria in New Product Development Gates," *Journal of Product Innovation Management* 20, 2003, pages 22–36, Figure 2.

the ability to manage multicultural research professionals? Are scientific personnel chosen locally or in concert with regional and central headquarters? How are they assigned projects to promote their own learning and growth?

As can be seen from the previous discussion, many questions must be resolved in developing and managing a global R&D effort. R&D is likely to increase in importance as multinationals increase their global manufacturing and marketing presence.

Summary

Three major issues for an international company are (1) deciding what new products to develop for global markets, (2) selecting the product line for individual foreign markets, and (3) deciding what foreign market to enter.

Several concepts are useful in developing new products: matching customer needs to a firm's knowledge base, basing products on core competence and common product platforms, and using both compression and experiential strategies in product development.

The starting point is consumer needs. Together with conditions of use and ability to buy, consumer needs indicate whether extension, adaptation, or completely new development of products and marketing mix is the appropriate strategy.

Ideas for new products should be sought in all major markets, both domestic and foreign. Distributors, licensees, joint-venture partners, and overseas subsidiary personnel are all potential sources. So are the competition, new patent filings, the plans of governments and international agencies, and the foreign buyer's consumption system.

Japanese product development approaches offer useful insights, particularly using supplier partnerships and working backward from a customer needs-based product configuration to actual product development.

The location of NPD activity is important. Multiple sites may prevent the "not-invented-here" syndrome (in which all "foreign" ideas are rejected on the basis of not having been invented at home) from taking hold.

Fast-moving technology requires specialized product development techniques, including the willingness to foster chaos and deliberate cannibalization of one's own products.

R&D is typically carried out in a firm's largest markets, provided the necessary scientific and technical personnel are available. R&D can be decentralized within a product line or across a product line. Basic R&D is sometimes carried out in one or two central locations, with applications of lesser importance conducted at more distant locations. R&D may be decentralized because of demands for local autonomy or in order to monitor technological developments in key lead markets. Government pressures and adaptation to the local market also influence the diffusion of R&D activity. Budgets and communication networks are tools helpful in coordinating geographically dispersed R&D labs.

New product ideas must be screened to select the most promising ones for further development. Screening may be done at the national, regional, and headquarters levels. Screening criteria should include production and marketing considerations, as well as legal factors, financial returns, logistics constraints, and government views.

Foreign-market testing is another essential step in launching new products internationally. Representative markets may be used as a surrogate for testing in potential foreign markets.

Product development through consortia and strategic alliances is becoming more common. Cooperation may lead to agreement on common standards and may arise because of a strategic fit among complementary skills.

Incremental innovation—keeping ahead of the competition through continuous improvements—is as important as implementing radical changes and introducing major new products.

Product testing in foreign markets may be necessary because of different use conditions and government regulations. There are also promotional benefits from testing specifically in foreign markets.

A general question in product-line management is whether to replicate a domestic product line in foreign markets. Market similarity and similar client needs support such product-line extension. Other determinants include competitive response, government regulation, level of economic development of the market, a firm's growth targets, and the length of time a firm has been in a market.

The mode of market entry also affects a product line. A joint-venture agreement, for example, may prohibit certain domestic products from being introduced. Adding and divesting products from a product line are equally important decisions. Legal matters are involved, as well as cost, competition, market, and other financial considerations.

The use of IPLC information helps in the identification of promising foreign markets. Technology diffusion and the presence of competing technologies are important elements in assessing foreign-market potential according to the product life cycle.

Market potential must be balanced with an assessment of market saturation. Markets should be chosen so that significant market share gains can be achieved.

Competitive audits are important in arriving at realistic market share targets. Government policies also delineate the extent to which foreign firm participation is encouraged.

Risk, competition, probable returns, and resource commitments suggest what foreign markets a firm should enter. Those factors form the basis of a list of questions used to screen for product launch.

Quality provides a marketer with an edge. Global benchmarking is one approach to ensuring that a new product does not fall far behind offerings from competitors. Obtaining world-class quality is an essential stage of product development. Meeting ISO 9000 certification is one way to ensure that processes resulting in quality production are in place.

Questions and Research

10.1 Explain how consumer needs, conditions of use, and ability to buy affect NPD.

10.2 Explain how Yamaha's attention to consumer needs enabled it to revitalize the worldwide piano market.

10.3 How are ideas diffused and new products adopted? How are those concepts relevant to NPD in international markets?

10.4 What are some potential sources of ideas for NPD? How can a firm obtain international inputs? Contrast the new product possibilities of a company that only exports with those of a company that has several wholly owned foreign plants.

10.5 Where should NPD activity be located? What are the advantages and disadvantages of decentralization?

10.6 What are some common patterns in global R&D? What pressures lead management to decentralize global R&D? How can such decentralized NPD be coordinated and controlled?

10.7 How and where should new product screening be done? What should be the role of the foreign subsidiary in this process?

10.8 How are marketing and production considerations used in screening new products for international markets?

10.9 Why are strategic alliances used in NPD?

10.10 Product testing must be done locally even when product development is centralized. Discuss.

10.11 Is market testing necessary before a firm introduces new products into foreign markets? Explain your answer.

10.12 What are the determinants of a firm's product line in foreign markets?

10.13 How does the nature of a firm's involvement in foreign markets affect the composition of its product line? Contrast the product-line alternatives open to an exporter with alternatives available to a licensor.

10.14 Discuss the decision to add or drop products to or from a product line in international markets

10.15 How does competition affect product-line composition? Illustrate your answer with reference to the luxury car segment in the United States.

10.16 What factors are relevant to the choice of foreign markets?

10.17 How does the use of IPLC information help a firm screen foreign markets for possible entry?

10.18 What is a competitive audit? How can it help in choosing foreign markets for possible entry?

10.19 Analyze how and why Coca-Cola has been rethinking its foreign market entry choices.

10.20 What are the implications of ISO 9000 for a firm developing products for international markets?

10.21 How should a firm use benchmarking in developing world-class products?

Endnotes

1. Ohmae, Kenichi. "Getting Back to Strategy," *Harvard Business Review*, November–December 1988.

2. "Why Heinz Went Sour in Brazil," *Advertising Age*, December 5, 1988.

3. "China's Buick Infatuation," *Wall Street Journal*, July 22, 2004.

4. Rogers, E. M. *Diffusion of Innovation*, 1995, New York: Free Press.

5. Normann, Richard and Rafael Ramirez. "From Value Chain to Value Constellation: Designing Interactive Strategy," *Harvard Business Review*, July–August 1993.

6. Meyer, Marc and J. M. Utterback. "The Product Family and the Dynamics of Core Capability," *Sloan Management Review*, Spring 1993, pages 1–19.

7. Halman, Johannes I. M., Adrian P. Hofer, and Win van Vuuren. "Platform-Driven Development of Product Families: Linking Theory With Practice" *Journal of Product Innovation Management*, Volume 20, 2003, pages 149–162.

8. Robertson, D. and K. Ulrich. "Planning for Product Platforms," *Sloan Management Review*, 1998, pages 19–31.

9. Normann, Richard and Rafael Ramirez. "From Value Chain to Value Constellation: Designing Interactive Strategy," *Harvard Business Review*, July–August 1993, page 76.

10. Eisenhardt, Kathleen and B. Tabrizi. "Accelerating Adaptive Processes: Product Innovation in the Global Computer Industry," *Administrative Science Quarterly*, Volume 40, Number 1, March 1995.

11. Kalyanaram, G. and V. Krishan. "Deliberate Product Definition: Customizing the Product Definition Process," *Journal of Marketing Research*, Volume 34, May 1997, pages 276–285.

12. Moskowitz, Howard R. and Sam Rabino. "Sensory Segmentation: An Organizing Principle for International Product Concept Generation," *Journal of Global Marketing*, Volume 8, Number 1, 1994.

13. http://www.sgi.com.

14. Prokesch, S. "Mastering Chaos at the High-Tech Frontier: An Interview with Silicon Graphics' Ed McCracken," *Harvard Business Review*, November–December 1993.

15. Thomke, Stefan and Eric von Hippel. "Customers as Innovators," *Harvard Business Review*, April 2002.

16. Morris, Charles and C. H. Ferguson. "How Architecture Wins Technology Wars," *Harvard Business Review*, March–April 1993; Shapiro, Carl and Hal Varian, "The Art of Standards Wars," *California Management Review*, Volume 41, Number 2, Winter 1999.

17. "Novartis to Acquire Hexal Ag and Eon Labs, Creating the World Leader in Generics," Novartis media release, February 21, 2005; "Sandoz AG Is Foraging for Additional Food Holdings," *Wall Street Journal*, February 21, 1995.

18. "Novartis and Alnylam Create Major Alliance to Discover RNAi Therapeutics," Alnylam press release, September 7, 2005.

19. "With Dry Pipelines, Big Drug Makers Stock Up in Japan," *Wall Street Journal*, November 24, 2003.

20. Kalagnanam, S. and S. K. Schmidt. "Analyzing Capital Investments in New Products," *Management Accounting*, January 1996, pages 31–36.

21. Sasaki, T. "How the Japanese Accelerated New Car Development," *Long Range Planning*, Volume 24, Number 1, 1991, pages 15–25.

22. Yamanouchi, Teruo. "Breakthrough: The Development of the Canon Personal Copier," *Long Range Planning*, Volume 22, Number 5, pages 11–21.

23. Harryson, Sigwald J. "How Canon and Sony Drive Product Innovation through Networking and Application-Focused R&D," *Journal of Product Innovation Management*, Volume 14, July 1997, pages 288–295.

24. Kamath, Rajan R. and J. K. Liker. "A Second Look at Japanese Product Development," *Harvard Business Review*, November–December 1994.

25. Aoshima, Yaichi. "Transfer of System Knowledge Across Generations in New Product Development: Empirical Observations from Japanese Automobile Development," *Industrial Relations*, Volume 41, Number 4, October 2002, pages 605–628.

26. Murray, Janet Y., Masaaaki Kotabe, and Joe Nan Zhou. "Strategic

Alliance-Based Sourcing and Market Performance: Evidence from Foreign Firms Operating in China," *Journal of International Business Studies,* Volume 36, March 2005, pages 187–208; Kotabe, Masaaki and K. S. Swan, "Offshore Sourcing: Reaction, Maturation, and Consolidation of U.S. Multinationals," *Journal of International Business Studies,* Volume 25, Number 1, First Quarter 1994, pages 115–140; Murray, Jane, M. Kotabe, and A. R. Wildt, "Strategic and Financial Performance Implications of Global Sourcing Strategy: A Contingency Analysis," *Journal of International Business Studies,* Volume 26, Number 1, 1995, pages 181–202; Swamidass, P. and M. Kotabe, "Component Sourcing Strategies of Multinationals: An Empirical Study of European and Japanese Multinationals," *Journal of International Business Studies,* Volume 24, Number 1, 1993, pages 81–99.

27. Zhao, Yushan and Roger J. Calantone. "The Trend towards Outsourcing in New Product Development: Case Studies in Six Firms," *International Journal of Innovation Management,* Volume 7, Number 1, March 2003, pages 51–66.

28. von Hippel, Eric and Ralph Katz. "Shifting Innovation to Users via Toolkits," *Management Science,* Volume 48, Number 7, July 2002, pages 821–833.

29. Takeuchi, H. and I. Nonaka. "The New New-Product Development Game," *Harvard Business Review,* January–February 1986.

30. Lint, Onno and Enrico Pennings. "An Option Approach to the New Product Development Process," *R&D Management,* Volume 31, Issue 2, 2001, pages 163–172; also see Lint, Onno and Enrico Pennings, "Finance and Strategy: Time-to-Wait or Time-to-Market," *Long Range Planning,* Volume 32, 1999, pages 483–493.

31. "Allied Domecq's Bet on Wine," *Wall Street Journal,* July 1, 2003.

32. Aaker, Jennifer L. "Dimensions of Brand Personality," *Journal of Marketing Research,* Volume 34, August 1997, pages 347–356.

33. "A Canny Move by Koc," *Financial Times,* July 5, 1994.

34. Quelch, John and David Kenny. "Extend Profits, Not Product Lines," *Harvard Business Review,* September–October 1994.

35. "The iPod Wannabees," *Wall Street Journal,* April 8, 2004.

36. Ryans, Adrian B. "Strategic Market Entry Factors and Market Share Achievement in Japan," *Journal of International Business Studies,* Fall 1988.

37. For background readings on benchmarking, see the following: Schmidt, Linda, G. Zhang, J. Herrmann, George Dieter, and P Cunniff. *Product Engineering and Manufacturing,* 2nd edition, Knoxville, TN: College House Enterprises, 2002; Zairi, Mohamed and R. Hutton, "Benchmarking: A Process-Driven Tool for Quality Improvement," *TQM Magazine,* Volume 7, Issue 3, 1995, pages 35–40; Walleck, A. S. et al, "Benchmarking World-Class Performance," *McKinsey Quarterly,* Number 1, 1991; Camp, R. C., "A Bible for Benchmarking by Xerox," *Financial Executive,* July/August 1993.

38. http://www.iso.org.

39. See http://www.iso.org/iso/en/iso9000-14000/understand/inbrief.html and Hayes, H. Michael. "ISO 9000: The New Strategic Consideration," *Business Horizons,* May–June 1994, pages 52–60.

40. Nichols, Nancy. "Scientific Management at Merck," *Harvard Business Review,* January–February 1994.

41. Henderson, Rebecca. "Managing Innovation in the Information Age," *Harvard Business Review,* January–February 1994.

42. Kim, K., J. H. Park, and J. E. Prescott. "The Global Integration of Business Functions," *Journal of International Business Studies,* Volume 34, July 2003, pages 327–344.

43. Cheng, Joseph L. C. and D. S. Bolon. "The Management of Multinational R&D," *Journal of International Business Studies,* Volume 24, Number 1, 1993, pages 1–18.

44. Pearce, Robert and M. Papanastassiou. "R&D Networks and Innovation: Decentralized Product Development in Multinational Enterprises," *University of Reading, Discussion Papers in International Investment and Business Studies,* Volume VIII, Series B, Number 204, October 1995.

45. Cooper, Robert G. *Product Leadership: Pathways to Profitable Innovation,* 2005, New York: Basic Books; Cooper, Robert G. "Stage-Gate Systems: A New Tool for Managing New Products," *Business Horizons,* May–June 1990, pages 44–54.

46. Hart, Susan, Erik Jan Hultink, Nikolaos Tzokas, and Harry R. Commandeur. "Industrial Companies' Evaluation Criteria in New Product Development Gates," *Journal of Product Innovation Management,* Volume 20, 2003, pages 22–36, Figure 2.

47. de Meyer, Arnoud. "Tech Talk: How Managers Are Stimulating Global R&D Communication," *Sloan Management Review,* Spring 1991; Bouteiller, Roman, Olivier Gassmann, and Maximilian von Zedtwitz, *Managing Global Innovation,* 2000, New York: Springer-Verlag.

Further Readings

Aaker, Jennifer L. "Dimensions of Brand Personality," *Journal of Marketing Research,* Volume 34, August 1997, pages 347–356.

Aoshima, Yaichi. "Transfer of System Knowledge Across Generations in New Product Development: Empirical Observations from Japanese Automobile Development," *Industrial Relations,* Volume 4, Number 4, October 2002, pages 605–628.

Bouteiller, Roman, Olivier Gassmann, and Maximilian von Zedtwitz. *Managing Global Innovation,* 2000, New York: Springer-Verlag.

Camp, R. C. "A Bible for Benchmarking by Xerox." *Financial Executive,* July–August 1993.

Cheng, Joseph L. C. and D. S. Bolon. "The Management of Multinational R&D," *Journal of International Business Studies,* Volume 24, Number 1, 1993, pages 1–18.

Cooper, Robert G. *Product Leadership: Pathways to Profitable Innovation,* 2005, New York: Basic Books.

Cooper, Robert G. "Stage-Gate Systems: A New Tool for Managing New Products." *Business Horizons,* May–June 1990, pages 44–54.

Eisenhardt, Kathleen, and B. Tabrizi. "Accelerating Adaptive Processes: Product Innovation in the Global Computer Industry," *Administrative Science Quarterly,* Volume 40, Number 1, March 1995.

Giddy, Ian H. "The Demise of the Product Life Cycle in International Business Theory," *Columbia Journal of World Business,* Spring 1978.

Green, Stephen, M. Ann Welsh, and Gordon E Dehler. "Advocacy, Performance, and Threshold Influences on Decisions to Terminate New Product Development," *Academy of Management Journal,* Volume 46, Number 4, 2003, pages 419–434.

Halman, Johannes I. M., Adrian P. Hofer, and Win van Vuuren. "Platform-Driven Development of Product Families: Linking Theory With Practice," *Journal of Product Innovation Management,* Volume 20, 2003, pages 149–162.

Harryson, Sigwald J. "How Canon and Sony Drive Product Innovation through Networking and Application-focused R&D," *Journal of Product Innovation Management*, Volume 14, July 1997, pages 288–295.

Hart, Susan, Erik Jan Hultink, Nikolaos Tzokas, and Harry R. Commandeur. "Industrial Companies' Evaluation Criteria in New Product Development Gates," *Journal of Product Innovation Management*, Volume 20, 2003, pages 22–36.

Hayes, H. Michael. "ISO 9000: The New Strategic Consideration," *Business Horizons*, May–June 1994, pages 52–60.

Henderson, Rebecca. "Managing Innovation in the Information Age," *Harvard Business Review*, January–February 1994.

Johansson, Johny K., S. P. Douglas, and I. Nonaka. "Assessing the Impact of Country-of-Origin on Product Evaluation: A New Methodological Perspective," *Journal of Marketing Research*, Volume 22, November 1985.

Johansson, Johny K., and Hans B. Thorelli. "International Product Positioning," *Journal of International Business Studies*, Volume 16, Number 3, Fall 1985.

Kalagnanam, S. and S. K. Schmidt. "Analyzing Capital Investments in New Products," *Management Accounting*, January 1996, pages 31–36.

Kalyanaram, G. and V. Krishan. "Deliberate Product Definition: Customizing the Product Definition Process," *Journal of Marketing Research*, Volume 34, May 1997, pages 276–285.

Kamath, Rajan R. and J. K. Liker. "A Second Look at Japanese Product Development," *Harvard Business Review*, November–December 1994.

Kashani, Kamran. "Beware the Pitfalls of Global Marketing," *Harvard Business Review*, September–October 1989.

Keegan, Warren. "Multi-National Product Planning: Strategic Alternatives," *Journal of Marketing*, January 1969.

Kim, K., J. H. Park, and J. E. Prescott. "The Global Integration of Business Functions," *Journal of International Business Studies*, Volume 34, July 2003, pages 327–344.

Kotabe, Masaaki and K. S. Swan. "Offshore Sourcing: Reaction, Maturation, and Consolidation of U.S. Multinationals," *Journal of International Business Studies*, Volume 25, Number 1, First Quarter 1994, pages 115–140.

Lint, Onno and Enrico Pennings. "An Option Approach to the New Product Development Process," *R&D Management*, Volume 31, Issue 2, 2001, pages 163–172.

Lint, Onno and Enrico Pennings. "Finance and Strategy: Time-to-Wait or Time-to-Market," *Long Range Planning*, Volume 32, 1999, pages 483–493.

Meyer, Marc and J. M. Utterback. "The Product Family and the Dynamics of Core Capability," *Sloan Management Review*, Spring 1993, pages 1–19.

Moskowitz, Howard R. and Sam Rabino. "Sensory Segmentation: An Organizing Principle for International Product Concept Generation," *Journal of Global Marketing*, Volume 8, Number 1, 1994.

Murray, Jane, M. Kotabe, and A. R. Wildt. "Strategic and Financial Performance Implications of Global Sourcing Strategy: A Contingency Analysis," *Journal of International Business Studies*, Volume 26, Number 1, 1995, pages 181–202.

Murray, Janet Y., Masaaaki Kotabe, and Joe Nan Zhou. "Strategic Alliance-Based Sourcing and Market Performance: Evidence from Foreign Firms Operating in China," *Journal of International Business Studies*, Volume 36, March 2005, pages 187–208.

Nichols, Nancy. "Scientific Management at Merck," *Harvard Business Review*, January–February 1994.

Normann, Richard and Rafael Ramirez. "From Value Chain to Value Constellation: Designing Interactive Strategy," *Harvard Business Review*, July–August 1993.

Ohmae, Kenichi. "Getting Back to Strategy," *Harvard Business Review*, November–December 1988.

Ohmae, Kenichi. "Planting for a Global Harvest," *Harvard Business Review*, July–August 1989.

Onkvisit, Sak and John J. Shaw. "An Examination of the International Product Life Cycle and Its Application within Marketing," *Columbia Journal of World Business*, Fall 1983.

Pearce, Robert and M. Papanastassiou. "R&D Networks and Innovation: Decentralized Product Development in Multinational Enterprises," *University of Reading, Discussion Papers in International Investment and Business Studies*, Volume VIII, Series B, Number 204, October 1995.

Peng, Mike W. *Global Strategic Management*, Mason, OH: Thomson Learning, 2005.

Prokesch, S. "Mastering Chaos at the High-Tech Frontier: An Interview with Silicon Graphics' Ed McCracken," *Harvard Business Review*, November–December 1993.

Quelch, John. *Global Marketing: A Casebook*, Hoboken, NJ: John Wiley & Sons, 2004.

Quelch, John and David Kenny. "Extend Profits, Not Product Lines," *Harvard Business Review*, September–October 1994.

Roberts, Edward B. "Benchmarking the Strategic Management of Technology—I," *Research-Technology Management*, Volume 38, Number 1, January/February 1995, pages 44–56.

Robertson, D. and K. Ulrich. "Planning for Product Platforms," *Sloan Management Review*, 1998, pages 19–31.

Rogers, Everett M. *Diffusion of Innovation*, 4th edition, New York: Free Press, 1995.

Root, Franklin. *Entry Strategies for International Markets*, Lexington, MA: Lexington Books, 1987.

Sasaki, T. "How the Japanese Accelerated New-Car Development," *Long Range Planning*, Volume 24, Number 1, 1991, pages 15–25.

Schmidt, Linda, G. Zhang, J. Herrmann, George Dieter, and P. Cunniff. *Product Engineering and Manufacturing*, 2nd edition, Knoxville, TN: College House Enterprises, 2002.

Shapiro Carl and Hal Varian. "The Art of Standards Wars," *California Management Review*, Volume 41, Number 2, Winter 1999.

Swamidass, P. and M. Kotabe. "Component Sourcing Strategies of Multinationals: An Empirical Study of European and Japanese Multinationals," *Journal of International Business Studies*, Volume 24, Number 1, 1993, pages 81–99.

Terpstra, Vern. "International Product Policy: The Role of Foreign R&D," *Columbia Journal of World Business*, Winter 1977, pages 24–32.

Thomke, Stefan and Eric von Hippel. "Customers as Innovators," *Harvard Business Review,* April 2002.

von Hippel, Eric and Ralph Katz. "Shifting Innovation to Users via Toolkits," *Management Science,* Volume 48, Number 7, July 2002, pages 821–833.

Walleck, A. S. et al. "Benchmarking World-Class Performance," *McKinsey Quarterly,* Number 1, 1991.

Yamanouchi, Teruo. "Breakthrough: The Development of the Canon Personal Copier," *Long Range Planning,* Volume 22, Number 5, 1989, pages 11–21.

Zairi, Mohamed and R. Hutton. "Benchmarking: A Process-Driven Tool for Quality Improvement," *TQM Magazine,* Volume 7, Issue 3, 1995, pages 35–40.

Zhao, Yushan and Roger J. Calantone. "The Trend towards Outsourcing in New Product Development: Case Studies in Six Firms," *International Journal of Innovation Management,* Volume 7, Number 1, March 2003, pages 51–66.

Case 10.1

BOEING AND AIRBUS: COMPETING PRODUCT LINES

In 2004, Airbus received 370 orders (for $34.4 billion) for its aircraft, giving the company 57 percent of the market. Airbus's leadership in market share was not a temporary phenomenon. In 1994, Airbus received 125 aircraft orders compared to 120 orders for Boeing, the first time in postwar history that Boeing did not have the leading market share. Over the next ten years, Airbus continued to gather orders from the world's leading airlines. Figure 10-9 summarizes the trends in market share for Being and Airbus since 1980.

Airbus has received government subsidies to conduct R&D to develop its new model of aircraft. Boeing has waged a continual campaign to reduce subsidies granted to Airbus, believing that those subsidies make it difficult to compete with Airbus and to earn sufficient cash flow and profits to fund the development of its own larger, new-generation jets. Nevertheless, Airbus has continued to launch new aircraft models and to gain significant global share. Boeing has survived in the aircraft industry for over 60 years, with capable and experienced management that has guided it through previous recessions in a cyclical industry. The company now faces the challenge of maintaining parity with Airbus's development of product line breadth and attractiveness to customers.

Airbus Industrie is a multinational consortium consisting of two state-owned enterprises, France's Aerospatiale (37.9 percent of Airbus) and Spain's CASA (4.2 percent of Airbus); the semiprivate Deutsche Airbus from West Germany (37.9 percent); and the wholly private British Aerospace (20 percent). All of them receive subsidies for aircraft development and customer financing of aircraft sales.

THE COMMERCIAL JET TRANSPORT INDUSTRY

The industry has been characterized as a "Sporty Game,"1 where introducing each new aircraft involves betting the continued survival of the company. The industry is now a duopoly, with Boeing and Airbus being the only manufacturers of large civilian jets. They work hand-in-glove with three aircraft engine manufacturers—GE (and its French joint venture GE-Snecma); Pratt & Whitney (a subsidiary of United Technologies), and Rolls-Royce, a British company. New airframe models typically require new engines. Estimated development costs of new airframes and engines are about $4 billion to $5 billion apiece, with total investment in the aircraft exceeding between $6 billion and $7 billion five to six years after the launch

Figure 10-9. Market Share of Boeing and Airbus Aircraft

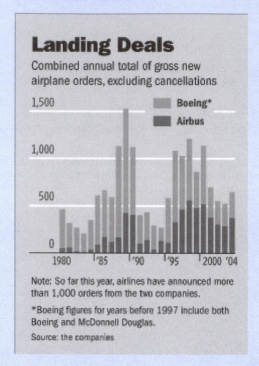

Source: "Boeing, Airbus Foresee Peak Year for Orders Despite Airline Woes," *Wall Street Journal*, September 20, 2005.

of a model. However, the Airbus A380, the largest civilian jet ever, is estimated to cost in excess of $10 billion to develop.

Development of new aircraft requires long lead times, with eventual sales volume amounting to one or two aircraft a day in a good year. Planning the introduction of a new aircraft involves looking ahead about 20 years: 5 years for the planning and a product life of 15 years or more. Hence, considerable market forecasting abilities are required, particularly since airline demand is highly cyclical.

Once an aircraft model moves beyond development into production, the cost of producing initial batches of aircraft will be far higher than, say, the 300th unit manufactured, owing to learning curve-driven cost reductions. Therefore, it is vital that the gamble represented by development of a new aircraft model be transformed into continuing sales. Commercial aircraft manufacturing can be highly profitable, as operating leverage beyond breakeven is high. It is the possibility of demand growth fueled by rising world incomes, trade, and airline traffic that attracts firms to this industry. If an aircraft model is successful, as in the case of Boeing's 747 (with virtually no competition for much of its life), profits can be enormous.

Introducing derivative aircraft models pushes back the payback period even further. Additional development costs are incurred, although they extend the life of the model. Thus, a company seeking to make commercial jets must be prepared to wait ten years or more to recover its investments—and even longer to make a profit. Price cutting by a less profit-oriented competitor will reduce margins and contribution, thereby pushing back the break-even point further. That practice affects the willingness of top management to approve funding for the development of new-generation aircraft. At the same time, lower prices and margins reduce cash flow and prejudice the ability of a firm to fund new aircraft development from internal sources.

Few aircraft have yielded sufficient volume sales to generate profits for their manufacturers. The De Havilland Comet, the pioneer jet introduced in 1952, sold only 112 units, while the Boeing 707, introduced in 1958, sold nearly 1,000 units. Given a break-even volume of about 600 units for the smaller jets,2 Boeing has achieved profitability with its 707 (1,010 sold), 727 (1,831 sold), and 737 (5,965 sold). In addition, the 747, with over 1,400 units sold, is profitable given its far higher unit price of between $150 million and $160 million and higher margins due to its erstwhile monopoly position. (As a consequence, break-even volume on the 747 is lower, at about 300 units.) Airbus may have reached breakeven with its A300/310 model (850 ordered through 2005), though development costs of extending the product family may have raised the break-even volume significantly. Its A320 is a success, with total orders exceeding 3,600 planes. Total orders for the A330/340 have reached about 900 planes; but it, too, has incurred development costs for several derivative models. At best, it is likely to achieve moderate financial returns. Despite those erratic results, Airbus has been able to develop its newest A380 model at an estimated cost of $10 billion. The company is also seeking launch aid from its governments to fund the development of another new aircraft, the A350.

Future growth and the bulk of the market for commercial aircraft would appear to lie overseas. U.S. traffic is expected to represent only about one-third of world traffic, with Europe, Canada, and the rest of the world representing another third each.3 Thus, foreign airlines will be the major customers for aircraft manufacturers, with government-owned airlines representing a significant share of the customer group. Political pressures could significantly affect a sale and hinder a private company that cannot obtain government help.

HOW DO AIRLINES BUY PLANES?

Airlines sell perishable commodities. An empty seat is revenue that is lost forever. Airlines would like to fly their planes with every seat sold, meaning they would like aircraft with different passenger capacities for different routes based on traffic demand patterns. Routes also vary in distance, with major transcontinental routes such as New York to Tokyo and London to Sydney requiring long-range aircraft. In addition, the gradual development of international hub-and-spoke systems means that different-sized but short-range aircraft may be needed depending on passenger density within each hub-and-spoke system.

Further, the larger the plane, the heavier the engine needs to be. Matching engine thrust to aircraft size determines fuel economy and speed, which become important as more airlines seek nonstop flight schedules. As the price of oil exceeded $65 a barrel in 2005, fuel costs approached 30 percent of total operating costs and aircraft buyers presumably placed a higher priority on fuel economy. Aging aircraft fleets are another factor where the costs of replacing fully depreciated aircraft must be balanced against fuel and maintenance costs that are comparatively higher with the older aircraft. Environmental controls and noise abatement provisions complicate this trade-off as freedom to operate older, noisier aircraft over crowded cities is gradually limited. Technical obsolescence of an existing fleet, with improved safety arising from advanced avionics, also color demand for new jet aircraft.

If existing models of planes are sufficiently discounted and cheap fuel reduces the economic gains to be had from the more expensive new-generation aircraft, airlines might prefer to buy the (cheaper) older models, hoping to squeeze the manufacturers into financing the aircraft at low risk to the consumers (the airlines). Thus, airlines buying jet aircraft are guided by their route structure and the balance of fuel versus labor versus capital costs. They would probably prefer a family of aircraft (of differing ranges and passenger capacity) from one manufacturer in order to economize on flight crew training, inventory of spare parts, spare engines, maintenance, and related expenses. But the business cycle and outlook for traffic growth influence the willingness of airlines to buy expensive new aircraft and add large amounts of long-term debt. Therefore, offering attractive aircraft financing and flexible delivery of aircraft becomes important. As in any new product launch, firms gamble that the product will appeal to the market. The risks of being wrong are magnified in the commercial jet market because the costs of development are so high.

In sum, aircraft product offerings from manufacturers must cater to market segments. Those markets are defined by the confluence of range, passenger capacity, and engine choices and with the requisite speed, fuel economy, and personnel savings—all at a reasonable and competitive price, while also matching financing terms offered by competitors.

AIRBUS AND BOEING: COMPETING PRODUCT PORTFOLIOS

Airframe manufacturers work within their customers' decision calculus to design and manufacture aircraft, relying on forecasts of expected modal route ranges and passenger densities. Current and proposed product offerings represent the outcome of that course of analysis. Table 10-8 sets out the current product portfolios of the two competing manufacturers. Commercial jet aircraft models—the A320 family, the A330, the A340, the A380, and the proposed A350 (all from Airbus) and the Boeing 787 and 777, the extended range 767s, and the 737 derivatives—can best be understood in light of two dimensions: range and passenger capacity. Other factors such as speed, fuel economy, number and type of engines, number of required flight crew, aircraft reliability, and financing terms also influence the choice between competing aircraft. However, range and capacity are central to demarcating broad product segments within which the factors mentioned above can play a further role.

Four groups emerge, although with some overlap, as follows:

- A crowded short-haul, short-capacity segment (the A320/Boeing 737 families)
- A competitive medium-haul, medium-sized segment (the A300/310 family and the Boeing 757/767 family)
- A long-range segment created by the Boeing 747, with competitors emerging after a long period, from the Airbus A380 with the higher passenger capacity and the A330/340 with fewer passengers. The Boeing 777 may also be seen as competing at the lower end.
- A fourth segment consisting of planes with 225 to 300 seats and flying extremely long distances, comparable to the 747 but with about 40 to 50 percent fewer seats. This segment has new entrants, including the A350 and the Boeing 787. The smallest-capacity Boeing 777 and A340 may also be competitive in this segment.

Boeing

Boeing has been successful because of its product forecasting ability. Its first product, the 707, was a success despite the fact that it came several years behind the British Comet. Since then, Boeing has offered jets to meet demand in a variety of segments, as follows:

- The 727 and 737 provide short-range, small-capacity routes. They compete against Airbus's A320. The 727 and 737 are two of the most successful aircraft ever introduced, with sales of about 1,800 and 6,000 units, respectively. The 727 has been withdrawn from production because of its outdated design, inefficient fuel consumption, and noise. The 737 is still in production, with several derivative model aircraft having been introduced recently—all in response to competition from Airbus.
- The 747 is used for large-capacity, long-range routes. Boeing pioneered this segment at the insistence of Pan Am, nearly bankrupting itself in the process. The aircraft is high-priced, currently at about $150 million each. It provided profit margins of 25 percent or more, principally because Boeing had a monopoly in this segment. The recent emergence of new offerings such as the A330/340 and the gigantic A380 provide competition in this segment, consequently eroding margins and profits. A further development is the Boeing 777, which is a competitive response to longer-range Airbus 330/340 aircraft.
- The 757 and 767 offer medium-range, medium- and small-capacity long-range routes. They were developed by Boeing in response to the Airbus A300/310 aircraft. They have a smaller capacity than the Airbus aircraft, but are two-engine fuel-efficient aircraft. The 767 gradually carved out a role in long-distance trans-Atlantic and trans-Pacific flights over water.
- As mentioned above, a new segment contains the Boeing 787 and the proposed Airbus 350.

As Airbus introduced planes to cover the principal market segments, Boeing's market share dropped in segments where competition from Airbus intensified. Table 10-9 breaks out orders by segments for each of the three manufacturers and further tracks orders over distinct time frames.

The market segments identified are not rigid, chiefly due to the ability to vary seating capacity on a

Table 10-8. Competitive Product Offerings from Boeing and Airbus

Features	Size: passengers	Range: nautical miles	Boeing: Model	Airbus: Model	Size: passengers	Range: nautical miles	Features
737s can cruise at 41,000 feet. Convertible freight version is also available.	110 to 132 126 to 149 162 to 189 177 to 189	3,200 3,200 3,200 3,200	737-600 737-700 737-800 737-900	A320 A321 A319 A318	150 185 124 107	3,000 3,000 3,700 3,250	Airbus's most successful "fly-by-wire" plane
First launched in 1969	416	7,260	747-400	A380	550	8,000	Long-range, double-deck aircraft; spacious and efficient
Two- or three-class configuration; freighter has 60-ton capacity with international capability	181-224 218-269 245-304	6,600 6,105 5,645	767-200ER 767-300ER 767-400ER	A300-600 A310	266 220	4,050 5,200	The original "Airbus" intended for European routes and European airlines
Fills gap between 767 and 747; stretched configuration; first delivery of three-class is in January 2006; freighter version in 2008	305 368 365 301	7,730 5,955 7,880 9,420	777-200ER 777-300 777-300ER 777-200LR	A330-300 A340-300 A340-500 A340-600	335 295 313 380	5,650 7,400 9,000 7,900	To compete with the Boeing 747, but longer range and smaller passenger capacity
Launched in 2003; GE and RR engines; production began in 2006 with entry into service in 2008	223-259 223-259 296	8,500 8,300 3,500	787-8 Dreamliner 787-9 Dreamliner 787-3 Dreamliner	A350-800 A350-900	253 300	8,800 7,500	Awaiting formal approval to compete against the 787 launched two years earlier

particular model of aircraft. Airlines have some flexibility in adapting capacity by offering one class or multiple classes of seating and by putting seats closer together. Aircraft manufacturers can adapt airframes by stretching them, literally extending the fuselage to hold more passengers. Further adaptations include upgrading the engines to provide more thrust for the now-heavier aircraft and redesigning the wings, using winglets, to increase aerodynamic efficiency and fuel burn.

Developing such *derivative* aircraft is less costly and, therefore, less risky. Boeing used this approach in offering the 747-400. Boeing's goal was to protect its monopoly position in the 747 segment and extend the product family, while conserving cash and reducing risk associated with developing a brand new plane.

But sticking to derivative aircraft, while safe, can allow a bolder competitor to pioneer a new aircraft model for a new market segment and develop a

Table 10-9. Boeing and Airbus Aircraft Orders in Units by Market Segments

Aircraft Segment	1970–1980	1981–1990	1991–2000	2001–2005	Total Order from Model Inception to September 2005
Short-Range, Small-Capacity					
Boeing 727 (first introduced in 1960)	960	50 (last order received was in 1983)			1,831
Boeing 737 (first introduced in 1965)	690	1,881	2,250	1,144	5,965
boeing total for segment	1,650	1,931	2,250	1,144	7,796
Airbus A320 family (first introduced in 1984)		680	2,120	840	3,640
Medium-Range, Medium-Capacity					
Boeing 757/767 (launched in 1978)	207	938	738	130	2,013
Airbus A300/A310 (launched in 1974)	300	435	155	69	959
Boeing 787 (first delivery scheduled for 2008)				250	250
Airbus 350 (first delivery scheduled for 2010)				125	125
Long-Range, Large-Capacity					
Boeing 747 (launched in 1966)	378	503	276	71	1,404
Airbus A330/A340 (launched 1988)		227	569	277	1,073
Airbus 380 (first delivery scheduled for 2006)				149	
A350 (awaiting formal launch)				125 (commitments)	

monopoly position, much like Boeing did with the 747. For example, Boeing was unable to prevent Airbus from gaining a significant presence in the 150-seat segment of the market. The launch success of Airbus's A320 may be traced, in part, to Boeing's strategy of delaying the launch of its competing similar-sized aircraft that utilized new technology, the 7J7, and ultimately canceling the project.

The 7J7 represents an interesting case of product development. Boeing decided to cancel the launch of the 7J7 for several reasons:

- Low fuel prices reduced the incentive to buy an expensive aircraft such as the 7J7 because its promised fuel economy was less attractive economically.
- Price was a factor because the 7J7 would compete with Boeing's own 737-400 and with Airbus's A320. Boeing estimated that the 7J7 should be priced at about $27 million (1987 dollars), about the price at which the 737 was being offered. Airlines seemed unwilling to pay more for the new technology under existing economic conditions. They did not want to commit the traditional one-third advance payment over the four-year development period.

- Airlines disagreed on the desired passenger capacity for a new aircraft, seeking somewhere between 150 and 170 seats.
- The version of the UHB engine's unducted fan that GE was to provide could not accommodate a stretched version of a 170-seat jet, which Boeing would have been likely to use. Therefore, waiting until the UHB engine was better defined seemed prudent both to Boeing and its customers.
- Because Boeing's backlog was high and employment was at almost 140,000 people, scarcity of human resources that could be committed to the 7J7 program became a constraining factor.

Instead, Boeing launched a derivative version of the 737, the 737-500. It had seating for between 100 and 125 passengers and had a range of between 1,700 and 2,800 nautical miles. In this segment of the market, Boeing faced competition from companies it did not usually consider its rivals. Those competitors were the manufacturers of small passenger jets, the Fokker F-100 and the BAE 146. However, those aircraft were intended mainly for short-range regional airline flights. Commuter airlines are becoming affiliates and subsidiaries of major carriers, the principal role of commuter airlines being that of providing feeder traffic for longer routes. The purchase of these smaller aircraft is subject to approval by the major airlines' partners. Commuter airlines began to use the small jet aircraft rather than turboprops. In response, other new manufacturers of small jets have emerged, such as Bombardier and Embraer.

Airbus

Airbus's product strategy has been one of catching up, and then surpassing, Boeing. Airbus's two central goals are to:

- Match Boeing's broad product range by providing an Airbus family of aircraft to meet a variety of range and passenger capacity needs: single- and twin-aisle aircraft for short-, medium-, and long-range flights. That is, Airbus had to grow beyond its two initial models (A300 and A310) and develop aircraft that could match Boeing's offerings across the entire product line.

- Utilize advanced technology, including the so-called "fly-by-wire" avionics and more fuel-efficient engines and airframe design. Those advances made Airbus's offerings efficient and attractive. In addition, the new aircraft could be flown by two-man crews. (The use of advanced cockpit instrumentation in the A300 and the follow-on A310 allowed the aircraft to be certified with a minimum crew of two pilots. That eliminated the need for a flight engineer and led to cost reductions in personnel.)

The Original Airbus: A300/A310

Airbus's initial product offerings were the A300 and the A310. The A300 was designed to meet a gap in the market for twin-engine medium-size aircraft designed for the routes needed by major European airlines. The 310 was a longer-range derivative introduced in 1978. Both aircraft were designed to suit the needs of European airliners. (Their routes did not cover long distances, but they needed passenger capacities of about 250 seats. Hence, the term airbus.) Cost reduction was achieved using the same jigs and tooling as the 300/310 program and a shared assembly line. However, the aircraft did not share the wing (one of the most expensive components). This initial focus on a narrow market reduced the appeal of the Airbus to U.S. airlines, which generally fly longer routes.

Hence, Airbus launched two derivatives, the long-range 310-300 with a fuel tank in the horizontal stabilizer and a stretched A300-600. With about 950 of the 300/310 aircraft sold, these programs have barely exceeded breakeven.

The A320

Despite average A300/310 sales, Airbus moved on to the 150-seat market with the A320, undergoing certification with fly-by-wire controls. Fly-by-wire refers to the use of computer-based controls of the aileron, rudder, and other aircraft mechanisms, replacing the more traditional mechanical controls. The A320 is a short-haul twin-engine aircraft, seating between 150 and 180 passengers in a single-aisle configuration. It uses tried and tested engines and achieves fuel economies with design innovations.

Given the lack of cash flow and profits from the A300/310 program, the A320 was entirely dependent on government funding for its development. But market prospects looked attractive as airlines would be replacing the aging DC9s and 727s. Airbus executives termed it "the hole in the sky." Because Boeing was deep in the launch of the 757/767 model family, it would be less able to launch yet another program for a new 150-seat aircraft model.

Airbus has been successful with the A320. It received 439 orders for the A320 by the time of its maiden flight on February 22, 1987, including 262 firm orders, 157 options, and 20 commitments. It followed up with the derivative launch of both larger and smaller versions of the A320. The A321 carried about 180 passengers; and the A319 carried 124 passengers, competing directly with Boeing's newest 737-500 aircraft. The A320 and the follow-on derivatives gathered more than 3,600 orders, thus becoming the first aircraft in the Airbus family to achieve commercial success. Even more importantly, airlines did not see Boeing's derivative 737s as fully matching the A320s fly-by-wire and other advanced technology capabilities. The A320 helped Airbus gain credibility as a technology leader.

The A330/340 Series

With the 150-seat and midsize (200–250 seats) segments covered, Airbus launched the high-capacity long-range A330/340 series. Again, the company shared design elements—the twin-aisle cross section of the A300/310, a variable camber high-efficiency wing, and a new final assembly line. Airbus's existing A300/310 aircraft needed new wings to improve range and efficiency; adapting the same wing to the A330 and A340 could further reduce development costs.

The A330, a high-capacity medium-range jet, can carry about 330 passengers. The jet has a range of about 5,500 miles. It was intended as a twin-engine replacement for aging wide-body tri-jets (three-engine jets) such as the DC-10 and the L-1011, with sufficient range to operate on transatlantic routes. The A340 was designed as a four-engine long-range aircraft for 260 to 290 passengers. It was capable of flying 7,650 nautical miles (or nonstop from New York to Hong Kong).

The A330/340 program was subsidized. While it is difficult to estimate the extent of subsidies made available to Airbus, total subsidies over the 1970–1990 period (covering the A300/310, the A320, and the A330/340 series) were between $12 billion and $15 billion, including launch. Airbus was certain of receiving government subsidies, and it had an early commitment from the French government to buy several newer models. Those facts may have emboldened Airbus to gamble on its obtaining enough unit volume to derive profits from launches of new aircraft, despite the presence of Boeing. Or perhaps Airbus reasoned that its government backing could enable it to sustain losses. Airbus's success with aircraft sales, particularly with the A320, complemented the subsidies, allowing it to lower total costs through economies of scale, thus enhancing its competitive position.

NEW PRODUCT DEVELOPMENT

The pace of new product development in the commercial jet industry might seem glacial compared to other fast-paced technology-intensive industries such as computers and networking. The necessary scale of R&D funding and the time to develop new jets explain why both Boeing and Airbus launch only one or two new models a decade. Since about 1990, only three new aircraft have been launched by the two competitors, with a fourth model on the verge of formal launch.

The B-777 Aircraft

Boeing's product-development effort during much of the 1990s was focused on developing and launching the Boeing 777. Airbus's A330/340 long-range but medium-capacity aircraft, which carried about 350 passengers, was first to market. (The A330/340 had less capacity than the 747, but a somewhat similar range.) It may have focused on the needs of the emerging Asian airlines. The response by Boeing was for its 777 to be the world's largest twinjet. In its initial version, the aircraft carried between 375 and 400 passengers, with a range of 4,200 nautical miles. Boeing intended the 777 to be positioned between the 767 and the 747, with an initial delivery scheduled for mid-1995. The 777 was planned as the widest and most spacious airline in its class, having great interior flexibility. Airlines could easily add, remove, and shift lavatories and galleys and change seating configuration as needed. The 777 was designed with folding wingtips so it could be parked at older airports. In building the 777, Boeing used Japanese suppliers. Mitsubishi, Kawasaki, and Fuji built about 20 percent of the airframe. Frank Schrontz, Boeing's then-CEO, noted, "We would rather have the Japanese with us than with Airbus."

United was the launch customer for the 777, buying 34 aircraft to replace its aged DC-10s. The initial version could replace tri-jets on U.S. domestic routes, on short transcontinental routes such as New York to London, and on regional routes in the Far East. Compared to the A330-300, the 777 would be more fuel-efficient and would carry more passengers. Cathay Pacific is typical of the airlines that ordered the 777. Offering several long flights from its hub in Hong Kong, Cathay Pacific ordered both the 777 and the Airbus A330s.

The "Superjumbo" Airbus A380

One of the interesting questions facing Boeing and Airbus was whether its customers, the airlines, needed planes that could carry more than 500 passengers, the outer limit of the Boeing 747. As Asian economies grew, demand from their larger populations could result in the need to carry more people at a time across Asian capitals separated by water, such as Singapore to Tokyo and Shanghai to Sydney. However, larger planes had be filled with people to operate profitably; and airlines might be concerned about their ability to fill 550-seat and larger planes at 75 percent capacity (the level at which the route would be profitable). Those planes would be heavy, require new engines, and incur large R&D costs (estimated at about $10 billion). Boeing decided not to pursue such an option, perhaps constrained by the need to deliver financial returns to its shareholders. Airbus did launch such a plane, the A380, making the announcement in 2002. The plane is a double-decker capable of carrying 550 passengers and flying 8,000 nautical miles nonstop. It is designed for long, high-density routes. For example, one of its customers is a start-up Indian airline, Kingfisher Air, which will operate the A380 with 496 seats in a three-class configuration from Mumbai (Bombay) to New York. Lufthansa, another customer, will use the A380 on high-density routes from Germany to cities such as New York, Singapore, Bangkok, and New Delhi. Other early customers are Thai Airways, Malaysia Air, and Qantas. The A380 had its maiden flight in April 2005. The first commercial deliveries to Singapore Airlines are scheduled for the second half of 2006. A freighter version will enter service in 2008.

The Boeing 787 Dreamliner

In 2003, Boeing launched a new aircraft, the 787 Dreamliner. It represented a different development direction from that of Airbus's A380. While the A380 will carry over 500 passengers and fly nearly halfway around the world nonstop, the Dreamliner 787 will be fuel-efficient and about half as large in terms of passenger capacity. The 787-8 Dreamliner and 787-9 airplanes will carry 223 to 259 passengers in tri-class configurations on routes of 8,500 and 8,300 nautical miles, respectively. A third 787 family member, the 787-3 Dreamliner, will accommodate nearly 296 passengers in a two-class configuration, optimized for routes of 3,500 nautical miles. Priced at $120 million, Boeing promised a 20 percent improvement in fuel efficiency per passenger. The 787 is aimed at replacing the 757 and the 767 and is intended to compete with the aging A300 and A330s. Most initial orders for the 787 have come from outside the United States. The two largest orders were placed by ANA (50 planes) and Japan Airlines (30 planes). The 787 will be available in 2008, two years ahead of the A350. By July 2005, Boeing had received orders for 252 of the Dreamliner 787 planes.

The A380 and the Boeing 787 represent different bets on the future direction of air travel. Airbus expects a major market of large-capacity planes that fly long distances. On the other hand, Boeing is banking on airlines and their customers wanting to fly long nonstop routes between smaller capitals and regional cities; however, there will be fewer passengers. This suggests that the international hub-and-spoke system will become less prevalent and that airlines and their customers will prefer to fly direct over long distances. Airlines can also reach breakeven with fewer customers when flying the smaller 787s.

Airbus's Proposed A350

Airbus's proposed A350 awaits final board approval, including $5 billion in funding (about a third to be received as government subsidies). Airbus plans two versions of the A350, the A350-800, which will seat 253 passengers and fly 8,800 nautical miles, and the A350-900, which will seat 300 passengers and fly up to 7,500 nautical miles. The aircraft will feature some of the innovations pioneered in the A380: a fuselage made of aluminium/lithium and carbon fiber wings, making it lighter in weight and leading to greater fuel efficiency. Both aircraft will offer spacious cabins with larger windows and more headroom, e-mail connectivity, and mood lighting. Deliveries of the A350 will begin at the end of 2012. Airbus noted that it would carry "30 more people eight percent more economically/seat than its closest competitor."

LOOKING TO THE FUTURE: THE GLOBAL AIR TRAFFIC ENVIRONMENT

Aircraft product cycles can easily extend beyond 20 years. Hence, aircraft manufacturers have to consider how the air traffic market will evolve over the long term. The major industry trend is faster growth outside the United States. Table 10-10 summarizes growth trends in global airline traffic.

As is the case of many other industries, higher rates of growth are occurring outside the United States. Table 10-11 summarizes long-term market forecasts prepared by Boeing and Airbus. Both airlines see significant growth in orders over the next two decades.

Table 10-10. Growth of Airline Passenger Traffic by Region

	Percentage Growth Rate						
	North America	Asia Pacific	China	Europe	Latin America	Middle East	Africa
2004–2023	4.2	6	8.2	5.2	4.9	7.1	4.5

Note: Growth rates are averages as traffic flows from one region to other geographic regions can vary; that is, traffic from North America to Southeast Asia is forecasted to grow at 7.3 percent; but traffic within North America, at 3.5 percent.

Source: Airbus Global Market Forecast 2004–2023.

Table 10-11. Manufacturers' Forecasts of Aircraft Market Size, 2005–2024

Manufacturer	Boeing (Forecast 2005–2024)	Airbus (Forecast 2004–2023)
Global Traffic Growth	4.8% per year	5.3% per year
Aircraft Demand (Number of Units)	25,700	17,328
Aircraft Demand (2004 Dollars)	$2.1 trillion	$1.9 trillion
Number of Aircraft in Fleet		
Beginning of Forecast Period	16,800 planes (2004)	10,838 passenger aircraft (end of 2003) and 1,506 freighter aircraft
End of Forecast Period	35,300 planes	21,759 passenger aircraft and 3,616 freighter aircraft

Note: Estimates differ because of different assumptions about growth rates, size of plane ordered, number of older planes replaced, and pricing.

Source: Boeing Market Outlook 2004 and Airbus Global Market Forecast 2004–2023.

Oversupply of Aircraft Capacity Relative to Demand

Is there a current oversupply of planes? Between 1985 and 1990, world traffic grew at 7 percent a year, aircraft orders rose at 30 percent a year, and production increased at 16 percent a year. Hence, airlines developed excess capacity. When recession hit Asia in 1997 and when a global recession unfolded in 2001, airline traffic dropped dramatically. As a consequence, domestic and international airlines reduced their capital spending, requesting aircraft delivery postponements. American, European, and Far Eastern airlines all implemented budget reductions. Despite subsequent recovery, airlines have been cautious in adding capacity and ordering new aircraft, preferring, instead, to fly older planes that have higher capacities.

Pacific-based airlines became the biggest source of aircraft orders as major U.S. airlines were noticeably reticent about ordering new planes. Bankruptcy of four of the major U.S. airlines diminished their ability to order new aircraft. Forecasts suggest that by 2015, about half of all wide-body jets will be flying Pacific routes and those routes will account for 70 percent of all wide-body seats. (The average number of seats on Pacific routes is likely to be around 350.) This boom in demand for aircraft that offer larger passenger capacity is reflected in the many orders that have come from the Pacific region. Airbus has received large orders from China and other Asian markets for its A380.

Financing Difficulties

Airline financing became harder to secure as airline balance sheets deteriorated. Reduced cash flow from a traffic decline due to terrorism fears and economic recession forced airlines and lenders to cut their capital spending budgets. Lenders became less willing to finance the purchase of aircraft to be flown on competitive routes, where rates of traffic growth and yields are low. However, funding is available for aircraft purchase for new routes in stable markets. Leasing of aircraft has also become more costly.

Upgrading Older Aircraft Instead of Replacing Them

Airlines have the option of cutting aircraft spending by upgrading older aircraft (retrofitting) and by using hush kits, thus preserving capacity without buying new aircraft. For example, Delta retrofitted 80 of its older 727-200 and 737-300 aircraft. Delta retrofitted its 727s with Honeywell's new glass cockpit avionics and Rolls Royce's Tay 670 engines, thus reducing crew from three to two. By doing so, Delta saved $400,000 per year per plane in labor and overhead. Retrofitted hardware costs between $15 million and $17 million compared to $30 million for a new aircraft. Such retrofitting meets noise reduction requirements and yields a 10 to 15 percent in fuel savings, provided the aircraft still has 12 or more years of economic life. In other words, about 35,000 to 40,000 cycles must still remain for the retrofitting to be economically viable.

When a major airline such as Delta proceeds to upgrade older aircraft, it legitimizes retrofitting as an alternative to buying in a poor economy. Of course, a sudden change in oil prices could make all of the older aircraft fuel obsolete and revive the demand for aircraft offering new technology. The rise in oil prices to $65 a barrel in 2005 could be a harbinger of a wave of retirement of older aircraft.

Responding to Subsidies Given to Airbus

In the face of competition from Airbus, Boeing has sought help from the U.S. government in limiting the subsidies for product development and export financing given to Airbus by the consortium member governments. Boeing has attempted to prevent Airbus gains in market share, particularly with long-established Boeing customers. In addition, Boeing has launched new aircraft models such as the 787. The U.S. government has threatened to file a complaint with the WTO. In turn, the European governments who back Airbus have noted that Boeing receives large subsidies in the form of military contracts. Boeing is one of the major U.S. defense contractors.

As the aircraft market recovers, continued government support has enabled Airbus to continue to develop new aircraft models. That has forced Boeing to consider how to counter new aircraft models offered by Airbus and how to fund and allocate R&D. Airbus has emerged as a viable competitor with a full product line. The global aircraft market is changing, with the Far East (especially China) becoming more important. Pressures from major markets such as China to conduct more in-country manufacturing are also affecting the nature of the aircraft industry. Understanding the changing world environment and responding to those changes will determine whether Boeing can continue to compete successfully in the global market.

QUESTIONS AND RESEARCH

1. What are the market segments within the commercial aircraft industry? How have Boeing and Airbus approached those segments?

2. Is Boeing the strongest company in the industry in terms of product line? Explain.

3. Compare Boeing's and Airbus's competing products.

4. Trace how Airbus has filled out its product line. Can its product introductions be seen as competitive responses to Boeing? Explain.

5. How do customers influence the aircraft product line?

6. What factors influence an airline's buying of jet aircraft?

7. What should Boeing do in response to Airbus's moves to launch the A380 and to receive European government aid for launching its new planes?

8. How relevant are subsidies in the aircraft industry? How should Boeing react to Airbus's subsidies in developing a new aircraft?

9. Will new competitors be entering the aircraft industry? If so, where will they come from and how should Boeing deal with this potential development?

10. Is U.S. government intervention necessary to enable Boeing to compete effectively in the global aircraft market? Explain.

CHAPTER 11

International Advertising and Promotion

Advertising, personal selling, sales promotion, and public relations are the major categories of promotion mix. Of all of them, advertising tends to get most of the attention when people think about or discuss marketing. As will be explained here, advertising is important; but it is only one component in an effective promotional strategy.

The main goals of this chapter are to

- Discuss how languages, regulations, and infrastructure impact promotion.

- Show how media diversity and media developments affect the options available in a market, with additional focus on the Internet as a promotion medium.

- Present criteria useful in selecting promotion agencies in those cases where a firm seeks outside help.

- Explore the ways in which personal selling varies in world markets, requiring different methods of recruitment and management of a sales force.

- Describe how different national cultures and requirements affect the possibilities for sales promotion in foreign markets.

- Detail special forms of sales promotion, such as trade fairs

- Explain the role of public relations in effective global promotion.

- Discuss promotion budgeting and strategy.

Promotion is the most visible as well as the most culture-bound of the marketing functions. In the other functions, a firm relates to the market in a quieter, more passive way. With the promotional function, a firm is standing up and speaking out, wanting to be seen and heard. **Promotion** is defined as "a firm's communication with its various audiences, with a view to informing and influencing them."

The subject of this chapter is not international promotion, but rather promotion in international marketing. Because relatively little promotion is truly international, this chapter is concerned primarily with the management of promotion in a number of nations. The international aspect is the coordination of the various national activities to make up the integrated international program. Promotion in international marketing plays the same role it does in domestic operations; that is, communication with a firm's audiences to achieve certain goals. Variations from country to country occur, however, in all three dimensions: means of communication, audience, and even company goals.

Promotion is aimed at selling products and enhancing a company's image. You have seen, however, that the situation of a company and its product line often are not the same from one country to another. Therefore, the promotional task is not the same in every market, either. Another dimension in the promotion mix is nationality; that is, a firm must decide whether to present itself as a local, foreign, or multinational company.

Integrated Marketing Communications

Promotion is communication; and communication, in almost any form, is a type of promotion. Global integrated marketing communications is a critical component to an effective marketing strategy. For a communication system to be truly integrated, the customers, suppliers, intermediaries, and firm must be in constant contact if the firm is to meet consumers' needs, satisfy relationships with suppliers and others, and remain profitable. Developing and maintaining an integrated marketing communication system is easier now than ever before because of technological advances in communication, data collection, management, and analysis. This section will briefly discuss each of the stakeholders in a firm's integrated marketing communications strategy—customers, intermediaries, and suppliers.

Customers

Enterprise systems have become sophisticated enough to provide almost instantaneous inventory information to manufacturers, which means that replenishment takes days, rather than months. That means customers can be assured of finding products, not empty shelves, in the stores they visit. Order tracking has long been available to manufacturers and intermediaries. Because consumers can now track products and packages as the items move through the system, they know when their products were built, shipped, and delivered. (Coincidently, this also frees up a firm's resources that might have gone to answering consumers' questions concerning their purchases.) Consumers can provide instantaneous feedback about products and services, suggest design modifications, and create customized products via the Web, in-store measurements, and interactive kiosks. For example, fliers sitting on a plane on an airport's tarmac can send complaints to the president of the company, using any number of handheld devices; send e-mail messages to friends about the lousy experience; possibly blog their ordeal; or if they are really angry, start a web site—xyzAirStinks.com.

Customer satisfaction is easier to solicit now than ever before because it can be accomplished electronically, which consumers seem to prefer over pen-and-paper mailed surveys or telephone interviews. Results of surveys are often the focus of marketing messages—for example, "J.D. Power and Associates ranks our car as number one in consumer satisfaction."

From movie stars' fan clubs to information about automobiles, just about any topic conceivable exists on the Internet. And anyone with access to a computer can post a web site or participate in blogging (online chatting that is complimentary or damning).

Intermediaries

Intermediaries have long depended on hardware and software to manage inventory. But as was stated previously, there are added levels of sophistication that allow intermediaries to react or be proactive more quickly than ever before. For example, the ability to determine what is on the shelves in a store or warehouse is important. But to be able to see what response a sales promotion is getting on an hour-by-hour basis, to be able to identify the consumers purchasing the items, and to know what the consumers are purchasing in addition to sales items is an exciting and relatively new addition to the marketing mix.

An example of well-targeted promotion is when Amazon.com contacts consumers who purchased a particular book, CD, or DVD to tell them that another item by the same artist is to be released next week. (Similarly, when someone places an order at Barnes & Noble's web site or at other online source, that person can receive suggestions of other items he or she might consider buying; for example, this pair of shoes goes well with those slacks or people who bought the item you ordered also purchased this product.) Intermediaries no longer have to reorder merchandise. As goods move into a customer's bag, the information is collected by a scanning device and sent directly to the manufacturer, not the warehouse. Thus, new items can be made as others are sold.

Sophisticated communications and design software also allow intermediaries to be more involved in the design and delivery of products and services. The furniture company Bombay, found in malls across America, helped design furniture that could be stored and shipped in relatively small spaces to accommodate limited inventory space. The ability to involve intermediaries in promotion can be helpful in markets where manufacturers do not have a physical presence. An intermediary becomes an extension of the firm and "speaks" for the consumer, providing the firm with much-needed input about customers' needs.

Suppliers

In the last half of the twentieth century, just-in-time inventory management meant having a few days' supply of materials and components sitting on a dock or in warehouses. Now it means that the parts needed for assembling a car come rolling in the backdoor 15 minutes before they become part of the car. Again, the communication technologies available allow suppliers and manufacturers to design and test compatibility of various construction steps together, before construction of the first item takes place. That reduces time-to-market for new products and reduces manufacturing costs. The integrated marketing communications systems in place today are a far cry from the systems in place only five years ago. Video-on-demand, the ability to download specific songs, and the ability to communicate synchronously and asynchronously in new ways make the manufacturer a partner with other interested constituents. Firms may be able to communicate better with consumers, but consumers also can communicate better with manufacturers. This chapter will demonstrate that promotion involves more than television advertising. The discussion will begin with advertising, but you will come to understand that promotion is broader and deeper and more powerful than advertising by itself.

Promotion Tools

Advertising is the paid communication of company messages through impersonal media. The messages may be audio, as in radio; visual, as in billboards or magazines; or audiovisual, as in the Internet, television, or movies. Advertising is used everywhere to achieve various marketing goals, which include paving the way for a sales force, gaining distribution, selling products, and improving brand image. In every country, advertising is just one element of the marketing mix. Its role depends on the other elements of the mix in that country. **Personal selling** is also paid communication, but it can be altered quickly and targeted at specific individuals or small groups of people.

Public relations, what some people think of as publicity, is often referred to as unpaid communications; but costs are certainly involved. Public relations people are salaried and exist in virtually every business entity. Other public relations expenses include entertainment for wining and dining media representatives, for example. Public relations has the benefit of being among the most powerful promotional tools. Those targeted view the people providing the message as impartial and, therefore, trustworthy. (People believe *Consumer Reports* because it accepts no paid advertising, for example.) The difficulty with public relations is that the message that people receive cannot be easily controlled, if at all, by a firm.

Sales promotion includes many things, and is sometimes referred to as the "all other" category of promotional tools. It includes coupons, directed e-mail and traditional mail, and sponsorship of events, among many other means of communicating with others. All of these promotional tools will be discussed in more depth. Because only the practice, not the principles, of promotion varies internationally, basic principles will not be covered in this text, the assumption being that you will remember them from previous courses you have taken.

International Promotional Environment

The international promotional strategy of a company is determined by two sets of constraints, one posed by the internal situation of the company and the other by the international environment. Important elements of the international environment will be presented first. Figure 11-1 illustrates some of the constraints on international marketing communication.

Languages: The Tower of Babel

Language was discussed in Chapter 2. Here language is examined for its significance in international promotion. Construction of the biblical Tower of Babel stopped when the workers could no longer communicate with one other. A manager of international promotion may feel a similar constraint when facing the diversity of languages in world markets. Although some languages are used in more than one country, there are many more languages than countries. An international marketer does not have to

Figure 11-1. Constraints on International Marketing Communications

know all of the languages of all markets, but the firm's promotion must communicate in those languages. Even in the few cases in which a product and its promotional appeals are universal, the language is not. In an attempt to minimize costs, in one promotional strategy, firms produce an advertisement or another promotional vehicle in one language and then dub it into another language. Mistakes have been made using this strategy, but studies show that it can be effective if applied carefully.[1]

Technical accuracy or perfect translations are insufficient. Persuasive messages must speak the "language of the heart"; and for that to occur, intimate local knowledge is required. Local help is of two kinds: (1) national personnel in countries in which a firm has subsidiaries and (2) the advertising agency located in the market. In both cases, a company benefits from having employees in whose language the company wants to promote itself and its products. In other markets, a firm may rely more on intermediaries for promotional assistance.

Another market factor is language overlap from market to market. One world language would obviously facilitate uniform international advertising. Fortunately for those who use the English language, English fills that role in many places. Of course, the present role of English does not allow universal international campaigns in English, except perhaps in the promotion of certain industrial goods or selected luxury items.

Although language overlap among countries does not allow for global campaigns, a few multilanguage areas do facilitate multinational advertising on a less-than-global basis. Examples are found in Europe, where the German language covers Austria, most of Switzerland, and Germany, and where the French language covers parts of Belgium, Switzerland, Luxembourg, Monaco, and France. More important examples include:

- The English-speaking world, covering up to 600 million people in dozens of nations.
- The French-speaking world, including the former

French colonies (including Quebec), in addition to the European countries mentioned above.
- The Spanish-speaking world, including most of the Americas south of the United States and the many Hispanic markets located throughout the United States. Even though not all residents of these areas are fluent in the dominant language, the role of the language is large enough to facilitate the internationalization of advertising.

Two examples illustrate the practical importance of language overlap. Unilever introduced its Radion detergent into Germany with a heavy ad campaign. Because several German media overlap into Austria, Austrian consumers sought Radion in Austrian stores. Because Radion had not yet been introduced into Austria, Unilever lost the benefit of the free advertising carryover.

In another example, Anheuser-Busch, a heavy advertiser of Budweiser beer in the United States, began marketing "Bud" in Canada, hoping for a 1 to 2 percent market share. It was pleasantly surprised to gain almost 8 percent of the market in a few months. One reason was the big carryover of U.S. TV commercials for "Bud" into the Canadian market.

A NOTE ON TRANSLATIONS

Language diversity does not, by itself, prevent the use of international appeals. When a translation is the only adaptation needed in a promotional message, it does not modify the similarity of the appeal. The humorous examples of translation errors—for example, General Motors' use of the model name Nova (meant to connote "bright and shining star") in a Spanish-speaking market where the name meant "does not go"—are recounted frequently because they make interesting copy; statistically, however, they are not significant.

David Kerr of the Kenyon & Eckhardt agency provides some guidelines for translation. He suggests that the English language used in international campaigns should be at a fifth- or sixth-grade vocabulary level and should contain no slang or idioms. Furthermore, copy should be short because other languages usually take more time or space to say what the English copy says. The growing use of visual presentations—pictures and illustrations—minimizes the need for translation. Thus, more marketers rely on the purely visual—showing something to evoke a mood—and then cite the company name. Simple illustrations are a way to get around the problem of illiteracy in poorer nations.

While visuals are one way to avoid translation problems, they can evidence translation problems of their own. For example, AT&T ran an international campaign using the thumbs-up illustration. To Russians and Poles, the illustration had a negative meaning because the palm of the hand was showing. With the help of YAR Communications, the thumbs-up illustration was retained, but with the back of the hand showing. YAR is one of the few agencies that specializes in translating cultural images, not just dialogue, to avoid such problems.

Role of Promotion in the Economy

In determining the marketing mix, another factor to consider is the importance of promotion in the national economy. Over half of the world's advertising expenditures were once in the United States. Since 1988, however, ad outlays abroad have surpassed those in the United States. While the United States still leads all countries in relative advertising expenditures, ad outlays in many overseas markets are growing faster than they are in the United States. For example, Spain, Korea, Taiwan, and Thailand have experienced advertising growth rates of 15 percent or more per year. Advertising in China grew over 50 percent per year in the years between 1990 and 2000, and media giants are flocking to those nations.[2]

The level of economic development is only one factor in determining advertising spending. Regulations on advertising and media, as well as other cultural factors, are also important. Colombia spends twice as much (relative to GDP) as most of its Latin American neighbors. Switzerland spends four times as much per capita as its neighbor Italy.

Media Availability

Some of the media used by advertisers in the United States may not be available abroad. Two factors are at work here. One is government regulation, which may limit commercials on specific media, such as radio, television, cell phones, or the Internet. Another variable is the communications infrastructure. For example, newspaper availabili-

ty includes one daily paper per 2 people in Japan, one daily paper per 4 people in the United States, one daily paper per 10–20 people in Latin America, and extreme cases such as one daily paper per 200 people in countries such as Bangladesh and most of Africa.

As another example, personal computer ownership ranges from more than 600 per 1,000 people (that is, 60 percent of the population) in Singapore, Sweden, and the United States to only 1 or 2 per 1,000 people in countries such as Chad, Malawi, and Niger.[3] Media availability will be discussed in more depth later in this chapter.

Government Controls

A problem for marketers everywhere is government regulation of promotional activities. U.S. marketers often find foreign countries more restrictive of different forms of promotion than their home market. Government regulations can affect the media, the message, the budget, and agency ownership. The following are specific limitations:

- Due to government regulation, some media are not available or are very limited for commercial use.
- Advertising messages have a variety of restrictions. Forty countries regulate the languages that can be used. Many countries have limits on comparative advertising, and about 25 countries require preclearance of certain commercials.
- The ad budget can draw government attention. India attacked the ad budgets of foreign tire companies in the country, and Britain made a similar attack on the ad budgets of resident Unilever and Procter & Gamble operations, which were considered too large. Developing countries are concerned about the ad budgets of drug firms for the same reasons.
- Some countries restrict ownership of ad agencies. Boddewyn found that 17 countries allowed only minority foreign ownership; Indonesia, Nigeria, and Pakistan allowed none.[4]

All governments have laws governing promotion. They are similar in some respects and quite different in others. For example, they are often similar in intent—to protect consumers. Therefore, it is common to see rules about truthful and credible promotional messages. Increasingly tobacco, liquor, arms, and pharmaceuticals are regulated product classes with regard to promotion.[5,6] Promotion aimed at children is regulated in many markets. There are also long lists of cultural taboos pertaining to the amount of nudity that is permitted, depiction of women or children in particular circumstances that are considered degrading or dangerous, and obscene language.

Many nations have privacy laws that dictate who may be contacted and when and how they may be contacted.

Certain laws dictate how marketers can collect, store, and use data about potential consumers.

(One web site that contains many links to foreign laws is Everything International at http://faculty.philau.edu/russowl/country.html#Law. For example, the Washburn University Law Library allows users to search by topic [privacy, for instance], country, or area. Its URL is http://www.washlaw.edu/forint/alpha/p/privacy.htm.)

Nationalistic policies also restrict advertisers' freedom. More countries are requiring local production of at least a portion of TV commercials in order to build their film industries and create more jobs.

Competition

The competitive situation is another environmental variable. In some markets, an international company competes against other international companies. In other markets, the competition is purely national. Sound promotional strategy in one market is not necessarily sound in another market facing a different set of variables. Furthermore, the approach of an international company provokes different reactions. In some countries, an international company causes national competitors to follow its course of action. For example, when a large competitor such as Wal-Mart enters a new market, established national competitors typically increase their advertising. During an economic crisis, some firms change their appeals, emphasizing the cheapness of their products, while others reduce their advertising budgets, not wanting to devalue their brand.

Agency Availability

Another constraint on the international advertiser is the availability of advertising, promotion research, and promotion agencies in different countries. Some countries may have only one advertising agency; for example, Bermuda, Iceland, and Mozambique. A number of countries have few; for example, Bolivia, Bulgaria, Ghana, and Zambia. But frequently the agencies are affiliates of the large international agencies, so the service may be better than the numbers suggest. At the other extreme are Japan, the United States, and the United Kingdom, all with literally hundreds of agencies, and semi-independent firms that specialize in specific media, promotional services, industries, or geographic areas. The quality of an agency's service corresponds roughly to the country's level of economic development and the size of its economy. Thus, India, a poor nation in per capita income, has several good agencies because its total market is large. However, promotional services are not as diverse as you would find in developed nations because the markets are not as devel-

oped. In China, an explosion of advertising and agencies has resulted in about 170 joint ventures between local and foreign agencies, as of this writing.

Strategic Promotion Decisions

Once environmental factors have been considered, the focus turns to the company's global marketing strategy. The international promotion manager must ensure appropriate campaigns for each market and try to get coordination among the various national programs. Seven decision-making areas in international promotion are presented next: (1) selecting the agency (or agencies), (2) choosing the message, (3) selecting the media, (4) determining the budget, (5) evaluating the effectiveness of promotion, (6) organizing for promotion, and (7) deciding whether to engage in cooperative promotion abroad.

Selecting the Agency

Many marketing functions are performed within a company. In the case of promotion, a firm often relies on expertise from an outside advertising or promotion agency. Agency selection is an important decision that a marketer has to make. Two major alternatives are available: (1) an international agency with domestic and overseas offices or (2) a local agency in each national market. Modifications of those alternatives are often available, especially with the formation of promotion conglomerates (for example, Omnicom Group Inc.), a trend that shows no signs of abating. Many larger agencies are acquiring local agencies to achieve global economies of scale and the ability to provide globally coordinated promotional campaigns for their clients, yet still provide the local expertise that many companies demand. (See Tables 11-1 and 11-2.)[7,8,9]

AGENCY SELECTION CRITERIA

Naturally, a firm should choose the agency or agencies that can best help it achieve its goals. Because that criterion is not easy to determine, a firm may want to identify derivative criteria to aid in its choice. First, agency alternatives should be identified. For example, what agencies are located in each market, and which agencies are preempted by competitors? Second, each agency should be evaluated using the following criteria:

- **Market Coverage**: Does the particular agency or package of agencies cover all of the relevant markets?
- **Quality of Coverage**: How effective is the job that the package of agencies does in each market?
- **Market Research, Public Relations, and Other**

Marketing Services: If a firm needs these services, how do the different agencies compare on their offerings?

- **Relative Roles and Compatibility of Company and Agency**: Some firms have large staffs that do much of the work of preparing promotional campaigns, while others have fewer in-house resources or expertise, leaving more to the agencies to perform.

- **Communication and Control**: When a firm wants frequent communication with agencies in foreign markets, it is inclined to hire a domestic agency that has overseas offices. The internal communications system of this agency network facilitates communication for the international marketer.

- **International Coordination**: Does a firm want its advertising tailor-made to each market? Or does it want coordination of national advertising with advertising done in other markets? One of the major differences among agency groups is their ability to aid in international coordination.

- **Size of Company's International Business**: The smaller a firm's international promotion expenditures, the less there is to be divided among different agencies. A firm's promotion volume may determine agency choice in order to ensure some minimum level of service. A small volume multiplied by a number of markets could interest an international agency even if it is of no interest to an agency in any one market.

- **Image**: Does a firm want a national or global image? If a firm wants local identification, it might choose a local agency rather than an international agency.

- **Company Organization**: Companies that are very decentralized, with national profit centers, might want to leave agency selection to the local subsidiary.

- **Level of Involvement**: In joint-venture arrangements, the international firm shares decision-making responsibilities. The national partner may have experience with a national agency, which could be the decisive factor. In licensing agreements, promotion is largely in the hands of the licensee. Selling through distributors also reduces the control of the international company. Generally, international marketers can choose only the agencies for the promotion paid for by their firms. Where a firm has a cooperative program with its distributors, it may have some voice in agency selection.

GLOBAL VERSUS LOCAL AGENCIES

The relentless growth of multinational agencies puts pressure on agencies that serve only one market. For example, mid-sized British agencies faced tough choices in planning for an integrated European market after 1992. They either

Table 11-1. Top Promotion Holding Companies

Name	Headquarters	2004 Revenues ($1,000 US)	Change over 2003 (%)
Omnicom Group	New York	9,747,200	13.1
WPP Group	London	8,243,00	12.6
Interpublic Group	New York	6,200,000	5.8
Publicis Groupe	Paris	4,930,000	-1.0
Dentsu	Tokyo	3,050,000	10.9

Source: "ADWEEK 22nd Annual Agency Report Cards," *ADWEEK*, April 25, 2005, page 57 (http://www.adweek.com/aw/industry_reports/index.jsp).

Note: Revenue figures in italics are estimates.

Table 11-2. Top American Advertising Agencies

Name (Holding Company)	Headquarters	2004 Revenues (US $1,000)	2004 Billings (US $1,000)
Grey (WPP)	New York	545,000	3,650,000
BBDO (OMC)	New York	540,000	3,625,000
JWT (WPP)	New York	534,000	3,600,000
Euro RSCG (Havas)	New York	523,000	3,600,000
DDB (OMC)	New York	523,000	3,380,000

Source: "ADWEEK 22nd Annual Agency Report Cards," *ADWEEK*, April 25, 2005, page 58 (http://www.adweek.com/aw/industry_reports/index.jsp).

Note: Revenue figures in italics are estimates.

had to forge a European network or had to sell out to one if they wanted to keep their clients who would be operating in the market. Similar integration pressures under NAFTA led U.S. agencies to acquire a number of Canadian agencies. Misfortunes have befallen single-country agencies that have multinational clients. Volkswagen advertising in the United States, for example, was handled very successfully by Doyle Dane Bernbach. When this U.S. agency opened an office in Germany, Volkswagen dropped its national agency and gave the account to the office of Doyle Dane Bernbach (DDB) in Germany.

National agencies are an alternative for the international marketer for several reasons. Although international agencies offer multimarket coverage, their networks are not always of even quality. Offices in some markets may be very strong, whereas offices in other markets may be only average. When a firm needs high-quality advertising in all of its markets, it may decide to use the best local agency in each market even if it does not belong to an international family.

Also, when a firm does not require coordination of its advertising in different markets, it has less need to employ an international agency. Similarly, the coordination provided by international agencies is often more apparent than real. Other reasons for choosing local agencies include the desire for local image and the desire to give national subsidiaries responsibility for their own promotions.

There is one more reason why local agencies survive in some countries—nationalism. Many countries resent the role that foreign firms play in their economies and restrict the firms in various ways. The restrictions often apply to the promotion industry, too. In the Philippines, for example, national agencies pressured the government to ban foreign agencies. They claimed that the multinationals would come to dominate the industry and that in spite of the qualifications of local agencies, the internationals' affiliates would win the major accounts because of their global ties with multinational clients. Thus, along with a dozen other countries, the Philippines allows only minority foreign ownership of agencies. Indonesia, Nigeria, and Pakistan allow no foreign ownership. That protectionism is one barrier to the growth of multinational agencies.

With an appropriate bow having been made to the independent national agencies, keep in mind the persistent trend toward the selection of international agencies by global companies. Although there will always be room for a certain number of quality independent agencies in each market, their relative importance is likely to decline.

FUTURE DEVELOPMENTS IN THE PROMOTION INDUSTRY

As the industry evolves, certain trends should continue. Those trends include:

- Further industry consolidation of agencies through mergers and acquisitions.
- Even greater internationalization, including more ties among U.S., Canadian, and Mexican agencies under NAFTA; more European networks, especially among new EU members; Asian consolidation and growth that mirrors rapid economic growth, especially in China, but also in India, Vietnam, and elsewhere in the region.
- An increasing demand for global coordination expertise and, therefore, demand for international agencies.
- Even more service from full-service internationals. In addition to advertising, such promotional conglomerates are acquiring capabilities in public relations, sales promotion, direct marketing, the Internet, and other marketing services.
- The Internet playing an increasingly important role in all phases and types of promotion, market research, mass customization of message, etc.
- Drastic erosion of the exclusive commission payment system, which had prevailed until recently in agency advertising. The majority of agencies are now on a fee basis, with some using a combination of fee plus commission..

Choosing the Promotional Message

A major decision for an international marketer is whether the firm should use national or international promotional appeals—a localized or standardized approach. The goal in either case is to fit the market. Although people's basic needs and desires are the same around the world, the way those desires are satisfied may vary from country to country.

LOCALIZED OR STANDARDIZED?

In the preparation of promotional campaigns, valid arguments exist for both a national and an international approach. The arguments reflect the self-interested evaluations of the parties involved as well as the objective factors in the situation. In general, two groups tend to be biased in favor of a separate national approach: management of the local subsidiary and the independent local agency. In each case, the argument depends in large part on the special local knowledge the agencies contribute. The more practical it is for an international firm to treat its international market like other markets, the smaller the role of the local subsidiary and the independent local agency. Because of this vulnerability, management of both the local subsidiary and the agency tend to be defensive about the uniqueness of the market and the need for special approaches therein. Both will argue in terms of objective factors, but their position is influenced by their perceived vulnerability.

Often the argument of local or globally standardized refers to the promotional message; but there is evidence that even something as targeted as personal selling can be standardized, at least to some extent.[10]

By way of clarification, the terms *localized* and *standardized* refer to the two extremes of the international promotion spectrum. Completely localized promotion has little similarity among countries. Completely standardized promotion is identical in all markets. Typically, neither extreme is practiced. The issue for a firm is the degree to which it should move toward one end or the other of the spectrum.

BUYER MOTIVATION

For a product that is used the same way and that meets the same needs from country to country, similar appeals are more feasible than localized campaigns. The international success of Coca-Cola, which takes a standardized approach in its advertising appeals, suggests that the product meets similar consumer desires everywhere. That is true for other consumer goods, too. A famous example is Nike's use of the swoosh symbol to promote its products globally.

Another consideration is the similarity of buying motives from country to country. The same product may be purchased for a mixture of functional, convenience, and status reasons, but with a different combination of motivations in each country. The more alike buying motives are, the more desirable the use of common appeals. This is often the case with industrial goods, but it is less common with consumer goods. Procter & Gamble learned that decay prevention was an important motive for buyers of its fluoride toothpaste in Denmark, Germany, and the Netherlands. In England, France, and Italy, however, cosmetic considerations were more important.

The Ford Motor Company promotes the same vehicles, using safety as the primary focus in some markets, fun and sportiness in others, and comfort in still others.

INTERNATIONAL MARKET SEGMENTS

Another factor is the existence of international market segments; that is, certain markets in a nation often have counterparts in a number of other nations. In many ways, the markets resemble their counterparts in other countries more than they do other markets in their own country. Wealthy people have similar motivations and tastes across national boundaries, for example. The youth market, made up of two segments (the adolescent group and the college-age group), is another prominent instance. The concerns of college students on all continents are remarkably similar. Such similarities among age groups can provide a truly global segment. There are numerous examples of successful appeals to national market segments that, together, constitute an international market for a product.

A final market consideration is the gradual development of the world or regional consumer. What is already seen in certain market segments will gradually expand to broader segments of the world's population. Advances in communication, transportation, and production will lead to an international democratizing of consumption. People are not alike; but market segments will become more international in scope, resulting in greater use of similar appeals in advertising. The EU is accelerating the emergence of the European consumer. In the United States, marketers speak of market segments on a national basis. They usually do not separate Michigan consumers from Maine or Missouri consumers, for example. The United States, in a sense, is merely one of the first of the regional groupings. As you know, advertising campaigns have been coordinated for groupings of countries. Industrial marketers such as Dell, Nokia, and Hyundai organize one campaign for a group of industrialized country markets and another campaign for a group of developing country markets.

ECONOMICS

Economic efficiency is another reason to consider whether to take a local or more standardized approach to promotion. As long as agencies were paid on a commission basis, no savings would seem to result from a uniform international message. Payment would be the same whether an international agency or separate national agencies were

used. Although that is true for commission payments, gains could still come in other areas. If a company uses a national approach to advertising, the quality of the creative work will probably vary greatly from country to country. Small markets have small agencies and small budgets for doing creative work, not to mention a shortage of skilled personnel.

A standardized approach would allow more money to be spent on developing a quality campaign with the best personnel. The best agencies in the larger markets could create the campaign, and that expenditure could then be "amortized" over many countries. A resource-based view is what allowed Shell Oil to leverage existing local strategies to a more global approach.[11] Others argue that a localized approach is more effective.[12]

As mentioned earlier, firms might choose to use little commentary and no spokesperson in an advertisement, instead using music and a clip of the product to invoke a feeling about the product. In this way, the ad can be duplicated in other countries, using a different voice-over, using different text placed at the end of the ad, or dubbing the ad in another language. Still another approach is to use universally recognized personalities or stars (for example, Johnny Depp and Beyonce Knowles). However, using celebrities can push production costs into the millions, while average production costs of 10- to 20-second commercials average approximately $100,000 in the United States.

TECHNOLOGY

Advances in communication—whether in media, devices used to transmit and receive messages, or software—have had a tremendous impact on promotion in the last 15 years. As more people spend more time on the computer, some project the end of television and television advertising.[13] There is no sign that this trend will abate, and one can only imagine what the world will be like in another 15 years. If the same media (the Internet, television, radio, print, etc.) were available everywhere, international campaigns would benefit greatly. The fact that that situation does not currently exist hampers an internationally similar approach. The media do "massage the message" to some degree, and a campaign prepared for a web site probably would not be identical to one prepared for radio or print media. The lack of media uniformity does not, in itself, prevent international campaigns, however, as is evidenced by domestic campaigns that use the same appeals simultaneously in several different kinds of media.

Similarity in international media conditions is increasing steadily. The Internet, satellite radio and television, and cell communications have become international media, bringing events such as the Olympic Games and the World Cup to the whole world. Print media is also international. Reader's Digest reaches 41 countries in each country's language; other magazines and newspapers also have international coverage (*The New York Times, Financial Times*, and *The Economist*). European print media are going more EU-wide, as well as beyond Europe. The internationalization of media ownership will reinforce that trend. Already, European groups are among the largest owners of U.S. magazines. Media internationalization will contribute to the internationalization of advertising messages.

Software that allows companies to manage consumer information—including contact information (e-mail addresses), purchase patterns (children's movies), frequency (more than once a month) and amounts (average purchase of $50 per order)—are able to direct messages tailored to very small segments of a target market. The more specialized the message, the more likely consumers are to read it and respond to it.

One reason television advertising is such a powerfully persuasive medium is because it involves participants on multiple levels and stimulates more than one human sense. People hear and we see what the marketers are trying to convey. Print media involves more sight (and less movement unless one includes moving displays that are sometimes seen in retail displays), while radio involves auditory stimulation alone. The Internet is superior to radio and print in that it, too, can involve sight and sound. But it offers more than current television technology in that customers can order items, interact with sales and technology staff for product specifications, learn about the company, and more—and by the way, be entertained in the process. Compare an advertisement for Ford in a newspaper around the turn of the last century (say, 1905) and the video for new cars on the *Motor Trend* web site. On the web site, going from one part of the site to another often triggers a short video commercial about the car mentioned in the article the reader was viewing. Customers can find out about new and used cars, play games (usually with fast cars), and communicate with other owners about specific models.[14]

vPods; iPods; and cell phones capable of receiving sports, entertainment, news, and other information make it possible for advertisers to communicate with consumers. They also allow companies to communicate instantaneously with suppliers and other constituents anywhere in the world.

CULTURE

Language, which was mentioned previously, plays a large role in communication. But as described in Chapter 3, culture encompasses more than language. The allure to Western (European and American) goods was high when Communism was practiced in Russia and other former Soviet Union nations. But today's Russians do not appreciate Western advertising because those creating the messages typically present ideals and images and make assumptions about gender roles and other important cultural traits that are incongruent with Russian culture. At

best, the intended messages either are not received or are misinterpreted; or they are perceived as offensive or ridiculous, at worst.[15]

Television advertisements and language tend to get most of the research attention, but researchers are now studying the effects of other cultural traits on newer media. For example, Cho and Cheon studied the interactivity of web sites, using Hofstede's cultural dimensions (see Chapter 3), in Japan, South Korea, the United Kingdom, and the United States. Among their findings was the fact that Western web sites tend to emphasize consumer-to-firm interactivity, whereas Eastern web sites highlight consumer-to-consumer interactions.[16]

REGIONAL OR GLOBAL PRODUCT INTRODUCTIONS

Companies are resorting to more uniform campaigns as they develop products for a regional or global market, introducing them simultaneously (or sequentially) in the region or the world. Adobe and, in particular, Microsoft have turned the announcement of new products into world-wide media events. Harry Potter books are delivered to retailers in armored cars, and Amazon.com must hold deliveries of new releases to coincide with brick-and-mortar retail releases. Whether planned or not, every small, medium, and large company that posts a web site is communicating on a global scale with potential customers—and some would argue that the Internet provides an important reason for small firms to learn about the opportunities and pitfalls of international business.

PRODUCT TYPE

Industrial products are generally more homogeneous than consumer goods. The appeal is generally rational and transcends personal tastes and needs. Therefore, marketers of industrial goods and services can generally implement standardized global campaigns. For example, Siemens of Germany has been working on internationally coordinated advertising in 52 foreign markets since 1955. By contrast, IBM did not run a globally integrated campaign until 1995. That ad was for its AS/400 computer workstation aimed at the industry segment.

Developing Promotional Strategies

All of the variables just discussed must be weighed in deciding what kinds of promotional appeals to use. Although agencies and subsidiaries in each country must help determine the appeals for their market, it is unlikely that a purely national approach will be taken in many markets. Some standardization will occur.

The task is not to find global uniformity, but to create the most effective advertising. Multimarket advertising on a regional basis may be desirable because of regional groupings, regional tourism, and media overlap. Or common appeals may be used in common language areas. In any case, by seeking common denominators and playing down national differences, a firm can be effective with similar appeals in many countries.

Selecting the Media

Another critical decision in international advertising is the selection of media for each market or market segment. The desirable media are those that reach the target markets efficiently. The target markets—the purchase decision influencers—are not always the same individuals or groups as in the domestic market. The relative roles of different family members in consumer buying or of the purchasing agent, engineer, or president in industrial procurement vary from country to country.

Those most familiar with the local scene—the agency and the company representative within the country—do much of the local media selection. Studies have found the greatest role of subsidiaries in advertising is in media selection. To the extent that subsidiaries do the job, international managers need not get involved. However, international managers might want to have some voice in local media selection. Through their experience in many countries, they may have insights to contribute.

Managers may also want to use international media alongside or in place of strictly national media. Because international media cover a number of markets, this combination required some centralization. Then, too, international managers may be able to contribute sophisticated techniques of media selection. International managers can ensure that those techniques are made available to all company operations in a truly integrated marketing communications system.

MEDIA DIVERSITY

International media selection is complicated by international differences in media availability. A successful media configuration cannot be taken from domestic operations and applied abroad because the same facilities often are not available. For instance, in nations where few people go to school and, therefore, are unable to read, the usefulness of print advertising is limited. When it is difficult to obtain addresses, direct mail may not be possible. Also discussed earlier was how nations differ in their communications infrastructure; that is, the availability of electricity for TV and radio. Due to those differences, how media are used for advertising also differs. The data in Table 11-3 illustrate that fact.

TV's share of advertising dollars spent ranges from US $693.0 million in Argentina to US $53.6 billion in the United States. Online advertising spending, in contrast, ranges from US $300,000 in Indonesia to nearly US $7.0

Table 11-3. Promotion Expenditures, Relative Importance of Media

Country	Television	Radio	Print	Cinema	Outdoor	Online	Total
North America							
Canada	2,069.2	841.5	2,883.6	10.7	261.9	...	6,066.9
Mexico	2,184.1	480.4	762.5	...	...	...	3,427.0
United States	53,642.0	19,181.0	62,775.0	263.0	4,352.0	6,955.0	147,168.0
Asia							
India	899.4	83.7	808.4	41.8	246.6	11.3	2,091.2
Indonesia	1,257.7	62.0	626.1	1.3	29.0	0.3	1,976.5
Japan	16,855.7	1,558.8	12,610.7	...	4,613.4	891.1	36,529.7
Europe							
France	3,372.3	820.5	5,156.7	81.3	1,249.4	88.0	10,768.2
Germany	5,008.8	680.6	13,480.3	180.6	893.9	303.6	20,547.7
Italy	4,820.4	434.5	3,016.8	73.4	344.2	93.7	8,73.0
United Kingdom	5,280.2	698.8	9,213.5	297.2	1,023.7	310.2	16,823.6
South America							
Argentina	693.0	94.1	759.1	25.9	101.1	25.2	1,698.3
Brazil	1,796.8	283.1	891.1	...	180.0	151.1	3,302.1
Venezuela	778.6	42.9	251.0	33.0	40.2	...	1,145.6

Media Expenditures, 2003 ($US millions)

Sources: International Marketing Data & Statistics, 2005, 29th edition, *Euromonitor*, page 128, Table 2.1; European Marketing Data and Statistics, 2005, 40th edition, *Euromonitor*, page 104, Table 2.1.

Note: The total amount does not equal 100 percent since cinema and other categories are not included. Categories other than those listed still accounted for only less than 2 percent of media expenditures.

billion in the United States. The amounts spent in each media category relative to the other categories are interesting, as well. Many assume that television accounts for the majority of ad spending; but in the United States, 36 percent of ad dollars was spent on television and 43 percent was spent on print. A similar pattern can be seen in the United Kingdom and France; while in Germany, print media absorbed 66 percent of all ad spending.

DIRECT MARKETING

Direct marketing, especially catalog sales, have been supplanted to some degree by electronic catalogs (they are much cheaper to produce and get into the hands of consumers) and by web sites. Relatively recent changes in privacy laws and the enactment of "opt-out" and "opt-in" laws in many nations limit the use of direct mail and telemarketing. Nevertheless, telemarketing and catalog sales contribute substantially to sales figures; and the impact can be measured more directly than with other media. In the United States, direct marketing accounts for more than 10 percent of GDP; and according to the Direct Marketing Association, it accounted for nearly 50 percent of U.S. ad spending in 2004.[17] Technology is driving down direct marketing costs drastically. Thus, despite laws regulating e-mail and other consumer contacts and all of the countertechnology spam and ad ware, companies are likely to continue spending a large proportion of their promotion budgets on direct marketing. Some firms, such as Herbalife, would not be able to expand as rapidly without the new technologies. (In 2005, Herbalife International, with the help of ExactTarget, which "delivers on-demand email software solutions for permission-based email marketing," won the award for Best Use of Email in an International Enterprise Environment.)[18]

Statistics for advertising spending for online media are still difficult to measure because doing so requires separating development costs of the advertising side of a company's web site from information for vendors, for example. Trends in the relative importance of the Internet as a medium for advertising bear careful attention as measurement techniques improve. New methods of communicating via the Internet are being developed every day. They are likely to prove more effective than many of the other media, and companies have been quickly adopting the new techniques.

While some experts predict the demise of both print and television as promotion media because of the Internet and technological developments such as on-demand programming, others contend that the media war is just beginning.[19,20,21] (See also "Old versus New" CNBC webcast in Endnote 13.)

MEDIA AVAILABILITY

Most people think of television (and perhaps the Internet) when discussing media. However, there are so many types of media that it is impossible to list them all. For that reason, the discussion that follows focuses on the main media outlets. Tables 11-4 and 11-5 provide statistics related to media availability. Be careful when interpreting the data. Few television sets in a country does not necessarily mean that few people watch television. Potential consumers (marketers think of people consuming entertainment as potential consumers) may gather in friends' homes or outside electronics stores to watch TV. And those people may pay more attention to the advertisements than people in areas with many televisions. Instead of owning personal computers, many people use computers found in local Internet cafés, which are located in nearly every city of the world. A nation reporting that it has many newspapers, magazines, or radio stations is not necessarily a good thing. It may mean that the markets are extremely well-defined and segmented, helping marketers budget their promotional spending more effectively. Or it may mean that there are many competitors in a fragmented market and to reach a broad audience, the marketer must advertise through all of the newspapers, magazines, and radio stations.

Many consumers no longer listen to the radio or watch television. People may just as easily watch a webcast of a news item on their cell phone or listen to music on their iPod. New technologies that have allowed mass customization of products are also part of media. Providers of entertainment have more outlets today than ever before, and those outlets tend to be targeted at audiences with better-defined characteristics. All of those factors make it more difficult to measure the effectiveness of media and complicate promotion budget decisions.

INTERNATIONAL OR LOCAL MEDIA?

When media availability differs from market to market, international marketers may have to decentralize media selection and adapt to local possibilities. Because local managers cannot follow media patterns used elsewhere, they must find the local media that reach their markets effectively.

In Peru, for example, it is more common to use a wide variety of media ranging from newspapers, TV, and radio to cinema and point-of-purchase materials. Outside the capital, Lima, using billboards makes sense because taxes on billboards are lower in the provinces. On the other hand, the use of cinema in the provinces is not very effective. A multinational marketing manager sometimes has the alternative of using national media or media that cover several markets; both print and broadcast media, for example, have multimarket coverage. Print media with international market coverage include U.S. general-interest magazines such as *Reader's Digest* and *TIME*, which reach most of the world's major markets. In addition, *Paris Match* and *Vision* reach several European and Latin American markets, respectively. *Elle*, the French women's magazine, has 28 editions worldwide. Numerous technical and

Table 11-4. Media Availability

Country	Televisions[a]	Media (per 1,000 people) Radios[b]	Daily Newspapers[c]	Personal Computers[d]
North America				
Canada	691	1,047	168	487
Mexico	282	330	94	82
United States	938	2,109	196	659
Asia				
India	83	120	60	7.2
Indonesia	153	159	23	12
Japan	374	795	62	54
Europe				
France	632	950	143	347
Germany	675	570	291	485
Sweden	965	2,811	410	621
United Kingdom	950	1,445	326	406
South America				
Argentina	326	697	40	82
Brazil	369	433	46	75
Venezuela	186	292	206	61

Source: *World Development Indicators, 2005*, The World Bank, "The Information Age," pages 310–313, Table 5.11.

Notes: a. number of sets in 2003; b. period covered is 1997–2003; c. period covered is 2000; d. period covered is 2003.

Table 11-5. Communication Infrastructure

Country	Television Stations[a]	Radio Stations[b]	Telephone Lines[c] (thousands)	Cell Phones[d] (thousands)	Internet Users[e] (millions)
North America					
Canada	80	245/582/6	19,951	13,222	16.1
Mexico	236	850/545/15	15,958	28.125	
United States	>1,500 (plus 9,000 cable systems)	4,854/8,950/18	181,599	158,722	159.0
Asia					
India	562	153/91/68	48,917	26,154	
Indonesia	41	678/43/82	7,750	11,700	
Japan	211	215/89/21	71,149	86,658	
Europe					
France	584	41/3,500/2	33,905	41,683	21.9
Germany	373	51/787/4	54,350	64,800	39.0
Sweden	169	1/265/1	6,579		5.12
United Kingdom	228	219/431/3	34,898	49,677	25.0
South America					
Argentina	42	260/NA/6	8,009	6,500	4.1
Brazil	138	1,365/296/161	38,810	46,373	14.3
Venezuela	66	201/NA/11	2,842	6,463	1.3

Source: *World Factbook, 2005*, The United States Central Intelligence Agency (http://www.odci.gov/cia/publications/factbook); accessed November 4, 2005.

Notes: a. number of stations not including local repeats of national networks, period covered is 1997–1999; b. AM stations/FM stations/shortwave, period covered is 2004; c. period covered is 2003; d. period covered is 2003; e. period covered is 2003.

trade publications (usually U.S.-based) in the engineering, chemistry, electronics, and automotive industries also have an extensive and influential worldwide circulation.

The amount of advertising in national media is greater than that in international media because national media offer certain advantages. National media offer more possibilities, ranging from newspapers, magazines, direct mail, cinema, and billboards to the broadcast media. National media use local languages and provide greater flexibility in market segmentation and test marketing. In general, local media do a better job of reaching and adapting to the local market, especially for consumer goods.

Disadvantages, however, occasionally arise in using local media. Although industrialized countries frequently offer the same media quality as that found in developed nations, in many other countries, print reproduction may be poor, rates may not be fixed, and audited circulation data may not be available. The need to place the advertising as well as pay for it locally can be a drawback when a firm has centralized control. Nevertheless, those disadvantages are not sufficient to seriously limit the use of local media.

Most companies do most of their advertising in the local media of the foreign market. Generally, the more decentralized a firm, the more it uses local campaigns; and the more a firm relies on local ad agencies, the more it uses local media.

Colgate knows how to use the local media in its foreign markets. It is credited with creating the Mexican soap opera, one of the more popular programs broadcast in Mexico. Thus, the company successfully carried to Mexico a form more commonly associated with its competitor, Procter & Gamble, in the United States.

The importance of local media is clear; yet the scope and sophistication of international media, especially the Internet, is rising steadily. Online, magazine, newspaper, and TV media are all expanding internationally. Bertelsmann, Disney, and Time Warner are among the communication giants that are acquiring other firms and consolidating the industry across media lines to include print, television, movie, and the Internet. Recently, AOL Time Warner purchased the web journal firm Weblogs as an extension of this philosophy.[22]

Measuring Media Reach and Effectiveness

Another factor hampering media decisions in many countries is the lack of reliable information on circulation and audience characteristics. Advertisers in developed nations are accustomed to having audited data about the size of the audience that various media reach. In addition, advertisers often get a breakdown on audience characteristics such as age, occupation, gender, education, and income level. Some media types are nearly impossible to measure. Word of mouth, text messaging and blogs, and so-called ephemeral media are based on the contact lists and perceived authority of the sender, relying in part on the gullibility of and acceptance by the recipient.[23] Online promotion is also difficult to measure or quantify. (When should page views, click-throughs, and hits be used?)[24] The availability and reliability of media data decrease rapidly with the level of economic development. The reliability of data is directly related to a nation's level of economic development—generally, the more developed a nation, the more reliable the data. Whether data is available is also related to economic development. Generalizing, the richer a nation, the more likely it is to collect data. Poorer countries tend to spend money on more essential needs. In many countries, the only figures are those supplied by the media themselves. Such unaudited figures are suspect.

Another consideration complicating media evaluation is that whatever figures are obtained for the circulation of a medium do not necessarily indicate the medium's true coverage. In countries where data can be obtained as to the number of TVs or radios, as mentioned, the true audience may be much larger than the figures suggest. For example, in countries with low literacy rates, the average number of viewers per TV set is likely to be at least twice as large as in the United States. That principle also applies to the number of radio listeners, especially in less developed countries, where a few receivers may reach a whole village. Media measurements often rely on samples of message recipients; for example, statements about television show viewership in the United States that are provided by Nielson are based on data from a small number of American homes. Technology has reached the point where some experts are suggesting moving away from samples and taking a census (that is, collecting data on the entire population!).[25]

Even with print media, average readership varies from country to country. In less developed countries, one literate villager will read a newspaper or magazine to illiterate neighbors. And in developed countries, one issue may pass from the initial purchaser to several other readers.

This lack of accurate media information makes media selection difficult. The answer in the long run is to expand media auditing services. In the short run, advertisers must depend on their own ingenuity. As firms gain experience in a market, they learn about the relative effectiveness of different media. Comparative analysis of similar markets can, again, be useful.

Setting the International Promotion Budget

Among the controversial aspects of promotion is determining the proper method for setting the budget. This is a problem domestically, as well as internationally.[26] But because an international marketer must try to find an optimum outlay for a number of markets, the problem is more complex on the international level. In theory, it is not difficult to state the amount of money a firm should put into promotion. In each of its markets, a firm should continue to put more money into promotion as long as a promotion dollar returns more than a dollar spent on anything else. In practice, that principle is difficult to apply because of the impossibility of measuring the returns accurately, not only from promotion, but also from other company outlays.[27]

Because of the difficulty in determining the theoretically optimum promotion budget, companies have developed more practical guidelines. This section will examine the relevance of those guidelines for the marketer. Although the principle noted previously is difficult to apply, it must, nevertheless, serve as an initial rough guide. In other words, a promotion budget is not set in a vacuum, but is just one element of the overall marketing mix. Therefore, it is necessary to have some idea as to whether a sum of money should go into advertising, personal selling, price reductions, product or package improvements, or something else.[28]

PERCENTAGE-OF-SALES APPROACH

An easy method for setting the promotion appropriation in a country is based on *percentage of sales*. Besides its convenience, that method has the advantage of relating promotion to the volume of sales in a country. This approach, perhaps the easiest to justify in a budget meeting, appeals to financially oriented managers who like to think in terms of ratios and costs per unit. And when a firm is selling in many markets, the percentage-of-sales approach has the further advantage of appearing to guarantee equality among them. Each market seems to get the advertising it deserves.

For a firm that centralizes control over global promotion, the percentage-of-sales approach is attractive. A manager at headquarters would have difficulty using any other budgeting approach for 50 or 100 markets. The Europeans favor this approach as much as the Americans do.

However, despite its positives, this approach has limitations. The purpose of promotion is to bring about sales, but this method perversely makes the volume of sales determine the amount of promotion. When sales are declining, promotion declines, although long-range considerations might suggest that promotion should be stepped up. When a firm is entering a foreign market, it may need a disproportionate amount of promotion to break into the market. Limiting the promotion to the same percentage-of-sales figure used elsewhere would be undesirable during a firm's first years in the market.

The same is true in the introduction of new products into a market. As firms expand, they introduce more products into their markets. The promotion budget for those introductions should relate to the introductory needs rather than to some percentage of sales applied to existing products—or to the same products being sold in other countries. Significant promotion outlays are usually required of firms that want to expand their presence in world markets.

When Panasonic tried to launch its batteries into the U.S. market, it set an ad budget that was a small fraction of those of its competitors. Its success was limited. By contrast, when Nike and Reebok entered Europe, they each had a promotion budget approximately twice that of the well-entrenched Adidas. They succeeded in sharing 50 percent of the market in a few years.

The major weakness in applying a standard percentage-of-sales figure for promotion in foreign markets is that this method does not relate to a firm's situation in each market. The examples given—entering a market and introducing new products—are just two illustrations of the need for special treatment in special situations. In some countries, a firm may be well established with no strong competitors; in other countries, a firm may have difficulty getting a consumer franchise. Promotional needs are different in those two instances. For example, European firms increased their promotion budgets for the entire EU, once the EU became a reality.

Until more sophisticated techniques are made operational, many companies will continue to use the percentage-of-sales method, despite its limitations. That is not necessarily bad if company experience shows the percentage to be reasonably successful and if the method is somewhat flexible, allowing different percentages to be applied in different markets according to need.

COMPETITIVE-PARITY APPROACH

Matching competitors' advertising outlays—the *competitive-parity approach*—is used by some companies. Although the competitive-parity approach may offer a firm the feeling that it is not losing ground to competitors, the merit of this approach is dubious in domestic operations; and it is to be challenged particularly in international marketing. As a practical matter, in most markets, a firm cannot determine competitors' promotion budgets or allocations.

Another danger in following the practice of competitors is that they are not necessarily right. In fact, an international firm is almost always a heavier promoter than national firms in the same industry. If anything, an international firm sets the standard for national competitors to follow, rather than the reverse. That was evident in Procter & Gamble's entry into Europe, for example. The fact that different competitors employ different promotional mixes also hampers the use of this approach. In the United States, for instance, Revlon is a heavy advertiser, whereas Avon relies more on personal selling. Who should follow whom?

A final limitation to the competitive-parity approach in foreign markets is the difference in the situation of the international firm. Since it is a foreigner in the market, its relationship with consumers may differ from that of national companies. This would be reflected in its promotion. Its product line and marketing program are also likely to differ from those of national competitors. For those reasons, it is improbable that matching competitors' outlays would prove to be a sound strategy in foreign markets.

OBJECTIVE-AND-TASK APPROACH

The weaknesses of the above approaches have led some marketers to the *objective-and-task method*. It begins by determining the promotion objectives, expressed in terms of sales, brand awareness, or something else, then ascertaining the tasks needed to attain those objectives, and finally estimating the costs of performing the tasks. If this approach includes a cost-benefit analysis, relating the objectives to the cost of reaching them, it is a desirable method.

The objective-and-task method is as relevant for markets abroad as it is for the home market. It logically seeks to relate the promotion budget to a firm's situation in a country and for the firm's goals there. To use it satisfactorily, however, a firm must know the local market so it can set appropriate objectives. Unfortunately, except where it has local subsidiaries, a firm does not have intimate knowledge of the market; so setting specific objectives and defining the task of promotion may be difficult. In those cases, a percentage-of-sales method may be more feasible. It may be more important to be operational than to be "scientifical-

ly correct." Europeans and North Americans display equally low usage of the objective-and-task method.

COMPARATIVE-ANALYSIS APPROACH

Between applying a uniform percentage to all markets and letting each market go its own way lies a middle ground: *comparative analysis*, in which markets are grouped into categories according to characteristics relevant to promotion. This method yields more flexibility than the uniform approach and more control than the laissez-faire approach. Categories might be based on size (markets with over $1 million in sales and markets with under $1 million in sales), media situation, or other pertinent characteristics. A firm might try different budgeting methods or percentages for each group. One country could serve as a test market for its group. This technique can be useful for the marketer who is faced with a large number of markets.

Selecting the Appropriate Promotional Tools

Marketers have a variety of promotional tools at their disposal. As mentioned earlier, when people hear the word *marketing*, they often think of advertising. But advertising is only one tool. There are also personal selling, public relations, and sales promotion, all of which have advantages and disadvantages. Selecting the proper tool and allocating promotional funds among the tools is another area of strategic decision making that marketers face. The

Table 11-6. Promotional Tools

Tool	Description	Advantages and Disadvantages	Conditions Conducive to Specific Tools
Advertising	Nonpersonal, sponsor-paid communication using mass media	Inexpensive per contact, nonpersonal (requires similar needs and fulfillment characteristics)	Big, homogeneous, and dispersed markets
Personal selling	Sponsor-paid communication that is personal (one-on-one, or one-on-few)	Expensive, but can be tailored to individual needs and the message can be changed quickly; immediate response, but dependent on salesperson's (inconsistent) skills	Expensive, new, and industrial products in concentrated markets
Publicity (public relations)	Nonpersonal, medium-paid communication using mass media	Effective and persuasive, but not easily controlled and effectiveness is difficult to measure	Damage control or introduction of new products
Sales promotion	Sponsor-paid communication in mass media as well as direct mail; generally short-term; "all else" category	Nonpersonal (changing), but effectiveness is easy to measure	Heavy brand switching, price-sensitive products with mass appeal

tools and their basic advantages and disadvantages are summarized in Table 11-6. However, because it is assumed that this is not your first marketing course, all aspects of these different tools will not be discussed.

ADVERTISING

Advertising is generally described as paid promotion of mass media messages. The concepts have changed little in some respects; but in other respects, advertising is quite different than it was just a decade ago. Marketers are now able to remove much of the "mass" from "mass media." One term used in manufacturing, *mass customization*, can also be applied to advertising. Technology in printing, programming, and Internet advertising allows a marketer to customize a message to ever smaller groups of people (and in the case of the Internet, almost down to the individual level). So while advertising is still a tool for which marketers must pay, the mass media message may no longer be one of the drawbacks of this tool.

Marketers must make many decisions with regard to advertising. Some of those decisions have already been discussed, such as what media to select and whether a firm should use a standard global approach or an adapted or local approach. There are many other decisions, though, some of which are strategic in nature; others are more tactical. For example, a firm may be able to develop an advertising campaign internally if it has the expertise, or it may seek additional outside help. The more markets a firm enters and the more diverse those markets are, the more likely the firm is to use outside expertise in developing an advertising campaign. Other decisions include the question of whether to use some form of cooperative advertising (as might be seen with a department store and a perfume manufacturer around big holidays), the timing of ads (for instance, windshield wiper blades when it's raining or toys around Christmas and other large gift-giving holidays), the message (rational or emotional), and the spokesperson (a character such as Garfield or a company president). (See "Global Marketing: The Wrong Message.") Those decisions are not unique to global marketing, but global campaigns complicate the decisions. For example, when Nike wants to identify its products with a sports figure, it must consider the national sport (baseball, soccer, skiing, etc.) and identify a person who will have instant name and face recognition. The top soccer player in Venezuela is likely to go unrecognized in South Korea. Children asking their parents to buy them the latest toy might work in the United States, but it will not work in many other countries where children "should be heard and not seen."

Internet audiences are global whether or not a company's intent was to go global. The following list of tips pertains to the development of web advertisements, as well as to all advertisements.

- Use simple language.

GLOBAL MARKETING

The Wrong Message

The time frame is early November; the place is somewhere in the United States; the television is tuned to a national program at 6:30 in the evening. The political advertisements outnumber the advertisements for cars; and as election day approaches, the ads take on a more negative tone. Candidates accuse one another of raising taxes; caring too little about the environment, the elderly, or children; or worse, having acted unethically in previous dealings with others.

A car drives through a winding, rain-soaked country road at a high rate of speed; but the driver is evidently in full control. The announcer's voice confidently states "our new tires are safe in all kinds of weather."

Ronald McDonald appears on the television screen, holding up a new grilled chicken sandwich. The commercial shifts to a group of people sitting around a table, talking and enjoying the new sandwich. The announcer states that three out of four people surveyed prefer this chicken sandwich over KFC's grilled chicken sandwich.

While those ads might be perfectly normal in the United States, they are not acceptable elsewhere. Some nations' laws about comparing products are so strict that no comparisons can be made between competing products. At one extreme, a tire company was sued because it made the claim that its tires were "strong as steel"— sued not by another tire manufacturer, but by the nation's steel industry because the statement put a negative light on steel products.

Researchers have found that negative and comparative advertisements are perceived differently around the world. One study found that East Europeans (in Poland, the Czech Republic, and Hungary) did not respond well to advertisements with negative or disparaging messages about competitors or their products.

Source: Orth, Ulrich R., Peter P. Oppenheim, and Zuzana Firbasova. "Measuring Message Framing Effects Across Europe," *Journal of Targeting, Measurement and Analysis for Marketing*, Volume 13, Issue 4, August 2005, pages 313–327.

- Avoid complicated sentence structures.
- Use the active voice.
- Avoid humor.
- Use graphics to help communicate written

concepts.
- Avoid complicated and unnecessary graphics.[29]

Other Forms of Promotion

Advertising is a major form of promotion in world markets, but it is not the only form of promotion. The following discussion presents alternatives in the use of promotional tools: personal selling, sales promotion, and public relations.

Although advertising is often the most prominent element in the promotional mix of an international marketer, for some firms, especially those in industrial marketing, it is a minor form of promotion. In any case, a sound promotional program involves more than advertising.

Personal Selling

Personal selling, a major promotional tool, is often more important in foreign marketing than in domestic marketing campaigns. That is, it consumes a greater percentage of the promotion budget, for two reasons: (1) Restrictions on advertising and media availability may limit the amount of advertising a firm can do, and (2) low wages in many countries allow a company to hire a larger sales force. The second reason is especially applicable in less developed nations. Working in the opposite direction is the low status associated with sales work in most countries.

The experience of Philip Morris in Venezuela illustrates the role personal selling can have. Low wages permitted the sales department to hire 300 employees. However, only one-third were salespeople. The rest were assistants who helped with deliveries, distribution of sales materials, etc. The younger sales assistants were provided with bikes, which were cheaper than four-wheeled transportation. The missionary-selling activities of the younger sales assistants provided a very effective complement to the regular sales force.

NATIONAL, NOT INTERNATIONAL
The subject considered here is essentially personal selling in a firm's foreign markets; it cannot really be called *international* personal selling. When discussing advertising, one could speak of international campaigns and international media; but personal selling involves personal contact and is more culture-bound than advertising. As a result, even though international business has expanded tremendously in recent decades, personal selling activities are still conducted primarily on a national basis. In fact, many national markets are divided into sales territories served by salespeople recruited only from their respective territories. The

salespeople do not even cover a national market.

A limited amount of personal selling does cross national boundaries, most commonly for industrial goods but big-ticket items in particular. However, as international as IBM is, it still uses national sales representatives in its markets. Although the growth of regionalism should encourage more international personal selling, economic integration is not the same as cultural integration. Experience in the EU shows that personal selling activities are very slow to cross cultural-political boundaries.[30] There are cultural boundaries that restrict personnel selling efforts, too. For example, in Japan, individual recognition of sales reps is still at odds with the cultural focus on group and team efforts; in Saudi Arabia, finding qualified sales reps is difficult because of a labor shortage and the low prestige of selling; and in India, sales force management is difficult in a market fragmented by language divisions and the caste system. Studies have also shown that training of a sales force is likely to differ from country to country while hiring practices are likely to be similar from market to market.[31]

One task of the international marketer is to determine the role personal selling should play in each market. Once the role of personal selling has been decided, administration of the sales force is similar to that in the home market. That is, the same functions must be performed: recruitment, selection, training, motivation, supervision, and compensation. A few of the international dimensions of administering a sales force are presented next.

Since sales task varies by country and personal selling takes place on a national basis, sales management must be decentralized to the national market. International marketers do not have a sales force; instead, they generally serve as advisors to national operations. For example, Manufacturing Data Systems, Inc. (MDSI), a producer of computer software, found that a sale in the United States requires an average of two calls per firm. In Europe, there are frequent callbacks, each involving of a higher level of management. That means more time and higher costs. In Japan, MDSI's selling requires even more time than in Europe. In other Asian markets, Electrolux finds its direct sales force requires an average of only five demonstrations to make a sale in Malaysia; but 20 demonstrations are needed in the Philippines.

RECRUITING, SELECTING, AND RETAINING THE SALES FORCE
Recruiting and selecting sales representatives are done in the local market by those who know the situation best. Three problems may arise in trying to find and retain salespeople in certain markets: (1) Selling is a low-status occupation in many countries; the most attractive candidates seek other employment; (2) finding people with the desired characteristics is often difficult; and (3) keeping

or retaining productive salespeople is difficult because they are in short supply and demand is high. When dealing with salespeople and their customers, it is important to remember, as described in Chapter 2, that the same motivation to sell or buy is different from culture to culture. Also, very often extra training is required, especially when a firm and its products are new to market. Although employee turnover is expensive, studies have identified strategies for reducing sales force turnover.[32] Add to that, though, the legal restrictions that exist in many countries that either limit or make it very expensive for a firm to fire salespeople for underperformance or other reasons—a potential disadvantage.

As an aid in recruitment and selection of salespeople, many companies develop job descriptions and specification lists. Both may vary internationally. In a foreign market, the sales job will be a function of a firm's product line, distribution channels, and marketing mix. Thus, the job will not be exactly the same in all markets. The greater the carryover from country to country, the more international direction is possible. The international marketer searches for similarities to aid supervision.

A question arises as to whether a universal "sales type" exists, even for one industry. As job descriptions and market situations vary from country to country, so do other cultural influences. In many markets, a variety of religious, educational, and racial or tribal characteristics must be considered. When markets are segmented along those dimensions, the sales force may have to be segmented as well. Just as German sales representatives generally are not used in France, so salespeople from one tribal or religious group often cannot sell to another group in their own country. The world is full of examples of group conflicts that can be reflected in sales force requirements: English versus Irish, French-speaking versus English-speaking Canadians, Hindu versus Muslim, Sinhalese versus Tamil, and Croat versus Serb.

In some parts of the world, a particular group is the major source of businesspeople, as were the Jews throughout Europe prior to World War II. The Chinese are prominent merchants in many Asian nations. Within the nation itself, a particular group or tribe may play this role. In many countries, the important commercial role played by a minority group, such as the Chinese, is resented by the majority. Laws may be passed that force greater hiring of the major national group. Although recruitment and selection are done in the host country, international marketers can make contributions. For example, they may introduce tests or techniques that have proved successful in domestic operations or in other subsidiaries. Each country is not completely different from all others, and some carryover of those techniques is possible. Through analysis of company experience and by collaboration with subsidiary personnel, international marketers should optimize the use of those experiences in local operations.

When industrial marketers enter a foreign market, they often find the lack of a local sales force to be an important barrier. To accelerate and ease their entry, they may find it desirable to join with—or acquire—a local firm for its sales force capability. In Japan, where relationships are so important, personal selling is especially critical. When Merck wanted to expand in Japan, it acquired Banyu Pharmaceutical, which enabled it to field a sales force of more than 1,000 people immediately!

IBM, long number one in Japan, dropped to number three, partly because it had only about 10,000 sales-engineer "hand holders," whereas Hitachi had 17,000 and Fujitsu had 23,000. Toyota has over 100,000 door-to-door salespeople in Japan, and Amway has over 1 million.

TRAINING THE SALES FORCE

The training of salespeople is done primarily in the national market. The nature of the training program is determined by the demands of the job and the previous preparation of the sales force. Those vary from country to country. Nevertheless, the international marketer has a voice in local training. Because of the similarity in company products from market to market, national training programs have common denominators.

Drawing on the firm's multinational experience, the international marketer seeks to improve each training program. That can be accomplished, in part, by supplying training materials, program formats, and ideas to each country. International meetings of subsidiary personnel responsible for sales training can also promote the exchange of experiences. Technology allows firms to train its sales force on new products and initiatives without taking employees to headquarters or to plant locations. Long-distance online programs are an alternative that allow employees the flexibility to learn new skills and earn higher-level degrees that often lead to advancement in the company. While motivation differs among various cultures, providing challenges and the opportunity to learn is a benefit that may mean the difference between a qualified and motivated sales force and a less effective sales force.

Bristol-Myers Squibb gives special attention to sales training in developing countries. Training programs are developed by the corporate medical affairs division and product planning division. The company has medical directors in its Latin American, Pacific, Indian, and Middle East regions who help in subsidiary training programs. All national salespeople receive basic training in anatomy, pharmacology, and diseases, as well as in sales. Then they receive detailed information on drug products, including contraindications and possible complications.

Another training technique is the traveling team of experts from regional or international headquarters. As a company finds new product applications, adds new products, or enters new market segments, the sales task might change. The new selling task usually requires additional training, which can be accomplished at a regional center, by a traveling team of experts, or via the Internet.

When a firm sells through independent distributors or licensees, it has little control over the sales force, except in the initial selection of the distributor. Firms have found, though, that using intermediaries to manage their foreign sales force is a quick and less expensive alternative to developing the sales force on their own. In those cases, it is not unusual for firms to provide specialized training to the sales staff of their distributors or licensees. This is generally done at no charge and turns out to be a profitable expenditure because of its contribution to sales as well as to relations with the licensee or distributor. A firm faces some challenges when using independent intermediaries, perhaps the most important of which was already mentioned—loss of control over the distribution network. Researchers have identified key areas that help ensure that a firm's relationship with sales force intermediaries is successful.[33] Careful evaluation of potential partners is one of those key factors.

As was mentioned previously, the demand for good salespeople is a particular problem that multinationals face in many markets. The best-trained sales staff tend to be "raided" by companies within the industry, as well as by noncompeting firms. That means firms must train more salespeople than they need or find some way of keeping their sales force, usually through higher compensation.

MOTIVATING AND COMPENSATING THE SALES FORCE

Motivation and compensation of the sales force are closely related to hiring and retaining good salespeople. Indeed, attractive compensation is often a primary motivator. Motivation can be more of a challenge abroad than at home, for two reasons: (1) the low esteem in which selling is held and (2) the cultural reluctance of prospective sales representatives to talk to strangers, especially to try to persuade them—two essential elements of selling.

Although compensation is a prime motivator, there are other ways to motivate. Since much depends on cultural factors, motivation must be designed to meet local needs. In countries where selling has especially low status, a firm must try to overcome this handicap. Training, titles, and perquisites are all helpful, as are financial awards. In addition, special recognition can help a salesperson's self-image. For example, Philip Morris in Venezuela publicizes the achievements of its best salespeople and gives them financial and other awards. Periodically the company gives a special party and banquet for its top four salespeople.

Foreign travel is another kind of reward employed by international companies. Few members of a sales force in foreign markets could afford a trip to the United States or Europe. Their ability to earn such a trip through good per-

formance is a strong incentive. In addition to providing access to tourist attractions, the company usually entertains the visitors at headquarters. International companies are able to do that because of their size and because their internal logistics facilitate such efforts. They also gain economies of scale by entertaining sales representatives from a number of countries at the same time. Electrolux rewards international trips to winning sales teams in Asia.

In motivating and compensating a sales force, one challenge is to find the mix of monetary and nonmonetary rewards appropriate for each market. Some nonmonetary factors are training, counseling, supervision, and the use of quotas and contests. In monetary compensation, the question usually arises as to whether payment should be a salary or a commission.

In many countries, salespeople are reluctant to accept an incentive form of payment such as a commission. They believe that it reinforces the cultural conflict and the negative image of personal selling. In those markets, a firm tends to rely on a salary payment rather than a commission. Some U.S. companies, however, have been able to introduce incentive elements into their sales representatives' remuneration package, even in those markets.

NCR, for example, pioneered the use of commission selling in Japan, a country where incentive payments were considered to be against the cultural pattern. However, a decade of experience in which NCR sales quadrupled and sales representatives were increasingly satisfied seemed to argue to the contrary. In fact, the evidence convinced others to follow. In addition to foreign firms such as IBM, even Japanese firms began to model commission systems on the NCR example.

CONTROLLING THE SALES FORCE

With a commission form of remuneration, close control over the sales staff is less necessary than with a straight salary. Regardless of the mode of payment, however, some control is necessary. Some control techniques are establishing sales territories, setting itineraries and call frequencies, using quotas, and reporting arrangements. Because the techniques must reflect local conditions, they must be determined, in part, at the local level. For example, when some territories are less attractive than others, a firm may offer extra rewards to ensure equal coverage. Philip Morris did that in Venezuela, offering higher commissions in rural provinces.

Even though the activity is decentralized, international managers should participate in establishing control techniques. They have contact with domestic operations, which are probably most sophisticated in using the techniques; and their experience can be a source of know-how for foreign markets. They can advise on establishing sales territories, norms for sales calls, and reporting arrangements.

The local knowledge of national management is complemented by the international knowledge of the international marketer. A comparative analysis of similar markets provides a better idea of what range of performance is possible. Thus, international managers can aid local managers in setting appropriate norms. Especially in the introduction of a new product, local management can learn from experience in the firm's other markets. In the United States, firms make comparisons among sales territories. With appropriate modifications, the same kind of comparative analysis should be conducted for foreign markets. The comparisons should be among groups of similar countries. That is one way managers can realize the benefits of multinational experience in sales force management.

EVALUATING SALES FORCE PERFORMANCE

Although far removed from selling activities in foreign markets, international marketers have a twofold interest in evaluating them. First, the performance of the sales force helps determine a firm's success in a market. International marketers want to be sure that local management is getting good performance. To do that, they help locals apply the best techniques of evaluation. They can assist with ideas, reporting forms, ratios, and other criteria used elsewhere in the company.

The second interest in evaluating performance is in making international comparisons. It is important to know not only how each country is performing in its local context, but also how it compares with other markets. Such comparisons identify the countries needing help. They can be used to motivate below-average markets to improve their performance. Some criteria used to compare countries include personal selling cost as a percentage of sales, number of salespeople per $1 million sales (to eliminate differences in wage costs), and units sold per sales representative.

Obviously, many differences hinder such comparisons. It is better that the comparisons be made explicitly, on the basis of criteria that take account of relevant differences. For example, the European division of Singer developed such a comparative framework for its 16 European subsidiaries, including such diverse countries as Sweden and Spain. That framework became operational in the sense that it was understood and accepted by management in the 16 subsidiaries.

Sales Promotion

Sales promotion is defined as "those selling activities that do not fall directly into the advertising, public relations, or personal selling categories, such as the use of contests, coupons, sampling, premiums, cents-off deals, and point-of-purchase materials." In the United States, sales promotion budgets have been larger than advertising budgets since 1980. The factors that created that situation are com-

GLOBAL MARKETING

McDonald's Tray Liners

McDonald's worked hard to train customers to clear their own tables. Today, when fast-food customers dine in and finish their meals, they take their trays to the trash bin, throw away the remains of the meal, and place the used tray in the receptacle above the trash bin. Although it's difficult to say how much money the fast-food industry saves by not having to hire workers to clean up after patrons (although workers still have to wipe down tables and sweep the floor), it is likely to be substantial. Part of the cleaning process is the tray liner—it makes cleanup fast and leaves less mess on the tray. Since so many people like to read while they eat, the tray liners also provide a vehicle for sales promotion.

Over the past half century, McDonald's has used the tray liner in many ways. Tray liners have served as a form of amusement for children, with games and puzzles printed on them; they have been used to announce new products; and they have been used to promote the image of McDonald's as a good corporate citizen. One example was when Mexico McDonald's wanted to promote pride in being Mexican and printed the Mexican flag on tray liners. That idea didn't work so well—drippings from food would fall on the tray liner, leading to comments from patrons that it was a desecration of a national symbol. More recently, in an effort to gain acceptance among Japanese (who were reluctant to try McDonald's menu items), the company included information about the caloric content of items. For example, the caloric content of a cheeseburger or a six-piece McNugget pack was compared to that of more traditional Japanese items, such as tonkatsu (fried pork) and gyodon (a beef, onion, and rice dish).

Sources: McDonald's web site, history (http://www.media.mcdonalds.com/secured/company/index.html); "McDonald's Comes Clean," Yahoo! Financial News (http://biz.yahoo.com/fool/051025/113027388625.html?.v=1); accessed October 26, 2005.

ing to other world markets, too. For example, in Colombia, two-thirds of spending goes to sales promotions and only one-third to media.

A firm is interested in promotional approaches that persuade customers to buy. Firms that use sales promotion in the United States generally find it as effective in other markets, if not more effective. When incomes are lower, people are usually more interested in "something for nothing," such as free samples, premiums, or contests.

Apart from economics, other constraints affect the international use of sales promotion, one of which is legal restrictions. Laws in foreign markets may restrict both the size and nature of the sample, premium, or prize. The value of the free item is often limited to a percent (say, 5 percent, as in France) of the value of the product. In other cases, the free item must be related to the nature of the product purchased, such as cups with coffee but not steak knives with detergent. Such restrictions are limiting but not always crippling. For example, Reader's Digest successfully used contests in Italy even though they are taxed there, giving away prizes such as automobiles. Vicks was able to distribute over 30 million samples of Oil of Olay in many countries.

Another constraint is cultural.[34] The premiums or other devices used must be attractive to the local consumer. For example, for many years, Procter & Gamble successfully used nativity scene characters in packages of detergent in the Spanish market. Premiums may require even greater adaptation than products.

Another problem involves the capabilities of local retailers. Many sales promotion activities require some retail involvement; that is, processing coupons, handling odd-shaped combination or premium packages, posting display materials, etc. Getting retailers to cooperate may be difficult when they lack appropriate facilities. Problems that arise with small retailers are that the retailers are difficult to contact, they have limited space, and they often handle the materials in a way that the producer did not intend.

The use of technology in sales promotions is becoming widespread and is taking on some unique properties.[35,36,37] A firm may send confirmation of an order to a customer via e-mail and include a "coupon" (typically a number that is to be entered on subsequent orders) or an invitation to participate in a special sales events. Those examples of sales promotion are more highly focused than coupons generated by registers that customers might receive in a grocery store. (Coupons generated in that fashion are often for products that relate to or compete with items that are scanned.) Consumers' inability to access computers will limit the use of electronically generated coupons, some voucher systems, and customer loyalty programs more commonly found in developed markets. A market's infrastructure and laws related to consumer privacy and the Internet must also be taken into account.

For a variety of legal and cultural reasons, sales promotions are primarily national rather than international. Even in Europe, for example, differences in advertising rules are not as great as differences in sales promotion rules. Thus, one sees more pan-European advertising than pan-European sales promotions.

The competitive situation in a market can also affect a firm's choice of sales promotions and their likelihood of success. GE provides an illustration: In Japan, GE had noticeable success in breaking into the air conditioning market. Two factors behind the successful entry were offering (1) overseas trips as prizes to outstanding dealers and (2) a free color TV set to purchasers of high-priced models.

The result was that the Japanese trade association drew up rules banning overseas trips as prizes for sales of air conditioners and setting a limit on the size of premiums that could be offered. Those rules were approved by the Japanese Fair Trade Commission. Company complaints led to a modification of the rules—no overseas trips as prizes for home electric appliance dealers.

An international firm should have some advantages over its national competitors in sales promotion. For example, economies of scale may exist in generating ideas and buying materials. Ideas and materials may be suitable for several markets. One country can be used as a test market for other similar countries. Analyzing the company's experience in different markets helps in evaluating sales promotion and setting budgets. Though sales promotion was discussed as a separate item, it obviously is part of overall promotion, as with Colgate in India, mentioned earlier.

Sponsorships, promotional events, sales, and other forms of sales promotion are similarly constrained for cultural, legal, and economic reasons. There are some very creative contests and events. Wal-Mart Germany developed an event that quickly spread across the country—singles night. Sales increased 15 percent between 6 p.m. and 8 p.m. on Friday nights (the scheduled day and time of these events). Perhaps as important, Wal-Mart received a lot of publicity for the stunt, which brought in even more customers—for which they didn't have to spend a cent.[38]

Public Relations—Publicity

Public relations is perhaps the most powerful of the promotion tools; unfortunately, it is the most forgotten or neglected. Public relations can raise a company's reputation to new heights—and as easily force it into bankruptcy.

WorldCom, Parmalat, Arthur Andersen, Tyco, and Enron were the focus of ethical scandals that came to light through publicity (bad publicity from the firms' perspective). Individuals working for those companies were found guilty of fraud and unethical practices that ruined the companies and people's lives. Schools' curriculums have been reshaped by those incidents; new laws have been enacted, such as Sarbanes-Oxley; and new products and industries have come into being. The effects will be long-lasting, and the names at the beginning of this paragraph will be repeated in business case studies for many years. As an example, the case at the end of this chapter deals with practices that a company engaged in a quarter century ago. The behavior was so out of character, so extraordinary, that it bears review even today.

History provides lessons, both good and bad, from which society can learn and benefit. Every day business news includes stories about companies' profits not meeting expectations or a new drug being denied approval or a product being recalled. Firms must be aware that this sort of publicity will occur; and with communication technology the way it is, the news spreads worldwide in a short period of time. Firms must include contingency strategies for managing bad publicity in their promotional plans. Of course, ethically and socially responsible firms face this dilemma less frequently than firms that are not good corporate citizens.

That's enough bad news. Publicity can also be good. Again, turning back the clock 25 years, an incident led to the tamperproof bottles and other containers used for most food products—and, incidentally, led to the company slogan "most trusted brand name in pain medication," which is still used today. The 1982 incident involved someone tainting Tylenol capsules with cyanide poisoning. Whether the person responsible wanted to actually kill someone or just gain attention may never be known (the person was never caught), but the response by Johnson & Johnson was immediate and decisive. The company recalled every bottle of Tylenol on every shelf in every store (at the time, about 250,000 bottles). That cost the company an untold amount of money, but the positive press from the incident was a boon to the company and is still used as a classic example of best corporate practices.[39,40]

Public relations is concerned with images. A firm attempts to present itself in a favorable light with one or more of its constituencies. Too often that has meant telling the world how good the company is or explaining away the company's mistakes. In an ideal sense, good public relations is corporate diplomacy—a firm seeking to relate constructively to its various stakeholders to the benefit of both parties. Thus, public relations involves more than corporate communications—it requires appropriate corporate behavior. (See Chapter 6.) Public relations is often more important in a foreign market than it is domestically.[41]

Public relations is not marketing, but good relations with the public are essential to marketing success. A firm that is seen as a bad citizen may find itself persona non grata in the marketplace; one reaction could be a boycott of its products. In another sense, public relations can be considered as the marketing of a product, the product being the firm itself. A firm's products can enjoy continued success only because of their performance. The image of the product cannot be maintained if product performance is inconsistent. The same reasoning applies to the image and behavior of a firm. Public relations cannot be more effective than the corporate behavior behind it.

Obviously, a firm must behave in a legal manner in all of its markets. It also must be perceived as behaving in an ethically correct and environmentally friendly way. (See Chapter 6.) A problem can arise because what is "ethically correct" and "environmentally friendly" may be defined somewhat differently by different observers. Those observers include a firm's various publics.

The publics of a firm are broader than its market. They include all of those who are affected by a firm's operations—and all of those who can have an effect on a firm's success. These publics, stakeholders, or constituencies include customers, suppliers, employees, intermediaries, stockholders, the general public, activist and special interest groups, governments, the financial community, and the media. The importance of any particular group varies from country to country. A firm's level of involvement in a market also affects the publics with which it must deal.

THE PUBLIC RELATIONS TASK TODAY

Just as the first job of marketing is to become familiar with the market, so the first task of international public relations is to become familiar with the firm's various publics in each market. This involves two processes: (1) seeing others as they see themselves, rather than using a foreign viewpoint or stereotype and (2) seeing the company as others see it. Thus, public relations should begin with market intelligence. By being informed, a firm can practice preventive medicine rather than being forced into drastic surgery after serious trouble has developed. Too often public relations is used to fight fires rather than prevent them. Inadequate intelligence can lead to many problems.

RESPONSE TO THE PUBLIC

The purpose of intelligence gathering is to serve as a basis for action. The appropriate action depends on the nature of the intelligence. Occasionally, the appropriate action involves a statement or press release by a firm; for instance, when false statements are circulating. In other instances, it may be a change in the behavior of the firm. When change is inevitable, initiating the change voluntarily is preferable to being forced to accept it. For example, Nestlé was reluctant to change its baby food marketing in developing countries. (See Case 11.1.) That led to a boycott of its products. On the other hand, Procter & Gamble immediately withdrew its Rely tampons from the market when unwanted side effects were discovered. That quick action minimized the problem and maintained customer goodwill. Avon Products took a proactive response to the rise of consumerism: (1) It created Avon Cares Network to respond to inquiries and complaints, (2) it published consumer information pamphlets, (3) it sought out consumer leaders and groups, (4) it held conferences on consumer issues, (5) it invited consumer leaders to meet Avon managers, and (6) it sought guidance from experts.

Noting host-country complaints about a "foreign" company is a helpful way to identify problems with which a firm must deal. In addition to problems that are peculiar to individual countries, certain complaints tend to appear in foreign markets. The complaints arise primarily because the international firm is a foreigner in the market, and the common thread is that the foreign firm takes unfair advantage of the host country and otherwise abuses its position as a guest. Those complaints are often expressed in emotional language, such as "imperialistic exploitation." A reasonable statement of the kinds of things a host country wants from a foreign firm is provided in Table 11-7.

Table 11-7. Public Relations—Things to Do

1. Maintain a high degree of local autonomy in decision making.
2. Retain some earnings within the country.
3. Allow and encourage exports.
4. Process the natural resources of the country locally.
5. Conduct research and development locally.
6. Search out and develop local sources of supply. (Use local content.)
7. Offer equity to national investors.
8. Provide employment and career opportunities at all levels.
9. Maintain fair prices locally and in transfer pricing.
10. Provide information and maintain transparency in company operations.

Source: Based on an advisory of the Canadian government.

The best defense is a good offense. An imaginative public relations program is the best way to reduce the probability of reaction against a company. There are numerous ways to learn about good corporate citizenship, which is defined as promoting ethically and socially responsible behavior. The mission of the World Bank's Corporate Governance and Corporate Social Responsibility division is to help firms meet those objectives. (The division even offers an online course). The OECD and the UN have multiple documents related to corporate codes of conduct—related to bribery, environmentalism, employment practices, economic development, corruption, and a host of other issues.

ORGANIZATIONAL ASPECTS

Because of its need to be sensitive to local publics, a firm must rely heavily on local staff. A firm can centralize policymaking, but day-to-day operations must be left to people in the local market. A firm has nationals on its staff and may use a local public relations agency. The international corporate communications manager ensures consistency from country to country and acts as a clearinghouse of ideas and experience. Aiding in this task is the increasing availability of international public relations firms, even in China and Russia. Such groups can aid coordination, much like the multinational agency does in advertising.

Public relations is important to effective marketing, but the two functions should be organizationally separate. Although public relations is a profitable activity, its purpose is not immediate sales. By lumping the public relations and marketing functions together, a firm runs the risk that public relations might take a short-run view, focusing on the annual profit-and-loss statement. Public relations should be sufficiently independent to be able to consider the interest of the public as well as the long-run interests of the firm.

Marketing Mix as Promotion

The principal elements of promotion have been discussed: advertising, personal selling, and sales promotion. The purpose of those activities is to induce consumers to purchase a company's products. As marketers well know, however, other factors also help persuade customers to buy—or not to buy—a firm's products. All elements of the marketing mix influence the sale of goods and services. Because the elements of the mix have a different influence from country to country, the appropriate mix for a given market should have some degree of individuality.

The idea of the complementarity and substitutability of the various elements of the mix is familiar to students of marketing. What are noted here are some of the international applications of the mix concept related to promotion. Since product policy, distribution, and the other elements of promotion have already been examined, the discussion will be brief.

Product

Although the quality of a product is presumably the major reason a consumer buys it, consumers' desires for a given product often differ from country to country. By modifying products for national markets, a firm can persuade more customers to buy. Affluent markets may demand more style and power or a larger size. Poorer markets may require smaller sizes, durability, and simplicity. Food products vary in the degree of sweetness or spiciness desired. Further differences are found in the form, color, and texture of products. In Britain, for example, Ocean Spray had to mix cranberry juice with black currant juice to gain acceptance.

PACKAGE

For many goods, the package is an important element of the product. Adapting packaging to the market may be effective promotion. In Latin America, Gillette sells Silkience shampoo in half-ounce plastic bubbles. In the Far East, Procter & Gamble sells most of its shampoo in single-use packets. In some markets, dual-use packages attract the consumer because they can be retained for some other use. Plastic containers are popular in some markets, whereas metal and glass are preferred elsewhere. Form and color are important, too. Ocean Spray, for example, had to change from bottles to juice boxes in Britain. The label on the package should also serve a promotional role in its design and color, in the language used, and in the text printed on it.

BRAND

Brand policy can affect a product's attractiveness. For some goods, an international brand name is more prestigious and trusted than a national brand. On the other hand, for many products, such as food and household items, individualized national brands are favored by international companies. Johnson Wax and CPC International are examples of firms that pursue primarily a national brand policy.

WARRANTY AND SERVICE

Many companies use warranties defensively; that is, they meet competitors' warranties. Warranties, however, can also be used aggressively to promote sales. If an international company offers better quality and a more reliable product than its competitors, it may gain a promotional edge through a more liberal warranty. Many producers of electrical and mechanical products have used a strong warranty as part of their entry strategy into foreign markets. When Chrysler reentered Europe, it offered a generous three-year/100,000-kilometer warranty.

Consumers everywhere are concerned about product service, which includes delivery, installation, repair and maintenance facilities, and spare parts inventories. International firms are handicapped in some markets because they are not represented well enough to offer service that is as good as what national firms offer. A weakness in this area can offset strengths in other areas. By the same token, a strong service capability can be effective promotion—a strength of Singer and IBM in many markets and of the German and Japanese auto producers in the U.S. market.

Distribution

Marketers are aware of the promotional implications of different distribution strategies. When convenience is important to the buyer, a firm must have widespread distribution. Where dealer "push" is important, more selective distribution is necessary. The same considerations apply to foreign markets. When an international firm sells through distributors, it usually provides an exclusive franchise to encourage support. This exclusive franchise is almost always necessary to get a distributor to cooperate.

When a firm goes from an indirect to a direct channel, the distribution system is bearing a greater part of the promotion. The more direct the channel, the greater the push it gives a product. Going direct can have a special significance for an international firm's level of involvement in a market. An indirect channel means that many intermediaries exist between producer and consumer. In international marketing, an indirect channel is exporting.

The way for a firm to go more direct in export markets is to establish its own presence there with a marketing subsidiary. As with any more direct method, the firm's cost will increase. Many benefits are associated with such a move, however, one of which is a favorable promotional effect. One way of illustrating the benefits is to note the disadvantages of exporting, which are usually overcome by establishing a local subsidiary.

Studies have shown the following complaints expressed by foreign buyers in dealing with U.S. exporters:

- U.S. exporters do not familiarize themselves with the market.
- Management gives less attention to foreign business. Foreign inquiries are sometimes ignored.
- There is a lack of reliability in delivery dates.
- Price quotations are FOB—U.S. plant.
- Little or no local language material describing the firm's products is available.
- Domestic customers get open account terms. Foreign buyers receive harsher terms, such as the requirement of a letter of credit.

The establishment of a foreign subsidiary is likely to eliminate those problems. It can be one of the most powerful promotional tools a firm can use.

Price and Terms

The idea behind the demand curve and the elasticity concept is that buyers are sensitive to price. By changing the price, the marketer affects the attractiveness of a product. In other words, pricing has promotional aspects. If consumers in different countries have differing degrees of price sensitivity, the marketer should try to adjust prices accordingly, if costs permit.

Price may be used promotionally in other ways. On products for which there is a price-quality association, a firm might want to price above its competitors to gain the quality image. Of course, that is most meaningful when the product actually has a quality advantage. In countries where purchasing power is low, prices might be reduced through modification of the product (for example, giving it fewer features and greater simplicity) or use of smaller sizes.

EXPORT PRICING

Export prices and terms can be used to promotional

advantage in several ways. One is in choosing the currency for the price quotation. Although exporters usually prefer to quote in their own currency, importers like price quotations in their currency because it protects them against variations in the exchange rate.

Another promotional aspect of export pricing is the specific quotation used. As noted in Chapter 12, FOB plant prices are favored by exporters. However, there is a promotional advantage in using a CIF quotation, which is preferred by importers.

A third promotional aspect of export pricing involves the terms extended to the buyer. Exporters often discriminate against foreign buyers. For example, domestic buyers may be given open account terms, whereas foreign importers have to pay by letter of credit. Foreign buyers would like the same terms as domestic buyers. Although that may not always be feasible, exporters who want to use pricing as a promotional tool will respond as best they can. They would move toward local currency price quotations, CIF pricing, and more liberal payment terms.

CREDIT

A final promotional aspect of payment terms is the use of credit. The credit needs of buyers vary from country to country. Sellers of industrial equipment often find that the factor determining the choice of supplier is the credit terms. For some, it has meant greater working capital to cover more liberal credit. Cincinnati Milacron lost a contract to supply equipment for a factory in Georgia even though it had the lowest bid. The factory chose a Japanese supplier because it offered a complete credit package.

For consumer goods marketers, credit extension can be directed at both channel members and consumers. In many countries, wholesalers and retailers are financially weak. The seller has to cover their credit needs in what seems to be a liberal fashion compared to domestic practices. Liberal credit may be needed to sell durable goods. For example, credit extension is one reason Singer has been able to maintain a market in sewing machines despite lower-priced competition.

Automobile dealers in Brazil found an ingenious way to sell cars without credit in a money-tight economy through a consorcio, or lottery. Each consorcio group member is guaranteed a new car within 60 months, and each group includes 120 people. The monthly payment is pegged to the price of the car divided by the number of members. Two winners are selected at a monthly drawing. The members pay for the whole 60 months, of course. Members avoid Brazil's high interest charges and the large down payment normally required. They pay a 10 percent administrative fee, however. Ford's Brazilian subsidiary parlayed those clubs into a major marketing tool. Ford ran 2,300 such consorcios and sold one-fifth of its total Brazilian output that way.

The promotional aspects of the elements of the marketing mix have been discussed in isolation up to this point. In reality, of course, those elements interact synergistically.

Summary

Several factors affect international promotion. Because languages vary by market, promotion must be in the local language. That requires local help from a local ad agency or subsidiary of the firm. Media availability (TV, radio, and newspaper) varies between countries, requiring a marketer to adjust. Governments place limits on advertised products, appeals, media use, and agency ownership. Competition in the local market influences a firm's promotion. Agency availability differs between markets for political and economic reasons. That can hinder a firm's ability to find a good agency or to get international coordination.

Major decisions involve selecting the agency, the message, and the media; determining the budget; evaluating the effectiveness of the promotion efforts; and determining the degree of centralization or decentralization that is appropriate.

Using its own international marketing criteria, a firm must choose an agency for each foreign market. The trend is to use multicountry agencies, which are gaining market share. However, some good local agencies survive in most markets.

In choosing a message, the issue is whether a firm should use local or international campaigns. The use of internationalized campaigns is affected by language requirements, the existence of international market segments, the use of local versus international agencies, and the degree of decentralization in the firm. To maximize similarities, many firms use a pattern, or prototype, approach.

A firm's media configuration often varies from country to country because of government restrictions or media infrastructure in the country. Some firms use international media for multicountry coverage, but local media predominate for most international marketers.

It is difficult to apply the various formulas for determining the ad budget for a firm's foreign markets. Therefore, the percentage-of-sales approach is the most common formula used. The ad budget for a country is a function of its overall promotional mix there, local media availability, and the firm's own level of involvement in the country.

Evaluating promotion effectiveness is more difficult in foreign markets than at home. For that reason, firms frequently use sales as a measure of effectiveness. The internationalization of research and advertising agencies is helping on this score.

A firm must also decide how to advertise in markets where it is represented by independent licensees or distributors. Should it rely on them, go it alone, or cooperate? Cooperative programs with the local licensee or distributor appear to be the most common and effective approach.

Personal selling is often more important in the promotional mix abroad than in the domestic market. Although personal selling is done almost entirely on a national basis, management at headquarters can contribute something to most of the tasks of sales force management in the firm's foreign markets: recruitment and selection, training, motivation, compensation, control, and evaluation. Successful techniques can be transferred from the home market to similar foreign markets. Economies of scale can be realized for some tasks. A firm will also frequently train or assist distributors' or licensees' sales forces. And international comparisons help in evaluating and, thus, improving international performance.

Sales promotion is usually effective in most foreign markets in spite of national restrictions. It must be adapted to meet local legal and cultural differences, but it plays the same role in the marketing mix abroad as it does at home.

Each of the four Ps of the marketing mix can attract the customer and therefore serve as promotion. Product modifications abroad (including package, brand, warranty, and service) can persuade customers to buy the firm's products. By going to more direct distribution abroad, the firm can usually increase sales and respond better to the local market. Various pricing and credit terms can make the firm's marketing more productive, such as C.I.F. quotes and open account terms.

Public relations is a very important and sensitive task for international marketing. The first step in successful public relations is conducting research so a firm becomes familiar with all of the constituencies that can affect its success in the market. The second is designing a company program and behavior appropriate to the market. Firms should not only respond to the communication environment, but also try to manage it, thus achieving more favorable outcomes in the marketplace through political power and public opinion—the "fifth P" of marketing.

Questions and Research

11.1 Discuss government controls and agency and media availability as constraints on the international advertising manager.

11.2 Home Care Products Co. just opened a marketing subsidiary in Spain. The company has been selling in 12 other European countries since 1950. The advertising manager at European headquarters must choose between the Madrid office of a large U.S. agency and a leading Spanish agency. What questions would you ask in advising her?

11.3 Why have international agencies been growing so strong?

11.4 Why do local agencies survive in view of the internationals' growth?

11.5 What factors encourage standardization of international advertising?

11.6 Why is it difficult for an international advertising manager to use the same media configuration in all markets?

11.7 Why does personal selling often play a proportionately larger promotional role in foreign markets than in the domestic market?

11.8 Why is personal selling done largely within national boundaries rather than internationally?

11.9 Since most of the task of sales force management must be done within the national market, what contributions can an international marketing manager make?

11.10 How can comparative analysis of a firm's foreign markets help an international marketer with local sales force management?

11.11 Explain how a multinational firm may have an advantage over local firms in training a sales force and evaluating its performance.

11.12 Discuss the influence of a firm's level of involvement on the personal selling function in foreign markets.

11.13 Discuss the potential competitive advantages of a multinational firm in sales promotion activities in foreign markets.

11.14 How does the establishment of local operations aid a firm's promotion in foreign markets?

11.15 Review the promotional services of the U.S. Department of Commerce. Who might use the services and how?

11.16 How might a firm take advantage of international trade fairs?

11.17 Discuss the role of the Washington representative in international marketing.

11.18 What are the elements of a sound public relations program?

11.19 What is the relationship of public relations to marketing?

Endnotes

1. Caruana, Albert and Monica Abdilla. "To Dub or Not to Dub: Language Adaptation of Global Television Advertisements For A Bilingual Community," *Journal of Brand Management*, Volume 12, Issue 4, April 2005, pages 236–249.

2. "Overseas Agencies Flocking to Korea," *Wall Street Journal*, July 9, 2002, page B2.

3. "World Development Indicators, 2005," *The World Bank*, Table 5.11, "The Information Age," pages 310–313.

4. Boddewyn, J. J. "Barriers to Advertising," *International Advertiser*, May–June 1989, pages 21, 22.

5. "Health (Government Urged to Implement Anti-Smoking Laws)," *Financial Times Information;* Global News Wire, Pakistan Press International Information Services Limited, May 11, 2005.

6. "Helping Consumers Make an Informed Choice," *Financial Times Information;* Global News Wire, Asia Africa Intelligence Wire; The Indian Express Online Media Ltd.; Financial Express, December 10, 2004.

7. "Still in the Hunt," *Business Week*, July 7, 2003, pages 42–44.

8. "Sir Martin's Shopping Spree," *Business Week*, October 4, 2004, pages 102–104.

9. "Predator to Prey," *The Economist*, September 25, 2004, pages 78–79.

10. Macquin, Anne, Dominique Rouzies, and Nathalie Prime. "The Influence of Culture on Personal Selling Interactions," *Journal of Euro-Marketing*, Volume 9, Issue 4, 2000, pages 71–94.

11. "Shell: An Advertising Success Story," *Strategic Direction*, Volume 21, Issue 9, September 2005, pages 15–19.

12. Okigbo, Charles, Drew Martin, and Osabuohien P. Amienyi. "Our Ads 'R US: An Exploratory Content Analysis of American Advertisements," *Qualitative Market Research*, Volume 8, Issue 3, 2005, pages 312–326.

13. "Old Versus New" CNBC, October 21, 2005, 1:00 PM PT (http://moneycentral.msn.com/cnbc/tv).

14. View Ford advertisements from the last century on the Ford Motor Company web site (http://www.ford.com). At the time this text was written, Ford made the ads available through a screen saver available on their "Ford Centennial" portion of the site, under "memorabilia." Compare those ads with the advertisements actually built into the ads on Motor Trend's web site (http://www.motortrend.com). An article might be about the latest Jaguar model. A window (rather than a pop-up or pop-under window) appears within the text, showing a short clip of the car in motion driving up a mountainside road.

15. Six, Irina. "What Language Sells: Western Advertising In Russia," *Journal of Language for International Business*, Volume 16, Issue 2, 2005, pages 1–11.

16. Cho, Chang-Hoan and Hongsik John Cheon. "Cross-Cultural Comparisons of Interactivity on Corporate Web Sites: The United States, the United Kingdom, Japan, and South Korea," *Journal of Advertising*, Volume 34, Issue 2, Summer 2005, pages 99–116.

17. Direct Hits It Big; Sales Driven by Direct Marketing Are Outstripping Overall Sales in the U.S., Attracting the Welcome Attention of C-Level Executives," *B to B*, October 10, 2005, page 29.

18. "500 Top Email Marketers Swap Ideas and Expertise at ExactTarget Global Conference: Five Customers Honored With ExactExcellence Awards," Business Wire, September 28, 2005.

19. "Long-Term Trends in the European Advertising Market," *International Journal of Marketing*, Volume 20, 2001, pages 545–547.

20. "Global Press Ad Trends," *International Journal of Advertising*, Volume 21, 2002, pages 551–553.

21. "WPP Chief Warns of 'Two-Speed' Advertising Industry," *Daily Telegraph*, Saturday, August 27, 2005, page 33.

22. Time Warner Corporate web site (http://www.timewarner.com/corp/aboutus/our_company.html); accessed November 9, 2005; "AOL to Buy Leading Blog Company," BBC News (http://news.bbc.co.uk/go/pr/fr/-/1/hi/business/4318732.stm), October 7, 2005; accessed November 10, 2005.

23. "The Unmeasurable," *PR Week*, Media Monitoring, September 23, 2005, page 25.

24. "Interim Online Ad Measures," *New Media Age*, September 22, 2005, page 14.

25. "A New TV Ratings Method: Bag Sample, Take Census," *Adweek*, July 18, 2005.

26. Fruchter, Gila E. and Shlomo Kalish. "Dynamic Promotional Budgeting and Media Allocation," *European Journal of Operational Research*, Volume 111, Issue 1, November 16, 1998, pages 15–27.

27. Yoo, Boonghee and Rujirutana Mandhachitara. "Estimating Advertising Effects on Sales in a Competitive Setting," *Journal of Advertising Research*, Volume 43, Issue 3, September 2003, pages 310–321.

28. Vancil, Richard C. "Marketing Budgets Are Earned, Not Granted," *B to B*, Volume 90, Issue 4, April 4, 2005, page 36.

29. Terpstra, Vern and Lloyd Russow. *International Dimensions of Marketing*, 1999, Mason, OH: South-Western College Publishing, page 16. (Adapted from Morelli, Laura. "Writing for a Global Audience," *Marketing News*, Volume 32, Issue 17, August 17, 1998).

30. Roman, Sergio and Salvador Ruiz. "A Comparative Analysis of Sales Training in Europe: Implications for International Sales Negotiations," *International Marketing Review*, Volume 20, Issue 3, 2003, pages 304–327.

31. Honeycutt, Earl D. Jr., John B. Ford, Robert A. Lupton, and Theresa B. Flaherty. "Selecting and Training the International Sales Force: Comparison of China and Slovakia," *Industrial Marketing Management*, Volume 28, Issue 6, November 1999, pages 627–636.

32. Darmon, Rene Y. "Controlling Sales Force Turnover Costs Through Optimal Recruiting and Training Policies," *European Journal of Operational Research*, Volume 154, Issue 1, April 1, 2004, pages 291–328.

33. Ingram, Thomas N., Thomas R. Day, and George H. Lucas, Jr. "Dealing With Global Intermediaries: Guidelines for Sales Managers," *Journal of Global Marketing*, Volume 5, Issue 4, 1992, pages 65–80.

34. Laroche, Michel, Maria Kalamas, and Qinchao Huang. "Effects of Coupons on Brand Categorization and Choice of Fast Foods in China," *Journal of Business Research*, Volume 58, Issue 5, May 2005, pages 674–675.

35. "Coupons and Samples 'Key' to E-Marketing," *Marketing Week*, January 27, 2005. page 17.

36. "Vouchers: Coupons Can Be Cutting-Edge," *Marketing Week*, June 23, 2005, page 45.

37. Best, Jeanette. "Online Coupons: An Engaging Idea," *Brandweek*, Volume 46, Issue 18, May 2, 2005, page 20.

38. "Everyone Agrees Singles Night Is a Good Way to 'Drive Sales,'" *Business and Industry, MMR*, Volume 21, Issue 20, December 13, 2004, page 110.

39. "The Brand You Save: Improving the Brand Is Cheaper Than Watching It Suffer a Slow Death," *Marketing Management*, Volume 13, Issue 3, May 2004, page 29.

40. George, John. "Tylenol Proves Resilient as It Adapts and Turns 50," *Philadelphia Business Journal*, November 6, 2005 (http://msnbc.msn.com/id/9954166); accessed November 11, 2005.

41. Lee, Suman. "The Emergence of Global Public and International Public Relations," *Public Relations Quarterly*, Volume 50, Issue 2, Summer 2005, pages 14–17.

Further Readings

Asugman, Gulden, Jean Johnson, and James McCullough. "The Role of After-Sales Service in International Marketing," *Journal of International Marketing*, Volume 5, Issue 4, 1997, pages 11–28.

Bang, Hae-Kyong, Mary Anne Raymond, Charles R. Taylor, and Young Sook Moon. "A Comparison of Service Quality Dimensions Conveyed in Advertisements for Service Providers in the USA and Korea: A Content Analysis," *International Marketing Review*, Volume 22, Issue 3, 2005, pages 309–326.

Dubinsky, Alan, J. and Abdalla Hanafg. "The Super Sales Force—Politicians in the World Market," *Journal of International Marketing*, Volume 4, Issue 3, 1996, pages 73–87.

Engle, Robert L. and Michael L. Barnes. "Sales Force Automation Usage, Effectiveness, and Cost-Benefit in Germany, England, and the United States," *Journal of Business & Industrial Marketing*, Volume 15, Issue 4, 2000, pages 216–240.

Grein, Andreas and Robert Ducoffe. "Strategic Responses to Market Globalisation among Advertising Agencies," *International Journal of Advertising*, Volume 17, Issue 3, 2003, pages 301–319.

Ha, Louisa. "Limitations and Strengths of Pan-Asian Advertising Media: A Review for International Advertisers," *International Journal of Advertising*, Volume 16, Issue 2, 1997, pages 148–163.

Hamill, Jim. "The Internet and International Marketing," *International Marketing Review*, Volume 14, Issue 5, 1997, pages 300–322.

Harker, Debra. "Analysis of Advertising Regulation in Five Countries," *International Marketing Review*, Volume 15, Issue 2, 1998, pages 101–118.

"Intel Accepts FTC's Cease-and-Desist Order in Japan," *Kyodo News International*, Friday, April 1, 2005.

"Internet Continues to Reshape Direct Marketing," *B to B*, October 10, 2005, page 30.

Mintu-Wimsatt, Alma and Jule B. Gassenheimer. "The Problem Solving Approach of International Salespeople: The Experience Effect," *Journal of Personal Selling & Sales Management*, Volume 24, Issue 1, 2004, pages 19–26.

Serringhaus, Rolf and Philip J. Rosson. "Management and Performance of International Trade Fair Exhibitors," *International Marketing Review*, Volume 15, Issue 5, 1998, pages 398–412.

Stafford, Marla Royne. "International Services Advertising (ISA): Defining the Domain

and Reviewing the Literature," *Journal of Advertising*, Volume 34, Issue 1, Spring 2005, pages 65–86.

Taylor, Charles R. "Moving International Advertising Research Forward: A New

Research Agenda," *Journal of Advertising*, Volume 34, Issue 1, Spring 2005, pages 7–16.

Thomas, Amos Owen. "Advertising to the Masses without Mass Media," *Journal of Global Marketing*, Volume 9, Issue 4, 1996, pages 75–88.

Whitelock, Jeryl and Jean-Christophe Rey. "Cross Cultural Advertising in Europe," *International Marketing Review*, Volume 15, Issue 4, 1998, pages 257–276.

"WPP Deal Puts Pressure on Havas." *Wall Street Journal*, Tuesday September, 2004. page B14.

Zalka, Lori, Meredith Downes, and Karen Paul. "Measuring Consumer Sensitivity to Corporate Social Performance across Cultures," *Journal of Global Marketing*, Volume 11, Issue 1, 1997, pages 29–42.

Zou, Shaoming. "Contributions to International Advertising Research:

Assessment of the Literature between 1990 and 2002," *Journal of Advertising*, Volume 34, Issue 1, Spring 2005, pages 99–110.

Zugelder, Michael T., Theresa B. Flaherty, and James P. Johnson. "Legal Issues Associated with International Internet Marketing," *International Marketing Review*, Volume 17, Issue 3, 2000, pages 253–270.

Recommended Web Sites

American Marketing Association (goes far beyond American borders). The association provides research, statistics, and networking for its members (http://www.marketingpower.com).

Federation of European Direct and Interactive Marketing (FEDMA) is a European direct marketing association that represents users, service providers, and media/carriers of direct marketing (http://www.fedma.org).

International Advertising Association. See especially the list of affiliated organizational members for advertising associations around the globe (http://www.iaaglobal.org).

Organisation for Economic Co-operation and Development; Observatory on Ethics Codes and Codes of Conduct in OECD Countries (http://www.oecd.org/document/12/0,2340,en_2649_34135_35532108_1_1_1,00.html).

POPAI is a nonprofit retail promotion association that provides industry information, performs market research, and provides a global network of firms involved in developing and manufacturing retail displays (http://www.popai.com/AM).

Web Marketing Today provides information and links to resources about Internet marketing (http://www.wilsonweb.com/research).

World Association of Internet Marketing provides information about Internet marketing (http://www.waim.org).

Case 11.1

NESTLÉ: MORE TROUBLE IN THE BABY MARKET

On October 12, 1988, the International Organization of Consumers Unions (IOCU) called for a renewal of the boycott against Nestlé, a Swiss firm. The boycott had been called in 1977 because of the deaths of babies in developing countries that were alleged to be related to the use of infant formula and reported unethical marketing practices. In 2000, abysmal sales for Nestlé's snack and juice products for children led to the products' withdrawal from the UK market; the 25-year-old boycott was blamed for the poor sales.

Shortly after the boycott was organized, Nestlé changed its marketing practices for infant formula, working with the industry and the WHO on a code for marketing infant formula and forming a prestigious committee to investigate the claims and advise Nestlé. By 1984, the company was perceived as a leading firm in support of the WHO code and the boycott was dropped.

Calls for a renewed boycott arose because some observers claimed that Nestlé and other firms were breaking the spirit of the code by supplying large amounts of free formula to hospitals in developing countries, with the result that too many mothers became dependent on formula and lost the ability to nurse their babies. Nestlé's response was that the WHO code allows for free distribution of supplies to hospitals that request it and that the amounts supplied were not excessive.

Nestlé in the U.S. Baby Market

The U.S. market for infant formula amounts to over $1.6 billion; and until 1988, none of it belonged to Nestlé. (Abbott and Bristol-Myers had 90 percent of the market between them.) In June 1988 Nestlé introduced Good Start H.A., which it said could prevent or reduce fussiness, sleeplessness, colic, rash, and other worrisome ailments because it was hypoallergenic—which the labels indicated in bold type. Carnation, Nestlé's U.S. subsidiary, introduced the product and called it "a medical breakthrough."

The market entry strategy for Good Start H.A. included the product differentiation feature of being hypoallergenic while having a taste similar to other infant formula products. By contrast, Nutramigen, another hypoallergenic product, had a distinctive, less pleasant taste. Good Start H.A. was priced competitively with the leading infant formula brands, although Bristol-Myers' hypoallergenic Nutramigen, a niche product, cost twice as much as Good Start H.A. To further speed market entry, Carnation broke with industry practice and publicized the hypoallergenic feature directly to parents without waiting for pediatricians to recommend it.

About three months after the introduction of Good Start H.A., there were scattered reports of severe reactions. Some mothers of severely milk-allergic babies tried the formula and reported that their babies vomited violently and went limp. Nestlé's competitors helped to publicize those incidents. Some leading pediatricians criticized Nestlé's marketing as misleading, and the American Academy of Pediatrics strongly protested against advertising directly to mothers and bypassing physicians. James Strain, director of the academy, said, "These ailments (fussiness, colic, etc.) happen to 90 percent of all babies and aren't really symptoms of anything. The advertising just raises the level of anxiety in mothers about something being wrong with their babies." One mother, Elizabeth Strickler, was interviewed by The Wall Street Journal.[1] Because her son, Zachary, hadn't tolerated other formulas well, she was eager to try Good Start H.A. After two weeks of use, Zachary experienced severe vomiting. She discontinued usage; but for two months, she had to feed him Maalox to soothe his gastrointestinal tract. "If you call something hypoallergenic, that means a lot to me," she said. "I thought it was the best thing, and that's why I bought it."

William Spivak, pediatrician and Mrs. Strickler's doctor, said, "My concern is that long after physicians realize that this formula isn't as hypoallergenic as claimed, parents with milk-allergic babies will be grabbing it off the shelf because of its attractive hypoallergenic labeling, and thereby exposing their babies to a potentially dangerous formula without physician supervision." Other pediatricians pointed out that while Good Start was easier to digest than ordinary milk-based formulas, it wasn't mild enough for the approximately 2 percent of babies who, like Zachary, were severely allergic to cows' milk. The mothers of those babies were most likely to be attracted by the hypoallergenic claim.

Good Start had received preliminary approval of the FDA before introductory marketing, but the FDA had asked for more data backing up the formula's extra claims that it could reduce allergies. After the severe reactions were reported, the FDA began a new investigation of the company's claims as well as of the six reports of severe reactions.

Following the widespread publicity given to the cases of severe reactions to the Good Start formula, several state attorneys general also began an investigation of Nestlé's Good Start marketing. The company had to submit copies of Good Start's print, radio, and TV advertising that had appeared in California, New York, and Texas. It also had to provide scientific studies supporting the formula's health and nutrition claims as well as studies showing consumer perception of the term *hypoallergenic*.

Robert Roth, an assistant attorney general in New York, said, "This case is a little unusual in that it involves the health of infants. We are pursuing it more urgently than we would a matter which is purely economic."[2]

In responding to the publicity and the criticisms, Nestlé and Carnation pointed out that all formulas have isolated cases of bad reactions. They argued that severe reactions to Good Start resulted from its misuse with highly milk-allergic babies. Pierre Guesry, a Nestlé vice president in Switzerland, said, "I don't understand why our product should work in 100 percent of cases. If we wanted to say it was foolproof, we would have called it allergy-free. We call it hypo- or less-allergenic."

A Product from Europe

Nestlé, which has the largest share of the infant formula market outside the United States, had introduced Beba H.A., a version of Good Start H.A., in Germany two years before bringing it to the U.S. market. While mothers are in the hospital after giving birth, Nestlé supplies them with information about hypoallergenic formulas and infant allergies. It doesn't name the company or the product, but Beba H.A. is the only major hypoallergenic brand available. Other formula makers also distribute information to mothers, but some critics say Nestlé goes too far. Judith Phillipoa of the Geneva Infant Feeding Association, an anti-Nestlé activist group, said, "In Europe, Nestlé is blowing up the allergy problem as a way of creating demand for their product. Now they're exporting this system to the United States."

Pierre Guesry said that Good Start was introduced in the United States because "we felt American babies should have the same rights to a good formula as German, Belgian, or French babies." He pointed out that no problems were reported in Europe as occurred in the United States and that most of the 40,000 U.S. babies who had tried Good Start had no problems with it.

Nestlé Responds

Nestlé's first response to the publicity and criticism was to remove the term *hypoallergenic* from the front of the can where it had been displayed in large type. Some critics were not satisfied because H.A. was still in the product name—Good Start H.A.—and *hypoallergenic* was in the fine print on the back of the can. Also, Good Start was still advertised in medical journals as a "breakthrough hypoallergenic infant formula."[3]

In July 1989, Nestlé reached a settlement with nine states' attorneys general about its Good Start marketing. The agreement specified that (1) Carnation could not use the word *hypoallergenic* in advertising Good Start, (2) it could not use expert endorsers that had been paid by the company, and (3) it could not make claims that were not scientifically supported. Carnation also agreed to pay $90,000 to cover the costs of the investigation.[4]

Nestlé also hired Ogilvy & Mather's public relations unit to help its relations with the FDA and the other publics involved. Among Ogilvy's proposals were these:

1. Get people into the groups organizing and supporting the boycott. This was meant to be an early warning system for Nestlé.
2. Create a Nestlé positive image campaign—a daily 12-minute news program to reach 8,000 high schools. This was not to advertise, but to buy public service time such as a "Nestlé News Network."
3. Create a Carnation image campaign to inoculate the Nestlé subsidiary from any negative effects of the boycott.

The game plan included a Carnation National Homework Help Line and a foster care fund for children with AIDS.

Nestlé has a special section on its web site devoted to public relations on this topic and on which its Infant Formula Policy is posted:

Breastfeeding is best for babies. Chemist Henri Nestlé stated this in his Treatise on Nutrition soon after founding our company in 1867, and it is still true today.

The company does:
- *encourage and support exclusive breastfeeding as the best choice for babies during the first months of life*
- *warn mothers of the consequences of incorrect or inappropriate use of infant formula*
- *believe that there is a legitimate market for infant formula 3 when a safe alternative to breast milk is needed*

- *believe that parents have the right to choose how their babies are to be fed on the basis of adequate and objective information*
- *comply with both the letter and the spirit of the World Health Organization's International Code of Marketing of Breast Milk Substitutes*
- *support efforts by governments to implement the International Code through legislation, regulation, or other appropriate measures*

The company does not:
- *advertise infant formula to the public*
- *permit staff whose responsibilities include the marketing of infant formula to make direct contact with mothers, except in response to consumer complaints*
- *give incentives to its staff based on infant formula sales*
- *use pictures of babies on its infant formula packs*
- *distribute free infant formula samples to mothers*
- *give financial or material incentives to health professionals for the purpose of promoting infant formula*
- *allow educational material relating to the use of infant formula to be displayed publicly in hospitals and clinics*
- *donate free infant formula for use by healthy new born babies except in exceptional social cases (e.g. where the government policy allows manufacturers to respond to a specific medical request, for example if the mother dies in child birth)*

Furthermore, the company includes the following statements: Nestlé will take disciplinary measures against any Nestlé personnel who deliberately violates this policy. Nestlé invites government officials, health professionals, and consumers, to draw to its attention any Nestlé infant formula marketing practices in developing countries which they consider are not in conformity with the above commitment.

QUESTIONS AND RESEARCH

1. Identify in some detail and evaluate Nestlé's marketing strategy (the four Ps) for entering the U.S. infant formula market.

2. Suggest a program for Nestlé to deal with its public relations problems, for example, the renewed boycott and the negative publicity about Good Start. Would you use the Ogilvy & Mather recommendations? Explain.

Sources: Nestllé web site (http://www.nestle.com/Our_Responsibility/Infant_Formula/Charter/The+Charter.htm); 1 *Wall Street Journal*, February 16, 1989, A1; 2 *Wall Street Journal*, February 24, 1989, B6; 3 *Wall Street Journal*, March 13, 1989, B6; 4 *Wall Street Journal*, July 7, 1989, B4; "Nestle's New Milk Run Reignites Old Debate," *Marketing Week*, June 27, 2002, page 20.

Case 11.2

EBERHARD FABER'S SPECIAL FORMS OF PROMOTION

The board of directors of Eberhard Faber, Inc., was discussing the matter of establishing a joint venture in a third world country. The joint venture was to supply the know-how to enable a local pencil company there to expand and improve its operations and to use Eberhard Faber's name. In return, Eberhard Faber would receive 35 percent equity of the local company, which could be expected to provide dividend income in the years ahead. However, no cash was required of Eberhard Faber for the equity position. The deal also envisaged that Eberhard Faber would supply equipment for the expected venture over a five-year period at a pretty good profit. After two years' effort, the deal was consummated in principle. Only the approval of the board was lacking.

The Company

Eberhard Faber, Inc., was founded in 1849 by the original Eberhard Faber. It is known for high-quality pencils as well as modeling (e.g., clay) and painting supplies. The company does business in many countries. In addition to the U.S. operation based in Wilkes-Barre, Pennsylvania, it had wholly owned subsidiaries in Canada and Germany and joint ventures in Venezuela and Colombia. There were also licensees using its name and know-how in Argentina, Brazil, Central America, Peru, Syria, and the Philippines. Eberhard Faber's board of directors has been on record for several years in favor of further expansion into foreign markets.

Following the board's policy of international growth, a substantial contract that included know-how for a factory to make Eberhard Faber products was signed with the Syrian government. Soon after, there was an expansion of the licensing agreement in Brazil. The proposed joint venture was the next step in this program of international development.

The company had a good reputation, both for product quality and business dealings. Recently, for example, it refused to ship large quantities of its newest pen because the quality didn't meet its standards—even though the company knew that its customers would accept the merchandise. The board of directors was concerned about the company's reputation.

The Board Meeting

After discussing the other major agenda items, Eberhard Faber, chairman and CEO, introduced the proposal for the joint venture with a ten-minute summary of the conditions of the deal. He explained that it would increase the year's budgeted profit by more than one-quarter. In addition, he mentioned that the local pencil company under consideration was paying off the government of its country in order to do business. Although the laws of the country prohibited bribery, it was a common and accepted practice there. Eberhard Faber, Inc., however, would be a minority shareholder in the venture; so there seemed to be no legal exposure. (Later it was confirmed by legal counsel that there was no legal exposure, and the company had informal advice from the IRS that its concern was primarily with U.S.-controlled companies that made illegal payoffs and deductions.)

A number of board members insisted that the problem was not the legal exposure but the ethics of taking an equity position in a company that was paying off its country's government. Faber argued, however, that aside from the rights and wrongs of payoffs in a country where they were common practice, the board's own company would be doing no paying off. Furthermore, it could not hope to change the practices of another company in which it held only a minority stock interest. Faber also said, "Don't you realize that if we adopt this type of policy, we'll be shut out of half the world? Don't you realize that our competition in Europe, if not the United States, won't have any such ethical qualms and will take over this opportunity in a flash, shutting us out of this market permanently? Whatever happened to our policy of international expansion?"

QUESTIONS AND RESEARCH

1. If you were a board member, what would your decision be? Why?

2. What guidelines for international business expansion would you suggest for Eberhard Faber, Inc.?

CHAPTER 12

Pricing in International Markets

This chapter examines price setting in international markets. International pricing is complex. It is influenced by differences in consumer behavior across markets, strategic goals, competitive response, a firm's cost structure and profit targets, and government regulation. Fluctuations in exchange rate add spice to the mixture.

Pricing is part of the marketing mix. Therefore, pricing decisions must be integrated with other aspects of the marketing mix. And since price is just one attribute of a product—along with quality, reliability, features, technology, service, and user satisfaction—trade-offs are necessary. A lower-priced product may offer lower quality or a less comprehensive warranty policy, for example. We will discuss such complexities of pricing in the following pages. A conceptual framework is developed for analyzing international pricing.

The main goals of this chapter are to

- Establish a framework that covers the broad principles governing international pricing. Determine the influence on pricing of foreign market variables such as competition, government, inflation, local demand, and costs.

- Discuss how a firm deals with the pressure to cut costs and prices caused by international competition and show how focusing on manufacturing location decisions and product redesign can help meet cost competition.

- Compare export prices to domestic prices. Explain why and how prices escalate in export selling. Explain how export price quotations are used in export marketing.

- Discuss how fluctuations in exchange rate challenge the export marketer. Discuss the importance of export credit and financing for successful export marketing.

- Explore the special roles and problems of transfer pricing in international marketing.

- Explore the dimensions and implications of countertrade, a sizable segment of world trade.

- Explain when and why coordinating prices is necessary in international marketing, and describe how it is done. Define gray markets and explain how to deal with them.

Factors in International Pricing

Several factors are important in international pricing:

- Setting strategic objectives for a market and monitoring their influence on pricing
- Monitoring price-setting behavior by competitors and assessing their strategic objectives
- Evaluating consumers' ability to buy in the various country markets
- Relating price to a firm's costs and profit goals
- Understanding the product-specific factors, including the product life cycle stage, that affect pricing. Generally, prices are reduced on mature products as they become more commodity-like and face increased competition.
- Recognizing differences in the country environment and their role in governing prices in each national market—factors such as differences in the legal and regulatory environment, the volatility of foreign exchange rates, market structure (especially distribution channels), and competitive environment.

Each of those differences influences a firm's price-setting behavior in its markets.[1] Table 12-1 illustrates the framework.

Because foreign market pricing is pricing for a national market, general pricing considerations are also relevant. Those considerations include pricing over the product life cycle, product-line pricing, first-time purchasers versus repeat sales, pricing to intermediaries, and market skimming versus market penetration strategies. However, because the markets are international, prices may need to be adapted to local market conditions and fluctuations in exchange rate. An additional consideration is that of coordinating pricing in multiple foreign markets, particularly choosing between standardizing prices and charging different prices in different markets.

Firm-Level Factors

Price, Competition, and Strategic Objectives

Pricing affects realized demand; hence, pricing is an influential tool in gaining market share. Or thinking in reverse, competitive objectives toward gaining market share determine pricing. Therefore, as market share and competitive positions differ from country to country, so do prices. A research study comparing U.S. and Korean price-setting practices considered market conditions and the importance of competitive position versus cost of goods sold in determining price. The study also considered how firm characteristics and export market characteristics, together with cost complexity, influenced pricing and, thus, performance. These characteristics, in turn, influenced the choice of alternative pricing – approached as dynamic pricing, marginal cost pricing, contribution margin pricing, and rigid cost-plus pricing. U.S. firms seem to place priority on cost and profit factors when setting price, while Korean firms appear more focused on pricing competitively. The study suggests that Korean firms seek market penetration in setting prices, while U.S. firms may be setting prices to emphasize contribution from export markets.[2]

Note that competitive objectives do not always demand that prices be lowered. In an oligopolistic environment with few competitors, for example, a company may attempt to head off ruinous price cutting by signaling its intent to keep prices steady or even raise them. A case in point is an airline that files a fare increase in a computer reservation system to see if its competitors raise prices, too. That signaling is part of the role prices play in affecting competitive position.

The strength of competition and a firm's objectives interact in determining how the firm sets its international prices. There are several types of pricing strategies:

- *Setting low prices that result in low margins.* The firm expects that elasticity of demand will result in increased volume so that overall contribution from the product (volume in units x margin per unit) is sufficient to meet profit and contribution targets for the product or product line. If the firm already has a large installed base and enjoys scale economies, this strategy hinders the competition from becoming strong.
- *Acting as price taker.* Stronger competitors set prices, and the firm follows and matches the price leader to the extent that it is capable of doing so. Its long-term viability in that product line is not endangered.
- *Pricing at a premium to the market.* The firm avoids the commodity end of the market and caters to niche segments, where a higher price is acceptable to customers in return for features and product characteristics that they need and want.
- *Pricing on a cost-plus basis.* Overall costs and a desired profit margin determine the level of prices. In the long run, prices should cover costs to yield a reasonable return on investment. Hence, in making a long-term decision such as whether to proceed with a new product proposal, the cost-plus pricing approach may play a role; that is, it may determine at what level prices should be set in order to earn a given rate of return (often the hurdle rate). In prac-

Table 12-1. Framework for International Pricing Strategy

Firm-Level Factors

Strategic Objectives : Market Share, Profits
Marketing Mix Elements: Segmentation, Product Positioning
                    Cost Structure:
Fixed Costs: Amortization of R&D, Manufacturing and Marketing
Fixed Costs
Manufacturing Costs: Productivity, Experience Curve, Scale Economies
Marketing and Related Costs: Inventory Levels, Promotion and Service
Shipping/Distance Costs:
Firm's Target Price
Forecasted Sales Volume, Cost Allocation
Transfer Pricing

Market-Specific Factors

Consumers
Income Levels, Ability to Buy, Information Seeking, Global
Account Management
Government Intervention
As Buyer: Countertrade Demands, Price and Profit Controls,
Transfer Price Controls, Barriers to Trade, Quotas, Tariffs,
Non-tariff Barriers, Subsidies
Distribution Channels
Multiple Channels and Price Differentiation, Channel Control,
Commission Structure
Local Advertising and Promotions: Local Cooperative Advertising
Macroeconomic Factors : Business Cycle Stage, Inflation
Competition:
Market Share Distribution, Competitive Goals
Price-Cutting
Cross-Subsidization of Markets
Price Signaling
Gray Markets : Product Flow between Markets

Effects of Exchange Rate
F/x volatility and impact on prices
Currency of Quote
S-T Hedging
Long-Term Impacts: Sourcing Reassessment

Product-Specific Factors

Local Demand: Elasticities, Cyclicality
Life Cycle Stage
Product Adaptation Costs
Substitutes
Other Product Attributes : Quality, Delivery, Service
Place in Product Line
Financing:
    Terms, Period, Interest Rate Subsidies
Price Unbundling : What Is Included in Price

International Market Price-setting: Decision Choices

Differential versus one global price

Market-based pricing
Cost-based pricing

Extent of exchange rate impact: pass-through versus dampening

Outsourcing and shift to low-cost manufacturing

Product redesign to lower costs

Product adaptation to balance price and product attributes

Product families: low to high end

Transfer price setting and administration

Focus on ownership costs over product life

Pricing for multinational clients Global account management policies

Client-specific pricing Discounting

Designing price band cafeteria pricing

Differential pricing by channel based on value-added services; volume discounts

Initiating countertrade and leasing

tice, this approach is possible only in industries with limited competition, such as regulated utilities. International long-distance rates come to mind, with the total market split between a few providers. Even in that instance, however, international call-back systems undercut the "cartel" price and force prices to respond to competition.

Firms can be clustered into groups by their strategic orientation that governs price setting. Organizational factors, venture-related factors, export market, and performance variables all determine the groups. Strategic orientation can have a market-based focus (on competition and demand) or a cost-based focus. When considerable customer segmentation exists, price differentiation is possible. Each segment can receive customized products suited to its needs, with additional value coming from tailoring that allows differential (higher) prices to be charged. A research study used factor analysis to derive five pricing dimensions as follows:

1. Nonprice competition
2. Focus on market intelligence
3. Price adaptation (a flexible approach, price differentiation across segments)
4. Cost-plus focus (rigid or variable-cost plus contribution margin)

5. Focus on new competition (sensitive to new competitive entry and pricing actions)

In studying how firms used those five dimensions to set their export prices, four clusters emerge. That is, based on their price-setting behavior, firms seem to fall into four types:

1. Highly centralized, experienced exporters: have standardized products, use a cost-plus approach, gather little marketing intelligence
2. Highly decentralized, experienced exporters: operate in less competitive export markets, offer differentiated products, delegate price setting to local managers, gather export market intelligence, and monitor new entrants
(The first two clusters are satisfied with their profitability.)
3. Less committed beginners: gather market intelligence, do not rely on cost-plus pricing, operate in moderately competitive markets
4. Experienced yet poor performers: are less successful, have little knowledge of their export markets

Figure 12-1 summarizes the price-setting behavior and related characteristics of those four clusters of firms.

Figure 12-1. Profiles of Firms and Their Export Pricing

Cluster	Organizational Characteristics	Export Market Environment	Strategic Orientations Derived from Stage 3 Analysis	Export Performance Outcomes
1 Highly centralized, experienced exporters (31%)	• Long experience in exporting • Decision making is centralized • High degree of commitment	• Operate in intensely competitive export markets	• Feature standardized products • Rely on cost-plus approach • Gather little market intelligence • Not concerned about new entrants	• Highly profitable • Consider the venture successful
4 Highly decentralized, experienced exporters (17%)	• Fairly experienced in exporting • Decision making is highly decentralized • High degree of commitment	• Operate in export markets not considered intensely competitive	• Feature differentiated products • In spite of operating in more friendly environments, gather much market intelligence and monitor new entrants • Avoid cost-plus approach	• Highly profitable • Consider the venture successful
2 Less committed beginners (23%)	• New-to-export companies • Low degree of commitment	• Operate in moderately competitive export markets	• Feature standardized products • Gather much market intelligence • Avoid cost-plus approach • Believe price affects performance	• Less profitable • Consider the venture not successful
3 Experienced, yet poor performers (29%)	• Fairly experienced to exporting • Reasonably committed	• Operate in moderately competitive export markets	• Feature differentiated products • Little emphasis on market intelligence and market segmentation • Avoid use of cost-plus approach • Believe price does not affect performance	• Less profitable • Consider the venture not successful

Source: S. Tamer Cavusgil, Kwong Chan, and Chun Zhang, "Strategic Orientations in Export Pricing: A Clustering Approach to Create Firm Taxonomies,: *Journal of International Marketing*, Volume 11, Number 1, 2003, pages 47–72.

The important point is that that there is no best way to set export prices to achieve export success. Multiple approaches can and should be used depending on the context.[3]

Firms that are faced with competitive price cuts may need to respond with a coordinated strategy in which pricing decisions are only one aspect of an overall marketing mix. In other words, lower prices alone are not the answer. Procter & Gamble, the giant U.S. manufacturer of products such as soap, detergent, shampoo, and food, had a minor presence in India while it focused on selling brand-name, higher-priced products in the U.S. and European markets. As India's economy showed sustained economic growth and the number of middle-class families began to increase, Procter & Gamble wanted to develop a stronger presence and market share there. Its initial strategy was to lower prices sharply (for example, cutting the prices of its detergent in half). However, it had to cope with a vigorous response from entrenched market leaders such as Unilever.

Unilever's subsidiary, Hindustan Lever, matched Procter & Gamble's price cuts in detergents and lowered its shampoo prices, as well. In addition, Hindustan Lever launched products suited to Indian consumer's needs, such as a cleaning powder that worked well with two buckets of water rather than the normal four, an important issue in a country in which running water is scarce in large cities. Hindustan Lever pioneered the use of small, affordable packets, sachets, of detergent, shampoo, and toothpaste, which could sell for as little as a penny apiece. The sachets provided a means for introducing Unilever products to low-income consumers across India.

Lever also enjoys a vast distribution system in India, built over many decades of Indian operations. It employs 20,000 wholesalers and distributors, who may, at times, make deliveries by bicycle. It reaches 2.5 million retail outlets across India in small, remote cities and rural areas. It began employing women, over 6,000 of them, to sell Unilever products door-to-door, planning to expand that sales force to 25,000 within two years. (Procter & Gamble has only about one-third the number of distribution points.) Lever also has a scale economy advantage with low manufacturing costs since it is ten times larger than Procter & Gamble in India, with $2.2 billion in Indian sales. Unilever's advertising is localized, with heavy use of Indian "Bollywood" stars. However, as a large global multinational, Procter & Gamble has the means to invest in India and to develop a similar marketing mix breadth adapted to Indian conditions. Procter & Gamble has no choice if it wants to develop a significant position in an Indian market expected to have 300 million middle-class consumers by about 2015, with a forecasted market for consumer goods (soap, detergent, and snack foods) of about $20 billion.[4]

In summary, the intensity of competition determines prices. Differentiating a product to command a higher price is more of a strategic positioning approach to reduce competition in order to gain greater leeway in setting prices.

MANUFACTURING COSTS

When products sold in a market are produced there, determining manufacturing costs is no problem. Questions arise, however, when a market is served by other production sources: How should fixed R&D and product development costs be allocated? If a firm has several plants, which plant's costs should be used? Should variable or full cost be used? What does "full cost" mean for a product coming from a plant in another country; that is, what portion of that country's costs should be allocated? Obviously, some costs, such as local advertising and marketing research, do not apply to products sold in another country.

MARKETING COSTS

Distribution and marketing costs also must be covered in the foreign market price. Because tariffs can be an important part of delivered cost, a subsidiary tends to prefer a source from a country having favorable tariff relations with its own. Thus, a subsidiary in the EU usually chooses another EU subsidiary because no tariff barriers exist.

Marketing costs in the foreign market price are generated primarily within the market by the national subsidiary. Occasionally, however, a firm incurs costs for marketing research or other services rendered by a regional division (or international division) for the subsidiary. Local marketing costs vary from one country to another. That variation derives, in part, from different product lines and company goals in each market.

SHIPPING AND TRANSPORTATION COSTS

Shipping and transportation are additional costs specific to international pricing. These added "distance" costs, if passed on as a price increment, are a deterrent to the gaining of market share in overseas markets.

The Firm's Costs and Profits: Target Pricing and Product Development

One way to be responsive to consumers' ability to buy is to use a target price approach. This approach was implemented by Canon in developing a personal copier for under $1,000. The company's decision to use the target price approach guided the entire product-development process. (See Chapter 10.) Such target pricing is a long-term pricing strategy because it envisions modulating the entire design, procurement, and manufacturing process in order to meet the target price. Implicit in the idea of a target price is the notion that the price is for a product for a certain market segment and that the product can achieve long-term profitability at the target price.

Another example of using target pricing comes from Japan's Olympus Optical Co., which made high-quality single-lens reflex cameras (SLRs). The market for SLRs began to erode as digital and compact cameras with auto-focus, built-in flash, and zoom lenses were sold at attractive prices. Olympus realized that the new generation of digital and compact cameras was determining what price consumers were willing to pay for cameras. Olympus also knew that it had to offer its cameras at that target price if it wanted to remain competitive and obtain market share. Working backward from the target price, Olympus developed (1) a set of features prioritized from must-have to nice-to-have; (2) the components and subassemblies needed to build such a camera; and (3) eventually, the target costs that had to be attained to sell the camera at the target price, allow dealer and distributor margins, and still have a satisfactory margin left over for the company. That approach is iterative, and products cannot always be designed to meet both the target price and the desired functionality at an acceptable cost. Olympus's efforts, however, demonstrate an approach to integrating product development, pricing, and targeted market share when product cycles are fairly short—about one year for a digital camera model.[5]

Figure 12-2 illustrates how a target-pricing approach interacts with product design and manufacturing to iteratively set product functionality and features so that target prices can be met. If careful study shows that target prices may have to be adjusted upward, the firm can then rethink whether satisfactory markets exist at the new target price. If not, it may consider canceling the particular product development effort.

Market-Specific Factors

Consumer's Ability to Buy

Incomes, cultural habits, and consumer preferences differ from country to country. Thus, for the same price in two different country markets, there may be demand for different amounts of products. The importance of pricing is seen in General Motor's attempt to capture minivan market share in China. A minivan priced at $5,000, the Wuling Sunshine, was manufactured in a joint venture (34 percent owned by General Motors) with SAIC (Shanghai Automotive Industry Corporation, 50.1 percent) and Liuzhou Wuling Automotive Company, (15.9 percent). The car got 43 mpg in city driving. The low price was made possible by using less powerful engines (one-fourth the horsepower of U.S. minivans), leading to weaker acceleration and a top speed of 80 mph, as well as thinner seats. Customers were mainly small businessmen who used the minivan to carry goods and transport their families. The Chinese government may pass regulation forcing better fuel utilization; thus, General Motors plays to the nation-

Figure 12-2. Target Pricing and Product Development

al interest. Instead of using robots, the Chinese factory uses many workers earning $60 a month—above-average wages for the region.[6]

However, shoppers in country markets that lack price competition and cut-priced distribution channels, for example, may not have formed the habit of comparing prices when shopping or waiting for sales when making large purchases.

GOVERNMENT

Governments also influence a firm's pricing in a variety of ways. When buyers choose winning bidders on government contracts, governments can dictate the acceptable price. Some influence is exerted via tariffs, non-tariff barriers, quotas, taxes, and competition policy. Some governments have specific legislation, such as that governing resale price maintenance or restraint of trade. Governments also have the power to control prices directly if they so choose, and they may use their power in varying degrees. In the United States, public utility pricing has been regulated and price freezes have been occasionally employed. Other governments also regulate specific prices (or occasionally all prices) in their countries.

In general, the purpose of price controls is to limit price increases. In such an environment, a manufacturer generally applies for a price increase with data to support the request (increased costs of energy or materials, higher wages, etc.). If the request is approved, a waiting period ensues before the price can be raised. Usually, a firm is limited to how frequently it can apply for a price increase.

Government controls obviously limit a firm's freedom in setting prices. They raise the cost of price administration by requiring more record keeping and management time. Such controls also may result in lower prices and less frequent price increases. The government limit to approved price increases may, in fact, be quite arbitrary. However, the greatest challenge to a firm arises when its request for a price increase is denied. A firm's inability to raise prices in an inflationary environment threatens its very survival.

Government price controls are often limited to select product groups. Some products are perceived as being more strategic or sensitive and are more susceptible to government regulation. Pharmaceuticals have the unenviable position of being most frequently subject to price controls. Even countries that don't control other prices usually control pharmaceutical prices. It is interesting to note, however, that drug firms manage to show consistently good profits.

DISTRIBUTION CHANNELS

A determinant of a firm's price to consumers in a foreign market is its distribution channels in those markets. The costs and margins of a given channel are not the same from country to country, suggesting that a channel decision may also be a pricing decision. A firm may be forced

Drug Pricing and Social Pressures

Health care accounts for about 15 percent of U.S. government spending, and health-care costs have risen at twice the rate of U.S. inflation. Controlling U.S. health-care costs, therefore, is a major national priority. Aside from economics, there is considerable social pressure against drug price increases, particularly when expensive life-saving drugs become out of reach of lower-income patients. Wellcome PLC's experience with AZT, an AIDS drug, is instructive.

Wellcome has been tagged as a corporate extortionist and AIDS profiteer by AIDS activists. Ironically, Wellcome is owned by the Wellcome Trust, a charitable organization. Initially, AZT was priced so a year's treatment cost about $8,000. As FDA tests verified the drug's efficacy and as production costs were lowered due to the experience curve and economies of scale, Wellcome began lowering the price to about $6,400 per patient per year by the end of 1989. The original research that developed AZT was done in the United States under U.S. government sponsorship—the U.S. government being one of the biggest purchasers of the drug through its Medicaid program.

Although activists want the drug price lowered and Congress held hearings, experts from the National Cancer Institute suggested that price control could be best achieved through competition. As competitors develop alternatives to AZT, market pressures could bring lower prices.

Sandoz, the Swiss drug firm, faced similar price control pressures over its schizophrenia treatment drug, Clorazil. Sandoz decided to market the drug only when tied to mandatory weekly blood tests performed by a company named Caremark, under contract with Sandoz. Annual patient costs approached nearly $9,000. As a result of the high cost, states have limited the availability of the drug under Medicaid, with only about 7,000 patients using it in 1990 in an estimated market of over 100,000 candidates. Sandoz instituted the weekly blood monitoring because of concern over potentially harmful side effects. Critics suggest that by limiting the blood monitoring to one company working for Sandoz, the total cost of using Clorazil is unduly high. As a result, 22 U.S. states filed suit against Sandoz, charging it with violating antitrust laws.

Gladwell cites the case of Nexium, a "new" version of Prilosec, a heartburn medication, from AstraZeneca. Prilosec's

continued

to choose a particular channel in a market to get the final consumer price it needs.

A research study looked at how a manufacturer con-trols a distributor's pricing decisions in export markets. The authors suggest that organizational factors—firm size, experience in exporting, asset specificity and dependence on distributors, and strategic factors (namely whether the firm is focused on cost based competition or differentia-tion)—will affect how much control is sought over the dis-tributor's pricing decisions. Large firms that are more experienced, that seek to compete strategically (whether based on cost position or product differentiation), and that devote assets specifically to export operations will seek to exercise greater control over a distributor's pricing deci-sions. In contrast, dependence on a distributor will reduce attempts to exert control over price. Further, a volatile local market economic environment can affect market perform-ance when manufacturers practice pricing control, as the distributor's flexibility is reduced. Pricing control may help manufacturers show a profit, but may affect the strategic performance (market share).[7]

Distribution channels also may differ across countries in the countries' relative demand for discounts. Customary business practices and long-standing relationships in a country may mean a series of additional discounts that reduce the ultimate price realized by the firm, the amount that Marn and Rosiello termed the pocket price.[8] Firms grant a variety of discounts for a number of reasons:

- Order size
- Co-op advertising
- Response to competitive price cuts
- Shipping charges
- Early payment
- Special customer relationships
- Cumulative volume
- Product-line promotions

Such discounts need not be offered to all customers in all markets. It is useful, however, to monitor the various dis-counts offered in each market and to establish norms under which the discounts are granted. Otherwise, the cus-tomer who negotiates additional discounts is the one who knows when and whom to call, asking for discounts. A firm that develops information on its price waterfall—the sequence of discounts leading to the pocket price—can more easily decide which customers are to be rewarded and which distribution channels should get the most dis-counts. Marn and Rosiello suggest that careful analysis can result in an overall reduction in discounting and signifi-cant gains in the pocket price achieved by the firm. Its sales margins will, therefore, be enhanced.

International Competition and Price-Cutting Pressures

Comparative-advantage concepts indicate that developing nations, with their lower labor costs, are likely to have an advantage in world competition in labor-intensive products. Those advantages also arise when foreign companies gain a technological advantage or obtain higher productivity. The resultant lower prices allowed can give the foreign firm a toe-hold in the market. Regardless of the source of comparative advantage, the end result is that foreign firms may have lower prices. The dilemma then facing the domestic (U.S.) firm is whether it should respond by also cutting prices. Suppose that a U.S. manufacturer of machine tools bids on an order. The salesperson calls the purchasing agent to check on the status of the bid. He or she is told that a Japanese company has submitted a lower bid and that the U.S. firm must cut its prices by a certain amount to get the order. The salesperson's boss, however, is adamant that company policy is not to compete on prices. The salesperson must convey to the client other advantages of the U.S. firm, such as its position as long-term supplier, its greater experience, its location closer to the client, and its reputation for better service.[9]

The problem is in judging how the role of price as an attribute of a product has changed. That is, as the technology inherent in a product is diffused, there are fewer differences in the product than there are between the U.S. firm and its foreign competitors. As the product becomes less differentiated, price cutting is more likely. Then if the foreign firms also match the U.S. firm on other attributes of the product, such as service, quality, and delivery terms, price becomes more influential in the decision to buy.

To generalize, U.S. firms must constantly monitor the prices charged by their foreign competitors and understand the reasons why foreign firm prices are lower. Are the price cuts of a temporary nature, designed to aid in initial market penetration? Or do they represent the net cost advantage enjoyed by the foreign competitors? In other words, price cutting is the symptom. The correct response to price cuts requires understanding the cause.

U.S. firms sometimes respond to lower-priced international competition by making allegations of dumping. Under U.S. international trade law, firms can petition the United States International Trade Commission (USITC) to declare that foreign competitors have dumped their goods in the U.S. market (that is, sold their goods in the United States at below fair value). If the U.S. firms can prove such dumping before the USITC panels, the firms can request relief in the form of imposition of countervailing duties. In a recent case, the USITC ruled that shrimp imports from six countries (China, Vietnam, India, Brazil, Thailand, and Ecuador) were being dumped in the United States. It recommended countervailing duties ranging from 2.35 to 67.8 percent depending on the specific importing firm's prices in the United States and its cost structure.[10]

Inflation

Most countries face some gradual increase in prices over time. However, continuing strong inflation characterizes a limited number of countries. In those markets where price levels rise by 20 percent or more every year, pricing presents some different issues. Selling in an inflationary market might well appear to be a marketer's dream. People are anxious to exchange their money for real assets that do not depreciate quickly. Indeed, it would be a good situation for sellers if it were not for other factors that usually accompany high rates of inflation. First, costs may go up faster than prices. Second, countries with high rates of inflation are usually those with strong price controls. Third, countries with rampant inflation usually have strict controls over foreign exchange. Profits earned in those countries may not be remittable, at least not until they have been eroded by the devaluations that usually accompany inflation.

Pricing for inflationary markets requires accounting for changing values over time. Material and other costs of a product must be recovered (plus a margin for profit) at the time of sale—or at the time of payment if credit is extend-

GLOBAL MARKETING

Tuna and Mango Prices in Japan: Price and Value

*A*s connoisseurs of fish, the Japanese are finicky about the quality of the raw fish used to make sashimi, a national favorite. Tuna is one of the major fish varieties used in sashimi. With both yellowfin and bigeye tuna found off the coast of Australia in the Coral Sea, the Australians have been encouraged to export chilled fresh tuna to Japan for consumption as sashimi. Chilled tuna must be exported by air, but auction prices in Japan are attractive—about A$80 (Australian dollar) per kilogram (in 1987) in Japan versus A$1 per kilogram in Australia. Clearly, the economic incentive is high. Australian exports of tuna have been low, however, even while Japanese fishing boats have been active in the waters.

The Australian fishing industry was discouraged by the high variation in prices received at the Tokyo fish auctions. Those price differences led them to believe that Japanese auction buyers colluded to keep Australia's imported fish out of the market, thereby favoring the Japanese fishing fleet in the Coral Sea. As a result, Australian researchers meticulously studied auction prices for 27 days in October 1985, attempting to relate prices (in yen per kilogram) to factors such as fish meat color, freshness, condition (degree of carcass damage, bruises, etc.), weight of the whole fish, and origin (whether the tuna was caught in the waters off Japan, the Philippines, Taiwan, or Australia). Since sashimi is eaten raw, consumers are willing to pay more for "good" meat color, such as the absence of a concentration of red meat pigments in the flesh of the tuna. They also want the freshest fish possible. (The degree of freshness can be measured by the presence of breakdown products such as adenosine triphosphate, which increase with length of time.)

Aside from the importance of freshness and color, the study found that auction prices were lower for bigeye tuna caught in non-Japanese waters. However, research could not determine the reason. Because bigeye tuna have a high fat content, one possibility was that the food organisms found in the particular feeding grounds off the waters of Taiwan and the Philippines are absorbed into the fat, yielding flavors that are less acceptable to the discerning Japanese palate. The main conclusion of the study, however, was that Japanese consumers

continued

choose raw fish for their sashimi on the basis of its appearance. Hence, buyers at auctions are willing to pay more for tuna that has good color. The implication, then, is this: If Australians want to get high prices, they must select tuna of the requisite freshness and meat color for export to the chilled tuna auction in Tokyo.

The researchers also found that although the Tokyo market accounted for nearly 60 percent of all chilled bigeye tuna sold in Japan, two other markets, Nagoya and Osaka, accounted for about 40 percent of all chilled yellowfin tuna, as compared to the Tokyo market's 16 percent. Thus, because of lack of information, the Australians were erroneously concentrating on the Tokyo market alone.

The market for tuna in Japan may be of little interest to most people. The principle that emerges from the study, however, is important: The price that people are willing to pay for a product depends on the value perceived. Careful market research can uncover what consumers in different countries look for in a product. The price set for a particular country market must be appropriate to the value delivered in that market if the company wants to avoid over- or underpricing the product.

Another Australian study focused on prices paid in Japan for wild shrimp exported from Australia to Japan. Wild shrimp are harvested at sea and used to be sold primarily to high-priced Japanese restaurants. Then Taiwanese research led to the cultivation of pond-reared, high-yield shrimp similar in taste to the Japanese kuruma ebi (a favorite among Japanese consumers), with about 25 to 30 shrimp per pound. The lower shrimp prices resulting from pond culture and higher yields increased Japanese demand considerably, with Japanese homemakers buying shrimp for home cooking and consumption. In 1990, Japan imported 287,000 tons of shrimp valued at $3.6 billion.

A direct consequence was that new producers, such as shrimp farmers from Vietnam, entered the market, and wild shrimp prices began dropping. Australian wild-shrimp fishing costs increased, while prices for their catch dropped 25 percent in Tokyo. Even so, wild shrimp prices were double farmed shrimp prices. While connoisseurs could distinguish between wild and farm shrimp, few consumers could, especially since shrimp is often cooked in spicy sauces, further masking the taste.

Australian shrimp producers began considering an advertising campaign to build a brand image for Australian shrimp. The campaign stressed that the shrimp was wild, that it had been harvested at sea in clean, cold, unpolluted waters; and that it had a distinctive and superior taste. The question was whether the expense of an advertising campaign could lead to a differentiated image for Australian shrimp and convince

Japanese consumers that Australian-origin shrimp justified a higher price. The Australian producers also considered other alternatives, including switching their export focus to less competitive markets in the United States and Europe. Doing so would further reduce Australian market share in Japan because Japanese shrimp dealers would not look kindly on suppliers who walked away from long-standing business arrangements. Another alternative was to form a Japanese distribution joint venture and sell directly to higher-priced Japanese restaurants whose chefs might be willing to pay higher prices for larger and more distinctive-tasting shrimp.

Another study on Japanese preferences for imported mangoes provides similar insights. The authors address the role of pricing in influencing the attractiveness of a new fruit unfamiliar to Japanese households and palates. Because most mangoes imported to Japan come from the Philippines and Mexico, Australia could be a new source. How can a new importer use price to compete against established import sources? Japanese consumers want premium quality and are willing to pay for it. Australian mangoes are relatively expensive in Japan and are positioned as "gift fruit"; if they were priced less expensively, home use would increase.

Sources: Yukiko Miyauchi and Chad Perry, "Marketing Fresh Fruit to Japanese Consumers: Exploring Issues for Australian Exporters," European Journal of Marketing, January 1, 1999, Volume 33, Issue 1/2; Stephen C. Williams and John W. Longworth, "Factors Influencing Tuna Prices in Japan and Implications for the Development of the Coral Sea Tuna Fishery," European Journal of Marketing, Volume 23, Number 3, 1989; and Steve C. Williams, "Prospects for Promotion of 'Wild' Shrimp in Japan: Implications for Australian Exporters," European Journal of Marketing, Volume 26, Number 10, 1992.

ed. If prices are stable, pricing can be a simple process of addition. If prices are rising rapidly, addition of the various cost elements at the time they were incurred will not ensure that the *current* value of the costs is recovered.

The following examples illustrate these contrasting situations.

Stable Currency Situation

Raw materials	250
Labor	100
Overhead	100
Packaging	50
Total costs	500
Gross profit (20%)	100
Selling price (cash sale)	600

INFLATION RATE OF 84 PERCENT PER YEAR

Assume that raw materials were purchased four months before being used in a product, labor costs were incurred one month before product sale, overhead was charged for a one-month period, and packaging materials were purchased three months before sale.

Raw materials	250 + 70 (28% inflation—4 months) = 320
Labor	100 + 7 (7% inflation—1 month) = 107
Overhead	100 + 7 (7% inflation—1 month) = 107
Packaging	50 + 10.5 (21% inflation—3 months) = 61
Total costs	595
Gross profit (20%)	119
Selling price (cash sale)	714

As shown in the preceding tables, selling price must be increased by 19 percent to reflect current cost levels.

In reality, many more cost elements go into a product than the four general headings shown above; for example, marketing costs are not mentioned. In addition, each of the cost elements has a rate of inflation different from the average (an increase of 84 percent a year in the general *price* level, as shown above). Finally, time may elapse between production and sale—as well as between sale and payment. That additional time is a further inflation cost that must be considered in the price.

Another problem arises if government price controls prevent raising the price. When a firm does have freedom to raise prices, it often fares better by making frequent small price increases rather than occasional large increases that jolt the consumer. Such was the experience of companies in Brazil. During one period, for example, companies raised their prices 7 percent on the first of every month. At one time, General Foods' Brazilian subsidiary, Kibon, had to raise prices on frozen treats from 10 cruzeiros (Brazil's former currency) to 60 cruzeiros in just two years. The buyers were mainly children, whose income had not risen anywhere near six times the product's original cost. Kibon tried to raise prices by small steps and undertook special promotions each time to minimize the shock. In one promotional program, those who bought the frozen treats and found a marked stick won a free bike.

Pricing in inflation is never easy, especially when there are price controls. However, certain guidelines can help:

- Good cost accounting is critical, especially in forecasting costs for pricing.
- It may be possible to source materials or components from lower-cost suppliers in other countries.
- Long-term contracts may need escalator or reopener clauses.
- Credit terms may be shortened.
- Product ingredients and/or the product line may be changed to items less subject to inflation or to government price control.
- It may be necessary to sacrifice short-term profits as the price of retaining market share, retaining customer goodwill, and keeping competition at bay.

Gray Markets

An additional pricing problem in international marketing is the incentive that the consumer price differential between countries creates for a given product in a country with lower prices. For example, it was common for planeloads of Japanese tourists (in times of economic prosperity in Japan) to take weekend shopping trips to Taiwan and Hong Kong. The tourists bought goods such as consumer electronics, perfumes, and clothes to take advantage of price differentials.

In international marketing, when a product can be manufactured in more than one location, currency fluctuations may make gray marketing profitable. **Gray marketing** is the unauthorized importing and selling of products intended for one market in another higher-priced market. When the dollar was appreciating in the early 1980s, dealers found it profitable to bring in unauthorized imports of Caterpillar tractors from Europe because of the weak European currency. In those cases, even after shipping and tariffs, the landed cost in the United States of the imported Caterpillar tractors was less than the price charged for U.S.-made Caterpillar tractors.[11]

The major problem with gray marketing is that established distributors lose motivation to sell their products because they see their margins eroded by low-overhead gray marketers. (Consider, for example, the mail-order computer resellers, whose main expense is telemarketing.) Meanwhile, the gray marketer is primarily interested in quick sales and short-term profits. Over time, a manufacturer could lose markets because the gray marketer competes only on price and drives away customers who seek after-sales service and other forms of support. This issue is particularly serious for industrial products. On the other hand, gray markets provide an outlet for excess production and, indeed, allow a firm to gain economies of scale by deliberately increasing production, some of which goes into the gray market. And when product life cycles are short, gray markets allow a firm to gain market share and not be stuck with obsolete inventories.

Ultimately, gray marketing arises because of unsustainable price differences between two markets. When a perfume manufacturer charges U.S. wholesale prices that are 25 percent higher than similar prices in Europe, it is not surprising that some of the product sold to European wholesalers leaks into the United States. (Such importing is legal under U.S. law.) Companies must carefully examine their pricing policies in different markets and their attempts to maintain a price differential. Otherwise, gray marketing is merely an efficient market response to ill-thought-out attempts to charge higher prices in certain markets.

Impact of Fluctuations in Exchange Rate

Currency instability presents one of the central challenges to a firm in its price-setting efforts in international markets. Table 12-2 shows how major currencies changed value against each other over the period June 2000 to June 2004.

The U.S. dollar lost value against every currency in the table, while the British pound gained value against every currency, appreciating as much as 8.3 percent against the U.S. dollar. The euro is the common currency adopted by 12 of the 25 EU members. It appreciated 3.5 percent against the U.S. dollar, but lost value against the three other major currencies, losing 4.3 percent against the Japanese yen, 2.6 percent against the Swiss franc, and 5.6 percent against the British pound.

As can be seen in Table 12-2, U.S. exporters, while keeping their U.S. dollar prices constant, have seen their products marketed for 3.5 to 8.3 percent less than what their major international trade partners charge. Normal price elasticities should cause demand for the U.S. products to rise. By the same token, Japanese, European, and Swiss exporters face loss of market share for products exported to the United States, as the exchange-related price rise reduces demand for their products. Within the EU, the euro lost value against the British pound. Given the EU's lack of internal trade barriers, this meant that French, German, and Italian producers could grab market share in competition against the British, without barriers such as customs duties and border controls. The U.S. dollar was the weakest currency during the period, falling in value against every other currency in the table. Table 12-2 clearly demonstrates that a world of volatile and fluctuating

exchange rates results in unexpected price rises and declines, even though exporters may not have changed list prices in their domestic currencies.

The data from Table 12-2 present an interesting decision for exporters. The average Japanese exporter faces a 7.6 percent price rise for its goods sold to the United States. It may lose some sales because of this price increase. It also may want to consider lowering its yen price so that the price increase in U.S. dollars is less than the total 7.6 percent appreciation of the yen against the dollar. Conversely, the U.S. exporter to Japan has the option of passing on the full 7.6 percent decline in the value of the dollar in the form of a price cut in yen. Or the U.S. exporter can allow the U.S. dollar price to rise somewhat, retaining some of the windfall gains from the appreciation of the yen. The U.S. exporter has to decide whether to gain market share or to increase its profit. On the other hand, the Japanese exporter's problem is to choose between losing U.S. market share or sacrificing profit to retain U.S. customers.

Strategies for Coping with Foreign Exchange Risk

Subaru of America (the U.S. distributor of Subaru cars) is an example of a company that was seriously affected by changes in the exchange rate. It was one of the most profitable companies in the United States for over a decade. Then the yen appreciated almost 50 percent against the dollar from the end of 1985 through 1987. As a result, the dollar price of Subaru cars had to go up because of yen appreciation. Suddenly, Subaru sales dropped by over 20 percent, and it began registering large losses. Chilean companies experienced similar problems when the Chilean peso appreciated significantly against the U.S. dollar, gaining 24 percent from 2003 to 2004. As a consequence, Chilean exporters of wine, fruit, and wood products saw their U.S. prices increase. They had to choose between maintaining their profit margins or maintaining U.S. mar-

Table 12-2. Potential Effects of Currency Movements on Sales Prices Percentage Changes in Exchange Rates, June 2000 to June 2004

	Euro	Japan	Switzerland	UK	United States
Euro	—				
Japan	+4.3	—			
Switzerland	+2.6	+1.7	—		
UK	+5.6	+0.8	+2.3	—	
United States		-3.5	-7.6	-6.0	-8.3	—

Source: Derived from exchange rates published in *The Economist*, June 26, 2004, page101.

Table is read as follows: Japanese yen gained 4.3 percent against the euro; thus, the euro lost 4.3 percent against the yen. Similarly, the U.S. dollar lost 3.5 percent against the euro, and the euro gained 3.5 percent against the U.S. dollar.

ket share but not raising U.S. prices by the extent of the Chilean peso appreciation.[12]

As the previous example shows, even highly profitable companies can be devastated by changes in the exchange rate. Three areas of risk are involved: transaction risk, competitive risk, and market portfolio risk.[13]

TRANSACTION RISK

When a firm makes a transaction denominated in a foreign currency (FC), it exposes itself to **transaction risk**, meaning that changes in the value of the FC may diminish the financial results of the firm. For example, if a firm purchases supplies from Germany totaling 100,000 deutsche marks (DMs) and the exchange rate is 2 DMs = $1, the dollar value of the purchase is $50,000. Further, if the period of credit granted is 90 days and the DM appreciates so that the rate at the end of 90 days is 1.80 DM = $1, the debt is now equal to $55,556. Thus, the importer is required to pay more dollars, raising its costs and reducing its profits. The exporter has gained by holding an asset denominated in DMs at a time when the DM has been appreciating against the dollar. A firm can guard against such transaction risk by hedging (using forward markets) and purchasing futures and options contracts.

COMPETITIVE RISK

The geographic pattern of a company's manufacturing and sales configuration, when compared to that of its key competitors, can result in **competitive risk**. Thus, if Firm A manufactures in a country with depreciating exchange rates and sells to a country with appreciating exchange rates, it stands to gain considerable market share without raising prices. Now suppose Firm B does exactly the opposite, manufacturing in a country with appreciating exchange rates and selling to a country whose exchange rate is depreciating. In that situation, Firm A could gain market share at the expense of Firm B without having to change its prices in its own domestic currency.

Subaru's problem in 1987 stemmed from the fact that it sourced its cars from Japan and sold them to the United States at a time when the dollar was weakening significantly against the yen. Thus, Subaru was influenced by the performance of two currencies, the yen and the dollar. All Japanese manufacturers importing cars from Japan for the United States had a greater competitive risk than European car makers, such as Volvo of Sweden. (The kroner did not appreciate as much as the yen against the dollar.) Chile faced similar problems with its grapes harvested in Chile and its wine made in Chile. It incurred costs in Chilean pesos, but principally exported to the United States.

MARKET PORTFOLIO RISK

The third kind of risk, **market portfolio risk**, arises from a firm's export markets as compared to the country-market portfolio of its global competitors. A more diversified company, one that sold to several country markets, would not be as influenced by changes in the yen/dollar rate. Subaru of America manufactured in Japan and sold 75 percent of its cars in the United States, with the remainder going to Canada and Europe. In contrast, BMW manufactured in Germany and derived only 36 percent of its sales from the United States. Since BMW manufactured in Germany, whereas Subaru manufactured in Japan, to the extent that the mark appreciated less than the yen, BMW would be less affected by the devaluation of the dollar. That is the difference in the two companies' competitive risk.

In addition, Subaru concentrated most of its export output to the U.S. market. By putting all of its eggs in one basket, therefore, it was more vulnerable to changes in the value of the yen versus the dollar. In contrast, BMW exported its output to other countries in addition to the United States, including Japan. Thus, its market portfolio risk was different from Subaru's since its foreign revenues were not affected only by the dollar's performance. BMW has a more diversified portfolio of markets and, hence, faces less risk. One solution for Subaru would be to similarly diversify markets, either by selling to more countries and/or by manufacturing in major markets. Subaru's decision to produce its new Legacy model in a U.S. plant is an example of such a solution.

Subaru, however, would not be likely to lose market share if all other car manufacturers were similarly affected. Subaru's problem was that it competed against U.S.-made subcompacts manufactured by U.S. car companies and by Japanese firms such as Mazda. In addition, imports of subcompact cars were also increasing from countries such as Brazil, Mexico, and South Korea. Those countries did not have the exchange rate disadvantage of Japanese manufacturing. In response, all of the major Japanese car companies began manufacturing cars in the United States. That changed their competitive and market portfolio risk, with all of the manufacturers seeing a reduction in their exposure to yen appreciation. That decision also changed their competitive risk compared to European competitors that did not have U.S. manufacturing facilities.

The problem of **pass-through** (how much of an exchange rate change to pass on in the form of adjusted domestic prices) is one that most international business exporting and importing firms face at some point in their operations. The issue is whether a firm wants to maintain some stability in local currency (LC) prices. Irandoust looked at whether car importers into Sweden attempted such LC price stabilization or passed on most of the foreign exchange rate appreciation. He found that Italian and British exporters were more likely to pass on the full impact of exchange rates than exporters from France, Japan, and Germany. He found that when an exporter had a large market share, exchange rate pass-through was higher. Thus, low market share holders are more willing to swallow some losses in order to retail or increase their low market share. The author looked at automobile prices in Sweden, adjusting price changes first for quality improvements ("hedonistic price adjustments"). Then he looked at the relationship between price level-adjusted exchange rates and the quality-adjusted automobile prices. The implication is that automobile manufacturers have target LC prices that they maintain by not passing through the full impact of exchange rate changes. Thus, the sellers of imported cars in Sweden are willing to reduce their profit margins, if necessary, in order to maintain market position within the set of competitors. A further implication is that manufacturers that are bringing in cars from countries whose currencies have not appreciated as much have a better chance of maintaining their profit margins and keeping their targeted market share.[14]

Adopting a more general perspective, Bodnar and his fellow economists considered how firms decide whether to pass through changes in exchange rates into FC prices and how doing so impacts their "exposure"; that is, the responsiveness of their profits to changes in exchange rate. To the extent that a firm does not pass through the exchange rate changes, its exposure is greater and its profits are affected. Bodner et al tested their models of optimal pass-through and exposure effects with Japanese exporters. They concluded that market share and the elasticity of substitution between the foreign-produced good and the home-produced good influenced the level of exchange rate pass-through.[15]

Product-Specific Factors and Their Relevance to Pricing

Demand

Demand for a firm's product or service will generally differ across markets. One implication of differing demand is that a firm may need to charge different prices in each market. Firms may have to choose between market skimming and penetration pricing. Market skimming involves setting prices at a high level and accepting lower sales volumes with higher margins per unit sold. That strategy assumes that as the market grows and evolves, prices will be cut gradually to make the product affordable to larger segments of the consuming population. Such a strategy also banks on the likelihood that costs will fall with accumulated volume production. Thus, margins can be held at attractive levels, with lower prices matched with lower costs. The opposite

strategy, penetration pricing, begins with lower prices, assuming that the lower prices will attract larger numbers of consumers and that the higher unit volumes will result in larger total profits even though margins per unit are lower. The strategy also banks on unit costs falling rapidly as sales volume grows, thus increasing margins as total volume increases. An additional benefit of the penetration pricing strategy is that a firm captures significant market share, making it difficult for competitors who enter the market later to capture equivalent market shares.

Demand for a firm's products is a function of the number of consumers; their ability to pay; their tastes, habits, and attitudes relating to the product; and the existence of competing products. Patterns of demand can also change in reaction to cyclical economic conditions within a country. Consider the evolution of U.S. goods and pricing in Japan. Imported U.S. goods such as brand-name sweaters, cosmetics, and software have all been set significantly above U.S. prices. Part of the reason for higher Japanese prices has been the higher local costs of rent, sales force, advertising, and multiple-layered distribution margins. However, when Japan underwent a deep recession, depressed incomes led Japanese buyers to seek bargains. Discounting and value-pricing strategies took hold. Gray market pressures and increased public consciousness of high Japanese prices also led to lowered prices, with U.S. companies following the general trend.[16]

Price and the Product Life Cycle

A product's price may be set with the goal of maximizing profits over the product life cycle rather than at every stage of the product's marketing. A company may deliberately price below costs in anticipation of reducing costs through increases in manufacturing volume, a variation of penetration pricing discussed previously. A classic example is the Japanese use of that method to penetrate the motorcycle industry.[17] Japanese firms gambled on gaining learning- and experience-curve efficiencies[18] to produce long-run profits. Note that price has several universal connotations as an indicator of quality and as a proxy for prestige. Negatively, price connotes with value consciousness, suggesting that high prices are not as desirable as equivalent quality with lower prices.[19]

Price and the Product Line

Products within a product line with less competition may be priced higher to subsidize other parts of the product line. Similarly, some items in the product line may be priced low to serve as loss leaders and induce customers to try the product, particularly if the company and its products are recent entrants into a country market. Another variant of such strategies is **price-bundling**—that is, setting a certain price for customers who simultaneously buy several items within the product line (for example, a season ticket price or a personal computer package with software and printer). In such cases, a key consideration is how much consumers in diverse country markets want to save money, to spend time searching for the "best buy," etc.

PRICE BUNDLING

Price bundling is the attempt to link prices, generally premium prices, with a variety of value-added services offered in conjunction with the product. Examples of price bundling come from the software industry, which has experimented with several innovative approaches to pricing:

- *Basing prices on the power of the processor utilizing the software.* Thus, a software package used on a mainframe or workstation would command a higher price than software used on a personal computer.
- *Using a metering approach.* A separate computer program keeps track of the number of users accessing a particular software package as well as the length of time they are using it, resulting in a variable price that generally increases with greater usage.
- *Offering a site license.* Individual corporate users negotiate a fixed lump-sum price, perhaps payable once a year, based on the organization's size, number of computers, and relative demand for computer utilization.
- *Selling "suites."* For Microsoft's Office suite, users get significant price concessions for buying a related set of different software packages from one vendor. In this case, the Microsoft Office suite contains word processing, spreadsheet, database, and other utility packages.

Price Unbundling and Flexible Service Offerings

With all of those approaches, prices are developed by assessing the value derived by the consumer from using the company's products or services.[20] A corollary of thinking in terms of value to the customer is to break out the total product offering into tiers of value and to charge price increments for delivering additional value beyond a base package provided to all customers. That approach, termed the *flexible service offering model*, allows users to pick the precise configuration of values they seek and to pay accordingly.[21] That approach allows a company to offer a bare-bones model at a lower price, attracting new customers who might then trade up and pay more for additional features. The sticking point here is how the bare-bones model is arrived at. If it is designed so that very few customers will settle for a bare-bones model but must add options to obtain an acceptable product, the pricing model might breed resentment and be seen as a transparent attempt to gouge the customer. If a company moves to the flexible service offering model, it must guard against

offering a baseline model for which there are no buyers.

In practice, all of those factors interact when prices are set. A study by Stottinger, based on interviews with the heads of export/foreign sales offices or managing directors of medium-sized manufacturing companies active in exporting in five industries in an EU country (systems, mechanical engineering, electrical engineering, plastics, and furniture), came to that conclusion. The objectives varied across firms, including maintaining market share and increasing international market coverage and profits. Experience and scale of exporting affected objectives—whether profits or market share and market position were emphasized. Financial targets were more likely to be used when independent distributors were used. In those cases, pricing adaptation (rather than uniform pricing) was more likely. Most sample companies had centralized international pricing, especially the larger companies. More experienced companies were more likely to be flexible in their use of cost-plus pricing, adapting to market conditions. Thus, market, industry, product, company, and management attitudes toward exporting and pricing were relevant. They influenced performance goal setting (market share and profits), centralization versus decentralization, standardization versus differentiation in pricing, and approaches to using cost-plus calculations in price setting—ultimately affecting satisfaction and whether pricing problems arose.[22]

Managers are often dissatisfied with their pricing strategies and choices, constantly revisiting those matters. When asked, managers point to a few difficult problem areas that require constant resolution:

- Commitment of adequate resources to export pricing efforts: conducting market research, gaining knowledge of the competition's pricing structure, assessing real demand, and analyzing the impact of foreign exchange fluctuations and inflation on price
- Centralized decision making: restricting local market pricing flexibility, working in the face of lack of detailed cost information (perhaps outdated), and being unable to quickly change local prices in reaction to changing market conditions
- Competition in the face of a high-cost position; cost-plus pricing based on higher-cost production and local channel costs; and unnecessary product features adding to costs, rendering products unaffordable given local market purchasing power.[23]

Price Standardization: Pressures for Uniform Pricing in International Markets

Customers of multinationals who pay different prices in different countries for essentially the same product or service can be expected to press for a global uniform price. Better information systems and sharing of data across national subsidiaries allow multinationals to see when different pricing exists, allowing them to pool their purchasing to command a single price and even volume discounts. In response, suppliers have begun a move to uniform pricing. A policy of keeping price variations across countries within a limited range also prevents gray marketing, such as when U.S. distributors ship products to Europe to take advantage of price differentials between the United States and Europe. Those approaches have been formalized in many companies through a program of *global account management.*

Uniform pricing also allows a firm to set pricing policy centrally and to decide the role that price should play in the overall marketing mix. Headquarters may then decide that the company will not indiscriminately cut prices to win market share. Doing so prevents inconsistencies from cropping up under which one subsidiary might cut prices excessively whereas another might prefer to cater to fewer clients at a higher margin.[24]

Hermann Simon suggests that pricing in a global setting consists of resolving the tension between the desire to charge different prices and the pressure to charge one price in all markets.[25] Multinational clients who want to buy all of their product needs at the lowest price prevalent within a group of countries and gray marketers indulging in price arbitrage are the two forces leading to a uniform price. Consumers in different markets may have different elasticities of demand, however, with some groups willing to pay higher prices.

As important, consumers may differ in the values and features they perceive in a product. Conjoint measurement allows a firm to see the differences in perceived value. Coupling that information with differing elasticities can justify higher prices in certain markets. The solution, according to Simon, is to set up an "international price corridor," within which band prices can vary across countries. The width of the band would be set centrally at headquarters. If some low level of gray marketing ensues, the firm can tolerate it. Simon emphasizes that "a global product and local price are incompatible"; and if low income and positioning strategies suggest that different prices need to be charged, then a multiple brand policy can prevent the low price from diluting the brand equity of the higher-priced brand.

Setting uniform prices across markets (that is, standardizing prices) is seen by some researchers as being influenced by the degree of similarity between home and host country—when viewed in terms of customer characteristics, legal environment, economic conditions, and stage of the product life cycle. Whether to standardize or adapt price may depend on:

- Macro environmental factors (convergence of economic, legal, cultural, physical, and demographic factors).
- Micro environmental factors such as similarity of customer characteristics; attitudes and behavior; structure and nature of competition; and availability, cost, and competence of intermediaries.
- Firm-specific factors including degree of centralization, international experience, strategic orientation, and subsidiary ownership structure.
- Product and industry factors such as life cycle stage, nature of product, product uniqueness, conditions of use, technology, and customer's degree of familiarity with the product.

Similarities of the economic environment, legal environment, distribution infrastructure, customer characteristics, purchasing behavior, and stage of product life cycle are most influential in determining the standardization of prices.[26]

Exchange Rate Volatility and Prices to the Consumer

Multinational clients can also force a company to share in exchange rate risk. That is, a large customer can insist that any windfall gains from exchange rate changes should be partially given back to the customer. For example, one U.S. drug manufacturer manufactured drugs in Ireland for a Japanese customer and invoiced in yen when the yen was 125 to the dollar. When the rate dropped to below 90 yen, the Japanese customer asked that yen prices be dropped. The same problem arises in transfer pricing, with a volatile currency changing the relative allocation of profit between the subsidiary and the parent company. In those cases, tax authorities in the jurisdiction where profits have dropped are likely to want prices to be adjusted so that profits and the tax payments remain constant.

One approach to uniform pricing in the face of exchange rate volatility is illustrated by Novell, which set a worldwide standard price in dollars. This places the onus on the distributor to decide how to adjust LC prices in response to exchange rate changes. Novell moved to its global uniform price because users could easily buy software in lower-priced markets. Once customers use Novell networking software, switching costs ensures that Novell retains a significant portion of its clients, resulting in a recurring income stream. Novell's competitor, 3Com, has a similar dollar-based pricing policy, with all customers being charged U.S. dollar prices. The impetus came when the company began receiving complaints from European customers who were sometimes charged 50 percent more than comparable U.S. prices for 3Com routers and hubs.[27]

Japanese semiconductor companies have developed an interesting response to the problem of price changes caused by shifts in exchange rates. Their client contracts include cost-sharing agreements. The Japanese companies know from internal profitability assessments that they can earn a reasonable rate of return on dollar-based contracts as long as the yen sells above 75 to the dollar. Hence, they negotiate contracts that guarantee a price as long as the yen remains between 75 and 95. If the yen falls below 75, however, the dollar price goes up. Similarly, if the yen rises above 95 to the dollar, the dollar price to the customer is cut. This flexibility is fair to both buyer and seller and enhances long-term relationships between supplier and client.[28] Of course, price changes also provide information about product characteristics to the customer. For example, do price reductions increase sales of high-quality brands more than lower-quality products? Under certain circumstances, price changes can affect consumer choices of the kind of product to consume and the specific brand chosen.[29]

Exchange rate volatility can also force firms to consider hedging strategies as part of overall pricing strategy. During 1995, for example, the yen appreciated from 100 yen to the dollar to nearly 80 yen to the dollar by mid-1995. Then the yen began depreciating, rising to above 100 yen to the dollar by year-end. Since Japanese corporations are major exporters, firms such as Nissan process $8 billion in foreign receivables. Such large foreign balances led many Japanese firms to hedge their foreign short-term assets (and liabilities). During 1995, however, a hedging strategy meant that Japanese firms may have locked in rates that prevented them from exploiting the dollar appreciation. For example, a hedge on dollar receivables at 90 yen to the dollar meant that the firm lost out on dollar appreciation to 107 yen to the dollar in January 1996. Because the Japanese fiscal year begins in April, treasurers all across Japan had to consider whether the steady weakening of the yen from mid-1995 was a secular trend reversing a decade-long strengthening of the yen or a short-term fluctuation.

Some firms such as Hitachi follow a simple decision rule: Always hedge half of all outstanding FC receivables.[30] Smaller firms may find even that degree of risk hard to accept, preferring a 100 percent hedging strategy. After all, hedging is about passing on FC risk to a third party. It is disingenuous for a firm to hope to pass on the downside risk but retain upside risk through simple hedges such as forward contracts. Hedging strategies such as selling FC "puts" do exist and incur costly premiums, but they can be used by a firm that wants to take on some degree of FC exposure.

Not every firm believes in hedging as a method of coping with exchange rate fluctuations. Peugeot is an example of a company that prefers to do nothing.[31] As the euro appreciated in 2003, Peugeot incurred losses nearing $600 million because of the rise of the euro against the British pound. Peugeot refuses to hedge as a matter of policy; CFO Yann Delabriere sees hedging as similar to gambling. He notes that "if markets move in your favor, you win, but if they turn against you, you lose". He also believes that "no-one can forecast currency movements correctly, so hedging means incurring a cost to run an equal chance of losing or winning." Peugeot runs the risk of being exposed to currency movements as a hedged company but avoids the hedge costs. Delabriere points out that while that results in volatility in earnings, the fluctuations even out in the long run. Peugeot reaped currency-based gains in 2002, when currency movements went in its favor.

CURRENCY OF QUOTATION

A firm has a choice in the currency used for the price quotation. U.S. firms price in U.S. dollars domestically and would like to do the same on exports. Quoting dollar prices is less risky and easier for the exporter. However, importers prefer all quotations in their own currency for easy comparison of the offers of various foreign and national suppliers. In addition, both exporters and importers would prefer to avoid the foreign exchange risk. If the importers' currency is susceptible to devaluation or depreciation, they would prefer the price quote in their own currency so that on the due date of their invoice, they will not have to pay a larger number of yen or euros for a given dollar amount. Similar reasoning lies behind U.S. exporters' preference for a dollar quote: Exporters do not want to receive fewer dollars when payment is finally made.

Assume, for example, that a U.S. exporter has a shipment for France worth $10,000, or 8600 euros, with payment due in euros in 90 days. If the euro depreciates by 15 percent during that period, the importer will still pay 8600 euros; but this now translates into only $8,500. In that case, the exporter experiences a big loss. Conversely, if the quote had been in dollars, the importer would still pay only $10,000, but this would now cost him or her 9890 euros instead of 8600. The importer would be the loser. Although each party could hedge its position in the forward exchange market, hedging has a cost.

How is the conflict resolved? The choice of currency for the price quotation depends partly on trade practice in the country and industry in question, but also partly on the bargaining position of the parties. In a buyer's market, the exporter is anxious for sales and tends to yield to the importer's desires. In a seller's market, the situation is reversed.

The advent of the euro, a single European currency, means that exchange risks in intra-European transactions disappear. That may reduce the volatility of the euro against the dollar, making international trade less subject to exchange rate fluctuations. A 1998 study considered differences in currency choice across countries. Factors affecting currency choice include avoidance of exchange rate exposure, relative bargaining power, predicted currency strength or weakness, market conditions, industry practices, and competition. After considering those factors, Samiee and Anckar divided the relevant factors into firm-level and market-based factors, a shown in Table 12-3.

In their global marketing efforts to hedge against exchange rate fluctuations, multinationals have developed some practical solutions:

- Reduce the time lag between order fulfillment and payment receipt to decrease exposure of accounts receivables; similarly, reduce payables exposure with timely payment.
- Since hedging is costly, consider balancing receipts in one currency with equal amounts of payables in that currency; that is, balance sales in a country with equal amounts of supplier sourcing in that country. Commodity hedges—owning commodities whose world price in LC will go up following a devaluation—can be a hedge against LC financial asset exposure. Similarly, real asset investments, such as those in land or plant, can be a hedge in an inflation/devaluation scenario.
- Hedge longer-term exposure, although the cost of hedging goes up with the period of coverage desired.
- Reassess sourcing decisions to switch to suppliers in weaker currencies when appropriate. This includes the possibility of switching internal sourcing to plants located in weaker-currency countries.
- Increase marketing in countries with strong currencies.
- Assess how exchange rate volatility affects competition. Which competitors are in a stronger or weaker market position, and how might they take advantage of it? Will they seek market share or higher profits?

Price Pressure and the Need to Cut Costs

If a U.S. firm must lower its prices, it will be able to do so only after cutting costs—either by redesigning the product to cut component and direct labor costs or by moving manufacturing overseas to a location with lower labor costs. However, this last, and seemingly obvious, choice can backfire on the company. Quality may be lower, and delivery may be delayed. The cost savings on the labor side may be eaten up by the need to maintain larger U.S. inventories; otherwise, the company may lose sales because its inventory is inadequate to meet orders on a timely basis. Manufacturing in a distant overseas location also makes it harder to respond to changing customer needs.

Consider the garment industry, in which low labor costs have led many U.S. firms to manufacture clothes in plants in the Far East. However, designs must be sent to the Far Eastern plants in the spring for clothes meant to be sold in the fall in the United States. Then in September, when the company finds out that certain designs are selling well, it is too late to attempt to increase production. As a result, potential sales are lost. Similarly, if some items are poor sellers, the company is stuck with excess inventory that must be sold off through sales at price discounts. The reduced profits caused by that discounting offset the gains from manufacturing overseas with lower labor costs.

A compromise between using overseas manufacturing and staying at home is the development of **maquiladora plants,** which are set up along the Mexican border by U.S. firms using Mexican labor that averages approximately $2 an hour. These workers perform assembly operations on parts and components imported from the United States; tariffs are paid when the completed product is brought back into the United States, but only on the value added by Mexican labor in Mexico. These factories allow U.S. firms to become more competitive with imports from low-wage countries in the Far East.

Table 12-3. Variables Affecting Currency Choice in Export Transactions

Firm-Level Factors	Market-Based Factors
Customer Orientation	Competition
Bargaining Power	Relative Importance of Product to Customer
Product Differentiation	Product Characteristics—Commoditization, Customization
Relative Price Control	
Relative Importance of Customer	
Firm and Transaction Characteristics	
Long-Term Nature of Relationship	

Source: Derived from S. Samiee and P. Anckar, "Currency Choice in Industrial Pricing: A Cross-National Evaluation," *Journal of Marketing,* Volume 62, July 1998, pages 112–127.

Maquiladoras are generally lower cost sources than U.S. factories and have the added advantage of being close to the U.S. customer. However, greater manufacturing efficiency and lower labor costs at more distant geographic sites can offset the advantage of Mexican maquiladoras. For example, it would seem counterintuitive to buy leather automobile seat covers from Thailand rather than from the nearer Mexican factories. Yet despite the longer supply chain, requiring a 12-week supply chain cycle and the need for safety stocks (additional inventory), a U.S. seat supplier to the auto industry chose to have his leather seat covers made in Thailand. This involved sending full containers of leather and other materials to northern Thailand to be sewed and completed. The finished leather seat covers were then sent back to the United States to be incorporated into the car seat for final delivery in a just-in-time (JIT) system to the automobile assembly line. Thailand was chosen over Mexico because of its lower labor costs and greater efficiency (that is, higher yield), which led to lower raw material (leather) costs per seat. Thus, despite higher logistics and inventory costs, Thailand became the preferred supplier. The relevant costs for the Mexican and Thai suppliers are listed in the table below.

Cost to Deliver One Leather Seat Cover, Mexico and Thailand

Cost elements	Mexico	Thailand
Labor	88	15
Leather (raw material)	199	185
Other materials	67	67
Packaging	2	6
Outbound logistics	4	21
Inbound logistics	2	8
Cost of inventory	—	3
Obsolescence allowance	—	9
Total costs	362	314

Source: "E. Rubesch and R Banomyong, "Selecting Suppliers in the Automotive Industry: Comparing International Logistics Costs," *Asia Pacific Journal of Marketing and Logistics*, Volume 17, Number 1, 2005 pages 61–69, Table 1.

Pricing Implications of International Manufacturing Decisions

Switching manufacturing locations to take advantage of lower labor costs or other factor costs is a long-run solution. It is costly and irreversible, but it is becoming increasingly common. For example, U.S. automobile companies sought to cut costs, but their union agreements made it difficult to shift jobs overseas. So the companies pressured their auto parts and subassemblies suppliers to lower their costs through outsourcing.[32] As noted earlier, price setting is partly determined by a company's cost structure. When competing in global markets, a firm must contend with the cost structure of its international competitors. Factor endowments and factor prices affect the cost structure of all companies. So an international competitor with lower-cost labor or capital can have a comparative advantage because its overall total costs are lowered to whatever extent its labor and capital costs affect its total cost of production.

However, while low-cost labor is an important factor affecting total costs, so are technology, the experience curve, and the capital intensity of manufacturing. As technology and capital equipment substitute for lower-cost direct labor, therefore, the paradoxical situation emerges that the country with the lowest-cost labor does not necessarily have the lowest total costs of production. A case in point is the example of the iron.[33] Table 12-4 gives the statistics, which show how innovative manufacturing can overcome higher labor costs.

Product Redesign and Pricing Implications

Table 12-4 compares the cost structure for irons manufactured by different companies in various locations. The irons are (1) Sunbeam's traditional product, the old iron; (2) a redesigned iron; (3) the Black & Decker iron,

Table 12-4. Cost Structure of Irons Manufactured at Various Locations

	Unit Cost	Materials	Labor	Manufacturing Overhead	Number of Parts	Number of Screws Needed
Sunbeam (old model)	9.50	4.32	1.06	4.12	73	13
Sunbeam (redesigned model)	6.66	4.10	.48	2.08	68	13
Black & Decker (Singapore)	5.98[a]	3.40	.53	1.25	74	19
Sunbeam (global model)	5.33	3.40	.35	1.58	52	3

a. Includes .80/unit of transportation costs.

Source: M. Therese Flaherty, "Emerging Global Business Environmental and Managerial Reaction to It," Paper COF-8, presented at the Ministry of International Trade and Industry Conference, Tokyo, 1988.

designed to be manufactured in Singapore; and (4) Sunbeam's latest product, the "global" iron, designed to be manufactured at low cost and sold around the world.

Sunbeam's old iron had an enormous cost disadvantage based on the design (using more materials) as well as the higher labor costs and manufacturing overhead. Black & Decker's approach was to manufacture an iron in Singapore, using almost the same design (the high number of parts needed and assembly operations indicated by the number of screws), but with lower-cost materials, overhead savings, and lower-cost labor. The unit cost advantage seems insurmountable. However, Sunbeam was able to respond to the competitive challenge with a multipart strategy:

- Redesign of the product to reduce the number of parts and assembly operations needed, thus reducing the use of direct labor
- Reduction in the cost of materials
- Reduction in the cost of direct labor (although overhead is higher than the case of Black & Decker in Singapore, reflecting the more capital-intensive nature of the manufacturing process)

Overall the data in the table underline the importance of cost structure when firms compete in product areas that are mature and subject to global competition where low-cost labor is significant. In those circumstances, pricing strategy becomes relevant only after the cost disadvantage can be overcome, which means paying attention to reducing labor cost, manufacturing overhead, and materials cost and redesigning the product so it can be manufactured at a lower cost. Thus, pricing strategy becomes closely linked to a firm's overall manufacturing strategy.

Changing manufacturing locations is, therefore, not the only way to cut costs. Product redesign and more capital-intensive manufacturing are other options. Baldor Electric, a manufacturer of industrial electric motors, faced severe competition from Taiwan, South Korea, and Japan; but it was unwilling to move to a low-wage overseas location. It feared that the quality of its product would go down and that a weakening dollar would diminish the gains from manufacturing overseas. Hence, Baldor tripled its rate of capital investment, using an adaptation of JIT manufacturing. Each worker assembles a complete motor from a full set of parts on a tray, with a computer printout providing information about the motor and how to assemble and test it. Four out of five workers attended in-house quality control seminars. The capital spending, new manufacturing methods, and focus on quality all helped Baldor innovate and stay in business while continuing to manufacture in the United States.

Remember, *pricing problems are symptoms*. In the short term, price cutting and adjustment might be the answer; but over the longer term, solutions lie in analyzing causes to the problems. As shown, exchange rates may be the initial cause of pricing problems; but a fundamental solution to the problems requires a firm to compare its structure with that of the competition, then taking action to reduce or nullify the effects of a cost disadvantage.

Export Prices in Relation to Domestic Prices

Should export prices be higher than, equal to, or less than domestic prices? If costs associated with export sales are greater than those associated with domestic sales, perhaps prices should be raised by incremental costs. For example, exports may require special packaging and handling. Extra costs may arise in translating and processing export orders, and credit and collection costs may be higher. If a company has an export department, operating costs may be higher as a percentage of sales.

Careful cost analysis is needed, however, before concluding that costs are higher for exports. Some costs allocated to domestic sales, such as domestic promotion or marketing research, do not apply to export sales. For example, foreign distributors may buy in larger quantities, assume warranty responsibility, and provide their own advertising and trade show support. Exports should bear only those costs for which the distributors are directly responsible plus, perhaps, a share of general overhead.

Even if export sales have higher costs, it does not necessarily follow that the export price should be higher than the domestic price. The best export price is the one that maximizes long-term profits. If foreign markets have lower income levels or more elastic demand curves, the most profitable export price may be lower than the domestic price. A firm may even find it necessary to modify a package or simplify a product to get the lower price needed for foreign markets.

EXPORT PRICE LESS THAN DOMESTIC

Setting the FOB plant price lower on exports than on domestic products favors export sales. Some good reasons exist for that approach:

- The lower income levels in some foreign markets may require a firm to set a lower price to achieve sales.
- Foreign competition may dictate a lower price.
- A firm realizes that even with a lower FOB plant price, the product can still be more expensive in the foreign market because of the transport and tariff costs and other add-ons. All of the add-ons can price the product out of the market if the FOB plant price is high.
- A firm may consider costs of export to be less because R&D, overhead, and other costs are already covered by domestic sales.

- A firm that sells abroad at less than domestic prices may be accused of **dumping**, selling goods in foreign markets at prices lower than those in the producer's home market. Recipient nations may complain because national producers claim that such low-price competition is unfair to them. To avoid this type of producer resentment, countries tend to penalize imports sold at dumping prices.

Marginal cost pricing for exports may be appropriate when there is excess capacity. If new investment is needed, however, company profit goals will dictate full cost pricing for exports. The excess capacity justification for lower export prices will no longer be reliable.

Another problem with export prices that are lower than domestic prices is that the producing division has less interest in export sales. Only when no domestic alternative presents itself do export sales become interesting.

MARKET-ORIENTED EXPORT PRICING

A good starting point for export price analysis is the determination of conditions in foreign markets: What are the demand and competitive situations in the target markets? Within what price range could a firm's product sell? By determining the demand situation in foreign markets, the export manager can get a base price for evaluating export opportunities. Having figured out what the market will pay, a firm must decide whether it can sell at that price, a determination it makes by working back from the market price (base price) to the cost structure of the firm. The various intermediary margins, taxes, duties, and transport and handling costs must be subtracted from the consumer price. The resulting figure will help determine the firm's FOB plant price for exports.

Price Escalation in Exporting

Because of the additional costs and steps involved in exporting, the final price to a consumer in the importing country often increases significantly. Incremental transportation and insurance costs and more intermediaries such as freight forwarders are involved in the channels of distribution. There are charges for export documentation, specialized packaging, and import duties. Table 12-5 illustrates this phenomenon.

The implication from Table 12-5 is that an exported product is typically sold for a higher price than the same product sold domestically. The higher price, in turn, raises two questions: (1) Can foreign consumers afford to buy the product at the higher price? If so, will demand be lowered because of it? (2) Will the higher price make imports less competitive against domestically produced products? The incremental distance costs associated with exporting allow domestic producer costs to be higher but to remain competitive.

Table 12-5. Export Price Escalation

	Export Price	Domestic Price
Manufacturer's FOB price	$ 9.60	$ 9.60
Ocean freight and insurance	1.08	
Landed or CIF value	10.68	
Tariff: 9% on CIF value	0.96	
CIF value plus tariff	11.64	
12% value-added tax (VAT)	1.40	
Distributor cost	13.04	9.60
Distributor markup @ 15%	1.96	1.44
Retailer cost	15.00	11.04
40% retail margin	10.00	7.36
Consumer price	25.00	18.40

In reality, shipping costs and tariffs totaling $2.04 in the table represent the true higher cost of the imported product. A manufacturer in the importing country can have higher production costs of up to $2.04 and still match the import price.

If, in fact, the manufacturer's costs in the importing country are only $1 higher, it can offer a price cut of about $2.20.[34] In that case, the exporter must consider several alternatives:

- It can discard exporting as an option, which may be a wise decision if it has plentiful opportunity for profitable growth in the domestic market.
- It can consider marginal cost pricing for exports if it has excess capacity that is expected to continue. This would allow exports to increase profits as long as more attractive domestic opportunities did not arise.
- It can try to shorten the distribution channel, for example, by selling direct to wholesalers or large retailers. Each step in the channel costs the firm something extra. Whether elimination of certain steps lowers costs for the exporting firm depends on how well it can perform the functions eliminated.
- It can modify the product to make it cheaper. A stripped-down model and smaller sizes or packaging are ways to achieve this. The company may also try to change the product for a lower duty classification.
- It can consider foreign manufacturing, assembly, or licensing as ways to tap foreign markets, avoiding many of the steps that inflate export prices. Although foreign manufacturing involves greater commitment, it could be the most profitable method if markets are large enough.

Export Price Quotations

Export price quotations include a range of possible costs associated with serving international markets, such as shipping costs and insurance. See Table 12-6 for a listing of terms.

Price quotations are important because they spell out the legal responsibilities of each party. Sellers favor a quote that gives them the least liability and responsibility, such as FOB their plant. In that case, exporters' responsibilities and liabilities end when the goods are put on carriers at their plants. Importer-buyers, on the other hand, favor a cost, insurance, and freight (CIF) to port of discharge price, which means that their responsibilities begin only when the goods are in their own country. Importers also favor CIF pricing because it facilitates price comparisons of different exporting nations and of national suppliers.

Generally, a market orientation indicates CIF (port of importation) pricing by the exporter. Note that the price quotation does not affect the total amount paid or received, but merely indicates the division of labor in providing for various transportation, handling, and insurance arrangements. The total burden of those arrangements may be lessened when exporters and importers do what they are most qualified to do. Exporters deal with their fellow nationals in arranging transportation to the port, insurance, and overseas shipping; whereas importers deal with their compatriots in unloading and transporting in their country. Occasionally, an importer is a large international organization—one of the Japanese trading companies, for example—that is better qualified to handle insurance and transportation than the exporter. That importer can gain economies of scale by taking the tasks out of the exporters' hands.

Table 12-6. Export Price Quotations

Ex (point of origin)
  Ex factory, ex mine, ex warehouse, etc.

FOB (free on board)
  FOB (named inland carrier)
  FOB freight allowed to (named point of exportation)
  FOB vessel (named port of shipment)
  FOB (named inland point in country of importation)

FAS (free alongside)
  FAS vessel (named port of shipment)

C&F (cost and freight)
  C&F (named point of destination)

CIF (cost, insurance, and freight)
  CIF (named point of destination)

Export Credit and Terms

Export credit and terms constitute another complex pricing area for the international market. The task is to choose payment terms that satisfy importers yet safeguard the interests of the exporter. On purely financial considerations, the exporter would favor very hard terms; that is, cash in advance of shipment—or even in advance of production for custom items. Because importers dislike bearing the financial burden implied in cash-in-advance terms, usually an exporter can demand prepayment only when producing merchandise to an importer's specifications.

In lieu of cash in advance, an export marketer can consider a range of terms that generally add to the convenience of the buyer while increasing the risks and financial burdens of the exporter. In order of increasing attractiveness to the importer are several common payment methods:

1. Cash in advance
2. Letters of credit
3. Time or sight drafts (bills of exchange)
4. Open account
5. Consignment

LETTERS OF CREDIT AND DRAFTS

Letters of credit and drafts are the most common forms of export financing. A **draft** is drawn by the exporter on the importer, who makes the draft a trade acceptance by writing the word accepted on it and signing it. The signature makes payment a legal obligation. The **letter of credit** is similar, except that it is drawn on a bank and becomes a bank acceptance rather than a trade acceptance. The bank's entrance into the payment process means greater assurance of payment for the exporter.

The terms of both are relatively strict and favor the exporter in that they spell out specific responsibilities and payment times for the importer, although they do not preclude credit extension. For example, time drafts are customarily drawn for periods ranging from 30 to 180 days after sight or after date. An exporter usually feels more secure with a letter of credit than with a draft. A letter of credit is safer for the exporter, but it is more costly for the importer.

OPEN ACCOUNT

In *open account* sales, terms are agreed to by the buyer and seller, but without documents clearly specifying the importer's payment obligations. Open account terms involve less paperwork and give more flexibility to both parties. However, the legal recourse of the exporter in case of default is less satisfactory than with the methods discussed previously. Open account sales are more attractive to the importer. But because of the risks to the exporter, open account sales tend to be limited to foreign subsidiaries, joint ventures and licensees, and foreign customers with whom the exporter has had long and favorable experience.

As a further precaution in open account sales, an exporter must consider the availability of foreign exchange in the importing country. In countries with tight foreign exchange positions, in foreign exchange allocation, imports covered by documentary drafts generally receive priority over imports on open account.

CONSIGNMENT

Since the exporter retains title until the importer sells the goods, consignment sales are not really sales. Because exporters own the goods longer in this method than in any other, their financial burdens and risk are great. In addition, legal recourse in case of misbehavior by importers and foreign exchange allocations are more difficult to obtain. Because of those problems, exporters tend to limit consignment arrangements to their subsidiaries abroad.

When exporters want to introduce goods to a new market, a consignment arrangement may be necessary to encourage importers to handle the merchandise. Furthermore, when exporters want to retain some control over the foreign market price, they can do so under a consignment contract. They can set the price when they own the goods, as they do under a consignment contract.

COMPANY-WIDE MODELS FOR REVENUE HEDGING

An innovative corporate-wide approach to managing the impact of volatile exchange rates is Merck's revenue hedging model of the mid-90s, shown in Figure 12-3.

The model attempts to gauge the impact of foreign exchange volatility on Merck's long-term capital and R&D expenditure programs. To do that, the model accepts as input the planned capital and R&D outlays and the forecasts of anticipated cash flows in multiple local currencies. It also adds forecasts of exchange rates for all relevant currencies over a five-year planning horizon and equations that link foreign exchange changes with forecasted earnings and cash flows. Stage 2 simulates the impact of different hedging strategies through the input of purchases and sales of foreign exchange forward contracts, as well as the use of theoretical option pricing models to calculate the value of the hedges purchased. Stage 3 is the actual simulation. For each iteration of estimated cash flows and forecasted foreign exchange rates, U.S. dollar cash flows are calculated and compared to programmed expenditures. Furthermore, the statistical distribution of earnings, both hedged and unhedged, are compared under different hedging and foreign exchange scenarios, possibly resulting

Figure 12-3. Merck's Revenue Hanging Model

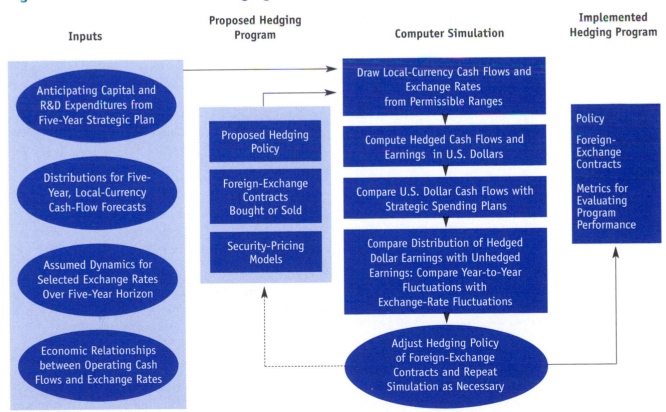

Source: Nancy A. Nichols, "Scientific Management at Merck: An Interview with CFO Judy Lewent," *Harvard Business Review* (January–February, 1994), 96.

in revised hedging strategies. The simulation model ends with a set of suggested hedging policies.[35]

Merck's model to cope with exchange rate volatility has many outstanding features, including a long-term simulation approach to measuring the impact of exchange rate volatility, the use of option pricing models to value hedged positions, and a recommended set of hedging policies as output. The model is not deterministic; instead, it provides executive users with a range of outcomes and a statistical probability distribution of the expected cash flows and earnings when the recommended hedging strategies are followed. The model is also heuristic in that it suggests new hedging strategies until a combination of strategies is found that matches simulated hedged cash flows with the amount of funds needed based on capital spending and R&D programs already committed to.

While the revenue hedging model is a headquarters model intended to approach the optimum for a company as a whole, Merck is also committed to using regional and national strategies to reduce the impact of foreign exchange volatility. For example, during the seventies, Merck had a range of controlled assembly operations across Latin America. They imported active chemical ingredients from Merck facilities in the United States and elsewhere and locally assembled the raw materials into tablets, capsules, and injections for local sale. During the eighties, the Latin American economic climate deteriorated, resulting in Merck's decision to pull out of manufacturing operations there. It preferred to license independent local companies that purchased the same raw materials, assembled them into pharmaceutical tablets and capsules, and sold them in Latin American markets. Once Latin economies moved to privatization—a reining in of inflation and government deficits and a greater reliance on the private sector—Merck once again changed course, buying back the rights to various Latin markets from its licensees and beginning again to manufacture for its own account. Merck's example suggests that foreign exchange rates have a deep strategic effect on long-term multinational operations.[36]

CURRENCY INCONVERTIBILITY

Most free-market economies follow a regime of freely floating exchange rates with complete convertibility of the currency. However, many countries, including key emerging markets such as China, still have restrictions on the convertibility of their currencies, allowing the governments to maintain artificial exchange rates that may diverge significantly from a freely floating or black-market exchange rate. Such currency inconvertibility also poses problems for multinationals seeking to integrate myriad multinational operations and transfer payments for goods and equipment supplied, as well as payment of dividends and capital repatriation.

Figure 12-4 provides an example of different approaches used by Pepsi in China. Shown are some of the stresses and creativity that currency inconvertibility fosters.

China's exchange controls are due to its desire to conserve scarce foreign exchange and use it for approved purposes such as imports of capital equipment and essential raw materials. The Chinese government prefers that multinationals become self-sufficient in foreign exchange by exporting sufficient amounts to generate the foreign exchange needed to pay for their imports and foreign-exchange outflows. Figure 12-4 shows some alternatives developed by Pepsi to handle exchange controls.[37]

Model A of Figure 12-4 shows how Pepsi can use surplus cash generated in one Pepsi subsidiary to fund the capital needs of another Pepsi subsidiary, thus obviating the need to send additional foreign exchange capital contributions into China. However, this runs up against the desire of Chinese states to conserve capital for use within the states. Thus, a state could prevent Pepsi from transferring capital out. More generally, such a solution works only as long as a multinational can use local funds to continue to expand within the country. Imports of machinery and components still have to be paid for with additional foreign exchange. In Pepsi's case, it needs to expand across China because soft drink consumption is still at low levels and there is considerable room for growth. Other companies, however, may not find enough attractive investment opportunities.

Model B shows how Pepsi can tap additional LC sources to meet its capital needs without having to bring in foreign exchange. In this instance, Pepsi relies on its connections with foreign banks to borrow hard currency (HC), which it then uses as collateral to borrow LC from a Chinese bank. As Pepsi's units generate funds from operations, the LC loans can be paid off. Paying off those loans releases the HC collateral, which, in turn, can be repaid to the foreign bank. The cost is higher because Pepsi has to pay interest on two loans, both the HC and the LC loans. However, this method prevents Pepsi from having to make additional HC contributions to its Chinese operations.

Model C is an illustration of how Pepsi might use surplus LC funds to source goods in China that can be used by Pepsi subsidiaries overseas. For example, Pepsi might use surplus LC to buy ingredients such as mushrooms for its international chain of Pizza Hut shops. Alternatively, Pepsi can use its surplus LC funds to invest in joint ventures with Chinese partners to start up new operations that supply goods to Pepsi's overseas subsidiaries or to use for general export purposes. China prefers this third alternative because it deepens China's business base and capabilities.

As the three models in Figure 12-4 show, getting paid becomes at least as important as making the basic pricing decision in major emerging markets. Pricing executives need to carefully consider how the foreign exchange situation can affect their pricing flexibility.

Figure 12-4. Pepsi in China: Dealing with Currency Volatility and Inconvertibililty

The problem: Inconvertibility of the Chinese currency (Renminbi) makes it difficult to remit dividends, repatriate capital, and import needed materials, parts, and capital goods.
The Chinese government solution: Earn export revenues sufficient to pay for imports and foreign currency outflows (dividends, imports, and capital repatriation).

A.

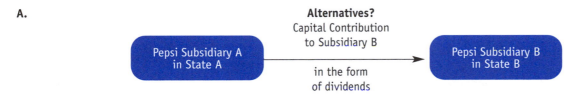

States Reluctant to Allow Interstate Transfers of Capital

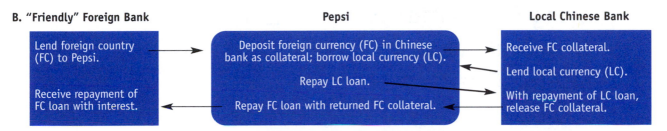

B. "Friendly" Foreign Bank

Net Cost to Company: Interest on FC and LC Borrowing, Less Interest Received on FC Collateral

C.

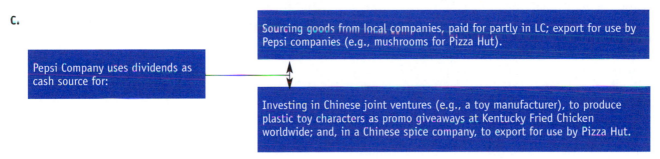

Source: Derived from "Learn from Russia," *Business China*, September 5, 1994, 1–3.

Options for Realizing Foreign Exchange Receivables[38]

Firms with export or foreign sales often face the problem of realizing their foreign client receivables. Normal commercial credit terms, when combined with additional delays in the international receivables collection process, can strain a company's working capital availability. Hence, many firms, especially smaller ones, seek to accelerate foreign receivables realization. Short-term receivables may be factored; that is, factors will exchange a receivable for cash at about 85 to 90 percent of the value, particularly if the transaction has been insured by an agency such as the Eximbank (Export-Import Bank of the United States). Upon collection, the company receives the balance less the factor's commission, which may be between 1 and 3 percent.

Forfaiting is more common with longer-term receivables, such as those associated with capital goods projects. Specialized forfait companies such as London Forfaiting work with receivables guaranteed by foreign banks and governments, charging a commission about 3 percent of the transaction value. Forfaiters often work with an exporter to determine the terms of the sale so the forfaiters' interests are covered, making the forfait agreement more likely. The exporter can then try to negotiate an export price that covers the forfaiter's commission. Forfaiters place the guarantee received from the foreign bank or government agency (known as avalizers) as an endorsement on the bill of exchange or other document evidencing the debt. This allows resale of the document on financial markets and enhances liquidity. A number of forfaited loans may be bundled together and sold on the secondary market to portfolio investors. This increases the total capacity of the world market for forfaits and reduces forfaiting commissions, making forfaiting more attractive to smaller firms. Forfaiting commission is also influenced by risk factors such as the debt rating for the debtor and its country, foreign exchange volatility, and overall debt service ratios. Forfaiting instruments are medium- to long-term instruments, with repayment in installments stretching over several years. The upfront fixed costs of setting up the forfait instrument and perhaps repackaging it to sell to secondary investors also sets a floor for transaction size, making forfaiting transactions economical only for large amounts over $1 million.

Financing International Sales: A Component of International Pricing

The terms of financing determine the final effective price paid by a buyer. If the cost of capital is 12 percent per year and a buyer is allowed to pay the bill in 90 days, that 90 days of free credit amounts to a 3 percent discount on the purchase price. When a purchaser perceives products from international competitors as being reasonably similar, the purchaser may choose the supplier that provides the best financing terms, resulting in the greatest effective discount. Thus, when Embraer, a Brazilian manufacturer of small aircraft, wanted to introduce its 19-seat commuter plane to the United States, it offered long-term (six years or more) financing at about 8 percent. Because Embraer was a state-owned enterprise, it could guarantee the availability of such credit. Fairchild Aircraft, a U.S. competitor, filed an "unfair trade practices" complaint with the USITC because of this low-interest-rate financing, offered at a time when U.S. interest rates were around 12 percent.[39]

Without government help, U.S. firms might find it impossible to offer the necessary financing. Ellicott Machine Corporation of Baltimore could not have sold its dredges to the former Yugoslavia without government help. The company had bid on a project to supply a dredge to mine coal near the Danube River, but the customer needed financing. Because Ellicott received a state of Maryland guarantee from the Maryland Industrial Development Financing Authority, it was able to offer 100 percent financing. Further, with the help of the Maryland Office of International Trade, Ellicott was able to get a Maryland State grant to offer training to customer personnel. That led to scholarships at the University of Maryland to train Yugoslav engineers in disciplines relevant to the project. Such government help led to an initial contract of $25 million awarded to Ellicott, with possible add-ons that could total nearly $100 million.

To successfully use financing as a competitive weapon in international marketing, two conditions are usually necessary:

1. A firm must have the ability to fund the long-term receivables at below-market interest rates. This condition usually favors state-owned enterprises and larger multinationals, which can borrow at lower rates and in countries where borrowing costs are low.
2. A firm must receive official government backing to subsidize the lower interest rates offered, as well as guarantee the loans. The government backing is necessary to match the best offers made by international competitors. Without government guarantees, private (U.S.) banks cannot make the loan; and without a government subsidy, below-market rates cannot be offered. Several nations have an established policy of offering such favorable financing as part of packages designed to promote exports from their countries.

A related problem for U.S. firms is that fewer commercial banks practice trade finance. Banks can make as much money on residential mortgages as they can on government-guaranteed export loans. Making export loans is also a labor-intensive business, requiring manager expertise. As a result, some money center banks have deliberately reduced their trade finance activities.

Twenty-two industrialized countries met in the early 1980s to limit such credit subsidies. The result was an agreement that specified minimum interest rates and maximum repayment periods for most categories of exports sold on credit terms of over two years.[40] However, a loophole is the use of **tied aid**, in which foreign aid is granted with the condition that a portion of the aid be used to buy goods from the aid-granting country. Thus, an exporter seeking a sale of $1 million might be able to allow the importer to use $100,000 of aid granted by the exporter's government to pay for part of the sale. That way, the exporter is offering a price cut of $100,000, or 10 percent, which is, in effect, equivalent to a direct interest rate or price subsidy. A 1989 Eximbank study estimated that $400 million to $800 million in potential U.S. exports were being lost because of tied aid in industries such as telecommunications, electric power systems, computers, and heavy earth-moving vehicles. Countries such as Canada, France, Germany, Italy, Britain, and Japan account for about 75 percent of all such credit subsidies.

While decrying such practices, the United States has, in self-defense, begun providing some tied aid on a limited scale. Yet the United States accounted for only about 2 percent of the world volume of tied aid. Eximbank is the main U.S. financing agency for international trade.

Other forms of government-supported trade development can help a firm bring in international sales. The U.S. Trade Development Agency offers funding to carry out market feasibility studies when matched with private funds. Thus, ABB Lummus of New Jersey obtained $300,000 in funds to study the feasibility of modernizing the Lukoil oil refinery in Russia. When the study was completed, Lukoil signed over $21 million in contracts for U.S. technology licenses and engineering services.

As suggested above, governments routinely offer tied aid as a means of export promotion. A Government Accounting Office study noted that OECD nations typically tied over half of their capital project aid to purchases from donor countries' firms. Compared to tied-aid percentages as high as 91 percent for Germany, 76 percent for Japan, and 73 percent for France, U.S. tied aid represented only 17 percent of capital project commitments over the 1988–1991 period.[41] In response, the U.S. Eximbank set up a war chest to counter other nations' tied-aid subsidies and was funded at $200 million in 1993. Eximbank disbursed war chest funds equal to about 30 percent of export value over the 1987–1993 period.

Transfer Pricing in International Marketing

Transfer pricing (intracorporate pricing) is an area that has special implications for international marketing. It refers to prices on goods sold within the corporate family; that is, from division to division or to a foreign subsidiary. (See "Global Marketing: Transfer Pricing at Hewlett-Packard.")

PRODUCT DIVISION TO INTERNATIONAL DIVISION

The transfer price paid by the international group to the producing division should have certain characteristics if it is to optimize corporate, rather than divisional, profit. For the producing division, the price should be high enough to encourage a flow of products for export. The transfer price does this if sales to the international division are as attractive as sales to other parties. The price to the international division may be even lower than to other parties if the services the international division renders (market research, promotion, etc.) warrant it.

For the international division, the transfer price should be low enough to enable it to be both competitive and profitable in the foreign market. Obviously, there is room for conflict. The producing division wants a high price, and the international division wants a low price. The transfer pricing mechanism must be such that the overall corporate interest is not ignored in the divisional conflict. A profit margin that is unattractive to one or the other division (or to both) may be worthwhile from the overall corporate viewpoint.

GLOBAL MARKETING

Transfer Pricing at Hewlett-Packard

*T*ransfer pricing plays a key role in coordinating numerous and distant profit centers at Hewlett-Packard, a multinational firm that gets over half of its sales from outside the United States. The company's transfer pricing objectives include (1) motivating local managers who want to show large profits, (2) minimizing the chances of a tax audit, and (3) moving profits to low-tax jurisdictions while satisfying tax authorities of the business reasons for those moves. Hewlett-Packard's accounting and finance manual describes the basis for transfer pricing, using either a list price minus a discount or a cost-plus method. The company typically uses cost plus 10 percent as the desired company rate of return. The Internal Revenue Service (IRS) generally advises corporations to base transfer pricing markups on a return on assets method.

Hewlett-Packard believes, however, that the return on assets method is more appropriate to capital-intensive and machinery-based industries. Hewlett-Packard and other high-tech companies spend an enormous amount on R&D, which is often expensed. Thus, capital assets may be understated. Hence, Hewlett-Packard argues that using a cost-plus method allows adequate return to R&D. Hewlett-Packard's tax department breaks down the profit from each product line and shows how it is allocated among R&D, manufacturing, and sales.

However, to avoid ongoing conflicts with the IRS over transfer pricing, Hewlett-Packard has considered whether to adhere to the new approach to transfer pricing, called advanced determination rulings (ADRs). The ADR method suggests that rather than wait for an audit to rule on the acceptability of a formula already in use, companies should submit proposed transfer pricing plans to determine whether they comply with IRS regulations. However, Hewlett-Packard believes that the ADR approach needs to be modified to make it more attractive. A few areas of concern exist:

- *The amount of detailed information and economic analysis required is enormous. (HP found this burden to be as great as the requirements of a tax audit.)*
- *The financial information disclosed can become available to competitors.*

continued

- *The information submitted would later be used by other parts of the IRS in a tax audit. Hewlett-Packard wanted the IRS department carrying out the ADR to be in a different jurisdiction from the one doing previous years' tax audits. Similarly, Hewlett-Packard wanted IRS agents involved in the ADR to agree not to disclose information gained from the ADR to agents conducting an audit.*

Given the importance of transfer pricing, ADRs look promising, especially because other countries use them (for example, Japan and Germany); and bilateral agreements are being developed. Under bilateral agreements between two countries, the results of one country's ADR investigations would be accepted in the other country.

Sources: "Hewlett-Packard: Making Transfer Pricing Work," *Business International*, November 12, 1990; "Hewlett-Packard: Jousting with the IRS over Transfer Prices," *Business International Money Report*, June 11, 1990.

Assume that the producing division makes a product at a full cost of $50. It sells that product to outside buyers for $60, but the transfer price to the international division is $58. The producing division may be unhappy because the markup is 20 percent lower to the international division ($8 versus $10). The international division adds its various export marketing expenses of $10, for an export cost of $68. For competitive reasons, the international division cannot sell the product for more than $72, or a $4 return. Since that is less than 6 percent of sales, the international division is also unhappy. However, the return to the corporation is $12 on $72, or almost 17 percent ($8 from the producing division plus $4 from the international division). The corporation may find that attractive, even though both divisions are unhappy with it.

Different approaches can be taken to solve that problem. One solution is to eliminate one division as a profit center. The producing division can be judged on the basis of costs and other performance criteria instead of profit. Then the producing division can sell to the international division at a price enabling it to become competitive in foreign markets. Market pricing will not be handicapped by internal markups of the transfer pricing process, and the total corporate profit will be given greater attention.

On the other hand, the international division can operate as a service center rather than as a profit center, thus eliminating one source of conflict. A question arises, however, about whether a selling organization can be as efficient and motivated when it is not operating under a profit constraint. A related possibility is to have the international division act as a commission agent for the producing divisions. When the international division is not a profit center, its expenses can be allocated back to the product divisions.

Transfer pricing can be established in three ways: at manufacturing cost, at arm's length, and at cost-plus.

Transfer at Manufacturing Cost

When profit centers are maintained, several alternatives are possible. At one extreme (and favoring the international division) is the transfer at direct manufacturing cost. This is the lowest cost, probably well under what the producing division could obtain from other customers. The producing division dislikes selling at manufacturing cost because it believes it is subsidizing the international division and thereby taking a loss when compared with other profit centers. A firm may offset this by an accounting or memorandum profit to the producing division on its sales for export. Such memorandum profits, unfortunately, are never as satisfactory as the real thing. When the product division is unhappy, the international division may get sluggish service because the product division is servicing more attractive domestic opportunities first.

Transfer at Arm's Length

The other extreme in transfer pricing is to charge the international division the same price any buyer outside the firm pays. This price favors the producing division because it does as well on internal as on external sales, sometimes even better. The services rendered by the international division and the elimination of the credit problem can make export sales especially profitable.

If the product has no external buyers, however, a problem occurs in trying to determine an arm's-length price. An artificial price must be constructed. Further difficulties arise because that price fails to take into account the services performed by the international division and because the international division may be noncompetitive with the price. Finally, there is no real reason why the price to foreign buyers should be determined by the domestic market.

Transfer at Cost-Plus

Between the transfer pricing extremes just discussed is a range of prices that involves a profit split between the producing and international divisions. Starting from the cost floor, cost-plus pricing attempts to add on some amount or percentage that will make the resulting price acceptable to both divisions. The "plus" may be a percentage negotiated between the divisions, a percentage of product division overhead, or a percentage return on product division investment. Further variation can be caused by using different definitions of cost. In any case, the pricing formula is less important than the results obtained. A good transfer pricing formula should consider total corporate profit and encourage divisional cooperation. It should also minimize the time that executives spend on transfer price disagreements and keep the accounting burden to a minimum.

Other factors affecting the transfer price charged include whether there are restrictions on capital outflows from a market; what level of customs tariffs exist in each market; and whether the two transacting parties are wholly owned by the firm or whether one of the two entities is a licensee, a joint-venture, or a minority-owned partner.

The Tax Authority's Interest

When countries have different levels of taxation on corporate profits, firms may want to accumulate profits in countries with low taxes. They would like to use a low transfer price to subsidiaries in low-tax countries and a high transfer price to subsidiaries in high-tax countries. U.S. companies, for example, are tempted to sell at low transfer prices to countries that have lower corporate tax rates than the United States. The IRS, however, is on guard against this because it does not want to lose taxable income to other countries. Therefore, it carefully scrutinizes the transfer prices of international companies to ensure that they are not too low. One specific demand of the IRS is that export prices bear a share of domestic R&D expenses. The IRS wants to be sure that an equitable portion of the income remains under U.S. tax jurisdiction. Transfer pricing cases can drag on for years. Therefore, corporations and the IRS have begun to establish procedures whereby firms set out the transfer pricing scheme they want to pursue and try to get the IRS to agree that the scheme results in a fair price. At the same time, the firms are anxious to prevent too much sensitive financial information from being handed over to the IRS. Similar problems confront firms using transfer pricing in other tax jurisdictions, especially when the tax authorities of various countries begin to share transfer pricing data and attempt joint regulation of transfer pricing.

An interesting approach is to use activity-based costing (ABC) in calculating costs. ABC allows for more rigorous allocation of costs and facilitates a company's ability to negotiate an advanced pricing agreement (APA) with tax authorities, whereby they approve a transfer pricing policy in advance, avoiding subsequent charges of tax avoidance. The key is to develop specific cost drivers for each activity. The ABC approach results in distinctly different profits being generated at different geographic locations, compared to use of a broader metric for cost allocation such as labor hours, even though total profitability remains the same under both methods. A company benefits when the ABC-based cost and profit derivation results in additional profits being generated in low tax areas in a manner that is recognized and accepted by tax authorities.[42]

Countertrade

As discussed previously, countertrade is a form of financing international trade wherein price setting and financing are tied together in one transaction. It is essentially barter, the exchange of goods for goods, but with some flexibility. In barter, the exact item to be exchanged is specified, such as oil for machinery. In countertrade, a range of specified goods can be taken in exchange for exports from a Western supplier. For example, Catalyst Research of Maryland began selling specialized batteries for pacemakers to Tesla, the Czech electronics collective. In 1986, Tesla bought the rights to manufacture the pacemaker battery, with Catalyst selling the equipment, supplies, and raw materials needed. As part of the agreement, Catalyst Research started buying product inventions from the Czech Academy of Sciences to fulfill its countertrade obligations.

A typical transaction might be as follows: A Polish apple juice factory may need new equipment, but it is unable to buy from a U.S. supplier because no U.S. bank will lend it money. However, an Austrian bank is willing to guarantee the factory's debt; hence, the order goes to an Austrian manufacturer. The Austrian bank undertakes to buy a large portion of the apple juice produced for resale to Western markets. It is able to do that because most Austrian banks have their own in-house trading companies. (Austria's proximity to the Eastern European countries has led to a concentration of countertrade expertise in Vienna.) Through this convoluted chain, the Polish factory gets the equipment, the Austrian manufacturer gets an order, and the bank makes fees from the loan guarantee and commissions on sale of the apple juice.[43]

The role of countertrade in world trade is increasing, accounting for about 15 percent of all world trade in 1996. Much of the growth in countertrade has occurred because of domination of the former Communist bloc economies by state trading. Such government monopolies use countertrade to make up for economic inefficiencies, while using their ability to control access to their domestic markets as a way to convince Western suppliers to agree to countertrade. Those trends have been exacerbated by uneven economic growth and shortages of FC caused by a lack of creditworthiness and past overborrowing.

There are several forms of countertrade:

- *Barter*, the simplest, is the direct exchange of goods for goods. It is cumbersome because each party must have goods in the exact quantities that the other party wants. It is the least attractive form of countertrade.
- *Counterpurchase* is reciprocal buying to be fulfilled over some future time period, with flexibility as to the actual goods to be purchased. In these transactions, a majority of the purchase price is paid in cash. An example of this is the way in which Lurgi,

a European construction and engineering firm, built a methanol plant for East Germany. In return for the 400 million DM contract to build the plant, Lurgi took back 408,000 tons a year of methanol, out of its total capacity of 800,000 tons. At the time the contract was signed, there was an excess supply, which eased only gradually as older, environmentally unacceptable plants were closed in Western Europe. Heinz Schimmelbusch, chair of Metallgesellschaft A.G., however, sees such deals as the major growth path for his Lurgi subsidiary because Eastern Europe is more willing to accept polluting plants if Western companies can solve their foreign exchange shortages.[44]

- *Offset* is similar to counterpurchase and is more likely at the government level. When dealing with government buyers, the other party has a generalized commitment to buy a certain percentage of the initial export transaction from the country. Thus, when Boeing sold AWACs to the British defense department, it agreed to buy 130 percent of the value of the transaction in British goods. A recent example of an offset deal is in South Africa, which purchased over $5 billion worth of arms from foreign defense companies on the condition that the suppliers would, in turn, "invest or spend on South African goods . . . three times as much as the weapons cost to buy." BAE/Saab, which won a $2.2 billion contract to supply fighter jets plans to open a timber plant, plans to generate $500 million in exports over the next decade, as part of a total commitment to create $8.7 billion of economic value by 2011.[45]

- *Buyback* occurs when capital equipment sales are sold with a counterpurchase clause that can be fulfilled by a firm buying some of the output of the plant that is set up with the imported capital equipment.

- *Switch trading* involves a third party, usually a specialized trading house with expertise in certain industrial sectors and with certain countries, usually centrally planned economies. Austria and Switzerland are two sources of expertise; several switch trading firms are located in those two countries.[46]

Countertrade involves forced sourcing, often from centrally planned economies and newly industrializing nations. Those sources of product may not have advanced technology and high-quality products. By default, then, countertrade forces an exporter to develop a strategic purchasing policy for countertrade opportunities. The Internet has led to the emergence of Internet-based online barter exchange companies such as BigVine and BarterTrust. They are seeking to attract small businesses to build up a global barter network. The difficulty is that the "currency" created by those barter exchanges is only usable within the

exchange. Therefore, it is not as useful until the network is large enough and has global reach so that the barter "currency" has wide and deep value.[47]

Before deciding to enter into countertrade, an exporter should scout firms in the targeted country to decide whether reliable suppliers (of raw materials or components) can be developed. It also should be willing to help upgrade the manufacturing capability of potential suppliers so that useful raw materials and components are obtained at reasonable prices as a result of the countertrade opportunity. Otherwise, the firm is likely to be stuck with poor-quality goods that are difficult to trade.

Countertrade, then, should be viewed as the initiation of a long-term relationship between a country and its firms. That, in turn, will satisfy the needs of the countries that resort to countertrade. Typically, such developing nations use countertrade for several reasons:

- They lack foreign exchange.
- They want as partners multinationals that will help sell their goods overseas.
- They hope that successful technology transfer will take place as multinationals work with domestic firms to transform them into reliable suppliers of high-quality raw materials and components.
- All of this, they hope, will increase domestic employment and incomes and lead to economic development.

Creativity in Countertrade

As countertrade evolves, Western firms often have to develop new forms of the countertrade model to adapt to changing circumstances in the FC-constrained buying nations. Several new forms of countertrade have been developed: the advance purchase model, the letter-of-credit model, the blocked evidence account, and the export prefinancing method.[48]

A new form of countertrade is the advance purchase model. A Western firm first buys locally manufactured goods from a company in a countertrade country such as an eastern European economy. This Western purchase provides HC. However, the HC is put into an escrow account with a Western bank. The local firm then buys goods from the Western firm, which is paid out of the escrow account. The local government may not be totally accepting of this advance purchase-escrow account model because it involves opening a foreign account in the name of a local citizen or entity. That can raise fears that the FC account will become a conduit for illegal payments and unauthorized retention of FC earnings. Governments may also be able to exercise sovereign authority and request sequestration of such accounts, blocking access to the account by both the local company and the Western firm.

Figure 12-5. The Export-Prefinancing Method of Countertrade

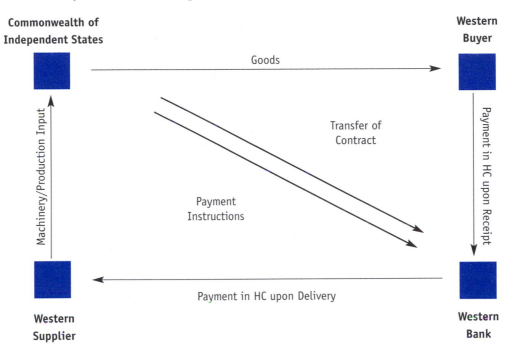

Source: "Countertrade," *Business Eastern Europe*, January 17, 1994.

A second approach to countertrade is the issuance of back-to-back letters of credit. Under this model, the Western firm opens an LC account in the name of the local firm but stipulates that funds may not be released until the local firm fulfills its side of the bargain. That is, the local firm must export the local goods under contract terms and furnish its own LC for purchase of the Western company's goods.

A third approach is the blocked evidence account, which allows a Western firm to transact multiple countertrade deals without having to balance each deal separately. The deposit by the Western company is "blocked," and the local company cannot get access to the funds until certain terms are met. A sequence of steps must occur:

1. The Western firm exports goods to the local firm.
2. The local firm receives goods from the Western firm and pays in LC into a blocked account with a local bank.
3. An independent trading company (acting as intermediary for the Western firm) buys goods from the local firm and pays with the LC in the account.
4. The trading company then pays for the goods in HC into the blocked account (possibly following successful export of the goods to a HC market).
5. The HC is received by the Western firm.

With such a complex chain of transactions, the main risk to the Western firm is that the local firm will not deliver to the trading company the goods contracted for. If that happens, the LC deposit in Step 2 can be used by the Western firm to purchase different goods for possible export.

A fourth method is the export prefinancing method, shown in Figure 12-5. This method is appropriate when a local firm has a Western buyer for its goods but needs help in setting up its manufacturing facility to produce the goods. The Western firm that can supply machinery and components to fulfill the order sells them in return for having the sales contract for final goods transferred to a Western bank. When the local firm produces and exports the final goods, the Western buyer then pays HC to the Western bank holding the sales contract. The bank, in turn, remits HC to the Western supplier of equipment and components.

While it is apparent that all of those methods are "second-best," tortuous, and cumbersome, they are creative responses to developing customers who have HC resource restraints.

In addition to being creative, success in countertrade requires a company to develop a strategic plan. Figure 12-6 outlines the major steps in implementing countertrade:

1. Ensure that the benefits outweigh the costs of carrying out countertrade.

Figure 12-6. Countertrade Implementation

2. Develop a countertrade strategy, including the development of foreign countertrade suppliers.
3. Get top management's support by explaining to them what task is involved and why countertrade will benefit the company.
4. Develop an organizational structure for countertrade. This includes deciding whether to rely on outside help or to keep the entire effort in-house. Outside help is particularly useful when goods obtained in countertrade are not needed by the exporting firm.

Separate contracts for the sale of goods and for the receipt of goods in countertrade can also help make the operation successful. The contract should specify the quality and the nature of goods to be received in countertrade. The contract should also clarify any restrictions that might be sought on the resale of Western goods and into what territories the goods may be resold. Penalty clauses and bank guarantees may be necessary to protect against non-compliance.[49]

It is difficult to ascertain the ultimate profit from a countertrade transaction. Several relevant payment streams must be examined:

- Net profit from the export of goods
- Plus/minus the profit or loss on disposition of goods received in countertrade (In the case of commodities such as oil, prices can fall rapidly, reducing the sales proceeds of the goods received in countertrade.)
- Less the imputed interest on the capital tied up in inventory of goods received in countertrade until disposed of
- Less the commissions paid to third parties, such as trading companies to help in disposing of goods received in countertrade (A World Bank study on countertrade deals in Indonesia found that about 85 percent of the total commissions went to brokers and intermediaries who arranged the various steps in the countertrade transaction.[50])
- Less the incremental marketing expenses associated with countertrade

Those factors help determine the short-term profit associated with a countertrade transaction. Generally, the profit will be lower than a straightforward market-based transaction, reflecting the second-best and inefficient nature of the countertrade approach. However, countertrade does have a strategic aspect—as a long-term source of materials and components and as a way of breaking into new markets. Hence, the opportunity costs of a countertrade transaction can be viewed as a strategic investment in gaining long-term market position. Countertrade as an isolated transaction makes little business sense.

Leasing in International Markets

Leasing—an alternative to outright purchasing—is an important pricing-financing-marketing device for expensive equipment. Offering competitive leasing terms can be crucial to winning orders in international markets.

For example, GPA Group Ltd., an aircraft leasing firm, placed a $16.8 billion order in 1989 for over 300 jet aircraft, one of the largest orders ever. Its order accounted for 10 percent of all aircraft built through 1995. Jet aircraft are expensive—at about $35 million for a modern Airbus A320 and climbing to $145 million for a long-range Boeing 747 (see Case 10.1). Given their high capital cost, leased aircraft appeal to small start-up airlines and to large carriers. In both cases, precious capital can be conserved for other areas, such as ground support, acquisition of aircraft gates, and a worldwide airline reservation system.

In effect, airlines are deciding that it is not necessary to own aircraft in order to provide airline service. The separation of ownership of aircraft from the airlines that operate them, however, raises questions. Will an adequate inventory of spares be kept? Will the lessee provide the same quality of maintenance services to leased aircraft? If leased planes are quickly available, will there be enough time for the training of flight crew? Aircraft manufacturers have traditionally relied on the airlines to provide information about their needs and market trends, which are used in designing new aircraft. If manufacturers cannot get direct market information from the airlines, deciding on the correct passenger capacity and flying range for a new model aircraft may be more difficult. Also, the emergence of a few large buyers such as GPA and International Lease Finance Corporation (ILFC), who then lease the purchased aircraft, results in an oligopoly on the buy side. Such clout can help drive down prices and reduce margins for aircraft manufacturers.

As the aircraft example shows, leasing is most likely with expensive capital equipment and undercapitalized purchasers in an environment in which credit is tight. Leasing can be seen as an opportunity; it is less risky to the purchaser, and firms can use that lower risk to convince would-be buyers to try new equipment. In new markets, leasing can be the avenue to obtaining the first few sales, thus providing an installed base. Then, subsequent sales prospects can be referred to the initial lease sales to get data on machine performance. In industrial selling, demonstrations of equipment in a practical real-life environment can be a powerful motivator to closing a sale.

Leasing can also help cope with downturns in an economy. Corporations might find it easier to take on moderate-sized lease payments if obtaining approval of large capital investments is not possible. A number of such leases can also lead to a predictable and recurring revenue stream in the form of lease payments. Another advantage to the lessee is the better maintenance that is available under a lease contract. In countries with shortages of trained service personnel, service facilities, and spare parts, maintenance service can be important. Finally, when product life cycles are short, customers may be unwilling to purchase high-priced equipment that might become obsolete. Leasing allows the sale to be made, with the manufacturer sharing a portion of the risk from obsolescence.

A complicating factor in international leases is the currency in which the lease is denominated. If LC leases are allowed, issues such as the expected pace of local inflation and expected future devaluations are relevant. Clauses allowing for adjustment to such anticipated or expected inflation and devaluation are a must. Also, the company must obtain the necessary permissions to ensure conversion into a foreign (hard) currency and repatriation of the lease payments to the parent company headquarters if desired. Again, competitive behavior should be a reference point. If competition does not press the local government to allow repatriation, but instead permits lease payments in LC to be accumulated in the economy for later local investment, the company may have no choice but to do the same thing. Then long-run strategic intent becomes important for the firm: Why is it in this particular country market? Why is it permitting leasing in this market? And what are its long-range strategic market share goals for the market? Needless to say, short-term leasing objectives should fit into the overall long-term market strategy.

Summary

Pricing in international markets is affected by a firm's strategic objectives, a firm's competitive behavior, consumers' ability to buy, the product life cycle stage, and market-specific environmental considerations such as government regulation.

Export prices should be set so that export sales are at least as rewarding as other sales outlets. Export sales prices may be less than domestic prices because of the additional costs involved and the need to keep the final consumer price affordable. In the short run, export prices can be set at just above marginal cost, though that can invite government accusations of dumping. Shipping and insurance costs, tariffs, market-specific taxes such as VAT, and distributor markups all add to the cost of exported products.

Exchange rate fluctuations can affect consumer prices, too. Offsetting such fluctuations may entail the sacrifice of profit margins to maintain market share. Quoting prices in a firm's domestic currency may seem to avoid problems related to the exchange rate. Whether buyers will accept such quotes, however, depends on the relative strength of demand and supply, as well as competitive behavior.

Export price quotations specify what services (for example, shipping, insurance, and documentation) are included in the quoted price.

When currencies appreciate, firms often raise prices by less than the amount of appreciation. Japanese firms are prone to such pricing behavior. Exchange rate risk can be classified as transaction risk, competitive risk, and market portfolio risk. Each of those risks suggests different strategic actions.

How sales are financed is crucial to winning export orders. Hence, financing terms and conditions form an integral part of international pricing policies. Government aid to exporters often comes in the form of subsidies that allow a firm to offer below-market rates of interest on customer receivables, thus offering a hidden price discount.

Transfer pricing becomes relevant when a product division in one country supplies another division located in a foreign market. Transfer prices must be set so they yield a satisfactory profit but are not so high as to discourage sales.

Common transfer pricing formulas are based on arm's-length market prices, cost-plus pricing, negotiated prices, and transfers at cost with shared profits. In all cases, motivation is as important as the profit accruing to each division.

Governments often intervene in international transfer pricing to ensure that prices are not set so low as to avoid taxes. Customs authorities may set a floor on the transfer price to prevent firms from avoiding tariffs.

International competition creates worldwide pressure to cut prices. Firms must rethink the role of price as a product attribute. Alternatives to matching price cuts are competing with differentiated products and relying on a technological or marketing edge.

If firms must match competitive price cuts, they need to cut their costs of production. A common solution is to shift production to low-cost overseas locations. Such cost reductions may be achieved, however, at the expense of new problems with quality and timely delivery.

Currency inconvertibility can affect the profitability of international operations and require creative solutions, as Pepsi's experience in China illustrates.

Better-informed multinational consumers prevent firms from charging different prices for the same goods in different markets, instead moving to uniform pricing.

Price differentials between country markets lead to arbitrage attempts. Gray marketing, the unauthorized import of cheaper goods from other foreign markets, can create problems with distributor channels and affect product image.

Product redesign is another avenue to providing customer value and cutting costs without necessarily competing with cheap labor manufacturing solutions.

Countertrade is a form of pricing because the sale is tied to accepting other goods in exchange. Creativity and a strategic plan for implementation are necessary for success. Countertrade is rapidly growing in importance and should be viewed as an opportunity to nurture a long-term source of quality raw materials and components.

International leasing is an alternative to outright sales and is important in the international capital goods market. To compete effectively, firms must be able to offer leasing alternatives as part of their international pricing policies.

To respond to competition, careful coordination is necessary to manage the conflicting demands of export pricing, foreign market pricing, and global pricing policies.

Questions and Research

12.1 What are some of the major factors affecting international pricing? In particular, how are prices influenced by a firm's strategy, a firm's competition, consumers' ability to buy, a firm's cost and market structure, and the complete product line?

12.2 What should be the relationship between export and domestic prices?

12.3 What are the consequences of charging an export price below the domestic market price?

12.4 Are there reasons why export prices should be higher than domestic prices? If so, what are the marketing implications of export price escalation?

12.5 How do exchange rates affect international pricing? Why might a firm with an appreciating currency not raise its export prices?

12.6 Is quoting export prices only in a firm's domestic currency a viable strategy to avoiding the impact of exchange rates?

12.7 What are the different ways in which export prices can be quoted?

12.8 What are the different risks that a firm marketing its products internationally faces because of exchange rate fluctuations? How might a firm cope with those categories of risk?

12.9 How and why are export credit financing terms and conditions relevant to international pricing?

12.10 How can governments help in financing international sales?

12.11 What is transfer pricing? Why is it a consideration in international pricing?

12.12 What are some useful formulas in setting transfer prices?

12.13 Why do tax authorities of both the parent country and the host country concern themselves with transfer prices? How might their intervention affect the multinational corporation?

12.14 How can the level of inflation affect the setting of prices in different country markets?

12.15 How should a firm cope with government price controls in foreign markets?

12.16 Why might international competition force a firm to consider price cuts? What other alternatives are open to a firm facing such price pressures in international markets?

12.17 What are the advantages and disadvantages of moving production offshore to a low-cost production site?

12.18 How is product redesign relevant to international pricing?

12.19 What is gray marketing? How does it affect international marketing and price setting?

12.20 What is countertrade? Why should firms be willing to consider countertrade arrangements in their international marketing efforts?

12.21 Why do countries seek countertrade? How can a firm assess the profitability of a proposed countertrade transaction?

12.22 How should a firm organize itself to deal in countertrade?

12.23 What are some creative ways to approach currency inconvertibility and countertrade?

12.24 How does international leasing form part of the global pricing decision?

12.25 What are some organizational issues relevant to international pricing?

12.26 What factors affect the prices received for export of tuna from Australia to Japan? What generalizations concerning pricing in foreign markets may be drawn from this illustration?

Endnotes

1. For reviews of pricing, see Monroe, Kent, Lan Xia, and Jennifer L. Cox. "The Price Is Unfair! A Conceptual Framework of Price Fairness Perceptions," *Journal of Marketing*, Volume 68, 2004; Davis, Scott, Akshay Rao, and Mark Bergen, "How to Fight a Price War," *Harvard Business Review*, March–April 2000; Rao, Vithala R., "Pricing Research in Marketing: The State of the Art," *Journal of Business*, Volume 57, 1984; and Tellis Gerard J., "Beyond the Many Faces of Price: An Integration of Pricing Strategies," *Journal of Marketing*, Volume 50, October 1986.

2. Raymond, Mary Anne, John F. Tanner, Jr., and Jonghoon Kim. "Cost Complexity of Pricing Decisions for Exporters in Developing and Emerging Markets," *Journal of International Marketing*, Volume 9, Number 3, 2001 pages 19–40.

3. Cavusgil, S. Tamer, Kwong Chan, and Chun Zhang. "Strategic Orientations in Export Pricing: A Clustering Approach to Create Firm Taxonomies," *Journal of International Marketing*, Volume 11, Number 1, 2003, pages 47–72.

4. "Unilever, P&G Wage Price War for Edge in India," *Wall Street Journal*, August 11, 2004.

5. Cooper, Robin and W. Bruce Chew. "Control Tomorrow's Costs through Today's Designs," *Harvard Business Review*, January–February 1996, pages 88–97.

6. Bradsher, Keith. "G.M. Thrives in China With Small, Thrifty Vans," *New York Times*, August 9, 2005.

7. Myers, Matthew B. and Michael Harvey. "The Value of Pricing Control in Export Channels: A Governance Perspective," *Journal of International Marketing*, Volume 9, Number 4, 2001, pages 1–29.

8. Marn, Michael and R. L. Rosiello. "Managing Price, Gaining Profit," *McKinsey Quarterly*, Number 4, 1992.

9. Karr, Mary. "The Case of the Pricing Predicament," *Harvard Business Review*, March–April 1988.

10. http://ia.ita.doc.gov/download/factsheets/factsheet-shrimp-brazil-ecuador-india-thailand-122004.pdf

11. Cespedes, F. V., E. Raymond Corey, and V. Kasturi Rangan. "Gray Markets: Causes and Cures," *Harvard Business Review*, July–August 1988.

12. "Peso Rise Squeezes Chile's Exports," *Wall Street Journal*, January 28, 2004.

13. Hertzell, Staffan and Christian Caspar. "Coping with Unpredictable Currencies," *McKinsey Quarterly*, Summer 1988.

14. Irandoust, M. "Exchange Rate Pass-Through in the Automobile Industry," *Journal of International Trade*, Volume 14, Issue 1, Spring 2000, pages 37–51.

15. Bodnar, Gordon M., Bernard Dumas, and Richard C Marston. "Pass-Through and Exposure," *Journal of Finance*, Volume 57, Issue 1, February 2002, pages 199–231.

16. "Luxury Prices for U.S. Goods No Longer Pass Muster in Japan," *Wall Street Journal*, February 8, 1996.

17. See "Note on the Motorcycle Industry," Harvard Business School Case Services, Number 578–210.

18. Boston Consulting Group, *Perspectives on Experience*, 1972, Boston: BCG; Dolan, Robert and Abel Jeuland, "Experience Curves and Dynamic Demand Models: Implications for Optimal Pricing Strategies," *Journal of Marketing*, Winter 1981.

19. McGowan, Karen M. and Brenda J. Sternquist. "Dimensions of Price as a Marketing Universal: A Comparison of Japanese and US Consumers," *Journal of International Marketing*, Volume 6, Number 4, 1998, pages 49–65.

20. Stremersch, Stefan and Gerard Tellis. "Strategic Bundling of Products and Prices: A New Synthesis for Marketing," *Journal of Marketing*, Volume 56, January 2002, pages 55–72.

21. Anderson, James C. and James A. Narus. "Capturing the Value of Supplementary Services," *Harvard Business Review*, January–February 1995, pages 75–83.

22. Stottinger, Barbara. "Strategic Export Pricing: A Long and Winding Road," *Journal of International Marketing*, Volume 9, Number 1, March 2000, pages 40–63.

23. Myers, Matthew B. "The Pricing of Export Products: Why Aren't Managers Satisfied with the Results?" *Journal of World Business*, Volume 32, Issue 3, 1997, pages 277–289.

24. "Is the Price Right?" *Business Europe*, February 6–12, 1995, pages 6–7.

25. Simon, Hermann. "Pricing Problems in a Global Setting," *Marketing News*, October 9, 1995.

26. Theodosiou, Marios and Constantine S. Katsikeas. "Factors Influencing the Degree of International Pricing Strategy Standardization of Multinational Corporations," *Journal of International Marketing*, Volume 9, Number 3, 2001, pages 1–18.

27. "Global Networks, Global Prices," *Data Communications*, July 1993, page 18.

28. Ostro-Landau, N. "Currencies, Prices, and Profits," *International Business*, Volume 83, Number 8, July 1995, pages 16–19.

29. Sivakumar K. and S. P. Raj. "Quality Tier Competition: How Price Change Influences Brand Choice and Category Choice," *Journal of Marketing*, Volume 61, July 1997, pages 71–84.

30. "As Yen Oscillates, Japanese Firms Mull Risks of Hedging Bets against Dollar," *Wall Street Journal*, February 8, 1996.

31. "Peugeot Won't Hedge Euro Risk, Despite Erosion in Earnings," *Wall Street Journal*, November 12, 2003.

32. "Big Three Outsourcing Plan: Make Parts Suppliers Do It," *Wall Street Journal*, June 10, 2004.

33. Flaherty, M. Therese. "Emerging Global Business Environment and Managerial Reaction to It," Paper COF-8, presented at the Ministry of International Trade and Industry Conference, Tokyo, 1988.

34. That is, $10.60 local manufacturer's price plus 12 percent VAT equals $11.87, plus 15 percent distributor markup equals $13.65, plus 40 percent retail margin on price equals $22.80. Since the import price is $25, the domestic manufacturer can undercut the import price by up to $2.20; that is, $25 minus $22.80, or $2.20.

35. Nichols, Nancy A. "Scientific Management at Merck: An Interview with CFO Judy Lewent," *Harvard Business Review*, January–February 1994, pages 89–99.

36. "Merck Renews Its Vows," *Business Latin America*, February 6, 1995.

37. "Learn from Russia," *Business China*, September 5, 1994, pages 1–3.

38. "Congratulations, Exporter! Now about Getting Paid . . ." *Business Week*, January 17, 1994; "Forfait," *Finance & Treasury*, July 17, 1995.

39. Sarathy, Ravi. "High-Technology Exports from Newly Industrializing Countries: The Brazilian Commuter Aircraft Industry," *California Management Review*, Volume 27, Number 2, Winter 1985, pages 60–84.

40. See *Trade Finance: Current Issues and Developments*, International Trade Administration, November 1988, Washington, DC: U.S. Department of Commerce, pages 34–43.

41. *International Trade: Competitors' Tied Aid Practices Affect U.S. Exports*, May 1994, Washington, DC: U.S. General Accounting Office, GAO/GGD-94-81; *Combating U.S. Competitors' Tied-Aid Practices*, May 1994, GAO/T-GGD-94-156.

42. Stevenson, Thomas H. and David W. E. Cabell. "Integrated Transfer Pricing Policy and Activity-based Costing," *Journal of International Marketing*, Volume 10, Number 4, 2002, pages 77–88.

43. Cohen, Stephen S. with John Zysman. "Countertrade, Offsets, Barter, and Buybacks," *California Management Review*, Volume 28, Number 2, Winter 1986, page 43.

44. Melloan, George. "Countertrade Suits Metallgesellschaft Fine," *Wall Street Journal*, August 2, 1988.

45. "Gunning for Profit," *The Economist*, November 22 2001.

46. Countertrade has become sufficiently important that DeBard, a Swiss company operating in Britain, has published *The Oxford International Countertrade Directory*, listing participants in the business worldwide.

47. "Barter's Latest Comeback," *The Economist*, October 19, 2000.

48. "Reinventing Countertrade," *Business Eastern Europe*, January 17, 1994.

49. Khoury, Sarkis. "Countertrade: Forms, Motives, Pitfalls, and Negotiation Requisites," *Journal of Business Research*, Volume 12, 1984.

50. "Too Much Barter Is Bad for You," *The Economist*, May 9, 1987.

Further Readings

Anderson, James C. and James A. Narus. "Capturing the Value of Supplementary Services," *Harvard Business Review*, January–February 1995, pages 75–83.

Bodnar, Gordon M., Bernard Dumas, and Richard C Marston. "Passthrough and Exposure," *Journal of Finance*, Volume 57, Issue 1, February 2002, pages 199–231.

Carter, Joseph R. and James Gagne. "The Do's and Don'ts of International Countertrade," *Sloan Management Review*, Spring 1988.

Cavusgil, S. Tamer. "Pricing for Global Markets," *Columbia Journal of World Business*, Winter 1996, pages 66–78.

Cavusgil, S. Tamer. "Unraveling the Mystique of Export Pricing," *Business Horizons*, May–June 1988, pages 54–63.

Cavusgil, S. Tamer, Kwong Chan, and Chun Zhang. "Strategic Orientations in Export Pricing: A Clustering Approach to Create Firm Taxonomies," *Journal of International Marketing*, Volume 11, Number 1, 2003, pages 47–72.

Cespedes, F. V., E. Raymond Corey, and V. Kasturi Rangan. "Gray Markets: Causes and Cures," *Harvard Business Review*, July–August 1988.

Cohen, Stephen S. with John Zysman. "Countertrade, Offsets, Barter, and Buybacks." *California Management Review*, Volume 28, Number 2, Winter 1986, page 43.

Cooper, Robin and W. Bruce Chew. "Control Tomorrow's Costs through Today's Designs," *Harvard Business Review*, January–February 1996, pages 88–97.

Davis, Scott, Akshay Rao, and Mark Bergen. "How to Fight a Price War," *Harvard Business Review*, March–April 2000.

Dolan, Robert and Abel Jeuland. "Experience Curves and Dynamic Demand Models: Implications for Optimal Pricing Strategies," *Journal of Marketing*, Winter 1981.

Hertzell, Staffan and Christian Caspar. "Coping with Unpredictable Currencies," *McKinsey Quarterly*, Summer 1988.

International Trade Administration, "*Trade Finance: Current Issues and Developments*, November 1988, Washington, DC: U.S. Department of Commerce.

Irandoust, M. "Exchange Rate Pass-through in the Automobile Industry," *Journal of International Trade*, Volume 14, Issue 1, Spring 2000, pages 37–51.

Khoury, Sarkis. "Countertrade: Forms, Motives, Pitfalls, and Negotiation Requisites," *Journal of Business Research*, Volume 12, 1984.

Marn, Michael and R. L. Rosiello. "Managing Price, Gaining Profit," *McKinsey Quarterly*, Number 4, 1992.

McGowan, M. and Brenda J. Sternquist, "Dimensions of Price as a Marketing Universal: A Comparison of Japanese and US Consumers," *Journal of International Marketing* 1998, Volume 6, Number 4, pages 49–65.

Monroe, Kent, Lan Xia, and Jennifer L. Cox. "The Price Is Unfair! A Conceptual Framework of Price Fairness Perceptions, *Journal of Marketing*, Volume 68, 2004.

Myers, Matthew B. "The Pricing of Export Products: Why Aren't Managers Satisfied with the Results?" *Journal of World Business*, Volume 32, Issue 3, 1997, pages 277–289.

Myers, Matthew B. and Michael Harvey. "The Value of Pricing Control in Export Channels: A Governance Perspective," *Journal of International Marketing*, Volume 9, Number 4, 2001, pages 1–29.

Nichols, Nancy A. "Scientific Management at Merck: An Interview with CFO Judy Lewent." *Harvard Business Review*, January–February 1994, pages 89–99.

Rao, Vithala R. "Pricing Research in Marketing: The State of the Art," *Journal of Business*, Volume 57, 1984.

Raymond, Mary Anne, John F. Tanner, Jr., and Jonghoon Kim. "Cost Complexity of Pricing Decisions for Exporters in Developing and Emerging Markets," *Journal of International Marketing*, Volume 9, Number 3, 2001 pages 19–40.

Sarathy, Ravi. "High Technology Exports from Newly Industrializing Countries: The Brazilian Commuter Aircraft Industry," *California Management Review*, Volume 27, Number 2, Winter 1985, pages 60–84.

Sivakumar, K. and S. P. Raj. "Quality Tier Competition: How Price Change Influences Brand Choice and Category Choice," *Journal of Marketing*, Volume 61, July 1997, pages 71–84.

Stevenson, Thomas H. and David W. E. Cabell. "Integrated Transfer Pricing Policy and Activity-based Costing," *Journal of International Marketing*, Volume 10, Number 4, 2002, pages 77–88.

Stottinger, Barbara. "Strategic Export Pricing: A Long and Winding Road," *Journal of International Marketing*, March 2000, Volume 9, Number 1, pages 40–63.

Stremersch, Stefan and Gerard Tellis. "Strategic Bundling of Products and Prices: A New Synthesis for Marketing," *Journal of Marketing*, Volume 56, January 2002, pages 55–72.

Tellis, Gerard J. "Beyond the Many Faces of Price: An Integration of Pricing Strategies," *Journal of Marketing*, Volume 50, October 1986.

Theodosiou, Marios and Constantine S. Katsikeas. "Factors Influencing the Degree of International Pricing Strategy Standardization of Multinational Corporations," *Journal of International Marketing*, Volume 9, Number 3, 2001, pages 1–18.

Walters, Peter G. P. "A Framework for Export Pricing Decisions." *Journal of Global Marketing*, Volume 2, Number 3, 1989.

Case 12.1

THE POWER OF LOW PRICES

In the far southwestern reaches of China, Anthony Le Corre, a French accountant in China, set up a small pizza restaurant in Kinming, the capital of Yunnan Province and a gateway to the Silk Road, close to the borders of Burma and Vietnam. He charged between $2.50 and $5.00 for pizzas, a relatively high price, making the pizza unaffordable for the masses. He sold that restaurant and opened another pizzeria in Chongqing, to the north and east of Kunming. Chongqing is a large port city at the confluence of the Yangtze and Jialing rivers and China's fourth-largest city. Le Corre's second restaurant, experiencing a similar fare, closed after a year, unable to be distinctive in a competitive local market. Two years later Le Corre opened a third restaurant in Shanghai, at the estuary of the Yangtze River. Shanghai is China's largest industrial city, as well as its largest financial and commercial center. This time he made some changes in the way he sold pizza. The Shanghai pizza restaurant, Hello Pizza, sold nine-inch pizza for 10 yuan, about $1.20. His most expensive pizzas sold for $4.20, still below the price of inexpensive pizzas sold at comparable restaurants, as shown in the table below.

In addition to three restaurants, Le Corre also has three pizza delivery locations, a bakery, and a catering business.

Low prices are an essential component of his business model. But to make a profit with low prices, he also has to achieve low costs, while maintaining quality. Le Corre learned his formula from reading a book about McDonald's, which achieved its success by combining low prices with consistent quality and service.

Le Corre's objective in Shanghai was to make inexpensive pizza that the Chinese could eat every day. In the evening, his staff chops green peppers and stores them in tiny resealable bags that hold exactly 30 grams of peppers. Similar small bags hold chopped eggplant, onions, sausage, and other ingredients designed to be used in making single pizzas. Salad boxes are prepared with lettuce, carrots, and a packet of salad dressing. Another employee rolls pizza crusts. All of those items are delivered to the restaurants the next morning.

The restaurants, seating about 25 customers, oper-

ate with four employees. One employee assembles the premixed salads while another employee sprinkles ingredients from the resealable bags onto the premade pizza crusts and begins baking them. A third employee serves the customers; the fourth employee is the cashier. Men on electric bicycles make deliveries, which are about half the business. The small staff, needing a limited skill set, can be well trained. To reduce turnover, the restaurants hire migrants from neighboring provinces who are likely to stay while they save money to take back on their visits home. Wage costs are $140 to $180 a month, nearly all local employees except for a French baker. Average Chinese urban income in 2003 was about 8,500 yuan, or a little over $1,000 a year.

Aside from low prices, Le Corre is careful to change menus and introduce new pizzas regularly, to cater to different tastes, and to offer new varieties to regulars, thus providing fewer reasons to go to other restaurants. His challenge is to grow the company and add restaurants while sticking to his formula and continuing to provide quality, low prices, and good service. Competition is intense, though, as noted above. The other foreign pizza establishments aim for a higher price point. By 2005, Pizza Hut had opened 160 restaurants across China in 40 cities. Young Chinese are attracted to those chains for the setting, the lifestyle it represents. Pizza Hut opened a Chinese call center in Hong Kong with an investment of HK$30 million (Hong Kong dollar) to help increase carry out sales by 20 percent. Two hundred workers take calls, which, at peak times, can number 10,000 per hour. Pizza Italia in Shanghai offers set menus to complement its pizza and pasta.

Hello Pizza is a departure from the normal foreign company approach that concentrates on higher-priced luxury products and brand names catering to the premium segment of the market. That segment may be narrow and competitive as all foreign companies occupy it, ignoring the masses of Chinese with moderate incomes. While margins may be higher in the premium segment, market share may be lower and growth circumscribed by the smaller size of the high-income segment. Offering low prices with quality and choices may represent a strategic alternative with considerable long-term promise.

Sources: "Lessons from a $1.20 Pizza," Wall Street Journal, February 10, 2004; "Pizza Hut Accelerates Expansion in China," China Daily, February 14, 2005.

Restaurant	Hello Pizza	Pizza Hut	Pizza Italia	Gino Cafe
Cheapest pizza ($)	1.2	5.4	6.6	4.3
Most expensive pizza ($)	4.2	6.6	9.0	9.2
Number of restaurants	3	28	3	12

Case prepared by Professor Ravi Sarathy for use in class discussion, © 2005, all rights reserved.

Adapted from "Lessons from a $1.20 Pizza," Wall Street Journal, February 10, 2004.

Case 12.2

PORSCHE EXPOSED

THUNDERBIRD
THE GARVIN SCHOOL OF
INTERNATIONAL MANAGEMENT

A06-04-0004

PORSCHE EXPOSED

BMW says that its decisions on where it locates production are driven by market needs, not currency considerations. Yet it has created natural hedges for itself by producing cars in America and Britain. By incurring costs in these markets, it greatly reduces the currency translation problem. Rival Porsche makes most of its cars in Germany, so its costs are mostly in euros. Yet a large chunk of its revenues come from sales of its sports cars in America. Lacking BMW's natural hedge, Porsche uses financial hedging to minimise the short-term impact of currency swings.
"Grappling with the Strong Euro," *The Economist*, June 5, 2003, p. 53.

The USA represents approximately 50 percent of our total business. There are a few other countries that also use US dollars. This situation will not change much in [the] future. That is why we are hedged against currency fluctuation for the next three to four years. In our books the dollar and the yen are above the actual rates. That allows us time to react to any currency movement.
"Porsche Roars Past Sales Targets," *Automotive News Europe*,
September 22, 2003, p. 20.

It was January 2004 and Porsche—the legendary manufacturer of performance sports cars—wished to reevaluate its exchange rate strategy. Porsche's management had always been unconcerned about the opinions of the equity markets, but its currency hedging strategy was becoming something of a lightning rod for criticism. Although the currency hedging results had been positive, many experts believed that Porsche had simply been "more lucky than good." There was growing concern among analysts that the company was actually speculating on currency movements. Analysts estimated that more than 40% of earnings were to come from currency hedging in the coming year. Porsche's President and Chief Executive Officer (CEO), Dr. Wendelin Wiedeking, now wished to revisit the company's exposure management strategy.

Porsche AG

Porsche was a publicly traded, closely held, German-based auto manufacturer. Dr. Wiedeking had returned the company to both status and profitability since taking over the company in 1993. Porsche had closed the 2002/03 fiscal year with €5.582 billion in sales and €565 million in profit, after-tax (see Appendix 1). Wiedeking and his team were credited with the wholesale turnaround of the specialty manufacturer. Strategically, the leadership team had now expanded the company's business line to reduce its dependence on the luxury sports car market, historically an extremely cyclical business line.

Although Porsche was traded on the Frankfurt Stock Exchange (and associated German exchanges), control of the company remained firmly in the hands of the founding families, the Porsche and Piéch families. Porsche had two classes of shares, *ordinary* and *preference*. The two families held all 8.75 million *ordinary shares*. Ordinary shares held all voting rights. The second class of share, *preference shares*, participated only in profits. All 8.75 million preference shares were publicly traded. Approximately 50% of all preference shares were held by large institutional investors in the United States, Germany, and the United Kingdom, 14% were held by the Porsche and Piéch families, and 36% were held by small private investors. As noted by the Chief Financial Officer, Holger Härter, "As long as the two families hold onto their stock portfolios, there won't be any external influence on company-related decisions. I have no doubt that the families will hang on to their shares."

Porsche was somewhat infamous for its independent thought and occasional stubbornness when it came to disclosure and compliance with reporting requirements. In 2002 the company had chosen not to list on the New York Stock Exchange after the passage of the Sarbanes-Oxley Act. The company pointed to the specific requirement of Sarbanes-Oxley that senior management sign off on the financial results of the company personally as inconsistent with German law (which it largely was) and illogical for management to accept.

Management had also long been critical of the practice of quarterly reporting, and had, in fact, been removed from the Frankfurt exchange's stock index in September 2002 because of its refusal to report quarterly financial results (it still only reports operating and financial results semi-annually). Porsche's public response to its removal from the MDAX was unapologetic as usual: "Of far more importance, from the investors' standpoint, than a continued presence in the internationally insignificant MDAX is the inclusion of Porsche's stock from the end of November 2001 in the Morgan Stanley Capital International index." Porsche's management continued to argue that the company believed itself to be quite seasonal in its operations, and did not wish to report quarterly. It also believed that quarterly reporting only added to short-term investor perspectives, a fire which Porsche felt no need to fuel. Porsche's brief press release announcing its decision not to list in New York is shown in Appendix 4.

Porsche also continued to report only under German accounting standards. German standards were often criticized for their lack of transparency, and allowed companies like Porsche to mix operating results with financial results, including foreign exchange operations. Many of its rivals, even German-based companies, were now reporting in accordance with either International Accounting Standards (IAS) or U.S. Generally Accepted Accounting Principles (GAAP). The refusal to expand reporting was seen as one more indicator of the company's stubbornness, particularly since all EU-listed companies were required to report in accordance with IAS beginning in 2005.

But, after all was said and done, the company had just reported record profits for the ninth consecutive year. Returns were so good, and had grown so quickly in the past two years, that the company had paid out a special dividend of €14 per share in 2002. That was in addition to increasing the size of the common regular dividend. The company's critics, of course, had argued that this was simply another way in which the controlling families drained profits from the company.

> *"With net cash of €1.1 billion at the end of 2002 and our forecast of strong cash flow generation, we believe that Porsche is unlikely to need to do a rights issue for some years, although it may choose to have one in order to fund a 4th or even a 5th model series—that is, unless there is a major liability or a severe and sustained weakening of the U.S. dollar. As a result, we think there is the potential risk that management may not rate shareholders' interests very highly."* [1]

The compensation packages of Porsche's senior management team were nearly exclusively focused on current-year profitability (83% of executive board compensation was based on performance-related pay), with no management incentives or stock option awards related to the company's share price. Porsche's leadership, however, had clearly built value for all shareholders in recent years. As illustrated in Exhibit 1, the current management team's tenure (beginning late 1993) had resulted in a significant increase over time in the share price, although the recent three-year period had been characterized by extreme volatility. Still, performance was nothing short of remarkable, particularly following the post-9/11 share price fall (2001) and the fact that it was a German-based company currently held captive by a strengthening euro (2003).

---

[1] "Porsche: Worth the Risk," UBS Investment Research, September 1, 2003, p. 54.

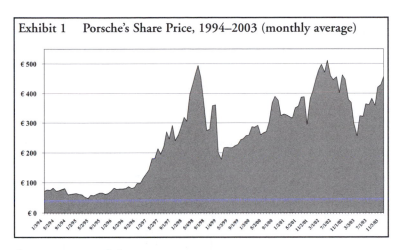

Exhibit 1   Porsche's Share Price, 1994–2003 (monthly average)

Porsche's Changing Portfolio

Porsche's product portfolio had undergone significant change as CEO Wiedeking pursued his promise to shareholders that he would grow the firm. The company had three major vehicle platforms: the premier luxury sports car, the *911*; the competitively priced *Boxster* roadster; and the recently introduced off-road sport utility vehicle, the *Cayenne*.

The 911 series was still the focal point of the Porsche brand, but many believed that it was growing old and due for replacement. Sales had seemingly peaked in 2001/02, and fallen back more than 15% in 2002/03. The 911 was a highly developed series with more than 14 current models carrying the 911 tag. The 911 had always enjoyed, and probably still did, nearly exclusive ownership of its market segment. Although its sales had been historically cyclical, 911 demand was not price-elastic. Management would not comment on rumors, but it was widely believed that the 911 series would be supplemented by a fourth platform in 2005.

The Boxster roadster had been introduced in 1996 as Porsche's entry into the lower price end of the sports car market, and had been by all measures a very big success. The Boxster was also considered an anticyclical move because the traditional 911 was so high-priced, its sales were heavily dependent on the disposable income of buyers in its major markets (Europe, the United States, and the United Kingdom). The Boxster's lower price made it affordable and less sensitive to the business cycle. It did, however, compete in an increasingly competitive market segment. Although the Boxster had competed head-to-head with the BMW Z3 since its introduction in 1996, the introduction of the Z4 in 2003 had drastically cut into Boxster sales. Volume sales were now only two-thirds of their peak 2000/01 levels.

The third major platform innovation was Porsche's entry into the sports utility vehicle (SUV) segment, the Cayenne. Clearly at the top end of the market (2002/03 Cayenne sales averaged more than $70,000 each), the Cayenne had been a very quick success, especially in the SUV-crazed American market. The Cayenne introduction had been hailed by many in the auto industry as one of the most successful new product launches in history, and had single-handedly floated Porsche sales numbers in this most recent fiscal year.

The Cayenne's success had been even more dramatic given much prelaunch criticism that the market would not support such a high-priced SUV, particularly one which shared a strong bloodline with the Volkswagen (VW) Touareg. The Porsche Cayenne and VW Touareg had been jointly developed by the two companies. The two vehicles shared a common chassis and, in fact, were both manufactured at the same factory in Bratislava, Slovakia. To preserve its unique identity, however, Porsche shipped the Cayenne chassis 17 hours by rail to its facility in Leipzig, Germany, where the engine, drivetrain and interior were combined in final assembly.[2] A new six-cylinder version was slated for introduction in 2004 and was expected to buoy Cayenne sales after the initial boom of the introduction year.[3] As illustrated by Exhibit 2, Porsche's platform innovations had been extremely successful in growing the firm's unit sales since 1995.

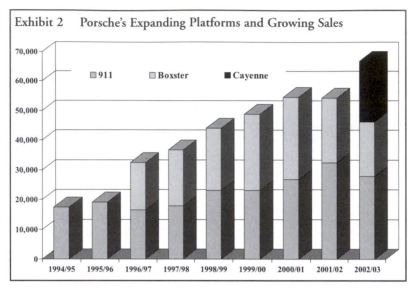

Exhibit 2   Porsche's Expanding Platforms and Growing Sales

Financial Health

Porsche's financial performance and health was, by all European auto manufacturer standards, excellent. It was clearly the smallest of the major European-based manufacturers with total sales of €5.6 billion in 2002. But, as illustrated in Exhibit 3, Porsche was outstanding by nearly every other financial performance metric: the highest revenue per vehicle, the highest operating margins (EBIT margin of 16.4%), the highest price-earnings ratio (16.5), the highest net operating profit after tax margin (NOPAT of 8.9%), and the highest return on invested capital (ROIC of 20.5%). The only category which was generally average by industry standards was invested capital turnover (2.3).

The company's low debt level was particularly notable, as Porsche had the second-lowest total debt-to-asset ratio. The company's superior operating cash flows had proven more than adequate to internally finance an aggressive capital expenditure and expansion program in recent years. In fact, Porsche's cash balances had reached a record level of €1.766 billion at the end of 2002/03 (see Appendix 2).

Porsche's view on debt was rather extreme compared to that held by most of the other major European-based automobile manufacturers. To quote CFO Härter: "We learnt the hard way that banks are there for you when you don't need them, and when you do need them, they're nowhere to be seen."[4] This antidebt philosophy was also consistent with the emphasis placed by Porsche on both cash flow and cash balances. Again, in the words of CFO Härter: "We need to optimize all of the cash we generate so that we're able to continue to finance our growth ourselves, and have the confidence that if anything happens in the future that is beyond our control, we'll always be able to survive. That's absolutely essential." Although long-term debt was readily available to a company of Porsche's financial health, debt was clearly anathema to current management.

---

[2] The engine was in fact the only part of the Cayenne which was actually manufactured by Porsche itself. All other components of the vehicle were either outsourced or built in conjunction with other manufacturers.
[3] The six-cylinder engine, however, was actually a Volkswagen engine which had been reconfigured. This led to significant debate, as Porsche was criticized for degrading the Porsche brand.
[4] Kersnar, Janet, "Hot Wheels," *CFO Europe.com*, November 2002.

Exhibit 3	Porsche's Competitive Positioning, 2002								
European Automaker	*Sales (billions)*	*Revenue per Vehicle*	*EBIT Margin*	*PE Ratio*	*NOPAT Margin*	*Debt to Assets*	*Moody's Rating*	*Invested Capital Turnover*	*ROIC*
Audi	€22.6	€27,000	6.6%	na	na	0.2%	na	na	na
BMW	42.3	32,221	8.0%	12.1	4.9%	47.5%	A1	2.3	11.3%
Fiat	€58.2	€25,829	1.6%	nm	-1.0%	31.3%	Ba3	2.9	-2.9%
Mercedes Benz	€50.2	€39,000	6.4%	na	na	na	na	na	na
Peugeot (PSA)	€54.4	€16,192	5.3%	5.9	3.5%	42.9%	A2	3.0	10.5%
Porsche	€5.6	€72,589	16.4%	16.5	8.9%	6.4%	na	2.3	20.5%
Renault	€36.3	€14,250	4.1%	7.5	2.2%	47.6%	Baa2	1.7	3.7%
Volkswagen	€86.9	€13,583	5.2%	6.4	3.4%	42.4%	A1	2.0	6.8%

Source: CreditSuisse/First Boston, December 16, 2003, p. 7; Commerzbank Securities, December 2003, company reports. For 2002, the two major U.S.-based auto manufacturers, GM and Ford, had EBIT margins of 0.1% each. EBIT = earnings before interest and tax; NOPAT = net operating profit after-tax; PE = share price/earnings per share; Debt to Assets = (short-term + long-term debt)/total assets; ROIC = return on invested capital. DaimlerChrysler does not report detailed financial results for Mercedes Benz. Audi and Porsche are not currently rated by either Moody's or Standard & Poor's; Mercedes Benz is not separately rated from DaimlerChrysler.

Foreign Currency Exposure

"Even if we sell a few or no cars at all in the U.S. we make money .... because we bought dollars cheap which we now sell expensively. Our hedging is extremely good; we are calculating with levels which are significantly below current levels, and today I know what I will get for the dollar in 2006. I am very relaxed."

Dr. Wiedeking in *Capital*, 2nd quarter, 2003.

"Porsche has the heaviest U.S. exposure (and this is increasing), yet it has the lowest level of natural hedging in the sector. Porsche's earnings will have a 43% contribution from hedging contracts in 2003/04E, the highest in the sector...."

Porsche, *Citigroup Smith Barney*, September 24, 2003, p. 5.

Among European-based automakers, BMW, Mercedes, Porsche, and VW were clearly the most exposed to exchange rate changes (primarily the dollar/euro). As illustrated by Exhibit 4, Porsche possessed the largest mismatch between where their automobiles were produced and where they were sold. With 42% of global sales in North American markets, and an additional 11% in the United Kingdom, Porsche possessed no manufacturing or assembly cost-bases in the countries of more than 50% of global sales.

Exhibit 4	United Kingdom and North American Sales and Production of Selected European Automakers as a Percent of Global Results, 2002			
	United Kingdom		*North American*	
Automaker	*Sales*	*Production*	*Sales*	*Production*
BMW	11%	15%	26%	11%
Fiat	6%	0%	0%	0%
Mercedes	9%	0%	19%	7%
Peugeot	12%	6%	0%	0%
Porsche	11%	0%	42%	0%
Renault	9%	0%	1%	1%
Volkswagen	7%	0%	13%	7%

Source: Company reports, authors' estimates.

All the European automakers, however, were cognizant and concerned over corporate currency exposures. BMW and Mercedes had announced plans to increase the amount of what analysts were calling *natural hedging* (the matching of dollar revenues with dollar costs). BMW planned to double the capacity of its Spartanburg, South Carolina manufacturing facility. Mercedes had similarly announced a capacity expansion for its Alabama manufacturing facility, while considering the downsizing of its Magna Steyr, Germany, operations. VW's continuing strategy to hedge its U.S. dollar exposure was a bit different. VW believed that if it increased its operating cost base in Brazil, it would be uniquely positioned to manage its U.S. dollar risks. In that pursuit, VW had announced it would be assembling all of its Bora line and the Fox small car in Brazil or Mexico, roughly 4% of VW's group output.

Porsche's exposure was clear—it was a global brand with a single-currency cost-base. The company produced in only two countries, Germany and Finland (the Boxster was assembled under a licensing agreement with Valmet of Finland). Both were euro-denominated economies. Porsche believed that the quality of its engineering and manufacturing were at the core of its brand, and leadership had not been willing to move production beyond the existing European footprint.

Porsche's sales by currency in 2002/03 were estimated as: European euro (€) 45%; U.S. dollar ($) 40%, British pound sterling (£) 10%, Japanese yen (¥) 3%, and Swiss franc (Sfr.) 2%. As illustrated in Exhibit 5, Porsche's non-euro sales were only expected to increase in the coming years.

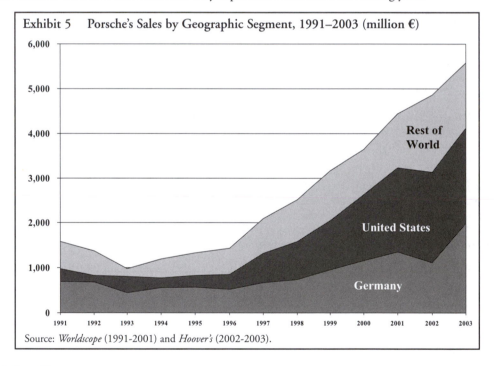

Exhibit 5   Porsche's Sales by Geographic Segment, 1991–2003 (million €)

Source: *Worldscope* (1991-2001) and *Hoover's* (2002-2003).

Pricing Pressures

Exchange rate pass-through, the process of passing through all or part of exchange rate changes to the final customer in price, was probably very product-specific for Porsche. The 911 series was largely considered price-inelastic, and could probably accommodate additional local currency (primarily U.S. dollar) price increases and maintain sales volumes. The Boxster, competing in a very price-intensive market segment, probably could not. And although the Cayenne had debuted at a very high level, Porsche was moving quickly to introduce the lower-powered, lower-priced version immediately, fearing the higher price segment of the market was not a growth segment. As illustrated in Appendix 5, all three vehicle platforms enjoyed at least attractive EBIT margins—some excessive compared to that of nearly every other auto manufacturer in the world. This portfolio could probably absorb some continued currency-induced pricing pressures in North America, but not the magnitudes some were forecasting for the euro's change against the dollar. Clearly, if the euro continued to rise, Porsche would be unable to absorb all of its movement in prices—margins would have to fall in North America.

The latest addition to the stable of 911 thoroughbreds, the 911 Carrera 4S Cabriolet, was symbolic of Porsche's growing pricing dilemma. A 320 horsepower, 3.6 liter six-cylinder engine convertible, the new Cabriolet had a top speed of 280 kilometers per hour and could go from zero-to-100 km/hr in 5.3 seconds. It was priced at a €85,900 in Continental Europe, not including value-added tax (VAT) or other country-specific taxes. Simultaneously, Porsche introduced the new Cabriolet in North American in July 2003 at $93,200. The price/exchange-rate relationship was then:

$$Price^\$ = Price^€ \times Spot\ rate^{\$/€}$$

This implied an exchange rate of $1.0850/€ when solving the relationship for the implied effective exchange rate:

$$Spot\ rate^{\$/€} = \frac{Price^\$}{Price^€} = \frac{\$93,200}{€85,900} = \$1.0850/€$$

This was a considerably stronger dollar than what was available on the open market at that time; the July 2003 monthly average was $1.1362/€. If the margins on the new Cabriolet were to be close to the similarly priced 911 Targa, which was currently averaging a 10.1% EBIT margin (see Appendix 5), these exchange rate changes and differentials from market could be quickly eliminated if not passed through to the dollar price. With the euro expected to rise to anywhere between $1.25/€ and $1.35/€ by July of 2004, Wiedeking and his staff did not believe even the 911 could absorb those currency price pressures that quickly.

In fact, Porsche's current belief was not to attempt to compete on price, but on quality and quantity. Porsche did not wish to let price clear the market. Its current contingency plans included production *stops* and production shifting. CEO Wiedeking was quite open about Porsche's ability to *stop* the Boxster production line within five hours of a simple phone call, under the production agreement with Valmet. Over the longer run, Porsche was considering shifting a large proportion of Boxster production from Valmet in Finland to Porsche's own Stuttgart facilities, shifting 911 production over to Boxster as 911 sales dropped. This would allow the company to sustain its operating margins under shifting product demand changes.

Current Hedging Strategy

Porsche, like some of its European counterparts, suffered the rather whimsical swings in the value of the dollar over the years. The company's aversion to dollar exposures was founded in the reality of the losses suffered in 1992 and 1993, when the combined global recession and weak dollar had caused Porsche's sales to drop 38% in one year. The memory of the resulting losses was a lasting one. Since that time, with new leadership and new business and financial aggressiveness, Porsche had centralized treasury functions and implemented a corporate-level currency hedging program.

Porsche's leadership had taken a very aggressive currency hedging strategy beginning in 2001 when the euro was at a record low against the U.S. dollar (see Appendix 8). With 45% of all sales in North America, and that percentage expected to climb with the growth of the Cayenne, the company was long-term *long dollars*. The 2003/04 year ended with $1.836 billion in gross dollar revenues, auto, financing, and engineering services combined, up from $1.60 billion in 2001/02 and $1.75 billion in 2002/03. Because the company incurred some local expenses in U.S. dollars, the net dollar exposure varied between 70% and 72% of the gross dollar amount.

Porsche began purchasing a series of put options on the U.S. dollar in 2000. These options would allow Porsche, if it desired, to exchange the U.S. dollars generated through North American sales into euros at specific exchange rates in the future. Described as a medium-term strategy, the company continued to increase its put option hedge purchases throughout 2002 and early 2003 so that it was 100% hedged for sales through the 2006 model year. To actually execute the strategy, Porsche created a three-year rolling portfolio of put options. Hedging net dollar exposures out three years required the company not to only forecast sales and subsequent exposures out three years, but to continually carry options possessing notional principals of a full three years of net exposure. Many analysts were highly critical of the cost of such a strategy.

Porsche had expected the dollar to fall in value (euro to rise). It therefore purchased put options with strike prices beginning at \$0.90/€, and rising in subsequent years to \$1.00/€. Only time would tell whether the put option strike rates chosen would provide significant profitability and protection. By locking in put option strike rates at the time of the euro's historical weakness, Porsche had acquired affordable protection against a strengthening euro for years to come—which was what Porsche both expected and feared. The gains from the hedging strategy were already materializing in 2002/03, and were expected to be even more substantial in the coming year. As illustrated in Exhibit 6, the impact of hedging activities on the basic earnings of the firm (EBIT margins) had not always been this successful.

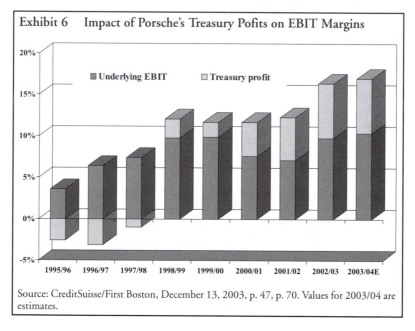

Exhibit 6   Impact of Porsche's Treasury Pofits on EBIT Margins

Source: CreditSuisse/First Boston, December 13, 2003, p. 47, p. 70. Values for 2003/04 are estimates.

Wiedeking and Härter did not make a practice of concerning themselves with the opinions or speculations of analysts. But many analysts were now separating Porsche's results into *underlying* versus *treasury*. For example, one investment banking firm had recently decomposed Porsche's forward-looking PE ratio into 18 *underlying* and 14 *treasury*, rather than crediting the firm with an aggregate PE of 32. Wiedeking and Härter wished to reconsider their current strategy. Was there a better long-term currency exposure management strategy out there for Porsche?

A06-04-0004

Appendix 1	Porsche's Consolidated Statement of Income (millions of euros)				
Income items	**1998/99**	**1999/00**	**2000/01**	**2001/02**	**2002/03**
Net sales	€ 3,161	€ 3,648	€ 4,441	€ 4,857	€ 5,582
Less cost of materials	(1,558)	(1,972)	(2,384)	(2,236)	(2,281)
Less personnel costs	(575)	(631)	(710)	(799)	(850)
Gross profit	€ 1,028	€ 1,045	€ 1,347	€ 1,822	€ 2,451
Gross margin (%)	32.5%	28.6%	30.3%	37.5%	43.9%
Other income	65	199	122	165	28
Less selling, G&A and other	(568)	(621)	(789)	(910)	(1,182)
EBITDA	€ 525	€ 623	€ 680	€ 1,077	€ 1,297
EBITDA margin (%)	16.6%	17.1%	15.3%	22.2%	23.2%
Less depreciation & amortization	(184)	(197)	(133)	(279)	(392)
Operating profit or income	€ 341	€ 426	€ 547	€ 798	€ 905
Operating margin (%)	10.8%	11.7%	12.3%	16.4%	16.2%
Income from investments	(2)	(23)	(7)	(3)	(2)
Interest income (expense), net	18	31	53	35	30
EBT	€ 357	€ 434	€ 593	€ 830	€ 933
Less corporate income taxes	(166)	(224)	(322)	(367)	(368)
Net income	€ 191	€ 210	€ 271	€ 463	€ 565
Return on sales (%)	6.1%	5.8%	6.1%	9.5%	10.1%
Effective tax rate (%)	46.5%	51.6%	54.3%	44.2%	39.4%
Shares (common & preferred)	17.5	17.5	17.5	17.5	17.5
Earnings per share	€ 10.93	€ 12.02	€ 15.51	€ 26.47	€ 32.29
EPS growth rate	34.9%	10.0%	29.0%	70.7%	22.0%
Dividends per share (common)		€ 1.48	€ 2.54	€ 2.94	€ 3.34
Extraordinary dividend				€ 14.00	
Dividends per share (preferred)		€ 1.53	€ 2.60	€ 3.00	€ 3.40

Source: Porsche AG, Morgan Stanley, December 8, 2003, p. 9.

Appendix 2	Porsche's Consolidated Balance Sheet (millions of euros)				
	1998/99	**1999/00**	**2000/01**	**2001/02**	**2002/03**
Assets					
Cash & cash equivalents	€ 730	€ 823	€ 1,121	€ 1,683	€ 1,766
Accounts receivable	148	204	248	171	211
Inventories	293	239	267	291	468
Prepaid expenses & other	72	67	81	50	42
Total current assets	1,243	1,332	1,717	2,195	2,487
Intangibles	16	76	108	214	346
Property, plant, and equipment	501	487	561	731	901
Leased vehicles	0	0	0	1,224	1,375
Financial assets	9	14	38	39	42
Other assets	149	295	443	1,006	1,163
Total Assets	€ 1,918	€ 2,204	€ 2,867	€ 5,409	€ 6,314
Liabilities & Equity					
Short-term borrowings	€ 54	€ 18	€ 159	€ 137	€ 88
Accounts payable	193	240	236	303	337
Total current liablities	247	258	395	440	425
Long-term debt	102	102	0	317	317
Other liabilities	124	111	132	1,469	1,729
Provision for risks and charges	856	951	1,312	1,716	2,088
Total long-term liabilities	1,082	1,164	1,444	3,502	4,134
Total liabilities	1,329	1,422	1,839	3,942	4,559
Stockholders' equity	589	782	1,028	1,467	1,755
Total liabilities & equity	€ 1,918	€ 2,204	€ 2,867	€ 5,409	€ 6,314

Source: Porsche AG, Morgan Stanley, December 8, 2003, p. 9.

Appendix 3	Porsche's Consolidated Statement of Cash Flow				
(millions of euros)	1998/99	1999/00	2000/01	2001/02	2002/03
Operating Activities					
Income before extraordinary items	€ 191	€ 210	€ 270	€ 462	€ 565
Depreciation, depletion, & amortization	184	197	133	138	196
Non-cash provisioning (excld pensions)	176	75	346	286	382
Change in net working capital	(76)	44	(76)	119	(183)
Cash flow from operating activities	€ 475	€ 526	€ 673	€ 1,005	€ 960
Investing Activities					
Capital expenditure	(153)	(257)	(294)	(410)	(591)
Cash flow from investing activities	(€ 153)	(€ 257)	(€ 294)	(€ 410)	(€ 591)
Financing Activities					
Change in short-term debt	0	0	37	339	(49)
Change in long-term debt	28	(36)	0	(102)	0
Payment of dividends	(22)	(22)	(26)	(45)	(297)
Cash flows from financing activities	€ 6	(€ 58)	€ 11	€ 192	(€ 346)
Exchange rate effect	1	4	2	(5)	0
Net change in cash	€ 329	€ 215	€ 392	€ 782	€ 23

Source: Porsche AG, Morgan Stanley, December 8, 2003, p. 9.

Appendix 4   Porsche Dispenses with Listing in New York

Stuttgart. The preferred stock of Dr. Ing. h.c. F. Porsche AG, Stuttgart, will continue to be listed exclusively on German stock exchanges. All considerations about gaining an additional listing in the U.S.A. have been laid aside by the Porsche Board of Management. The sports car manufacturer had been invited to join the New York Stock Exchange at the beginning of the year.

The Chairman of the Board of Management at Porsche, Dr. Wendelin Wiedeking, explained the decision: "The idea was certainly attractive for us. But we came to the conclusion that a listing in New York would hardly have brought any benefits for us and our shareholders and, on the other hand, would have led to considerable extra costs for the company." The crucial factor in Porsche's decision was ultimately the law passed by the U.S. government this summer (the "Sarbanes-Oxley Act"), whereby the CEO and the Director of Finance of a public limited company listed on a stock exchange in the U.S.A. have to swear that every balance sheet is correct and, in the case of incorrect specifications, are personally liable for high financial penalties and even up to 20 years in prison.

In Porsche's view, this new American ruling does not match the legal position in Germany. In Germany, the annual financial statement is passed by the entire Board of Management and is then presented to the Supervisory Board, after being audited and certified by chartered accountants. The chartered accountants are commissioned by the general meeting of shareholders and they are obliged both to report and to submit the annual financial statement to the Supervisory Board. The annual financial statement is only passed after it is approved by the Supervisory Board. Therefore, there is an overall responsibility covering several different committees and, as a rule, involving over 20 persons, including the chartered accountants. The Porsche Director of Finance, Holger P. Härter, made the following comments: "Nowadays in Germany, the deliberate falsification of balance sheets is already punished according to the relevant regulations in the Commercial Code (HGB) and the Company Act (Aktiengesetz). Any special treatment of the Chairman of the Board of Management or the Director of Finance would be illogical because of the intricate network within the decision-making process; it would also be irreconcilable with current German law."

Source: Porsche, News Release of October 16, 2002.

Appendix 5	The Porsche Platforms and Margins, 2002/03			
Boxster Roadster	**Boxster**	**Boxster S**		**Total Boxster**
Units sold	10,157	8,254		18,411
Average price	€ 41,380	€ 48,910		€ 44,756
Revenue (million)	€ 420.3	€ 403.7		€ 824.0
Less variable cost	(273.2)	(262.4)		(535.6)
Gross margin	147.1	141.3		288.4
Less fixed charges	(124.1)	(100.9)		(225.0)
EBIT	€ 23.0	€ 40.4		€ 63.4
EBIT margin	*5.5%*	*10.0%*		*7.7%*
911 Sports Car*	**C2 Cabrio**	**Targa**	**911 Turbo**	**Total 911**
Units sold	6,500	2,300	5,200	27,789
Average price	€ 82,877	€ 80,696	€ 124,038	€ 92,821
Revenue (million)	€ 538.7	€ 185.6	€ 645.0	€ 2,579.4
Less variable cost	(250.3)	(86.2)	(299.6)	(1,198.4)
Gross margin	288.4	99.4	345.4	1,381.0
Less fixed charges	(228.1)	(80.7)	(182.4)	(975.0)
EBIT	€ 60.3	€ 18.7	€ 163.0	€ 406.0
EBIT margin	*11.2%*	*10.1%*	*25.3%*	*15.7%*
Cayenne SUV	**Cayenne S**	**Cayenne Turbo**		**Total Cayenne**
Units sold	15,859	4,744		20,603
Average price	€ 59,165	€ 98,145		€ 68,145
Revenue (million)	€ 938.3	€ 465.6		€ 1,404.0
Less variable cost	(703.7)	(349.2)		(1,053.0)
Gross margin	234.6	116.4		351.0
Less fixed charges	(161.6)	(48.4)		(210.0)
EBIT	€ 73.0	€ 68.0		€ 141.0
EBIT margin	*7.8%*	*14.6%*		*10.0%*

*The 911 possesses 11 other models in addition to the three shown here.

Source: Citigroup Smith Barney, September 24, 2003, p.12.

Appendix 6	Currency Exposure Covered by Derivatives		
Automaker	*2003E*	*2004E*	*2005E*
BMW	90%	70%	35%
Mercedes	90%	60%	30%
Porsche	100%	100%	100%
Volkswagen	40%	70%	30%

E = estimate. Porsche's fiscal year ends in July while all others end in December.
Source: "European Autos Quarterly," Commerzbank Securities, January 7, 2004, p. 11.

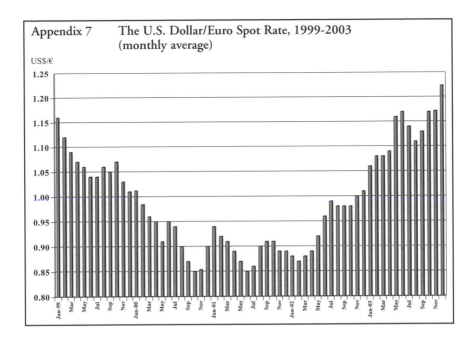

Appendix 7   The U.S. Dollar/Euro Spot Rate, 1999-2003
              (monthly average)

Appendix 8   The U.S. Dollar/Euro Exchange Rate and Selected Interest Rates and
              Volatilities, 1999-2003 (monthly)

Month/Year	Spot Rate (US$/€)	*Eurodollar LIBOR Rates by Maturity*			*Euro-LIBOR Rates by Maturity*		
		3-Month (percent)	6-Month (percent)	12-Month (percent)	3-Month (percent)	6-Month (percent)	12-Month (percent)
July-99	1.0371	5.310	5.610	5.771	2.676	2.897	3.031
July-00	0.9386	6.732	6.919	7.089	4.580	4.835	5.104
July-01	0.8616	3.751	3.791	4.001	4.467	4.386	4.310
July-02	0.9931	1.848	1.905	2.143	3.407	3.481	3.643
July-03	1.1362	1.110	1.123	1.201	2.127	2.090	2.077

Month/Year	Spot Rate (US$/€)	*US$/€ Volatility by Maturity*		
		One-Year (percent)	Two-Year (percent)	Three-Year (percent)
July-99	1.0371	9.01	12.95	14.80
July-00	0.9386	10.62	13.92	16.75
July-01	0.8616	11.55	15.68	18.08
July-02	0.9931	9.75	15.12	18.49
July-03	1.1362	9.44	14.13	17.83

Option volatilities are the mean for the 1-year, 2-year, or 3-year period ending with the listed date. For example, July 1999 one-year volatility is the mean of the August 1998–July 1999 period.

CHAPTER 13

Global Marketing of Services

T rade in services is growing faster than the international trade in goods. Services have unique characteristics that pose special problems in international marketing.

The main goals of this chapter are to

- Identify the characteristics that distinguish services from goods and that influence the way services are marketed internationally.

- Determine the basis of comparative advantage in service industries.

- Define the roles played by governments and WTO in the service trade.

- Discuss examples of services industries such as media and entertainment, sports, and other industries.

What are services? Industries such as wholesaling and retailing, communications, transportation, utilities, banking and insurance, tourism, and business and personal services are all service industries. Services account for the largest portion of output and employment in advanced industrialized countries. Services typically become more important as an economy becomes more developed. Thus, U.S. employment in service industries was 24 percent of total employment in 1870, 31 percent in 1900, 55 percent in 1950, and 72 percent in 1985, stabilizing around 75 percent in the mid-1990s. Similar increases were recorded in Japan, Germany, France, and Britain. The service industry as a whole has been increasing in importance in advanced industrialized nations for almost a century. Given their importance in national economies, it is not surprising that services are becoming increasingly important in world trade. Trade in services accounts for about one-third of all world trade, having grown at about 16 percent a year for the past several years. That figure is compared to an approximate 5–7 percent growth rate for merchandise trade.

U.S. services that have been exported include the following:

- Construction, design, and engineering services
- Banking and financial services
  - Insurance
  - Legal and accounting
  - Computer software and data
  - Training and education
  - Entertainment, music, film, and sports
  - Management consulting
- Franchising
- Hotel and lodging services
- Transportation services, including airline, maritime, and passenger and cargo services

As the list indicates, countries export a wide variety of services. It is interesting to note, however, that some major service sectors are not represented in the list. For example, the utility sector, auto repair services, and personal services (laundry, barbershops, home cleaning) are not well represented in service exports.

Because services often require the simultaneous presence of buyer and seller, services exports are likely to be quickly substituted with FDI and joint ventures, thereby facilitating the local delivery of services in various foreign markets. International marketing of services is done as much through FDI, franchising, and joint ventures as through exporting. The next section covers some service industry characteristics that make international trade difficult.

The growing convergence of tastes and the economies of scale stemming from standardization are the fundamental arguments for the increased company focus on international marketing. However, when it comes to services, standardization may be harder to sell. The reason is because cultural differences and market regulatory differences affect how services are designed and delivered. Further, as Silk and Berndt[1] note, services businesses may have fewer fixed costs. In addition, the higher ratio of variable costs to total costs may limit the scale and scope economies to be realized from globalization. Therefore, companies need to take into account the distinctive characteristics of services when planning to market them globally.

Services: How Are They Different From Products?

Services have been defined as "those fruits of economic activity that you cannot drop on your toe: banking to butchery, acting to accountancy."[2] Indeed, services are mostly intangible. The distinguishing characteristics of services include intangibility; heterogeneity; perishability; and, often, simultaneous production and consumption.[3] Those characteristics are outlined in Table 13-1 and are discussed below. Because of these characteristics, services are more difficult to price and measure than are products.

Intangibility

Services are often performances, such as conducting an audit, designing a building, and fixing a car. In that sense, they are intangible. Questions pertinent to the international marketing of services include whether (1) actions are being performed on people (for example, education) or things (for example, air freight),[4] (2) the customer needs to be physically present during the service or only at initiation and termination of the service, and (3) the customer can be just mentally present—that is, can the service be performed at a distance?

Heterogeneity

Different customers going to the same service company may not receive the same service. This quality of heterogeneity occurs because different people perform the service. Therefore, it is impossible to make sure that the service is performed the same way each time. One salesclerk may be less polite or amiable than another, resulting in consumer dissatisfaction. The implication of heterogeneity is that quality is difficult to control.

A logical response is to attempt to standardize the service. One way is to develop a detailed blueprint of the steps involved in providing the service, then analyzing results as the steps are taken to ensure that quality standards are maintained. This may mean changing the way the service is performed to reduce complexity and the possibility of divergence between different service providers.

Table 13-1. Services Characteristics and Their Implications for Globalization

Service Characteristics with Implications for Globalization

Intangibility: How to differentiate the service? Advertise mainly through word of mouth: Who are the influential opinion makers in each market? Validity of a *follow-the-client* strategy in entering international markets? Manage corporate image in multiple markets.

Heterogeneity: How to reduce across-country variations in service quality influenced by variations among service providers? Can all service personnel in several countries be trained to the same level and quality of performance? Impact of cultural differences affecting extent and kind of training in each market. *Develop ownership and control stake sufficient to influence recruitment and training.*

Perishability: Can excess capacity in one market be used to satisfy demand in another? How to forecast service demand patterns in different markets? Are there similarities in the model for service demand across countries? Can standardized incentives be used to manage demand across countries? *Create cross-country databases, raise switching costs, employ ownership, and franchise strategies.*

Inseparability: The simultaneity of production and consumption: Can service be provided at a distance internationally? *Enhancing role of technology and electronic delivery* (for example, ATMs—automatic teller machines). How much of service production can be placed in the "back office"? *Sharing of back-office functions across markets.* The need to find service providers places a constraint on the pace of international expansion. If technology cannot facilitate service exporting, then *franchising, licensing, joint venture, and foreign direct investment are better avenues.*

Service quality and consumer participation in service creation/delivery: How do consumers determine quality of service? It is a matter of consumer perceptions. Moreover, are customers in all markets equally willing to participate in the service creation process? What turns off the customer? (variations in customer defection rates across markets) How to ensure customer loyalty and repeat business? Developing market-specific plans to maintain customer loyalty. Customer perceptions of service quality may be affected by culture.

Implications of fixed-cost structure for pricing: Can scale economies lower costs of international entry? Will price-bundling strategies work in all markets? Can price discrimination be practiced across markets? Prioritizing markets by volume necessary to reach break-even. *Scale necessitates internationalization and, hence, foreign direct investment and joint ventures.*

Service as a process: Is the service concept culture-bound? Adaptation versus standardization of the service concept for overseas markets. Can standardized "scripts" for the service encounter be used across countries? *Franchising and licensing more appealing as greater adaptation is needed.*

Source: Adapted from R. Sarathy, "Global Strategy in Service Industries," *Long Range Planning,* Volume 27, Number 6, 1994.

But it is very difficult to standardize services when the personnel providing them must exercise a high degree of judgment. When a firm's advantage is based on customizing a service, any attempt at standardization means that the fundamental strategy of the business is being changed.

When extending the service to international markets, there is also the question of whether the service standardized for one national market will satisfy customers in other markets. For example, one way to standardize a service is to personalize the interaction between customer and service provider by training retail salespersons to greet customers by name and use certain standard conversational remarks. However, when employees must follow "scripts," cultural factors demand a somewhat different "script" for each country market.

The training of customer-contact personnel should also be conducted differently in different cultures. For example, the two-week training given to Kentucky Fried Chicken workers in Japan would be uneconomical in the context of high labor turnover in the United States. But the training is appropriate for Japan given the greater job loyalty among workers and, more importantly, the customers' expectations of politeness and courtesy from Japanese service workers.

Perishability

Services are perishable in that they cannot be inventoried, saved, or stored. Thus, a plane seat that sits empty when the flight takes off is lost forever. The perishability of seats makes it harder to adjust the supply of a service to fluctuating demand, especially during times of peak demand. Therefore, service companies seek innovations that allow the service to be "inventoried" in some fashion or that allow demand to be managed so that the supply of services is adequate and can be provided economically. An example is providing a restricted number of reduced-fare, advance-purchase seats on flights, with the number being increased if seats on the flight do not appear to be selling as forecast.

Marketing services internationally makes the task of forecasting demand more complex because the vagaries of individual national markets affect demand in unique ways. Further, service must match demand in many different markets. Idle capacity exists in some markets, while excess demand is encountered in other markets.

Simultaneous Production and Consumption

Production and consumption of a service often take place at the same time; that is, the producer and the seller of the service are often the same person. Moreover, the customer must often be present for the service to take place. Unlike products, services usually cannot be exported. So international marketing means that the service must be performed by the firm in the country market, whether through franchising, licensing, a direct investment, or an acquisition. Thus, the country in which the service is offered may affect the desirability of the service provider. Does country of origin matter to consumers when they select services? Javalgi and others suggest that the answer depends on the type of service being consumed. Specifically, customers seem to prefer core services from their home country (for example, medical care and travel). Supplementary services such as a warranty are more important when the country-of-origin effect is less favorable. Further, brand name recognition can make the country of origin less important, and cultural sensitivity can be an important adjunct of the country of origin of services.[5]

While country of origin may be important, the fundamental question is whether the service can be performed at a distance. If not, how should a firm position itself in a distant market when offering a service? An example is the use of ATMs (automated teller machines), which allow customers to conduct certain banking transactions without a teller being present.

Pricing Services

Services are difficult to price because calculating the cost of production is difficult.[6] Price can be set in relation to full costs, based on what the competition charges, or set at whatever the customer is willing to pay. Service businesses have a high fixed-cost ratio. Hence, if a service can be offered in many national markets without much modification, prices can be lower because the fixed costs have presumably been recovered in the home market. Therefore, some advantages of scale accrue to the company that is first to market a new service. For example, in the case of antivirus software U.S. firms have already recovered much of their fixed costs of developing the software, through sales in the United States. Hence, foreign prices can be lower because the firms do not have to incur the fixed costs of product development a second time.

Measuring Service Quality

Service quality is difficult to measure, particularly in cross-cultural settings. Smith and Reynolds emphasize the equivalence issues that need to be addressed in such cases.[7]

It is often unclear what the consumer expects. Yet quality is a matter of meeting customers' expectations. In other words, quality depends on consumer perception, which, in turn, is determined by the following:[8]

- The person doing the service
- The technical outcome of the service
- The overall image of the company whose employee is carrying out the service

Technical quality may be amenable to traditional quality-control approaches borrowed from a manufacturing setting, but only if the service process is standardized. If corporate image affects the perception of quality, the firm must decide whether the same corporate image is needed in all countries. Should all employees wear the same uniforms? Should the physical facilities look the same in all national markets?

Consumer dissatisfaction may result from unrealistic expectations. Other reasons for the gap between desired quality and perceived quality include a lack of understanding about what consumers expect from a service, an inability or unwillingness to meet customer expectations, problems with delivering the service, and communication gaps when a firm fails to communicate realistic expectations about what quality will be offered.[9] Quality of service is difficult to measure in cross-cultural settings.

Min and his coauthors make the crucial point that benchmarking allows service firms to assess performance gaps relative to their competitors and remedy those gaps in service quality. However, customers may change their perceptions of what attributes of service quality matter most. Responding to changing customer needs and perceptions of service quality, service providers must ensure continuous improvement. Min and his coauthors applied a dynamic benchmarking approach to luxury hotels in Seoul. They showed that hotels can improve customer desirability by using analytical hierarchy analysis to spot changes in customer perceptions of attributes considered important to overall service quality, then improve their service along those lines.[10]

While customer satisfaction and customer retention are seen as being linked, switching costs may stop customers from changing suppliers, in which case, retention may actually mask dissatisfaction. Lee and his coauthors studied this phenomenon among mobile phone users in France, separating switching costs into transactional (and search) costs, learning costs, and contractual costs. They found that switching costs do, indeed, mediate the satisfaction loyalty link, often creating hostages who would like to switch but are deterred by the total amount of switching costs—tangible and intangible.[11]

Importance of Customer Loyalty to Services

Because services cannot be stored, a basic marketing strategy is to ensure repeat business by generating loyalty in existing customers. Devices such as frequent-flier plans may be used to reward customer loyalty. But given that consumers have different characteristics in different countries, are such plans necessary for all national markets? Or should they be shaped mainly by competitive variations in each market? Loyalty can also be maintained and rewarded through pricing. The question for each national market is whether volume discounts and membership strategies work equally well in all markets.

Services can be segmented to focus on specific groups, as in the case of tourism. Tourists have many destinations from which to choose, and tourism marketers have to decide how to focus their advertising dollars to maximize benefits. Leisen suggests developing tourism customer segments based on similarity of perceptions among potential visitors of natural beauty, sociocultural features, recreational potential, and climate amenities at the destination sites. That allows managers to target specific segments whose top-ranking perceptions closely match the specific higher-ranking attributes of the particular tourism sites[12].

Additional Decision Areas

This section will discuss other relevant considerations, such as branding and advertising services, the impact of cultural variables on creating and marketing services, and organizational structure for managing services.

Branding Services

How services are branded should differ depending on whether the services are chosen based on comparative search and evaluation, (purchasing an expensive, durable service such as university education), previous experience (deciding on a restaurant), or established credibility (choosing a doctor). Some services may be chosen using multiple criteria. Moorthi's service branding model, set out in Figure 13-1, suggests that services branding will depend on how the brand is presented and perceived in the marketplace.[13]

Advertising Services

From branding services, it is a short and necessary step to advertising services, whose principal functions include making the services tangible, showing the service encounter, encouraging word-of-mouth communication (by satisfied users), and building the brand image. How are services best advertised—by word of mouth, direct mail, satisfied customer referrals, or ads in newspapers or on television? Are there national differences in the relative appeal of the different forms of advertising of services? What should be the focus of advertising? Which is more important—the image and name of the company providing the service or facets of the service being sold? Those questions must be answered for each country market.[14]

Mortimer noted that the traditional view of services advertising focused on making the service tangible, representing the service encounter, encouraging word-of-mouth communication, and building a strong brand image. In contrast, when advertising agencies were asked about services advertising, they emphasized that the advertising objective was what mattered. Agencies believed advertising was more influenced by the service being utilitarian (insur-

Figure 13-1. Services Branding Model

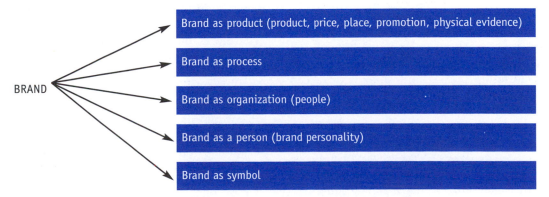

Source: Y.L.R. Moorthi, "An Approach to Branding Services," *Journal of Services Marketing,* 16(3), 2002, page 261.

ance) or experiential (leisure travel) and by the customer's level of involvement with the service.[15]

Culture affects the kind of information presented in services advertising. Comparing Hong Kong and the United States and drawing on Hofstede's cultural dimensions, Tai and Chan suggest that since price and status are connected, more price-based information is needed in cultures marked by high power distance (one of Hofstede's cultural dimensions). Cultures that score higher on the Hofstede masculinity dimension may need more performance-related information, as individuals in those cultures may connect success to achievement and status, therefore valuing performance information. The authors further suggest that people from less individualistic cultures value content that helps them protect group interests and reduce uncertainty in their purchasing decisions. In long-term oriented cultures, information on availability is valued. However, quality did not seem to be associated with specific cultural traits, suggesting that service quality could be a universal need.[16]

Organization for Marketing Services

A decentralized organization seems more fitting for service industries, given the inherent heterogeneity of the product and the customer base. But if a firm moves to standardize the service performance, can it do so without considerable centralization? That is a key decision for a firm that chooses to market its services internationally.

Cultural Variables

Because services generally involve close interaction between the service provider and the customer, cultural variables affect user satisfaction and loyalty to specific service providers. Cultural variables also affect service design and the nature of interaction with the customer. Patterson and Smith found that in collectivist cultures such as Thailand, where they did their study, consumers were less likely to switch service providers, particularly when they received special benefits in return for their loyalty. The authors go on to suggest that service providers need to make special efforts in collectivist cultures to provide special benefits, such as making appointments at the last minute and nurturing close relationships with specific service providers.[17]

An interesting illustration of the impact of cultural variables involves the signing of a book contract in Russia. Little, Brown, a U.S. publishing house, wanted to obtain the rights to Anatoli Rybakov's *Children of the Arbat*, a novel about life in Stalinist Russia. As was the norm in Russia at that time, Little, Brown had to negotiate with the state-owned copyright agency, VAAP, represented by a team of eight officials, two translators, and the author. Settling on the amount of advance was easy, but royalties created some difficulties. U.S. royalties are tied to the mode of selling; thus, they may be lower on discounted sales to book clubs, direct mail sales, and large wholesalers. But VAAP would accept a reduction only for paperback and book club sales. In addition, it wanted the right of approval over the translation, book jacket, flap copy, and promotional materials.

VAAP also wanted to insert a clause into the contract that the publisher would do no harm to "VAAP, the author, or the book." When Roger Donald of Little, Brown responded to that demand by discussing the acceptable amount of monetary damages, VAAP countered that that was not the meaning of injury to reputation. When Donald asked how the clause was to be enforced without a monetary provision, he was told that it would be based on honorable behavior. The difficulty was solved by inserting a clause vowing never to inflict "intentional harm." At the end of successful negotiations, when Donald invited the VAAP team to dinner, he discovered that all of them spoke English.[18]

Comparative Advantage and the Service Industries

Why do advanced industrialized nations dominate services exports? What factors lead a nation and its firms to have a comparative advantage in services? Clearly, each service industry is distinct, having a different production function; that is, each service industry uses technology, labor, capital, and management in different proportions to deliver its service. Still, certain factors of production play a role in service industries. Those factors of production are discussed next.

Labor

Service industries are generally labor-intensive, with both highly skilled and unskilled labor being used. Labor in retail stores, barbershops, and florists, for example, may not need much training and is likely to be low-paid. Countries with low labor costs have an advantage. At the other extreme are legal and accounting services that require highly educated and highly paid personnel. Advanced countries would likely have an advantage in offering those services. However, high-level skills may be country-specific and may not be easily transferable to other countries. Expertise in U.S. tax law may not be meaningful to tax practices in Europe. However, the *methodologies* used by U.S. law firms to research and argue tax issues may, indeed, be pertinent to the practice of tax law in advanced nations.

Capital

Traditionally, services have low capital-to-labor ratios. Lower amounts of capital are used per worker in service industries than in manufacturing industries. Service productivity has been lower than in manufacturing, and the future growth of service industries will require larger amounts of capital per worker to raise productivity and quality. In banking, for example, increased use of computers results in more productive workers, faster transactions, and more satisfied customers. If the trend continues, countries and firms with lower costs of capital will gain an advantage in international markets.

Technology

Services vary in their use of technology (although it is an increasingly pervasive influence in all industries). Services such as airlines and shipping, custom computer software, and banking can be termed high-tech services compared to, say, interior decorating, which uses less sophisticated technology.

Clearly, the capital investment in R&D that resulted in the technology-based services application leads to a comparative advantage for a company—and for a country. Both can use the technology to enter the global maintenance industry in a new fashion, bypassing former barriers.

Transfer of Information, Technology, Capital, and People

A global communications network is vital to the export of services. In essence, transborder data flows have created a whole new category of industries, meaning previously nontradable goods are now traded internationally. Providing custom software programming services over broadband networks and virtual private networks (VPNs) is an example of that phenomenon. Companies such as Microsoft, Siemens, Hewlett-Packard, and Texas Instruments have set up software development labs in India. Indian programmers develop, maintain, and upgrade software for the parent company and other clients in the United States by means of remote terminals and computers and telecommunications links.

Of course, services need not be provided solely through information transfer. FDI involves the transfer of capital and ideas, and often transferring the technology through which the service is provided. An example is the use of laser scanners, bar codes, and RFID tags, mentioned in Chapter 9. Those technologies are used to speed up logistics monitoring, inventory scanning, and checkout at warehouses, airports, grocery stores, and other retail outlets. Going a step further, companies such as Information Resources have developed proprietary databases of information gleaned from laser scanning the entire sales volume of a store. That data is analyzed and sold to companies seeking more information about their consumers. As companies begin selling such services outside the United States, they must ensure that bar code and laser scanning technologies are available in the countries and that the countries have the computer software need to analyze the raw data.

Thus, for services to be provided in foreign countries, there must be a transfer of information (or other intangible assets), technology, capital, and people—the service providers who interact with customers. However, barriers to labor mobility across countries exist. Thus, service firms often export capital, technology, and information to be combined with local labor.

Other Bases for Comparative Advantage

Javalgi and his coauthors examined whether firm-specific and location-specific factors affected the internationalization of service firms. They found that size and local market characteristics had the greatest influence in management attitudes toward operating internationally in service firms.[19] Other bases for comparative advantage include the following:

- Management skills specific to service industries
- Size
- Experience in a particular service sector
- The firm's global reputation

Thus, U.S. firms have been able to dominate the world software industry because of the experience and management skills developed over the years of being in business. U.S. firms have developed specific skills. Those skills include transforming custom software into packages that have the widest customer appeal, supervising the development of complicated software within large teams of programmers. Then, the software is marketed to an end-user base through indirect channels of distribution such as computer industry retailers and department stores.

In short, services can be more or less technology-intensive and capital-intensive and have greater or lesser reliance on skilled labor. Advanced industrialized nations such as the United States and France are likely to have a comparative advantage in service industry sectors that are more capital-intensive, skilled labor-intensive, and technology-intensive.

Sustainable Competitive Advantage in Services

Beyond country-specific advantages, service companies seek to build a *sustainable competitive advantage* in order to enhance long-term performance. Bharadwaj and others[20] have developed a conceptual framework that links the resources and capabilities of a service firm with the nature of the service offered and with certain characteristics of the firm. The result is a competitive positioning advantage. Whether the advantage can be sustained depends on whether barriers exist to the diffusion and imitation of firm-specific capabilities and resources. This model is shown in Figure 13-2.

Government Intervention in the Services Trade

As is true for goods, international trade in services is also subject to government interference and protection. Government actions can include the following:

- Rights of establishment (meaning the right to establish a branch or subsidiary in a foreign country; for example, many nations ban ownership of television stations by foreigners)
- Trade barriers, including limitations on the proportion of a market that a foreign company can serve and discriminatory taxation of services provided by a foreign company
- Foreign exchange controls; limits on remitting profits from service businesses
- Government procurement barriers because government buys services only from "national" companies
- Technical issues that serve to keep out foreign firms, such as the use of standards and certification conditions
- Government subsidies, countervailing duties, and high customs valuation of foreign services, leading to higher total tariffs
- Licensing regulations that impose unreasonable terms of entry or insist on licensing as the only mode of entry
- Restrictions on professional qualifications, including ban on entry of qualified service company personnel
- Tolerance of commercial counterfeiting

Other factors can include government support, preferential financing, and political or regional bias in public procurement. In addition, export restrictions, often for national security reasons, can be a barrier.

Mobile (cellular) phones are an example of an industry where governments can be influential. Governments may set national transmission standards, control entry, limit competition, set prices, and favor "national champions."

Fair Trade in Services

As services grow more important in world trade, nations have begun seeking a consensus on fair trade practices with regard to services. The WTO has paid special attention to protecting Intellectual Property (IP) rights. It has also addressed the issues of barriers to trade in services, national treatment of foreign firms, allowance of FDI in services without undue restrictions, temporary admission of foreign service workers, international agreement on the regulation of international data flows and ownership rights in international databases, and importation of materials and equipment necessary for providing services. Other thorny issues addressed by the WTO include establishing a framework to control restrictive licensing practices and the right of "nonestablishment," which is growing increasingly important as service firms deliver their services via electronic means or through the mail without being physically present in a country. The WTO regulations govern the conditions under which a foreign firm can be said to have established a presence in a foreign market. That, in turn, may determine whether the foreign firm qualifies for treatment as a domestic firm. Similarly, establishing a domestic presence is often necessary to qualify for protection under the laws of IP rights in a country.

The U.S. government offers specialized help to service industries. Within the Department of Commerce, the Office of Service Industries has divisions covering specific industry sectors such as information, transportation and tourism, and finance and management.

Selected Service Industry Sectors

The remainder of this chapter examines the global marketing of a variety of service industry sectors. Those sectors include the global media and entertainment industries, music and sports, the airline industry, hotels, professional services, and retail.

Figure 13-2. A Contingency Model of Sustainable Competitive Advantage in Service Industries

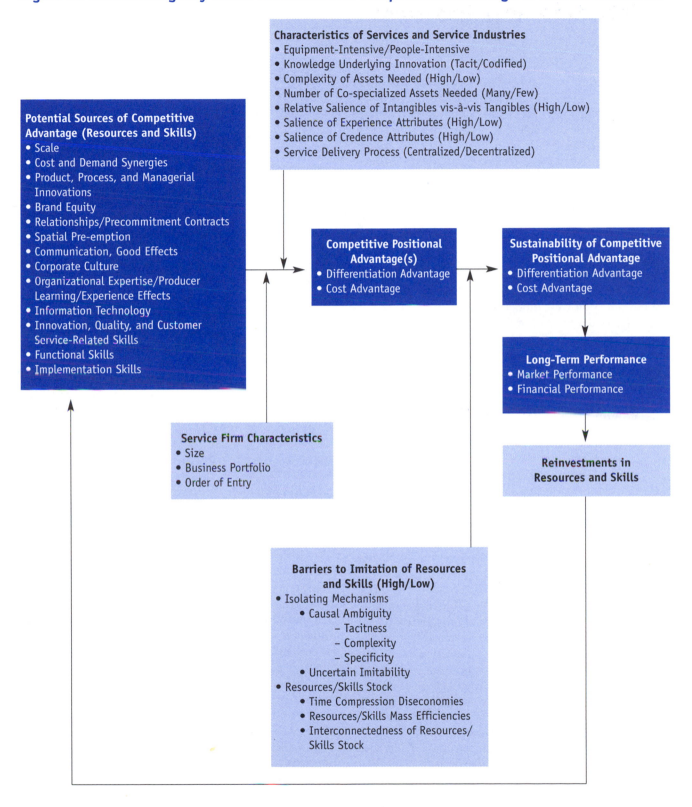

Source: From S.G. Bharadwaj, P.R. Varadarajan, and J. Fahy, "Sustainable Competitive Advantage in Service Industries: A Conceptual Model and Research Propositions," *Journal of Marketing*, October 1993, 85.

Global Media and the Entertainment Industry

In the United States, entertainment has always been one of the largest exports. The private enterprise system governing U.S. television and the burgeoning of alternative channels (first on pay TV, then on cable television, and now on satellite television and digital high-definition TV) have led to fierce competition. Each station seeks larger audiences in order to sell more commercials and charges higher prices for commercial time. That means showing the programs that attract the largest audiences. Over time, U.S. firms have become very adept in producing mass audience-pleasing programs. That is their competitive advantage in world markets.

Deregulation of U.S. television, the large U.S. population, the large number of available programming hours, and the many TV channels and theaters all combine to make it worthwhile for U.S. companies to invest additional resources in TV and film production. Those investments also become a comparative advantage because the U.S. industry enjoys economies of scale arising from a multiplicity of "customers," both in the number of TV channels and movie theaters and in the large English-speaking audience.

European Media Environment

In sharp contrast to the United States, European television was at one time largely government-controlled. Basically, government ownership of stations meant noncommercial television except for rare and restricted instances. In West Germany, for example, television advertising was restricted to 40 minutes a day; in Switzerland, 20 minutes a day.

Deregulation of European television has changed the competitive environment. The use of new technologies (satellite broadcasting, cable, and pay TV) has increased the number of channels. With more TV stations in Europe and Japan and more air time to fill, there is greater demand for TV programming. Also, deregulated TV stations show more commercials. As a result, advertising by firms seeking a European market share has increased, meaning more business for advertising agencies and their suppliers. The market for exports from U.S. producers of films and TV shows has grown. In response, the EU has attempted to create conditions favoring the emergence of a "European" TV industry. The French, in particular, have concerns about the loss of French culture. They have claimed a "cultural exception" to free trade in media and entertainment services, using their fears as a basis for limiting imports of U.S. TV shows and films.

Such changes broaden the scope of the media industry, which now encompasses broadcasting and production of TV and motion picture films. The industry also includes books and newspapers; video games; printing services; and alternative modes of information delivery, such as the creation and sale of proprietary databases. Information and entertainment can be delivered in many ways: by CD, through online digital files, by television and movie theater, in book form, and as data downloaded from online databases.

Satellite TV and a Pan-European Audience

Technology has played a key role in changing the nature of the television industry. New pan-European TV channels have been introduced through the use of high-powered direct broadcast satellite (DBS) systems that beam programs directly into homes from satellites via a small receiver. Satellite TV promises the possibility of creating a pan-European, cross-cultural audience. In response, European media companies have merged. U.S. media giants have acquired European media companies to obtain scale economies and distribution channels and to provide a better market to the growing European audience. (See Table 13-2.)

What decisions are involved in reaching a pan-European audience? First, firms must try to predict what programs are likely to appeal to viewers from different European countries. Second, firms must determine the appropriate forms of advertising for those viewers. Companies must also develop one brand name to push in their pan-European commercials. Thus, Unilever cannot easily advertise its cleaning fluid branded as Vif in Switzerland, Viss in Germany, Jif in the UK and Greece, and Cif in France. And nationalistic country managers must be persuaded to use standardized brand names and advertising channels. The proliferation of media can only motivate European firms to raise their spending on media.

Cable TV is not as widespread in Europe as it is in the United States, and it may never become as strong because of competition from DBS television. One of the more successful cable TV stations in Europe is MTV Europe, a joint venture of U.S. and European partners. Understanding why MTV has been successful is the key to understanding the potentials and pitfalls of a pan-European television network. So, let's examine its history.

MTV chairman and CEO Tom Freston has said, "Music crosses borders very easily, and the lingua franca of rock 'n roll is English. Rock is an Anglo-American form; German rock bands sing in English; Swedish rock bands sing in English." Not surprisingly, MTV is now available all across Europe and Asia. MTV's mission? According to Freston, "We want to be the global rock n' roll village where we can talk to youth worldwide."

However, MTV has taken pains to introduce a local flavor, with local video disc jockeys playing a mix of local acts and international (primarily U.S.) musical groups. The key to cross-national TV networks is language. People seeking entertainment are not likely to rely solely on foreign language shows. As *The Economist* stated, "Entertainment in a foreign language is seldom 'light.' " To overcome the language problem, cross-national TV channels must broadcast in dominant local languages and focus on special-interest programs, such as local sports, local business news, and first-run movies in local languages.[21]

Satellite TV and Cable TV in Asia

Over a dozen satellites are available to beam TV programs into Asia. Then the signals have to be received in the home through small antennas, "dishes," affixed outside the house or apartment or redistributed by cable TV operators. The latter is common in large apartment buildings in Singapore; Hong Kong; Taiwan; and, increasingly, China. Therefore, TV companies seeking to offer their programs may have to make alliances with local cable TV operators. Furthermore, as more moderate-income households become satellite and cable TV customers, they seek out entertainment in their native language. As a result, Star TV has focused on two programming segments, one aimed at India and the other aimed at China and surrounding countries. In addition to MTV, a new channel offering provides music in Chinese, Hindi, and other Asian languages. Advertisers prefer local programming because it is more likely to attract large audiences. Of course, no "right" formula exists. A mix of Western hits and sports with local appeal (such as cricket, soccer, and rugby), coupled with judicious international programming, may be the recipe for attracting and maintaining large audiences that, in turn, bring in advertising dollars.

Table 13-2. Global Media Empire Building: Major Acquisitions

Acquirer	Acquisition
Sony Corporation (Japan)	CBS Records, Columbia Pictures, Guber-Peters Productions. Entry into video games with PlayStation
Vivendi/Seagram (France)	Acquired 80 percent of MCA for $5.7 billion from Matsushita, which had earlier acquired MCA in response to Sony acquiring the media interests. Matsushita is reputed to have lost $3–$4 billion on purchase and sale of MCA. Seagram was then sold to Vivendi.
AOL Time Warner (U.S.)	Merger combining AOL online with books and magazines, pay and cable TV, film production, records, and movies. Previously acquired Turner Broadcasting, for its cable operations and film library, and CNN.
BMG Group/Bertelsmann (Germany)	Merger with Sony Music; RCA Records, Bantam Books, and Doubleday Books. Joint venture with Canal to develop digital pay TV in Europe. Similar accord with British Sky Broadcasting. Merger with Luxembourg-based CLT to gain presence in European over-the-air "free" TV.
News Corporation (Australia/United States) perhaps the best example of steady acquisition over 25 years to build a global media giant	Acquisition of DIRECTV to gain nationwide satellite TV presence in the United States; 20th Century Fox films and studios worldwide and several TV stations, both network and cable (The Fox network and specialized channels such as Fox Sports and National Geographic); British Sky Broadcasting (satellite TV) in Europe, *TV Guide* and Gemstar. Acquired control of Star TV, Asia's satellite TV channel. Joint venture with Televisa and Globo to launch a satellite direct-to-home TV service for Latin America. Book publishing, including HarperCollins, Avon Books, William Morrow.
Hachette (France)	Diamandis (magazines), Grolier (encyclopedias)
Disney/CapCities (U.S.)	Acquired CapCities and ABC for $19 billion, controlling both channels and content, with synergies in international markets and between cable and over-the-air TV networks in the United States. Main properties include ESPN, UK cable properties, and joint venture with Luxembourg-based CLT.
Viacom (U.S.)	Paramount Pictures acquisition, resulting in ownership of MTV Networks, Paramount Pictures, and Blockbuster Video stores.
GM-Hughes DIRECTV (U.S.)	Partnership with Cisneros (Venezuela), Abril (Brazil), and MVSMultivision (Mexico) to launch "Galaxy" Latin American satellite TV service. DIRECTV ultimately acquired by News Corporation.

Entertainment Industry Economics

The media industry has significant cost-structure characteristics that interact with the environmental changes discussed thus far to create the need for new global strategies.

First, entertainment is an industry with a high fixed-cost structure. Most costs are incurred in the production of programs and in the establishment of the distribution system (that is, the TV network, be it via satellite, on-air, cable, the Internet, or pay channels). These high fixed costs place a premium on obtaining a large subscriber base and creating high leverage, with handsome profits occurring once break-even levels are reached.

The media industry is also volatile, with sudden increases in revenue flowing from hit films, popular TV programs, blockbuster musical acts and CDs, and best-selling books and video games. Because it is difficult to plan for a hit, the result is a steady stream of releases, some of which become winners. Hence, the entertainment companies require abundant capital to finance production and to withstand fallow periods of few hits and possible negative cash flow. Controlling multiple distribution channels becomes an advantage, as the same content can be reformed and recycled as a book, videogame, TV program, or hit film with accompanying sound track.

The maturation of the U.S. market has brought lower growth rates and an abundant supply of TV channels compared to markets in Europe, Japan, and the Far East, where fewer channels are available and growth rates are higher because market saturation is low. That situation, together with the cyclical nature of the industry and its high fixed costs, results in a bias toward larger companies. A strategic advantage results for those able to control distribution channels as well as produce programs for them. That is, companies that own both channel and content (TV stations and TV film production companies) may enjoy higher profits, less risk, and faster growth rates.

Global Mergers in the Media Industry

A conjunction of environmental change and industry characteristics has led to globalization of the media industry. Conglomerates have resulted from the acquisitions of major U.S. media companies by foreign companies. Table 13-2 summarizes some of the major acquisitions that have taken place in the media industry in the past several years.

As the table shows, the bulk of acquisitions activity has been concentrated in the United States. Several reasons exist for that U.S. focus:

- The United States has had much experience in developing films and TV programs, and Hollywood and U.S. productions have enjoyed worldwide success. Owning the facilities delivers a stream of films and TV programs, books, records, and magazines to be marketed around the world.
- The U.S. market is huge, offering high potential profits. It is also a lead market, so programs successful in the United States can easily be sold in Europe.
- U.S. film and TV production technology is to be desired, as is the talent and experience of U.S.-based film and TV production crews. Rather than try to transport talent to European markets, companies often prefer to obtain it by acquiring a U.S. company.

The best example of this globalization phenomenon is News Corporation, controlled by Australian entrepreneur Rupert Murdoch. He first expanded from Australia to the United Kingdom, primarily in TV and newspapers. He built Sky Channel as a pan-European service using both cable and satellite delivery. Murdoch then developed a U.S. base, buying several independent TV stations and 20th Century Fox (along with its library of films), as the nucleus for creating a fourth U.S.-wide on-air TV network. The Fox network would distribute (show) films produced by 20th Century Fox, and the same movies could appear in England and Europe on Sky Channel. Then Murdoch acquired *TV Guide*, a vehicle used to appeal to the U.S. national TV audience and to further publicize his network. Finally, he acquired DIRECTV to give his company a nationwide satellite TV presence in the United States and to challenge cable TV firms such as Comcast.

News Corporation also purchased a majority stake in Star TV (from Hutchison Whampoa of Hong Kong) for $525 million, plus another $40 million for a similar stake in its programming affiliate, Media Assets Ltd. Star TV represented the missing piece in the creation of a global network. Star reaches an audience ranging from the Middle East to New Zealand that potentially includes two-thirds of the world's population. Star also complements Fox Broadcasting and DIRECTV in the United States and British Sky Broadcasting.

Murdoch's News Corporation is an example of the implementation of a globalization strategy in a global services industry. Controlling programming assets is just as important as creating a global network. News Corporation signed up Hollywood studios and international news programmers to supply content for the channels it controls. It also signed a contract with Taiwan-based Golden Harvest group to provide films, TV shows, and other programming in Chinese. A library of Chinese movies and programs will help News Corporation immeasurably in gaining audience share in mainland China and in the Chinese-speaking portions of Southeast Asia.

The principal points of Murdoch's strategy include (1) having a physical presence in the major markets of Europe, Asia, and the United States and (2) combining distribution channels, TV stations, and specialized cable channels with production facilities and "software" (the actual programs). Those will be in the form of a package of films and TV programs to be resold on a continuous basis.

Music

The music industry is also rapidly becoming global. The worldwide popularity of pop music and rock 'n roll owes much to MTV, with groups such as U2 representing this trend. BMG, a German company and music conglomerate, acquired RCA Records to sell pop music around the world. BMG saw the U.S. music industry as the primary source of innovation in the international music business. Upon acquiring RCA, Bertelsmann moved its music division headquarters to New York. Michael Dornemann, the company's then-CEO, followed a policy of "breaking" an artist into a country's market by launching the act on TV, on stage, and through publicity in newspapers and magazines. Only later would he begin to market CDs. That policy amounts to launching a separate marketing program for each artist for each country.

At the same time, there is rising demand for musical acts in local languages. Again, two big markets in Asia stand out: (1) music programs in Mandarin Chinese beamed from Hong Kong, Taiwan, and now mainland China to attract the vast numbers of Chinese speakers and (2) musical acts in Hindi aimed principally at the Indian subcontinent. Even Western channels such as MTV have become localized. Local hosts present shows that feature local acts singing in local languages. As explained earlier, entertainment is most appreciated when it is presented in one's native language. When TV channels were initially received primarily by upper-income segments, imported Western programs worked well because much of the audience had some understanding of English. But with the rapid spread of TV and the emergence of mass markets, local interests and local languages are becoming the key to gaining audience share. The reality TV phenomenon is easy to localize. The result has been the launching of local versions of well-known programs such *Who Wants To Be A Millionaire* and *Survivor*.

Trade Barriers in Entertainment

When foreign companies buy U.S. companies, they get market share as well as production capabilities. However, there is alarm in Europe and elsewhere about the domination of TV channels and air waves by U.S. products. That concern extends to U.S. culture, as well. As European governments respond to the opportunity they have created for new television programming, they have begun to favor home-grown shows. Smaller countries fear that their culture will be overrun by programs from countries with large internal markets, such as the United States. The French fear that English will become even more accepted as a world language. The European Community adopted a directive requiring that a majority of the shows on European television be European "where practicable." The effect of quotas and subsidies for production in Europe is that U.S. production companies, such as MTV Europe, increase their local production offices in Europe, injecting local tastes into their programs and deepening the media and entertainment industry capabilities in Europe.

European media companies do not necessarily welcome EU restrictions on the use of imported programs. From the perspective of major European media firms such as Havas, BMG, and BSkyB, the restrictions make it harder to provide attractive programs that will attract viewers; will increase advertising and subscriber revenues; and, ultimately, will enhance returns on investment.

Future Outlook for Globalization of Media and the Entertainment Industry

In summary, the globalization of the media industry, together with the proliferation of TV channels and other media overseas, presents large, growing markets for U.S.-made entertainment, sports, and news programming. Opportunities exist for U.S. firms to reap profits from their comparative advantage in the industry. So far, foreign companies have been aggressive in obtaining ownership in U.S. media properties. The emergence of global media has a ripple effect on a variety of industries, a notable example being the globalization of sports, which is examined next.

SPORTS

Sports is an area of the entertainment industry that is rapidly becoming globalized, principally because of the media industry itself. Global media enable local sporting events to be broadcast globally. That creates an international fan base for local teams and increases global fan interest in what were formerly local or regional sporting events such as baseball and basketball. (See Case 13.1 on Japanese baseball at the end of the chapter.). ESPN derives additional revenues overseas by broadcasting U.S. sports for which it has already obtained rights, such as games of the National Football League. At the same time, ESPN hopes to get rights to foreign sporting events and show them to viewers worldwide.

It is interesting to consider how the U.S. sports industry has been changed by the globalization of the media industry. A sporting event would generally be considered a nontradable good, perishable and temporary; yet TV media have made it commonplace for sporting events to be seen around the world. So now the sports industry has begun to ask, why not move players and games to foreign locations? Why not create global leagues? David Stern, commissioner of the National Basketball Association (NBA), noted that the NBA was "the world's largest provider of reality programming".[22]

While American football and basketball are being aggressively marketed around the world, equally significant is the rise of sports that have greater appeal in Asia. Football (or soccer as it is known in the United States) is the most widely played and watched sport in the world. The World Cup is truly a worldwide event as opposed to the so-called U.S. World Series in baseball. Cricket is played only in the former Commonwealth countries, and one would be hard-pressed even to find test match scores reported in U.S. newspapers or on ESPN. But cricket has huge appeal across India and other Commonwealth nations. With the advent of satellite TV and access to the middle class on the Indian subcontinent, ESPN and Star have begun broadcasting cricket games in both Hindi and English.

International Airline Industry

International marketing in the airline business consists mainly of offering air transportation services on foreign routes. However, foreign governments have traditionally regulated foreign competitors' access to domestic routes. Foreign governments have also regulated the rights of foreign airlines to offer service to international passengers. Such traffic rights have generally been subject to bilateral negotiation between governments.

Governments have also regulated what fares may be charged, what routes airlines may fly, and what airlines will be allowed to compete in the market. Many countries have one or two dominant airlines, either being owned by the government or enjoying quasi-public status. Those "flagship" carriers are given preference in the allocation of new routes, finances, and fare increases. Examples of those airlines are Lufthansa, Air France, Japan Air Lines, Royal Jordanian, and Air India. Thus, if a U.S. airline wants to compete for foreign passenger traffic, it has to wait for the U.S. government to negotiate a bilateral agreement.

Deregulation of the U.S. airline industry facilitated entry by foreign airlines and led many of them to seek a portion of U.S. air traffic. For example, KLM acquired a stake in Northwest Airlines and a joint marketing agreement was attained between British Airways and American Airlines. In that agreement, each airline agreed to use the other airline for ongoing service on complementary routes. The airlines also agreed to list each other's flights in the computer reservation system, which is the heart of competitive advantage in the industry. (Airlines that own such systems can more easily fill seats on flights.) Those agreements have gradually evolved into a series of formal global marketing coalitions. Examples include Star Alliance, whose members include United Airlines and Lufthansa; SkyTeam, which includes Air France, Delta Airlines, Continental Airlines, Northwest Airlines, and KLM; and AAadvantage, which includes American Airlines, British Airways, Quantas, and Cathay Pacific. Each of those global airlines attempts to provide seamless service by using alliance partners. The result is that they gain customer loyalty and market share and offer frequent-flier reward points for use across the alliance.

The major industry trend is for faster growth outside the United States. In such a regulated industry, the dilemma for U.S. airlines is how to obtain and increase market share in the fast-growing overseas markets when host governments seek to favor their domestic flagship carriers.

Table 13-3 summarizes growth trends in global airline traffic. Note that although the North American market is growing, it will register the lowest estimated rates of growth, while the East Asia/Pacific region will have some of the highest growth rates. Hence, airlines around the world will be seeking route authority to permit them to fly passengers on Pacific routes. Of course, factors such as airspace congestion and airport capacity limitations also hinder efforts by airlines to expand routes. Yet government regulation will not disappear overnight. Therefore, U.S. and other airlines must seek alliances with carriers from the Far East while requesting U.S. government help in obtaining fairer access to burgeoning markets.

Service quality is a particularly important issue for passengers choosing between airlines. Researchers Sultana and Simpson found that European and U.S. passengers

Table 13-3. Past Growth and Forecasted Growth Rates of Airline Passenger Traffic by Region

	North America	East Asia/Pacific	Europe	Latin America	Middle East	Africa
1976–1986	7.3%	9.5%	6.5%	8.1%	11.5%	8%
1986–1996	5.1%	6.8%	5.8%	6.4%	5%	5.5%
1996–2006	4.6%	6.5%	5.5%	6.3%	5.4%	5.5%
2006–2023	4.2%	6% (China at 8.2%)	5.2%	4.9%	7.1%	4.5%

differ in their expectations of service quality and in their assessment of whether airlines (European as well as American) meet their expectations. In general, European passengers seem to have higher service quality expectations and think that European airlines are closer to meeting those expectations. The authors speculate that those perceptions could be useful if "open skies" allow European airlines greater access to U.S. markets and to U.S. airline customers. The authors also suggest that global airline code-sharing alliances such as STAR (which includes United and Lufthansa) may face problems if service quality differs among the members of the alliance. Customers from different countries might rate members of the same alliance differently, causing dissatisfaction with the alliance as a whole.[23]

Air transportation also includes cargo traffic. The international express delivery market was estimated at about $20 billion in 2003. An example of global thinking in the industry is FedEx's acquisition of the Flying Tiger line in order to gain access to the worldwide delivery route system built over the course of 40 years. Tiger was the world's biggest heavy-cargo airline, flying from the West Coast of the United States to all of the Far East and Australia and from the East Coast to Brazil and Argentina, Europe, and the Persian Gulf. FedEx planned to use the acquired routes to offer global delivery of small packages, its major strength. Similarly, DHL, the global industry leader, formed an alliance with Blue Dart, the leading Indian air express company, to enhance market share and to offer better services to and from India, a major growth market. DHL also adopted a minority position in a joint venture with Sinotrans to capture market share in the fast-growing China air express market. In September 2005, Deutsche Post sought to reinforce its logistics business with the $6.7 billion acquisition of Exel Logistics. Deutsche Post hoped to balance an expected decline in its German business (due to deregulation and the opening up of its sector to competition) with contract logistics work for the world's largest multinationals gained through the Exel acquisition.[24]

International Professional Services

Professional services such as accounting and management consulting, legal counsel, advertising, and public relations are driven by growth among their business clients. Therefore, their international expansion is driven by the overseas growth of their clients. As their clients open offices and factories and set up joint ventures abroad, they will need help in the law, in advertising, in accounting, etc. At the same

GLOBAL MARKETING

Selling Telecommunications in China

China has a fast-growing economy, with average growth rates exceeding 8 percent a year since 1980. Its income has tripled, and it is modernizing rapidly. As part of its modernization, China needs telephones. There were approximately two telephone lines per 100 people in China, compared to about 51 lines per 100 people in the United States. A modern telephone system is essential for the smooth functioning of a country's economy, particularly its foreign trade and foreign investment activities. In 1995, China hoped to achieve ten lines per 100 people by around 2005. That meant the installation of over 100 million telephone lines, which represented between 20 and 30 percent of the world's demand for telecommunications equipment and also represented the world's largest market for telecommunications equipment.

All of the world's major telecommunications multinationals (including Ericsson; Siemens; NEC; and Alcatel, a French company) compete for the inviting Chinese market. When Alcatel purchased ITT's telecommunications business in 1987, it obtained a minority interest in Shanghai Bell, with China's telecommunications ministry owning 60 percent. Alcatel's factory in Shanghai's industrial zone had a production capacity of 4 million telephone lines annually, in 1993.

China favors local manufacturing over imports. At the same time, it wants technology transfer, even though that results in higher domestic prices. In response, Alcatel is manufacturing semiconductors for telecommunications use in a joint venture with Shanghai Belling Microelectronics. Alcatel expects that its local manufacturing will allow it to win a considerable number of Chinese government contracts for telecommunications equipment. Selling to any government is not easy. With the Chinese, Alcatel must deal with several decision makers, including the central government, the telecommunications ministry, other ministries, the cabinet ministers, provincial governments that control finances, and state-owned banks.

Political issues also affect Alcatel's chances of winning telecommunication contracts. France sold Mirage jet fighters to Taiwan, whereupon China closed France's consulate in

continued

Guangzhou. GEC Alsthom, half owned by Alcatel, had hoped to bid on a new $1 billion underground railroad in Guangzhou, but the fighter sale jeopardized bidding on and winning that contract.

While China is attractive to Western companies because of its growth potential, the Chinese government has been adept at obtaining Western technology and capital without giving up control of its telecommunications sector. China does not allow foreign ownership of its telephone networks. However, economic growth in China, exceeding 10 percent a year for several years, has strained its telephone capacity. The need to offer better and more phone service may be the reason why this ban is relaxed. Given the cost of $10 billion a year to add the 10 to 15 million new lines that China needs, the Chinese government may find it necessary to offer private Western capitalists more incentives to invest in the country. One approach that reduces risk is the "build-lease-service" approach. Western capital builds and leases the telephone network, receiving a rental income for use of the network while also getting paid to maintain it so that the network works as planned.

Motorola, which is a major supplier of cellular phone systems to China, faces similar pressures to transfer technology. It has invested $720 million in a semiconductor factory, together with 2,200 apartments, schools, and a management training program. Over time, that show of commitment, coupled with an early presence, could pay off as China modernizes and relaxes state control over key sectors such as telecommunications.

Sources: John Ure, "Telecommunications in China: More Than Was Bargained For?" Telecommunications Research Project, University of Hong Kong Working Paper 2001; "China's Telecom Industry: Hung Up," *The Economist*, July 22, 1995; "Tough at the Top," *The Economist*, January 6, 1996; "Alcatel in China: The Biggest Prize," *The Economist*, January 16, 1993.

time, as the foreign economies grow and begin to adopt professional management habits, they, too, will seek professional services with global networks. Again, the market growth will be higher and more attractive outside the United States. The question is, how can a firm market overseas?

How does a firm export legal services? Jones, Day, Reavis, & Pogue provide a model. Initially a regional law firm, it began by acquiring a New York law firm with a primarily international practice. Since then it has opened offices in Geneva, Hong Kong, London, Paris, and Riyadh, with new offices opening in Tokyo and Brussels. The firm's "product" strategy is interesting: "We are an American firm

using American methodology for solving legal problems." Foreign offices are staffed with U.S. citizens and foreign nationals with U.S. education and experience. For example, the company does not attempt to practice Japanese law for Japanese clients because local firms could do that more effectively. Instead, its goal is to provide a world view, helping Japanese clients in Europe and the United States and European clients in Japan. An in-house computerized communication system allows the firm's lawyers to contact one another around the world almost instantaneously.

International Retailing

Retailing, one of the major sectors of any economy, typically requires contact between retailer and seller. It is generally a labor-intensive and geographically diffused activity, with considerable national and regional variation in business practices. It is also an industry subject to government regulation. In addition, it is a major generator of jobs that requires substantial time and attention from management. This section discusses how internationalization of retailing services can proceed.

Two major avenues can be pursued. The first is to obtain control of retailing channels through direct investment. (Joint ventures and franchises are modified approaches to the overseas retailing industry.) The key objective is to have a degree of control over the retailing channel and to obtain from retailers as much information about consumers as possible. That control is often linked to a vertical integration strategy. However, retailing offers attractive returns in its own right as a means of participating in the growth of an economy. From that angle, a foreign retailer hopes to bring a competitive edge to the domestic industry in the form of more efficient management, greater worldwide purchasing clout, and superior retailing technology and information systems.

The second avenue for internationalization of retailing services lies in using technology to diminish the need for direct contact between retailer and customer, thus allowing for long-distance retailing. Computerized electronic shopping and direct mail are two instances of that approach. Foreign retailers can service domestic customers in another country market without physically entering the domestic retail industry.

The Changing Face of Retailing

In 1987, 3 percent of Taiwan's population shopped in modern supermarkets and grocery stores. Today over half of all shopping is done in modern department stores and supermarkets. All across Asia and Latin America, as incomes rise and more two-income families emerge, time has become scarce for consumers. Shopping at modern stores that offer large assortments of goods, fairly priced and fresh, and amenities such as debit card shopping and home delivery has caused a major shift in people's shopping habits and preferences. As shopping volumes increase, prices can be lowered as fixed costs of warehouses and computerization can be spread over a larger sales base. The net result is a virtuous cycle wherein low prices, convenience, more choices, and high quality combine to attract more customers, allowing owners to continually upgrade the shopping parameters that attracted shoppers initially. Western-style enclosed shopping malls, with their temperature-controlled, safe, well-lit ambience, offer variety and entertainment, attracting former patrons of small street-side shops.

China, for example, has seen the opening of stores by the Japanese chains Isetan and Yaohan and the Hong Kong-based chain A. S. Watson. There has also been an increase in local chains, such as Giordano. Those chains are adapting to the local culture, such as the traditional Chinese preference for "wet" markets, where shoppers can inspect live fish and chickens. Taiwan's local chain, Dairy Farm International, has seen competition from the European retailers Makro and Carrefour. Those two retailers stress the hypermarket model, offering a huge assortment and accepting very low margins. Makro, for example, sells groceries in bulk, office supplies, and computers to individuals as well as local wholesalers and small retailers. Regional integration has seen similar cross-border forays. Promodes from France has opened stores across Spain; and Wal-Mart, partnering with Cifra, is populating the Mexican countryside. One consequence of the proliferation of large chains is the gradual seeping of power from manufacturers to retailers. That is exemplified in rising sales of private, or store-brand, items – with the foremost exponents of private brands being the U.K. chains Tesco and Sainsbury. (See the discussions on private label versus branded goods and the implications for brand equity in Chapter 9, "Global Products and Global Branding" and Chapter 10, "Global Product Policy and New Product Development.")

The rapid expansion of retailing chains internationally raises this question: What are the critical steps in developing an internationalization strategy? The key variables requiring management's attention, in order of execution, are:

1. An understanding of the market obtained by careful observation over an extended period of time or through pilot expansion.
2. A measured pace of expansion within constraints of capital and management.
3. A clearly defined role for local partners after careful consideration of whether they are needed.
4. The importance of planning the assortment of goods to be carried, which should vary with the preferences of each local market. Stores such as Marks & Spencer carry a core of best-selling prod-

ucts across borders, supplemented by products adapted to local preferences.

5. The extent to which goods are sourced locally, which is affected by local quality and availability considerations, as well as exchange-rate volatility. For example, cost reduction pressures move Benetton toward centralization, with customization for individual markets happening at the last minute. At that point, up-to-date point-of-sale information is used to dye clothes in the colors that sell best in each market. Of course, that can work only if the basic product concept—namely, the style and design—have strong multicultural acceptability.
6. Scale economies, as evidenced by the merger of Kingfisher, a U.K. consumer electronics retailer, and Darty, a leading French retailer of consumer electronics and appliances (white goods) through warehouse-style stores, with 12 percent market share at the time of the merger.
7. The development of local management for day-to-day supervision as well as strategic expansion.
8. Reduction in cycle time, particularly with time-sensitive goods such as perishables and fashion items. Balancing in-house design and manufacture with outsourcing and just-in-time manufacturing shaped by information technology investments allow a firm to react quickly to changing market signals, such as shifts in fashion.

International Hotel Industry

The hotel industry is another sector whose growth is fueled by international business. As more businesspeople travel internationally, they demand lodging comparable to what they experience at home. Similarly, an increase in international tourism leads to greater demands for hotel beds, again with amenities comparable to what tourists have at home. In addition, there is a need for more hotels in towns of fast-growing countries in the Third World, in Eastern Europe, and in the smaller cities of Europe and Southeast Asia. There the demand is domestic, which can be satisfied by international hotel chains. Thus, business and leisure travel represent two major segments, as do foreign and domestic guests.

Hotels have a tangible side: their construction and ownership. The intangible side is their management, which includes marketing hotel rooms worldwide and providing the hotel service itself, as well as offering related services such as ongoing maintenance. The internationalization of the hotel industry means a separation of those two aspects. Domestic investors often build and own the hotel, while foreign hotel conglomerates provide hotel management services on a commission fee and profit-sharing basis.

As in the case of airlines, a key element in marketing hotel services worldwide is the use of computerized reserva-

Table 13-4. World's Major Global Banks

Position/Bank Name	Country	Assets
1 Mizuho Financial Group	Japan	1,285,471
2 Citigroup	USA	1,264,032
3 UBS	Switzerland	1,120,543
4 Credit Agricole Groupe	France	1,105,378
5 HSBC Holdings	UK	1,034,216
6 Deutscht Bank	Germany	1,014,845
7 BNP Paribas	France	988,982
8 Mitsubishi Tokyo Financial Group	Japan	974,950
9 Sumitomo Mitsui Financial Group	Japan	950,448
10 Royal Bank of Scotland	UK	806,207
11 Barclays Bank	UK	791,292
12 Credit Suisse Group	Switzerland	777,849
13 JP Morgan Chase & Co	USA	770,912
14 UFJ Holdings	Japan	753,631
15 Bank of America Corp	USA	736,445
16 ING Bank	Netherlands	684,004
17 Société Générale	France	681,216
18 ABN AMRD Bank	Netherlands	667,636
19 HBOS	UK	850,721
20 Indust. & Commercial Bank of China	China	637,829
21 HypoVereinsbank	Germany	605,525
22 Desdner Bank	Germany	602,461
23 Fortis Bank	Belgium	535,462
24 Robobank Group	Netherlands	509,352
25 Commerzbank	Germany	481,921

Source: The Banker, Top 1000 World Banks, July 2004.

tion services. It is a way to capitalize on brand image. Utilizing those systems, making one local phone call, a businessperson can book a room in any city in the world where the hotel chain has a presence. That convenience leads travelers to favor hotel chains such as Hyatt and Westin, giving them a competitive edge over more isolated hotels.

The other major variable is service. Top-notch service is labor-intensive and requires considerable training. Thus, Tokyo's Hotel Okura has 1,600 workers for 880 rooms, compared to about 1,000 workers for 1,008 rooms at the Helmsley Palace in Manhattan—both among the world's most prestigious hotels. Around-the-clock room service and a business center for sending international messages and translating documents are examples of the expected levels of service, even though those operations lose money.

International Financial Services

International financial services are also growing rapidly. In this segment, availability of low-cost capital is a critical advantage. Following clients as they enter foreign markets becomes a major influence on international expansion. Two other critical variables are innovation—coming up with ideas for new financial services—and technology—being able to deliver innovative services at arm's length, at a low cost, and of high quality. Twenty-four-hour trading, international bank lending, global foreign exchange trading, and the hedging of products to manage interest and currency exposure are services demanded by multinationals as they spread around the world. Japan, the United States, and the United Kingdom account for over 50 percent of all international bank lending and are the major financial centers of the world. Any company wanting to operate in the international financial services market must have a presence in those markets.

Table 13-4 lists the world's largest global banks by assets. Banks from many countries are represented, though it may seem surprising that only 3 of the top 25 are U.S. banks. Mitsubishi would become the largest bank in the world upon the completion of its announced merger with UFJ Holdings (Japan's fourth largest bank) in October 2005.[25] If one considers profitability, however, U.S. banks dominate, with an average return on capital of 29 percent. That is double the level of EU banks, with Japanese banks only earning 5.2 percent. U.S. banks may be smaller in size; but they are more numerous and competitive (and possibly focused), leading to greater profitability.

Global banks are interested in market share in key overseas markets, as is seen in the duel between Citicorp and HBSC. While HBSC branched out from its original Hong Kong base to acquire U.K. and U.S. banks, Citicorp was deepening its market share in Asia. As more people enter the middle class and become the newly rich, Citicorp and HBSC try to increase their business with this segment, selling credit cards, mutual funds, and smart cards. Both offer a form of specialized private banking services for more affluent clients, with amenities such as a personal banker and free advice. A particularly important segment is the entrepreneur who needs both business and personal banking.

Another aspect of banking is private banking, in which banks tailor their services to wealthy individuals. It is a labor-intensive business, with highly qualified and specialized employees developing customized financial packages for each client. U.S. banks are aggressively pursuing this opportunity, using their global networks to win clients by offering opportunities for investing globally and minimizing taxes.

International Investment Banking

Investment banking and brokerage services are another attractive international services industry. It is generally accepted that investment portfolios must be diversified internationally for superior performance. That means there is a need for information about and access to investing in foreign stock markets around the world. The question for U.S. brokerage houses is how to go about selling brokerage services in Europe, Japan, and other growing markets in the face of intense competition from local brokerage houses with extensive retail networks. It is expensive to do business in countries such as Japan. With high salaries, rent, and overhead costs, large volumes of business are needed to break even and to make a profit.

Foreign firms can concentrate on a specialty or, if they are large, offer a breadth of global investment opportunities. Accordingly, some large firms offer Japanese institutional clients the options of investing in U.S. Treasury securities, trading in futures and options, hedging currencies, and investing in major stock markets of the world. Smaller companies usually specialize. Because Japanese companies routinely issue warrants to buy their stocks, with Japanese bonds, some foreign companies have decided to specialize.

Over the past several years, Japanese financial markets have performed poorly. That fact has led Japanese investors to question the advice and returns delivered by their own, predominantly Japanese brokers and mutual funds. That is, Japanese protectionism had kept out technologically advanced and aggressive U.S. pension fund managers such as Fidelity. As Japanese investors began to seek better returns, pressure from them as well as from the U.S. government slightly opened up Japanese fund management markets. That allowed U.S. funds to offer their experience in global investing, their use of quantitative investing, and their skills in analyzing companies. Such liberalization points to another critical aspect of trade in services: Open markets are not always adhered to, and deregulating financial services can result in enhanced global market share.

Aside from the product, patience and cultural sensitivity are crucial to success (as in Japan) because personal relations with individual clients determine the volume of business. Local entities need autonomy and a local orientation. Local investment managers can leverage their personal contacts built over the years through professional and college ties. Their colleagues might manage the portfolios at Japan's life insurance and trust companies and, thus, determine the amount of institutional funds invested through foreign investment houses. A predominance of local managers also helps in recruiting young, qualified Japanese analysts and managers.

GLOBAL MARKETING

Designing Golf Courses for Southeast Asia

As Southeast Asia modernizes, incomes are rising, with per capita income reaching approximately $10,000 in countries such as South Korea, Taiwan, Singapore, and Hong Kong. Japan is the most prosperous country, with per capita income over $20,000. With the rise in disposable income, the Japanese have become more interested in leisure products and services. Golf falls within that consumption pattern, and designing new golf courses is a major growth business for U.S. golf course architects.

Japan is a mountainous country; all flat land is earmarked for agriculture. Thus, golf courses were built into hillsides, using the terrain as it was. That led to courses with steep holes. In one instance, golfers had to hold on to ropes to reach some holes. The Japanese first built golf courses as if they were highways, bulldozing away the earth and any obstacles. But once the Japanese began traveling and playing the world's famous courses at St. Andrew's, Pebble Beach, and Augusta, they raised their sights considerably. Hence, Japanese project developers began approaching U.S. architects (with their experience in building championship golf courses in the United States) to develop top-notch golf courses in Japan. Japanese developers vied for the services of U.S. architects, who are noted for their excellence in design.

J. Michael Poellot is one such architect. He has been involved in golf course projects that together total $1 billion in construction costs. He has built golf courses in swamps, in rice paddies, and near the Great Wall of China. He has had to move mountains, drain seas, and re-create the landscape to build world-class golf courses. All of that work raises costs; an average golf course in Japan may cost $30 million compared to $5 million in the United States. Poellot notes that Japanese golf courses are meant for golfers with high handicaps because Japanese golfers take up the game when they are older and have little time to practice. Because most Japanese live in cramped quarters, they want opulence during their leisure time. Clubhouses must be huge. Cramped living spaces may also explain why the wide-open expanse of golf courses has such an appeal for Japanese men. Another unusual feature of

continued

Japanese golf courses is the large reservoirs that hold water in case of torrential rainfall and typhoons, which are common.

Poellot got his start when serving in the military. His offer to review golf course plans for a Bangkok developer led to a meeting with Robert Trent Jones, one of America's foremost golf course designers. Poellot began working for Jones and became responsible for Asia/Pacific work. Japanese businessmen who played at the Gainey Ranch Golf Club, which Poellot designed, were sufficiently impressed to seek him out, offering a contract to design six golf courses. Poellot was on his way. Among his recent triumphs is a golf course for the Beijing Golf Club, which was voted the best new golf course in Asia. Poellot attributes some of his success to his love of nature and landscape, a feeling that reflects Japan's age-old traditions of formal gardens renowned for their meditative beauty.

As Japan begins importing rice, agricultural land will become available to build even more golf courses, a prospect that makes Poellot happy.

Source: Walter Roessing, "Master Planner," *Northwest Airlines Inflight Magazine.*

INTERNATIONAL PROJECTS

Many professional services are delivered as projects; for example, architectural projects and management consulting contracts. Marketing such projects internationally involves some unique aspects. For instance, projects are discrete, and each new project must be marketed separately, albeit building on established social and informational relationships. Trust may have to be built anew, tailored to the technical and financial needs of each project. A shifting cast of actors may be needed for each project, changing as project complexity and characteristics change. Thus, there is a strong interrelationship between networks (of actors, suppliers, and customers) and markets. As the territorial locus of a project changes, individual actors have to convince others in the network of their abilities, trustworthiness, ability to deliver, etc. That is accomplished through relationships, word of mouth, and references. Client-following firms can build on existing client-based networks, while market-following firms have to establish their networks more independently. A firm's locational advantage in a specific country may not be easily transferred to other geographic markets. Firms may have to establish themselves locally in order to learn the specific milieu of the new market and its rules, as well as to establish local relationships.[26]

International Insurance Markets

Insurance, another segment of the financial services industry, is growing much faster in international markets than in the U.S. market. The United States accounted for about 40 percent of premiums collected worldwide, but it is a saturated market, especially in life insurance. The potential for future growth lies primarily overseas, in markets where incomes are rising and individuals and heads of families are beginning to purchase insurance. The integration of Europe presents an opportunity for U.S. companies to offer lower prices and to take advantage of less efficient local competition.

Competition from European companies will be strong, however, and greater opportunities might be found in the Far East. U.S. insurance companies may face a fight for market share in advanced economies that have their own entrenched domestic insurance firms. Even so, this may be the right time to position themselves in the newly industrializing countries.

AIG IN CHINA

The market for life insurance in China is large and mostly untapped. The market is dominated by the state-owned People's Insurance Company of China (PICC), which has about 75 percent of the market. Founded in Shanghai in 1919, AIG operated in China until it was forced out in 1950. To win permission to reenter, it lavished attention on China, winning goodwill by setting up a $1 billion infrastructure fund and buying and restoring ancient pagoda windows for Beijing's Summer Palace. In 1992, AIG finally received permission to sell life insurance in China. As incomes increase and the middle class considers its future, the insurance market is expected to grow to $75 billion by 2006. To prepare for that potential market, AIG carefully screens and hires salespeople and then thoroughly trains them. Building on life insurance, AIG has formed an agreement with PICC, China's largest non-life insurance company, which has over 100,000 sales personnel, agents, and authorized representatives, to sell accident and health insurance.

Marketing Services Overseas: Major Findings

By way of review, Javalgi and White[27] outline their view of the major strategic challenges surrounding the international marketing of services, including the following:

- Overcoming barriers to trade in services
- Understanding the bases of international competitive advantage in services

- Understanding and overcoming country-of-origin effect in services
- Understanding how consumer ethnocentrism affects evaluation of services
- Understanding how culture affects service processes and service delivery
- Understanding how information content related to services is presented across cultures, especially between high-context and low-context cultures
- Using appropriate modes of entry in delivering services
- Forecasting and managing demand across markets
- Deciding whether to standardize or adapt services
- Understanding how service quality dimensions and their perceived importance vary across countries
- Conducting market research across nations in services industries

Through experience, firms have learned that because services are intangible, exporting them is often unfeasible without also exporting the personnel to provide them. Hence, FDI, licensing and franchising, and joint ventures are common vehicles for providing services in international markets.

Intangibility makes selling services overseas more difficult because the buyer must take the quality of service on faith. Corporate brand name and reputation sometimes help.

Financing the overseas expansion of services can be difficult, with the cost structure leaning toward fixed costs. Although heavy capital investments may not be necessary, working capital may be high initially, especially in regards to the personnel required to provide the service. That is another reason why joint ventures and strategic alliances are common when a firm seeks to sell services overseas.

Because direct interaction between buyer and service provider is essential to the marketing of services, cultural differences must be accounted for in seeking buyer satisfaction. For that reason, establishing a local presence and using local personnel are usually recommended. And if the service must be adapted to a foreign market, the interaction between buyer and foreign provider takes on additional importance because direct contact can facilitate cooperation and result in more appropriate adaptation.

Service markets are largest in the advanced industrialized countries. The U.S. market is generally saturated for a variety of services, making foreign expansion attractive for additional services revenue growth. Even with stiff competition in advanced industrialized nations, service markets, as a whole, offer greater unrealized potential than goods markets, especially for U.S. firms with their accumulated experience in service industry sectors.

However, service exports and foreign sales do not take place in a vacuum. They often accompany sales of goods.

GLOBAL MARKETING

McDonald's in Hungary, Russia, and Brazil

McDonald's began operations in Budapest, Hungary, on April 30, 1988. On its first day of operation, it broke a McDonald's record for the most transactions. Today it is one of the busiest McDonald's in the world, with 9,000 transactions a day.

Plans to establish a McDonald's in Hungary began with a joint-venture agreement in November 1986, although negotiations began back in 1985. McDonald's is a 50 percent owner, its partner being Hungary's Babolna Agricultural Cooperative.

McDonald's supplied all of the restaurant equipment, including equipment to established supply sources, such as a bakery to make hamburger buns. McDonald's also contributed something intangible: a standard of quality for the fast-food industry. It had to develop a supplier infrastructure by introducing new food-processing techniques and forcing development of new products in Hungary, as well as insisting on the improvement of existing products to meet world standards of quality. Products such as hamburger buns, the kind of cheese used in the cheeseburgers, and orange juice concentrate were unavailable in Hungary. Ketchup was available, but it did not meet McDonald's quality standards. It took over a year to develop supply sources. McDonald's experts in purchasing and quality control then worked with suppliers on a monthly basis to get the desired product and quality.

Locally produced food products are used. The exceptions are McCormick spices, which are used by McDonald's around the world, and sesame seeds, which cannot be grown in Hungary. Paper products, such as paper cups, are imported.

McDonald's opened with 7 partially trained managers and another 20 employees loaned from stores in other countries. Most of those employees returned home after a month, with the exception of a U.S. manager who stayed on as an advisor and trainer. New employees had training, but little experience. They had to learn while on the job, in the middle of huge crowds. During the first few days, a line wound outside the store. Some of the training focused on inculcating attitudes of customer service. In a country of shortages, where people are accustomed to waiting, customer service was, to

continued

some degree, an unfamiliar concept. McDonald's found it impossible to hire part-time help, which it relies on in most countries. However, having achieved one successful opening, in the next five years, McDonald's plans to open another five outlets in Budapest. Real estate is difficult to buy at any price, so the company must build its restaurants in existing buildings. McDonald's has not yet chosen franchisees, but plans to do so for perhaps three of the proposed five restaurants.

After its Hungarian experience, McDonald's natural response was to turn to Russia. McDonald's Russian entry was shepherded by its head of Canadian operations, George Cohon, who had made initial contact with some Russian delegation members during the Montreal Olympics in 1976. But the joint-venture agreement was not signed until April 1988 because of intervening events, one being the U.S. Olympic boycott. McDonald's Russian venture had some unusual features. McDonald's joint-venture partner, with a 51 percent ownership, was the food service department of the Moscow City Council. Normally, McDonald's worked with entrepreneurs; but in Russia in the late 1980s, the company had no choice but to work with a leading entity within the Communist party. The joint venture was also a "rubles-only" joint venture at a time when the ruble was inconvertible. That meant that McDonald's would sell its hamburgers to Russians for rubles and would buy mostly local supplies paid for in rubles. As in Hungary, the company had difficulty maintaining its reputation because of poor-quality local suppliers.

Ultimately, McDonald's had to invest over $40 million in setting up a raw material processing plant to supply the requisite buns, French fries, hamburger patties, etc. Amortizing that large injection of foreign capital at a time when the ruble was rapidly devaluing meant that McDonald's was making no money in the short run. It might well have been selling Ray Kroc's original dream of 15-cent hamburgers. But overall, McDonald's is hugely profitable and was planning to open over 2,000 restaurants outside the United States in 1995 alone. If one has faith in the long-term promise of Russia, losing money for a few years might seem a reasonable investment to ensure front-row seats for the Russian renaissance.

McDonald's has about 1,600 restaurants in Brazil. The Brazilian restaurants introduced interesting innovations, such as stand-alone ice cream kiosks. However, devaluation of Brazilian currency raised the price of dollar-linked ingredients such as bread and meat. As their prices rose, profits declined. McDonald's also became a luxury to a significant portion of the Brazilian population as unemployment rose and real incomes dropped. Disappointed franchisees began suing McDonald's management, complaining of high rents, oversaturation of the market, and general economic discontent. McDonald's began buying back distressed franchisees in order to help bring the Brazilian operations back to life.

Sources: "Joint Ventures in Hungary," *CW Informatika Ltd.* (Budapest), Volume 2, Number 1, 1989, pages 9–10; Peter Foster, "McDonald's Excellent Soviet Venture," *Canadian Business*, May 1991; "McDonald's Accelerates Store Openings in U.S. and Abroad, Pressuring Rivals," *Wall Street Journal*, January 18, 1996; and "McDonald's Faces Revolt in Brazil." *Wall Street Journal*, October 21, 2003.

Thus, if exports of goods are faltering, service sales will be affected. For example, billings of U.S.-based advertising agencies overseas depend somewhat on the success of their U.S. clients overseas. To the extent that a client such as IBM or Coca-Cola generates overseas sales growth, U.S. advertising agencies are more likely to have opportunities to increase their overseas billings.

This last point also suggests a path of least resistance for overseas growth: Follow the client. That strategy has been successful for Japanese auto parts companies in the United States and for Japanese banks providing yen-based financial software and services in Japanese to Japanese clients.

Concepts from the international marketing of goods can be carried over to services. For example, gap analysis (see Chapter 7) can be used to determine whether the actual market for a particular service (for example, the use of overnight parcel and small package delivery) is below the forecast potential. Similarly, the IPLC model can be used to predict, for example, when a developing nation will begin accelerating its consumption of long-distance phone and facsimile services based on the experiences of more developed nations.

Summary

Because international marketing of services differs from that of goods, issues such as acquisitions and joint ventures as part of a firm's overall strategy take on greater importance and complement pure marketing issues.

Services are offered by a number of industries, including wholesaling and retailing, communications, transportation, utilities, banking and insurance, tourism, and business and personal services. Because services account for an increasing portion of output and employment in industrialized nations, they are becoming increasingly important in international trade.

In the United States, nearly three out of four jobs outside of agriculture come from service industries. The most important service sectors in the United States (other than the government) are retail and wholesale trade, finance and insurance, health care, and business.

All of the major service exporters are developed/industrialized nations. Service exports do not tell the whole story, however, because many services can be provided only from within a foreign market.

Services are difficult to market because of their special characteristics: intangibility, heterogeneity, variability in service quality, perishability, simultaneity of production and consumption, and predominance of fixed costs.

Challenges in international services marketing include how to standardize services and how to manage demand to match supply and generate repeat business. Cultural variables are an important factor in user satisfaction.

Comparative advantage in services marketing can arise from labor, capital, technology, or management skills. Technology, in the form of computer hardware and software, and communication networks are useful in providing services at a distance. Services are information-intensive.

Government intervention in trade serves to keep foreign competition out of domestic markets. Restrictions are placed on the right of foreign firms to do business, sell to the government, repatriate profits, and transfer personnel. Trade barriers, licensing regulations, and divergent technical standards are also used to limit competition from foreign firms.

WTO talks on trade have focused on removing barriers to trade in services, with emphasis on protecting IP rights and setting parameters for government intervention in trade in services.

Entertainment is one of the largest U.S. exports. Deregulation of TV in Europe and elsewhere is increasing the demand for U.S. programs. However, European "local content" laws applying to TV programs may diminish market opportunities.

The emergence of a global entertainment industry has led to mergers, with multinationals jockeying to obtain global competitive advantage and representation in the key triad markets. All of the major firms seek to control production and distribution of entertainment programs, whether it be films, TV programs, sports events, or news and variety shows.

Foreign airline markets are growing faster than the U.S. market, with the highest growth occurring in the Pacific Rim area because of economic growth in Japan and its neighboring countries. Joint marketing and strategic alliances are being used to obtain market share.

Professional services are a growing market overseas, particularly as multinationals expand operations around the world, placing domestic professional service providers in various foreign markets.

Retailing offers considerable growth opportunities overseas as incomes rise around the world. Technological innovations allow retailers to offer their services at a distance. Acquisitions are the major mode of participation in retailing in foreign markets.

The international hotel industry is expanding because of growth in business and tourist travel internationally. Management skills and computerized global reservation systems provide U.S. hotel chains with a competitive edge.

The globalization of industry leads to growing demand for international banking services, such as global foreign exchange trading and international lending and hedging services to manage interest rate and currency exposure. Innovative new services and possession of a low-cost source of funds are critical to having a competitive advantage in overseas markets.

Firms can profit from targeting niches within financial services, such as private banking, credit cards, investment banking and brokerage services, and insurance. Because client contacts are important in finance, cultural sensitivity is as important as financial know-how.

Considerable untapped market potential exists for insurance products in the newly industrializing countries of Asia, in the EU, and in Japan. These foreign markets are characterized by high prices, and they have fewer innovative products available. Experienced U.S. insurance companies may have a competitive edge, although they have not been active in seeking foreign markets.

A few generalizations can be made about the service sector: (1) Foreign markets offer attractive growth prospects, (2) following domestic clients overseas is one way to gain foreign sales, and (3) some form of direct involvement in the foreign market is necessary to gain significant market share.

Questions and Research

13.1 What are services? Why are they important in industrialized nations?

13.2 Which service industry sectors are important in the U.S. economy? Can those sectors easily enter into foreign trade?

13.3 What are the major service-exporting nations? What might explain the number of advanced industrialized nations that appear on that list?

13.4 Explain the steps by which McDonald's was able to initiate operations in Hungary. What difficulties did the company face, and how did it solve them? What generalizations can you make from the McDonald's example?

13.5 What are some distinguishing characteristics of services? Explain why these characteristics make it difficult to sell services in foreign markets.

13.6 Discuss how culture can affect the sale of services overseas. Use the Little, Brown-Russian negotiations as an illustration.

13.7 What are the bases of comparative advantage in services? Explain how capital and technology have transformed global competition in services.

13.8 Why and how do governments intervene in services? How is the WTO attempting to create freer trade in services?

13.9 What is IP? Why is it the focus of WTO negotiations in the services area?

13.10 Why are U.S. firms dominant in the world entertainment industry?

13.11 How is environmental change in the European television industry creating opportunities – for U.S. firms?

13.12 How does the spread of satellite TV and cable TV affect pan-European advertising by multinational firms?

13.13 Why has MTV been successful in Europe?

13.14 Explain the reasons behind the rise in global mergers in the media industry. How do those mergers help the firms involved sell more entertainment services around the world?

13.15 Where is airline traffic growing the fastest? How should U.S. airlines respond in order to obtain a share of passenger traffic growth overseas?

13.16 What are the problems of expanding professional service operations overseas?

13.17 How can retailing services be expanded overseas? Why is acquisition a popular approach?

13.18 What are the forces creating greater demand for hotel services in foreign markets? How can multinational hotel chains profit from such growth?

13.19 How is banking becoming a global business?

13.20 Discuss how foreign brokerage and investment banking firms have marketed themselves in Japan. Why is culture important in selling financial services?

13.21 What are the prospects for the international marketing of insurance products and services?

13.22 What generalizations can be made about the international marketing of services?

Endnotes

1. Silk, Alvin J. and Ernst R. Berndt. "Cost Economies in the Global Advertising and Marketing Services Business," Chapter 11 in John Quelch and Rohit Deshpande, editors, 2004, *The Global Market*, Harvard Business School, San Francisco: Jossey-Bass, pages 217–257.

2. "Services Area in a Fog," *The Economist*, May 23, 1987.

3. Zeithaml, V., A. Parasuraman, and Leonard L. Berry. "Problems and Strategies in Services Marketing," *Journal of Marketing*, Volume 49, Spring 1985.

4. Lovelock, C. H. and George Yip. "Developing Global Strategies for Service Businesses," *California Management Review*, Volume 38, Issue 2, 1996, pages 64–86; Lovelock, Christopher, "Classifying Services to Gain Strategic Marketing Insights," *Journal of Marketing*, Volume 47, Summer 1983.

5. Javalgi, R. G., Bob D. Cutler, and William A. Winans. "At Your Service! Does Country of Origin Research Apply to Services?" *Journal of Services Marketing*, Volume 15, Issue 7, 2001, pages 565–582.

6. Guiltinan, Joseph P. "The Price Bundling of Services: A Normative Framework," *Journal of Marketing*, Volume 51, April 1987.

7. Smith, Anne M. and Nina L. Reynolds. "Measuring Cross-Cultural Service Quality: A Framework for Assessment," *International Marketing Review*, Volume 19, Number 5, 2001, pages 450–481.

8. Groonroos, C. "A Service Quality Model and Its Marketing Implications," *European Journal of Marketing*, Volume 18, Number 4, 1984.

9. Parasuraman, A., V. Zeithaml, and Leonard L. Berry. "A Conceptual Model of Service Quality and Its Implications for Future Research," *Journal of Marketing*, Volume 49, Fall 1985.

10. Min, Hokey, Hyesung Min, and Kyooyup Chung. "Dynamic Benchmarking of Hotel Service Quality," *Journal of Services Marketing*, Volume 16, Issue 4, 2002, pages 302–321.

11. Lee, Jonathan, Janghyuk Lee, and Lawrence Feick. "The Impact of Switching Costs on the Customer Satisfaction-Loyalty Link: Mobile Phone Service in France," *Journal of Services Marketing*, Volume 15, Issue 1, 2001, pages 35–48.

12. Leisen, Birgit. "Image Segmentation: The Case of a Tourism Destination," *Journal of Services Marketing*, Volume 15, Issue 1, 2001, pages 49–66.

13. Moorthi, Y. L. R. "An Approach to Branding Services," *Journal of Services Marketing*, Volume 16, Issue 3, 2002, pages 259–274.

14. Mortimer, Kathleen. "Integrating Advertising Theories with Conceptual Models of Services Advertising," *Journal of Services Marketing*, Volume 16, Issue 5, 2002, pages 460–468; Mortimer, K. and B. P. Mathews, "The Advertising of Services: Consumer Views vs. Normative Guidelines," *Service Industries Journal*, Volume 18, Number 3, 1998, pages 14–19.

15. Mortimer, Kathleen. "Services Advertising: The Agency Viewpoint," *Journal of Services Marketing*, Volume 15, Issue 2, 2001, pages 131–146.

16. Tai, Susan H. C. and Ricky Y. K. Chan. "Cross-Cultural Studies on the Information Content of Service Advertising," *Journal of Services Marketing*, Volume 15, Issue 7, 2001, pages 547–564.

17. Patterson, Paul G. and Tasman Smith. "Relationship Benefits in Service Industries: A Replication in a Southeast Asian Context," *Journal of Services Marketing*, Volume 15, Issue 6, 2001, pages 425–443.

18. Dudar, Helen. "Moscow Rights: Doing a Book Deal with the Soviets," *Wall Street Journal*, February 23, 1988.

19. Javalgi, R. G., D. A. Griffith, and D. Steven White. "An Empirical Examination of Factors Influencing the Internationalization of Service Firms," *Journal of Services Marketing*, Volume 17, Issue 2, 2003, pages 185–201.

20. Bharadwaj, S. G., P. R. Varadarajan, and J. Fahy. "Sustainable Competitive Advantage in Service Industries: A Conceptual Model and Research Propositions," *Journal of Marketing*, October 1993, pages 83–99.

21. "MTV's Passage to India," *Fortune*, August 9, 2004.

22. Wettheim, L. John. "The Whole World Is Watching," *Sports Illustrated*, June 14, 2004, page 76.

23. Sultan, Fareena and Merlin Simpson, Jr., "International Service Variants: Airline Passenger Expectations and Perceptions of Service

Quality," *Journal of Services Marketing*, Volume 14, Issue 3, 2000, pages 188–216.

24. "Exel Accepts German Bid," *International Herald Tribune*, September 19, 2005.

25. "Japan Recovery Aids Prospect of Merged Bank," *Wall Street Journal*, September 22, 2005.

26. Skaates, Maria Anne, H. Tikkanen, and K. Alajoutsijarvi. "The International Marketing of Professional Service Projects: To What Extent Does Territoriality Matter?" *Journal of Services Marketing*, Volume 17, Issue 1, 2003, pages 83–97.

27. Javalgi, R. G. and D. Steven White. "Strategic Challenges for the Marketing of Services Internationally," *International Marketing Review*, Volume 19, Number 6, 2002, pages 563–581.

Further Readings

"A Survey of Retailing: Change at the Checkout," *The Economist*, March 4, 1995.

Bertrand, Olivier, and T. Noyelle. *Human Resources and Corporate Strategy: Technological Change in Banks and Insurance Companies*, Paris: Organization for Economic Cooperation and Development, 1988.

Bharadwaj, S. G., P. R. Varadarajan, and J. Fahy. "Sustainable Competitive Advantage in Service Industries: A Conceptual Model and Research Propositions," *Journal of Marketing*, October 1993, pages 83–99.

"Fancy Free: A Survey of the Entertainment Industry," *The Economist*, December 23, 1989.

Feketekuty, Geza. *International Trade in Services: An Overview and Blueprint for Negotiation*, Cambridge, MA: Ballinger, 1988.

Foster, Peter. "McDonald's Excellent Soviet Venture," *Canadian Business*, May 1991.

Groonroos, C. "A Service Quality Model and Its Marketing Implications," *European Journal of Marketing*, Volume 18, Number 4, 1984.

Javalgi, R. G., Bob D. Cutler, and William A. Winans. "At Your Service! Does Country of Origin Research Apply to Services?" *Journal of Services Marketing*, Volume 15, Issue 7, 2001, pages 565–582.

Javalgi, R. G., D. A. Griffith, and D. Steven White. "An Empirical Examination of Factors Influencing the Internationalization of Service Firms," *Journal of Services Marketing*, Volume 17, Issue 2, 2003, pages 185–201.

Javalgi R. G. and D. Steven White. "Strategic Challenges for the Marketing of Services Internationally," *International Marketing Review*, Volume 19, Number 6, 2002, pages 563–581.

Lee, Jonathan, Janghyuk Lee, and Lawrence Feick. "The Impact of Switching Costs on the Customer Satisfaction-Loyalty Link: Mobile Phone Service in France," *Journal of Services Marketing*, Volume 15, Issue 1, 2001, pages 35–48.

Leisen, Birgit. "Image Segmentation: The Case of a Tourism Destination," *Journal of Services Marketing*, Volume 15, Issue 1, 2001, pages 49–66.

Lovelock, Christopher. "Classifying Services to Gain Strategic Marketing Insights," *Journal of Marketing*, Volume 47, Summer 1983.

Mann, Michael and Sylvia E. Bargas. "U.S. International Sales and Purchases of Private Services," *Survey of Current Business*, September 1995.

Min, Hokey, Hyesung Min, and Kyooyup Chung. "Dynamic Benchmarking of Hotel Service Quality," *Journal of Services Marketing*, Volume 16, Issue 4, 2002, pages 302–321.

Mortimer, K. and B. P. Mathews. "The Advertising of Services: Consumer Views vs. Normative Guidelines," *The Service Industries Journal*, Volume 18, Number 3, 1998, pages 14–19.

Mortimer, Kathleen. "Integrating Advertising Theories with Conceptual Models of Services Advertising," *Journal of Services Marketing*, Volume 16, Issue 5, 2002, pages 460–468.

Mortimer, Kathleen. "Services Advertising: The Agency Viewpoint," *Journal of Services Marketing*, Volume 15, Issue 2, 2001, pages 131–146.

Office of Technology Assessment. *International Competition in Services*, Washington, D.C.: Government Printing Office, 1987.

Parasuraman, A., V. Zeithaml, and Leonard L. Berry. "A Conceptual Model of Service Quality and Its Implications for Future Research," *Journal of Marketing*, Volume 49, Fall 1985.

Patterson, Paul G. and Tasman Smith. "Relationship Benefits in Service Industries: A Replication in a Southeast Asian Context," *Journal of Services Marketing*, Volume 15, Issue 6, 2001, pages 425–443.

Quelch, John and Rohit Deshpande, editors. *The Global Market*, Harvard Business School, San Francisco: Jossey-Bass, 2004.

Rubinfeld, Arthur and Collins Hemingway. *Built for Growth: Expanding Your Business Around the Corner or Across the Globe*, Wharton School Publishing, Upper Saddle River, NJ., 2005.

Sarathy, Ravi. "The Export Expansion Process in the Computer Software Industry." In *Managing Export Entry and Expansion*, Philip Rosson and Stan Reid, editors, New York: Praeger, 1987.

Sarathy, Ravi. "Global Strategy in Service Industries," *Long Range Planning*, Volume 27, Number 6, 1994.

Shelp, R. *Service Industries and Economic Development*, 1984, New York: Praeger.

Shostack, G. Lyn. "Service Positioning through Structural Change," *Journal of Marketing*, Volume 51, January 1987.

Skaates, Maria Anne, H. Tikkanen, and K. Alajoutsijarvi. "The International Marketing of Professional Service Projects: To What Extent Does Territoriality Matter?" *Journal of Services Marketing*, Volume 17, Issue 1, 2003, pages 83–97.

Smith, Anne M. and Nina L. Reynolds. "Measuring Cross-Cultural Service Quality: A Framework for Assessment," *International Marketing Review*, Volume 19, Number 5, 2001, pages 450–481.

Sultan, Fareena and Merlin Simpson, Jr. "International Service Variants: Airline Passenger Expectations and Perceptions of Service Quality," *Journal of Services Marketing*, Volume 14, Issue 3, 2000, pages 188–216.

Tai, Susan H. C. and Ricky Y. K. Chan. "Cross-Cultural Studies on the Information Content of Service Advertising," *Journal of Services Marketing*, Volume 15, Issue 7, 2001 pages 547–564.

Zeithaml, V., A. Parasuraman, and Leonard L. Berry. "Problems and Strategies in Services Marketing." *Journal of Marketing*, Volume 49, Spring 1985.

Case 13.1

BASEBALL: THE JAPANESE GAME

Babe Ruth toured Japan with an All-Star team in 1931. Professional baseball resumed in Japan after the war in 1950. Japanese teams play each other all the time. There are 12 professional teams divided into two leagues, the Pacific and the Central. The champion from each league plays in an end-of-season playoff, a Japanese "World Series." The teams are as follows:

Central League	Pacific League
Yomiuri Giants	Nippon Ham Fighters
Yakult Swallows	Orix BlueWave
Chunichi Dragons	Chiba Lotte Marines
Hanshin Tigers	Seibu Lions
Hiroshima Toyo Carp	Fukuoka Softbank Hawks
Yokohama Bay Stars	Kintetsu Buffaloes

Four of those teams are located in Tokyo, and four are located in Osaka; all of the teams are owned by corporations. The Yomiuri Giants are owned and run by Japan's leading newspaper chain, the Yomiuri. The Yokohama Bay Stars are owned by TBS, a Tokyo TV station. The Chunichi Dragons are owned by another newspaper chain. Two teams are owned by railroads: Hanshin and Kintetsu. Other team owners include Nippon Ham, a meat producer; Lotte, a Korean department store chain, Yakult, a yogurt and soft drink company; and Toyo Tire, which owns the Hiroshima Carp. The Central League is more popular, with an attendance of 12 million compared to 7 million for the Pacific League. The Yomiuri Giants are on TV five or six nights a week, and all 65 of their home games and most of their away games are covered. Similarly, both Yokohama and Yakult have TV connections; therefore, fan loyalty is strong and home attendance is high.

Japanese baseball stresses fundamentals. Bunting is common, and wa, or team spirit, is important. Managers are authoritarian, and teams practice extensively, working on fielding, covering bases, throwing to cut-off men, etc. Japanese players are small in size. They become professional baseball players the traditional way. They begin to play in high school, then moving on to Japan's only minor league team or to four years of college. Once in college, they cannot be drafted for four years. Japanese players know that American baseball players are better paid. They also accept that U.S. players are bigger, stronger, and faster and that U.S. players hit with more power than most Japanese players. Mike Lum, a hitting coach with the Kansas City Royals who played in Japan, noted, however, that Japanese pitching is good. It helps that the Japanese strike zone is wider and deeper, from below they player's belt to the armpits. Japanese pitchers pitch deeper into the game and, on average, pitch more innings over the course of a season.

As in the United States, TV has a strong influence on baseball. The Yomiuri Giants have a national following because of TV. With Sadaharu Oh (who has 868 career home runs), the team won nine straight national championships between 1965 and 1973. The team plays in the Tokyo Dome (which is modeled after the Metrodome in Minnesota), sharing it with the Nippon Ham Fighters.

Built by the Korakuen Corporation for about $280 million, the new Tokyo Dome produced first-year revenues of over $325 million. It draws on a population of nearly 30 million in a 100-square-mile radius (due to Japan's public transportation system). The 56,000-seat arena also hosts track meets, bicycle races (on which big bets are placed), rugby matches, and events as diverse as Michael Jackson concerts and Mike Tyson boxing matches.

To combat the greater financial strength of the Central League, the Pacific League began importing U.S. players. The practice is now standard in both leagues. Each team can have two active foreign players. Additional "imported" players are in the minor leagues and can be called up in case of injury. Japanese baseball offers an opportunity for young U.S. ballplayers who *almost* make the U.S. major league teams.

An example is Alfonso Soriano, the New York Yankee and Texas Ranger star. In 1984, he signed with the Hiroshima Toyo Carp at age 16. He went to Japan not knowing the language and knowing nothing about the country. In 1988, he came back to the United States, speaking Japanese and playing better baseball, and signed with the Yankees. His tutelage in Japan helped him become the first second baseman to hit 30 home runs and steal 30 bases, starting for the American League in the 2003 All Star game.

The foreign players, *gaijin senshu*, are well paid, with a strong yen making Japanese salaries look better. For example, in May 1998, Mike Easler signed with the Nippon Ham Fighters to play one year, making $975,000. He had been cut by the Yankees and, at age 37, saw Japan as his only chance to continue playing in the majors. Easler had played ten seasons of winter ball in Mexico and Venezuela, resulting in his becoming comfortable with foreign cultures. Other notable U.S. players who played in Japan include Orlando Merced, Kevin Mitchell, Tony Fernandez, and Reggie Jefferson. Managers such as Charlie Manuel (who played for six years in Japan) and Bobby Valentine have coached for Japanese teams, then moved on to coach U.S. major league teams.

Salaries for U.S. baseball players are high when compared with the average salaries for Japanese players. However, the pay difference is not a problem with the Japanese player. He knows that he is a company employee and that the company that owns the team will absorb him into the company culture, finding him a position if he decides to quit baseball.

The pay is good, but life is not easy for a U.S. ballplayer in Japan. For one thing, the entire team relies heavily on him. For another, although teams hire an interpreter to work with him, he and his family must adjust to the culture and deal with the scarce housing and the expensive way of life. Then there are the playing fields. The Tokyo Dome is first-class, as are three other stadiums that have artificial turf. But the remaining clubs have all-dirt infields and grass outfields or just all-dirt fields. When it rains, the field can be like a swamp. In contrast, playing during the hot season has been compared to playing on a basketball court. The work ethic, quintessentially Japanese, is often the undoing of an aging U.S. baseball player who comes to Japan expecting easy money. Faced with the demand to believe that the company or team is what matters and that the manager must not be questioned, many U.S. players quit after a year.

Randy Bass's story is an example of the culture gap. He became Japan's leading slugger, winning the Triple Crown in 1985 and 1986. He became the highest-paid player in Japan, but he left the Hanshin Tigers for San Francisco in May 1988, when his son was hospitalized. He was violating the Japanese cultural code that puts loyalty to the company above personal considerations. When he did not return to Japan by June 17, as he had agreed, he was released.

Unlike U.S. baseball, Japanese teams play each other frequently because each league has only six teams. Pitchers learn about batters. A pitcher's chief weapons are his curve, slider, and forkball—in other words, control. After facing a hitter so many times during the Japanese season (and studying him carefully), the pitcher has a distinct advantage. As Easler put it, "They know everything about you—what you can hit, what you can't. Before the game, you have a video of each team that you play. We go over everything in great detail. The practice habits and work habits here are just exceptional. . . . It's like spring training every day." One other difference is the stress on pitching complete games. Easler thinks that this builds confidence because the pitcher learns to bail himself out. "Patience

is the key to hitting in Japan. You are definitely going to have to hit the ball the other way. If you don't, you'll die here." Easler, who used to be a dead pull hitter (that is, a right-handed batter hitting to left field) returned to the spray hitting style (that is, hitting to all parts of the field, not just to left field) that he learned under Walter Hriniak with the Boston Red Sox.

Japanese Players to the United States

Most baseball fans have heard of Ichiro Suzuki. He plays for the Seattle Mariners, the first Japanese position player to sign with a major league club. Formerly a player for the Orix BlueWave, he broke George Sisler's 1920 record for most hits in a season, getting 262 hits in 2004—a sign of the extraordinary bat control that he possesses. He is only the first in a line of top Japanese baseball players who have begun to make an impact in the U.S. major leagues. Hideki Matsui is a mainstay slugger for the New York Yankees. Hideo Nomo has zig-zagged across the U.S. professional baseball landscape, pitching no-hitters and getting shelled.

A True World Series

What of the future? Because of the strong yen, Japanese clubs can bid more dollars for better U.S. players if they choose to do so. The concentration of teams in Tokyo and Osaka may hinder attempts to expand baseball in Japan by adding new teams in other cities. On the other hand, the success of the Tokyo Dome points to the possibility of moving franchises and creating expansion teams linked to new major league-quality stadiums. In March 2006, players will compete for their home countries in the World Baseball Classic, the first 16-nation world championship. Professional players will participate, making the event different from the Olympics, which allows only amateurs. Thus, Albert Pujols, Vladimir Gurrero, David Ortiz, and Pedro Martinez could all be playing for the team from the Dominican Republic. That type of international tournament will create a greater awareness of baseball globally and raise the quality of baseball elsewhere. Japan might consider increasing the size of team rosters from the present 25 men and raising the current ceiling for foreign players. Other nations might start larger and better-funded professional baseball leagues, thereby increasing market size for the better baseball players, bringing in more advertising dollars, and augmenting the economic stature of professional baseball.

Baseball Trade Opportunities

Selling U.S. baseball to the world is an "export" possibility. The popularity of Japanese players in the United States raises the audience for major league baseball games because Japanese fans want to see their favorite Japanese players succeed on the U.S. stage. TV rights for baseball games to be shown in Japan bring yen-based revenues for U.S. entrepreneurs. U.S. Major League Baseball announced a $275 million six-year deal selling television rights to its games to the Japanese advertising company Dentsu (three times what Major League Baseball received in its previous contract with Dentsu). Promotional opportunities for ballplayers in Japan are underexploited, currently under control of the company owning the team. And if baseball can be exported, can ownership rights be far behind? Would Sony buy a U.S. baseball team? After all, the owner of Nintendo was given permission by U.S. baseball team owners to purchase the Seattle Mariners when the team was up for sale. If the two richest markets in the world are baseball crazy, opportunities surely exist for further trade in baseball between those nations and others.

QUESTIONS AND RESEARCH

1. How is Japanese baseball marketed? How is that different from the way U.S. baseball is sold?

2. How would an aging U.S. baseball player market himself to a Japanese team? What about a rookie?

3. How is the growing popularity of baseball in Japan likely to affect U.S. baseball?

4. Does U.S.-Japanese collaboration change the market for U.S. and Japanese baseball players? How should the Major League Baseball Players Association (the union) react to protect its members' interests?

5. Why would U.S. entrepreneurs and agents be interested in Japanese baseball players?

6. Why would someone in Japan want to buy a U.S. baseball team? What are the implications of an internationalization of the baseball scene?

7. How can trade in baseball be seen as an example of trade in services?

Case prepared by Ravi Sarathy for use in classroom discussion. © 2005, all rights reserved. Based on Robert Whiting, "The Samurai Way of Baseball: The Impact of Ichiro," Warner Books 2005; "Major League Baseball Agrees to $275 Million Deal in Japan," *Wall Street Journal*, October 31, 2003; Warren Cromartie, "Slugging It Out in Japan," *Kodansha*, 1991; and a three-part series by Larry Whiteside, *Boston Globe*, July 17, 18, and 19, 1988. Also see http://baseballguru.com/bbjp1.html.

Case 13.2

SONY CORPORATION

Sony has long been known for its innovative consumer electronics products, such as the pioneering Walkman. Sony is an international corporation, with 70 percent of its sales coming from outside Japan and non-Japanese owners owning 23 percent of its stock. Sony manufactures about 20 percent of its output outside Japan. As of 1986, its sales mix was video equipment (VCRs), 33 percent; audio equipment (compact disc [CD] players), 22 percent; TVs (the Trinitron), 22 percent; and other products (records, floppy disk drives, and semiconductors), 17 percent. Sony has always emphasized R&D, spending about 9 percent of sales on it.

The Betamax Experience

Sony has seen increased competition from other Japanese companies and from countries with lower labor costs, such as Taiwan and South Korea. Its strategy of inventing new, advanced-technology products and then waiting for the market to buy seemed to be faltering. However, Sony's biggest failure was the VHS format. Having invented the Betamax format for VCRs, Sony refused to license the technology to other manufacturers. Betamax was higher-priced; and recording times were somewhat shorter than those of the competing VHS format, although image quality was better.

Sony's competitors—Matsushita (Panasonic), Hitachi, and Toshiba—all banded together around the VHS format. They licensed the format to any manufacturer who wanted it. Consequently, the total number of VHS sets produced and sold was far higher than the Betamax-format VCRs. That meant lower retail prices for the Betamax because of accumulated volume and resulting economies of scale. Also, far more "software" was available for the VHS format; that is, movie producers were more likely to use VHS tapes to make copies of their films available for purchase and rental. That further increased demand for VHS-format VCRs. The net result was that Betamax gradually faded. Sony stopped its production in 1988.

Rethinking Basic Strategy

The difficulty of selling advanced technology, coupled with the speed of imitation and the impact of low-wage country competitors, led Sony to change its basic corporate strategy. The CBS/Sony Group, Inc., a 50-50 joint venture between Sony and CBS, Inc., has grown dramatically over a 20-year period to become an industry leader in the multibillion yen Japanese music industry. On CD and other formats, the company releases recordings in Japan, Hong Kong, and Macau of popular Japanese artists as well as foreign artists.

Therefore, Sony's diversification into the global music industry is not unexpected. In January 1988, it agreed to buy CBS Records for $2 billion. But subsequent moves have dramatically transformed Sony as it moves to become more of a service company. Table 13-5 summarizes the major entertainment industry acquisitions made by Sony since 1988.

Table 13-5. From Electronics to Entertainment: Sony's Acquisitions since 1988

Date	Company Acquired	Price
October 1989	Guber-Peters Productions	$200 million
September 1989	Columbia Pictures	$3.4 billion
January 1989	Tree International (country music publishers)	$30 million
January 1988	CBS Records	$2 billion

Source: Sony Corporation news releases.

Sony's Diversification into the Entertainment Industry

The acquisitions are large, totaling over $5 billion, or about half of Sony's total assets. More interesting is the reasoning behind Sony's decision to acquire a slew of entertainment companies. A summary of the acquisitions follows.

- **CBS Records:** For $2 billion, Sony acquired control of the world's largest record company, CBS Records. CBS Records, Inc., consists of CBS Records (Domestic), CBS Masterworks, CBS Records International, CBS/Sony, Columbia House, and CBS Music Video. The acquisition gave Sony an immediate international presence in the music industry. Traditionally selling music hardware, Sony was one of the world's largest producers of CDs, tape recorders (including the phenomenally successful Walkman), and stereo television. But all of those products were subject to competition because innovative ideas could be imitated and prices could be cut. Sony realized that being in the music business allowed it to take advantage of the entire installed base of CD players around the world, not just those it manufactured. Imitation was impossible because each musical performance was unique. However, managing such a creative business required great cultural sensitivity and the use of local managers rather than predominantly Japanese management.

- **Columbia Pictures:** The major attraction of Columbia Pictures was its large library of movies, which earn revenues every time they are shown at cinemas and on video around the world. Columbia also had a profitable TV production and syndication business. Thus, through the acquisition, Sony could sell products to owners of TV sets and VCRs (similar to providing music on record and tape for owners of CD players and tape recorders).

There are two other reasons Sony found Columbia Pictures attractive. First, TV in Japan is being liberalized, with the number of TV stations and on-air time doubling because of the launch of satellite television. There will be a sudden increase in demand for products such as films and TV shows to fill air time on Japan's satellite stations. Sony will be in a position to supply those products at premium prices in yen at a time when demand is increasing. The second reason is hardware-related. Sony has been trying to establish its 8 mm camcorder format, competing with the VHS-C-based format from Japanese producers. This standards battle is reminiscent of Sony's experience with Betamax. This time, however, Sony realizes the need to build the installed base. Hence, it has licensed the 8 mm technology to other producers and is willing to manufacture the camcorders for others to sell under their brand names. Thus, Sony is making sure that volume sales of the 8 mm camcorder will be achieved, resulting in economies of scale and lower prices. The next step is to stimulate demand by making a variety of movies available in this format. Sony can do this by putting the entire Columbia Pictures catalog on 8 mm video, thus giving consumers a reason to buy the camcorder, which can also be used as a video player. Making the movie catalog available will be crucial to the success of Sony's newly introduced 8 mm video Walkman. The pocket-sized portable color TV will appeal to consumers as long as videos are available to use with it.

With the acquisitions of CBS Records and Columbia Pictures, Sony becomes one of the world's major producers of entertainment hardware and software: a producer of records and CD players, a leading manufacturer of TV sets, and an owner of a library of classic films.

- **Guber-Peters Productions:** When Sony purchased Columbia Pictures, it obtained a film library as well as a film production studio. Columbia had gone through four producers in five years, however, and needed more capable film production management. The logical step was to take over one of Hollywood's most successful film production companies, Guber-Peters Company (formerly Barris Productions). The company had produced Batman, one of Warner Communications' all-time best-selling films. In fact, Guber-Peters had signed a five-year exclusive agreement with Warner to produce movies on its behalf. Guber-Peter's expertise lay in spotting hot properties, signing them, and then convincing major studios to bankroll the films and distribute them. Guber-Peters had a unique culture-specific talent for working in and with Hollywood, producing successful films for the huge U.S. TV and film audience. Sony acquired Guber-Peters for over $200 million, or about five times Guber-Peters's latest-year revenues. The two key producers, Peter Guber and Jon Peters, received about $50 million for their stock in Guber-Peters, a 10 percent stake in future profits at Columbia Pictures, 8 percent of the future appreciation of Columbia Pictures' market value, and about $50 million in total deferred compensation.

Warner immediately sued Sony for acquiring Guber-Peters and refused to release Peter Guber from his long-term contract. Of course, Sony and Warner ultimately settled out of court, exchanging valuable assets such as a share of the movie studio and video rights. Clearly, Sony wanted the management talent—Americans who knew Hollywood and could hire the right people; had the appropriate financial and creative contacts; and, most importantly, knew how to make hit films.

- **Tree International:** Through CBS Records, Sony also acquired ownership of Tree International, the premier country music publishing company. Owning rights to several generations of hit country songs guaranteed a steady stream of revenue, especially as the catalog became popular around the world through Sony's music and video production divisions. This was a minor acquisition, but it may point to a trend toward acquiring other music publishing companies as a means to further control the software end of the entertainment business.

Sony's Future

Looking to the future, Sony's heavy involvement in new hardware technologies such as advanced high-definition TV, computer workstations, and compact disc interactive technology will require further research and development. Consumer acceptance of those products will depend on the availability of software products that showcase the new hardware products. Sony's long-term plans focus more on services and entertainment. Paradoxically, that focus will help the company become a stronger hardware company and reduce risk by smoothing revenue fluctuations and providing the stability of recurring earnings from sales of music, film, and videotapes. (The Sony case is continued on Cases 13.3 and 15.1).

QUESTIONS AND RESEARCH

1. What threats were facing Sony?
2. Trace the various entertainment industry acquisitions made by Sony. Why did Sony make these acquisitions? Have they helped the company compete more effectively in international markets?
3. What are the risks of Sony's strategy of buying U.S. entertainment companies?
4. What would you recommend that Sony do next? How do you think Sony's Japanese competitors might respond to its action?
5. Is Sony becoming a global company, or is it becoming a company with products adapted for each specific country market? Explain.
6. Based on Sony's experience, what generalizations can you make about the global service industry?

Sources: "Sony Sees More Than Michael Jackson in CBS," *The Economist*, November 28, 1987; "A Changing Sony Aims to Own the Software That Its Products Need," *Wall Street Journal*, December 30, 1988; "Sony Sets Pact with Coca-Cola for Columbia," *Wall Street Journal*, September 28, 1989; and "Dynamic Duo: Producers of 'Batman' Stir Whammo Battle over Future Services," *Wall Street Journal*, October 20, 1989.

Case 13.3

SONY IN 1996

In December 1994, Sony announced that it was taking a $2.7 billion write-off in connection with its 1989 acquisition of Columbia Pictures. Furthermore, Sony Pictures reported a loss of $500 million for the year. The combined losses of $3.2 billion were some of the largest losses incurred in Hollywood. Shortly thereafter, Matsushita, which had copied Sony by buying MCA, announced that it was selling MCA to Seagram, incurring a large loss in the process. MCA's top management had threatened to leave because Matsushita did not want to invest additional funds into MCA. MCA's main film-producing partner, Steven Spielberg, would have accompanied MCA's management and stopped distributing his films through MCA.

Meanwhile, back in Japan, an appreciating yen made Sony's consumer electronics products more expensive in its export markets. Sony was facing competition from producers in South Korea and Taiwan that could offer a basic VCR in U.S. stores such as Circuit City for $99, a price at which Sony could not compete.

Changes at the Top

Major changes occurred within Sony's top management ranks. Mr. Morita, Sony's founder, had suffered a stroke and was no longer involved in management. Mr. Ohga, the CEO, who had undergone a bypass operation, missed being able to chat with his mentor, Morita. The gradual decline in Sony's fortunes led him to think about what sort of person should lead Sony into the twenty-first century. Years earlier both Morita and Ohga had agreed to step down as president of the company at age 65. It was assumed that an engineer, Mr. Minoru Morio, the president of Sony's audiovisual products and head of Sony's digital video disc (DVD) efforts, would step in. Ohga, however, turned to a marketer, Mr. Nobuyuki Idei, as Sony's next president. Idei had worked for Sony in overseas locations and had been in charge of marketing Sony's audiovisual products. In 1990, Idei had become head of Sony's Design Center, responsible for Sony's merchandising and product promotions and corporate communications. As such, he represented Sony across the world at major trade shows and industry gatherings. His appointment signaled a major change in Sony's strategic direction and corporate vision. Idei was an enthusiastic proponent of digital video and saw opportunities for Sony in the convergence of entertainment, consumer electronics products, and computers.

The Digital Video Era

Digital video could be to VCRs and films on videotape what CDs were to older analog long-playing records (LPs). Digital video allows entire films to be stored on CD-ROM-sized discs, accessed at any point, manipulated, and reused. Sony had been working with the Dutch company Philips in developing a DVD standard that would be used in digital video devices. Sony's standard called for a single-sided disc containing about 3.7 gigabytes of information, equal to about 135 minutes of video.

Establishing an industry standard can be enormously profitable, as can be seen in the examples of Intel and Microsoft. Sony (and Philips) earned a nickel in royalties for each CD sold. But in 1993, Sony learned that Toshiba and Time Warner were working on a DVD standard of their own. Their Super Density, or SD, format would use both sides of the disk and store 5 gigabytes on each side. Time Warner was also able to get the attention of movie studios in Hollywood, learning what performance criteria they expected from DVD. (In contrast, Morio, who headed Sony's DVD effort, spoke little English and came from an engineering, not a marketing, background.) With mounting competition from Toshiba and Time Warner, Idei was asked to formulate a new DVD strategy, which he crafted by stressing the role of DVD as a format for multimedia computers. By January 1995, Matsushita had joined Hitachi, Pioneer, JVC, Thomson, and Mitsubishi in supporting the Toshiba SD standard. Possibly with the Betamax fiasco in mind, Sony ultimately compromised and agreed to work out a unified DVD standard.

New Business Directions

One of Sony's successes has been the Sony PlayStation, which competed against the Nintendo and Sega 16-bit game machines. However, it offered superior video and sound and faster speed through 32-bit processors. Planning for the PlayStation began in 1988. Ken Kutaragi, who was designing Sony workstations using advanced chips, realized that the price of the chips would fall to the point that it made sense to build a game machine around the 32-bit semiconductors. Features such as a CD-ROM input device and a superior graphics screen could also be added. However, game machines sell because customers want hit games that are exclusive to the platform. Hence, an executive from Sony Music, which was a distributor of Nintendo machines, suggested that Kutaragi think about building reusable modules that programmers could use to create entertaining and impressive new games quickly. Based on that suggestion, Kutaragi built a dictionary of images that could be combined on the fly to build game characters who exhibited subtle and lifelike movements, while cutting game development time by half. Sony also created a joint venture within the company with Sony Music to focus on selling hardware (the PlayStation) and software (newly developed games). That allowed the PlayStation to be priced at $299 in the United States, a full $100 below the competing Sega Saturn. (Sony's expectation was that a growing installed base would offer a fertile and captive market for the sale of high-margin hit games; the typical Nintendo owner purchased 6 to 12 games for a machine). In 1995, Sony's PlayStation became the best-selling 32-bit game machine in Japan and the United States. About a year later, when Nintendo introduced its N64 machine, both companies reduced prices of their game machines to under $150. Loyal Nintendo fans bought new Nintendo machine in large numbers. But Sony's lead and bigger selection of games meant that it continued to hold a larger market share over Nintendo in the new-generation video game segment of the market.

Under Idei's leadership, Sony entered into an alliance with Intel to make multimedia computers, what he termed "Intelligent TV." He visualized "the intelligence of computers, the access power of on-line communications, and the visual power of full-motion video integrated into a new form of viewing experience." Other new products that Sony targeted for the age of digital TV included wide-screen living room televisions that could access the Internet using web browsers, eyeglasses onto which TV and e-mail could be projected using wireless technology, and low-cost computers acting as web browsers. The new Sony computers could include PlayStation game-playing abilities as well as the ability to access digital TV programs and use screen savers featuring images and sound from Sony films and music acts. Moreover, Sony's library of 3,000 films and over 35,000 hours of TV programs would be a valuable resource for an age of digital TV.

Outside the United States, Sony saw strong growth possibilities in satellite TV. It formed a joint venture with Singapore-based Argos Communications to launch a Hindi satellite TV channel beamed to India. The channel featured Indian-produced shows and movies, as well as films and programs from Sony's library. Initially, the channel was offered free to cable TV operators who would redistribute it. Sony expected to generate revenues from sale of advertising time. Sony also became a partner in HBO Olç, a Spanish broadcast aimed at Latin America.

Management Shake-up in the United States

Mr. Schulhof, a physicist and jet pilot (like Ohga), was the head of Sony's U.S. operations and a close ally of Morita and Ohga. He had authorized payment of $200 million to buy Guber-Peters Entertainment and to buy out Guber's and Peter's contracts with Warner Brothers. He allowed Guber and Peters to choose their managers, sometimes resulting in the appointment of friends and associates. (Guber named his lawyer as the number two executive.) That may have resulted in an atmosphere where politics and the people one knew was important.

Guber and Peters had little experience in running a studio, but spent lavishly, updating the Culver City studios at a cost of $200 million. There were no cost controls, and several new film releases were expensive failures (Last Action Hero, Hudson Hawk, Geronimo, and Frankenstein). Schulhof also backed Sony's entry into programs for radio syndication and into theme parks featuring Sony characters and goods. He did not agree with the move into computers, which he characterized as a low-margin business with rapid change and short product cycles—an environment in which Sony had no experience. By the end of 1995, Schulhof had resigned from Sony as Idei moved to reestablish control by Japanese headquarters over Sony Pictures and U.S. operations.

Sony's Finances

Table 13-6 summarizes Sony's financial performance between 1986 and 1995. Sales grew dramatically, from $7.7 billion to over $46 billion. Sales in 1995 were nearly evenly distributed across Japan, the United States, and Europe, with sales of $12.3 billion, $13.9 billion, and $10.2 billion, respectively. However, net income was half the profitability levels of 1986, and long-term debt grew tenfold. In allocating its cash flow, Sony had to choose between the entertainment division and the support of R&D in the hardware divisions. In 1995, sales of TV, audio, and video equipment were about 58 percent of total sales (compared to about 20 percent from music and films). In 1995, U.S. revenues from consumer electronics actually exceeded U.S. revenues from music and film.

Alternatives for Sony's U.S. Entertainment Operations

Matsushita's sale of MCA immediately raised questions as to whether Sony should do the same. Idei remarked that Matsushita was shortsighted in selling its film division. In a digital age, content and copyrights can be distributed in many formats, and the large film library that came with the acquisition of

Table 13-6. Sony Corporation: 1986–1995 Financial Statements ($Billions)

	1986	1987	1988	1989	1990	1991	1992	1993	1994	1995
Sales	7.7	10.7	17.1	20.5	26.1	29.6	32.2	34.8	40.4	46.2
Operating income	0.2	0.4	1.2	2.1	2.1	1.4	1.0	0.9	-1.7	2.3
Net income	0.245	0.269	0.562	0.717	0.827	0.904	0.292	0.143	-2.97	0.683
Long-term debt	0.88	1.58	1.67	4.1	4.91	6.65	7.65	9.36	10.49	8.47
Net worth	3.7	5.2	6.9	9.1	10.4	11.6	12.4	12.6	11.7	10.7

Columbia Pictures was a valuable and scarce asset. Few Hollywood film studios remain for media companies to buy, wanting to enter into the software or content-generation side of the business. When Idei took over as president of Sony, he indicated that he wanted to hold on to the entertainment division in the United States. His priority, however, was to restore profitability to Sony Pictures. He wanted to see more pictures made with lower budgets, stressing cost controls. When Schulhof, head of Sony's U.S. operations, mentioned that Sony's market share was rising, Idei remarked that he was more interested in profits.

If Sony were to sell, several choices existed: Should it sell all of the entertainment business? If so, who should it sell to, mindful that it did not want to create a strong competitor down the road. Interested parties included GE, which owned NBC-TV; News Corporation, which already had Fox Studios; and overseas buyers such as Polygram and Bertelsmann, neither of which had a major Hollywood studio. Another alternative was to sell only part of the U.S. entertainment business. Options included selling a portion in a U.S. public stock offering or selling a stake in the company to a strategic partner.

Idei had specific ideas on how Sony should be run. He expressed little interest in buying media channels like Disney did with ABC. In his words, "Buying a network in a digital age with so many channels won't bring any benefits to us." He disliked the idea of selling the U.S. music and film business and taking on a partner. His fear was losing control and having to put up with interference from U.S. owners with different perspectives. "I also want to set a new future direction for our R&D so that it is not merely trying to extend our current business, but attempting to identify new opportunities for the 21st century. And of course DVD is a very high priority because setting a format standard energizes the company."

For a 2005 update on Sony, see Chapter 15, Case 15.1: Sony in 2005.

QUESTIONS AND RESEARCH

1. Evaluate the performance of Sony's U.S. entertainment division. Why did it do poorly?
2. What were the challenges facing Sony in 1996? Assess its strategy for coping with those challenges.
3. Looking back, would Sony have been better off not buying into the U.S. film and music businesses? Explain your answer.
4. What do you think of Mr. Idei's approach to running Sony?

Sources: "Ouster of Schulhof Leaves Focus Fuzzy at Sony Entertainment," *Wall Street Journal*, December 6, 1995; "Sony Heads Down Information Highway and Decides Not to Go It Alone," *Wall Street Journal*, April 14, 1995; "Sony President Rules Out Buying American Network," *Wall Street Journal*, November 21, 1995; "Sony May Sell Stake in U.S. Operations," *Wall Street Journal*, October 30, 1995; "Sony Resignation Brings Speculation about Possible Suitors for Movie Unit," *Wall Street Journal*, December 7, 1995; "Sony Unit Plans Venture to Launch Hindi-Language TV Channel in India," *Wall Street Journal*, August 14, 1995; "Sony President Seeks to Quash Rumors about Sale of U.S. Entertainment Unit," *Wall Street Journal*, January 15, 1996; "Sony's Heartaches in Hollywood," *Business Week*, December 5, 1994; "It's Nobuyuki Idei's Sony Now," *Business Week*, December 18, 1995; "Sony on the Brink," *FORTUNE*, June 12, 1995; "Lonesome Samurai," *Financial World*, May 23, 1995; and "Sony Outside, Intel Inside," *Financial World*, January 2, 1996.

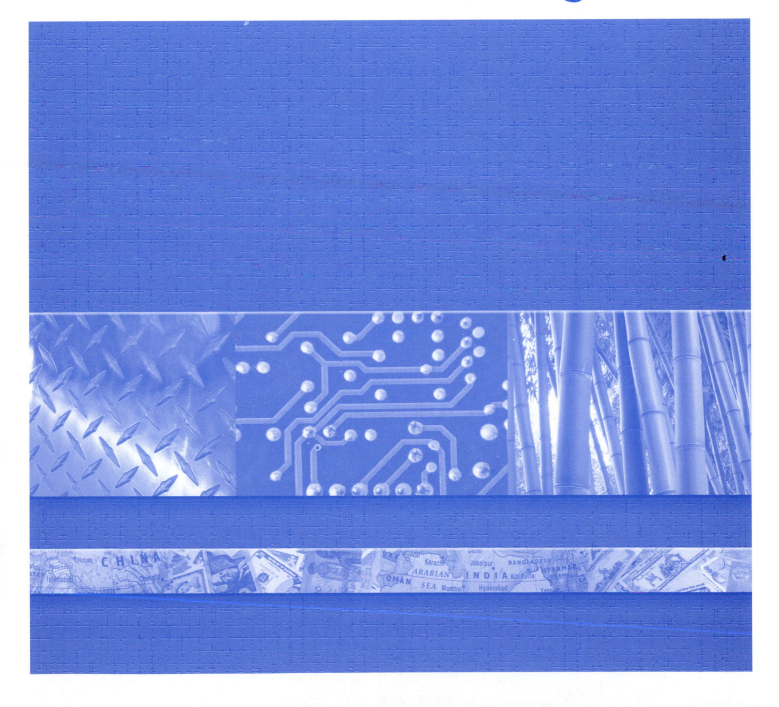

PART 3

Coordination and Control of Global Marketing

Part 1 looked at the world environment that shapes international marketing. Part 2 looks at how managers perform the functional tasks that constitute international marketing—that is, marketing intelligence, product development, pricing, etc. In conclusion, Part 3 deals with how the strategy and, then, separate functional tasks of organization, planning, and control are blended together into an effective international marketing mix.

Chapter 14 will discuss global strategy and its marketing implications. It deals at length with specifics of marketing internationally. However, the proof of the pudding is in the eating; a recipe alone does not yield a feast. The implementation of plans and strategies determines how well a firm functions in the global marketplace. Therefore, the following chapter (15), on Planning, Organization and Control of International Marketing, is concerned with such implementation. The Part then concludes with an Integrative Case Study on Sony Corp.

CHAPTER 14

Global Marketing Strategy

This chapter explains how a company can formulate international marketing strategy. Once a carefully thought-out strategy is in place, a company can take effective and consistent actions in the various areas of the marketing mix.

The main goals of this chapter are to

- Describe the process of formulating a global marketing strategy that is consistent with and integrated with a firm's overall global strategy.

- Delineate the steps involved in arriving at a global strategy.

- Explain how a global strategy relates to a product line and to individual country markets.

- Describe how firms compete in the global marketplace.

- Detail the effects of corporate goals on strategy formulation, such as a short-term orientation or the pursuit of market share.

- Discuss government influences and the impact of major trends such as the EU and the creation of the euro and the emergence of the triad economies of Europe, Asia, and the United States and the growing importance of China.

- Discuss the global automobile industry to provide a better understanding of how its global strategy unfolds.

To formulate market strategy, a marketer must consider the existence of global markets for the firm's products and take into account competitors who think and act globally. Worldwide competition is intense. As a result, firms must plan on obtaining significant market positions in all major developed country markets, where technology has become so widely diffused that "all developed countries are equally capable of doing everything, doing it equally well and doing it equally fast."[1] Widespread availability of information and volatile currencies pose additional challenges to a firm seeking leadership in a global industry.

A **global industry** can be defined as "an industry in which a firm's competitive position in one country is affected by its position in other countries, and vice versa." "If no one challenges a global competitor in its home market, the competitor faces a reduced level of rivalry; its profitability rises and the day when it can attack the home markets of its rivals is hastened."[2]

George S. Yip has developed an interesting framework for analyzing a company's global strategies.[3] He begins with environmental factors that lead an industry to become global. Terming them **industry globalization drivers**, Yip includes:

- Market factors.
- Cost factors.
- Competitive moves.
- Other environmental factors

In response to those environmental changes pushing a firm to develop global strategies, a firm can adopt a variety of strategic approaches, which Yip terms global strategy levers. They include:

- Participating in significant major markets.
- Offering a range of mostly standardized products worldwide.
- Configuring value-added activities across countries, based on the country's comparative advantage.
- Developing global marketing strategies.
- Developing a program of competitive moves integrated across countries.

Marketing and Its Links to Global Strategy

Marketing does not take place in isolation, but is inextricably linked to a firm's overall strategy. International marketing is likewise linked to its global strategy. Takeuchi and Porter use the term linkage to describe how technology development and manufacturing can make global marketing more effective and further enhance global competitive advantage.[4] Domestic marketing seeks to obtain and keep customers in the home market; likewise, the goal of international marketing is to create and retain customers in global markets. The customers may be global in character, or they may be limited to individual national markets. The added complexity is that a firm faces global competitors.

Global Strategy: A Framework

Firm-level global strategies cut across product lines. For example, global management of international financial flows can match cash inflows and outflows in a specific currency and integrate cash needs for specific currencies across product lines. If a company has several product lines in Japan, it can aggregate the surplus or deficit cash flow produced by each product line. Thus, it has a total deficit or surplus position in yen that must be financed and hedged. That procedure can reduce spending on hedging and reduce the firm's overall exchange rate risk. If a firm has organizationally distinct product-line divisions, (silos), however, deliberate planning is needed to achieve integration in managing foreign exchange.

Similarly, a multinational firm selling several distinct product lines within a country can gain economies of scale by performing a basic analysis of that country market's cultural, political, and economic structure. That analysis is done before the firm considers competition and demand profiles for individual product lines.

Another major influence that cuts across firms' product lines is management attitude. Management attitudes that lead to focusing on the domestic market and/or on a few foreign markets ("tunnel vision") without regard to global markets and competition hinder the formulation of global actions. The lack of global vision is one reason a firm's global strategies may be inadequate and may explain why the firm has not formulated a global strategy. The firm does not realize that it needs to think globally, consider all of the world's markets, and decide whether it wants to address each specific market, developing a plan for those objectives.

Global Strategy and the Product Line

Figure 14-1 sets out the framework for developing product-line global strategy. The three basic influences are the global environment, the industry, and the firm itself. In analyzing the firm, its **competitive advantage** is evaluated; that is, why the firm should be able to make a profit in its chosen line of activity in the face of competition and why customers should buy its product or service, preferring it to that of the competition. Competitive advantage can

Figure 14-1. Global Strategy at the Firm

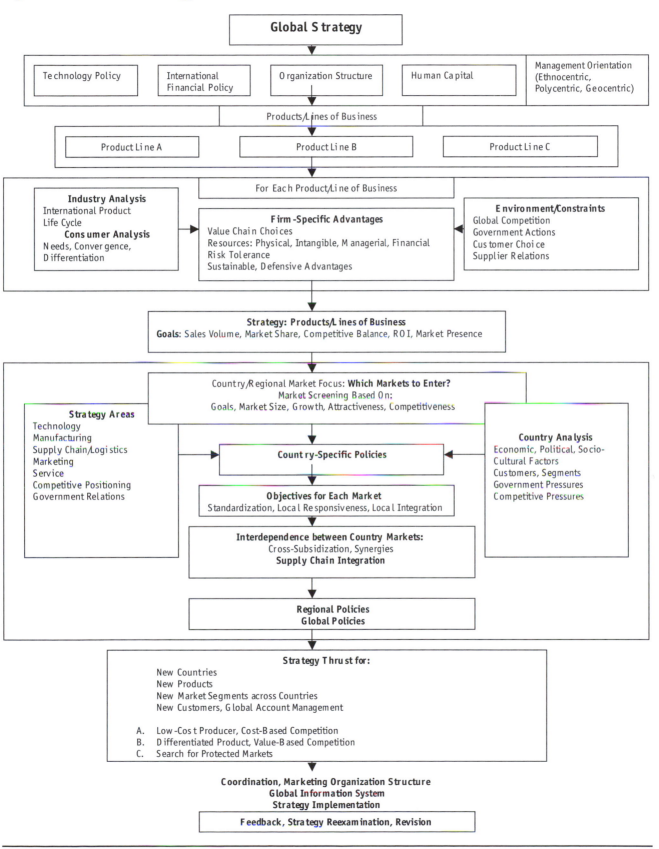

come from many sources: a firm's proprietary technology, its superior manufacturing, its skills in marketing or in managing global financial flows, or its overall management talent and organizational capabilities. Those sources of competitive advantage influence a firm when it comes time to determine what activities it will specialize in and implement; that is, how it will participate in the product's value-added chain. A firm is able to attract customers because of its superiority over its competitors in one or more elements of the value-added chain. That is, the firm attracts customers because of its superior technology, manufacturing, or marketing.

The second factor a firm must consider when attempting to formulate a strategy for competitive advantage involves several global environmental influences. Most important is the global competition that a firm faces. Then the firm must consider host-government actions, which vary from country to country and can affect the firm's freedom to carry out its strategy. Also important are the firm's customers, the reason for its being. Careful customer analysis is absolutely critical to developing competitive advantage. Finally, suppliers and their influence over a firm are relevant to strategy formulation.

Carpano et al studied the relationships among strategies, environments, and firm performance, using data on 75 firms in global and multidomestic industries.[5] They found that no one strategy was always superior, suggesting that the environment in which a firm finds itself dictates the appropriate strategy. Thus, mass-market standardized strategies are more effective in global industries than in multidomestic industries. One could use Yip's globalization drivers to determine whether an industry is becoming global; and if it is still in the multidomestic stage, strategies adapted to each country market might result in better performance.

The third major influence is the industry to which the product line belongs. Basic industry analysis is necessary to establish the product line's stage of growth, future prospects, and barriers to entry. A fundamental tool is the international product life cycle, which may be at different stages in different national markets. This life cycle is useful in forecasting demand and in selecting potential markets for future entry.

The rayon industry manufactures rayon fiber used to make yarn, then cloth, and then garments. As the garment industry concentrates in the low-wage countries of the Far East (China, India, Sri Lanka, and others), rayon manufacturers are motivated to locate their rayon factories near their customers, the garment-producing companies. Thus, more rayon factories are locating in the Far East, even though they are capital-intensive and seem unusual in low-wage countries. Companies such as Lenzing, whose home base is Austria, have gradually expanded their rayon manufacturing operations in Indonesia and China. Doing so allows the companies to be close to their markets and to possible sources of wood pulp, a key ingredient in the manufacturing of rayon.

The tables on the facing page summarize Philips' global sales by product line and by geographic area. Philips operates in six different lines of business, with lighting, consumer electronics, medical systems, and semiconductors being the largest. The company is also geographically diversified, though principally in Europe and the United States, with China increasing in importance. Not all of Philips' lines of business are profitable; semiconductors run at a loss. It is a strategically complex company, which sees itself as having three main foci: health care, lifestyle, and technology. Despite the size and breadth of operations, Philips' profitability is low, at only 1.7 percent of sales. Philips has to grapple with several questions in developing and implementing its global marketing strategy. Those questions include the viability of each line of businesses, the extent of differentiation, the competitiveness of its businesses, its cost structure, its geographical spread, and its long-term growth plans.

Product-Line Strategy for Individual Country Markets

After a firm has developed an initial strategy, it must begin to consider individual markets. Although global marketing involves considering all of a firm's markets with regard to their interdependence, a decision must be made about whether strategy will be the same in all markets or whether aspects of strategy, including global marketing strategy, will be adapted to fit individual countries. In part, this depends on the goals set for a product line within a particular country market. In some markets, a firm may seek market share, planning to obtain profits after market share has been established. In other cases, the goal may be to challenge strong global competitors as a means of preserving competitive balance across countries. In still other markets, a firm may simply want to establish a small market presence and wait until the market becomes more attractive. In more mature markets, a firm may actively seek profits and set up return-on-investment targets. The goals set for each country and for the product line as a whole determine which strategies are selected. As part of setting strategy, firms must choose which country markets to enter. Solberg sets up a range of strategies for markets, (nine "strategy windows") suggesting that the extent of globalization of an industry, together with the maturity of the individual market (whether early stage, growing, or saturated), should determine the broad characteristics of the strategy followed.[6] The

Global Marketing: Philips and Developing Global Marketing Strategy

Philips Electronics: Major Product Lines

Lighting	**Consumer Electronics**	**Domestic Appliances and Personal Care**	**Semiconductors**	**Medical Systems**
Lamps	Display	Shaving and Beauty	Consumer Systems	X-ray
Luminaries	Video	Oral Health Care	Communications	Computed Tomography
Lighting Electronics	Audio	Food and Beverage	Multimarket	Magnetic Resonance
Automotive and	Consumer	Home Environment Care	Semiconductors	Ultrasound
Special Lighting	Communications		Foundries	Nuclear Medicine
	Peripherals		Assembly and Test	Medical IT
	Accessories		Mobile Display	Cardiac and Monitoring
	Licenses		Systems	Systems
				Dictation and Speech
				Recognition Systems
				Personal Health Care
				Costumer Financing
				Document Management
				Systems
				Asset Management
				Services

Miscellaneous Products

Technology and Design
Corporate Investments
Shared Services
Navigation Technology
Optical Storage

Philips 2003 Results by Product Line (Millions of Euros)

	Sales	Income (loss) from Operations	As a % of Segment Revenues
Lighting	4,522	577	12.7
Consumer Electronics	9,188	248	2.7
DAP	2,131	398	18.5
Semiconductors	4,988	(342)	(6.6)
Medical Systems	5,990	431	7.2
Miscellaneous	2,218	(263)	(8.6)
Unallocated	—	(561)	
Total	**29,037**	**488**	
Income from Operations as a % of Sales		**1.7**	

Philips 2003 Results by Geographic Area (Millions of Euros)

	Sales (to third parties)	Total Assets	Net Operating Capital	Capital Expenditures	Depreciation
Netherlands	1,181	6,525	2,304	251	319
United States	7,532	7,458	3,554	140	444
Germany	2,184	1,675	259	90	134
France	1,952	2,267	(88)	40	62
United Kingdom	1,258	586	113	19	31
China	2,699	1,260	—	133	95
Other Countries	12,231	9,229	1,929	307	434
Total	**29,037**	**29,000**	**8,071**	**980**	**1,519**

Source: Philips 2003 *Annual Report.*

goals a firm sets for a market partly determine whether it will enter a particular country market.

Next, the firm must analyze whether it should change its marketing policies in a specific market because of government restrictions, competitive pressures, or differences in customer needs that may arise from economic and cultural differences. This choice between standardizing policies across markets or adapting them and becoming locally responsive is fundamental to international marketing. Not all aspects of global strategy need to be adapted for each market. Local responsiveness can vary across the marketing mix. Promotion and distribution may be tailored to individual national markets, while the same basic product and price strategies may be used for all markets.

The interaction between product-line goals and environmental analysis affects strategies in a variety of areas, including technology, manufacturing, marketing, customer service, competitive policy, and management of government relations. As shown in Figure 14-1, linkages exist between marketing strategy and strategy in other areas. Firms' consideration of these linkages leads to a more integrated strategy and, thus, more successful international marketing.

In addition, the interdependence of many national markets must be considered: When do changes in one market dictate changes to marketing strategy in other markets? A firm may develop standardized global policies for a product line in some aspects of strategy, such as making antilock brakes standard on all cars that it sells. But when it comes to introducing newer technologies, a firm may adopt a regional policy of first introducing the technology into a select group of countries. For example, automobile firms first included GPS-based navigational systems on all luxury cars sold in the countries of the EU. Over time, the navigation systems were introduced on lower-priced cars. However, it may be some time before the navigation systems become available in mass-market cars destined for countries such as India or China. In other areas, such as advertising and promotion, the same firm might adopt national policies tailored to each market's profile.

Although it is difficult to categorize strategies, in essence, they all try to determine what customers around the world want and then to satisfy those desires better than the competition. The basic strategy thrust, following Porter's classic framework, is (1) becoming the lowest-cost producer and competing on the basis of low prices or (2) providing a differentiated product and competing on the basis of providing unique value to the customer or (3) avoiding competition and seeking government help to operate in protected markets.

Finally, strategies must be implemented if they are to be of use. How well they are implemented depends on organizational structure and personnel assigned to a given country. Once implementation has begun, feedback on results is essential to monitor the plan and to decide when and how it should be changed.

Cavusgil and Zou examined the link between strategy and performance for a sample of 79 firms across 16 industries involved directly in 202 export ventures.[7] They analyzed firms along several dimensions, including export marketing strategy, firm characteristics, product characteristics, industry characteristics, and export market characteristics. They found that firms achieved better export performance when management was internationally competent, was committed to the export venture, adapted the

Table 14-1. Perspectives on Global Marketing Strategy

Perspective	Basic Logic	Key Variables	Antecedents	Effects
Standardization perspective	Scale economies Low-cost Simplification	Product standardization Promotion standardization Standardized channel structure Standardized price	Convergence of cultures Similarity of demand Low trade barriers Technological advances Orientation of firm	Efficiency Consistency Transfer of ideas
Configuration-coordination perspective	Comparative advantage Interdependency Specialization	Concentration of value-chain activities Coordination of value-chain activities	Low trade barriers Technological advances Orientation of firm International experience	Efficiency Synergies
Integration perspective	Cross-subsidization Competitive delocation Rationalization	Integration of competitve moves Global market participation	Low trade barriers Orientation of firm International experience Integrated markets	Effectiveness in competition Competitive leverage

Source: S. Tamer Cavusgil and Shaoming Zou, "Marketing Strategy-Performance Relationship: An Investigation of the Empirical Link in Export Market Ventures," *Journal of Marketing*, Volume 58, January 1994, Table 1.

product to meet export customer requirements, and provided strong support to their foreign distributors and/or subsidiaries. Looking more broadly at global marketing strategy, Zou and Cavusgil[8] state that three different perspectives—standardization, configuration-coordination, and integration—all come together to formulate a global marketing strategy. Table 14-1 explains how those three different perspectives together provide a rounded view of global marketing strategy.

Egelhoff raises the point that performance may be affected by how well the strategy is implemented rather than by how brilliant or unique the strategy is.[9] He studied Japanese semiconductor firms; and over the time frame that he examined, he suggested that their superior performance was due to better strategy implementation of rather ordinary strategies. Of course, more recent evidence suggests that Japanese semiconductor firms concentrating on high-volume memory chips have been beset by Korean competition. At the same time, U.S. firms have prospered by moving into high-margin specialized microprocessor chips for graphics, telecommunications, and multimedia applications. The difficulty with relating strategy to performance, therefore, may lie partly in the time frame over which the results are evaluated.

Competitive Advantage

As Figure 14-1 shows, competitive advantage provides the basis for choosing a strategy. Competitive advantage is achieved by matching a firm's capabilities with the chain of value-added activities. That is, a product line or service emerges following the completion of a series of activities such as technology development, manufacturing, logistics, marketing, and after-sales service. A firm with a competitive advantage in one or more activities that constitute the value-added chain is able to make a long-term profit by specializing in those activities. Table 14-2 illustrates the application of the value-added chain to a hypothetical global firm.

The Basic Questions: Which Activities and Where?

In a global industry, a firm must decide not only what value-added activities it will carry out, but also where (in what countries) to carry out those activities. Thus, two decisions are being made:

1. The firm decides what activities it will specialize in and what activities it will subcontract, thus adopting a make-or-buy decision on each of the activities that constitute the value-added chain. For example, a firm in the running shoe business might decide to develop a new type of running shoe in-house in its laboratories, using its own equipment and scientists. Then it might provide product specifications and ask another company to manufacture the product. After receiving delivery of the shoes, the firm might carry out its own marketing campaign in major markets around the world. Thus, it controls the technology and marketing activities while subcontracting the manufacturing value-added activity.

2. The firm must also decide where it will carry out the value-added activities it has chosen. In this regard, principles of comparative advantage come into play in deciding what activities are most appropriately carried out in what countries. A country typically has a comparative advantage in activities that use large amounts of its abundant factor of production. For example, a country with large quantities of unskilled labor might be an appropriate site for manufacturing products that use unskilled labor, such as garments or shoes.

Table 14-2. The Firm and the Global Value-Added Chain

Countries/ Markets	Technology	Purchasing	Manufacturing	Logistics	Marketing	Service
United States	X		X	X	X	X
Europe			X	X	X	X
Japan	X			X	X	X
Southeast Asia		X	X		X	X
LDCs					X	X
Eastern Europe					X	
Others						

LDCs = less developed countries; X = firm carries out the value-added activity in that country.

Note: The above represents a hypothetical firm's choices about countries and value-added activities, that is, configuration and coordination.

Going back to the example of the running shoe company, suppose that the company decided to let another independent company manufacture the shoes based on its technology and design. With the addition of the country factory, the company could decide not to subcontract the manufacturing of shoes, deciding to manufacture the shoes itself in another low-wage country by making an investment and managing a running shoe factory. The company could add manufacturing to its value-added chain by carrying out the activity in a different country. Moreover, if the company decides to continue to subcontract the manufacturing, it must decide which country's manufacturers to use as a source of supply. In choosing between competing subcontractors in different countries, the company will consider low delivery costs, quality, timely delivery, and low risk of supplies being interrupted.

Companies within the same industry can take different approaches to the value-added chain. Kogut cites the examples of Panasonic and Radio Shack in the consumer electronics industry.[10] Another example of the configuration of the value-chain is provided by the laptop industry. Laptop manufacturers such as Hewlett-Packard design their laptops and the manufacturing subcontract to Taiwan-based Quanta Computer Inc. Hewlett-Packard often identifies the location from which specific components should be sourced, ordering the components and having them shipped to Quanta's assembly locations. Thus, Hewlett-Packard buys microprocessors from the United States (Intel, AMD, and others); graphics processors from the United States and Canada; hard-disk drives from Japan, Singapore, and (increasingly) China; memory chips from South Korea, Taiwan, the United States, and Germany; LCDs for the computer screen from South Korea, Japan, Taiwan, and China; and power supplies and magnesium casings from China. In turn, Quanta has moved all of its laptop assembly operations to China to take advantage of low-cost but increasingly skilled labor. Quanta ships the assembled computers to a U.S. hub such as Memphis. There the individual laptops are packed to be sent directly to the customers. In contrast, Dell Computer prefers to perform the final assembly itself, after buying partly built laptops from contract manufacturers. Dell's laptop manufacturing approach is dictated by its business model, which relies on building laptops and computers to each customer's individual specifications, developed at Dell's web site. Dell's ability to meet each customer's configuration may rest partly on having significant control of the final assembly step. Thus, in the same industry, two prominent manufacturers have split up the value chain differently, based on their chosen strategy.[11]

A firm's decision making within the value-added chain is not a one-time exercise. The firm must constantly assess the shifting nature of comparative advantages across countries and its own competitive advantage when compared to that of its competitors. A firm can stay globally competitive only when it constantly reexamines and then changes its global strategy as needed.

Environmental Change and Value-Added Choices

Comparative advantage can shift over time as economies grow and acquire technology, capital, and skilled labor. Companies must change their value-added configuration to accommodate those shifts. If wage costs are important to a firm's competitive advantage and wages rise in its present manufacturing location, the company must consider whether to shift manufacturing to another lower-cost location, as discussed in the following example.

Micromotors are used in products such as cameras; hair dryers; cordless tools; and cars to run adjustable mirrors, central door locks, and fuel injection systems. Hong Kong's Johnson Electric Ltd. is the world's second-largest producer of micromotors. Because wages in Hong Kong have risen at a rate of 15 to 20 percent a year, Johnson has subcontracted its labor-intensive processes to factories in China, where wages are one-fifth those in Hong Kong. Johnson supplies equipment, technology, and components; Chinese partners provide land, labor, and the factory building. Johnson ships components by truck in the morning and receives subassemblies back by evening, with final assembly and quality control performed in Hong Kong. That subcontracting has allowed Johnson to increase output by 60 percent while reducing the number of employees in Hong Kong. Johnson has invested in automated equipment in Hong Kong. It works closely with customers such as Black & Decker, Kodak, and Sunbeam to design specialized value-added motors. As Johnson grows, it continues to stress quality. The China connection allows it to take advantage of low costs in competing with Mabuchi Motor, the Japanese company that is the global industry leader.[12]

Configuration and Coordination of the Value-Added Chain

Combining value-added chain analysis with the complexities of global markets requires firms to make decisions about both configuration and coordination.[13] Configuration refers to the decision about where a firm's value-added activities are carried out. Once the activities have been spread out (configured) in different countries, the firm must coordinate the activities to manage them effectively. **Configuration** decisions can result in a company having a presence in more than one national market. Let's distinguish between a global perspective, a multidomestic perspective, and a (domestic) market-extension perspective.

The **market-extension** idea, which is typically the way in which a small firm becomes involved in international marketing, represents an unplanned and short-term exploitation of foreign markets while the domestic market remains the focus of the company. Products developed for the home market are sold in one or more overseas markets to obtain incremental revenue, with little planning of the role of foreign markets in the firm's overall strategy.

A **multidomestic** perspective represents a careful consideration of foreign markets, but with a clearly separate orientation toward each country market. That is, the firm approaches each market on its own terms, and little effort is made to capitalize on interdependencies between various markets. Such an approach may be consistent with the nature of consumers and line of business.

An example is Fidelity's entry into the Japanese money management market. The Japanese save a considerable portion of their income—about 20 percent. That savings represents a rich pool of funds to be tapped by financial service firms such as banks, insurance companies, money management firms, and mutual funds. However, Japanese pension fund regulations had prevented foreign money management firms from access to this pool of funds. In addition, foreign mutual funds were prohibited from marketing their foreign funds to the Japanese. They were required to set up separate mutual funds to be marketed in Japan, which prevented them from relying on and advertising their past performance.

Changed Japanese government regulations have opened up the pension fund management market to foreign firms, and foreign mutual funds now market funds in Japan without having to set up new Japanese units. U.S. firms such as Fidelity expect that marketing a standardized product that has been time-tested in the United States will help them win significant market share in Japan. Another factor likely to influence Japanese investors is that Japanese financial markets have performed poorly from 1990–2003. Japanese investors may be looking to U.S. funds for superior returns. (The Japanese market began to register positive returns in 2005 after a ten-year period of stagnation.) Of course, a strong yen and exchange-rate volatility can affect the returns from foreign investments. That volatility is a factor that firms such as Fidelity and Merrill Lynch will have to manage if they are to retain Japanese accounts.

Thus, Fidelity obtains economies of scale by realizing that its research on U.S. companies can be sold to both American and Japanese customers. Scale economies could also be obtained by combining product development for several markets, by developing a regional or global brand, by running common advertising themes, or by centralizing manufacturing for sale to several markets. A multidomestic perspective is generally appropriate for industries with low economies of scale and major differences in customer profiles across national markets. Sometimes governments force a company to adopt a narrow single-country approach, deliberately encouraging local responsiveness, particularly in critical industries such as telecommunications and software. In those cases, corporate strategy might accommodate government pressures. In return, a company might negotiate for favors such as protection against foreign competition and fiscal incentives. However, if competitors are acting globally, a fragmented nationally responsive strategy will be less successful in the long term.

A **global perspective** is one in which the firm directs special attention to the interdependence among national markets and competitors' actions in those markets when formulating its own strategic plans. Such an approach can lead to economies of scale in technology development, manufacturing, and marketing and in making the appropriate competitive responses.

In the early 1960s, Komatsu was a small manufacturer of a narrow line of earth-moving equipment of indifferent quality, selling mainly in a protected Japanese market. When Caterpillar sought to enter the Japanese market through a joint venture with Mitsubishi, Komatsu quickly signed technology licensing agreements with U.S. firms to upgrade its products. Next, Komatsu launched an internal program, first to match Caterpillar in quality and then to reduce costs. Komatsu's corporate slogan became "Encircle Caterpillar."

Komatsu began to sell its products extensively in neighboring Asian countries and to the Middle East and third world countries, where much infrastructure development was taking place. It next embarked on a factory automation program and a new product development program. It also set up dealer networks in Europe and the United States. By 1980, it had begun to capture market share in the United States. When the dollar began gaining value, Komatsu cut prices, increasing its U.S. market share to about 25 percent by 1984 while Caterpillar experienced losses. In 20 years, Komatsu had become number two in the world in earth-moving equipment, the result of a carefully balanced global strategy with equal attention given to (1) configuration of value-added activities across global markets and (2) coordination of those growing and far-flung activities.[14]

Despite the theoretical and conceptualization emphasis on globalization, few of the world's largest multinationals have been successful in marketing globally. Rugman and Verbeke analyzed the geographic distribution of sales of 320 large multinationals. They showed that just over 80 percent of sales, on average, came from the home regions of the triad markets.[15]

In practice, the world's multinationals end up practicing a regional strategy, even though their intent is global. That suggests that even the world's largest firms have a long way to go before they achieve true globalization in their marketing activities.

It is unrealistic to discuss global marketing strategy without considering the extent of international business development within a firm. That is, firms pass through stages of internationalization. A company must first decide whether to sell internationally. If the company does so, it must then decide what markets to enter, how to be competitive in the global arena, and what mode of entry to adopt for a particular market. In the next stage, a firm must consider multiple international markets. The company has to choose between consolidating its market position in foreign country markets where it already has a presence or extending its sales and marketing reach to additional countries. In the third stage, a firm becomes truly global when it is established in several countries. It then faces the task of developing synergies across markets in marketing, manufacturing, R&D, and service and begins to change organizational structures to coordinate marketing decisions and aspects of the marketing mix across countries. Figure 14-2 presents this contingency approach to developing global marketing strategy. It can be considered an overlay to Figure 14–1. Depending on the international sophistication and development of a firm, different aspects of strategy should be emphasized.[16]

Why Should Firms Think Globally?

The following list provides a summary of reasons to plan for global markets and to compete on a global basis:
- Markets
- Technology, especially patents
- Production resources
- Competition
- Customers
- Governments
- Time factor; that is, speed of response

Global Markets

Markets are one reason a firm should think globally. A global orientation can exploit major markets around the world. Post-World War II economic development created three areas of roughly equal economic size: United States-Canada, Europe, and Asia.

Each of those blocs represents roughly one-third of the world market, so a company that sells only in the United States is ignoring roughly two-thirds of the potential world market. Further, as markets grow more alike, especially in developed countries, additional sales in Europe and Japan can be gained with a product that may have been initially designed for the U.S. market.

Figure 14-2. Phases in Global Market Evolution

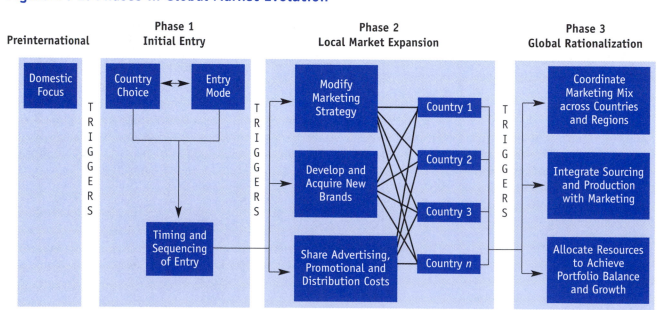

Source: Susan P. Douglas and C. Samuel Craig, "Evolution of Global Marketing Strategy," *Columbia Journal of World Business* Volume 24, no. 3 (Fall 1989). Copyright 1989. Used with permission.

The point is that there is a convergence of national markets, with European, Japanese, and U.S. markets for certain products displaying similar profiles. Hence, selling simultaneously to all of those markets can maximize sales, particularly when a company has introduced its products ahead of the competition. Overhead costs can be spread out over a larger volume base, allowing the firm to charge a lower price. When sales volume in the United States exceeds the breakeven point, R&D and other fixed costs have been amortized. In that case, a firm can capture a larger market share in overseas markets by charging lower prices because product-development costs have been recovered.

Most multinationals that market globally depend on certain critical markets for a stable source of profits and cash flow—usually their home market and other markets in which they have been long established. To have a global orientation, a firm must look beyond its familiar markets and recognize the need for a market presence in all major national markets, thereby protecting its position in the critical markets.

Certain markets are highly innovative "lead" markets.[17] A presence in a lead market helps a firm refine its products and services and learn lessons that can be transferred to other markets. Innovative ideas are not all that abundant, so being able to leverage new ideas across markets gives a global company an advantage over its national or regional competitors. As an example of the use of lead markets, large Japanese manufacturers and trading companies have made sizable equity investments in high-tech start-ups in California's Silicon Valley. Aside from an ownership share, the start-ups generally obtain exclusive product distribution rights for Japan and access to advanced technology. A small U.S. company benefits from the possibility of selling to the large but difficult Japanese market. However, a Japanese firm can license the technology and begin manufacturing in Japan, thus readying itself for the product cycle stage when low-cost competitors gain a competitive edge.

Global Technology Markets

One characteristic of lead markets is their function as a showcase for new technologies. Technology, a resource, is a critical element of the value-added chain, as are raw materials and skilled labor. Certainly, technology is an essential factor for firms seeking to compete in world markets using a differentiated product strategy thrust. Technology is expensive to develop, but patents can protect a firm's investment, allowing it to recoup development costs and make a profit.

U.S. firms that export products based on intellectual property rights suffer when their technological rights are pirated. Piracy reduces exports as well as domestic sales when imports based on pirated IP enter the United States. A 2002 estimate indicated that the piracy rate in China for U.S. films, home video, and television programs was about 91 percent! Piracy of DVDs in Russia was estimated at 92 percent in 2003.[18]

Global Production Resources

Production resources are another reason to think globally. Global sourcing of raw materials and scarce commodities can result in their timely delivery and reduced cost. A global strategy also allows firms to plan manufacturing configuration across countries to take advantage of the availability of another resource. That resource is labor, whether it be cheap unskilled labor or high-quality, technically skilled, and expensive labor (such as large pools of trained scientists). The laptop manufacturing example discussed earlier is a result of global production and logistics strategy.

Global Competition

A global competitor that is strong and unchallenged in its home market can undercut its competitors in their strong markets by deliberately channeling resources into those markets. The competitor buys market share with price cuts and accepts low profits (or even losses) for a while. Such threats can be countered only by similar tactics from a similar global position. That exchange of threats, or **cross-patrolling**, helps maintain the balance of power while firms go about further strengthening their competitive advantages. A global presence helps firms plan for both offensive and defensive strategic responses, as circumstances warrant.

Game theory can be useful in developing strategic competitive responses in international marketing through the development of both competitive and cooperative strategies.[19] To develop such strategies, firms need to develop a schematic map of all major global competitors and their interdependencies. Then before attempting strategy changes, the firm must identify how game players add value, the rules and tactics that each player follows, and the scope of those tactics.

TIME-BASED GLOBAL COMPETITION
Time is becoming an important factor in global competition. Speedy introduction of new products and rapid response to competitive actions are essential to maintain competitive strength. The ability to respond speedily is heightened when a firm has a global presence because it can draw on resources, ideas, and personnel from a variety of national markets.

Honda exemplifies that behavior. When faced with stiff competition from Yamaha in motorcycles, Honda responded by introducing 113 new models in just 18 months, equal to changing its entire product line twice over. Those rapid model changes had several consequences:

- Motorcycles came to be judged on fashion, with consumers expecting newness and freshness.
- Honda brought technology to the forefront, with four-valve engines, composite materials, direct drive, and other features.
- Although the number of new product introductions forced Honda's sales and service networks to work overtime, its bewildering variety of models left Yamaha in the dust, with over 12 months' inventory at one point. As Stalk put it, "Variety had won the war."[20]

How was Honda able to introduce over 100 models in 18 months? By managing time well, using flexible manufacturing and rapid-response systems, and stepping up the pace of innovation. Why does time-based competition work? Customers are willing to pay high prices for new products introduced in a timely fashion. Even small innovations introduced frequently can be appealing to consumers and can aid in sharpening product differentiation. If the customers are using just-in-time techniques, they are willing to pay more for timely delivery. Another reason is that a firm capable of speedy product development, manufacturing, and delivery can reduce costs by saving on inventory (particularly work in progress) and working capital. Time-based competition asks how quickly a product can be made for a given quality and price. Stalk believes that Japanese companies compete on the basis of time. The firm that gains competitive advantage is the one that can implement new product introductions quickly, manufacture a variety of products efficiently, move swiftly to sales and distribution, and do all of that faster than the competition.[21]

Global Customers

Customers also play a role in influencing a firm's global orientation. As customers become global, their first impulse is to continue to do business with established suppliers. For example, Hitachi Ltd. had sold few of its large mainframe computers in the United States. But when its Japanese customers started building factories and opening offices in the United States, Hitachi expanded its U.S. presence to maintain its relationships with those clients. Hitachi planned to use its U.S. operations to win business from new Japanese clients, such as the Japanese auto parts makers who followed the Japanese auto firms, and from firms such as Nomura Securities, which has been expanding its U.S. brokerage operations. To serve a potentially larger market, Hitachi expanded product development and

marketing in the United States, creating new software and augmenting consulting operations for Japanese clients. Such relationship building is particularly important in industrial marketing. But similar motivations can be found in consumer-oriented companies; for example, *The Wall Street Journal* began marketing a European edition partly because of the growing number of American managers in Europe. (Another factor was that European demand for American business news and stock quotes was growing.)

Government Actions

Government actions can have a big influence on global strategy. For example, governments can strengthen competitive advantage by subsidizing national firms. Such support can be helpful in the early stages of an industry's development, reducing risk and augmenting scarce resources.

Subsidies estimated at about $25 billion since the inception of Airbus in 1972 have allowed the European consortium firm to offer a family of new commercial jet aircraft. Without the subsidies, Airbus would have been unable to fund the development of its new models, the A320, the A330, the A340, and the "superjumbo" jet A380. Internal cash flow would have been inadequate because Airbus had not made a profit from its inception until 2003.[22] (and see Case Study 10.1)

Governments may also participate directly in competition through **state-owned enterprises (SOEs)**. Managers of those enterprises do not have to worry about profits because the companies are backed by the deep pockets of the national treasury. SOEs often have objectives such as maintaining employment and earning foreign exchange, which may lead to behavior quite at odds with maximizing profits. Private firms competing against these government-owned enterprises must worry about maintaining long-term profitability. In competing with Airbus, for instance, Boeing must maintain enough profits that allow it to set aside $10 billion or more to develop next-generation aircraft following the successful launch of the 777. Boeing does get some subsidies from the U.S. government for developing military aircraft and systems, but they are insufficient for financing the bulk of Boeing's research spending.

Corporate Goals and Global Strategy

Global strategy differs among multinational firms according to whether:

- The dominant orientation is short-term or long-term.
- Profits and return on investment are willingly sacrificed in return for higher market share.

- Global or national competitive position is more influential in determining competitive strategy and response.
- Time is given priority as a key goal, with corporations giving strategic importance to the timely formulation and implementation of strategy.

Modes of Global Competition

Are there standard approaches to global competition? In a broad sense, yes. That is, competition is based on low costs, offers differentiated products, and seeks protected markets.

COMPETING AS A LOW-COST PRODUCER

If a firm can produce its product or service at a lower cost than competitors, yet achieve comparable quality, it can lower its prices and still make an adequate profit. Or it can charge the same prices as its competitors and make higher profits because its costs are lower.

Low-cost production is typically linked to high-volume production. Economies of scale reduce costs; learning and experience curve factors also lead to cost reduction. **Learning curve economies** result from workers becoming more productive as they work at a job longer and learn from mistakes. Similarly, **experience curve economies** result from learning to better manage a line of business. As accumulated production grows, a company can manage its machines better, can reduce overhead, and typically finds that average cost per unit declines with each doubling of accumulated volume of production. Low cost and high market share are closely linked because the large market share allows for large-volume production.

COMPETING WITH DIFFERENTIATED PRODUCTS

Some firms rely on attracting customers with products that their competitors do not offer. Such differentiated products may have superior design or better performance, better quality and reliability, or more durability; they may be backed by better service; or they may simply appeal more to the consumer for aesthetic and psychological reasons. Examples abound: When initially faced with competition from Komatsu, Caterpillar said that its prices, which were 10 to 15 percent higher than Komatsu's, reflected the higher quality and value offered. When a luxury automobile such as BMW or Mercedes-Benz sells for over $80,000, the price reflects superior engineering and performance as well as a certain cachet. Buyers are willing to pay extra for the prestige a luxury automobile seems to bestow.

Firms competing on that basis must monitor world markets to ensure that the features that differentiate their product have not been copied by competitors. They must constantly work on new features because what is a differentiated product today will soon become a commodity. A global competitor must constantly stay ahead of the pack;

GLOBAL MARKETING

Corporate Goals and Global Strategy: Whirlpool in Europe

For most of its existence and through the eighties, Whirlpool was a U.S.-based manufacturer headquartered in rural Benton Harbor, Michigan. It focused mainly on selling to the U.S. market. Whirlpool acquired KitchenAid to enter the premium market; it also acquired Roper to gain entry in the value-oriented segment. However, Whirlpool saw little market share growth and slim margins in the U.S. market because of growing competition and concentration. The formation of the EU gave Whirlpool the impetus to consider expanding into the European market, with Asia as its second priority. Europe was attractive both for its consumer income levels and market size. It was also attractive because it had many small manufacturers and because the fragmented European industry would likely begin to consolidate in a fashion similar to that in the United States. Whirlpool reasoned that its experience in the consolidating U.S. market would help it be a winner in Europe. The company also believed that being an "insider" in Europe was essential, with established distribution and local market knowledge. Because a new independent venture would be expensive and time-consuming, Whirlpool began to look for a partner with the following parameters:

- *Strength in three core product areas: laundry, refrigeration, and cooking appliances.*
- *A strong presence across major European markets; Philips, for instance, was the second-largest manufacturer in Europe.*
- *A strong brand image across all segments; Philips had four brands (Philips, Bauknecht, Ignis, and Laden), all of which had a reputation for quality.*
- *Technological capabilities; Philips was strong in no-frost capability, insulation, and built-in appliances.*
- *A cultural fit with Whirlpool's managerial philosophy and practices.*

Based on the above factors, in 1989, Whirlpool initiated a joint venture with the Dutch Philips company. In 1991, Whirlpool acquired the firm from Philips, instantly transforming itself into a company that was rapidly globalizing. A plus

continued

was that Philips had a strong international presence with worldwide operations and sales, including an agreement with China. Whirlpool was then faced with the challenge of integrating European operations into a global framework. Whirlpool CEO David Whitwam described the need to unify two "parochial margin-driven" companies into "customer-focused organizations."

Whirlpool saw a competitive advantage in understanding how customers viewed the product, seeing products such as the microwave and kitchen range as part of appliances helping in better food preparation. From its usability lab in Italy, Whirlpool learned that consumers wanted a microwave to brown food, which led to the introduction of the best-selling VIP Crisp model. Whirlpool's challenge was to take the best practices wherever they arose and integrate them across its worldwide organization. As an example, the new entity adopted the European Philips' focus on ISO 9000 quality processes and integrated them with the U.S. focus on the Baldridge awards, together with ideas from other Whirlpool units from around the world. It then created a set of quality standards titled the "Whirlpool Excellence System."

In part, that meant developing common technology and manufacturing processes, then allowing regional manufacturing and marketing organizations to adapt product features and dimensions to local needs. An example is the formation of cross-border product development teams. For example, the CFC-free refrigerator was developed with insulation technology from Europe, compressor technology from Brazil, and manufacturing and design expertise from the United States.

The fundamental change was in organizational culture, convincing employees that they needed to learn to think glob-

ally. Above all, Whirlpool did not want to impose U.S. values or approaches on its worldwide organization. Whitwam commented that Whirlpool must avoid "the temptation to build Rome in a day . . . You may own the land but not the builders." The change involved a several-stage process. In Asia, for example, the local unit first learned about local consumers, building up local sales and overall capabilities. Then it built a regional distribution system centered around three regional offices: one for Singapore and Southeast Asia, another for greater China, and a third for Japan. That was followed by a design, engineering, and development center in Singapore, eventually extending to a manufacturing center in Asia.

At the same time, Whirlpool rationalized and unified European and U.S. operations and developed pan-European design teams that worked with U.S. designers on products sharing common platforms. That allowed distinct products such as the high-end Bauknecht, the broad-based Whirlpool brand, and the utilitarian Ignis all to share common interior components, saving costs. By 1996, Whirlpool expected 85 percent of its European appliances to share a common platform. Other rationalization moves included reducing European warehouses from 36 to 8, developing integrated regional European companies, cutting the number of Philips' suppliers by half, and rebranding products so former Philips' brand products were all sold under the Whirlpool name.

Sources: Regina Fazio Maruca, "The Right Way to Go Global: An Interview with Whirlpool CEO David Whitwam," *Harvard Business Review*, March/April 1994, pages 134–145; "Call It Worldpool," Business Week, November 28, 1994; and David Whitwam, "Whirlpool's Approach to the New Europe," *Journal of European Business*, September/October 1990, pages 5–8.

otherwise, the basis of its competitive advantage disappears. Once a product has become a commodity, the lowest-cost competitor will win.

COMPETING BY SEEKING PROTECTED MARKETS

Mentioned earlier was the fact that government is a key factor affecting global competition. One mode of competition, therefore, is to rely on government protection against foreign competition. That protection buys a company time by holding the efficient competitor at bay until the firm can lower its costs or develop a differentiated product. If the firm fails at those attempts, it can at least make a profit until the foreign competitor figures out a way to evade the protectionist barrier, perhaps by setting up manufacturing and sales facilities within the protected

sales market. Once that happens, of course, the inefficient, protected firm disappears.

Airbus was mentioned earlier as a firm receiving government subsidies and protection. After being in operation for 18 years, Airbus finally launched a commercially successful product, the A320, which received enough orders to take it beyond the breakeven point. Airbus seems to have used protection wisely to develop a family of competitive aircraft. In 1992, the U.S. and European governments agreed that subsidies for new aircraft development should not exceed 30 percent of producer costs. However, it is difficult to monitor implementation of such accords. The United States and the EU are disputing Airbus's intent to seek subsidies of 30 percent for the development of its newest plane, the A350, expected to cost $5 billion in R&D.

Where Do Global Competitors Come From?

New firms are constantly augmenting the pool of potential competitors. They do so through market extension, extension of product lines into new market segments, and forward or backward integration by suppliers. Competitors often emerge from their domestic markets to begin challenging established firms in major foreign markets. Komatsu emerged as a global competitor in that fashion. Firms from countries such as South Korea have begun competing in consumer electronics industries, where companies such as Samsung and the LG Group have gained market share in color televisions, cell phones, flat-panel displays, and semiconductors. In that case, market extension forms the basis for the entry of new competitors. South Korean companies have extended their reach to global markets after solidifying their position at home.

Firms may also diversify into new product markets to emerge as potent competitors. Examples abound in the biotech area, which is rich in small R&D-oriented start-up companies. It takes years to complete the research and to shepherd new drug applications through the FDA process, finally getting approval, after which time an approved drug may be marketed as a high-priced pharmaceutical. Large companies such as Pfizer have their own R&D labs. However, they are aware that their pace of innovation has slowed while it has become more costly and time-consuming to develop new blockbuster drugs. At the same time, the likelihood exists that a start-up biotech research outfit will develop innovative new drugs. Hence, it is becoming common for major pharmaceutical companies to take stakes in new biotech firms, often acquiring them if their R&D results in successful new drugs with sizable markets.

Existing competitors may also extend their product lines to enter new market segments. Japanese auto firms in the United States have followed that policy. Honda was the first; its high-priced Acura was marketed for the luxury car segment in the United States. Honda's action was promptly followed by Nissan and Toyota, with their Infiniti and Lexus lines, respectively. Such product extension moves by the Japanese auto industry affect the market share of Cadillac and Lincoln, as well as Mercedes, Volvo, Saab, and BMW.

Finally, competition can also develop from forward or backward integration by suppliers. That is happening in semiconductors. Manufacturers of memory chips and microprocessors are deciding to incorporate their semiconductor components into board-level and systems products, thus selling complete systems as opposed to components. Besides manufacturing digital imaging semiconductors, Omnivision is also is a leader in using those semiconductors in complete but inexpensive digital camera modules that can be incorporated into cell phones, giving them higher-quality picture-taking capabilities.

Such moves not only create competition for the cell phone manufacturing firm, but also affect its logistics position by creating uncertainty of supply. When shortages of critical components develop, will the supplier (Omnivision) prefer to feed its own manufacturing lines?

Assessing Global Competition

Global strategy must include a careful study of sources of competition and the likely responses of individual competitors in global markets. That analysis usually begins with an assessment of a competitor's strengths and weaknesses, its goals, and the way it should respond to the firm's actions. Much depends on the balance of competitive power; that is, whether the competitor is a leader in a particular product/market area. The same firm may hold a dominant market position in one national market and play catch-up in another. And within the same country/market, a firm may be a leader in one product line and hold a minor market share in another product line. Thus, how a firm reacts depends on its market position—whether it is a market leader; whether it seeks to challenge the market leader; or whether it is a follower, holding a small market position and using niche strategies to hold on to its market share.

A special place in global competition is held by **national champions**—firms that have dominant positions in their national markets and often receive government support. In the European auto industry, Fiat in Italy and Peugeot and Renault in France enjoy such a position, with their dominant market share in their home markets partly attributable to regulations that restrict Japanese auto imports. With continuing European integration, the position of nationally dominant firms becomes less secure as it becomes harder for national governments to justify favored treatment of national companies in a unifying Europe.

Impact of Government Actions on Strategy

Sometimes national governments come to the aid of their national champion firms, especially in industries in which a national presence is deemed important. As previously mentioned, the French government was eager to promote the merger of Sanofi with Aventis, both French drug companies, as a way of creating a French pharmaceutical company that would be among the world's largest. The government was quick to prevent any attempt by Aventis to find a merger partner in the open market, even after Novartis announced its willingness to explore such a merger at an attractive stock price.[23]

Much of what has been said about global strategy formulation assumes free markets. Government intervention in international business is quite common, however; and firms must temper their global strategies to accommodate government actions that serve to fragment a global outlook. Doz and Prahalad describe the juggling act in which corporations must engage in order to handle the conflicting demands of global integration and national responsiveness.[24] Changes in product and process technology, economies of scale, national factor cost advantages, and global distribution all require a global stance. Yet political processes and the interventionist policies of governments require firms to modify their global integration policies and accommodate government demands. That is, the underlying thrust is still global strategy, but temporary and shifting local accommodations are necessary for business to continue.

An example is Nissan in Europe, which faced problems due to protectionist pressures from European governments. Japanese automakers voluntarily agreed to restrict their European exports, with an import ceiling in the United Kingdom of about 11 percent of the total market and an even lower 3 percent share of the French market. In response, Nissan opened a small factory in Northern England, producing about 50,000 cars a year, with some of the output being exported to other European countries. Local content is about 70 percent; that is, the value-added chain in Britain accounts for about 70 percent of the car's value. France would not accept exports of those cars as European products, however, classifying them instead as Japanese autos subject to the 3 percent ceiling. An industry association headed by Umberto Agnelli of Fiat suggested that autos should have at least 80 percent local content to be classified as European.

France's two manufacturers, Renault and Peugeot, accounted for 23 percent of the market; and about one job in ten in France still relies, either directly or indirectly, on the auto industry. That may explain France's opposition to the Nissan imports from Britain. Imported Japanese parts used in engine assembly in Britain are being replaced with British-made parts. Nissan could obtain higher economies of scale if complete engines were imported from Japan because volume in a Japanese plant would be higher. The sacrifice of cost economies, however, is the price in terms of national responsiveness that Nissan paid to gain access to the European market.

Global Marketing Strategies

Clearly, global marketing strategy cannot be separated from overall corporate strategy. Decisions about technology, new product development, and manufacturing inevitably affect marketing decisions and marketing suc-

cess. Thus, a corporate strategy focused on time-based competition and speedy innovation requires a marketing division to plan for continued introduction of new products and to relay timely feedback on customer information to the product development department to help speed the innovation process. If a firm decides to focus on being the lowest-cost producer, low selling price becomes an essential element of the global marketing mix.

Standardization or Adaptation: Impact of Differences among National Markets

Keeping in mind the linkages between a firm's overall global strategy and global marketing strategy, a decision must be made between standardization and adaptation to local markets. Management complexity is reduced when a completely standardized marketing mix is applied without change to all national markets. Usually, some local adaptations are necessary to accommodate differences in consumer tastes, income levels, government regulations, and differences in distribution channels and structure of competition. In a broad review of a large number of scholarly studies on this topic, Theodosiou and Leonidou concluded that whether a firm will standardize or adapt largely depends on the specific circumstances of a particular foreign market at a specific point in time.[25]

When trying to decide what degree of adaptation is appropriate, a firm must consider the factors that distinguish between different national markets:

- Buyer profiles differ across countries; taste, income, culture, and buying decision processes are different.
- The marketing infrastructure differs from country to country, different kinds of media are available in different countries, and differences exist in what products and messages are acceptable in advertising.
- Variations in countries' transportation and communications systems affect marketing approaches, such as the use of mail order. Different legal provisions may govern conditions of sale.
- Distribution systems differ in the number of layers and in ease of access, and differences in the physical environment of various national markets may dictate changes in product design and sale.

Szymanski and his coauthors used the Yip framework of globalization drivers and strategy levers to formulate a model linking standardization to business performance; that is, to market share and profitability. (This model is described in Figure 14-3.) Their research covered U.S., UK, Canadian, and European markets. They found that "businesses may be better off standardizing their strategic resource mix to capture the benefits purported to be asso-

Figure 14-3. Global Drivers, Strategy Levers, and Business Performance

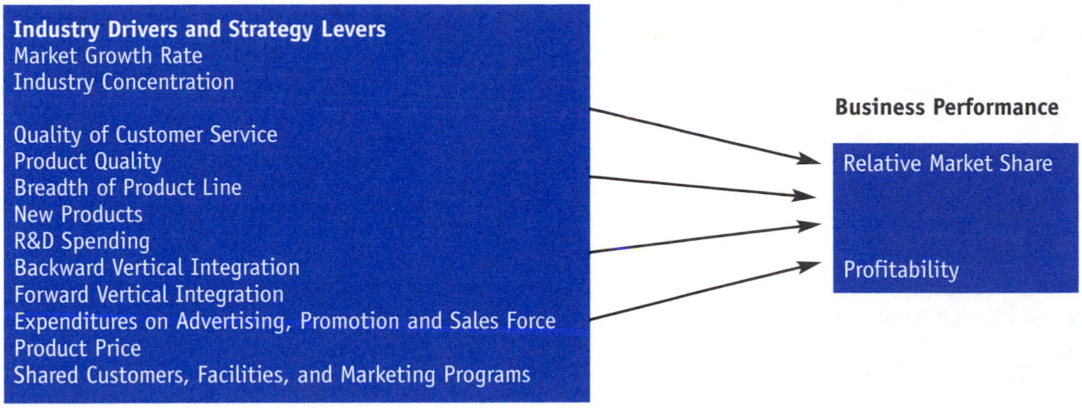

Industry Drivers and Strategy Levers
Market Growth Rate
Industry Concentration

Quality of Customer Service
Product Quality
Breadth of Product Line
New Products
R&D Spending
Backward Vertical Integration
Forward Vertical Integration
Expenditures on Advertising, Promotion and Sales Force
Product Price
Shared Customers, Facilities, and Marketing Programs

Business Performance
Relative Market Share

Profitability

Source: Figure 2 in D. Szymanski, S.G. Bharadwaj, and P.R. Varadarajan, "Standardization versus Adaptation of International Marketing Strategy," *Journal of Marketing* 57 (October, 1993), 4.

ciated with a standardized approach to serving multiple markets."[26] They also found that "offering a broad product line and selling high-quality products with high levels of customer service seem to be especially conducive to superior market share performance." They found, too, that marketing communications (advertising, promotion, etc.) was crucial to capturing market share, creating brand loyalty, and lowering susceptibility to price promotions by competitors. Laroche and others have similarly formulated a model to approach standardization of advertising in multinational corporations.[27]

Some Adaptation Is Necessary

The real question is not whether to adapt, but how much to adapt. Some elements of the marketing mix are more likely to be standardized than others. The basic product probably needs to be standardized in order to permit economies of scale in its manufacture. Firms are also likely to standardize brand names and the basic advertising message. Adaptation is more likely in areas such as packaging, pricing, sales promotion and media decisions, distribution channels, and after-sales service. Although management is motivated to standardize in order to reduce costs and management complexity, satisfying consumers in different markets and responding to competition should be the main criteria. Government restrictions can also circumscribe the degree of standardization possible. Hexter, Perez, and Perkins show that the same firm can adopt different strategies in a particular market (in this case, China) for different product lines.[28] They cite Danone's example, which used:

- A premium skimming strategy for its Evian water.
- A high-end market development approach for its Amoy line of foods. (Amoy was acquired by Danone.)

- A value-for-money proposition for the Danone biscuits line.

Hexter, Perez, and Perkins suggest that strategic success has a lot to do with choosing the right product line. That product line is characterized by immediate acceptance by a large base of consumers, high affordability, and robust economics to provide profit for market leaders even as competition increases. Products whose industries are marked by overcapacity or falling prices or those that require increasing amounts of promotional expenditures are unlikely to offer attractive profits. Achieving scale economies is also important, and firms may be better off investing in marketing and sales organization rather than hard assets. Finally, brand equity is helpful, particularly for first movers, in creating a sustainable competitive advantage.

The Global Marketing System

Doz and Prahalad (cited earlier) stress the importance of managing the global marketing system.[29] They focus on managing net prices in various markets in order to control global cash flow. The global marketing system, in their view, has three components:

- Presence in multiple markets in order to take advantage of their differences—that is, use high prices and cash flow in markets where the firm is dominant and competition is weak in order to subsidize market penetration by charging lower prices in other markets. (Of course, this assumes that leakage back into high-priced markets [of low-priced products introduced into new markets] is not a danger.)
- Global brand presence and strong distribution to help achieve target prices in various markets.
- Deployment of extended product lines and product

families across countries to gain economies of scope and greater competitive strength and allow opportunities for cross-subsidization across businesses and national markets.

Coordinating the Global Marketing System

As mentioned earlier, coordination of global marketing activities is as essential as configuring marketing activities across national markets. Table 14-3 summarizes various coordination issues, highlighting the adaptation-standardization dichotomy for various elements that enter into formulating a global marketing strategy.

Such coordination can take place in the following ways:[30]

- *Using similar methods to carry out marketing activities across countries.* Examples include Avon's door-to-door sales of cosmetics in different markets and companies' use of similar standards for warranty and after-sales service across countries.
- *Transferring marketing know-how and experience from one country to another.* This is particularly true in transferring information gained in lead markets to other countries.
- *Sequencing marketing programs.* This ensures that suc-cessful elements are gradually introduced into different markets, often in conjunction with evolution of the product life cycle in the various markets.
- *Integrating efforts across countries.* This ensures that international clients with operations in many countries can be offered the same service in each country. For example, a client may want to use the same computer equipment or software at all of its international subsidiaries. Closing that sale could require coordinating the sales effort in key markets where the largest subsidiaries are located. A clincher might be offering worldwide service with a maximum response time of 48 hours.

Organization Structure and Global Marketing Strategy

Strategy implementation occurs through managerial actions, and the roles and responsibilities of managers are delineated through the company's organization structure. If a firm's organization structure does not fit its strategy, implementation may suffer. Vorhies and Morgan found that marketing organization fit with strategic type is associated with marketing effectiveness in firms pursuing a variety of strategies, whether they be the prospector, defender, or analyzer type strategies.[31] Their model is shown in Figure 14-4.

Table 14-3. Global Marketing Strategy Choices

	Total Standardization					Complete Adaptation
New Product Development/ Product Line	X					
Marketing Mix						
Product Positioning					X	
Market Segmentation			X			
Brand Policy	X					
Packaging					X	
Advertising and Promotion		X				
Distribution Channels						X
Pricing				X		
Customer Service		X				
Country Markets						
Market 1	X					
Market 2			X			
•						
•						
•						
Market *n*						X

X = a hypothetical firm's choice.

Source: Adapted from John Queilch and E. Hoff, "Customizing Global Marketing," *Harvard Business Review,* May–June 1986.

Apple and the PC Industry

*A*pple has long distinguished itself in the personal computer world by making and selling computers based on a proprietary operating system standard. Until 1995, the company was unwilling to license its operating system to other manufacturers seeking to manufacture Apple-compatible clones. Because it had no clone competitors to innovate hardware and software advances, it had to spend more on R&D to keep up with developments in the industry. Apple must spread its R&D costs over the unit volume of computers sold; and because Apple held less than 3 percent of the total personal computer market as of 2003, its unit R&D cost was high.

Apple's early technological lead of a graphical user interface, the suitability of desktop publishing, the use of images, and digital video production and editing allowed the company to charge premium prices. But as the Intel/Windows standard began catching up and offering roughly comparable performance at lower prices, Apple found it hard to convince customers to pay a higher price for the privilege of using the Mac standard.

APPLE'S STRATEGIC PROBLEMS

For Apple to recover market share in global markets, it had to address solutions to several issues.

- Apple's R&D costs as a percentage of sales are high in relation to the Wintel standard.
- Apple incurs high marketing costs, about 15 percent of sales, to push and sustain the Apple brand; marketing costs of manufacturers of personal computers are 10 to 11 percent.
- Differentiation is being reduced as Microsoft's Windows XP became as easy to use as the Apple operating system.
- Computers in general are becoming a commodity; as a result, margins are falling.
- Apple has been forced to cut prices in the United States and elsewhere to compete against Wintel, cutting margins despite higher costs. As a result, its gross margins are under pressure.

- Once customers are lost to the Wintel standard, they do not come back because of lower prices and the investments in software and learning. They also become accustomed to the multiplicity of vendors from whom they can buy products and software.
- Apple is weak in the business market, a higher-end market segment with greater likelihood of repeat purchases and product upgrading.
- On occasion, Apple has experienced shortages of units in the retail channel at crucial selling seasons because it has underestimated demand.

As Apple declined through the 1990s and into the new millennium, the company went through several CEOs before calling back founder Steve Jobs (for the third time) as its new CEO. Jobs spun off several Apple products, including Newton, a handheld palmtop organizer, and concentrated on a newly designed Mac that would parallel the performance of the IBM PC-compatible world. His bold new design, transparent housing, green-gray color, and overall radically innovative look, coupled with a competitive price, won back many Apple fans.

Then Apple introduced its iPod and the iTunes service from which to download music legally. Those products have been enormous successes. The iPod has considerable memory capable of holding thousands of songs, it is elegant and compact, and it is easy to use. In addition, the iPod has a large store of downloadable music in a unique proprietary format. This allowed Apple to charge high prices and command attractive margins, thus regaining profitability while diversifying away from its personal computer base. As Apple attempts to spread its iPod franchise globally, it has to await governmental regulation of the downloadable music arena and conduct negotiations to license music that customer prefer in each major market. The heart of its marketing has been differentiation to the point of uniqueness, protected by proprietary standards and patents, and products that met consumer needs. That combination is difficult to achieve but is capable of obtaining huge success (and profits) when done right.

Sources: "Musical Chairs with the Big Boys," *New York Times*, March 4, 2004; "European Download Blues," *Wall Street Journal*, November 10, 2003; "EU Investigates 'Societies' Licensing Online Music," *Wall Street Journal*, May 4, 2004; "Apple Is Facing Widespread Shortages of Its Products," *Wall Street Journal*, August 11, 1995; and "Apple's Likely Loss May Spur Cutbacks, Merger," *Wall Street Journal*, December 18, 1995.

Figure 14-4. The Fit of Marketing Organization and Strategy

Source: Douglas W. Vorhies and Neil A. Morgan, "A Configuration Theory Assessment of Marketing Organization Fit with Business Strategy and Its Relationship with Marketing Performance," *Journal of Marketing*, Volume 67, January 2003, pages 100–105, Figure 1.

Targeting Individual Country Markets

Because management must determine the sequence in which to enter various global markets, an essential ingredient of global marketing is to assess the attractiveness of global markets. Criteria include current size and growth prospects, the product life cycle stage in the market, level of competition, similarity to existing markets, and the extent of government restrictions.

Corporate Goals and Choice of Markets

A firm's objectives help it decide which markets are attractive, as shown in Table 14-4. Three kinds of objectives are apparent:

- Short-term and long-term returns on investment in the form of profits and cash flow
- Market-share objectives, aimed partly at maintaining competitive balance and serving to provide credibility when exchanging threats with key global competitors
- Entry into lead markets, with learning objectives paramount, at least initially (A special case may be

protected markets; but even in that case, entry is based on attractive economic returns or on a global competitor's impact of gaining market share in the protected market.)

Firms primarily interested in profits seek high-growth markets where they encounter less competition and obtain higher margins. The firms may consider early entry into protected markets.

Firms that aggressively challenge their competitors prioritize markets based on growth and on market share held by key competitors. They enter markets that offer a chance of achieving reasonable market share, which can then be used as a deterrent in cross-patrolling (exchanging threats) with key global competitors. Firms seeking to establish a presence in lead markets choose markets based on growth prospects and product life cycle stage, but give little attention to competitors' market share or their own profit and prospects for market share. Firms seeking to enter protected markets first evaluate the likelihood of establishing cordial relations and favorable treatment from the local government.

A firm may have different objectives for different markets. Typically, it seeks strong profits and cash flow from one or two critical markets, including its home market. For emerging markets in which the competition is strong, it might adopt objectives for market share and competitive balance. Simultaneously, it might seek protected markets in large developing countries. Firms find it easy to devel-

Table 14-4. Market Characteristics and Corporate Objectives

	Goal			
Market Characteristics	Competitive Response/ Retaliation	Cash Flow/ Profits	Market Share	Lead Market Entry
Size/Market Potential				
Growth Prospects				
Margins				
Product Life Cycle Stage				
Similarity to Existing Markets				
Level of Competition				
Basis of Competition:				
Value-Added Chain Emphasis				
Government Attitudes				

op an integrated global strategy, however, by consciously tailoring objectives to country market characteristics. Risk perception and risk balancing play a considerable part in foreign market entry strategies. Brouthers suggests an integrated approach to risk management, wherein balancing high- and low-risk areas such as political and financial risk is appropriate.[32]

Market Positioning in the Triad Economies

When considering what national markets to enter, most firms seek to balance their market position in three major regional markets: North America, consisting of the United States, Canadian, and Mexican markets; Europe, variously called the Single Market and the European Union (even Euroland); and the Japan/Southeast Asia market, consisting of the high-income Japanese market and the fast-growing neighboring countries of China, Taiwan, Hong Kong, South Korea, Singapore, Thailand, and Malaysia. Those market regions are sometimes referred to as the **triad economies**. The former Communist nations of Eastern Europe represent another group of markets with considerable potential, particularly now that many of them have joined the EU. Certain nations and industries manifest a pattern in their expansion into foreign markets. For example, U.S. companies typically begin overseas expansion by branching into Canada, the United Kingdom, and then Europe. Studies of Japanese companies show distinct patterns of overseas market expansion. They typically begin by establishing themselves in the domestic Japanese market. Then one pattern of expansion is to refine international strategies in the developing countries neighboring Japan before moving into developed country markets such as the United States. That pattern has marked Japanese expansion in steel, petrochemicals, automobiles, watches, con-

sumer electronics, and cameras. A slightly different pattern emerges in high-tech industries such as computers, in which Japan expands into markets similar to the United States (for example, Australia) before entering U.S. and European markets.

Equally significant was the manner in which Japanese companies built a marketing network in foreign markets. Initially, they used independent distributors such as regional wholesale jewelers in the United States to sell watches. After sales had reached a reasonable level, they began establishing their own branches and sales companies, taking control of local advertising, promotion, and after-sales service. Subsequent steps included producing locally in developing and developed countries and eventually establishing a globally integrated manufacturing and sales network.

Responding to Regional Integration

Changing economic and political circumstances within a country can affect a firm's global strategies. The creation of the EU and NAFTA represent two key examples. Both are attempts at regional integration that reduce barriers between markets within a region, leading to market growth.

THE EU AND THE CREATION OF THE EURO
Companies responded to the formation of the EU in a variety of ways:

- By taking over other companies with significant market share and brand presence in major European markets
- By establishing manufacturing facilities and sales subsidiaries in the EU
- By integrating Europe into their global plans, such as developing products in Europe for the global market

Furthermore, the introduction of a single European currency, the euro, makes for greater pan-European competition and requires firms to rethink European pricing and hedging strategies. Cross-country comparison shopping becomes easier, facilitating cross-border pan-European direct marketing, with prices quoted in euros across the EU. In addition, the euro, with a common monetary policy across member nations, will provide impetus to common VAT rates and other forms of fiscal harmonization.

Acquiring firms with a dominant market position in a national market allows the acquiring company to expand sales into neighboring countries, capitalizing on and extending brand presence across national borders. It takes time to develop a brand presence and to develop distribution channels in the various European countries. Saving time while preempting the competition may be the most significant reason for such acquisitions. European union has added pressure on firms to establish a significant pan-European brand presence before the competition does so. Sometimes that requires developing manufacturing facilities across Europe, striking strategic alliances, or acquiring key firms in European nations where the firm has a weak market presence.

NAFTA

Reactions to this alliance have been similar, with the lowering of tariffs leading to a reshuffling of manufacturing activities. Large-volume manufacturing is being concentrated in the United States, with more specialized low- to medium-volume production being shifted to Canadian factories. Less skill-intensive assembly operations are increasingly locating in Mexico, with firms hoping to achieve cost reductions that could be used to lower prices and increase sales in the United States, Mexico, and Canada.

Marketing to Japan

The Japanese market is considered difficult to break into. It is highly competitive, usually requiring considerable adaptation, which is easier with well-informed local operations handling Japanese market research and advertising. Japanese distribution can be byzantine. Although it takes time to establish adequate control of distribution channels, the effort can be worthwhile. For example, both BMW and Mercedes-Benz successfully increased their Japanese market share by:

- Setting up their own independent dealer networks in Japan, replacing their former reliance on Japanese importers.
- Using financing as a marketing tool, offering low interest rates and long repayment periods. Their goal was for monthly payments on the costly imports to be about the same as payments for domestic cars.

- Using targeted and heavy advertising. Advertising stressed corporate image because Japanese buyers seem swayed more by the reputation of the company than by product-specific features.
- Utilizing price stability; that is, holding yen prices constant despite fluctuations in the exchange rate.

Strategy in the Global Automobile Industry: Competing for Position in China

How are the world's automakers responding to the maturity of the auto industry in many of the developed world markets, while China looms as a large and fast-growing market?

The global automobile industry is marked by global overcapacity and slow growth in the major auto markets of the United States, Europe, and Japan. The market is still highly fragmented, as shown in the following table.

Company	Global Production, October 2003 (millions of vehicles)	U.S. Sales, 2003 (millions of vehicles)	U.S. Sales, 2002 (millions of vehicles)
General Motors	8.79	4.7	4.8
Ford	7.60	3.5	3.6
Toyota	6.91	1.9	1.8
Daimler/Chrysler	6.05	2.3	2.4
Renault/Nissan	5.42	0.8	0.8
Volkswagen	5.06	0.4	0.4
PSA (Peugeot)	3.23	—	—
Honda	3.00	1.3	1.2
Suzuki	2.35	0.06	0.07
Hyundai	2.25	0.4	0.4

Source: "Eastern Drive," Wall Street Journal, December 8, 2003; "U.S. Car Makers Lose Market Share," Wall Street Journal, January 6, 2004.

Note: Mazda, BMW, Mitsubishi, and Subaru also sell between 184,000 and 275,000 units each in the U.S. market, while Porsche sells about 28,000 high-end vehicles.

Against the backdrop of a competitive and saturated U.S. market, China appears as an attractive market, with sales growth of 80 percent in 2003. Sales of passenger cars rose in China from 509,000 in 1998 to 2,040,000 in 2003. That can be compared to auto sales of 2,236,600 in Italy and of 2,579,100 in the UK. The Chinese market is forecast to be around 5 million units in 2008, making it the third-largest market after the United States and Japan. It is not surprising, then, to see the world's major automakers jockeying for competitive position in China.

However, the Chinese market is controlled by the Chinese government. Foreign auto companies must enter China through a joint venture and cannot own more than 50 percent of the company. The Chinese government exerts strong influence on the choice of partner; and their long-term plan is to make the auto industry a national one, controlled by Chinese companies. That is understandable from a national development perspective, as the automobile sector, with its ancillary industries, is an engine of economic growth, accounting for one in ten jobs. To that end, China has set a high price of entry, forcing companies eager to enter the market to offer significant transfer of technology, managerial skills, and financing and to work with local auto companies, which are often state-owned and likely to control marketing within China. Local sourcing is a must, with local content requirements beginning at about 40 percent. Since the Chinese government wants strong national players, it is pushing domestic consolidation, which means that there are few Chinese companies from which to choose. Hence, foreign competitors often find themselves in partnership with the same Chinese company. That fact facilitates the Chinese company's attempts to play off one foreign competitor against another, extracting better terms. The three main Chinese auto companies are SAIC (Shanghai Auto Industry Corporation), FAW (First Auto Works in Changchun), and Dongfeng.

Volkswagen was one of the first companies to enter China, initiating two joint ventures—one with SAIC and one with FAW. General Motors was allowed to enter China in 1997. Chosen over Ford, General Motors invested over $1.5 billion and brought technology and new models into a joint venture with SAIC. With China's entry into the WTO and the rapid growth of the auto sector from 1998 onward, other auto multinationals began seeking entry into the Chinese market. Toyota entered into a joint venture with FAW; Renault/Nissan, with Dongfeng. BMW, Ford, DaimlerChrysler, Honda, Hyundai, Mitsubishi, PSA Peugeot, and Suzuki are all in China. Their total production capacity totaled 2.6 million units, while actual production was 1.7 million units, for a capacity utilization of around 65 percent. However, domestic firms averaged only about 40 percent utilization.

Several new domestic companies—not state-owned and, hence, nimble—have entered the Chinese sector, seeking niche positions and often diversifying into the auto sector from other industries. For example, BYD Auto diversified from rechargeable batteries; its first car, the Flyer, had a 0.8-liter engine and sold for $4,000. BYD hopes to use its knowledge of rechargeable batteries to build an electric car in the future.[33] It is estimated that an additional 4 million to 5 million units of capacity will be added by 2006, raising the specter of overcapacity, resulting in price cutting and falling margins. Chinese governmental authorities introduced minimum capital restrictions to slow the growth of small firms entering the Chinese auto industry; consolidation is inevitable. New car designs are often quickly copied in China by newer, smaller domestic auto companies. A local company marketed a car labeled the Chery QQ at a price about 20 percent below General Motor's newly introduced Chevy Spark. SAIC, which owns 20 percent of Chery, had invested with General Motors in Daewoo Motors (Korea). Thus, SAIC may have been able to buy the design specs for the Daiwoo Matiz, on which General Motors's new Chevy Spark is based, thereby competing with its own joint venture with General Motors.[34]

The Chinese auto sector is quite profitable for the incumbents that dominate market share. In 2003, General Motors earned $437 million in profits on sales of 487,000 cars compared to North American profits of $811 million on sales of 4.5 million cars. Similarly, Volkswagen earned $561 million, or about 25 percent of its profits, on sales of 700,000 cars in China. Growing overcapacity will reduce such margins, and auto firms in China will have to consider strategic alternatives such as exporting from China, reducing capacity expansion, and increasing profits from financing. China allowed Volkswagen, General Motors, and Toyota to set up auto financing companies, with minimum capital requirements of $60 million.[35] A danger in that strategy is losses from high rates of payment default. Cars are still quite expensive in China relative to incomes, which averaged about $1,000 per annum, though incomes are higher on the coast. Despite China's lower wage rates, auto exports from China are not likely to be competitive. Auto manufacturing is a capital-intensive business where scale economies matter, and Chinese plants have to increase productivity and improve quality. Further, the major auto multinationals have considerable excess capacity worldwide, and exporting from China would only exacerbate problems elsewhere.

With the multitude of automobile companies in China, product differentiation is necessary. General Motors found that the Buick brand resonated with many Chinese customers because it had been sold in China since the early 1900s. It was known as the car of the elite—black sedans with whitewall tires. Sun Yat-sen as well the last emperor of China, P'u Yi, rode in Buicks. The car's image is contemporary, luxurious, safe, and elite; it is a car for weekend trips. Not surprisingly, General Motors sold about 141,000 Buicks in China in the first half of 2004, a bit under the 162,000 sold in the United States in the same period.[36] General Motors has used its local design center to cater to local tastes, such as a big washtub-shaped chrome grille, slanted headlights that allude to a smiling Buddha, leather seats, a DVD players built into the back-seat, and roomy backseats (as important passengers in China generally sit in the back). Lower-priced models include features such as a CD changer, a cooler in the glove compartment, and a drawer that holds comfortable shoes for women when they want to change from high heels.

Latecomers such as Toyota had to play catch-up with creative maneuvering. Toyota was in a partnership in Tianjin with an underperforming government-controlled Tianjin Automotive. Toyota decided to collaborate with First Automotive in Changchun to take over Tianjin, thus replacing a less desirable partner with a stronger local company that was larger and had a government permit to produce larger luxury vehicles.[37]

SUMMARY: OVERALL STRATEGY ISSUES IN THE GLOBAL AUTOMOBILE INDUSTRY

Based on the previous examples about China and its auto sector, the following steps may be necessary for developing a strong market position in automobiles in China:

1. Firms must develop the right car for the market in a timely fashion.
2. Firms must cut costs by designing cars with features most desired by customers. Fewer parts and fewer hours of production make the car affordable to a customer base whose incomes are still considerably below than those in developed nations.
3. Firms must attain national and regional market balance within China. Compliance with government regulations, alliances with local firms, and national distribution and service are all keys to long-term success.
4. Firms must transfer capitalization and technology and build brand equity and national distribution, forming part of a coherent set of strategic initiatives necessary for long-term success.
5. The Chinese government's auto industry policy, aimed at creating national champion firms of Chinese origin, requires multinationals to plan long-term strategies with a view to shared power and control as the price of long-term sustainable market presence.
6. While current margins are likely to decline, the potential of the Chinese market is such that multinationals with well-conceived strategic marketing plans can make China an integral part of their global marketing strategy.

Thus, auto companies are competing to enter and establish themselves in China for two reasons:

- Demand for their products in China is growing explosively and is likely to continue to grow faster than almost anywhere else in the world.
- They face global competition with most of their major developed country markets being mature and slow-growing.

GLOBAL
MARKETING

China: The Market at the End of the Rainbow

There are over 1.2 billion people in China, and incomes have been doubling every seven years since 1980. That means that growing numbers of Chinese citizens can afford to buy goods and services: prepared foods, clothes, motorcycles, refrigerators, insurance, and vacations. Consider orange juice, for instance. China is among the world's leading producers of oranges, but the Chinese drink little orange juice. Generally, it is drunk by adults at banquets and by children. Seagram's Tropicana division is one of North America's largest orange juice producers, owning large orange plantations in Florida and deriving nearly half of its sales from the United States. Because China looked like a huge market, Tropicana decided to enter the market there. Initially, Tropicana imported juice and concentrate, resulting in a luxury drink consumed mostly by foreigners. After much searching, it decided to set up an orange juice plant in southwestern China, near Zhongxian, high above the Yangtze River, in the region where the Three Gorges Dam is being built. But farmers had treated oranges as a low-cost side crop, leaving trees to grow on their own without fertilizer or irrigation. Tropicana wanted to get the farmers to plant over 1 million new trees, using seeds provided by Tropicana. The trees needed to be watered and fertilized and nurtured to yield sufficient quantities of high-grade orange juice. But the trees would not yield fruit for several years, raising the question of whether farmers would be willing to spend money initially in the hopes of seeing good returns after several years. Because the region was remote, Tropicana and its Chinese partner, the Chongqing Three Gorges Group, had to overcome poor infrastructure and a lack of roads in getting their juice to major markets, towns far to the east, such as Shanghai, Beijing, and Hong Kong. But Seagram was convinced that its $55 million investment would pay off, looking beyond the current Asian turmoil to a China 20 years later, a China likely to be far more prosperous.

China is equally attractive to overseas Chinese, such as the Wei brothers from Taiwan. Their firm, Ting Hsin International Group, owns the largest market share in China's instant noodle market. They have created a national brand, their logo a pot-bellied chef, Master Kang or Kang Shi Fu. A growing number of working couples made instant noodles a popular product. Initially, the instant noodles were priced 50 percent higher than local Chinese brands. The company decided to sell the package of noodles shrink-wrapped together with Styrofoam bowls, banking on a Chinese need to be able to eat clean food when traveling: "When do I eat and will it be clean?" Since hot water was easily found in a tea-drinking population, the noodles with a bowl could tap into a large market served only by expensive Japanese imports. When the Wei brothers saw that the product was successful, they expanded rapidly since the product was easy to copy and they wanted to cut production costs quickly, ahead of their imitators. Their Chinese roots allowed them to develop a large variety of noodles that catered to Chinese tastes. They also were able to project a high-quality image because they were seen as a foreign product featuring Taiwanese-style soup noodles.

The four Wei brothers control and run the company, splitting responsibilities for operations, finance, business relations, and marketing. A key tactic is their use of large numbers of sales agents who visit wholesalers across China on a regular basis. On those visits, the agents gather market information and learn about competitors' moves, such as promotional discounts. Ting Hsin, one of China's leading consumer food and beverage producers, advertises extensively on TV, a relatively new medium in China. The company continuously tests then launches new flavors; for example, chili noodles for the Sichuan palate, pork-free noodles for Muslim populations in western China, and small snack packages for children. While Ting Hsin also tests new lines such as biscuits and fried chicken outlets, noodles account for 80 percent of sales and remain the product line that will determine the firm's continuing success.

China's stunning growth has created large domestic enterprises that are beginning to look outward, even as their markets are being populated by foreign firms. Haier is China's leading manufacturer of white goods, products such as refrigerators, washing machines, air conditioners, and other home appliances. To compete with foreign firms' products in China, Haier knew that it had to offer superior technology, durability, and quality, all at a competitive price. That meant lowering costs with scale economies, efficiency in managing inventories, and a carefully planned sales campaign. Haier began with technology and specialized equipment for refrigerators obtained from Germany. Later, it procured industrial freezer technology from Italy, air conditioners through a joint venture with Mitsubishi, and Freon-free refrigerators from the U.S. Environmental Protection Agency (EPA). But Haier also set aside 4 percent of an estimated $750 million in revenues for in-house R&D, planning to raise the amount to 8 percent as finances permitted. That allowed the company to invent its own new products, such as Big Prince, an environmentally friendly and energy-saving refrigerator. The firm rewarded its employees for individual excellence, promoting them for superior performance. That was a change from the traditional mentality of state-owned companies that paid everyone equally regardless of performance. In a departure from the surly treatment of customers by state-owned monopoly sales outlets, Haier emphasized service, listening to customers, offering a toll-free hot line, and guaranteeing delivery and repair of its appliances within 24 hours. Offering 24-hour service was a serious undertaking in a country as geographically dispersed as China. Haier also regularly added and altered products to satisfy customers. For example, it introduced a mini washing machine that washes a small number of items, but is compact and cheap, fits into small flats, and requires little water (an important feature in a country in which interruptions of the water supply are frequent and the supply of running water is still scarce).

One of Haier's slogans says, "Never Say No to the Market." As a result, the firm is now beginning to take its products overseas, opening a factory in Indonesia, planning another for the Philippines, and planning additional overseas manufacturing for other Asian and Latin American countries. Haier's president, Zhang Ruimin, notes, "To build a name brand, you can't just stay in China." Haier had to combat the perception that goods made in China were of low quality. It responded to that challenge by placing two refrigerators (with their identifying marks removed, one a Haier product) before German retailers, asking them to identify the Chinese import. The test allowed Haier to convince the public of the quality of its products, leading to increased orders. Haier's long-term goal is to get one-third of production devoted to domestic sales, one-third to exports, and the remaining one-third to goods manufactured in overseas plants. The company is doing all it can to fulfill its other slogan, "Haier—Tomorrow's Global Brand Name."

Huawei, a Chinese telecommunications manufacturer, also focused on overcoming an image problem in an attempt to obtain foreign sales. In 1999, Huawei's sales of about $1.7 billion were concentrated in China. By 2004, sales had grown to $8 billion, 50 percent of which were international sales. However, the company had difficulties winning orders from major U.S. customers such as SBC and BellSouth. Huawei's U.S. problems included perceived contravention of IP rights, as it was sued by Cisco for copying Cisco's router software code. The lawsuit was settled after Huawei withdrew the offending products from the U.S. market.

Sources: "A Chinese Telecom Powerhouse Stumbles on Road to the U.S.," *Wall Street Journal*, July 28, 2005; "Tea and Tropicana: Seagram Wants Juice to Be Chinese Staple," *Wall Street Journal*, January 2, 1998; "Coals to Newcastle, Ice to Eskimos; now, Noodles to the Chinese," *Wall Street Journal*, November 17, 1997; "Would America Buy a Refrigerator Labeled Made in Qingdao?" *Wall Street Journal*, September 17, 1997.

Summary

Global marketing strategy must form part of and be consistent with a firm's overall global strategy. Linkages exist between the two in areas such as technology, manufacturing, organizational structure, and finance.

The formulation of a global strategy begins with corporate strategies that cut across product lines. Then product-line strategies are formed, influenced by the industry, the firm's competitive advantage, and its value-added chain. Other important influences are the environment, competition, government actions, and the firm's customers and suppliers. Next, the firm sets product-line strategy for individual markets. It also considers whether to standardize policies across markets or adapt them to individual markets.

Basic strategies are to become the lowest-cost producer, to provide a differentiated product, or to seek government protection against foreign competition. Configuration and coordination decisions follow. In configuring value-added activities, companies typically choose between market extension, a multidomestic perspective, or a global perspective.

Some of the variables firms must consider in adopting a global perspective include differences in global markets, customers, and competition; different host-government policies, technology, and production resources; and the time factor.

A government's policies can influence strategy by keeping foreign competition out and by subsidizing the global strategies of national champion firms, as is the case with Airbus.

A company may be willing to sacrifice short-term profits for higher market share, or it may emphasize its competitive position worldwide rather than in specific national markets. This suggests that a portfolio approach to individual national markets may be shortsighted, causing a firm to cede competitive position to other multinationals with longer-term orientations.

Global competitors emerge by (1) diversifying out of national markets that they dominate, (2) diversifying into new products, or (3) extending their product lines into new product segments. Suppliers are another source of competition.

Factors leading to adaptation in global marketing strategy include differences in customers; marketing infrastructure; legal, transportation, and communication systems; and distribution channels. In general, because national markets are sufficiently different, adaptation in some elements of the marketing mix is necessary.

Another component of a global marketing system is market position. Should a company aim to sell the same product to different segments in the various country markets or sell to the same segment in each country with some product adaptation?

Coordinating the global marketing system is a complex task. Some common methods include using similar marketing approaches across countries, transferring marketing know-how and experience, sequencing marketing programs across countries, and integrating approaches to multinational clients.

Management must decide what countries to target. Factors relevant to this decision include the size and growth of the market, the product life cycle stage in the market, the level of competition, the similarity to markets already served, and the influence of government restrictions. In general, multinationals seek market position in the triad economy regions: the United States, Europe, and Japan.

Another challenge is to respond to regional integration, such as the creation of Europe's Single Market. Alliances and acquisitions are two common approaches. The key goals are to obtain distribution and brand presence in a timely manner across Europe.

Another marketing challenge is selling to Japan. The critical issues are providing quality, overcoming the Japanese preference for domestic products, and working with complex distribution systems.

The unfolding of global strategy can be seen in the Chinese automobile industry.

Questions and Research

14.1 Why must companies think globally?

14.2 What is a global industry?

14.3 How is marketing strategy linked to global strategy?

14.4 What are some factors that affect global strategy at the level of a firm?

14.5 How can management attitude affect global strategy?

14.6 What are some factors that influence global strategy at the product-line level?

14.7 What is the value-added chain? How is it relevant to a firm in formulating a global strategy?

14.8 What are some goals that a firm might set for itself in individual country markets?

14.9 What are the basic strategies open to a firm in the global marketplace?

14.10 What does "configuring the value-added chain" mean? How do firms differ in their perspectives on configuring the value-added chain in different countries?

14.11 What are some factors that lead a firm to think globally?

14.12 What is a "lead" market? Why is it important?

14.13 Give an example of how time and speed of response affect global competition.

14.14 Why is it dangerous to adopt a portfolio approach in international marketing?

14.15 How can government policies affect a firm's ability to compete globally?

14.16 Explain why standardization versus adaptation is a fundamental issue in international marketing.

14.17 Highlight the key issues in coordinating the global marketing system.

14.18 How would a firm target individual country markets?

14.19 How do the EU and the euro affect a firm's global marketing strategy in Europe? Why have firms reacted by acquiring and merging with other European firms?

14.20 Discuss global competition and marketing strategy in the Chinese auto industry.

Endnotes

1. Drucker, Peter. "The Transnational Economy," *Wall Street Journal*, August 25, 1987.

2. Hamel, Gary and C. K. Prahalad. "Do You Really Have a Global Strategy?" *Harvard Business Review*, July/August 1985.

3. Yip, George S. *Total Global Strategy II*, 2002, Upper Saddle River, NJ: Prentice Hall.

4. Takeuchi, Hirotaka. "The Globalization of Markets Revisited" in *The Global Market*, John Quelch and Rohit Deshpande, editors, 2004, San Francisco: Jossey-Bass, pages 37–77; Takeuchi, Hirotaka and M. Porter, "Three Roles of International Marketing in Global Strategy"; Chapter 4 in *Competition in Global Industries*, M. Porter, editor, 1986, Boston: Harvard Business School Press.

5. Carpano, Claudio, James J. Chrisman, and Kendall Roth. "International Strategy and Environment: An Assessment of the Performance Relationship," Survey of U.S.-owned multinationals, *Journal of International Business Studies*, Volume 25, Number 3, 1994, pages 639–656.

6. Solberg, Carl Arthur. "A Framework for Analysis of Strategy Development in Globalizing Markets," *Journal of International Marketing*, Volume 5, Number 1, 1997, pages 9–30.

7. Cavusgil, S. Tamer and Shaoming Zou. "Marketing Strategy-Performance Relationship: An Investigation of the Empirical Link in Export Market Ventures," *Journal of Marketing*, Volume 58, January 1994, pages 1–21.

8. Zou, Shaoming and S. Tamer Cavusgil. "The GMS: A Broad Conceptualization of Global Marketing Strategy and Its Effect on Firm Performance," *Journal of Marketing*, Volume 66, October 2002, pages 40–56.

9. Egelhoff, William G. "Great Strategy or Great Strategy Implementation—Two Ways of Competing in Global Markets" (Illustrated by U.S. and Japanese semiconductor firms), *Sloan Management Review*, Volume 34, Winter 1993, pages 37–50.

10. Kogut, Bruce. "Designing Global Strategies: Comparative and Competitive Value-Added Chains," *Sloan Management Review*, Summer 1985, pages 15–27; "Managing the Transnational Value Chain: Strategies for Firms from Emerging Markets," with C. Samuel Craig, *Journal of International Marketing*, Volume 5, Issue 3, 1997.

11. "The Laptop Trail," *Wall Street Journal*, June 9, 2005.

12. "Lower Costs to Help Sales," *China Daily*, July 21, 2004; "Small Motors, Big Profits," *Forbes*, July 11, 1988.

13. Craig, C. Samuel and Susan P. Douglas. "Configural Advantage in Global Markets, *Journal of International Marketing*, 2000, Volume 6, Number 1, pages 6–25; M. Porter, "Competing in Global Industries: A Conceptual Framework," Chapter 1 in *Competition in Global Industries*, M. Porter, editor, 1986, Boston: Harvard Business School Press.

14. Komatsu Ltd., Harvard Business School Case Services #9-385-277.

15. Rugman, Alan M. and Alain Verbeke. "A Perspective on Regional and Global Strategies of Multinational Enterprises," *Journal of International Business Studies*, Volume 35, Number 1, 2004, pages 3–18.

16. Douglas, Susan P. and C. Samuel Craig. "Evolution of Global Marketing Strategy: Scale, Scope, and Synergy," *Columbia Journal of World Business*, Volume 24, Number 3, Fall 1989; "Developing Strategies for Global Markets: An Evolutionary Perspective," *Columbia Journal of World Business*, Volume XXXI, Number 1, Spring 1996.

17. Jeannet, Jean-Pierre and H. Hennessey. *Global Marketing Strategies*, 5th Edition, 2001, Boston: Houghton-Mifflin, 2001.

18. Senate Committee on Foreign Relations, *Evaluating International Intellectual Property Piracy*, Hearings before the Committee on Foreign Relations, U.S. Senate, June 9, 2004; U.S. International Trade Commission, "Foreign Protection of Intellectual Property Rights and the Effect on U.S. Industry and Trade," *Report to the U.S. Trade Representative*, Investigation No. 332-245, Publication 2065, February 1988.

19. Brandenburger, Adam M. and Barry J. Nalebuff. "The Right Game: Use Game Theory to Shape Strategy," *Harvard Business Review*, July/August 1995, pages 57–71.

20. Stalk, George. "Time—The Next Source of Competitive Advantage," *Harvard Business Review* July/August 1988; Stalk, George and Alan M. Webber, "Japan's Dark Side of Time," *Harvard Business Review*, July 1993.

21. Bower, Joseph L. and Thomas Hout. "Fast-Cycle Capability for Competitive Power," *Harvard Business Review*, November–December 1988; Stalk, George, Philip Evans, and Lawrence Shulman, "Competing on Capabilities: The New Rules of Corporate Strategy," *Harvard Business Review*, March 1992.

22. "Another Air Show, Another Row," *The Economist*, July 20, 2004; "Opening the Throttles," *The Economist*, July 8, 2004; "Enough Is Enough," *The Economist*, July 24, 2004; "Boeing's Complaints Move U.S. to Press Europe on Airbus Aid," *Wall Street Journal*, July 26, 2004; also see "All Shapes and Sizes: A Survey of the Civil Aerospace Industry," *The Economist*, September 3, 1988.

23. "In Face of French Resistance, Swiss Giant Enters Takeover Fray." *Wall Street Journal*, April 23, 2004.

24. Doz, Yves and C. K. Prahalad. *The Multinational Mission*, 1987, New York: Free Press.

25. Theodosiou, Marios and Leonidas C. Leonidou. "Standardization Versus Adaptation of International Marketing Strategy: An Integrative Assessment of Empirical Research," *International Business Review*, Volume 12, 2003, pages 141–171.

26. Szymanski, D., S. G. Bharadwaj, and P. R. Varadarajan. "Standardization Versus Adaptation of International Marketing Strategy," *Journal of Marketing*, Volume 57, October 1993, page 11.

27. Laroche, Michael, V. H. Kirpalani, Frank Pons, and L. Zhou. "A Model of Advertising Standardization in Multinational Corporations," *Journal of International Business Studies*, Volume 32, Number 2, 2001, pages 249–266.

28. Hexter, James, Javier Perez, and Anthony Perkins. "Gold from Noodles," *McKinsey Quarterly*, Number 3, 1998, pages 59–72.

29. Doz, Yves and C. K. Prahalad. "The Dynamics of Global Competition," in *The Multinational Mission*, 1987, New York: Free Press.

30. Takeuchi, Hirotaka and Michael Porter. "Three Roles of International Marketing in Global Strategy," in *Competition in Global Industries*, M. Porter editor, 1986, Boston: Harvard Business School Press.

31. Vorhies, Douglas W. and Neil A. Morgan. "A Configuration Theory Assessment of Marketing Organization Fit with Business Strategy and Its Relationship with Marketing Performance," *Journal of Marketing*, Volume 67, January 2003, pages 100–105.

32. Brouthers, Keith. "The Influence of International Risk on Entry Mode Strategy in the Computer Software Industry," *Management International Review,* Volume 35, Number 1, 1995, pages 7–28.

33. "Thanks, now move over," *Forbes,* July 26, 2004.

34. "Stolen Cars," *Forbes,* February 16, 2004.

35. "China Clears Car-Financing Ventures," *Wall Street Journal,* December 30, 2003.

36. "China's Buick Infatuation," *Wall Street Journal,* July 22, 2004.

37. "As Toyota Pushes Hard in China, A Lot Is Riding on the Outcome," *Wall Street Journal,* December 8, 2003.

Further Readings

Brandenburger, Adam M. and Barry J. Nalebuff. "The Right Game: Use Game Theory to Shape Strategy," *Harvard Business Review,* July/August 1995, pages 57–71.

Brouthers, Keith. "The Influence of International Risk on Entry Mode Strategy in the Computer Software Industry," *Management International Review,* Volume 35, Number 1, 1995, pages 7–28.

Carpano, Claudio, James J. Chrisman, and Kendall Roth. "International Strategy and Environment: An Assessment of the Performance Relationship" (Survey of U.S.-owned multinationals), *Journal of International Business Studies,* Volume 25, Number 3, 1994, pages 639–656.

Cavusgil, S. Tamer and Shaoming Zou. "Marketing Strategy-Performance Relationship: An Investigation of the Empirical Link in Export Market Ventures," *Journal of Marketing,* Volume 58, January 1994, pages 1–21.

Chee, Harold and C. West, *Myths About Doing Business in China,* 2005, Palgrove MacMilian.

Craig, C. Samuel and Susan P. Douglas. "Configural Advantage in Global Markets, *Journal of International Marketing,* Volume 6, Number 1, 2000 pages 6–25.

Dertouzos, Michael, Richard Lester, Robert Solow, et al. *Made in America,* 1989, Cambridge, MA: MIT Press.

Douglas, Susan and Dong Kee Rhee. "Examining Generic Competitive Strategy Types in U.S. and European Markets," *Journal of International Business Studies,* Volume 20, Fall 1989, pages 437–463.

Douglas, Susan P. and C. Samuel Craig. "Developing Strategies for Global Markets: An Evolutionary Perspective," *Columbia Journal of World Business,* Volume XXXI, Number 1, Spring 1996.

Doz, Yves and C. K. Prahalad. *The Multinational Mission,* 1987, New York: Free Press.

Egelhoff, William G. "Great Strategy or Great Strategy Implementation—Two Ways of Competing in Global Markets" (illustrated by U.S. and Japanese semiconductor firms). *Sloan Management Review,* Volume 34, Winter 1993, pages 37–50.

Ghoshal, Sumantra. "Global Strategy: An Organizing Framework." *Strategic Management Journal,* September–October 1987, pages 425–440.

Hamel, Gary and C. K. Prahalad. "Do You Really Have a Global Strategy?" *Harvard Business Review,* July/August 1985.

Hampton, Gerald M. and Erwin Buske. "The Global Marketing Perspective" in *Advances in International Marketing,* Volume 2, S. Tamer Cavusgil, editor, 1987, Greenwich, CT: JAI Press.

Hexter, James, Javier Perez, and Anthony Perkins. "Gold from Noo-

dles," *McKinsey Quarterly,* Number 3, 1988, pages 59–72.

Hout, Thomas, M. E. Porter, and E. Rudden. "How Global Companies Win Out," *Harvard Business Review,* September/October 1982.

Jeannet, Jean-Pierre and H. Hennessey. *Global Marketing Strategies,* 5th Edition, 2001, Boston: Houghton-Mifflin.

Kogut, Bruce. "Designing Global Strategies: Comparative and Competitive Value-Added Chains," *Sloan Management Review,* Summer 1985, pages 15–27.

Laroche, Michael, V. H. Kirpalani, Frank Pons, and L. Zhou. "A Model of Advertising Standardization in Multinational Corporations," *Journal of International Business Studies,* Volume 32, Number 2, 2001, pages 249–266.

Ohmae, Kenichi. *Triad Power: The Coming Shape of Global Competition,* 1985, New York: Free Press.

Peng, Michael, *Global Marketing Strategy,* 2005, Mason, OH, Southwestern.

Porter, M., editor. *Competition in Global Industries,* 1986, Boston: Harvard Business School Press, especially Chapter 1, "Competing in Global Industries: A Conceptual Framework."

Quelch, John A. and Edward J. Hoff. "Customizing Global Marketing," *Harvard Business Review,* May/June 1986.

Quelch, John and Rohit Deshpande, editors. *The Global Market: Developing a Strategy to Manage across Borders,* 2004, San Francisco: Jossey-Bass.

Rugman, Alan M. and Alain Verbeke. "A Perspective on Regional and Global Strategies of Multinational Enterprises," *Journal of International Business Studies,* Volume 35, Number 1, 2004, pages 3–18.

Senate Committee on Foreign Relations, *Evaluating International Intellectual Property Piracy,* Hearings before the Committee on Foreign Relations, U.S. Senate, June 9, 2004.

Solberg, Carl Arthur. "A Framework for Analysis of Strategy Development in Globalizing Markets," *Journal of International Marketing,* Volume 5, Number1, 1997, pages 9–30.

Stalk, George. "Time—The Next Source of Competitive Advantage," *Harvard Business Review,* July/August 1988.

Stalk, George and Alan M. Webber. "Japan's Dark Side of Time," *Harvard Business Review,* July 1993.

Szymanski, D., S. G. Bharadwaj, and P. R. Varadarajan. "Standardization versus Adaptation of International Marketing Strategy," *Journal of Marketing,* Volume 57, October 1993, pages 1–17.

Takeuchi, Hirotaka, "The Globalization of Markets Revisited" in *The Global Market,* John Quelch and Rohit Deshpande, editors, 2004, San Francisco: Jossey-Bass, pages 37–77.

Takeuchi, Hirotaka and M. Porter. "Three Roles of International Marketing in Global Strategy" in *Competition in Global Industries,* M. Porter, editor, 1986, Boston: Harvard Business School Press.

Theodosiou, Marios and Leonidas C. Leonidou. "Standardization versus Adaptation of International Marketing Strategy: An Integrative Assessment of Empirical Research," *International Business Review,* Volume 12, 2003, pages 141–171.

Vorhies, Douglas W. and Neil A. Morgan. "A Configuration Theory Assessment of Marketing Organization Fit with Business Strategy and Its Relationship with Marketing Performance," *Journal of Marketing,* Volume 67, January 2003, pages 100–105.

Yip, George S. *Total Global Strategy II,* 2002, Upper Saddle River, NJ: Prentice Hall.

Zou, Shaoming and S. Tamer Cavusgil. "The GMS: A Broad Conceptualization of Global Marketing Strategy and Its Effect on Firm Performance," *Journal of Marketing,* Volume 66, October 2002, pages 40–56.

Case 14-1

LION-NATHAN CHINA
by Prof. Delwyn Clark) from *Case Research Journal*

Lion Nathan China

Delwyn N. Clark
University of Waikato Management School

In China, anything is possible, everything is difficult.
Anonymous

This is not a destination in China, this is a journey.
This is going to be a forever thing.
Jim O'Mahony, Managing Director, Lion Nathan China

A good beginning is half way to winning.
The road ahead is long and rough, but step-by-step Lion Nathan will march to success.
Rheineck launch, Lion Nathan China Journal # 2

In April 1999, Paul Lockey, chief financial officer of the international brewing company Lion Nathan Limited (LN), was really quite perplexed as he prepared his midyear report for the board. With responsibility for corporate strategy and finance, Lockey realised that higher losses from their China operations were going to wipe out LN's profits from elsewhere. How would the New Zealand shareholders react? For how long would the board allow these losses to continue? When would the China operations break even? Competition was intensifying in the Chinese beer market, particularly at the higher-margin premium end. Markets were extremely volatile as consumers tried new brands, and the economy was cycling downwards. With overcapacity in the beer industry, consolidation was underway. Was the new deal to brew and market *Beck's* premium beer under license going to provide the leverage needed to survive the shake-out? How could Jim O'Mahony's China team deliver in the world's most exciting market?

COMPANY HISTORY

In 1999, Lion Nathan Limited (LN) was an international brewer with three geographic divisions in New Zealand, Australia, and China. With a portfolio of over 50 brands, the company owned and operated 10 breweries in these three countries.[1] To achieve greater international scale, LN also exported beer to 50 countries and licensed three brewers in Europe to produce and distribute Steinlager and

Originally prepared for the 6th Waikato Management School Case Competition in June 1999 from field research. The author thanks Paul Lockey and senior company executives for cooperation and support of this project and the anonymous reviewers for their helpful suggestions in developing this manuscript.

Castlemaine XXXX. Through its 45 percent Japanese equity partner, Kirin Brewing Company, LN was part of the fourth largest brewing group in the world.

Founded in New Zealand, LN origins went back 150 years. The company grew by mergers and acquisitions to become the largest brewer in New Zealand and one of the top-10 listed companies on the New Zealand stock exchange. From the mid-1980s, leadership of the series of expansion and consolidation strategies in the brewing company was provided by Douglas Myers, whose family involvement dated back to 1897. Building upon his international experience in the liquor industry, Myers developed Lion Corporation to include a portfolio of businesses in hotels, property, wine, and beer. Myers adopted an overarching strategic view of the New Zealand business and led the company with entrepreneurial drive and enthusiasm.[2]

Lion Nathan Limited was formed in 1988 when Lion Corporation merged with New Zealand's largest retailer, L.D. Nathan & Co. At this time, the chief executives of the two companies, Douglas Myers at Lion and Peter Cooper at Nathan, decided that the best thing to do was to get an outsider who came from neither culture to run it. As a result of an international search, Kevin Roberts was appointed in 1989 to manage the day-to-day operations as chief operating officer (COO). Roberts had significant international experience with consumer product brands from his days with companies such as Procter & Gamble, Gillette, and PepsiCo. Headhunted from Pepsi-Cola in Canada where he was president, Roberts also had knowledge of the beverage industry and hands-on leadership skills in high-performing organisations. Roberts brought Joe McCollum into the company at this time as HR director to help build the culture. Also at this stage, LN's corporate strategy was redefined, as Roberts explained:

It was very evident to me, after being here 10 seconds, that for a consumer products company to be exclusively dependent on New Zealand made no sense, because there were no consumers here. And that was not going to change. We were in a lot of businesses where we had no core competency. Our core competency, I decided, was going to be brand-building. Therefore, that meant the DEKA chain should go; the Woolworths chain should go. We wanted to build our Coke business, but Coke wouldn't give us any more territory, because they wanted to keep it for themselves. So, we sold off all noncore businesses. We decided that we had to go offshore, and the safest place to go was Australia. We also decided that ideally we needed brands that had a pedigree. In the soft drink business, we had to go with an established brand; therefore, go with Pepsi in Australia and New Zealand. We were able to get a deal—the Schweppes franchise for free. And to stay in beer, which was our core business in New Zealand. And buy established regional breweries—that was what we knew how to run. We acquired Alan Bond's breweries and transformed ourselves in a 12-month period from being a top-10 New Zealand conglomerate to the biggest beverage producer in Australasia. We simultaneously brought in a lot of international people to drive the culture, drive performance, and build brands and hired stellar people from offshore and New Zealand who became the core of the management group.

In 1993, with limited growth in the New Zealand and Australian markets, LN began looking further afield for growth opportunities in America, Europe, and Asia. Like many other multinational consumer product companies at this time, they found the world's largest consumer market—China. According to Roberts, "China represented the single best opportunity for a number of reasons, including size of market, growth potential, low barriers to entry, and no established big guy in there." Two years and 40 brewery evaluations later, LN entered this market in April 1995 with a 60 percent joint venture in Wuxi. This initial investment was made in one of the wealthiest cities in the heart of the Yangtze River Delta—China's fastest growing beer market (see Exhibit 1). Buoyed by success, LN increased its shareholding in this brewery to 80 percent in 1996 and made a major commitment to build a brand new $178 million[3] brewery 30 kilometres away in the Suzhou Industrial Park. Construction of this 200-million litre world-class brewery was completed $35.5 million under budget and 2 months ahead of schedule with "good planning, great people, combined with cooperation and teamwork." Commercial production began in February 1998, and the premium brand *Steinlager* was launched in September. In April 1999, LN announced a licensing agreement with German brewer Brauerei Beck and Co. to brew and market Beck's international premium beer. The addition of a high-margin brand to its portfolio was important to utilise brewing capacity at Suzhou and to extend its market reach beyond the Yangtze River Delta.

LN's ownership structure changed in April 1998 when the Japanese brewing group, Kirin Brewery Company, acquired a 45 percent share in the company. The composition of the board was changed at this time to allow participation by Kirin staff in LN's corporate governance. Kirin had its own small brewing and soft drink businesses in China and sold the Kirin lager beer in over 40 countries, particularly in North America, Europe, and Asia.

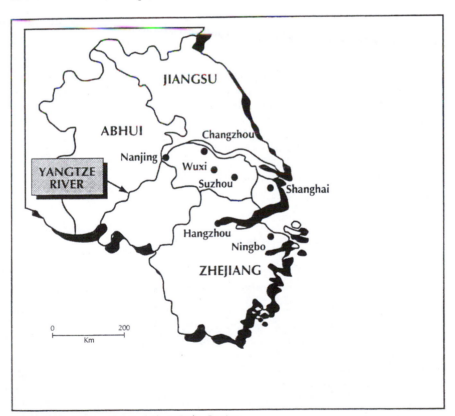

EXHIBIT 1 China: Yangtze River Delta Region

Gordon Cairns, who became CEO in April 1998 when Douglas Myers stepped up to chairman of the board, described LN's charter as "profitable growth." Business segment results for 1998 are shown in Exhibit 2. With growth of 5.5 percent in volume, 3.6 percent in revenue, and 7.5 percent in earnings, he called 1998 a "watershed year" for LN. Speaking at the company's annual meeting, Cairns reported:

> I believe these results are coming from a simple game plan that sets clear direction for each of our businesses. Australia is the engine of our business, where we expect profits to grow over the next 5 years, from modest share growth, stable pricing, and further cost reductions. In New Zealand, where our position is more dominant, the market less stable, the economy weaker, and there is a predatory third player, we are less ambitious in wanting to hold our position. In China, we are investing to develop the business, which will be generating profits in the medium term. Finally, provided there is a suitable buyer at a suitable price, we are actively seeking to divest Pepsi.
>
> As a shareholder, you obviously believe in the game plan. But let me draw to your attention five other reasons that differentiate us as a stock. First, we are virtually a pure beer company. Second, everywhere we compete, we are investing to build brands. Third, we believe beer is a regional business, with few truly global brands. Fourth, a key success factor is for us to be the lowest cost producer, everywhere we compete. Finally, we are measured, managed, and motivated by shareholder value, where what we do should earn greater than the cost of capital.

Financial comparisons and statistics for LN from 1994 to 1998 are provided in Exhibits 3 and 4. For the 6 months to February 1999, LN's profit was $83 million ($0.3 million more than the February 1998 profit figure) with strong results in the Australian business (7.8 percent EBIT increase). With difficult market conditions in China and prices under pressure, $20.4 million EBIT loss was reported (compared with $17.1 million loss in February 1998).

Exhibit 2 Lion Nathan Limited: Business Segments, 1998[a]

	New Zealand	Australia	China	Soft Drinks	Total
Assets ($M)	781.1	2,524.3	374.4	156.7	3,878.2[c]
Sales Revenue ($M)	414.5	1,106.3	56.2	229.4	1,806.4
Earnings ($M)[b]	100.1	286.0	(29.8)	0.3	346.3[d]
Market Share	61.1%[e]	41.3%	8.2%[f]	—	—
Staff	600	1,200	1,300		3,100

Notes [a] 1998 financial data in New Zealand dollars.

[b] Earnings Before Interest and Tax, EBIT.

[c] Total includes property/rental income and unallocated corporate overheads.

[d] Total includes property/rental income and unallocated corporate overhead.

[e] Share of LN/DB market.

[f] Market share in the Yangtze River Delta.

Source: Lion Nathan Limited, *Annual Report*, 1998.

Exhibit 3 Lion Nathan Limited: Financial Comparison,
Five-Year Review for Year Ended August 31 (dollar amounts in millions)

	1998	1997	1996	1995	1994
Total Net Revenue	**1,806.4**	**1,743.6**	**1,757.0**	**1,771.6**	**1,673.5**
Earnings					
Earnings Before Interest and Tax	346.3	333.0	378.3	382.2	378.8
Net Interest Expense	(102.9)	(105.4)	(131.7)	(151.0)	(169.1)
Earnings from Operations	243.4	227.6	246.6	231.2	209.7
Income Tax	(90.8)	(85.7)	(75.6)	(1.4)	8.9
Minority Interests	(0.8)	0.4	0.2	0.2	1.2
Goodwill Amortisation	(15.7)	(15.7)	(15.7)	(15.7)	(15.7)
Earnings After Tax & Before Ab. Items	136.1	126.6	155.5	214.3	204.1
Abnormal Items (net of tax)		(38.5)	(5.1)	(12.0)	17.0
Net Earnings	136.1	88.1	150.4	202.3	221.1
Distributions and Transfers	(87.6)	(87.6)	(87.0)	(93.5)	(86.8)
Retained Profits for the Year	48.5	0.5	63.4	108.8	134.3
Financial Position					
Current Assets	381.1[a]	355.8[b]	353.7	369.3	358.9
Current Liabilities	(413.5)	(366.6)	(366.2)	(442.8)	(413.6)
Working Capital	(32.4)	(10.8)	(12.5)	(73.5)	(54.7)
Deferred Taxation	(52.4)	(83.9)	(44.2)	(6.4)	(15.9)
Investments	124.7	124.8	132.1	106.0	117.7
Fixed Assets	1,159.2	1,010.6	937.5	996.3	1,057.9
Brands	1,993.7	1,964.3	2,011.9	2,052.6	2,142.0
Goodwill	220.1	235.8	251.5	267.0	282.0
	3,412.9	3,240.8	3,276.3	3,354.8	3,560.8
Financed by					
Paid in Capital	603.6	603.6	603.6	603.6	603.6
Reserves (incl. retained earnings)	1,466.8	1,308.6	1,350.8	1,305.6	1,286.4
Minority Interests	10.3	10.2	10.2	22.5	1.3
Noncurrent Liabilities	1,332.2	1,318.4	1,311.7	1,423.1	1,669.5
	3,412.9	3,240.8	3,276.3	3,354.8	3,560.8

Notes:[a] Includes inventories $124.2
   [b] Includes inventories $116.5

Source: Lion Nathan Limited, *Annual Report*, 1998, p. 62.

THE BREWING INDUSTRY IN NEW ZEALAND

Historically, the New Zealand brewing industry was highly concentrated.[4] In 1999, this industry was effectively a duopoly with the two major competitors, LN and DB Breweries, controlling about 97 percent of the beer market. Microbreweries accounted for a very small percentage. The two major players displayed a number of similarities. Both operated primarily on a national scale. DB had about 43 percent of the New Zealand market; LN, some 54 percent. Both companies had brewing capacities of around 200 million litres per year. Both companies were vertically integrated and enjoyed substantial ownership in companies that supply their raw materials. In addition, through forward integration they controlled wholesale distribution outlets. For example, DB owned Robbie Burns and Liquorland, and LN owned Liquor King. Competing products were similar, with differentiation based on marketing and price differences. Both companies enjoyed shelter from effective competition through the economies of scale and the very considerable capital costs of entering the industry. As both companies battled for leadership and control of a declining market, price competition was eroding profitability. Emerging developments in this industry included maturity of the beer market, proliferation of brands, growth of the premium beer brand, and changes in the location of consumption.

THE BREWING INDUSTRY IN AUSTRALIA

Historically, the Australian brewing industry was fragmented with a large brewery serving each local market. A gradual change in structure, in part the result of acquisition strategies, led to a situation in the mid-1980s where two national breweries, Carlton and United Breweries (CUB) and Bond Brewing, controlled almost 90 percent of the Australian beer market.[5] Government competition policy prevented any further concentration within this industry. Advertising and promotion expenditures increased as the competition between these two companies intensified. The financial difficulties of the Alan Bond empire led to its brewing operations (37.5 percent of the Australian market) being acquired by LN in 1990. CUB, with 52 percent market share, responded to this change by increasing investment in product development and marketing. LN's share of the Australian market increased to 46 percent in August 1993 with the acquisition of South Australian Breweries, after a CUB merger proposal for this company failed. LN's inherited portfolio of local brands provided the basis for its regional strategy and market leadership in Western Australia, South Australia, and Queensland. CUB worked to develop a national brand identity with several key brands including *Foster's Lager, Victoria Bitter, Foster's Light Ice,* and *Carlton Gold.* By 1999, as in New Zealand, demand growth was limited, per capita beer consumption was declining, and rising raw material costs were constraining profitability.

THE BREWING INDUSTRY IN CHINA

In 1998, there were over 600 brewers in the highly fragmented Chinese brewing industry, producing 17.8 million tonnes of beer. The sheer size of this beer market, servicing a population of 1.2 billion people, coupled with the growth potential due to increasing per capita consumption attracted many international brewers to China. However, growth rates had decreased dramatically from over 20 percent per year in the 1980s, to 12.5 percent on average between 1992 and 1997, and near 6 percent growth was projected from 1998 to 2001. Beer consumption had risen to average 14 litres per capita in 1998, but this was still low compared to average consumption of 30 to 40 litres in the Asian region, 87 litres in New Zealand, and 95 litres in Australia. The demand for beer was influenced by macroeconomic factors such as levels of unemployment and disposable income. Government rulings on items such as entertainment spending were also key to understanding beer consumption on public premises such as restaurants, bars and hotels. However, this aggregate level of analysis was of limited value in China, because there were quite different patterns of consumption throughout this vast country, particularly between urban and rural communities. For example, per capita beer consumption was 21 litres in the affluent urbanised Yangtze River Delta (YRD) region and closer to 29 litres within the leading city of Shanghai (the

Exhibit 4 Lion Nathan Limited: Financial Comparison, Statistics

	1998	1997	1996	1995	1994
Earnings After Tax and Before					
Abnormal Items Per Share (cents)	24.9	23.1	28.4	39.1	37.3
Net Asset Backing Per Share ($)	3.78	3.49	3.57	3.49	3.45
Current Assets to Current Liabilities (ratio)	0.9:1	1:1	1:1	0.8:1	0.9:1
Interest Cover (times)	3.2	3.0	2.9	2.5	2.2
Dividend Rate (excl supplements)(cents)	16.0	16.0	16.0	16.0	15.0
Dividend Cover (pre abnormals)(times)	1.6	1.4	1.8	2.4	2.4
Supplementary Dividend					
(foreign shareholder) (cents)	0.85	0.49	0.99	—	—
Dividend Imputation (%)	30.0	17.5	35.0	—	—
Net Debt/Net Debt & Equity (%)	38.7	40.5	40.9	44.1	48.0
Gearing (%)	63.2	68.0	69.1	78.9	92.4
Proprietorship Ratio (%)	53.6	52.2	52.5	49.3	47.7
Share Price 31 August (cents)	410	395	383	317	340
Highest During Year to 31 Aug. (cents)	550	412	389	338	430
Lowest During Year to 31 Aug. (cents)	340	322	305	261	295
Number of Shareholders	10,268	15,955	17,853	19,298	18,744
Number of Employees	4,072	3,741	3,624	3,690	3,140
Total Indirect Taxes Paid to Govt's. ($m)	1,069.0	864.4	880.5	869.9	885.5
Australian Dollar					
Period Closing Exchange Rate	0.873	0.873	0.873	0.859	0.809
Period Monthly Weighted Average	0.866				
Exchange Rate					
Chinese Renminbi					
Period Closing Exchange Rate	4.093	5.345	5.716	5.399	—
Period Monthly Weighted Average	4.854				
Exchange Rate					

Source: Lion Nathan Limited, *Annual Report*, 1998, p. 63.

"golden chalice"). Therefore, each region in China was considered a different market.Beyond the economic factors, provincial government requirements and limited transportation infrastructure for efficient distribution acted as specific constraints for multiregion or national participation. In addition, some uncertainty was created for foreign brewers by the government's signal of possible restriction of the proportion of beer sold by foreign firms to 30 percent, as it was not clear if, when,or how this would be implemented.

The major segments in the China beer market were linked to the quality and price of the beer. Exhibit 5 shows the key segments with their retail price points, market size in 1998, and market projections for 2001. Market share proportions for each segment in the Yangtze River Delta and Shanghai are shown in Exhibit 6.

Exhibit 5	China Beer Market Segments			
	Retail Price Points[a]	China 1998	China 2001	Examples
	(RMB)	(Tonnes)	(Tonnes)	
Imported Premium[b]	10.0	40,000	50,000	Heineken[c]
Premium	5.0-6.0	722,000	920,000	Beck's/Budweiser/Carlsberg
Mainstream	2.0-3.50	2,100,000	2,800,000	Reeb/Rheineck
Low End	Under 2.0[d]	14,900,000	14,500,000	GuangMing[e]
		17,762,000	18,270,000	
		========	========	

Notes   [a] Off-premise retail price points in Chinese reminbi (RMB), NZ1.00 = 4.67 RMB at 30 April 1999.

         [b] With 0.2% market share, this category was usually included in with other premium beer.

         [c] Retails for 12.50 RMB (NZ$2.67).

         [d] Most are priced close to 1.0 RMB (NZ$0.214).

         [e] Retails for 1.90 RMB (NZ$0.406).

Source: Lion Nathan China.

There were only 80 breweries in the country with capacity over 50 million litres; 18 of these had over 100 million litres capacity. The 10 largest domestic brewing groups accounted for less than 20 percent of the total market. Exhibit 7 shows the major international brewers operating in China in 1998 with their origin, type of investment, production capacity, and beer brands. Profiles of the major competitors are provided in Exhibit 8.

The low end of the China beer market was the largest segment served by several hundred small, state-owned domestic brewers. Many of these breweries suffered from problems of quality, were unable to achieve efficient operations, had insufficient capital for any improvements, and were unable to return a profit. With low-priced products and high distribution costs because of limited transportation networks, these brewers typically served a geographically limited, local market. The situation in this market segment was summarised by media commentator Denise McNabb as follows:

> Inefficient and undercapitalised, loss-making breweries are in their death throes as the government stops propping them up in line with cost-cutting reforms, which include the removal of housing and medical subsidies. Ugly price wars are expected to emerge as the tiny state-owned brewers make last-ditch efforts to stay alive by selling below cost on already thin margin prices of 1.9 renminbi (about NZ40 cents) for a 640 ml (quart) bottle.[6]

Brewers in the mainstream segment provided a higher quality beer at a slightly higher price (average 2.5 RMB, NZ$0.53). With higher margins but major executional challenges in sales and distribution, the mainstream segment attracted some of the more adventurous international brewers, including Asia Pacific Breweries with its Reeb (i.e., beer spelt backwards), Carlsberg with Karhu, Lion Nathan with Taihushui and Rheineck, and Suntory from the Japanese brewer Suntory (see Exhibits 7 and 8).

As Exhibit 6 illustrates, the mainstream and premium segments in the YRD and in Shanghai were significantly larger than the national average; Exhibit 5 shows that these segments were expected to continue to grow, while the overall market was static. In the coastal cities region the premium segment was estimated to be 7 percent of the market. Gross margins from 40 percent to 60 percent were needed in the brewing industry to cover marketing (30 percent to 100 percent), freight and warehousing (10 percent to 15 percent), and administration and other overhead expenses (10 percent to 40 percent). Assuming comparable production costs for mainstream and premium beer, the margins for premium beer were significantly higher (50 percent). However, profitability was elusive in this industry, with marketing expenses running between 30 percent to 120 percent of sales.

The premium segment was most attractive for international brewers because of the higher margins and the long-term potential in the China market. Most of the brewers were involved with joint ventures or licensing contracts for domestic brewing with local partners (see Exhibit 7). Exhibit 9 shows the premium market share for the top 10 brewers in China. By 1999, with overcapacity intensifying competition and economic growth declining, several of these foreign brewers were cutting back their involvement, putting breweries up for sale (e.g., Foster's), and reconsidering their future options in China (e.g., San Miguel). The imported premium segment was a niche segment for the most expensive beer brands. Rather than taking advantage of lower cost production within China, Heineken's premium beer was imported and, therefore, incurred higher transportation and production costs, but also realised a substantially higher selling price.

Seasonality had a major impact on the beer market in China. As Exhibit 10 shows, consumption of premium beer, primarily on licensed premises such as restaurants, bars, and hotels, did not show as much seasonal variation as sales of

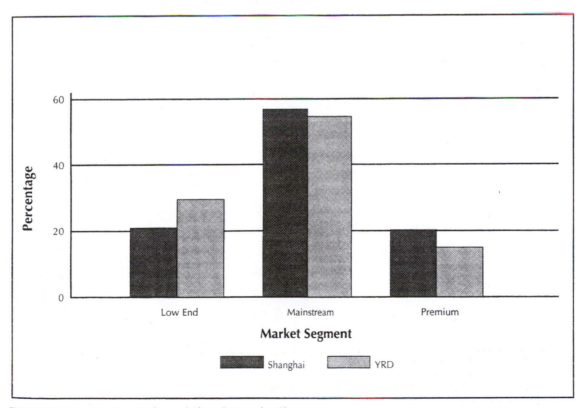

EXHIBIT 6 Yangtze River Delta and Shanghai Market Share

mainstream beer. However, to understand these beer consumption patterns, it was necessary to appreciate the perception of beer in China. Steve Mason, who had been LN's business development manager (China) and then marketing director in China for 2 years before becoming LN's corporate marketing director, explained:

Beer is seen to be a healthy drink, nutritive, low alcohol, no social downsides. Historically, strong alcohol beverages have been drunk, like white spirits or rice wine-based drinks that might be, say, 60 percent or 15 percent to 20 percent alcohol. Central government encouraged breweries as a moderation thing. So beer is seen as a beverage. It's not seen as a liquor or alcohol. So it's seen as a beverage choice. What will I have? A beer or a Pepsi or a cup of tea? With the communal society in China, there is a lot of emphasis put around meal times. Beer in conjunction with food is the habit. So you don't just go out to have a drink. Beer is an auxiliary to food.

Exhibit 7 Major Brewers and Brands in China, 1998

Brewers	Origin	Investment Type[c]	Capacity[a, b]	Premium	Mainstream Brands	Low End
Anheuser-Busch	USA	JV in Wuhan 5% in Tsingtao	250	Budweiser		
Asia Pacific	Singapore Holland	JV in Shanghai Imported JV in Hainan JV in Fuzhou	200 200 100	Tiger Heineken Heritage	Reeb	
Asahi	Japan	JV in Hangzhou	600	Asahi		
Beck's	Germany	JV in Fujian	150	Beck's		
Carlsberg	Denmark	JV in Shanghai	180	Carlsberg	Karhu	
Changzhou	Local					Guangyulan
Fosters	Australia	JV in Shanghai	120	Fosters Haoshun		Guangming Pujing Shanghai
Interbrew	Belgium	JV in Nanjing JV in Nanjing JV in Guangzhou	80 60		Jinling YaLi	
Linkman	Local				Linkman	
Lion Nathan	NZ	WFO in Suzhou JV in Wuxi	200 120	Steinlager Carbine	Rheineck Taihushui	
Kirin	Japan	JV in Shenyang	120	Kirin		
Miller	USA	JV in Beijing	200	Miller		
Pabst Blue Ribbon	USA	JV in Guangdong	350		Pabst	
San Miguel	Philippines	JV in Baoding	600	San Miguel		
South African	South Africa	5 breweries - North	950			Snowflake
Suntory	Japan	JV in Shanghai	200	Suntory	Suntory	
Tianmuhu	Jiangsu		50			Tianlun Tianmuhu Huaguang
Tsingtao[d]	Qingdao	5 breweries	800			Tsingtao
Zhanjiagang	Jiangsu		70	Dongwu		Zhangjiagang

Notes: [a] Capacity is in million litres.
[b] Capacity utilisation is generally low.
[c] International ownership varies for these joint venture partnerships.
[d] Largest local brewery in China.

Source: Lion Nathan China.

Exhibit 8 Key Players in the China Beer Industry

Although almost all of the world's major breweries have sought to establish a presence in China, there are significant differences in the competitive position and strategies of the various key players.

Anheuser-Busch

This American company was the world's largest brewer, selling its premium Budweiser brand in 60 countries around the world. The company was aiming for 20 percent of the world's market share. Anheuser-Busch entered the China market with a joint venture (80 percent) in Wuhan (on the Yangtze River for transportation access) in 1994. Anheuser-Busch was 1,160 km. by road and 1,400 km. by rail to Shanghai. Establishing a small stake in Tsingtao, China's largest domestic producer and exporter of beer, provided local connections for Anheuser-Busch and a status partner for Tsingtao. Budweiser was the leading premium beer brand with 30 percent of the China market in 1998. In China, the company built on high levels of ambient awareness of its brand from television, movies, sport, and sponsorship. In addition, Anheuser-Busch invested heavily in marketing to build brand equity; it also used its dominant international brand and resources to establish deals for access to on-premise retailers. By raising the costs to compete, Anheuser-Busch reduced the ability of most competitors to obtain profits from the premium beer segment in China, which lead to industry rationalisation.

Asahi

Founded in 1889, 90 percent of the Japanese Asahi Breweries' sales were from its flagship brand, Asahi Super Dry, which was marketed in over 30 countries. Asahi produced specialty beer, including a black draft, Asahi Kuronama, and a low-calorie beer for women, Asahi First Lady. The company also operated about 1 30 restaurants and sold other beverages, including soft drinks, wines, fruit juices, and whiskey. Growth in international activities through alliances was being developed in Europe and North America. In 1998, Asahi was a major player in the premium segment (estimated at 7 percent share of the China market) with very large-scale capacity (600 million litres). The company had joint ventures in Beijing, Quanzhou, and Hangzhou. Asahi was investing heavily in television and media to develop its premium brand; however, its foreign-image positioning was not as distinct as the American or European premium brands. Further development of distribution and trade networks was required to further increase sales volume.

Beck's

Founded in 1873 by a master builder with a passion for brewing beer, the German Brauerei Beck & Co. produced and sold its premium Beck's beer around the world. The company had a strong international focus with divisions in Finland, Greenland, Great Britain, the United States, Canada, Venezuela, Taiwan, and Puerto Rico. The Beck's brand was differentiated with a distinctive shaped bottle and positioned as a top-quality, world-class premium beer. The company had strict quality guidelines for raw materials and the brewing process, to achieve its unique quality and flavour. In China, Beck's beer was brewed under license at Putian [100 km. from Shanghai by road] and sold in over 40 cities, primarily located along the coast from Shenyang to Guangzhou. From mid-1999, the production and marketing of Beck's brand was to be taken over by Lion Nathan China.

Carlsberg

Carlsberg, a Danish company, had global brewing operations in 140 markets, brewing in 40 countries, and 80 percent of sales from overseas markets. The company's brewery construction division entered China in the mid-1980s, renovating 40 breweries. In 1994, Carlsberg established a joint venture brewery (with a Hong Kong trading partner) in Huizhou, Guangdong province, for its premium brand beer [1,600 km. from Shanghai by road]. The company built a new brewery in Shanghai in 1998 and successfully launched a new mainstream brand (Kaihu).

Foster's

This Australian brewer entered China in 1993 with joint ventures in Shanghai and Guangdong, adding a third brewery in Tianjin in 1995. Foster's strategic intent was to become the largest brewer in China with a national network of breweries, selling Foster's premium lager and several mainstream brands. In Shanghai, the company invested heavily in signage - the Foster's signs were in many key central city display areas, but the premium beer was not widely available. To curb continuing losses in Asia, Foster's admitted an "over aggressive" strategy in China and in 1998 announced plans to cut back. Sale of its breweries in Tianjin and Guangdong were announced in 1999, allowing the company to focus on the Shanghai market.

Heineken

Heineken, the largest European brewer, operated in over 170 countries, with shares in over 60 brewing companies. Heineken was a global beer brand with a high level of ambient awareness from television coverage, movies, sport, and sponsorship. In China, Heineken beer was imported and sold as super-premium, working with Asia Pacific Breweries joint ventures in Haikou (Hainan province) and Fuzhou. The company used local mainstream brands to achieve cost-efficient volumes while building its premium brand. Heineken was aiming for national coverage of key hotels in China and was prepared to wait while the premium segment grew, but it was not interested in lowering its prices to increase sales volume.

Kirin

Kirin, the fourth largest brewing group in the world, attempted initially to enter the Chinese market through a licensing arrangement, but then formed a joint venture with a local brewer at Zhuhai in Guangdong province. Kirin's premium beer was positioned as a high-quality beer because it was brewed with a single filtration process (and, therefore, had a higher extract loss than standard brewing processes). Kirin targeted Japanese expatriate consumers and their Japanese association. Kirin's beer was also produced under license at Shenyang, in northern China, by South African Breweries. Kirin, with a 45 percent equity stake in Lion Nathan, was planning to have some beer brewed under contract at Lion Nathan's brewery in Suzhou. Apart from its brewing operations, Kirin had joint ventures to produce and sell other beverages (e.g., soft drinks and fruit juices) in China. At home in Japan, Kirin had 15 breweries and captured 40 percent market share; it also sold over 300 beverage products in categories such as soft drinks, tea, coffee, wine, and spirits. Kirin had partnerships in pharmaceutical plants and research laboratories. Other joint venture and subsidiary businesses were in food service and restaurants, transportation, sports and recreation, engineering,building management, and business systems.

San Miguel

The largest brewer in the Philippines, San Miguel began a 5-year overseas expansion into the Asian region in 1998, aiming to brew the most beer in Asia and to be in the top 10 brewers in the world (by volume). The company had four breweries spread across China (including joint ventures in Baoding, Guangzhou, and Shunde) producing its premium beer, plus operations in Indonesia and Vietnam. Following the Asian economic crisis and losses in its China operations, San Miguel's new CEO announced plans (late 1998) to cut back loss-making businesses and focus on regaining market share in its domestic beer market. Talks with four international brewing companies (Anheuser-Busch, Carlsberg, Heineken, and South African Breweries) were underway to find a partner for its China breweries. San Miguel had a portfolio of businesses in food and beverages.

South African Breweries

South African Breweries had 16 brands providing 98 percent of the domestic beer market in South Africa and international operations spread throughout Africa, Asia, and Europe. The company's entry strategy in China involved buying into a local brewery with a joint venture agreement, then upgrading the operations and brands, rationalising costs, and building distribution infrastructure. This approach was replicated five times in the northern region of China, establishing large-scale capacity for local mainstream and low-end brands. In 1999, the company had two joint ventures in Shenyang and one in each of the following: Dalian, Chengdu, and Jilin. Each area was treated as an independent regional market. Bottled water was also produced and sold by its joint venture on the Hong Kong-Guangzhou border.

Suntory

Suntory was Japan's leading producer and distributor of alcoholic and nonalcoholic beverages. The company was also involved in pharmaceuticals, restaurant operation, sports, music and film, resort development, publishing, and information services. Approximately two-thirds of its annual international sales were from the food and nonalcoholic beverages and 20 percent from alcoholic beverages. In 1984, Suntory established China's first joint venture specialising in beer; in 1994, the company extended its alcoholic beverages to include whiskies and brandies. This company had a large joint venture brewery in Shanghai and a small brewery at Lianyungang (65 million litres). It sold a premium brand with very low volume; however, in the mainstream segment in Shanghai, Suntory was in second place (selling 50,000 tonnes in 1998), behind Asia Pacific's Reeb beer. The company used extensive market research to develop its positioning and promotion imagery.

Tsingtao

China's largest domestic brewer, Tsingtao was founded in 1903 by British and German businessmen and taken over by the Qingdao Municipal People's Government in 1949. From its head office and five major breweries in Qingdao in Shandong province, plus a few affiliates around the country, Tsingtao provided nearly 3 percent of the total Chinese beer production in 1998. In addition, Tsingtao exported beer to over 30 countries, which provided foreign exchange to import raw materials, packaging, technology, and equipment. The company responded to intensifying competition from foreign brewers by increasing its production capacity and revamping its sales and distribution network. Tsingtao beer was the best-selling domestic brand, sold at a premium to other domestic beer because of its popularity and reputation for award-winning quality taste.

Sources: Company, industry, and media reports.

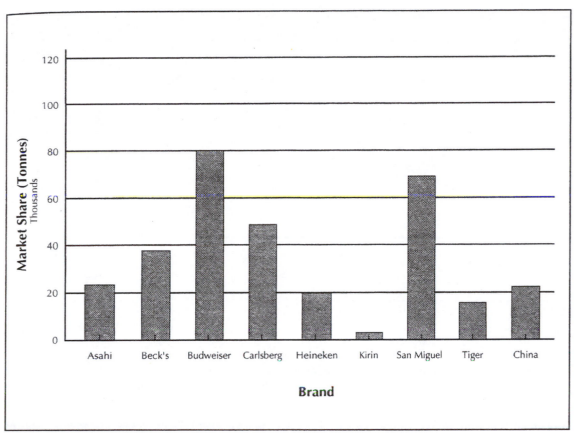

EXHIBIT 9 China Premium segment market share

Source: Lion Nathan China

Further, beer was a "cooling" beverage typically consumed warm, on a hot summer day. In winter, a "warming" drink such as rice wine was preferred, so sales of off-premise beer declined dramatically from October. Frank Gibson, who was the company's strategy director within China, elaborated on the nature of Chinese beer:

> *Chinese beer is clear and lager-like, drunk mainly in the humid summer months. This reflects its German heritage—the main brewery schools are still taught in the German mould. Even though more Chinese households now have refrigerators, it is not drunk cold, as this is considered unhealthy by Chinese.*

Mainstream beer was generally purchased in small quantities (one or two bottles) from a nearby street stall and carried to a multistory apartment block home. There was a myriad of small, off-premise retailers in China running kiosks, commonly known as "mom and pop" stores. Mason described the scale of these stores as follows:

> *The "retail outlet" is often nothing more than a shelving unit stuck to the front of someone's house. There are fewer than a dozen bottles of beer of various brands, some cans of soft drink, chewing gum, washing powder, sweets, and a shelf within a shelf containing packets of cigarettes and cheap lighters. In the doorway, an old lady sits knitting in the winter haze.*

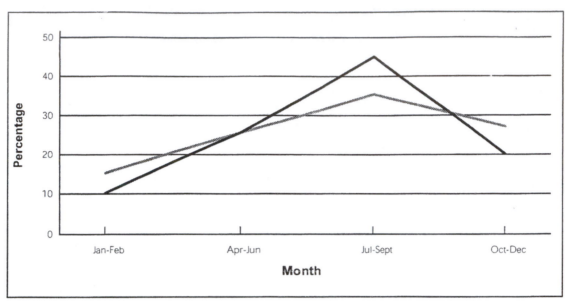

EXHIBIT 10 China Beer Market Seasonality

Source: Lion Nathan China

LNC sources estimated that there were 350,000 to 400,000 retailers of beer in the Yangtze River Delta region. Thirty local breweries operated in this region, servicing the population of 70 million via 200 to 300 distributors and 6,000 to 8,000 wholesalers. The structure of the YRD beer industry from production through to consumers is summarised in Exhibit 11.

Premium beer was primarily consumed in restaurants, bars, and hotels. Status was a major influence on consumption in this segment. Restaurants were prolific in this socialistic society. Steve Mason, who did LN's early research on the Chinese beer market and later became the chief marketing officer, explained, "As face is extremely important in China, you will drink internationally famous high-quality beer when entertaining clients or staff at restaurants." Therefore, the levels of government and corporate entertainment budgets acted as a driver for this segment of the beer market.

Market share statistics for the top brands in each beer segment for the five key cities in the YRD from 1996 to 1998 are shown in Exhibit 12. Even within this small regional sample, the volatility of the beer market was evident. New brands skyrocketed from obscurity to dominance within a few months with strong advertising, sales promotion, distribution, and support. However, with numerous competing brands and limited brand loyalty, leading brands could also disappear just as quickly. Developing brand equity was therefore a key challenge for competitors in this industry.

THE MACROENVIRONMENT IN CHINA

After record growth for nearly 2 decades, China's economic growth rate fell below the government's 8 percent of GDP target in 1998, with slower export growth, falling retail prices, and weaker consumption; the level of per capita GDP was $2,800 at this time. By comparison, Australia's economic growth estimate was 4.7 percent in 1998, with $23,600 GDP per capita; and New Zealand had -0.4 percent growth estimate and $18,500 per capita GDP.[7] However, the scale of expansion

Regional Market Architecture, Highly Fragmented

Brewery (local)	Distributors	Wholesalers	Retailers	Consumers
30	200-300	6,000-8,000	350,000-400,000	70 million
Servicing 100-250 distributors/ wholesalers/retailers	Servicing 50-80 wholesalers	Servicing 50-150 retailers	150-200 consumers	1,500 million litres
Average = 40 m. litres	Average = 300,000 crates	Average = 4,500 crates/ wholesalers	Average = 250 crates/ retailer	Average = 22 litres per capita
= 2,500,000 crates per year	= 1,500 truck loads per year	= 25 truck loads		= 33 bottles p.a.

China Update 4/98 10

EXHIBIT 11 Yangtze River Delta Beer Industry Structure

Source: Lion Nathan China.

that China offered as a consumer market was exponential. By 2000, there would be 160 cities with a population over 1 million people; 250 cities with annual income levels high enough to support consumerism; and 260 million people able to afford packaged consumer products, hence—the world's largest market in many categories including beer and biscuits.[8]

There were still many major challenges ahead for the Chinese government on the road to a free-market economy. The financial system was reported by *The Economist* to be a "mess," but the currency was not considered to be overvalued against a basket of its trading partners:

> There is no doubt that China is stuck with a cluster of financial time-bombs. Its state banks are insolvent, and they have few reliable borrowers. The competence and power of financial supervisors are stretched too thin, while mismanagement and fraud are stripping state assets. The central government has mounting financial liabilities, not least to pay for welfare and for infrastructure meant to sustain growth, but its grip on tax revenue is even shakier.[9]

Reforms were underway, and subsidies were being removed, but there were major performance problems in the state sector, as described in *Fortune* magazine:

> The major roadblock: a largely unreformed state manufacturing sector, numbering 300,000 enterprises, that employs 70 percent of the urban workforce (109 million workers), but generates only 30 percent of industrial output. Officially, around 40 percent of these enterprises are losing money; the true figure is certainly much higher.[10]

Reform packages typically included restructuring the state owned enterprise's (SOE's) operating systems and establishing social security systems and re-employment projects. However, allowing loss-making SOEs to continue operating avoided some of the social problems engendered by high unemployment levels. Nevertheless, the gap between rich and poor was increasing. There was an urban drift; according to a World Bank study, 80 million people had moved to the cities in search of work.

Exhibit 12 Yangtze River Delta Key Cities: Market Size for Key Brands, 1996–1998 (all figures in tonnes)

Shanghai 420,000

Premium (70,000)	1996	1997	1998	Mainstream (23,000)	1996	1997	1998	Low End (120,000)	1996	1997	1998
Budweiser	11,000	16,000	15,000	Reeb	133,152	88,154	70,182	Guangming	37,000	40,000	49,000
Beck's	18,600	18,800	10,836	Suntory	5,800	43,030	50,000	Zhonghua	8,000	6,000	7,000
Carlsberg	2,800	2,900	2,800	Rheineck	0	10,407	22,000	Qianjiang	6,600	4,000	4,500
San Miguel	1,800	1,500	1,400	Karhu	0	0	10,000	Shanghai	31,840	31,331	30,000
Tiger	2,335	2,961	3,903	Qingdaoa	26,000	24,200	25,000	Donghai	12,320	9,900	10,000
Heineken	650	700	750	Pabst	3,000	2,300	2,400	Swan	17,017	14,115	14,000
Kirin	600	620	600								

Suzhou 105,000

Premium (15,000)	1996	1997	1998	Mainstream (50,000)	1996	1997	1998	Low End (40,000)	1996	1997	1998
Budweiser	3,360	6,200	1,000	Taihushui	10,000	16,050	14,664	Zhangjiagang	30,000	27,696	8,000
Beck's	4,200	4,100	800	Linkman	2,000	1,500	500	Dongwu	7,000	6,200	4,000
Carlsberg	840	550	200	Rheineck	0	1,700	10,345	White Swan	15,000	12,602	6,000
San Miguel	240	650	200	Reeb	1,500	2,200	5,000	Shajiabang	14,000	12,200	4,000
Tiger	60	160	100	Sankong	5,000	4,720	1,000	Bawang	6,000	4,020	5,000
Heineken	60	220	200	Wumin	3,000	2,200	800	Weili	4,000	3,700	1,000
Qingdaoa	200	300	600	Pabst	100	100	100				

Wuxi 92,000

Premium (11,000)	1996	1997	1998	Mainstream (54,000)	1996	1997	1998	Low End (27,000)	1996	1997	1998
Budweiser	1,500	2,200	2,900	Taihushui	27,000	29,384	30,000	Zhangjiagang	15,000	13,800	12,000
Beck's	3,300	3,000	2,000	Shanjuan	10,000	10,916	10,000	Fuli	6,000	5,850	4,000
Carlsberg	500	450	234	Rheineck	0	3,550	2,934				
San Miguel	650	600	550	Linkman	2,000	1,800	1,000				
Heineken	100	130	156	Guanyulan	1,300	1,200	200				
Qingdaoa	400	500	700	Pabst	350	400	350				

Nanjing 114,000

Premium (26,000)	1996	1997	1998	Mainstream (70,000)	1996	1997	1998	Low End (18,000)	1996	1997	1998
Budweiser	4,300	6,000	11,500	Jinling	33,070	33,613	27,000	Zhangjiagang	800	500	300
Beck's	3,500	2,500	1,000	Yali	11,860	38,175	25,000	Tianmuhu	1,000	700	300
Carlsberg	1,200	800	400	Rheineck	0	1,700	17,000	Shenquan	10,000	9,500	9,000
San Miguel	1,200	800	400	Qingdaoa	2,900	2,950	3,000	Tiandao	4,000	4,500	5,000
Heineken	30	40	50	Pabst	6,400	3,000	1,500	Tianjin	3,000	3,500	4,000
Hansha	450	300	200								

Changzhou 70,000

Premium (4,000)	1996	1997	1998	Mainstream (36,000)	1996	1997	1998	Low End (30,000)	1996	1997	1998
Budweiser	800	1,200	1,000	Guangyulan	32,622	26,214	20,000	Tianmuhu	11,100	26,214	27,000
Beck's	1,500	1,400	1,400	Linkman	2,896	2,959	10,000	Zhangjiagang	2,400	2,300	2,400
Carlsberg	230	250	200	Taihushui	3,200	3,800	3,939				
San Miguel	150	280	250	Rheineck	0	40	1,659				
Heineken	15	25	20	Qingdaoa	500	350	400				
				Pabst	400	350	400				

[a] Qingdao is priced at RMB3.5 and is categorised as subpremium (overseas Chinese spelling is *Tsingtao*).

Source: Lion Nathan China.

China's landlocked hinterland remains, for the most part, an overcrowded world of poor peasants, rapacious officials, and indolent factory managers, with walk-on parts for disaffected ethnic minorities. It's here where foreign investment is thinnest that Premier Zhu Rongji must overcome the toughest resistance to reform.[11]

Improvements were being made to the transportation infrastructure, particularly between key cities in the coastal regions. However, difficulties with interregional and urban distribution were unlikely to be resolved quickly, as demand for transportation was increasing at a faster rate than the new capacity. With limited private ownership of motor vehicles and poor public transportation systems, the number of small-scale stores was increasing. The number of supermarkets was also increasing in the larger cities, but less than 10 percent of grocery sales were made in these "large format" stores.[12]

Patterns of consumer demand in China were found to vary by age and social activity. Price sensitivity increased with age. Consumers under 30 years of age were least sensitive to price and most responsive to marketing ". . . they are most likely to be familiar with advertising, especially on television, and to base their purchase decisions on its messages."[13] Within this segment, the majority were socially inactive, sticking close to home and family. The socially active minority group, who spent a lot of time on entertainment and travel, "perceive advertising as truthful, prefer branded products, and put a high value on attractive and comfortable retail environments."[14] The influx of new products to Chinese stores provided these consumers with endless opportunities to experiment with different products and brands. Consumers over 45 years of age, influenced by their experiences in China's Cultural Revolution, were "highly sensitive to price and respond negatively to new products and most forms of marketing."

Lifestyles and culture in China were strongly based upon relationships. Stemming from the Confucian view, family relationships were very important. This meant respect for elders, deference to authority, rank consciousness, modesty, ancestor worship, and harmony (avoidance of direct confrontation) were stressed. There was a cultural focus on team effort and enhancing group harmony. The group process was not just based on authority; it also strongly focused on consensus. For the collectivist Chinese, the family, including extended family and friends, was the prime group towards which allegiance was owed and paid. In the business context, having a good relationship (guanxi) network in China was the single most important factor for business success. Guanxi was the intricate, pervasive network of personal relationships that Chinese people cultivated with energy and imagination. Guanxi was not just a relationship network but one with obligations. In contrast to Western society where social order and business practices were regulated by law, the Chinese were willing to bend rules in order to get things done. It was regarded as reasonable and acceptable to find ways to avoid the consequences of rules, so that Chinese with guanxi connections could circumvent government regulations for their own benefit and for those to whom they owed an obligation.

China was a major player within the broader Asian region. Diplomats and other officials were lobbying actively for China's admission to the World Trade Organisation. Media commentators were optimistic that this would occur by 2002. Although rules for market access and tariff levels in many industries would be reviewed, increased uncertainty was expected during the transition period as new regulations and procedures were established. Throughout the Asian region, fluctuations in economic and political stability within specific countries created ripples for neighbouring nations, including China. For example, the economic crisis in Korea in 1997 had major impacts on trading partners throughout the region. Similarly, political instability in Indonesia had social and economic consequences extending beyond this country.

LION NATHAN CHINA, LNC

LN's research identified the Yangtze River Delta (YRD) as the best region for its entry to China. Ex-McKinsey consultant Paul Lockey, whose responsibilities included LN's corporate strategy and corporate finance, explained:

> *With a population of 70 million, the Delta is an area of relative wealth, high growth and above-average beer consumption. It has a rapidly developing infrastructure, including new highways along key corridors, express rail services, and a supply and service industry base suitable for foreign ventures.*

LN's entry strategy was to take a small, measured step into an existing brewery with an upgrade path, learn, and then build on the experience. The *Taihushui* Brewery at Wuxi was a profitable joint venture with good plant and astute management. LN's $50 million investment was used to double capacity to 120 million litres, improve the quality and the shelf life of the beer, introduce new packaging, expand distribution, and develop sales capabilities. David Sullivan, who was on LN's managing team for this joint venture and responsible for establishing processes, systems, and controls, explained LN's approach at Wuxi:

> *We brought in a sales director, who was an expatriate Hong Kong Chinese, out of Coca-Cola to try and build some sales skills into the workforce. We leveraged the expats like Steve Mason [LN's corporate marketing officer] to come in and improve the Taihushui brand, change the packaging a little bit, bring in new advertisements, look at how we communicated with the consumer, and do some research—basically, bringing Western sales and marketing practices into the business.*
>
> *We had a very good relationship. It started well. We valued the business at a fair price. We immediately doubled the size of it. We retained the workforce. We didn't do anything that created an unfair, unreasonable work environment for the local staff. We very much approached it from "We're here to learn and we're here to teach. You teach us about the local market, and we'll teach you about marketing." In the finance area, for example, we said, "This is what we want you to report, and this is how we want you to do it. Now, let's show you how to do it and teach you why it is important for us," rather than saying "Do this" or "Our guy will do this." We put a lot of trust in them, and they put a lot of trust in us.*

Confidence was developed from this first experience in China, the expansion programme was successful, sales and profits grew, and LN increased its ownership in this joint venture to 80 percent.

LN's second step into China was a bold commitment to build a large, world-class brewery in nearby Suzhou. Located within a 70-square-kilometre special development zone, Suzhou Industrial Park (SIP), established by the Chinese and Singaporean governments in 1994, enabled LN to create a privileged asset. Wholly-foreign ownership, which was highly restricted for breweries elsewhere in China, was a unique advantage that SIP offered for early investors. As Steve Mason, LN's chief marketing officer, explained:

To be able to talk about wholly-foreign owned sounds significant, but not particularly awesome. But in China it really, really is awesome. The autonomy to be able to make your own decisions and to be able to act on those decisions—the significance of that autonomy of action is absolutely awesome.

Efficient transportation links were available from Suzhou by air, road, rail, and canal to Shanghai and other key YRD cities. SIP provided utilities such as water, power, and telecommunications for industrial and residential usage. Other key support services for investors included a one-stop service for company incorporation and construction permits, local customs clearance, and warehousing and distribution.[15] This infrastructure and SIP's services were important for LN's "green field" project. The company also saved $50 million on import duties for plant and equipment; this duty-free policy ceased in 1997. A turnkey approach, driven by performance-based contracts and international sourcing of materials, enabled LN to complete the "single best facility in China" in just 16 months. Speaking at the official Suzhou opening ceremony in September 1998, Jim O'Mahony, managing director of Lion Nathan China, LNC, said, "We have built the capability to achieve our objective of being the leading brewer in the Yangtze Delta." Production capacity of the state-of-the-art brewery was 470 million bottles of beer per year or more than 1 million bottles per day.

LION NATHAN CHINA: STRATEGY

The vision of Lion Nathan China was "to become the leading brewer in the Yangtze River Delta by 2000 and the market leader in the Shanghai-Nanjing corridor." Three core values were emphasised in the company's formal and informal activities—passion, integrity, and realism. LNC's strategy for competing in China was updated in 1997 with input from the international strategy specialist consultancy firm, McKinsey & Co. LNC's five-point strategy involved (1) market leadership in the mainstream beer segment within the Shanghai-Nanjing corridor of the Yangtze River Delta, (2) developing a differentiated brand portfolio including premium and mainstream brands, (3) selling premium beer outside the YRD, (4) out-executing the competition, and (5) leading industry consolidation.

Reflecting on LNC's strategic position in February 1999, after 18 months as managing director for China, O'Mahony said:

We are focusing on five key cities in the Shanghai to Nanjing corridor, south of the Yangtze river. We are number 1 or number 2 in three of those cities already [in mainstream beer] . . . but Shanghai is going to be a real battle.

We have four brands now in our portfolio: Taihushui, meaning "water of lake Tai," is a high-quality mainstream beer for blue-collar workers; Rheineck, launched in 1997 with a foreign name and packaging linked to Germany, is positioned as a more outgoing mainstream beer for blue- and white-collar markets; Carbine is a dark, niche beer positioned at restaurants, so it's a beer with food. Then we have Steinlager, launched in September 1998, positioned as a trendy premium beer in a curvy bottle for sale in night venues and upmarket restaurants. The gap in our portfolio is a premium beer in the status segment occupied at the moment by Budweiser, Beck's, Tiger, San Miguel and Carlsberg. Our objective is to forge an alliance with another international player to get access to a major premium brand. We are just about ready to make an announcement. Then we'll have done the portfolio work.

We've been constrained in terms of moving outside the Delta because of lack of a premium brand that can actually do it for us. Apart from 3 million kiwis, nobody's ever heard of Steinlager. But when we announce the deal with the international alliance partner, as it is already a brand that's got presence throughout China, we'll have an immediate volume that we can "piggy back" Steinlager onto.

We started with a zero base, and we are building capabilities and developing infrastructure to compete in this region. This is proving to be as difficult as all the others. We've had a massive recruitment exercise followed by intensive training. We had no systems in place, so we had to build all the basic systems for the business including accounting systems, credit collection, invoicing, and sales reporting. But I think we are in line with plan. I think we are doing as well as anybody else in China.

We believe the long-term success of the beer industry in China is based on consolidation. Our alliance will not only achieve our goal but also lead the way for major consolidation. We are hoping there will be a domino effect to drive industry consolidation.

Adopting a regional strategy in the Yangtze Delta was not only consistent with the company's expertise in its home markets, but it also aligned closely with understanding of the economic drivers in brewing. CFO Lockey explained that LNC was "a small player in global terms, but we are the biggest where we are." He believed the company was "well positioned with the lowest cost position and amongst the largest capacity." However, continued growth was not without its problems, as Lockey elaborated:

Sustaining growth at 70 percent [as in 1998] is quite extraordinary. A lot of that growth has come from entering new cities. You have to recognise that there are only so many cities you can enter. At that point, you have to compete more aggressively in the cities you are already in. There are some dynamics about just how far you can go. In the mainstream market, for instance, you can only ship the beer about 300 kilometres before the freight costs just kill profits. In the premium market, it is a little bit different. The product is heavy relative to its value, unlike shampoo or microchips. Worldwide, this tends to be a business where local production is a dominant factor.

LION NATHAN CHINA: STRUCTURE AND SYSTEMS

In addition to the two breweries at Wuxi and Suzhou, LNC had a head office and sales team based in Shanghai. The profile of LNC staff in February 1999 is shown in Exhibit 13, and the structure chart is in Exhibit 14. Eight of O'Mahony's senior management team were located at the Shanghai office. Many of these key staff were relatively new to these executive positions. However, the company's staff rotation policy meant that expats from Australia or New Zealand had at least 5 years' experience in two or three breweries before joining the China team. In addition, all of the local Chinese managers had previous experience in the beverage or consumer products industries.

Monthly reporting systems and processes were established in China, leveraging the knowledge and expertise from throughout the company. A consultative team-based approach was used to deal with projects and problems. Corporate staff, including chief executive officer Gordon Cairns, chief financial officer Paul Lockey,

Exhibit 13 Lion Nathan China: Staff Profile, February 1999				
	Shanghai	**Suzhou**	**Wuxi**	**Consolidated**
Corporate Administration	8	2	0	10
Finance	20	21	12	53
Human Resources	9	11	5	25
Information Technology	1	8	2	11
Marketing	8	0	0	8
Operations	0	181	254	435
Other	3	2	51	56
Sales	174	144	137	455
Total	223	369	461	1,053[a]

[a] There are seasonal variations in the total number of staff employed; e.g., extra staff are needed in operations for the peak months from May-August.

Source: Lion Nathan China.

and chief marketing officer Steve Mason regularly visited the Shanghai office for performance review and problem-solving meetings. These visits provided invaluable learning opportunities, as well as being directional and driving. To keep track of the many projects that were in process, LNC appointed Julian Chen as programme manager in the head office team in 1997.

Computer systems for planning and control were developed and installed in China using expertise and technology from Australia and New Zealand. As David Sullivan, who was on the project team for Wuxi and Suzhou and served as LNC's finance director during 1997 and 1998, explained:

> We've got computerised systems in Suzhou. We've put in a full suite of systems that we have in our other breweries. We did it in 3 months because we want computerised record keeping. We want to be able to report back to our corporate office. Other brewers have gone in and said, "Oh, whatever you give us will be fine; as long as the bank statements are reconciled, that'll do." We've gone in and said, "We want information." So we do the same performance reporting in China that we do in New Zealand or Australia. All our internal standards are exactly the same . . . for beer quality, marketing approvals, pricing decisions, human resource policies—everything is using our Lion Nathan standard.

Taking an uncompromising stand on fundamental business practices was a feature of the corporate culture. Motivated by the desire for high performance, the corporate team initiated a project in 1996 to capture best practice and apply it universally across the business. The "Lion Nathan Way" was described by O'Mahony, who joined LN in 1991 and led this development, as follows:

> The Lion Nathan Way is the "way we do things around here." It says three things—what we do, how we do it, and why we do it. It covers marketing, sales, HR, operations, finance, IT. They're not intended to be big binders that sit on the shelf; they're intended to be live documents. Each of them has a self-paced training module that goes with it. This is something that spans the whole of Lion Nathan.

This resource was particularly useful for LNC with induction and training of new staff, and it also provided guidelines for the full range of core business processes and

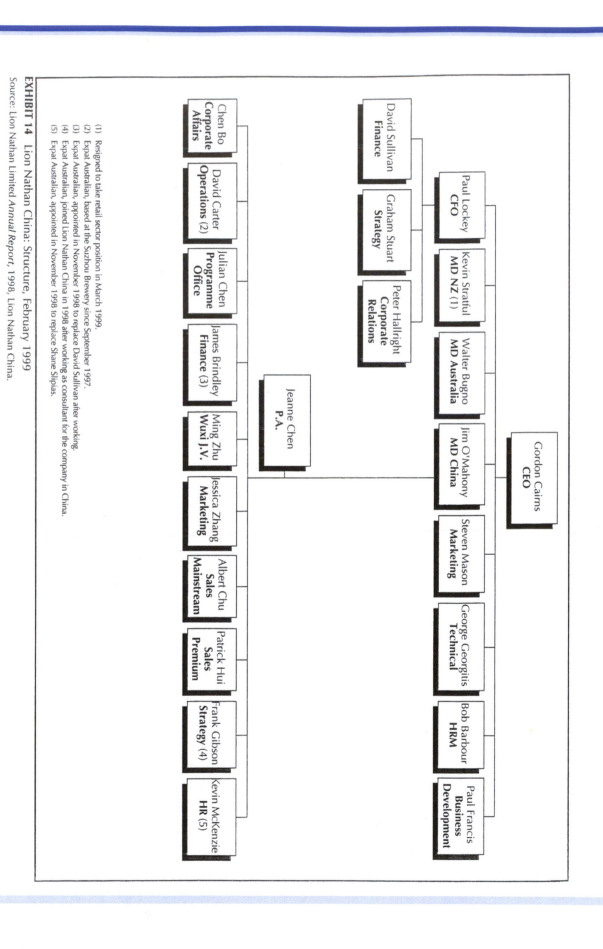

EXHIBIT 14 Lion Nathan China: Structure, February 1999

Source: Lion Nathan Limited Annual Report, 1998, Lion Nathan China.

(1) Resigned to take retail sector position in March 1999.
(2) Expat Australian, based at the Suzhou Brewery since September 1997.
(3) Expat Australian, appointed in November 1998 to replace David Sullivan after working.
(4) Expat Australian, joined Lion Nathan China in 1998 after working as consultant for the company in China.
(5) Expat Australian, appointed in November 1998 to replace Shane Slipias.

Gordon Cairns
CEO

David Sullivan
Finance

Paul Lockey
CFO

Kevin Stratful
MD NZ (1)

Walter Bugno
MD Australia

Jim O'Mahony
MD China

Graham Stuart
Strategy

Peter Hallright
Corporate Relations

Steven Mason
Marketing

George Georgitis
Technical

Bob Barbour
HRM

Paul Francis
Business Development

Chen Bo
Corporate Affairs

David Carter
Operations (2)

Julian Chen
Programme Office

James Brindley
Finance (3)

Jeanne Chen
P.A.

Ming Zhu
Wuxi J.V.

Jessica Zhang
Marketing

Albert Chu
Sales Mainstream

Patrick Hui
Sales Premium

Frank Gibson
Strategy (4)

Kevin McKenzie
HR (5)

activities, from financial reporting through to developing advertising copy and conducting consumer research.

LION NATHAN CHINA: HUMAN RESOURCES

People were critical for success of this business in China. Finding staff was not considered a problem by LNC in Shanghai; jobs were highly sought after in this progressive city as employment provided the work permits needed to relocate into this area. To select new staff, LNC looked for previous retail experience, ambition and ability of applicants. The company usually preferred recruits who were under 30 years of age and had more than 2 years' experience in another multinational corporation. Performance targets were established for each person, and a remuneration package including bonuses and rewards was negotiated. Status and loyalty were key elements of the Chinese culture, which influenced employment positions, promotions, and relationships, as Graham Stuart, LN's corporate strategy director (from February 1999) who had 5 years' experience working for LN in China, explained:

> *Ambitious young staff are prepared to work extremely hard toward long-term personal goals, especially those involving promotion and status. Western distinctions between personal and professional issues are not commonly understood in China. The hierarchical relationship between an employee and his/her boss is also intrinsically personal. Loyalty can be expected from employees as long as promises are kept. However, if they are dissatisfied, then they will feel this "contract" has been broken, and they may leave the company. Typically, they do not complain or ask for any explanation.*

According to Stuart, the main reasons for employees leaving jobs in China were (1) being offered more money elsewhere, (2) having pressures at work become too great, and (3) replacing expats with locals. The company had training systems in place to ensure that new staff not only understood their specific tasks, but also appreciated key corporate plans. Commenting on staff retention, Stuart said, "Retention of staff is not considered an issue for us in China, as we are still in a rapid growth phase."

Mindful of costs during the early stages of LNC's investment in China, the company leveraged knowledge and skills of key staff from Australia and New Zealand by flying them in for specific projects and then flying them home again. This project-based team approach was successful for introducing new systems and processes, as well as transferring and developing new skills within the local companies. This approach was also cost-effective because resident expatriates were significantly more expensive than local staff with their higher salaries, accommodation needs, and transport costs, plus needs for additional English-speaking support staff. Although the number of expatriates increased during the Suzhou construction phase, LNC's commitment to localise and build capabilities continued; by February 1999, LNC had only eight expatriate staff.

Rotating key staff throughout the company had many benefits for the company and the individuals concerned. Sullivan explained:

> *It transfers skills into the Chinese team, and it continually raises or benchmarks your standard against what we're doing back home. It's also development that the person then takes back home. Every person that we've sent to China from our business in Australia or New Zealand has come back saying they learnt so much. The environment is so different. They are so challenged. They're given a lot of*

responsibility to actually make things happen, and they've found it invaluable. This is why we've tended to try to use that project-based teamwork approach, rather than having a big bench of expats.

LION NATHAN CHINA: PRODUCTION

LNC's focus on brewing high-quality beer in Wuxi provided an initial source of differentiation in the mainstream market as the local breweries did not have the equipment, technology, or the systems to produce a consistent beverage. The addition of a large-scale, technologically advanced, world-class facility at Suzhou enabled LNC to produce at low cost. As LN's board chairman, Douglas Myers effused at the official opening of the Suzhou brewery in September 1998:

> *This brewery is a vital component in our China strategy. Without it, we would not have the capacity we need to continue our rapid growth. Nor would we have the capability to brew and package the high-quality premium brands necessary for profitability. The Suzhou Brewery is also an important asset as the beer market here undergoes very rapid change. It sets us apart as a brewery of the highest quality and lowest costs. Together with our first-class sales force, it gives us a strong position in the Yangtze River Delta.*

Capacity at Suzhou was also expandable as the plant design allowed for a mirror operation to be built on the same site. In 1998, LNC utilised one-third of the new plant's capacity (60,000 tonnes), which allowed for 100 percent volume growth in 1999. Brewing Beck's premium beer under license was expected to contribute a significant proportion of this new volume. LNC was also preparing to use some of this spare capacity for brewing Kirin's premium beer.

The process of brewing beer was well-known and documented. With sophisticated technological support, much of the craft of brewing had been routinised into precise scientific processes, which were able to be computer controlled. Fernando Coo, Suzhou's technical department manager, discussed LNC's brewing systems:

> *Our production systems are internally accredited with Class A ratings and externally validated by our ISO accreditation. The quality of raw materials is critical for beer attributes such as taste and colour. Availability and cost of raw materials have a major impact, too. Beer is made from malted barley, hops, yeast, and water. We get barley from Australia, Taiwan, Hong Kong, and Northern China; rice from Jiangsu province; and three different varieties of hops from New Zealand. Water, which is 90 percent of the beverage, is sourced locally (with assistance from SIP), filtered, and stored in tanks on site. Every beer has its own strain of yeast, which is grown from a 10 mL sample for 8 to 10 generations, and then a fresh batch is started. We are able to use the same suppliers for our breweries at Wuxi and Suzhou. At the other end of the process, we sell the grain residues that have been extracted as cattle feed.*

Quality was monitored at every stage of the brewing process. Further, to ensure that the consumer enjoyed consistent quality, the company worked to improve the shelf life of its beer and enforced strict rules for the product's life: LNC's beer was aged for 30 days before it was released, and it was destroyed if not sold within 84 days.

LION NATHAN CHINA: SALES AND DISTRIBUTION

Producing large volumes of top-quality beer to match local taste palettes was comparatively straightforward for LNC and other international brewers entering the China market. However, developing sales and distribution networks within this environment was significantly more challenging and complex than experiences elsewhere. LNC developed different systems for its two major market segments (see Exhibit 15): (1) selling mainstream brands for off-premise consumption through "mom and pop" stores and supermarkets; and (2) selling premium brands for consumption on-premise in restaurants, cafes, hotels, and bars.

LNC's off-premise system involved selling mainstream brands from five warehouses to 400 wholesalers, who then sold the beer to 70,000 retailers. Sales teams were established for the five YRD target cities, with account managers assigned to each wholesaler and merchandising managers providing the supporting merchandise (e.g., posters, price boards, shelf displays) for the retailers (to create consumer demand).

> The primary wholesaler is a man with a truck and a storage shed amid an enclave of houses down a track. He distributes the beer to the next-tier wholesaler, who stacks up a bike or rickshaw with heavy loads for distribution to small open-fronted shops (kiosks).[15]

Although beer sales in supermarkets were increasing (2 percent of total beer sales in 1998), the vast majority of off-premise beer was sold through "mom and pop" stores. These were typically small kiosks with a few shelves of basic household consumables such as soft drinks, beer, sweets, soap powder, and cigarettes. Located every few meters down many of the narrow streets, these cash-only stores provided a subsistence living. O'Mahony described the context for beer distribution:

> Most people in China go to the store next door, and they buy whatever they need to buy for that day or that half day. They go to the wet markets and buy what they need to buy in the wet market, the fruit market, or whatever. Now until that changes, we're not going to see much of a change in the distribution infrastructure in China. The people live in very concentrated areas. Public transport is ok, but people don't have cars. They can't afford taxis. So they are not going to carry bag loads of shopping long distances. They are going to buy very small quantities, frequently, and from the closest place to where they live as possible. We'll get in our car and drive 5 or 10 kms. to buy whatever we want. These guys won't. They will walk 100 metres. The normal quantity of beer purchased is one or two bottles at a time. Carrying one and a half kilos (which is two bottles) more than a short distance, if you are a frail old Chinese woman (the primary off-premise shopper) . . . is not something you are going to do.

The physical difficulties of frequent deliveries of crates of beer by tricycle through narrow, congested streets from the wholesaler to the retailer were handled by contractors. LNC negotiated contracts with wholesalers annually, but did not do direct store delivery of the returnable bottles and crates of mainstream beer.

Shanghai, a city of 13 million people in 6,340 square kilometres, was projected to be the leading consumer market in the twenty-first century. Although it offered a real challenge, LNC had 41,000 retail outlets systematically mapped and allocated to sales teams. Albert Chu, general manager for mainstream beer sales, had 160 permanent sales staff for this dynamic city. Chu outlined his ideas on this challenge as follows:

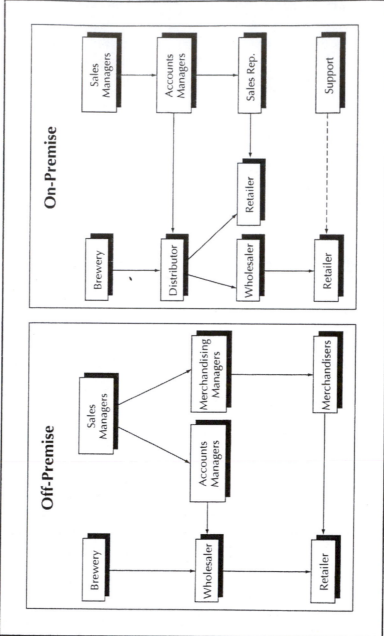

EXHIBIT 15 Lion Nathan China Sales Systems
Source: Lion Nathan China.

I was national sales director for Johnson & Johnson before joining LNC. I learned that increasing the proportion of stores stocking a product to 85 percent is needed to provide significant benefits from scale and market share. I am very keen to push the Rheineck brand to that level of coverage. I'd also like to increase our carton sales through supermarkets.

The process of making sales was highly social and time-consuming, requiring continuous communication, camaraderie, and cajoling. Major responsibilities were vested in regional sales managers to achieve aggressive sales targets. For example, Tommy Wang, one of LNC's top-performing regional sales managers, lead 71 staff servicing 84 wholesalers and 14,000 retailers in urban Shanghai; in Suzhou, Steven Zhu had a team of 68 staff for sales to 40 wholesalers, 250 secondary wholesalers, and 10,000 retailers. The on-premise system for selling premium brands involved the use of distributors to sell beer to wholesalers, as well as making some direct sales to large retail accounts (see Exhibit 15). LNC's sales managers had oversight of account managers who worked with the distributors. Sales representatives were employed to interact with wholesalers and retailers. Distributors typically carried a number of premium brands, with the exception of Anheuser-Busch specialists who were "voluntarily" exclusive. Selection of distributors and wholesalers was critical for success, as O'Mahony explained:

> There is always a big fight annually to get the best distributors and the best wholesalers. We have a system of annual contracts that run January through December. There is an annual rebate for hitting volume targets. We are in the middle of negotiating the 1999 contracts right now [2 February]. It is a competitive process. Distributors and wholesalers have catchment areas; they have loyal retailers, and then there are floating retailers. Capturing the best distributors and wholesalers is critical. After that, it's brand strength and how much support you are prepared to put into it. Off-premise retailers will stock a much wider range of brands than on-premise. Bars, particularly Western-style bars, may have 50 beers, but the regular restaurant will have only two or three beers.

Higher margins for premium beer attracted many international breweries to China; this gave retailers the power to choose from numerous foreign brands. In addition, consumers typically drank the beer recommended by the restauranteur or bar patron, as Frank Gibson, LNC's strategy director, reported:

> People go out to a good restaurant, and they want to impress their friends, so they want to buy a foreign beer. Unfortunately, at this point in time, they really don't care what sort of beer it is, as long as it's foreign. They don't care if it's Beck's, or Budweiser, or San Miguel, so the restauranteur has an enormous amount of power over what gets drunk. Research shows that nine out of 10 times the restauranteur can dictate what the consumer will drink. This gives the trade a lot of power. There is an increasing number of competitors, a very fragmented channel, and no brand equity, so the trade can exercise a lot of leverage over the breweries. They don't have to take your beer. You don't have to have every beer in a restaurant. You only have to have two, basically. Most have only two or three. In premium, the vast majority of restaurants will only have two, so they don't have to take your beer. This increases the cost of entry for any foreign players who want to get in. They've got to pay a lot of money below the line.

Higher margins for premium beer extended the distribution zones for these brands. Furthermore, improved intercity transportation infrastructure made it easier to supply beer to a broader region. Marketing Beck's, a top-tier premium brand, with LNC's other brands was expected to significantly improve LNC's access to retail outlets within the YRD and to springboard distribution well beyond the delta. Beck's was already sold in over 40 cities along the coast from Shenyang to Guangzhou. Distribution systems were generally a tablestake in most developed markets, but in China mastering logistical difficulties would be advantageous.

LION NATHAN CHINA: MARKETING

Like Procter & Gamble, LN had a portfolio of brands rather than a single brand based on its corporate name. This provided flexibility to select and adapt beer brands for Chinese markets. As O'Mahony noted, "Unlike Budweiser or Carlsberg or Foster's, we don't have to push a particular brand." Exhibit 16 shows the company's Chinese brands. Launching a new brand, even in just one region of China, was extremely costly. CEO Gordon Cairns reported at the annual general meeting that 37 cents out of every dollar earned in China was being invested in building brands. Steve Mason, chief marketing officer, explained the company's approach to marketing:

> We do market research and use very sophisticated psychographic profiling to position and promote our brands in all three countries. We are always measuring the health of our brands and monitoring the effectiveness of our advertising. Our approach has always been to study and learn iteratively about positioning in each market. We really try to build on our experiences.

In the mainstream segment, Taihushui, which was acquired with the Wuxi brewery, was upgraded and relaunched in 1996 as a high-quality local beer for everyday drinking with comfort and affiliation messages. According to Mason, these messages were designed to convey a sense of closeness and belonging—"because it is from around here, you should feel comfortable drinking it." Taihushui was a market leader in Wuxi and Suzhou and had the second highest market share in Changzhou (see Exhibit 9). Although a very strong performer, this brand was geographically locked.

Rheineck, which was from the New Zealand portfolio, was adapted and launched very successfully in 1997 as a pan-delta brand positioned as a beer "you drink with friends." LNC targeted a younger profile of more upwardly-mobile consumers, with images of good times with good friends. Rheineck was an affordable foreign lager beer, brewed locally. In this mainstream segment, the economics of returning bottles and crates constrained geographic expansion. As the market share figures in Exhibit 7 show, Rheineck rocketed into second or third place in these key YRD cities. Building on experience with Taihushui, LNC achieved significant volume growth within 12 months in Nanjing (17,000) and Shanghai (22,000). Sullivan described LNC's mainstream growth:

> We said there's growth . . . if we bring in a quality product and put in the right relationships with the wholesalers, do the right merchandising, get the brand out in front of the customer, and get consumer awareness, then there's market share available without going beyond price. We actually sell for a higher price than the local brands, and we've got significant growth in those markets.

Rapid turnover in popularity of beers was particularly obvious in the premium segment, where many major international competitors battled for on-premise market share; positioning of these international brands was generally based on status. Mason outlined LNC's promotional strategies for each premium brand, as follows:

> We launched Steinlager as a progressive premium beer for the "new generation" in Shanghai in September 1998. This was a New Zealand lager with German connections that we adapted for the Chinese palate. To differentiate this beer and position it as trendy, we used a curved green bottle, labeled it as an "international awards winner" and offered it in up-market Western-style bars, hotels, and restau-

EXHIBIT 16–LNC Beer Brands: China

Source: Lion Nathan Web site: *www.lionnathan.co.nz*, October 2000.

> *rants. We also had a dark-coloured niche beer, Carbine, which was sold in restaurants and positioned as "a beer with food." This was a mild stout beer, which was named using a brand from Queensland. This premium beer was reformulated and introduced to encourage winter consumption of beer using imagery of energy, warmth, and powerfulness.*

The addition of Beck's beer to the portfolio of premium brands that LNC brewed and marketed was expected to provide significant leverage in the future. Although *Beck's* volume and market share in the key YRD cities had declined significantly from

1997, the brand was still ranked number two behind Budweiser in four of these cities and was number one in Changzhou (see Exhibit 9).

Significant investments were involved to promote brands and obtain access to retail outlets. Image-building activities such as advertising, signage, event sponsorship, or merchandising to build brand equity were categorised as "above-the-line" expenditure. There were also "below-the-line" expenses for transactional deals with the trade, which were standard practice to gain access in China. With overcapacity in the on-premise segment, the costs to compete were increasing, as O'Mahony explained:

> A restaurant will typically stock two or three premium beers. They know that there are seven or eight producers of premium beer out there. It becomes an auction for which beers will be stocked. It comes down to who pays the most money. Therefore, the costs to compete have risen. You know whether it's a listing fee, or whether it's promotional support, whether it's paying for new signage, redecoration of the restaurant, whatever it happens to be. The other thing that has happened is the costs of TV advertising have risen as a result of demand. Again, when you've got seven or eight players looking for the same spot on TV, then you have to pay more for it.

Gibson described the below-the-line dealing required for access to restaurants:

> You're selling to restaurateurs; you're not selling to consumers. You're trying to convince the restaurateur to stock your beer and push it on to consumers. It's all sales driven. It's all about push. You get in there and you do deals with distributors who've got the best coverage, because you want the distributors who deal with the most restaurants directly. You go in there and do deals with the restaurateur. You give him push girls (who provide information and hand out promotion materials), and you give him so many ashtrays, and so many glasses, and so many beer mats, and uniforms. That's been the focus until now. Increasingly, the focus will be more on above-the-line marketing.

Increasing consumption and driving market share were critical activities for success in this market. LN's ex-COO Kevin Roberts, speaking in his new role as CEO of Saatchi & Saatchi, the worldwide advertising agency, described the status of brands in China:

> The Chinese have not been exposed to brands at all, so every brand promise that makes sense to them, hey, they'll try it immediately. They think it's cool. They believe it. They are not cynical. A brand to them screams quality, so the way to build brand equity is to advertise the living hell out of a property and communicate it. Have consistency of delivery, and become part of them. You cannot advertise down to them with Western characters.

Furthermore, Roberts advocated the Coca-Cola strategy to drive consumption: "Make it available everywhere, make it affordable, and make it acceptable."

LION NATHAN CHINA: FINANCIAL CONTROL

In 1998, sales revenue for LNC increased 91 percent to $56.2 million on volume growth of 73 percent; this result was impressive in a beer market growing at less than 5 percent. Performance data for LNC is provided in Exhibit 2, and the corporate financial results and statistics are included in Exhibits 3 and 4. James Brindley moved into LNC's finance director role in November 1998, after 6 months in Shanghai working as a planning manager for David Sullivan. Brindley's role included oversight of transaction processing, accounts payable, general ledger, and accounts receivable, plus credit control, statutory reporting, tax, funding, corporate reporting (including compliance with "a million" Chinese government regulations), and decision support. Corporate authorisation was required for capital expenditure by LNC over $2 million. Having a strong performance ethic in the company created continuous pressure for LNC to deliver on monthly volume and EBIT targets. Brindley was now in the hot seat. He recognised the need to balance shareholders' short-term needs and the company's long-term returns:

> We're playing in the premier league now. We've got to realise that it's a big game. We've got to act like a big player, not like a small amateur player, and that takes courage. Our NZ$30 million loss is nothing to the likes of Anheuser-Busch and the other big players. You know, beer in China is not a profitable business. Margins are very low and it's very competitive. The economy is in a terrible state. Pricing is very hard to maintain. All these things are stacked against us in the short term. But that could turn in 2 years with a few exits, income growth, the economy turning around . . . then we could be doing very well. Getting a partner is a great leap forward because it helps share the risk in these early years.

Commenting on the financial dilemma the company faced, CFO Lockey said:

> The faster we grow, the more we lose. In the broadest sense, the faster we grow, the more chance we have of winning, but in the short term, the more we would lose. We can improve our financial performance by slowing down.

Because margins for premium beer were 50 percent higher than mainstream beer, increasing the proportion of premium beer LNC sold was a top priority. Brewing Beck's beer under license in Suzhou would also help to utilise brewing capacity and accelerate break-even. Geographic expansion to new cities offered volume and sales growth, but there were major setup costs involved in establishing a sales force in a new city. As O'Mahony indicated, "Every time you open a sales office, you could be looking at $1 million loss in year one." This would typically be followed by achieving break-even in year 2 and making a profit in year 3. Another dynamic factor influencing profitability was the stage of brands in their life cycle; new brands required significantly more investment than older brands. LNC also faced challenges on a daily basis arising from the cash-flow nature of the beer business. Brindley explained:

> Most of the cash collection is by hand. Salespeople go to the wholesaler's office and collect a wad of cash, bring it back into the office, and deposit it. It's very high risk. It's very hard work, and it's a real challenge. Paying debts isn't a top priority here. We are really doing quite well on cash collection, but it's very hard work.

Seasonality was another major factor influencing this business. Brindley explained its impact on LNC as follows: "In August [summer], we sold 27 million litres of beer—nearly 1 million litres a day. In December, we sold 1 million litres of beer. So a month's sales equals a day's sales." There was a huge investment in bottles and crates to service peak sales; off-season (from October), the empties were returned and stacked high all around the plant. Bottles typically cost 0.8RMB, and 3 percent were written off annually (see Exhibit 17). Carton beer was more expensive because the bottles were not returned. Brindley was concerned about the

---

Exhibit 17 Lion Nathan China: Financial Data

Volumes

1,000 litres = 1 tonne
100 litres = 1 hectolitre

Bottles, Cans, and Kegs

The Yangtze River Delta beer market is split approximately 95% bottle, 2% can, and 3% keg.
Standard beer bottle size is 640 ml. and it costs RMB1.25; bottles are returnable; each trip averages RMB0.3.
Standard can holds 300ml and it costs about RMB1.
Standard keg holds 30 litres.

Most mainstream beer is sold in 24 slot returnable plastic crates, which cost RMB24 to produce.
Premium beer is sold in nonreturnable bottles of varying sizes.
Steinlager will be sold in shaped 700 ml. bottles and 300 ml. bottles.
Beck's also has nonstandard bottle shape.

LNC's Ex-Brewery Gate Prices (in standard 640 ml. bottles)

Taihushui	RMB1.90
Rheineck	RMB2.08
Carbine	RMB4.00
Steinlager	RMB5.50 (300ml); RMB5.70 (700ml)

LNC's Suzhou Packaging Capabilities

3 glass lines @ 36,000 bottles per hour each
1 canning line @ 400 cans per minute
1 kegging line @ 80 kegs per hour

Employee Remuneration in China

Average brewery worker	RMB2,000–15,000 p.a.
Seasonal contact workers (for peak periods)	RMB 800–1,000 per month
Good sales staff	RMB 24,000 p.a.
Good managers	Over RMB100,000 p.a.
Skilled local senior managers	Package over RMB500,000 p.a
Corporate executives (LN)	Up to 60% of pay package depends on individual and company performance.

Exchange Rates

NZ$1 at 30 April 1999

USA	Buy 0.5625	Sell 0.5510
Australia	Buy 0.8499	Sell 0.8366
China	Buy 4.6736	Sell 4.5340

Stock Performance

Stock performance (year ended 31 August 1998)	Return on stock outperformed NZSE40 index by 32% and Australian All Ord index by 11.5%.
LN's Share price (30 April 1999)	Buy NZ$4.55, Sell NZ$4.50 Movement +5, Volume sold 1,712,720

Sources: Company and industry sources.

financial implications of the government's ruling for beer to be sold only in approved new bottles:

By 1 April, every bottle has to be a B bottle made of safety glass. With the number of bottles in the marketplace and the actual glass-manufacturing capacity in China, it will take 11 years to make that number of bottles. But, they expect it to be done by 1 April. We may have to spend $10 million changing over our bottles. Mainstream beer is sold in returnable 640 ml. bottles, but it's impossible to get your own bottles back. Actually, we won't care whose bottle we get back as long as it has a B on it. The old labels are washed off in the washer anyway.

LION NATHAN CHINA: THE FUTURE?

With the partnership deal to brew and market Beck's beer signed on the table, LNC's strategy director, Gibson, reflected on the lengthy process that had been followed to put this international licensing agreement in place. He commented, "The strategy is all set now. We've nailed the final piece of the puzzle. My job is all done." Another key player, Graham Stuart, who had been actively involved in all the developments in China, moved in February 1999 from LNC's general manager sales and marketing to LN's corporate strategy director role. His brief was to look forward: "What's next for LN?" Stuart was excited to be beginning this task of searching for new opportunities and new horizons for LN.

However, the company's financial performance and future depended upon success in China. The competitive landscape was changing, competition was intensifying in the Chinese beer market, and the economy was slowing down. As CFO, Paul Lockey was concerned about the reaction of financial markets to the latest midyear results. In 1998, LNC had achieved record growth in volume and sales in this difficult market. However, Lockey recognised that the challenges in China were far from over. Could O'Mahony and his senior management team continue to deliver on aggressive growth targets? How was LNC going to ensure success in this volatile market? Was it time for another bold move? Could LNC lead consolidation in the Chinese brewing industry? If so, how?

Reflecting upon LNC's future options, Sullivan enthused:

What can we do to drive the industry forward? We can communicate with other brewers. We can talk about how we compete in a profitable way. We can look for alliances with other brewers that don't have competing portfolios. We could license other premium brands and produce them in Suzhou. We can leverage suppliers. We can raise the bar on quality, glass standards, labeling, and packaging. We can acquire other breweries. We can acquire other brands. We can encourage other brewers to acquire other brands. We don't look at Wuxi to grow massively; we look for growth outside of Wuxi. And then expanding out from the traditional base . . . trying to grow seasonality, or extending the shelf life, getting people drinking more beer in winter . . . getting premium products into more restaurants, and mainstream into more shops.

ENDNOTES

1. Lion Nathan International Limited Web site,*www.lion nathan.co.nz/companies_brands,cfm*

2. Kukutai, A., Cooper, A., and Gilbertson, D. Lion Nathan Ltd. *Innovation and Management in New Zealand: A Casebook*. Dunmore Press, Wellington, 1992, p.167.

3. Jones, S .R. H., and Paul, D. R. *Concentration and Regulation in the New Zealand Brewing Industry: 1870–1970*, 1987.

4. Lewis, G., Minchev, T., and Lebed, A. Foster's Brewing Group. In Lewis, G., Morkel, A., Hubbard, G., Davenport, S,. and Stockport, *G. Australian and New Zealand Strategic Management: Concepts, Texts and Cases*. 2d ed. Prentice Hall, Sydney, 1999, pp. 721–745.

5. McNabb, D. "World's Brewers Bleed in China's Beer Wars," *The Dominion*, 5 August 1998, Vol. 2, No. 21.

6. Anon. "Business: Economic Indicators," *Far Eastern Economic Review*, 162(6), 1999, pp. 58–59.

7. Ayala, J., and Lai, R. "China's Consumer Market: A Huge Opportunity to Fail?" *The McKinsey Quarterly*, Vol. 3, 1996, pp.56–71.

8. Anon. "Economic Dragon Staggers But Will Not Fall," *NZ Herald*, 17 February 1999, p. E2.

9. Tomlinson, R. "China's Reform: Now Comes the Hard Part," *Fortune*. 139(1), 1999, pp. 60–65.

10. Ibid.

11. Ayala, J., and Lai, R. "China's Consumer Market: A Huge Opportunity to Fail?" The *McKinsey Quarterly*, Vol. 3, 1996, pp. 56–71.

12. Landry, J. T. "Emerging Markets: Are Chinese Consumers Coming of Age?" *Harvard Business Review*, Vol. 76, No. 3, 1998, pp. 17–20.

13. Ibid.

14. Suzhou Industrial Park Administrative Committee, Suzhou Industrial Park, p. 18.

15. McNabb, D. "World's Brewers Bleed in China's Beer Wars," *The Dominion*, 5 August 1998, Vol. 2, p. 21.

CHAPTER 15

Planning, Organization, and Control of International Marketing

With global strategy covered in the preceding chapter, this chapter turns to considering how the separate functional tasks of organization, planning, and control are blended together into an effective international marketing mix.

The main goals of this chapter are to

- Identify the elements of the planning process.
- Describe how firms develop and coordinate plans for national markets.
- Describe the nature and role of long-range planning.
- Identify the variables that affect organizational design for international marketing.
- Describe the alternative designs available for international marketing organization.
- Study examples of how companies organize internationally and what roles headquarters can play.
- Discuss how companies control international marketing.
- Explain the role of the information system in international control.

Planning for Global Marketing

Planning consists of identifying systematic steps that will help a company formulate detailed actions to implement broad strategies. Thus, the stages of planning should mirror the steps used in formulating strategy, as set out in Figure 14-1 in Chapter 14. Planning can be for the short or long term. Typically, firms plan for three to five years, revising the long-term plan annually. The year immediately ahead then becomes the short-term plan, which involves more detailed strategies.

There is an advantage to having the annual plan be part of a longer planning horizon. It keeps planners from becoming shortsighted by forcing them to consider the impact of each year's operating plan. The short-range plan for international marketing can be composed of several elements, including, for example, a marketing plan for each foreign market, plans for individual product lines, and a plan for international product development.

There are several elements of the marketing plan:

- *Situation analysis: Where are we now?* The company must analyze its current environment in each market: What are the important characteristics of demand, competition, distribution, law, and government? What problems and opportunities are evident in the current situation?
- *Objectives: Where do we want to be?* Given an understanding of the firm's current situation in markets around the world, management can propose objectives that are appropriate for each country, market, and region. While those objectives should be challenging, they also need to be reachable. And they must be specific if they are to be operational.
- *Strategy and tactics: How can we best reach our goals?* Once the firm has identified concrete objectives for foreign markets, it must prepare a plan of action to meet the goals. The approach includes assigning specific responsibilities to marketing personnel and to the marketing functions.

Those three basic elements—situation analysis, objectives, and strategy and tactics—provide a framework for discussing the planning needs of the international marketing manager. The short-range planning task of the international marketer has two basic parts: (1) developing the plan for each foreign market and (2) integrating the national plans into a coherent international plan, both regional and global.

Developing Plans for Individual Markets

The mode of entry affects the extent to which a firm takes responsibility for and control of planning. Exporting may rely more heavily on export intermediaries for planning; similarly, licensing cedes principal control and responsibility to the licensee. In a joint venture, a partner may share or take a controlling role in planning, depending on how the joint venture has been structured. It is in wholly owned subsidiaries that a firm's planning role takes center stage.

SETTING OBJECTIVES FOR A SUBSIDIARY

As outlined in Chapter 14, a firm must first evaluate the environment and industry context, which can be unique for each subsidiary. It must also clarify the governmental actions and role that may affect the subsidiary and determine what competitors are up to—their strengths and weaknesses, the threats they pose, and their strategic actions and tactics. The firm can then set detailed subsidiary objectives, including:

- Target sales, in units, in local currency and in the parent company's home currency, possibly at a predetermined exchange rate.
- Target market share by product and line of business.
- Goals for distribution channel penetration, coverage, and extension to new distributors and channels.
- Goals for brand image creation and awareness.
- New product introduction plans, as appropriate, with detailed marketing plans for launch, covering issues such as pricing, positioning, channels, media plans and spending, target sales, logistics, and marketing service and support.
- Export and international marketing plans, including countries and regions to be addressed.
- Marketing research goals and specific programs.
- Marketing personnel training, hiring, and motivation, including sales force plans

FROM STRATEGY TO TACTICS AND BUDGETS

Each of the above planning goals can be broken down into more detailed targets, with operational plans spelling out details of implementation, budgets, and managerial responsibilities. At this stage, individuals within the marketing department can receive specific assignments, with details ironed out for working with third parties such as advertising agencies, market research firms, value-added distributors, product servicing companies, etc.

Stages in the Planning Calendar

Thus, a series of typical planning steps can be constructed:

1. *Market environment* analysis (macroeconomic and industry) to identify opportunities and threats and ways they will affect company objectives.
2. *Communication of company-wide goals,* subsequently broken down into global, regional, and country-specific goals and goals for product lines.
3. *Detailed country and product-manager* plans showing how goals such as market share, competition containment, and return on investment will be achieved.
4. *Aggregation of detailed country and product-line plans* to determine whether the overall result is compatible with corporate headquarters' goals.
5. *Translation of plans into budgets,* setting out quantitative and qualitative targets in terms of market share, unit volume growth, prices, target-market segments, distribution channels, advertising budgets, new product introductions, and personnel and training needs.
6. *Actions by product-line and country managers* based on plans and budgets, which also form the criteria used to judge performance.

Adapting Plans to Individual Countries

A centralized coordination of programs is necessary so, for example, global products can be introduced into different markets on a staggered basis. The experience of lead markets may be used to tailor product-introduction programs for other markets. In addition to country and product-manager initiatives, some programs may be initiated at headquarters and communicated to subsidiaries.

An example is Avon's planning process for Latin America. Local executives gather information and develop preliminary country business strategies. Scrutiny of the operating environment is given precedence, focusing on the political, economic, and regulatory environment in each market, as well as making forecasts for the next five years. Next, competitors are identified and their products, market share, strengths, and weaknesses assessed. Avon seeks to learn the sources of its competitors' competitive advantages and compare them with Avon's own competitive advantages. Out of such analysis emerges a plan designed to capitalize on opportunities and competitive weaknesses. Contingency planning is emphasized, the question being, what actions are necessary to achieve planned results in the face of unforeseen events?

The Avon planning process is initiated by top management, which visits each of the firm's key country subsidiaries over a period of two months. While each country subsidiary's general manager prepares the plan, a planning staff at headquarters, including a planning director, helps key markets with their plans. Once all of the plans are completed, they are forwarded to headquarters for review and integration. Country proposals are reviewed and prioritized; and through comparison, headquarters can detect unexploited opportunities and suggest imitation or adaptation of plans currently scheduled for implementation in one country.

WHAT DETERMINES WHETHER FORMAL GLOBAL MARKETING PLANS WILL BE DEVELOPED?

What factors influence whether a firm formally develops strategic marketing plans? As Figure 15-1 shows, Chae and Hill found:

- A corporate culture that believes in and is supportive of planning.
- Supply chain complexity.
- Complex and uncertain foreign environments.
- Higher levels of governmental involvement with and impact on the business environment.
- Higher levels of competition.

All of those factors influenced the degree of planning formality. Involvement by chief executive officers (CEOs) and firm size were not as important; furthermore, such formal planning generated competitive and organizational benefits.[1]

Figure 15-1. A Model of Global Strategic Planning Formality

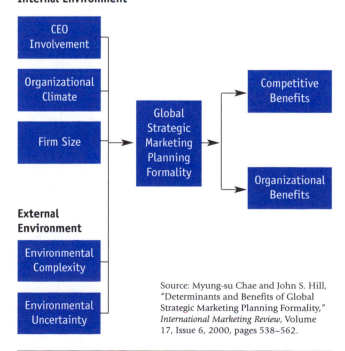

Source: Myung-su Chae and John S. Hill, "Determinants and Benefits of Global Strategic Marketing Planning Formality," *International Marketing Review,* Volume 17, Issue 6, 2000, pages 538–562.

Division of Labor in International Planning

Avon's approach, discussed earlier, highlights the importance of organizational arrangements in international marketing planning. How the company is organized will affect the quality of the plan and the likelihood of its implementation. Who contributes what to national operating plans? What are the respective roles of corporate headquarters and the national subsidiaries? Usually corporate headquarters can contribute planning know-how based on its domestic and international experience. That expertise would include planning guidelines, a planning schedule, and training of subsidiary personnel.

The national subsidiary should do most of the actual planning. Whereas the international parent has planning expertise, only the subsidiary has the intimate local knowledge needed. Most of the data for the plan, therefore, must be supplied locally. The resulting plan is more effective because of the complementary contributions of the two parties.

Nestlé provides an example of interactive planning, but with a bias toward decentralization. Some guidance comes from headquarters, but each national company prepares the annual marketing plan and budget. Once a year each affiliate meets at headquarters in Switzerland, to review the plan with specialists. Compromises and adjustments are made at that time.

International Coordination of National Plans

The final role of the international planner is to coordinate the national plans into an international plan. This coordination is not done after the national plans have been completed; rather, it is done at the beginning of the planning process. Otherwise, national plans will make conflicting claims on company resources and require time-consuming revision. Therefore, coordination begins with guidelines sent to each national operation at the beginning of the planning period. National plans may be modified during the planning process, but good communications will ensure that those changes can be coordinated within the overall international plan.

For example, assume that a company begins its planning cycle in August. Each country prepares its plan, which goes to its regional headquarters and then to international headquarters in the United States. Between September and November, continuing exchange of information might occur among the three levels. Final coordination takes place at area-wide meetings in December, where country managers, regional managers, and headquarters staff meet for one or two weeks. Those meetings are held in the critical area (for example, Europe or Latin America) and sometimes the United States.

Incorporating Government Policies in Global Marketing Planning

How should government policy be included in conducting marketing planning? LeClair uses the EU as an example to set out a model, including dimensions such as:
- Policy-making process.
- The broader policy climate.
- Categories of relevant legislation (EU regulations, directives, decisions, and recommendations and opinions).

Those dimensions should then be assessed for their effect on marketing objectives and strategy in areas such as market research, advertising, and promotion. Promotion includes communication strategy, product development, product liability, labeling, distance selling, data collection and privacy, and electronic commerce. Also broadly relevant are competition policy and the move toward monetary union (the Euro-zone) that affect choice of partners, channels, control over the entities, pricing, etc.[2]

Comparative Analysis for International Planning

As firms increase their multinational presence and the number of subsidiaries increases, regional and headquarters managers begin comparing subsidiaries against one another—by region, by product line, and by stage of evolution of their respective markets. Such comparisons can help determine whether targets set for individual subsidiaries represent challenging but achievable goals. Comparisons can be helpful when the subsidiaries being compared are similar in their markets and competitive environments and when they face roughly the same degree of governmental controls. Thus, it may make sense to compare plans for marketing razor blades in Brazil, Argentina, and Mexico, perhaps extending the marketing plan to Turkey and the Philippines. Nevertheless, including significantly poorer countries such as China and India, with their larger populations and lesser degree of infrastructure development, may blur the comparisons. Hence, care is necessary in choosing subsidiaries for comparison.

A-M International provides an example of how to plan for international markets by using an analytical approach. The company is a leader in the global graphics industry, with divisions selling offset presses, printing equipment, and engineering and architectural market graphics equipment. International sales are about 40 percent of total sales. A-M's strength is its worldwide sales and service infrastructure, having sales branches in countries on six continents and a worldwide base of installed equipment that is a continuing market for supplies and service. To manage this global business, the company operates warehouses, has a worldwide logistics system, and offers worldwide service capabilities (including training). A large portion of the costs of this infrastructure is fixed; hence, A-M's primary goal is to maximize sales from the worldwide infrastructure already in place. In practical terms, that means selling more products through the sales and service organization. To accomplish that, A-M analyzes the outlook for international markets for each of its market segments. Using that approach, A-M developed a new international presence in copiers, an area in which it had not been active previously. The A-M international division agreed to market the entire line of Konica copiers in Europe under the A-M label. This was part of the company's plan to leverage the existing distribution channel by taking on worldwide distribution rights to market "contiguous" products under the A-M brand name; A-M expected considerable overlap with its current customer base.

A-M further analyzed markets by geographic area, recognizing that growth rates of over 30 percent per year registered in the Asia/Pacific region would continue and should be exploited aggressively. At the same time, the above analysis, extended to include current market share and future potential, disclosed areas for further attention. Such comparative information gathering is the cornerstone of successfully planning for international markets.

Long-Range Planning

Long-range planning deals with the future of the company over a period of five to ten years. Uncertainty is high, and the level of detail that can be forecast is low. The major concern is determining the shape of future markets and competition. How will the environment change, how will competition change, how will the customer base change, and what will future needs be? A firm seeks to learn enough about the future to prevent unpleasant surprises that can reduce its competitive advantage.

The flavor of long-range planning can be seen in TRW's approach. It addresses questions such as the following: What markets should we be in at that time? What products should we be making then? What business and operations methods will be valid then? Those plans can be prepared at group headquarters by a planning and development department. It can draw on data assembled by the group's product divisions and foreign subsidiaries. The plan can cover several variables:

- Historical trends in the industry
- Forecasts of demand from end-user segments such as cars, trucks, and off-road vehicles
- Forecasts of the economies of the countries where the group has operations
- The competitive situation in those countries
- Possible future modes of transportation
- Possible future energy problems

GLOBAL MARKETING

Long-Range Scenario Building at Shell and at the Salim Group

Shell Oil (Royal Dutch/Shell) has long been renowned for using scenarios in its long-range planning. The oil industry requires long-term forecasts when examining investment decisions in new energy and exploration projects. An oil field can yield output for 20 years or more, and long-range scenarios covering that time period are common at Shell. The Middle East is critical to oil; hence, Shell's scenarios often study consequences for the oil industry of volatility in the Middle East. For example, when war broke out in Iraq, Shell's scenarios did not specifically address the war, but they did include unknown events leading to volatility in oil prices and supply uncertainty. As a result, Shell was able to implement contingency plans immediately—and did so when war broke out.

Shell typically develops global scenarios every two years, developing more detailed regional scenarios as needed. The scenarios address issues important to Shell's senior management. World experts work with in-house staff to develop "branching points" from which the business environment might be changed significantly. Plans are then developed to cope with shifts in the environment. The thinking is that if the business can be prepared to accept and live with major paradigmatic change, it can more easily accommodate lesser degrees of change. For example, recent scenarios addressed the growth of the environmental movement and the increase in mercantilism and protectionism by the world's leading economies. Other interesting scenarios might be a shift in the center of economic power to the Pacific Rim countries, the emergence of China as the world's largest economy, and another world war brought on by religious intolerance and conflict between the West and Moslem countries.

The Shell 2025 Global Scenarios discussed scenarios using three lenses: long-term predetermined trends, "the Jet Stream"; specific features of key regions influenced by the Jet Stream context, "the Weather system"; and market-level trends and turbulences. Scenario planning is designed to ensure both continuity and flexibility. Earlier, Shell used "TINA" (There Is No Alternative) as the basis for its 2001 scenarios to explore the impacts of globalization, market liberalization, and the "onrush of new technologies." In 2001, Shell

continued

was interested in understanding the tension between "efficiency on the one hand and values and social cohesion on the other. This resulted in the focal question, will the resolution to dilemmas arising from globalization be dominated by global elites or by the people of the heartland?

Between 2001 and 2005, Shell explored the consequences of 9/11 and the growing importance of security and trust in the marketplace. For 2005, they postulated a "Trilemma Triangle," with Market Incentives, Coercion and Regulation, and the Force of Community being the three apexes of the triangle, each pulling in a different direction. Market incentives prized efficiency, coercion and regulation stressed security, and community forces favored social cohesion as the driving objective. Shell saw trade-offs between the three points of the triangle and the ensuing objectives as critical in shaping its future planning.

Within scenarios, Shell uses econometrics and system dynamics models to study economic and energy situations in different countries. Users comment on the scenarios as they are developed. As a result, the scenario undergoes several iterations. The final result is a 100-page book for top management that summarizes the key scenarios, statistical data, and strategic implications for Shell's lines of business.

A different approach to long-range planning is illustrated by Indonesia's Salim Group, which starts with Indonesian government goals and national plans. Once the world's largest importer of rice, Indonesia became self-sufficient in rice before it began to import again, an amount equal to 8 percent of its needs in 1995. It would like to regain self-sufficiency, but a growing population has led to the loss of arable rice-growing land to urban development, even as rice consumption increases. Indonesia's national plans call for rice to be grown on less suitable swampy land in Borneo, asking Indonesia's conglomerates to help. The Salim Group responded by announcing plans to invest over $500 million in cultivating rice on about 300,000 hectares of land. That decision is of interest because Salim has palm oil and sugar plantations, but no experience with rice.

Salim also plans to diversify into supplying clean water to half of Jakarta. As part of a privatization move, the Salim Group was awarded a water utility franchise in a joint venture with the French water company Lyonnaise des Eaux and will invest $500 million to supply the western half of the capital city. The Salim Group is a family controlled company. Anthony Salim, the founder's eldest son, indicates that he is personally keen on the two projects just mentioned not because they are particularly profitable, but because they tackle essential needs of the country. Of course, such endeavors draw, in part, on close ties with political parties in power. Changes in government accompanied by loss of political allies can throw such planning into disarray. Recent political changes in Indonesia, with a movement toward democracy and away from the power of President Suharto illustrate the impact of such political changes.

Sources: Shell (http://www.shell.com/static/royal-en/downloads/scenarios/exsum_23052005.pdf); Paul J. H Schoemaker, "Scenario Planning: A Tool for Strategic Thinking," *Sloan Management Review,* Winter 1995, pages 25–40; "Shell Pioneers Use of Scenarios to Enhance Its Long-Range Planning," *Business International,* November 12, 1990; and "Indonesia's Salim Group Plans to Invest in Rice, Join Others on Water Project," *Wall Street Journal,* March 1, 1996.

Such short- and long-range plans will reflect a company's dependence on the plans of its key customer segments. Planners will rely heavily on contacts within customer companies for input to the plan.

Responding to Competition: Strategic Alliances

A central aspect of planning is responding to competition. In a global context, this may involve activities in more than one market, making integration of activities across markets essential. Response may be defensive or aggressive and may involve waiting for a competitor to act. Or, response may be preemptive, seeking to ward off competitors or warn them of actions such as price cuts, competitive product introductions, and expansion of dealer networks.

Being ready to respond to competition is partly a matter of contingency planning. Although a firm does not know what a competitor will do, it can make reasonable guesses about a competitor's options over the planning horizon. Planning should, therefore, include appropriate responses to those options.

Strategic response may sometimes entail cooperating with the competition; that is, forming a **strategic alliance**. This action is becoming increasingly popular as companies realize the importance of having a global strategy. The problem for many companies is that their global ambitions exceed their resources; and if they move too slowly in developing global markets, they may be swallowed up by stronger, already established global competition. Strategic alliances sometimes solve that problem. A review of a variety of strategic alliances follows, with examples from the pharmaceutical and tire industries.

COMPETITIVE RESPONSE IN THE PHARMACEUTICAL INDUSTRY

The pharmaceutical industry presents an interesting arena for competitive response. It is stable, with an aging population in the rich countries, boding well for growing demand. Major markets include the major economies of Japan, Europe, and the United States. Fast-growing developing countries such as India, China, and Brazil represent major markets of the future. International health-care crises such as the devastation rendered by the HIV/Aids crisis in Africa create ethical dilemmas for the industry, leading the companies to consider how to balance drug affordability criteria with shareholder wealth.

Developing a new drug is costly and time-consuming, exceeding $500 million and taking 10 to 15 years. Drug companies must be able to sell the drug quickly in all three major economic regions before their drug patents expire. Therefore, they may need partners to help market a drug or defray the cost of developing a new one. In addition, they may want partners who have something of their own to offer: ideally, a new drug, with marketing rights that can be swapped for the firm's own new drugs.

Drug companies also feel pressure to reduce costs because governments pay for many health-care costs and want to keep drug prices low. Hence, drug companies have to increase their sales volume to make up for lower margins. Generic drug companies also pose a threat, making drugs that are no longer protected by patents. Because generic drug companies do not have to invest in R&D, they can charge lower prices.

The global pharmaceutical industry has seen a changing environment in which customers are gaining power, forcing down prices and profit margins. The growth of large buyers such as health maintenance organizations (HMOs) has increased their power. Patents on many major drugs are expiring; and the industry is fragmented, with the largest company, Pfizer, controlling a little over 10 percent of the global market. The drug companies need to become larger in order to reap economies of scale, and they may need to diversify so they are not dependent solely on research success within pharmaceuticals.

Pfizer became the industry's largest company by acquiring the European company Pharmacia in an acquisition valued at nearly $60 billion. Other pharmaceutical companies have followed similar strategies of acquisition, as shown in Table 15-1.

The 1996 merger between Ciba-Geigy and Sandoz, which together became Novartis, illustrates why mergers have become the central strategic response to pharmaceutical industry change and globalization. It is instructive to consider the strengths and motivations that each company brought to the merger. Both companies were facing threats from generic drugs to their own lines, whose patents were expiring. They did not have blockbuster drugs

in their research pipeline, and Ciba had experienced negative clinical results in two major research efforts on acute heart disease and therapies to limit damage from head injuries and strokes. A merger would allow for elimination of redundancies and lead to cost reduction. Moreover, neither company would have to take on debt or spend large sums of money, as the merger was a friendly one.

Corporate culture clashes, while inevitable, might be reduced because of a shared Swiss culture, with companies headquartered in Basel, Switzerland. The merged company would be diversified, with 40 percent of total revenues coming from agricultural chemicals and human nutrition. Lastly, power would be shared, with each company contributing eight members to a joint executive board. Aside from those merger synergies, each company had certain strengths, as shown below (p.000):

Table 15-1. Pharmaceutical Company Acquisitions

Company	Strategic Moves
Sanofi	Acquired Aventis, another French pharmaceutical firm, to stay all-French and to become the third-largest drug firm in the world in 2004
Pfizer	Acquired Pharmacia for $60 billion, with resulting combined sales of $48 billion
Pharmacia	Acquired Monsanto in 2000
Monsanto	Acquired American Home Products (AHP), which was somewhat controversial; AHP is now Wyeth
Pfizer	Acquired Warner Lambert; the principal attraction was Lipitor, a statin to treat high cholesterol
Glaxo	Merged with Smith Kline, the second-largest pharmaceutical firm in the world
Merck	Acquired Medco Containment Systems to control the marketing of drugs in the United States and to build a detailed database of drugs
Novartis	Merger of Sandoz and Ciba-Geigy; holds one-third of Roche
Hoechst	Became a major drug company with the acquisition of Marion Merrell Dow
Roche Holding	Acquired U.S.-based Syntex and Japan's Chugai Pharma in 2001
Bristol-Myers Squibb	Merger of Bristol-Myers and Squibb
SmithKline Beecham	Merger of SmithKline and UK's Beecham; later merged with Glaxo
Pharmacia and Upjohn	Merger between Swedish and U.S. firms to gain size and to ward off hostile takeovers; later merged with Pfizer
American Home Products (AHP)	Acquired American Cyanamid including Lederle's drug division

Ciba-Geigy	Sandoz
Two strong divisions: over-the-counter medication and eye care	Strong gene therapy research
49% ownership of U.S. biotech leader Chiron	80% global market share in drugs to prevent rejection in organ transplants; $1 billion research on animal organ transplants in humans
Respected worldwide marketing capability	Owns Gerber Products (acquired in 1994 for $3.7 billion); strength in nutrition products for babies and aging population

The Sandoz/Ciba-Geigy merger illustrates one effect of globalization on strategy: Fragmented industries begin to consolidate in order to approach the requisite size and to obtain scale economies necessary to be competitive in the global arena.[3]

WHY FORM STRATEGIC ALLIANCES?

In a strategic alliance, firms join together in some area of their business to reduce risk, obtain economies of scale, and obtain complementary assets—often intangible ones such as market access, brand names, and access to government procurement. The allure of acquiring technology and the pressures of government are also reasons for such alliances. They are typically formed in one of three broad areas: technology, manufacturing, and marketing.

Another reason for alliances is that consumers are becoming alike in developed nations. Consumers tend to receive the same information, and their discretionary incomes are roughly equal. As a result, tastes are becoming homogenized. As Kenichi Ohmae put it, "Everyone in a sense wants to live and shop in California."[4] But no one company can expect to dominate all technologies and create entire product lines for the developing global market. A likely solution, therefore, is to swap products.

Another factor concerning alliances is that fixed costs account for a larger proportion of total costs. Global sales help a firm recover higher fixed costs even when lower prices are charged. (Volume compensates for a smaller contribution per unit.) The reason firms should lower prices and sell globally are that product life cycles are becoming short and fixed costs are more likely to be covered by resorting to global markets. It is difficult to exploit worldwide markets without global alliances, however. Short product life cycles mean that firms must move quickly to exploit their technological lead. Such a technology lead is actually a disappearing asset, diminishing in value with the passage of time. Strategic alliances allow a firm to penetrate several key markets simultaneously. Table 15-2 summarizes these motivations.

Alliances, however, require that each party has something to swap. In the tire industry, General Tire supplies Japanese auto companies in the United States on behalf of Japanese companies, which, in turn, supply companies in Japan on behalf of General Tire and Continental. Several alliances can be formed within the same country. IBM, for example, works in Japan with Ricoh to distribute its low-end copiers, with Nippon Steel to sell systems integration services, with Fuji Bank to sell financial systems, with OMRON to penetrate the computer-integrated manufacturing market, and with NTT to sell VANs.

Technology sharing, joint marketing, and supply arrangements are the main foci of such alliances. What is interesting is that these alliances often occur between companies that also compete with each other in other markets. In choosing such partners, several criteria are useful:[5]

- The competitor should have a competitive advantage—economies of scale, technology, or market access—and those areas should be critical in the value-added chain.
- The contributions of each partner should be complementary or balanced.
- The two partners should agree on what global strategy to follow.
- The risk should be low that the partner will become a future competitor.
- There should be a preemptive value in having the firm as a partner rather than a rival.
- There should be compatibility of organizations as well as top management of the two firms.

How should alliances in different market and cultural settings and with different management and organizational philosophies be managed? Speier, Harvey, and Palmer[6] suggest that alliances be treated as virtual relationships, a web of companies across the value chain. They propose five different approaches to managing such virtual global marketing organizations, as follows:

- A shared partnership, with nearly equal amounts of commitment
- A core/satellite organization, with a core firm providing the impetus to form the global network
- A virtual value chain to service the end customer
- An integrated firm model where the different companies agree to function as a single vertically integrated firm throughout the world
- An electronic market, with firms using technology as the means of interacting with end customers.

Such virtual organizations can be difficult to coordinate. Figure 15-2 sets out some areas for coordination essential to continuing success.

Table 15-2. Motivations to Form Joint Ventures and Strategic Alliances

Motivations	Results
Complement weaknesses in the value chain	Obtain complementary competencies in R&D (basic research and/or applications development) and manufacturing (scale/scope economies, new processes, and cost reduction)
Take defensive position to protect market	See examples from the pharmaceutical industry, such as the Sandoz/Ciba-Geigy merger
Be proactive by developing new businesses	Keep pace with new technologies and new customer segments
Focus on product line or geographic area	Enhance market access to specific countries, brands, distribution channels, and service capabilities; enhance product line with partners possessing complementary products and services
Think strategically of core and peripheral operations	Reduce dependency on alliance partner and possible hollowing out of the corporation
React to government-imposed regulations	Offer legally necessary ownership stakes in return for political ties and local influence, as in several Asian private energy infrastructure projects
Reduce/share risk	Reduce ownership with attendant reduction in share of profits and losses
Overcome resource scarcity with partner contributions	Obtain resources (materials, components, capital, management, and information technology, such as Computer Reservation Systems in airline and hotel businesses)
Learn from partner	Seek partners from related or unrelated industries, from supplier and customer segments, or from possible multiple partners and coalitions (for example, telecommunications firms bidding for licenses in the U.S. wireless industry)
Obtain fit with global strategy alternatives through licensing, foreign direct investment, and acquisitions	Act cautiously, for alliances are not the universal panacea (over half of all joint ventures and alliances are dissolved within a few years)

Figure 15-2. Virtual Organizational Models for Alliances

	Location	Work Cycle	Culture	Organizational Relationships	Virtual Management Issues
Shared Partnership (Model 1)	Often colocated, a spin-off approach	Often highly synchronized activities	Typically homogeneous cultures, although distinctive	Typically strong preexisting relationships	Challenge of adapting existing relationships on virtual management
Core/ Satellite (Model 2)	Typically not colocated unless performing physical job functions	Often highly synchronized activities	Less emphasis on culture, more use of contracting relationship	Established existing relationships	Ongoing assessment of old/new partners in constellation
Virtual Value Chain (Model 3)	Typically not colocated	Highly synchronized across adjoining members of the value chain	Some emphasis on culture across adjoining members, but more contractual	Often existing relationships limited to adjoining members only	Identifying alternative partners for expanding value chain globally
Integrated Firm (Model 4)	Often colocated or located in close proximity	Often highly synchronized with coordinated scheduling	Higher emphasis on culture as a competitive advantage	Strong existing relationships among at least some members	Initiating offensive, defensive, and existing strategies
Electronic Market (Model 5)	Rarely colocated	Highly responsive, but not necessarily highly coordinated	Similar service-oriented cultures, but not necessary	In many cases, few existing relationships	Auditing and exit strategies; competitive response

Source: Figure 2 from Cheri Speier, Michael G. Harvey, and Jonathan Palmer, "Virtual Management of Global Marketing Relationships," *Journal of World Business*, Volume 33, Issue 3, 1998, pages 263–276.

Organizing for Global Marketing

Whatever planning is done will be in vain unless the company is organized to implement the plans. Organizational structure determines who does what, including which employees exercise gatekeeping power in supporting or undermining decisions made by others. Furthermore, organizational structure determines how marketing activities will be implemented. Implementation should flow from strategy; that is, activities are carried out to implement strategy. Thus, a critical element of designing global marketing organization is to ensure that it is consistent with strategy, that it leads to activities that help implement strategy.[7] Organizational structure also sets up the rewards that motivate performance and determines the degree to which activities can be integrated. This is particularly important in global strategy since implementation must be carried out by subsidiaries in different countries, without many opportunities for face-to-face communication. Indeed, some of the worst problems facing international marketers result from the friction between headquarters and foreign subsidiaries.

The basic issue for all organizational structure in global corporations revolves around centralization versus decentralization. Global corporations need strong coordination at headquarters to provide and supervise implementation of global strategy. If local subsidiary managers may have different opinions, however, they may pull away from that strategy. Or pressures by the local government may require greater local responsiveness, even if it means diverging from global strategy. Thus, the major task for organizational structure is to mediate between the opposing needs for centralization and local responsiveness.[8]

Research has suggested that in some industries where consumers around the world buy essentially the same product, as in consumer electronics, centralization and large-scale manufacturing are the keys to success. In industries in which national consumers have distinct product preferences and much product adaptation, as in branded packaged goods (such as detergents), a large degree of national subsidiary autonomy is needed. Then there are industries in which scale economies demand centralized, large-scale manufacturing; and yet consumers have distinct product preferences, as in the telecommunications industry. Here, both centralization and local responsiveness are needed.[9]

GLOBAL MARKETING

Internationalizing the Company: Staffing Issues

Organizing the international marketing function is partly a matter of hierarchies, power, and control. But it is also about finding and putting the best people in key positions. Staffing international positions raises tricky issues not found in the domestic arena. Foremost is the danger that the executive assigned overseas will get "lost," forgotten by colleagues and bosses. The ability of executives posted overseas to function effectively is heavily influenced by whether their families, spouses, and children adjust well to the extended overseas assignment. Issues such as health care, education for children, and home cooking all loom large in family satisfaction. In turn, this makes re-entry into domestic operations difficult. Very often the returning expatriate finds no job available that makes use of the incremental international business skills gained during the overseas assignment. Overseas executives also supervise large staffs, enjoy high pay and fringe benefits, and have considerable autonomy. Returning to headquarters may mean lower pay and less prestige. Unless they have a mentor or champion at home who smooths re-entry and finds them a position commensurate with their new skills, returning managers often believe that their careers are at a dead end and that the firm does not appreciate or want them. Former overseas executives often resign, which is a loss to the firm because the international skills are hard-earned and necessary for the corporation to compete successfully in the global arena. Hence, firms need to set up programs that ensure that the best younger managers are selected for overseas assignments and that a clear career path is established, including identifying jobs that will be open and available for returning managers.

As the global economy continues to become more important, one prerequisite to attaining top management positions at large U.S. multinationals is substantial international experience. For example, all eight members of Tupperware's executive committee speak two to four languages and have worked overseas. Samir Gibara, CEO of Goodyear Tire & Rubber, spent 27 years in management positions outside the United States. The chief operating officer (COO) at the Gillette Company and the CEOs at Outboard Marine Corporation, Case Corporation, and ExxonMobil have all spent over half of their management careers outside the United States. Twenty-eight percent of all senior management searches now require inter-

continued

national experience. Companies seem to be looking for executives with substantial international experience who have spent several years overseas, immersing themselves in the culture while running operations. U.S. companies, in particular, seem to value experience in emerging markets such as China, India, and Brazil. The difficulty, of course, is how an executive who spends all of his or her time overseas become visible to headquarters' top management in the United States? The answer, presumably, is also to spend time at home in a job with significant managerial responsibilities.

Companies have also begun to assign executives from headquarters units to overseas locations based on the executives' origin and their cultural knowledge of those markets. Payless Shoe Source is one such company. It had set its strategy around expansion into Latin America. Payless, with its many U.S. stores in inner-city locations, appealed to Latin American immigrants to the United States who could afford the prices and liked the range of styles. Those people often gave Payless shoes as presents when they returned home to visit relatives. This practice created strong brand awareness and brand loyalty in the local population in these foreign markets.

In 2000, Payless began to expand by opening five stores in Costa Rica, increasing to almost 200 stores scattered throughout Central America, Trinidad, the Dominican Republic, Chile, Peru, and Ecuador. The company informed its U.S. employees of Latin American origin that it was willing to let some of them manage overseas stores in Central and Latin America. Many homesick expatriates were willing to accept such a job offer. One of those employee was Roxana Orellana, who had come to the United States when she was a child, smuggled into the country as a refugee from El Salvador during its civil war. Many years later she joined Payless, working her way up to manager of an outlet in Los Angeles. When the opportunity arose to go back home, she took it, despite a pay cut from $33000 to $15000. She was given charge of a new store in Sonsonate, a regional capital. Customers flocked to the store, which was air-conditioned, carried a full line of popular styles, attractively displayed a full range of sizes, and was decorated with mirrored panels with which to judge the potential new shoe purchases in a retail environment where such modern customer-friendly stores were uncommon. The stores became successful, partly because of the local managers who brought with them knowledge of both the U.S. corporate culture and the local culture.

Sources: "Deep Inside China: American Family Struggles to Cope," *Wall Street Journal*, August 2, 2005; "'Repats Help Payless Shoes Branch Out into Latin America," *Wall Street Journal*, December 24, 2003; "Grappling with the Expatriate Issue: Little Benefit to Careers Seen in Foreign Stints," *Wall Street Journal*, December 11, 1989; and "An Overseas Stint Can Be a Ticket to the Top," *Wall Street Journal*, January 29, 1996.

Approaches to Organizing International Operations

A company can organize its international operations as a separate *international division*, with further subunits within the international division consisting of regional and local entities. It may also prefer to create organizational units structured along *products and lines of business*. A third approach is to create *functional units*, with distinct *global* responsibilities for research, marketing, manufacturing, logistics, and other functions. Finally, a company may decide that proper planning and execution of tasks require cooperation between managers, thereby fostering such cooperation by resorting to a *matrix organization*. In the latter, responsibilities for achieving goals is jointly allocated to managers with country, functional, and product-line responsibilities.

The International Division

Creating a separate organizational unit to focus on international business and operations allows international expertise, personnel, and vision to be concentrated in one part of the company. It creates a unit whose sole focus is on international business, one that stands up for international operations and seeks human and capital resources for that activity. Such an approach is more common in companies with relatively limited international operations, where domestic concerns predominate, and where product-line complexity is limited. Figure 15-3 illustrates the international division structure.

However, a separate international division faces several problems. It may receive a lesser share of resources than its markets warrant, it may be perceived as a backwater that is less relevant to the future of the company, and it may have less political clout in the fight for attention and budget allocations from top management. Resolving international business issues without regard to their integration into the overall company's strategy may result in suboptimization.

STRUCTURING BY AREA

Rather than have a separate international division, a company may develop an organizational structure with distinct responsibilities for each major geographical area. What is "international" is not relegated to second-division status. Instead, world markets are broken up into a series of geographical divisions, one of which happens to include the company's home, or domestic, market.

When the company is structured by area, the primary basis for organization is by divisions for major regions of the world. For example, when CPC International reorganized from an international division to a world company

Figure 15-3. The International Division Organizational Structure

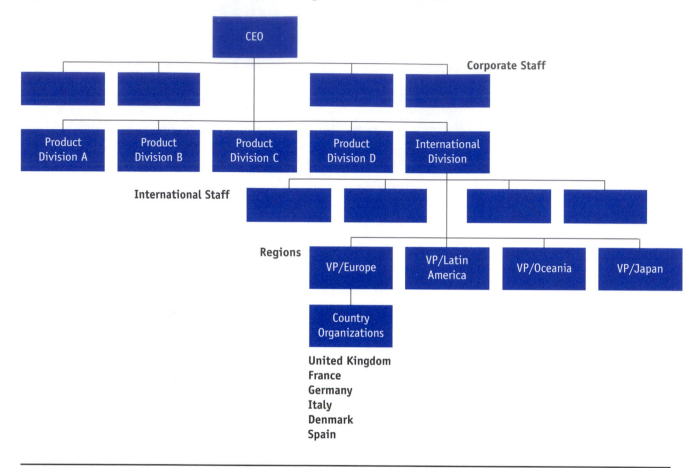

approach, it set up five operating companies—one for Europe, one for Latin America, one for the Far East, and two for North America (consumer products and industrial products). Although the structure is primarily a regional form of organization, the North American area is divided on the basis of product. Regional organization is used primarily by marketing-oriented companies that have relatively stable technology, such as those in consumer nondurables, pharmaceuticals, and automotive and farm equipment.

Several factors favor a regional approach to organization. The growth of regional groupings is one. As nations within a region integrate economically, it makes more sense to treat them as a unit. The proximity of countries provides one logical basis for organization. Certain kinds of expertise can be grouped within the region to enhance operations in the individual countries. Communication is easy, and coordination of product and functional know-how can take place in the region. A narrow product line and similarity in technology and methods of operation also favor regional organization. The greater the international similarity of the firm's products, the greater the importance of knowing the area.

In spite of its popularity, the regional organization has drawbacks. It ensures the best use of a firm's regional expertise, but it means less than optimal allocation of product and functional expertise. If each region needs its own staff of product and functional specialists, duplication—and inefficiency—may result if the best staff is not available for each region. Inefficiency is most likely when regional management is located away from corporate headquarters. When regional management is housed at corporate headquarters, a centralized staff can serve all regional units, providing some economies of scale. A regional organization may optimize performance within the region, but there is danger of global suboptimization when no coordination takes place among the regions. Each region must blend into a global operation. Figure 15-4 illustrates a regional organizational structure.

STRUCTURING BY PRODUCT

Organizing by product line means that product groups have global responsibilities for marketing; thus, it is a global company approach by product division. An international division can be organized along product lines, too;

Figure 15-4. The Worldwide Regional Organizational Structure

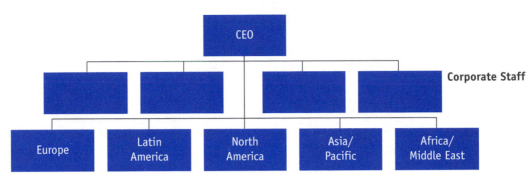

Figure 15-5. The Worldwide Product Organizational Structure

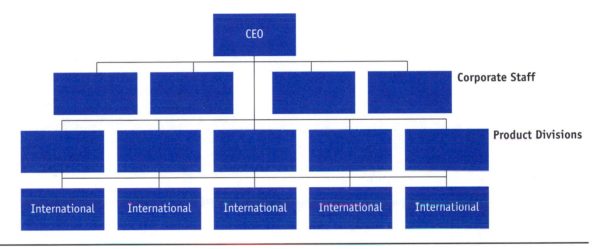

but by its very nature, this type of organizational structure also includes area expertise. Structuring by product line is most common for companies with several unrelated product lines because their marketing tasks vary more by product line than by region. As Figure 15-5 shows, the global product structure gives each product group what amounts to its own international division.

Structuring an organization along product lines has the merit of flexibility; a firm can add a new product division if it enters another business unrelated to its current lines. However, the product division approach has several potential limitations. When the domestic market is more important to a product division, international opportunities are likely to be missed. Limited area knowledge is a common weakness of product-structured organizations. Each product division cannot afford to maintain a complete international staff.

Another problem in a product-structured approach is the difficulty of achieving company-wide coordination in international markets. If each product division goes its own way, the firm's international development will encounter conflicts and inefficiencies. The organization

must provide global coordination to offset the sometimes contradictory international plans of individual product divisions. For example, it is probably unnecessary for each producing division to have its own advertising agency, service organization, and government relations staff in every market. When foreign plants manufacture products of different divisions, coordination among the divisions also is often a problem for a product organization.

Eaton provides an illustration of how companies with global product organization try to overcome some of its weaknesses. Eaton is highly diversified in the capital goods and automotive industries. It has five worldwide product groups, and each group has a managing director for European operations. To get a better overall corporate understanding and response to European problems in areas such as legislation, labor, and taxes, Eaton formed a European Coordinating Committee (ECC) composed of the five product division managing directors, several European staff, and one executive from world headquarters.

The responsibilities of the ECC's chair rotate among the managing directors, and meetings are held at different European facilities. Eaton established country coordinating committees to manage the product groups within each European country. It also formed a Latin American coordinating committee to achieve the same integration in Latin America.

STRUCTURING BY FUNCTION

A functional structure (whereby top executives in marketing, finance, production, etc, all have global responsibilities) is most suitable for firms with narrow, homogeneous product lines, when product expertise is not a variable. Also of benefit is when regional variations in operations are not great, thus lessening the need for regional expertise. Because those conditions are not usually met, the functional form of organization for international operations is not common among U.S. firms except in extractive industries, such as the oil and gas industry. The functional structure is more common in European companies. Although functional executives in U.S. firms do have international responsibilities, those responsibilities are usually in conjunction with a product or regional form of organization.

The Matrix Organization

One of the more interesting organizational developments in recent decades is the **matrix** form of organization. (See Figure 15-6.) Companies became frustrated with the shortcomings of unidimensional organizational structures (product, area, function) that were noted above. Therefore, they moved to a more complex organizational form that allowed two dimensions to have more or less equal weight in the organizational structure and decision making. A matrix organization has a dual rather than a single chain of command, meaning that many managers have two bosses. Matrix also involves lateral (dual) decision making and a chain of command that fosters conflict management and a balance of power. Product and market (geography) are the two dimensions receiving equal emphasis in matrix organizations in international business. For example, AGCO Corporation's 2004 matrix restructuring created operational control of sales, marketing, and engineering by geographic brand, with functional supervisory responsibility on a global basis.[10] Matrix can solve some problems of the simple product or area structure, but matrix organizations have many problems of their own arising from inherent conflicts and complexity.

Evolving to a Transnational Organization

To summarize, multinationals evolve from a structure consisting mainly of domestic operations with some overseas business to the multinational stage in which international business becomes more important. This typically results in independent, locally responsive subsidiaries that display greater sensitivity to local customers, governments, and culture and that are headed by local country managers with an entrepreneurial bent. At some point, competitive forces and environmental pressures from globalization of the industry lead headquarters to want greater global integration of relatively autonomous local subsidiaries. One solution is to implement a matrix approach. The problem, however, is that a global matrix organization is both com-

Figure 15-6. Matrix Organization

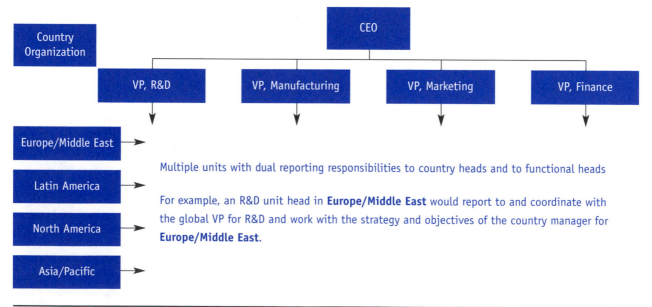

Multiple units with dual reporting responsibilities to country heads and to functional heads

For example, an R&D unit head in **Europe/Middle East** would report to and coordinate with the global VP for R&D and work with the strategy and objectives of the country manager for **Europe/Middle East.**

plex and bureaucratic with its two-boss structure. The possible consequence is conflict and confusion with overlapping responsibilities. Negotiation is necessary; and the organization may become bogged down with information, while multiple time zones and distances render the resolution of face-to-face conflict difficult. Hence, top management attempts to rein in national subsidiaries and begins to eliminate redundancies that may have developed in products, manufacturing sites, and staff functions.

Greater centralization focuses on developing global products and rationalized global manufacturing. Such steps require more central coordination and control. At this point, local managers begin to chafe against the dictates of central headquarters and market forces lead top management to realize that some local responsiveness and autonomy are necessary. *This leads to the emergence of the transnational form of organization*, with the goal of mediating between the conflicting drives of global integration and local responsiveness. Such an organizational form brings the added benefit of stimulating worldwide innovation because it also facilitates knowledge sharing and transnational cooperation.

The importance of local responsiveness is growing as multinationals increase their marketing in environments that are quite distinct from their home markets and from markets in other developed nations. Quelch points out that U.S. multinationals, in particular, have limited presence in Islamic countries and have few Muslims in upper levels of management. That limits the firm's ability to engage Islamic markets, take into account the sensibilities and culture of those markets, adapt products, and learn from the markets. He notes that Saudi Arabia is a lead market for film finishing. Saudi culture does not accept that women in the family be viewed by strangers. Therefore, there is a need for rapid film processing so that when men pick up their processed film, they can rest assured that strangers have not seen photographs of female family members. Thus, companies such as Fuji and Kodak are often first to introduce innovations in high-speed film processing in such markets. Quelch observes that more of this localization will be needed as such markets increase in importance.[11]

Why become transnational? The multinational can achieve scale and scope economies and obtain lower factor costs for raw materials, labor, and capital. At the same time, growing convergence of tastes allows the multinational to concentrate on developing global products and standards, with some local variation. The multinational is better able to confront global competitors with cross-subsidization of weaker or embattled subsidiaries with cash flow from stronger subsidiaries in healthy markets. Such a structure also allows the multinational to respond to environmental volatility, including discriminatory industrial policies by local governments, currency volatility, short product life cycles, economic cyclicality, and cultural differences. Because the environment is constantly changing, the challenge facing the transnational organization is to continue to stimulate worldwide innovation and organizational learning, while still maintaining organizational flexibility.[12]

Transnational corporations are the conceptual translation of the rule to "think local, act global." Transnationals often have products that require adaptation to the needs of local markets. At the same time, the size of transnationals results in benefits from the centralization or regionalization of functions such as finance and product development. And, as ideas can develop anywhere in the world in a large, far-flung corporation, the transnational form of organization creates communication links that encourage the sharing of information and ideas across entities, whether demarcated by function or geography or product line. Transnational organization is an evolution of the matrix form of organization; however, responsibility and authority are clarified.

Examples of Global Organization

It is difficult to appreciate arguments about organizational structure in the abstract. The subtleties of structure are more easily grasped in the context of a product and a market. Hence, this section presents specific examples of the evolution of organizational structure to show how market realities are incorporated in the process of organizational change.

REYNOLDS: EUROPEAN REGIONAL AUTONOMY

The EU has led many global corporations to reexamine how they structure their European operations. Reynolds Metals Company used to have 25 European subsidiaries report to the international division located at headquarters in Richmond, Virginia. That meant that each European country manager dealt directly with the United States and rarely attempted to coordinate operations with the other European countries. Thus, salespeople from different national units would compete against one another for the same multinational client. There were duplication of manufacturing operations and differences in cost and quality. The changes in Europe meant that Reynolds had to integrate European operations because it would be facing intense competition from pan-European companies such as Pechiney and Alusuisse.

Consequently, Reynolds created a European headquarters in Lausanne, Switzerland, to oversee all European operations so they would have a "single voice." Lausanne was headed by a top management team consisting of a president, a chief financial officer (CFO), an executive vice president in charge of manufacturing, and several vice presidents with responsibilities in areas such as marketing. The Lausanne location was chosen over others because Switzerland was viewed as a neutral site, unlikely to create regional tensions that a country with a strong national unit,

Bringing Global Vision into the Company

Global companies face a problem in that their top management is predominantly a national one; that is, most top managers at U.S. companies are Americans. In Japanese companies, top managers are predominantly Japanese. How can such companies not allow a purely nationalistic perspective to bias their attempts to develop a global vision in their planning? The answer may lie partly in adding nondomestic members to their board of directors. In 1989, only one-sixth of about 600 firms surveyed had one or more non-U.S. citizen directors. Because they have operated in international markets longer, European companies have a larger proportion of foreign directors. The difficulty lies in getting the closed-club world of top executives in one country to accept outsiders from another country. Then there is the matter of finding the appropriate people who are willing to serve. Firms need to establish criteria that are especially relevant for choosing a foreign director, such as close ties to local government, considerable experience in economic planning, or years of top management experience running a global company in a related industry. U.S. directors' liability laws can result in non-U.S. citizens being reluctant to serve. Scheduling meetings is another difficulty. A foreign director must fly to the United States for one- or two-day meetings several times a year.

Just as U.S. companies need Europeans and Asians to add a fresh perspective, Asian family-owned firms similarly need Western multinationals and their managers to bring in professional management techniques and a taste for open communication and meritocracy. Of course, as Asian firms begin to launch factories and sales offices across Europe and the Americas, Western contacts help them find their way. Cultural clashes abound, however, particularly in the contrast between the Asian emphasis on personal relationships in family businesses and the Western preference for legal contracts and agreements.

Sources: "Globalizing the Company with Foreign Board Members," *Business International*, March 4, 1991; "Asia's Family Empires Change Their Tactics for a Shrinking World," *Wall Street Journal*, April 19, 1995.

such as France or Germany, might. Reynolds (Europe) Ltd. had direct responsibility for manufacturing facilities.

Reynolds planned to focus on downstream, household-oriented products as well as the aluminum can market since European consumption of cans lagged far behind the 74 billion sold in the United States. Reynolds expected several benefits to flow from the organizational change:

- Rationalized manufacturing, resulting in lower costs
- Faster decision making
- A pan-European thrust in production, marketing, and advertising
- Greater influence in Brussels, a city fast becoming the seat of European government

UNILEVER: TRANSNATIONAL ORGANIZATION

In Unilever's transnational organization, product groups are responsible for profits in Europe and North America, while geographically based regional organizations have profit responsibility elsewhere in the world. Unilever's transnational organization is the result of a long evolution, lasting several decades. Initially, Unilever was organized as a series of relatively independent country subsidiaries with strong local management. Later, product groups took over worldwide profit responsibility, which was divided into three major groups: edible fats, frozen food and ice cream, and food and drinks such as tea and soup. Raw materials and distribution systems determined the makeup of those three groups. This change took many years of "patience, persuasion and even some early retirements."[13]

As markets changed, consumer-driven products such as low-calorie, health, and convenience foods and the use of natural ingredients became important. Unilever's response was to form an executive triad of three board directors responsible for all of Unilever's food businesses. Each director received profit responsibility for a group of countries in a region. Five strategic groups centered around edible fats, ice cream, beverages, meals, and professional markets. Today those groups advise the "food executive," providing product expertise; but they don't have profit center responsibilities. Unilever's newest transnational organization structure seeks to preserve unity within diversity. It well understands that current trends in major food markets such as global fast food, national foods that cross country boundaries (for example, Chinese and Mexican food), and purely national foods might require continued organizational evolution, which, in turn, means maintaining a flexible workforce.

Such flexibility is achieved by careful recruitment and training of managers. Unilever's managers constantly watch for young, bright local university graduates and scientists. Recruits go through in-house training programs on a continuing basis, maintaining contact with their peer cohorts around the world. Job rotation across product groups and countries and use of third-country nationals in high-level executive positions in country subsidiaries further cement informal transnational network ties across various country units. Unilever also uses international working groups to handle specific tasks and issues. Twice a year international conferences bring together managers from all over the world to listen to top management plans and to meet and renew old friendships.

In the pharmaceutical industry, Schering-Plough reorganized its U.S. and global marketing divisions into two major customer groups: primary care physicians and specialists Each group was in charge of certain drugs, based on who was most likely to understand the need for such drugs and had the power to prescribe them. Thus, the specialist group handled drugs to treat hepatitis C, Crohn's disease, brain tumors, and cardiovascular disease. Further, international pharmaceutical sales were subdivided by geography, with one subgroup in charge of Japan, Latin America, and the Far East and the other subgroup having responsibility for Europe, Canada, Africa, and the Middle East. The United States had it own domestic marketing division.[14]

GENERAL MOTORS: INCREASING CENTRALIZATION

As a company, General Motors has moved away from a decades-long philosophy of decentralized regional geographic subsidiaries. Previously, it set up European headquarters in Zurich. The heads of sales and marketing at its major product divisions in Europe Opel (Germany), Vauxhall (UK), and Saab—reported to the European sales and marketing chief based in Zurich. Similarly, the heads of production and product development at the three product divisions would report directly to Europe's COO in Zurich. Zurich coordinated European marketing, planning, and operations, with some division of tasks between national and European headquarters. Zurich focused on Europe-wide planning and strategy, environmental matters, personnel, and relations with the EU in Brussels and other European capitals.[15]

However, as global competition intensified, General Motors saw the need to coordinate product development in order to reduce the multitude of product variations and to reduce overall development and manufacturing costs. The company wanted to get away from its past approach where the global product plan was "four regional plans stapled together".[16] For example, this would allow General Motors to reduce the number of car radios from 270 to 50, leading to a 40 percent reduction in radio costs.

The example above refers to European organization alone. If global operations are considered, designing an organizational structure becomes even more difficult. This can be gauged by considering Toyota's global operations, as shown in Figure 15-7. Toyota has significant high-volume manufacturing operations in North America, Europe, and Asia; the heart of its operations is in Japan. Each location is a major source of exports. As a result, Toyota's organizational structure needs not only to manage and coordinate global manufacturing and supply chain, but also to link these sources of product with upstream global R&D and product development and with many downstream global markets, marketing subsidiaries, and distributors across the continents.

SHELL: RELYING ON MATRIX ORGANIZATION

The companies of the Royal Dutch/Shell Group, whose scenario planning we discussed earlier, also adopted a matrix structure, with the additional innovation of the matrix involving three dimensions: regions, industry sectors, and functions. Shell's several hundred operating companies, which are autonomous, draw on global resources of the "service" companies, including regional, sectoral, and functional management.

Shell has nine service companies providing specialized advice and services and consisting of executives who have considerable operating experience in the field. Thus, an operating company could call on experts in petroleum exploration techniques, in financial management, or in chemical plant management. The service companies include trading companies dealing in oil, chemicals, and coal.

The three dimensions of the service companies include five regional coordinators who monitor the profits of the operating companies and approve investments and six business sectors that consist of upstream oil and gas and downstream oil, including marketing, natural gas, chemicals, coal, and metals. Sectoral panels supervise strategy for national, regional, and worldwide lines of business. Further, nine specialized functional departments exist: finance, legal affairs, materials, planning, public affairs, research, safety and environment, information systems, and human resources and organization. The CEO of each operating company must draw up the annual plan, however, calling on any of the service companies for whatever assistance is need. The quality and experience of the service companies are what make the system work. A drawback, however, is the vast quantity of information that flows to headquarters. All in all, Shell believes that the gains from giving autonomy to operating companies provide a compensatory quick-response capability.[17]

Another example of matrix organization is the Radisson hotel chain, which is segmented by market and geographic area. The geographic segment focuses on North and South America, Europe, and Asia and the Pacific. The market segments include business travel, leisure travel, and group travel. The matrix structure leads to teams that can focus global resources on specific local properties.

PHILIPS: GLOBAL PRODUCT DIVISIONS

Philips, the Dutch electronics multinational, also stressed quick local responses and a marketing orientation as it

Figure 15-7. Toyota's Global Manufacturing Organization

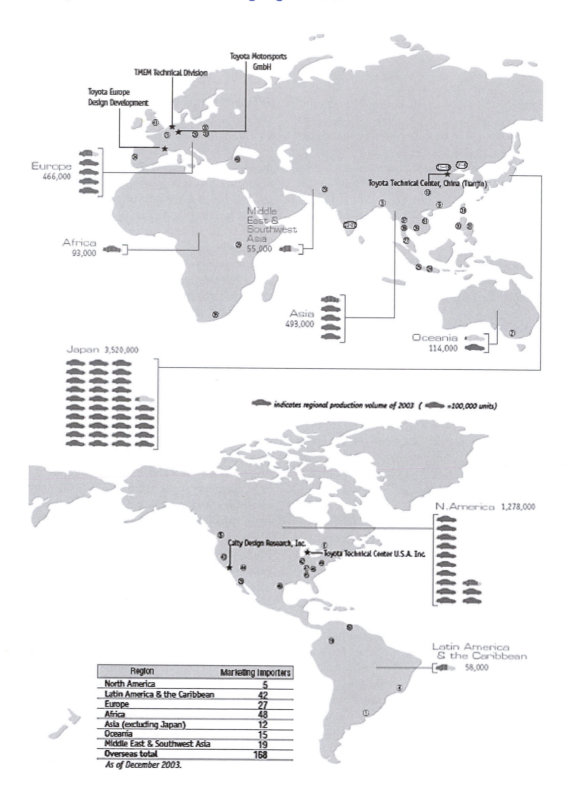

Region	Marketing Importers
North America	5
Latin America & the Caribbean	42
Europe	27
Africa	48
Asia (excluding Japan)	12
Oceania	15
Middle East & Southwest Asia	19
Overseas total	168

As of December 2003.

Source: Toyota Company web site, company worldwide organization (http://www.toyota.co.jp/en/about_toyota/manufacturing/worldwide.html); accessed April 27, 2005.

reorganized for global operations.[18] Philips reduced local subsidiary autonomy to focus on three core global product divisions: consumer electronics, electronic components, and IT/communications. National subsidiary autonomy was reduced to allow a global manufacturing and marketing strategy to be formulated for each product division. The importance of the product line is stressed by bringing product division directors on board. At the same time, central control allows for rationalized manufacturing on a global scale for each product line in order to gain economies of scale.

How can such a system not stifle local subsidiaries? Philips wants to be imaginative in creating new products and asks for input from key markets for this task. At the same time, central control is needed to prevent the creation of different national products for each market. Philips has located "competence centers" in crucial markets—car electronics in Germany and domestic appliances in Italy, for example. Also, the company uses multidisciplinary teams with expertise in development, design, manufacturing, and marketing, thus keeping in mind technical, manufacturing, and marketing considerations. As Dr. van Hamersveld, marketing manager at Philips, commented, "The international product axis underlies corporate policy, but the contribution of national organizations is vital for local marketing and distribution and in dealing with national regulations and handling relationships with governments."

Philips takes care to balance the opposing demands of centralization and local responsiveness over the stages of a product life cycle. In the early stage, product launch is centrally coordinated in Europe, the United States, and Japan, while centralized manufacturing and standardization reduce costs. In the maturity phase, local subsidiaries play a larger role, tailoring local marketing, possibly including some product modifications. In the decline phase, emphasis shifts to centralized manufacturing and cost saving. Local subsidiaries make the greatest contribution and have the greatest autonomy in choosing distribution channels, which Philips believes must be adapted to local conditions. The powerful distribution and dealer networks built up by local subsidiaries become a key competitive advantage in Philips' global strategy.

An important element in developing new products is the R&D lab. As firms try to decide whether to customize products for individual markets, they also must decide how to organize the R&D function. If R&D is centralized, organizational procedures must allow product customization requests to come in from the various subsidiaries, with a way to prioritize such requests and respond in a timely manner. One approach is to appoint a marketing executive to serve as liaison between marketing subsidiaries and the central R&D lab, channeling and prioritizing customization requests. Then the actual development can be carried out at the central lab or at

regional sites, serving specific clusters of markets. Such ventures also require the formation of virtual teams that are established on a project basis, using communication networks, e-mail, and videoconferencing to allow for exchange of information and debate on major issues.[19]

Organizational flexibility *will be* the necessary ingredient as organizations change to meet the challenges of a global economy and new forms of competition from knowledge-rich and Internet-based companies. Organizing to harness knowledge from around the world is the critical challenge. Building and using knowledge bases, motivating people to contribute to and use shared knowledge, and fostering interaction among virtual organizational units and teams that dominate specific forms of knowledge such as customer knowledge, business processes, and product-based knowledge are all part of these new organizational structures.

ORGANIZATIONAL RESPONSES TO ASIAN AND LATIN AMERICAN MARKETS

GE has 12 major lines of business in Asia; but unlike many Asian conglomerates that cross-subsidize their disparate lines of business, GE insists that each line of business be independent. In practice, this means that GE has a manager for each country. That manager can give a common face to all of GE's businesses in the country. However, the country manager at GE works in a matrix context, with each line of business evaluated on how it contributes to the global profits of that line of business and to the country unit's profits. Another critical element of GE's Asian focus is the rotation of managers across GE's various Asian country units. Human resources is a scarce and limiting factor, and the executives bring varied experience but a common GE perspective to each business to which they are assigned.[20]

Sometimes a company's situation and strategic need may dictate that it stop using mostly local managers and bring in more expatriates. For example, as China began to move to GSM-based cellular phones, Motorola saw its phone division sales drop precipitously. Because it did not have a GSM switch to sell with its phones, it lost out to competitors who could offer a complete turnkey system. To reverse the trend, Motorola brought back senior-level expatriates, replacing some high-level local managers. Motorola also began to sell older models at steep discounts so it could compete with traditional landline phones, increase its market share, and hold off competitors to give it time to upgrade its technologies. That involved licensing a local Chinese company, Da Tang, to produce CDMA switches, a new U.S. technology intended to replace the GSM standard that was becoming widespread in China.[21]

A similar matrix structure is used by DuPont in South America. Responding to the formation of Mercosur, DuPont integrated its South American operations, with headquarters outside of Sao Paulo, Brazil, where all prod-

Reorganization at Square D Company, AGCO, and Ciba-Geigy

*S*quare D Company is an example of the role of organizational structure in mediating headquarters and regional interests. Square D *manufactures electrical products in over 100 factories, including 31 outside the United States. Traditionally, international responsibility had been based at U.S. headquarters. The work was divided between vice presidents for international marketing and international manufacturing. U.S. products were sold overseas, foreign subsidiaries had little authority, and communication with the United States was infrequent.*

To implement a global strategy, the electrical group was divided into three business units: distribution equipment, power equipment, and controls. At the same time, five regional divisions were created: United States., Asia/Pacific, Canada, Europe, and Latin America. The result was a product/region matrix with the following structure:

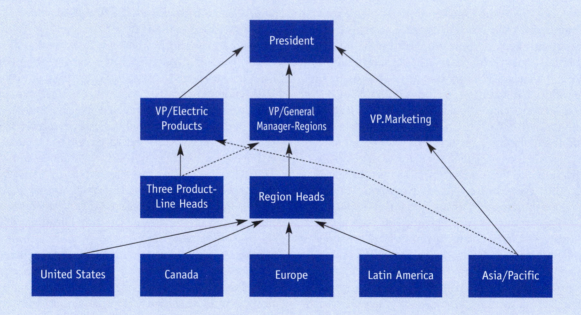

The matrix consists of product-line heads and regional managers, except for Asia/Pacific, which reports directly to a vice president of marketing because of Square D's limited manufacturing presence in Asia. Quarterly meetings are held in the United States with the product-line and regional heads as well as domestic marketing managers. Communications are emphasized through a quarterly videotape and an in-house magazine distributed worldwide.

The benefits from this reorganization included the following:

- *Greater regional autonomy with profit and loss responsibility*
- *Timely relay of market information about electrical standards, priorities for each market, and feedback on demand trends and competition—all to benefit manufacturing worldwide*
- *Ability to design a global product effectively and economically; the smooth flow of information from around the world helps determine global product requirements and allows pooling of manufacturing and engineering capabilities*
- *An emphasis on cooperation and global line responsibilities, fostering a global corporate culture*

continued

Ciba-Geigy presents an alternative approach to using regional managers. The company is divided into 14 major worldwide product lines and 34 profit centers. If a country has only one product subsidiary, that division reports directly to the worldwide product division manager. That person, in turn, reports to an executive committee member responsible for the product line. When countries have multiple product divisions, however, they are supervised by a regional manager, who reports to an executive committee member who has responsibility for a geographic area. Ciba-Geigy has three broad geographic areas: Europe, the Americas, and Asia/Australia. Thus, executive committee members have both product and geographic responsibilities. The company's regional managers oversee local management of areas such as legal, personnel, quality and security, management development, and performance measurement. The regional managers also represent the company in interaction with local governments, unions, and the media. The regional manager and the local product division manager are jointly responsible for profits. Bonuses for regional managers are based on a combination of local country profits and worldwide profits, as well as division profits in cases where the regional manager is responsible for the local product division.

Another recent example is AGCO Corporation, which designs, manufactures, and distributes agricultural equipment. It moved to a new matrix management structure, motivated by the need to focus on specific brands in specific geographic markets while also giving more authority and responsibility to functional heads, thus creating more control. The matrix was also intended to foster greater cooperation worldwide. It also allows the company to develop top management by giving managers an opportunity to gain hands-on international experience in operating positions.

Sources: "Square D Unites Managers to Compete Globally," *Business International*, September 21, 1987; "The Role of the Country Manager," *Business Europe*, March 27, 1995; and AGCO announces New Organization Structure as Part of Succession Planning," PR Newswire European, February 12, 2004.

uct-line managers are typically based. Each manager also has responsibility for a country in Mercosur and for smaller markets outside Mercosur. Such regional integration allows for the specialization of products by plants located in different countries with between-plant transfers of goods to meet various market needs.

An interesting issue in organizations where matrix structures exist and where country managers work closely with several product-line managers is how to measure per-

formance. Budgets can be set and performance against budget can be used to evaluate performance. Beyond financial targets, country managers are responsible for "soft" variables such as handling government relations, maintaining corporate culture, and nurturing managers. Each region and each country may have to develop specific measures adapted to the country's needs and cultures.[22]

Given the importance of organizational structure fitting with a firm's global marketing strategy, the organization will likely change as markets evolve and a company's strategy changes. Such organizational evolution can be seen in advertising agencies in China. Their initial customers, foreign multinationals in China, found that they needed to expand their marketing beyond the three largest cities of Beijing, Shanghai, and Guangzhou into smaller provincial capitals such as Fuzhou Fuijian. The multinationals needed advertising and communication services in these smaller, less well-known cities. The reason? They found themselves competing with larger local firms who were also attempting to establish their brands in these smaller cities in the face of growing local purchasing power and finicky customers. Such brand competition requires not only advertising, but also direct marketing, sales promotion, and an integrated communications strategy.

For the advertising agencies, both multinationals and local Chinese companies were important customers; local Chinese companies began to account for about half of all advertising spending. With continued growth, China was forecasted to become the second-largest advertising market in the world by 2010, from about $14.5 billion in 2003. This meant that advertising agencies had to expand rapidly beyond the three biggest cities into several smaller ones, providing advertising services, increasing their knowledge of local marketing and advertising issues, and adding local clients to their roster. This is a complex and difficult task to implement.

Not surprisingly, Ogilvy & Mather China, one of the largest foreign advertising agencies in China, sought to speed up this organizational expansion. It acquired a majority control of Fujian Effort, a large independent Chinese agency in Fuzhou, the capital of Fujian province. While this acquisition-based expansion met clients' needs, it also emphasized issues of corporate culture. Ogilvy had to grapple with merging the culture of Fujian Effort, a closely held Chinese company, with its own multinational advertising culture.[23]

Organizational Culture and Organizational Structure

As shown above in the example of Ogilvy in China, as a firm develops its international marketing organization, besides having to create a formal organizational structure (assigning roles, responsibilities, authority, accountability, and reporting relationships), it must also concern itself with spreading the organizational culture. As Schein notes,[24] organizational culture is deeply embedded in a group through its history and experiences and is embodied in the way in which that organization approaches problem solving.

A firm's or group's organizational culture consists of processes and values that all group members share. They agree that those values and processes, because they have been successful in the past, should continue to be used to solve problems in the future. The organizational culture determines how members are accepted by the group; how power is gained, exercised, and lost in the group; and how rewards and sanctions will be used by the group to motivate or deter certain behaviors. Such cultures can vary even within a large organization, with subcultures developing around functional roles, geographic or regional locales, professions, business units, etc. Thus, within a large U.S. organization, the marketing culture may be distinct from the organizational culture of an engineering and product development unit or a manufacturing site. Such differences are considerably exacerbated when the firm goes overseas to set up its international marketing organization. Many, if not most, of its employees in its overseas international marketing subsidiaries are likely to be local nationals or third-country nationals. In those cases, the company's organizational culture needs to be communicated and established; further, it needs to coexist with national culture.

For example, U.S. marketing organizations often use quotas of individual salespeople by territory. Receiving commissions based on sales performance and exceeding quotas can form a large (sometimes the biggest) share of total compensation. Salespeople may be given considerable autonomy to plan their sales calls and may report back to the head office once a week or less, communicating remotely and acting with a high degree of independence. Cold calling may be required; and salespeople may be expected to be highly productive, optimizing their time while in the field. Such behaviors are consistent with the broader U.S. culture that stresses individualism, material success, performance measurement, risk taking, and independence. However, such practices may be difficult to transfer to more traditional cultures where salespeople feel more comfortable being paid principally with salary, prefer close supervision and direction from sales managers, and are reluctant to initiate sales calls on clients to whom they have not been introduced or with whom they have no previous connection.

This suggests that the solution may lie in helping to socialize foreign salespeople gradually to the company's dominant organizational culture, beginning with careful recruitment to select individuals who may be a better fit with the company's values and processes. At the same time, the company should expect to adapt its processes to the changed environment and to the local culture while still maintaining its core values and core ethical stance. A recent study proposed that organizational culture differences could be disruptive in the formation and performance of an alliance, particularly when the underlying professional cultures (engineering and software design) were critical to value creation in the alliance.[25]

WHAT ROLE SHOULD HEADQUARTERS PLAY?

A constant theme running through the various attempts at creating an organizational structure appropriate for global strategy and marketing is the role that the parent company headquarters should take. Corporate headquarters can play three roles in its dealings with subsidiaries around the world: controller, coach, or orchestrator.[26]

A **controller** gives considerable autonomy to subsidiaries and uses measurements, such as profits by a small business unit, to determine when to intervene. This is classic management by exception.

The **coach** also decentralizes authority to subsidiaries but is available to provide support and advice, somewhat along the lines of the Shell example described previously. This means that the coach will intervene when necessary, attempting to strike the right balance between decentralization and central control.

The **orchestrator** is an interventionist with central control and responsibility for activities such as manufacturing, R&D, and finance. Subsidiary managers, therefore, have less autonomy. This style may be appropriate for industries for which global integration is important and investment needs are large, as in oil, steel, mining, and financial services.

In addition, headquarters can play two other temporary roles: surgeon and architect. When major upheavals threaten a firm and its industry, the company may have to be restructured, with many units divested, product lines dropped, and workers laid off. Responses to corporate raiders at companies such as Gillette are typical of such a stance. The other extreme is restructuring through acquisitions, as in the case of Sony, which reacted to the failure of the Betamax video format by deciding to emphasize "software"; that is, music and film production. This restructuring has led Sony to acquire U.S. record companies and film studios. This phase also requires strong central direction from the **architect**, who reshapes the company according to a global vision before returning to the mode of coach or orchestrator.

Company roles should be consistent with the nature of businesses within the global firm. The degree of synergy between the various lines of business in a firm, the level of risk facing the firm, and the intensity of competition determine which headquarters style is appropriate. (See Table 15-3.)

Table 15-3. Headquarters' Roles and Line-of-Business Characteristics

	Controller	Coach	Orchestrator
Synergy	Little/None	Medium	High
Risk	Low	Medium	High
Competition	Stable	Open	Intense

Source: M. Goold and A. Campbell, *Strategies and Styles*, United Kingdom: Ashridge Management Centre, 1989.

If a company's lines of business are such that both high and low risk are present, the task of headquarters becomes blurred. For a high-risk business, headquarters may have to play the role of orchestrator; for a low-risk business, a controller role is more appropriate. Unless the company restructures so that only one kind of business line profile prevails, the firm must live with multiple roles. This implies that no one organizational structure is appropriate for a global firm with many lines of business. This is the reason that large global firms seem to be constantly changing their organizational structure. As the profiles of the various lines of business change, new organizational structures are necessary.

Whatever the organizational structure, its success depends on the people filling the various positions created by the organizational structure. Difficulties arise because global marketing organizations are often headed by expatriates who are proven marketing executives with success in their home markets. As they move to new and distinct foreign markets, they are likely to bring with them assumptions and processes that may be wrong or inadequate for the new markets they are entering. Misapprehension or ignorance can cause flawed formulation and execution of a marketing strategy. Harvey and Novicevic suggest that such "pluralistic and probabilistic" ignorance can be countered with careful staffing, where the firm combines expatriate with "in-patriate" (host country nationals relocated to headquarters) management.[27] Such a staffing policy would allow the multinational firm to integrate missing context-specific knowledge. This approach would be particularly important for markets in developing countries where the cultural distance is large. Figure 15-8 shows what types of errors are likely and how enlightened staffing can correct them.

The Country Manager

A key element in the growing multinational company is the country manager (CM).[28] What does the CM do? The CM is often given local profit center responsibility, is responsible for multiple functional areas, and is the liaison with regional and headquarters management. Expected to be as much an entrepreneur as a manager, the CM seeks to increase local autonomy.

Factors changing the role of a CM include, for example, demands for greater global integration of R&D and manufacturing. Other factors include the subordination of national interests, the rise of product-based global organi-

Figure 15-8. Types of Errors Caused by Lack of Context-Specific Knowledge

Type of Ignorance	Type I Error	Type II Error	Type III Error	Type IV Error
Pluralistic ignorance	Management not recognizing the need to adopt existing strategies to local context of individual markets	Management implementing a strategic decision over the objections of an alliance partner more knowledgeable of the environment	Management not entering a market because there are too many government regulations... when demand was not large enough to support a new competitor	Management not correctly assessing market potential because of low per capita income... when there are a large number of people per household
Probablistic ignorance	Managers arguing that the global market is not attractive due to the need to contextualize marketing efforts to foreign markets	Managers not rejecting input from subsidiary management that local economic conditions prevent them from reaching their goals	Managers expecting to successfully compete in a country because there are only local competitors	Managers conducting a survey to collect data on consumers in developing countries without appropriate modification to research methodology

Source: Michael Harvey and M. M. Novicevic, "Staffing Global Marketing Positions: What We Don't Know Can Make a Difference," *Journal of World Business*, Volume 35, Issue 1, 2000, pages. 80–94, Table 1.

zations and global customers, and regional integration policies such as the EU and NAFTA. How do those forces impact on the CM? They tend to reduce the CM's local authority to implement global and regional policies in the national sphere. The CM's main focus becomes local sales and distribution, along with local planning, forecasting and budgeting, financial management and control, personnel and labor relations (including training local managers), and government relations. Public relations is another responsibility of the CM, particularly representing the parent company in meetings with local trade and industry officials and in community relations. However, the CM's autonomy may depend on the importance of the local subsidiary. This importance is typically determined by the subsidiary's size, age, and experience; total sales revenues and market position; overall performance; and the ability and effectiveness of local management. The cultural distance of the local subsidiary from its parent is also relevant.

As outlined below, the CM's responsibilities and roles change as the firm's international business position changes.

Stage of the Firm's Internationalization	CM's Role
International	*Trader*: The CM oversees sales and distribution of products principally exported from headquarters
Multinational	*Potentate*: A local czar with local products, manufacturing, profit and loss responsibility, particularly in countries with barriers to free trade
Transnational	*Cabinet Member*: A team player subordinating a local subsidiary to the needs of global integration; reduced authority in some areas (for example, R&D and manufacturing); greater role for regional manager
Global	*Ambassador*: The CM works with product and line-of-business global managers, focusing principally on the local government and trade issues; often a local national

CMs can draw on local roots to build businesses. For example, Richardson Hindustan's CMs were able to highlight the role of natural herbs used to formulate Vicks VapoRub cold medicine. That appealed to Indian consumers because they could see connections to the age-old Indian Ayurvedic system of medicine that also draws on native herbs and plants. At the same time, the parent company's transnational approach allows CMs to learn from local solutions and apply them in other national markets; for example, the success to be had from year-round advertising or from using traditional distribution systems in emerging markets.[29]

As was suggested previously, multinationals constantly change their organizational structure as environmental change and daily operations disclose weaknesses in the way the firm is organized. Organizational fashions can exist, such as the trend to develop worldwide product-line operations and to subordinate CMs to the product-line leaders. McKinsey[30] studied 43 U.S. consumer companies to see if organizational changes could be linked to international success. He found that superior international growth in sales and profits seemed to be linked to several traits:

- Centralized international decision making except in new product development
- Requirement that top management have international experience
- Use of videoconferencing and e-mail to link international managers
- Successful integration of international acquisitions
- Multiple product managers in a country reporting to a CM, as shown in the Ciba-Geigy example presented earlier.

The Informal Organization

Regardless of which organizational structure is chosen, the central problem is that organizational structure is static while the environment is dynamic. How can a multinational preserve strategic and organizational flexibility? *The answer is to go beyond the formal organization.* Beyond organizational structure, the firm must focus on communication channels, interpersonal relationships, and changing individual perceptions. The goal should be to let the informal organization bloom. Overall, an environment of intense competition, overcapacity, and technological change means that companies will succeed because of their clarity of corporate *purpose*, effective management *processes*, and ability to develop *people*—employee capabilities and perspectives. Instead of sweeping strategic visions, employees who believe in what the company is trying to achieve are more likely to move the company to success.[31]

FORMING INDUSTRY-WIDE "WEBS": GOING BEYOND A COMPANY'S ORGANIZATIONAL BOUNDARIES

Another facet of organizational structure is how a company is organized to deal with outsiders. As companies begin to work closely with entities such as suppliers and competitors, a network approach is becoming more common. Such network linkages go beyond purely commercial links; they encompass a larger relationship wherein the two partners attempt to share resources and to harmonize competitive strategies for competitive advantage. Such networks can include key suppliers and customers; competitors; and entities such as governments, unions, universities, research institutes, and trade associations.

Such networks are particularly interesting in technology-based industries where companies form a web without any formal agreement. Instead, the web is built around a common technological standard. One example is the number of companies developing software based on the Windows/Intel standard or, more recently, on the Explorer Internet browser. Coalescing around a technological standard reduces risk because there is greater assurance of larger market size. In addition, the web of informal linkages allows individual firms to focus their strategy and to concentrate on relatively narrow segments of the value chain. Because the technological standard reduces risk, the web shapers, who set the standard, have the option of keeping the standard to themselves (that is, creating a proprietary standard as Apple attempted to do with the Macintosh). The trade-off is whether to increase the size of the web by freely giving away the standard or to attempt to capture profits while reducing the size of the web. It is estimated that Microsoft captured only 4 percent of the total revenues created by the Wintel standard. It is debatable, however, whether the Wintel standard could have generated total web revenues of over $120 billion without facilitating creation of the web of Wintel companies. Webs are a further extension of the business networks idea, with the added complication that association is primarily voluntary. Companies join the web because of the profit potential they see in adhering to such voluntary webs.[32]

Implementation and Organization

A global strategy makes it inevitable that some intervention by headquarters will be necessary, ranging from informing to persuading, then coordinating and approving, and culminating in directing.[33] As headquarters moves from informing to directing, it is taking greater control and lessening autonomy at the subsidiary.

Headquarters' involvement may vary from country to country, with greater intervention occurring in regions experiencing troubles. However, greater autonomy may be given to some subsidiaries for certain elements of the marketing mix. Table 15-4 sets out a hypothetical example of how a company might arrange the role of headquarters in implementing strategy.

There are five modes of involvement, as follows:

1. *Informing*. Headquarters management informs subsidiaries of news, statistics, market research findings, corporate goals and objectives, and competitive developments. Successful experiences in a country or with a product line are disseminated throughout the organization, with top management relying on the business judgment of subsidiary managers to pick up relevant ideas for adaptation into their own lines of business. An example is Square D's use of a quarterly videotape to communicate developments in the electrical products group worldwide.

Figure 15-4. Global Marketing Strategy Implementation: Headquarters' Role

	Informing	Persuading	Coordinating	Approving	Directing
New-Product Development					X
Product Line					
Marketing Mix					X
Product Characteristics			X		
Product Segmentation			X		
Brand Policy			X		
Packaging				X	
Advertising			X		
Promotion		X			
Distribution Channels		X			
Pricing				X	
Customer Service			X		
Country Markets					
Market 1		X			
Market 2			X		
•					
•					
•					
Market *n*					X

Source: Adapted from John Quelch and E. Hoff, "Customizing Global Marketing," *Harvard Business Review*, May–June, 1986.

2. *Persuading*. The three-dimensional service groups used at Shell provide an example of this approach, with autonomy still resting at the subsidiary level. Much of matrix management involves persuasion, which can be a slow process. However, long-term results are more likely because the subsidiary managers will have been convinced of the merits of the actions taken.

3. *Coordinating*. Used by Avon, in this approach, subsidiary managers in Latin America develop their own plans, but headquarters coordinates the various country plans. Notably, Avon uses a bottom-up approach, preferring that plans originate with the national managers. That allows good managers to develop at subsidiaries and heightens the chances of their being retained.

4. *Approving*. Headquarters must approve plans drawn up by subsidiaries. This allows for global strategy, influenced by competitor response, to take precedence over plans tailored to the needs of a specific subsidiary.

5. *Directing*. Subsidiary managers do as they are told by headquarters. This approach may be necessary because of a critical situation, because of a lack of seasoned managers, or because the issue must be standardized on a global basis. The effect on manager motivation can be damaging. Those who are competent may chafe at the restraint and move on to other companies. It is also unlikely that decisions made by top management will always be right. What is lost in this approach is the sensitivity of local managers to the adaptation needs of the local market.

A global company needs strong local managers, but managers need experience to become strong. As Table 15-4 makes clear, some products, functions, and marketing activities can be safely left to subsidiary managers. Indeed, companies should seek to create some areas in which autonomy is fostered.

The extent to which a foreign subsidiary is allowed to practice greater or lesser independence in designing local marketing strategies is affected by the following:[34]

- The subsidiary's history of relationship with headquarters; for example, how much the subsidiary trusts headquarters, whether the subsidiary believes it is dependent on headquarters, whether the subsidiary believes it is part of the parent organization, how the subsidiary participates in setting local market objectives, and how much cooperation exits between the marketing manager and headquarters' marketing organization.

- Industry conditions; namely, whether the subsidiary is in a local market characterized by market turbulence and market concentration and whether the global industry is characterized by technological turbulence. A subsidiary may have more autonomy when the local market is turbulent. Also, a subsidiary is more likely to follow headquarters' direction when the local market is concentrated and when there is considerable technological turbulence.

- Economic and cultural distance. A subsidiary will have more autonomy when there is greater economic and cultural distance between the local market and the parent country.

Regional Headquarters: A Halfway House

You have considered decentralization in terms of the division of labor between corporate headquarters and the units in foreign markets. Frequently, however, as a firm's business in a region such as Europe or Latin America grows larger, the business becomes important enough to warrant separate attention. This can lead to the establishment of a new level in the organization between corporate headquarters and the foreign markets; that is, a regional headquarters. A **regional headquarters** is not necessarily located within the region, although it usually is for larger regions such as Europe. Many U.S. companies, for example, have their Latin American headquarters in Coral Gables, Florida, truly a halfway point between corporate headquarters and country operations. Regardless of location, however, regional headquarters gives undivided attention to the affairs of the region.

Almost all of the world's major computer companies find it necessary to have a regional headquarters in Asia for the important Asia/Pacific market. Firms such as Apple, Unisys, Hewlett-Packard, and Wang are based in Hong Kong. AT&T is in Singapore, IBM is in Tokyo, and ICL is in Australia.

Conclusions on Organizational Structure

From the preceding discussion, three generalizations can be made about organizational structure:

- The structure must be tailored to the situation and needs of the individual firm. No standard model exists.

- Changing conditions require the firm to adapt; as a result, organizational structures are in almost continual evolution.

- Perhaps the most important conclusion, though, is that firms are now recognizing that organizational structure can never be a complete and satisfactory means of coordinating their international operations.

Accordingly, they are now trying to incorporate the product, geographic, and functional dimensions into their decision making without changing their organizational structure. In other words, other approaches besides organizational structure can be used to coordinate international business.

Stopford and Wells studied structural changes but noted that "management skills" were more important than the formal organization structure.[35] In a later study, Bartlett found that many successful firms did not worry about structural change, but focused attention on the individual tasks they were facing. "Instead of joining the quest for the ideal structure, they looked at the connection between environment, strategy, and the 'way of managing.' " Hedlund found the same to be true of Swedish multinationals. Instead of introducing matrix structures, they complemented their simple organizational forms by making changes in information systems, budgeting, rotation of personnel, etc.[36]

As subsidiaries mature, they also evolve, developing their roles. Taggart has suggested that such evolution can result in four subsidiary configurations: as a confederation, as a strategic "auxiliary," as an autarchy, and as a detached unit. Birkinshaw also focuses on such evolution, with the path changing from that of being a sales subsidiary, to being involved in local sales and manufacturing, to being a regional hub, and then to developing a global scope with a world product mandate.[37]

Those evolutionary changes and what Bartlett calls the "way of managing" include a variety of approaches that can best be considered as control devices, the next topic.

Controlling International Marketing

Companies market internationally to attain certain corporate goals. The purpose of control is to direct operations to achieve desired objectives. Considered that way, control is the essence of management, consisting of establishing standards, measuring performance against the standards, and then suggesting and implementing corrective action for deviation from standards and plans.

Control is inextricably related to the previous topics, planning and organization. Management scholars Koontz and O'Donnell called planning and organization prerequisites of control systems. Planning involves setting standards and goals, the first step in the control process. The organization of a firm establishes the hierarchy, the division of labor, and the communications channels for management control. Furthermore, the degree of decentralization affects the control task. General control princi-

ples are as valid internationally as they are domestically. Special problems arise from different environments in which the operations occur. Communication gaps—distances between firms' different markets and differences in language, nationality, and culture—are the major causes of difficulty. Problems also arise from differences in financial and monetary environments. For example, government supervision, exchange controls, and differing rates of inflation limit a firm's ability to control transfer prices, remittances, and logistics; that is, inflation rates limit where it will buy and sell internationally.

Special Measurement Techniques

In addition to regular reporting, specialized techniques exist for evaluating marketing performance. Two of the most noteworthy are distribution cost analysis and the marketing audit.

Distribution cost analysis is a technique used to analyze the profitability of different parts of the marketing program. It can be used to study product lines, distribution channels, customers, or territories. Through comparative distribution cost studies of markets, international marketers can recognize weaknesses in marketing programs and find solutions to recommend to markets having problems.

The *marketing audit* is a methodical examination of the total marketing effort, often by some outside expert.[38] Such an audit may be done by international marketing managers for each market every few years. Certainly, the audit would add to management's understanding of the firm's foreign marketing and aid in improving it. A marketing audit is especially useful when a firm is changing its involvement in a country. At a higher level, an audit may be made of the total international marketing of a firm.

Organization

The purpose of organization is to facilitate management control. The organizational structure shows the lines of authority, the hierarchy of control. Going beyond organizational structure, a study by Doz and Prahalad emphasizes organizational context as a means of maintaining strategic control.[39] By *organizational context*, they mean that administrative mechanisms exist (apart from changing the organizational structure) that allow headquarters to maintain control in changing environments and circumstances. Table 15-5 gives an overview of these administrative mechanisms. Doz and Prahalad's argument is that headquarters must maintain strategic control if international operations are to be optimized. To achieve this, organizational context (the administrative mechanisms) is more effective than structural change. Dow, for example, refus-

Table 15-5. Administrative Mechanisms for Strategic Control

Data Management Mechanisms	Managers' Management Mechanisms	Conflict Resolution Mechanisms
1. Information systems	1. Choice of key managers	1. Decision responsibility assignments
2. Measurement systems	2. Career paths	2. Integrators
3. Resource allocation	3. Reward and punishment systems	3. Business teams
4. Strategic planning	4. Management development	4. Coordination committees
5. Budgeting process	5. Patterns of socialization	5. Task forces
		6. Issue resolution process

Source: Yves L. Doz and C.K. Prahalad, "Headquarter's Influence and Strategic Control in MNCs," *Sloan Management Review,* Fall 1981, 16. Copyright 1981 by the Sloan Management Review Association. All rights reserved.

es to create a written organization chart because it would de-emphasize the nonstructural methods the company uses to deal with competing strategic imperatives.

For example, in executive placement, it may be necessary to consider the propensity of individual managers to take a headquarters/business perspective versus a subsidiary/market perspective. Reporting relationships may be created to encourage greater or lesser local autonomy. Management accounting and reward systems may be used to enforce a strong national profit center mentality or to create an international perspective. Membership in critical committees may be adjusted to recognize either global or foreign national concerns. Critical functional staff groups may be centralized at headquarters or attached to local operating units. Table 15-6 provides additional positive and negative control mechanisms; in this case within the context of joint ventures.

Table 15-6. Control Mechanisms in Joint Ventures

Positive	Negative
Ability to make specific decisions	Board
Ability to design: planning process; appropriate requests	Executive committee
Policies and procedures	Approval required for:
Ability to set objectives for joint-venture general manager (JVGM)	Specific decisions
Bous of JVGM tied to parent results	Plans, budgets
Ability to decide on future promotion of JVGM (and other JV managers)	Appropriation requests
JVGM participation in parent's worldwide meetings	Nomination of JVGM
Relations with JVGM; phone calls, meetings, visits	Screening/No objection of parent before ideas or projects are discussed with other parent
Contracts: management; technology transfer; marketing; supplier	
Participating in planning or budgeting process	
Parent organization structure	
Reporting structure	
Staffing	
Training programs	
Staff services	
Feedback; strategy/plan budgets, appropriation requests	
Staffing parent with someone with experience with JV	
MNC level in Mexico	
Informal meetings with other parent	

Source: J.L. Schaan, "Parent Control and Joint Venture Success: The Case of Mexico," cited J.M. Geringer and L. Herbert, "Control and Performance of International Joint Ventures," *Journal of International Business Studies,* Summer 1989.

Budget

The budget is the basic control technique used by most multinationals. The control offered by the budget is essentially negative; it may prevent excessive expenditure, but it does not ensure that goals will be reached. Furthermore, if the foreign subsidiary is substantially independent financially, control from headquarters can be difficult. In that case, the administrative mechanisms mentioned by Doz and Prahalad become especially important.

Subsidiaries as Profit Centers

One way to minimize the control burden on corporate headquarters is to have each subsidiary operate as a profit center. Profit centers can take on varying degrees of responsibility. With a high degree of delegation, the subsidiary handles most control problems. Headquarters may enter the scene only when profits are unsatisfactory. Most U.S. companies operate their foreign subsidiaries as profit centers, but with differing degrees of decentralization.

The profit center approach to controlling subsidiaries has several advantages. It maximizes the use of local knowledge and on-the-spot decision making and minimizes the frictions of absentee management. It is good for subsidiary morale because local management likes to "run its own shop."

On the negative side, local management, evaluated on short-term profitability, may act in ways that endanger long-term profits. Autonomous subsidiaries are difficult to integrate into a coherent international operation. Therefore, a high degree of decentralization is most feasible when the subsidiaries are self-contained in buying and selling and have minimal reliance on the corporation for other inputs.

Information Systems for Control

Information is needed to plan, assess performance against plans, and monitor changes in the competitive and client environment. The company's planning and organizational structure determine what information is gathered and how it will be channeled through the organization. The amount of information collected can be enormous. (The topic of IT is presented in Chapter 5.)

Without information, global corporations cannot be integrated efficiently. Mattel, a U.S. toy company, is a good example. Toy sales are concentrated around the Christmas season, with 60 percent of sales occurring between late September and mid-December. Toy makers must stock sufficient quantities of the best-selling toys in order to do well. Mattel produces most of its toys in plants in the Far East and needs to be able to change production plans to take advantage of new sales forecasts, which are based on sales figures. That is, if a certain toy sells out in early November, Mattel needs to know so it can increase production in Hong Kong, then ship the toy where demand is greatest. Equally important, if a toy is not selling well, the company needs to know so it can stop production. Otherwise, the company may have to write off inventory.

Mattel also needs updated figures on toy inventory at its warehouses around the world so that it can shift excess inventory from slow-selling areas to high-demand markets. This requires a global computer and communication system that can track production of several thousand toys, inventories at warehouses in various countries, and all retail stock. Mattel built a global information system linking headquarters with distribution centers and its plants in the Far East. Now the company knows what finished goods are due from which plant on a daily basis and where inventory is located. This allows for "better alignment of the production schedule, market forecast, and real orders." Another benefit is that engineers can quickly communicate product specifications to plants, reducing the time it takes for an idea about a toy to become a finished product.

The global information system allows Mattel to update inventory, production schedules, and engineering specifications in a day, as opposed to between 7 and 30 days formerly. In addition, the system allows Mattel to reduce inventories significantly. Without this system, global strategy and its implementation would remain a dream.

Once such networks are in place, they can be used for other purposes. Communication through e-mail and videoconferencing allows for closer coordination of international marketing, making both local autonomy and centralized coordination achievable. Such systems also allow for close monitoring and the exchange of information about competitors from around the world, which can be invaluable in determining competitive response.

Summary

The basic elements of a marketing plan include the environment and the company situation in each market, the firm's objectives, and the strategy and tactics that will help the firm achieve its objectives.

Plans have a short-range and a long-range component. They should be developed for each foreign market and within the context of a global plan, integrating country markets and other areas of activity, such as manufacturing, technology planning, and R&D.

A comprehensive operating plan is necessary to help a firm achieve its short-term objectives. The plan should include elements such as detailed sales and market share targets, planned new distribution outlets, brand awareness goals, plans for new product introduction, test-marketing plans, and other market research activities. A planning calendar typically requires reconciliation of national plans with headquarters' goals. Once headquarters accepts the plan, budgetary targets are derived and become the basis for managerial action and evaluation.

Broad company-wide plans must be adapted to individual markets. Local participation is necessary, and additional information-gathering and analysis will ensure a plan that is better adapted to individual market realities.

Long-range planning deals with uncertainty. The focus is on developing scenarios in basic areas such as technology, market growth, competitive change, and a firm's resources. The goal is to be prepared for contingencies and to be alert for major opportunities.

Responding to competitive moves is another essential aspect of planning. This is contingency planning, with a firm deciding how it will react if the competition cuts prices, launches a new product, or strikes up a strategic alliance.

Paradoxically, the best way to counter competition may be through a strategic alliance with other competitors. Such alliances reduce risk, save time, provide access to technology and markets, and even secure supply sources. The main question is whether it is better to have a competitor as a partner. Generally, for a strategic alliance to work well, the competitor must possess a complementary asset.

Planning cannot work without a well-designed organizational structure to implement plans. The basic choice is between centralization and decentralization; in some cases, manufacturing may be centralized, with technology development, product adaptation, and marketing decentralized.

Multinational organizations can be structured along geographic, product, or functional lines. The chosen structure may then evolve to a matrix organization. As the environment changes, organizational structure also must change.

Examples of companies such as Reynolds Metals, Unilever, General Motors, Square D Company, Royal Dutch/Shell, the Salim Group, and Philips show that there is no one way to structure an international organization. The examples also show that firms do change their structure over time.

A central issue is the role that headquarters should play. One approach is to view headquarters as controller, coach, or orchestrator. In addition, when major changes are occurring in the environment, headquarters may play the role of surgeon or architect.

Further, headquarters' style must be consistent with the nature of the firm. Firms may be grouped according to three criteria: synergy between lines of business, level of risk, and intensity of competition facing the firm.

Headquarters can affect the quality of implementation, taking a stance that ranges from informing to persuading, coordinating, approving, and directing subsidiary actions. Headquarters must decide how much autonomy to grant subsidiaries. In some cases, it may want to direct new product development while using persuasion in the area of pricing.

Control is necessary to monitor progress against plans and budgets. The chief control tasks are establishing performance standards, measuring performance against standards, and taking corrective action in the case of deviations. Marketing audits are useful in looking at the performance of foreign markets.

Global information systems are a necessary component of international planning. A wide variety of information can be gathered and, if usefully organized, can help a firm increase sales and manage global factories and inventories, ultimately giving the firm a competitive edge.

Questions and Research

15.1 What basic elements should be included in a company's international marketing planning?

15.2 What distinguishes a short-range plan from a long-range plan? What sort of activities are appropriate for inclusion in a short-range plan?

15.3 How should a marketing plan be integrated with other aspects of the firm; for example, technology and manufacturing?

15.4 What elements would you include in a firm's operating plans for international markets?

15.5 What is the appropriate relationship between a national subsidiary's marketing plans and headquarters' broad goals?

15.6 Why should headquarters' broad plans uniquely be adapted to individual country markets?

15.7 Why should future scenarios be incorporated into a firm's long-range marketing plan?

15.8 How does competition affect international marketing planning?

15.9 Why would a firm consider forming a partnership with competitors?

15.10 Analyze the tire and pharmaceutical industries as examples of strategic alliance formation. What general principles emerge from your analysis?

15.11 How is a firm's organizational structure relevant to its international market planning?

15.12 Explain this statement: Organizational structure is essentially a choice between headquarters' centralization and local autonomy.

15.13 What are the merits of choosing functions, products, and geographic areas as the basis for organizational structure?

15.14 Compare the organizational structures chosen by Reynolds Metals, Unilever, General Motors, Square D Company, Royal Dutch/Shell, the Salim Group, and Philips. Explain why each organization has chosen a different path for its organizational structure. Is there an ideal structure? Explain.

15.15 How can headquarters influence the implementation of plans? Under what conditions will headquarters be more or less directive?

15.16 What is control? How is control related to multinational planning?

15.17 What are some measurements that could be useful in controlling a multinational marketing subsidiary?

15.18 What is a marketing audit? How might such an audit be useful in international markets?

15.19 What are the components of a global information system? How do such systems fit in with international market planning?

15.20 Explain how Mattel's global information system gives it a competitive edge in the global toy industry.

Endnotes

1. Chae, Myung-su and John S. Hill. "Determinants and Benefits of Global Strategic Marketing Planning Formality," *International Marketing Review*, Volume 17, Issue 6, 2000, pages 538–562.

2. LeClair, Debbie Thorne. "Marketing Planning and The Policy Environment In The European Union," *International Marketing Review*, Volume 17, Issue 3, 2000, pages 193–215.

3. "Chairman of Aventis Justifies Decision to Merge with Sanofi," *Les Echos*, June 14, 2004; "Pfizer Gains Final Approval to Buy Pharmacia," *New York Times*, April 15, 2003; "In Huge Drug Merger, Sandoz and Ciba-Geigy Plan to Join Forces," *Wall Street Journal*, March 7, 1996; "Multibillion-Dollar Creation of a Drug Colossus," *Wall Street Journal*, March 8, 1996.

4. Ohmae, Kenichi. "The Global Logic of Strategic Alliances," *Harvard Business Review*, March–April 1989.

5. Dyer, Jeffrey H., Prashant Kale, and Harbir Singh. "How to Make Strategic Alliances Work," *Sloan Management Review*, Summer 2001, pages 37–43; Porter, M. E. and Mark Fuller, "Coalitions and Global Strategy" in *Competition in Global Industries*, M. Porter, editor, 1986, Boston: Harvard Business School Press.

6. Speier, Cheri, Michael G. Harvey, and Jonathan Palmer. "Virtual Management of Global Marketing Relationships," *Journal of World Business*, Volume 33, Issue 3, 1998, pages 263–276.

7. Vorhies, Douglas W. and Neil A. Morgan. "A Configuration Theory Assessment of Marketing Organization Fit with Business Strategy and Its Relationship with Marketing Performance," *Journal of Marketing*, Issue 67, January 2003, pages 100–115.

8. See Bartlett, Christopher, Sumantra B. Ghoshal, and Julian Birkinshaw. *Transnational Management*, 4th Edition, 2004, New York: McGraw-Hill; Prahalad, C. K. and Yves Doz, *The Multinational Mission*, 1988, New York: The Free Press.

9. Bartlett, Christopher and Sumantra Ghoshal. "Managing across Borders: New Strategic Requirements," *Sloan Management Review*, Summer 1987.

10. "AGCO Announces New Organisation Structure as Part of Succession Planning," PR Newswire European, February 12, 2004.

11. Quelch, John. "Does Globalization Have Staying Power," *Marketing Management*, March–April 2002.

12. Bartlett, Christopher, Sumantra B. Ghoshal, and Julian Birkinshaw. *Transnational Management*, 4th Edition, 2004, New York: McGraw-Hill; Bartlett, C. and S. Ghoshal, "Organizing for Worldwide Effectiveness: The Transnational Solution," *California Management Review*, 1988.

13. Maljiers, Floris A. "Inside Unilever: The Evolving Transnational Company," *Harvard Business Review*, September–October 1992.

14. "Schering-Plough Reorganizes," *Pharmaceutical Executive*, August 2003.

15. "GM Plans Major Overhaul of Business in Europe," *Wall Street Journal*, June 17, 2004, Section A, page 3.

16. "Reversing 80 Years of History: GM Is Reining in Global Fiefs," *Wall Street Journal*, October 6, 2004.

17. "Shell: A Global Management Model," *Management Europe*, March 13, 1989.

18. "Philips: Thinking Global, Acting Local," *Management Europe*, April 10, 1989.

19. "Issues for the European CEO (4): New Products," *Business Europe*, February 12, 1997.

20. "GE's Asian Units: Rugged Individuals," *Crossboarder Monitor*, November 5, 1997.

21. "Comeback Kid in China," *Business China*, May 25, 1998.

22. "Mercosur: The Right Fit," *Business Latin America*, September 7, 1998.

23. "Ogilvy Builds China Presence beyond Three Largest Cities," *Wall Street Journal*, June 17, 2004.

24. Schein, Edgar. *Organizational Culture and Leadership*, 1988, San Francisco: Jossey-Bass.

25. Sirmon, David G. and Peter J Lane, "A Model of Cultural Differences and International Alliance Performance," *Journal of International Business Studies*, Volume 35, 2004, pages 306–319.

26. Goold, M. and A. Campbell. *Strategies and Styles*, 1989, United Kingdom: Ashridge Management Centre.

27. Harvey, Michael and M. M. Novicevic. "Staffing Global Marketing Positions: What We Don't Know Can Make a Difference," *Journal of World Business*, Volume 35, Issue 1, 2000, pages 80–94.

28. Quelch, John A. "The New Country Managers," *McKinsey Quarterly*, Number 4, 1992, pages 155–165.

29. Das, Gurcharan. "Local Memoirs of a Global Manager," *Harvard Business Review*, March–April 1993, pages 38–47.

30. "Study Sees U.S. Businesses Stumbling on the Road toward Globalization," *Wall Street Journal*, March 22, 1993.

31. Bartlett, Christopher and Sumantra Ghoshal. "Changing the Role of Top Management: Beyond Strategy to Purpose," *Harvard Business Review*, November–December 1994.

32. Hagel, John III. "A Web That Supports Rather Than Traps," *Wall Street Journal*, March 11, 1996.

33. Quelch, John and Edward Hoff. "Customizing Global Marketing," *Harvard Business Review*, Volume 64, Issue 3, May–June 1986, pages 59–68.

34. Hewett, K., M. S. Roth, and K. Roth. "Conditions Influencing Headquarters and Foreign Subsidiary Roles in Marketing Activities and Their Effects on Performance," *Journal of International Business Studies*, 2003, Volume 34, Issue 6, pages 567–585.

35. Stopford, John and Louis T. Wells, Jr. *Managing the Multinational Enterprise*, 1972, New York: Basic Books.

36. Bartlett, Christopher A. "Multinational Organization: Where to After the Structural Stages?" Cambridge, MA: Harvard Business School, 1981; Hedlund, Gunnar, "The Evolution of the Mother-Daughter Structure in Swedish Multinationals," *Journal of International Business Studies*, Fall 1984, Volume 15, Issue 2, pages 109–123.

37. Birkinshaw, Julian and Neil Hood, editors. *Multinational Corporate Evolution and Subsidiary Development*, 1998, London: Macmillan; Birkinshaw, Julian and Neil Hood, "Multinational Subsidiary Evolution: Capability and Charter Change in Foreign Owned Subsidiary Companies," *Academy of Management Review*, Volume 23, 1998, pages 773–795.

38. Kotler, Philip, W. T. Gregor, and W. H. Rodgers III. "The Marketing Audit Comes of Age," *Sloan Management Review*, Winter 1989.

39. Doz, Yves L. and C. K. Prahalad. "Headquarters' Influence and Strategic Control in MNCs," *Sloan Management Review*, Fall 1981, pages 15–29.

Further Readings

Bartlett, Chris and Sumantra Ghoshal. "Beyond Strategy to Purpose," *Harvard Business Review*, November–December 1994.

Bartlett, Chris and Sumantra Ghoshal. "Managing across Borders: New Strategic Requirements," *Sloan Management Review*, Summer 1987.

Bartlett, Chris and Sumantra Ghoshal. "Organizing for Worldwide Effectiveness: The Transnational Solution," *California Management Review*, 1988.

Bartlett, Chris, Sumantra Ghoshal, and Julian Birkinshaw. *Transnational Management*, 4th Edition, 2004, New York: McGraw-Hill.

Birkinshaw, Julian and Neil Hood, editors, *Multinational Corporate Evolution and Subsidiary Development*, 1998, London: Macmillan.

Birkinshaw, Julian and Neil Hood, "Multinational Subsidiary Evolution: Capability and Charter Change in Foreign Owned Subsidiary Companies," *Academy of Management Review*, Volume 23, 1998, pages 773–795.

Calantone, Roger and C. A. di Benedetto. "Defensive Marketing in Globally Competitive Industrial Markets," *Columbia Journal of World Business*, Fall 1988.

Chae, Myung-su and John S. Hill. "Determinants and Benefits of Global Strategic Marketing Planning Formality," *International Marketing Review*, Volume 17, Issue 6, 2000, pages 538–562.

Daniels, John D. "Bridging National and Global Marketing Strategies through Regional Operations," *International Marketing Review*, Autumn 1987.

Das, Gurcharan. "Local Memoirs of a Global Manager," *Harvard Business Review*, March–April 1993.

Dyer, Jeffrey H., Prashant Kale, and Harbir Singh. "How to Make Strategic Alliances Work," *Sloan Management Review*, Summer 2001, pages 37–43.

Goold, Michael and Andrew Campbell. *Strategies and Styles*, 1989, United Kingdom: Ashridge Management Centre.

Harvey, Michael and M. M. Novicevic. "Staffing Global Marketing Positions: What We Don't Know Can Make a Difference," *Journal of World Business*, Volume 35, Issue 1, 2000, pages 80–94.

Hewett, K., M. S. Roth, and K. Roth. "Conditions Influencing Headquarters and Foreign Subsidiary Roles in Marketing Activities and Their Effects on Performance," *Journal of International Business Studies*, Volume 34, 2003, pages 567–585.

Kotler, Philip, W. T. Gregor, and W. H. Rodgers III. "The Marketing Audit Comes of Age," *Sloan Management Review*, Winter 1989.

LeClair, Debbie Thorne. "Marketing Planning and the Policy Environment in the European Union," *International Marketing Review*, Volume 17, Issue 3, 2000, pages 193–215.

Maljiers, Floris A. "Inside Unilever: The Evolving Transnational Company," *Harvard Business Review*, September–October 1992.

Ohmae, Kenichi. "The Global Logic of Strategic Alliances." *Harvard Business Review*, March–April 1989.

Porter, M. E. and Mark Fuller. "Coalitions and Global Strategy" in *Competition in Global Industries*, M. Porter, editor, 1986, Boston: Harvard Business School Press.

Prahalad, C. K. and Yves Doz. *The Multinational Mission*, 1988, New York: The Free Press.

Quelch, John. "Does Globalization Have Staying Power?" *Marketing Management*, March–April 2002.

Quelch, John. "The New Country Managers," *McKinsey Quarterly*, 1992.

Quelch, John and Edward Hoff. "Customizing Global Marketing," *Harvard Business Review*, May–June 1986.

Schoemaker, Paul J. H. "Scenario Planning: A Tool for Strategic Thinking," *Sloan Management Review*, Winter 1995, pages 25–40.

Sirmon, David G. and Peter J. Lane. "A Model of Cultural Differences and International Alliance Performance," *Journal of International Business Studies*, Volume 35, 2004, pages 306–319.

Speier, Cheri, Michael G. Harvey, and Jonathan Palmer. "Virtual Management of Global Marketing Relationships," *Journal of World Business*, Volume 33, Issue 3, 1998, pages 263–276.

Verhage, Bronislaw and Eric Waarts. "Marketing Planning for Improved Performance," *International Marketing Review*, Spring 1988.

Vorhies, Douglas W. and Neil A Morgan. "A Configuration Theory Assessment of Marketing Organization Fit with Business Strategy and Its Relationship with Marketing Performance," *Journal of Marketing*, Volume 67, January 2003, pages 100–115.

Case 15.1

SONY IN 2005

In January 1997, as previously discussed in Chapter 13, Sony's stock was at $33.70. In August 2005, almost nine years later, Sony's stock price was $33.62. Over that period of time, Sony introduced new products such as the successful PlayStation computer game-playing console. Sony's stock price peaked at $111.5 in April 2000, before gradually declining back to early 1997 levels.

Sony is one of the best-known brand names in consumer electronics and is well regarded for its digital cameras, camcorders, TV sets, and computer game consoles. However, as its stock price performance suggests, Sony has not been able to achieve consistent growth and profits. As Tables 15-7 and 15-8 show, net income margins improved slightly. However, it is still low, at 2.3 percent for fiscal year 2005, with return on equity at approximately 6 percent. Those figures are not indicators of stellar performance.

Table 15-7. Sony Corporation's Income Statement ($Millions)

Year Ended March:	2005	2004	2003	2002	2001
Sales	66,912.0	72,081.0	63,264.0	57,117.0	58,518.0
Cost of Sales	40,673.0	42,175.0	40,672.0	34,993.0	38,901.0
Gross Margin	26,239.0	29,906.0	22,592.0	22,124.0	19,617.0
SG&A	18,856.0	22,152.0	15,402.0	16,612.0	13,071.0
EBITDA	7,383.0	7,754.0	7,190.0	5,512.0	6,546.0
Depreciation and Amortization	6,057.0	6,462.0	5,621.0	4,498.0	4,743.0
EBIT	1,326.0	1,292.0	1,569.0	1,014.0	1,803.0
Other Income	644.0	377.0	379.0	-301.0	79.0
Interest Expense	230.0	268.0	231.0	275.0	344.0
Minority Interest	15.0	23.0	56.0	-122.0	-123.0
Pretax Income	1,740.0	1,401.0	1,717.0	438.0	1,771.0
Income Taxes	150.0	507.0	684.0	491.0	924.0
Special Income/Charges	0.0	0.0	0.0	0.0	233.0
Net Income	1,575.0	871.0	978.0	70.0	970.0
Effect of Accounting Change	-44.0	-20.0	0.0	45.0	-836.0
Total Net Income	**1,531.0**	**851.0**	**978.0**	**115.0**	**134.0**
Net Income as a % of Sales	2.3%	1.2%	1.55%	0.2%	0.2%

Table 15-8. Sony Corporation's Balance Sheet ($Millions)

Year Ended March:	2005	2004	2003	2002	2001
Cash	7,269.0	8,165.0	6,036.0	5,154.0	4,858.0
Receivables	10,385.0	10,806.0	9,463.0	9,367.0	10,362.0
Inventory	5,890.0	6,409.0	5,297.0	5,076.0	7,543.0
Other Current Assets	9,635.0	6,960.0	5,904.0	5,556.0	5,057.0
Total Current Assets	7,269.0	8,165.0	6,036.0	5,154.0	4,858.0
Net Plant and Equipment	12,804.0	13,125.0	10,821.0	10,640.0	11,474.0
Intangibles	4,394.0	5,057.0	4,645.0	4,242.0	4,211.0
Other	38,249.0	36,888.0	28,690.0	21,662.0	19,119.0
Total Noncurrent Assets	55,447.0	55,070.0	44,156.0	36,544.0	34,804.0
Total Assets	**88,627.0**	**87,410.0**	**70,857.0**	**61,696.0**	**62,624.0**
Accounts Payable	6,965.0	7,809.0	7,315.0	6,554.0	6,460.0
S-T Debt	9,668.0	12,056.0	7,247.0	8,455.0	10,251.0
Other Current Liabilities	9,578.0	8,810.0	6,050.0	4,276.0	4,463.0
Total Current Liabilities	26,211.0	28,675.0	20,613.0	19,283.0	21,174.0
Long Term Debt	6,335.0	7,477.0	6,835.0	6,321.0	6,749.0
Other Noncurrent Liabilities	28,404.0	27,248.0	22,568.0	16,848.0	14,624.0
Total Noncurrent Liabilities (including deferred taxes, minority interest)	35,635.0	35,870.0	30,936.0	24,548.0	22,926.0
Total Equity	**26,780.0**	**22,865.0**	**19,308.0**	**17,866.0**	**18,524.0**
Total Liabilities and Stockholder Equity	88,626.0	87,410.0	70,856.0	61,699.0	62,624.0

Sony continued to invest in developing technology, with R&D spending averaging 7.5 percent of sales in the 2004 and 2005 fiscal years, up from 6.4 percent in 2003. Sony sold in markets all around the world, with sales split as follows: Japan (29.3 percent of sales), the United States (27.6 percent of sales), Europe (22.6 percent of sales), and the rest of the world (20.5 percent of sales).

Sony's Various Lines of Business

Sony had five major businesses:

- Electronics
- Sony Pictures
- Sony Music
- Games and Entertainment
- Financial Services division (a major cash generator)

Table 15-9 provides sales and operating profits for Sony's key lines of business.

Table 15-9. Sony's Sales and Operating Revenue by Line of Business

Year Ended March 31
¥ Millions

Sales	2003	2004	2005
Electronics	5,095,079	5,042,319	5,021,647
Games	955,031	780,220	729,754
Music	466,338	440,306	249,105
Pictures	802,770	756,370	733,677
Financial Services	537,276	593,544	560,557
Other	261,145	268,317	254,427
Operating Income			
Electronics	65,939	(6,824)	(34,305)
Games	112,653	67,578	43,170
Music	-28,261	-5,997	8,783
Pictures	58,971	35,230	63,899
Financial Services	22,758	55,161	55,490
Other	(28,316)	(12,054)	(4,077)

Some of Sony's top products and well-known brands include the PlayStation, the Wega and Bravia LCD, high-definition and projection TVs, the Walkman, the Vaio line of personal computers, and the Handycam video camera. Sony expected that in the future, it could link its various devices, offering consumers access to entertainment irrespective of their location; in other words, consumers did not need to be at home. For example, in the future, customers could wirelessly connect their digital cameras to TVs at home, access stored digital photos from anywhere, and share photos via connection to a proprietary Sony network site.

Sony also initiated a number of joint ventures, including the Sony Ericsson mobile phone manufacturing venture. In mobile phones sold, the joint venture sold about 43 million handsets. The GSM Association voted Sony's V800 model the best 3G handset. Sony also launched a Walkman phone and planned to draw on the company's entertainment assets to offer preloaded music and film clips on the phone.

In its TV business, Sony developed a joint venture with Samsung to source LCD panels to make large-screen LCD TVs. Sony also sourced parts from China to manufacture rear projection-screen TVs and high-definition TVs. (Seventy-five percent of products would support high definition by 2007.) Sony and BMG Music formed a music joint venture leading to a 25 percent global market share. Sony also formed a joint venture in semiconductors with Samsung to jointly produce amorphous thin film transistor liquid crystal display panels for new-generation big-screen TV sets. To make up for its inexperience in software, Sony set up operations in Bangalore, India, hiring 150 engineers initially and then rapidly increasing the number to over a thousand as it gained confidence in and success with developing critical software overseas.

Sony Appoints an American CEO

Sir Howard Stringer, a Welsh-born American, was appointed as CEO of Sony Corporation in April 2005. Following Nobuyuki Idei, who had been CEO since 1995, Stringer's appointment was unusual in that few large Japanese companies have foreign CEOs, with top management and boards dominated by senior Japanese executives. However, Stringer's appointment seemed consistent with Sony's maverick tradition. The company had been started in the rubble of the Second World War by Akio Morita and Masaru Ibuka, the inventor who led Sony into cassettes, Trinitron color TVs, and the Walkman. Morita, Sony's first CEO, had appointed Norio Ogha, an opera singer and symphony conductor, to succeed him. Ogha, in turn, appointed Idei as his successor. However, Ogha did not relinquish power and influence completely. He continued as chair and as a member of Sony's board of directors. At one point, in 1995, Sony had 40 directors, most of whom were insiders (that is, Sony executives). The appointment of Stringer, who did not speak Japanese, was a marked contrast to Sony's Japanese origins and tradition— and a shock to the largely Japanese employee base in the company's Japanese operations. It may also have been intended as a message from Idei to the Sony Japanese unit, underlining that business could not continue as usual.

In an address in New York, Stringer outlined how changing its organization could help increase Sony's competitiveness. (See Figure 15-9.)

Figure 15-9. Proposed Changes to Sony's Organization

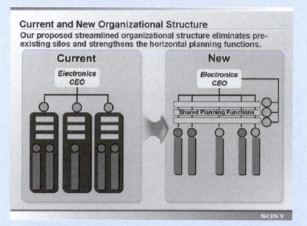

Source: Sony, Howard Stringer, CEO, corporate strategy presentation, New York, September 2005 (http://www.sony.net/SonyInfo/IR/info/Strategy/2005/Stringer/pre_index.html).

Stringer also announced a major restructuring at Sony to reduce the number of products by 20 percent, to reduce head count by 10,000 employees worldwide, and to reduce total costs by ¥200 billion. Sony would incur restructuring costs of ¥210 billion for closing down plants and related severance costs. In addition, Sony would attempt to sell nonstrategic surplus assets to raise ¥120 billion.

Sony's critical problems included:

- A silo organizational structure.
- Product lines that were becoming commodities.
- New products that customers found difficult to use, that were not widely adopted by customers, and that did not result in continued loyalty. (The exception was the PlayStation game machines.)
- Uncoordinated divisions that were acting semi-autonomously, making competing versions of the same product. For example, Sony's new PSX and another device named Sugoroku in Japan both included a combination of computer game and digital video recorder (DVR).
- Frequent changes in technology development strategy.

Sony's Electronics Division

The heart of Sony was its electronics division. That division had the highest sales; a strong global brand; and a variety of products ranging from color TVs, LCD TVs, flat panel TVs, and projector TVs to other products such as DVD players, camcorders, digital cameras, and commercial cinematography equipment. The division's strength was a well-regarded global brand, global marketing and advertising prowess, a strong global distribution system, and technological depth. The division's problem was that its technological advances were often quickly copied by competitors from Korea and China. That led to prices dropping quickly, making it difficult for Sony to maintain a premium pricing policy and to maintain higher operating margins in its electronics sector. Many of the division's innovations quickly became commodities, an arena in which scale economies and volume are critical to success. Those areas did not mesh well with Sony's competitive advantages. The division also had a number of fiercely independent, competitive businesses that did not cooperate well in developing new products—instead, often working at cross-purposes to each other. For example, Sony was developing the new PSP handheld game console, which could also store video, films, and music. However, another business in the electronics division developed the Sugoroku line, competing with the hybrid game player DVD recorder from the computer game division.

Part of Sony's restructuring was to merge such organizations so the company could focus on external competitors and develop a successful new product, rather than continue the in-fighting. The same organizational silos led to the introduction of a digital Walkman that could not directly play the common MP3 music files. A review of the new Walkman noted that its users were expected to use the SonicStage software (included with the digital Walkman) to convert the MP3s into a proprietary format, ATRAC3, the only format the Walkman could play. That conversion was a slow process that consumed precious hard disk space. The review also reported dissatisfaction with the user interface.

Figure 15-10 outlines some of the problems that Sony's electronics businesses faced.

Figure 15-10. Causes of Problems with the Electronics Line of Business

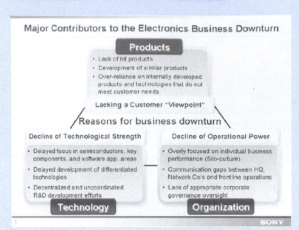

Source: Sony, Ryoji Chubachi, President and Electronics CEO, corporate strategy presentation, New York, September 2005 (http://www.sony.net/SonyInfo/IR/info/Strategy/2005/Chubachi/pre_index.html).

Executives of the electronics division discussed the following:

- The need for product interoperability and an attempt to shape industry standards.
- The consequent need to develop competence in software and networking, not just hardware.
- The need to divest of nonstrategic assets and businesses that were performing poorly.
- The need to work within the Japanese culture and organization while becoming and continuing to be a global company.
- The importance of emphasizing mobile entertainment.

Sony's top management recognized the importance of revitalizing the electronics business, Sony's largest. Many new ideas developed, such as the Connect initiative, to better integrate electronics, software, and service. The end result was Sony's emergent ability to provide location-independent TV and other products, such as its combination DVR and game console.

Hence, Ryoji Chubachi, the CEO of Sony's electronics division, outlined his proposed approach to solving the division's problems. (See Figure 15-11.)

Part of the solution involved reorganizing the organizational structure of the electronics division to overcome the consequences of silos. (See Figure 5-12.)

Sony's Computer Game Business

Sony's "newest" line of business was its computer game business, anchored by its PlayStation and PS2

Figure 15-11. A "Solution" for Electronics

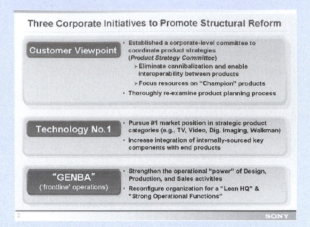

Source: Sony, Ryoji Chubachi, President and Electronics CEO, corporate strategy presentation, New York, September 2005 (http://www.sony.net/SonyInfo/IR/info/Strategy/2005/Chubachi/pre_index.html).

Figure 5-12. The Proposed New Electronics Organization

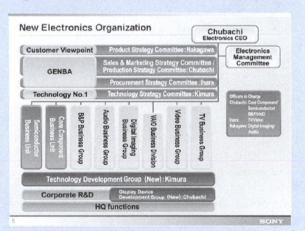

Source: Sony, Ryoji Chubachi, President and Electronics CEO, corporate strategy presentation, New York, September 2005 (http://www.sony.net/SonyInfo/IR/info/Strategy/2005/Chubachi/pre_index.html).

game machines. This business was a start-up within Sony, led by another maverick, Ken Kuratagi, who received Idei's assent to develop a game machine to challenge Nintendo, then the industry leader.

The computer game business was developed in a separate organization, independent of Sony's mainstream electronics business. Kuratagi's vision was to develop a proprietary chip for the game console and game software that would leap-frog Nintendo in game-playing quality and experience. Sony's games would be faster and more complex; players would have the ability to play games on the Internet against other Internet opponents. The PlayStation was successfully introduced with considerable marketplace demand, but Sony had difficulty manufacturing adequate quantities of the complex semiconductor chip, resulting in large losses in 2000. However, once the manufacturing difficulties were resolved, Sony began to dominate the computer gaming industry, gathering over 60 percent of the market share. Sony launched new products to compete with Microsoft, which entered the industry with its Xbox, and with Nintendo, the previous industry leader. By 2005, 200 million PS and PS2 models were shipped, accompanied by over 1.8 billion games. The PlayStation Portable, launched in late 2004, shipped over 6 million units. Sony's newest game machine, the PS3, would be launched in March 2006 to compete with Microsoft's latest Xbox model.

The computer entertainment (game) division's newer products included the PSX, containing a combined DVD recorder and game player. Sony planned to develop complex new-generation semiconductor chips in a joint venture with IBM and Toshiba for use in new-generation game machines and in other electronics products. The new semiconductor initiative, Cell, with IBM and Toshiba, was a supercomputer on a chip. It had 10 times the processing power of a standard computer and was designed for initial use in PS3, Sony's newest PlayStation game machine. Later applications would include real-time high-definition media processing. The computer entertainment (game) division, not the electronics division, would house the Cell development center under the leadership of its chief technology officer (CTO).

Sony Pictures and Music

Sony's third major business was Music and Entertainment. Based almost entirely in the United States, it included Sony Pictures and Sony/BMG Music. The division had over 7,500 films in its library, "about half of all color films ever made." The film library included hits such as the James Bond series, Spider Man, and The Wizard of Oz. However, sales declined as customers purchased fewer CDs and downloaded more music from the Internet, often for free. As a major producer of music and films, Sony was torn between embracing the delivery of digital media and opposing alternative forms of delivery for fear of rampant piracy of music CDs and films on DVD. Because Sony Pictures had recently acquired MGM and its film library, it saw an opportunity for synergies between computer games, films, and music; for example, a computer game drawing on the Spider Man film.

Sony saw promise in developing new ways of packaging and marketing film and music together. However, its film and music business, as well as its electronics business, had to cope with establishing new standards for the distribution of film and music on DVDs. Sony and its allies had developed the Blu-ray DVD format and were involved in a standards fight with the opposing and alternative standard, Toshiba's HD-DVD. While Microsoft had backed the Toshiba standard, Sony was attempting to establish its Blu-ray as the industry standard. As in a previous standards war with Toshiba over the VHS and Betamax standards for videotape, the prevailing standard will be determined by market forces. Toshiba "won" with its VHS standard because consumers liked it, therefore purchasing and renting more films in the that format.

Sir Howard Stringer's Years at Sony

Stringer had his roots in the media and entertainment industry, having come to Sony with a background in TV news production. He headed Sony Theaters and Sony's U.S. real estate divisions, then was appointed head of the film studio and music division before taking over as head of the music and pictures businesses. Idei said that Stringer was an excellent general manager and that he did not have to be an individual from the creative side of the business. Stringer was successful in cutting costs at the U.S. operations by over $600 million by 2005, an achievement that brought him to the forefront as a possible successor to Idei. When announcing Stringer's accession to the CEO position, Idei also revealed that he and six other insiders would be stepping down from Sony's board, that the board would be reduced in size, and that outside directors would now dominate the board by an 8 to 3 margin. The difficulty for Idei had been that Ogha, the former CEO, had continued to exercise influence from his position on the board, often undercutting Idei's attempts at change. For example, when Idei announced that Sony Insurance in Japan would be sold to GE Capital for $5 billion, the insurance business executives opposed the sale and enlisted Ogha's help. His opposition to the sale forced the board to reverse its decision.

Foreign CEOs in Japan

Another foreign CEO in Japan, Carlos Ghosn, who headed Nissan, noted that not speaking Japanese meant that all communication had to take place through translation. He added that change was possible in Japan; but for that to happen, it had to be clear what change was intended and how the change would be made. In addition, the CEO had to commit to results that would ensue from making the change. Ghosn emphasized that regardless of language, numbers were the same in any language and that performance spoke volumes, implying that achieving results helped support making changes.

The Challenge for Sony

After Stringer took over as CEO of Sony, he announced that about 10,000 jobs would be cut, 4,500 coming from Japan. He noted that because Japanese investors were against layoffs, he did not go as far as he would have liked. He pointed out that he had put several businesses on probation because those managers had promised results that never happened. Stringer had given the managers a year to show results, holding off further restructuring.

The broad challenge to Sony (and to many of its biggest competitors) came from the convergence of digital media across several forms of delivery. Modes of delivery included the TV, the personal computer, mobile phones (cell phones), music players, game machines, storage devices such as DVD players, and Tivo-like products. Digital content included the following: movies, new and old; music; digital pictures and digital video; data (business and personal); books, magazines, and newspapers; Internet content such as blogs and podcasting; and game software.

Convergence stems from the ability of content and modes of delivery to connect through the Internet, through broadband transmission across Internet networks, often wirelessly. The companies that can dominate that bridging can reap market share and profits and avoid the threat of commoditization. Microsoft is one such company. Its Windows software dominates. Microsoft is also attempting to use different versions of Windows in cell phones and in home electronics such as TV sets. Its hope is to achieve the success and dominance it has seen with Windows in the computer world.

Sony wanted to emulate Microsoft's success in leveraging its Windows platform. Sony could use Windows; but doing so would give some control to Microsoft, and Sony would have to pay license fees to Microsoft. Sony would be at greater risk from commoditization at the delivery device end. That explains Sony's attempts to develop advanced semiconductors (the Cell), a microprocessor and design distinct from Intel's Pentium architecture, and to develop Linux-based software for this microprocessor, relying on Linux's open source tradition.

The challenge for companies such as Sony is to mediate how such digital content is made available through the Internet broadband network to the variety of hardware delivery alternatives—as Sony puts it, how to capture a major role in the "broadband network society" of the twenty-first century.

QUESTIONS AND RESEARCH

1. Diagnose Sony's problems. How would you evaluate its performance?

2. Why did Sony succeed in the computer game business?

3. How does Sony's organization contribute to its difficulties?

4. What is your assessment of Mr. Chubachi's planned changes for the electronics division?

5. Why was Howard Stringer appointed CEO of Sony? What is he expected to achieve?

6. Why did Ken Kuratagi, Sony's "videogame whiz" not get the post of CEO?

7. If you were to advise Howard Stringer, what would you recommend?

8. What are the cultural and other difficulties Stringer is likely to face in turning Sony around?

Sources: "Sony's Sledgehammer Strategy" and "Sony Chief Wields His Ax with Sensitivity," *Financial Times*, September 26, 2005; "At Sony, Rivalries Were Encouraged, Then Came iPod," *Wall Street Journal*, June 29, 2005; "Inside the Shake-up at Sony," *Fortune*, April 4, 2005; "Sony, Lagging behind Rivals, Hands Reins to a Foreigner," *Wall Street Journal*, March 7, 2005; "Videogame Whiz Reprograms Sony after a 10-Year Funk," *Wall Street Journal*, September 2, 2004; "Sony's Digital Walkman Doesn't Best Apple's iPod," *Wall Street Journal*, July 28, 2004; "Sony: The Complete Home Entertainer," *The Economist*, March 1, 2003; "Sony Re-dreams Its Future," *Fortune*, November 25, 2002; "Sony Is Grooming Games Maverick for the Next Level," *Wall Street Journal*, April 18, 2002; Sony Corporation's web site (http://www.sony.net/SonyInfo/IR/info/Strategy/index.html).

Case prepared by Prof. Ravi Sarathy, ©2005, for use in class discussion.

Name/Company Index

Subject Index

Glossary

-A-

absolute advantage a country's ability to produce a good at a lower cost, in terms of real resources, than another country

adoption the fifth and final phase of new product introduction during which consumers assess their experience from first use and decide whether to continue using the product

advertising the paid communication of company messages through impersonal media

architect in dealing with subsidiaries, the person who reshapes his or her company according to a global vision before returning to the mode of coach or orchestrator

autarky national self-sufficiency with regard to economics

awareness the first stage of new product introduction that involves communicating the existence of a new product or innovation to potential adopters/consumers

-B-

balance-of-payments referring to summary statements of all of the economic transactions between one country and all other countries over a period of time, usually one year

balance of trade the difference between the total exports and total imports of a nation in one year

benchmarking the process during which a company compares its products to those of the competition, notes the dimensions along which the competitors' products are superior, and uses knowledge of those gaps to guide product improvement and future development

bimodal income distribution referring to a country in which most people are below the per capita income figure with a small wealthy group above it (that is, no middle class)

Born Global a term used to refer to companies that begin operations with both domestic and foreign sales from the outset

-C-

capital accounts a specific BoP account that includes flows such as direct and portfolio investments, private placements, and bank and government loans

caste a type of detailed, rigid social organization

change agents those that cause or effect change

choice cards used in an experimental design format to forecast market segments and market share on which respondents indicate their product preferences

civil (code) law law that is based on an extensive and, presumably, comprehensive set of laws organized by subject matter into a code

class groupings a type of loose, flexible social organization

coach the role of corporate headquarters in dealing with subsidiaries in which headquarters decentralizes authority to subsidiaries, but is available to provide support and advice

code of conduct guidelines that an organization agrees to follow

commercial infrastructure the availability and quality of supporting services such as banks and financial institutions, advertising agencies, distribution channels, and marketing research organizations

commercial policy government regulations that have a bearing on foreign trade

common law tradition-oriented law in that the interpretation of what the law means on a given subject is heavily influenced by previous court decisions as well as by usage and custom

common market a grouping of nations that seeks to standardize or harmonize all government regulations affecting trade

common territory a homeland; a neighborhood, a suburb, a city, or even a tribal grouping

comparative advantage a country's ability to produce a good at a lower cost, relative to other goods, compared to another country; a country tends to produce and export those goods in which it has the greatest comparative advantage and import those goods in which it has the least comparative advantage

competitive advantage why a firm should be able to make a profit in its chosen line of activity in the face of competition and why customers should buy its product or service, preferring it to that of the competition

competitive risk results from the geographic pattern of a company's manufacturing and sale configuration when compared to that of its key competitors

concept generation and screening the first stage of decision making that firms go through in introducing new products

configuration refers to decisions that result in a company having a presence in more than one national market

conflict diamonds diamonds that are sold to raise resources to purchase weapons and prolong conflict

consultation in the context of the WTO's use of the term, a principle that allows a forum for nations to compromise over trade disagreements rather than resort to arbitrary trade-restricting actions

contract manufacturing when a firm's product is produced in a foreign market by another producer under contract with the firm

controller the role of corporate headquarters in dealing with subsidiaries in which headquarters gives considerable autonomy to subsidiaries and uses measurements to determine when to intervene

Copenhagen Consensus in an example of how firms might prioritize their social responsibilities, this project has attempted to (1) rank some of society's major problems and (2) prioritize the problems based on the costs and benefits of developing solutions, then ranking the solutions based on what results in the greatest benefit for the least cost

core competencies the basis of effective product development

countertrade trade in which payment is made in goods or services

cross-patrolling the exchange of threats between global competitors; a strong global competitor undercuts its competitors in their strong markets by deliberately channeling resources into those markets; the competitor buys market share with price cuts and accepts low profits or losses; those threats are countered by similar tactics from a similar global position

cross-section comparison approach a way to gain a better understanding of market potential in countries with limited data; involves taking the known market size of a product in one country and relating it to some market indicator to obtain a ratio

culture a total pattern of behavior that is shared by a group of people, is consistent and compatible in its components, and is a learned behavior

current account a specific BoP account that is a list of trade transactions in manufactured goods and services, as well as a list of unilateral transfers

customer relationship marketing the purposeful development of systems and processes that allow for close contact between a firm and its customers

customer service level delivery times, availability of parts and service, and other elements required to meet customers' wants and needs

customs union similar to a free-trade area in that it has no tariffs on trade among members; it has the more ambitious requirement that members also have a uniform tariff on trade with nonmembers

-D-

database marketing analyzing and using knowledge about customers and potential customers to develop products and business strategies

data mining analysis of data to identify patterns for predictive purposes

deontological theory the school of thought that emphasizes means and the fact that people are entitled to be treated as ends in themselves

devolution the decomposition of national and regional groupings

direct exporting exporting that requires the use of intermediaries but in which a firm typically retains title (and assumes responsibility) for a longer period of time and has closer contact with the foreign buyer

divorce laws regulations that dictate the terms of separation between firms acting as intermediaries

draft a common form of export financing that is drawn by the exporter on the importer, who makes the draft a trade acceptance by writing the word *accepted* on it and signing it

dumping selling products in foreign markets at prices lower than those in the producer's home market

-E-

education the process of transmitting skills, ideas, and attitudes, as well as training, in particular disciplines

Electronic Data Interchange (EDI) the principal technical communication vehicle for the information exchange between a company and its business partners in the world

euro the common unit of currency used by members of the European Union

European Union (EU) as of May 1, 2005, the economic amalgamation of 25 European nations

evaluate the third stage of new product introduction during which consumers consider the knowledge they have gathered to decide whether to break old habits and take the risk of trying a new product

exchange control a scarcity of foreign exchange resulting in a government's rationing it out according to its own priorities

experience curve economies result from learning to better manage a line of business

exporting selling goods to other countries

export trading company (ETC) a service firm that provides expertise and assistance to other firms in moving products and services around the globe

-F-

foreign assembly a firm produces domestically all or most of the components or ingredients of its product and ships them to foreign markets for assembly

foreign exchange rate the domestic price of a foreign currency

foreign marketing marketing within foreign countries

franchise a business with the authority to sell or distribute a company's goods or services in a particular area

free-trade area an organization for economic integration in which member countries agree to have free movement of goods among themselves; that is, no tariffs or quotas are imposed against goods coming from other members

-G-

geographic proximity referring to the fact that countries that are neighbors are better trading partners than countries that are distant from each other

Global Compact endorsed by the UN, stating that "Businesses should work against corruption in all its forms, including extortion and bribery."

global environment referring to a business environment in which business transactions take place governed by conditions, constraints, events, and participants that represent the system

global industry an industry in which a firm's competitive position in one country is affected by its position in other countries, and vice versa

global marketing coordinating marketing in multiple markets in the face of global competition

global perspective the point of view that a firm takes when formulating its strategic plans by directing special attention to the interdependence among national markets and competitors' actions in those markets

Global Public Good (GPG) defined by the World Bank as "commodities, resources, services and systems of rules or policy regimes with substantial cross-border externalities that are important for development and poverty reduction, and that can be produced in sufficient supply only through cooperation and collective action by developed and developing countries"

gray marketing the unauthorized importing and selling of products intended for one market in another higher-priced market

gray markets unofficial markets in which goods destined for a particular geographic market are diverted to other markets, often through unauthorized distribution channels, to meet the needs of the alternative markets

grease payments money paid by companies to motivate officials to do jobs they are already supposed to be doing

gross national income (GNI) a measure of the total domestic and foreign value created by residents

-H-

hypernorms manifest, universal norms that represent principals so fundamental to human existence that they are reflected in a convergence of religious, philosophical, and cultural beliefs

-I-

indirect exporting a transaction in which a manufacturer has little control over the marketing strategy and there is little or no contact between the buyer and the manufacturer

individualism the second of Dr. Geert Hofstede's cultural indexes that refers to societies that place more emphasis and importance on individuals than on collectivistic societies

industry globalization drivers environmental factors that lead an industry to become global; markets factors, cost factors, competitive moves, and other environmental factors

infrastructure external facilities and services of an economy, including paved roads, railroads, energy supplies, and other communication and transport services

Integrative Social Contracts a theory that states that in the context of most local cultures, managers can apply ethical standards derived from the local context, principally from domestic firms, industries, professional associations, and other organizations

intellectual property protection (IPP) methods such as registration of trademarks and patents used to protect a firm's intellectual property

intensive distribution the policy of selling through any retailer that wants to handle the product

interest the second stage of new product introduction that relates to consumers obtaining detailed knowledge about a new product or innovation

international marketing marketing activities that involve identifying, understanding, and satisfying global customer needs better than the competition (both domestic and international)

International Monetary Fund (IMF) an organization that acts as a forum for monetary and fiscal discussions that affect the world economy and that supplies financial assistance (loans) and technical assistance (economic consultants)

international trade the cross-border movement of goods and services

Islamic law Shari'a; law of the religion of Islam

-J-

joint venture a foreign operation in which the international company has enough equity to have a voice in management but not enough to completely dominate the venture

-K-

kinship the social organization or structure of a group; the way people relate to other people

knowledge base knowledge, skills, resources, and competencies that a company possesses

-L-

launched the stage of decision making that firms go through in introducing new products after the product is tested in the marketplace

learning curve economies results from workers becoming more productive as they work at a job longer and learn from mistakes

legal environment a nation's laws and regulations pertaining to business

letter of credit a common form of export financing that is drawn on a bank and becomes a bank acceptance rather than a trade acceptance

licensing a way for companies that are unwilling to commit capital and management resources to marketing in foreign countries; results in less risk, less involvement, and lower returns for the firm

logistics management through the organization of an operation, international marketers can increase profits through cost reduction and market expansion

long-term orientation the fifth of Dr. Geert Hofstede's cultural indexes that describe people who believe that wisdom comes from age or longevity, that tradition and elders are to be valued, and that rewards come to those who make long-term commitments

-M-

manufacturing abroad a strategy undertaken by a firm to enlarge its customer base

maquiladora plants plants set up along the Mexican border by U.S. firms using Mexican labor that averages approximately $2 an hour

market-extension refers to an idea that represents an unplanned and short-term exploitation of foreign markets while the domestic market remains the focus of the company; is typically the way a small firm becomes involved in international marketing

marketing the collection of activities undertaken by a firm in order to assess and satisfy customer needs, wants, and desires

marketing information data and information about a market that is often gathered by a firm's partners abroad and that represents a major reason for seeking local partners

marketing management the planning and coordinating of activities to achieve a successfully integrated marketing program

market portfolio risk results from a firm's export markets as compared to the country-market portfolio of its global competitors

market size a consideration with regard to present markets and potential markets when a firm is examining world markets

masculinity the third of Dr. Geert Hofstede's cultural indexes that refers to societies that are male-dominated and in which a large separation exists between men and women

material culture the tools and artifacts in a society, excluding physical things found in nature unless they undergo some technological transformation

micromarketing the customization of marketing messages for small groups of people

multidomestic refers to a perspective that represents a firm's careful consideration of foreign markets, but with a clearly separate orientation toward each country market

multinational companies see *multinational corporation*

multinational corporation MNC; a company that manufactures and markets its products or services in several countries

-N-

national champions firms that have dominant positions in their national markets and often receive government support

national sovereignty a nation's right to govern itself without outside interference

natural resources a nation's actual and potential forms of wealth supplied by nature as well as its land area, topography, and climate

nondiscrimination in the context of the WTO's use of the term, a principal that calls for each contracting party to grant all other parties the same rate of import duty

non-tariff barriers (NTBs) trade barriers that include customs documentation requirements, marks of origin, food and drug laws, labeling laws, antidumping laws, "buy national" policies, and subsidies

North American Free Trade Agreement (NAFTA) a free trade agreement between Canada, the United States, and Mexico

-O-

orchestrator the role of corporate headquarters in dealing with subsidiaries in which headquarters is an interventionist with central control and responsibility for activities such as manufacturing, R&D, and finance

-P-

pass-through how much of an exchange rate change to pass on in the form of adjusted domestic prices

per capita income statistics most often used to describe a country economically; calculated as the total value of goods created divided by the total population of a geographic area

personal selling a promotion tool that is paid communication that can be altered quickly and targeted at specific individuals or small groups of people

piggybacking one form of indirect exporting in which one product "rides" on the back of another from one national market to another

point-of-sale (POS) refers to information systems that include data on sales sorted by brands, quantities, prices, package size, time of day and day of week, and month

political environment when referring to international business, any national or international political factor that can affect its operations

political influences a critical factor in trade relations

power distance the first of Dr. Geert Hofstede's cultural indexes that describes the degree to which power in a group is shared and that is the relative distance between the "most" and "least" powerful people

price bundling setting a certain price for customers who simultaneously buy several products within a product line

product everything a consumer receives when making a purchase

product innovation related to the needs of the home market in Phase 1 of the product life cycle

product life cycle when referring to international trade and product patterns, many products go through a trade cycle wherein one nation is initially an exporter, then loses its market exports, and finally may become an importer of the product

product platforms the layer of effective product development that is based on core competencies

product testing the stage of decision making that firms go through in introducing new products after ascertaining product viability and quality from an engineering and production standpoint

promotion a firm's communication with its various audiences, with a view to informing and influencing them

prototype refers to the stage of decision making that firms go through in introducing new products in which trial runs of new products are made

public relations publicity; a promotion tool that is considered unpaid communication, but with certain costs

-Q-

quotas quantitative restrictions that serve as barriers to imports

-R-

regional headquarters a level in an organization between corporate headquarters and foreign markets

regionalism economic cooperation within regions

repatriate to send home

resale price maintenance (RPM) the effect of rules imposed by a manufacturer on wholesale or retail resellers of its own products to prevent them from competing too fiercely on price and thus driving profits down from the reselling activity

risk avoidance a major factor in the low number of online shoppers

risk-based multistage production sequencing allows for development of production plans for the manufacturing process based on predictability or stability of demand

-S-

sales promotion sometimes referred to as the "all other" category of promotion tools; includes coupons, directed e-mail and traditional mail, sponsorship of events, and many other means of communicating with people

selective distribution choosing a limited number of resellers in a market area

social organization helps a group of people define their roles and the expectations they place upon themselves and others in the group

special interest group a kind of social grouping that may be religious, occupational, recreational, or political

state-owned enterprises (SOEs) enterprises, often corporations, owned by governments as a way to participate directly in competition

strategic alliance a relationship formed by a firm and the competition as a strategic response to developing global markets

sustainable economic development policies and programs designed to help developing countries by paying for or subsidizing the use of environmentally sound practices to reach economic goals

-T-

tariff a tax on products imported from other countries

tariff factory a term used when the primary reason a local plant exists is to get behind the tariff barriers of protected markets that it can no longer serve with direct exports

technology the techniques or methods of making and using that which surrounds us

teleological theory the school of thought that focuses on ends, choosing actions that maximize good and minimize harm for most people

tied aid foreign aid is granted with the condition that a portion of the aid be used to buy goods from the aid-granting country

time-series approach a way to gain a better understanding of market potential in countries with limited data; estimates the demand in the second country by assuming that it has the same level of consumption that the first country had at the same level of development

topography the surface features of a country's land, including rivers, lakes, forests, deserts, and mountains

transaction risk results from changes in the value of foreign currency that may diminish a firm's financial results

transfer pricing the price at which intercompany transfers take place

trend analysis the analysis showing which products are growing and which are fading, indicating potential threats and opportunities for a firm

triad economies the markets of North America, Europe, and Japan/Southeast Asia

trial the fourth stage of new product introduction during which a product is being used for the first time

-U-

uncertainty avoidance the fourth of Dr. Geert Hofstede's cultural indexes that measures a nation's tolerance for risk

United Nations Conference on Trade and Development (UNCTAD) a permanent organ of the United Nations General Assembly; its goal is to further the development of emerging nations

urbanization the number of people living in cities rather than rural locations

utilitarianism judges behavior in terms of the costs and benefits to society; it suggests choosing actions that result in the greatest net benefit or the lowest net cost

-V-

value-added networks communications networks that offer services, communications connections, and data transmission

-W-

World Bank an institution whose goal is to promote economic growth, to provide loans for infrastructure development, and to improve the living conditions of the world's population

World Trade Organization (WTO) an international body dealing with the rules of trade between nations

About NorthCoast Publishers

NorthCoast Publishers is a **Business Administration Publisher**, serving the Higher Education curriculum in the fields of International Business, Marketing, Management, and Entrepreneurial Studies.

"Quality publications at an affordable price" is our mantra. Thus, our publications will feature:

- a lower, more affordable price point than the competition;
- a fully supportive website for each product that acts as a "Portal" for the discipline and offers more educational substance and dialogic alternatives than the competition;
- an attractive, two-color design – primarily in paperback – with a full battery of teaching aids.
- the offering of modularized, "Custom" versions of our publications to those audiences comprised of 200 or more students that wish to use selected portions of our products.

The firm also provides close customer contact, offering hands-on editorial services, development of interactive software, securing of copyright clearances, timely manuscript editing and quality final production. This nimbleness and responsiveness extends to advanced and innovative marketing techniques – again, making use of the Web and electronic commerce.

We look forward to your participation in this exciting new endeavor and we would welcome any questions or suggestions you might have of us. Contact us at www.NorthCoastPub.com.

Sincerely,

Roger L. Williams
Publisher

Robert H. Vaughn
Vice-president, Operations

To find out about our new books, special offers and much more,
access our website at www.northcoastpub.com

From the authors of **this** book.
International Marketing, 9th (11\05)
Authors: Terpstra, Vern; University of Michigan,
Sarathy, Ravi; Northeastern University,
Russow, Lloyd; Philadelphia University
ISBN 1933583-177, 580 pp., paperback; $99.00

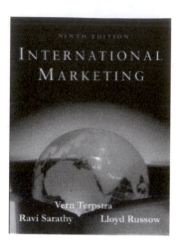

This is a Basic Text for courses in International Marketing and International Business. Relevant case studies are included for each section of the text. The Ninth Edition of this popular text has been completely revised, reflecting current developments in the field and the imperatives of dealing with an increasingly Globalized Economy. Drawing upon the extensive and unparalleled international marketing experience of its authors (one of whom is new to the Ninth Edition), *International Marketing* takes a comprehensive look at the environment, problems and practices of today's international marketing arena. This text gives students a real-world taste of this dynamic field, preparing them for entry into the marketing workplace of the 21st Century. Chapters on "Information Technology", and "Ethics", in particular, have been moved to the front section of the book, reflecting the widespread and pervasive impact of newer technologies and ethical questions on the marketing field.

Strategies in Entrepreneurial Finance (11\05)
Author: Stoller, Greg; Boston College
ISBN 1933583-118, 320 pp., paperback; $85.00

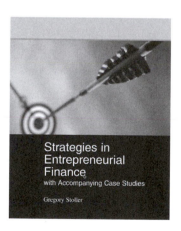

Strategies in Entrepreneurial Finance provides an in-depth casebook on the strategies required to build a company as viewed through the lens of entrepreneurial finance. It uses fourteen selected, original case studies describing the trials and successes encountered by real people as they started out as small business entrepreneurs. To add a real-world perspective to the cases and to round out the learning, the casebook also includes several sections that contain a multitude of qualitative and quantitative approaches and examples.

Globalization and International Business
Authors: He, Xiaohong; Quinnipiac University, *et. al.*
ISBN 1933583-428, paperback; Approx. 370 pgs., Preliminary ed 02/06; $92.00

Dr. He and her associates bring a wealth of real world international business experience, as well as years of college teaching to this exciting introductory textbook.. This groundbreaking work stands out in three respects from its competitors: 1.) it is *multi-disciplinary* and integrative in focus; 2.) truly international, it examines the issues from the point-of-view of both developed western countries and less developed nations; 3.) international business activities are placed within the context of history and globalization. Thus, there is ample detail on historical development, forms of government, social responsibility, and (importantly), *ethics*.

Managing Beyond Compliance: The Ethical and Legal Dimensions of Corporate Responsibility (12\05)
Authors: Marcus, Alfred; University of Minnesota
Kaiser, Sheryl; Loyola College
ISBN 1933583-290, 420 pp., paperback; $77.00

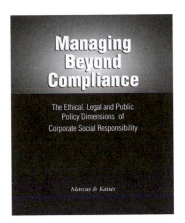

A thoughtful, contemporary treatise on Business Ethics, this text will provide a breath of fresh air for those professors wishing to combine current strands of thought in business ethics and corporate social responsibility. The text takes the position that the ethical dimension of business goes beyond business policy and regulation; it shapes and informs law and public policy. Rarely, however is the ethical dimension perfectly reflected in law; thus, "Managing Beyond Compliance" is a necessity.

Essentials Financial Accounting, I (6\05)
Author: Carter, C.P.; Univ. of Massachusetts
ISBN 1933583002, 320 pp., paperback; $65.00

The students' need to know about "resources and their sources" is the foundation for the presentation of the material. Each topic presented in the text is examined in terms of how it affects a company's resources (assets) and sources of resources (liabilities and stockholder equity). Once the effects of events have been examined, the text turns to journal entries in discussing the usual material in financial accounting. Accounting for business events through *debits* and *credits* is an important part of the text – as is a thorough coverage of the accounting cycle.

Order card

Book	ISBN	Price	Qty	Total
International Marketing, 9th	1933583177	99.00	_____	$_____
Entrepreneurial Finance	1933583118	85.00	_____	$_____
Globalization & International Bus	1933583428	92.00	_____	$_____
Managing Beyond Compliance:	1933583290	77.00	_____	$_____
Financial Accounting, vol I	1933583002	65.00	_____	$_____
Global Environment of Business	1933583185	52.00	_____	$_____
			Sub Total	$_____
	Shipping and Handling $7.00 x Qty			$_____
			Ohio Tax 8%	$_____
			Total	$_____

Or order on-line at www.northcoastpub.com
Call us toll free 866-537-0323

Global Environment of Business (8\05)
Authors: Terpstra, Vern; University of Michigan
Sarathy, Ravil Northeastern University
Russow, Lloyd; Philadelphia University
ISBN 1933583185, 302 pp., paperback; $52.00

This brief text gives students a real-world taste of this dynamic field, preparing them for entry into the global workplace of the 21st Century. "Information Technology", in particular, is featured — reflecting the widespread and pervasive impact of newer technologies on the field of international business.

NORTHCOAST PUBLISHERS INC
5063 TURNEY RD
GARFIELD HEIGHTS OH 44125